SECOND EDITION

PROTAGONISTAS

a communicative approach

Charo Cuadrado
Pilar Melero
Enrique Sacristán

VISTA®
HIGHER LEARNING
Boston, Massachusetts

Publisher: José A. Blanco
Editorial Development: Judith Bach, Emily Bates, Jo Hanna Kurth
Project Management: Brady Chin, Sally Giangrande
Rights Management: Ashley Dos Santos, Annie Pickert Fuller
Technology Production: Egle Gutiérrez, Paola Ríos Schaaf
Design: Radoslav Mateev, Gabriel Noreña, Andrés Vanegas
Production: Manuela Arango, Oscar Díez, Alejandro Rojas

Original title: Protagonistas
© Charo Cuadrado; Pilar Melero; Enrique Sacristán
© Ediciones SM, Madrid

Student Text (Perfectbound) ISBN: 978-1-68004-975-6

Instructor's Annotated Edition ISBN: 978-1-68004-985-5

Library of Congress Control Number: 2016947901

2 3 4 5 6 7 8 9 RW 21 20 19 18 17

Introduction

Welcome to **PROTAGONISTAS, Second Edition,** your gateway to the Spanish language and the vibrant cultures of the Spanish-speaking world. **PROTAGONISTAS** is adapted for North American college students from an innovative text used in Spain. It includes ground-breaking features to keep you engaged and motivated, and to make language-learning accessible.

Original, hallmark features

- A curriculum built around individuals from all over the Spanish-speaking world, presenting vocabulary and grammar through the context of their daily lives

- Coverage of the entire Spanish-speaking world

- An emphasis on real-life language use

- Practical, high-frequency vocabulary in meaningful contexts

- Clear, concise grammar explanations with high-impact graphics and other special features that make structures easier to learn and use

- Ample guided, focused practice to reinforce the vocabulary and grammar you are learning

- Abundant opportunities to interact with a classmate, small group, the full class, and your instructor

- Thirty-six "bite-sized" lessons, each of which is organized exactly the same way

- Careful development of your reading, writing, and listening skills, incorporating learning strategies and a process approach

- Integration of an appealing video series

- An easy-to-navigate design built around recurring sections that appear either completely on one page or on spreads of two facing pages

- Thorough learning support through on-the-spot sidebars and suggestions, models and guides to conversation, grammar clarifications, and language-learning tips

- A complete set of print and electronic supplements to help you learn Spanish

To familiarize yourself with the program's organization, turn to page xiii and take the **PROTAGONISTAS** at-a-glance tour.

NEW! to the Second Edition

- Online chat activities for synchronous communication and oral practice

- Customizable study lists for vocabulary words

- Integrated performance assessment

- Assignable oral testing

Apéndice

Grammar Reference Table of Contents

The Appendix includes a thorough grammar reference section, conveniently cross-referenced with the **Gramática funcional** presentations in each lesson.

Supersite

The sections of your textbook come with activities on the **PROTAGONISTAS** Supersite, most of which are auto-graded for immediate feedback. Plus, the Supersite is iPad®-friendly*, so it can be accessed on the go! Visit **vhlcentral.com** to explore this wealth of exciting resources.

Functional Context sections

- Audio activities
- Textbook activities
- Additional activities for extra practice
- Chat activities for conversational skill-building and extra practice

Protagonistas section

- Audio activities
- Textbook activities
- Additional activities for extra practice
- Chat activities for conversational skill-building and extra practice

Gramática funcional

- Animated grammar tutorials
- Textbook activities
- Additional activities for extra practice

Vocabulario

- Vocabulary list with audio
- Customizable study lists

Avance

- Textbook activities
- **Proyecto** composition activity written and submitted online
- Chat activities for conversational skill-building and extra practice
- Streaming video of **Flash Cultura** series, with instructor-managed options for subtitles and transcripts in Spanish and English

Plus! Also found on the Supersite:

- All textbook and Student Activities Manual audio MP3 files
- Communication center for instructor notifications and feedback
- Live Chat tool for video chat, audio chat, and instant messaging without leaving your browser
- A single gradebook for all Supersite activities
- WebSAM online Student Activities Manual
- vText online interactive student edition with access to Supersite activities, audio, and video

*Students must use a computer for audio recording and select presentations and tools that require Flash or Shockwave.

The **Unit Opener** presents the protagonists you will encounter and the communicative functions you will learn in the two lessons of the unit.

Unidad 5

Salma Hayek, más que una cara bonita

Communicative functions are summarized at the beginning of the unit, so you know from the start what you will be able to accomplish by the end of each lesson.

Juanita y Bernardo, dos abuelos muy activos

La casa de Frida

Every unit concludes with **Avance,** a section containing review strategies and activities or readings, as well as the **Flash Cultura** cultural video series.

Each lesson features a protagonist from the Spanish-speaking world, someone who will show you how Spanish is used in real-world situations.

Supersite resources for each lesson are available at **vhlcentral.com**. Icons show you which textbook activities are also available online, and where additional practice activities are available. The description next to the icon indicates what additional resources are available: videos, tutorials, and more!

Each lesson features two **Functional Context** sections presenting vocabulary and structures.

Mi experiencia activities provide conversation outlines that guide you to use lesson vocabulary and structures for meaningful, personalized communication.

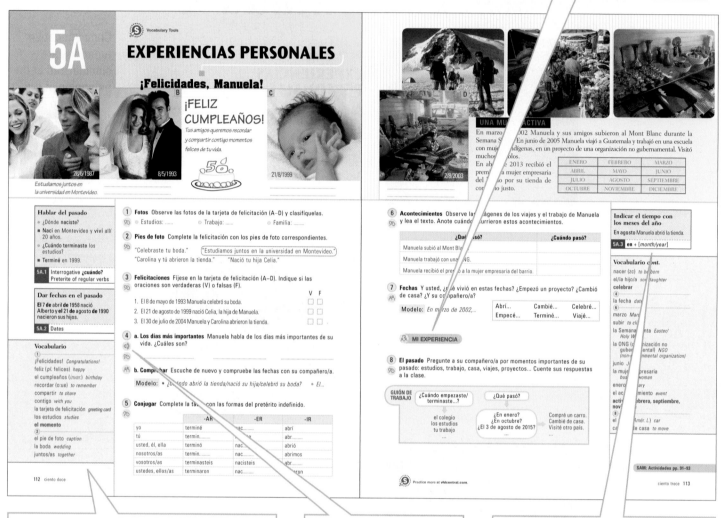

Active vocabulary is presented in **Vocabulario** sidebars, organized in order of appearance, with reference to the relevant activity. Cognates are provided without translation. Active vocabulary is also summarized at the end of the lesson.

Audio icons call out listening activities with available audio recordings.

Communicative functions are summarized in sidebars throughout the lesson. Cross-references guide you to the **Gramática funcional** reference section at the end of each lesson.

Textbook activities

Additional online-only practice activities

Chat activities for conversational skill-building and oral practice

Each **Functional Context** section is self-contained, providing you with the tools and references you need to communicate in Spanish in specific real-world contexts.

Pair and group icons highlight communicative activities.

Photos, colorful graphics, and varied activity formats expose you to different cultural contexts and ways of using the language.

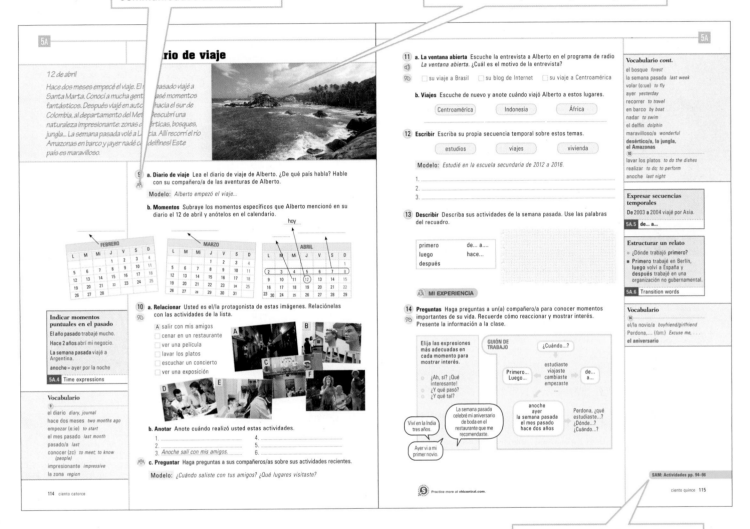

References in the footer show you exactly which pages in the **Student Activities Manual** correspond to each presentation.

Textbook activities
Additional online-only practice activities
Chat activities for conversational skill-building and oral practice

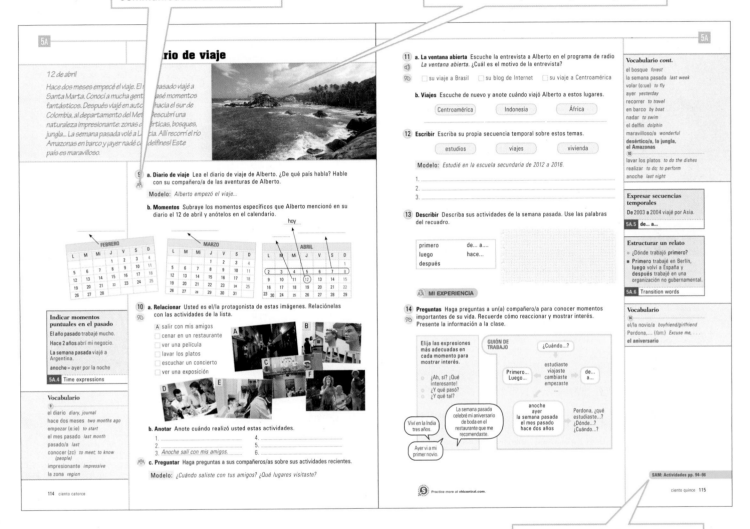

The next section of each lesson features a **protagonista** from the Spanish-speaking world whose job or lifestyle ties in to the lesson themes.

The protagonists (main characters) come from countries all over the Spanish-speaking world. They provide a personal connection and a practical application for the language you are learning.

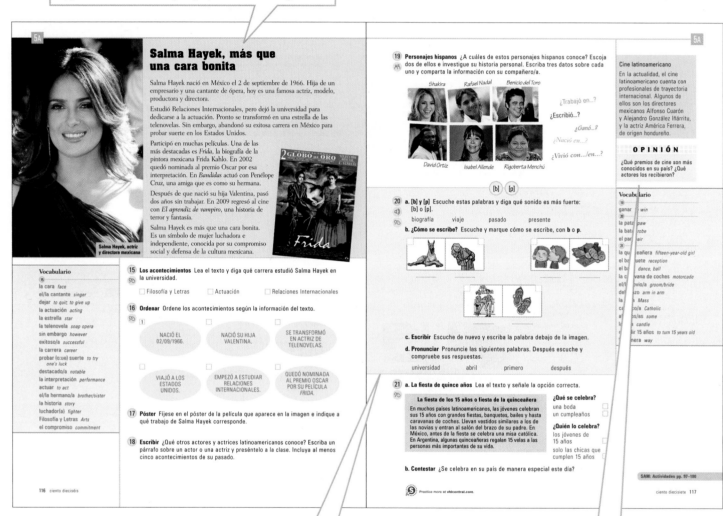

Units 1–6 include pronunciation practice. Units 7–18 feature expanded reading and writing practice.

Green and yellow sidebars provide additional cultural information, conversation topics, and communication strategies.

Textbook activities
Additional online-only practice activities

Tarea final and **Yo puedo...** bring together the lesson's cultural and communicative goals.

Tarea final
group projects give you the opportunity to apply the lesson structures and vocabulary in meaningful, real-life situations.

5A

TAREA FINAL

Biografía de la clase

Escriba cinco momentos importantes de su vida e indique cuándo ocurrieron.

- estudiar
- cambiar de casa/de ciudad
- empezar un proyecto
- viajar
- trabajar
- comprar una casa/un coche

Pregunte por los momentos importantes de la vida de su compañero/a.

¿Qué momentos importantes recuerdas de tu vida? ¿Cuándo...?

Comente con su compañero/a si hay algunas coincidencias en sus datos.

Elijan tres fechas y averigüen qué pasó en la vida de tres o cuatro compañeros de clase en esas fechas.

YO PUEDO...

- Puedo hablar de mi vida y de la de otras personas en el pasado.
  Escriba tres datos sobre su pasado con sus referencias personales.

- Puedo referirme a fechas en el pasado para contar acontecimientos.
  Escriba dos fechas sobre otras personas y qué pasó.

  ....

  ....

- Puedo nombrar los meses del año.
  Nombre tres meses.

  ....

- Puedo hablar de etapas en la vida.
  Describa brevemente dos etapas de su vida.

| El año pasado .... |
| Hace .... |
| La semana pasada .... |

| De .... |
| a .... |
| De .... |
| a .... |

Yo puedo... self-assessment gives you the opportunity to check your understanding of the lesson's communicative functions, and identify any areas where you need further review and practice.

Gramática funcional offers contextualized explanations of the structures behind the lesson's communicative functions.

Grammar explanations are organized according to the related communicative function in the lesson.

If you need further support, Grammar Reference numbers direct you to traditional grammar explanations in the appendix.

¡Póngalo en práctica! activities give you a chance to practice these structures right away.

GRAMÁTICA FUNCIONAL ⑤ Tutorials

5A.1 Talk about the past

Interrogative ¿cuándo? 9
The preterite of regular verbs 5.2.1

- Use the interrogative ¿Cuándo? to ask when an event occurred in the past.

  ¿Cuándo terminaste la escuela secundaria?
  When did you finish high school?

- Note that ¿Cuándo? asks *When?* in a general sense, whereas ¿A qué hora? prompts you to answer with a specific time of day.

- Use the preterite (**pretérito indefinido**) to express actions or states completed in the past. Spanish uses two simple tenses, the preterite and the imperfect, to talk about events in the past.

- Viajar, nacer, and vivir exemplify the conjugation patterns of regular -ar, -er, and -ir verbs in the **pretérito indefinido**.

	VIAJAR	NACER	VIVIR
(yo)	viajé	nací	viví
(tú)	viajaste	naciste	viviste
(usted, él, ella)	viajó	nació	vivió
(nosotros/as)	viajamos	nacimos	vivimos
(vosotros/as)	viajasteis	nacisteis	vivisteis
(ustedes, ellos/as)	viajaron	nacieron	vivieron

  ¿Cuándo **viajaste** a El Salvador?
  When did you travel to El Salvador?

  Mi hermana **nació** en 2002.
  My sister was born in 2002.

- The endings for regular -er and -ir verbs are identical in the preterite.

  Nadia **conoció** a su novio el día que **cumplió** 18 años.
  Nadia met her boyfriend the day she turned 18.

¡OJO!

Note that the **yo** and **usted/él/ella** forms of all three conjugations have written accents on the last syllable to show that it is stressed. If you forget to include the accent, it can change the meaning of the word entirely! **viajo** = *I travel*
viajó = *you/he/she traveled*

- The preterite **nosotros/as** forms of regular -ar and -ir verbs are identical to their present-tense forms. The context can indicate which tense is being used.

  Cada año **pasamos** las vacaciones en Puerto Vallarta.
  Every year, we spend our vacation in Puerto Vallarta.

  Pasamos cuatro noches en Puerto Vallarta en mayo.
  We spent four nights in Puerto Vallarta in May.

¡Póngalo en práctica!

G1 **Relacionar** Elija la forma del pretérito indefinido que corresponde a cada sujeto.

celebrar		
1. ellas		a. celebrasteis
2. nosotros		b. celebraron
3. vosotros		c. celebraste
4. usted		d. celebré
5. tú		e. celebramos
6. yo		f. celebró

subir		
1. ustedes		a. subió
2. yo		b. subisteis
3. tú		c. subí
4. él		d. subieron
5. nosotros		e. subimos
6. vosotras		f. subiste

G2 **Completar** Complete las oraciones con la forma correcta del verbo en el pretérito indefinido.

1. ¿Cuándo .... (nacer) tu hermana?
2. Nosotros .... (vivir) en Cuernavaca diez años.
3. Gonzalo .... (terminar) sus estudios en 2005.
4. Tú .... (recibir) el premio de poesía.
5. Mis padres .... (abrir) una tienda.
6. Gabriela y tú .... (viajar) a Lima en diciembre.

G3 **Crear oraciones** Escriba oraciones completas usando el pretérito indefinido.

1. Damián / trabajar / para una ONG
   ....
2. Laura y Beatriz / estudiar / en la UNAM
   ....
3. Analía y tú / abrir / una tienda de ropa
   ....
4. yo / subir / el Aconcagua
   ....
5. nosotros / visitar / muchos pueblos bonitos
   ....
6. tú / comprar / unas gafas de sol
   ....

⑤ Practice more at vhlcentral.com. ciento diecinueve **119**

Explanations in English, abundant examples, and graphics like charts and tables make the grammatical structures accessible.

¡OJO! boxes offer further explanation or clarification about structures and usage.

Animated grammar tutorials
Textbook activities
Additional online-only practice activities

Vocabulario summarizes all active vocabulary in the lesson.

Vocabulary is grouped by section, and listed in alphabetical order by part of speech.

VOCABULARIO · Vocabulary Tools

¡Felicidades, Manuela!

¡Felicidades!	*Congratulations!*
el acontecimiento	*event*
la boda	*wedding*
el carro (*Amér. L.*)	*car*
el cumpleaños (*invar.*)	*birthday*
enero	*January*
los estudios	*studies*
febrero	*February*
la fecha	*date*
el/la hijo/a	*son/daughter*
junio	*June*
marzo	*March*
el momento	*moment*
la mujer empresaria	*businesswoman*
noviembre	*November*
la ONG (organización no gubernamental)	*NGO (non-governmental organization)*
el pie de foto	*caption*
la Semana Santa	*Easter/Holy Week*
septiembre	*September*
la tarjeta de felicitación	*greeting card*
contigo	*with you*
cambiar de casa	*to move*
celebrar	*to celebrate*
compartir	*to share*
nacer (zc)	*to be born*
recordar (o:ue)	*to remember*
subir	*to climb*
activo/a	*active*
feliz (*pl.* felices)	*happy*
juntos/as	*together*

Diario de viaje

en barco	*by boat*
hace dos meses	*two months ago*
Perdona, ... (*fam.*)	*Excuse me, . . .*
el Amazonas	*Amazon River*
el aniversario	*anniversary*
el bosque	*forest*
el delfín	*dolphin*
el diario	*diary, journal*
la jungla	*jungle*
el mes pasado	*last month*
el/la novio/a	*boyfriend/girlfriend*
la semana pasada	*last week*
la zona	*region*
conocer (zc)	*to meet; to know (people)*
empezar (e:ie)	*to start*
lavar los platos	*to do the dishes*
nadar	*to swim*
realizar	*to do; to perform*
recorrer	*to travel*
volar (o:ue)	*to fly*
desértico/a	*desert-like*
impresionante	*impressive*
maravilloso/a	*wonderful*
pasado/a	*last*
anoche	*last night*
ayer	*yesterday*

Salma Hayek

del brazo	*arm in arm*
la actuación	*acting*
el baile	*dance, ball*
el banquete	*reception*
la bata	*robe*
el/la cantante	*singer*
la cara	*face*
la caravana de coches	*motorcade*
la carrera	*career*
el compromiso	*commitment*
la estrella	*star*
Filosofía y Letras	*Arts*
el/la hermano/a	*brother/sister*
la historia	*story*
la interpretación	*performance*
la manera	*way*
la misa	*Mass*
el/la novio/a	*groom/bride*
el par	*pair*
la pata	*paw*
la quinceañera	*fifteen-year-old girl*
la telenovela	*soap opera*
la vela	*candle*
actuar	*to act*
cumplir 15 años	*to turn 15 years old*
dejar	*to quit; to give up*
ganar	*to win*
probar (o:ue) suerte	*to try one's luck*
algunos/as	*some*
católico/a	*Catholic*
destacado/a	*notable*
exitoso/a	*successful*
luchador(a)	*fighter*
sin embargo	*however*

Variación léxica

la cara ↔ el rostro

el carro (*Amér. L.*) ↔ el coche (*Esp.*) ↔ el auto(móvil) (*Amér. L.*)

el/la chico/a ↔ el/la chavo/a (*Méx.*) ↔ el/la chaval(a) (*Esp.*) ↔ el/la botija (*Uru.*) ↔ el/la chamo/a (*Ven.*) ↔ el/la chamaco/a (*Amér. L.*)

la telenovela ↔ el culebrón (*Esp.*) ↔ la novela (*Arg.*) ↔ la teleserie (*Chi.*)

Variación léxica highlights alternate words and expressions used throughout the Spanish-speaking world. Active vocabulary is indicated in blue type, while the most high-frequency word or expression is listed first.

Vocabulary is listed in convenient column format that allows for easy studying.

Audio for all vocabulary items
Customizable study lists

Even-numbered units include **Estrategias** and **Competencias** activities in the **Avance** section for review.

Estrategias' tiered presentation reviews language-learning and communication strategies from the preceding two units.

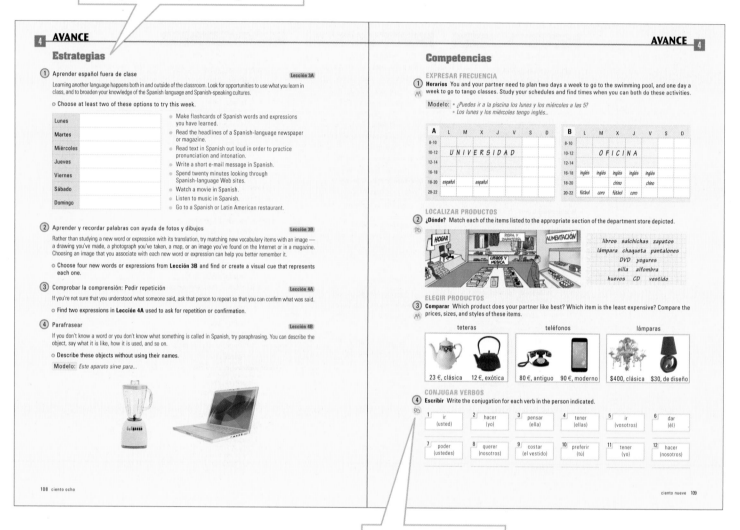

Competencias activities review vocabulary and structures presented in the preceding two units.

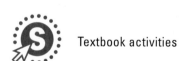
Textbook activities

Odd-numbered units feature **Lectura**, which presents literary and cultural readings that gradually increase in length and difficulty.

Vocabulario útil provides words and expressions to help you understand and talk about the reading.

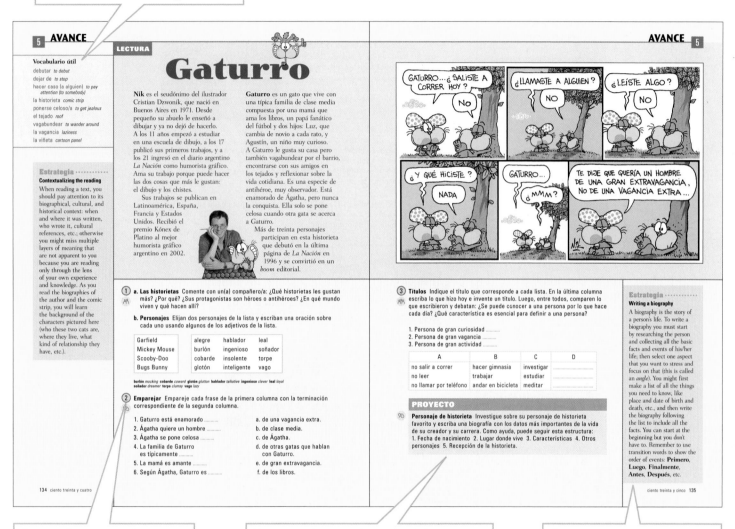

Pre-reading and reading comprehension activities help you better understand the text.

Proyecto gives you the opportunity to apply oral or written presentation strategies in the context of the reading and the unit themes.

Strategies give you tools to aid in reading comprehension, and written and oral expression.

Textbook activities
Composition engine for **Proyecto** writing activities

Each unit ends with a **Flash Cultura** video episode featuring fun and entertaining cultural information from around the Spanish-speaking world.

Listening and viewing strategies help you get the most out of the videos.

Flash Cultura episodes address unit themes from a different cultural perspective.

Video

La casa de Frida

Ya leyó sobre la carrera de Salma Hayek y sobre las familias en el mundo hispano. En este episodio de **Flash Cultura** va a ver la casa de la artista mexicana que Hayek interpretó en el cine: Frida Kahlo, una mujer que vivió una vida de película y tuvo un matrimonio inusual.

1. **Preguntas** Con un(a) compañero/a, hable de las siguientes preguntas: ¿Es importante el lugar donde vivimos? ¿Qué cosas expresa la decoración de una casa sobre sus habitantes? ¿Cuál puede ser el lugar más personal de una casa? ¿Por qué es interesante conocer la casa de los artistas? ¿Qué esperan encontrar en la casa de Frida?

2. **Mirar** Mire este episodio de **Flash Cultura**. Recuerde que el museo que va a ver es en realidad una casa, por lo que la visita empieza en la puerta principal y termina en el dormitorio de Frida.

Esta casa tiene varios detalles que revelan el amor de esta mexicana por la cultura de su país.

Uno de los espacios más atractivos de esta casa es este estudio...

3. **¿Verdadero o falso?** Indique si las oraciones son verdaderas (**V**) o falsas (**F**). Después, en parejas, corrijan las falsas.

1. Diego Rivera se casó dos veces con Frida.
2. Frida nunca tuvo una mascota en su casa.
3. El jardinero conoció a Diego.
4. El museo de Frida se llama Casa Amarilla.
5. Frida usó silla de ruedas varias veces.

4. **Guía de recorrido** Con un(a) compañero/a, escriba una breve guía de recorrido para el museo de Frida Kahlo. Luego lean su guía a la clase.

Modelo: *La casa es de color... El patio está en el centro de la casa y tiene... El jardinero trabaja allí desde hace... Frida pintó... En la cocina hay... Finalmente, llegamos al...*

Practice more at vhlcentral.com.

Streaming video of **Flash Cultura**
Textbook activities
Additional online-only practice activities
Chat activities for conversational skill-building and oral practice

The **Grammar Reference** in your textbook appendix provides additional support in the form of traditional explanations organized by grammar topics.

Grammatical structures are grouped and presented by part of speech.

Convenient cross-references direct you to the lessons where these structures are covered.

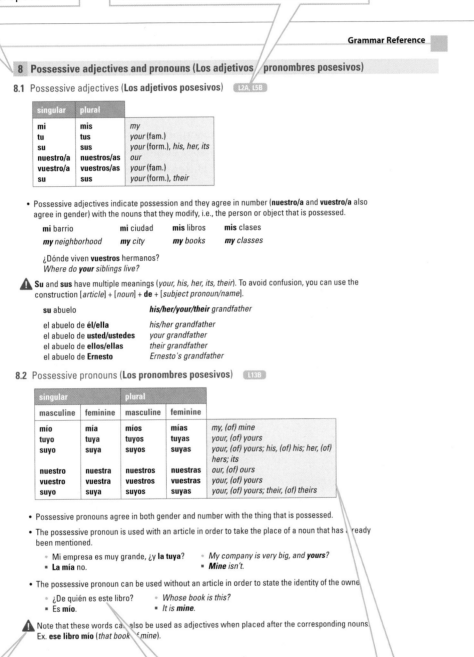

8 Possessive adjectives and pronouns (Los adjetivos y pronombres posesivos)

8.1 Possessive adjectives (**Los adjetivos posesivos**) `L2A, L5B`

singular	plural	
mi	mis	*my*
tu	tus	*your* (fam.)
su	sus	*your* (form.), *his, her, its*
nuestro/a	nuestros/as	*our*
vuestro/a	vuestros/as	*your* (fam.)
su	sus	*your* (form.), *their*

- Possessive adjectives indicate possession and they agree in number (**nuestro/a** and **vuestro/a** also agree in gender) with the nouns that they modify, i.e., the person or object that is possessed.

mi barrio	**mi** ciudad	**mis** libros	**mis** clases
my neighborhood	*my* city	*my* books	*my* classes

¿Dónde viven **vuestros** hermanos?
*Where do **your** siblings live?*

⚠ **Su** and **sus** have multiple meanings (*your, his, her, its, their*). To avoid confusion, you can use the construction [*article*] + [*noun*] + **de** + [*subject pronoun/name*].

su abuelo ***his/her/your/their*** grandfather

el abuelo de **él/ella** *his/her grandfather*
el abuelo de **usted/ustedes** *your grandfather*
el abuelo de **ellos/ellas** *their grandfather*
el abuelo de **Ernesto** *Ernesto's grandfather*

8.2 Possessive pronouns (**Los pronombres posesivos**) `L13B`

singular		plural		
masculine	feminine	masculine	feminine	
mío	mía	míos	mías	*my, (of) mine*
tuyo	tuya	tuyos	tuyas	*your, (of) yours*
suyo	suya	suyos	suyas	*your, (of) yours; his, (of) his; her, (of) hers; its*
nuestro	nuestra	nuestros	nuestras	*our, (of) ours*
vuestro	vuestra	vuestros	vuestras	*your, (of) yours*
suyo	suya	suyos	suyas	*your, (of) yours; their, (of) theirs*

- Possessive pronouns agree in both gender and number with the thing that is possessed.
- The possessive pronoun is used with an article in order to take the place of a noun that has already been mentioned.

  ▪ Mi empresa es muy grande, ¿y **la tuya**? ▫ *My company is very big, and **yours**?*
  ▪ **La mía** no. ▪ ***Mine** isn't.*

- The possessive pronoun can be used without an article in order to state the identity of the owner.

  ▫ ¿De quién es este libro? ▫ *Whose book is this?*
  ▪ Es **mío**. ▪ *It is **mine**.*

⚠ Note that these words can also be used as adjectives when placed after the corresponding nouns. Ex. **ese libro mío** (*that book of mine*).

A65

Attention icons highlight exceptions and structures that are often difficult for beginning Spanish students.

Examples that highlight the target structure provide ample models of proper usage.

Charts and tables consolidate information for easy reference.

Learning Spanish with PROTAGONISTAS

PROTAGONISTAS, Second Edition, offers a communicative approach to learning Spanish that is rich in contemporary culture and focuses on Spanish in everyday life. The **PROTAGONISTAS** approach is extremely practical and will enable you to use Spanish in real-life situations quickly. Each lesson has what is referred to as a "notion" or context, such as grocery shopping or housework and a few "functions" within that notion, such as asking how much food items cost and dividing up chores with a roommate.

Lessons are short, and each one integrates new vocabulary and grammar into the activities and readings and then places that new information in a broader context—all of which help make your experience learning Spanish successful and enjoyable. Different types of classroom activities— pair work, small-group work, class circulation, information gap, and so forth—help you learn to communicate effectively from the very first lesson of the program.

PROTAGONISTAS offers an easy-to-use layout with each lesson organized in the same way: three presentation spreads where vocabulary and communicative functions are presented through readings and activities, followed by review and self-evaluation activities and the **Gramática funcional** and **Vocabulario** reference sections at the end. Additional support is provided through the **Grammar Reference** and the bilingual glossary in the appendix, as well as Supersite activities for extra practice and communication.

In addition, easy-to-identify cross-references and repeated features provide support at every step of the process.

Sidebars

Vocabulario sidebars list the active vocabulary presented on that spread with English translations.

Communicative functions are called out in convenient sidebars, including examples of usage and reference to the grammatical structures being practiced.

¡OJO! notes provide clarification or further linguistic or cultural information to help you better use the new structures in context.

Cultural notes offer supplementary cultural readings to help you contextualize the lesson themes.

Estrategias provide you with linguistic tools and learning strategies to help you navigate reading, writing, listening to, and conversing in Spanish.

Opinión sidebars present questions geared toward stimulating personalized conversation about the lesson themes.

Studying Vocabulary

PROTAGONISTAS takes an innovative approach to teaching vocabulary. You learn the words that you need in order to complete the communicative task at hand.

Vocabulary is presented at three different levels. First, convenient **Vocabulario** sidebars list the active words on the spread where they are used, in the order in which they are used. English translations are provided for easy reference, and cognates are listed in bold without translations, to help you see the connections between Spanish and English.

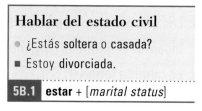

The **Vocabulario** page at the end of each lesson summarizes the active vocabulary presented in that lesson. Here, all words are listed with their English translation, and words are grouped alphabetically by part of speech.

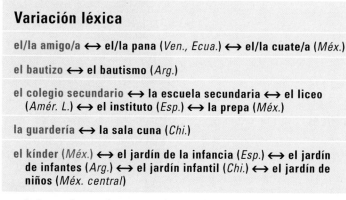

Finally, the Spanish-English and English-Spanish glossaries in your textbook appendix list all the text's active vocabulary with convenient references to the lesson where each word is presented.

In addition, most lessons include a **Variación léxica** feature that provides alternate words and expressions used throughout the Spanish-speaking world. Note that only those terms listed in blue are considered active vocabulary.

Studying Grammar

Grammar structures are also presented at three levels in **PROTAGONISTAS**.

Sidebars in the lesson provide examples of the language structures you need in order to complete the communicative function presented on the page.

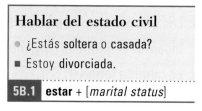

These structures are explained in their functional context in the **Gramática funcional** reference section at the end of each lesson, together with examples of usage and practice activities to reinforce what you have learned.

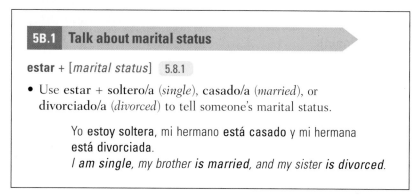

Finally, the **Grammar Reference** in your textbook appendix offers a thorough traditional grammar reference where topics are organized by part of speech.

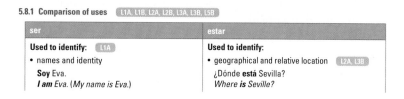

Flash Cultura Video Program

The dynamic, engaging **Flash Cultura** video program draws from the cultural themes addressed in the text and provides an entertaining conclusion to the **Avance** section of each unit. Young people from all over the Spanish-speaking world share aspects of life in their countries with each other. The similarities and differences among Spanish-speaking countries that come up through their exchanges will challenge you to think about your own cultural practices and values.

The segments provide valuable cultural insights as well as linguistic input; the episodes will expose you to a wide variety of accents and vocabulary.

Here are the **Flash Cultura** episodes featured in **PROTAGONISTAS**.

Unidad 1: Encuentros en la plaza (Argentina)

Unidad 2: Los estudios (Mexico)

Unidad 3: ¡Fútbol en España! (Spain)

Unidad 4: Comprar en los mercados (Costa Rica)

Unidad 5: La casa de Frida (Mexico)

Unidad 6: ¿Estrés? ¿Qué estrés? (Spain)

Unidad 7: El mundo del trabajo (Ecuador)

Unidad 8: Arquitectura modernista (Spain)

Unidad 9: Las fiestas (Puerto Rico)

Unidad 10: La salud (Argentina)

Unidad 11: Machu Picchu: encanto y misterio (Peru)

Unidad 12: Las relaciones personales (Spain)

Unidad 13: Inventos argentinos (Argentina)

Unidad 14: La comida latina (U.S.A.)

Unidad 15: Las alpacas (Peru)

Unidad 16: Puerto Rico, ¿nación o estado? (Puerto Rico)

Unidad 17: Lo mejor de Argentina (Argentina)

Unidad 18: Palacios del arte (Spain)

Icons and Resources

Familiarize yourself with these icons that appear throughout **PROTAGONISTAS**.

(S) Supersite content available	◁)) Listening activity/section	Chat activity
(∞) Activity available on Supersite	Pair activity	
(S) Additional activities available on Supersite	Group activity	

The SAM Activities tab on each presentation spread shows you exactly which pages in your Student Activities Manual practice the topics presented on that spread.

SAM: Actividades pp. 69–71

Student Ancillaries

- **Student Activities Manual**

    The Student Activities Manual (SAM) provides additional practice of the vocabulary and grammar in each textbook lesson. The SAM integrates written and audio activities, as well as reading comprehension and self-assessment for every lesson. Audio activities build listening comprehension, speaking, and pronunciation skills.

- **SAM MP3s**

    The SAM MP3s provide the recordings to be used in conjunction with the audio activities in the Student Activities Manual. These recordings are available on the **PROTAGONISTAS** Supersite.

- **Textbook MP3s**

    The Textbook MP3s are the recordings for the listening activities in each lesson of **PROTAGONISTAS**, as well as the active vocabulary in each end-of-lesson **Vocabulario** list. These recordings are available on the **PROTAGONISTAS** Supersite.

- **Supersite**

    Practice from the textbook, additional practice, as well as all audio and **Flash Cultura** video materials related to the **PROTAGONISTAS** program are available on the Supersite. An online Student Activities Manual (WebSAM) also appears on the Supersite. See page xxviii for additional information on the **PROTAGONISTAS** Supersite.

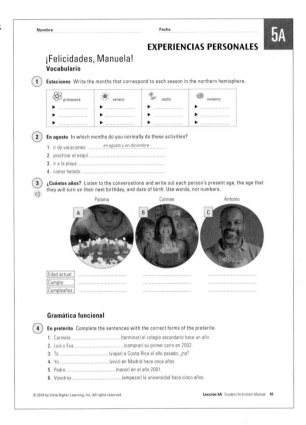

Instructor Ancillaries

- **Instructor's Annotated Edition**

    The IAE contains a wealth of information and resources to support classroom teaching.

- **PROTAGONISTAS Instructor Supersite**

    In addition to full access to the student Supersite, the password-protected Instructor Supersite offers a robust course-management system that allows instructors to assign activities and track student progress. Instructor Supersite access includes:

- Gradebook and course management
- Communication center for instructor notifications and feedback
- Textbook and SAM audio MP3s
- **Flash Cultura** episodes in streaming video
- Video scripts and translations
- Audio scripts
- Testing Program RTFs, PDFs, MP3s
- Detailed Lesson Plans
- Interactive Worksheets
- Answer Keys

Supersite

The **PROTAGONISTAS, Second Edition,** Supersite provides a wealth of resources for both students and instructors. Icons indicate exactly which resources are available on the Supersite for each section of every lesson. Plus, the Supersite is iPad®-friendly*, so it can be accessed on the go!

For Students

Student resources, available through an access code, are provided with the purchase of a new student text. Here is an example of what you will find at **vhlcentral.com:**

- Activities from the student text, most with auto-grading
- Chat activities for conversational skill-building and oral practice
- Additional practice for all textbook sections
- Record & Compare audio activities
- All audio material related to the **PROTAGONISTAS** program
- Animated grammar tutorials
- The **Flash Cultura** video program, in streaming video
- MP3 files for the complete **PROTAGONISTAS** textbook and SAM Audio Program
- Customizable study lists for vocabulary words
- vText online interactive student edition with access to Supersite activities, audio, and video

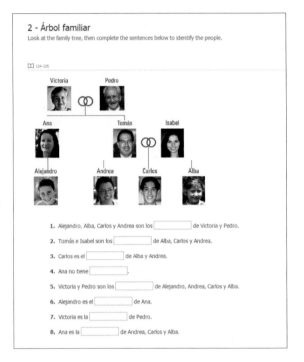

For Instructors

Instructors have access to the entire student site, as well as these key resources:

- The entire Instructor Ancillary package, including Testing Program and Lesson Plans, in downloadable and printable formats
- A robust course management system
- Voice Board capabilities for you to create additional activities
- And much, much more…

*Students must use a computer for audio recording and select presentations and tools that require Flash or Shockwave.

Acknowledgments

On behalf of its authors and editors, Vista Higher Learning expresses its sincere appreciation to the instructors and college professors across the U.S. who contributed their ideas and suggestions.

PROTAGONISTAS, Second Edition, is the direct result of extensive reviews and ongoing input from both students and instructors using the First Edition. Accordingly, we gratefully acknowledge those who shared their suggestions, recommendations, and ideas as we prepared this Second Edition.

Reviewers

Carol A. Anderson
Jamestown Community College, NY

Laura K. Anderson
Jamestown Community College, NY

Theresa R. Baginski
Jamestown Community College, NY

Richard Bailey
Seabury Hall, HI

Sandra Caballero, MA
Christopher Newport University, VA

Danielle Cahill Velardi
Christopher Newport University, VA

Elizabeth Ann Giannone
Portland State University, OR

Rocío Gordon
Christopher Newport University, VA

Helena Hernández
Georgia Southern University, GA

Melissa Katz
Albright College, PA

Alice A. Miano
Stanford University, CA

Elaine M. Miller
Christopher Newport University, VA

Dr. Margaret L. Morris
South Carolina State University, SC

Camelia Rivera Deller
Christopher Newport University, VA

Janice E. Rodriguez
Albright College, PA

Judy L. Rodriguez
California State University, Sacramento, CA

Laura Ruiz-Scott
Scottsdale Community College, AZ

Albert Shank
Scottsdale Community College, AZ

Víctor Tijerina
University of Texas–Pan American, TX

Dr. Ingrid Watson-Miller
Norfolk State University, VA

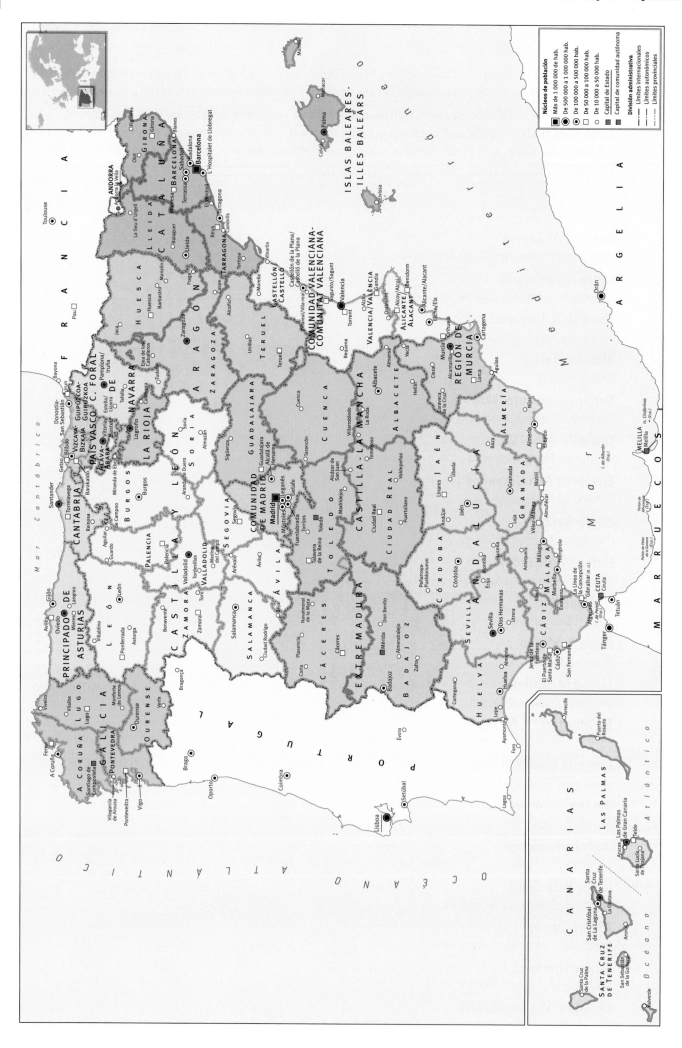

Map of Latin America

Núcleos de población

- ■ Más de 3 000 000 de hab.
- ⊙ De 1 000 000 a 3 000 000 de hab.
- ▫ De 500 000 a 1 000 000 de hab.
- ○ Menos de 500 000 hab.
- ■ Capital de Estado

A. y B. Antigua y Barbuda	**S. L.** Sta. Lucía	
C. y N. S. Cristóbal y Nieves	**V. y G.** S. Vicente y las Granadinas	
D. Dominica	**G.** Granada	

PROTAGONISTAS

Benicio del Toro,
San Juan (Puerto Rico)
¡Buenos días!
1A

Joan Fusté,
Barcelona (España)
¡Hola!
1B

Juan Tomás Álvarez,
Ciudad de Panamá (Panamá)
¿Qué tal?
2A

Rosa Iglesias,
Haro (España)
¡Buenas tardes!
2B

Pablo Linares,
Colonia (Uruguay)
¡Buenas!
3A

Carmen Abreu,
La Romana (República Dominicana)
¡Buenas noches!
4B

Olga Piedrahita,
Bogotá (Colombia)
Hola, ¿qué tal?
3B

Paco Suárez García,
Madrid (España)
¿Qué pasa?
4A

Greet people

- ¡Hola!
- ¡Buenos días!
- ¡Buenas tardes!
- ¿Qué tal?
- ¡Buenas noches!
- ¡Buenas noches!

0.1 Greetings

Vocabulario

(1)

Buenos días. *Good morning.*

Hola. *Hi.*

¿Qué tal? *How are you?; How's it going?*

Buenas tardes. *Good afternoon.*

Buenas. (*fam.*) *Hi.*

¿Qué pasa? *What's up?*

Buenas noches. *Good evening.; Good night.*

Estrategia

Vocabulario lists the active vocabulary that you learn and use in each activity, in the order in which it is presented. These words and expressions are summarized on the last page of each lesson.

---

1 **Hola** Listen to these greetings and indicate the order in which you hear them.

..... ¡HOLA!   ..... ¿QUÉ TAL?

..... BUENOS DÍAS.   ..... HOLA, BUENAS TARDES.

2 **Protagonistas** In this lesson, you will meet the **protagonistas** (*protagonists*) you will encounter throughout this text. Look at the photos and read the labels. Now, listen to the recording. You will hear the names of five **protagonistas.** Check off the names you hear.

3 **Países** The **protagonistas** come from all over the Spanish-speaking world. Look at their hometowns. Then, with a partner, take turns matching these cities and towns to the corresponding country.

1. Bogotá ....
2. Haro ....
3. San Juan ....
4. Madrid ....
5. La Romana ....
6. Ciudad de Panamá ....
7. Barcelona ....
8. Colonia ....

¿Cómo te llamas?

Salma Hayek, Coatzacoalcos (México)

Hola, soy Salma. ¿Cómo te llamas? **5A**

Bernardo Maldonado y Juanita Rodríguez de Maldonado, McAllen, Texas (Estados Unidos)

Yo me llamo Bernardo y ella se llama Juanita. Encantados. **5B**

Domingo Buendía, Quito (Ecuador)

Yo soy Domingo Buendía. Mucho gusto. **6A**

Felipe Daza, Santiago de Chile (Chile) y Julia Navarro, Vancouver (Canadá)

Se llama Julia. Se llama Felipe. **6B**

Jorge Drexler, Montevideo (Uruguay)

Me llamo Jorge Drexler. Encantado. **7A**

Guadalupe Rodríguez Córdoba (Argentina)

Soy Guadalupe. Encantada. **7B**

Justo Gallego, Mejorada del Campo (España)

Buenas tardes, me llamo Justo Gallego. **8A**

Introduce yourself

- ¿Cómo te llamas?
- **Me llamo** Andrés Rodríguez Sánchez. **Encantado.**
- **Encantada.**

- ¿Cómo se llama usted?
- **Me llamo** Emiliana. **Mucho gusto.**

0.2 The verb **llamarse**

Vocabulario

④

¿Cómo te llamas? (*fam.*) *What is your name?*

(Yo) soy... *I am . . .*

(Yo) me llamo... *My name is . . .*

(Él/Ella) se llama... *His/Her name is . . .*

Encantado/a. *Pleased to meet you.*

Mucho gusto. *Pleased to meet you.*

Él/Ella es... *He/She is . . .*

¿Y tú? (*fam.*) *And you?*

¿Y usted? (*form.*) *And you?*

¿Cómo se llama? (*form.*) *What is your name?*

---

4 **Combinar** Match words from the two categories to show the different ways of telling people's names.

se
me
te

llamas
llamo
llama

5 **Encantado** Decide whether these **protagonistas** would say **encantado**, **encantada**, or **encantados**. Check your answers with a partner.

1. Salma Hayek ....
2. Felipe Daza ....
3. Héctor y Gabriela ....
4. Jorge Edwards ....
5. Carlos y Lola ....
6. Juanita Rodríguez de Maldonado
....

6 **a. Me llamo...** Greet a partner and introduce yourself. Then, switch partners and introduce yourself to another classmate.

Modelo:
- ¡Hola! Me llamo Juan Domínguez. ¿Cómo se llama usted?
- Lisa Scanlon.
- Encantado.
- Encantada.

b. Se llama... Now introduce yourself and your classmates to the rest of the class. Listen carefully so you can remember the names of those who were introduced before you.

Me llamo Fabricio.

Se llama Fabricio, me llamo Alice.

Se llama Fabricio, se llama Alice, me llamo Didier...

Fernanda Pimentel y Alberto Tapia,
San Salvador (El Salvador)

Yo soy Fernanda y él es Alberto. Encantados.

8B

Luis Soriano,
La Gloria (Colombia)

Me llamo Luis Soriano. ¿Y tú?

9A

Lola Sanz,
Oviedo (España)

Hola, soy Lola. ¿Qué tal?

9B

Carlos Salazar,
La Habana (Cuba)

Buenos días. Me llamo Carlos Salazar.

10A

Jorge Edwards,
Santiago de Chile (Chile)

Me llamo Jorge Edwards. Y usted, ¿cómo se llama?

10B

José Carlos Segura Prados,
San Juan (Puerto Rico)

Hola, yo soy José Carlos. Encantado.

11A

Gabriela Bettini y Héctor Varela,
El Calafate (Argentina)

Yo soy Héctor y ella se llama Gabriela. Mucho gusto.

11B

hotel	aeropuerto	señorita	taxi	jamón
café	bar	mercado	paella	España
metro	restaurante	banco	leche	moneda
mañana	museo	policía	azúcar	chocolate

(7) **a. Palabras en español** Look at these Spanish words. Which ones are similar in English? Do you know the English equivalent of any of these words?

b. El alfabeto Now look at the letters of the Spanish alphabet. Which letter doesn't exist in English? Which of the words above use this letter?

(8) **a. Letras** Listen to the pronunciation of each letter of the Spanish alphabet. Repeat the letters after the speaker.

b. Palabras Now listen to the pronunciation of the words listed above. Which pronunciations surprise you? Listen again and say each word aloud after you hear it.

c. Palabras adicionales Listen to the pronunciation of these words, and pay close attention to the letters marked in red. Repeat the words after the speaker.

La Habana   paella   Chile   Ibiza   jamón   Toledo

Spell

A	(a)	Ñ	(eñe)
B	(be)	O	(o)
C	(ce)	P	(pe)
D	(de)	Q	(cu)
E	(e)	R	(erre)
F	(efe)	S	(ese)
G	(ge)	T	(te)
H	(hache)	U	(u)
I	(i)	V	(ve)
J	(jota)	W	(doble ve)
K	(ka)	X	(equis)
L	(ele)	Y	(i griega)
M	(eme)	Z	(zeta)
N	(ene)		

0.3 The Spanish alphabet

MI EXPERIENCIA

(9) **¿Qué tal?** Greet and introduce yourself to your classmates.

GUIÓN DE TRABAJO

Hola.
Buenos días.
Buenas tardes.
Buenas noches.
¿Qué tal?
¿Qué pasa?

→ Me llamo...
(Yo) soy...

→ ¿Y tú?
¿Y usted?

Encantado/a.
Mucho gusto.

Estrategia · · · · · · · · · · ·

Mi experiencia activities guide you through conversations with your classmates that will help you review and reinforce the lesson vocabulary and structures in a meaningful, personalized context.

¡Hasta pronto!

Ricardo Hernández,
México, D.F. (México)

¿Cómo se escribe *Marifé*? ¡Gracias!

12A

Marifé Cester,
Salamanca (España)

Eme-a-erre-i-efe-e con acento.

12B

Nelson Morales, Lima (Perú)
y Edgar Hugo Torrico, La Paz (Bolivia)

¿Cómo se escribe *Rubio*?

13A

Cristina Rubio,
Monterrey (México)

Con be de *burro*.

13B

Acacio Maye Ocomo,
Malabo (Guinea Ecuatorial)

Adiós, hasta mañana.

14A

Macarena Berlín,
Madrid (España)

¡Buenas noches!

14B

Evaristo Acebedo,
Miami, Florida (Estados Unidos)

¡Nos vemos!

15A

Ask for clarification

- ¿Cómo se escribe *Acebedo*?
- A-ce-e-be-e-de-o.

0.4 Questions for clarification

Say goodbye

- ¡Hasta luego!
- ¡Adiós!
- ✦ ¡Hasta mañana!

0.5 Farewells

Vocabulario

10

Hasta pronto. *See you soon.*

¿Cómo se escribe...? *How do you spell . . . ?*

con acento *with an accent*

¡Gracias! *Thank you!*

Adiós. *Goodbye.*

Hasta mañana. *See you tomorrow.*

¡Nos vemos! *See you!*

Hasta la vista. *See you later.*

Chau. *Bye.*

Hasta luego. *See you later.*

el saludo *greeting*

la despedida *farewell*

12

el nombre *name*

el país *country*

la ciudad *city*

el burro *donkey*

la vaca *cow*

---

10 **Saludos y despedidas** Listen to the recordings and decide whether each person is saying hello (**saludos**) or goodbye (**despedidas**).

	saludos	despedidas
1	☐	☐
2	☐	☐
3	☐	☐
4	☐	☐

11 **a. ¿Cómo se escribe...?** With a partner, look at maps of Spain and Latin America. Find where each of the **protagonistas** is from, and take turns asking each other how to spell the names of different cities and countries.

> **Modelo:** ● ¿Cómo se escribe *Arequipa*?
> ■ A-erre-e...

b. Lista Together, make a list of city and country names for five letters in the alphabet. Are there any letters for which you can't find examples?

12 **Nombres, países y ciudades** As a class, try to come up with a name (**nombre**), a country (**país**), or a city (**ciudad**) that starts with or contains each letter in the alphabet.

> **Modelo:** *Eñe... ¡España!*

LETRA	NOMBRE	PAÍS	CIUDAD

Marina Sánchez, Caracas (Venezuela)
¡Hasta la vista!
15B

Ingrid Betancourt, Bogotá (Colombia)
¡Adiós!
16A

Estela Salvador, Ciudad de Guatemala (Guatemala) y Mario Martínez, Managua (Nicaragua)
¡Hasta mañana!
16B

Marián Rico, San José (Costa Rica)
¡Hasta pronto!
18B

Salvador Moncada, Tegucigalpa (Honduras)
Adiós, buenas tardes.
17A

Rubén Sosa, Buenos Aires (Argentina) y Amanda Roa, Asunción (Paraguay)
¡Chau!
17B

Rafael Nadal, Manacor (España)
¡Hasta luego!
18A

YO PUEDO...

- **Puedo saludar a la gente.**
  Write three expressions you have learned to greet people.

  ....

- **Puedo presentarme y responder a una presentación.**
  Complete this conversation.

  - ¿Cómo te ....?
  - Me .... Javier.
  - Mucho gusto.
  - ....

- **Puedo deletrear en español.**
  Practice spelling these words in Spanish.

  - saludo   • mañana
  - México   • encantado

- **Puedo preguntar cómo se escribe una palabra o un nombre.**
  - ¿ .... hotel?
  - Con hache.

- **Puedo despedirme de la gente.**
  Write three expressions you have learned to say goodbye.

  ....

¡OJO!

In Spanish, the letters **b** (be) and **v** (ve) are pronounced the same. To distinguish between the two, many Spanish speakers call **b** be de burro (*donkey*) and **v** ve de vaca (*cow*). In Spain, the letter **v** is called **uve**, so this distinction is not necessary.

Estrategia ··············

Yo puedo activities at the end of each lesson help you review the communicative functions you have learned in the lesson. These activities show you how much you learned and can help you identify which functions you need to review.

GRAMÁTICA FUNCIONAL

0.1 Greet people

Greetings; Interrogative words 9

- Use expressions such as **Hola**, **¿Qué tal?**, and **¿Qué pasa?** to greet people in an informal context. Note that Spanish uses both opening and closing question marks.

  - **Hola**, Ana, **¿qué pasa?**
    Hi, Ana, what's up?

  - **Hola**, Jaime, **¿qué tal?**
    Hi, Jaime, how's it going?

- In both formal and informal contexts, use the expressions **Buenos días** (*Good morning*), **Buenas tardes** (*Good afternoon*), or **Buenas noches** (*Good evening*) to greet people according to the time of day.

  - **Buenos días**, señor Martínez.
    Good morning, Mr. Martínez.

  - **Buenos días**.
    Good morning.

0.2 Introduce yourself

The verb **llamarse** 5.7   Reflexive pronouns 5.7.1

- To ask someone's name, say **¿Cómo te llamas?** in an informal context or **¿Cómo se llama (usted)?** in a formal context.

- To answer, say **Me llamo** + [*name*] or **(Yo) soy** + [*name*].

  - Hola, **¿cómo te llamas?**
    Hi. What's your name?

  - Hola, **soy Marta**.
    Hi, I'm Marta.

  - Buenas tardes. **¿Cómo se llama usted?**
    Good afternoon. What is your name?

  - **Me llamo** Jorge García.
    My name is Jorge García.

- When meeting someone for the first time, say **Encantado** if you are male or **Encantada** if you are female. Both men and women can also say **Mucho gusto**.

0.3 Spell

The Spanish alphabet 1.1

- Review the Spanish alphabet on page 3. Note that the letter **ñ** does not appear in the English alphabet and the letters **k** and **w** are used only in words of foreign origin.

- **Ch (che)** and **ll (elle)** are no longer considered letters in the Spanish alphabet; they are included under **c** and **l** in alphabetized lists. When spelling aloud, **ch/c-h** and **ll/doble l** will be equally understood.

0.4 Ask for clarification

Questions for clarification
Prepositions: **con** 10.4   Interrogative words 9

- To ask how a word is spelled, say **¿Cómo se escribe** + [*word*]? Be sure to say **¡Gracias!** (*Thank you!*) when someone helps you.

  ¿Cómo se escribe *Montevideo?*
  How do you spell Montevideo?

- To explain that a word is spelled with a certain letter, or that a letter takes a written accent, use the word **con** (*with*).

  con hache   a **con acento**
  with an h   *with an accent on the a*

¡Póngalo en práctica!

G1 **Diálogos** Complete the dialogues with appropriate words or expressions.

- Hola, María, ¿(1)......................... tal?
- ¡(2)........................., Teresa!

- (3)................ noches, señora Gutiérrez.
- Buenas (4)................, señor Ríos.

- Buenos (5)........................., Martín.
- Hola, Gladys, ¿qué (6).........................?

G2 **Conversación** Complete the conversation.

¿Cómo (1)................................... llamas?

Me (2)................................... Raúl Soria. ¿Y tú?

Yo (3)................................... Clara, Clara Esteban.

(4)................................... .

G3 **El alfabeto español** Practice spelling these words in Spanish.

¿Cómo se ....?

paella	café
jamón	azúcar
Canadá	taxi
señorita	hotel
chocolate	Guatemala
aeropuerto	restaurante

¡ .... !

GRAMÁTICA FUNCIONAL

0.5 **Say goodbye**

Farewells; Exclamation points **1.5**

- Use expressions such as ¡**Adiós!** (*Goodbye!*), ¡**Hasta luego!** (*See you later!*), ¡**Chau!** (*Bye!*), and ¡**Hasta pronto!** (*See you soon!*) to say goodbye in Spanish. Note that Spanish uses both opening and closing exclamation marks.

  - ¡Hasta luego, Luisa!
    See you later, Luisa!
  - Adiós. ¡Hasta mañana!
    Goodbye. See you tomorrow!

- ¡**Buenas noches!** (*Good evening; Good night*) can be used as both a greeting and a farewell.

¡Póngalo en práctica!

G4 **Completar** Write the missing words or punctuation.

1. ¡............................ luego!
2. ¡............................ noches!
3. ¡............................ pronto!
4. .... Adiós!

 Practice more at **vhlcentral.com**.

VOCABULARIO 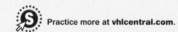 Vocabulary Tools

Protagonistas

Buenas. (*fam.*)	Hi.
Buenas noches.	Good evening.; Good night.
Buenas tardes.	Good afternoon.
Buenos días.	Good morning.
Hola.	Hi.
¿Qué pasa?	What's up?
¿Qué tal?	How are you?; How's it going?

¿Cómo te llamas?

¿Cómo te llamas? (*fam.*)	What is your name?
¿Y tú? (*fam.*)	And you?
¿Cómo se llama? (*form.*)	What is your name?
¿Y usted? (*form.*)	And you?
(Yo) me llamo...	My name is . . .
(Yo) soy...	I am . . .
(Él/Ella) se llama...	His/Her name is . . .
Él/Ella es...	He/She is . . .
Encantado/a.	Pleased to meet you.
Mucho gusto.	Pleased to meet you.
el aeropuerto	airport
el azúcar	sugar
el banco	bank; bench
el bar	bar; café
el café	coffee; café
el chocolate	chocolate
el hotel	hotel

el jamón	ham
la leche	milk
el mercado	market
el metro	subway
la moneda	coin
el museo	museum
la paella	paella
la policía	police
el restaurante	restaurant
la señorita	young lady; Miss
el taxi	taxi
mañana	tomorrow

¡Hasta pronto!

Adiós.	Goodbye.
Chau.	Bye.
Hasta la vista.	See you later.
Hasta luego.	See you later.
Hasta mañana.	See you tomorrow.
Hasta pronto.	See you soon.
¡Nos vemos!	See you!
¿Cómo se escribe...?	How do you spell . . . ?
con acento	with an accent
¡Gracias!	Thank you!
el burro	donkey
la ciudad	city
la despedida	farewell
el nombre	name
el país	country
el saludo	greeting
la vaca	cow

Países y ciudades

Argentina	Argentina
Bolivia	Bolivia
Canadá	Canada
Chile	Chile
Ciudad de Guatemala	Guatemala City
Ciudad de Panamá	Panama City
Colombia	Colombia
Costa Rica	Costa Rica
Cuba	Cuba
Ecuador	Ecuador
El Salvador	El Salvador
España	Spain
Estados Unidos (EE.UU.)	United States (U.S.A.)
Guatemala	Guatemala
Guinea Ecuatorial	Equatorial Guinea
Honduras	Honduras
La Habana	Havana
México	Mexico
México, D.F.	Mexico City
Nicaragua	Nicaragua
Panamá	Panama
Paraguay	Paraguay
Perú	Peru
Puerto Rico	Puerto Rico
República Dominicana	Dominican Republic
Uruguay	Uruguay
Venezuela	Venezuela

SPANISH TERMS for direction lines and classroom use

Below is a list of useful words and expressions that appear in the direction lines of your text, as well as expressions your instructor might use in class.

¿Cómo se dice...?	How do you say . . . ?
¿Qué significa...?	What does . . . mean?
No entiendo.	I don't understand.
Más despacio, por favor.	Slower, please.
Competencia	Competence; Ability
Estrategia	Strategy
Lectura	Reading
Mi experiencia	My experience
¡Ojo!	Be careful!
Protagonistas	Protagonists
Yo puedo...	I can . . .
el acontecimiento	event
la actividad	activity
el/la alumno/a	student
el anuncio	ad(vertisement)
el cartel/el póster	poster
la casilla	(check) box
el/la compañero/a	classmate
los datos	information; data
el diálogo/ la conversación	dialogue/ conversation
el ejemplo	example
la entrevista	interview
la fecha	date
el final	end, ending
el folleto	brochure
la foto(grafía)	photo(graph)
la frase	phrase
la hoja (de papel)	sheet (of paper)
la imagen	picture, image
el juego	game
el libro	book
la lista	list
el modelo	model
el número	number
la oración	sentence
la página	page
la palabra	word
el párrafo	paragraph
la pregunta	question
la prueba	test
el recuadro	box
la respuesta	answer
(el resto de) la clase	(the rest of) the class
la tabla	table/chart
la tarea	homework
la terminación	ending
el texto	textbook; reading

el titular	title/headline
la viñeta (cómica)	cartoon panel
el/la/los/las siguiente(s)...	the next/following . . .
que falta(n)	missing
(in)correcto/a	(in)correct
¿Verdadero o falso?	True or false?
¿Masculino o femenino?	Masculine or feminine?
antes	before
después	after
luego...	then . . .
de nuevo/otra vez	again
¿Cómo...?	How . . . ?
¿Cuál(es)...?	Which . . . ?
¿Cuándo...?	When . . . ?
¿Dónde...?	Where . . . ?
¿Por qué...?	Why . . . ?
¿Qué...?	What . . . ?
¿Quién(es)...?	Who . . . ?
En parejas/grupos...	In pairs/groups . . .
Adivine(n)...	Guess . . .
Agrupe(n)...	Group/Organize . . .
Anote(n)...	Write down . . .
Añada(n)...	Add . . .
Averigüe(n)...	Find out . . .
Busque(n)...	Look for . . .
Calcule(n)...	Calculate . . .
Clasifique(n)...	Classify . . .
Coloque(n)...	Place . . .
Comente(n)...	Discuss . . .
Compare(n)....	Compare . . .
Comparta(n)...	Share . . .
Complete(n)...	Complete . . .
Compruebe(n)...	Check/Verify . . .
Conjugue(n)...	Conjugate . . .
Construya(n)...	Create/Build . . .
Conteste(n)/ Responda(n) (a)...	Answer . . .
Cuente(n)...	Tell . . .
Decida(n)...	Decide . . .
Describa(n)...	Describe . . .
Descubra(n)...	Discover/Learn . . .
Dibuje(n)...	Draw . . .
Diga(n)...	Say . . .
Diseñe(n)...	Design . . .
Elabore(n)...	Create/Make . . .
Elija(n)...	Choose . . .
Escriba(n)...	Write . . .
Escuche(n)...	Listen . . .

Exponga(n)...	Display/Post . . .
Fíje(n)se en...	Look at . . .
Forme(n)...	Form/Create . . .
Haga(n)...	Do/Make . . .
Imagíne(n)se que...	Imagine that . . .
Informe(n)...	Tell/Inform . . .
Lea(n)...	Read . . .
Localice(n)...	Locate/Find . . .
Marque(n)...	Mark/Check off . . .
Mencione(n)...	Mention . . .
Mire(n)...	Look at . . .
Muestre(n)...	Show . . .
Nombre(n)...	Name . . .
Observe(n)...	Observe . . .
Obtenga(n)...	Get/Obtain . . .
Ordene(n) ...	Put in order . . .
Organice(n)...	Organize . . .
Piense(n) en...	Think about . . .
Ponga(n) atención (a)...	Pay attention (to) . . .
Practique(n)...	Practice . . .
Pregunte(n)...	Ask . . .
Presente(n)...	Present/Introduce . . .
Pronuncie(n)...	Pronounce . . .
Recuerde(n)...	Remember . . .
Redacte(n)...	Write . . .
Relacione(n)...	Relate/Match . . .
Rellene(n)...	Fill in . . .
Repita(n)...	Repeat . . .
Represente(n)/ Escenifique(n)...	Role-play . . .
Resuma(n)...	Summarize . . .
Reúna(n)...	Gather . . .
Revise(n)...	Review . . .
Rodee(n)...	Circle . . .
Seleccione(n)...	Select . . .
Señale(n)...	Indicate . . .
Subraye(n)...	Underline . . .
Sustituya(n)...	Substitute . . .
Tache(n)...	Cross out . . .
Transforme(n)...	Transform . . .
Use(n)/Utilice(n)...	Use . . .

Unidad 1

Benicio del Toro, un actor puertorriqueño

Joan, un catalán políglota

Encuentros en la plaza

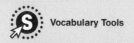
Vocabulary Tools

¡Bienvenidos!

Imágenes y palabras

1 | 2 | 3 | 4

Numerar

0	cero	7	siete
1	uno	8	ocho
2	dos	9	nueve
3	tres	10	diez
4	cuatro	11	once
5	cinco	12	doce
6	seis		

1A.1 Numbers 0–12

Identificar y especificar

● ¿Qué es?
■ Es Madrid. Es una ciudad.

● ¿Quién es?
■ Es Isabel Allende. Es una escritora.

1A.2 Indefinite article **un(a)**
Interrogatives ¿qué?, ¿quién?

Vocabulario

1

la imagen *picture, image*
¿Quién es? *Who is it?*
¿quién? *who?*
¿Qué es? *What is it?*
el/la arquitecto/a *architect*
la comida *food*
la isla *island*
el pueblo *town*
el/la escritor(a) *writer*

3

la playa *beach*
la biblioteca *library*
el personaje *important figure*
el monumento, la música

---

1 **a. Relacionar** Match each photo to a section of the wheel on page 11. Write the number of the photo in the corresponding section of the wheel.

b. Escribir Write out the numbers.

1	5	4	3	2	6
....	....	....	....	....	....

c. Comprobar Check your answers with a partner.

Modelo: • *"Uno." ¿Quién es?*
• *Es Vargas Llosa. Es un escritor.*

2 **a. Sumar** Add the numbers showing on each pair of dice and write out the sum.

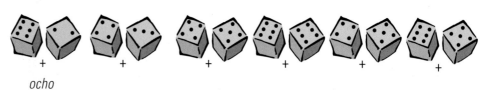

+   +   +   +   +   +

ocho ....

b. Tirar los dados Now use real dice. With a partner, take turns rolling the dice and giving the sum of the numbers showing.

Modelo: *Seis más dos: ¡ocho!*

3 **¿Un o una?** Write the correct indefinite article. Refer to the sections of the game wheel and pay attention to the last letter of each word.

1. *un* hotel
2. .... música
3. .... comid**a**
4. .... monument**o**

5. .... playa
6. .... metro
7. .... isla
8. .... pueblo

9. .... biblioteca
10. .... arquitect**a**
11. .... escritor
12. .... personaje

¿QUIÉN ES?

ANTONI GAUDÍ, UN ARQUITECTO

BUENOS AIRES, UNA CIUDAD

GUACAMOLE, UNA COMIDA

¿QUIÉN ES?

¿QUÉ ES?

PUERTO RICO, UNA ISLA

(1) VARGAS LLOSA, UN ESCRITOR

ALBARRACÍN, UN PUEBLO

¿QUÉ ES?

---

4 a. Lugares Listen to the conversation and write down the place names that are mentioned. Use letters from the boxes.

A – Z – G – H – A – R – K – A – O – T – Z – U

....

T – H – I – N – F – A – E – E – S – R – U – E

....

b. Dos ciudades Study the map in your text on page xxxii and write out the names of two cities in Latin America.

5 Deletrear Choose two names from the wheel and spell them out loud. Your partner will write them out.

🔲 **MI EXPERIENCIA**

6 Adivinar Think of a city, food, or person from a Spanish-speaking country. Your partner must guess whom or what you are thinking about.

> **Deletrear**
> - ¿Cómo se escribe *Toledo*?
> - Te - o - ele - e - de - o.
> - ¿Cómo se escribe *Ana*? ¿Con una ene o con dos enes?
> - Con una ene.
> - ¿Cómo se escribe *música*?
> - Con acento en la *u*.
>
> **1A.3** Interrogative ¿cómo?

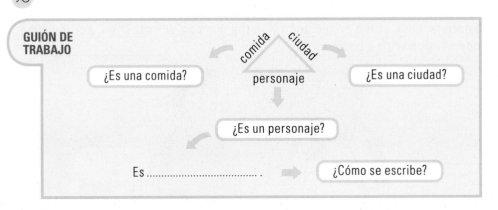

GUIÓN DE TRABAJO

comida — ciudad

personaje

¿Es una comida? ¿Es una ciudad?

¿Es un personaje?

Es .... → ¿Cómo se escribe?

SAM: Actividades pp. 5–7

Practice more at vhlcentral.com.

once **11**

Yo soy de Madrid, ¿y tú?

Vocabulario

7

Yo soy de Madrid. *I'm from Madrid.*

¿y tú? *and you?*

muy bien *very well*

bien *well*

¿De dónde eres? *Where are you from? (fam.)*

¿De dónde es usted? *Where are you from? (form.)*

sí *yes*

Portugal, Brasil, no

9

el origen *origin*

el interés *interest*

el fútbol *soccer*

el esquí *skiing*

el tenis, la salsa, el hip-hop, el teatro, el concierto

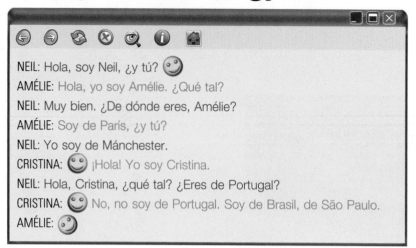

NEIL: Hola, soy Neil, ¿y tú? 😊

AMÉLIE: Hola, yo soy Amélie. ¿Qué tal?

NEIL: Muy bien. ¿De dónde eres, Amélie?

AMÉLIE: Soy de París, ¿y tú?

NEIL: Yo soy de Mánchester.

CRISTINA: 😊 ¡Hola! Yo soy Cristina.

NEIL: Hola, Cristina, ¿qué tal? ¿Eres de Portugal?

CRISTINA: 😊 No, no soy de Portugal. Soy de Brasil, de São Paulo.

AMÉLIE: 😊

Hablar del origen

(informal)

● ¿De dónde eres?

■ Soy de España, de Bilbao. ¿Y tú?

● Yo soy de Chile.

■ ¿Eres de Bogotá?

● No, no soy de Bogotá. Soy de Cali y Ana María es de Quito, Ecuador.

(formal)

● ¿De dónde es usted?

■ Soy de Zaragoza. ¿Y usted?

1A.4 Interrogative **¿de dónde?**
The verb **ser** (singular forms)
ser + de

Afirmar y negar

Sí, soy de León.

No, no soy de Cuenca. Soy de Córdoba.

1A.5 **sí /no, no** + [*verb*]

---

7 **¿Sí o no?** Read this chat between Spanish students from all over the world and write whether each statement is true. Correct any false statements.

1. Amélie es de Londres.	*No, Amélie no es de Londres. Es de París.*
2. Neil es de Mánchester.	
3. Cristina es de Portugal.	

8 **Completar** Fill in the table with the missing form or subject pronoun.

yo	
	eres
usted	es
él/ella	

9 **a. Intercambio** Read this information card for a language exchange and answer the questions. Which words do you know already? How do you know them?

○ ¿De dónde es esta persona?

○ ¿Cómo se llama?

> **Nombre:** Raúl
>
> **Origen:** Pamplona
>
> **Intereses:** fútbol, tenis, esquí, música (salsa, hip-hop), teatro y conciertos

🔊 **b. Raúl** Listen to the conversation between Raúl and the person he meets. What is his exchange partner's name? Where is she from?

10 **Historieta** Look at the comic and fill in the missing words. Then, act out the conversation with a partner.

¿.................................
.................................?

No, no soy de Madrid. Soy de Alicante. ¿Y tú? ¿.......... de Barcelona?

No. Soy de Madrid.

11 **a. Situaciones** Look at the photos and decide in which situation people are using **tú** and in which situation they are using **usted**. Which situation is more formal? Which is more informal?

 A

 B

b. ¿Formal o informal? Listen to the recording and complete the questions.

> ○ ¿De dónde .... ?
>
> ○ ¿De dónde ....?

12 **Preguntas** Which question should be used in each situation? Write the appropriate question under each photo.

○ *¿De dónde eres?*

○ *¿De dónde es usted?*

 A

....

 B

....

 C

....

🗣 MI EXPERIENCIA

13 **a. Ciudades** Listen to the names of these cities. How are they similar in English?

b. ¿De dónde...? Use both **tú** and **usted** to ask your classmates where they are from. Before you begin, study the maps on pages xxxi and xxxii in your text to find the Spanish names of several cities.

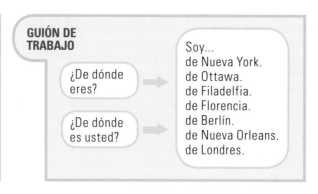

NUEVA YORK

OTTAWA

BERLÍN

FLORENCIA

FILADELFIA

LONDRES

NUEVA ORLEANS

GUIÓN DE TRABAJO

¿De dónde eres? →

¿De dónde es usted? →

Soy...
de Nueva York.
de Ottawa.
de Filadelfia.
de Florencia.
de Berlín.
de Nueva Orleans.
de Londres.

Tú o usted

In Spanish, you can address an individual as **tú** or **usted**. Use **usted** with people who are older than you, people you don't know, and authority figures. Use **tú** with close friends and family, and with children. The informal **tú** is used much more widely in Spain than in Latin America. In Spain, **tú** is often used among people of all ages, in the workplace, at stores, etc.

Vocabulario

(13)

Nueva York *New York*
Nueva Orleans *New Orleans*
Filadelfia *Philadelphia*
Los Ángeles *Los Angeles*
Londres *London*
Ottawa, Toledo

SAM: Actividades pp. 8–10

 Practice more at **vhlcentral.com**.

Benicio del Toro, un referente de la comunidad latina.

Benicio del Toro, un actor puertorriqueño

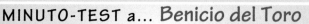

MINUTO-TEST a... *Benicio del Toro*

- Una ciudad: Los Ángeles
- Una isla: Puerto Rico
- Una comida: Mallorcas
- Un barrio: Santurce
- Un personaje: Luis Buñuel

Película *Traffic*

Películas

- *Guardianes de la galaxia* (2014), director: James Gunn
- *Che, el argentino* (2008), director: Steven Soderbergh
- *La ciudad del pecado* (2005), directores: Frank Miller, Robert Rodríguez
- *21 gramos* (2003), director: Alejandro González Iñárritu
- *Traffic* (2000), director: Steven Soderbergh

Vocabulario

14

puertorriqueño/a *Puerto Rican*
el actor/la actriz *actor/actress*
el minuto *minute*
la mallorca *Puerto Rican pastry*
el barrio *neighborhood*
la comunidad *community*
la película *movie*
el test, el/la director(a)

15

¿Qué... eliges? *Which . . . do you choose?*

---

14 **a. Protagonista** Look at the photo of this lesson's protagonist and answer the questions.

- ¿Quién es?
- ¿De dónde es?

b. Minuto-test Read Benicio del Toro's Minute Test and add a caption to each photo.

c. Asociar Now it's your turn to take the Minute Test. What people, places, and things do you associate with Spanish-speaking countries?

MINUTO-TEST a _____

- Una ciudad: ....
- Una isla: ....
- Una comida: ....
- Un pueblo: ....
- Un personaje: ....
- Un barrio: ....

15 **Tabla** Ask two classmates what people, places, and things they chose in the Minute Test, and write their answers in the chart.

Modelo: *¿Qué ciudad/isla/comida/pueblo/personaje/barrio eliges?*

		....	....
REFERENTES CULTURALES	una ciudad		
	una isla		
	una comida		
	un pueblo		
	un personaje		
	un barrio		

16 Adivinar Choose a photograph. Your partner has to guess which photo you chose.

Modelo: *¿Es de España? ¿Es una isla? ¿Es ....?*

comida • paella • España

ciudad • Santiago de Chile • Chile

isla • Ibiza • España

comida • asado • Argentina

([c]) ([g])

17 a. [c] Listen to these words. Is the letter **c** always pronounced the same?

Caracas - comida - Cuba / centro - ciudad

b. [g] Now listen to how the letter **g** is pronounced.

Galápagos - golf - guacamole / Gerona - Gibraltar

c. [c] y [g] Which vowels come after **c** and **g** in each case?

18 Referentes latinos What do you know about Latin America? Complete the sentences about these photos, then match the photos to the corresponding descriptions.

Caracas es una .... (A)

El ceviche .... ◯

Salma Hayek .... ◯

Cuba .... ◯

OPINIÓN

What people, places, and foods do your classmates associate with Spanish-speaking countries? Discuss your ideas with a partner.

Vocabulario

16
la paella *Spanish rice dish*
el asado *barbecue*
17
el centro *center; downtown*
el golf, el guacamole
18
el referente latino *Hispanic icon*
el ceviche *marinated seafood dish*

TAREA FINAL

Palabras, palabras...

Create a portfolio of your Spanish vocabulary!

 First, brainstorm ideas with the class. What Spanish words do you know for each letter of the Spanish alphabet?

A ....

B ....

C ....

D ....

. . .

Find photos to represent your words and assemble them in a notebook or online portfolio. Add words, photos, and other materials to your portfolio throughout the Spanish course.

YO PUEDO...

- **Puedo nombrar y especificar ciudades, comidas y personajes.**
  Name two cities, foods, and people.

- **Puedo preguntar cómo se escribe una palabra y deletrearla (*spell it*).**
  Spell out the names of these two cities.

- **Puedo decir cómo me llamo y de dónde soy.**
  Write out your personal information.

- **Puedo preguntar a alguien de dónde es, en situaciones formales e informales.**
  Look at the photo and complete the question.

Oviedo

....

Santo Domingo ....

....

....

....

....

¿De dónde ....?

GRAMÁTICA FUNCIONAL Tutorials

1A.1 Use numbers 0–12

Numbers 0–12   13.1

0 **cero**	4 **cuatro**	7 **siete**	10 **diez**
1 **uno**	5 **cinco**	8 **ocho**	11 **once**
2 **dos**	6 **seis**	9 **nueve**	12 **doce**
3 **tres**			

• Use **uno** (*one*) when counting or after a noun. Use **un** before masculine nouns and **una** before feminine nouns.

la Unidad **uno**	**un** hombre	**una** mujer
Unit **one**	**one** man	**one** woman

• Use **más** (*plus*) to give sums.

Tres **más** siete: diez. (3 + 7 = 10)

1A.2 Identify and specify

Singular indefinite article **un(a)**   3.2
Interrogatives **¿qué?, ¿quién?**   9

• All Spanish nouns are either masculine or feminine. To say *a, an,* or *one,* use **un** with masculine nouns (which usually end in **-o**) and **una** with feminine nouns (which usually end in **-a**). Pay attention to gender as you learn nouns, as there are many exceptions.

un pueblo	**una** comida	**un** hotel	**una** ciudad
a/one town	**a/one** food	**a/one** hotel	**a/one** city

• To ask what something is, say **¿Qué es?** To answer, use **Es** + [*indefinite article*] + [*noun*]. **Es** is the 3rd person singular form of the verb **ser** (*to be*). There is no Spanish equivalent to the subject pronoun *it*. To say *It is,* use **Es**.

¿Qué es?	**Es** una isla.	**Es** un barrio.
What is it?	*It's an island.*	*It is a neighborhood.*

• To ask who someone is, say **¿Quién es?** To respond, use **Es** + [*name*].

¿Quién es?	**Es** Luis Buñuel.
Who is it?	*It's Luis Buñuel.*

1A.3 Spell

Interrogative **¿cómo?**   9

• To ask how a Spanish word is spelled, say **¿Cómo se escribe?**

¿Cómo se escribe Albarracín?
How do you spell Albarracín?

• Use the word **con** (*with*) to clarify spellings.

Con be.	**Con** dos erres.	**Con** acento en la i.
With a b.	*With two r's.*	*With an accent on the i.*

• Note that Spanish questions use both opening (¿) and closing (?) question marks and that all interrogatives take a written accent.

¿Qué es?	**¿Quién** es?	**¿Cómo** se escribe?
What is it?	*Who is it?*	*How do you spell it?*

¡Póngalo en práctica!

G1 **Adición** Write out these sums.

Modelo: **3 + 4** *Tres más cuatro: siete.*

1. **5 + 3** ....
2. **9 + 0** ....
3. **2 + 2** ....
4. **3 + 8** ....
5. **4 + 6** ....
6. **10 + 2** ....
7. **1 + 6** ....
8. **2 + 3** ....

G2 **¿Qué es?** Use the cues to answer the questions.

¿Qué es?

1. biblioteca ....
2. monumento ....
3. playa ....
4. barrio ....
5. pueblo ....
6. comida ....
7. personaje ....

¿Quién es?

8. Benicio del Toro ....
9. Penélope Cruz ....
10. Mario Vargas Llosa ....

G3 **¿Cómo se escribe?** Match each word in the box to the clarification about its spelling.

¿Cómo se escribe?

ceviche	esquí	Brasil
Ottawa	hip-hop	fútbol

1. Con acento en la i. ....
2. Con ce. ....
3. Con dos tes. ....
4. Con acento en la u. ....
5. Con ese. ....
6. Con hache. ....

GRAMÁTICA FUNCIONAL

1A.4 Talk about where people are from

Interrogative **¿de dónde?** 9
The verb **ser** (singular forms) 5.1.2, 5.8.1

- To ask where someone is from, say **¿De dónde** + [*form of* **ser**] + [*subject*]?

¿De dónde eres tú?	¿De dónde es Carolina?
Where are you from?	*Where is Carolina from?*

- To tell where someone is from, say [*subject*] + [*form of* **ser**] + **de** + [*city/country*].

Yo **soy de** Guayaquil.	Ella **es de** Paraguay.
I am from Guayaquil.	*She is from Paraguay.*

- The singular subject pronouns in Spanish are **yo** (*I*), **tú** (*you*, fam.), **usted** (*you*, form.), **él** (*he*), and **ella** (*she*). As with all verbs, **ser** (*to be*) has a set of forms corresponding to the different subjects.

SER (Formas singulares)	
(yo)	**soy**
(tú)	**eres**
(usted, él, ella)	**es**

- Unlike in English, subject pronouns are not required in Spanish and are usually omitted.

¿De dónde eres?	Soy de Miami.
*Where are **you** from?*	*I'm from Miami.*

¡OJO! Both **tú** and **usted** mean *you*. Use **tú** when addressing a friend, a family member, or someone younger than you. Use **usted** to address a person with whom you have a more formal relationship. Note that **usted** is used with the same verb forms as **él** and **ella**.

1A.5 Answer yes-or-no questions

sí/no, no + [*verb*] 12.1, 12.2

- To answer a question in the affirmative, say **Sí,** + [*verb*].

¿Es usted Antonio García?	**Sí, soy** Antonio García.
Are you Antonio García?	*Yes, I am Antonio García.*

- To answer a question negatively, say **No, no** + [*verb*]. To make a negative statement, always place the word **no** directly before the verb.

¿Es usted de Canadá?	**No, no soy** de Canadá.
Are you from Canada?	*No, I am not from Canada.*
¿Te llamas Pablo?	**No, no me llamo** Pablo.
Is your name Pablo?	*No, my name is not Pablo.*

- To answer negatively and provide the correct information, you can also say **No,** + [*correct information*]: **No, me llamo Pedro.** (*No, my name is Pedro.*)

G4 **¿De dónde...?** Ask where each of these people is from.

1. usted ....
2. Gustavo ....
3. el escritor ....
4. tú ....
5. ella ....
6. Gabriela ....
7. él ....
8. la arquitecta ....

G5 **Un diálogo** Complete the conversation.

> Inés, ¿de (1) .... eres?

> Yo (2) .... de Cartagena.
> Y (3) ...., ¿de dónde eres?

> Soy (4) .... Barranquilla.

> ¡Qué lindo! Shakira (5) .... de Barranquilla, ¿no?

> Sí, (6) .... es de Barranquilla.

G6 **¿Sí o no?** Answer these questions about yourself. Use complete sentences.

1. ¿Es usted estudiante?
   ....
2. ¿Es usted de Estados Unidos?
   ....
3. ¿Eres escritor(a)?
   ....
4. ¿Eres María?
   ....
5. ¿Eres de Puerto Rico?
   ....
6. ¿Es usted arquitecto/a?
   ....

S Practice more at **vhlcentral.com**.

VOCABULARIO  Vocabulary Tools

Imágenes y palabras

¿Qué es?	What is it?
¿Quién es?	Who is it?
¿quién?	who?
el/la arquitecto/a	architect
la biblioteca	library
la comida	food
el/la escritor(a)	writer
la imagen	picture, image
la isla	island
el monumento	monument
la música	music
el personaje	important figure; character
la playa	beach
el pueblo	town

Yo soy de Madrid, ¿y tú?

¿De dónde eres?	Where are you from? (fam.)
¿De dónde es usted?	Where are you from? (form.)
Yo soy de Madrid.	I'm from Madrid.
¿y tú?	and you?
el concierto	concert
el esquí	skiing
el fútbol	soccer
el hip-hop	hip-hop
el interés	interest
el origen	origin
la salsa	salsa
el teatro	theater
el tenis	tennis
Brasil	Brazil
Filadelfia	Philadelphia
Londres	London
Los Ángeles	Los Angeles
Nueva Orleans	New Orleans
Nueva York	New York
Ottawa	Ottawa
Portugal	Portugal
Toledo	Toledo
bien	well
muy bien	very well
sí	yes
no	no; not

Benicio del Toro

¿Qué... eliges?	Which. . . do you choose?
el actor/la actriz	actor/actress
el asado	barbecue
el barrio	neighborhood
el ceviche	marinated seafood dish
el centro	center; downtown
la comunidad	community
el/la director(a)	director
el golf	golf
el guacamole	guacamole
la mallorca	Puerto Rican pastry
el minuto	minute
la paella	Spanish rice dish
la película	movie
el referente latino	Hispanic icon
el test	test
puertorriqueño/a	Puerto Rican

Variación léxica

el barrio ⟷ el vecindario ⟷ la vecindad ⟷ la colonia (*Méx.*)

el fútbol ⟷ el futbol (*Amér. C., Méx.*)

la mallorca (*P.R.*) ⟷ la ensaimada (*Esp.*)

el test ⟷ la prueba

1B

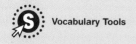
Vocabulary Tools

LENGUAS

Hablamos

Helen, ¿qué lenguas estudias tú?

Pues, sí. Hablamos alemán, francés y ¡un poco de español!

¿Vosotros habláis tres lenguas? ¿De verdad?

Peter, ¿qué lenguas hablas?

Hablo inglés y estudio español.

Yo estudio italiano y español.

Informar sobre las lenguas que uno habla y estudia

- ¿Tú **hablas** francés?
- No, no **hablo** francés. Yo **hablo** español.
- Fernando **no habla** inglés.
- ¿Qué lenguas **estudiáis** vosotros?
- **Estudiamos** español y japonés.
- Jaime y Lola **hablan** italiano y alemán.

1B.1 Regular **-ar** verbs: **estudiar, hablar**

Vocabulario
①

hablar *to speak*

¿Qué lenguas hablas? *What languages do you speak?*

el inglés *English*

estudiar *to study*

el español *Spanish*

el italiano *Italian*

el alemán *German*

el francés *French*

el chino *Chinese*

el portugués *Portuguese*

el coreano *Korean*

el japonés *Japanese*

---

1 Las lenguas Look at the photo and listen to the conversation. In the chart, indicate which languages the students speak or study.

	ESPAÑOL	INGLÉS	FRANCÉS	ALEMÁN	ITALIANO
hablan					
estudian					

2 Relacionar Match each subject to a verb ending.

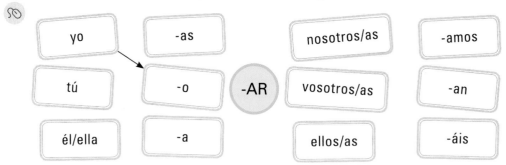

yo — -as — nosotros/as — -amos
tú — -o — **-AR** — vosotros/as — -an
él/ella — -a — ellos/as — -áis

3 Conjugar Write the correct form of each verb. Compare your answers with a partner's.

(yo)	(tú)	(él)	(ella)	(nosotros)	(vosotros)	(ellos)
hablar	**hablar**	**estudiar**	**estudiar**	**estudiar**	**hablar**	**hablar**
hablo						

4 Entrevista Interview your partner. What languages does he/she speak and study?

Modelo: *¿Hablas chino? ¿Estudias francés?*

INTERCAMBIO DE CONVERSACIÓN en la CAFETERÍA BABEL
Plaza San Juan, 6. Barcelona
Día 28 de abril a las 18:00 h

5 **a. Nacionalidades** Indicate each person's nationality in the photo captions.

| chino | alemana | inglés | coreana | portugués | francesa | italiano |

b. Yumi Yumi enters the café. Read the conversation and fill in the information.

- ¡Buenas tardes! ¿Cómo te llamas?
- Yumi.
- ¿Y de dónde eres, Yumi?

- Soy de Tokio, Japón.
- Muy bien. ¿Qué lenguas hablas?
- Hablo japonés e inglés. Y bueno, estudio español y francés.

Nombre: .... Nacionalidad: .... Lenguas: ....

c. Conversación Now you enter the café. Practice the conversation with a partner.

6 **¿Verdadero o falso?** Listen to Yumi and Jordi, and indicate whether each statement is true (**verdadero**) or false (**falso**).

1. Yumi habla japonés. ......
2. Jordi estudia francés. ......
3. En Barcelona se hablan español y catalán. ......
4. En Tokio se habla japonés. ......

7 **Se habla...** Have you been to any of these cities? What languages are spoken there?

Modelo: *En Montevideo se habla...*

PEKÍN   MONTREAL
MONTEVIDEO   BUENOS AIRES

MI EXPERIENCIA

8 **¿Qué lenguas?** Ask your classmates what languages they speak and study.

GUIÓN DE TRABAJO

¿Eres...?

¿Qué lenguas hablas?

¿Hablas...?

alemán
inglés
francés
italiano

español
chino
coreano
portugués

¿Qué lenguas estudias?

¿Qué lengua se habla en tu país/familia?

Vocabulario

5
estadounidense *American*
canadiense *Canadian*
el intercambio *exchange*
la cafetería *café; cafeteria*
la plaza *square*
abril *April*
18:00 h *6:00 p.m.*
chino/a *Chinese*
alemán/alemana *German*
inglés/inglesa *English*
coreano/a *Korean*
portugués/portuguesa *Portuguese*
francés/francesa *French*
e *and (before i or hi + consonant)*
la nacionalidad *nationality*
la conversación, italiano/a

6
se habla(n) *is/are spoken*
el catalán *Catalan*
el idioma *language*

7
Pekín *Beijing*

Indicar la nacionalidad

- ¿Eres **alemana**?
- No, soy **estadounidense**.
- ¿Y él? ¿Es **francés**?
- No, es **canadiense**.

1B.2 ser + [*nationality*]

Informar sobre las lenguas que se hablan en un país

En México se habla español.

En Canadá se hablan dos lenguas.

1B.3 en + [*country/city/place*]
se habla(n) + [*language(s)*]

SAM: Actividades pp. 15–16

Profesiones y trabajos

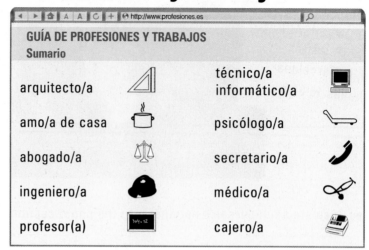

GUÍA DE PROFESIONES Y TRABAJOS
Sumario

arquitecto/a		técnico/a informático/a	
amo/a de casa		psicólogo/a	
abogado/a		secretario/a	
ingeniero/a		médico/a	
profesor(a)		cajero/a	

9 **Guía** Read the guide to jobs and identify which occupations are centered around interacting with people. Discuss your answers with a partner.

Contacto con personas: ....

10 **Blanca y Juana** Read this conversation and decide whether each statement is true (**verdadero**) or false (**falso**).

- Somos Blanca y Juana. Trabajamos en un hospital. Blanca es psicóloga y yo, médica. ¿Y tú? ¿A qué te dedicas? ¿También eres médica?
- No, yo soy secretaria.
- ¡Qué interesante! ¿Y vosotros?
- Nosotros somos arquitectos.

	V	F
1. Blanca y Juana son ingenieras.	☐	☐
2. Ellos son arquitectos.	☐	☐
3. Juana es médica.	☐	☐

11 **Una profesión** Listen to the radio program. What do these people do for work, and how do they describe their profession?

	una profesión...	... divertida.
....		... estresante.
		... interesante.
		... aburrida.

12 **Oraciones** In pairs, take turns using words from each group to form sentences.

Modelo: *Ellos son profesores.*

vosotras nosotros ellos ellas nosotras vosotros	somos sois son	cajeros profesores psicólogas amas de casa secretarios abogadas

13 **a. Fotos** Choose three photos and say the numbers you see aloud. Your partner should then identify which photo you are talking about.

Modelo: *Es la foto...*

b. Escribir Write out the numbers you see in each photo on the line below.

1

....

2

....

3

....

4

....

5

....

6

....

14 **a. Números de teléfono** Listen to the recording of these phone numbers and write them down. Pay close attention to how the numbers are grouped.

Irene: .... Daniel: .... Cristina: ....

b. Intercambiar Exchange phone numbers with a partner.

Modelo: • *¿Cuál es tu número de teléfono?*
• *0160-4458679: cero, uno, seis...*

🎏 **MI EXPERIENCIA**

15 **Preguntar** Ask your classmates about their studies and their jobs.

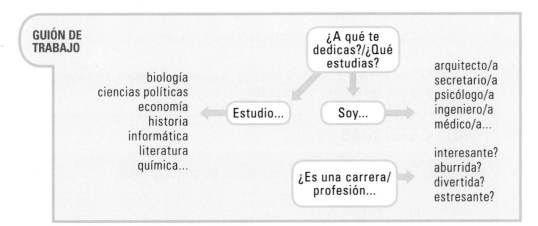

GUIÓN DE TRABAJO

¿A qué te dedicas?/¿Qué estudias?

biología
ciencias políticas
economía
historia
informática
literatura
química...

Estudio...

Soy...

arquitecto/a
secretario/a
psicólogo/a
ingeniero/a
médico/a...

¿Es una carrera/ profesión...

interesante?
aburrida?
divertida?
estresante?

Numerar

- ¿Cuál es tu número de teléfono/celular?
- Es el seis, noventa y nueve, trece, cuarenta, treinta y uno. (6 99 13 40 31)

12	doce	33	treinta y
13	trece		tres
14	catorce	...	
15	quince	40	cuarenta
16	dieciséis	41	cuarenta
17	diecisiete		y uno
18	dieciocho	42	cuarenta
19	diecinueve		y dos
20	veinte	43	cuarenta
21	veintiuno		y tres
22	veintidós	...	
...		50	cincuenta
30	treinta	60	sesenta
31	treinta y	70	setenta
	uno	80	ochenta
32	treinta y	90	noventa
	dos	100	cien

1B.6 Numbers 12–100

Vocabulario

14

¿Cuál es tu número de teléfono? *What is your phone number?*

el (teléfono) celular *cell phone*

15

la biología *biology*

las ciencias políticas *political science*

la economía *economics*

la historia *history*

la informática *computer science*

la literatura *literature*

la química *chemistry*

la carrera *major*

Joan Fusté, 28 años.
Guía turístico y
estudiante de idiomas.

Joan, un catalán políglota

Museu
Picasso

Joan Fusté
Guía turístico

FORO DE LENGUAS

Joan

Registrado: 20-Sep
Mensajes: 1

Título del mensaje: **Intercambios de conversación**   Citar
Publicado: 20-Sep

¡Hola! Me llamo Joan Fusté. Soy de Barcelona. Hablo catalán y español. Trabajo en el Museo Picasso. Soy guía y, claro, con los turistas hablo inglés, francés, italiano... Es un trabajo muy interesante, ¡y divertido! También estudio alemán. Busco personas para practicar idiomas...

LENGUAS

Like many countries in the Spanish-speaking world, parts of Spain have two official languages: Spanish and the regional language. For example, **catalán** is spoken in Cataluña, **euskera** is spoken in **País Vasco**, and **gallego** is spoken in Galicia.

Vocabulario
(17)

políglota *multilingual*

el foro *forum*

el/la guía (turístico/a) *(tour) guide*

claro *of course*

el/la turista *tourist*

buscar *to look for*

la persona *person*

País Vasco *Basque Country*

el euskera *Basque (language)*

el gallego *Galician (language)*

(16) **Protagonista** Look at the photo of Joan and his name tag. What city does he live in? Where does he work? Have you ever been there?

(17) **Foro de lenguas** Read Joan's post on the language forum and complete the information below.

- Nombre y apellido: ....
- Ciudad: ....
- Profesión: ....

(18) **Contestar** Answer the questions.
1. ¿Qué lenguas habla Joan? ¿Qué lenguas estudia?

2. ¿Ser guía turístico es un trabajo interesante para Joan?

(19) **Escribir** Write an answer to Joan's posting. Include your name, nationality, job, major, and any languages you speak or study.

FORO DE LENGUAS

Respuesta

Registrado: 20-Sep
Mensajes: 1

Título del mensaje: **Intercambios de conversación**   Citar
Publicado: 20-Sep

¡Hola, Joan! ....
....
....

20 **a. Una clase de español** Look at the photo next to the e-mail message. What do you think the e-mail will say? Read it.

○○○   Mensaje nuevo

Enviar   Chat   Adjuntar   Agenda   Tipo de letra   Colores   Borrador

De: | Anna
Para: | Pablo Fernández
Asunto: | CLASES DE ESPAÑOL

Hola, Pablo, ¿qué tal?
Te envío una foto de mi clase de español. ¡Sí, estudio español! Es una clase muy divertida y muy internacional. Somos seis: un inglés, una francesa, dos italianas, un portugués y yo. En clase hablamos español. Carla y Paola, las italianas, trabajan en un banco. Son abogadas.

b. Completar Fill in the missing information about the students mentioned in the e-mail.

Nombre: Valérie Renoir
Profesión: técnica informática
Nacionalidad: ....
Idiomas: francés, inglés

Nombre: Carla Conte
Profesión: ....
Nacionalidad: ....
Idiomas: ...., inglés

Entonación

21 **a. Entonación** Listen to these sentences and repeat after the speaker. Pay special attention to the intonation.

Estudio español.   ¿Hablas inglés?   ¿Estudias idiomas?

b. Escuchar Listen to these sentences and draw the intonation you hear on a separate sheet of paper.

22 **a. Lenguas** You have read about the variety of languages spoken in Spain. Now think about where Spanish is spoken in the Americas. In which of these countries is Spanish not an official language? Circle it/them.

- ☐ Ecuador
- ☐ México
- ☐ Colombia
- ☐ Estados Unidos
- ☐ Chile
- ☐ Uruguay
- ☐ Perú
- ☐ Argentina
- ☐ Cuba
- ☐ Brasil
- ☐ Venezuela
- ☐ Guatemala

b. Países Listen to the recording and check off the countries that are mentioned. These are the most populous countries in Latin America.

c. Quechua y guaraní Now listen to the recording to learn in which countries **quechua** and **guaraní** are spoken in addition to Spanish.

El quechua se habla en ...., Ecuador, Bolivia, Colombia, Argentina y Chile.
El guaraní se habla en Paraguay, ... y Bolivia.

Machu Picchu, Perú

Vocabulario *cont.*

el nombre *name*
el apellido *last name*

20

la clase *class*
la foto(grafía) *photo(graph)*
internacional *international*
el banco *bank*

OPINIÓN

¿Qué lenguas se estudian más en su país?
Se estudian más...

¿Qué lenguas se estudian en su universidad?
Se estudian...

¿Qué otras lenguas o dialectos se hablan en su país?
Se habla(n)...

Vocabulario

22

indígena *indigenous, native*
el quechua *Quechua*
el guaraní *Guarani*

SAM: Actividades pp. 19–24

TAREA FINAL

Compañeros de clase

Gather information about a classmate.
Answer his/her questions as well.

¿Cómo te llamas? ¿De dónde eres?
¿Qué lenguas hablas/estudias?
¿A qué te dedicas? ¿Cuál es tu número de teléfono? ...

Fill in your partner's information on this card.

> ○ Nombre: ....
>
> ○ Nacionalidad: ....
>
> ○ Lenguas que habla y estudia: ....
>
> ○ Profesión/Carrera: ....
>
> ○ Teléfono: ....

Share your partner's information with the rest of the class.

YO PUEDO...

• **Puedo decir el nombre de distintas lenguas.**
List five languages.

• **Puedo informar sobre las lenguas que hablo y estudio.**
Answer these questions.

• **Puedo rellenar una ficha de inscripción con mis datos.**
Complete this card with your information.

• **Puedo nombrar diferentes profesiones y carreras.**
List four professions and four academic majors.

• **Puedo comprender y dar números de teléfono.**
Write out your phone number(s).

> ¿Qué lenguas hablas?
> ....
> ¿Qué lenguas estudias?
> ....

> Nombre: ....
> Nacionalidad: ....
> Profesión/Carrera: ....

> Mi número de teléfono es:
> ....
> ....

GRAMÁTICA FUNCIONAL $\mathcal{S}$ Tutorials

1B.1 **Talk about the languages you speak and study**

Regular **-ar** verbs 5.1.1

- Use the verbs **hablar** (*to speak*) and **estudiar** (*to study*) to talk about the languages people speak and study.

  ¿Qué lenguas **hablas**?
  *What languages **do you speak**?*

  Hablo inglés y **estudio** español.
  *I **speak** English and I **study** Spanish.*

- **Estudiar** and **hablar** are regular -ar verbs. In order to conjugate these verbs, drop the -ar ending from the infinitive and add the endings that correspond to the different subject pronouns. All regular -ar verbs use the same set of endings.

	ESTUDIAR	HABLAR
(yo)	estudio	hablo
(tú)	estudias	hablas
(usted, él, ella)	estudia	habla
(nosotros/as)	estudiamos	hablamos
(vosotros/as)	estudiáis	habláis
(ustedes, ellos/as)	estudian	hablan

- Since all regular -ar verbs follow this pattern, you can tell the subject of the verb by looking at the ending. As you saw in 1A.4, this allows you to omit the subject pronoun.

  Hablas portugués e inglés, ¿no?
  *You **speak** Portuguese and English, right?*

- In 1A.4, you learned the singular subject pronouns **yo, tú, usted, él,** and **ella.** The plural subject pronouns are **nosotros/as** (*we*), **vosotros/as** (*you*, fam.), **ustedes** (*you*, form. and fam.), and **ellos/as** (*they*).

  Nosotros estudiamos español y **ellos** estudian chino.
  We study Spanish and they study Chinese.

- The feminine forms **nosotras, vosotras,** and **ellas** are used only when all members of the group are female. For groups of mixed gender or groups that are all male, use the masculine forms **nosotros, vosotros,** and **ellos.**

  Clara y Mónica = **ellas**

  Clara y Roberto = **ellos**

  Roberto y Daniel = **ellos**

¡OJO!

Both **vosotros/as** and **ustedes** mean *you* and are used to address a group of people. In Spain, **vosotros/as** is used in informal contexts, similar to when **tú** is used. However, in Latin America, **ustedes** is used to address groups in both formal and informal contexts.

¡Póngalo en práctica!

G1 **¿Ellos o ellas?** Decide whether each group should be called **ellos** or **ellas**.

1. Rubén y Carlos
2. Raquel y Daniel
3. Ana y Rosa
4. Tomás y David
5. Gloria, Teresa y Ramón

G2 **Emparejar** Match each form of **hablar** to its corresponding subject pronoun.

	1. usted	a. hablas
	2. nosotras	b. hablan
	3. ellos	c. hablo
	4. tú	d. habla
	5. vosotros	e. hablamos
	6. yo	f. habláis

G3 **¿Qué lenguas estudian?** Use the cues to state what languages these people study.

  Modelo: Eduardo / chino
           Eduardo estudia chino.

1. nosotros / coreano
   ....
2. ustedes / francés
   ....
3. yo / español
   ....
4. vosotras / italiano
   ....
5. tú / japonés
   ....
6. tú y yo / alemán
   ....
7. Miguel y Elena / catalán
   ....
8. Mauricio y tú / portugués
   ....

1B.2 Identify nationalities

ser + [*nationality*]   4.1; 5.8.1

- To indicate a person's nationality, use **ser** + [*nationality*]. Unlike in English, adjectives of nationality are not capitalized in Spanish.

> Nuno **es portugués.**
> *Nuno is Portuguese.*
>
> Chiara **es italiana.**
> *Chiara is Italian.*

- Most Spanish adjectives have multiple forms. An adjective must match the person it describes in gender and number. When the masculine form ends in -o, form the feminine by changing the -o to -a.

> Iván es colombian**o** y Eugenia es colombian**a.**
> *Iván is Colombian and Eugenia is Colombian.*

- When the masculine form ends in -e, there is no change for the feminine form.

> Scott es canadiens**e** y Laura es canadiens**e.**
> *Scott is Canadian and Laura is Canadian.*

- When the masculine form ends in a consonant, form the feminine by adding -a. If the masculine form has a written accent on the final syllable, drop the accent mark for the feminine form.

> Pierre es franc**és** y Julie es franc**esa.**
> *Pierre is French and Julie is French.*

1B.3 Indicate the languages spoken in a country

en + [*country/city/place*]   10.12

se habla(n) + [*language(s)*]   5.12.1

- To ask which languages are spoken in a given place, say ¿Qué lenguas se hablan en [*place*]?

> **¿Qué lenguas se hablan en** Chile?
> *What languages are spoken in Chile?*

- Use **en** (*in*) before the name of a city, country, or other place to talk about what happens there.

> ¿Qué lenguas se hablan **en** Barcelona/**en** clase?
> *What languages are spoken in Barcelona/in class?*

- To tell what languages are spoken in a place, say **En** + [*place*] + **se habla(n)** + [*language(s)*]. Use **habla** for one language and **hablan** for more than one.

> En Santiago de Chile **se habla** español.
> *In Santiago, Chile, Spanish is spoken.*
>
> En Santiago de Compostela **se hablan** español y gallego.
> *In Santiago de Compostela, Spanish and Galician are spoken.*

- Use only the 3rd-person forms of a verb (**habla, hablan**) after **se**.

¡Póngalo en práctica!

 G4 **Adjetivos** Give the missing form of each adjective.

masculino	femenino
1. japonés	
2.	alemana
3. canadiense	
4. italiano	
5.	coreana
6. inglés	
7.	francesa
8. portugués	

 G5 **Es...** Use the cues to tell people's nationalities.

Modelo: Chiara / Italia
Chiara es italiana.

1. Sonia / Portugal
2. Rafael / Estados Unidos
3. Pierre / Francia
4. Carmen y Carlos / España
5. James / Canadá
6. Ángela y Valentina / Colombia
7. Ming / China
8. Josef y Konrad / Alemania

 G6 **Se habla...** Say what language(s) is/are spoken in each place.

Modelo: Marruecos / árabe
En Marruecos se habla árabe.

1. Bolivia / español

....

2. Canadá / inglés y francés

....

3. Corea / coreano

....

4. Alemania / alemán

....

5. Suiza / alemán, italiano y francés

....

6. Hong Kong / chino e inglés

....

 Practice more at **vhlcentral.com.**

GRAMÁTICA FUNCIONAL

Talk about professions

ser + [*profession*] 5.8.1

Plural of nouns 2.2

The verb **ser** (plural forms) 5.1.2

- Use the question **¿A qué se dedica?** (*form.*) or **¿A qué te dedicas?** (*fam.*) to inquire about a person's job or profession.

> ¿A qué te dedicas, Manuela?
> *What do you do, Manuela?*

- To answer, use **ser** + [*profession*].

> Soy profesora de español.
> *I'm a Spanish teacher.*

- Most names of professions have different masculine and feminine forms.

masculino	femenino
el arquitecto	la arquitecta
el ingeniero	la ingeniera
el profesor	la profesora
el técnico informático	la técnica informática

> José Luis es ingeniero y Claudia es ingeniera.
> *José Luis is an engineer and Claudia is an engineer.*

- Use the plural forms of **ser** to talk about more than one person. Unlike **hablar** and **estudiar**, **ser** is an irregular verb. This means it does not follow a regular conjugation pattern and you must memorize the forms.

SER			
(yo)	**soy**	(nosotros/as)	**somos**
(tú)	**eres**	(vosotros/as)	**sois**
(usted, él, ella)	**es**	(ustedes, ellos/as)	**son**

- Use plural nouns with the plural forms of a verb. When a noun ends in an unaccented vowel, form the plural by adding -s.

> Somos ingenieros, arquitectos y médicos.
> *We are engineers, architects, and doctors.*

- When a noun ends in a consonant, form the plural by adding -es. If the final syllable has a written accent, drop the accent mark when forming the plural.

> profesor - profesores   profesión - profesiones
> *teacher - teachers*   *profession - professions*

- As with adjectives, when a noun represents a group of mixed gender, use the masculine form.

> Darío es psicólogo y Cati es psicóloga. Darío y Cati son psicólogos.
> *Darío is a psychologist and Cati is a psychologist. Darío and Cati are psychologists.*

¡Póngalo en práctica!

G7 **Plurales** Write the plural of each noun.

Modelo: conversación
conversaciones

1. idioma ....
2. trabajo ....
3. carrera ....
4. nacionalidad ....
5. psicóloga ....
6. celular ....
7. turista ....
8. cafetería ....

G8 **Completar** Complete the sentences with the appropriate forms of **ser**.

1. Luis .... técnico informático.
2. David y yo .... ingenieros.
3. Ustedes .... médicos, ¿no?
4. Luis Miguel y Alberto .... secretarios.
5. Yo .... médico.
6. Esteban y tú .... abogados.

G9 **Un diálogo** Complete the conversation using appropriate words and expressions.

> Jorge, ¿a qué (1) .... dedicas?

> Soy (2) .... en el Hospital 12 de Octubre. Y tú, ¿a qué te (3) .... ?

> (4) .... profesora de biología.

> ¡Qué interesante! Mi amigo David también es (5) .... de biología.

> ¿David Ramírez?

> ¡Sí!

> ¡Qué casualidad! David y yo (6) .... colegas en el Instituto La Paz.

| 1B.5 | Give opinions about professions and majors |

ser + [*adjective*]   5.8.2

- Use **ser** + [*adjective*] to give your opinion about a profession, class, or other experience.

aburrido/a	estresante
divertido/a	interesante

Eres ingeniero, ¿no? ¿Es una profesión **aburrida**?
*You're an engineer, right? Is that a **boring** profession?*

No, no **es** una profesión **aburrida. Es interesante.**
*No, it's not a **boring** profession. It's interesting.*

| 1B.6 | Use numbers 12–100 |

Numbers 12–100   13.1

12 doce	**17** diecisiete	**40** cuarenta	**90** noventa
13 trece	**18** dieciocho	**50** cincuenta	**100** cien
14 catorce	**19** diecinueve	**60** sesenta	
15 quince	**20** veinte	**70** setenta	
16 dieciséis	**30** treinta	**80** ochenta	

- Form numbers 21–29 by combining **veinti-** + [*numbers 1–9*]: **veintiuno, veintidós,** etc. Note that **veintidós** (*twenty-two*), **veintitrés** (*twenty-three*), and **veintiséis** (*twenty-six*) have a written accent.

  Hay **veinticinco** estudiantes en la clase.
  *There are **twenty-five** students in the class.*

- Form numbers 30 and higher as three separate words: **treinta/ cuarenta,** etc. + **y** + [*numbers 1–9*]: **treinta y uno, treinta y dos,** etc.

- For numbers that end in **uno,** use **un** before masculine nouns and **una** before feminine nouns.

  cuarenta y **un** abogados   cincuenta y **una** cajeras
  forty-one lawyers   *fifty-one cashiers*

- Use **cien** before nouns or when counting. For numbers over one hundred, use **ciento.**

  Hay **cien** técnicos y **ciento cinco** arquitectos.
  *There are **one hundred** technicians and **one hundred five** architects.*

¡OJO!   In Spanish, phone numbers are frequently given in pairs of numbers, such that the number **616 23 45 18** would be pronounced **seis, dieciséis, veintitrés, cuarenta y cinco, dieciocho.**

¡Póngalo en práctica!

G10 **Carreras** Use adjectives to give your opinion of these majors.

Modelo: ciencias políticas
Ciencias políticas es una carrera estresante.

1. química
2. historia
3. economía
4. literatura
5. biología
6. informática

G11 **Números** Write out these numbers.

Modelo: **96**
noventa y seis

1. **48** ....
2. **72** ....
3. **28** ....
4. **81** ....
5. **55** ....
6. **63** ....

G12 **Números de teléfono** Practice giving these phone numbers.

915 44 24 13

614 81 90 90

523 68 55 26

937 70 33 51

802 22 18 04

025 70 20 90

S Practice more at **vhlcentral.com**.

VOCABULARIO 🔊 Ⓢ Vocabulary Tools

Hablamos

¿Qué lenguas hablas?	What languages do you speak?
se habla(n)	is/are spoken
18:00 h	6:00 p.m.
abril	April
el alemán	German
la cafetería	café; cafeteria
el catalán	Catalan
el chino	Chinese
la conversación	conversation
el coreano	Korean
el español	Spanish
el francés	French
el idioma	language
el inglés	English
el intercambio	exchange
el italiano	Italian
el japonés	Japanese
la nacionalidad	nationality
Pekín	Beijing
la plaza	square
el portugués	Portuguese
estudiar	to study
hablar	to speak
alemán/alemana	German
canadiense	Canadian
chino/a	Chinese
coreano/a	Korean
estadounidense	American
francés/francesa	French
inglés/inglesa	English
italiano/a	Italian
portugués/ portuguesa	Portuguese
e	and (before i or hi + consonant)

Profesiones y trabajos

¿A qué te dedicas?	What do you do (for work)?
¿Cuál es tu número de teléfono?	What is your phone number?
¡Qué interesante!	How interesting!
el/la abogado/a	lawyer
el amo/a de casa	homemaker
la biología	biology
el/la cajero/a	cashier
la carrera	major
las ciencias políticas	political science
la economía	economics
la guía	guide(book)
la historia	history
el hospital	hospital
la informática	computer science
el/la ingeniero/a	engineer
la literatura	literature
el/la médico/a	doctor
la profesión	profession
el/la profesor(a)	teacher
el/la psicólogo/a	psychologist
la química	chemistry
el/la secretario/a	secretary
el sumario	table of contents
el/la técnico/a informático/a	computer technician
el (teléfono) celular	cell phone
el trabajo	job
trabajar	to work
aburrido/a	boring
divertido/a	fun
estresante	stressful
interesante	interesting
también	too

Joan, un catalán políglota

el apellido	last name
el banco	bank
la clase	class
el euskera	Basque (language)
el foro	forum
la foto(grafía)	photo(graph)
el gallego	Galician (language)
el guaraní	Guarani
el/la guía (turístico/a)	(tour) guide
el nombre	name
País Vasco	Basque Country
la persona	person
el quechua	Quechua
el/la turista	tourist
buscar	to look for
indígena	indigenous, native
internacional	international
políglota	multilingual
claro	of course

Variación léxica

claro ↔ por supuesto ↔ desde luego

el euskera ↔ el vasco

la lengua ↔ el idioma

el/la médico/a ↔ el/la doctor(a)

políglota ↔ plurilingüe

Vocabulario útil

¿Qué onda? *What's up?*

¿Cómo te va? *How are you doing? (fam.)*

¿Cómo le va? *How are you doing? (form.)*

el/la amigo/a *friend*

el abrazo *hug*

el apretón de manos *handshake*

el beso *kiss*

el ayuntamiento *city hall*

Saludos y besos
en los países hispanos

In Spanish-speaking countries, kissing on the cheek is a customary way to greet friends and family members. Even when people are introduced for the first time, it is common for them to kiss, particularly in non-business settings. Whereas North Americans maintain considerable personal space when greeting, Spaniards and Latin Americans tend to decrease their personal space and give one or two kisses (**besos**) on the cheek, sometimes accompanied by a handshake (**apretón de manos**) or a hug (**abrazo**). In formal business settings, where associates do not know one another on a personal level, a simple handshake is appropriate.

Greeting someone with a **beso** varies according to gender and region. Men generally greet each other with a hug or warm handshake, with the exception of Argentina, where male friends and relatives lightly kiss on the cheek. Greetings between men and women, and between women, generally include kissing, but can differ depending on the country and context.

Estrategia

Using charts and tables

Charts and tables are a helpful way to organize and summarize information in an easy-to-reference format. They allow you to see patterns in data and can provide interesting supplementary information to a reading. Creating your own tables can also be a useful study method. For this reading, you can create a table with the countries mentioned and list the common greetings next to the country names. You can later use the table you created to study and review the readings.

① **Saludos** How do you greet different people?

	beso	abrazo	apretón de manos
un amigo			
una amiga			
un abogado			
una profesora			

② **Saludos y besos** Indicate how these people are likely to greet each other according to the reading.

un abrazo	un beso
un apretón de manos	dos besos

Matías y Marcos, amigos (Argentina)

Marta y Eduardo, abogados (Bolivia)

John y Lauren, amigos (EE.UU.)

In Spain, it is customary to give **dos besos**, starting with the right cheek first. In Latin American countries, including Mexico, Costa Rica, Colombia, and Chile, a greeting consists of a single "air kiss" on the right cheek. Peruvians also "air kiss," but strangers will simply shake hands. In Colombia, female acquaintances tend to simply pat each other on the right forearm or shoulder.

Tendencias

País	Beso	País	Beso
Argentina	💋	España	💋💋
Bolivia	💋	México	💋
Chile	💋	Paraguay	💋💋
Colombia	💋	Puerto Rico	💋
El Salvador	💋	Venezuela	💋 / 💋💋

▶ **La plaza principal**
In the Spanish-speaking world, public space is treasured. Small city and town life revolves around the **plaza principal.** Often surrounded by cathedrals or municipal buildings like the **ayuntamiento,** the pedestrian **plaza** is designated as a central meeting place for family and friends. During warmer months, when outdoor cafés usually line the **plaza**, it is a popular spot to have a leisurely cup of coffee, chat, and people watch. One of the most famous town squares is the **Plaza Mayor** in the university town of Salamanca, Spain. Students gather underneath its famous clock tower to meet up with friends or simply take a coffee break.

(3) **Representar** Two of the people in the photos in **Actividad 2** meet in a **plaza**. With a partner, write a brief conversation between them and act it out.

Estrategia ··········

Doing Internet research in Spanish

When you do Internet research in Spanish, in addition to using Spanish search words, you can adjust the settings of your browser so that it only searches sites that contain Spanish content. If you do not know the Spanish for the keywords you are looking for, use a good online dictionary. Avoid conducting your search in English and using an automatic translator to get the information in Spanish.

PROYECTO

Mapa de saludos
As you have learned, greetings can vary quite a bit from country to country. Prepare a greetings map to share with the class.

• Choose the region you will focus on (the world, Latin America, etc.).

• Research greetings in countries other than those in the reading.

• Add labels in Spanish for countries and greetings.

• Include a photo of two people from one of the countries greeting each other.

Estrategia

Looking at labels

When you are watching **Flash Cultura** episodes, pay attention to the labels that appear on the screen. These will point out important information and names of places and monuments. You can pause the video and write down the labels. This video is about socializing in the city squares in Buenos Aires. As the different squares appear on the screen, what labels do you expect to see?

Vocabulario útil

la aventura *adventure*

el/la presentador(a) *presenter, host*

¡Qué bueno verte! *So good to see you!*

¡Cuánto tiempo! *Long time no see.*

Video

Encuentros en la plaza

You have learned about greetings and **plazas**. In this episode of **Flash Cultura**, you will learn more about how people greet each other in Argentina and about the plazas in Buenos Aires.

1. **Saludos** Where do you and your friends meet up? Are there public places where you get together? How do you greet people when you first meet them? Discuss your experiences with a partner.

2. **Mirar** Watch this **Flash Cultura** episode. While you watch the video, pay attention to the on-screen labels.

Today we are at the Plaza de Mayo.

—Hola.
—¿Cómo estás?
—¡Cuánto tiempo!

3. **Señalar** Mark the words and phrases that you heard in the video.

1. Chau. ☐
2. Hola. ☐
3. ¿Qué tal? ☐
4. Buenos días. ☐
5. Mucho gusto. ☐
6. Adiós. ☐

4. **¿Verdadero o falso?** Indicate whether each statement is true (**verdadero**) or false (**falso**).

	V	F
1. La presentadora habla inglés.	☐	☐
2. Gonzalo es de Estados Unidos.	☐	☐
3. Mark es de Estados Unidos.	☐	☐
4. Gonzalo estudia en la Universidad de Buenos Aires.	☐	☐

5. **Diálogo** With a partner, prepare a brief dialogue in which two people who have not seen each other in a while meet in a **plaza**.

Modelo: • ¡Pedro!
              ■ Hola, Martín. ¡Cuánto tiempo! ¿Qué...?

Estrategia

Using synonyms

When greeting someone or saying goodbye, use a variety of expressions. If the other person asks **¿Cómo estás?**, after responding, you can ask him/her **¿Qué tal?** instead of repeating the original question. If you have learned colloquial expressions from different countries, remember to use them in an appropriate context!

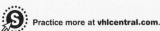

Practice more at **vhlcentral.com**.

Unidad 2

Juan Tomás, un taxista de Panamá

Rosa, camarera del bar El rey de la tapa

Los estudios

2A

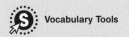

ENTRE EL NORTE Y EL SUR

¡Viva Guatemala!

Plaza de la Constitución, Ciudad de Guatemala

Distancias Entre Capitales de América Central

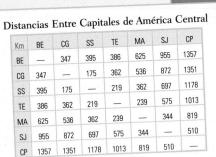

Km	BE	CG	SS	TE	MA	SJ	CP
BE	—	347	395	386	625	955	1357
CG	347	—	175	362	536	872	1351
SS	395	175	—	219	362	697	1178
TE	386	362	219	—	239	575	1013
MA	625	536	362	239	—	344	819
SJ	955	872	697	575	344	—	510
CP	1357	1351	1178	1013	819	510	—

Situar lugares

- ¿Dónde está Tegucigalpa?
- Está en el sur de Honduras.

2A.1 Interrogative ¿dónde? The verb **estar**

Expresar cantidades

100	cien
121	ciento veintiuno/a
200	doscientos/as
300	trescientos/as
400	cuatrocientos/as
500	quinientos/as
600	seiscientos/as
700	setecientos/as
800	ochocientos/as
900	novecientos/as
1000	mil

2A.2 Numbers 100–1,000

Vocabulario

(1)

entre *between*

el norte *north*

el sur *south*

¡Viva...! *Long live . . . !*

el este *east*

el oeste *west*

la distancia *distance*

¿Dónde (está)...? *Where (is) . . . ?*

(2)

estar a... kilómetros de... *to be . . . kilometers from . . .*

(4)

cerca de *near*

lejos de *far from*

muy *very*

---

1 **Coordenadas** Look at the map and circle the option that best completes each statement.

1. Guatemala está en el norte / sur / este de América Central.

2. Panamá está en el norte / sur / oeste de América Central.

3. Managua está en el norte / este / oeste de Nicaragua.

2 **Ciudades y distancias** Listen to the recording and complete each statement with the missing city and distance.

1. .... está a .... kilómetros de Managua.

2. .... está a .... kilómetros de Tegucigalpa.

3. .... está a .... kilómetros de San José.

4. .... está a .... kilómetros de San José.

5. .... está a .... kilómetros de Managua.

6. .... está a .... kilómetros de San Salvador.

3 **Preguntar** Refer to the distance chart and ask a partner about distances between pairs of cities in Central America.

Modelo: • ¿Cuál es la distancia entre Managua y Belmopán?
• *Seiscientos veinticinco kilómetros.*

4 **¿Verdadero?** Read these statements and check the ones that are true.

1. El Salvador está muy cerca de Honduras. ☐
2. Ciudad de Guatemala está lejos de Ciudad de Panamá. ☐
3. Panamá está muy cerca de Belice. ☐
4. Tegucigalpa está cerca de Ciudad de Guatemala. ☐

Ciudad de Guatemala, 26 de mayo

Hola, Lupe: Estoy en el sur de Guatemala, en Ciudad de Guatemala, la capital. Está lejos de México, D.F., a 1060 kilómetros. Es una ciudad muy bonita, con lugares fantásticos: la Plaza de la Constitución (o Parque Central), la catedral y grandes edificios como el Palacio Nacional de la Cultura. El hotel es muy agradable y está en el Centro Histórico, un barrio típico muy antiguo en el centro. ¡Es una pequeña ciudad antigua en el corazón de una ciudad moderna! El centro de la ciudad es precioso. ¡Ah! Y los guatemaltecos ¡son muy simpáticos!

Un beso, Hugo

Sra. Guadalupe Henríquez

Avenida de la Paz, 4564

34453 México, D.F.

MÉXICO

Indicar distancias e intensificar

San Salvador **está cerca de** Guatemala.

San Salvador **está lejos de** Belmopán.

San Salvador **está muy lejos** de San José.

San Salvador **está a** 697 km **de** San José.

2A.3 | **estar cerca/lejos de**
muy + [*adjective/adverb*]

---

5 **¿Verdadero o falso?** Read the postcard and indicate whether each statement is true (**verdadero**) or false (**falso**), according to Hugo. Compare your answers to a partner's.

	V	F
1. Hugo está en Ciudad de Guatemala.	☐	☐
2. El Centro Histórico es precioso.	☐	☐
3. La Plaza de la Constitución y el Parque Central son dos parques.	☐	☐
4. El hotel está en un barrio moderno.	☐	☐
5. Los guatemaltecos son muy simpáticos.	☐	☐

6 **Seleccionar** Choose the correct form of **ser** or **estar** to complete each sentence.

1. Antigua **es/está** una ciudad bonita.
2. Chichicastenango **es/está** cerca de Ciudad de Guatemala.
3. Tikal **es/está** en Guatemala.
4. Cobán **es/está** una ciudad histórica.

7 **Oraciones** Use these elements to write complete sentences with forms of **ser**.

Modelo: *El parque es romántico.*

el	la	parque	hotel	ciudad		es		agradables	famoso
los	las		guatemaltecos			son		simpáticos	preciosa
		plazas		barrios				romántico	bonitas

MI EXPERIENCIA

8 **Mi ciudad** Tell a classmate about your city or town.

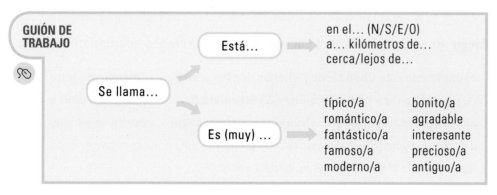

GUIÓN DE TRABAJO

Se llama...

Está... → en el... (N/S/E/O) a... kilómetros de... cerca/lejos de...

Es (muy) ... → típico/a bonito/a
romántico/a agradable
fantástico/a interesante
famoso/a precioso/a
moderno/a antiguo/a

Presentar y describir lugares

Ciudad de Guatemala es **una** ciudad fantástica.

El Palacio Nacional de la Cultura es **un** edificio famoso.

Los guatemaltec**os** son simpátic**os**.

2A.4 | Article-noun-adjective agreement

2A.5 | **ser/estar**
ser + [*descriptive adjective*]

Vocabulario

5

mayo *May*

señora (Sra.) *Mrs.*

la avenida *avenue*

la paz *peace*

bonito/a *pretty*

el lugar *place*

el parque *park*

la catedral *cathedral*

el edificio *building*

agradable *pleasant*

típico/a *typical*

antiguo/a *old*

el corazón *heart*

precioso/a *lovely*

el/la guatemalteco/a *Guatemalan*

simpático/a *nice*

el beso *kiss*

la capital, fantástico/a, moderno/a

7

famoso/a, romántico/a

SAM: Actividades pp. 25–27

Practice more at vhlcentral.com.

Cerca de casa

SAN JOSÉ HOY

CARTAS AL DIRECTOR

Vivo en el centro de la ciudad, cerca de la catedral. Mi barrio tiene unos lugares preciosos: museos, el ayuntamiento, la plaza, iglesias. Mi calle tiene bares y cafeterías... Todo es muy bonito y muy romántico, pero vivir en el centro también tiene problemas. Tenemos pocos parques y el tráfico es horrible. Mi casa está cerca de una discoteca y tenemos un ruido insoportable. Mi familia vive muy lejos, en la periferia, y su barrio es muy diferente: tiene parques, centros comerciales, polideportivos... y es tranquilo. ¡Mi esposo y yo vivimos en el centro, pero no somos unos privilegiados!

Lucía Olivas Gómez, San José

(Editorial de *SAN JOSÉ HOY*, 26 de mayo)

Hablar del lugar de residencia

- ¿**Vives** en el centro?
- No, **vivo** en la periferia.
- Nosotros **vivimos** en el centro y ellos **viven** en la periferia.

2A.6 Regular **-ir** verbs: **vivir**

Expresar posesión

Tengo unas postales de Nicoya.

San José **tiene unos** barrios muy bonitos.

2A.7 The verb **tener**
Indefinite articles (plural)

Vocabulario

9

la carta al director *letter to the editor*
el ayuntamiento *city hall*
la iglesia *church*
todo *everything, all*
pocos/as *few*
pero *but*
vivir *to live*
tener *to have*
la calle *street*
la discoteca *disco, nightclub*
el ruido *noise*
insoportable *unbearable*
la periferia *suburbs*
el centro comercial *shopping mall*
el polideportivo *sports center*

---

9 **Títulos** Read Lucía's letter to the editor and choose a title for it. Propose another title for the letter.

"EL CENTRO DE LA CIUDAD"   **"VIVIR EN EL CENTRO"**

"BARRIOS CON PROBLEMAS"

10 **a. Contestar** Answer the questions using complete sentences.

- ¿Dónde vive Lucía?
- ¿Dónde vive la familia de Lucía?

b. Preguntar Now ask your partner about his/her neighborhood.

Modelo:
- *¿Dónde vives?*
- *Vivo en... Vivo cerca/lejos de...*

11 **Conjugar** Complete the chart with the missing forms of **vivir** from the letter.

yo	tú	usted, él, ella	nosotros/as	vosotros/as	ustedes, ellos/as
	vives			vivís	viven

12 **a. Problemas** What problems does Lucía describe in her letter?

Modelo: *El centro tiene... / no tiene...*

b. Tener Underline all the forms of **tener** used in the letter.

13 **Elegir** Read the summary of Lucía's letter and circle the appropriate articles.

El *centro* de San José tiene (1) unos/los lugares muy románticos, pero (2) un/el centro también tiene (3) el/un tráfico horrible y las calles con discotecas tienen (4) el/un ruido insoportable. La periferia es muy diferente; tiene (5) los/unos centros comerciales y polideportivos. Está lejos, pero no tiene (6) un/el ruido del centro.

Iglesias | *Parques* | *Cafeterías y restaurantes*

Museos

Centros comerciales

Polideportivos

14 **a. Los barrios** Look at the photos and ask your partner what attractions his/her neighborhood has. Then, tell your partner about your neighborhood.

Modelo: *¿Tu barrio tiene...?*

b. Su barrio Now tell the class about your partner's neighborhood.

Modelo: *Su barrio tiene... / no tiene...*

15 **Una carta al director** Work with a partner to write a letter to the editor about two problems in your neighborhood. Share your letter with the class.

Sr. Director:

MI EXPERIENCIA

16 **Describir** Describe your ideal neighborhood or town.
Before completing the activity, decide whether each of the words listed is masculine or feminine, and list them under the appropriate definite articles.

museo, iglesia, parque, plaza, discoteca, centro comercial, polideportivo, catedral, ayuntamiento

el	la

GUIÓN DE TRABAJO

Mi barrio ideal

tiene...
- museos
- parques
- plazas
- centros comerciales
- polideportivos
- ayuntamiento

no tiene...
- ruido
- tráfico
- problemas
- tranquilidad
- discotecas
- monumentos

Expresar posesión

Mi barrio no tiene parques.
¿Tu barrio está en el centro?
¡Su ciudad es preciosa!

2A.8 Possessives (singular)

Vocabulario *cont.*

el/la privilegiado/a *privileged person*
el problema, el tráfico, horrible, la familia, diferente, tranquilo/a
⑯
la tranquilidad *peace, tranquility*
ideal

Lugares de encuentro

Most cities in Spanish-speaking countries have a central **plaza,** where important government and religious buildings are located, where official ceremonies and celebrations are held, and where people gather to socialize or hold markets. Famous **plazas** in San José include **Plaza de la Cultura** and **Plaza de la Democracia**.

SAM: Actividades pp. 28–30

Juan Tomás, un taxista de Panamá

Juan Tomás: *El tráfico en Ciudad de Panamá no es muy bueno, la verdad. El centro de la ciudad tiene problemas de tráfico, de ruido, de obras... pero es muy bonito y tiene de todo: restaurantes, monumentos, paseos, tiendas... Vivir en Panamá es fantástico, con sus fiestas, su gente, su buen tiempo... La vida aquí es muy cómoda; tienes mucha calidad de vida.*

Entrevistador: Juan Tomás, ¿y cómo es el trabajo de taxista en Ciudad de Panamá?

Juan Tomás: *Bueno... Es un trabajo agradable, muy bonito. Escucho la radio, hablo con la gente: panameños, turistas...*

Entrevistador: ¿Y tienes clientes extranjeros?

Juan Tomás: *¡Claro! Un abrazo a todos los extranjeros y para los panameños y las panameñas. ¡Viva Panamá!*

Juan Tomás, taxista en Ciudad de Panamá desde 2001, enamorado de su ciudad y su profesión.

Vocabulario

(17)

desde *since*

enamorado/a de *in love with*

..., la verdad *to tell the truth*

las obras *construction*

el paseo *walkway*

la tienda *store*

la fiesta *festival*

la gente *people*

el buen tiempo *good weather*

cómodo/a *comfortable*

mucho/a *much, a lot*

la calidad de vida *quality of life*

¿Cómo es...? *What is . . . like?*

bueno... *well . . .*

escuchar la radio *to listen to the radio*

hablar con la gente *to talk to people*

el/la panameño/a *Panamanian*

extranjero/a *foreign*

el abrazo *hug*

la central *main office*

n.° (el número) *number*

el domicilio *home address*

el/la cliente, la licencia

(19)

ocupado/a *busy*

allí *there*

perfecto/a

17 Contestar Look at Juan Tomás's taxi license and answer these questions.

1. ¿Dónde vive? ....
2. ¿Dónde trabaja? ....
3. ¿Cuál es el número de su licencia? ....

18 Preguntas Read the interview and answer the questions.

1. ¿Qué problemas tiene el centro de la ciudad?
2. ¿Qué lugares interesantes tiene?
3. ¿Cómo es vivir en Ciudad de Panamá?

19 Radio-Taxi Listen to the call from the Radio-Taxi dispatch and answer the questions.

Central: Central de Radio-Taxi. ¿Dónde estás?
Taxista: Estoy en el centro, muy cerca de la Universidad, en la Avenida José de Fábrega.
Central: ¿Estás ocupado?
Taxista: No.
Central: Hay un cliente en la calle 53 Oeste, número 43.
Taxista: Estoy cerca; estoy allí en tres minutos.
Central: Perfecto. Gracias.

1. ¿Dónde está el taxista? ....
2. ¿Dónde está el cliente? ....

20 Representar In pairs, practice reading the interview aloud, taking turns with the different roles. Then role-play a similar conversation for the class.

21 Entrevista Interview a classmate to find out what he/she thinks about his/her city or region. Also answer his/her questions.

Modelo: *¿Estás orgulloso/a de tu ciudad?*

MUNICIPIO DE PANAMÁ

CENTRAL DE RADIO-TAXI

LICENCIA DE TAXISTA:
N.° 00-BA-957

Nombre:
Juan Tomás Álvarez
Domicilio:
Calle Colón, 3
Ciudad de Panamá

22 **a. México, D.F.** Read the excerpt from a tourbook about Mexico City. Underline the key pieces of information.

MÉXICO, D.F.

Ciudad: *México, D.F.*
Población: *8 874 700 habitantes*
Clima: *calor en verano y frío en invierno*
Superficie: *1485 km²*
País: *México*

México, D.F. es la capital de México. Está en el centro del país, al este del océano Pacífico y al oeste del golfo de México. Tiene barrios muy típicos, como Coyoacán, San Ángel y Chapultepec, y una universidad muy antigua, la UNAM. También tiene monumentos importantes: el Ángel de la Independencia, el Monumento a Benito Juárez, el Monumento a la Revolución Mexicana y el Monumento a los Niños Héroes. El ambiente es único: universitarios, jóvenes, turistas, etc. La gente es muy agradable. Además, muy cerca de la ciudad están las pirámides de Teotihuacán, y se pueden visitar las ruinas.

b. Adjetivos How does this guide describe Mexico City? List the adjectives used in the description.

c. Describir Imagine you work in a travel agency. Choose a city you know well and describe it to a client. Tell him/her where it is and follow the model description of Mexico City to describe your preferences and any places of interest.

○ *La ciudad es…*   ○ *Tiene…*   ○ *Está…*   ○ *La gente es…*

([b])─([v])

23 **a. [b] y [v]** Listen to these place names. What sound do they have in common?

Parque Berlín   Avenida de Buenos Aires   Hotel Sevilla
Plaza de Bogotá   Catedral de Valencia   Barrio de Río Abajo

• In Spanish, **b** and **v** are pronounced the same.

b. Repetir Now repeat the words to practice their pronunciation.

24 **a. Ciudades** Many city names are repeated in several Spanish-speaking countries. Use the maps on pages xxxi–xxxii of your text and the Internet to identify at least two countries where you can find cities with each of these names.

Córdoba	Toledo	Trujillo
Santiago	Mérida	Santa Cruz
Guadalajara	San José	Trinidad

b. ¿Dónde está…? Ask a partner questions about the information he/she found.

Modelo: ● *¿Dónde está Córdoba?*
■ *Córdoba está en .... y ....*

Vocabulario

21
orgulloso/a *proud*

22
la población *population*
el/la habitante *inhabitant*
el clima *climate*
el calor *heat*
el verano *summer*
el frío *cold*
el invierno *winter*
la superficie *area*
la universidad *university*
el ambiente *atmosphere*
único/a *unique*
el/la universitario/a *college student*
joven (*pl.* jóvenes) *young*
los jóvenes *young people*
además *in addition*
importante, la pirámide, las ruinas

SAM: Actividades pp. 31–34

Practice more at **vhlcentral.com.**

T A R E A   F I N A L

Su ciudad ideal

Think: what is your ideal city like?

Es...   Tiene...   Está...   Las personas son/La gente es...

List the characteristics of the city and describe what it does and does not have.

Compare your list with a partner's, and create a combined list.

Draw a map of your city, including labels for the sites and features you chose.

Write a description of your city and present your map to the class.

Y O   P U E D O . . .

• **Puedo hablar de la localización geográfica de una ciudad.**
  Think of a city in your country and say how far it is from other cities or towns.

• **Puedo indicar la localización de mi vivienda.** - - - - - - - - - - - - - - - - - ▸
  Tell where your home is.

• **Puedo hablar de diferentes aspectos de una ciudad o un lugar.**
  Talk about a city. Describe three interesting aspects.

• **Puedo indicar posesión o pertenencia.** - ▸
  Name three of your favorite things in your city or neighborhood.

Write three sentences.

Mi casa ....
....
....
....

Mis lugares preferidos:
....
....
....

GRAMÁTICA FUNCIONAL Ⓢ Tutorials

2A.1 Indicate places

Interrogative **¿dónde?** 9
The verb **estar** 5.1.2, 5.8.1

- To ask where a city or place is located, say **¿Dónde está** + [*place*]? To answer, say [*place*] **está** + **en** + [*location*].

¿Dónde está Santander?	Santander está en el norte.
Where is Santander?	*Santander is in the north.*

- Use the verb **estar** (*to be*) to express location. **Estar** is an irregular verb, so you must memorize its forms.

ESTAR

(yo)	estoy	(nosotros/as)	estamos
(tú)	estás	(vosotros/as)	estáis
(usted, él, ella)	está	(ustedes, ellos/as)	están

Fernando, ¿dónde estás?	Estoy en Antigua.
Fernando, where are you?	*I'm in Antigua.*

2A.2 Express quantities

Numbers 100–1,000 13.1

- These are the hundreds 100 to 1,000. Note the spelling changes in 500, 700, and 900.

Números del 100 al 1000

100	cien, 121 ciento...	600	seiscientos/as
200	doscientos/as	700	setecientos/as
300	trescientos/as	800	ochocientos/as
400	cuatrocientos/as	900	novecientos/as
500	quinientos/as	1000	mil

- The numbers 200 through 999 agree in gender with the noun they modify.

San José está a trescient**os** cuarenta y cuatro kilómetr**os** (doscient**as** catorce mill**as**) de Managua.

San José is three hundred forty-four kilometers (two hundred fourteen miles) from Managua.

2A.3 Indicate distances and intensify

estar + **cerca/lejos** + **de** 5.8.1, 11.7
muy + [*adverb/adjective*] 11.4

- Use **estar** + **cerca/lejos** + **de** to express relative distance.

Colón **está cerca de** Ciudad de Panamá.
Colón is near Panama City.

Canadá **está lejos de** Guatemala.
Canada is far from Guatemala.

- To intensify the meaning of an adjective or adverb, place **muy** (*very*) immediately in front of the adjective or adverb.

La playa es **muy bonita** y está **muy cerca** de la ciudad.
The beach is very pretty and it is very close to the city.

¡Póngalo en práctica!

G1 **Ciudades** Complete each sentence with the appropriate form of **estar**.

1. Managua y León .... en el oeste de Nicaragua.
2. Puntarenas .... en Costa Rica.
3. Yo .... en San Diego.
4. ¿Dónde .... el lago de Nicaragua?
5. Magdalena y tú .... en Colón.
6. Tú .... en Panamá.
7. ¿Dónde .... Miguel y Jesús?
8. Ricardo y yo .... en California.

G2 **Números** Write out these numbers.

1. 339 ....
2. 437 ....
3. 555 ....
4. 738 ....
5. 945 ....
6. 226 ....

G3 **Distancias** Write out these distances in **millas** or **kilómetros**.

1. 222 km ....
2. 333 mi ....
3. 500 mi ....
4. 780 km ....
5. 850 km ....
6. 160 mi ....

G4 **¿Cerca o lejos?** Use the cues to write complete sentences.

1. Puebla / cerca / la Ciudad de México

   ....

2. Cuba / muy lejos / España

   ....

3. Maracaibo / lejos / Arequipa

   ....

4. Ciudad Juárez / muy cerca / El Paso

   ....

GRAMÁTICA FUNCIONAL

2A.4 / 2A.5 Present and describe places

Definite articles **3.1**   **ser** + [*adjective*] **5.8.1**
Gender agreement with articles and adjectives **3.1, 4.1**

- Use a definite article (**el**, **la**, **los**, or **las**) to refer to a specific noun. The definite article must correspond to the gender and number of the noun it modifies.

	singular	plural
masculino	el parque	los parques
femenino	la plaza	las plazas

- Adjectives must also agree with nouns in gender and number.

  La plaza es bonit**a**.   **Los** barrios son bonit**os**.
  The square is pretty.   *The neighborhoods are pretty.*

- Use **ser** + [*adjective*] to describe the characteristics of a person, place, or thing.

2A.6 Talk about your place of residence

Regular -ir verbs: **vivir** **5.1.1**   Prepositions: **en** **10.12**

- Use the regular verb **vivir** (*to live*) to talk about where people live. Other regular **-ir** verbs follow this same conjugation pattern.

VIVIR

(yo)	vivo	(nosotros/as)	vivimos
(tú)	vives	(vosotros/as)	vivís
(usted, él, ella)	vive	(ustedes, ellos/as)	viven

- Use **¿Dónde** + [**vivir**]**?** to ask where someone lives. To answer, say [**vivir**] + **en** + [*place*].

  ¿Dónde vives, Ángel?   **Vivo en** San Juan.
  Where do you live, Ángel?   *I live in San Juan.*

2A.7 / 2A.8 Express possession

The verb **tener** **5.1.2**   Indefinite articles (plural) **3.2**
Possessive adjectives (singular) **8.1**

- Use the irregular verb **tener** (*to have*) to express possession.

TENER

(yo)	tengo	(nosotros/as)	tenemos
(tú)	tienes	(vosotros/as)	tenéis
(usted, él, ella)	tiene	(ustedes, ellos/as)	tienen

- Use the plural indefinite article **unos/as** to express the idea *some*.

  Madrid tiene **unas** plazas bonitas y **unos** parques tranquilos.
  *Madrid has **some** pretty squares and **some** quiet parks.*

- Use the possessive adjectives **mi** (*my*), **tu** (*your*), and **su** (*your* [form.]/*his/her/its*) with singular nouns to indicate to whom something belongs.

  mi barrio   **tu** ciudad   **su** pueblo
  my neighborhood   *your city*   *your/his/her/its town*

¡Póngalo en práctica!

G5 **Describir** Form sentences with the words provided. Remember to include a definite article and the correct form of the verb **ser**.

> Modelo: calles / modernas
> *Las calles son modernas.*

1. chicos / simpáticos

   ....

2. ciudad / única

   ....

3. monumentos / antiguos

   ....

4. plaza / agradable

   ....

5. tráfico / horrible

   ....

G6 **Conversación** Complete the conversation using the appropriate forms of **vivir**.

- ¿Dónde (1)................. María José?
- (2)................. en Sevilla.
- Y tú, ¿dónde (3).................?
- (4)................. en Dublín. Vosotros, ¿dónde (5)................. ?
- (6)................. en Córdoba.
- ¡Qué bien! Es una ciudad preciosa.

G7 **Vivir aquí** Complete each sentence with the appropriate possessive adjective.

1. Vivo aquí; es .... casa.
2. Usted vive aquí; es .... ciudad.
3. Tú vives aquí; es .... calle.
4. José vive aquí; es .... pueblo.

G8 **Completar** Complete the conversation with the appropriate form of **tener** and indefinite articles.

- Yo (1)............... una casa en Miami.
- Mi amigo Antonio también (2)............... una casa en Miami. Es una ciudad fascinante.
- Sí, tiene (3)............... barrios muy interesantes y (4)............... playas preciosas.

 Practice more at vhlcentral.com.

VOCABULARIO 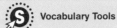 Vocabulary Tools

¡Viva Guatemala!

¿dónde?	where?
¿Dónde está...?	Where is . . . ?
estar a... kilómetros de...	to be . . . kilometers from . . .
señora (Sra.)	Mrs.
¡Viva...!	Long live . . . !
la avenida	avenue
el beso	kiss
la capital	capital
la catedral	cathedral
el corazón	heart
la distancia	distance
el edificio	building
el este	east
el/la guatemalteco/a	Guatemalan
el kilómetro	kilometer
el lugar	place
mayo	May
el norte	north
el oeste	west
el parque	park
la paz	peace
el sur	south
agradable	pleasant
antiguo/a	old
bonito/a	pretty
famoso/a	famous
fantástico/a	fantastic
moderno/a	modern
precioso/a	lovely
romántico/a	romantic
simpático/a	nice
típico/a	typical
cerca de	near
entre	between
lejos de	far from
muy	very

Cerca de casa

el ayuntamiento	city hall
la calle	street
la carta al director	letter to the editor
el centro comercial	shopping mall
la discoteca	disco, nightclub
la familia	family
la iglesia	church
la periferia	suburbs
el polideportivo	sports center
el/la privilegiado/a	privileged person
el problema	problem
el ruido	noise
el tráfico	traffic
la tranquilidad	peace, tranquility
todo	everything, all
tener	to have
vivir	to live
diferente	different
horrible	horrible
ideal	ideal
insoportable	unbearable
pocos/as	few
tranquilo/a	calm, quiet
pero	but

Juan Tomás

bueno...	well . . .
..., la verdad	to tell the truth
¿Cómo es...?	What is . . . like?
escuchar la radio	to listen to the radio
enamorado/a de	in love with
hablar con la gente	to talk to people
el abrazo	hug
el ambiente	atmosphere
el buen tiempo	good weather
la calidad de vida	quality of life
el calor	heat
la central	main office
el/la cliente	client
el clima	climate
el domicilio	home address
la fiesta	festival
el frío	cold
la gente	people
el/la habitante	inhabitant
el invierno	winter
los jóvenes	young people
la licencia	license
n.º (el número)	number
las obras	construction
el/la panameño/a	Panamanian
el paseo	walkway
la pirámide	pyramid
la población	population
las ruinas	ruins
la superficie	area
la tienda	store
la universidad	university
el/la universitario/a	college student
el verano	summer
cómodo/a	comfortable
extranjero/a	foreign
importante	important
joven (pl. jóvenes)	young
mucho/a	much, a lot
ocupado/a	busy
orgulloso/a	proud
perfecto/a	perfect
único/a	unique
allí	there
además	in addition
desde	since

Variación léxica

el ayuntamiento ⟷ la intendencia (*Arg., Uru.*) ⟷ la municipalidad

la periferia ⟷ las afueras

el polideportivo ⟷ el complejo deportivo ⟷ el parque de recreación y deportes

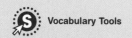
Vocabulary Tools

ESPECIALIDAD DE LA CASA

Café con leche

CAFETERÍA LEVANTE

DESAYUNO N° 1:   3€
- Café (solo o con leche) o té
- Tostada con mantequilla y
  mermelada, cruasán o churros

DESAYUNO N° 2:   4€
- Chocolate con churros

- Zumo de naranja natural   2€

¡Hola, buenos días! ¿Qué desean?

Un café solo y una tostada con mantequilla y mermelada, por favor. ¡Ah, y un zumo de naranja natural!

Y yo... ¡un chocolate con churros!

¿Cuánto es?

Son 9 euros.

Pedir y pagar en una cafetería

- ¿Qué desea tomar?
- Un té y un cruasán.
- ¿Cuánto es?
- Son 3 euros.

2B.1 Interrogative **¿cuánto?**

Vocabulario

(1)

el té *tea*

el desayuno *breakfast*

la tostada *toast*

la mantequilla *butter*

la mermelada *jam, marmalade*

por favor *please*

el cruasán *croissant*

el zumo/jugo de naranja (*Esp./Amér. L.*) *orange juice*

natural *fresh*

¿Qué desean tomar? *What would you like (to have)?*

el café solo *black coffee*

¿Cuánto es? *How much is it?*

Son 9 euros. *It's 9 euros.*

el queso *cheese*

el pan *bread*

el aceite de oliva *olive oil*

el/la compañero/a *partner*

los cereales, los churros, el sándwich, el yogur

(2)

el/la camarero/a *waiter/waitress*

---

1 **a. Cafetería Levante** Alicia and Carmen are having breakfast at a café in Alicante, Spain. Read their conversation with the waitress, and check off the items they order.

un café solo		un sándwich de jamón y queso	
un té		churros	
un café con leche		cereales	
un chocolate		un cruasán	
un zumo de naranja		una tostada con mantequilla y mermelada	
un yogur		pan tostado con aceite de oliva	

b. El desayuno What would you order for breakfast at **Cafetería Levante**? And your partner?

- YO: - MI COMPAÑERO/A:

2 **Completar** Look at the menu and read each mini-conversation; then fill in the blanks to tell what each person ordered at **Cafetería Levante**.

- Por favor, camarero, ¿cuánto es?   ■ Son 3 euros.

  Café con .... y tostada con .... y ....

- ¿Cuánto es, por favor?   ■ Son 6 euros.

  .... con .... y zumo de ....

3 **Representar** In groups of three, role-play a conversation at a café.

Hola, ¿qué........................... ....?

Yo ....

Yo ....

Son ....

¿Cuánto ....?

1001 Cafés

Normalmente, los españoles desayunan poco; beben una taza de café o té y siempre comen algo dulce: *galletas*, *bollería* o una *tostada* con *mantequilla y mermelada*. A veces desayunan una tostada con *aceite de oliva o cereales y yogur*. También beben *zumo de naranja natural*. Tienen muchas formas de tomar café: café solo, café con leche, largo de café (el doble de café), corto de café (poco café), descafeinado (sin cafeína), cortado (con unas gotas de leche), café con hielo... El fin de semana es frecuente desayunar algo especial. Por ejemplo, en Madrid, chocolate con *churros* y, en Andalucía, *pan tostado con aceite y tomate*.

4 **a. El café** What types of coffee are listed in the reading?

1. .... 3. .... 5. .... 7. ....
2. .... 4. .... 6. ....

b. Relacionar Match the words in italics to the items shown in the photo.

1. .... 4. .... 7. .... 10. ....
2. .... 5. .... 8. .... 11. ....
3. .... 6. .... 9. ....

5 **Escribir** Find the forms of the verb **beber** and write the missing verb endings on the coffee cups.

BEB-

-........   -ÉIS

-O   -E   -........   -........

6 **Los hábitos de Lucía** Listen to the interview and connect items from each column to show what you learned about Lucía's dining habits.

MI EXPERIENCIA

7 **Preguntas** Ask a partner about his/her eating habits and report your findings to the class.

Hablar de las comidas del día y expresar frecuencia

- Nosotros **bebemos** té. ¿Y vosotros?
- Yo **bebo** café y ella **bebe** jugo de naranja.
- Pedro, ¿dónde desayunas?
- **Siempre** desayuno en casa.
- ¿Usted **almuerza** en casa?
- Normalmente almuerzo en un restaurante. **A veces**, ceno fuera.

2B.2	Regular **-er** verbs: **beber**
2B.3	Adverbs of frequency **almorzar** (o:ue)

Vocabulario
4

normalmente *normally*
desayunar *to eat breakfast*
beber *to drink*
la taza *cup*
siempre *always*
comer *to eat*
algo *something*
dulce *sweet*
la galleta *cookie*
la bollería (*Esp.*) *pastries*
poco/a *little*
la gota *drop*
el hielo *ice*
(el fin de) semana (*f.*) *week(end)*
frecuente *common*
el doble, la cafeína, el descafeinado, especial
6

a veces *sometimes*
almorzar (o:ue) *to eat lunch*
cenar *to eat supper*
en casa *at home*
fuera *out*

SAM: Actividades pp. 35–37

2B.4 otro/a; algo/nada más

Pedir y pagar en un restaurante

- ● ¿Qué desea?
- ■ De **primer plato**, lentejas, y de **plato principal**, dorada, por favor.
- ● ¿De beber?
- ■ Agua.
- ...
- ■ ¡Camarero!, por favor, **otra** botella de agua.
- ...
- ■ **De** postre, un flan.
- ● ¿Desea **algo más**?
- ■ No, **nada más**, gracias. La cuenta, por favor.

Vocabulario

8

¿Algo más? *Anything else?*

Nada más, gracias. *Nothing else, thanks.*

la cuenta *bill*

el menú del día *fixed-price menu*

el primer plato *first course*

el plato principal *main course*

el postre *dessert*

la bebida *beverage*

la ensalada de la casa *house salad*

las lentejas con chorizo *lentils with chorizo (sausage)*

el arroz con verduras *rice with vegetables*

la sopa de pescado *fish soup*

la dorada *sea bream (type of fish)*

el filete de ternera *fillet of veal*

la patata (*Esp.*) *potato*

la albóndiga *meatball*

el bacalao en salsa *cod with sauce*

el helado *ice cream*

la fruta *fruit*

el flan *flan (custard)*

IVA incluido *tax included*

9

las verduras *vegetables*

las legumbres *legumes*

el pescado *fish*

la carne *meat*

10

el vino *wine*

la cerveza *beer*

la botella *bottle*

vale (*Esp.*) *OK*

Menú del día

Restaurante Casa del Pescador
Calle del Puerto, 4 (Santander)

Menú del día

PRIMER PLATO
- Ensalada de la casa
- Lentejas con chorizo
- Arroz con verduras
- Sopa de pescado

PLATO PRINCIPAL
- Dorada con ensalada
- Filete de ternera con patatas
- Albóndigas
- Bacalao en salsa

POSTRE
- Helado
- Fruta
- Flan

PAN Y BEBIDA

15 € (**IVA incluido**)

8 **a. Platos** Which of the dishes at **Casa del Pescador** have you tried? What other Spanish dishes do you know? Share your answers with a partner.

b. Contestar *¿Dónde está la* **Casa del Pescador***?*

9 **Clasificar** With a partner, categorize the foods on the menu as vegetables and legumes, fish, or meat. Ask your instructor if you aren't sure.

Modelo: *¿Las albóndigas son pescado o carne?*

VERDURAS Y LEGUMBRES	PESCADOS	CARNES
ensalada		

10 **a. Laura y Enrique** Listen to Laura and Enrique's conversation with the waiter. Circle the items they order.

1. De primer plato, Laura come lentejas con chorizo/ensalada de la casa y Enrique, sopa de pescado /arroz con verduras.

2. De plato principal, Laura come albóndigas/dorada con ensalada y Enrique, bacalao en salsa/filete de ternera.

3. Bebidas: Laura y Enrique beben vino/agua/cerveza.

4. De postre, Laura come flan/helado y Enrique, flan/fruta.

b. Bebidas Now listen to the rest of their conversation and circle what else they order.

5. otra cerveza/una botella de agua

6. un café/té

11 a. Casa del Pescador Listen to these customers' opinions of **Casa del Pescador** and match each question to the response you hear.

1. ¿Qué tal está el pulpo?
2. ¿Qué tal está el queso?
3. ¿Qué tal están las gambas?
4. Y los calamares, ¿qué tal están?

a. Un poco soso.
b. Están un poco saladas.
c. Muy ricos.
d. Está un poco picante.

b. Positivo o negativo Categorize the opinions as positive or negative.

😊 positivo: ....

☹ negativo: ....

12 Tapas Mónica and Cristián are having tapas at **Casa del Pescador**. What do they order? Work with a partner to complete this conversation creatively, including the waiter's lines from the box at the right.

- ¿Tomamos unas tapas?
- Vale. ¡Camarero, por favor!
- ....
- Una ración de .... y una de ....
- Y una ración de ....
- ....
- Dos cervezas, por favor.
[...]
- Camarero, otra .... de pulpo, ¡está .... rico!
- ....
- No, ... más, gracias. La ...., por favor.

¿Qué desean?
¿Y para beber?
¿Algo más?

13 Representar With a partner, role-play a similar situation at **Casa del Pescador**.

Modelo:
- ¡Hola, buenas tardes!
- Hola, ¿qué desean?

MI EXPERIENCIA

14 En un restaurante What do you normally eat and drink at restaurants? Ask your classmates. Before you begin, use an idea web to organize your thoughts.

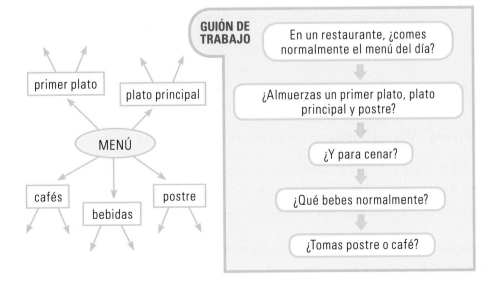

GUIÓN DE TRABAJO

En un restaurante, ¿comes normalmente el menú del día?

¿Almuerzas un primer plato, plato principal y postre?

¿Y para cenar?

¿Qué bebes normalmente?

¿Tomas postre o café?

primer plato · plato principal · MENÚ · cafés · bebidas · postre

TAPAS Y RACIONES

Jamón serrano 14 € · Aceitunas 5 €

Queso 8 € · Gambas 9 €

Pulpo 15 € · Calamares 9 €

Valorar la comida
- ¿Qué tal está el pulpo?
- (Está) un poco picante, pero muy rico.

Adjetivos:

rico/a 😊   salado/a
picante 🌶   soso/a

2B.5 estar + muy/un poco + [adjective]

Vocabulario

(11)

la ración *portion*
el jamón serrano *Serrano ham*
la aceituna *olive*
la gamba *shrimp*
el pulpo *octopus*
los calamares *calamari, squid*
¿Qué tal está(n)...? *How is/are...?*
un poco *a little*
rico/a *tasty*
picante *spicy*
salado/a *salty*
soso/a *bland, lacking salt*
la tapa, positivo/a, negativo/a

SAM: Actividades pp. 38–40

Rosa, camarera del bar El rey de la tapa

DIARIO

LA RIOJA

Rosa Iglesias en El rey de la tapa.

PREMIO A "LA CAMARERA DE LA RIOJA" MÁS PROFESIONAL Y SIMPÁTICA

Rosa Iglesias tiene 35 años y vive en Haro (La Rioja, España). Trabaja como camarera en el popular bar El rey de la tapa en la calle Mayor, 4. Rosa recibe este premio por su profesionalidad y simpatía.

El rey de la tapa es un bar especializado en tapas y vinos: la tortilla española, los pimientos, el jamón, el pulpo y los caracoles son muy ricos, los vinos de La Rioja son excelentes... pero para los clientes, la especialidad de la casa es la simpatía de Rosa.

Premio a LA MEJOR CAMARERA DE LA RIOJA
D.ª *Rosa Iglesias Redondo*
Bar "El rey de la tapa"
Gremio de hosteleros de La Rioja

Tapear

Going out for **tapas** is a Spanish tradition; it's an opportunity to get together with friends and have a good time. According to legend, **tapas** get their name from the piece of bread that bartenders used to put over a glass of wine to cover (**tapar**) and protect it. Over time, these slices of bread were served with a piece of ham, **chorizo**, or cheese, and that's how **tapas** were born.

Vocabulario

(17)
el premio *award*
el año *year*
recibir *to receive*
la profesionalidad *professionalism*
la simpatía *friendliness*
especializado/a en *specializing in*
la tortilla española *Spanish potato omelet*
el pimiento *(bell) pepper*
el caracol *snail*
tapear *to eat tapas*
el bar, profesional, popular
(18)
económico/a *affordable*

---

15 **a. La Rioja** What product is commonly associated with the region of La Rioja?

Aceitunas   Pescado   Vino   Jamón

b. En el mapa Find La Rioja on a map of Spain. Then, take turns asking a partner: *¿Está lejos o cerca de* ....?

16 **Foto** Look at the photo of Rosa and answer the questions.

- ¿Dónde está?
- ¿Toma tapas con amigos o trabaja?

17 **Anotar** Read the article from the local paper and take notes on information about Rosa and the bar where she works.

Rosa	El rey de la tapa
• Tiene 35 años.	• Está en la calle Mayor, 4.
•	• ....
•	• ....
•	• ....
•	•

18 **Premio** Why did Rosa receive an award? Check off the correct answer.

- Por la tapa más rica: la tortilla de patatas. ☐
- Por el restaurante más económico de La Rioja. ☐
- Por ser la camarera más simpática y profesional. ☐

19 **Tapas** Read the paragraph about tapas and discuss these questions with a partner.

- ¿Existe esta costumbre en su país?
- ¿Hay bares de tapas en su ciudad?

20 **Pirámide de alimentos** Study this food pyramid and write down how many times per week you eat each of these foods.

azúcar, dulces
aceite
carnes, huevos, pescado
verduras y legumbres
frutas
leche, yogur, queso
pan, pasta, arroz, cereales

Modelo:
- Alimentos: *leche*
- Veces por semana: *siete*

Stressed syllable

21 **a. Sílabas acentuadas** Listen to these words and underline the stressed syllable.

mantequilla filete bacalao postre arroz lentejas tostada
patata dorada jamón helado churro ternera albóndigas chorizo

b. Contestar Which syllable is most often stressed: the last, the second-to-last, or the third-to-last?

22 **Tortillas** Read the text about **tortillas** and answer the question.

América Latina tiene muchas tradiciones gastronómicas. Por ejemplo, en México son muy típicos los tacos, las tortillas de maíz con carne o verduras y la salsa muy picante. Las tortillas mexicanas y las tortillas españolas son muy diferentes. Una palabra, dos comidas distintas.

- What are the names for these foods in Spain?

AMÉRICA LATINA	ESPAÑA
jugo de naranja	....
papas	....

23 **Ingredientes** Find a recipe for **tortilla española** and one for **tortilla mexicana** and write a list of the ingredients in Spanish. Compare your recipes with a partner's.

Modelo: *La tortilla española tiene...*

Vocabulario

20
- el dulce *sweet, candy*
- el huevo *egg*
- el arroz *rice*
- los alimentos *food*
- **la pasta**

22
- mexicano/a *Mexican*
- gastronómico/a *gastronomic, culinary*
- el maíz *corn*
- la naranja *orange*
- la papa (*Amér. L.*) *potato*
- **el taco, la tradición**

OPINIÓN

¿Tiene usted una cafetería, un bar o restaurante habitual?

¿Conoce restaurantes españoles en su ciudad?
- ¿Tienen menú del día?
- ¿Tienen tapas?
- ¿Los camareros son profesionales y simpáticos?

tortilla mexicana

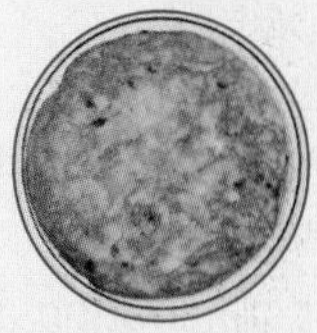
tortilla española

SAM: Actividades pp. 41–46

TAREA FINAL

Un restaurante español

Open a Spanish restaurant! Working with a partner, first choose a name.

Bar La tortilla española, Bar El pulpo...

Create a menu of breakfast items and **tapas**.

Desayunos	Precio	Tapas	Precio
Café + tostada	*$4*		

Write a dialogue between a customer placing an order and a waiter/waitress who tells the customer about the dishes.

Role-play your dialogue for the class.

YO PUEDO...

- **Puedo pedir un desayuno y preguntar por el precio.**

  In groups of three, use the menu you created in **Tarea final** to practice ordering food.

- **Puedo hablar de costumbres en relación con la comida y expresar frecuencia.**

  Write a blog posting about your eating habits.

- **Puedo pedir un menú del día y la cuenta.**

  De bebida, ...
  De primer plato, ...
  De plato principal, ...
  De postre, ...
  Por favor, ...

- **Puedo valorar la comida.**

  Use these words: **salado/a, soso/a, rico/a.**

- ¿Dónde y qué desayuna normalmente?
- ¿Almuerza en el trabajo, en casa, en un restaurante?
- ¿Cena el fin de semana en casa o en un restaurante?

En el restaurante Casa del Pescador normalmente:

- la ensalada está

  ....

- los calamares están

  ....

- la carne está

  ....

GRAMÁTICA FUNCIONAL (S) Tutorials

2B.1 Order and pay at a café

Interrogative **¿cuánto?** **9**   Regular -ar verbs: **desear** **5.1.1**

- To take someone's order at a restaurant or café, ask **¿Qué desea?** if there is one client or **¿Qué desean?** for more than one.

  ¿Qué desea, señorita?
  What would you like, miss?

  ¿Qué desean, señores?
  What would you like, gentlemen?

- To ask how much you owe at a café, say **¿Cuánto es?** (*How much is it?*) To answer, say **Son X euros/dólares/pesos**, etc.

2B.2 Talk about daily meals

Regular -er verbs: **beber, comer** **5.1.1**

- Use the verbs **comer** (*to eat*) and **beber** (*to drink*) to talk about your meals. **Comer** and **beber** are regular -er verbs; all regular -er verbs follow the same conjugation pattern.

	COMER	BEBER
(yo)	como	bebo
(tú)	comes	bebes
(usted, él, ella)	come	bebe
(nosotros/as)	comemos	bebemos
(vosotros/as)	coméis	bebéis
(ustedes, ellos/as)	comen	beben

Yo normalmente **bebo** un café por las mañanas y **como** unas galletas.
I usually drink a coffee in the morning and I eat some cookies.

2B.3 Express frequency

Adverbs of frequency **11.8**
Stem-changing verbs o→ue: **almorzar** **5.1.1**

- Use the adverbs **siempre** (*always*), **normalmente** (*normally*), and **a veces** (*sometimes*) to talk about frequency. Place the adverbs directly before the verb.

  Normalmente desayuno en casa; **siempre** almuerzo fuera.
  Normally, I have breakfast at home; I always have lunch out.

- To discuss the meals of the day, use **desayunar** to talk about breakfast (**el desayuno**), **almorzar** to talk about lunch (**el almuerzo**), and **cenar** to talk about supper (**la cena**). **Desayunar** and **cenar** follow the regular -ar conjugation pattern.

  Tú desayun**as** galletas y Ramón desayun**a** tostada.
  You have cookies for breakfast and Ramón has toast.

- **Almorzar** is an o→ue stem-changing verb; this means that the stressed -o- in the stem changes to -ue- in every form except the **nosotros/as** and **vosotros/as** forms. Note that the endings still follow the conjugation pattern of regular -ar verbs.

ALMORZAR			
(yo)	almuerzo	(nosotros/as)	almorzamos
(tú)	almuerzas	(vosotros/as)	almorzáis
(usted, él, ella)	almuerza	(ustedes, ellos/as)	almuerzan

¡Póngalo en práctica!

G1 **Completar** Complete the conversation logically.

- Buenos días.
- Buenos días. ¿(1).................... .... ?
- Un café con leche y un cruasán.
- Muy bien. Aquí tiene.
- ¿(2).................... .... ?
- (3).................... tres euros.
- ¡Muchas gracias!

G2 **Beber o comer** Complete the sentences with the appropriate forms of **beber** or **comer**.

1. Lorenzo .... pan tostado.
2. Tú .... zumo de naranja natural.
3. Mateo y yo .... café con leche.
4. ¿.................... ustedes los churros?
5. Vosotras .... un café cortado.
6. Adela .... una taza de chocolate.
7. Yo siempre .... flan de postre.
8. Antonio y Jorge .... té con el desayuno.
9. Gabriela y yo .... pan con mermelada.
10. ¿.................... (tú) las galletas?

G3 **Reordenar** Unscramble the words to write complete sentences. Remember to conjugate the verbs.

1. a veces / desayunar / café / Joaquín
2. en casa / almorzar / siempre / mis amigos
3. nosotros / fuera / a veces / cenar
4. almorzar / en la cafetería / tú y Manolo / siempre
5. yogur / normalmente / yo / desayunar

GRAMÁTICA FUNCIONAL

2B.4 Order and pay at a restaurant

otro/a 6.5 **algo/nada más** 6.5

- To inquire about specials or items on a menu at a restaurant, ask **¿Qué tienen de** + [menú/primer plato/postre, etc.]?

  ¿Qué tienen de primer plato?
  What do you have as a starter?

- When ordering, say **De primer plato/plato principal/postre...** for food, and **Para beber...** for drinks.

  De plato principal, el arroz con pollo, y **para beber**, una botella de agua.
  As a main dish, the rice with chicken, and to drink, a bottle of water.

- Use **otro/a** (*another*) to request more items. **Otro/a** must agree in gender and number with the noun it modifies, and is never used with an indefinite article.

  Otro café y **otra** botella de agua, por favor.
  Another coffee and another bottle of water, please.

- To ask customers if they would like anything else, say **¿Desea(n) algo más?** If you do not want anything more, say No, **nada más**.

  ¿Desea algo más?
  Would you like anything else?

  No, **nada más.**
  No, nothing else.

2B.5 Give your opinion on food

estar + muy/un poco + [*adjective*] 5.8.1, 11.4

- To inquire about the quality of food that someone is eating, ask **¿Qué tal está(n)** + [*food*]?

  ¿Qué tal están las lentejas?
  How are the lentils?

- To explain how the food is, say **Está(n)** + [*adjective*]. Remember, the adjective must agree in gender and number with the food you are describing.

  La sopa **está rica**, pero el arroz **está soso**.
  The soup is tasty, but the rice is bland.

- Use **muy** to intensify a description, and use **un poco** to soften the impact of negative opinions.

  Los pimientos están **muy ricos**, pero los calamares están **un poco salados**.
  The peppers are delicious, but the calamari is a bit salty.

¡OJO!

Use **estar** + [*adjective*] to describe how food tastes on a specific occasion: **El queso está muy salado.** (*The [This] cheese is really salty.*) Use **ser** + [*adjective*] to describe the general characteristics of a food: **Los jalapeños son picantes.** (*Jalapeño peppers are spicy.*)

¡Póngalo en práctica!

G4 Un diálogo Complete the dialogue.

¿Qué (1).........................?

¿Qué tienen como (2).........................?

(3)........................... primer plato, tenemos arroz con verduras, ensalada o sopa de pescado. De (4)..........................., bacalao en salsa o filete de ternera.

De (5)..........................., sopa de pescado, y de (6)..........................., filete de ternera.

¿Desea (7)........................... más?

Sí, (8)........................... café y la (9)..........................., por favor.

G5 Las comidas Use the cues to write complete sentences with **estar**. Change adjectives when necessary for agreement.

Modelo: la sopa / un poco / salado
La sopa está un poco salada.

1. el pescado / un poco / soso
....

2. los calamares / muy / rico
....

3. el pulpo / un poco / picante
....

4. las albóndigas / un poco / salado
....

5. el queso / un poco / salado / pero / rico
....

6. las gambas / muy / rico
....

7. el chorizo / un poco / picante
....

8. todo / muy / rico
....

VOCABULARIO Vocabulary Tools

Café con leche

¿Qué desean tomar?	What would you like (to have)?
por favor	please
¿Cuánto es?	How much is it?
Son 9 euros.	It's 9 euros.
el aceite de oliva	olive oil
la bollería (*Esp.*)	pastries
el café solo	black coffee
la cafeína	caffeine
el/la camarero/a	waiter/waitress
los cereales	cereal
los churros	churros
el/la compañero/a	partner
el cruasán	croissant
el desayuno	breakfast
el descafeinado	decaf coffee
el doble	double
el fin de semana	weekend
la galleta	cookie
la gota	drop
el hielo	ice
el jugo de naranja (*Amér. L.*)	orange juice
la mantequilla	butter
la mermelada	jam, marmalade
el pan	bread
el queso	cheese
el sándwich	sandwich
la semana	week
la taza	cup
el té	tea
la tostada	toast
el yogur	yogurt
el zumo de naranja (*Esp.*)	orange juice
algo	something
almorzar (o:ue)	to eat lunch
beber	to drink
cenar	to eat supper
comer	to eat

desayunar	to eat breakfast
dulce	sweet
especial	special
frecuente	common
natural	fresh
poco/a	little
a veces	sometimes
en casa	at home
fuera	out
normalmente	normally
siempre	always

Menú del día

¿Algo más?	Anything else?
Nada más, gracias.	Nothing else, thanks.
¿Qué tal está(n)...?	How is/are . . . ?
un poco	a little
IVA incluido	tax included
vale (*Esp.*)	OK
la aceituna	olive
la albóndiga	meatball
el arroz con verduras	rice with vegetables
el bacalao en salsa	cod with sauce
la bebida	beverage
la botella	bottle
los calamares	calamari, squid
la carne	meat
la cerveza	beer
la cuenta	bill
la dorada	sea bream (type of fish)
la ensalada de la casa	house salad
el filete de ternera	fillet of veal
el flan	flan (custard)
la fruta	fruit
la gamba	shrimp
el helado	ice cream
el jamón serrano	Serrano ham
las legumbres	legumes
las lentejas con chorizo	lentils with chorizo (sausage)

el menú del día	fixed-price menu
la patata (*Esp.*)	potato
el pescado	fish
el plato principal	main course
el postre	dessert
el primer plato	first course
el pulpo	octopus
la ración	portion
la sopa de pescado	fish soup
la tapa	tapa
las verduras	vegetables
el vino	wine
negativo/a	negative
picante	spicy
positivo/a	positive
rico/a	tasty
salado/a	salty
soso/a	bland, lacking salt

Rosa Iglesias

los alimentos	food
el año	year
el arroz	rice
el bar	bar
el caracol	snail
el dulce	sweet, candy
el huevo	egg
el maíz	corn
la naranja	orange
la papa (*Amér. L.*)	potato
la pasta	pasta
el pimiento	(bell) pepper
el premio	award
la profesionalidad	professionalism
la simpatía	friendliness
el taco	taco
la tortilla española	Spanish potato omelet
la tradición	tradition
recibir	to receive
tapear	to eat tapas
económico/a	affordable
especializado/a en	specializing in
gastronómico/a	gastronomic, culinary
mexicano/a	Mexican
popular	popular
profesional	professional

Variación léxica

almorzar ⟷ comer (*Esp., Méx.*)	el jugo (*Amér. L.*) ⟷ el zumo (*Esp.*)
la bollería (*Esp.*) ⟷ la pastelería (*Amér. L.*) ⟷ las facturas (*Arg.*)	el sándwich ⟷ el bocadillo (*Esp.*) ⟷ la torta (*Méx.*)
el/la camarero/a ⟷ el/la mesero/a (*Amér. L.*)	la tortilla española ⟷ la tortilla de patatas (*Esp.*)
el cruasán ⟷ la medialuna (*Arg.*)	De acuerdo ⟷ ¡Vale! (*Esp.*)

Estrategias

① Deducir nuevas palabras a través de cognados

Lección 1A

Recognizing Spanish words that are similar to words you already know in English or another language can help you expand your vocabulary.

○ Read these words and identify the English cognates.

aeropuerto	restaurante	idea	radio	música	teléfono

○ Make a list of other cognates you have learned in **Unidades 1 y 2**.

② Crear palabras a partir de reglas de formación

Lección 1B

You can use patterns of word formation to recognize the relationships between words and help expand your vocabulary. For example, if you know that **pintar** means to *paint* and that the suffix **-or(a)** can be added to a verb stem to create the name of a profession, you can see that **un(a) pintor(a)** is a painter.

○ Match words from the word bank to the related words below to see how the names for some professions are formed. Use a dictionary if necessary.

cartero/a	periodista	recepcionista	trabajador(a)	zapatero/a
librero/a	pescador(a)	taxista	vendedor(a)	

+ -ista	+ -ero/a	+ -dor(a)
el periódico	la carta	pescar ....
la recepción	el libro	trabajar ....
el taxi	el zapato	vender ....

③ Hacer listas y fichas de palabras

Lección 2A

Creating vocabulary lists and flashcards can be a helpful way to study new words and expressions. Think of different ways to organize the words: in alphabetical order, by part of speech, or by where and how you use them.

○ Make flashcards for the words you learned in **Lección 2A**.

④ Hacer redes de palabras

Lección 2B

Making word maps is a helpful way to organize and learn vocabulary. They allow you to visually organize words into thematically related groups to help you learn words in context.

○ Fill in this word map about breakfast.

Competencias

LENGUAS

(1) **Se habla...** What languages are spoken in these five countries? Find their names in the word search **(sopa de letras)**. Then write each name under its flag.

C	T	I	E	S	P	A	Ñ	O	L	I
M	U	P	É	S	Y	S	B	U	S	T
F	R	R	A	L	E	M	Á	N	U	A
Y	R	A	Z	H	R	T	E	I	G	L
G	O	A	N	X	K	Ñ	R	A	T	I
A	V	Z	N	I	N	G	L	É	S	A
U	R	U	R	C	A	E	Z	G	S	N
K	R	M	O	R	É	T	X	Á	P	O
Ñ	O	W	B	C	U	S	V	S	H	D

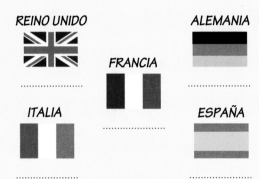

REINO UNIDO

....

FRANCIA

....

ALEMANIA

....

ITALIA

....

ESPAÑA

....

CIFRAS

(2) **Números** Write out the numbers in words and the words in numerals.

diecinueve años .... 555 pesos .... los años ochenta .... Madrid-Barcelona 630 km

....

HABLAR DE REFERENTES DE UNA CULTURA CONCRETA

(3) **Completar** Complete these sentences with the appropriate indefinite article and adjective ending.

- El guacamole es .... comida mexican........... .
- Cuba es .... isla muy bonit........... .
- La Puerta de Alcalá es .... monumento muy famos........... de Madrid.
- Varadero es .... playa fantástic........... de Cuba.

DAR DATOS PERSONALES

(4) **Preguntar** Choose card A or B, and ask your partner questions to fill in the missing information.

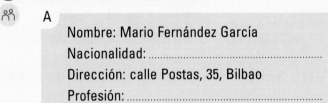

A

Nombre: Mario Fernández García
Nacionalidad: ....
Dirección: calle Postas, 35, Bilbao
Profesión: ....

B

Nombre: ....
Nacionalidad: español
Dirección: ....
Profesión: arquitecto

PEDIR Y PAGAR EN UN CAFÉ

(5) **Diálogo** Look at the illustration and work with a partner to create a dialogue about this situation.

HABLAR DE UN LUGAR

(6) **Ser o estar** Complete each sentence with an appropriate form of **ser** or **estar**.

- ¿Dónde .... Sucre?
- ¿..................... una ciudad boliviana?
- ¿..................... lejos o cerca de La Paz?
- Sucre .... una ciudad histórica.

Video

Los estudios

You have learned about several Latin American cities, including **México, D.F.** Now you will learn about the **UNAM**, Mexico's largest university. You will meet several students, learn about their majors, and hear about some of the **UNAM's** most famous alumni.

1 **Mi universidad** What is the name of your school or university? What degree program are you in? What are your favorite classes? Share your experiences with a partner.

2 **Mirar** Watch this **Flash Cultura** episode.

Estudio derecho en la UNAM.

¿Conoces algún profesor famoso que dé clases en la UNAM?

3 **Relacionar** Match each sentence starter with the appropriate ending.

1. Los estudiantes de la UNAM no viven ....
2. México, D.F. es ....
3. La UNAM es ....
4. La UNAM ofrece ....

a. una universidad muy grande.
b. 74 carreras de estudio.
c. en residencias estudiantiles.
d. la ciudad más grande de América Latina.

4 **Comparar** Create an idea web to summarize what you learned about the **UNAM**. Then, create another idea web about your school or college and write a paragraph comparing and contrasting the two institutions. Use the word **pero** in your contrasts and the word **también** in your comparisons.

Modelo: *La UNAM está en una ciudad muy grande, pero mi universidad está...*

Estrategia

Brainstorming questions before viewing

Before you watch a cultural video, think about what information you expect to learn and what questions you would like to have answered. What do you already know about Mexico City? What do you know about the university system in Mexico? In what ways is the **UNAM** similar to your school or university? Write down your questions, and as you watch this **Flash Cultura**, take notes on the answers you see and hear.

Vocabulario útil

¿Cuál es tu materia favorita? *What it is your favorite subject?*

¿Cuántos años tienes? *How old are you?*

la carrera de medicina *medical degree program, major*

las ciencias de la comunicación *communications*

el derecho *law*

la facultad *(academic) department*

ofrecer (zc) *to offer*

la residencia estudiantil *dorm(itory)*

Estrategia

Using idea webs to make comparisons

An idea web is a useful way to graphically summarize information relating to a given topic. When you take notes, try not to write out complete sentences. Instead, write only key facts, words, and phrases, and use circles, lines, and arrows to show the relationships between ideas. Later, you can use these categories to make comparisons.

Practice more at **vhlcentral.com**.

Unidad 3

Pablo Linares, dos ritmos de vida

Olga Piedrahita, la moda en Colombia

Fútbol en España

3A

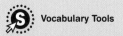

RITMO DE VIDA

Horarios

ABRIL

lunes	martes	miércoles	jueves	viernes	sábado	domingo
			1	2	3	4
5	6	7	8	9	10	11
12	13	14	15	16	17	18
19	20	21	22	23	24	25
26	27	28	29	30		

Atención: personas del mundo de las finanzas, profesionales, jóvenes, niños...

La Bolsa de Comercio de Buenos Aires les invita al

DÍA DE PUERTAS ABIERTAS

el 13 de abril
de 08:30 h a 18:00 h

Visitas con guía cada 20 minutos

Sarmiento 299
C1041AAE Buenos Aires

Contacto:
visitasguiadas@bcba.sba.com.ar

Hablar de horarios y días de la semana

Abre de diez de la mañana a ocho y media de la noche.

- ¿Qué hora es? (14:20)
- Son las dos y veinte de la tarde.
- ¿Y en Santiago? (13:20)
- Es la una y veinte de la tarde.
- ¿Qué día abre la Bolsa?
- El martes 13 de abril.

01:00 h-11:00 h: 1-11 de la mañana
12:00 h: 12 del mediodía
13:00 h-19:00 h: 1-7 de la tarde
20:00 h-00:00 h: 8-12 de la noche

en punto

menos cuarto — y cuarto

y media

El lunes/martes/miércoles...

3A.1 Telling time
Days of the week

Vocabulario

1

el horario *schedule*

el mundo de las finanzas *world of finance*

el/la niño/a *boy/girl*

la bolsa (de comercio) *stock exchange*

abierto/a *open*

el 13 de abril *April 13*

Vocabulary Tools

1 **Calendario** What day of the week is the **Día de Puertas Abiertas**?

2 **a. La Bolsa** What are the opening hours of the Buenos Aires stock exchange?

La Bolsa abre de .... a ....

b. Horas When the Buenos Aires stock exchange opens, what time is it in these other cities? Mark the times on the clocks and write them out in words.

1. Nueva York (-1 hora)   2. Tokio (+12 horas)   3. Londres (+4 horas)   4. Madrid (+5 horas)

....

....

3 **¿Qué hora es?** Write the time displayed on each clock.

18:25 ......Son las seis y veinticinco de la tarde.

12:45 ....

06:40 ....

22:00 ....

4 **Relacionar** Match each day to its common abbreviation.

L	M	Mi	J	V	S	D

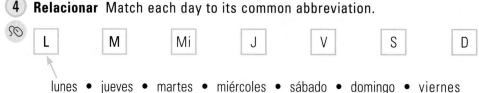

lunes • jueves • martes • miércoles • sábado • domingo • viernes

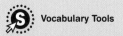

Elsa, veterinaria

Vicente, músico

Vocabulario *cont.*

el día de la semana *day of the week*

el lunes *Monday*

el martes *Tuesday*

el miércoles *Wednesday*

el jueves *Thursday*

el viernes *Friday*

el sábado *Saturday*

el domingo *Sunday*

el/la profesional, el calendario

② ──────────────

abrir *to open*

③ ──────────────

¿Qué hora es? *What time is it?*

el reloj *clock; watch*

de la mañana *a.m., in the morning*

de la tarde *p.m., in the afternoon*

de la noche *p.m., at night*

5 **a. Adivinar** A Spanish radio program interviews Vicente and Elsa about their daily routines. Before you listen, look at their photos and guess at what time they do each activity.

Vicente	Rutinas	Elsa
	desayunar	
	ir a trabajar	
	comer	
	llegar a casa	
	cenar	

◁)) **b. La rutina** Now listen to the recording and check the accuracy of
👓 your guesses.

Hablar de rutinas

● ¿Cuándo vas al gimnasio?

■ Voy los lunes por la mañana y los jueves por la tarde.

● ¿A qué hora va Marta a clase?

■ Va a clase a las 8:00 h.

Por la mañana/tarde/noche...
Los lunes/jueves/sábados...

3A.2	Time expressions The verb **ir**; a + el = al

6 **Preguntas** Use elements from each column to create original questions.

(usted)	¿Vais	los sábados	por la mañana	al cine?
(vosotros)	¿Van	los martes	por la tarde	al parque?
(ustedes)	¿Va	los lunes	por la noche	al mercado?

7 **Describir** Choose one of the three people listed and describe his/her daily
👥 routine. Your partner should guess whom you are describing.

○ Un(a) niño/a   ○ Una persona de 80 años   ○ Un(a) vigilante nocturno/a

Vocabulario

⑤ ──────────────

la rutina diaria *daily routine*

¿A qué hora...? *At what time . . . ?*

ir a trabajar *to go to work*

llegar a casa *to arrive home*

por la mañana *in the morning*

por la tarde *in the afternoon*

por la noche *in the evening, at night*

el programa de radio, el/la veterinario/a, el/la músico/a, el gimnasio

⑥ ──────────────

el cine *movie theater*

⑦ ──────────────

una persona de 80 años *an 80-year-old person*

el/la vigilante nocturno/a *night security guard*

👥 **MI EXPERIENCIA**

8 **Entrevista** What are your classmates' daily routines like? Interview a partner and report your findings to the class. Whose routines are most similar?

GUIÓN DE TRABAJO

👓 ¿A qué hora desayunas/almuerzas/cenas?
¿Cenas a las ocho/nueve de la noche...?
¿Vas al gimnasio? ¿Cuándo?
¿Trabajas?
¿Estudias?
¿A qué hora vas al trabajo/a la universidad?
¿A qué hora llegas a casa?

Por la...

mañana
tarde
noche

los lunes
los martes
los miércoles
los jueves
los viernes

los sábados
los domingos
el fin de semana

SAM: Actividades pp. 47–49

Ⓢ Practice more at **vhlcentral.com**.

Agenda semanal

- Verónica, ¿qué haces después de clases?
- Todos los días tengo una o dos actividades. Los lunes por la tarde, a las ocho, hago yoga. Los martes colaboro en una asociación del barrio de nueve a diez o diez y media de la noche.
- ¿Todos los martes?
- Sí, todos, y los miércoles de ocho a nueve y media, Ana y yo hacemos un curso de informática. ¡Ah!, y los jueves de ocho a nueve tengo clase de francés...
- ¿Qué haces los viernes?
- Los viernes por la noche, Emilio y yo salimos; vamos al cine.
- ¿Salís todos los viernes?
- Sí, normalmente sí. El sábado por la mañana hago las compras en el centro comercial y el domingo salimos a pasear con la familia... ¿Y tú?

Expresar frecuencia

- Jorge, ¿qué **haces** por la tarde?
- **Salgo** con los niños y voy al parque.
- ¿Todos los días?
- Sí, **todas las tardes**. Después **hago** deporte.
- ¿Y no **vas** al cine o a un restaurante...?
- Sí, los viernes mi mujer y yo **hacemos** algo especial o **salimos** con amigos.
- Yo **nunca salgo** los viernes.

Todos los días, todas las tardes, todos los jueves...

> **3A.3** Verbs with irregular **yo** forms: **hacer, salir**
> Expressions of frequency

Vocabulario

9

la agenda (semanal) *(weekly) planner*

hacer *to do; to make*

la mujer *woman; wife*

todos los días *every day*

colaborar *to participate*

el curso *class, course*

tener clase *to have class*

salir (con amigos) *to go out (with friends)*

hacer las compras *to do the shopping*

pasear *to go for a walk*

el yoga

9 a. **El horario de Verónica** Verónica and Nuria are college students. Read and listen to their conversation over coffee. Write down the missing information in Verónica's weekly planner.

	lunes	martes	miércoles	jueves	viernes	sábado	domingo
POR LA MAÑANA	clases	clases	clases	clases	clases	....	día familiar
POR LA TARDE/ NOCHE	....	asociación	informática	....	....		....

b. **Conjugar** Underline the forms of **hacer** and **salir** in the conversation above and complete the chart with the missing forms.

	yo	tú	usted, él, ella	nosotros/as	vosotros/as	ustedes, ellos/as
HACER			hace			hacen
SALIR	salgo	sales	sale			salen

10 a. **Completar** Listen to this interview with a teenager on the street in Madrid. How often does he do each activity?

1. Hacer deporte: ....
2. Salir con amigos: ....
3. Hacer algo en casa: ....

b. **Preguntar** How often do you do these activities? Ask a partner about his/her habits.

Modelo: *¿Con qué frecuencia vas al cine? ¿Tienes clases todos los días?*

- hacer deporte
- ir al teatro o al cine
- salir con amigos
- cenar fuera
- hacer las compras

ANDRÉS

Lunes **1** Agosto	Jueves **4** Agosto
Reunión 8:00-18:00. Escribir	*Presentación del proyecto 8:00-*
informes. 19:00 Gimnasio	*18:00. Reunión. Informática e inglés.*
Martes **2** Agosto	Viernes **5** Agosto
Entrevista 8:00-12:00. Escribir informes	*8:00-18:00. Escribir informes,*
13:00-17:00 Informática e inglés.	*hacer llamadas.*
Miércoles **3** Agosto	Sábado **6** Agosto
Equipo de trabajo 8:00-18:00.	*Gimnasio 13:00*
Escribir informes. Gimnasio	
Viajes de negocios: No	Domingo **7** Agosto
	Vacaciones: del 8 al 23

AGOSTO 2016

INÉS

Lunes **1** Agosto	Jueves **4** Agosto
Visita a clientes 8:30-16:00.	*Visita a clientes 8:30-16:00.*
	21:00 Cena con Teresa.
Martes **2** Agosto	Viernes **5** Agosto
Visita a clientes 8:30-16:00.	*Visita a clientes 8:30-12:00. Escribir*
	informes. Curso de Informática
Miércoles **3** Agosto	Sábado **6** Agosto
Visita a clientes 8:30-16:00.	*Al cine con Carlos.*
Viaje a Sevilla y Córdoba.	
Reservar billete para el viaje a Londres	Domingo **7** Agosto
	Vacaciones: del 8 al 30

AGOSTO 2016

11 **Agendas** Read Andrés's and Inés's planners and compare them.

Modelo: *Inés hace más viajes que Andrés.*

12 **Comparar** Now compare your answers to **Actividad 10b** with your partner's.

Modelo: *Hago deporte todos los días y tú haces deporte los sábados.*
→ *Hago más deporte que tú.*

13 **Comparaciones** Compare this information about Spain with your country.

EN ESPAÑA
- Los trabajadores tienen 22 días de vacaciones al año.
- El calendario tiene 14 días festivos.
- En julio y agosto los niños no van al colegio.
- El horario de trabajo es normalmente de 8:00/9:00 h a 18:00/20:00 h.

MI EXPERIENCIA

14 **Los horarios** Ask your partner about his/her activities. Compare your schedules and present your findings to the class.

GUIÓN DE TRABAJO

¿A qué hora vas a la universidad /a trabajar? → A la(s)...

¿A qué hora sales de clases/ trabajar? → A la(s)...

¿Qué haces por las tardes? → Hago teatro. Voy a clase de... Salgo con...

¿Con qué frecuencia? → Todos los días. Todos los martes. Todas las tardes.

Mi compañero/a:
trabaja más/menos horas que yo.
hace más/menos deporte que yo.

Comparar
- ¿Dónde trabajas?
- En un gimnasio; trabajo por la mañana y por la tarde.
- ¡Trabajas **más** horas **que** yo!
- Sí, ¡y hago **menos** deporte **que** tú!

3A.4 Comparatives
más/menos + que

Vocabulario

10
la entrevista *interview*
el ritmo de vida *pace of life*
¿Con qué frecuencia? *How often?*
hacer deporte *to exercise*
hacer algo en casa *to do something at home*
hacer la cama *to make the bed*
terminar *to end*

11
el viaje de negocios *business trip*
las vacaciones *vacation*
tres veces al año *three times a year*
la vez (*pl.* veces) *time*
más que *more than*
menos que *less than*

13
el/la trabajador(a) *worker*
el día festivo *holiday*
julio *July*
agosto *August*
el colegio *school*
el horario de trabajo *work schedule*

14
salir de *to leave*

SAM: Actividades pp. 50–52

Practice more at **vhlcentral.com**.

Pablo Linares, dos ritmos de vida

EL **BLOG** DE Pablo

Nombre: Pablo Linares
Edad: 35 años
Ciudad: Buenos Aires/Colonia
<u>Ver datos completos</u>

HOME	COMENTARIOS	DATOS

"Trabajo y descanso" Lunes, 8 de diciembre, 22:30 h.

Escribir este blog es terapia; trabajo mucho y no hablo con otras personas.

Soy de Colonia, Uruguay, pero vivo en Buenos Aires porque trabajo en la bolsa. Salgo de casa a las siete y media de la mañana, desayuno en una cafetería y a las ocho en punto entro en el trabajo. Por la noche llego a casa a las nueve. Hago aproximadamente 50 llamadas de teléfono al día. El ritmo de vida es muy intenso, ¡no paro un segundo! Todos los días hago lo mismo: trabajar, leer prensa económica, comer en diez minutos y media hora de deporte por la noche en el gimnasio. Los miércoles ceno con compañeros en un restaurante y hablamos, naturalmente, de la bolsa.

Los viernes por la tarde salgo de la bolsa a las seis, tomo el ferry y a las ocho y media estoy en Colonia. Soy persona de campo y quiero estar al aire libre. Mi familia tiene una estancia muy tranquila cerca de Colonia.

En la estancia, el celular no funciona, no tengo tele, no tengo Internet...

Tengo el río, mis libros, amigos, más tiempo que en la ciudad, menos estrés que de lunes a viernes y más paz. ¡Los sábados y domingos tengo otro ritmo de vida!

Bolsa de Comercio de Buenos Aires

Nombre: Pablo
Apellidos: Linares García
D.N.I.: 22.756.240

Vocabulario

(15)

el descanso *rest*
diciembre *December*
la terapia *therapy*
entrar en *to enter*
aproximadamente *approximately*
la llamada (de teléfono) *(phone) call*
parar *to stop*
la prensa económica *financial press*
el deporte *sport(s)*
tomar el ferry *to take the ferry*
el campo *country(side)*
al aire libre *outdoors*
la estancia (*Cono S.*) *ranch*
la tele(visión) *television*
el río *river*
el tiempo *time*
el estrés *stress*
el DNI (Documento Nacional de Identidad) *national identity card*
el blog, intenso/a

---

15 **Un blog** What type of text does Pablo Linares write? Choose the best category for this type of blog.

☐ Biografía ☐ Informe profesional ☐ Diario personal

16 **Fotos** Which photos represent Pablo during the week? And on the weekends?

 A

 B

 C

○ Durante la semana: .... ○ Los fines de semana: ....

17 **Contestar** Reread the blog and write your answer to the question on a separate piece of paper.

○ ¿Qué hace Pablo Linares normalmente los fines de semana?

18 **El blog de Pablo** Relate each of the words from Pablo's blog with the corresponding day(s) of the week.

bolsa · paz · gimnasio · estancia · celular · río · Buenos Aires · Colonia · prensa económica · estrés · blog · compañeros

lunes
martes
miércoles
jueves
viernes
el fin de semana

19 a. Los ritmos de vida Many families have an intense daily schedule. Read this magazine article and write down the activities that homemakers and children do. Compare notes with a partner.

¡RITMOS DE VIDA DIFERENTES, PERO TODOS INTENSOS!

Un empleado de bolsa tiene un ritmo de trabajo muy intenso, pero no es el único caso. Otro ejemplo de ritmo de vida intenso son las amas y los amos de casa. En su agenda semanal está: llevar a los niños al colegio, hacer las compras, cocinar, limpiar... Son muchas horas y todos los días. Es importante programar la vida y tener tiempo para uno mismo, hacer deporte, salir con amigos, etc. ¿Y los niños? Muchos niños también tienen un ritmo de vida intenso: clases de 8:00 a 16:00 h (una hora de pausa para comer de 12:00 a 13:00 h) y por la tarde mil actividades: los lunes y los martes clase de música, los miércoles, piscina, los jueves, clase de karate, los viernes, pintura, informática...

b. Profesiones What other professions tend to require an intense daily schedule? Think of the professions you learned in **Lección 1B.**

(ch)(ll)(ñ)

20 a. ch, ll, ñ Listen to these words; pay attention to the pronunciation of **ch, ll,** and **ñ.**

| mañana | ocho | llegar | montaña | ellos | chocolate |
| noche | llamada | coche | La Coruña | niño |

b. Palabras Write three more words you have learned with these letters.

21 Pronunciación Listen to these sentences and repeat them after the speaker.

1. En La Coruña voy a la montaña por la mañana.
2. Ellos llaman porque llegan a las ocho.
3. Por la noche, muchos van en coche.

22 Asociar Listen to the recording and match the comments with these photos.

1. "El ritmo de vida aquí es muy relajado" (...)
2. "Después de la cena, la zona colonial tiene otro ritmo" (...)
3. "El ritmo de vida es muy acelerado" (...)

Santo Domingo, República Dominicana

Santiago, Chile

Costa Rica

Practice more at vhlcentral.com.

Vocabulario

19

el/la empleado/a *employee*

llevar a los niños al colegio *to take the kids to school*

cocinar *to cook*

limpiar *to clean*

programar *to plan*

tiempo para uno/a mismo/a *time for oneself*

la clase de música *music class*

la piscina *swimming pool*

la pintura *painting*

el karate

20

el coche (*Esp.*) *car*

la montaña *mountain*

llegar *to arrive*

21

ir en coche *to go by car*

22

relajado/a *relaxed*

la zona colonial *the colonial area*

aprender español *to learn Spanish*

fuera de clase *outside of class*

participar en *to participate in*

ver películas *to watch movies*

viajar *to travel*

el chat

O P I N I Ó N

¿Le interesan los blogs?

¿Usted lee o escribe blogs?

¿Tiene usted diferentes ritmos de vida?

Estrategia ....

Consider ways that you can learn Spanish outside of class. Which options are most interesting to you?

☐ hacer un intercambio

☐ participar en un chat en español

☐ ver películas en español

☐ hacer un blog en español

☐ viajar a países hispanohablantes

☐ escuchar música en español

☐ ....

SAM: Actividades pp. 53–56

TAREA FINAL

Un plan para la semana

Choose a profession or a type of person and think about his/her lifestyle.

Un(a) ejecutivo/a, un(a) universitario/a, un(a) niño/a...

Discuss your person with a partner. Choose either your partner's person or yours.

Take notes on the weekly activities of that person and create a schedule for him/her.

Trabaja/Estudia todos los días de 9:00 h a 18:00 h.
Por las tardes...
Por las noches...

Share the schedule you created for that person with the class without revealing the type of person or profession.

Va a trabajar a las diez de la noche. Todos los meses viaja al extranjero...

Listen to your classmates' presentations and guess what type of person or profession they chose.

YO PUEDO...

- **Puedo preguntar e informar sobre la hora.**
  Complete the conversation.

- **Puedo hablar de horas y rutinas.**
  Write an e-mail to a Spanish-speaking friend and tell him/her about your typical day. Answer these questions.

- **Puedo rellenar una agenda.**
  Write a schedule of the things you have planned for next week.

- **Puedo hacer una comparación.**
  Think of a friend of yours and write three comparisons between your life and his/hers.

- Perdone, ¿.............. ....
  ....?
- .... la una y media. /........
  las dos menos ....

- ¿Estudia/Trabaja por la mañana, por la tarde, por la noche?
  ¿A qué hora va a clases/al trabajo?
- ¿Hace deporte? ¿Sale con sus amigos?

- ¿Estudia/Trabaja más o menos horas que yo?
- ¿Hace más o menos deporte?

GRAMÁTICA FUNCIONAL (S) Tutorials

3A.1 Talk about schedules and days of the week

Telling time, days of the week 2.1, 5.8.1

- To ask what time it is, say ¿Qué hora es? To answer, say Es + [la una/el mediodía/la medianoche] or Son + [other times]. To specify, use en punto (sharp), de la mañana (a.m.; in the morning), de la tarde (p.m.; in the afternoon), and de la noche (p.m.; at night).

Es la una.	Son las dos en punto.	Son las seis de la tarde.
It's 1 o'clock.	*It's 2 o'clock sharp.*	*It's six p.m.*

- For times up to the half hour, say y + [minutes]. For other times, subtract minutes from the next hour: menos + [minutes].

Son la siete **y diez**.	Son las diez **menos veinte**.
It's 7:10.	*It's 9:40.*

- Use **y quince** or **y cuarto** to say *quarter past*, use **menos cuarto** to say *quarter to*, and **y treinta** or **y media** to refer to a half hour.

Son las tres **y media**.	Son las dos **menos cuarto**.
It's 3:30.	*It's 1:45.*

- The 24-hour clock is commonly used in writing, though you should not use it when speaking. Instead, use the 12-hour clock and specify **de la mañana, de la tarde,** etc.

- The week on most Spanish calendars begins on Monday (**lunes**). All days of the week are masculine, and they are not capitalized.

lunes	martes	miércoles	jueves	viernes	sábado	domingo

3A.2 Talk about times of day and routines

The verb **ir** 5.1.2   The contraction **al** 10.1
The preposition **por** 10.16

- Use the irregular verb **ir** (*to go*) to talk about your daily routine.

IR			
(yo)	voy	(nosotros/as)	vamos
(tú)	vas	(vosotros/as)	vais
(usted, él, ella)	va	(ustedes, ellos/as)	van

- **Ir** is often used with the preposition **a** (*to*). When **a** precedes the masculine article **el**, the words combine to form the contraction **al**.

Vamos **al** gimnasio a las tres.
*We're going **to the** gym at three.*

- To ask what time an event takes place, say ¿A qué hora...? To tell what time an event takes place, say **a la(s)** + [*time*].

● ¿A qué hora vas a clases?	■ Voy a clases **a las ocho**.
What time do you go to class?	*I go to class **at eight**.*

- To indicate a general time of day, use **por** + [la mañana/ la tarde/la noche].

Van a la universidad **por la mañana**.
*They go to the university **in the morning**.*

¡Póngalo en práctica!

G1 **¿Qué hora es?** Write what time it is.

> **Modelo:** 11:05 p.m.
> *Son las once y cinco de la noche.*

1. **4:00 a.m.** ....
2. **7:20 p.m.** ....
3. **12:45 p.m.** ....
4. **9:30 p.m.** ....
5. **10:35 a.m.** ....
6. **3:30 p.m.** ....
7. **12:00 a.m.** ....

04:00 19:20 12:45 21:30

10:35 15:30 24:00

G2 **Completar las horas** Unscramble the cues to tell the time using complete sentences.

1. cuarto / mañana / menos / cinco
....
2. ocho / punto / noche
....
3. tarde / seis / media
....
4. once / noche / catorce / y
....
5. menos / una / mañana / veinte
....
6. nueve / noche / y / quince
....

G3 **¿Adónde vas?** Complete each sentence with the appropriate form of **ir**.

1. Pedro .... a la universidad en coche.
2. Gonzalo y Analía .... al centro por la mañana.
3. Claudia y yo .... a trabajar.
4. Mariana y tú .... al cine.
5. Tú .... a la discoteca.

G4 **Completar** Complete the conversation.

- Gloria, ¿vas (1)................ cine esta noche?
- Sí, José María y yo (2)................ a ver una película.
- ¡Qué bien! ¿(3)................ qué hora es la película?
- A (4)................ ocho (5)................ media. ¿Tienes planes?
- Sí, hoy tengo la clase de yoga (6)................ la noche.

- Use **el** + [*day of the week*] to say that something will happen on that day. Use **los** + [*day of the week (plural form)*] to talk about recurring events that happen on that day of the week. Note that only **sábado** and **domingo** add an -s to form the plural; the other days are invariable.

Voy a Cali **el martes**.	Tengo yoga **los jueves**.
*I'm going to Cali **on Tuesday**.*	*I have yoga **on Thursdays**.*

3A.3 Express frequency

Verbs with irregular **yo** forms: **hacer, salir** 5.1.2
Expressions of frequency 13.3

- Use the verbs **hacer** (*to make; to do*) and **salir** (*to go out*) to talk about activities. Both verbs have irregular **yo** forms ending in **-go**; the rest of the forms follow the regular conjugation patterns for **-er** and **-ir** verbs, respectively.

	HACER	SALIR
(yo)	hago	salgo
(tú)	haces	sales
(usted, él, ella)	hace	sale
(nosotros/as)	hacemos	salimos
(vosotros/as)	hacéis	salís
(ustedes, ellos/as)	hacen	salen

Los domingos **hago** la tarea o **salgo** con los amigos.
*On Sundays, **I do** homework or **go out** with friends.*

- To indicate that something happens every day/week/morning, etc., use **todos/as** + **los/las** + [*time designation*]. Always use a plural noun with this construction.

  Elena hace deporte **todos los días** y sale **todos los fines de semana**.
  *Elena works out **every day** and goes out **every weekend**.*

3A.4 Compare

Comparatives: **más/menos + que/de** 12.7

- To compare two experiences, use the construction **más/menos** + [*noun*] + **que**. Use **más** (*more*) to indicate a greater degree and **menos** (*less*) to indicate a lesser degree.

  Trabajas **más horas que** yo, pero tengo **menos vacaciones que** tú.
  *You work **more hours than** I do, but I have **less vacation than** you do.*

- To compare two actions or activities, use the construction [*verb*] + **más/menos** + **que**.

  Laura **estudia menos que** Jaime, y Jaime **sale más que** ella.
  *Laura **studies less than** Jaime, and Jaime **goes out more than** she does.*

- To express *more/less than* a number, use **más/menos** + **de**.

  Julia estudia **más de cuatro** horas al día.
  *Julia studies **more than four** hours a day.*

  Antonio va al gimnasio **menos de una** vez al mes.
  *Antonio goes to the gym **less than once** a month.*

¡Póngalo en práctica!

G5 **Planes** Complete the conversation.

- ¿Qué planes tienes para (1).................... jueves?
- Normalmente, voy al gimnasio (2)................... martes y los jueves. ¿Por qué?
- Ah, (3)................ jueves voy a un concierto de jazz con Lucía y Guillermo.

G6 **Relacionar** Choose the correct ending to complete each sentence.

	1. Tomás y yo	a. hacéis deporte.
	2. Clara	b. hacemos las compras.
	3. Vosotras	c. sales de casa.
	4. Yo	d. sale con amigos.
	5. Ustedes	e. hacen planes.
	6. Tú	f. salgo el viernes.

G7 **Oraciones** Use the cues to form sentences with **todos/as**.

  Modelo: yo / hacer la cama / día
  Yo hago la cama todos los días.

1. Raquel / hacer deporte / fin de semana
   ....

2. David y Jorge / hacer las compras / semana
   ....

3. tú / salir de casa / mañana
   ....

4. yo / salir con amigos / viernes
   ....

G8 **Comparar** Complete the conversation.

  Yo tengo quince días de vacaciones y tú tienes diez, ¿no?

  Sí, tú tienes (1)................ días de vacaciones (2)................ yo.

  Bueno, pero yo trabajo todas las tardes y tú no. Trabajas menos (3)................ treinta horas por semana.

  Es verdad, yo trabajo (4)................ (5)................ tú.

Practice more at vhlcentral.com.

Horarios

¿Qué hora es?	What time is it?
¿A qué hora...?	At what time . . . ?
una persona de 80 años	an 80-year-old person
el día de la semana	day of the week
el lunes	Monday
el martes	Tuesday
el miércoles	Wednesday
el jueves	Thursday
el viernes	Friday
el sábado	Saturday
el domingo	Sunday
el 13 de abril	April 13
la bolsa (de comercio)	stock exchange
el calendario	calendar; schedule
el cine	movie theater
el gimnasio	gym
el horario	schedule
el mundo de las finanzas	world of finance
el/la músico/a	musician
el/la niño/a	boy/girl
el/la profesional	professional
el programa de radio	radio program
el reloj	clock; watch
la rutina diaria	daily routine
el/la veterinario/a	veterinarian
el/la vigilante nocturno/a	night security guard
abrir	to open
ir a trabajar	to go to work
llegar a casa	to arrive home
abierto/a	open
de la mañana	a.m., in the morning
de la tarde	p.m., in the afternoon
de la noche	p.m., at night

por la mañana	in the morning
por la tarde	in the afternoon
por la noche	in the evening, at night

Agenda semanal

¿Con qué frecuencia?	How often?
todos los días	every day
tres veces al año	three times a year
más que	more than
menos que	less than
la agenda (semanal)	(weekly) planner
agosto	August
el colegio	school
el curso	class, course
el día festivo	holiday
la entrevista	interview
el horario de trabajo	work schedule
julio	July
la mujer	woman; wife
el ritmo de vida	pace of life
el/la trabajador(a)	worker
las vacaciones	vacation
la vez (pl. veces)	time
el viaje de negocios	business trip
el yoga	yoga
colaborar	to participate
hacer	to do; to make
hacer algo en casa	to do something at home
hacer deporte	to exercise
hacer la cama	to make the bed
hacer las compras	to do the shopping
pasear	to go for a walk
salir (con amigos)	to go out (with friends)
salir de	to leave
tener clase	to have class
terminar	to end

Pablo Linares

tiempo para uno/a mismo/a	time for oneself
el blog	blog
el campo	country(side)
el chat	chat room
la clase de música	music class
el coche (Esp.)	car
el deporte	sport(s)
el descanso	rest
diciembre	December
el DNI (Documento Nacional de Identidad)	national identity card
el/la empleado/a	employee
la estancia (Cono S.)	ranch
el estrés	stress
el karate	karate
la llamada (de teléfono)	(phone) call
la montaña	mountain
la pintura	painting
la piscina	swimming pool
la prensa económica	financial press
el río	river
la tele(visión)	television
la terapia	therapy
el tiempo	time
la zona colonial	the colonial area
aprender español	to learn Spanish
cocinar	to cook
entrar en	to enter
ir en coche	to go by car
limpiar	to clean
llegar	to arrive
llevar a los niños al colegio	to take the kids to school
parar	to stop
participar en	to participate in
programar	to plan
tomar el ferry	to take the ferry
ver películas	to watch movies
viajar	to travel
intenso/a	intense
relajado/a	relaxed
al aire libre	outdoors
aproximadamente	approximately
fuera de clase	outside of class

Variación léxica

el carro (Amér. L.) ↔ el coche (Esp.) ↔ el auto (Cono S.)

el colegio ↔ la escuela

el ferry ↔ el transbordador

la finca ↔ la hacienda ↔ la estancia (Cono S.)

la mujer ↔ la esposa

la piscina ↔ la alberca (Méx.) ↔ la pileta (Arg.)

el DNI ↔ la cédula de identidad ↔ la cédula de ciudadanía (Méx.)

3B

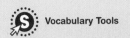
CENTRO COMERCIAL

¡Regalos fantásticos!

¿Necesita un regalo original y diferente?

¡EN ESTE REGALO HAY TODOS ESTOS REGALOS!

Con este cheque-regalo, esta semana...

CENTRO COMERCIAL OVIEDO:
Perfumería García • Regalos Amigos • Librería García Márquez • Discos América

CHEQUE-REGALO
N°: 868H
1000 PESOS
Centro Comercial Oviedo

Identificar y especificar

- ¿**Este** libro de **aquí** es de fotografía?
- No, **ese** libro de **ahí** es de fotografía.

3B.1 Demonstratives and adverbs of location

Hablar de la existencia

- ¿Qué tiendas **hay** en la calle comercial?
- **Hay** una librería y una zapatería.

3B.2 The verb **haber: hay**

Vocabulario

①

el regalo *present*
la perfumería *perfume/cosmetics shop*
la librería *bookstore*
el cheque-regalo *gift voucher*
la chaqueta *jacket*
caro/a *expensive*
la colección, original, el perfume, personal

②

el abanico *(hand-held) fan*
las gafas *glasses*
práctico/a *practical*
feo/a *ugly*

---

1 **a. Los regalos** Carmela and Jorge are buying a present for a friend. Listen to their conversation with the sales clerk and answer the questions.

1. ¿De qué regalos hablan Carmela y Jorge?
2. ¿De qué regalo habla el vendedor?

b. Cerca o lejos Listen to their conversation again and associate the words in each column.

| este/esta | lejos/ahí | estos/estas | cerca/aquí |
| ese/esa | cerca/aquí | esos/esas | lejos/ahí |

2 **a. Cheque-regalo** Look at the **cheque-regalo** and circle the items available this week.

| Hay... | libros | abanicos | perfumes | coches |
| | colección de CD | teléfonos celulares | gafas |

b. Comentar Use these adjectives to discuss the **cheque-regalo** in pairs.

bonito/a • original • personal • diferente • práctico/a • moderno/a • feo/a

3 **Las tiendas** Match each item to the store where it is sold.

1. libros ....
2. perfume ....
3. chaqueta ....
4. zapatos ....
5. CD ....

a. zapatería
b. tienda de ropa
c. librería
d. perfumería
e. tienda de discos

Localizar

¿Dónde está el bolígrafo?

Está en la mesa,
al lado del libro.

Está a la derecha
del libro.

Está a la izquierda
del libro.

Está debajo
del libro.

Está detrás
del libro.

Está delante
del libro.

Está entre el libro
y el teléfono.

Está encima
del libro.

3B.3 estar + [*prepositional phrase*]; de + el = del

4 **a. Identificar** Look at the gift shop window and identify the items described.

1. Están a la derecha de los libros: *las gafas de sol*
2. Está encima de la agenda: ....
3. Está a la izquierda de los CD: ....
4. Están a la derecha de la lámpara: ....
5. Está detrás de los zapatos: ....
6. Está delante de la chaqueta: ....

b. ¿Dónde están? Choose three items in the store and tell your partner where they are. Your partner will identify the items.

Modelo: • *Está entre el perfume y el paraguas.*
           • *¿El marco?*

5 **Describir** In pairs, use the adjectives from **Actividad 2b** to describe these gifts.

Modelo: *El reloj es muy práctico.*

MI EXPERIENCIA

6 **Elaborar** Create a **cheque-regalo**. Choose two gifts for this week, the stores that will participate, and a price. Explain your offer to the class.

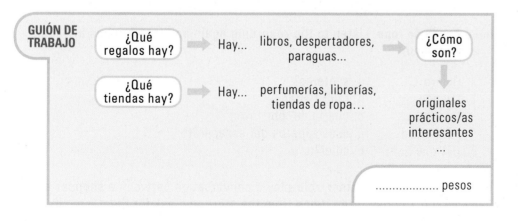

Vocabulario

③
el zapato *shoe*
la zapatería *shoe store*
la tienda de ropa *clothing store*
la tienda de discos *music store*
④
el bolígrafo *pen*
la mesa *table*
al lado de *next to*
a la derecha de *to the right of*
a la izquierda de *to the left of*
debajo de *under*
detrás de *behind*
delante de *in front of*
encima de *on (top of)*
del (= de + el) *of the*
el despertador *alarm clock*
el pañuelo *scarf; handkerchief*
la lámpara *lamp*
las gafas de sol *sunglasses*
el marco *picture frame*
el paraguas *umbrella*
la tienda de regalos *gift shop*
el objeto *object*
⑤
el reloj (de pulsera) *(wrist)watch*

SAM: Actividades pp. 57–59

Practice more at **vhlcentral.com**.

Prendas de moda

Leticia lleva una camiseta anaranjada, una falda negra y unas zapatillas de deporte rojas.

Carlos lleva una chaqueta anaranjada, una camiseta amarilla y unos pantalones azules.

Sara lleva una camiseta verde y unos pantalones grises. Ángel lleva una camiseta anaranjada y unos jeans azules.

Juanjo lleva un traje marrón, una camisa azul y una corbata roja, y Mireia lleva un vestido blanco con unas botas marrones.

Indicar el color

Una chaqueta blanca.

Un bolso blanco.

Unas zapatillas blancas.

Unos pantalones blancos.

3B.4 Colors

Hablar de la ropa

Marta lleva un vestido verde y unos zapatos verdes.

3B.5 The verb llevar

Solicitar productos

Quiero una camisa azul.

Quería unos zapatos negros.

¿Tienen jeans de señora?

3B.6 Stem-changing verbs
e→ie: querer

Vocabulario

(7)

la prenda *garment*

llevar *to wear*

la camiseta *T-shirt*

anaranjado/a *orange*

la falda *skirt*

negro/a *black*

las zapatillas de deporte *running shoes, sneakers*

rojo/a *red*

amarillo/a *yellow*

los pantalones *pants*

azul *blue*

7 **a. Prendas de moda** Read the descriptions and write the photo number that corresponds to each person or pair.

☐ Leticia   ☐ Sara y Ángel   ☐ Carlos   ☐ Juanjo y Mireia

b. Los colores For each color, list the articles of clothing that appear in the description.

marrón	gris	blanco/a	negro/a

rojo/a	verde	azul	amarillo/a	anaranjado/a

8 **La ropa** Describe what your classmates are wearing.

Modelo: *Anne lleva unos pantalones azules...*

9 **a. Escuchar** Listen to these conversations in a clothing store and circle the three items mentioned.

vestido	falda	traje	pantalones	zapatos	suéter

b. La tienda de ropa Listen to the recording again and match items in each column.

1. Quiero ....   a. suéteres?
2. ¿Tienen ....   b. talla tiene?
3. Quería ....   c. una falda, por favor.
4. ¿Qué ....   d. esos zapatos del escaparate.
5. ¿De qué ....   e. color?

10 **Representar** With a partner, role-play a conversation between a shopper and a salesperson. Choose three items from the store and ask for them, specifying the size and color you want.

Cliente: Hola, quería esta camisa.
Vendedora: ¿Qué talla tiene?
Cliente: La talla L. ¿La tiene blanca?
Vendedora: Sí, aquí está.
Cliente: También quería estos pantalones, ¿los puedo ver?
Vendedora: Sí, claro, aquí los tiene.

Cliente: Y estas gafas de sol... ¿Las tiene marrones?
Vendedora: No, las tengo negras.
Cliente: Ese suéter, ¿lo tiene verde?
Vendedora: No, lo siento. Lo tenemos en azul.
Cliente: Gracias, ¿puedo pagar con tarjeta?
Vendedora: Sí, por supuesto.

11 a. En la tienda Read the conversation and write the clothing item each question refers to.

1. ¿La tienen blanca? *la camisa*
2. ¿Los puedo ver? ....
3. ¿Las tiene marrones? ....
4. ¿Lo tiene verde? ....

b. Reescribir Rewrite the questions, substituting the underlined words with **lo**, **la**, **los**, or **las**.

1. Quería este suéter negro. ¿Tienen <u>el suéter negro</u> en la talla M?
   ¿Lo tienen en la talla M?

2. Quería estas gafas. ¿Tienen <u>estas gafas</u> en otro color? ....

3. Quería unos pantalones. ¿Tiene <u>pantalones</u> negros? ....

4. Me gusta esta camiseta. ¿Tienen <u>esta camiseta</u> en la talla L? ....

12 Relacionar Now it's time to pay. Match the expressions with the method of payment.

- en efectivo ....
- con tarjeta ....

MI EXPERIENCIA

13 Mi ropa favorita What are your favorite colors and clothes?

First, review clothing vocabulary and associate words with pictures. Then draw a picture of your favorite clothing item.

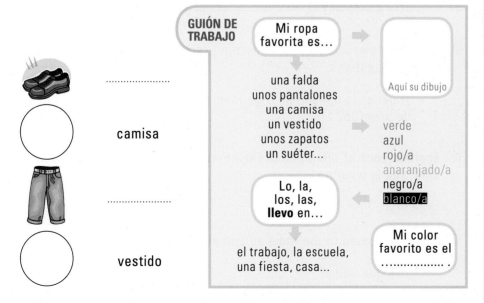

 camisa

vestido

GUIÓN DE TRABAJO

Mi ropa favorita es...

una falda
unos pantalones
una camisa
un vestido
unos zapatos
un suéter...

➡ verde
azul
rojo/a
anaranjado/a
negro/a
blanco/a

Aquí su dibujo

Lo, la, los, las, **llevo** en...

el trabajo, la escuela, una fiesta, casa...

Mi color favorito es el ....

Vocabulario *cont.*

verde *green*
gris *gray*
el traje *suit*
marrón *brown*
la camisa *shirt*
la corbata *tie*
el vestido *dress*
blanco/a *white*
la bota *boot*
el bolso *bag*
la marca *brand*
el color, los jeans
⑨
el suéter *sweater*
querer (e:ie) *to want*
el escaparate *shop window*
¿De qué color (*m.*)? *What color?*
¿De qué talla (*f.*)? *What size?*

Referirse a un objeto ya mencionado

Lo llevo siempre. (el reloj)
La quería marrón. (la falda)
Los tengo en azul. (los pantalones)
¿Las puedo ver? (las camisetas)

3B.7 Direct object pronouns

Pedir permiso y aceptar

● ¿**Puedo** ver esos pantalones?
■ Por supuesto.
● ¿**Puedo** pagar con tarjeta?
■ Sí, claro.

3B.8 Stem-changing verbs
o→ue: poder
Adverbs of affirmation

Vocabulario

⑪
¿Los puedo ver? *Can I see them?*
ver *to see*
Lo siento. *I'm sorry.*
con tarjeta *with a credit card*
⑫
en efectivo *in cash*
⑬
preferido/a *favorite*
el dibujo *drawing*
la escuela *school*

SAM: Actividades pp. 60–62

Practice more at **vhlcentral.com**.

ESCAPARATE

Noviembre n.º 11

Edición especial
La moda en Colombia

Olga Piedrahita

Tiendas de moda en Colombia
Moda infantil
Decoración práctica
Regalos originales
Viajes diferentes

Olga Piedrahita, la moda en Colombia

ESCAPARATE

"Para mí, la moda es comunicación. La moda es arte."

Moda colombiana

Olga Piedrahita es una importante diseñadora colombiana. Estudió Bellas Artes en Estados Unidos y ahora trabaja en Colombia. Pertenece a un grupo de diseñadores llamados "intelectuales" que hacen moda artística y creativa. La diseñadora colombiana representa a Colombia en la **LatinoAmérica Fashion** en el marco del Salón Internacional de la Moda de Madrid.

Olga Piedrahita presenta una interesante colección para la mujer contemporánea. Sus trabajos son personales y prácticos; su lema, "arte para llevar". Sus camisas, faldas, vestidos o pantalones reflejan magia, poesía y humor, y los colores son verdes, marrones, azules y grises.

Vocabulario

(14)

la edición especial *special edition*
la moda *fashion*
el/la diseñador(a) *designer*
colombiano/a *Colombian*
estudió *she/he studied*
pertenecer (zc) *to belong*
el Salón Internacional de la Moda *International Fashion Fair*
contemporáneo/a *contemporary*
el lema *motto*
la moda infantil *children's fashion*
la portada *cover*
el viaje *trip*
la comunicación, el arte, la decoración

(16)

el/la modelo *(fashion) model*

---

(14) Escaparate Look at this magazine cover and answer the questions.

1. ¿Qué tipo de revista es?

☐ de moda ☐ de decoración ☐ de viajes

2. ¿Cuándo sale la revista?

☐ todos los días ☐ todas las semanas ☐ todos los meses

3. ¿Cuáles son los temas de la revista?

☐ moda ☐ viajes ☐ cine ☐ regalos ☐ decoración

(15) a. Contestar Answer these questions about Olga Piedrahita.

○ ¿De dónde es? ○ ¿Cuál es su profesión?

b. ¿Están de acuerdo? With a partner, reread the article and answer these questions.

○ ¿Cuál es la opinión de Olga Piedrahita sobre la moda? ¿Están ustedes de acuerdo?

(16) Escribir Look at the photo of Olga Piedrahita and write a brief description of what she is wearing.

Modelo: *Olga Piedrahita lleva...*

(17) Escuchar Listen to the radio ad and answer the question.

○ ¿De qué habla?

CONSUMO RESPONSABLE

Muchos productos que compramos todos los días, como por ejemplo, la ropa, los complementos, la comida y la artesanía, vienen de países en vías de desarrollo. Las organizaciones internacionales de comercio justo quieren garantizar un sueldo digno al productor y proteger los derechos de los niños y de las mujeres en estos países. Otro objetivo de estas organizaciones es hacer conscientes a los consumidores del origen de los productos que compran.

18 **a. Consumo responsable** Read the text and answer these questions.

1. ¿De qué productos habla el texto?

2. ¿De dónde vienen los productos de este tipo de comercio?

3. ¿Cuál es el objetivo del comercio justo?

b. Comentar Discuss your answer to question 3 with a partner. Do you agree?

[j] [g]

19 **a. [j] y [g]** Listen to these words. Underline the sound they have in common.

gimnasio   traje   joven   agenda   rebajas   objetivo

origen   ecológica   jirafa   tarjeta   mujeres   justo

b. Organizar Now organize the words according to how this sound is spelled.

ja	je/ge	ji/gi	jo	ju
rebajas				

20 **a. Relacionar** These are some typical products from Latin America. Match each product to its country of origin.

puros habanos

yerba mate

tapices

café

(**C**) Perú   ( ) Cuba   ( ) Colombia   ( ) Argentina

b. Más productos What other products from Latin America can you name?

Vocabulario

18

el consumo *consumption*
los complementos *accessories*
la artesanía *crafts*
venir *to come*
en vías de desarrollo *developing*
el comercio justo *fair trade*
garantizar *to guarantee*
el sueldo *wage*
digno/a *decent*
el/la productor(a) *producer*
proteger (j) *to protect*
el derecho *right*
el objetivo *goal, objective*
hacer consciente *to make aware*
el/la consumidor(a) *consumer*
comprar *to buy*
**responsable, el producto,
la organización**

¡OJO!

Venir is an irregular verb in the present indicative similar to **tener**: **vengo, vienes, viene, venimos, venís, vienen.**

Vocabulario

19

la rebaja *discount*

20

el puro habano *Cuban cigar*
la yerba mate *mate (infusion)*
el tapiz (*pl.* tapices) *tapestry*

OPINIÓN

¿Sigue usted la moda?

¿Cree que la moda es una forma de arte?

¿Compra usted por Internet? ¿Qué tipo de productos? ¿Por qué prefiere esta opción?

SAM: Actividades pp. 63–68

TAREA FINAL

Tienda de regalos

Make a list of the types of stores you have seen in this lesson.

With a partner, choose a type of store. Give the store a name and decide what products it will sell.

Come up with a special of the month and make a poster advertising the items and their prices.

Hang the posters in your classroom, and, as a class, vote on who has the best promotion.

YO PUEDO...

- **Puedo hablar sobre las tiendas y los artículos que hay en ellas.**
  Choose a store you know and list what items are sold there.

- **Puedo localizar objetos en el espacio.**
  Choose an item near you and say where it is located, using prepositions of location.

- **Puedo identificar diferentes prendas de ropa y especificar su color.**
  Write the name and color of each article of clothing.

- **Puedo pedir un artículo en una tienda y solicitar información sobre la forma de pago.**
  Complete this dialogue.

Tienda: ....
Artículos: ....
....
....
....

....

....

- Buenos días, ...
  unos pantalones azules.
- Por supuesto.
- ¿.............. pagar
  ....?

GRAMÁTICA FUNCIONAL (S) Tutorials

3B.1 Identify and specify items

Demonstratives and adverbs of location 7.1, 7.2, 11.7

- When referring to specific objects, use the adjectives **este/a/os/as** (*this/these*), and **ese/a/os/as** (*that/those*) to identify precisely which object(s) you are talking about.

    Este pañuelo cuesta $50, pero **ese** pañuelo cuesta $30.
    This scarf costs $50, but that scarf costs $30.

- **Este/a/os/as** and **ese/a/os/as** must agree in gender and number with the nouns they modify. Place these adjectives before nouns.

(aquí)		(ahí)	
este libro estos libros	esta lámpara estas lámparas	ese libro esos libros	esa lámpara esas lámparas

- For added emphasis and precision, use the expressions **de aquí** (*over here*) and **de ahí** (*over there*) to specify which item(s) you are talking about.

    Esta agenda **de aquí** es muy práctica.
    This planner (over) here is very practical.

    Ese paraguas **de ahí** es muy original.
    That umbrella (over) there is very original.

- **Este/a/os/as** and **ese/a/os/as** can also be used on their own, as pronouns. Remember that the pronoun should match the gender and number of the noun or person it represents.

    Esta es la vendedora.
    This is the saleswoman.

    Esos son los libros de García Márquez.
    Those are the books by García Márquez.

3B.2 Express existence

The verb **haber: hay** 5.1.2, 5.9

- Use the verb **hay** (*there is/are*) to express that something exists.

    Hay tres libros encima de la mesa.
    There are three books on the table.

- Note that **hay** is invariable; it is used both for a single item and for multiple items.

    Hay una lámpara.   **Hay** cuatro marcos.
    There is a lamp.   *There are four picture frames.*

- Use **hay** in questions to mean *is/are there*.

    ¿**Hay** discos de Juanes?
    Are there (any) CDs by Juanes?

    ¿Qué **hay** en la tienda de regalos?
    What is there in the gift shop?

¡Póngalo en práctica!

G1 **De aquí y de ahí** Write the appropriate form of **este/a/os/as** or **ese/a/os/as** for each item.

(de aquí)	(de ahí)
1. .... regalos	6. .... marco
2. .... tienda	7. .... libros
3. .... perfumerías	8. .... chaquetas
4. .... abanico	9. .... escaparate
5. .... colección	10. .... librería

G2 **Elaborar** Write a sentence identifying each person or object.

> Modelo: (aquí) Juan
> *Este es Juan.*

1. (ahí) las gafas
2. (aquí) los paraguas
3. (aquí) Ana y Jorge
4. (ahí) el perfume
5. (ahí) la zapatería
6. (aquí) el cheque-regalo

G3 **Inventario** Look at the inventory for the gift shop and write four sentences describing what can be found there.

OBJETO	CANTIDAD
abanico	32
pañuelo	14
marco	21
lámpara	8
libro	55
gafas de sol	10

3B.3 Identify relative location

estar + [*preposition/prepositional phrase*]   5.8.1, 10.5, 10.17
de + el = del

en / encima de	•	debajo de	⊤
a la derecha de	I•	delante de	▪▪
a la izquierda de	•I	detrás de	▪▪

- To describe where something is in relation to something else, use **estar** + [*preposition/prepositional phrase*].

  Las gafas de sol **están al lado de** la lámpara.
  The sunglasses are next to the lamp.

  El coche **está delante de** la librería.
  The car is in front of the bookstore.

- When **de** is followed by the masculine article **el**, combine the words to form the contraction **del**.

  Los CD están a la derecha **del** despertador.
  The CDs are to the right of the alarm clock.

3B.4 Indicate colors

Colors   4.1   The plural   4.2

- Use colors to specify and add detail to a description. Place adjectives of color after the nouns they modify.

rojo/a/os/as	anaranjado/a/os/as	amarillo/a/os/as
verde(s)	azul(es)	blanco/a/os/as
negro/a/os/as	gris(es)	marrón/marrones

- Some nouns, such as **café**, **rosa**, and **naranja**, can be used as invariable adjectives to refer to the colors brown, pink, and orange, respectively. They are most commonly used with the noun **color**.

  Irene lleva un suéter **color naranja** y unos pantalones **rosa**.
  *Irene is wearing an **orange** sweater and **pink** pants.*

3B.5 Talk about clothing

The verb **llevar**   5.1.1

- Use the verb **llevar** (*to wear*) to talk about the clothes people wear. **Llevar** is a regular **-ar** verb.

LLEVAR			
(yo)	llevo	(nosotros/as)	llevamos
(tú)	llevas	(vosotros/as)	lleváis
(usted, él, ella)	lleva	(ustedes, ellos/as)	llevan

  Héctor y Lourdes **llevan** unas zapatillas de deporte blancas.
  *Héctor and Lourdes **are wearing** white sneakers.*

- As you saw in **Lección 3A**, **llevar** can also mean *to take*.

  Llevo mis libros a clase.
  *I **take** my books to class.*

¡Póngalo en práctica!

G4 **¿Dónde está?** Say where each item is in relation to the other.

> **Modelo:** la tienda de regalos I• la librería
> *La tienda de regalos está a la derecha de la librería.*

1. el CD ⊤ el libro
   ....
2. el despertador ▪▪ la lámpara
   ....
3. el marco • el pañuelo
   ....
4. el abanico I• los CD
   ....
5. el celular •I la chaqueta
   ....
6. los jeans ▪▪ los suéteres
   ....

G5 **En la tienda** Complete the paragraph using the correct form of each adjective.

En el escaparate de la tienda hay unos pantalones (1)..................... (azul), un suéter (2)..................... (verde), una camisa (3)..................... (rojo) y unos zapatos (4)..................... (marrón). También hay un bonito vestido (5)..................... (rosa), unas faldas (6)..................... (amarillo) y una corbata (7)..................... (negro).

G6 **Llevar** Complete each sentence with the appropriate form of **llevar**.

1. Manolo siempre .... una corbata.
2. Celia y Rebeca .... unas camisetas verdes.
3. Yo .... un suéter bonito.
4. Tú .... unos jeans negros.
5. Ustedes .... unas gafas de sol elegantes.
6. Carlos y yo .... unos zapatos nuevos.
7. Mi madre siempre .... prendas de marca.
8. El cajero y tú .... el mismo suéter.

 Practice more at **vhlcentral.com**.

GRAMÁTICA FUNCIONAL

3B.6 Request products

Stem-changing verbs e→ie: querer 5.1.1
Demonstrative adjectives and pronouns 7.1, 7.2

- Use the verb **querer** (*to want*) to request products.

  Hola, **quiero** estos zapatos, por favor.
  *Hello, **I want** these shoes, please.*

- **Querer** is an **e→ie** stem-changing verb; the **e** in the stem changes to **ie** in all forms except for the **nosotros/as** and **vosotros/as** forms. You saw a similar pattern with **almorzar** in **2B.3**.

QUERER			
(yo)	quiero	(nosotros/as)	queremos
(tú)	quieres	(vosotros/as)	queréis
(usted, él, ella)	quiere	(ustedes, ellos/as)	quieren

  ¿Quieres el vestido verde o este azul?
  ***Do you want** the green dress or this blue one?*

  Quiero este de aquí, por favor.
  ***I want** this one here, please.*

- To make a polite request, use **quería** (*I wanted*) instead of **quiero**.

3B.7 Refer to a previously mentioned object

Direct object pronouns 6.2.1

- To avoid unnecessary repetition, use a direct object pronoun to refer to something that has been mentioned previously.

  Quería esta falda. ¿**La** tienen verde?
  *I'd like this skirt. Do you have **it** in green?*

- A direct object is a noun that receives the action of a verb. In the statement *I'm wearing jeans*, the direct object is *jeans*; it answers the question *What am I wearing?*

SUBJECT	VERB	DIRECT OBJECT
Esperanza	lleva	una camiseta azul.
Esperanza	*is wearing*	*a blue T-shirt.*

- Direct object pronouns agree with the nouns they replace.

	singular	plural
masculino	lo	los
femenino	la	las

  Luis compra **los zapatos**. ⟷ Luis **los** compra.
  *Luis buys **the shoes**. ⟷ Luis buys **them**.*

  Queremos **la lámpara**. ⟷ **La** queremos.
  *We want **the lamp**. ⟷ We want **it**.*

- Place a direct object pronoun directly before the conjugated verb.

  Lo tengo y **lo** llevo siempre.
  *I have **it** and I wear **it** all the time.*

¡Póngalo en práctica!

G7 **De compras** Complete the conversation with the appropriate forms of **querer**.

> Buenos días, nosotras (1)............... unos vestidos de fiesta.

> Muy bien. ¿De qué colores los (2)........................ ?

> Yo (3).................... un vestido azul. Manuela (4)........... ese vestido negro de ahí.

> Lo siento mucho; no tenemos vestidos azules. ¿(5)........... usted ver otro color?

> Ay, no, gracias. Yo realmente (6)........... uno azul.

G8 **Completar** Complete the conversations with the appropriate direct object pronouns.

- Hola, quería unos zapatos marrones.
- ¿De qué número (1)........... quiere?
- (2)........... quiero del número 42, por favor.

- Buenas tardes, quería una falda nueva.
- ¿De qué color (3)........... quiere?
- ¿(4)........... tienen roja?
- Sí, (5)........... tenemos roja y negra también.

G9 **Reescribir** Rewrite each sentence using a direct object pronoun.

1. Concepción lleva la camiseta.
   ....

2. Germán y tú queréis las gafas negras.
   ....

3. Claudia y yo queremos los zapatos elegantes.
   ....

4. La tienda tiene los jeans nuevos.
   ....

5. ¿De qué talla quiere la camiseta?
   ....

6. Quiero el suéter gris.
   ....

GRAMÁTICA FUNCIONAL

3B.8 Request and grant permission

Stem-changing verbs o→ue: poder   5.1.1
Infinitive constructions   5.10
Adverbs of affirmation   11.2

- Use the verb **poder** (*to be able to*) to request and grant permission.

  ¿Podemos ver ese reloj?
  Can we see that watch?

- **Poder** is an o→ue stem-changing verb. As with other stem-changing verbs, the stem change occurs in all forms except the **nosotros/as** and **vosotros/as** forms.

PODER			
(yo)	puedo	(nosotros/as)	podemos
(tú)	puedes	(vosotros/as)	podéis
(usted, él, ella)	puede	(ustedes, ellos/as)	pueden

  ¿Puedo pagar con tarjeta?
  Can I pay with a credit card?

- **Poder** is often used in combination with another verb; in this construction, use the conjugated form of **poder** followed by the infinitive of the second verb.

  Sí, usted **puede pagar** con tarjeta.
  Yes, you can pay with a credit card.

- **Querer** is also frequently used in combination with an infinitive.

  Quiero ver esa camiseta.
  I want to see that T-shirt.

- When you use a direct object pronoun with an infinitive construction, the direct object pronoun can be placed before the conjugated verb or it can be attached to the end of the infinitive.

  ¿La puedo ver? / ¿Puedo **verla**?
  Can I see it?

- Use affirmative expressions such as **claro** and **por supuesto** (*of course*) to add emphasis and variety to your conversations.

- ¿Puedo pagar con tarjeta?   ▪ Sí, **por supuesto.**

¡Póngalo en práctica!

G10 **Relacionar** Match each sentence starter with the appropriate ending.

1. Silvia y yo...
2. El vendedor...
3. Tú...
4. Yo...
5. Gabriel y Daniel...

a. .... puedes pagar con tarjeta.

b. .... puede vender los regalos.

c. .... pueden comprar las gafas.

d. .... podemos hacer las compras.

e. .... puedo llevar mi nuevo vestido.

G11 **Oraciones** Rewrite each sentence using a direct object pronoun.

> **Modelo:** ¿Podemos comprar las gafas de sol?
> *¿Podemos comprarlas?* OR *¿Las podemos comprar?*

1. ¿Puedo ver el paraguas?

....

2. ¿Quiere comprar los CD?

....

3. Puedes llevar los zapatos negros.

....

4. Los niños pueden llevar jeans al restaurante.

....

G12 **Comprando** Use phrases from the word bank to complete this conversation.

Claro, aquí tiene.	Sí, por supuesto.
Solo en efectivo.	¿Lo puedo ver?
¿Puedo pagar con tarjeta?	

- Buenos días. Quería este suéter.
  (1)...

▪ (2)... Aquí está.

- ¿Lo tienen en la talla M?

▪ (3)...

- Muchas gracias. Es muy elegante; lo quiero comprar.
  (4)...

▪ Lo siento, no. (5)...

 S Practice more at **vhlcentral.com.**

VOCABULARIO 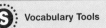 Vocabulary Tools

¡Regalos fantásticos!

el abanico	(hand-held) fan
el bolígrafo	pen
la chaqueta	jacket
el cheque-regalo	gift voucher
la colección	collection
el despertador	alarm clock
las gafas (de sol)	(sun)glasses
la lámpara	lamp
la librería	bookstore
el marco	picture frame
la mesa	table
el objeto	object
el pañuelo	scarf; handkerchief
el paraguas	umbrella
el perfume	perfume
la perfumería	perfume/cosmetics shop
el regalo	present
el reloj (de pulsera)	(wrist)watch
la tienda de discos	music store
la tienda de regalos	gift shop
la tienda de ropa	clothing store
el zapato	shoe
la zapatería	shoe store

caro/a	expensive
feo/a	ugly
original	original
personal	personal
práctico/a	practical

a la derecha de	to the right of
a la izquierda de	to the left of
al lado de	next to
debajo de	under
delante de	in front of
detrás de	behind
encima de	on (top of)

del (= de + el)	of the

Prendas de moda

¿De qué color (m.)?	What color?
¿De qué talla (f.)?	What size?
Lo siento.	I'm sorry.
¿Los puedo ver?	Can I see them?

la bota	boot
el bolso	bag
la camisa	shirt
la camiseta	T-shirt
el color	color
la corbata	tie
el dibujo	drawing
el escaparate	shop window
la escuela	school
la falda	skirt
los jeans	jeans
la marca	brand
los pantalones	pants
la prenda	garment
el suéter	sweater
la talla	size
el traje	suit
el vestido	dress
las zapatillas (de deporte)	running shoes, sneakers

llevar	to wear
querer (e:ie)	to want
ver	to see

amarillo/a	yellow
anaranjado/a	orange
azul	blue
blanco/a	white
gris	gray
marrón	brown
negro/a	black
preferido/a	favorite
rojo/a	red
verde	green

en efectivo	in cash
con tarjeta	with a credit card

Olga Piedrahita

estudió	he/she studied
el arte	art
la artesanía	crafts
el comercio justo	fair trade
los complementos	accessories
la comunicación	communication
el/la consumidor(a)	consumer
el consumo	consumption
la decoración	decoration
el derecho	right
el/la diseñador(a)	designer
la edición especial	special edition
el lema	motto
la moda	fashion
la moda infantil	children's fashion
el/la modelo	(fashion) model
el objetivo	goal, objective
la organización	organization
la portada	cover
el producto	product
el/la productor(a)	producer
el puro habano	Cuban cigar
la rebaja	discount
el Salón Internacional de la Moda	International Fashion Fair
el sueldo	wage
el tapiz (pl. tapices)	tapestry
el viaje	trip
la yerba mate	mate (infusion)

comprar	to buy
garantizar	to guarantee
hacer consciente	to make aware
pertenecer (zc)	to belong
proteger (j)	to protect
venir	to come

colombiano/a	Colombian
contemporáneo/a	contemporary
digno/a	decent
en vías de desarrollo	developing
responsable	responsible

Variación léxica

el bolígrafo ⟷ la pluma (*Méx.*) ⟷ la birome (*Arg.*) ⟷ la lapicera (*Uru., Arg.*)

la camiseta ⟷ el polo (*Ven.*) ⟷ la playera (*Méx.*) ⟷ la remera (*Arg.*) ⟷ la polera (*Chi.*)

la falda ⟷ la pollera (*Cono S.*) ⟷ la saya (*Cub.*)

las gafas ⟷ los lentes ⟷ los anteojos ⟷ los espejuelos (*Cub.*)

los jeans ⟷ los vaqueros (*Esp.*) ⟷ los bluyines (*Cub.*)

el suéter ⟷ el jersey (*Esp.*) ⟷ el pulóver ⟷ la chompa (*Per.*)

las zapatillas (de deporte) ⟷ los (zapatos de) tenis ⟷ las deportivas (*Esp.*)

LECTURA

Vocabulario útil

alentar (e:ie) *to cheer, to root for*

el campeón/la campeona *champion*

la Copa Mundial *World Cup*

la cuna *cradle*

el equipo *team*

ganador(a) *winning*

el/la jugador(a) *player*

junto/a *together*

paralizar *to paralize*

el partido *game*

el pasatiempo *pastime*

el/la seguidor(a) *follower*

Estrategia ....

Using a bilingual dictionary

Language learners often make the mistake of using the first option given in a bilingual dictionary without consulting the other options. Always pay attention to the examples and information provided to differentiate word meanings in your dictionary. Look at the photo in the article. What is it about? Which meaning of the word **partido** will apply in this case?

1 *Pol* party

2 *Dep* match, game

Dos idiomas, dos camisetas, un campeón

El fútbol en España es pasión de multitudes. Los dos equipos más conocidos de este país son el Real Madrid y el Barça (que oficialmente se llama Fútbol Club Barcelona). Un partido entre estos dos equipos paraliza Madrid y Barcelona. Los seguidores del Real Madrid llevan camisetas blancas y alientan

 1 **Preguntas** Discuss these questions with a partner.

 ¿Qué deportes practicas? ¿Qué deportes miras en la televisión? ¿Vas al estadio para ver algún deporte? ¿Qué rivalidades deportivas importantes conoces? ¿De qué color es la camiseta de tu equipo favorito?

2 **¿Verdadero o falso?** Indicate whether each statement is **verdadero** or **falso**.

1. El fútbol no es muy popular en España.

2. En Madrid, la gente habla catalán.

3. Los jugadores del Real Madrid llevan camisetas blancas.

4. El equipo nacional español no tiene jugadores del Barça.

5. España es el país ganador de la Copa Mundial 2010.

6. En México, el hockey sobre césped es popular entre las chicas de escuela secundaria.

7. En el mundo hispanohablante, los deportes son parte del programa de estudios universitario.

8. Las estudiantes argentinas y españolas practican hockey habitualmente.

Rivalidades del fútbol

Argentina:	Boca Juniors vs River Plate
Perú:	Universitario vs Alianza
México:	Águilas del América vs Chivas del Guadalajara
Chile:	Colo colo vs Universidad de Chile
Guatemala:	Comunicaciones vs Municipal
Uruguay:	Peñarol vs Nacional
Colombia:	Millonarios vs Independiente Santa Fe

a su equipo en español. Los seguidores del Barça llevan camisetas rojas y azules y alientan a su equipo en catalán.

Trece jugadores del Barça y diez del Real Madrid participaron° en la Copa Mundial de 2010 (seis del Barça y cinco del Real Madrid en el equipo nacional español, el campeón mundial ese año; el resto en equipos de otros países). Madrid y Barcelona hablan idiomas diferentes y son rivales en el fútbol, pero juntas son cuna de campeones.

participaron *participated*

► **Los estudiantes y el deporte**

En los países hispanohablantes no es común practicar deportes como parte del programa de estudios universitario. Algunas universidades tienen equipos deportivos, pero esto no es muy habitual. En general, los estudiantes practican deportes como pasatiempo fuera de la universidad.

En la escuela secundaria, los estudiantes practican deportes en la escuela y fuera de la escuela. En Argentina, los chicos practican fútbol y rugby, mientras que° entre las chicas es muy popular el hockey sobre césped°. En México, Colombia y España, el fútbol y el baloncesto° son

populares entre los chicos. Las chicas mexicanas y colombianas practican baloncesto y vóleibol, mientras que las españolas practican vóleibol y hockey. En América Central y el Caribe, el béisbol es muy popular entre los estudiantes.

mientras que *while*
hockey sobre césped *field hockey*
baloncesto *basketball*

---

 ③ Entrevista In pairs, improvise an interview with a high school student about the sports he/she practices at school and out of school. Use some of the words and expressions in the box.

deporte	favorito/a	partido
en la escuela	fuera de la escuela	practicar

PROYECTO

Rivalidades

Choose two sports rivals and prepare a poster or a presentation about them to show in class.

- Choose two sports rivals (it can be two professional teams, two college teams, etc.).
- Introduce each of the teams (what sport they play, what city/state/country they are from).
- Include other relevant information: their stadiums, their jersey colors, etc.
- Illustrate your presentation with photos.

Estrategia ············

Conducting interviews

When conducting an interview, start by introducing yourself (**Hola, soy Pedro Gómez de Conexión Deportiva**). Then introduce the person you are interviewing (**Hoy estamos con Juan Ramírez, estudiante de.../Hoy entrevistamos a.../Hoy está con nosotros Juan Ramírez, estudiante de..., para hablar de...**). After asking all the questions you need to ask, thank your interviewee (**Juan, gracias por participar en esta entrevista./Gracias por hablar con nosotros.**)

Video

¡Fútbol en España!

Many famous players have played for **Real Madrid** and **Barça** over the years. In this **Flash Cultura**, you will learn about the intense rivalry between these two teams. Did you know that Lionel Messi, one of the stars of the 2014 World Cup, currently plays for **Barça**?

Flash CULTURA

Vocabulario útil

la afición *fans*
el/la aficionado/a *follower, fan*
celebrar *to celebrate*
la estrella *star*
ganar *to win*
el/la jugador(a) *player*
perder (e:ie) *to lose*

FIFA WORLD CUP Brasil

1 Comentar Discuss these questions with a partner.

¿Qué comes cuando vas a un estadio a ver deportes? ¿Qué jugadores de fútbol famosos conoces? ¿Cómo celebran los aficionados las victorias en tu país?

2 Mirar Watch this **Flash Cultura** episode. While you watch the video, listen for the Spanish words you have already learned.

(Hay mucha afición al fútbol en España.)

¿Y quién va a ganar?

3 ¿Qué oye? Mark the statements you hear in the video.

1. El fútbol en España es muy importante. ☐
2. Nunca pierde el Real Madrid. ☐
3. ¿Quieres sal? ☐
4. Sí, un poquito. Muchas gracias. ☐
5. También quiero palomitas de maíz. ☐
6. ¿Cuál es tu equipo preferido? ☐

4 Entrevista With a partner, prepare a brief interview with a sports fan in a stadium.

Modelo: • ¿Quién gana hoy?
■ Los Red Sox, por supuesto.
• ¿Qué comes?

 Practice more at **vhlcentral.com**.

Unidad 4

Paco, amigo del Rastro

Carmen Abreu, fundadora de Caribe Propiedades

AVANCE

Comprar en los mercados

S Vocabulary Tools

BARRIOS CON CARÁCTER

La Latina en directo

La Latina es un barrio de Madrid, especial, auténtico, único... Está en el centro de la ciudad, al lado de la calle Toledo, la Puerta de Toledo y la calle Mayor. En el barrio vive gente de distintas nacionalidades: indios, pakistaníes, marroquíes, chinos... Tiene iglesias y calles muy bonitas, mercados tradicionales, muchas tiendas, muchos bares, restaurantes, teatros y también bancos y cibercafés muy modernos.

Dar y pedir opinión

- ¿Qué piensas de tu barrio?
- Pienso que es un barrio con carácter.

4A.1 Stem-changing verbs e→ie: pensar

Vocabulario

①
el carácter *atmosphere*
en directo *live*
distinto/a *different*
indio/a *Indian*
paquistaní *Pakistani*
marroquí *Moroccan*
el cibercafé *Internet café*
visitar *to visit*
auténtico/a, tradicional

②
pensar (e:ie) de *to think of*
gustar *to like*
exótico/a

⑤
el/la vecino/a *neighbor*

1 **La Latina** What is **La Latina** like? Read the newspaper article above to learn about this neighborhood.

- ¿Dónde está La Latina?
- ¿Qué gente vive en el barrio?
- ¿Es un barrio tradicional o moderno? ¿Por qué?

2 **María y Roberto** Listen to María and Roberto's opinions about their neighborhood, **La Latina.** Then, correct the answers to the questions below.

- ¿Qué piensa María de La Latina?
- Piensa que no es auténtico.
- A María no le gusta vivir en este barrio.

- ¿Qué piensa Roberto de La Latina?
- Piensa que es un barrio romántico.
- Piensa que es un barrio moderno y también muy exótico.

3 **Opiniones** Read these opinions about **La Latina** from some of the neighborhood's residents. With a partner, discuss what aspects of **La Latina** each pair likes or doesn't like.

OPINIONES

Nos gusta La Latina porque es muy moderno. Tiene muchas tiendas, bares, restaurantes, cibercafés... Y todo en el centro de Madrid.

(Teresa y Lola)

A mí me gusta este barrio porque es típico de Madrid, con mucho carácter. A Paloma no le gustan los edificios porque son muy antiguos y no le gusta el tráfico.

(Adrián y Paloma)

OPINIONES

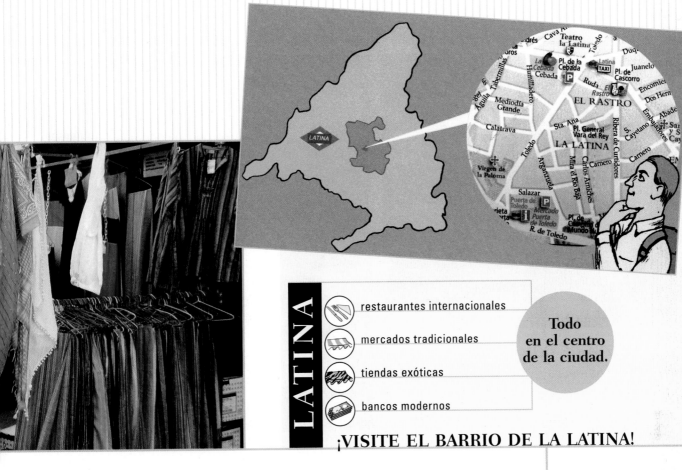

LATINA

restaurantes internacionales

mercados tradicionales

tiendas exóticas

bancos modernos

Todo
en el centro
de la ciudad.

¡VISITE EL BARRIO DE LA LATINA!

4 **No me gusta...** And you? What aspects do you like or dislike about neighborhoods like **La Latina**? Write them down and compare your answers with a partner's.

A mí (no) me gusta   +   [singular noun].
A mí (no) me gustan   +   [plural noun].

MI EXPERIENCIA

5 **Preguntar** Ask a classmate about where he/she lives, and write down the answers. Then, report your findings to the class.

GUIÓN DE TRABAJO

¿Dónde vives?

¿En una ciudad?
¿En qué barrio?

¿Qué hay?
¿Hay muchos restaurantes?
¿De qué nacionalidad?
¿Qué tiendas hay?
¿Tiene teatros?
¿Mercados?
¿Bancos?

¿En un pueblo?
¿Cómo se llama?

¿Dónde está
tu barrio?

¿En el centro?
¿Al lado de qué calles?

¿Dónde está
tu pueblo?

¿Cerca o lejos
de la ciudad?

¿Cómo es?

¿Es un barrio/pueblo moderno o tradicional?
¿Es un barrio/pueblo con carácter? ¿Por qué?

¿Te gusta?

¿Qué te gusta o no te gusta de tu barrio/pueblo? ¿Por qué?
Y a tus vecinos... ¿qué les gusta de tu barrio/pueblo?

**Expresar gustos
y preferencias**

A mí me gusta mi barrio.

A ti te gusta tu barrio, ¿verdad?

A él le gusta La Latina.

A María no le gustan los barrios modernos.

A usted le gustan también los barrios típicos.

A nosotras no nos gusta vivir en el centro.

A vosotros os gusta vivir en La Latina.

A ellos les gustan los barrios con carácter.

4A.2 The verb **gustar**
Indirect object pronouns

SAM: Actividades pp. 69–71

Hacer las compras

LISTA DE COMPRAS

pasta	refrescos	yogures
huevos	tomates	salchichas
leche	manzanas	patatas fritas

Indicar cantidades y envases

un kilo de manzanas

una botella de leche

un paquete de salchichas/galletas

una docena/media docena de huevos

una bolsa de patatas

4A.3 The preposition **de** with quantities and units of measurement

Vocabulario

6

la lista de compras *shopping list*

el refresco *soft drink*

la manzana *apple*

la salchicha *sausage*

las patatas fritas (*Esp.*) *potato chips*

el tomate

7

la cantidad *quantity*

el kilo *kilogram*

medio kilo *half a kilogram*

el paquete *package*

la docena *dozen*

media docena *half a dozen*

la bolsa *bag, sack*

6 **Fotos** Look at the photos of these two people doing their grocery shopping in different types of stores. Then, answer the questions.

- ¿Qué le gusta comprar a ella?
- ¿Dónde compra ella?
- ¿Qué le gusta comprar a él?
- ¿Dónde compra él?

7 **Las compras** Listen to the conversations with the young man and the woman. What quantities of groceries did each of them buy?

8 **Lista de compras** Something is wrong with this shopping list. Correct the list so that each item is listed in an appropriate quantity or container. Compare your answers with a partner's.

Modelo: *No es una botella de tomate, es una lata de tomate.*

1. Botella de tomate
2. Lata de salchichas
3. Kilo de vino
4. Bolsa de huevos
5. Docena de manzanas
6. Paquete de patatas

9 Conversación Decide which line (of **a–k**) matches each part of the shopper's interaction with the grocer (**1–3**). Then, with a partner, role-play the conversation with these or other products.

a. ¿A quién le toca ahora?

b. Me toca a mí.

c. ¿Qué le doy?

d. Una botella de leche y una docena de huevos, por favor.

e. Una docena, ¿verdad?

f. Sí.

g. ¿Algo más?

h. Sí, también me da una bolsa de patatas, por favor. ¿Cuánto es todo?

i. 16 pesos.

j. 16 pesos, ¿no?

k. Sí. Muchas gracias.

1 Los primeros productos que solicita el cliente. .....

2 El cliente añade un producto más y pregunta el precio total. .....

3 El cliente indica que es su turno de compra. .....

10 ¿Cuánto cuesta? Write down how much of each of these products you will need for the next two weeks. Calculate the total price of your groceries and compare your answers with a partner's.

Modelo: *Dos botellas de leche.*
La botella de leche cuesta 5 pesos.
Total 10 pesos.

Leche: $5 botella
Tomates: $8,50 kilo
Manzanas: $5,50 kilo
Huevos: $4,80 docena
Salchichas: $5,20 paquete

MI EXPERIENCIA

11 Entrevista Interview a classmate. Does he/she like to shop for groceries? Write down his/her answers.

Before you begin the interview, review the conversation in **Actividad 9** and identify the expressions that you can use to ask for clarification.

○ Una docena, ¿verdad?

○ 16 pesos, ¿no?

GUIÓN DE TRABAJO

¿Te gusta hacer las compras? ¿Qué productos compras normalmente?

Leche, tomates...

¿Dónde haces las compras normalmente?

¿En un mercado tradicional?
¿En un supermercado?
¿En tiendas del barrio?
¿En Internet?

Preguntar y responder por el turno

● ¿A quién le toca?
■ Me toca a mí.

4A.4 Verbs used with object pronouns: **tocar**

Solicitar un producto

● ¿Qué le doy?
■ Me da tres manzanas, por favor.
● ¿Qué le pongo?
■ Me pone medio kilo de tomates.

4A.5 Verbs with irregular **yo** forms: **dar** and **poner**

Preguntar y responder por el precio

● ¿Cuánto cuestan dos botellas de leche?
■ Cuestan 10 pesos.

4A.6 Stem-changing verbs o→ue: **costar**

Vocabulario

9

¿A quién le toca? *Whose turn is it?*
Me toca a mí. *It's my turn.*
¿verdad? *right?*
Me da/pone... *Give me . . .*
dar *to give*
poner *to put*
¿Cuánto cuesta(n)...? *How much does/do . . . cost?*
costar (o:ue) *to cost*
solicitar *to request*
añadir *to add*

¡OJO!

Most Spanish-speaking countries use kilograms (**kilos**) rather than pounds (**libras**). Remember that **1 kilo = 1000 gramos** (*grams*).

SAM: Actividades pp. 72–74

Paco Suárez García, 38 años. Tiene un puesto en el Rastro de Madrid.

Paco, amigo del Rastro

Vives en La Latina, ¿verdad?
Sí, vivo en la calle Toledo.

¿Te gusta este barrio?
¡Me gusta mucho! Está en el centro y es muy típico.

El domingo trabajas en el Rastro. ¿Y los otros días de la semana?
Trabajo en el Mercado de la Cebada, en una tienda de alimentación.

¿Qué tienes en tu puesto del Rastro?
Pues muchas cosas típicas de Madrid: pósters, abanicos, postales, libros...

¿Qué te gusta del Rastro?
Me gusta todo: la gente, las calles, las tiendas, los puestos...

¿Piensas que el Rastro es un lugar único?
Sí. ¡Es un lugar único y especial!
[...]

El Rastro
El Rastro es un mercado al aire libre muy popular de Madrid. Está en el barrio de La Latina. Las tiendas del Rastro generalmente están en la calle y se llaman "puestos".

Vocabulario
12

la tienda de alimentación *grocery store*

el puesto *stand (in a market)*

la cosa *thing*

el póster
13

la edad *age*

OPINIÓN

¿Le gusta ir a mercados como el Rastro? ¿Por qué?

¿Qué venden en estos mercados?

¿Qué compra cuando va a estos mercados?

¿Hay un mercado como el Rastro en su ciudad/pueblo? ¿Cómo es?

---

12 **¿Verdadero o falso?** Indicate whether each statement is true (**verdadero**) or false (**falso**).

1. Paco no vive en La Latina. ....

2. Paco trabaja todos los días en el Rastro. ....

3. Paco no vende libros. ....

4. A Paco le gustan la gente, las calles y las tiendas. ....

5. Paco piensa que el Rastro es único y especial. ....

13 **Rellenar** Fill in this information sheet about Paco.

- Nombre y apellidos: ....
- Edad: ....
- Domicilio: ....
- Lugar de trabajo (lunes a sábado): ....
- Lugar de trabajo (domingos): ....

14 **Comentar** In pairs, discuss what you have learned about Paco. What is he like? What things does he like? Do you know anyone like Paco?

15 **En el puesto** Imagine that you and your partner have a stand at a street market, like Paco. What typical products from your city or region would you sell?

16 Anotar Read this information from a Buenos Aires guidebook and fill in the notes below. Then, compare your answers with a partner's.

La Feria de San Telmo

Probablemente es la feria al aire libre más conocida de Argentina. Se celebra todos los domingos en la Plaza Dorrego en el barrio de San Telmo. Encuentras de todo: artesanía, antigüedades, objetos curiosos, souvenirs... También puedes ver espectáculos de tango y turistas de muchas nacionalidades.

Los vendedores en general son muy simpáticos y amables. A veces es posible regatear y conseguir precios más bajos.

La Plaza de Mayo, uno de los lugares clave de Buenos Aires, está muy cerca. En San Telmo también puedes disfrutar comidas muy ricas y puedes tomar un café en una de las tradicionales confiterías de la zona.

El mejor medio de transporte es el subte. Para llegar a San Telmo, toma la línea A (estación: Plaza de Mayo) o la línea E (estación: Belgrano).

Horario y lugar: _los domingos en_ _____

Cómo llegar: _____

Productos: _____ _____

Actividades recomendadas: _____

Vendedores: _____

Lugares cerca: _Plaza de Mayo_

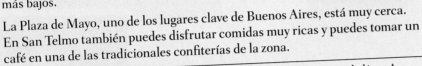

([r]) ([rr])

17 a. [r] y [rr] Listen to these series of words. Which sound do you hear: [r] or [rr]?

a. barrio, ricas, Dorrego   [   ]

b. bar, carácter, mercado   [   ]

b. Barrios de Buenos Aires Read aloud the names of these neighborhoods in Buenos Aires. Circle the words that have the [r] sound and underline the words that have the [rr] sound.

Puerto Madero   *Retiro*   *Montserrat*   *Recoleta*   *Palermo*

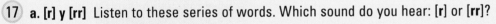

18 Productos Read this paragraph about Cuban produce markets. Can you find these foods where you live? Work with a partner to write a list of typical products from your region. Then, present your list to the class.

El agromercado cubano

En Cuba es muy típico hacer la compra en los agromercados. Los cubanos compran en estos mercados papayas, yucas, frijoles y papas, entre otras cosas. Es también un lugar donde a la gente le gusta hablar de la calidad de los productos, de los precios y de las noticias del mundo.

A veces la fruta y los alimentos tienen nombres diferentes en América Latina y España. Por ejemplo:
- papa (patata)   • frijol (alubia)

Vocabulario

16

probablemente *probably*
más conocido/a *best-known*
se celebra *is held*
encontrar (o:ue) *to find*
la antigüedad *antique*
el objeto curioso *curiosity, knickknack*
el espectáculo *show*
en general *generally*
es posible *it's possible*
regatear *to bargain*
conseguir (e:i) *to get, to obtain*
el precio *price*
bajo/a *low*
el lugar clave *landmark*
disfrutar (de) *to enjoy*
la confitería (*Arg.*) *café*
el medio de transporte *means of transportation*
el subte(rráneo) (*Arg.*) *subway*
la estación *station*
recomendado/a *recommended*
la nota, el souvenir, la línea

Internet
Cada vez son más los hispanos, sobre todo los jóvenes, que hacen las compras por Internet. Entre los productos más vendidos en la red están los de alimentación, discos y libros. ¿Y en su país? ¿Compra usted a través de Internet? ¿Qué productos?

Vocabulario

18

el agromercado *produce market*
la yuca *yucca*
el frijol *bean*
la noticia *news*
el mundo *world*

SAM: Actividades pp. 75–78

TAREA FINAL

Un mercado en la clase

Make a list of five items you have at home that you would like to sell.

Discos, sellos...

 Tell the other members of your group which products you are selling.

Un disco de Shakira. Me gusta, pero quiero comprar un CD nuevo.

Set a price for your products.

Disco, $6

Ask about at least four products being sold by another group. Try to bargain for a lower price.

Share with the class the items that you bought, as well as the purchase price.

Una camiseta de Plaza Sésamo, $20

YO PUEDO...

• **Puedo hablar de mi barrio.**

Write a letter to a friend, giving him/her information about your neighborhood.

¿Dónde está? ¿Qué actividades puedes hacer? ¿Qué opiniones hay sobre el barrio? ¿Qué le gusta a la gente de esta zona? ¿Qué no le gusta?

• **Puedo escribir una lista de compras.**

Add containers and units of measurement to this shopping list.

• **Puedo mantener un diálogo en español en una tienda.**

Complete the dialogue.

• **Puedo describir tres aspectos de mercados del mundo hispanohablante.**

Answer these questions.

¿Dónde está el Rastro? ¿Qué puedes comprar en la Feria de San Telmo? ¿Qué puedes comprar en un agromercado cubano?

| 3 .... de patatas |
| 1 .... de azúcar |
| 1 .... de huevos |
| 2 .... de leche |

| • ¿A quién le toca? |
| ■ .... |
| • ¿Qué le doy/pongo? |
| ■ .... |
| • ¿Algo más? |
| ■ .... |
| • 14 pesos. Gracias. |

GRAMÁTICA FUNCIONAL (S) Tutorials

4A.1 Ask for and give opinions

Stem-changing verbs e→ie: pensar 5.1.1

- Use the verb **pensar** (*to think*) to ask for and give opinions. **Pensar** is an **e→ie** stem-changing verb. You saw the same stem-changing pattern with **querer** in **3B.6**. Remember that the **nosotros/as** and **vosotros/as** forms don't have a stem change.

> ¿Qué **piensan** ustedes de Valparaíso?
> *What **do you think** of Valparaíso?*

> **Pensamos** que es una ciudad encantadora.
> *We think it is a charming city.*

- To ask someone's opinion about something or someone, use **pensar + de +** [*noun*].

> ¿Qué **piensas del** mercado de la fruta?
> *What **do you think of** the fruit market?*

- To give an opinion about something or someone, use **pensar + que +** [*verb*].

> **Pienso que es** exótico.
> *I think it's exotic.*

PENSAR

(yo)	p**ie**nso	(nosotros/as)	pensamos
(tú)	p**ie**nsas	(vosotros/as)	pensáis
(usted, él, ella)	p**ie**nsa	(ustedes, ellos/as)	p**ie**nsan

4A.2 Express tastes and preferences

The verb **gustar** 5.11
Indirect object pronouns 6.2.2

- Use the verb **gustar** (*to like*) to express likes and dislikes. Unlike in English, the person or thing that is liked is the grammatical subject of the sentence in Spanish. Therefore, **gustar** is most commonly used in the 3rd person singular or plural.

> ¿Te **gusta** mi barrio?
> *Do you like my neighborhood?*

- Use **gusta** with a singular noun or a verb in the infinitive; use **gustan** with a plural noun.

> Sí, me **gusta** vivir en el centro; me **gustan** los barrios dinámicos.
> *Yes, I like living downtown; I like lively neighborhoods.*

- Always use an indirect object pronoun (**me, te, le, nos, os,** or **les**) before **gusta(n)** to indicate who likes a certain object or activity.

> ¿**Les** gusta la Feria de San Telmo?
> *Do you like the San Telmo market?*

> Sí, **nos** gusta muchísimo.
> *Yes, we like it a lot.*

¡Póngalo en práctica!

G1 **Completar** Complete the conversation.

- ¿Qué piensas (1) .... Buenos Aires?
- (2) .... (3) .... Buenos Aires es una ciudad muy interesante.
- ¿Y Andrea y Sebastián?
- Los dos (4) .... que Buenos Aires tiene barrios muy especiales.
- ¡Bien! ¡Todos nosotros (5) .... igual!
- ¿Cuándo vamos a Argentina?

G2 **Contestar** Answer the questions using the cues.

> **Modelo:** ¿Qué piensan los clientes de la tienda? (única)
> *Los clientes piensan que la tienda es única.*

1. ¿Qué piensa Ramón del mercado? (divertido)
2. ¿Qué piensan los vecinos de este barrio? (dinámico)
3. ¿Qué piensan ustedes del museo? (interesante)
4. ¿Qué piensas tú de los edificios? (tradicionales)

G3 **Me gusta...** Complete the conversation.

> ¿Te (1)......................... mi barrio?

> ¿Tu barrio? Sí, mucho. Me (2)......................... los edificios, las calles, las tiendas...

> ¿Y a Brenda?

> A Brenda y a mí (3)......................... gusta vivir en el centro de la ciudad.

> ¿Pero (4)......................... gusta a los dos este ambiente?

> (5)......................... me gusta, pero a Brenda no. Y a ti, ¿qué (6)......................... de tu barrio?

- For emphasis or clarification, use a + **mí, ti, usted, él, ella, nosotros/as, vosotros/as, ustedes, ellos/as,** or a person's name.

> **A mí** me gusta hacer las compras en el mercado, pero **a Martín** no le gusta. ¿Y **a ti**?
> *I like to shop at the market, but Martín doesn't. How about you?*

a mí	me	
a ti	te	
a usted, a él, a ella	le	
a nosotros/as	nos	**gusta(n)**
a vosotros/as	os	
a ustedes, a ellos/as	les	

Me gust**a** mi barrio.
Me gust**an** las tiendas.
Me gust**a** vivir aquí.

gust**a**	+	[*singular noun*]
gust**an**	+	[*plural noun*]
gust**a**	+	[*infinitive*]

4A.3 **Indicate quantities and units of measurement**

The preposition **de** with quantities and units of measurement 10.5

- Use the preposition **de** when indicating quantities. Use the formula [*number*] + [*unit of measurement*] + **de** + [*item or product*].

> Quiero **dos kilos de naranjas.**
> *I want **two kilograms of oranges**.*

- These are some common units of measurement.

una **bolsa de** patatas fritas
un **paquete de** azúcar
una **botella de** leche
un **kilo / medio kilo de** manzanas, tomates...
una **docena / media docena de** huevos

4A.4 **Ask and tell whose turn it is**

Verbs used with object pronouns: **tocar** 6.2.3

- To indicate whose turn it is in a line or a game, use the idiomatic construction [*indirect object pronoun*] + **toca** + a + [**mí, ti,** etc., or a *person's name*].

> ¡Me toca a mí!   ¡Nos toca a nosotros!
> *It's my turn!*   *It's our turn!*

- **Toca** is the 3rd person singular form of the verb **tocar** (*to touch*).

> ¿Te toca a ti ahora?   No, le toca a María Jesús.
> *Is it your turn now?*   *No, it's María Jesús's turn.*

me		(a mí)
te		(a ti)
le		(a usted, a él, a ella)
nos	**toca**	(a nosotros/as)
os		(a vosotros/as)
les		(a ustedes, a ellos/as)

¡Póngalo en práctica!

G4 **A ella le gusta...** Answer the questions using the cues.

1. ¿A Mauricio le gustan los barrios con carácter? (sí)

2. ¿A Valeria y a Diego les gusta la comida marroquí? (no)

3. ¿A ustedes les gusta vivir en el centro? (no)

4. ¿A los vecinos les gustan las tiendas exóticas? (sí)

5. ¿A vosotros os gusta hacer las compras en el mercado? (no)

6. ¿Te gusta ir al centro comercial? (no)

7. ¿Al señor Martínez le gusta la pasta con tomate? (sí)

G5 **Un kilo de tomates** Complete the requests.

> Por favor, me pone una (1) .... de patatas fritas, un (2) .... de azúcar, una (3) .... de vino y una (4) .... de huevos.

> Buenos días. Quiero (5) .... (500 gr) de tomates y (6) .... de huevos.

> Muy buenas. Queremos dos (7) .... de pasta, dos (8) .... de refresco y un (9) .... de cebollas, por favor.

G6 **Mi turno** Complete the conversation.

- Buenos días. ¿A quién le toca ahora?
- Me (1) .... a mí.
- Perdone, pero (2) .... toca a nosotros.
- Es verdad, (3) .... toca a ellos.

G7 **¿A quién le toca?** Match each sentence starter with the correct ending.

	1. Nos toca	a. a mí.
	2. Te toca	b. a ustedes.
	3. Les toca	c. a nosotras.
	4. Le toca	d. a ti.
	5. Me toca	e. a vosotros.
	6. Os toca	f. a Marcos.

 Practice more at vhlcentral.com.

GRAMÁTICA FUNCIONAL

4A.5 Ask for a product

Verbs with irregular **yo** forms: **dar** and **poner** 5.1.2

- Use the verbs **dar** (*to give*) and **poner** (*to put*) to ask for items. Both **dar** and **poner** have irregular **yo** forms.

> ¿Me **da/pone** una botella de agua, por favor?
> *Would you give me a bottle of water, please?*

¡OJO! **¿Qué le doy?** is the most commonly used expression for orders. **¿Qué le pongo?** is used primarily in Spain.

- The **yo** form of **dar** is **doy**. The other present-tense forms follow the regular pattern for -ar verbs.

> ¿Qué le **doy**?
> *What would you like?*

DAR			
(yo)	**doy**	(nosotros/as)	damos
(tú)	das	(vosotros/as)	dais
(usted, él, ella)	da	(ustedes, ellos/as)	dan

- As you saw with **hacer** and **salir** in 3A.3, some verbs have irregular **yo** forms ending in **-go**. The **yo** form of **poner** is **pongo**. The other present-tense forms follow the regular pattern for **-er** verbs.

> ¿Qué le **pongo**?
> *What would you like?*

PONER			
(yo)	pon**g**o	(nosotros/as)	ponemos
(tú)	pones	(vosotros/as)	ponéis
(usted, él, ella)	pone	(ustedes, ellos/as)	ponen

- When you use **dar** or **poner** to ask for items, use an indirect object pronoun to specify *to* or *for whom* the items are being requested. As you have seen in 4A.2 and 4A.4, the Spanish indirect object pronouns are **me, te, le, nos, os,** and **les**. These pronouns correspond to *to/for me, you, him/her, us, you (pl., fam.), them/you (pl.)* in English.

> ¿**Te** doy algo más, Dani?
> *Would you like anything else, Dani?*

- Place indirect object pronouns before the conjugated form of the verb.

> Sí, **me** das medio kilo de arroz, por favor.
> *Yes, please give me half a kilogram of rice.*

¡Póngalo en práctica!

G8 **Un diálogo** Complete the conversation.

> ¿Qué (1)........................
> (2)........................?

> (3)........................ (4)........................ un kilo de tomates, por favor.

> ¿Qué (5)........................ pongo, señoritas?

> (6)........................ (7)........................ dos botellas de agua fría, por favor.

G9 **Reordenar** Unscramble the words to write complete sentences.

1. un paquete de salchichas / me / pone / por favor

2. doy / les / algo más / ¿?

3. nos / una botella de leche / por favor / pone

4. un paquete de pasta / me / da / por favor

G10 **Dar o poner** Complete the statements with the correct form of **dar** or **poner**.

1. El vendedor me .... (dar) dos kilos de tomates.

2. Tú me .... (dar) un paquete de galletas.

3. Yo les .... (dar) los refrescos.

4. Ustedes nos .... (dar) las papas fritas.

5. Nosotros te .... (poner) las bebidas.

6. El camarero nos .... (poner) el desayuno.

GRAMÁTICA FUNCIONAL

4A.6 Ask and tell how much something costs

Stem-changing verbs o→ue: costar 5.1.1

- Use the verb **costar** (*to cost*) to request and give information about prices. Like **poder** (see **3B.8**), **costar** is an **o→ue** stem-changing verb.

    ¿Cuánto **cuesta** el pañuelo?
    *How much **does** the scarf **cost**?*

- Use **costar** only in the 3rd person singular (to talk about one item) or the 3rd person plural (to talk about more than one item).

    Los zapatos **cuestan** 300 pesos.
    *The shoes **cost** 300 pesos.*

¡Póngalo en práctica!

G11 **¿Cuánto cuesta...?** Complete the conversation.

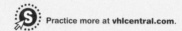

- Por favor, ¿cuánto cuesta este abanico?
- El abanico (1)........................ 50 euros.
- Y ¿(2)........................ cuestan estas postales?
- Las postales (3)........................ 2 euros.

Practice more at **vhlcentral.com**.

SÍNTESIS

Look at the photographs and write a short conversation for each of them using the words and expressions provided.

1.

barrio	calle	gustar	tradicional

- _____
- _____
- _____
- _____

2.

Me da...	más	kilo	tomates

- _____
- _____
- _____
- _____

3.

costar	euros	pasta	todo

- _____
- _____
- _____
- _____

VOCABULARIO ◁)) (S) Vocabulary Tools

La Latina en directo	
el carácter	atmosphere
el cibercafé	Internet café
el/la vecino/a	neighbor
gustar	to like
pensar (e:ie) de	to think of
visitar	to visit
auténtico/a	authentic
distinto/a	different
en directo	live
exótico/a	exotic
indio/a	Indian
marroquí	Morroccan
paquistaní	Pakistani
tradicional	traditional

Hacer las compras	
¿A quién le toca?	Whose turn is it?
¿Cuánto cuesta(n)...?	How much does/do . . . cost?
Me da/pone...	Give me . . .
Me toca a mí.	It's my turn.
¿verdad?	right?
la bolsa	bag, sack
la cantidad	quantity
la docena	dozen
el kilo	kilogram
la lista de compras	shopping list
la manzana	apple
media docena	half a dozen
medio kilo	half a kilogram
el paquete	package
las patatas fritas (Esp.)	potato chips
el refresco	soft drink
la salchicha	sausage
el tomate	tomato
añadir	to add
costar (o:ue)	to cost
dar	to give
poner	to put
solicitar	to request

Paco, amigo del Rastro	
es posible	it's possible
se celebra	is held
el agromercado	produce market
la antigüedad	antique
la confitería (Arg.)	café
la cosa	thing
la edad	age
el espectáculo	show
la estación	station
el frijol	bean
la línea	line
el lugar clave	landmark
el medio de transporte	means of transportation
el mundo	world
la nota	note
la noticia	news
el objeto curioso	curiosity, knickknack
el póster	poster
el precio	price
el puesto	stand (in a market)
el souvenir	souvenir
el subte(rráneo) (Arg.)	subway
la tienda de alimentación	grocery store
la yuca	yucca
conseguir (e:i)	to get, to obtain
disfrutar (de)	to enjoy
encontrar (o:ue)	to find
regatear	to bargain
bajo/a	low
más conocido/a	best-known
recomendado/a	recommended
en general	generally
probablemente	probably

Variación léxica

Me da... ←→ Me pone... (Esp.)

la confitería (Arg.) ←→ la terraza (Esp.)

el frijol ←→ la alubia (Esp.) ←→ el poroto (Cono S.)

la lista de compras ←→ la lista de la compra (Esp.)

el mercado ←→ la feria ←→ el mercadillo (Esp.) ←→ el mercado de pulgas

las patatas fritas (Esp.) ←→ las papas fritas

el refresco ←→ la gaseosa ←→ la soda (Amér. L.)

el souvenir ←→ el recuerdo

el subte (Arg.) ←→ el metro

la tienda de alimentación ←→ la tienda de abarrotes (Méx.) ←→ el almacén (Arg.) ←→ la tienda de abasto(s) (Ven.)

4B CON VISTAS AL MAR

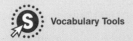

Apartamento de alquiler

1 Alquiler. Apartamento 60 m². 1 dormitorio, salón, cocina y 1 baño. Amueblado. Terraza. Vistas al mar. Piscina a 5 minutos. **Precio: $1200 /mes**

2 Alquiler. Casa 190 m². 4 dormitorios, 3 baños, salón, cocina. 2 terrazas. Vacía. Jardín y garaje. Bien comunicada. Playa a 2 kilómetros. **Precio: $2000 /mes**

3 Venta. Apartamento 90 m². 1 dormitorio principal y 2 dormitorios más, 2 baños, salón-comedor, cocina. Vacío. Terraza. Garaje. Mucho sol. Centro de La Libertad. Estación de autobús a 3 minutos. **Precio: $270 500**

Hablar de viviendas

- ¿**Cuántos** dormitorios tiene?
- Tiene tres.
- ¿Qué **hay** cerca del apartamento?
- **Hay** un colegio, un parque…
- ¿**Está** bien comunicado?
- Sí, el metro **está** a 5 minutos.

4B.1 hay/estar ¿cuántos/as?

Informar del precio

El precio del apartamento **es** $456 000.

1000	mil
10 000	diez mil
100 000	cien mil
200 000	doscientos/as mil
1 000 000	un millón
2 000 000	dos millones

4B.2 Numbers 1,000 and higher

Vocabulario

①

el alquiler *rental; rent*
el dormitorio *bedroom*
el salón *living room*
el comedor *dining room*
la cocina *kitchen*
el baño *bathroom*
amueblado/a *furnished*
la terraza *balcony*
la casa *house*

La Palma, Islas Canarias, España

1 Una habitación Find these things on the floor plan.

baño	salón
dormitorio	cocina
principal con baño	dormitorio
	balcón

Modelo: *El 1 es el baño…*

2 a. Viviendas Read the real-estate listings and choose one of the homes. Then, try to figure out which listing your partner chose. Ask him/her what the home has, where it is, and what is close by.

- ¿Cuántos/as .... tiene?
- ¿Dónde está?
- ¿Qué hay cerca?

- Tiene…
- Está…
- Hay…

b. De alquiler Which home would be appropriate for a family with three children? And a couple with no children?

- Una familia con tres niños puede alquilar .... porque ....
- Una pareja sin hijos puede alquilar .... porque ....

3 Los precios Match each price to one of the homes listed.

1. El precio del apartamento 1 es ……	a. mil doscientos dólares al mes.
2. El precio del apartamento 3 es ……	b. dos mil dólares al mes.
3. El precio de la casa es ……	c. doscientos setenta mil quinientos dólares.

4 **a. Fotos** Mercedes and Luis are looking for a home. Look at the available homes in photos A, B, and C. What types of homes are they?

1. apartamento ....   2. estudio ....   3. casa ....

b. Mercedes y Luis Listen to the recording and complete the questions with **qué** or **cuál**.

○ ¿............ tipo de vivienda es: un estudio, un apartamento, una casa?

○ ¿............ es la otra oferta?

○ Perfecto. Calle Mayor, ¿............ número?

c. Anotar Listen to the recording again and take notes about each home.

○ A: *La casa está* ....

○ B: ....

○ C: ....

5 **Anuncios** Write your own real-estate listing. Compare your ad with a partner's, and answer these questions.

○ ¿Qué vivienda es de alquiler? ¿Cuál está a la venta?

○ ¿Qué vivienda tiene más habitaciones? ¿Cuál es más cara?

MI EXPERIENCIA

6 **Mi vivienda ideal** Ask your partner about his/her ideal home. Then, share your findings with the class.

GUIÓN DE TRABAJO

¿Está cerca de la playa?   ¿Cuántos dormitorios tiene?
¿Está cerca de la montaña?   ¿Cuántos metros cuadrados tiene?

¿Cómo es tu vivienda ideal?

¿Tiene garaje, terraza, jardín…?   ¿Cuál es el precio del alquiler/de venta?

¿Qué hay cerca?

Vocabulario *cont.*

vacío/a *empty*

el jardín *yard*

bien comunicado/a *easily accessible*

la venta *sale*

principal *main*

el salón-comedor *living room-dining room*

el sol *sun*

el autobús *bus*

¿Cuántos/as? *How many?*

el balcón *balcony*

el apartamento, el garaje

Identificar

¿**Qué** casas le gustan?

¿**Cuál** es de alquiler?

¿Y **cuáles** tienen piscina?

4B.3 ¿**qué**? + [*noun*] + [*verb*]
¿**cuál/cuáles**? + [*verb*]

Vocabulario

② —————
el anuncio *ad*

④ —————
la inmobiliaria *real-estate agency*
el estudio *studio apartment*
¿Cuál(es)? *Which one(s)?*

⑤ —————
a la venta *for sale*
la habitación *room*

⑥ —————
la vivienda ideal *ideal home*
los metros cuadrados (m²) *square meters*

SAM: Actividades pp. 79–81

Su casa, su estilo

1. Mesa funcional: $480
2. Sillón cómodo: $530
3. Silla sencilla: $150
4. Sofá de diseño: $2000
5. Lámpara moderna: $310
6. Armario práctico: $950
7. Cama clásica: $2675
8. Alfombra elegante: $370

Describir objetos, tamaños y cualidades

- ¿Cómo es la cama?
- Es una cama de matrimonio **ancha, larga** y muy **moderna**.

Tamaño: pequeño/a, grande, ancho/a, largo/a

Cualidades: sencillo/a, práctico/a, clásico/a, cómodo/a, moderno/a, elegante, antiguo/a, funcional, de diseño

4B.4 **ser** + (**muy**) + [*adjective*]

Hablar de preferencias

- ¿Qué estilo **prefieren**?
- **Preferimos** el estilo clásico.

- ¿Te gusta esta silla negra?
- **Prefiero** la silla blanca.

4B.5 Stem-changing verbs **e→ie: preferir**

Vocabulario

⑦

el estilo *style*
los objetos domésticos *furnishings*
el sillón *armchair*
la silla *chair*
el diseño *design*
el armario *closet*
la cama *bed*
la alfombra *rug*
funcional, el sofá, clásico/a

---

7 **En mi casa** Look at the furnishings listed in this catalogue. Where do you have each of these items in your home? Compare your answers with a partner's.

en la cocina	en el salón	en el dormitorio
una mesa		

8 **Describir** Choose three objects from the photo of the living room and write a sentence to describe each one.

Modelo: *La lámpara es roja, sencilla y funcional.*

9 **a. Los objetos domésticos** Listen to these three young people as they choose furnishings for their apartment. Then, decide whether each statement is **verdadero** or **falso**.

	V	F
1. Las chicas prefieren las sillas rojas.	☐	☐
2. El chico prefiere las sillas negras.	☐	☐
3. El chico prefiere una alfombra moderna, de colores alegres.	☐	☐
4. Los tres prefieren una alfombra clásica.	☐	☐

b. Contestar Listen to the end of the conversation and answer the question.

- ¿Qué compran?

10 **Entrevista** Which furnishings do you like? What is your style? Interview your partner to find out his/her preferences.

- ¿Qué muebles y objetos prefieres?
- ¿Cuál es tu estilo?

ESTE TELEVISOR SIRVE PARA TODO

Ahora tiene tres aparatos en uno.

¡COMPRE AHORA SU TELEVISOR!

11 Anuncio Look at this ad. What can this television set do?

Sirve para...

1. ver la televisión. ☐
2. ver películas en DVD. ☐
3. escribir correos electrónicos. ☐
4. escuchar música. ☐

12 Servir Match each form of the verb **servir** to the corresponding subject(s). Then, underline the forms with an **e→i** stem change.

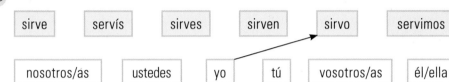

| sirve | servís | sirves | sirven | sirvo | servimos |

| nosotros/as | ustedes | yo | tú | vosotros/as | él/ella |

13 Expresar utilidad Choose one of these objects and write several sentences describing its characteristics and function(s). Then, switch papers with a partner and try to figure out which object he/she chose.

👥 **MI EXPERIENCIA**

14 Test de estilo What is your partner's home style? Write down his/her answers, and share your findings with the class.

Before you begin the activity, read the definition on the left and write the word being defined.

Es un mueble.
Está en el dormitorio.
Es para una o dos personas y es muy cómoda. Sirve para dormir, leer y ver la tele.

Es ....

Escriba las definiciones de:
ARMARIO LÁMPARA

GUIÓN DE TRABAJO

TEST DE ESTILO

1. ¿Cómo son los muebles de su apartamento/casa?
   a. funcionales
   b. modernos
   c. antiguos

2. Prefiere los muebles y objetos porque...
   a. sirven para algo y son económicos.
   b. son de diseño.
   c. son elegantes.

3. ¿Cómo es su salón?
   a. blanco
   b. azul
   c. amarillo

4. ¿Qué estilo prefiere?
   a. práctico y sencillo
   b. de diseño y diferente
   c. elegante y tradicional

Muchas a: Su casa es funcional.
Muchas b: Tiene una casa moderna.
Muchas c: Su casa es clásica.

Expresar utilidad

- ¿**Para qué sirve** este aparato?
- Es muy práctico, **sirve para** hacer pan en casa.
- ¿Y estos botones?
- **Sirven para** encender el aparato.

4B.6 Stem-changing verbs **e→i: servir** **servir para** + [*infinitive*]

¡OJO!

Note that **el televisor** is a television set, while **la televisión** refers to broadcasting.

Vocabulario

8
grande *big*
pequeño/a *small*
la cama de matrimonio *double bed*
ancho/a *wide*
elegante
9
alegre *bright*
11
¿Para qué sirve? *What is it used for?*
servir (e:i) para... *to be good for . . .*
el televisor *television (set)*
el aparato *device*
la función *function*
la película en DVD *movie on DVD*
el correo electrónico *e-mail*
el botón *button*
encender (e:ie) *to turn on*
13
la computadora, la radio

SAM: Actividades pp. 82–84

Carmen Abreu, fundadora de Caribe Propiedades

Carmen Abreu,
34 años.
Directora de una
inmobiliaria.

CARIBE PROPIEDADES

Esta agencia inmobiliaria nace en un bonito pueblo de la costa dominicana: La Romana. Carmen Abreu, su fundadora y directora, explica el origen de Caribe: "Me gusta vivir cerca del mar, pero también viajo mucho por el mundo. En vacaciones, no me gustan los hoteles, todos son iguales; prefiero los apartamentos: es más cómodo, privado y barato. Esta es la idea de mi proyecto. Hay muchos turistas que también prefieren pasar las vacaciones en un buen apartamento en la costa caribeña, un apartamento con muebles funcionales, cómodo, bien comunicado, económico y, naturalmente, con terraza y vistas al mar."

¿Cuál es su opción: estudio, apartamento o casa? ¿Alquiler o compra?
CARIBE OFRECE LO MEJOR

CARIBE PROPIEDADES

Carmen Abreu
Directora

Trinitaria esq. Santa Rosa
Bayahibe, La Romana
Tel.: 809-688-1234
c.abreu@caribeprop.com.do

Vocabulario

15

el/la fundador(a) *founder*
el mar Caribe *Caribbean Sea*
privado/a *private*
barato/a *cheap*
el proyecto *project*
pasar las vacaciones *to spend one's vacation*
caribeño/a *Caribbean*
ofrecer (zc) *to offer*
lo mejor *the best*
la costa, la idea, el mapa

16

el puesto *job, position*

15 **Mapa** Look at the map and find La Romana. What is the name of the beach nearby?
- Isla Catalina
- Playa Caleta
- Rancho Arriba

16 **Carmen** What is Carmen's position at the agency? How can she be reached?
- Puesto: ....
- Información de contacto: ....

17 **Elegir** Choose the option that best completes this statement.
El proyecto de Carmen, la inmobiliaria, nace porque...
- ☐ su familia tiene muchos apartamentos en La Romana y los quiere alquilar.
- ☐ los hoteles de la costa dominicana no tienen muchas habitaciones.
- ☐ en vacaciones, Carmen prefiere alquilar un apartamento.

18 **Características** What characteristics does Carmen consider important in an apartment? Underline relevant words and phrases in the reading. Do you agree?

19 **Rellenar** You are looking for an apartment by the beach. Fill in this form for Carmen's real-estate agency.

○ Busco:

○ Lugar:
○ Características:

○ Nombre:
○ Teléfono:

20 **a. Titulares** Read the text and choose the best headline for each paragraph.

> La isla de Mallorca es uno de los principales destinos turísticos. También la Familia Real pasa allí las vacaciones de verano. Al aeropuerto de su capital, Palma, llegan en la temporada alta más de 100 000 personas al día. Los atractivos de las islas son el clima, la cultura, el arte y la gastronomía. Otro atractivo turístico es su naturaleza, y la calidad y belleza de sus playas. Mallorca también es un paraíso ecológico, por eso es necesario proteger el medio ambiente.

> En el año 2001 nace la "ecotasa" en las Islas Baleares. Es un impuesto que pagan los hoteles y apartamentos para financiar el mantenimiento del medio ambiente. Unos meses más tarde, en octubre de 2003, se elimina por la presión de los hoteleros.

"Un destino turístico... y ecológico"   *"Todos a Mallorca"*

"Mallorca: la isla preferida de los turistas"   *"Impuesto ecológico: ¿Sí o no?"*

b. Definiciones Match each word with its synonym or definition.

1. destino ......
2. atractivo ......
3. proteger ......
4. medio ambiente ......
5. paraíso ......

a. naturaleza
b. defender del peligro
c. lugar de viaje o de vacaciones
d. elemento interesante
e. lugar ideal

c. Opiniones Are you in favor of an ecotax? Do you consider Mallorca a vacation destination? What about your classmates?

Modelo: *Yo pienso que la ecotasa...*

([c]) ([qu]) ([k])

21 **[c], [qu] y [k]** The [k] sound is represented by these consonants. Listen to the words and fill in the table with other words you have learned with the [k] sound.

- c + a, o, u: casa, cosas, cualidad
- qu + e, i: pequeño, quiero
- k in foreign words: kiwi, karate, kilómetro

c	qu	k
casa cocina	alquiler parque	kilómetro

22 **Equivalentes** Compare these listings from Argentina and Mexico to the listings on page 98. Which words are different? Write the equivalent term you have learned.

SE ALQUILA DEPARTAMENTO

Buenos Aires, zona centro.
Departamento de 3 ambientes.
Amoblado. Living de 20 m². 2 baños.
Cochera. $4200

Argentina	Equivalente
departamento	*apartamento*
ambiente	
amoblado	
living	
cochera	

CASA EN EL D.F.

Casa con 5 recámaras. Sala de 30 m².
Alberca y jardín. $45 000 000

México	Equivalente
recámara	
sala	
alberca	

Vocabulario

20

los destinos turísticos *tourist destinations*
la Familia Real *the royal family*
la temporada alta *high season*
los atractivos *attractions*
la gastronomía *gastronomy, cuisine*
la naturaleza *nature*
la belleza *beauty*
el paraíso *paradise*
el medio ambiente *environment*
las Islas Baleares *Balearic Islands*
el impuesto *tax*
financiar *to finance*
el mantenimiento *maintenance*
la presión *pressure*
el/la hotelero/a *hotel manager*
la agencia de viajes *travel agency*
la experiencia *experience*

O P I N I Ó N

¿Busca su apartamento de vacaciones por Internet?

¿Cree que las buenas ofertas están en Internet o en las agencias de viajes?

¿Tiene experiencias de alquiler en España o América Latina?

SAM: Actividades pp. 85–90

S Practice more at **vhlcentral.com**.

TAREA FINAL

Intercambio de casa

Write two descriptions, one of your home, and one of a home you would like to rent somewhere in Spain or Latin America.

Apartamento, 90 m², centro de la ciudad...

Choose which home you are going to offer for the house exchange.

Tu apartamento porque tiene vistas al parque...

Tell the class about the home you are offering.

Es una casa...

Choose your favorite home exchange destination.

YO PUEDO...

- **Puedo hablar de mi vivienda.**
  Write to a friend and describe your home: number of rooms, size, nearby attractions, price, etc.

- **Puedo identificar algo a través de preguntas.**
  Look at the illustration and ask questions to identify one piece of furniture.

- **Puedo describir un mueble y preguntar por sus características.**
  Describe your favorite sofa.

- **Puedo hablar de mis preferencias.**
  Which of the homes pictured on page 99 is your favorite?

- **Puedo referirme a la utilidad de algo.**
  What are these items used for?

¿.................?

¿Qué tamaño, características y estilo tiene?

....

....

Un libro

....

Un televisor

....

GRAMÁTICA FUNCIONAL 🅢 Tutorials

4B.1 Talk about houses and homes

hay/estar; ¿cuántos/as? `5.9; 9`

- Use **hay** to talk about the existence of something. As you learned in 3B.2, **hay** can be followed by a singular or plural noun.

  En mi barrio, no **hay** muchos apartamentos de alquiler.
  *In my neighborhood, **there are** not many apartments for rent.*

- Use **estar** to describe where something is located.

  La casa de mi tía **está** a cinco minutos de la playa.
  *My aunt's house **is** five minutes from the beach.*

- Use **¿cuántos/as?** to ask how many of something there are. Remember to use **cuántos** with masculine nouns and **cuántas** with feminine nouns. To answer, say **Tiene...**

  ¿Cuántas habitaciones tiene el apartamento?
  How many rooms does the apartment have?

4B.2 Talk about prices

Numbers 1,000 and higher `13.1`

- Use multiples of one thousand (**mil**) and one million (**un millón**) to talk about housing prices.

1000	mil	**Note:**
10 000	diez mil	EE.UU. = 1,000,000.00
100 000	cien mil	México = 1,000,000.00
200 000	doscientos/as mil	España = 1.000.000,00
1 000 000	un millón	Este texto = 1 000 000,00
2 000 000	dos millones	

- Numbers ending in **-cientos/as** agree in gender with the nouns they modify, even when followed by **mil**.

  Setecientas mil libras son **ochocientos** mil euros.
  700,000 pounds are 800,000 euros.

- When **millón/millones** is followed by a noun, use **de** before the noun.

  La casa de Coyoacán cuesta **cinco millones de** pesos.
  *The house in Coyoacán costs **five million** pesos.*

4B.3 Identify which item you are talking about

¿qué? vs. ¿cuál(es)? `9`

- Use **¿qué?** or **¿cuál(es)?** to identify which item(s) a person is talking about. Remember that question words take an accent.

  ¿Qué casa tiene piscina? **¿Cuál** es la más grande?
  Which house has a swimming pool? Which one is the biggest?

- Use **qué** + [*noun*] + [*verb*] to ask *which*.

  ¿Qué apartamento te gusta?
  Which apartment do you like?

- Use **cuál** + [*verb*] to ask *which one* and **cuáles** + [*verb*] to ask *which ones*. Never use a noun immediately following **cuál(es)**.

  De estas casas, **¿cuáles** tienen garaje?
  *Of these houses, **which ones** have a garage?*

¡Póngalo en práctica!

G1 **¿Hay o estar?** Complete each sentence with **hay** or the correct form of **estar**.

1. .... tres casas a la venta.
2. El estudio .... cerca del centro.
3. Estas casas .... lejos de la estación.
4. En tu barrio, ¿........... muchas casas grandes?

G2 **Una conversación** Complete the conversation.

- Lola, ¿(1) .... un parque cerca de tu casa?
- No, pero tenemos un jardín.
- ¿Dónde (2) .... tu casa?
- (3) .... a diez minutos de la playa.
- ¿(4) .... dormitorios tiene?
- (5) .... dos, un salón, baño y cocina.

G3 **¿Cuánto cuesta?** Say how much each of these homes costs.

Modelo: *La casa en El Paso cuesta trescientos veinte mil dólares.*

CASA	APARTAMENTO
Santa Bárbara:	Nueva York:
$2 100 000	$5 000 000

ESTUDIO	APARTAMENTO
Miami:	Santa Fe:
$150 000	$400 000

APARTAMENTO
Londres:
£530 000

G4 **Identificar** Complete the questions.

¿cuál?

¿qué?   ¿cuáles?

1. De estas casas, ¿........... es de alquiler?
2. ¿........... apartamento está en el centro?
3. ¿........... os gustan más: los modernos o los clásicos?
4. ¿........... barrio te gusta?
5. ¿........... estilo les gusta a ustedes?
6. ¿........... es más caro?

GRAMÁTICA FUNCIONAL

¡Póngalo en práctica!

4B.4 | Describe objects, sizes, and characteristics

ser + (**muy**) + [*adjective*] 5.8.2

- Use **ser** + [*adjective*] to describe the size and characteristics of an object. Remember that adjectives must agree in gender and number with the noun they modify.

  La mesa es **grande** y **moderna**.
  *The table is **large** and **modern**.*

- Add **muy** before an adjective to intensify its meaning.

  El sofá es **muy cómodo**.
  *The sofa is **very comfortable**.*

4B.5 | Talk about preferences

Stem-changing verbs **e→ie: preferir** 5.1.1

- Use the verb **preferir** (*to prefer*) to talk about preferences. Like **querer** (3B.6) and **pensar** (4A.1), **preferir** is an **e→ie** stem-changing verb.

  ¿Ustedes **prefieren** los sillones verdes o los azules?
  *Do you **prefer** the green armchairs or the blue ones?*

- Remember that the **nosotros/as** and **vosotros/as** forms don't have a stem change.

  Nosotros **preferimos** las lámparas modernas.
  *We **prefer** modern lamps.*

PREFERIR			
(yo)	prefiero	(nosotros/as)	preferimos
(tú)	prefieres	(vosotros/as)	preferís
(usted, él, ella)	prefiere	(ustedes, ellos/as)	prefieren

4B.6 | Explain how things are used

Stem-changing verbs **e→i: servir** 5.1.1
servir + **para** + [*infinitive*] 10.15

- Use the verb **servir** (*to serve*) to ask and explain how something is used. **Servir** is an **e→i** stem-changing verb. As with other stem-changing verbs, the **nosotros/as** and **vosotros/as** forms don't have a stem change.

  Los teléfonos **sirven** para hacer llamadas.
  *Telephones **are used** to make calls.*

- To ask what something is used for, say, **¿Para qué sirve(n)?** To answer, use **sirve(n)** + **para** + [*infinitive*].

  ¿Para qué sirve este aparato?
  What is this device for?

SERVIR			
(yo)	sirvo	(nosotros/as)	servimos
(tú)	sirves	(vosotros/as)	servís
(usted, él, ella)	sirve	(ustedes, ellos/as)	sirven

G5 **Las casas** Use words from the list and other adjectives to write two sentences describing each house.

muy	cómodo/a	pequeño/a
no	moderno/a	sencillo/a

G6 **Preferir** Complete the conversation with the correct forms of **preferir**.

¿Qué (1).................. usted: un sofá o tres sillones?

(2).................. un sofá.

Y ustedes, ¿(3).................. las sillas blancas o negras?

(4).................. el color blanco.

G7 **¿Para qué sirve?** Write the correct forms of **servir**; then match each sentence starter with the most logical ending.

1. Los televisores ....
2. El bolígrafo ....
3. El metro y el autobús ....
4. La taza ....
5. La radio ....
6. Las guías ....

a. ___ para ir al centro.
b. ___ para ver películas.
c. ___ para tomar el café.
d. ___ para escribir.
e. ___ para dar información turística.
f. ___ para escuchar música.

 Practice more at **vhlcentral.com**.

VOCABULARIO 🔊 Ⓢ Vocabulary Tools

Apartamento de alquiler	
¿Cuál(es)?	Which one(s)?
¿Cuántos/as?	How many?
el alquiler	rental; rent
el anuncio	ad
el apartamento	apartment
el autobús	bus
el balcón	balcony
el baño	bathroom
la casa	house
la cocina	kitchen
el comedor	dining room
el dormitorio	bedroom
el estudio	studio apartment
el garaje	garage
la habitación	room
la inmobiliaria	real-estate agency
el jardín	yard
los metros cuadrados (m²)	square meters
el salón	living room
el salón-comedor	living room-dining room
el sol	sun
la terraza	balcony
la venta	sale
la vivienda ideal	ideal home
a la venta	for sale
amueblado/a	furnished
bien comunicado/a	easily accessible
principal	main
vacío/a	empty

Su casa, su estilo	
¿Para qué sirve?	What is it used for?
la alfombra	rug
el aparato	device
el armario	closet
el botón	button
la cama	bed
la cama de matrimonio	double bed
la computadora	computer
el correo electrónico	e-mail
el diseño	design
el estilo	style
la función	function
los objetos domésticos	furnishings
la película en DVD	movie on DVD
la radio	radio
la silla	chair
el sillón	armchair
el sofá	sofa
el televisor	television (set)
encender (e:ie)	to turn on
servir (e:i) para...	to be good for . . .
alegre	bright
ancho/a	wide
clásico/a	classic
elegante	elegant
funcional	functional
grande	big
pequeño/a	small

Carmen Abreu	
la agencia de viajes	travel agency
los atractivos	attractions
la belleza	beauty
la costa	coast
los destinos turísticos	tourist destinations
la experiencia	experience
la Familia Real	the royal family
el/la fundador(a)	founder
la gastronomía	gastronomy, cuisine
el/la hotelero/a	hotel manager
la idea	idea
el impuesto	tax
las Islas Baleares	Balearic Islands
el mantenimiento	maintenance
el mapa	map
el mar Caribe	Caribbean Sea
el medio ambiente	environment
lo mejor	the best (thing)
la naturaleza	nature
el paraíso	paradise
la presión	pressure
el proyecto	project
el puesto	job, position
la temporada alta	high season
financiar	to finance
ofrecer (zc)	to offer
pasar las vacaciones	to spend one's vacation
barato/a	cheap
caribeño/a	Caribbean
privado/a	private

Variación léxica

la alfombra ⟷ el tapete (Méx.)	el autobús ⟷ el colectivo (Arg.) ⟷ la guagua (Car.) ⟷ el bus (Amér. L.)
el alquiler ⟷ la renta (Méx.)	el dormitorio ⟷ la recámara (Méx.) ⟷ la pieza (Arg.)
amueblado/a ⟷ amoblado/a (Arg.)	el garaje ⟷ la cochera (Arg.)
el anuncio ⟷ el aviso (Amér. L.)	la habitación ⟷ el ambiente (Arg.)
el apartamento ⟷ el departamento (Amér. L.) ⟷ el piso (Esp.)	el salón (Esp.) ⟷ la sala (de estar) (Amér. L.) ⟷ el living (Arg.)

Estrategias

(1) Aprender español fuera de clase `Lección 3A`

Learning another language happens both in and outside of the classroom. Look for opportunities to use what you learn in class, and to broaden your knowledge of the Spanish language and Spanish-speaking cultures.

○ **Choose at least two of these options to try this week.**

Lunes	
Martes	
Miércoles	
Jueves	
Viernes	
Sábado	
Domingo	

- Make flashcards of Spanish words and expressions you have learned.
- Read the headlines of a Spanish-language newspaper or magazine.
- Read text in Spanish out loud in order to practice pronunciation and intonation.
- Write a short e-mail message in Spanish.
- Spend twenty minutes looking through Spanish-language Web sites.
- Watch a movie in Spanish.
- Listen to music in Spanish.
- Go to a Spanish or Latin American restaurant.

(2) Aprender y recordar palabras con ayuda de fotos y dibujos `Lección 3B`

Rather than studying a new word or expression with its translation, try matching new vocabulary items with an image — a drawing you've made, a photograph you've taken, a map, or an image you've found on the Internet or in a magazine. Choosing an image that you associate with each new word or expression can help you better remember it.

○ **Choose four new words or expressions from Lección 3B and find or create a visual cue that represents each one.**

(3) Comprobar la comprensión: Pedir repetición `Lección 4A`

If you're not sure that you understood what someone said, ask that person to repeat so that you can confirm what was said.

○ **Find two expressions in Lección 4A used to ask for repetition or confirmation.**

(4) Parafrasear `Lección 4B`

If you don't know a word or you don't know what something is called in Spanish, try paraphrasing. You can describe the object, say what it is like, how it is used, and so on.

○ **Describe these objects without using their names.**

Modelo: *Este aparato sirve para...*

Competencias

EXPRESAR FRECUENCIA

1 **Horarios** You and your partner need to plan two days a week to go to the swimming pool, and one day a week to go to tango classes. Study your schedules and find times when you can both do these activities.

Modelo: • ¿Puedes ir a la piscina los lunes y los miércoles a las 5?
• Los lunes y los miércoles tengo inglés...

A	L	M	X	J	V	S	D
8-10							
10-12	U	N I V E R S	I D A D				
12-14							
16-18							
18-20	español		español				
20-22							

B	L	M	X	J	V	S	D
8-10							
10-12	O	F I C I N A					
12-14							
16-18	inglés	inglés	inglés	inglés	inglés		
18-20			chino		chino		
20-22	fútbol	coro	fútbol	coro			

LOCALIZAR PRODUCTOS

2 **¿Dónde?** Match each of the items listed to the appropriate section of the department store depicted.

libros   salchichas   zapatos
lámpara   chaqueta   pantalones
DVD   yogures
silla   alfombra
huevos   CD   vestido

ELEGIR PRODUCTOS

3 **Comparar** Which product does your partner like best? Which item is the least expensive? Compare the prices, sizes, and styles of these items.

teteras

23 €, clásica   12 €, exótica

teléfonos

80 €, antiguo   90 €, moderno

lámparas

$400, clásica $30, de diseño

CONJUGAR VERBOS

4 **Escribir** Write the conjugation for each verb in the person indicated.

1 ir (usted)   2 hacer (yo)   3 pensar (ella)   4 tener (ellas)   5 ir (vosotros)   6 dar (él)

7 poder (ustedes)   8 querer (nosotros)   9 costar (el vestido)   10 preferir (tú)   11 tener (yo)   12 hacer (nosotros)

4

 Video

Comprar en los mercados

You have learned how to talk about and shop for food in Spanish. In this episode of **Flash Cultura**, you will learn about shopping in the markets in San José, Costa Rica.

Estrategia ············

Using visual cues

When you are watching a video in Spanish, be sure to look for visual cues that will orient you to the content and purpose of the video. Before viewing **Flash Cultura**, look at the video stills. What do you think this episode will be about? What Spanish words do you think they will use?

1. **Mercados** Have you ever been to an open-air market? What did you buy? Have you ever negotiated a price? What did you say? What words and expressions do you already know in Spanish that you could use for bargaining? Discuss your experiences with a partner.

2. **Mirar** Watch this **Flash Cultura** episode. While you watch the video, pay attention to the on-screen labels.

...pero me hace
un buen descuento.

Vocabulario útil

el camarón (*Amér. L.*) *shrimp*

colones (*pl.*) *currency from Costa Rica*

¿Cuánto vale? *How much does it cost?*

el descuento *discount*

No hay problema. *No problem.*

¡Pura vida! (*C.R.*) *Cool!, Alright!*

el regateo *bargaining*

suave *soft*

el/la tico/a *person from Costa Rica*

¿Qué compran en el
Mercado Central?

3. **Seleccionar** Select the description that best summarizes this episode.

A. Randy Cruz va al mercado al aire libre para comprar papayas. Luego va al Mercado Central. Les pregunta a los clientes qué compran, prueba platos típicos y busca la heladería.

B. Randy Cruz va al mercado al aire libre para comprar papayas y pedir un descuento. Luego va al Mercado Central para preguntarles a los clientes qué compran en los mercados.

Estrategia ············

Making polite requests

When asking someone for directions, use expressions such as **Disculpe** or **Perdón** (*Excuse me*) before making your request, and be sure to say ¡**Gracias**! at the end. If you do not understand, ask for confirmation using expressions such as ¿no? and ¿verdad?

4. **Diálogo** With a partner, prepare a brief dialogue in which one person asks for directions to an ice cream shop (**una heladería**). Then, present your dialogue to the class.

Modelo: • *Disculpe, ¿dónde está la heladería?*
■ *A ver... la heladería está a la derecha de...*

110 ciento diez

 Practice more at **vhlcentral.com**.

Unidad 5

Salma Hayek, más que una cara bonita

Juanita y Bernardo, dos abuelos muy activos

La casa de Frida

Vocabulary Tools

EXPERIENCIAS PERSONALES

¡Felicidades, Manuela!

A

28/6/1987

B

8/5/1993

¡FELIZ CUMPLEAÑOS!

Tus amigos queremos recordar y compartir contigo momentos felices de tu vida.

5

C

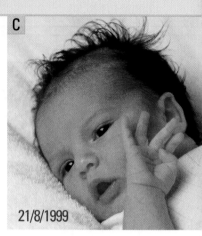

21/8/1999

Estudiamos juntos en la universidad en Montevideo.

....

....

....

....

Hablar del pasado

- ¿Dónde naciste?
- Nací en Montevideo y viví allí 20 años.
- ¿Cuándo terminaste los estudios?
- Terminé en 1999.

5A.1 Interrogative **¿cuándo?** Preterite of regular verbs

Dar fechas en el pasado

El 7 de abril **de** 1958 nació Alberto y **el 21 de** agosto **de** 1990 nacieron sus hijos.

5A.2 Dates

Vocabulario

①

¡Felicidades! *Congratulations!*
feliz (*pl.* felices) *happy*
el cumpleaños (*invar.*) *birthday*
recordar (o:ue) *to remember*
compartir *to share*
contigo *with you*
la tarjeta de felicitación *greeting card*
los estudios *studies*
el momento

②

el pie de foto *caption*
la boda *wedding*
juntos/as *together*

---

1 **Fotos** Observe las fotos de la tarjeta de felicitación (A–D) y clasifíquelas.

- Estudios: ......
- Trabajo: ......
- Familia: ....

2 **Pies de foto** Complete la felicitación con los pies de foto correspondientes.

"Celebraste tu boda."　　"Estudiamos juntos en la universidad en Montevideo."
"Carolina y tú abrieron la tienda."　　"Nació tu hija Celia."

3 **Felicitaciones** Fíjese en la tarjeta de felicitación (A–D). Indique si las oraciones son verdaderas (V) o falsas (F).

	V	F
1. El 8 de mayo de 1993 Manuela celebró su boda.	☐	☐
2. El 21 de agosto de 1999 nació Celia, la hija de Manuela.	☐	☐
3. El 30 de julio de 2004 Manuela y Carolina abrieron la tienda.	☐	☐

4 **a. Los días más importantes** Manuela habla de los días más importantes de su vida. ¿Cuáles son?

....　　.................................　　.................................

b. Comprobar Escuche de nuevo y compruebe las fechas con su compañero/a.

Modelo: • ¿Cuándo abrió la tienda/nació su hija/celebró su boda?　• El...

5 **Conjugar** Complete la tabla con las formas del pretérito indefinido.

	-AR	-ER	-IR
yo	terminé	nac........	abrí
tú	termin........	naciste	abr.........
usted, él, ella	terminó	nac........	abrió
nosotros/as	termin........	nac........	abrimos
vosotros/as	terminasteis	nacisteis	abr.........
ustedes, ellos/as	terminaron	nac........	abrieron

2/8/2003

....

....

UNA MUJER ACTIVA

En marzo de 2002 Manuela y sus amigos subieron al Mont Blanc durante la Semana Santa. En junio de 2005 Manuela viajó a Guatemala y trabajó en una escuela con mujeres indígenas, en un proyecto de una organización no gubernamental. Visitó muchos pueblos.

En abril de 2013 recibió el premio a la mujer empresaria del barrio por su tienda de comercio justo.

ENERO	FEBRERO	MARZO
ABRIL	MAYO	JUNIO
JULIO	AGOSTO	SEPTIEMBRE
OCTUBRE	NOVIEMBRE	DICIEMBRE

6 Acontecimientos Observe las imágenes de los viajes y el trabajo de Manuela y lea el texto. Anote cuándo ocurrieron estos acontecimientos.

¿Qué pasó?	¿Cuándo pasó?
Manuela subió al Mont Blanc.	
Manuela trabajó con una ONG.	
Manuela recibió el premio a la mujer empresaria del barrio.	

7 Fechas Y usted, ¿qué vivió en estas fechas? ¿Empezó un proyecto? ¿Cambió de casa? ¿Y su compañero/a?

Modelo: *En marzo de 2002,...*

Abrí...	Cambié...	Celebré...
Empecé...	Terminé...	Viajé...

MI EXPERIENCIA

8 El pasado Pregunte a su compañero/a por momentos importantes de su pasado: estudios, trabajo, casa, viajes, proyectos... Cuente sus respuestas a la clase.

GUIÓN DE TRABAJO

¿Cuándo empezaste/ terminaste...?

el colegio
los estudios
tu trabajo
...

¿Qué pasó?

¿En enero?
¿En octubre?
¿El 3 de agosto de 2015?
...

Compré un carro.
Cambié de casa.
Visité otro país.
...

Indicar el tiempo con los meses del año

En agosto Manuela abrió la tienda.

5A.3 en + [*month/year*]

Vocabulario *cont.*

nacer (zc) *to be born*

el/la hijo/a *son/daughter*

celebrar
4
_____

la fecha *date*
6
_____

marzo *March*

subir *to climb*

la Semana Santa *Easter/ Holy Week*

la ONG (organización no gubernamental) *NGO (non-governmental organization)*

junio *June*

la mujer empresaria *businesswoman*

enero *January*

el acontecimiento *event*

activo/a, febrero, septiembre, noviembre
8
_____

el carro (*Amér. L.*) *car*

cambiar de casa *to move*

SAM: Actividades pp. 91–93

Diario de viaje

12 de abril

Hace dos meses empecé el viaje. El mes pasado viajé a Santa Marta. Conocí a mucha gente y pasé momentos fantásticos. Después viajé en autobús hacia el sur de Colombia, al departamento del Meta. Descubrí una naturaleza impresionante: zonas desérticas, bosques, jungla... La semana pasada volé a Leticia. Allí recorrí el río Amazonas en barco y ¡ayer nadé con delfines! Este país es maravilloso.

9 **a. Diario de viaje** Lea el diario de viaje de Alberto. ¿De qué país habla? Hable con su compañero/a de las aventuras de Alberto.

> **Modelo:** *Alberto empezó el viaje...*

b. Momentos Subraye los momentos específicos que Alberto mencionó en su diario el 12 de abril y anótelos en el calendario.

....

FEBRERO						
L	M	Mi	J	V	S	D
			1	2	3	4
5	6	7	8	9	10	11
12	13	14	15	16	17	18
19	20	21	22	23	24	25
26	27	28				

....

MARZO						
L	M	Mi	J	V	S	D
			1	2	3	4
5	6	7	8	9	10	11
12	13	14	15	16	17	18
19	20	21	22	23	24	25
26	27	28	29	30	31	

.....hoy.....

....

ABRIL						
L	M	Mi	J	V	S	D
						1
2	3	4	5	6	7	8
9	10	11	12	13	14	15
16	17	18	19	20	21	22
23 30	24	25	26	27	28	29

10 **a. Relacionar** Usted es el/la protagonista de estas imágenes. Relaciónelas con las actividades de la lista.

- [A] salir con mis amigos
- [ ] cenar en un restaurante
- [ ] ver una película
- [ ] lavar los platos
- [ ] escuchar un concierto
- [ ] ver una exposición

b. Anotar Anote cuándo realizó usted estas actividades.

1. ....
2. ....
3. *Anoche salí con mis amigos.* ....
4. ....
5. ....
6. ....

c. Preguntar Haga preguntas a sus compañeros/as sobre sus actividades recientes.

> **Modelo:** *¿Cuándo saliste con tus amigos? ¿Qué lugares visitaste?*

Indicar momentos puntuales en el pasado

El año pasado trabajé mucho.

Hace 2 años abrí mi negocio.

La semana pasada viajé a Argentina.

anoche = ayer por la noche

5A.4 Time expressions

Vocabulario

9

el diario *diary, journal*

hace dos meses *two months ago*

empezar (e:ie) *to start*

el mes pasado *last month*

pasado/a *last*

conocer (zc) *to meet; to know (people)*

impresionante *impressive*

la zona *region*

11 a. La ventana abierta Escuche la entrevista a Alberto en el programa de radio *La ventana abierta*. ¿Cuál es el motivo de la entrevista?

☐ su viaje a Brasil   ☐ su blog de Internet   ☐ su viaje a Centroamérica

b. Viajes Escuche de nuevo y anote cuándo viajó Alberto a estos lugares.

(Centroamérica)   (Indonesia)   (África)

....

12 Escribir Escriba su propia secuencia temporal sobre estos temas.

(estudios)   (viajes)   (vivienda)

Modelo: *Estudié en la escuela secundaria de 2012 a 2016.*

1. ....
2. ....
3. ....

13 Describir Describa sus actividades de la semana pasada. Use las palabras del recuadro.

primero	de... a....
luego	hace...
después	

MI EXPERIENCIA

14 Preguntas Haga preguntas a un(a) compañero/a para conocer momentos importantes de su vida. Recuerde cómo reaccionar y mostrar interés. Presente la información a la clase.

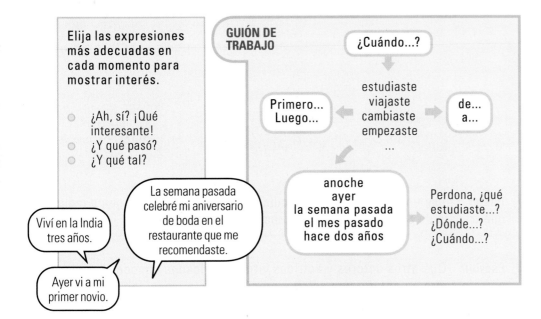

Elija las expresiones más adecuadas en cada momento para mostrar interés.

○ ¿Ah, sí? ¡Qué interesante!
○ ¿Y qué pasó?
○ ¿Y qué tal?

Viví en la India tres años.

Ayer vi a mi primer novio.

La semana pasada celebré mi aniversario de boda en el restaurante que me recomendaste.

GUIÓN DE TRABAJO

¿Cuándo...?

Primero... Luego... ← estudiaste viajaste cambiaste empezaste ... → de... a...

anoche ayer la semana pasada el mes pasado hace dos años → Perdona, ¿qué estudiaste...? ¿Dónde...? ¿Cuándo...?

Vocabulario *cont.*

el bosque *forest*
la semana pasada *last week*
volar (o:ue) *to fly*
ayer *yesterday*
recorrer *to travel*
en barco *by boat*
nadar *to swim*
el delfín *dolphin*
maravilloso/a *wonderful*
desértico/a, la jungla, el Amazonas
10
lavar los platos *to do the dishes*
realizar *to do; to perform*
anoche *last night*

Expresar secuencias temporales

De 2003 a 2004 viajé por Asia.

5A.5 **de... a...**

Estructurar un relato

● ¿Dónde trabajó **primero**?
■ **Primero** trabajé en Berlín, **luego** volví a España y **después** trabajé en una organización no gubernamental.

5A.6 Transition words

Vocabulario
14
el/la novio/a *boyfriend/girlfriend*
Perdona,... (*fam.*) *Excuse me, . . .*
el aniversario

SAM: Actividades pp. 94–96

Salma Hayek, actriz y directora mexicana

Salma Hayek, más que una cara bonita

Salma Hayek nació en México el 2 de septiembre de 1966. Hija de un empresario y una cantante de ópera, hoy es una famosa actriz, modelo, productora y directora.

Estudió Relaciones Internacionales, pero dejó la universidad para dedicarse a la actuación. Pronto se transformó en una estrella de las telenovelas. Sin embargo, abandonó su exitosa carrera en México para probar suerte en los Estados Unidos.

Participó en muchas películas. Una de las más destacadas es *Frida*, la biografía de la pintora mexicana Frida Kahlo. En 2002 quedó nominada al premio Oscar por esa interpretación. En *Bandidas* actuó con Penélope Cruz, una amiga que es como su hermana.

Después de que nació su hija Valentina, pasó dos años sin trabajar. En 2009 regresó al cine con *El aprendiz de vampiro*, una historia de terror y fantasía.

Salma Hayek es más que una cara bonita. Es un símbolo de mujer luchadora e independiente, conocida por su compromiso social y defensa de la cultura mexicana.

Vocabulario

(15)

la cara *face*

el/la cantante *singer*

dejar *to quit; to give up*

la actuación *acting*

la estrella *star*

la telenovela *soap opera*

sin embargo *however*

exitoso/a *successful*

la carrera *career*

probar (o:ue) suerte *to try one's luck*

destacado/a *notable*

la interpretación *performance*

actuar *to act*

el/la hermano/a *brother/sister*

la historia *story*

luchador(a) *fighter*

Filosofía y Letras *Arts*

el compromiso *commitment*

15 **Los acontecimientos** Lea el texto y diga qué carrera estudió Salma Hayek en la universidad.

☐ Filosofía y Letras ☐ Actuación ☐ Relaciones Internacionales

16 **Ordenar** Ordene los acontecimientos según la información del texto.

☐ 1
NACIÓ EL 02/09/1966.

☐
NACIÓ SU HIJA VALENTINA.

☐
SE TRANSFORMÓ EN ACTRIZ DE TELENOVELAS.

☐
VIAJÓ A LOS ESTADOS UNIDOS.

☐
EMPEZÓ A ESTUDIAR RELACIONES INTERNACIONALES.

☐
QUEDÓ NOMINADA AL PREMIO OSCAR POR SU PELÍCULA *FRIDA*.

17 **Póster** Fíjese en el póster de la película que aparece en la imagen e indique a qué trabajo de Salma Hayek corresponde.

18 **Escribir** ¿Qué otros actores y actrices latinoamericanos conoce? Escriba un párrafo sobre un actor o una actriz y preséntelo a la clase. Incluya al menos cinco acontecimientos de su pasado.

19 **Personajes hispanos** ¿A cuáles de estos personajes hispanos conoce? Escoja dos de ellos e investigue su historia personal. Escriba tres datos sobre cada uno y comparta la información con su compañero/a.

Shakira

Rafael Nadal

Benicio del Toro

David Ortiz   Isabel Allende   Rigoberta Menchú

¿Trabajó en...?

¿Escribió...?

¿Ganó...?

¿Nació en...?

¿Vivió con.../en...?

Cine latinoamericano

En la actualidad, el cine latinoamericano cuenta con profesionales de trayectoria internacional. Algunos de ellos son los directores mexicanos Alfonso Cuarón y Alejandro González Iñárritu, y la actriz América Ferrera, de origen hondureño.

OPINIÓN

¿Qué premios de cine son más conocidos en su país? ¿Qué actores los recibieron?

[b] [p]

20 **a. [b] y [p]** Escuche estas palabras y diga qué sonido es más fuerte: [b] o [p].

biografía   viaje   pasado   presente

b. ¿Cómo se escribe? Escuche y marque cómo se escribe, con **b** o **p**.

....

....

c. Escribir Escuche de nuevo y escriba la palabra debajo de la imagen.

d. Pronunciar Pronuncie las siguientes palabras. Después escuche y compruebe sus respuestas.

universidad   abril   primero   después

21 **a. La fiesta de quince años** Lea el texto y señale la opción correcta.

La fiesta de los 15 años o fiesta de la quinceañera

En muchos países latinoamericanos, las jóvenes celebran sus 15 años con grandes fiestas, banquetes, bailes y hasta caravanas de coches. Llevan vestidos similares a los de las novias y entran al salón del brazo de su padre. En México, antes de la fiesta se celebra una misa católica. En Argentina, algunas quinceañeras regalan 15 velas a las personas más importantes de su vida.

¿Qué se celebra?

una boda ☐
un cumpleaños ☐

¿Quién lo celebra?

los jóvenes de 15 años ☐
solo las chicas que cumplen 15 años ☐

b. Contestar ¿Se celebra en su país de manera especial este día?

Vocabulario

19
ganar *to win*
20
la pata *paw*
la bata *robe*
el par *pair*
21
la quinceañera *fifteen-year-old girl*
el banquete *reception*
el baile *dance, ball*
la caravana de coches *motorcade*
el/la novio/a *groom/bride*
del brazo *arm in arm*
la misa *Mass*
católico/a *Catholic*
algunos/as *some*
la vela *candle*
cumplir 15 años *to turn 15 years old*
la manera *way*

SAM: Actividades pp. 97–100

 Practice more at **vhlcentral.com**.

TAREA FINAL

Biografía de la clase

Escriba cinco momentos importantes de su vida
e indique cuándo ocurrieron.

- *estudiar*
- *cambiar de casa/de ciudad*
- *empezar un proyecto*
- *viajar*
- *trabajar*
- *comprar una casa/un coche*

Pregunte por los momentos importantes de la vida de
su compañero/a.

*¿Qué momentos importantes recuerdas de tu vida?
¿Cuándo…?*

Comente con su compañero/a si hay algunas coincidencias
en sus datos.

Elijan tres fechas y averigüen qué pasó en la vida
de tres o cuatro compañeros de clase en esas fechas.

YO PUEDO...

- **Puedo hablar de mi vida y de la de otras personas en el pasado.**
  Escriba tres datos sobre su pasado con sus referencias personales.

- **Puedo referirme a fechas en el pasado para contar acontecimientos.**
  Escriba dos fechas sobre otras personas y qué pasó.

  ....

  ....

- **Puedo nombrar los meses del año.**
  Nombre tres meses.

  ....

- **Puedo hablar de etapas en la vida.**
  Describa brevemente dos etapas de su vida.

El año pasado ....

....

Hace ....

....

La semana pasada ....

....

De ....
a ....

....

De ....
a ....

....

GRAMÁTICA FUNCIONAL ⚙ Tutorials

Interrogative ¿cuándo? 9
The preterite of regular verbs 5.2.1

- Use the interrogative ¿Cuándo? to ask when an event occurred in the past.

  ¿Cuándo terminaste la escuela secundaria?
  When did you finish high school?

- Note that ¿Cuándo? asks *When?* in a general sense, whereas ¿A qué hora? prompts you to answer with a specific time of day.

- Use the preterite (pretérito indefinido) to express actions or states completed in the past. Spanish uses two simple tenses, the preterite and the imperfect, to talk about events in the past.

- Viajar, nacer, and vivir exemplify the conjugation patterns of regular -ar, -er, and -ir verbs in the pretérito indefinido.

	VIAJAR	NACER	VIVIR
(yo)	viajé	nací	viví
(tú)	viajaste	naciste	viviste
(usted, él, ella)	viajó	nació	vivió
(nosotros/as)	viajamos	nacimos	vivimos
(vosotros/as)	viajasteis	nacisteis	vivisteis
(ustedes, ellos/as)	viajaron	nacieron	vivieron

  ¿Cuándo viajaste a El Salvador?
  When did you travel to El Salvador?

  Mi hermana nació en 2002.
  My sister was born in 2002.

- The endings for regular -er and -ir verbs are identical in the preterite.

  Nadia conoció a su novio el día que cumplió 18 años.
  Nadia met her boyfriend the day she turned 18.

¡OJO!

Note that the yo and usted/él/ella forms of all three conjugations have written accents on the last syllable to show that it is stressed. If you forget to include the accent, it can change the meaning of the word entirely! viajo = *I travel* viajó = *you/he/she traveled*

- The preterite nosotros/as forms of regular -ar and -ir verbs are identical to their present-tense forms. The context can indicate which tense is being used.

  Cada año pasamos las vacaciones en Puerto Vallarta.
  Every year, we spend our vacation in Puerto Vallarta.

  Pasamos cuatro noches en Puerto Vallarta en mayo.
  We spent four nights in Puerto Vallarta in May.

¡Póngalo en práctica!

G1 **Relacionar** Elija la forma del pretérito indefinido que corresponde a cada sujeto.

celebrar		
	1. ellas	a. celebrasteis
	2. nosotros	b. celebraron
	3. vosotros	c. celebraste
	4. usted	d. celebré
	5. tú	e. celebramos
	6. yo	f. celebró

subir		
	1. ustedes	a. subió
	2. yo	b. subisteis
	3. tú	c. subí
	4. él	d. subieron
	5. nosotros	e. subimos
	6. vosotras	f. subiste

G2 **Completar** Complete las oraciones con la forma correcta del verbo en el pretérito indefinido.

1. ¿Cuándo .... (nacer) tu hermana?
2. Nosotros .... (vivir) en Cuernavaca diez años.
3. Gonzalo .... (terminar) sus estudios en 2005.
4. Tú .... (recibir) el premio de poesía.
5. Mis padres .... (abrir) una tienda.
6. Gabriela y tú .... (viajar) a Lima en diciembre.

G3 **Crear oraciones** Escriba oraciones completas usando el pretérito indefinido.

1. Damián / trabajar / para una ONG
   ....
2. Laura y Beatriz / estudiar / en la UNAM
   ....
3. Analía y tú / abrir / una tienda de ropa
   ....
4. yo / subir / el Aconcagua
   ....
5. nosotros / visitar / muchos pueblos bonitos
   ....
6. tú / comprar / unas gafas de sol
   ....

- **-Ar** and **-er** verbs with a present-tense stem change are regular in the preterite. That is, they do *not* have a stem change.

	PRESENTE	PRETÉRITO INDEFINIDO
recordar (o:ue)	Recuerdo tu boda.	Recordé tu boda.
	I remember your wedding.	*I remembered your wedding.*
encender (e:ie)	Encienden las luces.	Encendieron las luces.
	They turn on the lights.	*They turned on the lights.*

- However, **-ir** verbs with a stem change in the present do have a stem change in the preterite in the **usted/él/ella** and **ustedes/ellos/ellas** forms only.

- Verbs with an **e→i** stem change, such as **servir**, maintain the e→i stem change in these two forms of the preterite. Verbs with an **o→ue** stem change, such as **dormir** (*to sleep*), have an **o→u** stem change in the preterite.

	SERVIR	DORMIR
(yo)	serví	dormí
(tú)	serviste	dormiste
(usted, él, ella)	sirvió	durmió
(nosotros/as)	servimos	dormimos
(vosotros/as)	servisteis	dormisteis
(ustedes, ellos/as)	sirvieron	durmieron

- Verbs ending in **-car**, **-gar**, and **-zar** have a spelling change in the **yo** form of the preterite.

	PRACTICAR	LLEGAR	EMPEZAR
(yo)	practiqué	llegué	empecé

- The verbs **creer** (*to believe*), **leer** (*to read*), and **oír** (*to hear*) follow the same pattern of spelling changes in the preterite: the **i** in the ending carries an accent, and changes to **y** in the **usted/él/ella** and **ustedes/ellos/ellas** forms.

	CREER	LEER	OÍR
(yo)	creí	leí	oí
(tú)	creíste	leíste	oíste
(usted, él, ella)	creyó	leyó	oyó
(nosotros/as)	creímos	leímos	oímos
(vosotros/as)	creísteis	leísteis	oísteis
(ustedes, ellos/as)	creyeron	leyeron	oyeron

- The verb **ver** is regular in the preterite, but its forms do not take a written accent.

    Vi la nueva película de Almodóvar.
    I saw Almodóvar's new film.

- Note that several common verbs, such as **ir**, **ser**, **estar**, **hacer**, **tener**, **poder**, **poner**, and **querer**, have irregular preterite forms. You will learn these forms in coming lessons.

¡Póngalo en práctica!

G4 **Conjugar** Escriba las formas del pretérito indefinido que faltan.

1. Juan	empezó	
2. Lourdes y yo		
3. tú		pensaste
4. ustedes	empezaron	
5. yo		pensé
6. vosotras		

G5 **Párrafo** Complete el párrafo con el pretérito indefinido de los verbos.

En marzo de este año, Luis (1) .... (viajar) a México. Antes del viaje, (2) .... (leer) la guía de viajes entera. (3) .... (comprar) el pasaje en la agencia de viajes y (4) .... (llamar) al hotel para hacer la reserva. El día del vuelo, (5) .... (salir) de su casa a las ocho, (6) .... (tomar) un taxi y (7) .... (llegar) al aeropuerto a las nueve. (8) .... (entrar) en el aeropuerto, (9) .... (tomar) un café en el bar y (10) .... (pagar) en efectivo. Luego (11) .... (subir) al avión, la auxiliar de vuelo le (12) .... (servir) un refresco y Luis (13) .... (empezar) su maravilloso viaje.

G6 **Componer** Use las expresiones para escribir oraciones originales sobre usted mismo/a.

1. nacer ....
....

2. terminar la escuela secundaria ....
....

3. empezar la universidad ....
....

4. cumplir 10 años ....

5. viajar a otro estado por primera vez ....

6. visitar un museo ....
....

 Practice more at **vhlcentral.com**.

GRAMÁTICA FUNCIONAL

5A.2 Give dates in the past

Dates 10.5

- When answering the question ¿Cuándo?, you will often need to provide a date. To give the date in Spanish, say el + [day] + de + [month] + de + [year].

  ¿Cuándo naciste? **El veintitrés de marzo de 1995.**
  When were you born? *March twenty-third, 1995.*

- When referring to the first of the month, use **el primero** (*the first*); for all other days, use the cardinal numbers you have already learned (**dos, tres, cuatro,** etc.).

- In Spanish, always pronounce the year as a single number; do not separate it into two pairs. Use the article **el** for the year 2000 (**el dos mil**).

  El **primero** de julio de mil **novecientos noventa.**
  *July **first, nineteen ninety.***

- Unlike in English, when dates are written in numerical format in Spanish, the day precedes the month.

Español:	17/2/1982	El 17 de febrero de 1982.
English:	*2/17/1982*	*February 17, 1982.*

5A.3 Specify with months and years

en + [*month/year*] 10.12

- Months are not capitalized in Spanish.

enero	abril	julio	octubre
febrero	mayo	agosto	noviembre
marzo	junio	septiembre	diciembre

- To tell when something happened by specifying the month or the year, use **en** + [*month*] or **en** + [*year*].

  ¿Cuándo empezaste a estudiar español?
  When did you start studying Spanish?

  En septiembre. / En 2009.
  In September. / In 2009.

5A.4 Specify moments in the past

Time expressions 5.2.3, 11.6

- Use these expressions to tell when events happened in the past.

el año **pasado**	ayer
el mes **pasado**	anoche
la semana **pasada**	**hace** dos días/un año...
el jueves **pasado**	el 3 **de** agosto **de** 1995

- Use **el/la** + [*time designation*] + **pasado/a** to say *last week/month*, etc. Use **hace** + [*time period*] to express *ago*.

  Silvia abrió la tienda **hace tres años.**
  *Silvia opened the store **three years ago.***

¡Póngalo en práctica!

G7 **Las fechas** Escriba estas fechas con palabras.

1. 3/5/1988

2. 20/6/2000

3. 12/12/2002

4. 1/9/1860

5. 12/10/1492

6. 30/7/1997

7. 18/8/1932

8. 6/11/1808

G8 **Oraciones** Escriba oraciones completas en el pretérito indefinido.

1. Ana / terminar los estudios / junio
....

2. David y Marcos / viajar a Texas / enero
....

3. tú / recibir el premio / 2002
....

4. Laura y yo / abrir la tienda / 1999
....

5. yo / cambiar de casa / mayo
....

G9 **Conversación** Complete la conversación con palabras y expresiones adecuadas.

- Jaime, ¿saliste (1)..................? Te llamé (2).................., pero no contestaste.

- Sí, Raquel y yo cenamos en el restaurante mexicano de la calle Limón. Mi padre comió allí el mes (3).................. y nos lo recomendó. Cenamos allí la semana (4).................., y nos gustó tanto que volvimos.

- ¡Es muy bueno ese restaurante! Cené allí (5).................. dos semanas.

Practice more at **vhlcentral.com**. ciento veintiuno **121**

GRAMÁTICA FUNCIONAL

5A.5 Express time sequences

de... a... 10.1, 10.5

- To specify the timing of an event or activity, use **de** + [*starting point*] + **a** + [*end point*].

> Estudié en la UNAM **de** 2005 **a** 2009.
> *I studied at the UNAM from 2005 to 2009.*

> Trabajé en la heladería **de** junio **a** agosto de 2008.
> *I worked at the ice cream shop from June through August, 2008.*

5A.6 Structure a narrative

Transition words 11.6, 14.12

- Use transition words such as **primero** (*first*), **luego** (*then*), and **después** (*then, afterward*) to show the time relationship between events.

> Pilar estudió biología **primero, luego** hizo el doctorado y **después** consiguió trabajo en un hospital.

> *First, Pilar studied biology, then she got her Ph.D., and later she got a job at a hospital.*

¡Póngalo en práctica!

G10 **Escribir** Escriba oraciones completas.

1. Ramón / vivir en Quito / 1998–2000

2. tú / estudiar francés / septiembre–diciembre

3. los chicos / viajar por Europa / julio–octubre

4. nosotros / trabajar en el banco / 2003–2007

G11 **Desarrollar** Use **primero, luego** y **después** para combinar estas oraciones.

1. Juan estudió literatura.
2. Escribió una novela.
3. Ganó un premio.

....

....

....

SÍNTESIS

Mire las fotos y escriba una breve conversación para cada una usando las palabras y expresiones del recuadro.

1.

nacer	2013	hijo	celebrar tu boda	2010

- _____
- _____
- _____
- _____

2.

de... a...	estudiar	trabajar	primero	después

- _____
- _____
- _____
- _____

¡Felicidades, Manuela!

¡Felicidades!	*Congratulations!*
el acontecimiento	*event*
la boda	*wedding*
el carro (*Amér. L.*)	*car*
el cumpleaños (*invar.*)	*birthday*
enero	*January*
los estudios	*studies*
febrero	*February*
la fecha	*date*
el/la hijo/a	*son/daughter*
junio	*June*
marzo	*March*
el momento	*moment*
la mujer empresaria	*businesswoman*
noviembre	*November*
la ONG (organización no gubernamental)	*NGO (non-governmental organization)*
el pie de foto	*caption*
la Semana Santa	*Easter/Holy Week*
septiembre	*September*
la tarjeta de felicitación	*greeting card*
contigo	*with you*
cambiar de casa	*to move*
celebrar	*to celebrate*
compartir	*to share*
nacer (zc)	*to be born*
recordar (o:ue)	*to remember*
subir	*to climb*
activo/a	*active*
feliz (*pl.* felices)	*happy*
juntos/as	*together*

Diario de viaje

en barco	*by boat*
hace dos meses	*two months ago*
Perdona, ... (*fam.*)	*Excuse me, . . .*
el Amazonas	*Amazon River*
el aniversario	*anniversary*
el bosque	*forest*
el delfín	*dolphin*
el diario	*diary, journal*
la jungla	*jungle*
el mes pasado	*last month*
el/la novio/a	*boyfriend/girlfriend*
la semana pasada	*last week*
la zona	*region*
conocer (zc)	*to meet; to know (people)*
empezar (e:ie)	*to start*
lavar los platos	*to do the dishes*
nadar	*to swim*
realizar	*to do; to perform*
recorrer	*to travel*
volar (o:ue)	*to fly*
desértico/a	*desert-like*
impresionante	*impressive*
maravilloso/a	*wonderful*
pasado/a	*last*
anoche	*last night*
ayer	*yesterday*

Salma Hayek

del brazo	*arm in arm*
la actuación	*acting*
el baile	*dance, ball*
el banquete	*reception*
la bata	*robe*
el/la cantante	*singer*
la cara	*face*
la caravana de coches	*motorcade*
la carrera	*career*
el compromiso	*commitment*
la estrella	*star*
Filosofía y Letras	*Arts*
el/la hermano/a	*brother/sister*
la historia	*story*
la interpretación	*performance*
la manera	*way*
la misa	*Mass*
el/la novio/a	*groom/bride*
el par	*pair*
la pata	*paw*
la quinceañera	*fifteen-year-old girl*
la telenovela	*soap opera*
la vela	*candle*
actuar	*to act*
cumplir 15 años	*to turn 15 years old*
dejar	*to quit; to give up*
ganar	*to win*
probar (o:ue) suerte	*to try one's luck*
algunos/as	*some*
católico/a	*Catholic*
destacado/a	*notable*
exitoso/a	*successful*
luchador(a)	*fighter*
sin embargo	*however*

Variación léxica

la cara ⟷ el rostro

el carro (*Amér. L.*) ⟷ el coche (*Esp.*) ⟷ el auto(móvil) (*Amér. L.*)

el/la chico/a ⟷ el/la chavo/a (*Méx.*) ⟷ el/la chaval(a) (*Esp.*) ⟷ el/la botija (*Uru.*) ⟷ el/la chamo/a (*Ven.*) ⟷ el/la chamaco/a (*Amér. L.*)

la telenovela ⟷ el culebrón (*Esp.*) ⟷ la novela (*Arg.*) ⟷ la teleserie (*Chi.*)

5B

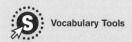
Vocabulary Tools

MI GENTE

Foto de familia

Una pareja feliz

Dolores y Ramón están casados. El próximo mes celebran ¡40 años de matrimonio! Son una pareja feliz; están jubilados y ahora tienen mucho tiempo libre. Tienen tres hijos maravillosos: Manuel, Mario y Marisa.

Manuel está soltero. Mario está casado con Paula y juntos tienen una hija, Lucía, de 5 años. Marisa está divorciada y vive con su hijo Sergio, de 3 años.

Los fines de semana, Dolores hace una rica comida para sus hijos y nietos. A los dos nietos les gusta mucho ir a casa de sus abuelos.

padre + madre = padres
abuelo + abuela = abuelos
nieto + nieta = nietos
hermano + hermana = hermanos
tío + tía = tíos
primo + prima = primos
hijo(s) + hija(s) = hijos

.... Dolores
.... ← Mario / ....
.... Sergio

Hablar del estado civil

- ¿Estás **soltera** o **casada**?
- ■ Estoy **divorciada**.

5B.1 **estar** + [*marital status*]

Vocabulario

①

mi gente *my folks*
casado/a *married*
el próximo mes *next month*
el matrimonio *marriage*
la pareja *couple; partner*
jubilado/a *retired*
el tiempo libre *free time*
soltero/a *single*
divorciado/a *divorced*
los fines de semana *on weekends*
los nietos *grandchildren*
los abuelos *grandparents*
el árbol genealógico *family tree*
los padres *parents*
el/la abuelo/a *grandfather/
  grandmother*
el/la nieto/a *grandson/
  granddaughter*
los hermanos *siblings*
el/la tío/a *uncle/aunt*
el/la primo/a *cousin*

① **a. Foto de familia** Fíjese en la fotografía. ¿Cuál es el tema de este artículo? Lea el texto y complete el árbol genealógico.

b. ¿Quién es quién? Complete las oraciones.

1. Manuel, Mario y Marisa son ....
2. Paula y Mario son los .... de Lucía.
3. Lucía y Sergio son los .... de Ramón y Dolores.

② **Agrupar** Agrupe a los miembros de esta familia según su estado civil. Compruebe las respuestas con su compañero/a.

Está soltero/a.	Está casado/a.	Está divorciado/a.
	Dolores,	

③ **La familia de Laura** Laura habla sobre su familia con una compañera de trabajo. Anote cuántos hermanos tiene y cuántos nietos tienen sus padres.

Tiene .... hermanos y sus padres tienen .... nietos.

④ **Enrique** Observe la ilustración. ¿Cuál es el estado civil de Enrique?

¿Nombre? — Enrique
¿Edad? — 45
¿Estado civil? — Ayer soltero, hoy casado, mañana ¿divorciado?

Recuerdos de familia

"Aquí estamos el abuelo y yo con vuestros padres y el hijo de mi hermana." ☐

"Este es nuestro hijo Mario con dos años. Lucía, este es tu padre." ☐

"Estos son mis hermanos, los tíos de vuestros padres." ☐

"Sergio, esta es tu madre con sus compañeros de clase en el colegio." ☐

---

5 **a. Fotos** Dolores enseña a sus nietos el álbum de familia. Relacione las oraciones con las fotografías antiguas.

b. ¿Quién? Diga quién aparece en cada una de las fotografías.

1. *Es su hijo.* 2. .... 3. .... 4. ....

c. Los posesivos Revise las formas de los posesivos.

1. (yo) ......*mis*...... hijos /.................. hijas
2. (tú) .... tíos /.................. tías
3. (usted, él, ella) .... hermanos /.................. hermanas
4. (nosotros/as) .... padres /.................. madres
5. (vosotros/as) .... abuelos /.................. abuelas
6. (ustedes, ellos/as) .... nietos /.................. nietas

6 **La familia** ¿Quién es para Dolores su familia? ¿Y para usted?

Modelo: *Para Dolores, su familia son los padres, los hijos...*

👥 **MI EXPERIENCIA**

7 **Describir** ¿Cómo es la familia de su compañero/a? Anote sus respuestas. Luego cuente al resto de la clase sus averiguaciones.

GUIÓN DE TRABAJO

¿Cómo es tu familia? ¿Es una familia grande/pequeña? ¿Tienes hermanos? ¿Están casados, solteros, divorciados...?

Descríbela.

¿Y tú? ¿Estás casado/a? ¿Soltero/a? ¿Divorciado/a? ¿Tienes pareja? ¿Tienes hijos?

Para mí, una familia es...

...una pareja con o sin hijos.
...una madre o un padre y su hijo...

Hablar de los familiares

¿**Su marido** trabaja mucho?

¿**Tus padres** están jubilados?

Nuestras nietas son pequeñas.

Vuestros hermanos, ¿dónde viven?

Sus abuelos son de Bogotá.

5B.2 Plural possessives

Vocabulario

② ——————————

el miembro *member*

el estado civil *marital status*

⑤ ——————————

el recuerdo *memory; souvenir*

enseñar *to show; to teach*

el marido *husband*

el álbum

⑦ ——————————

el nacimiento *birth*

último/a *last*

la adopción, adoptar

Hijos

La mayoría de las parejas españolas tienen un solo hijo. Hay pocos nacimientos, pero el número de adopciones aumentó. El 75% de los niños que se adoptaron durante los últimos años nacieron en otros países, como China, Rusia y Etiopía.

SAM: Actividades pp. 101–103

Ⓢ Practice more at **vhlcentral.com**.

Mis amigos, mi otra familia

MI CUMPLEAÑOS

Mario ....

Mis amigos
de la universidad en
el día de mi cumpleaños

EN LA OFICINA

.... Jaime

Mis compañeros de trabajo,
mi otra familia

Hablar de conocidos

- ● ¿**Conoces** a Laura? Es una amiga de Montevideo. La conozco **desde** pequeña.
- ■ No, no la **conozco**.
- ● Este es Pedro, un amigo del trabajo, ¿lo **conoces**?
- ■ Sí, lo **conozco desde hace** unos días.

5B.3	Irregular verbs -zc- **conocer a** + [people] **conocer** + [places/things]
5B.4	**desde** **desde hace**

Vocabulario

8

el/la compañero/a de
   trabajo *coworker*

desde hace *for (and until now)*

desde pequeño/a *since childhood*

10

cronológicamente *chronologically*

---

8 **a. Los amigos de Jaime** Escuche a Jaime hablar con su hija sobre sus amigos. ¿Cómo se llaman? Escriba sus nombres en la foto.

b. Dónde y cuándo ¿De dónde los conoce y desde cuándo?

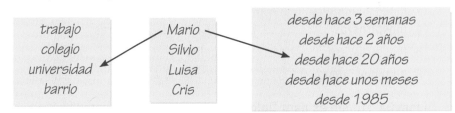

> trabajo
> colegio
> universidad
> barrio

> Mario
> Silvio
> Luisa
> Cris

> desde hace 3 semanas
> desde hace 2 años
> desde hace 20 años
> desde hace unos meses
> desde 1985

Modelo: *A Mario lo conoce de la universidad, desde hace 20 años.*

9 **Conocer** Complete la conversación. ¿Cuándo se usa **conocer a**?

- ● Luisa, yo no (1)............... el Museo Nacional, ¿tú lo (2)...............?
- ● No, pero mi amigo Julio lo (3)............... muy bien. ¿(4)............... a Julio?
- ● Sí, lo (5)............... de la universidad.
- ● ¿Ah, sí?

10 **a. Dos amigos** Escriba el nombre de dos amigos. Su compañero/a le pregunta de dónde y desde cuándo los conoce.

Modelo: *A tu amigo Sebastián, ¿lo conoces del colegio?*

b. Ordenar ¿Dónde conocemos normalmente a los amigos? Ordene los lugares cronológicamente.

trabajo	colegio	barrio	universidad	...

barrio - .... - .... - ....

11 **a. Memorias** Este es un fragmento de las "memorias" de Marisa. ¿Qué título le parece más adecuado?

"Laura, una amiga muy especial"

"Laura, mi hermana"

"Viajar con amigos"

[...] Mi amiga Laura es como una hermana. La veo poco; ella vive en Veracruz con su marido y su hija. Hablamos mucho por teléfono; es una relación de amistad muy especial. No olvidamos los momentos que vivimos juntas. De 1999 a 2004, estudiamos Economía en la Universidad de Guadalajara. ¡Qué tiempos aquellos! En la Navidad de 2007 fuimos de viaje a Perú y estuvimos en muchas ciudades. ¡Fue una experiencia increíble! Un año más tarde yo estuve de profesora en Lima y ella estuvo en Chile. Mi hijo nació tres años más tarde y cuatro años después de eso nació su hija. Nuestras vidas tienen muchos puntos en común. ¡Es una gran amiga!

b. Fechas ¿Qué pasó según las memorias de Marisa en las siguientes fechas?

2007   1999–2004   2008

2011   2015

c. Verbos Fíjese en el texto y complete la terminación de estos verbos.

ella est........... / nosotras fui........... / ellas fue........... / yo est...........

12 **Con amigos** Piensen en experiencias con amigos. ¿Qué pasó? ¿Cuándo?

En 20...
De 20... a...

fuimos a...
estuvimos en...

viaje
universidad
América Latina
aventura

MI EXPERIENCIA

13 **Mis amigos** Primero relacione las palabras de las dos listas de la derecha para repasar el vocabulario. Luego presente sus amigos a un(a) compañero/a.

GUIÓN DE TRABAJO

¿Quiénes son tus amigos?

Compañeros de estudios, de trabajo, hermanos, ...

¿De dónde conoces a tus amigos?

Del trabajo, de los viajes, del barrio,...

¿Desde cuándo conoces a tus amigos?

Desde hace...

¿Están casados, solteros, ...? ¿Tienen pareja?

¿Qué momentos importantes viviste con ellos?

Fui con .... a ....
Estuve con .... en ....

Hablar de viajes y de experiencias en momentos concretos

- ¿Adónde **fuiste** el año pasado?
- **Fui** a Argentina con un amigo.
- ¿Dónde **estuviste**?
- **Estuvimos** una semana en Buenos Aires y desde allí **fuimos** en avión a la Patagonia. **Fue** un viaje inolvidable.

5B.5 Irregular preterite forms **ir, ser, estar**

Vocabulario

11
las memorias *memoirs*
parecer (zc) *to seem*
adecuado/a *appropriate; suitable*
la relación *relationship*
la amistad *friendship*
olvidar *to forget*
¡Qué tiempos aquellos! *Those were the days!*
la Navidad *Christmas*
increíble *incredible*
el punto en común *point in common*
gran (grande) *great*
inolvidable *unforgettable*
12
la aventura *adventure*

¡OJO!

The adjective **grande** drops the final **-de** before a singular noun. **Gran** before a noun means *great*. **Grande** following a noun means *large* or *big*. So, **un gran país** refers to *a great country*, whereas **un país grande** refers to *a big country*.

1. soltero .... a. madre
2. padre .... b. hijo
3. tíos .... c. mujer
4. marido .... d. primos
5. hija .... e. casado

SAM: Actividades pp. 104–106

Juanita y Bernardo, dos abuelos muy activos

Bernardo y Juanita, abuelos a tiempo completo

Juanita y Bernardo son una pareja de jubilados de 81 y 84 años, respectivamente. Viven en el estado de Texas; Bernardo es de Texas y Juanita nació en el estado de Tamaulipas, México. Hace mucho tiempo, decidieron formar una familia grande... ¡y lo lograron! Tienen 6 hijos y 21 nietos.

Juanita, ¿en qué ocupan su tiempo de lunes a viernes?
Yo hago las compras, cocino y limpio la casa. Mi marido me ayuda y además cuida el jardín. También cuidamos a nuestro nieto más pequeño: lo recogemos del kínder y lo llevamos a la alberca.

¿Y por la noche?
Miramos la televisión. ¡Nos encantan las películas viejas y las telenovelas! Algunas noches cenamos con amigos. Bernardo pasa horas contando chistes. ¡Es una persona muy alegre!

¿Y los fines de semana?
Los sábados paseamos y caminamos en el parque. ¡Nos mantiene sanos! Los domingos descansamos y vamos a la iglesia. También tenemos diversos acontecimientos familiares. ¡En los últimos dos años celebramos 5 bodas, 4 fiestas de quinceañera y 6 bautizos!

Vocabulario

14

el estado *state*
lograr *to achieve*
ocupar *to spend; to take up*
ayudar *to help*
cuidar (a/de) *to take care of*
recoger (j) *to pick up*
el kínder (*Méx.*) *kindergarten*
llevar *to take*
la alberca (*Méx.*) *pool*
encantar *to love, to get a kick out of*
viejo/a *old*
el chiste *joke*
alegre *happy*
caminar *to walk*
mantener *to keep*
sano/a *healthy*
descansar *to rest*
diverso/a *various*
el bautizo *baptism*

17

el placer *pleasure*
la obligación, compatible

14 a. Foto Mire la foto. ¿Qué relación familiar tienen estas personas?

b. Juanita y Bernardo Ahora lea el texto. ¿Qué hacen Juanita y Bernardo de lunes a viernes?

1. Están en la cama hasta las once de la mañana. ☐
2. Recogen al nieto del kínder. ☐
3. Almuerzan con amigos. ☐
4. Hacen las compras. ☐
5. Van a la iglesia. ☐
6. Limpian la casa. ☐

15 Entrevista Con un(a) compañero/a, imaginen una entrevista con Juanita o Bernardo. Hagan preguntas sobre el fin de semana pasado. Luego presenten su entrevista a la clase.

16 Familiares Pregunte a su compañero/a si tiene abuelos, hermanos o primos. ¿Pasa mucho tiempo con ellos? ¿Pasó usted mucho tiempo con sus abuelos u otros familiares?

17 ¿Obligación o placer? ¿Conoce a abuelos como Juanita y Bernardo? ¿Cree usted que para Juanita y Bernardo es una obligación estar con su nieto? ¿Por qué?

18 **La familia** Mire el siguiente estudio del Centro de Investigaciones Sociológicas (CIS) de España sobre la familia. ¿Está de acuerdo con estas afirmaciones? Marque después si las oraciones son verdaderas (**V**) o falsas (**F**).

¿Está usted muy, bastante, poco o nada de acuerdo?	Muy de acuerdo	Bastante de acuerdo	Ni de acuerdo ni en desacuerdo	Poco de acuerdo	Nada de acuerdo
Cuando alguien no puede valerse, es mejor pedir ayuda a los Servicios Sociales que a la familia.	10,4 %	19,6 %	14,7 %	38,0 %	16,4 %
Si necesita dinero, pide un crédito a un banco, no a la familia.	14,7 %	29,7 %	14,3 %	28,3 %	11,6 %
Prefiere llevar a los hijos a una guardería a llevarlos con los abuelos o familiares.	16,1 %	32,3 %	16,1 %	25,0 %	8,9 %

www.cis.es

V F

1. Muchos españoles tienen más confianza en la familia que en los Servicios Sociales. ☐ ☐

2. Pocos españoles prefieren pedir créditos al banco. ☐ ☐

3. La mayoría de los españoles están de acuerdo con el papel de abuelos de Juanita y Bernardo. ☐ ☐

[c] [z]

19 **a. [c] y [z]** Luis busca el número de teléfono y la dirección de un amigo. Fíjese: **c + e, i** y **z + a, o, u** representan el mismo sonido. Escuche y marque ese sonido en estas palabras.

Cela, Cerezo, Cid... Aquí está: Cifuentes Cubero, Zulma.

Su dirección es: calle Zárraga, 8, Villa Ortúzar

b. Marcelo Ahora escuche a Marcelo repetir las mismas frases. ¿Qué diferencia nota entre las dos formas de pronunciar la **c** y la **z**?

20 **a. La comunidad latinoamericana** La comunidad latinoamericana más numerosa en España es la ecuatoriana. Doris llegó con su marido hace un año. Escuche la entrevista y escriba los términos que ella usa para hablar de su familia y amigos.

Una familia ecuatoriana

España	Ecuador
padres	*mamá y papá*

b. Preguntar Pregunte a su compañero/a y compare con el resto de la clase.

¿Conoces a familias latinoamericanas? ¿De qué países son?

Practice more at vhlcentral.com.

¡Gracias, abuelos!
Cada vez más familias funcionan gracias a los abuelos: llevan a sus nietos al colegio, los cuidan cuando están enfermos y en verano pasan con ellos las vacaciones si los padres trabajan.

Vocabulario
18
estar de acuerdo *to agree*
bastante *quite a lot*
alguien *someone*
valerse *to be self-sufficient*
pedir (e:i) ayuda *to ask for help*
la ayuda *help*
los Servicios Sociales *Social Services*
pedir (e:i) un crédito *to ask for a loan*
la guardería *day care*
el familiar *relative*
estar en desacuerdo *to disagree*
tener confianza en *to trust in*
el papel de *role of*
gracias a... *thanks to. . .*
enfermo/a *sick*
20
la mamá *mom*
el papá *dad*
el/la esposo/a (*Amér. L.*) *husband/wife*
la mayoría *most; majority*
el/la inmigrante *immigrant*

¡OJO!
The letters **c** (before **e** and **i**) and **z** are pronounced as [s] in southern Spain and in Latin America (**seseo**), but as [z] (like the *th* in *think*) in most of Spain (**ceceo**).

El 43% de los inmigrantes que viven en España nacieron en América Latina. Los países más destacados son Ecuador (13%), Colombia (8%), Bolivia (6%), Perú (5%), República Dominicana (2%) y Argentina (2%).

SAM: Actividades pp. 107–112

TAREA FINAL

Nuestro álbum de amigos y familiares

Piense en un familiar o amigo/a.
Hermano/a, amigo/a de la universidad, del barrio...

Escriba un texto breve con la información más importante.
Nombre, relación, experiencias vividas en el pasado...

Presente su familiar o amigo/a a sus compañeros de grupo.
Se llama..., lo conozco de..., es..., estuvimos en...

Organicen un álbum de fotos de amigos y familiares del grupo y escriban los datos sobre ellos.
Este es Nelson...

YO PUEDO...

- **Puedo hablar de mi familia.**
  Dibuje un árbol genealógico de su familia y descríbalo en un pequeño texto. Hable del estado civil de sus hermanos, primos...

- **Puedo hablar sobre conocidos.**
  Complete la conversación.

● ¿Conoces a Marta?
■ Sí, es una amiga del colegio.
● Ah, yo no la ....

- **Puedo contar una experiencia compartida con amigos o familia.**
  Complete las oraciones, anotando una experiencia del pasado.

Estuve en ....
Fui a ....
Fui ....

- **Puedo hablar de distintos modelos de familia.**
  ¿Qué modelos de familia son especialmente frecuentes en su país?

GRAMÁTICA FUNCIONAL Tutorials

5B.1 | Talk about marital status

estar + [*marital status*] 5.8.1

- Use estar + **soltero/a** (*single*), **casado/a** (*married*), or **divorciado/a** (*divorced*) to tell someone's marital status.

  Yo **estoy soltera**, mi hermano **está casado** y mi hermana **está divorciada**.
  I am single, my brother is married, and my sister is divorced.

¡OJO! In many Spanish-speaking countries, it is also possible to use **ser** with marital status (**Soy casado/a**).

5B.2 | Talk about family relationships

Possessive adjectives (plural) 8.1

- In 2A.8, you learned to use the possessive adjectives **mi**, **tu**, and **su** to express possession of individual objects. Here are the possessive adjectives to use with all combinations of people and things.

	singular	plural
(yo)	**mi** hijo/hija	**mis** hijos/hijas
(tú)	**tu** amigo/amiga	**tus** amigos/amigas
(usted, él, ella)	**su** hermano/hermana	**sus** hermanos/hermanas
(nosotros/as)	**nuestro** padre **nuestra** madre	**nuestros** padres **nuestras** madres
(vosotros/as)	**vuestro** tío **vuestra** tía	**vuestros** tíos **vuestras** tías
(ustedes, ellos/as)	**su** abuelo/abuela	**sus** abuelos/abuelas

- Possessive adjectives match the person or thing *possessed* in gender and number, not the *possessor*.

  Nuestra tía vive en San Diego y nuestros primos, aquí.
  Our aunt lives in San Diego and our cousins live here.

- Note that su(s) can mean *your*, *his*, *her*, *its*, or *their*. Use context to determine who the possessor is, and be sure to provide enough information to ensure that your meaning is clear.

  Está con **sus** tías.   Los padres hablan con **su** hijo.
  She's with her aunts.   *The parents talk to their son.*

5B.3 / 5B.4 | Talk about people you know

Irregular verbs **c→zc** 5.1.2   **a personal** 10.1

- Use the verb **conocer** (*to know*) to talk about people, places, or things you are familiar with. **Conocer** has an irregular **yo** form.

CONOCER			
(yo)	conozco	(nosotros/as)	conocemos
(tú)	conoces	(vosotros/as)	conocéis
(usted, él, ella)	conoce	(ustedes, ellos/as)	conocen

  Conozco bien Ciudad de Guatemala.
  I know Guatemala City well.

  ¿**Conoces** a mi primo, Marcos?
  Do you know my cousin, Marcos?

¡Póngalo en práctica!

G1 **¿Soltero, casado o divorciado?** Complete la conversación.

- ¿(1).................. casado?
- No, tengo pareja, pero no estamos (2)..................
- ¿Y Juana?
- Está (3)..................; le gusta vivir sola.
- María (4).................. casada y tiene dos hijos, ¿no?
- No, está (5).................. y, sí, tiene dos hijos; viven con ella. El ex marido está (6).................. La nueva esposa se llama Marcela.

G2 **Posesivos** Complete la tabla con las formas que faltan.

	singular	plural
1.	su nieto	
2.		mis primas
3.	nuestro amigo	
4.		vuestras abuelas
5.		tus vecinos
6.	su hijo	

G3 **Conversaciones** Complete las conversaciones de forma lógica.

- (1).................. tíos, los hermanos de mi padre, se llaman Roberto y Paz, como (2).................. padres.
- ¡Qué coincidencia! (3).................. tía también se llama Paz, igual que mi abuela materna.
- (4).................. padres no nos comprenden.
- ¡Uf! ¡(5).................. madre piensa que tenemos cinco años!
- Pero, por lo menos (*at least*), (6).................. padre trabaja con jóvenes como nosotros y entiende (7).................. problemas.

G4 **Conocer** Complete las oraciones con la forma adecuada de **conocer** en el presente.

1. Guillermo .... a mi hermana.
2. Claudia y yo .... el Museo del Prado.
3. Julieta y tú .... al hermano de Germán.
4. Tú .... la ciudad, ¿verdad?
5. Yo .... a Javier desde pequeño.
6. Mis padres .... al arquitecto.

- To express that a person is known, use **conocer** + a + [*person*]. This usage is called the **a personal**, and is required whenever a person is the direct object of a verb.

    Conocemos **a** la directora. ¿Conocen ustedes **a** María?
    We know the director. Do you know María?

¡OJO! Spanish has two words that mean *to know*: **conocer** and **saber**. You will learn to use the verb **saber** in **6B.1**.

desde, desde hace, hace + que   `10.7, 10.8`

- Use **desde**, **desde hace**, or **hace** + **que** with a present-tense verb to tell how long something has been happening. Use **desde** + [*specific time in the past*] to mean *since*.

    Conozco a Luisa **desde** 2002/el año pasado/pequeña.
    *I've known Luisa **since** 2002/last year/I was little.*

- To specify the length of time something has been going on, use **desde hace** + [*span of time*].

    Conocemos a su madre **desde hace** una semana/dos años.
    *We've known her mother **for** a week/two years.*

- Express the same meaning with the construction **hace** + [*span of time*] + **que**.

    Hace una semana/dos años **que** conocemos a su madre.
    *We've known her mother **for** a week/two years.*

- Use **hace** with a verb in the **pretérito indefinido** to mean *ago*.

    Conocí a Mireia **hace** tres semanas.
    *I met Mireia three weeks **ago**.*

5B.5 Talk about trips and experiences at specific times

Irregular preterite: ir, ser, estar   `5.2.2, 5.2.3`

- The verbs **ir**, **ser**, and **estar** are irregular in the **pretérito indefinido**. Note that these irregular forms do not have written accents.

	IR/SER	ESTAR
(yo)	**fui**	**estuv**e
(tú)	**fuiste**	**estuv**iste
(usted, él, ella)	**fue**	**estuv**o
(nosotros/as)	**fuimos**	**estuv**imos
(vosotros/as)	**fuisteis**	**estuv**isteis
(ustedes, ellos/as)	**fueron**	**estuv**ieron

- **Ir** and **ser** have the same conjugation in the preterite, so you must use context to clarify meaning. Remember that the verb **ir** is often followed by **a**.

    Fuimos a una fiesta en casa de Pedro. **Fue** una noche divertida.
    We went to a party at Pedro's house. It was a fun evening.

¡Póngalo en práctica!

G5 **Completar** Complete las oraciones con **desde**, **desde hace** o **hace**.

1. Miguel conoce a Elena .... quince años.
2. Conocemos a Patricia .... el año pasado.
3. Mi tío trabaja aquí .... el martes.
4. .... muchos años que Magda y Carlos conocen Londres.
5. Valeria vive en Colón .... tres meses.

G6 **Desde o hace** Complete las oraciones con **desde** o **hace**.

1. Vivimos en Guayaquil .... mayo.
2. Viajaron a Puebla .... cinco años.
3. Escribe poesía .... la universidad.
4. Mi tío terminó sus estudios .... 20 años.
5. Raúl conoció a Verónica .... tres semanas.

G7 **Escribir** Escriba oraciones completas.

1. Tomás / junio / conocer / Juanita / desde

....

2. desde hace / yo / 5 años / Acapulco / conocer

....

3. conocer / nosotras / Felipe / hace 2 semanas

....

4. Pablo / conocer / desde pequeño / las vecinas

....

G8 **Relacionar** Elija los finales correctos.

	1. Vosotros...	a. fui a México en mayo.
	2. María...	b. estuvisteis juntos en Oaxaca.
	3. Mis sobrinos...	c. fuiste la ganadora del concurso.
	4. Yo...	d. estuvieron en la fiesta anoche.
	5. Tú...	e. fue al mercado por la mañana.

G9 **Ser o ir** Indique si el verbo conjugado es una forma de **ser** o de **ir**.

SER IR

☐ ☐ 1. Juan fue al parque con sus hermanos.
☐ ☐ 2. Mario y yo siempre fuimos buenos amigos.
☐ ☐ 3. ¿Ustedes fueron a la fiesta de cumpleaños?
☐ ☐ 4. Carla y tú fuisteis buenas estudiantes.

 Practice more at **vhlcentral.com**.

Foto de familia

los fines de semana	(on) weekends
mi gente	my folks
el próximo mes	next month
el/la abuelo/a	grandfather/ grandmother
los abuelos	grandparents
la adopción	adoption
el álbum	album
el árbol genealógico	family tree
el estado civil	marital status
los hermanos	siblings
el marido	husband
el matrimonio	marriage
el miembro	member
el nacimiento	birth
el/la nieto/a	grandson/ granddaughter
los nietos	grandchildren
los padres	parents
la pareja	couple; partner
el/la primo/a	cousin
el recuerdo	memory; souvenir
el tiempo libre	free time
el/la tío/a	uncle/aunt
adoptar	to adopt
enseñar	to show; to teach
casado/a	married
divorciado/a	divorced
jubilado/a	retired
soltero/a	single
último/a	last

Mis amigos, mi otra familia

desde pequeño/a	since childhood
¡Qué tiempos aquellos!	Those were the days!
la amistad	friendship
la aventura	adventure
el/la compañero/a de trabajo	coworker
las memorias	memoirs
la Navidad	Christmas
el punto en común	point in common
la relación	relationship
olvidar	to forget
parecer (zc)	to seem
adecuado/a	appropriate; suitable
gran (grande)	great
increíble	incredible
inolvidable	unforgettable
cronológicamente	chronologically
desde hace	for (and until now)

Juanita y Bernardo

gracias a..	thanks to. . .
la alberca (Méx.)	pool
la ayuda	help
el bautizo	baptism
el chiste	joke
el/la esposo/a (Amér. L.)	husband/wife
el estado	state
el familiar	relative
la guardería	day care
el/la inmigrante	immigrant
el kínder (Méx.)	kindergarten
la mamá	mom
la mayoría	most, majority
la obligación	obligation
el papá	dad
el papel de	role of
el placer	pleasure
los Servicios Sociales	Social Services
alguien	someone
ayudar	to help
caminar	to walk
cuidar (a/de)	to take care of
descansar	to rest
encantar	to love, to get a kick out of
estar de acuerdo	to agree
estar en desacuerdo	to disagree
llevar	to take
lograr	to achieve
mantener	to keep
ocupar	to spend; to take up
pedir (e:i) ayuda	to ask for help
pedir (e:i) un crédito	to ask for a loan
recoger (j)	to pick up
tener confianza en	to trust in
valerse	to be self-sufficient
alegre	happy
compatible	compatible
diverso/a	various
enfermo/a	sick
sano/a	healthy
viejo/a	old
bastante	quite a lot

Variación léxica

el/la amigo/a ⟷ el/la pana (Ven., Ecua.) ⟷ el/la cuate/a (Méx.)

el bautizo ⟷ el bautismo (Arg.)

el colegio secundario ⟷ la escuela secundaria ⟷ el liceo (Amér. L.) ⟷ el instituto (Esp.) ⟷ la prepa (Méx.)

la guardería ⟷ la sala cuna (Chi.)

el kínder (Méx.) ⟷ el jardín de la infancia (Esp.) ⟷ el jardín de infantes (Arg.) ⟷ el jardín infantil (Chi.) ⟷ el jardín de niños (Méx. central)

LECTURA

Gaturro

Estrategia ············

Contextualizing the reading

When reading a text, you should pay attention to its biographical, cultural, and historical context: when and where it was written, who wrote it, cultural references, etc.; otherwise you might miss multiple layers of meaning that are not apparent to you because you are reading only through the lens of your own experience and knowledge. As you read the biographies of the author and the comic strip, you will learn the background of the characters pictured here (who these two cats are, where they live, what kind of relationship they have, etc.).

Nik es el seudónimo del ilustrador Cristian Dzwonik, que nació en Buenos Aires en 1971. Desde pequeño su abuelo le enseñó a dibujar y ya no dejó de hacerlo. A los 11 años empezó a estudiar en una escuela de dibujo, a los 17 publicó sus primeros trabajos, y a los 21 ingresó en el diario argentino *La Nación* como humorista gráfico. Ama su trabajo porque puede hacer las dos cosas que más le gustan: el dibujo y los chistes.

Sus trabajos se publican en Latinoamérica, España, Francia y Estados Unidos. Recibió el premio Kónex de Platino al mejor humorista gráfico argentino en 2002.

Gaturro es un gato que vive con una típica familia de clase media compuesta por una mamá que ama los libros, un papá fanático del fútbol y dos hijos: Luz, que cambia de novio a cada rato, y Agustín, un niño muy curioso. A Gaturro le gusta su casa pero también vagabundear por el barrio, encontrarse con sus amigos en los tejados y reflexionar sobre la vida cotidiana. Es una especie de antihéroe, muy observador. Está enamorado de Ágatha, pero nunca la conquista. Ella solo se pone celosa cuando otra gata se acerca a Gaturro.

Más de treinta personajes participan en esta historieta que debutó en la última página de *La Nación* en 1996 y se convirtió en un *boom* editorial.

① **a. Las historietas** Comente con un(a) compañero/a: ¿Qué historietas les gustan más? ¿Por qué? ¿Sus protagonistas son héroes o antihéroes? ¿En qué mundo viven y qué hacen allí?

b. Personajes Elijan dos personajes de la lista y escriban una oración sobre cada uno usando algunos de los adjetivos de la lista.

Garfield	alegre	hablador	leal
Mickey Mouse	burlón	ingenioso	soñador
Scooby-Doo	cobarde	insolente	torpe
Bugs Bunny	glotón	inteligente	vago

burlón *mocking* **cobarde** *coward* **glotón** *glutton* **hablador** *talkative* **ingenioso** *clever* **leal** *loyal* **soñador** *dreamer* **torpe** *clumsy* **vago** *lazy*

② **Emparejar** Empareje cada frase de la primera columna con la terminación correspondiente de la segunda columna.

1. Gaturro está enamorado ....   a. de una vagancia extra.

2. Ágatha quiere un hombre ....   b. de clase media.

3. Ágatha se pone celosa ....   c. de Ágatha.

4. La familia de Gaturro es típicamente ....   d. de otras gatas que hablan con Gaturro.

5. La mamá es amante ....   e. de gran extravagancia.

6. Según Ágatha, Gaturro es ....   f. de los libros.

(3) **Títulos** Indique el título que corresponde a cada lista. En la última columna escriba lo que hizo hoy e invente un título. Luego, entre todos, comparen lo que escribieron y debatan: ¿Se puede conocer a una persona por lo que hace cada día? ¿Qué característica es esencial para definir a una persona?

1. Persona de gran curiosidad ....
2. Persona de gran vagancia ....
3. Persona de gran actividad ....

A	B	C	D
no salir a correr	hacer gimnasia	investigar	....
no leer	trabajar	estudiar	....
no llamar por teléfono	andar en bicicleta	meditar	....

PROYECTO

Personaje de historieta Investigue sobre su personaje de historieta favorito y escriba una biografía con los datos más importantes de la vida de su creador y su carrera. Como ayuda, puede seguir esta estructura: 1. Fecha de nacimiento 2. Lugar donde vive 3. Características 4. Otros personajes 5. Recepción de la historieta.

Video

La casa de Frida

Ya leyó sobre la carrera de Salma Hayek y sobre las familias en el mundo hispano. En este episodio de **Flash Cultura** va a ver la casa de la artista mexicana que Hayek interpretó en el cine: Frida Kahlo, una mujer que vivió una vida de película y tuvo un matrimonio inusual.

1. **Preguntas** Con un(a) compañero/a, hable de las siguientes preguntas: ¿Es importante el lugar donde vivimos? ¿Qué cosas expresa la decoración de una casa sobre sus habitantes? ¿Cuál puede ser el lugar más personal de una casa? ¿Por qué es interesante conocer la casa de los artistas? ¿Qué esperan encontrar en la casa de Frida?

2. **Mirar** Mire este episodio de **Flash Cultura**. Recuerde que el museo que va a ver es en realidad una casa, por lo que la visita empieza en la puerta principal y termina en el dormitorio de Frida.

Esta casa tiene varios detalles que revelan el amor de esta mexicana por la cultura de su país.

Uno de los espacios más atractivos de esta casa es este estudio...

3. **¿Verdadero o falso?** Indique si las oraciones son verdaderas (**V**) o falsas (**F**). Después, en parejas, corrijan las falsas.

1. Diego Rivera se casó dos veces con Frida.
2. Frida nunca tuvo una mascota en su casa.
3. El jardinero conoció a Diego.
4. El museo de Frida se llama Casa Amarilla.
5. Frida usó silla de ruedas varias veces.

4. **Guía de recorrido** Con un(a) compañero/a, escriba una breve guía de recorrido para el museo de Frida Kahlo. Luego lean su guía a la clase.

Modelo: *La casa es de color... El patio está en el centro de la casa y tiene... El jardinero trabaja allí desde hace... Frida pintó... En la cocina hay... Finalmente, llegamos al...*

 Practice more at **vhlcentral.com**.

Unidad 6

Domingo Buendía, maestro de yoga

Julia y Felipe, amor a distancia

¿Estrés? ¿Qué estrés?

6A

EL ARTE DE VIVIR

Tiempo libre

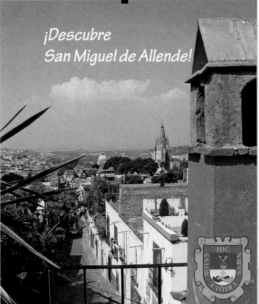

¡Descubre San Miguel de Allende!

¡Bienvenidos todos!

Colaboramos un año más con el Instituto Nacional de las Personas Adultas Mayores (INAPAM) para ofrecer el mejor viaje.

Este año estamos en San Miguel de Allende, en el centro de nuestro país, México.

Con esta carta les entregamos un folleto con los lugares y actividades más interesantes de la ciudad para disfrutar al máximo de su tiempo libre.

¡Gracias por su participación!

Cuantificar

- ¿Vas **mucho** al cine?
- Sí, voy **mucho**. ¿Y tú?
- Yo voy **bastante**.

- ✦ ¿Miras **mucho** la televisión?
- No, **poco**. ¿Y tú?
- ✦ Yo **casi nada**.

6A.1 Adverbs of quantity

Negar

- Yo estudio alemán y bailo tango. ¿Y tú?
- Yo **no** estudio alemán **ni** bailo tango, pero leo mucho.
- ✦ Yo **no** practico deporte **nunca**.

6A.2 Double negatives

Vocabulario

①

las personas mayores *the elderly*
la exposición *exhibition*
la fiesta popular *festival*
el descuento *discount*
estar dirigido/a a *to be aimed at*
la excursión

②

el ocio *leisure*

---

1. **Tiempo libre** Lea el texto de la carta. ¿A quiénes están dirigidas las actividades de tiempo libre? ¿Qué edad cree que tienen los participantes?

2. **a. Clasificar** Clasifique las actividades y los lugares de ocio y compare sus respuestas con las de su compañero/a.

   ○ actividades culturales   ○ actividades gastronómicas
   ○ actividades de diversión

   b. ¿Cuál? ¿Hay alguna actividad o lugar de ocio en dos o más grupos? ¿Cuál?

3. **a. Preguntar** Seleccione en la lista las tres actividades que usted realiza con más frecuencia y pregunte por ellas a su compañero/a.

   Modelo: • ¿Vas mucho al teatro?
             • Sí, voy bastante.

   b. Nunca ¿Cuáles son las actividades que usted no hace nunca?

4. **a. La encuesta** Escuche la encuesta a los participantes del viaje y marque cuántas veces mencionan estas actividades.

estar con la familia	X X X	mirar la televisión	
salir con los amigos		navegar por Internet	
cocinar		ir al cine	
ir de compras		practicar deporte	

   b. Actividades ¿Cuál es la actividad que más realizan estas personas? ¿Y la que menos realizan?

| 1 | 2 | 3 | 4 | 5 | 6 |

¿Te gusta…
- cocinar?
- pintar?
- bailar?
- hacer cerámica?
- hacer yoga?
- hacer excursiones?

HORARIOS DE LAS ACTIVIDADES						
HORA	L	M	Mi	J	V	S
16:00–17:30	Yoga	Pintura	Excursión	Cocina	Yoga	Excursión
17:30–19:00	Pintura	Baile	Salsa	Baile	Pintura	Baile
19:00–20:30	Cocina	Cerámica	Cocina	Cerámica	Cerámica	Visita ciudad

5 Indicar Indique la actividad de cada foto.

1. .... 3. .... 5. ....
2. .... 4. .... 6. ....

6 Horario ¿Qué actividades se organizan con estas frecuencias?

una vez a la semana	
dos veces a la semana	
tres veces a la semana	

7 ¿Con qué frecuencia? ¿Realiza usted o alguna persona que conoce estas actividades? ¿Con qué frecuencia? Hable con su compañero/a.

Modelo: *Tengo una amiga que hace yoga dos veces a la semana.*

8 Mirar la tele Una de las principales actividades de ocio de la gente es mirar la tele. ¿Mira usted mucho la tele? ¿Cree que es una buena manera de ocupar su tiempo? Comente con su compañero/a los aspectos positivos y negativos de esta actividad de ocio pasiva.

MI EXPERIENCIA

9 Actividades de ocio Encuentre a compañeros de clase que practican las mismas actividades de ocio que usted. Presenten el resultado al grupo.

GUIÓN DE TRABAJO

¿Qué haces en tu tiempo libre? → ¿Viajas mucho? ¿Vas mucho al cine?

bailar
hacer yoga
viajar
estar con la familia
estar con los amigos
ir al cine
hacer deporte
…

una vez…
dos veces…

a la semana
al mes
al año
…

Preguntar e indicar frecuencia

- ¿Cuántas **veces al mes** van de excursión?
- Yo, **dos veces al mes.**
- Yo, **una vez a la semana.**
- Yo no voy **nunca.**
- Yo **a veces…**

6A.3 Expressions of frequency

Vocabulario *cont.*

la diversión *fun*
3
mucho *a lot*
nunca *never*
casi nunca *hardly ever*
4
mirar *to watch; to look at*
navegar por Internet *to surf the Internet*
5
pintar *to paint*
bailar *to dance*
hacer cerámica *to make pottery*
6
una vez a la semana *once a week*
dos veces al mes *twice a month*
organizar
8
pasivo/a

SAM: Actividades pp. 113–115

Un día perfecto

CUESTIONARIO DE BIENESTAR

		Sí	No
1	¿Ha dormido bien hoy?	☐	☐
2	¿Ha tomado un buen desayuno hoy?	☐	☐
3	¿Ha dado un paseo esta semana?	☐	☐
4	¿Ha hablado con un amigo hoy?	☐	☐
5	¿Ha reído en su trabajo o en casa?	☐	☐
6	¿Ha leído un libro interesante este mes?	☐	☐
7	¿Ha comido bien hoy?	☐	☐
8	¿Ha aprendido algo este año?	☐	☐

- 8 veces Sí: ¡Felicitaciones!
- De 5 a 7 veces Sí: No está mal.
- Menos de 5 veces Sí: Un consejo: menos trabajo y más tiempo para usted.

Describir su día

- ¿Hoy has dormido bien?
- Sí, gracias, he dormido muy bien.
- ✦ Mi hija hoy no ha dormido nada.

- ¿Habéis tomado ya un café esta mañana?
- No, todavía no hemos tomado café.

6A.4 Present perfect
Expressions of time
hoy, esta semana, este mes, este año, ya/todavía no

Vocabulario

(10)
el bienestar *well-being*
hoy *today*
dar un paseo *to take a walk*
esta semana *this week*
reír (e:i) *to laugh*
este mes *this month*
este año *this year*
¡Felicitaciones! *Congratulations!*
el consejo *piece of advice*
el cuestionario *questionnaire*
(12)
ya *already*
todavía no *not yet*

---

10 a. **Cuestionario** Responda al cuestionario y comente los resultados con el grupo.

b. **Un día perfecto** Mencione tres actividades que hace usted para tener un "día perfecto". Compare su lista con las de sus compañeros y elaboren una lista común.

Modelo: *leer un libro, dar un paseo, salir con amigos...*

11 a. **Elegir** Elija la forma del verbo **haber** que corresponde a cada persona.

ha	habéis	han	has	he	hemos

1. yo .... reído
2. tú .... reído
3. usted, él, ella .... reído
4. nosotros/as .... reído
5. vosotros/as .... reído
6. ustedes, ellos/as .... reído

b. **Relacionar** Relacione cada participio con su infinitivo.

1. habla**do** ....   2. le**ído** ....   3. dorm**ido** ....
a. le**er**   b. dorm**ir**   c. habl**ar**

12 a. **Hoy** ¿Qué actividades de la lista de la **Actividad 10b** ya ha realizado o todavía no ha realizado hoy?

b. **¿Cuándo?** Anote cuándo las ha realizado. Compare sus respuestas con las de su compañero/a.

(hoy)   (esta semana)   (este mes)

13 **Todavía no** Escuche el mensaje telefónico y marque en la columna adecuada.

Susana ...	ya	todavía no
ha llamado a Antonio.	✔	
ha recibido el correo electrónico.		
ha contestado el correo electrónico.		
ha leído el libro.		
ha hablado con Antonio.		

14 **Problemas** Fíjese en la imagen. ¿Es una situación normal? ¿Quién tiene problemas y cuáles son? ¿Qué consejos recibe? Añada otros consejos.

15 **a. Consejos** Relacione cada situación con su consejo correspondiente.

> Hoy he dormido muy poco.

> ¿Por qué no organizas el día para tener tiempo libre?

> He trabajado todo el día.

> Tienes que reservar un día a la semana para hacer ejercicio.

> Esta semana no he practicado deporte.

> ¿Por qué no duermes la siesta?

b. Situaciones Proponga un consejo para estas situaciones.

1. Su amigo solo come carne.
2. Su amiga siempre va a todos los lugares en coche.
3. Su hijo mira mucho la tele.

16 **Tres consejos** Ofrezca a su compañero/a tres consejos para tener un día perfecto a partir de sus respuestas al cuestionario de la **Actividad 10**.

Modelo: *Tienes que… / ¿Por qué no…?*

👥 MI EXPERIENCIA

17 **Esta semana** ¿Cómo ha sido su semana? Primero, aprenda recursos para controlar una conversación. Escriba las respuestas de su compañero/a.

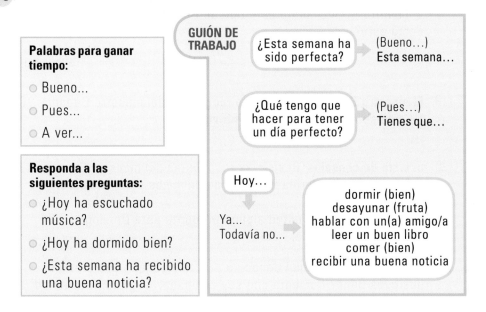

Palabras para ganar tiempo:

○ Bueno…
○ Pues…
○ A ver…

Responda a las siguientes preguntas:

○ ¿Hoy ha escuchado música?
○ ¿Hoy ha dormido bien?
○ ¿Esta semana ha recibido una buena noticia?

GUIÓN DE TRABAJO

¿Esta semana ha sido perfecta?

(Bueno…) Esta semana…

¿Qué tengo que hacer para tener un día perfecto?

(Pues…) Tienes que…

Hoy…

Ya… Todavía no…

dormir (bien)
desayunar (fruta)
hablar con un(a) amigo/a
leer un buen libro
comer (bien)
recibir una buena noticia

Dar consejos

● Estoy muy cansado…
■ **Tienes que** descansar un poco más.
✦ **¿Por qué no** trabajas menos?

6A.5 Expressions to give advice

Vocabulario

14
¿Por qué no…? *Why don't you . . .?*
tener que *to have to*
cansado/a *tired*

15
todo el día *all day*
hacer ejercicio *to exercise, to work out*
reservar *to set aside*
dormir (o:ue) la siesta *to take a nap*
la siesta *nap*

17
pues *well*
a ver *let's see*

SAM: Actividades pp. 116–118

Domingo Buendía, maestro de yoga

TU PERIÓDICO.com Los internautas preguntan

Lunes, 19 de noviembre

Domingo Buendía (Quito, Ecuador, 1948) es médico y psicólogo, y dirige desde 1981 en Quito uno de los centros de yoga más importantes de América Latina. Ha viajado a muchos países orientales, principalmente a la India, y ha entrevistado a los principales maestros de psicología oriental y relajación. Ha publicado muchos libros sobre la meditación, el yoga y la autoayuda.

El maestro Buendía ha participado en la sección "Los internautas preguntan" del blog de *Tu Periódico* y ha hablado con ellos.

18:08 Matías

Maestro, he leído muchos de sus libros y todos me han encantado. Soy director de una empresa, trabajo muchas horas al día y practico yoga desde hace unos años, pero no encuentro equilibrio ni tranquilidad. ¿Qué me aconseja?

18:10 Maestro Buendía

¿Por qué no organizas tu ocio? Hay tiempo para todo. Tiempo para trabajar y tiempo para descansar. Tienes que aprender a decir "no".

18:13 Alejandro

Practico mucho yoga y hago mis ejercicios todos los días, pero no duermo casi nada.

18:14 Maestro Buendía

El yoga no es solo una serie de ejercicios físicos relajantes. Es una ciencia del alma que busca la paz del espíritu. El cuerpo y la mente tienen que estar en conexión.

18:20 Luz

Voy a clase de yoga dos veces a la semana. ¿Cuál es el mejor momento del día para practicar?

18:30 Maestro Buendía

Cada persona es un mundo diferente y el momento del día no es muy importante. Es más importante encontrar un lugar tranquilo y en silencio para escuchar la voz de nuestra mente.

Vocabulario

(18)

el/la maestro/a *master; teacher*
el/la internauta *Internet user*
dirigir (j) *to run; to manage*
la autoayuda *self-help*
la empresa *company*
el equilibrio *balance*
aconsejar *to advise*
relajante *relaxing*
la ciencia *science*
el alma (f.) *soul*
el espíritu *spirit*
el cuerpo *body*
la mente *mind*
estar en conexión *to be connected*
la relajación, físico/a

(18) **Foro** Observe el texto en el que participa el maestro Buendía. ¿Dónde encuentra normalmente este tipo de textos? ¿Participa usted en foros como este?

☐ libros   ☐ Internet   ☐ televisión

(19) **El maestro Buendía** Lea la nota biográfica del maestro Buendía. ¿Cuál ha sido su formación? ¿Dónde ha viajado?

(20) **a. Lista de consejos** Revise las respuestas del maestro Buendía a los internautas y escriba una lista de consejos para relajarse.

b. Preguntar ¿Tiene usted alguna pregunta para Domingo Buendía? Escríbala.

(21) **El yoga** ¿Usted o algún conocido practica yoga? ¿Qué efectos positivos tiene? Comente con sus compañeros. ¿Qué hace usted para mantener equilibrio en su vida?

22 **a. Leer** Lea el artículo sobre la jornada laboral en España. ¿Qué es la jornada flexible? ¿Existe en su país? ¿Cuál es el horario laboral de su país?

TIEMPO PARA TODO

España es uno de los países europeos que más horas dedica al trabajo. ¿Cómo se puede mejorar la productividad sin trabajar tanto tiempo? Algunas de las recomendaciones son flexibilizar los horarios y limitar las horas de trabajo en la oficina.

La flexibilidad horaria permite a los trabajadores decidir la hora de entrada y salida del trabajo para conciliar la vida personal y la profesional.

Limitar las horas de trabajo es otra posibilidad. Un ejemplo es la política de "luces apagadas". Establece una hora de salida exacta, y el trabajador tiene que organizarse mejor para hacer su trabajo antes de esa hora.

Para muchos trabajadores tener un buen horario es más importante que tener un buen sueldo. No tener el suficiente tiempo libre es un factor de estrés muy importante que nos hace rendir menos en el trabajo.

b. Anotar Anote las conclusiones del artículo.

1. Algunas recomendaciones para mejorar el horario laboral son...
2. La política de "luces apagadas" establece...
3. Para muchos trabajadores es más importante...

c. Calendario Marque en el calendario su tiempo de ocio y de trabajo. Compare su calendario semanal con el de un(a) compañero/a. ¿Quién tiene mayor equilibrio?

	lunes	martes	miércoles	jueves	viernes	sábado	domingo
9:00 h–17:00 h							
17:00 h–22:00 h							

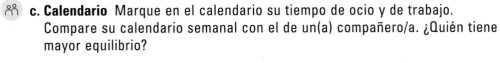

23 **[p] y [t]** La **p** y la **t** en español tienen los siguientes sonidos. Escuche estos trabalenguas y después intente repetirlos.

"Tres tristes tigres comen trigo en un trigal."
"El que poca papa gasta, poca papa paga."

24 **a. El mate** Lea el texto e indique qué tipo de actividad de ocio describe.

☐ cultural ☐ deportiva ☐ social

Reunirse con la familia y los amigos a tomar mate es una costumbre social en varios países de América Latina, especialmente Argentina y Uruguay. La yerba mate es una hierba que se bebe en infusión, su origen es muy antiguo y tiene propiedades estimulantes.

b. Contestar ¿Qué es el mate? ¿En qué países se toma especialmente? ¿Conoce otros ritos sociales particulares del mundo hispano?

Vocabulario *cont.*

la voz (*pl.* voces) *voice*
oriental, la India, la psicología, la meditación, el silencio
⑲
la formación *education*
㉑
el efecto
㉒
la jornada flexible *flexible workday*
mejorar *to improve*
flexibilizar *to make flexible*
la flexibilidad horaria *schedule flexibility*
la entrada *arrival*
la salida *departure*
conciliar *to reconcile*
la política *policy*
la luz apagada *lights off*
establecer (zc) *to establish*
mejor *better*
suficiente *enough*
rendir (e:i) *to perform*
menos *less*
europeo/a, dedicar, la productividad, la recomendación, limitar, la oficina, decidir, la posibilidad, exacto/a, el factor

Comparar experiencias

● Para ti, ¿es **mejor** tener un buen sueldo o un buen horario?
■ Para mí, el horario flexible es **más importante que** el dinero.

6A.6 Comparatives: adjectives/adverbs

Vocabulario
㉓
el trabalenguas *tongue twister*
㉔
deportivo/a *sporting*
reunirse *to meet, to gather*
el mate *mate*
la hierba *herb*
la propiedad *property*
estimulante *stimulating*
el rito *ritual*
la lluvia *rain*
cultural, social, la infusión

SAM: Actividades pp. 119–122

Ⓢ Practice more at **vhlcentral.com.**

TAREA FINAL

Vivir el arte

Escriba una lista de tres actividades de ocio que ha realizado últimamente.

Teatro, cine, libros, música…

 Pregunte a su compañero/a por las actividades de su lista.

¿Has ido al cine a ver…?

Recomiende a su compañero/a alguna de las actividades de su lista.

Tienes que leer…

Elijan tres actividades ideales para un fin de semana con lluvia.

YO PUEDO...

• **Puedo hablar de mis actividades de ocio.**

Complete el horario semanal con sus actividades de ocio.

	lunes	martes	miércoles	jueves	viernes	sábado	domingo
por la mañana							
por la tarde							
por la noche							

• **Puedo expresar frecuencia.**

Escriba con qué frecuencia realiza las siguientes actividades.

• **Puedo describir mi día.**

Relate en un diario sus actividades de esta semana.

• **Puedo dar consejos.**

Responda con un consejo.

Ir al cine.

....

Estar con los amigos.

....

Ir a la montaña.

....

"He comido muy mal."

....

"Esta semana he dormido poco."

....

GRAMÁTICA FUNCIONAL

 Tutorials

6A.1 Express quantity

Adverbs of quantity 11.4

- Use the adverbs **mucho** (*a lot*), **bastante** (*enough; quite a bit*), and **poco** (*little, seldom*) to say how often people perform different activities.

> Corro **bastante**, pero voy **poco** al gimnasio.
> *I run **quite a bit**, but I **rarely** go to the gym.*

- Place these adverbs immediately following the verb they modify. Remember that adverbs are invariable, so they never change form.

> ¿Vas **mucho** a ese restaurante?
> *Do you **often** go to that restaurant?*

- Use **no** + [*verb*] + (**casi**) **nada** to express *not at all*.

> ¿Bailas mucho?
> *Do you dance a lot?*
>
> No, no bailo **casi nada**.
> *No, I **hardly** dance **at all**.*

6A.2 Express negation

Double negatives 12.3

- Use the expressions **ni... ni...** (*neither . . . nor . . .*), **nunca** (*never*), and **nada** (*nothing*) to make negative statements. Say **no** + [*verb*] + [*negative expression*].

> **No** me gusta **ni** el cine **ni** el teatro.
> *I **don't** like the movies **or** the theater.*

¡OJO!

Unlike in English, you must use double (or sometimes triple!) negatives in this construction. This means you might use a negative expression in Spanish (**nunca, nada**) in cases where you would use an indefinite word in English (*ever, anything*).

- When making a negative statement, always place a negative word before the conjugated verb. Remember that when a statement begins with **no**, **nunca**, etc., all elements of that statement must be negative.

> ¡**No** le gusta hacer **nada**!
> *He **doesn't** like to do **anything**!*

> Pedro **no** termina **nunca** la tarea.
> *Pedro **doesn't ever** finish the homework.*

- You can also place the negative expression at the beginning of a sentence, before the verb.

> **Nunca** vamos a la playa.
> *We **never** go to the beach.*

- Use **ni... ni...** when listing several items, activities, etc.

> No quiero **ni** bailar **ni** cantar **ni** escuchar música.
> *I don't want to dance, sing, **or** listen to music.*

¡Póngalo en práctica!

G1 **Ordenar** Ordene las palabras para escribir oraciones completas.

1. bastante / Juan / viajar
....

2. poco / bailar / nosotros
....

3. trabajar / Mariela y tú / mucho
....

4. casi nada / tú / comer
....

5. ir a clase de yoga / poco / yo
....

6. navegar por Internet / ustedes / mucho
....

G2 **Completar** Complete las oraciones.

> no   ni
> nada   nunca

1. Maite .... va .... a la biblioteca.
2. Tú .... comes .... fruta .... verduras.
3. El profesor .... llega tarde.
4. Juliancito .... come ....
5. .... vamos .... al museo .... al concierto.
6. Ramón .... sale .... los jueves.
7. ¡Mi madre .... entiende ....!
8. .... quiero comprar .... este suéter .... ese otro.

G3 **No me gusta nada** Responda a las preguntas con negaciones dobles.

1. ¿Te gusta el tango o la salsa?
....
2. ¿Haces deporte con frecuencia?
....
3. ¿Bebes té o café en el desayuno?
....
4. ¿Pedro trabaja o estudia?
....
5. ¿Vosotros vais de excursión con frecuencia?
....
6. ¿Ustedes saben mucho de informática?
....

 Practice more at **vhlcentral.com**.

6A.3 Ask about and indicate frequency

Expressions of frequency 11.8

- Use the word **vez** (*time*) to talk about frequency. Note the spelling change in the plural, **veces**.

  > Roberto va a yoga tres **veces** a la semana.
  > *Roberto goes to yoga three **times** a week.*

- Use the construction [*number*] + **vez/veces** + **al/a la** + [día/semana/mes/año, *etc.*] to say how often something happens.

  > Viajamos a México **dos veces al año.**
  > *We travel to Mexico **twice (two times) a year.***

- As you learned in 2B.3, **a veces** means *sometimes*.

  > **A veces** vamos a la playa, pero nunca vamos a la piscina.
  > ***Sometimes** we go to the beach, but we never go to the pool.*

¡OJO!

You have learned three words in Spanish to say *time*: **el tiempo, la hora,** and **la vez.** Use **el tiempo** to discuss time in a general sense: ¿Qué haces en tu tiempo libre? Use **la hora** to refer to a time of day: ¿Qué hora es? Use **la vez** to talk about an instance or occasion: ¿Cuántas veces has visto *El Señor de los Anillos?*

6A.4 Describe your day

Present perfect 5.3, 5.3.1

Expressions of time 11.6

- Use the present perfect (**el pretérito perfecto**) to talk about past actions that are connected to the present. The **pretérito perfecto** tells what a person *has done*.

  > ¿Alguna vez **has leído** *Cien años de soledad?*
  > *Have you ever **read** One Hundred Years of Solitude?*

- The **pretérito perfecto** is a compound tense composed of two parts: **haber** + [*past participle*]. **Haber** is an irregular verb.

HABER			
(yo)	he	(nosotros/as)	hemos
(tú)	has	(vosotros/as)	habéis
(usted, él, ella)	ha	(ustedes, ellos/as)	han

- Form the past participle of regular verbs by adding -ado to the stem of -ar verbs and -ido to the stem of -er and -ir verbs.

hablar		hablado
comer	→	comido
vivir		vivido

¡Póngalo en práctica!

G4 **Oraciones** Escriba oraciones completas usando las pistas. Agregue **al** o **a la** para formar expresiones de frecuencia.

1. Ángeles / 4 veces / ir a la piscina / semana

2. 1 vez / tú y yo / mes / ver una película

3. mis padres / comer verduras / día / 2 veces

4. año / tú y Luis / viajar a Caracas / 3 veces

5. mes / yo / ir de excursión / 2 veces

G5 **Relacionar** Elija la opción correcta para completar cada oración.

1. Mi hermana y yo...   4. Usted...
2. Tus vecinos...   5. Yo...
3. Tú...   6. Vosotros...

	a. ha conocido al presidente.
	b. habéis estudiado química.
	c. han viajado a Canadá.
	d. hemos alquilado esta película tres veces.
	e. he comido dos platos de arroz.
	f. has dormido la siesta hoy.

G6 **El participio** Escriba el participio de cada verbo.

1. tomar ....
2. recibir ....
3. aprender ....
4. dar ....
5. hablar ....
6. leer ....

Practice more at **vhlcentral.com.**

GRAMÁTICA FUNCIONAL

- When the stem of an **-er** or **-ir** verb ends in **-a, -e,** or **-o,** add a written accent mark to the **i** of the **-ido** ending.

  Hemos **reído** mucho.
  *We have **laughed** a lot.*

- You will learn irregular past participles in **7B.1.**

- The past participle does not change in form depending on the subject; only the form of **haber** changes.

  Ustedes **han ido** a Puerto Rico y yo también **he ido** a Puerto Rico.
  *You **have gone** to Puerto Rico and I **have gone** to Puerto Rico, too.*

- Use the **pretérito perfecto** with time expressions such as **alguna vez** (*ever*), **ya** (*already*), and **todavía no** (*not yet*) to talk about things people have or have not done.

  ¿Alguna vez has estado en San Miguel de Allende?
  *Have you **ever** been to San Miguel de Allende?*

  Yo **ya** he estado, pero Beatriz **todavía no** ha ido.
  *I've **already** been, but Beatriz has **not** gone **yet**.*

- Never place these expressions between **haber** and the past participle; unlike in English, the two components of the **pretérito perfecto** cannot be separated.

  Ya hemos conocido a la novia de Luis.
  *We have **already** met Luis's girlfriend.*

- The **pretérito perfecto** can also be used to refer to the recent past, especially in a context that is still connected to the present (*this morning, this week*, etc.). Expressions such as **hoy, esta semana, este mes,** and **este año** often accompany this usage.

  ¿Dónde **has estado** hoy?
  Te **he llamado** y no **has contestado.**
  *Where **were** you today?*
  *I **called** you and you **didn't answer.***

  Ay, **he dejado** el celular en casa.
  Esta tarde **he ido** al médico.
  *Oh, I **left** my cell phone at home.*
  *This afternoon I **went** to the doctor.*

- To form the present perfect of **hay,** use **ha habido.**

  Ha habido algunos problemas con la productividad del equipo.
  *There **have been** some problems with the team's productivity.*

¡OJO!

The **pretérito perfecto** is widely used in Spain, especially in reference to the recent past. However, its use is limited in Latin America, and in some countries the **pretérito indefinido** exclusively is used in all contexts presented here.

¡Póngalo en práctica!

G7 **Conversaciones** Complete las conversaciones con **ya, alguna vez,** o **todavía no.**

- Silvia, ¿(1)........................ has ido a Bolivia?
- No, (2)........................ he ido, pero me gustaría ir.

- ¿Ustedes (3)........................ han ido a ver la exposición de Chillida?
- Sí, la vimos ayer. ¿Tú no?
- No, (4)........................ he ido.

G8 **El pretérito perfecto** Escriba oraciones completas usando el pretérito perfecto.

1. ¿? / alguna vez / (usted) / estudiar física
....

2. cenar en ese restaurante / ya / esta semana / (nosotros)
....

3. Gloria / conocer al amor de su vida / todavía no
....

4. (tú) / ¿? / ya / estar en México
....

5. ir al dentista / ¿? / (tú y Carlos) / ya / este año
....

G9 **Hoy** Complete el párrafo de manera lógica.

Hoy (yo) (1)........................ llamado a Antonio y (2)........................ comido juntos. Después Antonio ha (3)........................ (ir) a trabajar y yo (4)........................ comprado el periódico y he (5)........................ (leer) todas las noticias. A las seis, mis hermanos (6)........................ llegado y hemos (7)........................ (preparar) la cena para la familia. Luego a las siete y media (8)........................ cenado todos juntos.

6A.5 Give advice

Expressions to give advice 5.10, 9

- Use the question **¿Por qué no** + [*verb*]? to offer someone advice.

    ¿Por qué no descansas un poco?
    Why don't you rest for a bit?

- To be more assertive in your recommendation, use the construction **tener + que +** [*infinitive*].

    Tienes que descansar.
    You have to rest.

- Use **tener + que +** [*infinitive*] to express other sorts of obligations.

    Tengo que pasar por el banco esta tarde.
    I have to go by the bank this afternoon.

6A.6 Compare experiences

Comparatives: adjectives/adverbs 4.4.2, 12.7

- Use the construction **más/menos +** [*adjective/adverb*] **+ que** to compare some characteristic of two people, items, or experiences.

    La salud es **más importante que** el dinero.
    *Health is **more important than** money.*

    Ariel corre **menos a menudo que** Ramón.
    *Ariel runs **less often than** Ramón.*

- When comparing two nouns, make sure the adjective agrees in gender and number with the first noun.

    Mi tía es **más seria que** mi tío.
    *My aunt is **more serious than** my uncle.*

- Some adjectives have irregular comparative forms. Use these forms instead of **más +** [*adjective*].

ADJETIVO	COMPARATIVO
bueno/a	**mejor**
malo/a	**peor**
grande	**mayor**
pequeño/a	**menor**
joven	**menor**
viejo/a	**mayor**

    Este hotel es **mejor que** ese hotel.
    *This hotel is **better than** that hotel.*

- When **grande** and **pequeño/a** refer to age, use the irregular comparatives **mayor** and **menor**; for size, use the regular comparatives.

    Yo soy **mayor que** Carlos.   Esta casa es **más grande que** esa.
    *I'm **older than** Carlos.*   *This house is **bigger than** that one.*

- The adverbs **bien** (*well*) and **mal** (*badly*) have the irregular comparative forms **mejor** and **peor**.

    Marisol baila **peor** que yo, pero canta **mejor**.
    *Marisol dances **worse** than I (do), but she sings **better**.*

¡Póngalo en práctica!

G10 **Transformar** Transforme las oraciones usando **¿Por qué no...?** o **tener + que.**

1. Tienes que dormir más.
   ....
2. ¿Por qué no estudia en la biblioteca?
   ....
3. Tienen que comer más verduras.
   ....
4. ¿Por qué no tomáis unas vacaciones?
   ....
   ....

G11 **Comparar** Escriba oraciones comparativas con **más** o **menos.**

   Modelo: la computadora / cara / el televisor
   La computadora es más cara que el televisor. OR *La computadora es menos cara que el televisor.*

1. el tren / económico / el avión
   ....
2. bailar / divertido / pintar
   ....
3. mis padres / serios / yo
   ....
4. practico deporte / frecuentemente / tú
   ....
5. haces yoga / a menudo / Ignacio
   ....
6. llegamos / temprano / los vecinos
   ....

G12 **Comparativos irregulares** Complete las oraciones con comparativos irregulares.

1. El profesor habla .... (bien) que yo.
2. Su hermano es .... (joven) que yo.
3. Mis abuelos son .... (viejo) que ese hombre.
4. Clara baila .... (mal) que Daniel.
5. Los calamares son .... (malo) que las gambas.
6. Estas naranjas son .... (bueno) que esas.
7. Tengo dos hermanos .... (grande).
8. En este restaurante sirven .... (bueno) tapas que en el otro.

 Practice more at **vhlcentral.com.**

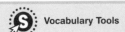
Tiempo libre

estar dirigido/a a	to be aimed at
el descuento	discount
la diversión	fun
la excursión	excursion
la exposición	exhibition
la fiesta popular	festival
el ocio	leisure
las personas mayores	the elderly
bailar	to dance
hacer cerámica	to make pottery
mirar	to watch; to look at
navegar por Internet	to surf the Internet
organizar	to organize
pintar	to paint
pasivo/a	passive
casi nunca	hardly ever
dos veces al mes	twice a month
mucho	a lot
nunca	never
una vez a la semana	once a week

Un día perfecto

a ver	let's see
¡Felicitaciones!	Congratulations!
¿Por qué no...?	Why don't you...?
pues	well
el bienestar	well-being
el consejo	piece of advice
el cuestionario	questionnaire
la siesta	nap
dar un paseo	to take a walk

dormir (o:ue) la siesta	to take a nap
hacer ejercicio	to exercise, to work out
reír (e:i)	to laugh
reservar	to set aside
tener que	to have to
cansado/a	tired
esta semana	this week
este año	this year
este mes	this month
hoy	today
todavía no	not yet
todo el día	all day
ya	already

Domingo Buendía

el alma (f.)	soul
la autoayuda	self-help
la ciencia	science
el cuerpo	body
el efecto	effect
la empresa	company
la entrada	arrival
el equilibrio	balance
el espíritu	spirit
el factor	factor
la flexibilidad horaria	schedule flexibility
la formación	education
la hierba	herb
la India	India
la infusión	infusion
el/la internauta	Internet user
la jornada flexible	flexible workday

la lluvia	rain
la luz apagada	lights off
el/la maestro/a	master; teacher
el mate	mate
la meditación	meditation
la mente	mind
la oficina	office
la política	policy
la posibilidad	possibility
la productividad	productivity
la propiedad	property
la psicología	psychology
la recomendación	recommendation
la relajación	relaxation
el rito	ritual
la salida	departure
el silencio	silence
el trabalenguas	tongue twister
la voz (pl. voces)	voice
aconsejar	to advise
conciliar	to reconcile
decidir	to decide
dedicar	to dedicate
dirigir (j)	to run; to manage
establecer (zc)	to establish
estar en conexión	to be connected
flexibilizar	to make flexible
limitar	to limit
mejorar	to improve
rendir (e:i)	to perform
reunirse	to meet, to gather
cultural	cultural
deportivo/a	sporting
estimulante	stimulating
europeo/a	European
exacto/a	exact
físico/a	physical
oriental	oriental
relajante	relaxing
social	social
suficiente	enough
mejor	better
menos	less

Variación léxica

la siesta ⟷ el camarón (Ven.) ⟷ el motoso (Col.)

el trabajo ⟷ el camello (Col.) ⟷ el curro (Esp.) ⟷ el laburo (Arg.) ⟷ la pega (Chi.)

mirar la televisión (Amér. L.) ⟷ ver la televisión (Esp.)

¡Felicitaciones! (Amér. L.) ⟷ ¡Felicidades! ⟷ ¡Enhorabuena! (Esp.)

6B

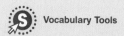
AMOR A DISTANCIA

Planes de viaje

 Viajes de ida y vuelta

¿Viaja usted en...?	✈ ☐ avión	🚇 ☐ tren	
	🚗 ☐ coche	🚲 ☐ bici	
¿Compra billete de...?	↪ ☐ ida	🔄 ☐ ida y vuelta	
¿Pasa la noche en un...?	🏕 ☐ camping	🛏 ☐ hotel	
	🏙 ☐ apartamento	🏘 ☐ albergue	
¿Reserva el hotel y el vuelo en...?	🌐 ☐ Internet	🌍 ☐ una agencia de viajes	

¿Va usted a...?	🏙 ☐ ciudades	
	🏘 ☐ pueblos	
	🏖 ☐ playas	
¿Qué hace usted?	🏄 ☐ hacer deporte	
	🏛 ☐ ver monumentos	
	📷 ☐ tomar fotos	

Hacer planes

- ¿Qué **vas a hacer** estas vacaciones?
- ■ **Voy a viajar.** Tengo unos amigos en Caracas pero no **sé** si voy a ir allí. Y, después, **voy a ir** a la playa. Y tú, ¿qué planes tienes?
- No sé...

6B.1	**ir + a +** [*infinitive*] **saber**

Vocabulario

(1)

ida y vuelta *round-trip*
el avión *plane*
el tren *train*
la bici(cleta) *bike (bicycle)*
el billete *ticket*
pasar la noche *to spend the night*
el camping *campsite*
el albergue *hostel*
el vuelo *flight*
tomar fotos *to take pictures*

(2)

el castillo *castle*
el paseo a caballo *horseback ride*
el caballo *horse*
con encanto *charming*

(3)

el puente (*Esp.*) *long weekend*
el dinero *money*

---

1 **Cuestionario** ¿ Qué tipo de viajes hace usted normalmente? Complete el cuestionario y compare sus respuestas con las de su compañero/a.

> Modelo: *Yo normalmente viajo en avión y él/ella en coche...*

2 **Oferta** Fíjese en la oferta de la agencia Ida y vuelta. ¿Qué actividades le gustan?

Viajes
IDA y VUELTA

★ *Pueblos de Castilla Fines de semana con encanto*

Información y reservas:

Agencia de viajes **IDA Y VUELTA:**
C/ Alcalá, 51.
Teléfono: 91 435 06 88

www.idayvuelta.com

- Paseos por el campo
- Excursión a los castillos (Sepúlveda, Pedraza, Turégano)
- Paseos a caballo
- Hoteles con encanto

3 **Planes** Escuche la conversación de estas tres personas. ¿Qué planes tienen?

	Jaime	Elisa	Tomás
Va a ir a unos pueblos de Segovia con una amiga.			
Va a hacer un viaje por Europa en verano.			
Va a descansar.			
Va a dar un paseo a caballo.			
Va a comer con su familia.			
No va a salir de Madrid.			

4 **Las vacaciones** Imagine que tiene una semana de vacaciones. Pregunte a su compañero/a qué planes tiene. Puede decir **Voy a..., No sé si...**

¿Cómo vais a ir a Pedraza?

Vamos a ir en coche, primero a Segovia y después de Segovia, a Pedraza.

¿Vais a pasar por Sepúlveda?

Sí, vamos a pasar por Turégano y después por Sepúlveda.

---

5 **Destinos** Lea la conversación entre Ana y Tomás y observe el mapa. ¿Adónde van Ana y su prima? ¿Por qué pueblos pasan en su ruta?

6 **Preposiciones** Observe la ruta del mapa y escriba las preposiciones que faltan.

Vamos .... Madrid .... Santander .... Burgos.
Vamos .... coche.

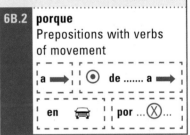

7 **Una ruta interesante** Organice una ruta interesante por su país para una persona que está de visita por una semana. Su compañero/a le pregunta cómo ir y qué lugares visitar.

MI EXPERIENCIA

8 **Planes de viaje** Pregunte a sus compañeros sus planes para los próximos viajes. ¿Tienen planes similares?

Hablar de viajes y medios de transporte

- ¿Cómo vais a ir a España?
- Vamos a ir **en** coche porque no me gusta el tren. Vamos **de** París **a** Lyon. Después vamos **de** Lyon **a** Madrid y pasamos **por** Barcelona.

6B.2	**porque** Prepositions with verbs of movement

Vocabulario

5

¿Cómo vas? *How are you going there?*

ir en... *to go by (means of transportation)*

pasar por *to go via*

la ruta *route*

8

volver (o:ue) *to return*

¡OJO!

The preposition **en** is used to talk about means of transportation, as in **en avión, en coche/carro, en tren.** An important exception is **a pie** *(on/by foot).*

SAM: Actividades pp. 123–125

Practice more at **vhlcentral.com**.

Reservas

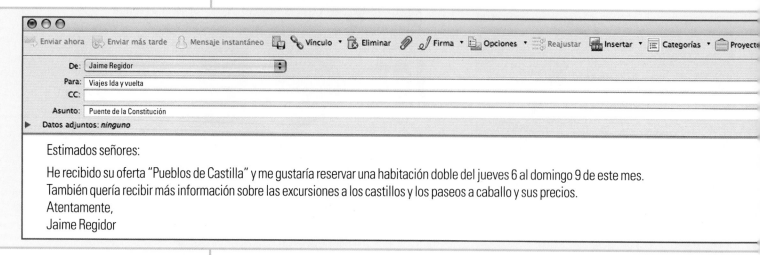

De: Jaime Regidor
Para: Viajes Ida y vuelta
CC:
Asunto: Puente de la Constitución
▶ **Datos adjuntos:** *ninguno*

Estimados señores:

He recibido su oferta "Pueblos de Castilla" y me gustaría reservar una habitación doble del jueves 6 al domingo 9 de este mes.
También quería recibir más información sobre las excursiones a los castillos y los paseos a caballo y sus precios.
Atentamente,
Jaime Regidor

Empezar y terminar una carta

Estimados/as señores/as:
Atentamente,

6B.3 Formulas for written correspondence

Solicitar información o un servicio

- Hola, buenos días. **Me gustaría reservar** una habitación.
- Muy bien. **¿Quería** una habitación doble o individual?
- Doble, por favor.

6B.4 me gustaría + [*infinitive*]
quería + [*noun/infinitive*]

Vocabulario

⑨

el reencuentro *reunion*
Estimados señores: *Dear Sirs:*
estimado/a *dear*
el/la señor(a) *sir/madam*
reservar *to reserve; to book*
la habitación doble *double room*
Atentamente, *Sincerely,*
la reserva *reservation*
la habitación individual
single room
confirmar

---

⑨ **Pueblos de Castilla** Lea el correo electrónico de Jaime y señale en la tabla las respuestas correctas.

Jaime escribe para...	reservar un billete.	reservar una habitación.	confirmar la reserva.
Quiere una habitación...	individual.	doble.	triple.
Quiere información sobre...	excursiones.	ofertas para el verano.	hoteles.

⑩ **Relacionar** Relacione las frases con la información de los recuadros.

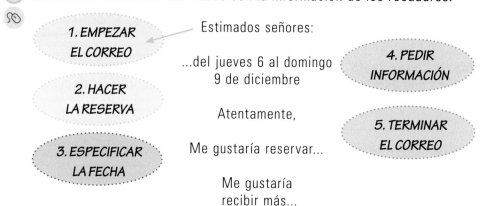

1. EMPEZAR EL CORREO

2. HACER LA RESERVA

3. ESPECIFICAR LA FECHA

Estimados señores:

...del jueves 6 al domingo 9 de diciembre

Atentamente,

Me gustaría reservar...

Me gustaría recibir más...

4. PEDIR INFORMACIÓN

5. TERMINAR EL CORREO

⑪ **Escribir** Escriba un correo a uno de estos hoteles para reservar una habitación. Indique fechas, tipo de habitación, y pida información de precios.

HOTEL AGUADULCE (ALMERÍA)

HOTEL VISTANEVADA (CANDANCHÚ, PIRINEOS)

HOTEL TOLEDO (TOLEDO)

De:
Para:
CC:
Asunto:
▶ **Datos adjuntos:** *ninguno*

(12) **a. Llamada** Ana llama a su amiga Carmen que está en Galicia. Ordene el diálogo. Luego escuche la conversación y compruebe si el orden es correcto.

- ¿Diga? `1`
- ¡Ah, perfecto! Bueno, pues nada. Nos vemos pronto. ☐
- ¡Buen viaje! ☐
- Genial. Oye, una cosa... ¿Ya has reservado la habitación? ☐
- Hola, Carmen, soy Ana. ¿Qué tal? ¿Tienes ya el billete? ☐
- Sí, soy yo. ☐
- ¿Está Carmen, por favor? ☐
- Sí, ya lo he comprado. Voy a llegar a las nueve y media de la noche. ☐
- Sí, he reservado una habitación doble. ☐
- Estupendo. Voy a buscarte a la estación y vamos a cenar. ☐

b. Subrayar Subraye cómo se contesta el teléfono y cómo se pregunta por alguien.

(13) **Representar** Imagine que tiene tres días de vacaciones. Llame a un(a) amigo/a por teléfono para organizar el transporte y el alojamiento de un fin de semana en Barcelona. Represente la conversación con un(a) compañero/a.

MI EXPERIENCIA

(14) **La agencia de viajes**
Prepare un viaje con un(a) amigo/a para el fin de semana. Llame a una agencia de viajes para reservar todo.
Su compañero/a es el/la empleado/a de la agencia.

Observe el billete y subraye la información clave del viaje.

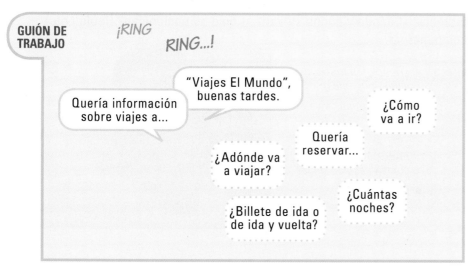

GUIÓN DE TRABAJO

¡RING RING...!

"Viajes El Mundo", buenas tardes.

Quería información sobre viajes a...

¿Cómo va a ir?

¿Adónde va a viajar?

Quería reservar...

¿Billete de ida o de ida y vuelta?

¿Cuántas noches?

**Hablar por teléfono
Proponer un plan y aceptar una propuesta**

- ¿Diga/Dígame/Hola/Bueno?
- ¿Está Carmen, por favor?
- Sí, soy yo./Sí, (con) él/ella habla.
- ¿**Vamos** a cenar el jueves?
- Vale/De acuerdo, perfecto.
- ¡Genial!

6B.5	Expressions for phone conversations
6B.6	ir + a + [infinitive/noun]

Vocabulario

(12)
¿Diga?/¿Dígame?/¿Hola?/¿Bueno? *Hello?*
¿Está Carmen? *Is Carmen there?*
genial *great*
estupendo/a *wonderful*

(13)
el alojamiento *lodging*
el parador nacional *state-run hotel in a Spanish historic building*
el paisaje *landscape*
a pesar de *despite*
acondicionado/a *equipped*
asequible *affordable*
el convento, histórico/a

Paradores nacionales
Son hoteles con mucho encanto.
Algunos son antiguos castillos o conventos. Están situados en lugares históricos o con paisajes impresionantes. Son muy populares, porque a pesar de ser hoteles muy bien acondicionados, los precios son asequibles.

SAM: Actividades pp. 126–128

Julia y Felipe, amor a distancia

Felipe y Julia son novios pero viven en países diferentes, a miles de kilómetros. Él es chileno, vive en Santiago y trabaja en un banco. Julia vive en Vancouver y trabaja en un colegio. Los dos buscan la manera de estar juntos, pero no es fácil.

Entrevistador: *Felipe, ¿dónde conociste a Julia?*

Felipe: En Canadá, en Vancouver. Fue el año pasado en un viaje de trabajo. La conocí allá en una cena, con mis compañeros... Así pasó.

Entrevistador: *Entonces, desde el año pasado no están juntos. Es mucho tiempo, ¿no?*

Julia: Sí, sí, mucho tiempo.

Entrevistador: *¿Y cómo es una relación a esta distancia?*

Felipe: Pues... chateamos, hablamos por teléfono, nos comunicamos con la cámara web, pero no siempre es fácil por la diferencia de horario. Pero tenemos planes para esta Navidad.

Entrevistador: *¿Ah, sí? ¿Qué planes tienen para estas vacaciones?*

Felipe: Vamos a estar acá, en Chile, tres semanas porque Julia tiene vacaciones en el colegio. Claro, es un viaje muy largo.

Entrevistador: *¿Van a viajar por Chile o van a estar todo el tiempo en Santiago?*

Felipe: Para Julia es la primera vez en Chile y acá es verano, un tiempo fantástico para viajar. Vamos a ir a la playa, a Viña del Mar con mi familia y después, vamos a ir al sur, a visitar los lagos y el volcán Osorno.

Julia: Y a mí me gustaría también ir al Parque Pumalín, pero está un poco lejos. Vamos a ver...

Felipe Daza y Julia Navarro, muy enamorados, en el aeropuerto de Santiago de Chile.

Vocabulario

(15)

el amor a distancia *long-distance love*

el amor *love*

los novios *sweethearts*

los miles *thousands*

los/las dos *both*

fácil *easy*

allá *there*

chatear *to chat (on the Internet)*

la cámara web *webcam*

acá *here*

el lago *lake*

el volcán

OPINIÓN

¿Alguna vez ha tenido un(a) novio/a a distancia?

¿Qué es lo más importante para mantener una relación a distancia?

15 **Amor a distancia** ¿De qué habla Felipe en esta entrevista?

1. de las tradiciones navideñas en Chile ☐
2. de sus planes para la visita de Julia ☐
3. del paisaje de Chile ☐

16 **Julia y Felipe** Responda a las preguntas.

1. ¿Cuándo y dónde conoció Felipe a Julia?
2. ¿Tienen planes para estas vacaciones? ¿Qué van a hacer?
3. ¿Cuánto tiempo va a estar Julia en Chile?
4. ¿Por qué se titula la entrevista "Amor a distancia"?
5. ¿Cómo se comunican Felipe y Julia?

17 **Relaciones a distancia** ¿Tiene usted amistades o relaciones familiares a distancia? ¿Cuándo y dónde se ven? ¿Cómo se comunican? Hable con su compañero/a.

Modelo:
- *¿Tienes familiares que viven muy lejos?*
  - *Sí, mis primos viven en Tokio.*
- *¿Ah, sí? ¡Qué interesante! ¿Y cómo te comunicas con ellos?*
  - *Pues, ...*

PARQUE PUMALÍN, CHILE

El parque tiene una extensión de unas 325 mil hectáreas. Allí están los últimos bosques vírgenes del sur de Chile. Nuestra excursión en kayak nos permite entrar en una parte del parque, correspondiente a la zona de Chiloé Continental, que tiene fiordos rodeados de vegetación, cascadas, termas a orillas del mar y lagos escondidos.

Duración: *5 días / 4 noches*
Lugar: *Patagonia Norte, Chile*
Dificultad: *moderada*
Época: *octubre a abril*
Salida: *Puerto Montt*
Alojamiento: *cabañas y campamento*
Actividades del viaje: *kayak de mar, trekking, observación de flora y fauna*
Fechas: *del 23 al 27 de enero*
          del 01 al 05 de febrero
          del 01 al 05 de marzo
          del 31 de marzo al 03 de abril
Otros viajes:

[CONSULTAS]   [RESERVAS]

Vocabulario

18

la extensión *area*
el bosque virgen *virgin forest*
permitir *to allow*
rodeado/a de *surrounded by*
la cascada *waterfall*
las termas *hot springs*
la orilla *shore*
escondido/a *hidden*
la dificultad *difficulty*
moderado/a *moderate*
la época *time of year*
la cabaña *cabin*
el campamento *campsite*
el trekking *hiking*
la observación de flora y fauna *wildlife viewing*
las consultas *questions*
la publicidad *advertisement*
la hectárea, el kayak, el fiordo, la vegetación, la duración, la Patagonia

20

el pasaje de avión *plane ticket*
el auto *car*
regalarse *to give oneself*

18 **Parque Pumalín, Chile** Lea la publicidad de Internet y responda a las preguntas.

1. ¿De qué lugar habla esta publicidad?
2. ¿Qué tipo de turismo ofrece?

    ☐ turismo natural   ☐ turismo monumental   ☐ turismo de aventuras

3. ¿Dónde podría realizarse este tipo de turismo en su país?

[d] y [j] finales

19 **a. [d] y [j] finales** Algunos hablantes de español pronuncian las [d] y [j] finales muy relajadas. Escuche las palabras terminadas en [d] y [j] y repítalas.

    Madrid   *ciudad*   *reloj*

b. Repetir Al formar los plurales o cuando la palabra siguiente empieza con vocal, la [d] y la [j] deben pronunciarse claramente. Escuche las palabras y repítalas.

    ciudades   *Madrid está en España.*   *El reloj es bonito.*

c. Practicar Practique esta conversación con su compañero/a.

> He dejado el reloj en el hotel de Madrid.

> Yo también olvidé un reloj en un viaje a Valladolid.

20 **Variación léxica** ¿Cómo se dice? Complete esta actividad con las palabras relacionadas con el transporte que figuran en el recuadro.

.... España
.... México
.... Argentina

.... España
.... Caribe
.... Argentina

.... España
.... América Latina

auto	coche
autobús	colectivo
billete	guagua
carro	pasaje

Practice more at vhlcentral.com.

SAM: Actividades pp. 129–134

TAREA FINAL

Un viaje con la clase

 ¿Por qué no se regala un viaje con sus compañeros de clase?

 ¿Qué lugares de interés van a visitar? ¿Qué actividades van a hacer? Hable con un(a) compañero/a.

Vamos a ir...
Vamos a ver...
Vamos a...

 Hablen de sus viajes y elijan uno. A continuación piensen en cómo llegar (transporte y ruta). Organicen la reserva de los billetes y de las habitaciones.

¿Vamos a ir en bici? ¿En avión?
¿Vamos a ir de... a...?
¿Vamos a pasar por...?

 Pregunten por sus planes de viaje y juntos decidan cuál es el mejor.

¿Qué planes tienen para el viaje con la clase?

YO PUEDO...

- **Puedo hablar de mis planes de viajes con otras personas.** - - - - - -
  Anote sus planes para las próximas vacaciones.

- **Puedo decir cómo llegar a un destino, con qué tipo de transporte y a través de qué ruta.**
  Describa una ruta por su país.

- **Puedo escribir un correo electrónico para reservar una habitación en un hotel.** - - - - - -
  Escriba un breve correo electrónico indicando sus datos de viaje.

- **Puedo hablar por teléfono.** - - - - - -
  ¿Cómo se contesta el teléfono y se pregunta por alguien? Escríbalo.

Las próximas vacaciones ......
....
....
....

....
....
....
....

¿...?
¿...?

GRAMÁTICA FUNCIONAL

 Tutorials

6B.1 | Make plans

ir + a + [*infinitive*] `5.16.1`
saber `5.1.2`

- To ask someone what he/she is going to do, say **¿Qué va(s) a hacer?** Answer using the construction **ir + a +** [*infinitive*] to talk about plans.

> Maribel, **¿qué vas a hacer** este verano?
> Maribel, **what are you going to do** this summer?

> En agosto, **voy a viajar** a Acapulco.
> In August, **I'm going to travel** to Acapulco.

- As with other infinitive constructions, remember to conjugate the first verb (**ir**), and use the second verb in the infinitive.

- Use the verb **saber** (*to know*) to express your degree of certainty about plans. **Saber** has an irregular **yo** form.

SABER

(yo)	**sé**	(nosotros/as)	sabemos
(tú)	sabes	(vosotros/as)	sabéis
(usted, él, ella)	sabe	(ustedes, ellos/as)	saben

> **¿Sabes si** vienen Juana y Pepe?
> **Do you know** if Juana and Pepe are coming?

- Use **no + saber + si +** [*verb*] to express uncertainty.

> Cristián quiere ir a la fiesta, pero **no sabe si puede.**
> Cristián wants to go to the party, but **he doesn't know if he can.**

- Use **saber** to talk about knowledge of facts and **conocer** to talk about familiarity with people, places, and things.

> **Conozco** a Julián, pero **no sé** si viene hoy.
> **I know** Julián, but **I don't know** if he's coming today.

6B.2 | Talk about trips and means of transportation

Prepositions with verbs of movement `10.1, 10.5, 10.12, 10.16`

- Use the prepositions **a** (*to*), **de** (*from*), **en** (*in; by*), and **por** (*via, through*) with verbs of movement to add detail.

> Vamos **de** Boston **a** Chicago **en** autobús y pasamos **por** Buffalo.
> We go **from** Boston **to** Chicago **by** bus and we pass **through** Buffalo.

- Common verbs of movement are **ir, viajar, pasar,** and **volver** (*to return*). **Volver** has an o→ue stem change.

- Use **porque** (*because*) to give explanations.

> Vamos en autobús **porque** es caro viajar en avión.
> We're going by bus **because** it's expensive to travel by plane.

Practice more at vhlcentral.com.

¡Póngalo en práctica!

G1 **Completar** Complete las oraciones para contar qué va a hacer cada persona.

1. Luisa .... (comprar) un carro nuevo.
2. Ignacio y Teresa .... (visitar) a Iván.
3. Yo .... (ir) a la boda de mi prima.
4. Laura y yo .... (pasar) el día en la playa.
5. Tú .... (trabajar) en esa heladería.
6. ¿Ustedes .... (salir) esta noche?
7. Julia .... (hacer) un viaje en avión.
8. Ricardo y tú .... (tomar) el ferry para Menorca.

G2 **Saber** Complete la conversación con las formas correctas de **saber**.

> Armando, ¿(1)...................... si Sara viene a la cena esta noche?

> Mmm, no (2)...................... Me ha explicado que no (3)...................... si tiene que trabajar esta noche.

> ¿Y Carla y Alberto (4)...................... a qué hora vamos a empezar?

> Mmm, no (5)...................... Ahora llamo a Carla para preguntarle.

G3 **Preposiciones** Complete las oraciones con **a, de, en** o **por**.

1. Mis padres siempre viajan .... tren.
2. Compramos un billete para ir .... Lima.
3. ¿Vas a pasar .... Miami?
4. Ana viaja .... autobús porque cuesta menos.
5. Voy a salir .... Guadalajara por la mañana.
6. ¿Van a ir .... coche o .... pie?
7. Felipe vuelve .... casa el viernes.
8. Nuria y yo vamos a pasar .... la farmacia.
9. Todos los miércoles voy .... Buenos Aires .... Montevideo.

GRAMÁTICA FUNCIONAL

6B.3 Begin and end a letter

Formulas for written correspondence

- Begin a formal letter with **Estimado/a(s)** + [*name*].

  Estimados Álvaro y Eva: **Estimada** Sra. Martínez:
  Dear Álvaro and Eva,   *Dear Mrs. Martínez,*

- If you are writing to an unknown or unspecified recipient, write **Estimados señores:** (*Dear sirs:*).

- Close a letter by writing **Atentamente,** (*Sincerely,*).

6B.4 Request information or services

Formulas of courtesy 5.10, 5.11

- Use the formulas **Me gustaría** + [*infinitive*] and **Quería** + [*noun/infinitive*] to request services and information.

  Me gustaría reservar una habitación doble. También **quería** información sobre excursiones al Parque Pumalín.
  I'd like to reserve a double room. I'd also like information about trips to Pumalín Park.

- These expressions are considered more polite than saying **Quiero** (*I want*).

6B.5 Talk on the phone

Expressions for phone conversations

- Use the expressions **¿Diga?, ¿Dígame?** (primarily in Spain), **¿Hola?,** or **¿Bueno?** to answer the phone.
- To ask if someone is home or available, say **¿Está** + [*name*], **+ por favor?**
- To **answer** *Speaking/This is (s)he,* say **Sí, soy yo** or **Sí, (con) él/ella habla.**

• ¿Hola?	• *Hello?*
▪ ¿Está Gladys, por favor?	• *Is Gladys there, please?*
• Sí, soy yo. / Sí, con ella habla.	• *Yes, this is she.*

6B.6 Propose a plan and accept

Irregular verbs 5.1.2 ir a + [*infinitive*] 5.16.1

- Use **ir + a** + [*noun/infinitive*] to propose a plan.

  ¿Vamos al Museo Picasso?   **¿Vamos a** esquiar?
  Shall we go to the Picasso   *Shall we go skiing?*
  Museum?

- Use affirmative expressions such as **De acuerdo, Perfecto, Genial, Estupendo, Vale,** or **Muy bien** to agree.

¡OJO! In **3A.2**, you learned to use **ir + a** + [*place*] to talk about physically going to a place. Use **ir + a** + [*infinitive*] to say what you are *going to do*.

¡Póngalo en práctica!

G4 **Correo electrónico** Complete el correo electrónico.

(1)........................ señores:

Quería información sobre sus visitas guiadas a Valparaíso porque voy a viajar a Chile en agosto.

(2)........................ ,
Joaquín Ramírez

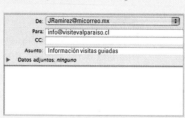

De:	JRamirez@micorreo.mx
Para:	info@visitevalparaiso.cl
CC:	
Asunto:	Información visitas guiadas
▶ Datos adjuntos:	*ninguno*

G5 **Pedir información** Pida información o ayuda para cada situación.

1. comprar un billete

....

2. información sobre los paseos a caballo

....

3. reservar una habitación doble

....

4. un mapa de Chile

....

5. tomar el ferry

....

G6 **Conversación telefónica** Complete la conversación telefónica.

a	estupendo	vamos
de acuerdo	Hola	vas
está	soy yo	

- • ¿(1) ....?
- ▪ Hola, ¿(2) .... Verónica, por favor?
- • Sí, (3) ....
- ▪ Verónica, soy Carolina. ¿Qué tal?
- • Muy bien, ¿y tú?
- ▪ Bien. Oye, ¿a qué hora (4) .... a llegar esta noche?
- • El autobús llega a las 7:20.
- ▪ Genial. Voy (5) .... buscarte a la estación y luego vamos a cenar, ¿de acuerdo?
- • (6) ...., pero ¿(7) .... a casa primero? Así me cambio de ropa.
- ▪ Muy bien. Nos vemos a las 7:20 en la estación.
- • (8) .... ¡Hasta luego!

 S Practice more at **vhlcentral.com**.

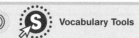
Planes de viaje

¿Cómo vas?	How are you going there?
ida y vuelta	round-trip
el albergue	hostel
el avión	plane
la bici(cleta)	bike (bicycle)
el billete	ticket
el caballo	horse
el camping	campsite
el castillo	castle
el dinero	money
el paseo a caballo	horseback ride
el puente	long weekend
la ruta	route
el tren	train
el vuelo	flight
ir en...	to go by (means of transportation)
pasar la noche	to spend the night
pasar por	to go via
tomar fotos	to take pictures
volver (o:ue)	to return
con encanto	charming

Reservas

Atentamente,	Sincerely,
¿Diga?/¿Dígame?/ ¿Hola?/¿Bueno?	Hello?
¿Está Carmen?	Is Carmen there?
Estimados señores:	Dear Sirs:
el alojamiento	lodging
el convento	convent
la habitación doble	double room
la habitación individual	single room
el paisaje	landscape
el parador nacional	state-run hotel in Spanish historic building
el reencuentro	reunion
la reserva	reservation
el/la señor(a)	sir/madam
confirmar	to confirm
reservar	to reserve; to book
acondicionado/a	equipped
asequible	affordable
estimado/a	dear
estupendo/a	wonderful
genial	great
histórico/a	historic
a pesar de	despite

Julia y Felipe

el amor a distancia	long-distance love
el amor	love
el auto	car
el bosque virgen	virgin forest
la cabaña	cabin
la cámara web	webcam
el campamento	campsite
la cascada	waterfall
las consultas	questions
la dificultad	difficulty
los/las dos	both
la duración	duration
la época	time of year
la extensión	area
el fiordo	fjord
la hectárea	hectare
el kayak	kayak
el lago	lake
los miles	thousands
los novios	sweethearts
la observación de flora y fauna	wildlife viewing
la orilla	shore
el pasaje de avión	plane ticket
la Patagonia	Patagonia
la publicidad	advertisement
las termas	hot springs
el trekking	hiking
la vegetación	vegetation
el volcán	volcano
chatear	to chat (on the Internet)
permitir	to allow
regalarse	to give oneself
escondido/a	hidden
fácil	easy
moderado/a	moderate
rodeado/a de	surrounded by
acá	here
allá	there

Variación léxica

aquí ⟷ acá (*Amér. L.*)

el billete ⟷ el boleto (*Méx.*) ⟷ el pasaje (*Amér. L.*)

el camping ⟷ el campamento

¡Genial! ⟷ ¡Chévere! (*Amér. C.*) ⟷ ¡Chido! (*Méx.*) ⟷ ¡Fenomenal!

la reserva (*Esp., Arg.*) ⟷ la reservación (*Amér. L.*)

tomar una foto ⟷ hacer una foto (*Esp.*) ⟷ sacar una foto (*Amér. L.*)

Estrategias

(1) Mostrar interés en la conversación Lección 5A

If you want to improve your conversational skills, show interest in what the other person is saying! Use expressions such as **¿Ah, sí?**, **¡Qué interesante!**, or **¿Y qué pasó?** to improve communication and make the conversation more interesting.

○ Un(a) amigo/a le cuenta lo siguiente. Reaccione. Muestre interés.

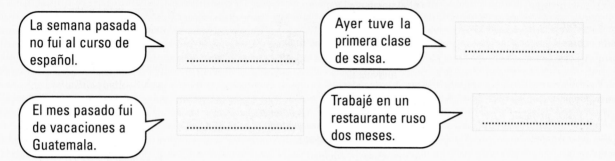

(2) Aprender vocabulario con ayuda de grupos de palabras Lección 5B

One strategy for learning and remembering new vocabulary is to study pairs or groups of words together: antonyms, masculine and feminine forms, synonyms, or related words.

○ Revise el vocabulario nuevo que ha aprendido en la Lección 5B y cree grupos de palabras para retenerlas mejor.

(3) Ganar tiempo para pensar Lección 6A

Sometimes it is helpful to hesitate or "buy time" in a conversation in order to give a more thoughtful response. In these cases, you can use filler words or expressions, such as **bueno**, **pues**, and **a ver**, that give you time to formulate your answer.

○ Escuche de nuevo la conversación de la **Actividad 4a** de la **Lección 6A** y fíjese cómo usan palabras de relleno los interlocutores para ganar tiempo.

(4) Subrayar palabras clave Lección 6B

You don't need to know every word and detail in a text in order to understand its meaning. Focus on the words and expressions you already know and then look up the key words that are central to the text's meaning.

○ Subraye las palabras y la información clave en este texto.

HOTEL LA BARRANCA (ESCAPADA ROMÁNTICA)

Pase un fin de semana romántico en un entorno natural muy especial.

Fines de semana de mayo y junio descuentos en habitaciones dobles.

La Barranca es un acogedor hotel a solo 30 minutos de Madrid, en un valle al pie de La Maliciosa, en plena Sierra de Guadarrama, donde podrá disfrutar de un ambiente tranquilo en compañía de su pareja. El hotel se encuentra a 40 minutos del aeropuerto Madrid-Barajas, a 30 de Segovia, a 15 del Monasterio de El Escorial y a 15 minutos de las pistas de esquí. Aquí puede disfrutar de unos días de relax en un hotel de montaña rodeado de naturaleza.

Organizamos excursiones por la sierra y visitas a las localidades cercanas.

Competencias

HABLAR DE PARENTESCOS

1 **Mi familia** Responda ¿quién es?

1. El padre de mi madre: ....

2. La hermana de mi padre: ....

3. La hija de mi hijo: ....

4. El hijo de mi madre: ....

5. La madre de mi padre: ....

HABLAR DEL PASADO Y FUTURO

2 **Clasificar** Clasifique las formas verbales en el siguiente cuadro.

	Pretérito perfecto	Pretérito indefinido	Futuro
ser			
estar			
ir			

he estado
voy a ir
fui
estuve
he ido
voy a ser
voy a estar
he sido
fui

NARRAR BIOGRAFÍAS

3 **Javier Bardem** Elija el texto A o el texto B y pregunte los datos que faltan a su compañero/a.

A

Javier Bardem nació en Las Palmas (Islas Canarias, España) en (1)................ . Antes de trabajar en el cine, estudió (2)................... y jugó al rugby en la selección nacional. Sus primeras películas fueron *Jamón, jamón* y (3).......................... . En (4)............... recibió el premio del público al mejor actor europeo. Ha trabajado con importantes directores como Almodóvar y (5)..................... .
En febrero de 2008 ganó un Oscar por su actuación en una película de (6)......................... .

B

Javier Bardem nació en (1) ....
.... en 1969.
Antes de trabajar en el cine, estudió pintura y jugó (2) .... en la selección nacional. Sus primeras películas fueron (3) .... y *Huevos de oro*. En 1997 recibió el premio del (4) .... Ha trabajado con importantes directores como (5) .... y .... En febrero de (6) .... ganó un Oscar por su actuación en una película de los hermanos Coen.

HABLAR DE VIAJES EN PASADO

4 **Preposiciones** Complete el texto con la preposición apropiada.

El verano pasado estuvimos (1) .... Mallorca de vacaciones. Primero fuimos (2) .... Valencia (3) .... tren y allí tomamos un barco (4) .... la isla. La vuelta fue (5) .... avión, directamente (6) .... Mallorca (7) .... Ginebra. ¡Fue fantástico!

HACER PLANES

5 **Nuestros planes** Señale qué actividades van a hacer mañana. Pregunte a su compañero/a por sus planes y anótelos en la tabla.

Actividades	Yo	Mi compañero/a
ir al cine		
estudiar español		
cenar con amigos		
trabajar		
estar en casa		
hacer las compras		
ir de viaje		
leer un libro		

 Video

¿Estrés? ¿Qué estrés?

Ya ha visto cómo aprovechar el tiempo libre y buscar el bienestar cada día en actividades de ocio y con sus amigos. En este episodio de **Flash Cultura** va a conocer cómo el estrés afecta la vida de los madrileños y qué opciones tienen para relajarse.

Estrategia

False cognates

From time to time you will come across some *false friends* or *false cognates* (words that appear to mean the same in English and Spanish but actually don't) such as **librería**, which means *bookstore* in Spanish, not *library*. So be very careful or you might misinterpret the whole sentence! Can you think of another example of a false friend?

(1) Preguntas Hable con un(a) compañero/a de las siguientes preguntas. ¿Durante las vacaciones les gusta viajar a ciudades grandes para visitar museos y teatros o a lugares pequeños para disfrutar de la naturaleza? ¿Cuál es su lugar de retiro favorito para descansar del trabajo y el estrés?

(2) Mirar Mire este episodio de **Flash Cultura**. No se distraiga (*Don't get distracted*) cuando escuche muchas voces al mismo tiempo. Concéntrese en las preguntas del presentador y en las respuestas.

Siempre hay cola para todo.

Vocabulario útil

el bullicio *hubbub*
la cola *line*
combatir *to fight*
con prisa *in a hurry*
mantenerse sano/a *to stay healthy*
remar *to row*
el retiro *retreat*
trotar *to jog*

Para mantenerse sano es importante aprender a luchar contra el estrés.

Estrategia

Filler words

In Spanish, as in English, many people use filler words (*muletillas*) when they speak: when you don't know how to continue in a sentence you may use **este, o sea,** or **es/quiero decir**. Also, when you need to get your thoughts together or want to rephrase a sentence you may use **pues,** or **a ver/veamos/vamos a ver**.

(3) Indicar A partir de lo que vio en el video, clasifique las siguientes actividades en la columna correspondiente.

caminar por la calle   conseguir entradas para un espectáculo
ir al trabajo   pasear con tu perro   recibir un mensaje
remar en el Retiro   tomar una siesta   tomar un baño árabe
trotar   viajar en autobús   visitar un museo

Da estrés	Combate el estrés

(4) Escribir Con un(a) compañero/a, escriba una conversación entre dos amigos que planean visitar Madrid; uno/a está muy entusiasmado/a, el/la otro/a es pesimista.

Modelo: • *¿Por qué no vamos al museo?*

 Practice more at **vhlcentral.com**.

Unidad 7

Jorge Drexler, cantautor uruguayo

Guadalupe Rodríguez, una nueva etapa

AVANCE

El mundo del trabajo

7A

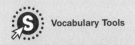 **Vocabulary Tools**

HOY POR HOY

El día a día

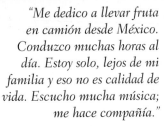

Profesión y vocación

"Me dedico a llevar fruta en camión desde México. Conduzco muchas horas al día. Estoy solo, lejos de mi familia y eso no es calidad de vida. Escucho mucha música; me hace compañía."

Carlos. San Antonio, Texas (EE.UU.)

"Enseño inglés a niños, pero mi verdadera vocación es la traducción. Por las tardes traduzco literatura juvenil inglesa. Me gusta trabajar sola."

Gabriela. Santa Fe (Argentina)

"Soy bombero; es mi vocación desde pequeño. El trabajo en equipo y la preparación física y psicológica son muy necesarios. Es una profesión de riesgo."

Pedro. A Coruña (España)

"Nuestros espectáculos son el motor de nuestras vidas. El trabajo de bailaoras es el trabajo de un gran equipo, pero viajamos mucho y es difícil compaginar familia y trabajo."

Ana y Carmela. Granada (España)

Hablar del trabajo

- ● ¿A qué te dedicas?
- ■ Me dedico a la traducción. Traduzco textos literarios.

7A.1	**dedicarse a** + [*noun/ infinitive*] Verbs with irregular **yo** forms: **traducir, conducir**

Vocabulario

①

el día a día *daily life*

dedicarse a (hacer) algo *to do something (for a living)*

el camión *truck*

conducir (zc) *to drive*

solo/a *alone*

(hacer) compañía *(to keep) company*

el/la bombero/a *firefighter*

en equipo *as a team*

el riesgo *risk*

traducir (zc) *to translate*

juvenil *for young people*

el/la bailaor(a) *flamenco dancer*

difícil *difficult*

compaginar *to combine*

el/la camionero/a *truck driver*

apagar *to put out*

① a. Profesión y vocación El trabajo marca nuestro día a día. ¿Qué profesiones representan las fotografías del reportaje?

b. ¿A qué te dedicas? Compruebe sus hipótesis. Lea los textos y relacione las oraciones.

1. Soy camionero. ......
2. Son bailaoras. ......
3. Es profesora. ......
4. Soy bombero. ......

a. Me dedico a apagar incendios.
b. Me dedico a transportar fruta en camión.
c. Se dedican al baile flamenco.
d. Se dedica a la enseñanza.

c. Asociar ¿Con qué profesiones del texto asocia estas características?

Lejos de la familia	Trabajar en equipo	Profesión de riesgo	Preparación física	Trabajar solo/a
camionero				

② Transformar Transforme estas oraciones como en el ejemplo.

> **Modelo:** Estoy jubilado, cuido de mis nietos.
> *Me dedico a cuidar de mis nietos.*

1. Es bailarina, baila tango.
   ....
2. Eres diseñador, haces diseño gráfico.
   ....

③ a. Completar ¿A qué se dedican Gabriela y Carlos? Complete las oraciones.

1. Gabriela: "También .... (traducir) textos del inglés al español."
2. Carlos: " .... (Conducir) un camión de 14 toneladas."

b. Responder ¿Quiénes de los entrevistados cree usted que trabajan por vocación? ¿Quiénes no, y por qué?

UN DÍA DE ESPECTÁCULO

- [ ] "A las 21:00 h me visto y me maquillo para el espectáculo."

- [ ] "El ensayo es a las 18:00 h. Después descanso un poco y me ducho."

- [ ] "Después del espectáculo cenamos y a medianoche me acuesto."

- [ ] "Me despierto a las 7:00 h, el resto del grupo se despierta más tarde."

---

4 **Un día de espectáculo** Observe la vida de la bailaora Carmela, un día de espectáculo. Asocie las oraciones con las imágenes y compare sus respuestas con las de su compañero/a.

5 **a. Bomberos** ¿Cuál es la rutina de un bombero? ¿Cree que ve mucho a su familia?

b. La rutina de un bombero Escuche a la mujer de Pedro, el bombero, en un programa de radio. Lea el texto y seleccione la opción correcta.

> Los horarios de mi marido son diferentes de los del resto de la familia. Cuando los niños se acuestan /se despiertan, mi marido se acuesta/ se despierta. A veces los niños ven a su padre cuando se viste de bombero/ desayuna. ¡Les gusta mucho!

6 **Las rutinas** Describa la rutina de uno de los entrevistados. Su compañero/a debe adivinar de quién se trata.

🎤 MI EXPERIENCIA

7 **Mi día a día** Describa su día a día a su compañero/a.

GUIÓN DE TRABAJO

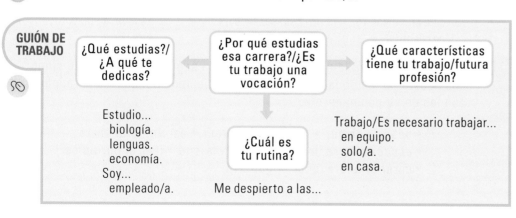

¿Qué estudias?/ ¿A qué te dedicas?

¿Por qué estudias esa carrera?/¿Es tu trabajo una vocación?

¿Qué características tiene tu trabajo/futura profesión?

Estudio...
biología.
lenguas.
economía.
Soy...
empleado/a.

¿Cuál es tu rutina?

Me despierto a las...

Trabajo/Es necesario trabajar...
en equipo.
solo/a.
en casa.

Describir hábitos

- ¿A qué hora **se acuesta** usted?
- **Me acuesto** tarde y me **despierto** temprano. **Me visto** en cinco minutos.

7A.2 **despertarse (e:ie)**
acostarse (o:ue)
vestirse (e:i)

Vocabulario *cont.*

el incendio *fire*
el baile flamenco *flamenco dance*
la enseñanza *teaching*
la vocación, transportar
② ――――――――――――
el bailarín/la bailarina *dancer*
el diseño gráfico *graphic design*
③ ――――――――――――
por vocación *by vocation*
④ ――――――――――――
vestirse (e:i) *to get dressed*
maquillarse *to put makeup on*
el ensayo *rehearsal*
ducharse *to shower*
acostarse (o:ue) *to go to bed*
despertarse (e:ie) *to wake up*
tarde *late*
temprano *early*
levantarse *to get up*
el hábito
⑤ ――――――――――――
la rutina

SAM: Actividades pp. 135–137

Intereses

Hablar de acciones que ocurren en este momento

- ¡Hola, Carmela! ¿Qué **estás haciendo**?
- ¡Hola, Ana! **Me estoy vistiendo**. ¿Y tú?
- **Estoy desayunando**. ¿Salimos a correr más tarde?

7A.3 **estar** + [*present participle*]

Vocabulario

8

estar haciendo algo *to be doing something*
jugar (u:ue) *to play*
al mismo tiempo *at the same time*

10

atender (e:ie) *to attend to*
el pasatiempo *pastime*
el trabajo voluntario *volunteer work*

> No puedo hacer dos cosas al mismo tiempo, primero una cosa y después otra, jefe.

---

8 **a. Fotos** ¿Qué están haciendo en estas fotos el bombero, el camionero, las bailaoras y la profesora de inglés de la Actividad 1 (pág. 164)?

> "Aquí estoy leyendo con mi hijo. Le estoy enseñando inglés."
>
> **4**

> "Aquí estoy durmiendo la siesta en el jardín de mi casa."

> "Ahora mismo estamos haciendo deporte."

> "En este momento estoy jugando con mi hija."

b. Gerundios Complete las formas del gerundio regular.

1. jugar - jug............. 2. hacer - hac............. 3. conducir - conduc.............

9 **a. Acciones** ¿Qué están haciendo las personas en estas imágenes?

Está durmiendo. ☐
Están leyendo. ☐
Está yendo a clase. ☐

b. Gerundios irregulares Ahora, complete las formas del gerundio irregular.

1. ir - .... 2. dormir - .... 3. leer - ....

10 **Escuchar** Un cliente llama a una empresa. ¿Por qué está ocupada la Sra. Aguilera? Escuche al secretario y ordene sus respuestas.

☐ Está atendiendo a un cliente. ☐ Está saliendo de la oficina. ☐ Está hablando por otra línea.

11 **a. Observar** Fíjese en la historieta. Observe la segunda viñeta. ¿Qué cinco cosas está haciendo la persona al mismo tiempo? Compare sus respuestas con las de su compañero/a.

> • beber • comer • conducir • dormir • escribir una carta
> • escuchar la radio • hablar por teléfono • leer el periódico
> • mirar la tele • tocar la guitarra

Está mirando la tele, ...

b. Contestar Y usted, ¿puede hacer muchas cosas a la vez? ¿Qué está haciendo ahora?

- le(s) encanta(n)...
- le(s) interesa(n)...
- le(s) preocupa(n)...

> estar en forma

> la literatura juvenil

> dormir la siesta

> los riesgos de su profesión

> traducir

> jugar con sus hijos

> la música

> estar lejos de la familia

12 **Intereses** ¿Qué cree usted que les encanta, les interesa y les preocupa a nuestros profesionales?

1. A Pedro, el bombero, le preocupan...

2. A Carmela y a Ana, las bailaoras, les interesa...

3. A Carlos, el camionero, le gusta...

4. A Gabriela, la profesora, le encanta...

13 **a. Encuesta** Escuche la encuesta que le hacen a un joven universitario en la calle y anote la información.

Gustos	Intereses	Preocupaciones
el tailandés, ...		

b. Responder ¿Qué le encanta, le interesa y le preocupa a usted? ¿Y a su compañero/a?

14 **Por ejemplo...** Termine las oraciones con ejemplos. Pregunte a su compañero/a qué ejemplos usó y por qué.

1. Me interesan todos los deportes, por ejemplo...

2. Una comida latinoamericana que me encanta es, por ejemplo...

3. Me preocupan muchas cosas, por ejemplo...

15 **Mi profesor(a)** ¿Qué está haciendo su profesor(a)? ¿Qué cree que le interesa/preocupa?

MI EXPERIENCIA

16 **Preguntas** ¿Qué es lo que más le gusta de aprender español? ¿Qué aspecto le parece más interesante? ¿Qué es lo más difícil de aprender una lengua? Compare sus respuestas con las de su compañero/a.

Hablar de intereses

- ¿Qué **te** interesa y qué **te** preocupa?
- **Me** interesa la literatura. **Me** encantan las siestas y **me** preocupa estar lejos de casa.
- Y a tu madre, ¿qué **le** interesa y **le** preocupa?

7A.4 Verbs like **gustar: encantar, interesar, preocupar**

Estrategia

Dar ejemplos
Me encanta la música, **por ejemplo**, el flamenco, la rumba...

Vocabulario

12

interesar *to be of interest*

estar en forma *to be fit, in (good) shape*

preocupar *to worry; to concern*

13

la preocupación *worry; concern*

dar un ejemplo *to give an example*

el tailandés *Thai*

Tailandia *Thailand*

la trompeta *trumpet*

la salud *health*

el jazz, los cómics

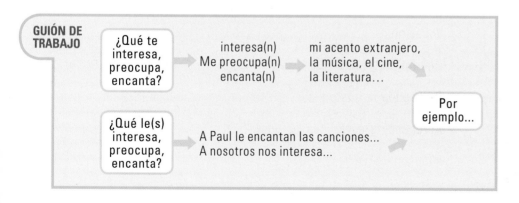

GUIÓN DE TRABAJO

¿Qué te interesa, preocupa, encanta? → interesa(n) Me preocupa(n) encanta(n) → mi acento extranjero, la música, el cine, la literatura... →

¿Qué le(s) interesa, preocupa, encanta? → A Paul le encantan las canciones... A nosotros nos interesa... → Por ejemplo...

SAM: Actividades pp. 138–140

Practice more at **vhlcentral.com.**

Jorge Drexler tocando la guitarra

Jorge Drexler, cantautor uruguayo

Jorge Drexler nació en Montevideo en 1964. Como él dice, es hijo de un judío alemán y de una uruguaya. Estudió medicina como sus padres y hermanos, pero su verdadera vocación siempre fue la música. Desde los 30 años escribe letras de canciones y compone música.

En 1995 llegó a España, donde vive desde entonces. Ha editado una decena de discos, ha escrito canciones para otros músicos y también para el cine. Ganó un Oscar en 2005 por la canción *Al otro lado del río*, compuesta especialmente para la película *Diarios de motocicleta* de Walter Salles. Actualmente está preparando un nuevo disco y está dando conciertos por muchos países europeos y americanos.

Su día a día cambia si tiene conciertos o se dedica a componer en casa. Cuando no está de viaje, se despierta temprano y lleva a su hijo al colegio. Eso sí, siempre se acuesta tarde.

Últimamente está colaborando con una ONG, Puente al sur, que se dedica a proyectos culturales y solidarios para el desarrollo en Uruguay.

Expresar acciones en desarrollo

- ¿Qué estás haciendo ahora?
- Actualmente estoy escribiendo nuevas canciones.

7A.5 actualmente, últimamente

Vocabulario

17

el/la cantautor(a) *singer-songwriter*
decir *to say; to tell*
el/la judío/a *Jew*
uruguayo/a *Uruguayan*
la letra *lyrics*
la canción *song*
componer *to compose*
desde entonces *since then*
entonces *then*
editar *to edit; to release*
el disco *album*
especialmente *specially*
actualmente *currently*
dar un concierto *to give a concert*
estar de viaje *to be away*
últimamente *lately*
preparar

18

madrugar *to get up early*
la variedad *variety*
la diversidad *diversity*

---

17 a. **Jorge Drexler** Observe la foto. ¿Conoce a nuestro protagonista? ¿Es actor? Lea su biografía y compruébelo.

b. **¿Verdadero o falso?** Indique si las oraciones son verdaderas (**V**) o falsas (**F**).

	V	F
1. A Jorge Drexler le encanta la música, pero se dedica a la medicina.	☐	☐
2. Jorge Drexler, médico de profesión, se dedica a la música.	☐	☐
3. Es un cantautor uruguayo, pero actualmente vive en España.	☐	☐
4. Colabora con una ONG porque le interesan los temas sociales.	☐	☐

c. **Años** ¿Qué representan estos tres años en su vida?

1. 2005 ....
2. 1995 ....
3. 1994 ....

18 **Completar** Escuche la entrevista a Jorge Drexler del año 2009 y complete su ficha. Escuchará la entrevista dos veces.

Profesión: ....

Vocación: ....

Día a día: ....

De España le gustan: ....

Actualmente está: ....

Idiomas: ....

19 **El acento uruguayo** ¿Recuerda qué dice Jorge Drexler sobre su acento uruguayo? Escuche de nuevo estos fragmentos de la entrevista y fíjese cómo pronuncia las palabras marcadas.

> "Yo **empecé** a estudiar música con **cinco** años y luego estudié otra carrera. Estudié **medicina**."

> "Estoy sobre todo descansando, viendo amigos, **leyendo**, viendo películas."

20 **a. Leer** Lea estos reportajes sobre tres artistas hispanos.

Silvio Rodríguez es un cantautor, guitarrista y compositor cubano. A él le gusta llamarse "trovador". A pesar de que su carrera comenzó hace unos 50 años, dice que todavía le asustan las luces y las cámaras. Este artista participa de manera activa en la política. En muchas ocasiones ha usado su arte para defender los ideales en los que cree.

Julieta Venegas es una de las cantautoras más famosas de América Latina. Nació el 24 de noviembre de 1970 en Tijuana, una ciudad mexicana que queda muy cerca de la frontera con los Estados Unidos. Por eso habla desde pequeña tanto español como inglés y tiene un gran conocimiento de las dos culturas. Toca varios instrumentos e interpreta diferentes estilos musicales.

Joan Manuel Serrat, el Nano, es un cantautor de origen catalán. Siempre le gustó tocar la guitarra, pero nunca pensó en convertirse en músico profesional. De hecho, ¡es ingeniero agrónomo! Al comienzo de su carrera solo interpretaba canciones catalanas, pero luego decidió escribir canciones en español. Con el tiempo, se convirtió en uno de los artistas más influyentes del mundo hispano.

b. Contestar ¿Qué tienen en común estos artistas?

1. Tienen aproximadamente la misma edad. ☐
2. Son cantautores. ☐
3. Hablan varios idiomas. ☐

21 **Escribir** Elija otro cantautor hispano y escriba un breve reportaje sobre su vida. Si lo desea, puede llevar a la clase una de sus canciones y compartirla con sus compañeros/as.

Vocabulario *cont.*

rico/a *rich*

el hebreo *Hebrew*

la energía, vital

20

el/la guitarrista *guitarist*

el/la trovador(a) *troubadour*

a pesar de que *in spite of the fact that*

asustar *to frighten*

la frontera *border*

tanto... como *both . . . and*

interpretar *to perform*

convertirse (e:ie) en *to become*

el/la (ingeniero/a) agrónomo/a *agronomist*

de hecho *in fact*

influyente *influential*

░ O P I N I Ó N ░

¿Qué profesión valora usted más: médico o cantante? ¿Por qué?

Vocabulario

21

elegir (j) (e:i) *to choose*

22

el periódico *newspaper*

el conflicto *conflict*

22 **Oraciones** En grupos, formen oraciones lógicas con los siguientes elementos. Gana el grupo que consigue hacer más oraciones en menos tiempo.

Estamos (dormir) poco...

Estamos (colaborar) con la Cruz Roja...

Estamos (aprender) español...

Estamos (leer) el periódico...

Estamos (buscar) una casa en Acapulco...

Estamos (escuchar) música...

ÚLTIMAMENTE

ACTUALMENTE

... porque nos (interesar) la actualidad.

... porque nos (preocupar) los países en conflicto.

... porque nos (encantar) la música latina.

... porque nos (preocupar) muchas cosas.

... porque nos (interesar) los países hispanos.

... porque nos (encantar) ir allí en verano.

TAREA FINAL

¿Qué estamos haciendo?

Lleve fotos u objetos a clase relacionados con la carrera que está estudiando, sus intereses y sus preocupaciones actuales.

Hable de ello con su compañero/a.

Quiero ser guía turístico/a porque me encanta viajar. En esta foto estoy visitando las pirámides mayas.

Compartan con la clase lo que aprendieron sobre su compañero/a.

Preparen un cartel o una presentación sobre las profesiones, vocaciones, gustos e intereses de la clase.

YO PUEDO...

- Puedo hablar del trabajo.
  ¿A qué se dedican sus familiares?

- Puedo describir hábitos.
  Describa hábitos característicos de una profesión.

- Puedo expresar lo que estoy haciendo y lo que está pasando en este momento.
  Imagine qué están haciendo ahora sus familiares o amigos.

- Puedo hablar de gustos, intereses y preocupaciones.
  ¿Qué le interesa, preocupa, encanta...?

- Puedo expresar lo que hago actualmente.
  ¿Está haciendo algo especial últimamente?

GRAMÁTICA FUNCIONAL Tutorials

7A.1 Talk about work

dedicarse a + [*noun/infinitive*] 5.7.1
Verbs with irregular **yo** forms: **traducir, conducir** 5.1.2

- In **1B.4**, you learned how to inquire about a person's job or profession using the question **¿A qué se/te dedica(s)?** (*form./ fam.*). To answer, use **dedicarse a** + [*noun/infinitive*].

- The verb **dedicarse** is reflexive, so a reflexive pronoun (**me, te, se,** etc.) must be used; this is placed directly in front of the conjugated verb. You will learn more about reflexive verbs in **7A.2**.

DEDICARSE

(yo)	**me** dedico	(nosotros/as)		**nos** dedicamos
(tú)	**te** dedicas	(vosotros/as)		**os** dedicáis
(usted, él, ella)	**se** dedica	(ustedes, ellos/as)		**se** dedican

- You have already learned to talk about someone's profession using **ser** + [*profession*]. With **dedicarse a,** use an infinitive or the noun that describes the profession.

  ¿A qué se dedica tu tío?
  What does your uncle do?

  Se dedica a pintar casas.
  He paints houses.

  Y tú, **¿a qué te dedicas?**
  And you, what do you do?

  Me dedico al diseño gráfico.
  I work in graphic design.

- In **5B.3**, you learned the verb **conocer** (*to know*). **Conocer** has an irregular **yo** form, **conozco.** The verb **traducir** (*to translate*) also has an irregular **yo** form that undergoes the same **c→zc** change; the rest of the forms follow the regular conjugation pattern for **-ir** verbs.

TRADUCIR

(yo)	tradu**zco**	(nosotros/as)	traducimos
(tú)	traduces	(vosotros/as)	traducís
(usted, él, ella)	traduce	(ustedes, ellos/as)	traducen

  ¿Qué lenguas **traduces?**
  What languages do you translate?

  Traduzco del francés al español.
  I translate from French into Spanish.

- The verb **conducir** (*to drive*) has the same **c→zc** change in the **yo** form as **traducir.**

CONDUCIR

(yo)	condu**zco**	(nosotros/as)	conducimos
(tú)	conduces	(vosotros/as)	conducís
(usted, él, ella)	conduce	(ustedes, ellos/as)	conducen

  Conduzco un camión todos los días.
  I drive a truck every day.

¡Póngalo en práctica!

G1 **Elegir** Elija la opción correcta para completar cada oración.

1. Nosotros...   4. Vosotros...
2. Inés...   5. Tú...
3. Yo...

...... a. me dedico a la enseñanza.

...... b. te dedicas a la arquitectura.

...... c. nos dedicamos a apagar incendios.

...... d. os dedicáis al baile flamenco.

...... e. se dedica a cuidar de niños.

G2 **Traducir** Complete las oraciones con la forma correcta de **traducir.**

1. Los estudiantes .... las oraciones del inglés al español.

2. En mi trabajo, a veces .... cartas para mi jefe.

3. Nosotros .... mucho en la clase de latín.

4. Luciana quiere .... este documento del español al portugués.

5. Iván se dedica a .... artículos académicos.

6. ¿Qué lengua .... tú?

G3 **Diálogo** Complete la conversación con las formas correctas de **dedicarse, traducir** y **conducir.**

¿A qué (1)........................ usted?

(2)........................ a la literatura: soy escritor y traductor.

¿Qué lenguas (3)........................ usted?

(4)........................ textos del portugués al español. Y usted, ¿a qué se dedica?

Soy camionero. (5)........................ un camión para una empresa multinacional. (6)........................ a transportar cereales.

GRAMÁTICA FUNCIONAL

Reflexive verbs: **despertarse, acostarse, vestirse** `5.7`
Reflexive pronouns `5.7.1`

- Use the reflexive verbs **despertarse** (*to wake up*), **acostarse** (*to go to bed*), and **vestirse** (*to get dressed*) to describe daily habits. You will know a verb is reflexive when you see the pronoun **se** attached to the infinitive.

	DESPERTARSE	ACOSTARSE	VESTIRSE
(yo)	**me** desp**ie**rto	**me** ac**ue**sto	**me** v**i**sto
(tú)	**te** desp**ie**rtas	**te** ac**ue**stas	**te** v**i**stes
(usted, él, ella)	**se** desp**ie**rta	**se** ac**ue**sta	**se** v**i**ste
(nosotros/as)	**nos** despertamos	**nos** acostamos	**nos** vestimos
(vosotros/as)	**os** despertáis	**os** acostáis	**os** vestís
(ustedes, ellos/as)	**se** desp**ie**rtan	**se** ac**ue**stan	**se** v**i**sten

- **Despertarse, acostarse,** and **vestirse** are stem-changing verbs with e→ie, o→ue, and e→i changes, respectively.

  > **Nos acostamos** a la misma hora, pero (yo) **me despierto** más temprano.
  > *We go to bed at the same time, but I wake up earlier.*

- Reflexive verbs indicate that the subject both performs and receives the action of the verb, showing that the subject is doing something for or to himself, herself, or itself. Place the reflexive pronoun (**me, te, se,** etc.) directly in front of the conjugated verb.

  > **Me visto** en cinco minutos y preparo el desayuno.
  > *I get dressed (I dress myself) in five minutes and I prepare breakfast.*

- Note that **se** is the reflexive pronoun for both the third-person singular and plural forms of reflexive verbs.

  > Raquel **se** acuesta a las 22:00 h, y sus padres **se** acuestan a las 23:00 h.
  > *Raquel goes to bed at 10:00 p.m., and her parents go to bed at 11:00 p.m.*

- You can also use other reflexive pronouns with the infinitive in appropriate contexts.

  > Después de **despertarme**, me visto.
  > *After I wake up, I get dressed.*

- Many reflexive verbs can also be used non-reflexively, but with slightly different meanings. **Me despierto** means *I wake up*, but **despierto a mi hermano** means *I wake my brother up*. Since the person doing the waking is not the recipient of the action, the reflexive pronoun is not used.

  > Mi amiga Carla **se despierta** a las 7:00 h durante la semana.
  > *My friend Carla **wakes up** at 7:00 a.m. during the week.*

  > **Despierto** a mi hermano porque tiene clase a las 8:00 h.
  > *I wake up my brother because he has class at 8:00 a.m.*

¡Póngalo en práctica!

G4 **Pronombres** Escriba el pronombre reflexivo que corresponde a cada verbo conjugado.

1. .... vestimos
2. .... acuesto
3. .... despierta
4. .... vestís
5. .... despiertas
6. .... visten
7. .... acuesta
8. .... visto

G5 **Completar** Complete las oraciones con las formas correctas de los verbos reflexivos.

1. Pablo .... (despertarse) temprano todos los días.
2. En general, nosotros .... (despertarse) a las 7:30 h.
3. Cuando trabajan de noche en el hospital, Adriana y Carmen .... (acostarse) a las 6:00 h de la mañana.
4. Rafael siempre .... (acostarse) muy tarde los viernes.
5. ¿A qué hora .... (acostarse) tú?
6. Los lunes por la mañana .... (vestirse), tomo el desayuno y salgo temprano para clase.

G6 **Los reflexivos** Complete la conversación con la forma correcta del verbo reflexivo.

- ¿A qué hora (1)......................... (acostarse, tú) los sábados?
- (2)......................... (Acostarse, yo) muy tarde y los domingos (3)......................... (despertarse, yo) a las 11:00 h. (4)......................... (ducharse, yo) y después (5)......................... (vestirse, yo) y voy a dar un paseo. ¿Y tú?
- (6)......................... (acostarse, yo) tarde también los sábados, pero los domingos (7)......................... (levantarse, yo) temprano para estudiar. Mi hermana siempre (8)......................... (despertarse) más tarde que yo.

G7 **Verbos reflexivos** Complete las oraciones con la forma correcta de los verbos reflexivos ilustrados.

1. Mario .... temprano.

2. Yo .... y canto.

3. Marta y Raquel .... a la misma hora.

4. Tú .... para ir a la escuela.

 Practice more at **vhlcentral.com.**

GRAMÁTICA FUNCIONAL

7A.3 **Talk about actions that are happening right now**

The present progressive 5.14

- Use the present progressive (**el presente progresivo**) to talk about an action that is currently in progress.

  Estoy preparando la cena.
  I am preparing dinner.

- The **presente progresivo** is a compound tense that consists of two parts: **estar** + [*present participle*]. The present participle (**el gerundio**) of regular verbs is formed by adding **-ando** to the stem of **-ar** verbs and **-iendo** to the stem of **-er** and **-ir** verbs.

habl**ar**	habl**ando**
com**er** →	com**iendo**
viv**ir**	viv**iendo**

- Verbs that end in **-ir** and have a stem change in the present tense also undergo a change in the present participle.

Infinitive	Present tense	Present participle
referir	e:ie refiero	e:i refiriendo
conseguir	e:i consigo	e:i consiguiendo
dormir	o:ue duermo	o:u durmiendo

- If the stem of an **-er** or **-ir** verb ends in a vowel, the present participle ends in **-yendo**. For example: **leer→leyendo**; **oír→oyendo**; **traer→trayendo**.

- **Ser**, **tener**, and **ir** are rarely used in the present progressive. The present participle of the verb **ir** is **yendo**; the present participles of **ser** and **tener** are regular.

7A.4 **Talk about interests**

Verbs like **gustar**: **encantar, interesar, preocupar** 5.11.1

- In **4A.2**, you learned to use **gustar** to express likes. The verbs **encantar** (*to love; to enjoy*), **interesar** (*to be of interest*), and **preocupar** (*to worry*) follow the same pattern. Like **gustar**, they are also used most commonly in the third-person singular and plural with indirect object pronouns.

(a mí)	**me**	encanta
(a ti)	**te**	interesa → + [*singular noun/ infinitive(s)*]
(a usted, a él, a ella)	**le**	preocupa
(a nosotros/as)	**nos**	encantan
(a vosotros/as)	**os**	interesan → + [*plural noun*]
(a ustedes, a ellos/as)	**les**	preocupan

A mí me **encanta** el flamenco, pero a mis padres no **les interesa**.
I love flamenco, but my parents aren't interested in it.

G8 **El gerundio** Escriba el gerundio de cada verbo.

1. reír ....
2. dar ....
3. tomar ....
4. leer ....
5. viajar ....
6. conducir ....
7. compartir ....
8. servir ....

G9 **El presente progresivo** Complete las oraciones con las formas correctas del presente progresivo.

1. Los niños .... (jugar) en la sala.
2. Tomás .... (comer) un sándwich.
3. Yo .... (leer) una novela.
4. Raquel y yo .... (escuchar) la radio.
5. Mi jefa .... (traducir) el documento.
6. Tú y Gustavo .... (hacer) deporte.

G10 **Conversaciones** Complete las conversaciones con la forma correcta del verbo y un pronombre de objeto indirecto.

- Nuria, ¿te interesa la política?
- No, pero (1)........................ (encantar) la historia.

- ¿Les preocupa estar lejos de la familia?
- Sí, (2)........................ (preocupar) bastante.

- ¿A Vicente (3)........................ (interesar) la música clásica?
- No, no (4)........................ (gustar) mucho.

- ¿A José (5)........................ (interesar) los deportes?
- No, no (6)........................ (preocupar) estar en forma.

- Remember that in this construction, the object or activity that is *liked/of interest/worrisome* is the subject of the verb.

> **Me interesa el cine,** pero me encantan **las telenovelas.**
> *I'm interested in film, but I love soap operas.*

- As you learned in **4A.2** with **gustar,** use **a + mí, ti, usted, él, ella, nosotros/as, vosotros/as, ustedes, ellos/as,** or **a** + [*person's name*] for emphasis or clarification.

> **A Samuel** le interesa la política internacional, pero **a su hermana,** no.
> *Samuel is interested in international politics, but his sister isn't.*

> (A mis amigos y a mí) **nos interesan** los deportes.
> *Sports are of interest to us.*

- Note that the third-person singular is used with an infinitive or a series of infinitives.

> A Susana **le encanta** jugar con su hijo.
> *Susana loves playing with her son.*

> **Me encanta** cantar, bailar y escuchar música.
> *I love to sing, dance, and listen to music.*

7A.5 Describe ongoing actions

Adverbs 11

- Adverbs (**adverbios**) modify verbs, adjectives, or other adverbs, and are invariable. Many adverbs in Spanish are formed by adding **-mente** to the feminine form of the adjective, much like the English ending *-ly*.

adjective (*fem. sing.*)		adverb
exacta		**exactamente**
preferible	**+ mente**	**preferiblemente**
difícil		**difícilmente**

> **Actualmente** estoy componiendo canciones.
> *Currently I am composing songs.*

- When the adjective has a written accent, the accent is maintained in the adverb as well.

> **Últimamente** estoy trabajando hasta muy tarde.
> *Lately I am working very late.*

- Some common adverbs ending in **-mente** have an equivalent form in the construction **en** + [*adjective*].

en concreto	concretamente
en general	generalmente
en especial	especialmente
en particular	particularmente

¡Póngalo en práctica!

G11 **Escribir** Escriba oraciones completas.

1. a Federico y a Delia / interesar / los edificios modernos

....

2. a ti / preocupar / el examen de matemáticas

....

3. a Consuelo y a Rodrigo / encantar / ir a la playa

....

4. a nosotros / interesar / las novelas inglesas

....

5. a mí / encantar / la clase de yoga

....

6. a Esteban / preocupar / las decisiones importantes

....

7. a Paco / interesar / estudiar otras lenguas

....

8. a vosotros / encantar / viajar

....

G12 **Los adverbios** Escriba el adverbio que corresponde a cada adjetivo.

1.	práctico	
2.	triste	
3.	fácil	
4.	seguro	
5.	frecuente	

G13 **Transformar** Cambie los adjetivos a adverbios y complete las oraciones con el adverbio apropiado. Use cada adverbio una sola vez.

general   paciente   lento   inmediato   actual

1. Esperé al doctor .... por una hora.

2. Leo .... cuando estudio porque quiero entender bien el material.

3. .... estoy trabajando en el restaurante de mi tío, pero me interesa el teatro.

4. .... la gente de mi pueblo va a trabajar en autobús, pero algunas personas van en coche.

5. Cuando Juan escuchó la alarma de incendio, llamó .... a los bomberos.

 Practice more at **vhlcentral.com.**

VOCABULARIO Vocabulary Tools

El día a día

el día a día	daily life
el/la bailaor(a)	flamenco dancer
el bailarín/la bailarina	dancer
el baile flamenco	flamenco dance
el/la bombero/a	firefighter
el camión	truck
el/la camionero/a	truck driver
el diseño gráfico	graphic design
el ensayo	rehearsal
la enseñanza	teaching
el hábito	habit
el incendio	fire
el riesgo	risk
la rutina	routine
la vocación	vocation
acostarse (o:ue)	to go to bed
apagar	to put out
compaginar	to combine
(hacer) compañía	(to keep) company
conducir (zc)	to drive
dedicarse a (hacer) algo	to do something (for a living)
despertarse (e:ie)	to wake up
ducharse	to shower
levantarse	to get up
maquillarse	to put makeup on
traducir (zc)	to translate
transportar	to transport
vestirse (e:i)	to get dressed
difícil	difficult
juvenil	for young people
solo/a	alone
en equipo	as a team
por vocación	by vocation
tarde	late
temprano	early

Intereses

los cómics	comics
el jazz	jazz
el pasatiempo	pastime
la preocupación	worry; concern
la salud	health
el tailandés	Thai
Tailandia	Thailand
el trabajo voluntario	volunteer work
la trompeta	trumpet
atender (e:ie)	to attend to
dar un ejemplo	to give an example
estar en forma	to be fit, in (good) shape
estar haciendo algo	to be doing something
interesar	to be of interest
jugar (u:ue)	to play
preocupar	to worry; to concern
al mismo tiempo	at the same time

Jorge Drexler

tanto... como	both . . . and
el/la (ingeniero/a) agrónomo/a	agronomist
la canción	song
el/la cantautor(a)	singer-songwriter
el conflicto	conflict
el disco	album
la diversidad	diversity
la energía	energy
la frontera	border
el/la guitarrista	guitarist
el hebreo	Hebrew
el/la judío/a	Jew
la letra	lyrics
el periódico	newspaper
el/la trovador(a)	troubadour
la variedad	variety
asustar	to frighten
componer	to compose
convertirse (e:ie) en	to become
dar un concierto	to give a concert
decir	to say; to tell
editar	to edit; to release
elegir (j) (e:i)	to choose
estar de viaje	to be away
interpretar	to perform
madrugar	to get up early
preparar	to prepare
influyente	influential
rico/a	rich
uruguayo/a	Uruguayan
vital	vital
actualmente	currently
de hecho	in fact
desde entonces	since then
entonces	then
especialmente	specially
últimamente	lately
a pesar de que	in spite of the fact that

Variación léxica

conducir ⟷ manejar (*Amér. L.*)

dar un ejemplo ⟷ poner un ejemplo

elegir ⟷ escoger

vestirse ⟷ ponerse la ropa

7B

CAMBIO DE VIDA

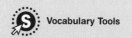 **Vocabulary Tools**

Madre trabajadora

SOBRE RUEDAS
MENSAJES ECOLÓGICOS

HEMOS TRAÍDO
UN PAQUETE PARA TI

○○○   Mensaje nuevo

Enviar   Chat   Adjuntar   Agenda   Tipo de letra   Colores   Borrador

De: Carla
Para: Marta
Asunto: Vuelta al trabajo

📎 Folleto sobre ruedas

Querida Marta:

¿Cómo estás? He estado cuatro meses de baja por maternidad y esta semana he vuelto al trabajo. ¡Cuántos cambios! Me ha gustado ver a mis compañeros. Los he visto estupendos. Esta semana he tenido mucho trabajo, así que he dejado al niño con mis padres… He puesto al día mi agenda y ¡hoy he escrito más de cincuenta correos!

Te envío el nuevo folleto de mi empresa. Lo hemos actualizado.

¿Qué has hecho tú esta semana? Me ha dicho Rosa que has estado de vacaciones fuera de España.

Un beso,

Carla

Hablar de experiencias recientes

- ¿Qué has **hecho** hoy?
  ¿Has **visto** a Carla?
- No, no **la** he visto. Pero he hablado con ella.

7B.1 Present perfect with direct object pronouns
Irregular past participles

Vocabulario

1

la madre trabajadora *working mother*

traer *to bring*

la baja por maternidad (*Esp.*) *maternity leave*

dejar *to leave behind*

poner al día *to bring up to date*

enviar *to send*

actualizar *to update*

estar de vacaciones *to be on vacation*

la mensajería *courier company, messenger company*

3

la entrada *ticket*

el taller (mecánico) *repair shop*

el frigorífico (*Esp.*) *refrigerator*

---

1   **a. Folleto** Fíjese en la imagen del folleto. ¿A qué cree que se dedica esta empresa? ¿Conoce una empresa similar?

     b. Correo Lea el correo de Carla. ¿Por qué ha sido una semana especial?

2   **Madre trabajadora** Subraye en el texto qué ha hecho Carla esta semana. Relacione las formas irregulares con su infinitivo.

1. vuelto ……	4. escrito ……	a. hacer	d. decir
2. visto ……	5. hecho ……	b. escribir	e. volver
3. puesto ……	6. dicho ……	c. ver	f. poner

3   **a. ¿Qué han hecho?** Carla habla por la noche con su marido sobre lo que han hecho en el día. Escuche la conversación. ¿Qué ha hecho cada uno?

	Carla	Ángel
- sacar las entradas para el teatro		
- llamar a sus padres		
- llevar el coche al taller		
- hacer las compras		

     b. Fragmento Represente con su compañero/a este fragmento de la conversación.

> - ¿Has sacado las entradas para el teatro?
> - Sí, <u>las</u> he sacado para el sábado por la noche. He pasado un momento por allí después del trabajo y antes de llevar el coche al taller.
> - ¿<u>Lo</u> has llevado? ¡Menos mal! ¡Ah! ¿Y has llamado a tus padres? Yo no he podido llamar…
> - Pues yo sí, <u>los</u> he llamado esta mañana.

     c. Indicar Indique a qué se refieren las palabras subrayadas.

     d. Representar Con un(a) compañero/a, represente una conversación sobre lo que han hecho durante el día. Usen **la, las, lo** y **los** para referirse a cosas o personas ya mencionadas.

Quiénes somos

Silvio Villa y Pedro Simón, mensajeros

¿Ya he repartido el último paquete de hoy? No sé… Creo que no…

El sábado dejo a Leo con mis padres… Un poco difícil, pero es posible.

Sara Santos, directora

Somos compañeros y amigos.

Quiero llevar a Sara al cine, pero es mi jefa… Quizás es un problema, pero creo que sí quiere venir conmigo.

Manolo García, mecánico

Carla López, auxiliar administrativa

---

4 **a. Quiénes somos** Fíjese en la imagen. ¿A qué se dedican los empleados de Sobre ruedas?

b. Subrayar Lea lo que están pensando los empleados y subraye las expresiones para hacer hipótesis.

5 **Hacer hipótesis** Lea lo que están pensando Manolo y Sara. ¿Qué relación existe entre ellos? Con un(a) compañero/a, haga hipótesis.

> Modelo: • *Quizás a Manolo le gusta Sara.* • *Es posible.*

6 **Reaccionar** ¿Cree que sus compañeros/as han hecho algo especial esta semana? Reaccione ante las hipótesis de sus compañeros/as.

> Modelo: • *Yo creo que John ha ido a un concierto…* • *No sé, quizás…*

MI EXPERIENCIA

7 **Adivinar** Piense en una actividad laboral ideal y explique a sus compañeros/as qué ha hecho esta semana. Sus compañeros/as adivinan qué profesión es.

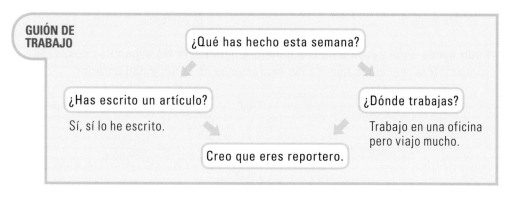

GUIÓN DE TRABAJO

¿Qué has hecho esta semana?

¿Has escrito un artículo?

Sí, sí lo he escrito.

¿Dónde trabajas?

Trabajo en una oficina pero viajo mucho.

Creo que eres reportero.

Hacer hipótesis

- **Quizás** Carla tiene trabajo y ha olvidado enviar el correo.
- **Creo que sí, es posible.**

7B.2 creo que sí/no, quizás, es posible

Vocabulario

4

repartir *to deliver*

Creo que sí./no. *I think so./not.*

el/la auxiliar *assistant*

el/la mecánico, administrativo/a

7

la actividad laboral *job*

la licencia por maternidad *(Amér. L.) maternity leave*

el/la reportero/a

Baja por maternidad

En España las mujeres tienen 4 meses de licencia por maternidad. Los hombres casi no toman licencias para cuidar a los hijos. En muchos casos lo hacen los abuelos. En otros, se buscan trabajos que dejan más tiempo para la familia.

SAM: Actividades pp. 145–147

Ⓢ Practice more at **vhlcentral.com.**

Un día negro

Mi perfil
Nombre: Silvio Villa
Nacionalidad: colombiano
Edad: 32 años

Un día negro

Hoy he tenido un día negro en la oficina, de esos en los que todo va mal.

La co................ no funciona, la com................ va muy lenta y la im................ no puede imprimir. No puedes recibir ni enviar co................, un virus ha invadido la red y todos los ar................ han desaparecido. El ra................ está bloqueado y tampoco puedes llamar al servicio técnico porque el teléfono no funciona, pero... ¡no hay problema!, para eso tienes tu ce................ ...sin batería.

He perdido mucho tiempo y ¡no he podido entregar los paquetes a tiempo!

Pedir y ofrecer ayuda

- ● ¿Puedes ayudarme?
- ■ Sí, claro. ¿Qué necesitas?

- ● ¿Me ayudas?
- ■ ¡Claro! Por supuesto.

- ● ¿Te puedo ayudar?
- ■ Sí, por favor.

- ● ¿Te ayudo?
- ■ No, gracias. Estoy bien.

7B.3 **poder** + [*infinitive*]
ayudar, necesitar

Vocabulario

8

ir mal *to go wrong*
la (foto)copiadora *photocopier*
funcionar *to function, to work*
lento/a *slow*
la impresora *printer*
imprimir *to print*
el archivo *file*
el ratón *mouse*
bloqueado/a *locked; blocked*
¡No hay problema! *No problem!*
perder (e:ie) *to lose*
a tiempo *in/on time*
el ordenador (*Esp.*) *computer*
la batería

9

Estoy bien. *I'm OK.*

10

mandar *to send*
guardar *to save*
el fax

---

8 **a. Un día negro** Lea el blog de Silvio Villa y busque en el recuadro las palabras incompletas.

> archivos • celular • computadora • copiadora • correo • impresora • ratón

b. Comparando ¿Sabe qué palabras se usan en España (Esp.) y cuáles en Latinoamérica (LA.)? Márquelas.

	Esp.	LA.		Esp.	LA.		Esp.	LA.
la computadora			el móvil			la copiadora		
el ordenador	✓		el celular			la fotocopiadora		

9 **a. Ordenar** Escuche las conversaciones y ordénelas.

1
A. Silvio, ¿puedo ayudarte? ☐
B. ¡Por supuesto! ☐
C. Sí, por favor. En esta oficina no funciona nada y tengo mucho trabajo: mi computadora está loca... ¿puedes venir un momento, por favor? ☐

2
A. Sí, claro. ¿Necesita el móvil o el fijo? ☐
B. Perdone, ¿puede decirme el teléfono del Sr. Mur? ☐
C. El móvil, por favor. ☐

b. Relacionar Relacione las preguntas con las respuestas.

1. ¿Puedes decirme el teléfono de Sonia? ....
2. Perdone, ¿puedo ayudarlo? ....
3. ¿Puedes ayudarme un momento? ....
4. ¿Me ayudas? ....

a. Sí, ¿qué necesitas?
b. Sí, claro. Es el 897 38 97.
c. Por supuesto.
d. Sí, por favor.

10 **Pedir ayuda** Pida ayuda a su compañero/a para hacer las siguientes cosas. Su compañero/a reacciona usando las expresiones de la actividad anterior.

> 1. mandar un fax   2. guardar un archivo   3. escribir un correo en español

> 4. usar la impresora   5. llamar al servicio técnico

Cuando trabajé por primera vez con españoles, me llamó la atención una cosa en concreto: la costumbre del tuteo. La gente en el trabajo se habla de *tú*, especialmente los colegas, y muchas veces el jefe y sus empleados también se hablan de *tú*.

Eso es imposible en mi país, Colombia, donde incluso los colegas se hablan de *usted*.

En España, en general la gente se habla de *tú* con los vecinos, en la calle y en las tiendas. Con las personas mayores, sin embargo, normalmente se habla de *usted*. Yo ahora ya me he acostumbrado, y me gusta.

11 **a. El blog de Silvio** Lea el blog de Silvio. ¿Qué le llamó la atención en España?

b. Completar Observe las siguientes expresiones y complete el recuadro.

	concretamente
	generalmente
en especial	
	particularmente

12 **a. Comentar** Una española y dos latinoamericanos hablan sobre las formas de tratamiento (*forms of address*) que usan generalmente. Observe el resumen y comente las diferencias con un(a) compañero/a.

Con.... hablo de...	Sara, española	Lucas, colombiano	Marta, uruguaya
los compañeros de clase	tú	tú	vos*
el jefe	usted	usted	usted
los vecinos	tú	tú	vos*
mis padres	tú	usted	vos*
las personas mayores	usted	usted	vos*

* El uso de **vos** en lugar de **tú** es común en varios países de Sudamérica y América Central, en particular en Uruguay y Argentina.

b. Horarios laborales Lea la nota sobre los horarios laborales en España. ¿Son iguales en su país?

MI EXPERIENCIA

13 **Un día de trabajo** Piense en un día de trabajo en una oficina y anote las situaciones o problemas que ocurren. Pida y ofrezca ayuda en estas situaciones.

GUIÓN DE TRABAJO

La impresora no funciona. Esto es un problema, especialmente si tienes una reunión urgente porque...

¿Puedes ayudarme? ¿Me puedes ayudar?

Sí, ¿qué necesitas?

Generalmente es difícil... Especialmente... En concreto...

¿Puedo ayudarte? ¿Te puedo ayudar?

Sí, por favor.

Vocabulario

11

en concreto *in particular*

el tuteo *use of* tú

hablarse de *tú* to address somebody as tú

el/la colega *colleague*

hablarse de *usted* to address somebody as **usted**

concretamente *specifically*

generalmente *generally*

en especial *especially*

13

la reunión *meeting*

laboral *working*

Estrategia

Generalizar y matizar

Generalmente la gente se habla de **tú**, especialmente en el trabajo. El trato es, en general, informal.

Horarios laborales

En los países hispanos la jornada laboral es normalmente partida, es decir, con una parada para comer de una o dos horas. En América Latina la pausa de la comida es normalmente a las 12:00 o las 13:00 h. En España, descansan entre las 13:00 y las 15:00 h. En las empresas españolas existe generalmente la jornada reducida en verano.

Horario Oficina
Lunes a Jueves
8:00-12:00 A.M. 1:30-5:00 P.M.
Viernes 8:00-12:00 A.M.

SAM: Actividades pp. 148–150

Guadalupe Rodríguez, una nueva etapa

En Villahermosa del Río, un pueblo ubicado en las montañas de la provincia de Castellón, vive y trabaja desde hace cuatro años Guadalupe Rodríguez con su familia. La vida de esta mujer argentina nacida en Córdoba y su marido escocés ha cambiado completamente desde que se mudaron de un apartamento céntrico en Londres a una masía en España.

"En algunos aspectos vivimos como hace cien años."

Guadalupe habla de su experiencia: "El invierno es muy duro y a veces no se puede salir de la masía para llegar al pueblo por la nieve. La casa es muy

Guadalupe Rodríguez y sus dos hijas en su casa de Villahermosa del Río

antigua y hemos abandonado muchas de las comodidades de la ciudad, pero esto nos gusta.

¿Estamos locos? Quizás... Aquí se puede respirar aire puro, tener animales, vivir en contacto con la naturaleza y ser autosuficiente. Esto no se puede hacer en la ciudad.

"Tengo más tiempo para mis hijas."

Este año ha sido muy intenso. Hemos hecho muchas cosas nuevas: hemos arreglado la casa, la hemos pintado... Además hemos empezado nuestro proyecto: La Ecocesta, un sistema de reparto de productos ecológicos a domicilio. Trabajamos con otros agricultores de la zona."

Expresar posibilidad

Aquí **no se puede** ir al cine o salir a cenar... pero sí **se puede** tener una vida más saludable.

7B.4 (no) se puede

Vocabulario

14

escocés/escocesa *Scottish*
cambiar *to change*
mudarse *to move (from home)*
céntrico/a *in the center of town*
la masía *country house (Cataluña)*
duro/a *hard; tough*
No se puede... *You/One can't...*
abandonar *to leave; to give up*
las comodidades *comforts*
loco/a *crazy*
respirar *to breathe*
autosuficiente *self-sufficient*
ecológico/a (*Esp.*) *organic*
arreglar *to repair*
el reparto a domicilio *home delivery*
el/la agricultor(a) *farmer*
el negocio *business*
la provincia, el aspecto, el aire, puro/a, el animal

---

14 a. Una nueva etapa ¿Cómo ha cambiado la vida de Guadalupe? ¿Por qué es una nueva etapa?

b. El negocio de Guadalupe ¿En qué consiste el negocio de Guadalupe?

15 Villahermosa del Río ¿Qué se puede y qué no se puede hacer en el pueblo de Guadalupe?

16 Escuchar Escuche a Guadalupe y marque **verdadero (V)** o **falso (F)**. V F

1. A las niñas les gusta más vivir en el pueblo que en la ciudad. ☐ ☐
2. En el pueblo donde viven hay muchos niños. ☐ ☐
3. Sus padres no tienen tiempo para estar con ellas. ☐ ☐

17 En mi pueblo ¿Cómo es la vida en el lugar donde usted vive? Haga una lista de las posibilidades que ofrece y coméntelas con su compañero/a.

Modelo: • En mi ciudad/pueblo se puede vivir tranquilo.
• En mi ciudad/pueblo no se puede ir al cine.

18 Cambios ¿Cuál de estos cambios de vida prefiere? Explique por qué.

| mudarse a otro país   cambiar de trabajo   cambiar de carrera |
| hacerse vegetariano/a   desconectarse de la tecnología |

Modelo: *Prefiero cambiar de trabajo porque se puede conocer gente nueva.*

19 **La Ecocesta** Lea el folleto de La Ecocesta y complete la información.

La Ecocesta

Una dieta ecológica es mejor para el medio ambiente y para tu salud. En La Ecocesta hay todo lo que se necesita para una alimentación sana y equilibrada: verduras, frutas y otros productos naturales (leche, pan, huevos, queso). Nuestros alimentos son totalmente ecológicos, sin productos químicos y sin manipulación genética. Nuestro servicio a domicilio lleva la ecocesta a tu casa. Se puede elegir entre tres tipos diferentes de cesta y cambiar el pedido hasta 24 horas antes de la entrega. Escríbenos un correo electrónico o llámanos. ¡Estamos a tu servicio!

TIPOS DE CESTA	PRECIOS
Estándar: 3 kg de fruta y otros productos variados	30 €
Frutimix: 4 kg de fruta	12 €
Verdumix: 4 kg de verdura	10 €

FORMAS DE PAGO
Transferencia bancaria o en efectivo.

1. Las formas de pago son ....
2. Las posibilidades que ofrece el servicio son ....
3. Los productos ecológicos son ....

20 **a. Foto** Observe la foto. ¿Conoce el nombre de estos productos en español?

b. Productos ecológicos ¿Cree que los productos ecológicos son mejores para la salud? ¿Conoce un sistema de compra parecido en su país? ¿Lo utiliza?

21 **Escribir** Escriba un correo a La Ecocesta para hacer un pedido. Detalle su listado de alimentos, cantidad y forma de pago. Recuerde estas expresiones útiles.

Estimados señores: Quería solicitar…   Un saludo,

22 **a. Leer** Lea esta información sobre la agricultura ecológica en México. ¿Cómo es la situación en su país?

La agricultura ecológica crece en el mundo entre el 20% y el 25% al año. En México en los últimos 10 años, el área cultivada aumentó de 21 000 a unas 500 000 hectáreas, y es el primer productor y exportador mundial de café orgánico. También produce miel, bebidas, frutas y hortalizas, carne, leche y queso. Casi el 85% de los alimentos orgánicos que se producen en México se exportan a Europa, los Estados Unidos y Japón.

b. Responder ¿En qué tipo de países se consume la mayor parte de los alimentos ecológicos producidos en México? ¿Por qué cree que esto es así?

Vocabulario

18
cambiar de vida *to change one's life*
cambiar de trabajo *to change jobs*
hacerse vegetariano/a *to become a vegetarian*
desconectarse *to disconnect (oneself)*
19
equilibrado/a *balanced*
la cesta *basket*
el pedido *order; request*
la entrega *delivery*
a tu servicio *at your service*
variado/a *assorted*
el pago *payment*
la transferencia bancaria *bank transfer*
la dieta, la manipulación genética, estándar
22
crecer (zc) *to grow*
cultivar *to grow; to cultivate*
mundial *global, worldwide*
la miel *honey*
la hortaliza *vegetable*
orgánico/a, exportar

OPINIÓN

¿Qué piensa de la opción que eligieron Guadalupe Rodríguez y su familia? ¿Cree que se puede cambiar de vida fácilmente?

¡OJO!

Primero and **tercero** drop their final **o** when used before masculine singular nouns, as in **el primer capítulo** or **el tercer año**. This rule does not apply to **primera** and **tercera**. So you should say, for example, **la primera vez** and **la tercera calle**.

SAM: Actividades pp. 151–156

 Practice more at vhlcentral.com.

23 Preguntas Juegue con sus compañeros/as. Tiren dos dados para decidir qué grupo empieza la serie de preguntas y respondan a la pregunta de la casilla correspondiente.

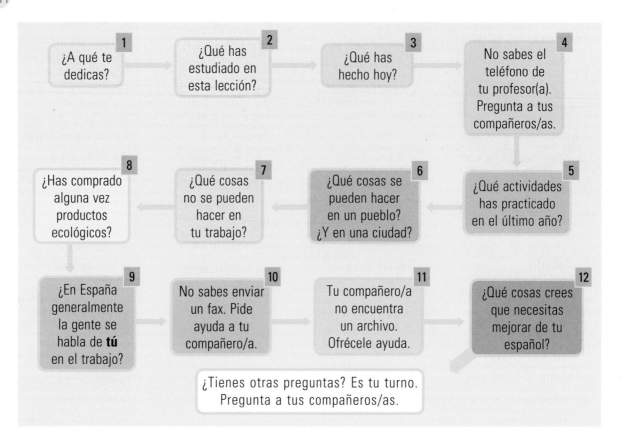

1 ¿A qué te dedicas?

2 ¿Qué has estudiado en esta lección?

3 ¿Qué has hecho hoy?

4 No sabes el teléfono de tu profesor(a). Pregunta a tus compañeros/as.

8 ¿Has comprado alguna vez productos ecológicos?

7 ¿Qué cosas no se pueden hacer en tu trabajo?

6 ¿Qué cosas se pueden hacer en un pueblo? ¿Y en una ciudad?

5 ¿Qué actividades has practicado en el último año?

9 ¿En España generalmente la gente se habla de **tú** en el trabajo?

10 No sabes enviar un fax. Pide ayuda a tu compañero/a.

11 Tu compañero/a no encuentra un archivo. Ofrécele ayuda.

12 ¿Qué cosas crees que necesitas mejorar de tu español?

¿Tienes otras preguntas? Es tu turno. Pregunta a tus compañeros/as.

TAREA FINAL

Una nueva vida

Hagan una lista de lugares conocidos (pueblos, ciudades…). Elijan uno de ellos.

Decidan a qué se quieren dedicar y dónde quieren vivir.

Hagan una pequeña descripción de su nueva vida. Cuenten al grupo, por ejemplo, lo que han hecho los últimos días.

Elijan la alternativa más original.

YO PUEDO...

- **Puedo hablar sobre experiencias recientes.**
  Escriba una lista de todo lo que ha hecho hoy antes de ir a la clase de español.

- **Puedo hacer hipótesis.**
  Piense en una hipótesis sobre algo dudoso.

- **Puedo pedir y ofrecer ayuda.**
  Cree una conversación. Alguien le pide ayuda y otro la ofrece.

- **Puedo expresar posibilidad.**
  Escriba una lista de cosas que se puede y no se puede hacer en su trabajo.

GRAMÁTICA FUNCIONAL

 Tutorials

5.3.2

7B.1 Talk about recent experiences

Irregular past participles 5.3.2
Present perfect with direct object pronouns 5.3.3

- In 6A.4, you learned to use the present perfect (**el pretérito perfecto**) to talk about past actions that are connected to the present. Remember that the **pretérito perfecto** is a compound tense composed of two parts: **haber** + [*past participle*]. You have already learned how to form the past participle with regular verbs. Several common verbs have irregular past participles.

abrir	→	**abierto**	poner	→	**puesto**
decir		**dicho**	ver		**visto**
escribir		**escrito**	volver		**vuelto**
hacer		**hecho**			

Marta ya ha **vuelto** a casa, pero no ha **hecho** la tarea.
Marta already came home, but she hasn't done her homework.

- The two components of the **pretérito perfecto** always appear together and cannot be separated by another word. When you use a direct object pronoun, place it before the conjugated form of **haber**. As you saw in 3B.7, direct object pronouns (**lo, la, los, las**) are used to refer to people or things that have been mentioned previously.

¿Has hecho la comida?   Sí, **la** he hecho.
Have you made the food?   *Yes, I have made it.*

- Likewise, when you use a reflexive verb in the **pretérito perfecto**, place the reflexive pronoun before the conjugated form of **haber**.

Yo ya **me** he duchado, pero Julia no **se** ha levantado todavía.
I have already showered, but Julia hasn't gotten up yet.

- Note that past participles may also be used as adjectives, in which case the normal rules of agreement apply.

Las ventanas están **abiertas**.
The windows are open.

7B.2 Make hypotheses

creo que sí/no; quizás; es posible 11.5

- Use **quizás** (*perhaps; maybe*) to speculate or make hypotheses.

Quizás Manolo ya ha hecho las compras.
Maybe Manolo has already done the shopping.

- To agree with someone's speculation, say **creo que sí** (*I think so*); to show some agreement, say **es posible** (*it's possible*); and to disagree, say **creo que no** (*I don't think so; I think not*).

Quizás Analía tiene un nuevo novio.
Maybe Analía has a new boyfriend.

Creo que sí./Es posible./Creo que no.
I think so./It's possible./I don't think so.

¡Póngalo en práctica!

G1 **El pretérito perfecto** Complete la conversación con las formas correctas del pretérito perfecto.

- ¡Hola, Paula! ¿Qué (1)........................ (hacer) este verano?
- Bueno, este verano (2)........................ (volver) al pueblo y (3)........................ (ver) a mis amigos de la infancia.
- ¿Y qué (4)........................ (hacer) Antonio y Clara esta semana?
- Esta semana (5)........................ (volver) de sus vacaciones. (6)........................ (Escribir) un blog sobre su viaje al Caribe.
- ¡Qué bien! Mi tía me (7)........................ (decir) que quiere hablar con ellos sobre su viaje.
- Sí, ellos me (8)........................ (comentar) lo mismo. La van a llamar pronto.

G2 **Pronombre de objeto directo** Complete las oraciones con un pronombre de objeto directo.

1. • ¿Has comprado los billetes?
   ▪ No, no .... he comprado.
2. El reportero ha escrito un artículo y .... ha enviado a su jefe.
3. • ¿Habéis visto a Carla?
   ▪ Sí, ... hemos visto.
4. La torta está muy rica. ¿.............. has probado?
5. • ¿Ha comprado Toño el libro de español?
   ▪ No, no .... ha comprado.
6. Has hecho una comida muy rica. .... hemos comido con mucho gusto.

G3 **Completar** Complete las conversaciones de manera lógica.

creo que sí   **quizás**
creo que no   **es posible**

- ¿Crees que Marisa dejó su trabajo?
- No, (1)........................
- Paula es de Colombia, ¿no?
- Sí, (2)........................
- ¿Dónde está Raquel? No la he visto hoy.
- (3)........................ está enferma.
- Sí, (4)........................

GRAMÁTICA FUNCIONAL

7B.3 Ask for and offer help

poder + [*infinitive*]; **ayudar**; **necesitar** 5.1.1, 5.10
Placement of object pronouns 6.2.4

- Use the construction **poder** + [*infinitive*] (*to be able to; can*) to ask for and offer help.

  ¿Puedes imprimir estos documentos?
  Can you print these documents?

  Por supuesto, los **puedo imprimir**.
  Of course, I can print them.

- **Poder** is often used with the regular -ar verb **ayudar** (*to help*) to ask for or offer help.

  ¿Te puedo **ayudar**?   ¿Me puede **ayudar**?
  Can I help you?   *Can you help me?*

- When using an object pronoun with an infinitive construction, the object pronoun may be placed before the conjugated verb or attached to the end of the infinitive.

  ¿Nos puedes ayudar?/¿Puedes ayudar**nos**?
  Can you help us?

- **Ayudar** can also be used on its own in a question or a statement offering or asking for help. Place the object pronoun before the conjugated verb.

  ¿Te **ayudo**?   ¿Me **ayudas**?
  Can I help you?   *Can you help me?*

- Use the verb **necesitar** (*to need*) to ask what a person needs. **Necesitar** is a regular -ar verb.

  ¿Me puedes ayudar?   Sí, ¿qué **necesitas**?
  Can you help me?   *Yes, what do you need?*

7B.4 Express possibility

(no) se puede 5.12.1

- Use the expressions **se puede** (*you/one can*) + [*infinitive*] and **no se puede** (*you/one can't*) + [*infinitive*] to tell what can and cannot be done or what is or is not allowed.

  Aquí **se puede** esquiar, pero **no se puede** patinar.
  Here you can ski, but you can't skate.

- Use this construction to talk about possibilities in general, not tied to a specific person. As with other infinitive constructions, the second verb is always in the infinitive.

  En un pueblo pequeño **se puede** jugar en la calle, pero normalmente **no se puede** hacer compras en un centro comercial.
  In a small town, you can play in the street, but generally you can't go shopping at a mall.

G4 **Conversaciones** Complete las conversaciones con la forma correcta de **poder, ayudar** o **necesitar**.

- ¿(1)....................... venir un momento?
- Sí, ¿qué (2).......................?
- ¿Me (3)....................... con la traducción de esta carta?
- Claro, te puedo (4).......................
- ¡Muchas gracias por tu ayuda!

- ¿Los puedo (5).......................?
- Sí, por favor.
- ¿Qué (6).......................?
- ¿(7)....................... decirnos la dirección?
- Sí, claro.

G5 **Escribir** Escriba preguntas completas.

  Modelo: yo / ayudar / (a ustedes) / ¿?
              ¿Los ayudo?

1. yo / ayudar / (a ti) / ¿?
   ....
2. usted / ayudar / (a mí) / ¿?
   ....
3. nosotros / ayudar / (a vosotros) / ¿?
   ....
4. tú / ayudar / (a nosotros) / ¿?
   ....
5. ustedes / ayudar / (a mí) / ¿?
   ....

G6 **Transformar** Transforme las oraciones usando **se puede** y **no se puede**.

1. No podemos fumar (*smoke*) aquí.
   ....
2. Podemos imprimir en esta oficina.
   ....
3. Puedes cenar tarde en este restaurante.
   ....
4. No podemos usar esta computadora.
   ....
5. Puedo ir en autobús.
   ....
6. No podemos comer en la clase.
   ....
7. Puedes mirar televisión en español.
   ....

S Practice more at **vhlcentral.com**.

VOCABULARIO 🔊 ⓢ Vocabulary Tools

Madre trabajadora

Creo que sí./no.	I think so./not.
la actividad laboral	job
el/la auxiliar	assistant
la baja por maternidad (Esp.)	maternity leave
la entrada	ticket
el frigorífico (Esp.)	refrigerator
la licencia por maternidad (Amér. L.)	maternity leave
la madre trabajadora	working mother
el/la mecánico/a	mechanic
la mensajería	courier company, messenger company
el/la reportero/a	reporter
el taller (mecánico)	repair shop
actualizar	to update
dejar	to leave behind
enviar	to send
estar de vacaciones	to be on vacation
poner al día	to bring up to date
repartir	to deliver
traer	to bring
administrativo/a	administrative

Un día negro

Estoy bien.	I'm OK.
¡No hay problema!	No problem!
el archivo	file
la batería	battery
el/la colega	colleague
el fax	fax

la (foto)copiadora	photocopier
la impresora	printer
el ordenador (Esp.)	computer
el ratón	mouse
la reunión	meeting
el tuteo	use of **tú**
funcionar	to function, to work
guardar	to save
hablarse de *tú/usted*	to address somebody as **tú/usted**
imprimir	to print
ir mal	to go wrong
mandar	to send
perder (e:ie)	to lose
bloqueado/a	locked; blocked
laboral	working
lento/a	slow
a tiempo	in/on time
concretamente	specifically
en concreto	in particular
en especial	especially
generalmente	generally

Guadalupe Rodríguez

No se puede...	You/One can't . . .
el/la agricultor(a)	farmer
el aire	air
el animal	animal
el aspecto	aspect
la cesta	basket
las comodidades	comforts
la dieta	diet

la entrega	delivery
la hortaliza	vegetable
la manipulación genética	genetic modification
la masía	country house (Cataluña)
la miel	honey
el negocio	business
el pago	payment
el pedido	order; request
la provincia	province
el reparto a domicilio	home delivery
la transferencia bancaria	bank transfer
abandonar	to leave; to give up
arreglar	to repair
cambiar	to change
cambiar de trabajo	to change jobs
cambiar de vida	to change one's life
crecer (zc)	to grow
cultivar	to grow; to cultivate
desconectarse	to disconnect (oneself)
exportar	to export
hacerse vegetariano/a	to become a vegetarian
mudarse	to move (from home)
respirar	to breathe
autosuficiente	self-sufficient
céntrico/a	in the center of town
duro/a	hard; tough
ecológico/a (Esp.)	organic
equilibrado/a	balanced
escocés/escocesa	Scottish
estándar	standard
loco/a	crazy
mundial	global, worldwide
orgánico/a (Amér. L.)	organic
puro/a	pure
variado/a	assorted
a tu servicio	at your service

Variación léxica

los alimentos ecológicos (*Esp.*) ⟷ los alimentos orgánicos (*Amér. L.*)

la baja por maternidad (*Esp.*) ⟷ la licencia por maternidad (*Amér. L.*) ⟷ **el permiso por maternidad**

la cesta (*Esp.*) ⟷ **la canasta** (*Amér. L.*)

la computadora (*Amér. L.*) ⟷ **el ordenador** (*Esp.*)

la copiadora (*Cub., Méx.*) ⟷ **la fotocopiadora** (*Esp., Arg.*)

poner al día ⟷ **actualizar**

el ratón ⟷ **el mouse** (*Arg.*)

el refrigerador ⟷ **la nevera** (*Esp.*) ⟷ **el frigorífico** (*Esp.*) ⟷ **la refrigeradora** ⟷ **la heladera** (*Arg.*)

Vocabulario útil

la baja (*Esp.*)/el permiso/la licencia por enfermedad *sick leave*

el día libre *day off*

faltar (al trabajo) *to be absent, to take time off work*

los feriados (*Amér. L.*)/los días festivos (*Esp.*) *holidays*

librar (*Esp.*) *to have the day off work*

los logros *achievements*

estar en el paro (*Esp.*); estar desocupado/a *to be unemployed*

el paro (*Amér. L.*)/la huelga *strike*

el sindicato *union*

tomarse (las vacaciones) *to take (a vacation)*

Estrategia · · · · · · · · · · · ·

Types of information

When reading a text, start by identifying what type of information is provided: definitions, problems and solutions, cause and effect, or comparison and contrast. Then, you can list the facts using a diagram, chart, or graphic organizer in order to compare or match the different concepts; organizing ideas this way will help you make sense of the information. In the article above, what type of information do you find? What are the important pieces of information in the text? Are there numbers, names, and specific terms?

Beneficios
en los empleos

Alguien dijo que lo mejor del trabajo son las vacaciones… En algunos países hay más días libres y beneficios laborales° que en otros. En Estados Unidos se otorga° una licencia por maternidad de doce semanas, pero puede ser pagada o no: eso depende de cada empresa. En algunos

países latinoamericanos, la ley° se ocupa de que esta licencia sea pagada°. Por ejemplo, Venezuela ofrece veintiséis semanas de licencia a las madres trabajadoras y les pagan el 100% de su salario durante° ese tiempo. En el otro extremo se encuentra Paraguay, que concede° solo la mitad° del salario y únicamente durante nueve de las doce semanas de licencia por maternidad.

1 **Conversar** Converse con un(a) compañero/a: ¿Todos los años usted se toma vacaciones? ¿Qué prefiere: un trabajo interesante con pocas vacaciones o un trabajo aburrido con más vacaciones? ¿Alguna vez se tomó un día libre con la excusa de estar enfermo/a? ¿Ha participado en alguna huelga o manifestación laboral o estudiantil?

2 **Identificar** A partir de la lectura, identifique el país de origen de las personas que dicen estas oraciones.

1. Estoy disfrutando de seis meses de licencia por maternidad.

2. Ella está preocupada porque recibe la mitad de su salario durante la licencia y ahora tiene un bebé.

3. Me interesa festejar Navidad porque para mí este feriado es algo nuevo.

4. Hoy he terminado mis veintidós días de vacaciones anuales.

5. En mi país, tenemos licencia por maternidad, pero mi empresa no me paga el salario durante ese tiempo.

6. Estamos planeando las vacaciones para los veinte días feriados de este año.

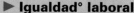

También es importante considerar las fiestas nacionales y religiosas que suman días de vacaciones en distintos momentos del año. En España los empleados típicamente tienen veintidós días de vacaciones pagadas y otros catorce días festivos al año. Puerto Rico disfruta de veinte días feriados en su calendario porque celebra los días no laborables de Estados Unidos, los días festivos del calendario católico y algunas fiestas exclusivas del país. En México, en cambio, hay ocho feriados nacionales. Hay ocho también en Cuba, donde el día de Navidad es fiesta solo desde la visita del papa Juan Pablo II a la isla en 1998.

beneficios laborales *job benefits* **se otorga** *is given* **ley** *law* **sea pagada** *is paid*
durante *throughout* **concede** *it grants* **mitad** *half*

El currículum vítae

- El currículum vítae° contiene información personal y tiene que ser muy detallado°.
- Normalmente incluye° la educación completa, todos los trabajos que ha tenido e incluso sus gustos personales y pasatiempos.
- También puede incluir detalles que no se suele incluir° en los Estados Unidos: una foto, su estado civil e incluso si tiene coche y de qué tipo.

currículum vítae *résumé* **detallado** *detailed* **incluye** *it includes*
no se suele incluir *aren't usually included*

DATOS PERSONALES

Nombre y apellidos:	**Carmelo Roca**
Fecha de nacimiento:	**14 de diciembre de 1992**
Lugar de nacimiento:	**Salamanca**
DNI:	**7885270-R**
Dirección:	**Calle Ferrara 17, 5**
	37500 Salamanca
Teléfono:	**923 270 118**
Correo electrónico:	**rocac@teleline.com**

FORMACIÓN ACADÉMICA
- 2015-2016 Máster en Administración y Dirección de Empresas, Universidad Autónoma de Madrid
- 2010-2015 Licenciado en Administración y Dirección de Empresas por la Universidad de Salamanca

CURSOS Y SEMINARIOS
- 2015 "Gestión y Creación de Empresas", Universidad de Córdoba

EXPERIENCIA PROFESIONAL
- 2013-2014 Contrato de un año en la empresa RAMA S.L., realizando tareas administrativas
- 2012-2013 Contrato de trabajo haciendo prácticas en Banco Sol

IDIOMAS
- INGLÉS Nivel alto. Título de la Escuela Oficial de Idiomas
- ITALIANO Nivel medio

INFORMÁTICA / COMPUTACIÓN
- Conocimientos de usuario de Mac / Windows
- MS Office

(3) **Puestos vacantes** Se está entrevistando gente para cubrir puestos de trabajo. Hable de hipótesis y posibilidades con un(a) compañero/a.

Modelo: • *¿Crees que ella puede obtener ese trabajo?*
■ *Creo que no. No se puede trabajar en Oxfam con ropa de diseñador.*

1. Puesto vacante: recepcionista en la United Fruit Company
   Candidata: una mujer muy tímida a la que no le gusta hablar por teléfono
2. Puesto vacante: domador de leones (*lion tamer*)
   Candidato: un hombre valiente que trabajó en un zoológico por 20 años
3. Puesto vacante: niñera (*babysitter*)
   Candidata: una joven maestra que tiene dos hermanos pequeños
4. Puesto vacante: asistente en el Ministerio de Salud
   Candidato: un hombre que fuma (*smokes*) todos los días

PROYECTO

Currículum vítae Escriba su currículum vítae siguiendo el esquema. Luego intercambie lo que escribió con su compañero/a y corrijan los errores.

1. Datos personales: nombre y apellido, edad, dirección, etc.
2. Antecedentes: qué ha estudiado, dónde ha trabajado, qué sabe hacer.
3. Información adicional: describir pasatiempos, deportes que practica, intereses personales, logros importantes (trofeos, concursos), etc.

Video

El mundo del trabajo

Ya han leído sobre las profesiones, los intereses y las actividades en el mundo hispano; este episodio de **Flash Cultura** muestra a qué se dedican cada día los habitantes de Quito, Ecuador, y cómo a veces pueden unir el trabajo con el placer... y a veces no.

(1) Los trabajos Hable con un(a) compañero/a. ¿Prefiere un trabajo con mucha rutina en una oficina o una actividad variada en contacto con la gente? ¿Le interesa trabajar ayudando a los demás? ¿Qué trabajo le parece horrible? ¿Puede ser divertido trabajar en la calle o viajando?

(2) Mirar Mire este episodio de **Flash Cultura**. Mucha gente opina en el video; preste atención al contexto para poder interpretar correctamente las palabras de cada uno. ¿Quiénes no dicen la verdad? ¿Por qué?

¿Cuántos años lleva usted en la profesión?

¿Te gusta tu trabajo?

(3) Completar Complete las oraciones sobre el video.

1. Los policías solo tienen tres horas de .... diario.
2. Todos los jefes pueden ser muy amables o muy ....
3. A través del turismo es posible .... las maravillas de Ecuador.
4. El trabajo de cada persona ayuda al .... del país.
5. En Klein Tours se .... excursiones de andinismo y viajes de exploración.

(4) Diálogo En parejas, escriban un diálogo entre un(a) consejero/a (*adviser*) escolar que propone alternativas profesionales y un(a) alumno/a que debe decidir a qué se quiere dedicar. Luego compartan el diálogo con la clase.

Modelo:
● *A ti te interesa el ejercicio... quizás puedes ser policía.*
■ *No me gusta ese trabajo porque los horarios son muy complicados*

Estrategia

Pay attention to context

When watching a video, pay attention to the context, the parts of the message that surround a given word or phrase, because there you may find clues to the meaning of unknown words and phrases. Try to identify the speaker's tone of voice and mood. Does the speaker sound angry, confused, happy, nervous, sad, or scared? Is he/she really speaking his/her mind, using irony, or joking?

Vocabulario útil

el andinismo *hiking; mountain climbing*
dar a conocer *to make known*
demostrar (o:ue) *to show*
el desarrollo *development*
el descanso *break*
desenvolverse (o:ue) *to manage*
exigente *demanding*
fastidioso/a *fussy*
realizar *to make*
el sombrerazo *big hat*

Estrategia

Saying *You're welcome*

When someone says **Gracias** to you, you might answer back either **De nada** or **No hay de qué**; also, you may say **Un placer** or **Encantado/a**, meaning that you are pleased to have done whatever the person is thanking you for. When there's been a reciprocal service (for example, when you buy something), the answer should be **Gracias a ti/usted** or **A ti/usted**.

 Practice more at vhlcentral.com.

Unidad 8

Justo Gallego, manos a la obra

Fernanda y Alberto, dueños de un negocio salvadoreño

Arquitectura modernista

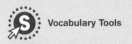
Vocabulary Tools

HECHO A MANO

Habilidades

BANCO DE TIEMPO
Córdoba
INTERCAMBIO DE HABILIDADES

Categorías

- Música y baile
- Cuidado de personas
- Educación: clases
- Bricolaje: hogar y jardín
- Cocina
- Tecnología
- Motor
- Salud

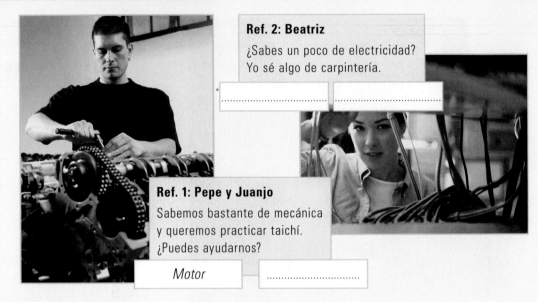

Ref. 2: Beatriz
¿Sabes un poco de electricidad?
Yo sé algo de carpintería.

....

Ref. 1: Pepe y Juanjo
Sabemos bastante de mecánica
y queremos practicar taichí.
¿Puedes ayudarnos?

Motor   ....

Hablar de habilidades

- ¿**Sabes** tocar la guitarra?
- **Sé** un poco. ¿Y tú?
- Yo **nada**, pero **sé bastante de** música y mis hijos **saben** tocar el piano **muy bien**.

8A.1	**saber (de)** **algo, bastante...**

Vocabulario

(1)

el bricolaje *do-it-yourself*

el hogar *home*

la cocina *cooking*

saber (algo) de *to know (something) about*

la carpintería *carpentry*

la habilidad, la educación, la tecnología, la electricidad, la mecánica, el taichí

(2)

saber *to know*

regular *so-so*

nada *at all*

tocar (un instrumento) *to play (an instrument)*

el piano

---

1 **a. Página web** Observe la página web. ¿Qué servicio ofrece?

b. Categorías Relacione las categorías con los anuncios de las dos páginas. Compare sus respuestas con las de su compañero/a.

2 **a. Mis habilidades** ¿Qué habilidades tiene usted? Fíjese en las estructuras e indique su grado de habilidad.

Sé...	algo/un poco, bastante, mucho de... cocina.
	cocinar... algo/un poco, (muy) bien, regular.

No sé...	nada, mucho de... cocina.
	cocinar bien, nada.

Modelo: *Sé tocar el piano muy bien, pero no sé mucho de cocina.*

b. Conversar Comparta sus habilidades con su compañero/a.

Modelo: • *Yo sé cocinar muy bien. Y tú, ¿sabes cocinar?*
• *Sí, sé un poco.*

3 **Escribir** ¿Quiere hacer un intercambio? Escriba un anuncio para la página web Banco de tiempo. Pregunte a su compañero/a por su anuncio.

Ref.: ....
....
....
....
....

Ref. 3: Antonio

Sé tocar el piano y la guitarra.
¿Quién sabe informática?

....

Ref. 5: Felipe

¿Sabéis hacer muebles de
madera? Consejos de jardinería
a cambio.

....

Ref. 6: Silvia

¿Sabes cocinar? Yo sé bailar
flamenco muy bien.

....

Ref. 4: Estelle

Doy clases de francés a cambio de
cuidado de niños (4 y 7 años).

....

---

4 a. Anuncios Escuche la conversación entre Estelle e Inés y lea los anuncios.
 ¿Con cuál de los anuncios la relaciona?

b. Corregir Escuche de nuevo y corrija las informaciones falsas.

Estelle ha quedado con Inés... para ir al cine/en la plaza de las Tendillas/
el martes/a las 17:00 h.

5 Propuestas Escriba propuestas con los elementos de los recuadros.

Si > querer / poder > ir al cine / hacer un intercambio | tomar un café / estudiar español

6 Responder Responda a los siguientes
mensajes de texto. Usted tiene clase
de español hasta las 21:00 h.

✉ ¿Quedamos
para ir al cine
esta noche?

1 2 3

✉ Si quieres,
vamos a cenar
mañana.

1 2 3

🗣 **MI EXPERIENCIA**

7 Intercambiar Busque a una persona para intercambiar habilidades y quede
con ella.

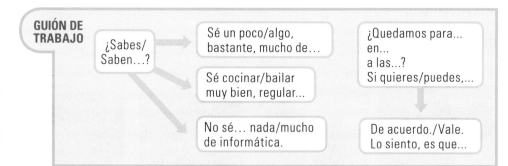

**GUIÓN DE
TRABAJO**

¿Sabes/
Saben...? →

Sé un poco/algo,
bastante, mucho de...

Sé cocinar/bailar
muy bien, regular...

No sé... nada/mucho
de informática.

¿Quedamos para...
en...
a las...?
Si quieres/puedes,...

De acuerdo./Vale.
Lo siento, es que...

Quedar

¿Quedamos a las 18:00 h para
nuestro intercambio?

Quedamos con Martín en la plaza.

....
8A.2 quedar + para/en/a/con

**Hacer propuestas;
Aceptar y rechazar
propuestas**

● Si queréis, quedamos esta
tarde.

■ Lo siento, no puedo. Es que
tengo una clase.

● Si puedes, quedamos a las
14:00 h.

■ De acuerdo./Vale.

....
**8A.3 si quieres/puedes...
vale; lo siento, es que...**

Vocabulario
④

dar clases (de algo) *to give [subject]
classes*
a cambio de *in exchange for*
el mueble *piece of furniture*
la madera *wood*
la jardinería *gardening*
quedar *to (arrange to) meet*
la guitarra
⑦
intercambiar *to exchange*

SAM: Actividades pp. 157–159

Trucos para el hogar

¿Los electrodomésticos no funcionan?

¿Tienes que montar o arreglar un mueble?

¿No sabes qué hacer con las plantas del jardín?

Si las actividades con las manos son muy difíciles para ti, si eres un *manazas*, estos consejos prácticos te pueden ayudar.

Para limpiar los vidrios...

utiliza agua con limón.

Para abonar tus plantas...

guarda los posos del café.

Para eliminar los parásitos...

mete cerillas en las macetas.

Dar instrucciones

Utiliza agua con limón para limpiar los vidrios.

Mete cerillas en las macetas.

Añade limón a las verduras.

8A.4 Regular commands (**tú**)

Hablar de materiales

- ● ¿De qué es este cinturón?
- ■ Es de metal y de cuero.
- ● ¿Y esta lámpara?
- ■ Es de tela y de plástico.

8A.5 **ser** + **de** + [*material*]

Vocabulario

⑧

el truco *trick*

el electrodoméstico *appliance*

montar *to assemble*

el/la manazas (*Esp.*) *clumsy person*

el vidrio *(pane of) glass*

abonar *to fertilize*

meter *to put*

la cerilla *match*

la maceta *flowerpot*

el jabón *soap*

conservar *to keep*

sujetar *to hold*

clavar *to nail down*

el clavo *nail*

el peine *comb*

el cajón *drawer*

la planta, el parásito

---

⑧ **Trucos para el hogar** Los trucos se han desordenado. Ordénelos y reescriba las oraciones.

1. Usa ~~cerillas~~ para limpiar los vidrios. → *Usa agua con limón para limpiar los vidrios.*

2. Mete agua con limón en las macetas para eliminar los parásitos. →

3. Guarda jabón para abonar tus plantas. →

4. Añade los posos del café a las verduras para conservar su color natural. →

5. Sujeta con limón para clavar un clavo. →

6. Usa un peine para abrir los cajones. →

⑨ **a. Objetos** Relacione los objetos con el material y compare sus respuestas con las de su compañero/a.

1	papel
	cerámica
	madera
	plástico
	tela
	cuero
	metal
	vidrio

8 botella
1 hoja
7 pañuelo
2 caja
3 taza
4 cinturón
5 bolígrafo
6 lata

Modelo: • ¿De qué es la hoja? • *Es de papel.*

b. Materiales Piense en otros objetos y pregunte a su compañero/a de qué material son.

⑩ **Gazpacho** Complete las instrucciones de esta receta de gazpacho.

(Pelar) los tomates y el pepino y (cortar) el pimiento.

(Añadir) sal, aceite de oliva, ajo y pan duro.

(Batir) bien la mezcla.

Y (meter) la sopa en el refrigerador. ¡Buen provecho!

mete

Para conservar el color natural de las verduras...

añade limón.

Para clavar clavos...

sujeta el clavo con un peine.

Para abrir los cajones de madera fácilmente...

usa jabón.

11 **Trucos** ¿Sabe usted algún truco? Consulte primero con su grupo y después compartan sus trucos con la clase.

de bricolaje	de limpieza	de decoración
de jardinería	de cocina	de belleza

12 **a. Escuchar** Observe y escuche a estas dos personas. ¿Cuál es el problema?

Mira...

1

¡Dale!

2

b. Expresiones Escuche de nuevo. ¿Para qué se usan las expresiones anteriores?

para animar a la acción ☐   para introducir la explicación ☐

c. Grados de habilidad **Manitas** y **manazas** son palabras que se usan en España para describir diferentes grados de habilidad de una persona. En su casa, ¿quién es un(a) **manitas**? ¿Quién es un(a) **manazas**?

13 **Dar instrucciones** Pida ayuda y dé instrucciones a su compañero/a para estas situaciones.

Su computadora no funciona.	Su celular no se oye.

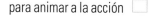 **MI EXPERIENCIA**

14 **Compartir** Comparta con sus compañeros los trucos que sabe.

GUIÓN DE TRABAJO

¿Qué sabes hacer? → Sé bricolaje, cocinar, decorar...

¿Sabes algún truco de bricolaje? → Utiliza aceite para abrir las puertas fácilmente.

 Practice more at **vhlcentral.com.**

Estrategia ···········

Introducir una explicación y animar

● Mira, te voy a explicar algo.

■ ¡Dale!/¡Venga! (*Esp.*)/ ¡Sale! (*Méx.*)

Vocabulario

⑨
la hoja   *sheet; leaf*
la caja   *box*
el cinturón   *belt*
la tela   *(piece of) cloth, fabric*
el cuero   *leather*
el material, el plástico, el metal
⑩
el plato   *dish; plate*
la receta (de cocina)   *recipe*
pelar   *to peel*
el pepino   *cucumber*
la sal   *salt*
el aceite   *oil*
el ajo   *garlic*
batir   *to beat*
¡Buen provecho!   *Enjoy your meal!*
el refrigerador
⑫
Mira...   *Look...*
¡Dale!/¡Venga! (*Esp.*)/¡Sale! (*Méx.*)   *Come on!*
el frasco   *jar*
el/la manitas (*Esp.*)   *handyperson*
la goma elástica   *rubber band*
alrededor   *around*
la tapa de rosca   *screw top*

SAM: Actividades pp. 160–162

Justo Gallego, manos a la obra

Justo Gallego (n. 1925) construye desde hace cincuenta años una catedral con sus propias manos. Está en Mejorada del Campo (Madrid) y su cúpula tiene 40 metros° de alto.

Utiliza materiales reciclados que recoge de la basura. No sabe nada de construcción, no tiene planos ni proyecto y no recibe dinero de la administración. Lo ha hecho casi todo solo, sin ayuda de nadie. Ha cumplido su sueño: construir una catedral para Nuestra Señora del Pilar. Justo explica que "es un acto de fe°".

Es increíble pensar que alguien puede hacer algo así, pero Justo lo ha logrado y ahora es famoso: su obra se ha expuesto en el MoMA de Nueva York y una marca de refrescos ha usado la imagen de Justo para una exitosa campaña de publicidad. El mensaje es claro: "Las posibilidades del ser humano son ilimitadas".

Si alguien quiere ver la catedral, puede visitar Mejorada del Campo. La construcción es el mayor interés turístico de este lugar. "Ahora soy famoso", dice Justo Gallego, pero no tiene celular, y su coche es una bicicleta. ¡Nadie ha visto nunca nada igual!

40 metros *131 feet* **fe** *faith*

Justo Gallego delante de la catedral que ha construido.

Hablar de personas o cosas indeterminadas

¿**Alguien** que ha construido una catedral solo? ¡Es **algo** increíble! **Nadie** ha visto nunca **nada** igual.

8A.6 **alguien/nadie, algo/nada**

Vocabulario

15

manos a la obra *(Let's) Get to work!*
la mano *hand*
alto/a *high; tall*
reciclado/a *recycled*
la basura *garbage*
nadie *nobody*
el acto de fe *matter of faith*
la obra (de arte) *work of art*
el ser humano *human being*
ilimitado/a *unlimited*
el plano, la administración

19

Dios *God*

---

15 **Foto** Observe la imagen de la construcción. ¿Qué tipo de edificio es?

castillo ☐   iglesia ☐   catedral ☐   museo ☐

16 **a. Manos a la obra** Mire al protagonista. ¿A qué cree que se dedica? ¿Qué relación tiene con la construcción? Lea el texto y compruebe.

b. Responder ¿Cómo cree que Justo Gallego ha podido construir esta catedral solo?

17 **Palabras clave** Elija palabras o frases clave de cada párrafo y explique a su compañero/a por qué las eligió.

18 **Elegir** Elija la opción correcta.

> Justo ha hecho **algo/nada** increíble. **Alguien/ Nadie** ha visto **nada/algo** igual. Si **nadie/alguien** no lo cree, solo tiene que visitar la catedral.

19 **a. Refranes** Escuche la entrevista a Justo Gallego. ¿Cuál de estos refranes resume mejor el mensaje de la entrevista? ¿Por qué?

> Nadie es profeta en su tierra°.

> Querer es poder.

> A quien madruga, Dios lo ayuda.

No man is a prophet in his own land.

b. Escribir Con su compañero/a, escriban tres preguntas para hacerle a Justo.

20 **Contestar** ¿Alguien de su familia o amigos ha hecho algo especial o importante? ¿Conoce a un artista como Justo Gallego?

21 **Títulos** Lea el texto y relacione los títulos con los párrafos.

Catedrales

Santiago de Compostela

Buenos Aires

Sevilla

León

☐ Las catedrales antiguas se realizaron con pocos medios técnicos gracias a un gran esfuerzo colectivo. Además de su valor religioso, fueron símbolos sociales y culturales de nuestras ciudades y hoy en día son <u>monumentos históricos</u>.

☐ Actualmente las catedrales son lugares de culto, pero también tienen un valor artístico y turístico. Para <u>visitar las catedrales</u>, hay que respetar ciertas normas, por ejemplo estar en silencio y apagar el celular.

☐ En España se destacan° las catedrales de Sevilla, Burgos, Toledo, León y Santiago de Compostela, donde termina la famosa ruta del <u>Camino de Santiago</u>.

☐ Las catedrales europeas han sido <u>modelos para la construcción</u> de las grandes catedrales de América Latina. Algunas de las más importantes son las de Santo Domingo, México, D.F., Lima y Buenos Aires.

se destacan *stand out*

Vocabulario

21

el esfuerzo *effort*

colectivo/a *collective*

el lugar de culto *place of worship*

el símbolo, religioso/a, respetar, la religión

24

el Patrimonio de la Humanidad *World Heritage (Site)*

el piso *floor, story*

la ingeniería *engineering*

la arquitectura

---

1. Religión y arte	2. Maravillas arquitectónicas	3. Influencia europea	4. La ruta de las catedrales

22 **Preguntar** Haga preguntas a su compañero/a sobre las frases subrayadas en el texto.

Modelo: *¿Cuál es tu monumento histórico preferido y por qué? ¿De qué estilo arquitectónico es?*

23 **Monumentos** ¿Conoce las catedrales que menciona el texto? ¿Y otras? ¿Qué monumentos famosos o importantes hay en su ciudad?

24 **La arquitectura** Aquí tiene algunas muestras de la arquitectura del mundo hispano. Lea las características de las obras. ¿Qué imagen las representa?

1. **Luis Barragán** (Guadalajara, México). Su casa estudio, en México, D.F. es una de las obras arquitectónicas contemporáneas más importantes en el contexto internacional y es también Patrimonio de la Humanidad de la UNESCO.

2. **Bernardo Fort-Brescia** (Lima, Perú). Es el autor junto con su esposa, Laurinda Spear, del Hotel Westin en Manhattan, Nueva York. Tiene 45 pisos y 873 habitaciones.

3. **Santiago Calatrava** (Valencia, España). Sus creaciones son mitad arquitectura, mitad ingeniería. Están en ciudades de todo el mundo como Valencia, Mérida, Bilbao, Buenos Aires y Venecia.

SAM: Actividades pp. 163–166

Practice more at **vhlcentral.com.**

25 **a. Tortilla de patata** Complete y ordene las instrucciones para hacer una tortilla de patata. El grupo más rápido gana. Después escuche el audio y compruebe sus respuestas.

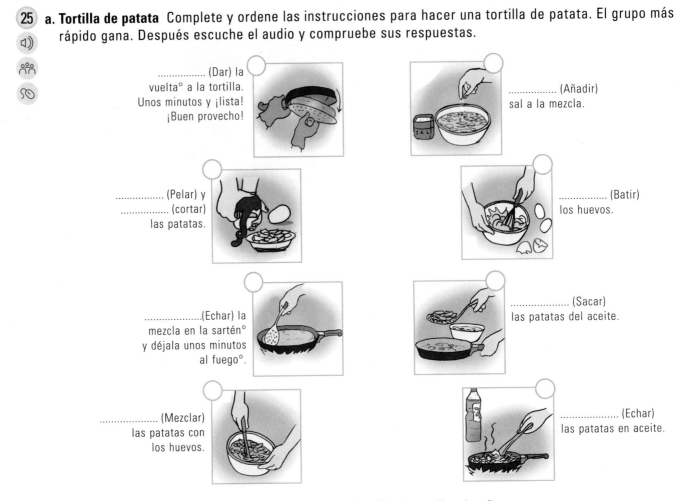

.... (Dar) la vuelta° a la tortilla. Unos minutos y ¡lista! ¡Buen provecho!

.... (Añadir) sal a la mezcla.

.... (Pelar) y .... (cortar) las patatas.

.... (Batir) los huevos.

................(Echar) la mezcla en la sartén° y déjala unos minutos al fuego°.

.... (Sacar) las patatas del aceite.

.... (Mezclar) las patatas con los huevos.

.... (Echar) las patatas en aceite.

dar la vuelta *to flip; to turn over* **la sartén** *frying pan* **el fuego** *heat; fire*

b. Una receta de cocina Con su grupo, elijan una receta de cocina y escriban las instrucciones en diferentes tiras de papel. Otro grupo debe ponerlas en orden. Luego comprueben si el orden es correcto.

TAREA FINAL

Banco de tiempo del español

Elabore un cuestionario sobre habilidades y conocimientos relacionados con el español. (gramática, pronunciación, cultura...)

Conteste el cuestionario y complételo con la información de sus compañeros.

Organicen un intercambio de habilidades en español. Creen una tabla con las habilidades y los nombres de los alumnos.

Quede con uno o varios compañeros para intercambiar sus habilidades.

YO PUEDO...

- **Puedo hablar de habilidades.**
  Describa una de sus habilidades.

- **Puedo quedar con alguien.**
  Cree una conversación para realizar alguna actividad relacionada con la clase de español.

- **Puedo hacer propuestas.**
  Escriba un mensaje de texto con una propuesta de actividad.

- **Puedo dar instrucciones.**
  Explique a un(a) amigo/a las instrucciones de un truco para el hogar.

- **Puedo hablar de objetos y materiales.**
  Elija tres objetos y diga de qué materiales son.

- **Puedo hablar de personas o cosas indeterminadas.**
  Escriba oraciones sobre personas o cosas que no conoce.

GRAMÁTICA FUNCIONAL ⓢ Tutorials

8A.1 Talk about skills

saber (de) 5.10
Adverbs of quantity and negation 11.1, 11.4, 12.3

- Use the verb **saber** (*to know [how]*) to talk about skills or abilities. **Saber** has an irregular **yo** form: **sé**.

    Sé tocar muy bien la guitarra.
    I know how to play the guitar very well.

- Use **saber** + [*infinitive*] to tell what someone knows how to do. Use adverbs like **algo**, **un poco**, and **(muy) bien** to indicate skill.

    Luisa **sabe tocar un poco** el piano.
    Luisa knows how to play the piano a bit.

- To indicate what someone knows *about* a topic, use **saber** + [**algo/un poco/bastante/mucho**] + **de** + [*noun*].

    Sabemos bastante de política.
    We know a lot about politics.

- Use **no saber** + [**nada/mucho**] + **de** + [*noun*] or **no saber** + [*infinitive*] + [**bien/nada**] to express what someone does not know how to do, or do well.

    No sé nadar **bien**.
    I don't know how to swim well.

8A.2 Meet with people

quedar + a/con/en/para 10.1, 10.4, 10.12, 10.15

- Use the verb **quedar** to make plans to meet people. **Quedar** is a regular verb.

    Quedamos en la parada de autobuses a las ocho.
    Let's meet at the bus stop at eight.

- Give more information about your meeting using **en** + [*place*], **con** + [*person*], **a** + [*time*], or **para** + [*activity (infinitive)*].

    Quedamos con mis primos **para** ir al cine.
    We're meeting (with) my cousins to go to the movies.

8A.3 Propose, accept, and decline plans

Si quieres/puedes... 12.9
De acuerdo./Lo siento, es que... 14.14

- To propose plans, say **Si quieres/puedes** + [*plan*]. Be sure to match the form of **querer** or **poder** to your listener(s).

    Si quieren, pueden cenar en mi casa esta noche.
    If you want, you can have supper at my house tonight.

- To accept, say **¡De acuerdo!** or **¡Vale!** (*Esp.*). To politely decline, say **Lo siento, es que** + [*excuse*].

    Lo siento, es que tengo que lavarme el pelo.
    I'm sorry, I have to wash my hair.

¡Póngalo en práctica!

G1 Oraciones Escriba oraciones completas con los elementos dados. Haga todos los cambios necesarios.

1. Pedro / algo / saber / tango

2. muy bien / saber / jugar al tenis / Miriam y Laura

3. saber / hacer adornos preciosos / vosotras

4. jardinería / (tú) / no / ¿? / saber / mucho

5. cocinar / regular / yo / saber

G2 Escoger Empareje cada comienzo de oración con el final apropiado.

	1. Pedro quedó con Ana para	a. las tres en la oficina.
	2. Quedé con	b. ayudarme a estudiar.
	3. Quedamos para	c. Manuel para cenar.
	4. Usted quedó a	d. un restaurante.
	5. Quedaste conmigo para	e. vernos pronto.
	6. Quedaron en	f. llevarla a bailar.

G3 Planes Complete la conversación.

- Sofía, si (1)............................, vamos a cenar.

- (2)............................, es que tengo que estudiar español.

- Yo sé mucho español. Si (3)............................, puedo ayudarte.

- (4)............................ Podemos hacer un intercambio. Yo sé cocinar muy bien.

- (5)............................ quieres, puedo estar en tu casa a las 7, ¿de acuerdo?

- Sí, genial.

ⓢ Practice more at **vhlcentral.com**.

GRAMÁTICA FUNCIONAL

8A.4 Give instructions

Regular commands (tú) 5.18.2

- Use commands to give someone instructions.

    Sujeta la puerta con una madera.
    Hold the door with a piece of wood.

- Regular **tú** commands have the same form as the present-tense **usted/él/ella** form of the verb.

    Usted **lava** los platos con jabón. ➔ **Lava** (tú) los platos.
    *You **wash** the plates with soap.*   ***Wash** the plates.*

- You will learn other command forms, including irregular and negative **tú** commands, in **9B.2**, **11A.1**, and **16B.1**.

8A.5 Talk about materials

ser + de + [material] 10.5

- Use **ser + de + [material]** to tell what an object is made of.

    La mesa **es de madera** y las sillas **son de metal**.
    *The table **is made of wood** and the chairs **are made of metal**.*

- Use **de + [material]** as an invariable adjective.

    Las botellas **de vidrio** son muy frágiles.
    ***Glass** bottles are very fragile.*

8A.6 Talk about unidentified people or things

alguien/nadie, algo/nada 6.5, 12.3

- Use the indefinite pronouns **alguien** (*someone; anyone*) and **algo** (*something; anything*) to refer to people or objects that are unspecified.

    ¿Hay **alguien** en casa?   Quiero comer **algo**.
    *Is there **anyone** at home?*   *I want to eat **something**.*

- Use **alguien** and **algo** in affirmative statements. For negative statements, use **nadie** (*nobody; anybody*) and **nada** (*nothing; anything*). As you saw in **6A.2**, all indefinite words in a negative statement must be negative (**no, nada, nadie, nunca...**).

    No veo a **nadie**.   No queremos beber **nada**.
    *I don't see **anyone**.*   *We don't want to drink anything.*

- Remember to use the **a personal** when **alguien** or **nadie** is the direct object of a verb. (See **5B.3**.)

    ¿Viste **a alguien** cuando entraste?
    *Did you see **anyone** when you came in?*

- These pronouns can also be used as the subject of a sentence.

    ¿**Alguien** sabe **algo** de finformática?
    *Does **anyone** know **anything** about computing?*

    No, **nadie** sabe **nada**.
    *No, **nobody** knows **anything**.*

¡Póngalo en práctica!

G4 **Completar** Complete las oraciones con el verbo en imperativo.

1. .... (Batir) los huevos.
2. .... (Añadir) la harina y el azúcar.
3. .... (Revolver) bien la mezcla.
4. .... (Utilizar) un molde grande.
5. .... (Meter) la fuente al horno.
6. .... (Esperar) que se enfríe.

G5 **Escribir** Escriba oraciones completas para indicar de qué material es cada objeto.

    Modelo: el cinturón *El cinturón es de cuero.*

1. las tazas ....
2. la sartén ....
3. las ventanas *(windows)* ....
4. el periódico ....
5. los zapatos ....
6. el vestido ....

G6 **Conversación** Complete la conversación.

- ¿Llamaste a (1)...................... ayer?
- No, ayer no llamé (2)......................
  (3).......................
- ¿Miraste (4)...................... en la televisión?
- No, (5)...................... miro (6)...................... en la televisión.
- ¡Yo siempre encuentro (7)...................... interesante en la tele!
- ¿En serio? Yo nunca encuentro (8)...................... divertido.

G7 **Pregunta o respuesta** Responda a las preguntas con una negación o escriba las preguntas para las respuestas.

1. ¿Te ha ocurrido algo?
2. No, no llegó nadie todavía.
3. ¿Sabe tu hermano algo de música?
4. ¿Quieres algo?
5. No, no conozco a nadie aquí.
6. ¿Alguien te ofreció algo?
7. ¿Le contaste algo a alguien?
8. No, no leí nada interesante.

 Practice more at **vhlcentral.com**.

VOCABULARIO ◁)) Ⓢ Vocabulary Tools

Habilidades

el bricolaje	do-it-yourself
la carpintería	carpentry
la cocina	cooking
la educación	education
la electricidad	electricity
la guitarra	guitar
la habilidad	ability
el hogar	home
la jardinería	gardening
la madera	wood
la mecánica	mechanics
el mueble	piece of furniture
el piano	piano
el taichí	tai chi
la tecnología	technology
dar clases (de algo)	to give [subject] classes
intercambiar	to exchange
quedar	to (arrange to) meet
saber (algo) (de)	to know (something) (about)
tocar (un instrumento)	to play (an instrument)
a cambio de	in exchange for
nada	at all
regular	so-so

Trucos para el hogar

¡Buen provecho!	Enjoy your meal!
¡Dale!/¡Venga! (Esp.)/¡Sale! (Méx.)	Come on!
Mira...	Look...
el aceite	oil
el ajo	garlic
la caja	box
el cajón	drawer
la cerilla	match
el cinturón	belt
el clavo	nail
el cuero	leather
el electrodoméstico	appliance
el frasco	jar
la goma elástica	rubber band
la hoja	sheet; leaf
el jabón	soap
la maceta	flowerpot
el/la manazas (Esp.)	clumsy person
el/la manitas (Esp.)	handyperson
el material	material
el metal	metal
el parásito	parasite
el peine	comb
el pepino	cucumber
la planta	plant
el plástico	plastic
el plato	dish; plate
la receta (de cocina)	recipe
el refrigerador	refrigerator
la sal	salt
la tapa de rosca	screw top
la tela	(piece of) cloth, fabric
el truco	trick
el vidrio	(pane of) glass

abonar	to fertilize
batir	to beat
clavar	to nail down
conservar	to keep
meter	to put
montar	to assemble
pelar	to peel
sujetar	to hold
alrededor	around

Justo Gallego

manos a la obra	(Let's) Get to work!
el acto de fe	matter of faith
la administración	administration
la arquitectura	architecture
la basura	garbage
Dios	God
el esfuerzo	effort
el fuego	heat; fire
la ingeniería	engineering
el lugar de culto	place of worship
la mano	hand
la obra (de arte)	work of art
el Patrimonio de la Humanidad	World Heritage (Site)
el piso	floor, story
el plano	plan
la religión	religion
la sartén	frying pan
el ser humano	human being
el símbolo	symbol
dar la vuelta	to flip; to turn over
respetar	to respect
alto/a	high; tall
colectivo/a	collective
ilimitado/a	unlimited
reciclado/a	recycled
religioso/a	religious
nadie	nobody

Variación léxica

la cerilla (Esp.) ⟷ el fósforo (Amér. L.) ⟷ el cerillo (Méx.)

¡Dale! ⟷ ¡Venga! (Esp.) ⟷ ¡Sale! (Méx.)

el intercambio ⟷ el trueque ⟷ el canje

el refrigerador ⟷ la nevera (Esp.) ⟷ la heladera (Arg.) ⟷ el frigo (fam.)

el vidrio ⟷ el cristal (Esp.)

8B

HORIZONTES

Emigrantes

1

☑ *"En 1905 mis abuelos fueron desde Canarias a Caracas en barco, como muchos otros españoles. Ellos se quedaron en Caracas, otros hicieron fortuna y volvieron."*

☐ *"Somos salvadoreños, de Intipucá. En 1980, cuando comenzó la guerra en nuestro país, hicimos las maletas y vinimos a California. Aquí tuvimos a nuestros hijos. Ellos hablan inglés desde niños."*

☐ *"En los años 60 dejé mi finca en Bolivia para buscar trabajo en Chimbote, una ciudad industrial de Perú. Mi señora y mis hijos se quedaron en el campo por un tiempo. Luego vinieron conmigo."*

☐ *"Soy química. En 2001 vine a Londres con una beca de investigación. Tuve suerte y me quedé."*

☐ *"En 1937, con 6 años, vine a Veracruz como niño de la guerra. Hubo españoles que volvieron de mayores, otros no quisimos o no pudimos, mi vida está aquí, en México."*

Hablar de experiencias

- Tu padre **vino** a México y ¿qué **hizo**?
- **Tuvo** suerte y **pudo** trabajar de camionero.

8B.1	Irregular preterite verbs

Vocabulario

①

quedarse *to stay*

hacer fortuna *to make a fortune*

salvadoreño/a *Salvadoran*

hacer las maletas *to pack*

la maleta *suitcase*

tener un hijo *to have a child*

desde niño(s) *since childhood*

los años 60 *the sixties*

la finca *farm*

el/la químico/a *chemist*

la beca *scholarship; grant*

la investigación *research*

la suerte *(good) luck*

la guerra *war*

a finales del siglo XIX *toward the end of the 19th century*

a principios del siglo XX *at the beginning of the 20th century*

la guerra civil *civil war*

---

① **a. Emigrantes** Lea los testimonios de la exposición *Emigrantes* y escriba el número de la foto correspondiente.

b. Relacionar Relacione las fotos con los siguientes titulares.

(Europa: finales del siglo XIX–principios del siglo XX) Emigración a Latinoamérica. ☐4

(España: 1936–1939) Exilio a Europa y Latinoamérica por la guerra civil española. ☐

(Latinoamérica: años 60 y 70) Migración del campo a la ciudad. ☐

(El Salvador: años 80) Exilio a los Estados Unidos y otros países de América por la guerra civil salvadoreña. ☐

(Latinoamérica: 2000–actualidad) Nietos de inmigrantes vuelven al país de sus abuelos. ☐

② **Verbos** Marque en los textos los verbos en pretérito indefinido y clasifíquelos.

Regulares	Irregulares
se quedaron,...	*fueron,...*

③ **Testimonio** Complete el testimonio de una visitante a la exposición usando el pretérito indefinido de estos verbos.

casarse • emigrar • poder • tener • venir

Soy argentina y ahora vivo en España. En 1920 mi abuelo (1)............................ a Buenos Aires. Allá (2)............................... con mi abuela y (3)........................... dos hijos: mi mamá y mi tío Alfonso. Nunca (4)............................... a España; no (5)............................. regresar a su querida Galicia.

4 **a. Foto** Antes de escuchar a Faustino, un boliviano que emigró a Perú en los años sesenta, fíjese en la foto 5. ¿Por qué hay tantas chimeneas?

b. Faustino Escuche a Faustino y a su mujer, y marque la opción correcta.

1. Hace casi cincuenta años desde que...
   a. Faustino emigró a Perú.　　　b. Faustino vino de Perú.
2. Desde 1962 hasta 1965...
   a. estuvo con su familia en Bolivia.　　b. vivió solo en Perú.
3. Estuvieron juntos en Perú durante...
   a. cuarenta años.　　　　b. treinta y siete años.

c. Responder ¿Conoce a otros emigrantes como Faustino? ¿Qué pasó en sus vidas?

5 **Titulares** Lea de nuevo los titulares de la **Actividad 1b** y complete estas oraciones con **desde, hasta, durante** y **desde que**.

1. .... los primeros emigrantes fueron a Latinoamérica han pasado más de cien años.
2. .... el año 1960 .... el año 1973 hubo migraciones del campo a la ciudad.
3. .... la guerra civil, muchas personas salieron de El Salvador.

6 **Preguntar** ¿Desde cuándo vive en su ciudad o pueblo? ¿Cuánto tiempo hace que estudia español? Pregunte a su compañero/a.

MI EXPERIENCIA

7 **En el extranjero** ¿Ha vivido usted, su familia o un(a) amigo/a en el extranjero? Hable con su compañero/a de la experiencia.

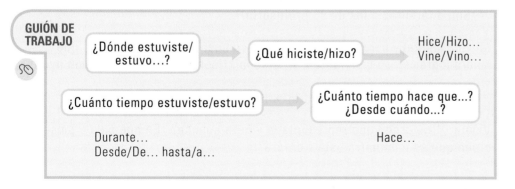

GUIÓN DE TRABAJO

¿Dónde estuviste/estuvo...? → ¿Qué hiciste/hizo? → Hice/Hizo... Vine/Vino...

¿Cuánto tiempo estuviste/estuvo? → ¿Cuánto tiempo hace que...? ¿Desde cuándo...?

Durante... Desde/De... hasta/a... Hace...

Indicar duración

- ¿Desde cuándo/Cuánto tiempo hace que vives aquí?
- Viví en Bogotá **durante** cinco años. **Desde** 1965 **hasta** 1970.
- ¿Desde cuándo vives aquí en Belice?
- **Desde que** me jubilé hace diez años.

8B.2 **durante, desde/de... hasta/a, desde que**

Vocabulario *cont.*

el/la obrero/a *worker*

en la actualidad *today; nowadays*

el horizonte, el/la emigrante, el testimonio, industrial, la emigración, el exilio, la migración

3

el/la visitante *visitor*

casarse *to get married*

regresar *to return*

4

la chimenea *chimney*

la fábrica *factory*

5

¿cuánto tiempo (hace)? *how long (have/has)?*

desde/de... hasta/a *from... until/to*

desde que *since*

pasar *to happen*

¡OJO!

Usually, when the preposition **de** is followed by the article **el**, the two words combine to form the contraction **del**. However, if the article **el** is part of a proper name (**El Salvador**), this contraction does not occur: **Somos de El Salvador**.

SAM: Actividades pp. 167–169

Nuevas formas de vida

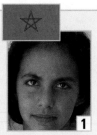

1

España tuvo un pasado emigrante y actualmente recibe personas de todo el mundo. Aproximadamente el 10% de la población es de otros países.

Entre los colectivos de inmigrantes más numerosos en España están los marroquíes, rumanos, ecuatorianos, colombianos, británicos, alemanes y argentinos.

Muchos quieren estar en España temporalmente y enviar dinero a sus familias. Otros quieren vivir allí para siempre. Los nuevos ciudadanos trabajan en la agricultura, el servicio doméstico, el comercio, los transportes, la hostelería o la construcción, y muchos abren su propio negocio. También hay médicos, profesores de idiomas o directivos de empresas. Otros no trabajan; son inmigrantes jubilados que quieren disfrutar del buen clima y el estilo de vida todo el año.

Vocabulario

8

temporalmente *temporarily*

para siempre *forever*

el/la ciudadano/a *citizen*

el servicio doméstico *domestic service*

el comercio *commerce*

el/la directivo/a *manager*

la bandera *flag*

la procedencia *origin*

la población migrante *migrant population*

el Reino Unido *United Kingdom*

10

el futuro

Expresar intenciones

- ¿Qué **quiere hacer** en los próximos años?
- **Quiero ganar** dinero para viajar por el mundo.

8B.3 **querer** + [*infinitive*]

EL ROTO

8 **a. Nuevas formas de vida** Busque en el texto cómo se llaman los ciudadanos de estos países. Escríbalos al lado del país correspondiente.

1. Marruecos *marroquíes*
2. Rumania ....
3. Ecuador ....
4. Reino Unido ....

5. Colombia ....
6. Alemania ....
7. Argentina ....

b. Relacionar Las banderas representan la procedencia de la población migrante más numerosa en España. Relaciónelas con los países.

9 **Responder** ¿A qué se dedican estos nuevos ciudadanos? ¿De dónde es la población migrante que vive en su país? ¿A qué se dedica?

10 **a. Intenciones** Escuche a estas dos personas en una clase de español para extranjeros. ¿Cuáles son sus intenciones de futuro?

1. Amina quiere...
2. Neil quiere...

- vivir mucho tiempo en España.
- disfrutar del sol.
- conocer otras ciudades.
- ayudar económicamente a su familia.

b. Amina y Neil ¿En qué coinciden Amina y Neil? Los dos quieren ....

c. Liuba Fíjese en el acento y la entonación de Liuba, la profesora cubana. ¿Son diferentes a los de su profesor(a)?

11 **Mi vida laboral y personal** Hable con su compañero/a de tres cosas que quiere lograr en su vida laboral y personal. Usen estas palabras como ayuda.

casa • hijo/a • horario • mujer/marido • sueldo • viajar

12 **Viñeta** ¿Qué creen que representa la viñeta cómica? ¿En qué país o países creen que se encuentra esta frontera?

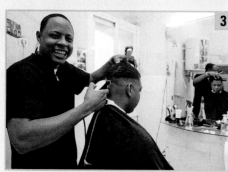

una peluquería dominicana

una tienda china

un locutorio latino

un bazar marroquí

una panadería ecuatoriana

una tetería turca

un restaurante indio

13 Fotos Observe las imágenes. ¿A qué negocios corresponden?

14 La comunidad china Escuche a esta persona que habla sobre un tipo de tienda que abre la comunidad china en España. ¿Qué características tiene?

1. Muchas veces no tienen nombre, es decir, ...
2. Tienen un horario amplio, es decir, ...
3. Venden de todo, o sea, ...

15 a. Reformular Reformule con su compañero/a estas oraciones usando **o sea** o **es decir.**

1. En las zonas donde viven inmigrantes hispanos hay muchos negocios latinos, o sea,...
2. Los locutorios ofrecen distintos servicios, es decir,...

b. Negocios ¿Hay restaurantes típicos de otros países en su barrio/pueblo? ¿Cuáles son los negocios más comunes de comunidades inmigrantes?

MI EXPERIENCIA

16 Mi negocio Usted quiere abrir un negocio diferente en su país. Descríbalo a su compañero/a.

GUIÓN DE TRABAJO

¿Qué negocio quieres abrir? → ¿Cómo? ¿Una tetería?

Quiero abrir... → Sí, o sea, un lugar para tomar té.

un bar de tapas, una tetería turca, ...

Estrategia

Reformular

¿Hay un cíber cerca? O sea, ¿un locutorio? Es decir, ¿un sitio donde pueda hacer llamadas al extranjero y usar Internet?

Vocabulario

13
la peluquería *hair salon*
el locutorio *call center; Internet café*
la panadería *bakery*
la tetería *tearoom*
el bazar
14
reformular *to restate*
o sea *that is*
es decir *in other words*
el juguete *toy*
15
la comunidad inmigrante *immigrant community*

Practice more at vhlcentral.com.

SAM: Actividades pp. 170–172

Fernanda y Alberto, dueños de un negocio salvadoreño

http://www.redempresariosmigrantes.com

El portal de los empresarios migrantes

REGISTRO	EMPRESAS ▶	• Hostelería • Comercio • Servicios • Construcción	FORO	NOTICIAS	CONTACTO

Fecha: 24 de julio

Título: Un sueño hecho realidad

Mi nombre es Fernanda Pimentel y soy de San Salvador. Mis abuelos llegaron de España a El Salvador en los años 30. Yo emigré igual que ellos. Vivo en East Boston, Massachusetts, desde hace seis años. Acá hay oportunidades, pero no es tan fácil encontrar un buen trabajo inmediatamente. Estuve en el servicio doméstico durante dos años y también cuidé a niños y a ancianos.

Mi esposo vino hace cuatro años y comenzó en la construcción. Hace seis meses, con todos los ahorros de estos años y mucho esfuerzo, hicimos realidad nuestro sueño: pudimos abrir una pequeña tienda-pupusería.

El negocio funciona bien; en la zona viven muchos salvadoreños y a los estadounidenses también les gustan nuestras pupusas. Tenemos muchos clientes estadounidenses que practican su español con nosotros cuando vienen a comprar. Además tenemos otros productos como leche, arroz, pasta... Ahora queremos traer a nuestros tres hijos. ¡El esfuerzo tiene su recompensa!

Vocabulario

17

el/la dueño/a *owner*

el/la empresario/a *businessperson*

el sueño *dream*

la oportunidad *opportunity*

comenzar (e:ie) *to start*

los ahorros *savings*

hacer realidad *to make something happen*

la pupusería *store where **pupusas** are sold*

la pupusa *Salvadoran filled tortilla*

la recompensa *reward*

tantos/as *as many*

tan/tanto... como *as much/ many... as*

vender *to sell*

la sección

Comparar formas de vida

- ¿Hay muchas diferencias entre San Salvador y Boston?

■ Allá hay **tantas** panaderías **como** acá, pero no hay **tanto** dinero y no es **tan** fácil abrir un negocio.

8B.4 tan/tanto... como

17 **a. Observar** Observe el portal de Internet. ¿Qué secciones tiene? ¿Qué información cree que da? ¿Qué países están representados?

b. Empresarios migrantes Lea el texto y fíjese en la foto. ¿Qué tipo de negocio es?

1. una tetería ☐

2. una pupusería y tienda de alimentación ☐

3. un bar ☐

c. Contestar ¿Qué productos vende?

18 **Buscar** Busque en el texto estos datos de Fernanda y Alberto.

1. ¿En qué trabajó Fernanda al principio?

2. ¿Cuánto tiempo hace que Fernanda vino a los Estados Unidos?

3. ¿Desde cuándo vive con su esposo en Boston?

19 **Dos formas de vida** San Salvador y Boston: dos formas de vida. Relacione y compare.

1. Fernanda trabaja tanto ....   a. como en San Salvador.

2. En San Salvador no tuvieron tantas oportunidades de trabajo ....   b. como Alberto.

3. Con sus hijos en Boston, la familia va a ser tan feliz ....   c. como en Boston.

20 **Fernanda y Alberto** ¿Cree que Fernanda y Alberto están felices con su nueva vida? ¿Qué intenciones tienen para el futuro?

21 a. Leer Lea el texto y observe la gráfica.

Información para la igualdad

Cada año, llegan a los Estados Unidos más de un millón de inmigrantes. Estas personas tienen una gran importancia para la economía nacional y, al parecer, son muy emprendedoras. Según informes recientes, los inmigrantes son propietarios del 18% de los negocios que hay en los Estados Unidos. Los sectores más elegidos para trabajar son el entretenimiento, el transporte, el comercio, la educación y la salud.

La presencia de los inmigrantes no es igual en todos los estados. En la gráfica siguiente se ve cuáles son los estados que los inmigrantes eligen para abrir sus negocios.

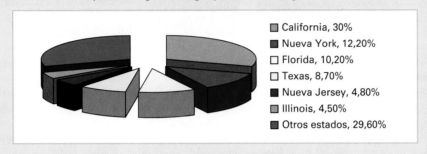

- ■ California, 30%
- ■ Nueva York, 12,20%
- □ Florida, 10,20%
- □ Texas, 8,70%
- ■ Nueva Jersey, 4,80%
- ■ Illinois, 4,50%
- ■ Otros estados, 29,60%

b. Completar Complete las oraciones con las palabras del recuadro. Puede usarlas más de una vez.

| más | más de | más que |

1. Cada año, los Estados Unidos reciben .... 1 millón de inmigrantes.
2. California es el estado que .... inmigrantes eligen para abrir sus negocios.
3. Los inmigrantes que eligen Texas para abrir sus negocios son .... los que eligen Nueva Jersey.
4. Los negocios de inmigrantes de Nueva York son casi tres veces .... los de Illinois.

c. Responder ¿Cuál cree usted que es la procedencia de la mayoría de los inmigrantes que tienen negocios en su ciudad? ¿Por qué?

22 Escribir Participe en el foro. Escriba sus comentarios y preguntas para Fernanda y Alberto.

23 a. Alimentos latinoamericanos Lea el recuadro de la derecha y observe las fotos. ¿Conoce alguno de estos alimentos?

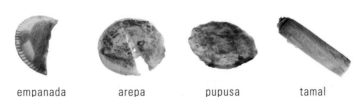

empanada   arepa   pupusa   tamal

b. Alimentos extranjeros ¿Ha probado alguno de ellos? ¿Qué otros alimentos extranjeros son populares en su país?

Practice more at vhlcentral.com.

Vocabulario

21

la igualdad *equality*
al parecer *apparently*
emprendedor(a) *enterprising*
el/la propietario/a *owner*
el entretenimiento *entertainment*
el millón, el sector, la presencia

23

hacerse *to become*
el país receptor *host country*

▪▪▪▪ O P I N I Ó N ▪▪▪▪

¿Cree que es fácil encontrar trabajo en su país? ¿Hay oportunidades profesionales para las personas de procedencia extranjera?

Comidas latinoamericanas

Cuando las personas migran de un país a otro, llevan sus costumbres, sus tradiciones ¡y sus recetas! Muchas veces, esos alimentos se hacen populares en el país receptor. Estas son algunas de las muchas comidas conocidas en los Estados Unidos:

Argentina: empanadas
Colombia: arepas, pandebono
El Salvador: pupusas
México: enchiladas, tacos, tamales
Perú: ceviche

SAM: Actividades pp. 173–178

24 **Los países receptores** Imagine que participará en un programa de estudios en el extranjero. Diga a sus compañeros qué país eligió y por qué.

Modelo: *Elegí Ecuador porque quiero estudiar las tortugas de las islas Galápagos.*

Argentina

China

Ecuador

Reino Unido

Colombia

Chile

Alemania

España

Cuba

México

TAREA FINAL

El origen de mi familia

Piense en el origen de su familia y en los lugares donde han vivido ustedes hasta ahora, y complete esta ficha.

familiar	procedencia	destino

Presente la historia personal de migraciones de su familia al grupo. Haga un esquema y marque los itinerarios y etapas.

Haga preguntas a sus compañeros sobre los motivos de sus migraciones.

Reflexione con sus compañeros acerca de las causas principales que motivan estas migraciones.

YO PUEDO...

• Puedo hablar sobre experiencias pasadas.
Cuente en qué lugares ha vivido o hable de la última vez que viajó a un país extranjero.

• Puedo indicar la duración de una experiencia.
Indique la duración de las experiencias anteriores.

• Puedo expresar intenciones.
Exprese sus intenciones sobre su lugar de residencia y su trabajo.

• Puedo comparar formas de vida.
Compare las formas de vida de los diferentes lugares donde ha vivido, o los diferentes trabajos que ha tenido.

GRAMÁTICA FUNCIONAL S Tutorials

8B.1 **Talk about experiences**

Irregular preterite verbs 5.2.2

- Many common verbs are irregular in the preterite. These verbs use an irregular preterite stem and a common set of endings.

VENIR			
(yo)	**vin**e	(nosotros/as)	**vin**imos
(tú)	**vin**iste	(vosotros/as)	**vin**isteis
(usted, él, ella)	**vin**o	(ustedes, ellos/as)	**vin**ieron

- These are the preterite stems and conjugations of some common irregular verbs.

estar	→	estuv-	→	estuve, estuviste, estuvo, estuvimos, estuvisteis, estuvieron
poder	→	pud-	→	pude, pudiste, pudo, pudimos, pudisteis, pudieron
poner	→	pus-	→	puse, pusiste, puso, pusimos, pusisteis, pusieron
saber	→	sup-	→	supe, supiste, supo, supimos, supisteis, supieron
tener	→	tuv-	→	tuve, tuviste, tuvo, tuvimos, tuvisteis, tuvieron
hacer	→	hic-	→	hice, hiciste, **hizo**, hicimos, hicisteis, hicieron
querer	→	quis-	→	quise, quisiste, quiso, quisimos, quisisteis, quisieron
conducir	→	conduj-	→	conduje, condujiste, condujo, condujimos, condujisteis, **condujeron**
decir	→	dij-	→	dije, dijiste, dijo, dijimos, dijisteis, **dijeron**
traducir	→	traduj-	→	traduje, tradujiste, tradujo, tradujimos, tradujisteis, **tradujeron**
traer	→	traj-	→	traje, trajiste, trajo, trajimos, trajisteis, **trajeron**

- Note that the **c** in the stem of **hacer** changes to **z** in the usted/él/ella form, in order to maintain the same sound.

   Yo **hice** la ensalada y Ramón **hizo** el pastel.
   I made the salad and Ramón made the cake.

- For **j**-stem verbs such as **conducir** and **traducir**, drop the **i** from the ending of the ustedes/ellos/ellas form.

   Ustedes **condujeron** desde San Salvador, ¿verdad?
   You drove from San Salvador, right?

- The preterite form of **hay** is **hubo**. As with **hay**, use **hubo** with both singular and plural objects.

   Hubo tormentas anoche y el vuelo no salió.
   There were storms last night and the flight didn't leave.

8B.2 **Indicate duration**

Prepositions of duration 10.5, 10.7, 10.8, 10.11, 10.14

- To ask how long something has been happening, say **¿Desde cuándo** + [*present-tense verb*]?, **¿Desde hace cuánto tiempo** + [*present-tense verb*]? or **¿Cuánto tiempo hace que** + [*present-tense verb*]?

   ¿Desde cuándo viven en Boston?
   How long have you lived in Boston?

- To say *since* some prior action or event, use **desde que** + [*verb in preterite*].

   Vivo aquí **desde que** me casé.
   I've lived here since I got married.

¡Póngalo en práctica!

G1 **Completar** Complete las oraciones con la forma correcta del verbo en el pretérito indefinido.

1. ¿...................... (Poder) resolver el problema tú solo?

2. Mi amigo y yo .... (conducir) por turnos durante el viaje.

3. Mis padres .... (saber) aprovechar las oportunidades.

4. Yo siempre .... (querer) viajar por Latinoamérica.

5. Sonia .... (hacer) realidad su deseo de poner un negocio.

6. ¿Ustedes .... (venir) en autobús?

7. Dos expertos .... (traducir) el libro al español.

8. Tú .... (estar) en Guadalajara, ¿no es cierto?

G2 **El día de ayer** Vuelva a escribir la oración en el pretérito indefinido, sobre el día de ayer.

   Modelo: Tengo que ir al médico.
   Tuve que ir al médico ayer.

1. Hay un descuento en este producto hoy.

   ....

2. Jimena se pone la chaqueta.

   ....

3. Ellos conducen muchos kilómetros.

   ....

4. Tú haces unos postres deliciosos.

   ....

5. Hay mucho tráfico.

   ....

6. Estamos paseando en el campo.

   ....

7. Vosotros podéis salir temprano hoy.

   ....

G3 **Conversación** Complete la conversación.

- ¿Desde cuándo (1)................ (vivir, tú) en California?

- Desde que (2)................ (casarse) en 2005.

- ¿Y cuánto tiempo hace que (3)................ (poner) tu propio negocio?

- (4)................ tres años.

- ¿Por qué crees que tienes tanto éxito?

- Tal vez porque (5)................ llegué no paro de trabajar.

- Use **durante** to indicate duration.

> **Durante** diez años viví en el extranjero.
> *For ten years I lived abroad.*

- To specify the beginning and end of a time period, use **desde/de** + [*start time*] + **hasta/a** + [*end time*]. Be sure to use **desde** and **hasta** together and **de** and **a** together, and remember to form the contractions **del** and **al** when necessary.

> Trabajé en esa empresa **desde** 2003 **hasta** 2007.
> *I worked for that company **from** 2003 **to** 2007.*

> Estuve de viaje **del** primero de julio **al** primero de agosto.
> *I was traveling **from** July first **to** August first.*

8B.3 Express intentions

querer + [*infinitive*]   5.10, 6.2.4

- Use **querer** + [*infinitive*] to express desires or intentions. Remember to conjugate only the first verb (**querer**) in infinitive constructions.

> **Quiero mirar** la tele esta noche. ¿Qué **quieres hacer** tú?
> *I **want to watch** TV tonight. What **do you want to do**?*

- When you use a reflexive pronoun or other object pronoun with this construction, place the pronoun before the conjugated verb or attach it to the end of the infinitive. You saw this pattern with direct object pronouns in **3B.8**.

> Mañana quiero levantar**me** más tarde.
> Mañana **me** quiero levantar más tarde.
> *I want to **get up** later tomorrow.*

8B.4 Compare lifestyles

Comparisons of equality   4.4.3, 12.7

- Comparisons of equality express the degree to which two people, items, or experiences are similar. Use **tan** + [*adjective/adverb*] + **como** to compare descriptions with adjectives and adverbs.

> Las pupusas son **tan ricas como** las empanadas.
> *Pupusas are **as tasty as** empanadas.*

- Use **tanto/a(s)** + [*noun*] + **como** to compare amounts or quantities. **Tanto/a** must agree in gender and number with the noun it modifies.

> Preparé **tantos tamales como** Alberto.
> *I made **as many tamales as** Alberto.*

- Use [*verb*] + **tanto como** for comparisons with verbs. Note that **tanto** is invariable in this construction.

> Martín trabaja **tanto como** Eduardo.
> *Martín works **as much as** Eduardo (does).*

- Use **tan** and **tanto/a(s)** for emphasis when the second point of comparison is not specified.

> ¡Trabajo **tantas** horas, preparo **tanta** comida y estoy **tan** cansada!
> *I work **so many** hours, I make **so much** food, and I am **so** tired!*

¡Póngalo en práctica!

G4 **Escribir** Escriba oraciones completas en pasado usando **desde/de..., hasta/a** o **durante.**

1. nosotros / no poder viajar / enero–julio
2. yo / conducir / dos días
3. ellos / estar casados / 1999–2006 /
4. tú / tener el mismo carro / cinco años
5. él /hacer las entrevistas / lunes–jueves
6. ustedes /querer tener su propia casa / 20 años
7. Marcelo / estudiar inglés / tres años

G5 **Deseos e intenciones** Escriba oraciones completas para expresar deseos o intenciones.

1. Juan / conseguir un buen trabajo
   ....
2. tú / nunca / levantarse / temprano
   ....
3. ustedes / hacer fortuna con este invento
   ....
4. nosotros / tener un hijo el año próximo
   ....
5. ellos / dedicarse más al estudio
   ....
6. yo / acostarse temprano
   ....

G6 **Tanto como** Complete la conversación.

- Tomás, ¿tú trabajas (1)........................ horas como Pedro?
- No, yo no trabajo (2)........................
- Pero su trabajo no es (3)........................ cansador (4)........................ el tuyo.
- Es cierto, él no camina (5)........................ como yo.

G7 **Oraciones** Escriba oraciones completas usando **tan** o **tanto/a(s).**

1. inmigrantes / Florida / establecerse / Nueva York
   ....
2. ¡! / los inmigrantes / emprendedores
   ....
3. (yo) / viajar / ahora / no / para ir al trabajo
   ....
4. Isabel / dedicarse al trabajo / Diana
   ....
5. Mauricio / Mariana / conducir / rápido
   ....

 Practice more at **vhlcentral.com.**

VOCABULARIO 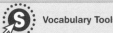 Vocabulary Tools

Emigrantes	
a finales del siglo XIX	toward the end of the 19th century
a principios del siglo XX	at the beginning of the 20th century
¿cuánto tiempo (hace)?	how long (have/has)?
los años 60	the sixties
la beca	scholarship; grant
la chimenea	chimney
la emigración	emigration
el/la emigrante	emigrant
el exilio	exile
la fábrica	factory
la finca	farm
la guerra	war
la guerra civil	civil war
el horizonte	horizon
la investigación	research
la maleta	suitcase
la migración	migration
el/la obrero/a	worker
el/la químico/a	chemist
la suerte	(good) luck
el testimonio	testimony
el/la visitante	visitor
casarse	to get married
hacer fortuna	to make a fortune
hacer las maletas	to pack
pasar	to happen
quedarse	to stay
regresar	to return
tener un hijo	to have a child
industrial	industrial
salvadoreño/a	Salvadoran
desde/de... hasta/a	from... until/to
desde niño(s)	since childhood
desde que	since
en la actualidad	today; nowadays

Nuevas formas de vida	
es decir	in other words
o sea	that is
la bandera	flag
el bazar	bazaar
el/la ciudadano/a	citizen
el comercio	commerce
la comunidad inmigrante	immigrant community
el/la directivo/a	manager
el futuro	future
el juguete	toy
el locutorio	call center; Internet café
la panadería	bakery
la peluquería	hair salon
la población migrante	migrant population
la procedencia	origin
el Reino Unido	United Kingdom
el servicio doméstico	domestic service
la tetería	tearoom
reformular	to restate
para siempre	forever
temporalmente	temporarily

Fernanda y Alberto	
los ahorros	savings
el/la dueño/a	owner
el/la empresario/a	businessperson
el entretenimiento	entertainment
la igualdad	equality
el millón	million
la oportunidad	opportunity
el país receptor	host country
la presencia	presence
el/la propietario/a	owner
la pupusa	Salvadoran filled tortilla
la pupusería	store where **pupusas** are sold
la recompensa	reward
la sección	section
el sector	sector
el sueño	dream
comenzar (e:ie)	to start
hacer realidad	to make something happen
hacerse	to become
vender	to sell
emprendedor(a)	enterprising
al parecer	apparently
tan/tanto...como	as much/many...as
tantos/as	as many

Variación léxica

el/la dueño/a ⟷ el/la propietario/a

la maleta ⟷ la valija (*Arg.*)

regresar ⟷ volver

Estrategias

1 Dar ejemplos
Lección 7A

Including examples in a conversation allows you to explain your ideas more clearly.

○ **Añada ejemplos donde corresponda en estas conversaciones.**

- ¿Quedamos mañana por la noche?
- Dale, ¿qué quieres hacer?
- Si quieres, podemos ir a cenar a un restaurante exótico...
- ¡Buena idea!

- La vida en el campo me encanta.
- ¿No es un poco aburrida?
- No, es posible hacer muchas cosas...

2 Generalizar y matizar
Lección 7B

Making generalizations (**generalmente/en general**) and explaining nuances (**especialmente/en especial**, **particularmente/en particular**) help you to be more precise in your communication.

○ **Sustituya los iconos** ⬮ **por expresiones para generalizar o matizar según convenga.**

En mi país, la gente en el trabajo ⬮ se tutea, ⬮ los colegas de la misma categoría. Hay otros contextos que son más formales ⬮. Por ejemplo, si hablas con una persona que no conoces, ⬮ usas el **usted**, ⬮ si la persona es mayor.

3 Introducir una explicación y animar
Lección 8A

Expressions such as **¡Mira!** to begin an explanation and **¡Dale!** to offer encouragement let you communicate more naturally.

○ **Complete el texto con *¡Mira!* o *¡Dale!* y ordene las ilustraciones.**

- ¡........................! Así se hace un álbum de fotografías.
  Corta° la cartulina de las tapas°.
  Forra° las tapas con el papel deseado.
  Corta las hojas del álbum.
  Realiza agujeros° y une las hojas con el cordón°.
  Por último, pega° el interior del álbum a la tapa interior.
- Parece fácil...
- ¡........................! Ahora tú.

corta *cut* **la tapa** *cover* **forra** *cover (v.)* **agujero** *hole* **cordón** *string* **pega** *glue*

4 Reformular
Lección 8B

Restating ideas in mid-conversation will help you gain fluency and confidence in your communication.

○ **Reformule las informaciones correctas o inexactas.**

- ¿Qué hora es?
- Son las 10:00 h.

- ¿Qué día es hoy?
- Es casi fin de semana.

JUNIO						
L	M	M	J	V	S	D
					1	2
3	4	5	6	7	8	9
10	11	12	13	(14)	15	16
17	18	19	20	21	22	23
24	25	26	27	28	29	30

Competencias

HABLAR DE TRABAJO, HÁBITOS Y ACCIONES QUE OCURREN EN EL MOMENTO

(1) **Oraciones** Forme oraciones con estas palabras.

> **Modelo:** colegio, todos los días, madrugo, niños, llevo
> *Todos los días madrugo y llevo a los niños al colegio.*

a. dedicarse, cantautora, escribir canciones, o sea, yo _____

b. vestimos, levantamos, 15 minutos, duchamos _____

c. conduce un camión, filosofía, verdadera vocación, Carlos _____

d. leyendo el periódico, Sandro, este momento _____

HABLAR DE EXPERIENCIAS RECIENTES

(2) **Completar** Javier y Fernando se encuentran en el Zócalo, en México, D.F. Complete la conversación con un verbo de la lista en la forma correcta del pretérito perfecto.

decir ● dejar ● escribir ● hacer ● leer ● olvidar ● pasar ● traer ● ver ● volver

● ¡Hola! Esta mañana te (1) _____ un mensaje de texto para quedar más temprano. ¿No lo (2) _____? Hace casi media hora que espero.

■ Lo siento, Javier. Mi celular está sin batería y lo (3) _____ en casa.

● No hay problema. ¿(4) _____ las entradas para el concierto?

■ Oh, no, ¡las (5) _____! Es que (6) _____ muchas cosas hoy y no (7) _____ por casa.

● Pero te (8) _____ que las necesito. El concierto es hoy.

■ Perdona, por favor. Apenas esta mañana (9) _____ de mis vacaciones. ¿(10) _____ un bar donde tomar algo? Yo invito.

DAR INSTRUCCIONES

(3) **Consejos** Con su compañero/a, escriban algunos consejos para ayudar a estas personas.

1. entrevista de trabajo

2. viaje a un país extranjero

> **Modelo:** ● *Llega temprano a una entrevista de trabajo.*

HABLAR DE EXPERIENCIAS E INDICAR DURACIÓN

(4) **Testimonio** Complete el testimonio de Tania.

abrí	aprendo	cantautor	cuidé	desde hace	doméstico	exótico
fue	mi	nuestros	panadería	soy	vivo	vocación

Soy dominicana, pero (1) _____ en Barcelona (2) _____ cuatro años. Mi primer trabajo (3) _____ en el servicio (4) _____. Después (5) _____ a ancianos. Pude ahorrar algo de dinero y (6) _____ una peluquería con una amiga. ¡(7) _____ tan feliz! Esta es (8) _____ verdadera vocación.

Video

Arquitectura modernista

Para todas las personas es importante cumplir sus sueños: algunas construyen cosas bellas para hacer un mundo mejor. Este episodio de **Flash Cultura** presenta las creaciones de los arquitectos catalanes que hicieron realidad sus sueños en la ciudad de Barcelona.

Estrategia

Getting the gist

When watching a video, try to get the gist by listening first for a statement about the general topic. Concentrate on words you know instead of fixating on unfamiliar words. The title is a good clue for predicting what the video will be about. Before watching this **Flash Cultura** episode, make one or two hypotheses based on the title **Arquitectura modernista**.

① Preguntas Hable con un(a) compañero/a:
¿Cuáles son los edificios más famosos de su país? ¿Dónde están? ¿Han visitado o conocen ciudades con edificios importantes? ¿Creen que un edificio solamente tiene que ser útil y cómodo o también debe ser bonito? ¿Qué es más importante?

② Mirar Mire este episodio de **Flash Cultura**. Trate de identificar cada lugar concentrándose en una característica o en un detalle; no se preocupe por entender toda la descripción.

Vocabulario útil

el baldosín *ceramic tile*
brillar *to shine*
la calavera *skull*
el encargo *job, assignment*
la escama *scale*
la escalera *staircase*
la fachada *front of building*
el hierro forjado *wrought iron*
el hueso *bone*
inacabado/a *unfinished*
el tejado *roof*

Antonio Gaudí... también creó un extraordinario espacio público donde la gente puede disfrutar...

Estrategia

Connotations

Remember that in Spanish, as in English, some words may have figurative uses. Metaphors, similes, and personifications appear not only in poetry, but also in everyday language. For example, (Está que) se lo/la lleva el diablo or (Está que) echa chispas, do not mean that a person is about to be taken away by the devil or to explode; these phrases express (colloquially) that the person is extremely angry.

La Sagrada Familia es el edificio más visitado y emblemático de la ciudad.

③ Escoger Una la primera columna con la segunda para completar las oraciones.

1. La zona del Paseo de Gracia...	.... a. fue encargo de un chocolatero.
2. La Casa Batlló de Gaudí...	.... b. es una obra inacabada de Gaudí.
3. La Casa Amatller...	.... c. se conoce como la Manzana de la Discordia.
4. El banco ondulado del Parque Güell...	.... d. fue punto de encuentro de jóvenes artistas modernistas.
5. La Sagrada Familia...	.... e. representa la leyenda de San Jorge y el dragón.
6. El café Los cuatro gatos...	.... f. tiene forma de serpiente colorida.

④ Propuestas Con un(a) compañero/a, hable de propuestas para hacer un mundo mejor; acepte o rechace cada una y escriba las que aprobó. Después, comparta el resultado con la clase.

  Practice more at **vhlcentral.com**.

Unidad 9

Luis Soriano, creador del Biblioburro

Lola, la del quiosco del barrio

Las fiestas

9A

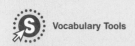
Vocabulary Tools

ETAPAS DE LA VIDA

¡Qué tiempos!

¿Dónde estabas en 2005?

¿Estudiabas en la Escuela Primaria N.º 3?

¿Qué hacías cuando estudiabas?

¿Qué hacían tus compañeros de curso?

¿Conocían el club El progreso?

¿Compartían otras actividades además de la escuela?

Si la respuesta es sí, eres uno de los compañeros de Cristina y Carlos.

En Punto de encuentro puedes volver a ver a tus compañeros de la promoción de 2005.

Sábado 12 de febrero. 22:00 h.

Punto de encuentro

Un programa de TV para el pasado y para el presente.
Para reencontrar a amigos de la infancia
y a compañeros de la escuela primaria.

Describir hábitos y situaciones del pasado

- ¿Qué **hacías** en la época de la escuela primaria?

- **Tenía** clases por la mañana. **Compartía** el autobús escolar de regreso a casa con Nico y Mario. **Estaba** siempre con ellos: **estudiábamos** juntos y **jugábamos** en el mismo equipo de fútbol.

9A.1 | Imperfect

Vocabulario

① ────────

la etapa *stage*

la escuela primaria *elementary school*

el punto de encuentro *meeting point*

la promoción *graduating class*

reencontrar (o:ue) *to meet again*

la infancia *childhood*

la época *time, period*

egresar *to graduate*

el programa, la TV

③ ────────

estar callado/a *to be silent*

---

① **a. Punto de encuentro** Lea el anuncio. ¿Qué es *Punto de encuentro*?

b. El pretérito imperfecto Localice en los textos las formas del pretérito imperfecto y complete la tabla.

	ESTAR	HACER	COMPARTIR
yo	estaba	hacía	compartía
tú			compartías
usted, él, ella	estaba	hacía	compartía
nosotros/as	estábamos	hacíamos	compartíamos
vosotros/as	estabais	hacíais	compartíais
ustedes, ellos/as	estaban		

c. Conjugar Localice otros verbos en pretérito imperfecto. ¿Cuál es su infinitivo? Escriba su conjugación.

② **Contestar** ¿A quiénes buscan Cristina y Carlos? ¿Qué características identifican a los compañeros de su curso?

③ **a. Cristina y Carlos** Escuche a Cristina y a Carlos en el programa. ¿Quién hacía estas cosas?

1. Tomaba clases de guitarra. Su hermano tenía un grupo de música y ella soñaba con tocar con ellos. ....

2. Vivía cerca de Juan y muchas veces salían en bici a la hora de la siesta. Jugaba al fútbol con sus amigos en el club El progreso. ....

b. Juntos Escuche otra vez y marque qué hacían ellos juntos.

Hacían la tarea juntos. ☐   Tomaban el mismo autobús escolar. ☐

Veían películas juntos. ☐   Estudiaban francés juntos. ☐

④ **Responder** ¿Qué hacía usted hace cinco años? ¿Cuántos años tenía? ¿Dónde vivía? ¿Qué estudiaba? ¿A qué jugaba? ¿Qué música le gustaba?

Los invitamos este sábado a compartir el antes y el ahora.

Cuando éramos pequeños, nos reuníamos en alguna casa a jugar o caminábamos juntos a la escuela. ¡Hasta llevábamos a nuestra vecinita al jardín! Vivíamos muchas cosas juntos…

Ahora ya somos jóvenes hechos y derechos, con nuevas responsabilidades, pero si lo queremos ¡podemos vivir juntos muchas cosas más!

---

5 Fotos Observe las imágenes y lea los textos. ¿Cómo eran antes y cómo son ahora estas personas?

6 Antes y ahora Escuche a un compañero que llama al programa. ¿Cómo era antes? ¿Adónde iba? ¿Y ahora?

7 Verbos Fíjese en las formas de los verbos regulares. Luego escriba los sujetos para las formas del pretérito imperfecto de estos dos verbos irregulares.

SER			
1. .... éramos	4. .... era
2. .... erais	5. .... eran
3. .... era	6. .... eras

IR			
1. .... íbamos	4. .... ibais
2. .... iba	5. .... iba
3. .... ibas	6. .... iban

8 Mi vida ¿Ha cambiado mucho la vida desde que usted era pequeño/a? ¿Cómo era antes y cómo es ahora? Dé algunos ejemplos.

👥 **MI EXPERIENCIA**

9 Hace diez años ¿Cómo era su vida hace diez años? Pregunte a su compañero/a.

GUIÓN DE TRABAJO

	Hace 10 años...	Ahora...
vivienda	vivía	vivo
edad		
estudios		
aficiones		

¿Dónde estudiabas? ¿Qué hacías? ¿Cómo eras?

Y ahora... ¿Qué haces? ¿Cómo eres?

Comparar el pasado con el presente

• Yo antes **era** más inseguro. Ahora sé lo que quiero.

■ Pues yo antes **iba** a conciertos de rock, y ahora también voy.

9A.2 Irregular imperfect verbs

Vocabulario

(5)
el/la joven hecho/a y derecho/a *all grown-up*
la responsabilidad *responsibility*
antes *before*

(6)
la mochila *backpack*
la carpa *tent*
aventurero/a *adventurous*
guapo/a *good-looking*
el pelo *hair*
el canal *channel*

La televisión en el mundo hispano

Dos de los grupos audiovisuales hispánicos más importantes son Televisión española (TVE), y Televisa, en México. Ambos tienen canales de proyección internacional.

SAM: Actividades pp. 179–181

Ⓢ Practice more at **vhlcentral.com.**

Segunda juventud

Seguro que tienes muchas cosas interesantes que compartir:

algún viaje, alguna canción, alguna noticia, algún amor...

Queremos escucharte.

somos-todo-oídos
Televisión para mayores de 65

Referirse a cantidades indefinidas

- ¿Hay **algún** documental en la tele?
- Sí, creo que hay **alguno**.
- ¿Hay **alguna** serie hoy?
- Sí, creo que hay **alguna**.
- ¿No hay **ningún** debate ahora?
- No, **ninguno**.
- ¿No hay **ninguna** entrevista?
- No, **ninguna**.

9A.3 | **algún, ningún alguno/a, ninguno/a**

Vocabulario

(10)

la juventud *youth*
Seguro que... *I'm sure (that)...*
algún *some, any*
alguno/a *some, any*
ser todo oídos *to be all ears*
mayor de *older than*
el/la camarógrafo/a *cameraperson*
el documental

(12)

ninguno/a *no, not any, none*
ningún *no, not any*

Estrategia ···········

Ganar tiempo mientras pensamos

- ¿Sabe alguna canción?
- ¿Alguna canción? Mmm... bueno, pues, no sé... a ver... ¿cómo era?

---

10 **a. Foto** Observe la imagen de la izquierda. Describa qué está pasando.

b. Publicidad ¿Qué anuncia la publicidad?

c. Responder ¿Mira usted la televisión? ¿Algún programa en especial?

11 **Algún, alguna** Fíjese en el texto del anuncio. Relacione los elementos de los grupos.

algún
alguna

amor
canción
viaje
noticia

12 **a. En directo** Escuche a esta persona a la que han entrevistado en directo en el programa de televisión y marque los temas que menciona.

¿Algún/Alguna...?	Sí, alguno/a.	No, ninguno/a.
viaje	✓	
canción		
noticia		
amor		
persona		

b. Formas para ganar tiempo Escuche de nuevo y localice las formas para ganar tiempo antes de responder.

13 **Alguna información** Comparta con el grupo alguna información sobre estos temas para colaborar con el programa.

| algún viaje | alguna canción | alguna noticia | algún amor |

| alguna persona | alguna experiencia con el español | otros... |

Modelo: • ¿Sabes alguna canción?
• Pues, no sé... a ver...

TV Hoy — Programación

 9:00 h Informativo *¡Buen día, país!*
10:00 h Tertulia política en *Todas las voces.*
11:00 h La información deportiva en *Charlas de fútbol.*
12:00 h *El magacín de la tele* con informativos, pronóstico del tiempo y temas de sociedad.
14:00 h *Los jóvenes tienen la palabra* con la participación de los televidentes.
15:00 h *Trotamundos* Viajes y ritmos del mundo.
16:00 h *Somos todo oídos* para mayores de 65.

---

14 Programación Lea la programación de televisión y clasifique los programas de acuerdo a estas categorías.

> deporte • música • noticias • política • sociedad • viajes

15 a. Mi opinión Dé su opinión de los programas.

El más...   El menos...

> aburrido • completo • divertido • interesante • útil

b. El mejor y el peor Con un(a) compañero/a, elija el mejor y el peor tipo de programa.

El mejor...   El peor...

16 La TV La televisión acompaña la vida de muchas personas. ¿Qué programas son los más vistos en su país? ¿Cuáles son sus preferidos? ¿Por qué?

MI EXPERIENCIA

17 Preferencias Piense en los medios de comunicación que prefiere para estas situaciones, y qué programas le parecen los más interesantes en cada caso.

GUIÓN DE TRABAJO

Situaciones	Programas	Medios
entretenerse	documentales	Internet
escuchar música	información deportiva	radio
informarse	informativos	televisión
participar en debates	programas musicales	
sentirse acompañado/a	pronóstico del tiempo	

Para mí, la televisión es el mejor medio para informarse. → ¿Conoces algún programa/alguna página web para escuchar música?

↓

No, ninguno.
Sí, hay algunas muy buenas en Internet.

Expresar preferencias

- ¿Qué programa de televisión prefieres?
- Para mí, **el más interesante** es la tertulia política.
- Ese es **el más aburrido**. Para mí, **el mejor** es el programa de viajes.
- ¿Y **el peor**?
- **El peor**, las charlas de fútbol.

9A.4 el más/menos...
el mejor/peor...

Vocabulario

14

el informativo *news (program)*
la tertulia *roundtable; talk show*
la charla *chat*
el magacín *news and talk show*
el pronóstico *weather forecast*
la sociedad *society*
el/la televidente *TV viewer*
el/la trotamundos *globetrotter*

15

el/la más/menos *the most/least*
el/la mejor/peor *the best/worst*
útil *useful*
completo/a

16

acompañar *to keep company*

17

los medios (de comunicación) *media*
entretenerse *to amuse oneself*
sentirse (e:ie) acompañado/a *to feel accompanied*

SAM: Actividades pp. 182–184

Luis Soriano, creador del Biblioburro

Cada fin de semana, el profesor Luis Soriano lleva su biblioteca ambulante Biblioburro a pequeñas aldeas rurales del departamento del Magdalena (Colombia). Montado en sus burros, Alfa y Beto, recorre hasta veinte kilómetros cargando unos 200 libros, entre cuentos infantiles, novelas, diccionarios y enciclopedias.

Luis lleva más de veinte años con este proyecto. "Tuve la idea del Biblioburro cuando mis alumnos de las veredas cercanas llegaban a la escuela sin hacer la tarea porque no tenían libros en la casa. No podían investigar, ¡no podían hacer nada!", dice el profesor. Pero su proyecto es también a largo plazo: estos niños van a ser los futuros adolescentes y es importante despertarles la inquietud de la lectura para formar mentes constructivas e imaginativas.

Cuando comenzó, tenía dos burros y setenta libros. Ahora su colección cuenta con más de 4800 títulos. En esta biblioteca hay que respetar dos reglas: tocar los libros con las manos limpias y no escribir en las páginas. Para Luis, lo mejor de todo es cuando algún niño le pregunta "¿Cuándo va a regresar, maestro?" Lo peor es que algunas veces los libros que presta nunca vuelven.

Hoy el Biblioburro ya es parte de la red nacional de bibliotecas. Además, el proyecto se extendió a otras zonas y desde 2006 también funciona en la Sierra Nevada de Santa Marta.

El profesor Luis Soriano con su burro cargado de libros

Hablar de la cantidad de tiempo

Luis Soriano **lleva toda una vida** como maestro.

Lleva más de veinte años con el Biblioburro.

El proyecto también **lleva diez años** funcionando en la Sierra Nevada de Santa Marta.

9A.5 llevar + [*length of time*]

Vocabulario

18

la biblioteca ambulante *traveling library*

la aldea *village*

el/la burro/a *donkey*

cargar *to load; to carry*

montar *to ride*

la vereda (*Col.*) *rural neighborhood*

a largo plazo *in the long term*

despertar (e:ie) la inquietud *to stir up interest*

la inquietud *interest*

contar (o:ue) con *to include*

prestar *to lend*

la red *network*

gracioso/a *funny*

el/la adolescente

19

la sede *headquarters*

la devolución *return*

---

18 **Luis Soriano** Lea el texto. Describa la actividad que realiza Luis Soriano. ¿Por qué realiza esta actividad? ¿Qué es gracioso acerca del nombre de los burros?

19 **a. Completar** Conozca más detalles del profesor Luis Soriano. Escuche qué dice de estos temas y anótelo. Luego compruebe las respuestas con su compañero/a.

La sede de la biblioteca: ....

Su criterio para elegir qué lugares visita con el Biblioburro:

....

La recepción en los pueblos:

....

Los libros más pedidos: ....

La devolución de los libros: ....

b. Tú o usted Escuche nuevamente y diga si la entrevistadora y el profesor hablan de **usted** o de **tú**. ¿Por qué cree que esto es así?

c. Relacionar Lea estas oraciones sobre el Biblioburro. Las palabras subrayadas se usan en Colombia. Relaciónelas con su significado.

a. niño, muchacho (*fam.*)   b. llevar   c. barrio rural

1. Es una biblioteca para los niños que viven en esta <u>vereda</u>. ......
2. Los <u>peladitos</u> que viven al lado de la carretera ven gente que pasa y eso les va dejando algo de enseñanza. ......
3. *La Ilíada* no lo devolvieron porque les gustó mucho y dijeron "Este me lo <u>cargo</u>". ......

20 a. Platero y yo Uno de los libros que Luis Soriano lleva a veces en su Biblioburro es *Platero y yo*. En este clásico de la literatura infantil y juvenil, el escritor español Juan Ramón Jiménez narra su tierna relación con un burrito. Lea el texto y busque las palabras que tienen estos significados.

1. con mucho pelo ....
2. tierra con hierba para alimentar a los animales ....
3. parte de la cabeza de algunos animales donde están la boca y la nariz ....
4. forma de caminar del caballo o del burro ....

Platero es pequeño, peludo, suave; tan blando por fuera, que se diría° todo de algodón, que no lleva huesos. Sólo los espejos de azabache° de sus ojos son duros cual dos escarabajos° de cristal negros.

Lo dejo suelto°, y se va al prado, y acaricia tibiamente con su hocico°, rozándolas° apenas, las florecillas rosas, celestes y gualdas°... Lo llamo dulcemente: "¿Platero?", y viene a mí con un trotecillo alegre que parece que se ríe, en no sé qué cascabeleo° ideal...

que se diría *you would say he's* **azabache** *jet (black stone)* **cual dos escarabajos** *like two beetles* **suelto** *loose* **hocico** *snout* **rozándolas** *gently touching them* **gualdas** *yellow* **cascabeleo** *jingle*

Juan Ramón Jiménez (1881–1958)

b. Contestar ¿Qué actividades hace Platero y cuáles hace su dueño?

21 Comparar Según el autor, Platero es tan blando como el algodón. Complete las comparaciones con sus propias ideas. Use un diccionario si lo necesita.

1. tan transparente como ....
2. tan negro como ....
3. tan brillante como ....
4. tan alto como ....
5. tan duro como ....

22 Responder ¿Por qué son importantes los animales para los seres humanos? ¿Y los seres humanos para los animales? Describa a su mascota o a algún animal. ¿Cómo es físicamente? ¿Cómo es su personalidad?

23 Escribir ¿Cuáles son los cuentos que más le gustaban en su infancia? ¿Por qué? Escriba una breve reseña de uno de sus cuentos preferidos en esa época.

24 [c] y [ll] Escuche el segundo párrafo de *Platero y yo* leído por un español y un argentino. Fíjese en cómo pronuncian estas palabras y apunte las diferencias.

acaricia	rozándolas	llamo	trotecillo
hocico	florecillas	dulcemente	parece

Vocabulario *cont.*

el/la campesino/a *rural worker*
la donación
20
tierno/a *affectionate*
peludo/a *shaggy*
la tierra *land, dirt*
el prado *meadow*
la boca *mouth*
la nariz *nose*
blando/a *soft*
el algodón *cotton*
el hueso *bone*
el espejo *mirror*
el ojo *eye*
acariciar *to caress*
celeste *light blue*
el clásico, trotar
21
brillante *bright*
transparente
23
la reseña *summary; review*
la lancha *boat*
flotante *floating*

Promover la lectura
Todo sirve para promover la lectura. Hay bibliobuses en España, un biblioavión interactivo en México, bibliolanchas en Argentina y bibliotecas flotantes en el Amazonas. ¿Hay alguna biblioteca no convencional en su ciudad o región?

SAM: Actividades pp. 185–188

25 **Actividades** Descubra más sobre usted mismo/a. Anote el número de las tres actividades que más le interesan. Comparta el resultado con sus compañeros. ¿Hay alguna coincidencia?

jardín

viajes

lectura

deporte

ONG

actividades artísticas

familiares y amigos

cursos

Resultados:

2, 4, 5: Le encanta descubrir lugares nuevos y conocer a personas nuevas.

4, 2, 1: Tiene mucha energía física.

3, 8, 6: Siempre quiere aprender más.

5, 7, 8: Le gusta compartir su tiempo con otros.

6, 1, 3: Lo que más le gusta es expresarse.

Mi resultado:

Para mí, las más interesantes son

....

....

....

T A R E A   F I N A L

Un programa de televisión

Definan qué tipo de programa de TV quieren hacer. Dividan el programa en secciones y trabajen en grupos pequeños o en parejas.

Escriban el guión del programa: redacción de noticias, canciones, anuncios, etc.

Presenten los contenidos al grupo.

Y O   P U E D O . . .

• Puedo describir hábitos del pasado.

¿Dónde vivía hace diez años?

• Puedo comparar el pasado con el presente.

Compare su vida de hace cinco o diez años con la de ahora en estos aspectos: vivienda, estudios, familia.

• Puedo referirme a cantidades indefinidas.

¿Hay algún estudiante en clase que vive cerca de usted?

• Puedo expresar preferencias.

Anote cuál es la mejor y la peor noticia del año según su opinión.

• Puedo hablar de la cantidad de tiempo.

Indique cuánto tiempo lleva con esta autoevaluación.

GRAMÁTICA FUNCIONAL ⓢ Tutorials

9A.1 Describe habits and situations in the past

Imperfect of regular verbs 5.4.1, 5.4.3

- You have learned that Spanish uses two simple tenses, the preterite and the imperfect, to talk about events in the past. Use the imperfect (**el pretérito imperfecto**) to express repeated or habitual actions in the past, or to describe past situations.

> Cuando **estaba** en la escuela primaria, **jugaba** al fútbol.
> *When **I was** in elementary school, **I played** soccer.*

- **Estudiar**, **tener**, and **vivir** exemplify the conjugation patterns of regular -ar, -er, and -ir verbs in the **pretérito imperfecto**.

	ESTUDIAR	TENER	VIVIR
(yo)	estudi**aba**	ten**ía**	viv**ía**
(tú)	estudi**abas**	ten**ías**	viv**ías**
(usted, él, ella)	estudi**aba**	ten**ía**	viv**ía**
(nosotros/as)	estudi**ábamos**	ten**íamos**	viv**íamos**
(vosotros/as)	estudi**abais**	ten**íais**	viv**íais**
(ustedes, ellos/as)	estudi**aban**	ten**ían**	viv**ían**

- The **yo** and **usted/él/ella** forms are the same in all conjugations of the imperfect, so you should use context to clarify. Additionally, the endings of **-er** and **-ir** verbs in the imperfect are the same.

> Yo **estudiaba** periodismo y Juan **estudiaba** biología.
> *I **studied** journalism and Juan **studied** biology.*

- Use the imperfect to describe habitual or repeated actions, actions that were in progress, physical characteristics, mental or emotional states, age, and to tell time.

> ¿Cuántos años **tenías** cuando **tomabas** clases de francés?
> *How old **were you** when **you took** French classes?*

- Use the imperfect of **haber** (**había**) to talk about the existence of things. As with **hay** in the present, **había** is used with singular or plural objects.

9A.2 Compare the past with the present

Imperfect of irregular verbs 5.4.2

- The verbs **ser**, **ir**, and **ver** have irregular forms in the **pretérito imperfecto**.

	SER	IR	VER
(yo)	**era**	**iba**	**veía**
(tú)	**eras**	**ibas**	**veías**
(usted, él, ella)	**era**	**iba**	**veía**
(nosotros/as)	**éramos**	**íbamos**	**veíamos**
(vosotros/as)	**erais**	**ibais**	**veíais**
(ustedes, ellos/as)	**eran**	**iban**	**veían**

> En la universidad mis amigos y yo **íbamos** todos los domingos al cine.
> *In college, my friends and I **used to go** to the movies every Sunday.*

- All other verbs are regular in the imperfect. Note that there are no stem changes in the imperfect.

 Practice more at **vhlcentral.com**.

¡Póngalo en práctica!

G1 **Elegir** Elija la forma del pretérito imperfecto que corresponde con cada sujeto.

viajar		
	1. ella	a. viajabas
	2. nosotros	b. viajabais
	3. tú	c. viajaba
	4. vosotras	d. viajábamos
	5. ellos	e. viajaban

escribir		
	1. ustedes	a. escribías
	2. él	b. escribíamos
	3. nosotras	c. escribían
	4. vosotros	d. escribía
	5. tú	e. escribíais

G2 **Párrafo** Complete las oraciones con la forma correcta del verbo en el pretérito imperfecto.

Cuando mi madre (1)................ (tener) diez años, (2)................ (vivir) en un pueblo pequeño cerca de la costa. Ella y sus dos hermanos (3)................ (caminar) a la escuela todos los días y (4)................ (volver) a casa para almorzar. Mis abuelos (5)................ (trabajar) en un café y todos los veranos la familia entera (6)................ (pasar) mucho tiempo en la playa. Mi hermana y yo siempre (7)................ (querer) visitar el pueblo porque nuestra madre nos (8)................ (contar) historias interesantes de su infancia.

G3 **Completar** Complete las oraciones con la forma correcta del verbo en el pretérito imperfecto.

1. Cuando .... (ser) pequeños, vivíamos con nuestra familia en las montañas.

2. Francisco y Manuel .... (ir) a la costa todos los veranos cuando vivían en Buenos Aires.

3. Yo .... (ir) a la biblioteca después de clases.

4. La casa de campo de los abuelos de Maribel .... (ser) amplia y luminosa.

5. Durante la universidad, tú y yo nos .... (ver) todos los días.

6. Tú y Javier .... (ser) muy tímidos durante la secundaria.

GRAMÁTICA FUNCIONAL

9A.3 Refer to undefined quantities

algún; ningún; alguno/a(s); ninguno/a 6.5

- Use **algún, alguno/a(s)** (*a/an; any; some*) and **ningún, ninguno/a** (*no; none; not any*) to talk about undefined quantities. These adjectives must agree with the nouns they modify. Always use a negative expression (**ningún, ninguno/a**) in a negative sentence.

  ¿Tienes **alguna** película para recomendarme?
  *Do you have **a** movie to recommend to me?*

  No hay **ninguna** canción buena en este CD.
  *There are **no** good songs on this CD.*

- Use **algún** and **ningún** before masculine singular nouns.

  ¿Miras **algún** programa de noticias por la mañana?
  *Do you watch **a** news program in the morning?*

- **Alguno/a(s)** and **ninguno/a** can also function as pronouns.

  Ayer había un buen programa, pero hoy no hay **ninguno**.
  *Yesterday there was a good show on, but today there aren't **any**.*

9A.4 Express preferences

Superlatives: adjectives 4.4.1, 4.4.2

- Use **el/la/los/las + más/menos +** [*adjective*] to describe a characteristic that surpasses all others (**el superlativo**).

  El Aconcagua es **la** montaña **más alta** de las Américas.
  *Aconcagua is **the highest** mountain in the Americas.*

  Los programas **menos interesantes** son los concursos.
  The least interesting programs are game shows.

- Use the preposition **de +** [*group*] to mean *in/of +* [*group*].

  Miguel es el más listo **de la clase**.
  *Miguel is the smartest **in the class**.*

- Some adjectives have irregular superlative forms.

  | bueno/a(s) → **el/la mejor; los/las mejores** |
  | malo/a(s) → **el/la peor; los/las peores** |

  El perro es **el mejor** amigo del hombre.
  *Dog is man's **best** friend.*

9A.5 Talk about length of time

llevar + [*length of time*] 5.1.1

- Use the construction **llevar +** [*length of time*] to tell how long you have been doing something.

  llevar + [*length of time*]
  en + [*place*]
  como + [*profession*]
  + [*present participle*]
  con + [*other noun*]

  Llevo dos años en Canarias.
  I have been in the Canaries for two years.

  Llevo cinco años como traductor.
  I have been a translator for five years.

¡Póngalo en práctica!

G4 Conversaciones Complete las conversaciones.

- ¿Hay (1)......................... documental en la tele esta noche?
- Sí, creo que hay (2).........................
- ¿No hay (3)......................... programa de música clásica en la radio?
- No, no hay (4).........................
- ¿Escuchaste (5)......................... noticia interesante hoy por la tele?
- No, no escuché (6).........................
- ¿Conoces (7)......................... canción popular de España?
- Sí, conozco (8).........................

G5 El superlativo Escriba oraciones completas usando el superlativo.

1. Rhode Island   estado   + pequeño   Estados Unidos
   ....

2. lunes   día   + malo   semana
   ....

3. tertulia política   programa   – divertido   canal
   ....

4. María y Ana   + bueno   estudiante   clase
   ....

5. el Amazonas   río   + largo   mundo
   ....

G6 Diálogo Complete la conversación.

- ¿Cuánto tiempo (1)......................... Carmela (2)......................... la danza?
- (3)......................... casi quince años (4)......................... bailarina.
- ¿Y sus padres viven aquí hace mucho tiempo?
- Sí, (5)......................... diez años (6)......................... Caracas.
- Yo (7)......................... solo cinco años en la capital.

S Practice more at **vhlcentral.com**.

VOCABULARIO   Vocabulary Tools

¡Qué tiempos!

el canal	channel
la carpa	tent
la época	time, period
la escuela primaria	elementary school
la etapa	stage
la infancia	childhood
la mochila	backpack
el pelo	hair
el programa	program
la promoción	graduating class
el punto de encuentro	meeting point
la responsabilidad	responsibility
la TV	TV
egresar	to graduate
estar callado/a	to be silent
reencontrar (o:ue)	to meet again
aventurero/a	adventurous
guapo/a	good-looking
el/la joven hecho/a y derecho/a	all grown-up
antes	before

Segunda juventud

el/la más/menos	the most/least
el/la mejor/peor	the best/worst
Seguro que...	I'm sure (that)...
el/la camarógrafo/a	cameraperson
la charla	chat
el documental	documentary
el informativo	news (program)
la juventud	youth
el magacín	news and talk show
los medios (de comunicación)	media
el pronóstico	weather forecast
la sociedad	society
el/la televidente	TV viewer
la tertulia	roundtable; talk show
el/la trotamundos	globetrotter
acompañar	to keep company
entretenerse	to amuse oneself
sentirse (e:ie) acompañado/a	to feel accompanied
ser todo oídos	to be all ears
algún	some, any
alguno/a	some, any
completo/a	complete
mayor de	older than
ningún	no, not any
ninguno/a	no, not any, none
útil	useful

Luis Soriano

el/la adolescente	adolescent, teenager
la aldea	village
el algodón	cotton
la boca	mouth
la biblioteca ambulante	traveling library
el/la burro/a	donkey
el/la campesino/a	rural worker
el clásico	classic
la devolución	return
la donación	donation
el espejo	mirror
el hueso	bone
la inquietud	interest
la lancha	boat
la nariz	nose
el ojo	eye
el prado	meadow
la red	network
la reseña	summary; review
la sede	headquarters
la tierra	land, dirt
la vereda (Col.)	rural neighborhood
acariciar	to caress
cargar	to load; to carry
contar (o:ue) con	to include
despertar (e:ie) la inquietud	to stir up interest
montar	to ride
prestar	to lend
trotar	to trot
a largo plazo	in the long term
blando/a	soft
brillante	bright
celeste	light blue
flotante	floating
gracioso/a	funny
peludo/a	shaggy
tierno/a	affectionate
transparente	transparent

Variación léxica

la biblioteca ambulante ↔ la biblioteca itinerante ↔ la biblioteca móvil

egresar ↔ graduarse (Amér. L.)

gracioso/a ↔ chistoso/a

el informativo ↔ el noticiero (Amér. L.) ↔ el telediario (Esp.) ↔ el noticiario

el magacín ↔ el programa de variedades

el/la niño/a ↔ el/la peladito/a (fam., Col.)

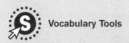
HISTORIAS DE LA CALLE

Caras del barrio

EL UNIVERSO DEL BARRIO

Su periódico semanal gratuito   Viernes, 3 de diciembre

Concurso "LAS CARAS MÁS POPULARES DEL BARRIO" ¡AQUÍ ESTÁN LOS FINALISTAS!

Algunos de ellos llevan toda la vida en el barrio, como Paqui la vendedora de lotería, la de la calle Palma, la que reparte suerte y simpatía desde hace muchos años, ¡casi cincuenta! Otros viven con nosotros desde hace poco tiempo, como Hugo Valdez, el del locutorio de la calle Paloma, que llegó de República Dominicana en busca de nuevas experiencias.

¡VOTEN POR SU FAVORITO O FAVORITA!

"El negocio era de mis padres, y antes de mis abuelos."
—Antonio Campos

"He repartido muchos premios y ¡dos gordos!"
—Paqui Ruiz

Identificar por una característica

El de la frutería se llama Antonio.
Norma es **la que** tiene el estanco.
Los de la panadería son ecuatorianos.

9B.1	el/la/los/las + de/que

Vocabulario

① ────

gratuito/a *free (of charge)*

el/la vendedor(a) de lotería *lottery ticket seller*

el gordo *jackpot; first prize*

gordo/a *fat*

el universo, el/la finalista, el/la favorito/a

② ────

la agencia de lotería *lottery ticket booth*

el estanco (*Esp.*) *tobacconist shop*

la frutería *fruit shop*

la juguetería *toy store*

la papelería *stationery store*

③ ────

el sorteo *drawing*

la telefonía *phone service*

el establecimiento *store; establishment*

---

1 **Observar** Observe el documento. ¿Qué tipo de publicación es? ¿En qué consiste el concurso?

2 **a. El universo del barrio** ¿Qué negocios representan la vida de este barrio? Márquelos.

> agencia de lotería • bar • estanco • frutería • juguetería
> (locutorio) • panadería • papelería • tienda de alimentación

b. Identificar Identifique a los finalistas del concurso por el negocio que tienen.

Norma Hugo Paqui Antonio	es	el que vende fruta. la que tiene la agencia de lotería. la del estanco. el del locutorio.

3 **Relacionar** Relacione estas explicaciones con las declaraciones de los finalistas.

> [2] El gordo es el mayor premio del sorteo de la lotería de Navidad.

> Los locutorios ofrecen servicios de telefonía, Internet o envío de dinero, especialmente para las comunidades de extranjeros.

> En los mercados de barrio, los negocios pasan muchas veces de padres a hijos.

> Los estancos son los establecimientos oficiales para vender tabaco en España.

4 **a. Adivinar** Identifique a las personas del barrio y adivine de quién habla su compañero/a.

b. Responder ¿Quién es su favorito para ganar el concurso? ¿Por qué?

Los 10 establecimientos imprescindibles del barrio

"La ley antitabaco ha afectado mucho a mi negocio. ¡Ahora necesito vender más chicles y regalitos!"—Norma Sánchez

"Llegué a España y abrí este negocio. Muchos extranjeros llaman desde aquí a sus familias."—Hugo Valdez

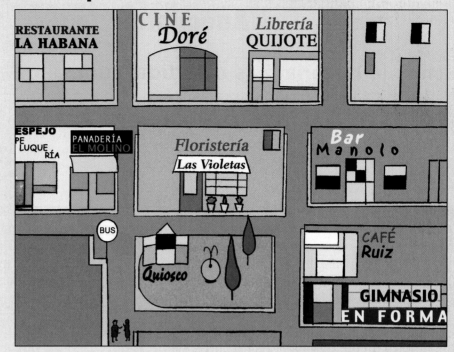

(5) **Escuchar** Escuche la conversación. ¿Qué dos establecimientos busca una de las personas? Señale en el plano el camino que debe recorrer.

(6) **a. El imperativo** Marque las formas verbales del imperativo. ¿Se hablan de **tú** o de **usted**?

> • Perdone, ¿hay una librería cerca?
> • Sí, mire, tome esta calle, siga todo recto y vaya hasta la plaza, luego gire la tercera a la derecha.

> • Perdona, ¿sabes dónde está el restaurante La Habana?
> • Mira, toma esta calle, sigue recto y ve hasta la plaza. Después, gira a la izquierda.

b. Completar Observe los ejemplos anteriores y complete la tabla. ¿Qué verbo es irregular?

	GIRAR	RECORRER	SEGUIR	IR
tú	gira			ve
usted		recorra	siga	

MI EXPERIENCIA

(7) **Mi establecimiento** Sitúe en el plano un nuevo establecimiento e indique la dirección a su compañero/a.

GUIÓN DE TRABAJO

> ¿Cuál es el establecimiento?
>
> Es la papelería Papiro.

> ¿Dónde está?
>
> Sigue recto y...

Indicar el camino

● Perdone, ¿hay una cafetería cerca?

■ Sí, **siga** usted **todo recto** y **gire** la segunda a la derecha. **Vaya** hasta el final de la calle y allí, **al lado del** gimnasio, hay una...

9B.2 Affirmative commands (singular forms) **ve/vaya**, directions

Vocabulario

5
el chicle *chewing gum*
la floristería *florist (shop)*
el quiosco *kiosk*

6
perdone (*form.*) *excuse me*
tomar *to take*
seguir (e:i) *to continue, to keep going*
recto *straight*
girar *to turn*
a la derecha *(to the) right*
a la izquierda *(to the) left*

Estrategia ···········

Llamar la atención

● Perdona, ¿sabes dónde está la parada de autobús?

■ Perdone, ¿sabe dónde hay un locutorio?

SAM: Actividades pp. 189–191

Practice more at **vhlcentral.com**.

Anécdotas

Escriba la historia más divertida, curiosa o increíble del barrio

Participe en el concurso

1 "Era el día antes del sorteo de Navidad. Había un número 'feo' que nadie quería: el 00.101. De repente llegó un autobús de turistas y compraron todos los billetes de este número y les tocó el gordo."

Francisca (Paqui) Ruiz,
vendedora de lotería de la calle Palma

2 "Una vez intentaron comprar el tradicional Mercado de San Miguel para hacer oficinas. Entonces había crisis y los negocios no funcionaban. Todos vendieron, menos dos que decidieron no vender y salvaron el mercado."

Antonio Campos,
frutero del Mercado de San Miguel

3 "El otro día estábamos en la plaza tomando un café. De repente apareció mucha gente y empezaron a rodar la escena de una película. Necesitaban extras para el rodaje y participamos. Entonces conocimos al director y a todos los actores. Fue muy curioso ser actores por un día."

Ana López,
vecina de la plaza del Carmen

Relatar en pasado

El otro día **era** mi cumpleaños. **Estaba** en mi oficina y, de repente, ¡vinieron todos mis compañeros con un ramo de flores!

| 9B.3 | Preterite vs. imperfect **el otro día, de repente...** |

Vocabulario

8

salvar *to save*

el/la frutero/a *fruit seller*

el otro día *the other day*

de repente *suddenly*

rodar (o:ue) *to shoot, to film*

entonces *then*

el ramo *bouquet*

la anécdota

¡OJO!

December 28 is the Feast of the Holy Innocents, which began as a religious observance but now is a prank-filled day known as **Día de los Inocentes**, similar to April Fool's Day. The prankster usually ends his joke by exclaiming "**¡Inocente palomita!**"

---

8 **a. Relacionar** Relacione las anécdotas con alguna de estas características.

> curiosa • divertida • increíble • interesante

b. Clasificar Localice los verbos de las anécdotas y clasifíquelos.

Pretérito indefinido	Pretérito imperfecto
llegó, ...	*era, ...*

c. Indicar ¿Pretérito imperfecto o pretérito indefinido? Indique qué tiempo usamos en cada caso.

- Para describir situaciones pasadas usamos...
- Para relatar acciones pasadas usamos...

9 **Construir** Fíjese en las imágenes y construya estas anécdotas.

SITUACIONES

ACCIONES

El otro día...
Una vez...

.... (ser) de noche, ... (hacer) calor y yo no .... (poder) dormir.

Entonces...
De repente...

(levantarse) de la cama y .... (ir) a dormir en el parque.

....

yo .... (ir) por la calle solo. Todo el mundo me .... (mirar) y yo no .... (saber) por qué.

Una persona .... (señalar) el muñeco de papel de mi espalda. ¡Claro, era el 28 de diciembre, Día de los Inocentes!

....

10 Viñeta Lea la viñeta cómica. ¿Conoce al personaje famoso? ¿Conoce usted a alguien famoso? ¿A quién?

11 a. Anécdotas Escuche las dos anécdotas. ¿En cuál de las dos la persona se sorprende positivamente?

b. Escuchar Escuche de nuevo y ordene las anécdotas.

1

¿Ah, sí? ¿Y qué pasó? ☐

Yo una vez iba a casa y me encontré un billete de lotería. ☐

¿De verdad? ¡Increíble! ¡Qué suerte! ☐

¡Al día siguiente gané el premio! ☐

2

¡Anda ya! ☐

No, ¿qué te pasó? ☐

¿Sabéis qué me pasó el otro día? ☐

¡Llegué a la oficina y no había nadie… ¡Era domingo! ☐

12 Reaccionar En parejas, lean las frases y reaccionen.

En San Valentín recibí una nota anónima.

Conocí a un chico muy guapo.

Gané un viaje a Europa.

Mi padre me regaló un coche.

MI EXPERIENCIA

13 Contar anécdotas Piense en una anécdota real o inventada y cuéntesela a su compañero/a.

GUIÓN DE TRABAJO

¿Sabes qué me pasó/ a quién conocí/ con quién estuve…? → Un día/El otro día/ Una vez estaba… y de repente/entonces…

¿Qué te pasó? ¿A quién conociste? → ¿De verdad? ¡No me digas! ¡Increíble!

Contar anécdotas

- ¿Sabes qué me pasó el otro día?
- No, ¿qué te pasó?
- Participé en un concurso de radio y gané un viaje al Caribe.
- ¿De verdad? ¡Increíble! ¿Cuándo debes recoger los pasajes?

9B.4 ¿Sabes/Sabe/Saben/ Sabéis qué…? ¿De verdad?...

Vocabulario

10

comprar (billetes de) lotería *to buy lottery tickets*

¿De verdad? *Really?*

¡No me digas! *You don't say!*

¡Increíble! *Unbelievable!*

11

¡Anda ya! (*Esp.*) *Come on!*

12

jugar (u:ue) a la lotería *to play the lottery*

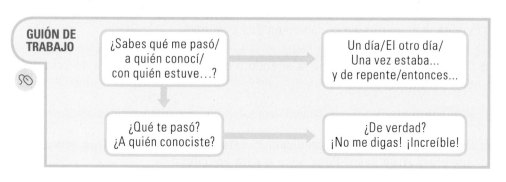

Juegos de azar
Jugar a la lotería es una costumbre muy extendida en el mundo hispano. En España, de todos los sorteos, el de Navidad es el más popular. Se celebra el 22 de diciembre. Existe la creencia de que algunas agencias traen suerte y la gente hace cola durante horas para comprar el número de la suerte. El mejor premio se llama **el gordo**.

SAM: Actividades pp. 192–194

Lola, la del quiosco del barrio

Lola Sanz, 35 años. Quiosquera, como su madre y su abuela

Lola, tú eres una de las "caras" del barrio. ¿Cuándo empezaste a trabajar en el quiosco?

Desde pequeña, lo normal en un negocio familiar, pero hace cinco años empecé a llevarlo sola porque mi madre se jubiló.

¿Ha habido muchos cambios desde que se abrió el quiosco?

Sí, antes mi madre y mi abuela vendían solo prensa. Ahora vendo muchas cosas más: películas, libros, postales, souvenirs, chicles... especialmente desde que hay periódicos gratuitos.

¿Y cómo es tu jornada laboral?

Empiezo a trabajar a las 6:30 h de la mañana; recibo la prensa diaria y la coloco en el puesto. Abro el quiosco de 7:00 h a 14:00 h, voy a comer a casa y por la tarde abro de 16:30 h a 20:00 h. Los domingos abro solo por la mañana.

¿Qué se vende más: periódicos, revistas, cómics...?

Aquí hay gente que compra el periódico todos los días, pero el del domingo es el que más se vende. Muchas mujeres compran las revistas del corazón todas las semanas.

¿Y las colecciones?

Las de los niños sí se venden: los cromos de fútbol, los cuentos, los DVD... pero la gente se cansa de coleccionar y, al final, es caro.

Y con tanta promoción, ¿te falta sitio en el quiosco?

Bueno, yo tengo uno de los grandes, tengo suerte. Los quioscos aquí en Oviedo ahora son más pequeños.

¿Te gusta este barrio?

Sí, es mi barrio de toda la vida, nací y crecí aquí. Vivo muy cerca; cruzo esta calle, sigo recto cien metros y a la derecha está mi piso.

Expresar el inicio de una acción

- ¿Cuándo **empezaste a trabajar** en el quiosco?
- Hace cinco años.

9B.5 **empezar** + **a** + [*infinitive*]

Vocabulario

(14)

llevar (un negocio) *to run (a business)*

la prensa *press*

la postal *postcard*

colocar *to place*

la revista (del corazón) *(gossip) magazine*

el cromo (de fútbol) *(Esp.) (soccer) trading card*

el cuento *short story*

---

14 Contestar Observe la foto y conteste las preguntas.

1. ¿Qué vende Lola en el quiosco?
2. ¿Dónde está el quiosco: en una ciudad, en un pueblo, en un lugar turístico...?
3. ¿Hay quioscos así en su ciudad?

15 a. Completar Lea la entrevista a Lola y complete estas oraciones.

Hace cinco años...

A las 6:30 de la mañana...

b. La jornada laboral ¿Cómo es la jornada laboral de Lola?

16 Los clientes Lola sabe qué productos compra más la gente de su barrio. ¿Pueden imaginar ustedes cómo son sus clientes?

17 a. La clienta de Lola Escuche la anécdota que cuenta una clienta de Lola y elija un título.

    a. Visita real   b. Nuevo vecino   c. Vida cotidiana

b. Reaccionar ¿En qué establecimiento estaba esta persona? ¿Qué quería comprar? ¿Qué pasó? Reaccione a esta anécdota.

18 **a. Leer** Lea el título de este artículo. ¿Qué significa **prensa digital** y **prensa en papel**?

¿Prensa digital o en papel?

Leer la prensa en Internet es hoy una práctica habitual. Los principales periódicos tienen versiones en línea. Los que más se leen en español son los periódicos de deportes, como *Marca* (España) y *Ovaciones* (México). También se pueden leer en Internet periódicos de economía, como *Portafolio* (Colombia) y *Diario Financiero* (Chile). Y si se busca información general, se pueden visitar diarios como *El País* (España), *La República* (Perú) y *La Prensa* (Bolivia).

La prensa rosa o las revistas del corazón como *¡HOLA!* (España, México, Argentina, Perú, Ecuador, Puerto Rico) o *Gente* (Argentina) también tienen una versión en línea pero se visitan menos, quizás porque el periódico se lee con rapidez para informarse de las noticias del día, y las revistas se leen con más tiempo.

Los periódicos digitales aprovechan las posibilidades multimedia: voz, música, video... y las noticias se actualizan varias veces al día como en la radio o la televisión. Además, permiten a las personas que viven fuera de su país mantenerse informados.

La prensa en papel se puede leer en el metro, en el sofá en casa o en un parque y no solo delante de la computadora. Además, los periódicos del domingo traen muchos suplementos, y para muchas personas es un ritual desayunar en casa o en una cafetería con la prensa dominical.

....

....

....

b. La prensa Anote los tipos de prensa en las imágenes correspondientes.

| deportes • economía • información general |

c. Versiones digitales ¿Tienen todas las publicaciones versión digital? ¿Cuáles son las más leídas? ¿Cuáles no? ¿Por qué?

19 **Ventajas y desventajas** Busque en el texto los aspectos positivos de la prensa digital y la prensa en papel. ¿Qué otras ventajas y desventajas tienen? Comente con su compañero/a.

20 **Responder** ¿Qué tipo de prensa lee usted? ¿Por qué? Explique.

21 **a. Profesiones que se heredan** Lea la información sobre profesiones que se heredan. ¿Existe esta costumbre en su país?

b. Mi opinión ¿Conoce algún caso? ¿Cuál es su opinión al respecto?

Vocabulario *cont.*

cansarse de (algo) *to get tired/ bored of (something)*

el sitio *room; space*

crecer (zc) *to grow up*

el/la quiosquero/a *kiosk attendant*

el DVD, coleccionar, la promoción, el dispensador
⑱

en línea *online*

la prensa rosa *gossip press*

el suplemento dominical *Sunday supplement*

la versión, digital, multimedia, informado/a
⑲

la ventaja *advantage*

la desventaja *disadvantage*
㉑

heredar *to inherit*

O P I N I Ó N

¿Cómo compra la prensa: en el quiosco, en un dispensador de periódicos, por suscripción? ¿Por qué? ¿Hay prensa gratuita en su ciudad o pueblo?

Profesiones que se heredan

Muchos negocios o empresas familiares se heredan de padres a hijos. Los hijos, desde pequeños, aprenden la profesión de los padres y continúan el negocio. Esta costumbre ya no es tan frecuente como antes, pero todavía hay muchos casos.

SAM: Actividades pp. 195–200

22 **a. Juego** Elija el tiempo verbal adecuado (pretérito indefinido o imperfecto) y complete la anécdota. Gana el grupo que termina primero la anécdota correctamente.

El año pasado... → yo _buscaba_ (buscar) otro trabajo, → y .... (enviar) mi currículum a muchas empresas. → Un día .... (recibir) la llamada de una empresa.

.... (ser) una empresa muy importante.

Yo .... (estar) muy interesado.

.... (empezar) a hacer entrevistas...

y .... (superar) todas las pruebas.

La última entrevista .... (ser) con el director general en un restaurante.

Todo .... (ir) bien y...

de repente yo .... (ver) que en la mesa de al lado .... (estar) mi jefa.

No .... (saber) qué hacer...

entonces .... (decidir) contar la verdad.

Y al final los tres .... (hablar) animadamente.

Yo .... (conseguir) el trabajo y mi antigua jefa .... (empezar) a colaborar con nosotros. ¡Cosas de la vida!

b. Anécdota de la clase Forme un círculo con todos sus compañeros. Escriba en una hoja las primeras dos oraciones de una anécdota. Doble la hoja para que solo se vean las últimas palabras. Luego, pásela a su compañero/a de la derecha. Esa persona debe continuar la anécdota con otras dos oraciones y doblar la hoja antes de pasarla. Al completar el círculo, lean la anécdota en voz alta.

TAREA FINAL

Nuestro periódico

Hablen de anécdotas o noticias que ocurrieron ayer. La información puede ser real o no, con noticias del mundo exterior o de la clase.

Elijan un tipo de publicación y elaboren la portada (titular, noticias más importantes, imágenes, etc).

Presenten su portada a la clase.

YO PUEDO...

- Puedo identificar a alguien por una característica.
  Identifique a personas de su barrio.

- Puedo indicar el camino.
  Explique cómo ir de su casa a un establecimiento cercano.

- Puedo relatar en pasado.
  Cuente una historia que le ocurrió hace tiempo.

- Puedo contar anécdotas.
  Escriba una conversación o una anécdota real o inventada.

- Puedo expresar el inicio de una actividad.
  Hable de cuándo empezó a estudiar español.

GRAMÁTICA FUNCIONAL (S) Tutorials

9B.1 **Identify with a characteristic**

el/la/los/las + de/que 3.1.1

- Use the construction **el/la/los/las de** + [*noun*] or **el/la/los/las que** + [*verb*] to refer to people or things based on some other point of reference.

> Jorge es **el del** restaurante cubano.
> *Jorge is **the man (the one) from** the Cuban restaurant.*

> Gabriela y Elena son **las que** trabajan en la librería.
> *Gabriela and Elena are **the women (the ones) who** work in the bookstore.*

- The definite article in this construction (**el/la/los/las**) must agree in gender and number with the people or things that are being identified.

9B.2 **Give directions**

Affirmative commands (singular forms) 5.18.2a, 5.18.3a
Prepositions of place 10.17

- Use affirmative commands to give directions.

> **Gira** a la derecha.　**Gire** (usted) a la izquierda.
> *Turn right.*　*Turn left.*

- As you learned in 8A.4, regular **tú** commands have the same form as the third-person form of the present. The affirmative **usted** command is formed by dropping the final **-o** of the **yo** form of the present tense. For **-ar** verbs, add **-e**; for **-er** and **-ir** verbs, add **-a**.

	GIRAR	RECOGER	SEGUIR
(tú)	gir**a**	recog**e**	sigu**e**
(usted)	gir**e**	recoj**a**	sig**a**

- The formal and informal commands undergo the same stem changes as verbs in the present tense. (Yo **sigo** → **Siga** usted.)

> **Sigue/Siga** todo recto.
> *Continue straight ahead.*

- The verb **ir** has irregular forms in both the formal and informal commands.

	IR
(tú)	**ve**
(usted)	**vaya**

> **Vaya** hasta el cine y gire a la derecha.
> *Go to the movie theater and turn right.*

- Use expressions such as **todo recto** (*straight ahead*), **la primera/segunda calle** (*the first/second street*), **a la derecha/izquierda**, (*to/on the right/left*), **al final de** (*at the end of*), and **enfrente de** (*across from*) when giving directions.

> Sigue **todo recto** y gira **a la derecha al final de** esta calle. La panadería está **enfrente del** restaurante.
> *Continue **straight ahead** and turn right **at the end of** this street. The bakery is **across from** the restaurant.*

(S) **Practice more at vhlcentral.com.**

¡Póngalo en práctica!

G1 **Completar** Complete las oraciones.

1. Juana es .... trabaja en la frutería.
2. Hugo es .... locutorio.
3. • ¿Qué bar ofrece el mejor café del barrio?
   - Creo que .... ofrece el mejor café es .... la plaza, el bar Colombia.
4. • ¿Quién es Marina?
   - Es .... tiene el bar El Rincón.
5. Héctor es .... la panadería.

G2 **Imperativo afirmativo** Escriba las formas correctas del imperativo afirmativo.

	tú	usted
1. pasar		
2. compartir		
3. volver		
4. mirar		
5. escuchar		
6. pensar		

G3 **Conversaciones** Complete las conversaciones con la forma correcta del imperativo formal o informal. Seleccione el verbo apropiado.

> seguir　　girar　　ir

- Perdone, ¿sabe dónde hay una librería?
- Sí, mire, (1)........................ todo recto y (2)........................ a la izquierda. (3)........................ hasta la plaza. Enfrente hay una librería.

> tomar　　seguir　　girar

- Hola, ¿sabes dónde hay un restaurante por aquí cerca?
- En este barrio hay muchos. Mira, (4)........................ esta calle hasta la floristería, (5)........................ a la derecha y allí hay una pizzería y un restaurante tailandés. También, Casa Lucía tiene menú del día y está cerca. (6)........................ la primera calle a la izquierda y el restaurante está enfrente del quiosco.

9B.3 Narrate in the past

Preterite vs. imperfect 5.2.3, 5.4.3, 5.6

- Use the **pretérito indefinido** to narrate past actions that belong to a period of time that has ended.

  > Hugo **llegó** a España hace cinco años.
  > *Hugo arrived in Spain five years ago.*

- Use time expressions such as **el otro día** (*the other day*), **una vez** (*once*), **de repente** (*suddenly*), and **[y] entonces** (*[and] then*) with the **pretérito indefinido**.

  > **Una vez** viajamos a Portugal en autobús.
  > *Once we traveled to Portugal by bus.*

- Use the **préterito imperfecto** to tell about habitual or repeated actions in the past.

  > Cuando **vivía** en ese barrio, siempre **compraba** el periódico en el quiosco de la plaza.
  > *When I lived in that neighborhood, I always bought the newspaper at the kiosk in the square.*

- Use the **préterito imperfecto** to describe past situations, causes, and circumstances that establish the background details of a past event. The **préterito imperfecto** and the **pretérito indefinido** are often used together to narrate in the past.

  > **Hacía** frío y **llovía** mucho, así que **decidimos** ir al cine.
  > *It was cold and it was raining a lot, so we decided to go to the movies.*

- Use **mientras** (*while*) with the imperfect to describe what was happening at the same time as another action (imperfect) or when an interrupting action occurred (preterite).

9B.4 Tell anecdotes

Questions and interjections 14.13

- To introduce an anecdote, say **¿Sabe(s) qué (me pasó)?** or **¿Sabéis/Saben qué?** (*Guess what!*)

- Use expressions such as **¿Y qué pasó?** (*And what happened?*) or **¿A quién viste?** (*Who did you see?*) to show interest in the anecdote and encourage the speaker to continue.

- **¡No me digas!**, **¡Increíble!**, **¿De verdad?**, and **¿Ah, sí?** express surprise or skepticism.

9B.5 Express the beginning of an action

empezar + a + [infinitive] 5.10

- Use the construction **empezar + a + [infinitive]** to indicate the beginning of an action or an event. **Empezar** has an **e→ie** stem change in the present, and the **yo** form of the **pretérito indefinido** has a **z→c** spelling change to maintain the same pronunciation.

  > Ayer **empecé a trabajar** en el restaurante; mi hermana **empieza** mañana.
  > *I started working in the restaurant yesterday; my sister starts tomorrow.*

- Use **empezar** in the **pretérito indefinido** to tell when past actions began.

¡Póngalo en práctica!

G4 **Oraciones** Complete las oraciones con la forma correcta del pretérito indefinido o el pretérito imperfecto.

1. Yo .... (estar) en casa limpiando el salón y entonces .... (encontrar) debajo de la alfombra unas cartas de amor del año 1920.

2. Ayer Sabrina .... (caminar) a la frutería cuando, de repente, ... (ver) a una amiga de la infancia.

3. Tío Ramón nos .... (llamar) mientras .... (preparar, nosotros) la cena.

4. Alejandro .... (tener) dieciocho años cuando .... (conocer) a Celia.

5. .... (ser) las doce de la noche cuando Pedro y Alicia .... (volver) del teatro.

6. De niña, Leila siempre .... (leer) un poco en la cama y .... (acostarse) temprano.

7. El otro día mi abuela .... (escuchar) una anécdota curiosa del barrio cuando .... (estar) en el mercado.

8. De joven, yo .... (querer) ser astronauta y tú siempre .... (hablar) de trabajar con animales.

G5 **Emparejar** Empareje cada oración con su respuesta lógica.

1. ¿Sabes qué me pasó ayer?	**a.** ¿Y qué pasó?
2. El otro día estaba viajando en tren cuando subió Benicio del Toro.	**b.** ¡No me digas!
3. ¡Mi hermano ganó el gordo de Navidad!	**c.** No, ¿qué te pasó?

G6 **Empezar** Complete la conversación con el verbo **empezar**.

- ¿Cuándo (1)................. (vosotros) a trabajar en el mercado?

- (2)................. en 1991, pero mi padre (3)................. a vender fruta en el barrio hace cincuenta años.

- ¿Cuándo(4) .... (tú) a trabajar en el quiosco?

- (5)................. a ayudar a mis padres a los dieciséis años y la semana que viene (6)................. a trabajar sola.

 Practice more at **vhlcentral.com**.

VOCABULARIO 🔊 Ⓢ Vocabulary Tools

Caras del barrio

perdone (*form.*)	*excuse me*
la agencia de lotería	*lottery ticket booth*
el chicle	*chewing gum*
el establecimiento	*store; establishment*
el estanco (*Esp.*)	*tobacconist shop*
el/la favorito/a	*favorite*
el/la finalista	*finalist*
la floristería	*florist (shop)*
la frutería	*fruit shop*
el gordo	*jackpot; first prize*
la juguetería	*toy store*
la papelería	*stationery store*
el quiosco	*kiosk*
el sorteo	*drawing*
la telefonía	*phone service*
el universo	*universe*
el/la vendedor(a) de lotería	*lottery ticket seller*
girar	*to turn*
seguir (e:i)	*to continue, to keep going*
tomar	*to take*
gordo/a	*fat*
gratuito/a	*free (of charge)*
a la derecha	*(to the) right*
a la izquierda	*(to the) left*
recto	*straight*

Anécdotas

¡Anda ya! (*Esp.*)	*Come on!*
¿De verdad?	*Really?*
¡Increíble!	*Unbelievable!*
¡No me digas!	*You don't say!*
la anécdota	*anecdote*
el/la frutero/a	*fruit seller*
el ramo	*bouquet*
comprar (billetes de) lotería	*to buy lottery tickets*
jugar (u:ue) a la lotería	*to play the lottery*
rodar (o:ue)	*to shoot, to film*
salvar	*to save*
de repente	*suddenly*
el otro día	*the other day*
entonces	*then*

Lola

el cromo (de fútbol) (*Esp.*)	*(soccer) trading card*
el cuento	*short story*
la desventaja	*disadvantage*
el dispensador	*dispenser*
el DVD	*DVD*
la postal	*postcard*
la prensa	*press*
la prensa rosa	*gossip press*
la promoción	*promotion*
el/la quiosquero/a	*kiosk attendant*
la revista (del corazón)	*(gossip) magazine*
el sitio	*room; space*
el suplemento dominical	*Sunday supplement*
la ventaja	*advantage*
la versión	*version*
cansarse de (algo)	*to get tired/bored of (something)*
coleccionar	*to collect*
colocar	*to place*
crecer (zc)	*to grow up*
heredar	*to inherit*
llevar (un negocio)	*to run (a business)*
digital	*digital*
en línea	*online*
informado/a	*informed*
multimedia (*invar.*)	*multimedia*

Variación léxica

la agencia de lotería ⟷ la administración de lotería (*Esp.*) ⟷ el expendio de lotería	perdone ⟷ disculpe
el chicle ⟷ la goma de mascar	el quiosco ⟷ el kiosco
el cromo ⟷ la figurita (*Amér. L.*)	el/la quiosquero/a ⟷ el/la kiosquero/a
la floristería ⟷ la florería (*Arg., Cub.*)	recto ⟷ derecho
girar ⟷ doblar	tomar ⟷ coger (*Esp.*)
multimedia ⟷ multimediático/a	el/la vendedor(a) de lotería ⟷ el/la lotero/a (*Esp.*)

Vocabulario útil

la creencia *belief*

los desfiles *parades*

festejar *to celebrate*

el fiel *faithful (person)*

hoy en día *nowadays*

mismo/a *same*

perdurar *to remain*

por entonces *in those days*

rezar *to pray*

Estrategia ············

Making the connection

When reading a text about traditions in another country, try to connect what you read with what you already know about that culture and related traditions. Start by building your background knowledge of the place: Where are celebrations held? What kind of culture is this? What words and expressions do you expect to encounter? Compare your traditions and your own experiences in similar situations, and ask yourself: What do I already know about this topic?

Semana Santa:
vacaciones y tradición

Procesión de Semana Santa, España

Hay muchas celebraciones importantes en España, pero la Semana Santa° es una de las más espectaculares. Se festeja la semana antes de Pascua°, cuando los cristianos recuerdan la Pasión de Jesucristo. Generalmente, la gente tiene unos días de vacaciones en esa semana. Algunas personas aprovechan° estos días para viajar, pero otras prefieren participar en los desfiles en la calle y ver a los "capuchones". Esta antigua tradición perdura desde la época de la Inquisición: por entonces las personas castigadas° por motivos religiosos debían usar túnicas y sombreros°

① **Preguntas** ¿Ha participado de alguna fiesta religiosa? ¿Se celebra alguna fiesta parecida a las de España y Guatemala en su país? ¿Qué tradiciones populares festejaban sus padres de jóvenes? ¿Qué tradiciones están vivas hoy en su país?

② **¿Verdadero o falso?** Indique si las oraciones son **verdaderas** o **falsas**. Luego, en parejas, corrijan las falsas.

1. En Semana Santa, la gente puede disfrutar toda esa semana de vacaciones.

....

2. La tradición de los capuchones perdura desde la época de la Inquisición.

....

3. Por entonces, la gente debía usar todo el tiempo grandes sombreros cónicos.

....

4. En las procesiones, los fieles desfilan con imágenes y faroles.

....

5. Unos elementos importantes para las celebraciones religiosas son las flores y las velas.

....

6. La tradición del Vía Crucis es original de Guatemala.

....

cónicos que les cubrían° la cara. Hoy en día, los miembros de las cofradías° de Semana Santa usan esos mismos sombreros mientras desfilan el Viernes Santo°. Los fieles llevan faroles° o velas encendidas y sacan imágenes religiosas a las calles. Estas imágenes van sobre plataformas decoradas con muchas flores y velas.

Alfombra de flores en Antigua, Guatemala

En **Antigua, Guatemala**, las personas hacen alfombras de flores y altares; también organizan Vía Crucis° y danzas°. La tradición llegó con los misioneros españoles de Sevilla y luego evolucionó° a lo largo de los años.

En **Ayacucho, Perú**, además de alfombras de flores y procesiones, hay una antigua tradición llamada "quema de la chamiza"°.

En **Iztapalapa, Ciudad de México**, el famoso Vía Crucis del cerro° de la Estrella es una representación del recorrido° de Jesucristo con la cruz°.

En **Popayán, Colombia**, en las procesiones "chiquitas", los niños llevan copias pequeñas de las imágenes que llevan las personas mayores.

Si visitas algún país hispano durante la Semana Santa, debes ver un desfile. Las playas pueden esperar hasta la semana siguiente.

Semana Santa *Holy Week* **Pascua** *Easter* **aprovechan** *take advantage of* **castigados** *punished* **sombreros** *hats* **cubrían** *covered* **cofradías** *brotherhoods* **Viernes Santo** *Good Friday* **faroles** *lamps* **Vía Crucis** *Stations of the Cross* **danzas** *dances* **evolucionó** *evolved* **quema de la chamiza** *burning of brushwood* **cerro** *hill* **recorrido** *route* **cruz** *cross*

▶ **Otras celebraciones famosas**

- *Oruro, Bolivia*: Durante el carnaval de Oruro se realiza la famosa Diablada, una antigua danza que muestra la lucha° entre el bien y el mal: ángeles contra° demonios.

- *Panchimalco, El Salvador*: La primera semana de mayo, Panchimalco se cubre de flores y de color. También hacen el Desfile de las palmas° y bailan danzas antiguas.

- *Quito, Ecuador*: El mes de agosto es el Mes de las Artes. Danza, teatro, música, cine, artesanías y otros eventos culturales inundan° la ciudad.

- *San Pedro Sula, Honduras*: En junio se celebra la Feria Juniana. Hay comida típica, bailes, desfiles, conciertos, rodeos, exposiciones ganaderas° y eventos deportivos y culturales.

lucha *fight* **contra** *versus* **palmas** *palm leaves* **inundan** *flood* **exposiciones ganaderas** *cattle shows*

---

(3) **Cartel de promoción turística** En parejas, armen un cartel de promoción turística de alguna de las fiestas mencionadas en esta página para presentar en la clase. Deben señalar los datos importantes (pueden buscar más información en Internet).

lugar • época del año • qué se celebra • cómo se celebra

Usen frases de esta lista.

| Venga a disfrutar... | Viva la fiesta en... | Anímese a conocer... |
| No se puede perder... | Visite... | |

PROYECTO

Una fiesta popular Elija una fiesta popular que se celebre en su país (el Día de San Patricio, el Día de Acción de Gracias, el Carnaval en Nueva Orleans, etc.) y escriba una breve descripción desde un punto de vista subjetivo. Luego preséntelo a la clase. Puede guiarse por estas preguntas.

1. ¿Cuándo se celebra?
2. ¿Cómo y cuándo se inició la costumbre?
3. ¿Tiene el mismo significado hoy en día?
4. ¿Cuáles son las características más importantes del festejo?
5. ¿Tiene influencias de otros países?

Estrategia ············

Descriptive text
The main purpose of a descriptive text is to give information about a place, an event, an object, or a person. You must make use of your five senses to explain how it looks, smells, and tastes, to show the noises and textures involved. You might take an objective point of view and give facts (accurate and precise information) or you might take a subjective point of view and give opinions (expressing your own feelings, likes, and dislikes).

Video

Las fiestas

Ya ha visto que algunas cosas cambian con el tiempo; pero otras se hacen siempre de la misma manera: las fiestas populares de Latinoamérica reviven cada año la tradición de todo el pueblo. Este episodio de **Flash Cultura** presenta la fiesta de San Sebastián que se realiza en Puerto Rico.

(1) Preguntas ¿Se hacen desfiles y ferias en las calles de su ciudad? ¿Cómo se festejan la Navidad y el Año Nuevo en su país? ¿Qué otras fiestas importantes hay? ¿Cuánto tiempo duran los festejos? Coméntenlo en parejas.

(2) Mirar Mire el video. Preste atención a las palabras que suenan conocidas, como **máscaras, procesión, competir,** etc. ¿Adivina su significado?

La fiesta comienza con una misa (...) y una procesión...

Llevo viniendo como quince años.

(3) Completar Complete las oraciones.

1. San Sebastián fue un soldado y ahora es un...
   a. mártir cristiano.   b. cabezudo.
2. Las estatuas de los tres santos reyes son...
   a. las más populares.   b. las más coloridas.
3. La fiesta de San Sebastián es...
   a. antes de Navidad.   b. al final de Navidad.
4. En lugar de ser totalmente religiosas, las fiestas son...
   a. eventos de pueblo.   b. misas.

(4) Conversación Dos personas conversan en la fiesta: una cuenta anécdotas y la otra quiere contar algo más impresionante. Con un(a) compañero/a, escriban la conversación. Luego, preséntenla a la clase.

Modelo: • ¿Sabes qué me pasó una vez? ¡Me encontré con el fantasma de Elvis Presley! Yo iba en la procesión y él me saludó desde el balcón.
   • ¡No me digas! Yo tengo una historia más interesante. Llevo años viniendo, y...

 Practice more at **vhlcentral.com.**

Unidad 10

Carlos Salazar, médico de familia en La Habana

Jorge Edwards, recuerdos de un escritor

La salud

AL MAL TIEMPO BUENA CARA

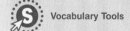 Vocabulary Tools

El tiempo y la salud

El tiempo en Venezuela hoy

sábado 30 de abril

Hace sol y buen tiempo en el norte del país, como en Sucre y en Isla Margarita, con temperaturas entre los 23 °C y 30 °C.

Está nublado en los estados del oeste como Táchira y Apure, y hace 15 °C de temperatura.

Nieva en el Pico Bolívar en Mérida. Llueve y hace frío en el estado de Bolívar.

Última actualización a las 13:36 h

Hablar del tiempo

- ¿Qué tiempo hace?
- En el norte **hace sol** y **buen tiempo**. **Hace 30 °C de temperatura.** En el sur **llueve**, **está nublado** y **hace frío**.

10A.1 **hace, llueve, nieva, está nublado**

Vocabulario

1

el tiempo *weather*

hacer sol *to be sunny*

hacer buen/mal tiempo *there is good/bad weather*

nublado/a *cloudy*

nevar (e:ie) *to snow*

llover (o:ue) *to rain*

hacer frío/calor *to be cold/hot out*

¿Qué tiempo hace? *What's the weather like?*

hace 30 °C de temperatura *the temperature is 30 °C*

la temperatura

2

tomar el sol *to sunbathe*

menos mal *thank goodness*

por fin *at last*

4

la estación (del año) *season*

la primavera *spring*

el otoño *fall*

---

1 **a. El tiempo en Venezuela** Observe el mapa de Venezuela. ¿Qué información da? Relacione los símbolos que aparecen en el mapa con las expresiones para hablar del tiempo.

....

Hace sol.
Está nublado.
Llueve.
Nieva.

b. En Sucre ¿Qué tiempo hace en Sucre? ¿Y en el Pico Bolívar?

2 **¿Qué tiempo hace?** Escuche estas conversaciones sobre el tiempo que hace hoy. ¿Qué tiempo hace en Caracas?

- *Hace...*

3 **El tiempo en España** ¿Qué tiempo hace en España un 16 de febrero? Mire el mapa y pregunte a su compañero/a.

Modelo:
- *¿Qué tiempo hace en el sur?*
- *Hace...*

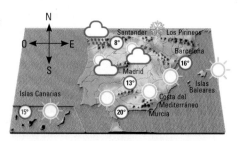

4 **En mi región** ¿Qué tiempo hace hoy en su ciudad o región? ¿Y en las diferentes estaciones del año?

En primavera	En verano	En otoño	En invierno

....

¿CÓMO SE ENCUENTRA? Tome este test para saber cómo le afecta el tiempo.

En primavera

a. Me encuentro muy bien.

b. Tengo alergia y estoy cansado/a.

c. Depende, algunos días bien y otros mal.

Cuando hace calor

a. Tengo que beber mucha agua, pero me encuentro bien.

b. Estoy muy cansado/a y no tengo energía.

c. Me encuentro muy bien. Me encanta el verano.

En un día de lluvia

a. Me encanta, es muy romántico.

b. Me duelen la cabeza y los huesos.

c. Me encuentro mal. Salgo sólo si es necesario.

En otoño

a. Me encuentro bien después del verano.

b. Tengo frío y siempre estoy resfriado/a.

c. Me gusta salir y disfrutar de los colores del otoño.

Mayoría de respuestas a

Usted se encuentra bien en todos los climas. ¡Felicidades!

Mayoría de respuestas b

Usted es muy sensible al tiempo y a los cambios en general, pero piense que el clima no es lo más importante para ser feliz.

Mayoría de respuestas c

Usted necesita sol y calor para ser feliz. Prefiere el buen tiempo, pero se adapta cuando hace mal tiempo.

---

5 **¿Cómo se encuentra?** Responda al test. ¿Influye el tiempo en su estado físico y anímico? ¿Qué tiempo es mejor para usted? Hable con un(a) compañero/a.

6 **Observar** Observe las imágenes. ¿Cómo se encuentran estas personas?

1. Le duele la cabeza. [F]
2. Le duelen las muelas. [ ]
3. Le duele el estómago. [ ]
4. Le duele la garganta. [ ]
5. Está resfriado. [ ]
6. Tiene fiebre. [ ]

7 **Remedios** ¿Para qué casos son más adecuados estos remedios? ¿Conoce algún otro remedio?

- TOMAR leche con miel / antibióticos / una aspirina / una manzanilla
- IR al dentista / al médico
- OTROS: descansar / darse un baño / dormir

🗣 MI EXPERIENCIA

8 **Las estaciones del año** Piense en cómo se encuentra en las diferentes estaciones del año. Pregunte a su compañero/a y compartan los remedios más adecuados para cada síntoma o dolencia.

GUIÓN DE TRABAJO

¿Cómo te encuentras en primavera, verano...? → Si hace buen tiempo, me encuentro... En primavera siempre estoy...

¿Qué remedios conoces? → Si tengo gripe, tomo té con miel...

Describir síntomas y dolencias

- ¿Qué te pasa?
- Estoy enfermo. Me duele la garganta y tengo frío.
- ¿Tienes fiebre?
- No sé, me encuentro mal. Estoy resfriado.

10A.2 **doler, encontrarse (o→ue)** **tener + [noun]** **estar + [adjective]**

Vocabulario

5

encontrarse (o:ue) to feel

depender (de) to depend (on)

doler (o:ue) to hurt

la cabeza head

tener frío/calor to be cold/hot

estar resfriado/a to have a cold

ser sensible a to be sensitive to

el estado físico physical condition

el estado anímico state of mind

la alergia, adaptarse

6

la dolencia ailment

el síntoma symptom

la muela molar

el estómago stomach

la garganta throat

la fiebre fever

7

la manzanilla chamomile tea

darse un baño to take a bath

el remedio, el antibiótico, la aspirina, el/la dentista, la infección

SAM: Actividades pp. 201–203

Salud, divino tesoro

Consultorio de salud

1

Desde hace meses me duele mucho la espalda. A veces tomo dos aspirinas diarias durante tres o cuatro días y me encuentro mejor, pero después me duele otra vez. Otras veces me duelen las piernas; trabajo muchas horas sentada. ¿Qué puedo hacer?

Raquel García, 40 años, Montevideo

2

Trabajo con mi marido desde hace unos meses y últimamente discutimos mucho. Creo que esto afecta mi salud. Me encuentro mal y me duele el estómago. ¿Es una buena idea trabajar con la pareja? ¿Qué debería hacer?

Carmen Jiménez, 33 años, Las Palmas de Gran Canaria

3

Dirijo una pequeña empresa y siempre he disfrutado mucho con mi trabajo. Pero ahora no me gusta ir a trabajar; estoy nervioso y tenso. Me duele la cabeza muy frecuentemente. ¿Qué me aconseja?

Joaquín Simón, 58 años, San José

Pedir consejos

- ● Tengo estrés en el trabajo. ¿Qué puedo hacer?
- ■ Trabaja menos horas.

- ● Me duele la cabeza. ¿Qué me aconseja? ¿Qué debería hacer?
- ■ Tome una aspirina.

10A.3 ¿Qué puedo/debería hacer? ¿Qué me aconseja(s)?

Vocabulario

9

el consultorio *advice column; doctor's office*
la espalda *back*
la pierna *leg*
el dolor *pain*
afectar, nervioso/a, tenso/a

10

el oído *ear*
el brazo *arm*
el pie *foot*

11

¿Qué te/le pasa? *(fam./form.)*
    What's wrong?
el analgésico *painkiller*
por cierto *by the way*
a propósito *incidentally; by the way*

Estrategia ··········

Añadir información a una conversación
Por cierto, el otro día escribí a un consultorio.
A propósito, ¿habéis escrito alguna vez a uno?

---

9 **Las consultas** Lea las consultas en este consultorio de salud y elija un título para cada una.

> Estrés en el trabajo   Dolores de espalda   Problemas de pareja

10 **a. Partes del cuerpo** ¿Qué partes del cuerpo mencionan los textos? Sitúelas en la imagen. Sitúe después el resto de las palabras del recuadro.

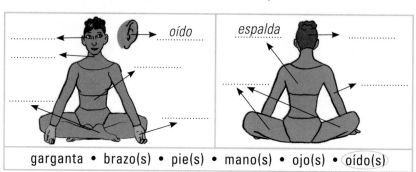

oído   espalda

> garganta • brazo(s) • pie(s) • mano(s) • ojo(s) • oído(s)

b. Subrayar Busque y subraye en los textos las formas para pedir consejo.

11 **a. Consultorio de salud** Escuche la llamada a este programa de televisión sobre la salud. ¿Cuál de las tres personas del consultorio llama?

b. Relacionar Escuche y relacione las preguntas con las respuestas.

1. ¿Qué le pasa? ......
2. ¿Ha intentado hacer ejercicio? ......
3. Ya… Por cierto, ¿duerme bien?......
4. ¿Hay algo que le preocupa? ......
5. A propósito, ¿ha probado algún remedio natural contra el estrés? ......

a. Sí, pero no me ayuda.
b. Me duele mucho la espalda.
c. No, no mucho.
d. La verdad es que no.
e. He tenido problemas con mi pareja.

c. Anotar Fíjese en las preguntas y apunte las expresiones para añadir información nueva a la conversación.

d. Preguntas Haga sus propias preguntas a la paciente.

Modelo: • *Por cierto, ¿ha probado la natación?*

Consejos para una vida sana

1. Levántate media hora antes para hacer un poco de gimnasia.
2. Dúchate con agua fría. Es bueno para la circulación y para tu piel.
3. Desayuna alimentos con mucha fibra y toma jugos naturales.
4. ¿Tienes bicicleta? Utilízala para ir al trabajo o a clases.
5. Toma té y no café. Tómalo por las mañanas en el desayuno.
6. Come despacio y siempre a la misma hora. ¡Olvida la comida basura!
7. Trabaja menos. Deberías disfrutar más de tu familia y de tus amigos.
8. Acuéstate temprano. Deberías dormir por lo menos ocho horas.

12 **a. Leer** Lea los consejos de arriba. ¿Lee usted este tipo de artículos sobre la salud? ¿Qué consejos asocia con las imágenes? Lea el texto y compruebe.

b. Preguntar Lea los consejos y pregunte a su compañero/a por estos y otros hábitos saludables.

13 **a. Completar** Fíjese en la formación del imperativo informal de los verbos reflexivos y complete la tabla.

	Presente	Imperativo
LEVANTARSE	te levantas	levántate
DUCHARSE		
ACOSTARSE		

b. Señalar Lea estas frases del texto y diga a qué se refieren.

○ Utilízala para ir al trabajo. ○ Tómalo por las mañanas.

c. Adivinar Piense en un problema de salud y anote consejos para solucionarlo. Su compañero/a debe adivinar qué problema es.

MI EXPERIENCIA

14 **Hábitos y consejos** Piense en sus hábitos de vida y haga una lista de cosas positivas y cosas no tan positivas. Compárela con la de su compañero/a y ofrezca consejos.

GUIÓN DE TRABAJO		
	¿Llevas una vida sana?	→ Bueno... como sano, pero no duermo mucho...
	¿Qué me aconsejas? ¿Qué puedo/debería hacer?	→ Acuéstate temprano. Deberías hacer ejercicio. Por cierto, prueba el yoga.

Dar consejos

¿Llevas una vida sana?
Levántate temprano y disfruta de la vida.
También **deberías hacer** ejercicio.
Si tienes bicicleta, **utilízala**.

10A.4 The imperative with pronouns
deberías + [infinitive]

Vocabulario *cont.*

el/la paciente *patient*
la natación *swimming*
el/la especialista, el ejercicio
12
hacer gimnasia *to exercise*
la piel *skin*
la fibra *fiber*
despacio *slowly*
la comida basura *junk food*
llevar una vida... *to lead a . . . life*
la circulación

¡OJO!

Spanish uses different words to talk about the inner ear and the outer ear. Use **el oído** to refer to the inner ear and your sense of hearing: **Tengo fiebre y me duelen los oídos.** Use **la oreja** to talk about the outer ear: **Mi abuelo tiene las orejas muy grandes.**

SAM: Actividades pp. 204–206

Carlos Salazar, médico de familia en La Habana

Carlos Salazar, médico de familia en el Hospital Salvador Allende en La Habana

La Habana, 26 de enero

Carlos Salazar, médico de familia en La Habana, nos habla de su día a día

La sala de Medicina General del hospital es uno de los servicios que atiende a más personas.

En este servicio trabaja Carlos Salazar como médico de familia desde hace un año porque, como él mismo dice: "Me gusta poder ayudar donde es más necesario."

Hace cinco años, Carlos participó en un programa de intercambio con Venezuela y trabajó dos años en la Clínica Popular El Valle, en Caracas. Su misión era enseñar nuevas técnicas de prevención a un grupo de médicos venezolanos.

"La medicina cubana es muy prestigiosa. Por eso, nuestro país recibe a pacientes de todo el mundo. Hay que atender a más de ochenta pacientes en un día. No podemos dedicarles mucho tiempo, y a veces es difícil; por eso también hay que educar en salud. Las medicinas no son siempre la única solución, y hay que informar a los pacientes sobre hábitos de vida sanos y remedios naturales para cuidarse y sentirse bien de salud."

Cuando le preguntamos sobre el aspecto más importante de su trabajo, Carlos responde con una gran sonrisa: "Sin duda la gente, las personas... el aspecto humano. En mi trabajo hay que saber escuchar. Esto llega a las personas. Mi trabajo es duro a veces, pero me encanta."

Expresar obligación

En un día normal **hay que solucionar** muchos problemas y **hay que hacerlo** con rapidez.

10A.5 hay que + [*infinitive*]

Vocabulario

15

el/la médico/a de familia *family doctor*

la sala *ward*

atender (e:ie) *to see (a patient), to examine*

la sonrisa *smile*

solucionar *to solve*

la clínica, la misión, la prevención, la medicina, prestigioso/a

17

el/la doctor(a)

---

15 **a. Carlos Salazar** Fíjese en la imagen del protagonista y en el título del artículo. ¿Qué sabe del sistema de salud en Cuba?

b. Médico de familia ¿Sabe qué es un "médico de familia"? Haga sus hipótesis. ¿Existe un equivalente en su país?

c. Elegir Ahora lea el texto y elija un título para el artículo. Justifique su elección.

"Mejor prevenir que curar"

"Programas de intercambio profesional"   "Tu médico, tu amigo"

16 **Problemas y soluciones** Marque en el texto con un color los problemas que Carlos tiene a diario y con otro color las soluciones que encuentra. ¿Tiene alguna otra idea para solucionar sus problemas? Hable con su compañero/a.

17 **Escuchar** Escuche la conversación entre este compañero venezolano de Carlos Salazar en la Clínica Popular El Valle y una de sus pacientes, y complete la tabla.

Síntomas	Tratamiento

18 Clasificar Lea estas recomendaciones de viaje de la revista *Excursionista* y clasifíquelas.

ANTES DEL VIAJE: ....   DURANTE EL VIAJE: ....
DESPUÉS DEL VIAJE: ....

RECOMENDACIONES PARA UN VIAJE DE AVENTURA

1. Visite a su médico de familia e infórmese de los medicamentos que necesita.

2. Lleve ropa y calzado adecuados al clima del país de destino. Lleve calzado cómodo, botas de *trekking*, ropa para el frío (chaqueta, pantalones largos...), para el calor (pantalones cortos, gorro), y para la lluvia (impermeable).

3. Infórmese sobre el sistema de asistencia sanitaria del país de destino.

4. Algunas enfermedades tropicales no se manifiestan inmediatamente. Si tiene síntomas como fiebre, diarrea, dolor de cabeza, picazón, etc., informe a su médico.

5. Coma solo alimentos cocinados.

6. Báñese en zonas de la playa donde haya un salvavidas.

7. Beba mucha agua. Bébala en botella, sin hielo.

8. Vacúnese contra las enfermedades peligrosas de los países de destino (fiebre amarilla, hepatitis...) y tome la medicación contra el paludismo si es necesario.

9. Cuando coma fruta, siempre lávela y pélela antes.

10. Prepare un botiquín con medicamentos básicos: desinfectante para heridas, crema solar protectora, repelente de mosquitos, etc.

Vocabulario
18

el medicamento *medicine*
el calzado *shoes*
el gorro *cap*
el impermeable *raincoat*
la asistencia sanitaria *health care*
la enfermedad *illness; disease*
la picazón *itch*
bañarse *to swim*
el/la salvavidas (*invar.*) *lifeguard*
vacunar *to vaccinate*
peligroso/a *dangerous*
la fiebre amarilla *yellow fever*
el paludismo *malaria*
el botiquín *first-aid kit*
la herida *injury; wound*
la crema solar protectora *sunscreen*

la diarrea, la hepatitis, la medicación, el desinfectante, el repelente, el mosquito

OPINIÓN

Piense en el sistema de asistencia sanitaria de su país. ¿Qué aspectos positivos y negativos tiene?

19 Categorías Busque en el texto palabras relacionadas con estas categorías.

enfermedades • síntomas • medicamentos • ropa

20 Recomendaciones Para usted, ¿cuáles son los tres consejos más importantes ofrecidos en el artículo? ¿Le sorprende alguno? ¿Ha viajado alguna vez a algún destino que ha requerido precauciones especiales?

21 Escribir Escriba al consultorio de salud, exponga un problema que tiene y pida consejo.

Nombre: ....   Edad: ....
Enfermedades: ....
Alergias: ....

Comentarios: *Últimamente duermo poco, y me duele la espalda...*

22 Expresiones Escuche de nuevo al doctor y a su paciente y fíjese en estas expresiones propias del habla venezolana. ¿Qué cree que significan? ¿Ha escuchado alguna vez un acento similar en español?

○ Ahorita.   ○ ¿Cómo anda?   ○ ¿Cómo me la tratan?   ○ ¡A la orden!

SAM: Actividades pp. 207–210

Practice more at **vhlcentral.com**.

23 **Viaje** Formen dos grupos y viajen por América Latina. Tiren el dado° y avancen por los países. Si contestan correctamente, pueden seguir el viaje.

1 ¿Qué tiempo hace en Isla Margarita?

2 Viajan al Amazonas. ¿Qué hay que hacer contra el paludismo?

3 Viajan de Belém (Brasil) a Montevideo (Uruguay). ¿Qué transporte utilizan? Pidan consejo.

4 Aconsejen actividades interesantes para hacer en Buenos Aires (Argentina).

5 ¿Qué ropa hay que llevar a los Andes?

6 Están en Chile. Un compañero está resfriado. Describan los síntomas.

7 ¿Qué tiempo hace en La Paz (Bolivia)?

8 Están en Perú y una compañera se encuentra mal. Piensen en remedios para el dolor de estómago.

9 Están en Colombia. Una compañera perdió su pasaporte. ¿Qué pueden hacer?

tiren el dado *roll the die* **la embajada** *embassy*

TAREA FINAL

Receta para ser feliz

Haga una lista de seis recomendaciones para ser feliz.

Disfruta de tu familia.

....

 Compare su lista con la de su compañero/a y elijan diez recomendaciones.

 Compártanlas con sus compañeros. Escojan las recomendaciones más brillantes y escriban la receta para ser feliz.

YO PUEDO...

- Puedo hablar del tiempo.
  ¿Qué tiempo hace hoy?

- Puedo expresar dolencias y síntomas.
  ¿Cómo se siente si está resfriado/a?

- Puedo pedir consejos.
  Usted tiene fiebre: pida consejo.

- Puedo dar consejos.
  Escriba consejos para un amigo que tiene estrés.

- Puedo expresar obligación.
  ¿Qué hay que hacer para llevar una vida sana?

GRAMÁTICA FUNCIONAL ⓢ Tutorials

10A.1 Talk about the weather

hace; llueve; nieva; está nublado `5.12.2`

- To inquire about the weather, say **¿Qué tiempo hace?** or **¿Qué tal (está) el tiempo?** (*How's the weather?*).

- To describe the weather, use these impersonal expressions, which do not have an expressed subject (equivalent to *it* in English).

Hace frío.	**Hace buen tiempo.**	**Nieva.**
Hace calor.	**Hace mal tiempo.**	**Está nublado.**
Hace sol.	**Llueve.**	

- To ask the temperature, say **¿Qué temperatura hace?** To answer, say **Hace** + [*number*] + **grados (centígrados/Fahrenheit).**

10A.2 Describe symptoms and ailments

doler; encontrarse/estar + bien/mal/[*adjective*], tener + [*noun*] `5.8.2, 5.11.2`

- The verb **doler** (*to hurt*) undergoes an **o→ue** stem change. Like **gustar,** it is conjugated in the third person and used with indirect object pronouns. Use the verb in the singular or plural form in order to make it agree with the subject.

DOLER		
(a mí)	**me**	
(a ti)	**te**	
(a usted/él/ella)	**le**	
(a nosotros/as)	**nos**	d**ue**le(n)
(a vosotros/as)	**os**	
(a ustedes, a ellos/as)	**les**	

- As with **gustar** (4A.2), use **a + mí, ti, usted, él, ella, nosotros/as, vosotros/as, ustedes, ellos/as,** or a person's name for clarification.

- Unlike in English, use the definite article (**el, la, los, las**) and not the possessive adjective with parts of the body.

  Me duele la cabeza. A Hugo le duelen los hombros.
  My head hurts. *Hugo's shoulders hurt.*

- Use the reflexive verb **encontrarse** (*to feel*) to express how someone is feeling. **Encontrarse** has an **o→ue** stem change.

  Estoy cansada hoy, pero **me encuentro** bien.
  *I am tired today, but **I feel** well.*

- When **encontrar** is used non-reflexively, it means *to find*.

- Use the construction **tener** + [*noun*] to express certain states. Remember to use **tener** + **frío/calor** to say that someone feels hot or cold and **hace** + **frío/calor** to talk about the weather.

tener calor	*to be hot*	**tener hambre**	*to be hungry*
tener frío	*to be cold*	**tener sed**	*to be thirsty*
tener fiebre	*to have a fever*	**tener sueño**	*to be sleepy*
tener gripe	*to have the flu*	**tener dolor de. . .**	*to have a . . . ache*

- Use **estar** + **bien/mal/**[*adjective*] to describe other states, as in **estoy resfriado/a** (*I have a cold*) or **estoy enfermo/a** (*I am sick*).

¡Póngalo en práctica!

G1 **Completar** Complete el diálogo.

- ¿Qué tiempo (1).................... hoy en Caracas?

- (2).................... sol y buen tiempo.
  ¿Qué tal el (3).................... en Mérida?

- (4).................... mal tiempo.
  (5).................... nublado y (6)....................
  mucho frío.

- ¿Qué (7).................... hace?

- Hace tres (8).................... centígrados.

G2 **Conversaciones** Complete las conversaciones con la forma correcta de **doler, encontrarse** y **tener.** Incluya el pronombre reflexivo o el pronombre de objeto indirecto si es necesario.

- ¿Qué te pasa? ¿Cómo (1)....................?

- Me encuentro mal. (2).................... las muelas.

- ¿Cómo está María?

- Pues no muy bien; (3).................... gripe,
  (4).................... la cabeza y (5).................... fiebre.

- ¿Y a usted qué le pasa? ¿Cómo (6)....................?

- Mal; (7).................... calor y (8)....................
  el estómago.

G3 **Escoger** Empareje el comienzo de cada oración con el final apropiado.

	1. Gabriela está un poco	a. enfermo.
	2. Leo tiene	b. piernas.
	3. Mi hermano está	c. resfriada.
	4. Me duelen las	d. garganta.
	5. A Marcela le duele la	e. frío.

ⓢ **Practice more at vhlcentral.com.**

GRAMÁTICA FUNCIONAL

10A.3 Ask for advice

¿Qué puedo/debería hacer?; ¿Qué me aconseja(s)? 5.17.3

- Say **¿Qué puedo hacer?** (*What can I do?*) or **¿Qué debería hacer?** (*What should I do?*) to ask for advice.

  > Doctor, tengo fiebre. ¿Qué **debería** hacer?
  > *Doctor, I have a fever. What **should** I do?*

- You can also use the verb **aconsejar** (*to advise*) with an indirect object pronoun to ask someone's advice.

  > Tengo un problema. **¿Qué me aconseja?**
  > *I have a problem. **What would you advise me to do?***

10A.4 Give advice

The imperative with pronouns;
debería(s) + [*infinitive*] 5.17.3, 5.18.4a, 5.18.5a

- You learned how to form singular affirmative commands, both formal and familiar, in **8A.4** and **9B.2**. With affirmative commands, reflexive and object pronouns are always attached to the end of the imperative form. When a pronoun is attached to an affirmative command with two or more syllables, add an accent mark to maintain the original stress.

  > Dúch**ate** y vís**te**te.   Bebe el agua. Béb**ela**.
  > *Shower and get dressed.*   *Drink the water. Drink it.*

- You can also give advice using the construction **deberías** + [*infinitive*] in familiar contexts (**tú**) and **debería** + [*infinitive*] in formal situations (**usted**).

  > **Deberías** hacer deporte.   **Usted debería** descansar.
  > ***You should** exercise.*   ***You should** rest.*

- **Debería** is the conditional form of the verb **deber** (*must; ought to*). Use **debería** + [*infinitive*] to express what you should do.

- Use **deber** in the present tense to express an obligation or strong suggestion.

  > Tienes un examen mañana y **debes** estudiar.
  > *You have an exam tomorrow and you **must** study.*

10A.5 Express obligation

tener que + [*infinitive*]; **hay que** + [*infinitive*] 5.10

- In **6A.5**, you learned the construction **tener + que +** [*infinitive*] to express obligation.

  > **Tengo que hacer** algunas llamadas.
  > *I **have to make** some phone calls.*

- Another way to express obligation is the construction **hay que** + [*infinitive*]. **Hay que** expresses an impersonal obligation and it is invariable.

  > **Hay que** repartir las tareas.
  > *We/One must distribute the tasks.*

¡Póngalo en práctica!

G4 **Consejos** Complete las preguntas.

1. ¿Qué me .... para llevar una vida sana?
2. Estoy muy estresada. ¿Qué .... hacer?
3. No duermo bien. ¿Qué puedo ....?
4. ¿Qué .... aconsejas para sacar mejores notas?
5. Doctor, mi hermano siempre tiene sueño. ¿Qué le ....?
6. Quiero comer bien, pero no tengo tiempo para preparar la comida todos los días. ¿Qué .... hacer?

G5 **Imperativos informales** Escriba el imperativo informal de cada verbo.

(1) .... (Cambiar) tus hábitos de vida; (2) .... (levantarse) temprano, (3) .... (practicar) deportes y (4) .... (comer) sano. (5) .... (Acostarse) temprano y (6) .... (dormir) ocho horas como mínimo.

G6 **Transformar** Transforme cada oración al imperativo usando el pronombre de objeto directo apropiado.

> **Modelo:** Deberías beber la leche.
> *Bébela.*

1. Deberías utilizar la bicicleta para ir al trabajo. ....
2. Deberías comer las verduras. ....
3. Toma el jugo. ....
4. Deberías leer estos libros. ....
5. Deberías probar el yoga. ....
6. Usted debería tomar la manzanilla. ....
7. Usted debería levantarse temprano. ....
8. Usted debería evitar la comida basura. ....

G7 **Oraciones** Complete las oraciones usando **hay que** o la forma correcta de **tener que**.

1. Para llevar una vida sana, ... hacer ejercicio.
2. Un médico .... atender a muchos pacientes.
3. Lucas e Iván .... terminar el proyecto.
4. .... meter goles para ganar el partido.
5. ¿Qué .... hacer para aprender un idioma?
6. El paciente .... hablar con el médico ahora.

El tiempo y la salud

menos mal	thank goodness
por fin	at last
estar resfriado/a	to have a cold
hace 30 °C de temperatura	the temperature is 30° C
hacer buen/mal tiempo	there is good/bad weather
hacer frío/calor	to be cold/hot out
hacer sol	to be sunny
¿Qué tiempo hace?	What's the weather like?
la alergia	allergy
el antibiótico	antibiotic
la aspirina	aspirin
la cabeza	head
el/la dentista	dentist
la dolencia	ailment
la estación (del año)	season
el estado anímico	state of mind
el estado físico	physical condition
el estómago	stomach
la fiebre	fever
la garganta	throat
la infección	infection
la manzanilla	chamomile tea
la muela	molar
el otoño	fall
la primavera	spring
el remedio	remedy
el síntoma	symptom
la temperatura	temperature
el tiempo	weather
adaptarse	to adapt
darse un baño	to take a bath

depender (de)	to depend (on)
doler (o:ue)	to hurt
encontrarse (o:ue)	to feel
llover (o:ue)	to rain
nevar (e:ie)	to snow
ser sensible a	to be sensitive to
tener frío/calor	to be cold/hot
tomar el sol	to sunbathe
nublado/a	cloudy

Salud, divino tesoro

a propósito	incidentally; by the way
llevar una vida...	to lead a . . . life
por cierto	by the way
¿Qué te/le pasa? (fam./form.)	What's wrong?
el analgésico	painkiller
el brazo	arm
la circulación	circulation
la comida basura	junk food
el consultorio	advice column; doctor's office
el dolor	pain
el ejercicio	exercise
la espalda	back
el/la especialista	specialist
la fibra	fiber
la natación	swimming
el oído	ear
el/la paciente	patient
el pie	foot
la piel	skin
la pierna	leg

afectar	to affect
hacer gimnasia	to exercise
nervioso/a	nervous
tenso/a	tense
despacio	slowly

Carlos Salazar

tiren el dado	roll the die
la asistencia sanitaria	health care
el botiquín	first-aid kit
el calzado	shoes
la clínica	clinic
la crema solar protectora	sunscreen
el desinfectante	disinfectant
la diarrea	diarrhea
el/la doctor(a)	doctor
la embajada	embassy
la enfermedad	illness; disease
la fiebre amarilla	yellow fever
el gorro	cap
la hepatitis	hepatitis
la herida	injury; wound
el impermeable	raincoat
la medicación	medication
el medicamento	medicine
la medicina	medicine
el/la médico/a de familia	family doctor
la misión	mission
el mosquito	mosquito
el paludismo	malaria
la picazón	itch
la prevención	prevention
el repelente	repellent
la sala	ward
el/la salvavidas (invar.)	lifeguard
la sonrisa	smile
atender (e:ie)	to see (a patient), to examine
bañarse	to swim
solucionar	to solve
vacunar	to vaccinate
peligroso/a	dangerous
prestigioso/a	prestigious

Variación léxica

centígrados ⟷ grados Celsius

la comida basura ⟷ la comida chatarra (Arg., Méx.)

el consultorio ⟷ la consulta (Esp.)

la crema solar protectora ⟷ el protector solar (Amér. L.)

la malaria ⟷ el paludismo

el medicamento ⟷ la medicina (Amér. L.) ⟷ el remedio (Arg.)

la picazón ⟷ el picor (Esp.) ⟷ la comezón

el/la salvavidas ⟷ el/la guardavidas (Arg.) ⟷ el/la socorrista (Esp.)

solucionar ⟷ resolver

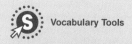

Vocabulary Tools

MEMORIAS

Imágenes de la memoria

Madrid, 16 de junio de 1977

Primeras elecciones democráticas

Los españoles votaron ayer, 15 de junio, en las primeras elecciones democráticas de los últimos 40 años. Fue un día histórico y la gente estaba emocionada.

Bogotá, 21 de octubre de 1982

Premio Nobel de Literatura para García Márquez

Anoche estaba en su casa de Ciudad de México y un periodista lo llamó para entrevistarlo. Así recibió la noticia.

Hablar de memorias

García Márquez **estaba** en su casa y **recibió** la noticia por teléfono.

Hoy **hemos votado** por primera vez. La gente **estaba** emocionada.

10B.1 Preterite
Present perfect
Imperfect

Vocabulario

1

el Premio Nobel *Nobel Prize*

el/la periodista *journalist*

emocionado/a *excited*

la memoria, las elecciones, democrático/a, votar

3

el/la testigo *witness*

el entusiasmo *enthusiasm*

emocionante *exciting; moving*

el optimismo *optimism*

decisivo/a, la generación

4

la moneda *currency*

dejar de *to stop*

desaparecer (zc) *to disappear*

el torneo *tournament*

1 a. **Fotos** Tome unos momentos para observar las imágenes de las dos páginas. Cierre el libro. ¿Qué imagen recuerda en primer lugar? ¿Recuerda las otras?

b. **Imágenes de la memoria** ¿Qué otra imagen quiere añadir a la exposición *Imágenes de la memoria*?

2 a. **Memorias** Lea las noticias de las dos páginas y anote ejemplos para cada tiempo verbal.

1 pretérito indefinido	2 pretérito perfecto	3 pretérito imperfecto

b. **Tiempos** Indique cuál de los tiempos anteriores usamos para:

- expresar acciones pasadas. ☐
- describir situaciones en el pasado. ☐
- expresar acciones pasadas conectadas con el presente. ☐

3 a. **Historia de España** Escuche a estos españoles que hablan de un momento importante de la historia de España. ¿De qué momento hablan?

b. **Datos** Escuche de nuevo y anote estos datos.

	¿Dónde y con quién estaban?
Mateo	
Celia	
Julián	

c. **Responder** ¿Ha vivido alguno de los momentos de las fotografías? ¿Cuál? ¿Dónde estaba y qué hacía cuando sucedió?

1.º de enero de 2000

Cambio de milenio

Varias horas antes de la medianoche, cientos de miles de personas de todo el mundo se reunieron frente a los monumentos representativos de cada ciudad para celebrar.

1.º de enero de 2002

El euro (EUR o €) ha entrado hoy en circulación como moneda única de la Unión Europea

En España, la peseta dejó de ser la moneda oficial hace tres años, pero se usó hasta ayer. Va a desaparecer como moneda física el 28 de febrero de 2002.

11 de julio de 2010

España ha ganado la Copa Mundial de Fútbol

Después de participar trece veces en el campeonato, la selección española (La Roja) ha ganado su primera copa del mundo en Sudáfrica.

---

4 **a. Antes o después** Lea estas informaciones. ¿Ocurrieron antes o después de los momentos de las imágenes? Complete las oraciones.

> Gabriel García Márquez publicó *Cien años de soledad* en 1967.
> *El escritor colombiano recibió el Nobel* ....

> El dictador español Francisco Franco murió el 20 de noviembre de 1975.
> *Las primeras elecciones democráticas se celebraron* ....

> La peseta dejó de ser la moneda oficial de España el 1.º de enero de 1999.
> *La peseta dejó de ser la moneda oficial de España tres años antes de* ....

b. Otros hechos Añada otros hechos que ocurrieron antes y después de los que se representan en las cinco fotografías.

ꝏ MI EXPERIENCIA

5 **Un hecho histórico** Piense en un hecho histórico que ha vivido. Cuente a su compañero/a qué recuerdos tiene de ese día. Exprese las acciones y describa las situaciones.

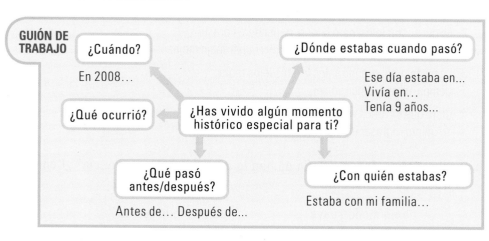

Relacionar momentos pasados

El Muro de Berlín se derribó veintiocho años **después de su construcción**.

Antes de retirarse, el ciclista español Miguel Ángel Indurain ganó el Tour de Francia cinco veces.

10B.2 antes/después de + [*infinitive/noun*]

Vocabulario *cont.*

morir (o:ue) *to die*
la muerte *death*
el hecho *event*
el Muro de Berlín *Berlin Wall*
derribar *to knock down, to demolish*
el milenio, la Unión Europea

MERCOSUR

En 1985, Argentina y Brasil firmaron un acuerdo que dio origen al Mercosur (Mercado Común del Sur), creado oficialmente en 1991 por Argentina, Brasil, Paraguay y Uruguay. Este mercado integra económica, política y culturalmente países muy diferentes y, al mismo tiempo, muy cercanos. Es el mayor productor de alimentos del mundo. Los miembros más recientes son: Bolivia, Chile, Colombia, Ecuador, Perú y Venezuela.

SAM: Actividades pp. 211–213

Chile en la memoria

Tan lejos y tan cerca

Hola a todos los chilenos y chilenas. Soy Elizabeth. Vivo y trabajo en Europa, en Bélgica. Estoy contenta acá. Solo tengo un problema: todavía no he conocido a ningún chileno para hablar de nuestro país. Quiero estar en contacto con otros compatriotas y creo que esta es una bonita oportunidad. ¿Creen que es posible?

Espero sus noticias. ¡Hasta pronto!

¡Hablamos!

Comentarios recientes

Hernán ¡Hola, Elizabeth y compatriotas chilenos en el mundo! Opino que este blog es fantástico. Llevo en París diez años. Llegué por trabajo y todavía no he vuelto a mi tierra. Para mí es un poco difícil estar lejos de mis familiares. ¿Y para ustedes?

Carolina Yo salí en momentos muy duros en mi país, por motivos políticos. Los años pasan rápido... Ya soy abuela y estoy en paz, pero mi corazón está todavía en Chile. En mi opinión, el propio país no puede olvidarse nunca. Y ustedes, ¿qué opinan? ¿Están de acuerdo?

Pedir y dar opiniones

- ● ¿**Creen que** vivir afuera es difícil?
- ■ Yo **creo que** sí.
- ✦ **Para mí**, tiene muchas ventajas. ¿Están de acuerdo?
- ● **En mi opinión**, es mejor estar en tu propio país. ¿Qué opinan?

10B.3	creer/opinar que..., para mí; en mi opinión...

Vocabulario

6

Bélgica *Belgium*

el/la compatriota *countryman/ countrywoman*

estar en paz *to be at peace*

no puede olvidarse *cannot be forgotten*

vivir afuera *to live abroad*

la esperanza *hope*

la nostalgia *homesickness; nostalgia*

la tristeza *sadness*

la decepción *disappointment*

En mi opinión,...

Estrategia ············

Minimizar el desacuerdo

- ● Es duro estar lejos, **pero** bueno, depende... para mí es una oportunidad.
- ■ Claro que es difícil, **pero** no imposible.

---

6 **a. Chile en la memoria** Fíjese en el blog y lea los textos. ¿Qué tienen en común los testimonios de estos chilenos? Márquelo.

> **Sienten...** esperanza • nostalgia • tristeza • decepción

b. Motivos Para Hernán y Carolina, ¿cuáles fueron los motivos para salir de Chile?

7 **a. Subrayar** Subraye en el texto las formas para pedir una opinión.

b. Completar Complete estas opiniones a partir del texto. Identifique quién dice cada una.

- ○ Opino que este blog ....
- ○ Creo que esta es ....
- ○ En mi opinión, el propio país ....
- ○ Para mí es un poco difícil ....

8 **a. Experiencias** Escuche a dos chilenos que hablan de sus experiencias en otros países. ¿A quién corresponden estas intervenciones?

	Diego	Sofía
1. Para mí es muy duro estar acá, lejos de mi país.	✓	
2. Es duro estar lejos, pero bueno, depende... Para mí ha sido una oportunidad para encontrar un trabajo mejor.		
3. En mi opinión, cuando sales y estás lejos tanto tiempo, es muy difícil volver.		
4. Claro que es difícil volver a veces, pero no imposible. Yo quiero regresar un día.		

b. Diego y Sofía ¿Diego y Sofía opinan lo mismo de su experiencia? ¿Cómo expresan su desacuerdo?

de un modo suave ☐   de un modo fuerte ☐

9 **Vivir afuera** ¿Qué opina usted de vivir y trabajar afuera? ¿Cuáles cree que son los aspectos positivos y negativos?

FORO CHILE EN LA MEMORIA

Entrada: Carlos Vallejo   23-09

Amigos, quiero compartir con ustedes algunas reflexiones de nuestros queridos escritores chilenos.

«La experiencia es como un billete de lotería comprado después del sorteo. No creo en ella.»

(GABRIELA MISTRAL)

«Vengo del llamado tercer mundo. (¿Cuál es el segundo?)»

(ISABEL ALLENDE)

«Algún día en algún lugar vas a encontrarte a ti mismo, y esa puede ser la más feliz o la más amarga de tus horas.»

(PABLO NERUDA)

Carolina: No estoy de acuerdo con Gabriela Mistral. Para mí la experiencia es esencial. ¿No creen?

Leonardo: Yo tampoco estoy de acuerdo con Gabriela Mistral. Creo que no tiene razón. La experiencia enseña muchas cosas.

Sandra: Pues yo sí estoy de acuerdo con ella. Yo tampoco creo en la experiencia.

Pablo: Es verdad, Sandra, tienes razón. La experiencia no sirve para nada.

Carolina: Para mí la frase de Isabel Allende es la mejor. Es la mejor escritora de Chile.

Pablo: ¡Ah! En esto no estoy de acuerdo. No es verdad. Neruda es el mejor.

---

10 **a. Escritores chilenos** ¿Conoce a estos escritores? Lea sus frases. ¿Le gustan? ¿Por qué?

b. Comentarios Lea los comentarios del foro. ¿Cuáles muestran estar de acuerdo y cuáles en desacuerdo? Subráyelos con colores distintos.

c. También o tampoco Complete las oraciones con **también** o **tampoco**.

- Estoy de acuerdo.
- Yo ....
- No estoy de acuerdo.
- Yo ....

11 **Opiniones** ¿Con qué opiniones del foro están de acuerdo y con cuáles no?

12 **Escribir** ¿Está de acuerdo con el mensaje que transmite cada uno de estos refranes? ¿Por qué? Explíquelo por escrito, dando ejemplos concretos de momentos pasados de su vida en los que estos refranes se aplicaron o no.

> Mejor malo conocido que bueno por conocer.

> El que guarda siempre tiene.

> Después de la tormenta viene la calma.

MI EXPERIENCIA

13 **Tres personajes** Vote con el resto de sus compañeros para elegir los tres personajes más representativos y carismáticos de la historia.

GUIÓN DE TRABAJO

> Yo creo que Teresa de Calcuta es la más representativa... En mi opinión,...

→ Estoy de acuerdo. Para mí también es... Tienes razón.

→ No estoy de acuerdo. No es verdad. Yo tampoco estoy de acuerdo.

Expresar acuerdo y desacuerdo

- Neruda tiene razón.
- Estoy de acuerdo.
- Sí, yo también.
- Neruda es el mejor escritor chileno.
- No es verdad. No estoy de acuerdo.
- Yo tampoco.

10B.4 **(no) estar de acuerdo, (no) tener razón, (no) ser verdad también, tampoco**

Vocabulario

8
el desacuerdo *disagreement*
10
amargo/a *bitter; painful*
tampoco *not ... either, neither*
tener razón *to be right*
ser verdad *to be true*
12
la tormenta *storm*

Jorge Edwards, recuerdos de un escritor

> "El hombre es historia, es memoria y es, a la vez, como se sabe, desmemoria."

Jorge Edwards, escritor chileno

Buenos Aires, 1.º de abril de 2008

El escritor chileno Jorge Edwards ha ganado el II Premio de Narrativa Iberoamericana Planeta-Casamérica

"*La casa de Dostoievski* toma el nombre de un edificio en ruinas de Santiago de Chile donde vivía un grupo de poetas y pintores a mediados del siglo XX", ha declarado el feliz autor después de conocer la noticia.

Jorge Edwards es uno de los principales representantes de la narrativa chilena. Ha ganado el Premio Nacional de Literatura de Chile en 1994 y el Premio Cervantes en 1999.

Estudió Derecho y representó a Chile como diplomático en Cuba y París. Allí se relacionó con algunos grandes del *boom* de la literatura latinoamericana, como Gabriel García Márquez, Julio Cortázar y Mario Vargas Llosa. Después del golpe de estado de Pinochet, abandonó su vida diplomática y se exilió en Barcelona, donde empezó su labor editorial. Actualmente, Jorge Edwards es escritor, editor y también colabora en diversos periódicos de Europa y América Latina como crítico literario.

Entre sus obras principales se encuentra la biografía *Adiós, poeta...* (1990). En esta obra, el escritor recuerda una parte de la vida de Pablo Neruda en el contexto cultural, social y político de la historia de Chile.

También ha publicado, entre otras muchas obras: *Persona non grata* (1973), donde el autor recuerda su período como representante del gobierno chileno en La Habana; *Machado de Assis* (2002), sobre el escritor brasileño Joaquim Machado de Assis, y *El sueño de la historia* (2000), de gran éxito entre la crítica, en la que recuerda la historia de Chile.

Expresar qué se recuerda

El escritor **recuerda** la historia de Chile.

10B.5 recordar (o→ue)

Vocabulario

14

el/la representante *representative*

la narrativa *fiction*

relacionarse *to run in the same circles*

el golpe de estado *coup d'état*

exiliarse *to go into exile*

la nota de prensa *press release*

representar, colaborar, el/la crítico/a literario/a

OPINIÓN

¿Ha leído alguna obra de algún escritor latinoamericano o español? ¿Cuál? ¿Le ha gustado? ¿Por qué?

---

14 **a. Jorge Edwards** Observe la imagen y lea el titular. ¿A qué se dedica nuestro protagonista?

b. Nota de prensa Lea la nota de prensa sobre Jorge Edwards. ¿Cuál es el motivo de la información que se publica sobre él?

15 **La biografía** Anote otros datos de su biografía que se mencionan.

- Países donde ha vivido. ¿Por qué motivos?: ....
  ....
- Actividad profesional: ....
- Libros publicados: ....

16 **a. Indicar** Indique qué recuerda el autor en algunas de sus obras.

b. Recuerdos ¿Y usted qué recuerda? Piense en un período pasado de su vida. ¿Dónde vivía? ¿Con quién? ¿Qué hacía?

17 **a. Explicar** Lea la cita de Jorge Edwards y explique con otras palabras su significado.

b. Responder ¿Qué datos de la biografía del protagonista le han llamado la atención? ¿Le parece un personaje interesante? ¿Están sus compañeros de acuerdo?

18 **a. El discurso** Lea este discurso de Jorge Edwards. ¿Qué hecho relata?

○ una aventura   ○ un encuentro   ○ un recuerdo de Cuba

«Tres o cuatro años después, en una casa de lo que ya se llamaba el barrio alto, el dueño, un arquitecto avanzado para el Chile de esos tiempos, se acercó al grupo de adolescentes del que yo formaba parte y nos presentó a un poeta de voz nasal, de tez aceitunada, vestido con un traje de gabardina de color verde botella. Era una casa diferente de todas las que había visto antes, con un cuadro del entonces joven Roberto Matta encima de un piano de cola negro, con dos dibujos de Pablo Picasso en una esquina.

"A la edad de ustedes", nos dijo el poeta, cuyo nombre, Pablo Neruda, sonaba tan extraño como su voz, "yo estudiaba matemáticas en un banco del Cementerio General, debajo de grandes magnolias, y le tenía un miedo pánico a los exámenes…".
Ya conocía el primero de sus *Veinte poemas de amor*, otro de mis textos de iniciación, y devoré cada una de sus palabras como un maná.»

EDWARDS, Jorge:
Discurso en la recepción del Premio Cervantes.

tez:	Cara. Tez aceitunada: Cara de color aceituna, verdoso.
gabardina:	Tipo de tela.
banco:	Asiento en que pueden sentarse varias personas, en un parque, por ejemplo.
cementerio:	Lugar donde se entierran los muertos.
magnolias:	Flores de un gran árbol, el magnolio.
devorar:	Comer con mucha hambre.
maná:	Alimento sagrado, según la Biblia.

b. Palabras Escriba una definición o descripción para estas palabras.

1. acercarse:...

2. verde botella:..

3. el miedo pánico:...

19 **Escribir** Escriba un relato breve sobre un encuentro. Use estos elementos del texto anterior.

Hace tres o cuatro años…

era…   conocí a…

dijo…

y…

20 **a. Poetas** ¿Conoce a Gabriela Mistral y a Pablo Neruda? Lea el texto y busque más información sobre estos escritores chilenos en Internet.

Gabriela Mistral

Gabriela Mistral, poetisa chilena, fue la primera escritora de América Latina que ganó el Nobel de Literatura, en 1945. Algunas de sus obras son *Sonetos de la muerte* (1914) y *Lagar* (1954).

Pablo Neruda ganó el Nobel en 1971. Algunas de sus obras son, por ejemplo, *Veinte poemas de amor y una canción desesperada* (1924), o *Confieso que he vivido* (1974), un libro de memorias donde el escritor recuerda hechos históricos de Chile.

Pablo Neruda

b. Escritores latinoamericanos ¿Qué otros escritores latinoamericanos conoce? ¿De dónde son? ¿Qué obras han escrito? Comparta sus conocimientos con su compañero/a.

Vocabulario

18
el encuentro *encounter*
el/la poeta/la poetisa *poet*
el piano de cola *grand piano*
cuyo/a *whose*
el miedo *fear*
nasal, el poema
20
el soneto
21
la dictadura *dictatorship*

Estrategia ············

Using a monolingual dictionary
When you come across a new word in Spanish, consult a monolingual dictionary. A monolingual Spanish dictionary describes meaning using descriptions, synonyms, and examples in Spanish rather than translations. Reading Spanish definitions will help you learn related words, and will keep you thinking in Spanish only.

El *boom* latinoamericano
En las décadas de 1960 y 1970, Gabriel García Márquez, Mario Vargas Llosa, Guillermo Cabrera Infante, Julio Cortázar, José Donoso y Carlos Fuentes, entre otros escritores latinoamericanos, revolucionaron la manera de contar historias. En las novelas del *boom*, las cosas irreales se describen como reales, los hechos no siempre están en orden cronológico, hay una mezcla de narradores y abunda el interés en la historia y la política.

SAM: Actividades pp. 217–222

 Practice more at **vhlcentral.com**.

21 **a. Juego** Tiren el dado y decidan quién empieza el juego. Hagan la pregunta con **qué, cuándo, dónde** o **quién** al equipo contrario, según el color. Tapen las respuestas. Si la respuesta no es correcta, pasa el turno al equipo contrario. Gana el grupo que más respuestas correctas recuerde.

1. ¿La Roja ganó la Copa Mundial?	2. ¿Huracán° Katrina?	3. ¿España 1977?	4. ¿Igualdad en el matrimonio en los EE.UU.?	5. ¿*Cien años de soledad*?	6. ¿Juegos Olímpicos de 1992?

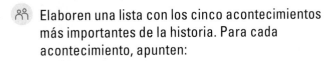

15. ¿Primera presidenta en Chile?		7. ¿1.° de enero de 2000 en el mundo?
14. ¿*Boom* de la literatura latinoamericana?		8. ¿Neruda, *Veinte poemas de amor…*?

¿Qué?   ¿Dónde?

¿Cuándo?   ¿Quién?

13. ¿Entrada en circulación del euro?	12. ¿Primera chilena que ganó Nobel de Literatura?	11. ¿Ganó Edwards en 1999?	10. ¿Nobel de Literatura 1971?	9. ¿Dictadura militar de Pinochet?

Respuestas

14. Décadas de 1960 y 1970	11. El Premio Cervantes	13. Unión Europea	15. Michelle Bachelet
8. 1924	7. Cambio de milenio	9. Chile	12. Gabriela Mistral
4. 2015	3. Primeras elecciones democráticas	6. Barcelona	10. Pablo Neruda
1. 2010		2. EE.UU.	5. Gabriel García Márquez

el huracán *hurricane*

 b. Otras preguntas Haga con su grupo otras preguntas sobre América Latina y España al grupo contrario.

T A R E A   F I N A L

Acontecimientos de la historia

Elaboren una lista con los cinco acontecimientos más importantes de la historia. Para cada acontecimiento, apunten:

- quién participó
- qué pasó
- cuándo pasó
- dónde estuvieron

Justifiquen la elección y presenten la lista al grupo.

Evalúen las elecciones de otros grupos y voten todos por el acontecimiento más importante.

Y O   P U E D O . . .

- Puedo hablar de memorias.

  ¿Qué hacía, dónde estaba y cómo era hace diez años?

- Puedo relacionar momentos pasados.

  Anote los momentos más importantes de su biografía relacionándolos entre sí temporalmente.

- Puedo pedir y dar opiniones.

  Comparta con sus compañeros de clase su opinión sobre el personaje más carismático de su país.

- Puedo expresar acuerdo y desacuerdo.

  Cree un diálogo en el que se expresa acuerdo y desacuerdo con las opiniones formuladas en la actividad anterior.

- Puedo expresar recuerdos.

  Anote un recuerdo agradable de algún período en su vida.

GRAMÁTICA FUNCIONAL Tutorials

10B.1 Talk about memories

Preterite, imperfect, and present perfect 5.6

- You know three tenses to talk about the past: the **pretérito indefinido**, the **pretérito imperfecto**, and the **pretérito perfecto.**

- Use the **pretérito perfecto** to talk about past events that are connected to the present.

> Ya **hemos probado** la sopa: está muy rica.
> *We've already **tried** the soup: it's very tasty.*

- Use the **pretérito indefinido** to describe completed actions in the past. Also use the **pretérito indefinido** if the actions occurred during a specific period of time.

> La familia de Eduardo **viajó** a Brasil el año pasado.
> *Eduardo's family **traveled** to Brazil last year.*

- Use the **pretérito indefinido** for a series of completed actions.

> Me **levanté**, me **vestí** y **preparé** el desayuno.
> *I **got up**, **got dressed**, and **prepared** breakfast.*

- Use the **pretérito imperfecto** to describe habitual or repeated actions in the past, or to provide the background details.

> **Estaba** aburrido y no **tenía** planes. Por eso, **acepté** su invitación.
> *I **was** bored and **didn't have** plans, so I **accepted** his invitation.*

- These two tenses are often used together when one action interrupts another action in progress. Use the **pretérito indefinido** for the action that interrupts the other.

> Tomás **leía** el periódico cuando **sonó** el teléfono.
> *Tomás **was reading** the newspaper when the phone **rang.***

- Use the **pretérito imperfecto** to describe simultaneous actions in the past with **mientras** (*while*). Use the preterite with **mientras** when an action interrupts an ongoing action.

> Gabriela **miraba** la televisión **mientras** Julián **cocinaba**.
> *Gabriela **watched** television **while** Julián **cooked**.*

> Toni **llegó** mientras yo **miraba** la tele.
> *Toni **arrived** while **I was watching** TV.*

- Use the **pretérito imperfecto** when describing age, weather, time of day, and physical and emotional states.

> **Eran** las dos de la tarde, **hacía** calor y **tenía** mucha sed.
> *It **was** two o'clock, it **was** hot out, and **I was** very thirsty.*

- To form the past progressive, use the imperfect of **estar** + [*present participle*].

> Guillermo **estaba charlando** con Elisa cuando empezó a llover.
> *Guillermo **was chatting** with Elisa when it started to rain.*

10B.2 Relate past events

antes/después de + [*infinitive/noun*] 10.3, 10.10, 12.13

- Use the prepositions **antes de** (*before*) and **después de** (*after*) before infinitives and nouns.

> Juan Carlos fue rey **antes de** aprobarse la Constitución.
> *Juan Carlos became king **before** the Constitution was approved.*

> **Después de** la muerte de Franco, empezó la democracia.
> *After Franco's death, democracy began.*

¡Póngalo en práctica!

G1 **Párrafos** Complete los párrafos con la forma correcta de los verbos.

Hoy (1)......................... (yo, ir) al barrio donde (2)......................... (yo, nacer) y (3)......................... (yo, ver) a uno de mis vecinos. Cuando mi familia y yo (4)......................... (dejar) el barrio, yo (5)......................... (tener) 18 años. Mis padres (6).........................,... (vivir) ahí por más de veinte años.

La caída del Muro de Berlín en 1989 (7)......................... (ser) un acontecimiento histórico muy importante. Yo (8)......................... (ser) muy joven, pero recuerdo que la gente (9)......................... (estar) muy emocionada. Cuando (10)......................... (llegar) la noticia, mi familia y yo (11)......................... (estar) cenando. Un amigo de mis padres nos (12)......................... (llamar) y mi familia entera (13)......................... (dejar) de comer para ir a ver las primeras imágenes por televisión.

G2 **Escribir** Complete las oraciones con las formas correctas de los verbos en el pretérito indefinido o el pretérito imperfecto.

1. Natalia .... (dormir) cuando .... (sonar) la alarma.

2. Los hombres .... (hablar) en el bar mientras .... (tomar) café.

3. Cuando .... (empezar) la democracia en España, Javier .... (tener) doce años.

4. Yo .... (preparar) las maletas, ... (tomar) el taxi y .... (llegar) al aeropuerto a tiempo.

G3 **Completar** Complete las oraciones sobre la vida de José usando **antes de** y **después de**.

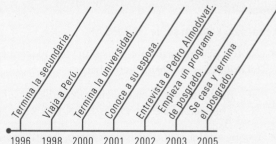

1. José viajó a Perú .... terminar la secundaria.

2. Conoció a su esposa .... la universidad.

3. .... entrevistar a Almodóvar, terminó la universidad.

4. Se casó .... empezar el posgrado.

 Practice more at **vhlcentral.com.**

¡Póngalo en práctica!

10B.3 Ask for and give opinions

creer/opinar + que; para mí/en mi opinión `10.15, 12.8`

- Use the verbs **creer** (*to think, to believe*) and **opinar** (*to think*) to ask for and express opinions. These verbs are often followed by the conjunction **que** (*that*). **Creer** and **opinar** are regular **-er** and **-ar** verbs, respectively.

> ¿Qué **opinas**?
> *What do you think?*

> ¿**Crees que** es difícil vivir en otro país?
> *Do you think it is difficult to live in another country?*

- To introduce a personal opinion, say **para mí** (*for me*) or **en mi opinión** (*in my opinion*).

> **En mi opinión,** Diego Maradona jugaba mejor que Pelé.
> *In my opinion, Diego Maradona played better than Pelé.*

10B.4 Express agreement and disagreement

(no) estar de acuerdo; (no) tener razón; (no) ser verdad; también, tampoco `11.2`

- To agree or disagree with a statement or idea, use a form of **(no) estar de acuerdo** (*to [not] agree*), **(no) tener razón** (*to [not] be right*), or **(no) ser verdad** (*to [not] be true*).

> —Picasso es el mejor pintor de la historia.
> —**Estoy de acuerdo.**
> —*Picasso is the best painter in history.*
> —*I agree.*

- Use **también** to agree with an affirmative statement and **tampoco** to add information to a negative statement. If **tampoco** precedes the verb, the word **no** is not used.

> Yo estoy de acuerdo **también.**
> *I agree, too.*

> No estoy de acuerdo **tampoco.**   **Tampoco** estoy de acuerdo.
> *I don't agree either.*   *I don't agree either.*

10B.5 Talk about what you remember

recordar, acordarse de `5.1.1, 5.7.1`

- Use the verb **recordar** (*to remember*) to talk about memories. **Recordar** has an **o→ue** stem change.

> **Recuerdo** muy bien el viaje a Costa Rica.
> *I remember the trip to Costa Rica very well.*

- A synonym for **recordar** is **acordarse**. **Acordarse** also has an **o→ue** stem change and it is used reflexively. It is used with the preposition **de**.

> **Me acuerdo de** muchas cosas de mi infancia.
> *I remember many things from my childhood.*

¡Póngalo en práctica!

G4 **Conversación** Complete la conversación.

> ¿Qué (1)....................... (vosotros, opinar) de la entrada del euro en España?
> ¿Creéis (2)........................ es positivo?

> (3)........................ (yo, creer) que sí.

> Pues en mi (4)........................, ha traído muchos problemas.

> (5)........................ mí, es muy positivo.

G5 **Diálogo** Complete la conversación.

- Creo que Gabriel García Márquez es el mejor autor latinoamericano. Y tú, Julio, ¿(1)........................ de acuerdo?

- Sí, creo que (2)........................ razón. Yo (3)........................ pienso que escribía muy bien. ¿Qué opinas, Alba?

- Yo no estoy de (4)........................ . Para mí, hay otros escritores más talentosos.

- ¡(5)........................ verdad! Julio Cortázar fue un escritor excelente, por ejemplo, y me encanta la poesía de Mario Benedetti. Yo (6)........................ estoy de acuerdo con ustedes.

G6 **Oraciones** Complete las oraciones con la forma correcta de **recordar** y **acordarse** en el presente.

1. ¿........................ (acordarse, tú) del profesor Álvarez de la secundaria?

2. Siempre .... (recordar, nosotros) el maravilloso viaje a Portugal.

3. Martín .... (acordarse) del fin de la dictadura en Argentina.

4. Los estudiantes .... (acordarse) del primer día del colegio.

5. Nunca .... (recordar, yo) las fechas de cumpleaños de mis amigos.

 Practice more at vhlcentral.com.

Imágenes de la memoria

las elecciones	elections
el entusiasmo	enthusiasm
la generación	generation
el hecho	event
la memoria	memory
el milenio	millennium
la moneda	currency
la muerte	death
el Muro de Berlín	Berlin Wall
el optimismo	optimism
el/la periodista	journalist
el Premio Nobel	Nobel Prize
el/la testigo	witness
el torneo	tournament
la Unión Europea	European Union
dejar de	to stop
derribar	to knock down, to demolish
desaparecer (zc)	to disappear
morir (o:ue)	to die
votar	to vote
decisivo/a	decisive
democrático/a	democratic
emocionado/a	excited
emocionante	exciting; moving

Chile en la memoria

En mi opinión,...	In my opinion, . . .
no puede olvidarse	cannot be forgotten
Bélgica	Belgium
el/la compatriota	countryman/ countrywoman
la decepción	disappointment
el desacuerdo	disagreement
la esperanza	hope
la nostalgia	homesickness; nostalgia
la tormenta	storm
la tristeza	sadness
estar en paz	to be at peace
ser verdad	to be true
tener razón	to be right
vivir afuera	to live abroad
amargo/a	bitter; painful
tampoco	not . . . either, neither

Jorge Edwards

el/la crítico/a literario/a	literary critic
la dictadura	dictatorship
el encuentro	encounter
el golpe de estado	coup d'état
el miedo	fear
la narrativa	fiction
la nota de prensa	press release
el piano de cola	grand piano
el poema	poem
el/la poeta/la poetisa	poet
el/la representante	representative
el soneto	sonnet
colaborar	to collaborate
exiliarse	to go into exile
relacionarse	to run in the same circles
representar	to represent
cuyo/a	whose
nasal	nasal

Variación léxica

el *boom* ⟷ el auge ⟷ el éxito

los Juegos Olímpicos ⟷ las Olimpíadas ⟷ las Olimpiadas

la nostalgia ⟷ la morriña (*fam., Esp.*)

vivir afuera (*Amér. L.*) ⟷ vivir fuera (*Esp.*) ⟷ vivir en el extranjero

Estrategias

(1) Ganar tiempo mientras pensamos Lección 9A

Every language has certain words and expressions its speakers use to "buy time" while they are thinking. Learning the expressions used in Spanish will help you gain fluency, as well as maintaining the interest of the person with whom you are speaking.

○ En parejas, cada uno representa el papel de la ficha. Intercambien los papeles después.

Estudiante A	**Estudiante B**
Objetivo: Pensar en una anécdota y responder a las preguntas de su compañero/a.	**Objetivo:** Preguntar a su compañero/a por una anécdota que ha vivido. Hacer preguntas constantemente y mostrar interés.

(2) Llamar la atención Lección 9B

Use expressions such as **Perdona** (*fam.*) or **Perdone** (*form.*) to politely get someone's attention.

○ Relacione las columnas.

Perdona,...
Perdone,...

¿me trae la cuenta, por favor?
¿qué hora tienes?
¿me permite pasar?
¿está ocupado este asiento?
¿me prestas tu bolígrafo un momento?

(3) Añadir información a una conversación Lección 10A

Expressions such as **por cierto** or **a propósito** are used to add related information or to change topics of conversation.

○ Lea lo que dice esta persona y añada información a la conversación.

Ayer estaba en el trabajo y empezó a dolerme una muela; llamé al dentista y...

....
....

He leído una novela muy buena de un escritor chileno —se llama Luis Sepúlveda y...

....
....

(4) Minimizar el desacuerdo Lección 10B

Part of polite conversation is being able to express disagreement without offending the person you are speaking with. Use expressions such as **bueno; vale; depende;** or **sí, claro, pero** to soften the force of your opinions and give a cooperative tone to the conversation.

○ Esta persona está un poco enfadada. Minimice su desacuerdo y ayúdela a sentirse más relajada en la conversación.

- "No estoy de acuerdo, una sopa de ajo no es lo mejor para curar el resfriado." ....
- "No comparto tu opinión: si llueve, no podemos hablar de buen tiempo." ....
- "Mi opinión es que los periódicos tienen demasiada publicidad." ....
- "La memoria nunca es objetiva, en absoluto." ....

Competencias

CONJUGAR VERBOS

1 **Pretérito imperfecto** Escriba la forma verbal del pretérito imperfecto para cada verbo en la persona indicada. Compare sus respuestas con las de su compañero/a.

1 estudiar (nosotros)	2 estar (yo)	3 hacer (tú)	4 compartir (vosotros)	5 ser (nosotros)	6 ir (ustedes)

7 compartir (él)	8 conocer (vosotros)	9 estar (ellas)	10 ir (ella)	11 ser (yo)	12 hacer (usted)

INDICAR EL CAMINO

2 **Mapa** Imagine que está en el lugar que indica la cruz (**X**) del mapa. Pregunte a un(a) compañero/a cómo ir a tres establecimientos. Luego intercambien papeles. Recuerden practicar el uso de **tú** y **usted**.

1. Frutería
2. Locutorio
3. Estanco
4. Panadería
5. Quiosco
6. Agencia de lotería

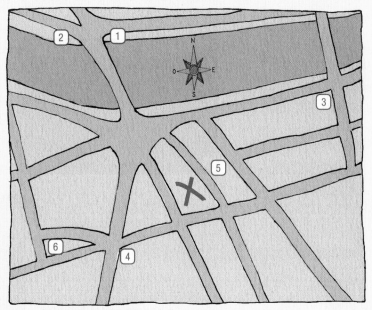

DESCRIBIR SÍNTOMAS Y DOLENCIAS, PEDIR Y DAR CONSEJOS

3 **En el consultorio** Imagine que se encuentra mal y está en un consultorio. Describa sus síntomas y las posibles causas. Después cambie su descripción con la de un(a) compañero/a y proponga remedios adecuados.

Modelo: *Me encuentro mal hoy. Me duele...*

CONTAR ANÉCDOTAS

4 **El otro día** ¿Pretérito indefinido o pretérito imperfecto? Complete la conversación con la forma correcta del verbo.

- ¿Sabes qué me (1) _____ (pasar) el otro día?

- ¿Qué te (2) _____ (pasar)?

- (3) _____ (Estar) en la puerta del auditorio porque (4) _____ (querer) escuchar el concierto de Julieta Venegas. (5) _____ (Llevar) casi una hora en la cola para sacar la entrada. Y cuando me (6) _____ (tocar) a mí, (7) _____ (acabarse) las entradas.

- ¿De verdad?

- (8) _____ (Estar) muy triste porque (9) _____ (tener) muchas ganas de escucharla. De repente, la persona que (10) _____ (estar) parada delante de mí en la cola (11) _____ (recibir) una llamada al celular y (12) _____ (tener) que irse. Pero antes, (13) _____ (acercarse) a mí y me (14) _____ (regalar) su entrada. (15) _____ (Ser) para la primera fila. Increíble, ¿no?

- ¡Sí, increíble!

Video

La salud

Ya ha leído sobre los cuidados necesarios para la salud y ha aprendido cómo opinar y expresar su acuerdo o desacuerdo. Este episodio de **Flash Cultura** muestra un aspecto del sistema de salud en Argentina que puede llevar a una reflexión sobre el tema.

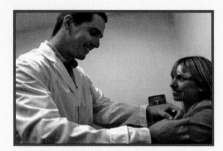

Estrategia

Note-taking

When watching a video, you can take notes to help you remember what you saw. Good notes are short sentences and key words: pay attention to the main points. From the title, you can infer the topic of this episode of **Flash Cultura**. Focus on that, and be ready to take notes!

Vocabulario útil

acompañar *to go with*

ser atendido/a *to be seen (by a doctor)*

chocar *to collide with*

la cita previa *scheduled appointment*

golpeado/a *beaten up*

estar de guardia *to be on duty*

grave *serious*

lastimado/a *injured*

la tos *cough*

Estrategia

Interjections

Interjections are short exclamations, words, or phrases typical of spoken language, and often used to express emotion or a reaction. Many interjections have meanings that can vary depending on context and intonation, and also depending on the country. For example, as a warning you might hear **¡Cuidado!** or **¡Ojo!** in any Spanish-speaking country, but you wouldn't hear **Híjole** outside of Mexico or **Jolín** outside of Spain (both are used to express surprise). To express encouragement, you should use **¡Dale!** in Argentina, but **¡Sale!** in Mexico and **¡Venga!** in Spain.

1 **Preguntas** ¿Qué opina del sistema de salud de su país? ¿Conoce el sistema de salud de algún otro país? ¿Cree que la atención de la salud es un derecho de todos los ciudadanos? ¿Por qué?

2 **Mirar** Mire este episodio de **Flash Cultura**. Preste atención a los puntos más importantes. ¿Qué cosas encuentra sorprendentes o distintas de su experiencia?

Aquí siempre hay médicos que están de guardia las 24 horas, noche y día.

¡No cuesta nada! Nuestro sistema de salud es público.

3 **¿Sí o no?** Indique en la lista los pasos que son necesarios y los que no lo son para recibir atención en un hospital público de Argentina.

Sí No

☐ ☐ 1. Enfermarse o tener un accidente

☐ ☐ 2. Ir a un hospital público

☐ ☐ 3. Ser argentino/a

☐ ☐ 4. Tener cita previa con un doctor

☐ ☐ 5. Dar los datos personales en recepción

☐ ☐ 6. Sacar turno con un número

☐ ☐ 7. Conocer al doctor Corbo

☐ ☐ 8. Esperar en la Sala de Guardia

4 **Conversación** En parejas, escriban una conversación entre un turista que sufrió un accidente (pueden elegir el país) y una persona que le aconseja qué hacer.

Modelo: • *Usted está lastimado: tiene que ir a un hospital.*

• *No quiero gastar dinero, y por cierto, no me duele mucho...*

 Practice more at **vhlcentral.com**.

Unidad 11

José Carlos, encantado de ayudarlo

Héctor y Gabriela, propietarios de Patagonia Natural

AVANCE

Machu Picchu: encanto y misterio

11A

DE VIAJE

Cambiar de aires

VIAJA
Especial
Semana Santa

**VIAJA
TE RECOMIENDA
LOS MEJORES
LUGARES**

Sal de casa,
ve a un lugar especial
y haz una pausa en tu vida.

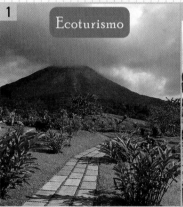

1 Ecoturismo

**Parque Nacional Volcán
Arenal, Costa Rica**

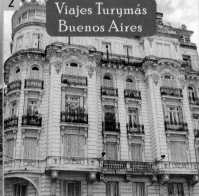

2 Viajes Turymás
Buenos Aires

hotel + avión + espectáculo de tango
Precios reducidos a grupos

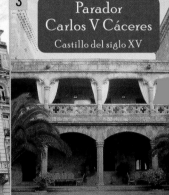

3 Parador
Carlos V Cáceres
Castillo del siglo XV

**Con la garantía de Paradores
de Turismo de España**

Recomendar

- **Haz** una pausa y **sal** de la rutina. **Ven** y disfruta del sol.
- ¿**Me recomiendas** ir al mar o a la montaña?
- Yo **te recomiendo** tranquilidad.

11A.1	Affirmative commands: irregular **tú** forms **recomendar** + [*infinitive/noun*]

Vocabulario

①

el cambio de aires *change of scenery*

el Parador de Turismo de España *state-run hotel in a Spanish historic building*

boricua *Puerto Rican*

el encanto *charm*

el ecoturismo, la garantía, el eslogan

¡OJO!

Puerto Ricans (**puertorriqueños/as**) often refer to themselves as **boricuas** (both males and females) or **borinqueños/as**. These words are derived from **Borinquen**, the Taino name for the island before the arrival of Columbus.

---

1 **a. Eslóganes** Observe los anuncios y elija un eslogan para cada uno. Compare sus propuestas con las de su compañero/a.

Sé aventurero.

Disfruta del sol boricua.

Vive el encanto del mar desde adentro.

Ven a la naturaleza.   Da un paseo por la historia.

Pon ritmo de tango a tus vacaciones.

b. Responder ¿Ha visitado estos lugares u otros similares? ¿Qué opción le parece más interesante?

2 **a. Relacionar** Localice los imperativos irregulares en los textos de esta página y relaciónelos con estos infinitivos.

1. salir: ___sal___   3. venir: ....   5. poner: ....
2. ser: ....   4. ir: ....   6. hacer: ....

b. Crear Cree su propio eslogan con alguno de los verbos anteriores. Piense en un hotel, una ciudad, una región o un espectáculo.

3 **Recomendar** Pregunte a su compañero/a por sus gustos y hábitos de viaje, y recomiéndele un destino de los anteriores o algún otro.

Modelo: *Si te gusta visitar ciudades, ve a... / te recomiendo ir a...*

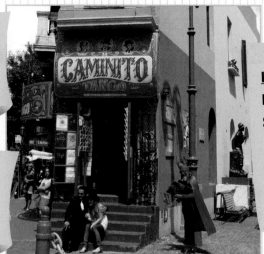

Información hotel

Dirección: Avenida Rosario 234

Desayuno 7:00-10:00 h

Cena 20:00-24:00 h

Información actividades

Salida del hotel: 21:30 h

Espectáculo de tango:
sábado 22:00 h

Información vuelos

Llegada a Buenos Aires vuelo AA 956

Salida de Buenos Aires vuelo AA 957

Recepción en el aeropuerto: 14:30 h

Llegada al hotel: 15:15 h

---

4 **De viaje** Observe las notas de la guía turística. ¿A qué viaje de la página anterior corresponde?

5 **a. Escuchar** Escuche a la guía. ¿En qué momento del viaje se encuentran, al principio o al final?

b. Indicar Escuche de nuevo y marque lo que ha dicho la guía.

Ha dicho que…		Ha preguntado…	
el hotel no está muy lejos.	☐	si tenemos los pasaportes a mano.	☐
vamos todos juntos en ómnibus al hotel.	☐	si queremos ir al espectáculo de tango.	☐
el equipaje llega mañana.	☐	cuándo queremos cenar.	☐

6 **Transmitir mensajes** Transmita estos mensajes a su compañero/a.

En su ausencia ha llamado:
Carlos Herrero

Mensaje:
¿Cuándo tienes
vacaciones?

En su ausencia
ha llamado: Marta

Mensaje:
He comprado ya
los pasajes de avión.

En su ausencia ha llamado:
Alejandro

Mensaje:
Tengo el pasaporte en
regla. ¿Y tú?

MI EXPERIENCIA

7 **Recomendaciones** ¿Qué viaje recuerda con especial cariño? Recomiéndeselo a su compañero/a. Cuente al grupo la recomendación de su compañero/a.

GUIÓN DE TRABAJO

Te recomiendo…

Ve…
Haz…
Reserva…

Lugar: mar, montaña

Transporte: avión…

Alojamiento: hotel, parador…

Mi compañero/a ha dicho que… (hay un lugar…)

Transmitir palabras de otros

- "Ya tengo los pasajes."
- Marta **dice/ha dicho que** ya tiene los pasajes.
- "¿Cuándo quieren viajar? ¿Pueden viajar en septiembre?"
- En la agencia de viajes **me han preguntado cuándo** queremos viajar y **si** podemos viajar en septiembre.

11A.2 Reported speech

Vocabulario

④

la recepción *pickup*

la llegada *arrival*

⑤

el equipaje *baggage*

⑥

en regla *in order; valid*

favorecer (zc) *to favor*

los ingresos *income*

el PIB (producto interior bruto) *GDP (Gross Domestic Product)*

la ausencia

El turismo

El turismo es una industria muy importante que ha favorecido a la economía de Latinoamérica. Algunos de los países que reciben mayores ingresos por turismo en la región son: República Dominicana (14,8% de su PIB), Costa Rica (12,9% de su PIB), México (12,6% de su PIB) y Argentina (10,3% de su PIB).

SAM: Actividades pp. 223–225

Experiencias de viaje

LIBRO DE QUEJAS

Lugar y fecha

En: Ponce, Puerto Rico   Fecha: 26 de junio

Datos del cliente

1.er apellido: Suárez   2.° apellido: Abiega   Nombre: Laura

D.N.I.: 51065258   Dirección: C/ Pozas 23, Bilbao, España

Datos del establecimiento

Nombre: Hotel Playas Doradas   Dirección: 111 Calle Villa, Ponce 00733, Puerto Rico

Motivo de la queja

En primer lugar, el hotel está cerca del aeropuerto y hay mucho ruido. Hemos pedido una habitación con vistas al mar y nos han dado una con vistas... ¡al aparcamiento! La atención al cliente me parece pésima. Después, la piscina no está abierta y el jardín está en obras, y por último, el restaurante no tiene menú infantil y en general la comida no es buena. ¡En un hotel de cuatro estrellas! ¡Es increíble!

Expresar protestas

- ¿Qué te parece este hotel?
- No es muy bueno. Las instalaciones me parecen **muy malas** y el servicio es **pésimo**.

11A.3 **estar/parecer + bien/mal**
estar/parecer + bueno/a, malo/a, pésimo/a

Vocabulario

(8)

el libro de quejas *complaint form*

la queja *complaint*

la vista *view*

el aparcamiento *parking lot*

pésimo/a *dreadful*

estar en obras *to be under construction*

el hotel de cuatro estrellas *four-star hotel*

la instalación *facility*

Estrategia ···········

Ordenar la información

En primer lugar, la habitación es pequeña, **después**, no hay servicio de habitaciones y **por último**, la piscina está cerrada.

---

8 **a. Experiencias de viaje** Observe los documentos de las dos páginas. ¿En cuál expresa la cliente opiniones negativas y en cuál positivas?

b. Libro de quejas Lea el libro de quejas y marque qué le parece mal a la cliente.

1. atención al cliente ☐   5. tranquilidad ☐

2. vistas ☐   6. habitaciones ☐

3. instalaciones ☐   7. restaurante ☐

4. decoración ☐   8. calidad/precio ☐

9 **a. En la terraza** Escuche esta conversación en la terraza de un bar. ¿Por qué protesta el cliente? Numere sus intervenciones.

- Me parece pésimo. ☐   ○ Creo que hay un error en la cuenta. [1]
- Esto no está bien. ☐   ○ Quiero el libro de quejas. ☐

b. Responder ¿Qué le parece la forma en que reacciona el cliente?

10 **Escribir** Elija una de estas situaciones y complete el libro de quejas.

Restaurante La Perdiz. Menorca	Hotel La Playa. República Dominicana
Ha esperado una hora la comida.	La habitación es muy pequeña.
La comida es mala.	El aire acondicionado no funciona.
La cuenta tiene errores.	Hay muchos mosquitos.

Datos del cliente

Nombre: Apellidos:

Datos del establecimiento

Nombre: Lugar:

Motivo de la queja

En primer lugar,
Después,
Por último,

Cuestionario de satisfacción Grandes Vuelos

¡AYÚDENOS A MEJORAR!

SERVICIOS	Muy bueno/a	Bastante bueno/a	No muy bueno/a	Nada bueno/a
la reserva en línea			X	
la facturación		X		
la puntualidad	X			
el personal	X			
la comida	X			

11 **a. Servicios** Lea el cuestionario y fíjese en los servicios de esta compañía aérea. ¿Cuáles le parecen más importantes? ¿Puede añadir otros?

b. Cuestionario de satisfacción Observe la puntuación que dio el viajero en el cuestionario de satisfacción y marque con cuál de estas opiniones coincide.

1. "Estoy encantado. ¡El servicio de reserva en línea es muy bueno!"

2. "El único problema, la facturación. Hay que esperar mucho."

3. "Me alegro de haber elegido esta compañía. Estoy muy contento con la puntualidad y el personal, y el menú es estupendo. ¡Qué bien!"

12 **Reaccionar** ¿Cómo reacciona usted ante estas situaciones?

1. Está probando una comida muy buena en un restaurante. ¡ .... !

2. Está visitando un monumento muy atractivo. ¡ .... !

3. Su vuelo no tiene retraso. ¡ .... !

¡Qué bonito! • ¡Qué bien! • ¡Qué rico!

13 **Completar** Recuerde su último viaje en avión y complete el cuestionario de satisfacción según su experiencia.

14 **Contestar** ¿Usted consulta guías, páginas web o revistas para viajeros? ¿Alguna vez siguió una recomendación que no coincidía con la realidad?

MI EXPERIENCIA

15 **Preguntar** Elabore un cuestionario con los aspectos más importantes de un viaje y pida a su compañero/a que lo complete.

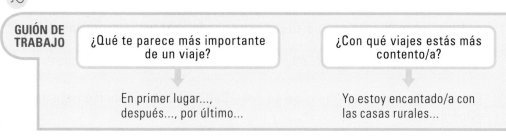

GUIÓN DE TRABAJO

¿Qué te parece más importante de un viaje?

¿Con qué viajes estás más contento/a?

En primer lugar..., después..., por último...

Yo estoy encantado/a con las casas rurales...

Expresar satisfacción

- ¿Están contentos con el servicio?
- Sí, estamos encantados.
- ¡Qué bien! ¡Me alegro de saberlo!

11A.4 **estar contento/a, encantado/a alegrarse (de) ¡qué + [adjective/adverb]!**

Vocabulario

9
la protesta *complaint*
protestar *to complain*
el error

10
el aire acondicionado *air conditioning*

11
la facturación *check-in*
la puntualidad *punctuality*
el personal *staff*
la compañía aérea *airline*
la puntuación *score, evaluation*
el/la viajero/a *traveler*
estar encantado/a *to be delighted*
alegrarse (de) *to be glad (that)*
contento/a *happy*
la satisfacción

12
el retraso *delay*

14
rural

SAM: Actividades pp. 226–228

Practice more at **vhlcentral.com**.

José Carlos, encantado de ayudarlo

En esta ocasión hablamos con José Carlos Segura Prados,
empleado del mes en el Hotel El Convento, ubicado en
San Juan, Puerto Rico.

¿Está contento con la mención de "Mejor empleado del mes"?
Estoy encantado, pero todo mi equipo es fantástico. Este premio es para todos.

> Estimado cliente:
> El **Hotel El Convento** le da la
> bienvenida y le desea una feliz estancia.
> Estamos encantados de ayudarlo.
>
> La Dirección

**José Carlos Segura Prados, 37 años. Jefe del
Departamento de Recepción.**

**Háblenos del hotel. Es
un edificio muy elegante
y también parece muy antiguo...**
*Efectivamente. ¡Se empezó a construir en 1646! Fue un convento
carmelita hasta fines de 1903. Comenzó a funcionar como hotel en
el año 1962.*

¿Y qué ofrece El Convento?
*Nuestras claves son el entorno histórico y la atención personalizada.
Además, ofrecemos habitaciones lujosas, cuatro restaurantes, un gimnasio,
una biblioteca, una playa privada, piscina... En fin, ¡muchas cosas!*

¿Lo mejor y lo peor de su trabajo?
*El trato con el público. Es gratificante y también difícil. Son las dos caras
de la misma moneda.*

¿Recuerda algún momento especial?
*Sí, claro, ¡muchos! Nuestro hotel es un lugar especial para mucha gente
porque aquí han celebrado momentos importantes... Estamos encantados
de poder contribuir a esa alegría.*

**Dar la bienvenida y
expresar buenos deseos**

¡Bienvenida a casa!

¡Bienvenidos a El Convento!

Le(s) damos la bienvenida a
nuestro hotel.

Le(s) deseo una feliz estancia.

11A.5 bienvenido/a(s); desear

Vocabulario

(16)

ubicado/a *located*
carmelita *Carmelite*
el entorno *environment, surroundings*
lujoso/a *luxurious*
gratificante *rewarding*
personalizado/a

(18)

la bienvenida *welcome*
dar la bienvenida *to welcome*
desear *to wish*
¡Feliz estancia! *Have a nice stay!*
la estancia *stay*
¡Bienvenido(s)/a(s)! *Welcome!*

---

16 a. **Conventos** ¿Sabe qué es un convento? ¿Conoce alguno?

b. **Leer** Lea la entrevista. ¿Qué tiene de especial el hotel?

17 a. **Contestar** ¿Qué ha dicho José Carlos que le ha llamado la atención?

Modelo: *Ha dicho que...*

b. **Expresión** Localice esta expresión en el texto. ¿Qué cree que significa?

"Son las dos caras de la misma moneda."

18 a. **José Carlos** Anote esta información de José Carlos.

○ nombre y apellidos   ○ puesto de trabajo   ○ lugar de trabajo

b. **Tarjeta del hotel** Fíjese en la tarjeta del hotel. ¿Dónde se encuentran
normalmente estas tarjetas? Marque las expresiones para dar la bienvenida
y expresar buenos deseos. Relaciónelas con estas equivalentes.

○ ¡Feliz estancia!   ○ ¡Bienvenido!

c. **Situaciones** Piense en qué situaciones puede usar estas expresiones.

¡Felicitaciones! • ¡Buen viaje! • ¡Felicidades! • ¡Felices vacaciones!

19 **Escuchar** Escuche este mensaje de José Carlos. ¿Qué tipo de mensaje es?
¿Qué dice?

20 **Anuncios** Observe los anuncios que hay en la recepción del Hotel El Convento.

Ecoturismo: El Yunque
A solo una hora de San Juan hay un verdadero paraíso tropical: El Yunque. En este bosque de 100 km² vas a encontrar unas 240 especies de árboles, 50 clases de orquídeas, hongos fluorescentes, animales exóticos y otras maravillas de la naturaleza. Ideal para los amantes del trekking.

El Viejo San Juan
Recorre el distrito histórico de la capital de Puerto Rico. El paseo incluye el Fuerte San Felipe del Morro, La Fortaleza, la Catedral, la Casa de los Contrafuertes y muchos rincones fuera del circuito habitual. Haz tu reserva con antelación. Con este cupón recibirás un descuento del 10%.

La noche sanjuanera
¿Quieres divertirte esta noche? Puedes ir a los bares y discotecas de Isla Verde. O quizás prefieres visitar los hoteles de Condado. Si lo que estás buscando es *janguear* como un verdadero boricua, debes ir a la Placita de Santurce. Hay una fiesta abierta todos los fines de semana. ¡Ven!

21 **a. Transmitir** Transmita uno de los anuncios a su compañero/a.

Modelo: *El anuncio dice que...*

b. Responder ¿Qué propuesta es más interesante para usted? ¿Por qué?

22 **Escribir** Piense en un(a) amigo/a o familiar a quien le pueda interesar alguna de las propuestas del Hotel El Convento y envíe un correo electrónico para transmitirle el anuncio. Explique por qué le parece interesante.

Modelo: *Mamá, he encontrado este anuncio en mi hotel...*

23 **Paradores de Turismo** Lea el texto e indique si las afirmaciones son verdaderas (**V**) o falsas (**F**).

La Red de Paradores de Turismo
Una de las maneras más interesantes de conocer España es a través de la Red de Paradores de Turismo. Hay construcciones modernas pero también castillos, palacios, conventos y otros edificios históricos restaurados.

Entre los paradores más conocidos está el Hostal de los Reyes Católicos, ubicado cerca de la catedral de Santiago (Galicia). Es el hotel más antiguo del mundo y también uno de los más lujosos. Nació como Hospital Real en 1499 para albergar a los peregrinos que visitaban Santiago. Más de 500 años después, continúa recibiendo a viajeros de todo el mundo.

	V	F
1. La Red de Paradores de Turismo ofrece alojamiento.	☐	☐
2. Los paradores siempre son edificios antiguos restaurados.	☐	☐
3. El Hostal de los Reyes Católicos se construyó hace más de 500 años.	☐	☐

Practice more at **vhlcentral.com**.

Vocabulario
20
la orquídea *orchid*
el hongo *mushroom*
incluir (y) *to include*
el fuerte *fort*
la fortaleza *fortress*
el rincón *spot, place*
con antelación *in advance*
sanjuanero/a (*P.R.*) *from San Juan*
janguear (*fam., P.R.*) *to hang out*
fluorescente
23
restaurar *to restore*
albergar *to accommodate*
el/la peregrino/a *pilgrim*
el hostal

¡OJO!
Incluir has a spelling change in most forms of the present indicative: incluyo, incluyes, incluye, incluimos, incluís, incluyen.

OPINIÓN
¿Cómo se siente en los hoteles?
¿Qué le gusta encontrar en un alojamiento?

SAM: Actividades pp. 229–232

24 **Juego** Fíjense en la imagen que ilustra el juego. Hagan un círculo y piensen en una anécdota breve. Una persona transmite la información a su compañero/a y así sucesivamente. ¿Cuál es el mensaje final?

robar *to steal*

TAREA FINAL

Nuestros viajes favoritos

Piense en los lugares más especiales que ha conocido. Lleve a la clase fotografías o información que conserva de ellos.

Recomiende estos lugares a sus compañeros y hábleles de ellos.

Preparen entre todos un álbum de viaje de estos lugares.

YO PUEDO...

• Puedo expresar recomendaciones.

Recomiende una actividad de interés en su ciudad o región.

• Puedo transmitir palabras o información de otros.

Transmita las palabras de Laura: "El profesor no puede venir mañana."

• Puedo expresar protestas y quejas.

Piense en una experiencia de viaje negativa y exprese sus protestas.

• Puedo expresar satisfacción.

Piense que está de vacaciones en el hotel donde trabaja José Carlos y su experiencia es muy positiva. Exprese satisfacción.

• Puedo dar la bienvenida y expresar buenos deseos.

Imagine que da la bienvenida a un(a) compañero/a que hace tiempo que no ha ido a la clase de español.

GRAMÁTICA FUNCIONAL 🅢 Tutorials

11A.1 Give recommendations

Affirmative commands: irregular **tú** forms 5.18.3a
recomendar + [*infinitive/noun*] 5.1.1, 5.10, 6.2.4

- Use the imperative to give strong suggestions or recommendations. In 8A.4 and 9B.2, you learned regular **tú** commands. Several common verbs have irregular **tú** commands.

DECIR	HACER	IR	PONER	SALIR	SER	TENER	VENIR
di	haz	ve	pon	sal	sé	ten	ven

Haz la tarea.	**Sé** bueno.	**Di** la verdad.
Do the homework.	*Be good.*	*Tell the truth.*

- To make recommendations, use [*indirect object pronoun*] + **recomendar** + [*infinitive/noun*]. **Recomendar** has an e→ie stem change.

Te **recomiendo** ir.	Le **recomiendo** el hotel.
I recommend that you go.	*I recommend the hotel.*

11A.2 Communicate other people's words

Reported speech 12.10   **decir** 5.1.2

- Use **el estilo indirecto** (*indirect discourse*) to tell what another person has said. Use verbs such as **decir, comentar, explicar,** and **preguntar** in the present or the present perfect.

DIRECT SPEECH	REPORTED SPEECH
Declaration:	**decir/explicar** + **que** + [*present tense*]
"Hay una habitación libre."	Dice/Ha dicho **que hay** una habitación libre. *He says/said **that there is** a room available.*
Information question:	**preguntar** + **qué/cuándo/dónde...** + [*present tense*]
"¿Dónde está el museo?"	Pregunta/Ha preguntado **dónde está** el museo. *She asks/asked **where** the museum **is**.*
Yes-or-no question:	**preguntar** + **si** + [*present tense*]
"¿Tenéis habitaciones libres?"	Pregunta/Ha preguntado **si tenemos** habitaciones libres. *He asks/asked **if we have** rooms available.*

- When reporting a question, be sure to include the written accent in **qué** (*what*), **cuándo** (*when*), **dónde** (*where*), etc.

   Silvia me ha preguntado **cuándo** llegará Felipe.
   *Silvia asked me **when** Felipe will arrive.*

- Often it is necessary to change the person of the verb when relaying information in reported speech. Use an indirect object pronoun to indicate to whom the speaker is talking.

   "¿Queréis ir?"→(Me) Pregunta si **queremos** ir.
   *"Do **you** want to go?"→He's asking (me) if **we want** to go.*

- **Decir** (*to say, to tell*) is an irregular verb. Its past participle is **dicho**.

DECIR			
(yo)	**digo**	(nosotros/as)	decimos
(tú)	dices	(vosotros/as)	decís
(usted, él, ella)	dice	(ustedes, ellos/as)	dicen

¡Póngalo en práctica!

G1 Completar Complete la conversación entre dos amigos con la forma correcta del verbo.

> Voy a hacer un viaje a Puerto Rico. César, ¿qué me (1)........................ (recomendar)?

> (2)........................ (Ir) a la playa,
 (3)........................ (hacer) excursiones y
 (4)........................ (poner) ritmo a tu viaje.

> Para moverme por la isla ¿me (5)........................ (recomendar) ir en carro o en autobús?

> Te (6)........................ (recomendar) el autobús. Después de tu viaje, ¡(7)........................ (venir) a verme para contarme cómo lo pasaste!

G2 Transformar Transforme las oraciones al estilo indirecto.

1. "Hay varios hoteles cerca de la playa."

   Me .... (explicar) que .... varios hoteles cerca de la playa.

2. "¿Queréis una habitación con vistas al mar?"

   Me .... (preguntar) .... una habitación con vistas al mar.

3. "¿Cuándo queréis la reserva?"

   Me .... (preguntar) .... la reserva.

4. "Pueden hacer muchas excursiones interesantes."

   Me .... (decir) que .... hacer muchas excursiones interesantes.

5. "¿A qué hora empieza el espectáculo?"

   Me .... (preguntar) a .... hora .... el espectáculo.

6. "Queremos reservar una habitación doble."

   Me .... que .... una habitación doble.

 Practice more at vhlcentral.com.

11A.3 Make complaints

estar/parecer + bien/mal; estar/parecer + bueno/a, malo/a, pésimo/a 5.11.1, 11.1

- Use **estar** and **parecer** (*to seem*) to express a positive or negative judgment. With **parecer**, use the construction [*indirect object pronoun*] + **parece(n)** + [*adjective/adverb*].

  > El servicio **me parece bueno,** pero las instalaciones **me parecen malas.**
  > *The service **seems good**, but the facilities **seem bad** (to me).*

- Use the adverbs **bien** and **mal** to describe an event or situation when using an infinitive.

  > **Me parece/Está mal cerrar** la piscina si hace calor.
  > *It's not right to close the pool if it's hot out.*

- Use adjectives such as **bueno/a, malo/a,** and **pésimo/a** when assessing objects or experiences. Remember that adjectives must agree in gender and number with the nouns they modify.

  > La comida **está buena,** pero los camareros **me parecen pésimos.**
  > *The food **is good**, but I think the waitstaff **is awful.***

11A.4 Express satisfaction

estar contento/a, encantado/a 5.8.2
alegrarse de 5.7.1, 5.10   **¡Qué + [*adjective/adverb*]!** 12.5

- Use **estar contento/a** and **estar encantado/a** to describe positive emotions. Use these expressions followed by **con** + [*noun*] to tell what makes the person happy.

  > Los clientes **están** muy **contentos** con la excursión.
  > *The clients **are** very **happy** with the excursion.*

- Use the reflexive verb **alegrarse** (*to be happy/glad*) on its own or followed by **de** + [*infinitive*].

  > **¡Me alegro** mucho!   **¡Me alegro de** saberlo!
  > *I am so happy!*   *I am glad to hear it!*

- Use the exclamation **¡qué** + [*adjective/adverb*]! to express an opinion.

  > **¡Qué** interesante!   **¡Qué** bien!   **¡Qué** guapa!
  > *How interesting!*   *That's great!*   *How pretty!*

11A.5 Welcome people and wish them well

bienvenido/a(s); desear with object pronouns 6.2.4

- The adjective **bienvenido/a** (*welcome*) must agree with the gender of the person or people you are welcoming. Alternatively, use the construction [*indirect object pronoun*] + **dar** + **la bienvenida.**

  > **¡Bienvenidas,** chicas!   **Les damos la bienvenida.**
  > *Welcome, girls!*   *We welcome you.*

- Use the verb **desear** (*to wish*) with an indirect object pronoun to wish someone well.

  > **Te deseo** un buen viaje.
  > *I hope you have a good trip.*

¡Póngalo en práctica!

G3 **Conversación** Complete la conversación.

> ¿Qué te (1)............... el hotel?

> El hotel no me gusta. La información de esta guía es (2)............... porque no es real. Me parece (3)............... dar información falsa. ¡No (4)............... bien mentir a la gente!

> ¡Qué pena! Y las instalaciones, ¿qué tal?

> Me (5)............... bastante malas. No hay servicio de habitaciones y no podemos usar la piscina. Hay un restaurante, pero la comida (6)............... mala.

> ¡Qué lástima! No me (7)............... bien pasar las vacaciones en un hotel tan malo.

G4 **Oraciones** Complete las oraciones de forma lógica. Conjugue los verbos en el presente.

1. Los turistas .... (estar encantado) con el nuevo hotel en el centro.

2. • Mañana nos vamos de vacaciones al Caribe.
   ■ ¡....................... bien!

3. Norma .... (alegrarse) de viajar a Buenos Aires para su trabajo.

4. Estamos muy contentos con la comida del hotel. ¡....................... rica!

5. Me alegro .... conocer tantos lugares interesantes en este viaje.

6. Mis padres estaban encantados .... su habitación con vistas al mar.

7. María .... (estar contento) con el hotel que le recomendé.

8. Los niños .... (alegrarse) de estar de vacaciones esta semana.

G5 **Escribir** Escriba oraciones completas. Conjugue los verbos en el presente.

1. bienvenido / hotel / Sr. García

2. nosotros / dar / bienvenida / estudiantes nuevos

3. (a ti) / desear (yo) / unas felices vacaciones

4. bienvenido / Barcelona / Camila y Ramón

Practice more at **vhlcentral.com.**

Cambiar de aires

la ausencia	absence
el cambio de aires	change of scenery
el ecoturismo	ecotourism
el encanto	charm
el equipaje	baggage
el eslogan	slogan
la garantía	guarantee
los ingresos	income
la llegada	arrival
el Parador de Turismo de España	state-run hotel in Spanish historic building
el PIB (producto interior bruto)	GDP (Gross Domestic Product)
la recepción	pickup
favorecer (zc)	to favor
boricua	Puerto Rican
en regla	in order; valid

Experiencias de viaje

el aire acondicionado	air conditioning
el aparcamiento	parking lot
la compañía aérea	airline
el error	error
la facturación	check-in
el hotel de cuatro estrellas	four-star hotel
la instalación	facility
el libro de quejas	complaint form
el personal	staff
la protesta	complaint
la puntuación	score, evaluation
la puntualidad	punctuality
la queja	complaint
el retraso	delay
la satisfacción	satisfaction
el/la viajero/a	traveler
la vista	view
alegrarse (de)	to be glad (that)
estar en obras	to be under construction
estar encantado/a	to be delighted
protestar	to complain
contento/a	happy
pésimo/a	dreadful
rural	rural

José Carlos

¡Bienvenido(s)/a(s)!	Welcome!
¡Feliz estancia!	Have a nice stay!
la bienvenida	welcome
el entorno	environment, surroundings
la estancia	stay
la fortaleza	fortress
el fuerte	fort
el hongo	mushroom
el hostal	hostel
la orquídea	orchid
el/la peregrino/a	pilgrim
el rincón	spot, place
albergar	to accommodate
dar la bienvenida	to welcome
desear	to wish
incluir (y)	to include
janguear (fam., P.R.)	to hang out
restaurar	to restore
carmelita	Carmelite
fluorescente	fluorescent
gratificante	rewarding
lujoso/a	luxurious
personalizado/a	personalized
sanjuanero/a (P.R.)	from San Juan
ubicado/a	located
con antelación	in advance

Variación léxica

el aparcamiento (Esp.) ⟷ el estacionamiento (Amér. L.)
⟷ el parqueadero (Bol., Col.) ⟷ el parking (Esp.)

con antelación ⟷ con anticipación

facturar (el equipaje) ⟷ registrar (el equipaje) (Amér. L.)

el libro de quejas ⟷ la hoja de reclamaciones (Esp.)

la queja ⟷ el reclamo ⟷ la reclamación (Esp.)

el PIB (producto interior bruto) ⟷ el PBI (producto bruto interno)

ubicado/a ⟷ situado/a

11B INICIATIVAS

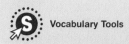
Pasión y profesión

Mi afición, mi trabajo: ¿es posible?

¿Es usted feliz en su trabajo?

No siempre es fácil cambiar de profesión, pero hay opciones creativas. Su afición puede ser una alternativa. Un talento escondido puede servir para empezar un nuevo proyecto laboral. ¿Le gusta la moda? ¿Ha pensado en trabajar como diseñador?

Nunca pensamos en nuestras aficiones como un medio de vida, pero son las cosas que más nos gusta hacer, y las que mejor hacemos.

Para María, Jorge y Javier, su afición es ahora su trabajo, y son ejemplos de que es posible reciclarse profesionalmente.

María, antes ama de casa, trabaja desde hace un año en su propia tienda de ropa. "Siempre me ha gustado la moda, es mi pasión, pero no pensaba en ella como un trabajo."

Jorge antes era profesor de historia. Su afición, el senderismo, es ahora su trabajo: vive en Puntarenas, Costa Rica, y es guía en el Parque Nacional Carara. "La decisión no fue fácil, pero ha valido la pena."

Presentar un contraargumento

- ● ¿Cambiar de profesión? Es muy difícil.
- ■ Tienes razón, **pero** no es imposible.
- ◆ Estoy de acuerdo, **pero** hay que intentarlo.

11B.1 **pero**

Vocabulario

1

la afición *hobby*

el/la diseñador(a) (de moda) *(fashion) designer*

el medio de vida *way of life*

reciclar(se) *to recycle (oneself)*

el senderismo *hiking*

valer la pena *to be worth it*

el talento

2

el submarinismo *scuba diving*

el/la biólogo/a marino/a *marine biologist*

---

1 **a. Reciclaje profesional** Fíjese en el título del reportaje y las fotos. ¿Qué entiende usted por "reciclaje profesional"?

b. Aficiones Lea el artículo. ¿Qué aficiones tienen estas personas que ahora son su trabajo?

2 **a. Relacionar** Relacione cada afición con una profesión.

submarinismo	moda	senderismo	arte

diseñador(a)	guía	biólogo/a marino/a	propietario/a de una tienda de artesanía

b. Lista Haga una lista de sus aficiones y posibles empleos alternativos.

3 **a. Reacciones** Lea estas reacciones al texto y relacione cada frase con la terminación apropiada.

1. "Creo que es bastante difícil ......
2. "Yo creo que los estudios son importantes, ...
3. "Creo que las empresas prefieren a personas jóvenes, ...

a. pero la experiencia es fundamental."
b. pero últimamente valoran mucho la experiencia de la gente mayor."
c. pero no imposible convertir una afición en una profesión."

b. Comentar ¿Es posible convertir una afición en una profesión? Hable con un(a) compañero/a de las ventajas y desventajas.

Modelo: *Yo creo que no es fácil, pero es posible. Si tú...*

CURRÍCULUM VÍTAE

DATOS PERSONALES

Nombre: Javier Ezequiel Farías
Dirección: 25 de Mayo 677
(C1002ABM) Buenos Aires

Correo electrónico: javierito@mimail.com
Lugar de nacimiento: Montevideo

ESTUDIOS

marzo 2001 – diciembre 2006	Estudios de Administración de Empresas en la UBA
marzo 2007 – diciembre 2009	Máster en Relaciones Internacionales
marzo 2010 – diciembre 2012	Máster en Márketing
abril 2015 – noviembre 2016	Curso de fotografía profesional

EXPERIENCIA PROFESIONAL

agosto 2012 – octubre 2016	Asesor financiero en OCA-Internacional, Montevideo
septiembre 2016	Reportaje fotográfico en la revista *Trabajo argentino*

IDIOMAS

Dominio del inglés
Conocimientos de italiano y francés

Javier ya no trabaja como asesor financiero. Empezó a tomar fotos hace unos años y sigue con ello. Es fotógrafo profesional. "Cambié de vida. Ya no gano tanta plata, pero soy más feliz."

---

4 **a. Currículum** Lea el currículum de Javier. ¿Cuál es su experiencia laboral? ¿Y su formación académica?

Modelo: *De 2001 a 2006 estudió en la universidad...*

b. Localizar ¿En qué parte del currículum aparece esta información?

| de dónde es | qué lenguas habla | dónde ha trabajado |

5 **a. La entrevista** Javier se presenta a una entrevista de trabajo. Escuche la entrevista y diga qué trabajo solicita.

b. Señalar Vuelva a escuchar el audio y señale los datos correctos.

1. Javier sigue en Montevideo. ☐   3. Ya no trabaja como asesor financiero. ☐
2. Ha cambiado de ciudad. ☐   4. Su primer trabajo fue de fotógrafo. ☐

c. Cambios ¿Y usted, ha cambiado algo en su vida en los últimos cinco años?

Modelo: *Ya no tomo clases de guitarra, pero sigo jugando al fútbol.*

MI EXPERIENCIA

6 **Contar** Cuente a su compañero/a los cambios que ha habido en sus costumbres y aficiones. Escuche a su compañero/a y busque su talento escondido.

| **GUIÓN DE TRABAJO** | ¿Qué has cambiado de tu vida? | → | He cambiado de trabajo dos veces...
Ya no vivo en...
Sigo en mi empresa. |
| | Creo que tu talento escondido es... | → pero... → | necesitas formación.
tienes que ser constante. |

Hablar de cambios

- ¿Has **cambiado de** ciudad/casa?
- No, **sigo** allí.
- ¿**Ya no** trabajas?
- Sí, pero **he cambiado de** trabajo.

11B.2 **cambiar de, seguir, ya no**

Vocabulario

4

el/la asesor(a) *advisor*
financiero/a *financial*
seguir (e:i) *to go on, to keep (on)*
el/la fotógrafo/a *photographer*
ganar *to earn*
la plata (*fam.*, *Amér. L.*) *money*
el currículum (vítae) *résumé*
el lugar de nacimiento *birthplace*
la experiencia profesional
　professional experience
las Relaciones Internacionales
　International Relations
fotográfico/a

5

volver (o:ue) a... *to do . . . again*
aficionado/a *amateur*
trabajar como *to work as*

SAM: Actividades pp. 233–235

Cartas al director

DIARIO DE SEVILLA

CARTAS AL DIRECTOR

Mi mujer y yo estamos buscando piso desde hace dos años, pero es difícil porque los precios son altísimos. Ahora vivimos en un piso de alquiler, pero preferimos comprar, y ¿ha visto los anuncios de minipisos que publica su periódico? Son pisos pequeñísimos a precios muy altos. Si un piso de 30 metros cuadrados es tan caro, la vivienda de nuestros sueños es imposible. ¿Cuándo van a bajar los precios?

Eduardo Pérez y Ana Díaz, Alcalá de Guadaíra

Las Rosas

Pisos modernísimos en el centro, con todas las comodidades. ¡Ven a visitarnos!

VENTA

35 m²
salón-cocina
1 baño
1 dormitorio

Expresar valoraciones en grado máximo

- Las viviendas son pequeñísimas.
- Sí, y son muy muy caras.
- Sí, encontrar un piso económico es superdifícil.

11B.3 -ísimo/a, super-..., muy muy...

Vocabulario

7

altísimo/a *excessive; very high*
de alquiler *rental*
el minipiso *tiny apartment*
pequeñísimo/a *tiny*
la vivienda *home; housing*

8

superdifícil *extremely difficult*

9

u *or (before a word beginning with o or ho)*
incomodísimo/a *extremely uncomfortable*

Estrategia ············

Mostrar interés en la conversación

- Los pisos son carísimos.
- Sí, la verdad que sí. Mi piso tiene 25 m² y ha costado muchísimo.
- ¿Sí? ¿En serio?

---

7 **Carta** Lea la carta al director de un periódico español. ¿Por qué se escribe este tipo de cartas? ¿En su país es igual? ¿Por qué escriben Ana y Eduardo?

8 **a. Superlativos** Escriba la forma superlativa de los adjetivos, siguiendo el modelo.

1. moderno/a: *modernísimo/a*
2. caro/a: ....
3. bueno/a: ....
4. cómodo/a: ....
5. fácil: ....
6. alto/a: ....

b. Anotar Observe estas formas más coloquiales y anote un adjetivo en grado superlativo (-*ísimo/a*) equivalente.

El piso es muy muy pequeño. ....

Es superdifícil encontrar casa. ....

9 **Describir** Describa las imágenes. Utilice los adjetivos del recuadro u otros.

grandísimo/a • pequeñísimo/a • carísimo/a • (in)comodísimo/a

10 **a. La vivienda** Escuche cómo describen Ana y Eduardo la situación de la vivienda y explíquelo.

- La situación es...
- Los precios son...
- El alquiler es...

b. Contestar ¿Cuál es su alternativa?

c. Señalar Vuelva a escuchar el diálogo y señale las expresiones para mostrar interés en la conversación.

Sí, ya... ☐   ¿No? ☐   ¿De verdad? ☐   ¿Sí? ¿En serio? ☐   ¿Y qué? ☐

11 **Responder** Piense en Ana y Eduardo. ¿Conoce a alguien con el mismo problema? ¿Hay también dificultades para encontrar vivienda en su región?

INMOBILIARIA SU CASA

¿Dónde le encantaría vivir?
¿Cómo es la casa de sus sueños?

- con varios baños ☐
- con terraza ☐
- bien comunicada ☐
- cerca del trabajo ☐
- cerca de supermercados ☐
- al lado de una zona verde ☐
- en una zona tranquila ☐
- en el centro ☐

12 **Mi vivienda ideal** Mire las fotos del anuncio. ¿Como es su vivienda ideal?

13 **a. Cuestionario** Complete el cuestionario de la inmobiliaria. Elija los tres aspectos más importantes para usted. Añada otros si lo necesita.

b. Preferencias Pregunte a su compañero/a por sus preferencias.

Modelo: *A mí me gustaría vivir cerca del centro, ¿y a ti?*

c. Lista Pongan en común sus preferencias y hagan una lista de los aspectos más populares de los estudiantes en la clase.

- A muchos les encantaría…
- A algunos les gustaría…

14 **Vivienda propia** Lea la nota sobre la vivienda propia en España. ¿Cómo es en su país? ¿Es habitual comprar o alquilar? ¿Cuándo forman los jóvenes su hogar propio?

MI EXPERIENCIA

15 **¿Dónde?** Haga su hipótesis y piense dónde le gustaría vivir a su compañero/a.

GUIÓN DE TRABAJO

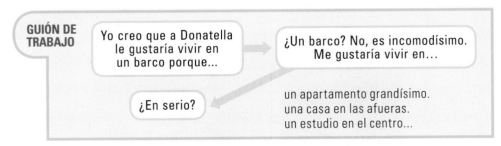

Yo creo que a Donatella le gustaría vivir en un barco porque...

¿Un barco? No, es incomodísimo. Me gustaría vivir en...

¿En serio?

un apartamento grandísimo.
una casa en las afueras.
un estudio en el centro...

Formular deseos

- ¿Dónde te gustaría vivir?
- ■ **Me gustaría** vivir en una casa con jardín. ¿Y a ustedes?
- **Nos encantaría** vivir en el campo, pero a los niños no.

11B.4 **me, te, le... gustaría/ encantaría** + [*infinitive*]

Vocabulario

14
la falta *lack*
el empleo *employment*
15
las afueras *outskirts*

Vivienda propia

Según datos del Consejo de la Juventud de España, aún viven con sus padres el 80% de los jóvenes españoles menores de 30 años. Las principales causas son la falta de empleo estable y el alto costo de las viviendas.

SAM: Actividades pp. 236–238

Practice more at **vhlcentral.com**.

Héctor y Gabriela, propietarios de Patagonia Natural

Héctor Varela y Gabriela Bettini, sonrientes en la posada que es también su hogar

Estamos con Héctor y Gabriela, un matrimonio porteño que hace cinco años decidió abrir una posada acá, en El Calafate. ¿Por qué decidieron dejar Buenos Aires?

Bueno, yo trabajaba en una empresa, pero me quedé desocupado hace siete años y en Buenos Aires no encontraba trabajo. Es dificilísimo si tenés más de cuarenta años, así que decidimos abrir nuestro propio negocio, que es también nuestra casa.

Ya no viven en una gran ciudad. ¿Cómo es vivir aquí en la Patagonia?

Es un lugar inhóspito a veces, aunque la ciudad puede serlo mucho más... No, en serio, es lindísimo acá.

En primer lugar, tenemos la vida que queremos. Además, mi esposa y yo seguimos haciendo las cosas que nos gustan... leer, sacar fotos, pasear, practicar deportes... y sobre todo disfrutar de la naturaleza. La verdad, encontramos nuestro sitio en el mundo.

Gabriela, ¿decoró la casa personalmente? *Sí, sí...*

La vi y es muy linda. El *living* es impresionante. ¿Es decoradora profesional?

No, en absoluto. Siempre me gustó la decoración, pero allá en Buenos Aires no tenía tiempo... ni espacio. Nuestro departamento era muy chico. Acá fue facilísimo tener ideas. Solo es cuestión de paciencia.

¿Pueden contarles a nuestros lectores qué ofrece su posada?

Tenemos un paisaje espectacular y además organizamos excursiones. Por ejemplo, mañana vamos a ir al Parque Nacional Los Glaciares con cinco turistas. Y pasado mañana vamos a recorrer el bosque petrificado La Leona. ¡Son dos paseos fantásticos!

Añadir información

Tenemos la vida que queremos.
Además, acá es lindísimo, **sobre todo** por el paisaje.

11B.5 **además, sobre todo**

Vocabulario

16

el matrimonio *married couple*

la posada *inn*

desocupado/a *unemployed*

inhóspito/a *inhospitable*

el sitio *place*

lindo/a *lovely*

chico/a (*Amér. L.*) *small*

pasado mañana *the day after tomorrow*

petrificado/a *petrified*

el/la decorador(a), espectacular, el glaciar

---

16 **a. Patagonia Natural** Fíjese en el título del artículo. ¿Qué puede ser Patagonia Natural?

b. Héctor y Gabriela Lea la entrevista y piense por qué son Héctor y Gabriela los protagonistas de la lección. ¿Cuál es su historia personal?

c. Resumen Escriba un resumen de los motivos que llevaron a Héctor y a Gabriela a vivir en la Patagonia. Use expresiones como **además** y **sobre todo**.

17 **a. Así se dice en Argentina** ¿Sabe el significado de estas palabras del habla argentina? Escriba un equivalente.

1. acá: ....
2. esposa: ....
3. allá: ....
4. chico: ....
5. lindo: ....
6. tenés: ....

b. Contestar ¿Qué otras formas del habla argentina reconoce?

18 **Publicidad** Escuche la publicidad y marque en el mapa los lugares que nombra.

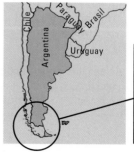

CAMBIE DE AIRES

¿Le gustaría hacer un viaje diferente? Lo invitamos a explorar un lugar mágico entre lagos, ríos, montañas, valles y bosques, lejos de la civilización: el Parque Nacional Los Glaciares, declarado Patrimonio Mundial por la UNESCO en 1981.

Está ubicado al sudoeste de la provincia de Santa Cruz, justo en la frontera con Chile, y tiene una superficie de 7178 km². Allí se pueden ver los enormes glaciares que forman el manto de hielo más grande después del continente antártico. Uno de ellos es el Perito Moreno, famoso por estar continuamente en movimiento.

Pero ese no es el único atractivo del parque; también va a poder apreciar las altísimas cumbres del monte Fitz Roy (3405 m) y del cerro Torre (3102 m), la extraordinaria riqueza de la flora y de la fauna, y la inmensidad del lago Argentino y el lago Viedma. No se pierda esta experiencia única. ¡Lo esperamos!

19 **Leer** Lea el artículo sobre el Parque Nacional Los Glaciares, ubicado en la Patagonia argentina. Haga una lista de los adjetivos usados y subraye los de grado superlativo.

20 **Preguntas** Haga a su compañero/a cinco preguntas sobre el texto y responda también a las de su compañero/a.

> Modelo: *¿Has estado en la Patagonia? ¿Y en Argentina? ¿Recuerdas un alojamiento especial?*

21 **Escribir** ¿Le gustaría a usted desarrollar un proyecto similar al de Héctor y Gabriela? Escríbales un correo electrónico y pregunte lo que le gustaría saber.

> Estimados Héctor y Gabriela:
> He sabido de la existencia de su posada y les escribo porque me gustaría desarrollar un proyecto...
>
> Saludos cordiales,

22 **a. Excursiones** Héctor organiza excursiones por la región. Escuche a Héctor en una de estas excursiones. ¿Qué lugar describe? ¿Le gustaría visitar ese lugar?

b. Lugares especiales ¿Conoce algún otro lugar en América Latina muy especial para usted? ¿Qué lugares de América Latina le gustaría conocer? Busque información en Internet y coméntela con sus compañeros.

¡OJO!

In the dialect spoken in Argentina and Uruguay (known as Rioplatense Spanish), **vos** replaces **tú** as the second-person singular pronoun (**voseo**). The pronoun **vos** has its own set of verb conjugations. Therefore, in this dialect, people say **vos tenés** instead of **tú tienes**. Although **vos** is also used in other countries, such as Paraguay, Bolivia, Chile, Colombia, Guatemala, Ecuador, and Nicaragua, in those places its use is normally limited to informal contexts.

Vocabulario

19

explorar *to explore*

el Patrimonio Mundial *World Heritage*

el manto de hielo *ice sheet*

la riqueza *richness*

la inmensidad *immensity*

No se pierda... *Don't miss . . .*

el valle, la civilización, el continente, extraordinario/a

OPINIÓN

¿Le gustaría vivir en otro lugar muy diferente de donde vive ahora? ¿Dónde? ¿Por qué?

SAM: Actividades pp. 239–244

Practice more at **vhlcentral.com**.

23 **Indicar** Observen estas dos series de imágenes e indiquen cómo ha cambiado la vida de Héctor y Gabriela. Utilicen las estructuras que han aprendido en la unidad.

| seguir • ya no… • cambiar de |

Antes

Ahora

TAREA FINAL

La vivienda de sus sueños

Realicen una encuesta en la clase para saber los deseos del grupo en cuanto a vivienda.

En parejas, piensen en una promoción inmobiliaria según las respuestas de la mayoría de la clase.

- características de la vivienda
- localización
- precio

Realicen el plano de la vivienda y redacten un anuncio con las características principales.

Presenten al grupo su proyecto. ¿Qué vivienda responde mejor a los deseos de la clase?

YO PUEDO...

- **Puedo presentar un contraargumento.**

  Conecte estas dos ideas sobre encontrar trabajo:
  Es difícil. No es imposible.

- **Puedo hablar de cambios en la vida.**

  Piense en sus actividades recientes, actividades que han cambiado, que ya no hace o que siguen igual. Escriba cinco oraciones sobre ellas.

- **Puedo expresar valoraciones en grado máximo.**

  Diga de otra manera que México, D.F. es muy grande y muy lindo.

- **Puedo formular deseos.**

  Nombre tres cosas que le gustaría hacer ahora mismo.

- **Puedo añadir información.**

  Complete con su opinión la situación de la vivienda en su ciudad.
  La situación de la vivienda es…
  Además…
  Sobre todo…

GRAMÁTICA FUNCIONAL Tutorials

11B.1 Present a counterargument

pero 12.8

- Use the conjunction **pero** (*but*) to introduce information that contrasts with previous information.

> Me dedico a la fotografía, **pero** no tengo formación.
> *I work in photography, **but** I do not have a degree.*

> Marta estudia Economía, **pero** también le interesa la pintura.
> *Marta studies Economics, **but** she's also interested in painting.*

11B.2 Talk about changes

cambiar de, seguir 5.15
ya no 11.2

- Use **cambiar de** + [*noun*] to expresses change.

> Marcelo **cambió de trabajo** el mes pasado.
> *Marcelo **changed jobs** last month.*

- Use **seguir** + [*adverbial phrase*] to express the idea that someone continues to do something.

> **Sigo** con mi trabajo.
> *I am **still** at my job.*

- Use **seguir** + [*present participle*] to express a continued action.

> Carina **sigue trabajando** en el banco.
> *Carina **is still working** at the bank.*

- **Ya no** (*no longer; [not] anymore*) signals that an action has ended.

> Ramiro **ya no** trabaja en el restaurante.
> *Ramiro does **not** work at the restaurant **anymore**.*

11B.3 Express the highest degree

The absolute superlative 4.5

- The absolute superlative (**el superlativo absoluto**) describes a quality without making reference to other people or things. It is equivalent to adding *extremely*, *super*, or *very* to an adjective in English. You learned the superlative to distinguish one among many in **9A.4**.

> Fue un viaje **carísimo**, pero valió la pena.
> *It was a **really expensive** trip, but it was worth it.*

- To form the absolute superlative, drop the final vowel of the adjective (if there is one) and add -**ísimo/a(s)**.

¡Póngalo en práctica!

G1 **Emparejar** Empareje el comienzo de cada oración con el final apropiado.

1. Quiero vivir en el centro,	a. pero no tengo experiencia de administración.
2. No tienes formación en la fotografía,	b. pero los apartamentos allí son muy caros.
3. Me gustaría abrir una posada,	c. pero no ganas suficiente para pagar un alquiler.
4. Te gustaría salir de la casa de tus padres,	d. pero has hecho varias exposiciones.

G2 **Conversación** Complete la conversación con la expresión **ya no** o con la forma correcta de **cambiar** o **seguir**.

- ¡Cuánto tiempo sin verte, Benjamín! ¿Qué tal estás? ¿(1)....................... trabajando en la inmobiliaria?

- No, (2)....................... trabajo allí. (3)....................... de trabajo. Abrí mi propio negocio. ¿Y tú? ¿(4)....................... en el banco?

- Sí, (5)....................... allí, pero (6)....................... estoy tanto tiempo en la oficina; ahora viajo mucho.

- ¡Qué bien! Me alegro mucho. A veces es necesario (7)....................... de vida o de trabajo. Ahora que tengo mi propio negocio, (8)....................... viajo tanto como antes, pero ahora tengo menos estrés.

G3 **Adjetivos** Escriba el adjetivo correspondiente a cada superlativo absoluto.

1.	suavísimos
2.	llenísima
3.	grandísimo
4.	comodísimo
5.	riquísima
6.	modernísimas

pequeño/a	→	pequeñísimo/a
grande	→	grandísimo/a
difícil	→	dificilísimo/a

La nueva casa en la playa es **grandísima**.
*The new beach house is **very big**.*

- The -ísimo/a(s) ending always carries an accent mark, so an adjective that already has a written accent will undergo a change in pronunciation.

- Note that adjectives like **grande** and **difícil** have only one singular form, but they have distinct masculine and feminine forms in the absolute superlative.

- Words whose stem ends in -c, -g, or -z undergo a spelling change to preserve the original pronunciation of the adjective.

rico	→	riquísimo
largo	→	larguísimo
feliz	→	felicísimo

- In colloquial language, other superlative constructions are used, such as **muy muy** (*very, very; really*) and **super-** (*super, extremely*).

Es **super**difícil encontrar un apartamento en este barrio.
*It is **extremely** difficult to find an apartment in this neighborhood.*

11B.4 Express wishes

me, te, le... gustaría/encantaría + [*infinitive*] 5.17.3

- Use the conditional construction [*indirect object pronoun*] + **gustaría/encantaría** + [*infinitive*] to express wishes. You have already seen **me gustaría** + [*infinitive*] used as an expression of courtesy in 6B.4.

A muchos **les encantaría** vivir en un edificio moderno.
Y a ti, ¿qué **te gustaría**?
*Many people **would love** to live in a modern building.
And you, what **would you like**?*

11B.5 Add information

además, sobre todo 11.3

- Use the adverbs **además** (*furthermore; besides; as well*) to add information, and **sobre todo** (*above all; especially*) to both add and highlight information.

El apartamento es grandísimo y **además** está muy cerca del centro.
*The apartment is extremely big and **furthermore** it is very close to downtown.*

Los parques de Madrid son muy bonitos, **sobre todo** en primavera.
*The parks in Madrid are very pretty, **especially** in spring.*

¡Póngalo en práctica!

G4 **El superlativo absoluto** Complete las oraciones con el superlativo absoluto.

1. Los apartamentos en ese edificio nuevo son .... (caro).

2. La comida en el restaurante de la esquina siempre está .... (rico).

3. El examen que tenemos mañana va a ser .... (fácil).

4. Héctor y Gabriela están .... (contento) con su nueva posada en la Patagonia.

5. Mi tía vende ropa .... (elegante) en un negocio en el centro.

6. La profesora de historia del arte es .... (inteligente).

7. Estoy leyendo un libro .... (interesante) sobre personas que cambian de vida y de profesión.

8. El paisaje de la Patagonia es .... (bello).

G5 **Completar** Complete las oraciones.

- ¿Dónde (1)......................... (gustar) vivir?
- Me (2)......................... (encantar) vivir en una casa con jardín.

A mí (3)......................... (encantar) ir de vacaciones a España, pero a mi marido (4)......................... (gustar) ir a México.

G6 **Párrafo** Complete el párrafo con **además** y **sobre todo**.

Ahora vivimos en el campo. Nos gusta estar aquí. (1)................................ la vida aquí es más fácil. Pero (2)................................ nos gusta lo que hacemos. Abrimos una posada y nos gusta recibir visitas de todo el mundo. Es interesante el trabajo y (3)................................ podemos trabajar y vivir en la misma casa. ¡No extrañamos para nada la vida de la ciudad!

Pasión y profesión

la afición	hobby
el/la asesor(a)	advisor
el/la biólogo/a marino/a	marine biologist
el currículum (vítae)	résumé
el/la diseñador(a) (de moda)	(fashion) designer
la experiencia profesional	professional experience
el/la fotógrafo/a	photographer
el lugar de nacimiento	birthplace
el medio de vida	way of life
la plata (fam., Amér. L.)	money
las Relaciones Internacionales	International Relations
el senderismo	hiking
el submarinismo	scuba diving
el talento	talent
ganar	to earn
reciclar(se)	to recycle (oneself)
seguir (e:i)	to go on, to keep (on)
trabajar como	to work as
valer la pena	to be worth it
volver (o:ue) a...	to do . . . again
aficionado/a	amateur
financiero/a	financial
fotográfico/a	photographic

Cartas al director

las afueras	outskirts
el empleo	employment
la falta	lack
el minipiso	tiny apartment
la vivienda	home; housing
altísimo/a	excessive; very high
de alquiler	rental
incomodísimo/a	extremely uncomfortable
pequeñísimo/a	tiny
superdifícil	extremely difficult
u	or (before a word beginning with o or ho)

Héctor y Gabriela

No se pierda...	Don't miss . . .
la civilización	civilization
el continente	continent
el/la decorador(a)	decorator
el glaciar	glacier
la inmensidad	immensity
el manto de hielo	ice sheet
el matrimonio	married couple
el Patrimonio Mundial	World Heritage
la posada	inn
la riqueza	richness
el sitio	place
el valle	valley
explorar	to explore
chico/a (Amér. L.)	small
desocupado/a	unemployed
espectacular	spectacular
extraordinario/a	extraordinary
inhóspito/a	inhospitable
lindo/a	lovely
petrificado/a	petrified
pasado mañana	the day after tomorrow

Variación léxica

el buceo ⟷ el submarinismo

pequeñísimo/a ⟷ minúsculo/a ⟷ diminuto/a

la plata (fam., Amér. L.) ⟷ el dinero ⟷ la marmaja (fam., Col. y Méx.) ⟷ el pisto (fam., Amér. C.) ⟷ la pasta (fam., Esp.) ⟷ la lana (fam., Méx.)

quedar desocupado/a (Amér. L.) ⟷ quedarse en paro (Esp.) ⟷ quedar desempleado/a

valer la pena ⟷ merecer (zc) la pena (Esp.)

Vocabulario útil

la altura *height*
el apunamiento *altitude sickness*
el Camino Inca *Inca Trail*
el/la excursionista *hiker*
a pie *on foot*
el recorrido *journey*
la subida *climb*

Estrategia ···········

Make a chart

When reading a text, start by identifying the general organization of the reading. Use a chart to write down each event or topic mentioned. You will find different chronological sequences in this reading, all of them providing information about the Inca Trail. Make three columns: one for Larry's trip, one for the history of the Inca Empire, and one for events in the present, so you don't miss any details.

El Camino Inca

Larry se levanta muy temprano, desarma° el campamento, desayuna y comienza su día. Ayer, él y su grupo caminaron siete millas (once kilómetros) hasta una altura de 9700 pies (2956 metros); hoy, los excursionistas deben recorrer otras siete millas hasta casi 14 000 pies (4267 metros), todo el tiempo con mochilas de cincuenta libras (veintidós kilos y medio) a la espalda. Para otros puede resultar dificilísimo completar este recorrido, pero Larry está haciendo el viaje de su vida: el Camino Inca.

Entre 1438 y 1533, durante el apogeo° del poderoso imperio incaico, los incas construyeron una compleja red de caminos por los Andes que llevaban hasta Cuzco, la capital del imperio. Actualmente, cientos de miles de turistas viajan a Perú todos los años para recorrer los caminos que aún existen y disfrutar de paisajes espectaculares.

(1) **a. Preguntas** Discuta con un(a) compañero/a: ¿Qué clase de viajes prefiere hacer en sus vacaciones? ¿Alguna vez ha ido a acampar? ¿Le interesan las civilizaciones antiguas? ¿Por qué? ¿Cuáles son los lugares más extraños del mundo sobre los que ha oído hablar o leído?

b. Recomendaciones Hagan juntos una lista de tres recomendaciones para un amigo que va de excursión a las montañas (qué llevar, etc.).

Modelo: *Te recomiendo...*

(2) **Completar** Complete las oraciones con el vocabulario de la lista.

1. A Machu Picchu puedes subir en pocas horas en tren o en autobús, pero llegar hasta lo alto de la montaña .... es más emocionante.
2. Los .... recorren el .... en cuatro días, acompañados de guías especializados.
3. No se puede hacer el .... a Machu Picchu en cualquier momento: es necesario .... lugar con anticipación.
4. La .... comienza en un puente colgante y termina en la entrada de Machu Picchu.
5. Es importante tener un buen estado físico para resistir las dificultades del terreno; además, la gran .... puede producir ...., con dolor de cabeza y mareos.

El famoso Camino Inca va desde Cuzco hasta la antigua ciudad de montaña Machu Picchu. Muchos visitantes hacen un itinerario guiado de cuatro días, que comienza en un puente colgante° sobre el río Urubamba y termina en Intipunku, la entrada a Machu Picchu. Los guías organizan los campamentos y las comidas para los viajeros, y también una estancia de una noche en un hostal durante el recorrido.

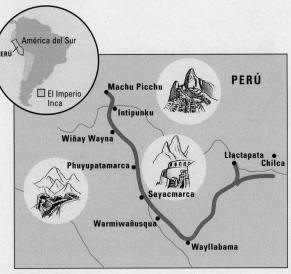

Ruta de cuatro días

Para conservar el Camino Inca, el Instituto Nacional de Cultura de Perú limita a quinientos por día el número de visitantes a pie. Quienes hacen el viaje deben reservar su lugar con anticipación y necesitan un buen estado físico para soportar las dificultades del terreno y la altitud, que genera apunamiento. Las abundantes lluvias en enero de 2010 provocaron graves inundaciones°: ocho personas murieron y tres mil quinientos turistas fueron evacuados en helicópteros hacia Cuzco. Puentes, caminos y la vía férrea° quedaron dañados° y se suspendieron los viajes durante un tiempo. Afortunadamente el 1.° de abril de 2010 se reabrió Machu Picchu a los turistas de todo el mundo que esperan visitarla.

desarma *breaks down* **apogeo** *height* **puente colgante** *suspension bridge*
inundaciones *floods* **vía férrea** *railroad track* **dañados** *damaged*

▶ **Destinos populares**

- Las playas del Parque Nacional Manuel Antonio (Costa Rica) ofrecen la oportunidad de nadar y luego caminar por el bosque tropical°.

- Teotihuacán (México). Desde antes de la época de los aztecas, aquí se celebra el equinoccio° de primavera en la Pirámide del Sol.

- Puerto Chicama (Perú), con sus olas° de cuatro kilómetros de largo°, es un destino para surfistas expertos.

- Tikal (Guatemala). Aquí puedes ver las maravillas de la selva° y ruinas de la civilización maya.

- Las playas de Rincón (Puerto Rico) son ideales para descansar y observar a las ballenas°.

bosque tropical *rain forest* **equinoccio** *equinox* **olas** *waves* **de largo** *in length* **selva** *jungle* **ballenas** *whales*

---

(3) **Presentación de bienvenida** Con un(a) compañero/a, elijan uno de los lugares que se mencionan en la unidad y armen una presentación de bienvenida a un grupo de turistas. Organicen un discurso, usando **En primer lugar...**, **después...**, **por último...** Pueden seguir este esquema:

1. Presentación personal y bienvenida a los visitantes: agradezcan su presencia allí.
2. Mencionen la ocasión: vacaciones, fiesta, luna de miel, reinauguración (Machu Picchu), etc., y señalen por qué es el lugar indicado para eso.
3. Hablen del lugar y de sus beneficios: playas, ruinas arqueológicas, posibilidad de hacer deportes, etc. Pueden añadir que algo ha cambiado recientemente (remodelación del hotel, construcción de un centro comercial, etc.), usando: **Además, actualmente... Sobre todo ahora, con la nueva...**
4. Finalicen con buenos deseos para la visita.

PROYECTO

El viaje de mis sueños Para participar en un concurso de viajes, debe escribir sobre su viaje soñado. Escriba un texto breve contando por qué desearía ir a ese lugar, cómo supo que existía (si alguien le contó o lo vio en un programa de televisión, un libro, etc.), cómo le han dicho que es y qué espera encontrar allí. Luego, presente su descripción a la clase.

Estrategia ············

Writing a speech

A speech must be engaging, entertaining, clear, and concise. To write a speech, begin by establishing who you are, what your purpose is, and whom the speech is for (i.e., that you are a hotel manager welcoming guests). You might include jokes, anecdotes, interesting facts, examples, or quotations to grab the audience's attention and make your point. At the end, remember to include a conclusion to remind listeners of your main purpose. When speaking in a formal setting in Spanish, remember to address your listeners using **ustedes.**

 Video

Machu Picchu: encanto y misterio

Ya ha leído sobre gente que quiere pasear, hacer deportes, ver bellos paisajes y tomar fotos; algunos lo hacen viajando, otros deciden convertir eso en su forma de vida. Este episodio de **Flash Cultura** nos lleva a uno de los lugares más hermosos del mundo que ofrece todo esto y más: las ruinas incas de Machu Picchu en Perú.

1 **Preguntas** ¿Le gustaría hacer un viaje de aventura? ¿Qué cosas pueden ser difíciles o peligrosas en un viaje a un lugar lejano? ¿Adónde no iría nunca? ¿Por qué?

2 **Mirar** Mire este episodio de **Flash Cultura.** Aunque opinan distintas personas, hay un solo tema principal y todo lo que dicen añade información sobre ese tema. Preste atención y apunte la nueva información que aprende. ¿Qué es lo más importante de Machu Picchu?

Aún hoy es asombroso ver cómo lograron construir en la cima de la montaña...

Esta cultura quechua hizo muchas grandes obras...

3 **¿Verdadero o falso?** Indique qué oraciones son **verdaderas** y cuáles son **falsas.** Corrija las falsas.

1. Machu Picchu fue descubierta hace solo cien años.
2. En quechua, significa "símbolo inca".
3. No sabemos por qué la ciudad fue abandonada.
4. Machu Picchu fue aislada por la conquista española.
5. En la ciudadela no hay dos bloques de piedra iguales.
6. Todas las construcciones son religiosas.

4 **Conversación** En parejas, escriban una conversación: una persona desea hacer un viaje para conocer una antigua civilización, pero el/la agente de viajes desea venderle un viaje a otra parte.

Modelo:
• *Me encantaría conocer Atenas. Me han dicho que es preciosa.*
• *Los hoteles están muy caros, es ruidosa y no es buena época porque hace mucho calor. Le recomiendo pensar en algo diferente...*

 Practice more at **vhlcentral.com.**

Estrategia

Summarizing

As you are watching a video, try to organize and repeat back in your own words what has been said. State only the important points. Try to summarize as you go (don't wait until the end, or you may lose track!).

Vocabulario útil

el borde *brink*
la bruma *mist*
la ciudadela *citadel*
contratar *to hire*
la cordillera *mountain range*
el depósito *warehouse*
evitar *to prevent*
la intrepidez *determination*
labrado/a *carved*
la orilla *bank*
la sangre *blood*
tallado/a *carved*

Estrategia

The word *cool* is common in English; but if you look it up in a bilingual dictionary, chances are you'll find **fresco.** In Spanish, you can use the words **genial, estupendo, fenomenal, bueno,** or **buenísimo,** but expressions used in certain countries also convey a similar meaning. In Mexico, you can say **¡Qué chido! ¡Qué padre!** (or **¡Padrísimo!**); in Argentina, you might say **¡Qué copado!** or **¡Qué bárbaro!**; in Spain, **¡Qué guay!**; in Perú, Colombia, Venezuela, Chile, and Ecuador **¡Qué bacán!**; and in many Caribbean countries you would hear **¡Qué chévere!** Just remember that slang is time-sensitive and expressions are updated all the time.

Unidad 12

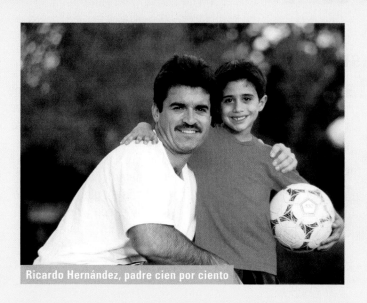
Ricardo Hernández, padre cien por ciento

Marifé, vendedora de ilusiones

Las relaciones personales

SEGUNDA OPORTUNIDAD

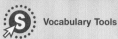

Vocabulary Tools

Vida en común

Querida Matilde:

He conocido a una chica en la universidad. Me encanta porque es divertida, inteligente, culta, responsable, realista y muy atractiva. Es pelirroja y tiene los ojos verdes... El problema es que ella tiene novio, pero no está contenta con su relación. ¿Qué puedo hacer? Gracias por tu ayuda.

Antonio

El consultorio de Matilde

Hola, Matilde:

Quiero hacerte una consulta. En la residencia de estudiantes donde vivo hay un chico que me gusta mucho. Se llama Rafa, es muy simpático, cariñoso, alegre, siempre está de buen humor y es muy optimista. Físicamente es mi tipo: es moreno, alto, guapo... Pero yo soy muy tímida y no sé qué hacer para invitarlo a salir. Espero tu consejo.

Eva

Describir el carácter y el aspecto físico

● ¿Cómo es tu novio?

■ Bueno, pues **es inteligente, cariñoso** y un poco **pesimista**. Físicamente **es bajo, moreno, tiene los ojos negros y usa gafas.**

12A.1 **ser, tener, usar**

Vocabulario

(1)

culto/a *educated*

pelirrojo/a *red-haired*

hacer una consulta *to ask somebody's advice*

la residencia de estudiantes *dorm*

cariñoso/a *affectionate*

de buen/mal humor *in a good/bad mood*

moreno/a *dark-haired*

tímido/a *shy*

inteligente, realista, atractivo/a, optimista, el tipo

(2)

el carácter *character, personality*

el aspecto físico *physical appearance*

pesimista

---

1 **El consultorio de Matilde** Fíjese en el título de esta sección de la revista y en la imagen. ¿Cuál es el tema? Lea los textos. ¿Por qué escriben a Matilde?

2 **a. Consultas** En las consultas hay descripciones del carácter y del aspecto físico. Anote los adjetivos.

Carácter: *divertido/a*	← SER →	Aspecto físico: *atractivo/a*

b. Adjetivos Clasifique los adjetivos anteriores por sus terminaciones.

-o/a	*divertido/a*	-e		-ista	

3 **Describir** ¿Cómo es físicamente su pareja real o la persona de sus sueños? ¿Y de carácter?

¿Es...

pelirrojo/a? rubio/a?

¿Es...

alto/a? bajo/a?

¿Tiene los ojos...

azules? castaños?

¿Tiene el pelo...

blanco y liso? moreno y rizado?

¿Usa... ¿Tiene...

gafas? barba y bigote?

¿Tiene el pelo...

largo? corto?

La historia de Eva continúa: comienza a salir con Rafa, se gradúa, y junto con dos amigas alquila su primer apartamento.

FIESTA DE INAUGURACIÓN
de nuestro apartamento
viernes 5 de septiembre a las 9 h

Queridos amigos:

Después de nuestra graduación, hemos dejado la casa de nuestros padres y hemos alquilado un apartamento para las tres en el centro. Estamos muy ilusionadas (...y un poco asustadas también).

Otra buena noticia: nuestro apartamento tiene balcón con vista a la calle. Queremos inaugurarlo con ustedes. ¡Los esperamos!

Eva, Laura y Daniela

Estamos muy preocupados: ahora que tienen un apartamento en el centro, ¿van a olvidar a sus amigos?

¡Felicidades! ¡Estamos encantados con esta decisión!

Lucía y Juanma

¡Felicitaciones, amigas!
Estoy muy contento con la noticia, pero un poco enfadado porque no puedo celebrarlo con ustedes. Tengo que trabajar ese día.

¡Mis mejores deseos!

Pedro

---

4 Invitación Fíjese en la invitación y en las felicitaciones. ¿Qué celebran? ¿Existe la misma costumbre en su país?

5 ¿Cómo se sienten? ¿Cómo se sienten Eva, Laura y Daniela? ¿Y sus amigos?

| Eva, Laura y Daniela Pedro Juanma y Lucía | ESTAR | contento/a(s) ilusionado/a(s) encantado/a(s) de buen humor | enfadado/a(s) preocupado/a(s) asustado/a(s) de mal humor |

6 Eva Escuche la conversación entre Eva y una amiga. ¿Verdadero o falso?

	V	F
1. Eva se siente asustada.	☐	☐
2. Eugenia está triste porque no tiene pareja.	☐	☐

	V	F
3. Eva está ilusionada.	☐	☐
4. Las dos amigas están contentas.	☐	☐

7 a. Estados de ánimo ¿Cómo está usted de ánimo ahora? ¿Por qué? ¿Y sus compañeros?

b. Situaciones ¿En qué situaciones se siente contento/a? ¿Y enfadado/a?

MI EXPERIENCIA

8 Una persona querida Piense en una persona muy querida por usted. Descríbala.

GUIÓN DE TRABAJO

¿Quién es? → ¿Cómo es físicamente? ¿Y de carácter? → ¿Cómo cree que se siente actualmente?

Es mi amigo/a...

Es alto/a... Tiene el pelo rubio... Usa gafas...

Creo que está muy contento/a porque...

Expresar el estado de ánimo
- ¿Cómo te sientes?
- Estoy un poco asustada pero muy ilusionada.

12A.2 sentirse (e→ie), estar

Vocabulario

3
rubio/a *blond(e)*
bajo/a *short*
castaño/a *brown*
liso/a *straight*
rizado/a *curly*
la barba *beard*
el bigote *mustache*
largo/a *long*
corto/a *short*

4
graduarse (*Amér. L.*) *to graduate*
la inauguración *housewarming*
ilusionado/a *excited*
asustado/a *frightened*
inaugurar *to open; to inaugurate*
preocupado/a *worried*
enfadado/a *angry*

6
triste *sad*

7
el estado de ánimo *state of mind, mood*

SAM: Actividades pp. 245–247

Relaciones personales

FOTONOVELA

1 Adela busca de nuevo el amor y decide escribir un anuncio.

Me llamo Adela. Soy una mujer independiente y optimista. Vivo en Monterrey y quiero conocer a un hombre para una relación seria, enamorarme y casarme.
Celular 8113208982

2 Norberto llama...

SÍ, SOY REGIOMONTANO Y RESIDO AQUÍ. NO, ESTOY SOLTERO. MUY BIEN, ENTONCES EL JUEVES A LAS SIETE.

3 Y empiezan a salir y conocerse...

SÍ, EL NIÑO TENÍA DOS AÑOS. DESPUÉS ÉL SE CASÓ DE NUEVO. MI EX ES UN BUEN PADRE. NOS LLEVAMOS BIEN.

¿TE DIVORCIASTE PRONTO DE TU EX ESPOSO?

Hablar de relaciones personales

Mi hermana Juana **se enamoró y se casó**, pero no **se llevaban bien** y un año más tarde **se separaron**. Ahora **sale** con César.

12A.3 **enamorarse, separarse, llevarse bien/mal**

Vocabulario

9

la fotonovela *photo story*

enamorarse *to fall in love*

regiomontano/a *born in Monterrey*

divorciarse *to get divorced*

el/la ex esposo/a *ex-husband/wife*

llevarse bien/mal *to get along/not to get along*

separarse *to split up, to separate*

independiente, serio/a

Estrategia ··········

Cerrar una cita

● Lucía, ¿vienes el sábado a la cena?

■ Sí, claro.

● **Entonces**, hasta el sábado.

■ **De acuerdo, nos vemos.**

---

9 **a. Título** ¿Qué le sugiere el título "Fotonovela"? ¿Alguna vez ha leído una fotonovela?

b. Resumir Lea esta fotonovela y resuma qué ocurre.

c. Ordenar ¿En qué orden suelen pasar estas acciones?

divorciarse ☐   casarse ☐   salir con alguien ☐
enamorarse ☐   separarse ☐

10 **Adela** Complete la ficha de Adela.

Nombre: *Adela* ....

Lugar de residencia: ....

Estado civil: ....

Otra información: ....

11 **a. La llamada** Escuche la primera llamada telefónica de esta pareja. ¿Cuál es la historia sentimental de cada uno de ellos? Márquelo en el recuadro.

	Se enamoró.	Se casó.	Se separó.	Tuvo una relación seria.	Se divorció.
Norberto	✓				
Adela					

b. Ordenar Escuche el final de la conversación y ordene las frases.

● De acuerdo, nos vemos el jueves. Adiós, Adela. ☐

● Muy bien, a las siete en el Faro del Comercio y ¿damos un paseo? ☐

● Entonces, hasta el jueves, Norberto. ☐

● Sí, es un lugar precioso. ☐

● Muy bien, ¿el jueves a las siete? ☐

c. Cerrar una cita Fíjese en cómo indican que cierran una cita. ¿Se hace de la misma forma en su lengua?

FIN

12 **La fotonovela** Lea la fotonovela de esta página. ¿Cómo sigue la historia de amor?

Son buenos amigos. ☐   Se enamoran. ☐   Se casan. ☐

13 **Contestar** ¿Qué es importante para Adela en la vida y en una pareja?

Es importante... estar enamorados/la moda/su carrera profesional/
su hijo/viajar/disfrutar de la vida/tener salud.

14 **Expresar afecto** Fíjese en las formas para expresar afecto y ordene la
conversación entre dos amigas con estas frases.

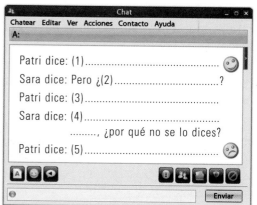

- ¿realmente lo quieres?
- Bueno, si estás tan enamorada de él
- No puedo. Creo que Luis quiere a otra mujer.
- Estoy muy enamorada de Luis.
- Sí, lo quiero muchísimo. Es el hombre de mi vida.

MI EXPERIENCIA

15 **Valorar** ¿Qué es importante para usted? Compártalo con su compañero/a.

GUIÓN DE TRABAJO

¿Qué es importante para ti...

...en la vida?
...en una relación?

Es importante el amor,
la salud, quererse...

Valorar la importancia y expresar afecto

- ¿Qué es importante en una relación?
- Para mí, es importante llevarse bien. ¿Y para ti?
- Es importante el amor, quererse... ¿Me quieres?
- Sí, te quiero mucho. Estoy enamorada de ti.

12A.4 **es importante +** [*noun/infinitive*] **estar enamorado/a de, te quiero**

Vocabulario

12

estar enamorado/a (de) *to be in love (with)*

14

el afecto *affection*

querer (e:ie) a alguien *to love someone*

el hombre/la mujer de mi vida *the man/woman of my dreams*

SAM: Actividades pp. 248–250

Practice more at **vhlcentral.com**.

Ricardo Hernández, padre cien por ciento

Asociación Mexicana de Padres de Familia Separados

Boletín informativo N.° 61, junio

Mi nombre es Ricardo Hernández, estoy divorciado y vivo en México, D.F. Mi hijo Néstor tiene siete años y vive con su mamá desde que nos separamos hace cuatro años. Me llevo bien con mi ex esposa y tenemos una buena comunicación. Es muy importante ser respetuoso entre padres separados porque esto ayuda a los hijos. Normalmente paso todos los fines de semana y las vacaciones con Néstor.

La vida me dio una segunda oportunidad y el año pasado me enamoré de Virginia, una mujer muy buena, inteligente, cariñosa y muy alegre. Hace seis meses que salimos y estoy muy contento. Mi hijo se lleva muy bien con ella y, por eso, para mí ahora es muy importante tener custodia compartida. Mi ex esposa está de acuerdo y también cree que es importante compartir la custodia. Hoy quiero compartir esta decisión con ustedes a través de este boletín, ¡estoy muy emocionado!

Les envío una foto de Néstor; es del fin de semana pasado. Como ven, nos parecemos mucho; es alto y tiene el pelo negro, como yo, ¡pero es más guapo!

Hoy es el tercer domingo de junio, Día del Padre en México. ¡Felicidades a todos!

Ricardo Hernández, 37 años. Padre de Néstor.

Hablar de parecidos

- ● ¿Te pareces a tu padre o a tu madre?
- ■ Físicamente **me parezco** mucho a mi madre pero en el carácter **soy como** mi padre.

12A.5 **parecerse (zc) a**
ser/tener... como

Vocabulario

(16)

cien por ciento *one hundred percent*

respetuoso/a *respectful*

la custodia compartida *joint custody*

parecerse (zc) a alguien *to look like somebody*

el parecido *resemblance*

la asociación, separado/a, el divorcio

---

16 **a. Foto** Observe la foto. ¿Qué relación tienen? ¿En qué se nota?

b. Ricardo Esta asociación quiere ayudar a los padres separados. ¿Por qué Ricardo es un ejemplo para ellos? Lea el texto.

c. Padres de familia separados ¿Hay alguna asociación como esta en su país? ¿Conoce a algún padre o a alguna madre en esta situación?

17 **a. La carta de Ricardo** Lea la carta de Ricardo. ¿Qué sabe de su vida?

> Lugar de residencia: .... Estado civil: ....
> Relaciones personales: ....
> Estado de ánimo hoy: ....

b. Día festivo ¿Qué día escribe Ricardo la carta? ¿Qué se celebra ese día? ¿Cuándo es el Día del Padre en su país?

18 **El Día del Padre** Escuche a Néstor, que felicita a su padre en el Día del Padre. ¿Cómo lo hace? ¿Qué le dice al final?

19 **a. Ricardo y Néstor** Mire la foto de Ricardo y su hijo. ¿Se parece Néstor a su padre?

b. Hablar de parecidos ¿A quién se parece usted en el físico y en el carácter? ¿Y su compañero/a?

20 **a. Leer** Lea el texto. ¿De qué trata?

En el mundo hispano es común usar el nombre de pila del padre cuando hay que elegir un nombre para el primogénito, o hijo mayor. Para diferenciar a uno del otro en el ámbito familiar, se suele aclarar "padre" o "hijo" después del nombre, o bien referirse al hijo con diminutivos como Carlitos o Anita. Fuera del ámbito familiar, hay otra tradición que ayuda a diferenciar entre los tocayos. En España y en Latinoamérica también es común tener doble apellido, es decir, un apellido compuesto por el primer apellido del padre y el de la madre, en ese orden. De este modo, Néstor, hijo de Ricardo Hernández Perlera y Clara Sánchez Uribe, se llama Néstor Hernández Sánchez. Esta tradición europea traída a América por los españoles se usa actualmente en muchos países, como Chile, Colombia, México, Perú y Venezuela.

b. Los nombres Complete las oraciones que resumen el texto anterior.

1. En el mundo hispano, cuando se elige el nombre de pila de un primogénito a veces se usa ....

2. Si en una misma familia el padre y el hijo se llaman Adolfo, quizás los familiares se refieren al hijo como ....

3. El doble apellido está formado por ....

4. Alejandro González Iñárritu es un famoso director de cine mexicano. Según la tradición descrita en el texto, puede deducir que el apellido de su padre es .... y el de su madre es ....

21 **Escribir** Escriba qué es importante para usted en las relaciones entre padres e hijos.

> *Para mí, es importante...*

22 **a. El náhuatl** Lea el texto sobre el náhuatl. ¿Cuál es el origen de esta lengua? ¿Dónde se habla?

Una de las palabras que Ricardo podría usar para referirse a su hijo es *chamaquito*, un nahuatlismo habitual en la lengua coloquial de México y otros países de Centroamérica. El náhuatl es una lengua azteca, y es la cuarta lengua indígena de América por el número de personas que la hablan, después del quechua, el aimara y el guaraní. El español tiene numerosos nahuatlismos: *aguacate*, *cacahuate*, *chamaco*, *chicle*, *chile*, *chocolate*, *cuate*, *guacamole*, *tomate*, *coyote*, *cacao*, *chipotle*, etc.

b. Palabras ¿Cuáles de estas palabras existen también en su lengua?

Vocabulario

20

el nombre de pila *first name*

el/la primogénito/a *firstborn*

en el ámbito familiar *among family*

o bien *or otherwise*

el diminutivo *diminutive, nickname*

el/la tocayo/a *namesake*

el doble apellido *two last names*

22

el/la chamaquito/a (*dim. de* el/la chamaco/a) (*Amér. L.*) *kid, youngster*

azteca *Aztec*

el aimara *Aymara*

el aguacate *avocado*

el cacahuate (*Méx.*) *peanut*

el/la cuate/a (*fam., Méx.*) *friend, pal*

el náhuatl

23

el romanticismo *romanticism*

el amor (no) correspondido *(un)requited love*

SAM: Actividades pp. 251–254

Practice more at **vhlcentral.com**.

23 **a. Poema de amor** Gustavo Adolfo Bécquer fue el máximo protagonista del romanticismo español. Escribió memorables poemas de amor que publicó en sus *Rimas*. Lea el siguiente poema de este autor y marque de qué tema trata.

☐ el amor correspondido

☐ el amor no correspondido

b. Describir ¿Cómo son físicamente y de carácter las dos primeras mujeres con las que habla el poeta? Use los adjetivos del recuadro en su descripción.

tierna apasionada morena rubia

 c. Comentar ¿A cuál de las tres mujeres elige el poeta? Hable con su compañero/a sobre por qué el poeta elige a esa mujer.

RIMA XI

—Yo soy ardiente°, yo soy morena,
yo soy el símbolo de la pasión,
de ansia de goces° mi alma está llena.
¿A mí me buscas?

—No es a ti; no.

—Mi frente° es pálida°, mis trenzas° de oro°,
puedo brindarte° dichas sin fin°.
Yo de ternura° guardo un tesoro.
¿A mí me llamas?

—No; no es a ti.

—Yo soy un sueño, un imposible,
vano fantasma° de niebla y luz°;
soy incorpórea°, soy intangible:
No puedo amarte.

—¡Oh, ven; ven tú!

BÉCQUER, Gustavo Adolfo
(1836–1870)

ardiente *passionate* **goces** *pleasures* **frente** *forehead*
pálido/a *pale* **trenzas** *braids* **de oro** *golden*
brindarte *give you* **dichas sin fin** *endless happiness*
ternura *tenderness* **fantasma** *ghost* **niebla y luz** *fog and light*
incorpórea *without a body*

T A R E A   F I N A L

Reglas para una buena vida en común

 Pregunte a su compañero/a qué cosas son importantes para la vida en común.

Hagan una lista común entre todos y decidan cuáles son los diez principios más importantes.

Es importante...

    1. comunicarse.

    2. el respeto.

    3. ...

Escriban en una hoja sus principios. Las pueden pegar en la pared de la clase y también en su propia casa.

Y O   P U E D O . . .

• **Puedo describir el carácter y el aspecto físico de una persona.**

Describa el carácter y el aspecto físico de un(a) amigo/a suyo/a.

• **Puedo expresar el estado de ánimo.**

Imagine que hoy es el aniversario de una fecha importante para usted. ¿Es una ocasión feliz o triste? Describa su estado de ánimo.

• **Puedo hablar de relaciones personales.**

Piense en un familiar y describa la relación que los une.

• **Puedo valorar la importancia de algo y expresar afecto.**

Señale qué es importante para tener una buena relación y piense en una forma de expresar afecto o amor.

• **Puedo hablar de parecidos.**

Busque parecidos entre uno de sus compañeros y una persona famosa o familiar.

12A.1 Describe personality and physical traits

ser, tener, usar 4.1, 5.1.1, 5.1.2, 5.8.2

- Use **ser** + (**muy/un poco**) + [*adjective*] to describe people's personality and physical traits.

> Leonardo **es** divertido pero un poco tímido.
> *Leonardo is a fun guy, but he is a bit shy.*

> **Es** muy atractivo, moreno y alto.
> *He is very attractive, dark-haired, and tall.*

- As you saw in **2A.4,** adjectives must agree with the noun that they modify. Adjectives that end in -**e** and adjectives that end in -**ista** do not have distinct masculine and feminine forms.

> Emilio es **responsable** y **optimista**; Adriana también es **responsable** y **optimista**.
> *Emilio is **responsible** and **optimistic**; Adriana is also **responsible** and **optimistic**.*

- Use **tener** + **el pelo/los ojos** + [*adjective*] to describe people's appearance. To say that someone wears glasses, use the verb **usar**.

> Marisa **tiene** los ojos verdes y **usa** gafas.
> *Marisa **has** green eyes and **wears** glasses.*

12A.2 Express mood

sentirse, estar 5.1.1, 5.1.2, 5.7.1

- Use **sentirse** to talk about feelings and states of mind. To ask someone how he/she feels, say **¿Cómo se/te siente(s)? Sentirse** is a reflexive verb that undergoes an e→ie stem change.

> Elena **se siente** de buen humor.
> *Elena **is** in a good mood.*

SENTIRSE			
(yo)	**me** siento	(nosotros/as)	**nos** sentimos
(tú)	**te** sientes	(vosotros/as)	**os** sentís
(usted, él, ella)	**se** siente	(ustedes, ellos/as)	**se** sienten

- Also use **estar** + [*adjective*] to talk about people's feelings.

> Alejandro y Susana **están** muy ilusionados y un poco nerviosos.
> *Alejandro y Susana **are** very excited and a bit nervous.*

12A.3 Talk about personal relationships

enamorarse, separarse, llevarse bien/mal 5.7.1, 11.1

- Use the verbs **enamorarse, casarse, separarse, divorciarse,** and **llevarse bien/mal** to talk about personal relationships.

> Los padres de Candela **se divorciaron**.
> *Candela's parents **got divorced**.*

- **Enamorarse, separarse,** and **divorciarse** are used with the preposition **de,** and **casarse** and **llevarse bien/mal** are used with **con** when you explicitly mention the other person in the relationship.

> Leonor **se enamoró de** Sebastián y **se casó con** él en 2003.
> *Leonor **fell in love with** Sebastián and **married** him in 2003.*

¡Póngalo en práctica!

G1 **Completar** Complete la conversación. Use cada palabra solamente una vez.

rubio	pesimista	tiene
usa	simpático	pelo

> ¿Cómo es Enrique?

> Es muy (1)........................ pero un poco (2)........................

> ¿Y físicamente?

> Es (3)........................, (4)........................ los ojos azules y (5)........................ gafas. Hace mucho tiempo que tiene el (6)........................ largo.

G2 **¿Sentirse o estar?** Complete las oraciones con la forma correcta de **sentirse** o **estar**, o con la forma correcta del adjetivo.

1. Mañana es tu cumpleaños; ¿cómo .... (sentirse)?

2. Josefina está muy .... (enfadado) porque tiene que trabajar todo el día.

3. ¡Felicidades a los dos! ¿Cómo .... (sentirse)?

4. Benjamín y Sofía .... (estar) muy contentos.

5. Hoy Héctor .... (estar) de muy mal humor.

6. Estoy muy ilusionada, pero un poco .... (asustado) antes de hacer el viaje.

G3 **Conversaciones** Complete las conversaciones.

- ¿Qué sabes de nuestra compañera Isabel?
- Sé que se (1)........................ de un chico mexicano muy guapo y (2)........................ casó (3)........................ él.

- ¿Sabes si Elena se separó (4)........................ su marido?
- Sí, ellos no se llevaban (5)........................, así que (6)........................ divorciaron el año pasado.

 Practice more at vhlcentral.com.

GRAMÁTICA FUNCIONAL

12A.4 Assess importance and express affection

es importante + [*noun/infinitive*] 5.12.3
estar enamorado/a de; te quiero 5.8.2, 6.2.1

- Use **es importante** + [*noun/infinitive*] to talk about what is important.

  > En una relación, **es importante** llevarse bien.
  > *In a relationship, **it is important** to get along well.*

- Use **estar enamorado/a (de)** (*to be in love [with]*) to describe someone who has fallen in love.

  > Carlos **está enamorado de** Liliana.
  > *Carlos **is in love with** Liliana.*

- Use the prepositional pronouns **mí, ti, él, ella, usted, nosotros/as, vosotros/as, ustedes,** or **ellos/as** after **de** to refer to the person who is loved.

  > Tomás está enamorado **de mí,** y yo estoy enamorada **de él.**
  > *Tomás is in love **with me,** and I am in love **with him.***

- Use **querer a alguien** (*to love someone*) to express feelings of love. You can also use a direct object pronoun before **querer** in this construction. Direct object pronouns are used when a person directly receives the action of the verb.

	singular		plural
me	*me*	**nos**	*us*
te	*you* (fam.)	**os**	*you* (fam., Esp.)
lo	*you* (m., form.); *him*	**los**	*you* (m.); *them* (m.)
la	*you* (f., form.); *her*	**las**	*you* (f.); *them* (f.)

  > **Te quiero,** Lucía. Estoy enamorado de ti.
  > *I love you, Lucía. I am in love with you.*

12A.5 Talk about resemblances

parecerse a 5.7.1   **ser/tener... como** 5.1.2

- To talk about resemblances, use the reflexive verb **parecerse (a)**. **Parecerse** undergoes a **c→zc** spelling change in the **yo** form. The other forms follow the regular conjugation pattern for **-er** verbs.

- As with **de**, use prepositional pronouns after the preposition **a** in this construction.

  > **Me parezco** a mi hermana.   Ella **se parece a mí.**
  > *I look like my sister.*   *She looks like me.*

- Use **nos parecemos** to say *we resemble each other*.

  > Mis hermanos y yo **nos parecemos** mucho.
  > *My siblings and I **resemble each other** quite a lot.*

- Use **ser como** (*to be like*) to talk about resemblances and similarities. Use the construction **tener** + [*noun*] + **como** to compare physical characteristics.

  > **Eres como** tu padre.   **Tienes** los ojos **como** tu madre.
  > *You are like your father.*   *You have your mother's eyes.*

G4 **Diálogo** Complete la conversación de manera lógica.

hablar	llevarse	quiero	tener

> Para ti, ¿qué es importante en una relación?

> Para mí, es importante la comunicación y (1)........................ bien.

> Para mí, es importante (2)........................ tiempo para estar juntos y decirle a mi pareja que la (3)........................ También es importante (4)........................ de los problemas.

G5 **Pronombres** Complete las oraciones con el pronombre correcto.

1. Manuel quiere mucho a Patricia. Está enamorado de ....
2. Mi novia dice que está enamorada de .... Yo también .... quiero.
3. • ¿ .... quieres, Dolores?
   ▪ Sí, Emilio, ... quiero. Estoy enamorada de ....
4. Claudio y Ana tienen once nietos y .... quieren mucho.
5. Dalia quiere casarse con su novio; está totalmente enamorada de ....

G6 **Parecidos** Complete las conversaciones.

• ¿A quién (1)................ pareces?
▪ Físicamente me (2)................ muchísimo a mi padre, pero en el carácter soy (3)................ mi madre.

• Daniela (4)................ parece mucho a su abuela, ¿no?
▪ Sí, (5)................ la nariz como ella.

• Mario y yo nos (6)................ a nuestro padre. Los dos tenemos el pelo (7)................ él.
▪ Sí, también (8)................ como él porque son alegres, inteligentes y trabajadores.

 Practice more at **vhlcentral.com**.

Vida en común

el aspecto físico	physical appearance
la barba	beard
el bigote	mustache
el carácter	character, personality
el estado de ánimo	state of mind, mood
la inauguración	housewarming
la residencia de estudiantes	dorm
el tipo	type
graduarse (*Amér. L.*)	to graduate
hacer una consulta	to ask somebody's advice
inaugurar	to open; to inaugurate
asustado/a	frightened
atractivo/a	attractive
bajo/a	short
cariñoso/a	affectionate
castaño/a	brown
corto/a	short
culto/a	educated
enfadado/a	angry
ilusionado/a	excited
inteligente	intelligent
largo/a	long
liso/a	straight
moreno/a	dark-haired
optimista	optimistic
pelirrojo/a	red-haired
pesimista	pessimistic
preocupado/a	worried
realista	realistic
rizado/a	curly
rubio/a	blond(e)
tímido/a	shy
triste	sad
de buen/mal humor	in a good/bad mood

Relaciones personales

el afecto	affection
el/la ex esposo/a	ex-husband/wife
la fotonovela	photo story
el hombre/la mujer de mi vida	the man/woman of my dreams
divorciarse	to get divorced
enamorarse	to fall in love
estar enamorado/a (de)	to be in love (with)
llevarse bien/mal	to get along/not to get along
querer (e:ie) a alguien	to love someone
separarse	to split up, to separate
independiente	independent
regiomontano/a	born in Monterrey
serio/a	serious

Ricardo Hernández

cien por ciento	one hundred percent
en el ámbito familiar	among family
o bien	or otherwise
el aguacate	avocado
el aimara	Aymara
el amor (no) correspondido	(un)requited love
la asociación	association
el cacahuate (*Méx.*)	peanut
el/la chamaquito/a (*dim. de* el/la chamaco/a) (*Amér. L.*)	kid, youngster
el/la cuate/a (*fam., Méx.*)	friend, pal
la custodia compartida	joint custody
el diminutivo	diminutive, nickname
el divorcio	divorce
el doble apellido	two last names
el náhuatl	Nahuatl
el nombre de pila	first name
el parecido	resemblance
el/la primogénito/a	firstborn
el romanticismo	romanticism
el/la tocayo/a	namesake
parecerse (zc) a alguien	to look like somebody
azteca	Aztec
respetuoso/a	respectful
separado/a	separated

Variación léxica

cien por ciento ⟷ ciento por ciento (*Amér. L.*) ⟷ cien por cien (*Esp.*)

enfadado/a (*Esp.*) ⟷ enojado/a

graduarse (*Amér. L.*) ⟷ licenciarse (*Esp.*) ⟷ recibirse (*Arg., Chile*) ⟷ terminar la carrera

liso/a ⟷ lacio/a

el maní ⟷ el cacahuate (*Méx.*) ⟷ el cacahuete (*Esp.*)

rizado/a ⟷ chino/a (*Méx.*) ⟷ colocho/a (*Amér. C.*) ⟷ enrulado/a (*Arg.*) ⟷ crespo/a

12B

SIN LÍMITES

Voluntarios

Médicos Sin Fronteras colaborará en proyectos de salud en más de sesenta países.

Aldeas Infantiles SOS ofrecerá una familia y un hogar estable a miles de niños en todo el mundo.

A partir de ahora, Cimientos repartirá más becas escolares entre niños y jóvenes de pocos recursos en Argentina.

Hablar de compromisos futuros

Médicos Sin Fronteras **llegará** a sesenta países.

Aldeas Infantiles SOS **ofrecerá** ayuda a miles de niños.

Cimientos **repartirá** más becas escolares en Argentina a partir de ahora.

....

12B.1 Simple future (regular forms)
a partir de...

Vocabulario

①

el/la voluntario/a *volunteer*
a partir de *from, starting*
repartir *to distribute*
la beca (escolar) *scholarship*
los recursos *resources, means*
la campaña *campaign*
a favor de *in favor of*
el/la enfermero/a *nurse*
el tratamiento *treatment*
la vacuna *vaccine*
estable, defender (e:ie), la crisis, futuro/a

③

la emergencia

---

1 **ONG** Lea los carteles de las organizaciones no gubernamentales (ONG) y relaciónelos con estas afirmaciones. ¿Conoce estas ONG? ¿Existen estas u otras parecidas en su país?

1. Cimientos ......
2. Médicos Sin Fronteras ......
3. Aldeas Infantiles SOS ......

a. Defiende los derechos de los niños en todo el mundo.
b. Ofrece educación de calidad en lugares sin recursos. Organiza campañas a favor de la educación.
c. Sus médicos y enfermeros ayudan en zonas de crisis. Ofrecen tratamiento médico, vacunas y alimento.

2 **Futuro simple** Fíjese en las formas de **colaborar** y complete las series que faltan del futuro simple.

COLABORAR	colabora**ré**, colabora**rás**, colabora**rá**, colabora**remos**, colabora**réis**, colabora**rán**
OFRECER	
REPARTIR	

3 **a. Proyectos** ¿En qué otros proyectos colaborarán estas organizaciones en el futuro? Exprese estos proyectos usando el futuro simple.

1. Dar formación profesional a jóvenes. *Cimientos dará formación...*
2. Enviar médicos a zonas de guerra.
3. Recoger y repartir medicinas.
4. Crear aldeas infantiles y dar una nueva familia a muchos niños.
5. Abrir hospitales de emergencia.

b. Voluntarios ¿Conoce otras ONG o asociaciones de voluntarios en su país, ciudad o barrio? Explique a sus compañeros lo que hacen.

Médicos Sin Fronteras

Paula Fernández

Puerto Príncipe, lunes 3 de octubre

Hoy ha sido un día muy largo. En este trabajo lo difícil es saber cuándo parar... Es que nuestra labor de atención médica a veces no es suficiente y eso es frustrante. Es lo malo de este trabajo. Lo bueno es que ves el resultado del esfuerzo día a día.

Hace semanas que no hablo con mi madre... tengo que llamarla más. Lo más importante es la familia. A veces lo olvido.

A partir de ahora, llamaré más a casa y estaré más en contacto. Intentaré pasar más tiempo con ellos.

---

4 **El diario de Paula** Lea el diario de Paula. ¿En qué organización de las anteriores trabaja Paula? ¿En qué país? ¿Qué compromisos personales de futuro tiene?

5 **Valoraciones** ¿Cómo valora Paula su trabajo y su vida? Complete las frases.

1. Lo difícil...   2. Lo bueno...   3. Lo malo...   4. Lo más importante...

6 **Lo bueno y lo malo** ¿Cómo valora usted su carrera/trabajo? Compare sus respuestas con las de su compañero/a.

Modelo: • *Lo bueno de mi carrera/trabajo es...*   • *Lo malo es...*

7 **Intenciones** Escuche la llamada de Paula a su madre y marque sus intenciones.

1. Llamará más a su madre. ☐
2. Recordará el cumpleaños de su hermano. ☐
3. Volverá a casa en enero. ☐

MI EXPERIENCIA

8 **Compromisos** Y usted, ¿cuál de estos u otros compromisos asume más frecuentemente? ¿Y su compañero/a? Valore estas acciones.

GUIÓN DE TRABAJO

pasar más tiempo con mi familia/
dejar de fumar/practicar más deporte/
trabajar menos/no dejarlo todo para el último minuto/
organizar mejor mi tiempo/
aprender a cocinar/ahorrar...

Yo siempre digo: "A partir de ahora, practicaré más deporte." → Yo también; lo importante es tener tiempo.

Expresar valoraciones

Lo importante es la familia.
Lo bueno es que me gusta mi trabajo.
Lo difícil es tener tiempo para todo.
Lo malo son los horarios.

12B.2 lo bueno/malo... es/son

Vocabulario

4
Puerto Príncipe *Port-au-Prince*
la labor *work, task*
frustrante *frustrating*
lo malo/bueno *the bad/good thing*
el resultado *result*
estar en contacto *to be in touch*

8
asumir *to assume, to take*
dejar de fumar *to quit smoking*
el último minuto *the last minute*
ahorrar *to save*

SAM: Actividades 255–257

Practice more at **vhlcentral.com**.

Hablar de deseos personales

Deseo encontrar un trabajo.
Quiero integrarme en la sociedad.
Espero lograr mi independencia.

12B.3 **querer, desear, esperar** + [*infinitive*]

Vocabulario

9

el congreso *conference*
sordo/a *deaf*
esperar *to hope; to wait for*
la barrera *barrier*
integrarse *to be integrated; to fit into*
la independencia

10

la rueda de prensa *press conference*
sufrir *to suffer*
la marginación *marginalization*
discapacitado/a *disabled*
el grupo marginado *marginalized group*
estar adaptado/a *to be adapted*
la discapacidad *disability*
quería decir... *I meant . . .*

Estrategia ··············

Tomar la palabra

● Perdón, quería decir que lo importante es informar a la sociedad.

■ Sí, y además...

✦ Una cosa más...

Querer es poder

CONGRESO PARA LA IGUALDAD

Mercedes es sorda y trabaja como profesora en una escuela para niños sordos: "Quiero ayudar a estos niños."

Marta Torre, abogada: "Quiero ser independiente. Deseo ayudar a mis hijos y espero lograrlo. Lo malo son las barreras físicas."

9 **Expresión** ¿Qué significa la expresión *querer es poder*? ¿Y para estas personas? ¿Qué desean y esperan?

10 **a. La rueda de prensa** Primero, lea esta lista. Luego, escuche la rueda de prensa con los organizadores del congreso e indique qué temas mencionan.

- ○ La marginación de personas discapacitadas ☐
- ○ Otros grupos marginados en la sociedad ☐
- ○ Los edificios públicos no están adaptados a personas con discapacidades. ☐
- ○ Informar a la sociedad de sus problemas ☐
- ○ El gobierno no da suficiente ayuda económica a las familias. ☐
- ○ Hay muchas personas marginadas. ☐

b. Ordenar Escuche de nuevo y diga en qué orden se mencionan en el audio estas expresiones para tomar el turno de palabra.

- ○ Perdón, quería decir que... ☐
- ○ Una cosa más... ☐
- ○ Sí, y además... ☐

11 **Viñeta** Mire esta viñeta. ¿A qué tipo de persona critica el personaje de la imagen? ¿Cree que hay motivos para esta crítica? ¿Por qué?

12 **Deseos personales** Y usted, ¿qué cosas desea en su vida? Compare su respuesta con la de su compañero/a.

SENDRA

MANIFIESTO DE LOS PARTICIPANTES

Queremos integrarnos a la sociedad y por eso pedimos:

1 la aceptación de la sociedad

2 la eliminación de barreras físicas y mentales en pueblos y ciudades

3 puestos de trabajo para personas con discapacidades

4 ayuda económica para nuestras familias

5 escuelas con programas especiales de integración para nuestros hijos

Miguel Sanz, carpintero:
"Deseo tener un trabajo como el resto de la gente. Quiero integrarme a la sociedad."

---

13 **Clasificar** Lea el manifiesto del congreso y clasifique las peticiones de los participantes.

trabajo	educación	ciudad/pueblo	sociedad	familia
3	☐	☐	☐	☐

14 **Relacionar** Relacione las partes de la izquierda con las de la derecha para formar oraciones lógicas. Obtendrá un resumen del manifiesto de los participantes.

El gobierno los representa

Participar es formar parte

por eso

pido la eliminación de barreras.

pedimos la participación.

Quiero ser independiente

piden compromiso a los gobernantes.

15 **Peticiones** Imagine que es portavoz del congreso. Formule con su compañero/a otras peticiones.

MI EXPERIENCIA

16 **Deseos** Exprese sus deseos y peticiones personales. Compártalos con su compañero/a y juntos hagan peticiones para sus deseos comunes.

GUIÓN DE TRABAJO

¿Qué quieres/deseas/esperas?

¿Qué piden?

de la sociedad/ de la vida/ del trabajo...

de la sociedad/ de la vida/ del trabajo...

Deseamos encontrar un trabajo,...

por eso...

pedimos el apoyo del gobierno.

Hacer peticiones y expresar consecuencias

Queremos puestos de trabajo y **por eso pedimos** medidas de integración.

12B.4 **pedir (e→i)**
por eso

Vocabulario

13

el manifiesto *manifesto*

pedir (e:i) *to ask for*

la aceptación *acceptance*

el puesto de trabajo *job*

el/la carpintero/a *carpenter*

el resto de *the rest of*

la petición *request*

la consecuencia *consequence*

la eliminación, mental, la integración

14

el/la gobernante *ruler, leader*

15

el/la portavoz *spokesperson*

SAM: Actividades 258–260

Marifé, vendedora de ilusiones

Marifé en su puesto de la ONCE junto a su marido

Entrevista a Marifé Cester

En este número de nuestra revista hemos seleccionado a Marifé Cester con motivo de su décimo aniversario como vendedora del cupón del sorteo de la ONCE en la Plaza de San Justo, en el casco viejo de Salamanca.

Ciega desde los once años, su discapacidad no le ha impedido hacer una vida completamente normal. Está casada con Manuel y es madre de dos hijos.

Marifé, gracias a la ONCE encontraste en la venta del cupón una forma de mantener a tu familia y ser independiente. ¿Puedes hacer balance de tu trabajo?

Me encanta: soy independiente, no tengo jefe, y me gusta el trato con el público. Lo malo es que estoy muy poco con mi familia, pero me encanta mi trabajo. Espero seguir con este trabajo muchos años más.

Marifé, ¿cómo te imaginas los próximos diez años?

Intentaré trabajar menos y estaré más con mi familia. Buscaré una persona para las tardes.

Día a día Marifé vende el cupón de la ONCE con la misma ilusión que sus clientes cuando le piden: "¡Uno para esta noche, Marifé!". Ella siempre contesta: "¡Mucha suerte y buen día!".

Expresar buenos deseos

- Colaboraré con una ONG en otro país.
- Ah, ¡buen viaje y buena suerte!

12B.5 buen viaje
buena/mucha suerte

Vocabulario

(17)

la ilusión *hope; excitement*

con motivo de *on the occasion of*

décimo/a *tenth*

el cupón *(lottery) ticket*

el sorteo *lottery, drawing*

la ONCE *Spanish National Organization of the Blind*

el casco viejo *historic neighborhood*

ciego/a *blind*

impedir (e:i) *to prevent; to stop*

hacer balance de *to take stock of*

el/la jefe/a *boss*

el trato *interaction*

la sigla *acronym*

nacional

---

17 **ONCE** Observe la fotografía. ¿Sabe qué significa la sigla *ONCE*? Construya el nombre completo.

> Ciegos   Organización   Españoles   Nacional

O................   N................de   C................   E................

18 **Título** ¿Qué cree que significa el título "vendedora de ilusiones"? ¿Qué relación cree que tiene con la ONCE? Lea la entrevista y compruebe sus hipótesis.

19 **Marifé** ¿Qué cree Marifé que es lo bueno y lo malo de su trabajo? Haga una lista de los compromisos de Marifé para el futuro.

20 **a. Buenos deseos** ¿Qué les dice a sus clientes nuestra protagonista para expresar buenos deseos?

b. Expresiones Asocie estas expresiones con los contextos correspondientes. ¿Cuándo se usa cada una? En parejas, hagan una lista.

> ¡Buen viaje!   ¡Adiós, mucha suerte!

21 **El cupón** Observe el cupón y escuche el anuncio de la ONCE. ¿Cuál es el premio?

Perros guía

Aquí está Lola, una futura perra guía de la ONCE, con sus educadores, Jacobo y Belén.

> "Queremos educar a una gran perra guía."

> "Somos educadores de Lola, no sus dueños. Sabemos que Lola se irá."

> "Lo bueno es que podemos llevarnos a Lola al trabajo. Tuvimos que pedir permiso, pero es una perra muy buena y nunca hemos tenido ningún problema."

Jacobo y Belén son los educadores de Lola, una cachorra de la Fundación ONCE del Perro Guía (FOPG). Jacobo nos contó cómo empezó su interés por los perros guía. "Queríamos tener un perro, pero por nuestro trabajo y tipo de vida no podíamos. Descubrimos la opción que ofrece la ONCE y lo intentamos." La ONCE paga todos los gastos de Lola; a cambio, Belén y Jacobo educan a la cachorra.

> "Educar a Lola no es fácil pero es una labor de voluntariado muy gratificante: sabemos que ayudará a alguien."

Después de doce meses, Lola volverá al centro y empezará su verdadera educación como perro guía. Estará de seis a ocho meses más y se graduará para ayudar a una persona ciega. Lola será sus ojos. ¡Buena suerte, Lola!

Vocabulario

22
el/la perro/a guía guide dog
el/la educador(a) trainer (of dogs)
educar to train; to educate
irse to leave
pedir (e:i) permiso to ask permission
el/la cachorro/a puppy
a cambio in return
verdadero/a real

24
el/la deportista athlete
la medalla medal
el bronce bronze
el/la pintor(a) painter
el/la atleta track-and-field athlete
el oro gold
la plata silver
los Juegos Paralímpicos Paralympic Games

25
el socorro help
el atentado attack; offense

OPINIÓN

¿Existe alguna organización similar a la ONCE en su país?

¿Juega habitualmente a la lotería?

¿Ha ganado algún premio alguna vez?

¡OJO!

ONCE is an acronym, or **sigla**, that stands for **Organización Nacional de Ciegos Españoles**. Note that **la sigla** is either an acronym or each of the initials that make up an acronym, while **el siglo** refers to a century. What is the difference in meaning for these pairs: **la derecha/el derecho**; **la libra/el libro**?

22 **Preguntar** Lea el texto y haga estas preguntas a su compañero/a.

- ¿Quiénes son? - ¿Qué hacen? - ¿Para qué? - ¿Cómo? - ¿Dónde?

23 **Escribir** Elija una de estas categorías y escriba una petición.

- trabajo - educación - sociedad

> Quiero... por eso...

24 **Personajes** ¿Conoce a estos personajes? Relaciónelos con la información. Elija el más interesante para usted y busque más información en Internet. ¿Conoce a alguien con una discapacidad y con una vida autónoma?

Jorge Luis Borges

Saúl Mendoza

Francisco de Goya

Nilda Gómez López

- ☐ Deportista puertorriqueña, medalla de bronce en tiro en los Juegos Paralímpicos de Beijing 2008.
- ☐ Pintor español sordo.
- ☐ Atleta mexicano, medallas de oro y plata en los Juegos Paralímpicos de Atenas 2004.
- ☐ Escritor argentino ciego.

SAM: Actividades pp. 261–266

25 **a. Relacionar** Fíjese en los eslóganes de estas ONG. ¿Qué le sugieren? Relaciónelos con las categorías del recuadro.

educación • asuntos sociales • política • voluntariado • medio ambiente

Cruz Roja:
Tu ayuda vale mucho para el socorro ante desastres.

....

Amnistía Internacional:
Defendemos los derechos humanos en todo el mundo.

....

Asociación Conciencia:
Educando jóvenes para una sociedad democrática.

....

Greenpeace:
Para proteger y defender activamente el planeta de los atentados que se cometen contra la naturaleza.

....

Desarrollo y asistencia:
Tú tienes mucho. Muchos no tienen nada. Por eso da. Porque merece la pena.

....

 b. Responder Piensen en la labor que realiza cada una de estas ONG. ¿Con cuál desearían colaborar? ¿Por qué? ¿Cómo colaborarían? Elija una de estas organizaciones y busque oportunidades para colaborar con ella en su región.

 T A R E A   F I N A L

Nuestra ONG

Haga una lista de las ONG y asociaciones que conoce. Busque ideas en Internet o hable con un club o asociación de voluntariado de su universidad.

Explique a su compañero/a la labor que realizan estas ONG o asociaciones.

Compartan y elijan las ideas más interesantes para crear su propia ONG o asociación.

Elijan un eslogan y una sigla.

Presenten su ONG o asociación a la clase. Expliquen a sus compañeros la labor que realizarán en el futuro.

Y O   P U E D O . . .

- Puedo hablar de mis compromisos para el futuro.
  Piense en algo que quiere cambiar de su vida y escriba los compromisos para hacerlo.

- Puedo expresar valoraciones.
  Piense qué es lo bueno y qué es lo malo de: su trabajo, sus estudios, su ciudad...

- Puedo hablar de deseos personales.
  Escriba tres deseos personales.

- Puedo hacer peticiones y expresar consecuencia.
  Describa una situación y, como consecuencia de esta, exprese una petición.

- Puedo expresar buenos deseos.
  Un(a) compañero/a se va de viaje. ¿Qué le dice?

GRAMÁTICA FUNCIONAL Ⓢ Tutorials

12B.1 Talk about future commitments

The simple future (regular forms) 5.16.2a
a partir de... 10.2

- To express actions and events in the future, such as anticipated plans or objectives, use the simple future (**el futuro simple**).

    La universidad **ofrecerá** más clases de noche este año.
    *The university **will offer** more classes at night this year.*

- In 6B.1, you learned to use **ir + a +** [*infinitive*] to talk about what someone is going to do in the near future. Use the **futuro simple** to express a firm intention for the future.

- For regular verbs, the endings of the **futuro simple** are added to the infinitive. The endings are the same for **-ar**, **-er**, and **-ir** verbs.

	TRABAJAR	SER	VIVIR
(yo)	trabajar**é**	ser**é**	vivir**é**
(tú)	trabajar**ás**	ser**ás**	vivir**ás**
(usted, él, ella)	trabajar**á**	ser**á**	vivir**á**
(nosotros/as)	trabajar**emos**	ser**emos**	vivir**emos**
(vosotros/as)	trabajar**éis**	ser**éis**	vivir**éis**
(ustedes, ellos/as)	trabajar**án**	ser**án**	vivir**án**

    Trabajaremos juntos a partir de marzo.
    We will work together starting in March.

- Note that all **futuro simple** endings have a written accent except the **nosotros/as** form.

    Ellos **irán** de viaje y nosotros **nos quedaremos** en casa.
    They will take a trip and we will stay home.

- Use **a partir de** + [*time expression*] to express *from* + [*time expression*] + *on*.

12B.2 Express opinions

lo bueno/lo malo... es/son 3.3.1

- To assess something based on its general characteristics, use **lo** with the masculine singular form of an adjective. Say **lo** + [*adjective*] + **es** followed by a singular noun or an infinitive.

    Lo bueno es tener un horario flexible.
    The good thing is having a flexible schedule.

    Lo importante es la familia.
    The important thing is family.

- Use **lo** + [*adjective*] + **son** followed by a plural noun.

    Lo malo son las grandes distancias.
    *The long distances **are the bad part**.*

- With a conjugated verb, use **lo** + [*adjective*] + **es** + **que**.

    Lo difícil es que no tengo tiempo para todo.
    The difficult part is that I don't have time for everything.

¡Póngalo en práctica!

G1 Futuro simple Escriba la forma correcta del futuro simple.

1. defender (yo) ....
2. pedir (ustedes) ....
3. esperar (vosotros) ....
4. desear (tú) ....
5. educar (ellas) ....
6. lograr (Juan) ....
7. compartir (tú y yo) ....
8. ver (usted) ....

G2 Oraciones Complete las oraciones con la forma correcta del futuro simple.

Quiero hacer algo por la sociedad. He decidido que (1)........................ (colaborar) con una ONG.

La empresa ha prometido que a partir de este año (2)........................ (subir) los salarios a los trabajadores. A cambio, los trabajadores (3)........................ (ser) eficaces y (4)........................ (cumplir) los objetivos.

Este año muchas ONG (5)........................ (trabajar) en zonas de catástrofe. Las organizaciones (6)........................ (llevar) comida, agua y medicamentos a los más afectados.

Nosotros hemos decidido poner más atención al estudio. Por eso, (7)........................ (ir) con más frecuencia a la biblioteca y (8)........................ (estudiar) juntos.

G3 Diálogos Complete los diálogos.

- ¿Qué es (1)........................ importante en la vida?
- Lo (2)........................ es la salud.

- ¿Qué es lo bueno y lo malo de tu trabajo?
- Lo bueno (3)........................ que me gusta. Lo malo (4)........................ los horarios.

- ¿Qué es lo mejor y lo peor de vivir en otro país?
- Lo mejor (5)........................ poder aprender cosas nuevas todos los días. Lo peor es (6)........................ no puedo viajar muy frecuentemente a mi país.

 Practice more at **vhlcentral.com**.

GRAMÁTICA FUNCIONAL

12B.3 Talk about desires and hopes

querer/desear/esperar + [*infinitive*] 5.10

- Use the verbs **querer**, **desear**, and **esperar** followed by an infinitive to express hopes and desires.

> **Quiero ir** de vacaciones pronto.
> *I want to go on vacation soon.*

> **Esperamos verte** de nuevo.
> *We hope to see you again.*

- **Querer** has the stem change **e→ie**, as you learned in 3B.6. **Desear** and **esperar** are regular **-ar** verbs.

12B.4 Make requests and express consequences

pedir 5.1.1 **por eso** 12.8

- Use the verb **pedir** (*to ask for*) + [*noun*] to make requests. **Pedir** has an **e→i** stem change.

> **Pido** la participación de todos.
> *I ask for everyone's participation.*

PEDIR			
(yo)	pido	(nosotros/as)	pedimos
(tú)	pides	(vosotros/as)	pedís
(usted, él, ella)	pide	(ustedes, ellos/as)	piden

- Note that no preposition is used between **pedir** and the noun in Spanish. Other common verbs that require a preposition in English but not in Spanish include **buscar** (*to look for*) and **esperar** (*to wait for*).

> Estoy buscando las llaves; espérame.
> *I'm looking **for** the keys; wait **for** me.*

- To show consequences, use **por eso** (*that's why; therefore*).

> Queremos ayudas económicas y programas especiales, **por eso** pedimos el compromiso del gobierno.
> *We want economic assistance and special programs; **that's why** we are asking for a commitment from the government.*

12B.5 Express well wishes

buen viaje, buena/mucha suerte 4.6

- To wish someone a good trip, say **buen viaje**. To wish someone luck, say **buena/mucha suerte**.

> —Mañana tengo una entrevista.
> —**¡Mucha suerte!**
> —*I have an interview tomorrow.*
> —*Good luck!*

- The adjective **bueno** drops the final vowel **-o** in front of a singular masculine noun. Another example of this shortened adjective is in the expression **buen provecho** (*Bon appetit!*).

- When **bueno** is followed by a feminine noun or a plural noun, it is not shortened: **buena suerte**; **buenos días**; **buenas noches**.

¡Póngalo en práctica!

G4 **Escribir** Escriba oraciones completas según las pistas.

1. (yo) querer / aprender / español
   ....

2. (nosotros) esperar / tener / buena salud
   ....

3. Paola / desear / mejorar / sus notas
   ....

4. Raúl y Mónica / querer / encontrar / trabajos interesantes
   ....

5. Florencia / desear / estudiar / física
   ....

G5 **Completar** Complete las oraciones con **por eso** o la forma correcta de **pedir**.

- ¿Qué quieres de tu trabajo?
- Quiero un trabajo interesante; (1)......................... (2)......................... proyectos participativos y creativos. Y vosotros, ¿qué queréis?

Queremos puestos de trabajo dignos para todos y (3)......................... (4)......................... la eliminación de barreras físicas y mentales.

- Los ciudadanos quieren una ciudad limpia; (5)......................... (6)......................... más recursos. ¿Qué más pueden (7).........................?
- Es importante la participación de todos; (8)......................... hay que ir a votar.

G6 **Buenos deseos** Responda a cada situación con una expresión de buenos deseos.

1. —Mañana tengo un examen.
   —¡.............................!
2. —Me voy de vacaciones mañana.
   —¡.............................!
3. —Voy a dar una presentación esta semana en mi trabajo.
   —¡.............................!
4. —Voy a comer una ensalada.
   —¡.............................!
5. —Son las once de la noche y me voy.
   —¡.............................!

Practice more at **vhlcentral.com**.

VOCABULARIO

Vocabulary Tools

Voluntarios

a favor de	in favor of
lo malo/bueno	the bad/good thing
la beca (escolar)	scholarship
la campaña	campaign
la crisis	crisis
la emergencia	emergency
el/la enfermero/a	nurse
la labor	work, task
Puerto Príncipe	Port-au-Prince
los recursos	resources, means
el resultado	result
el tratamiento	treatment
el último minuto	the last minute
la vacuna	vaccine
el/la voluntario/a	volunteer
ahorrar	to save
asumir	to assume, to take
defender (e:ie)	to defend
dejar de fumar	to quit smoking
estar en contacto	to be in touch
repartir	to distribute
estable	stable
frustrante	frustrating
futuro/a	future
a partir de	from, starting

Querer es poder

el resto de	the rest of
quería decir...	I meant . . .
la aceptación	acceptance
la barrera	barrier
el/la carpintero/a	carpenter
el congreso	conference
la consecuencia	consequence
la discapacidad	disability
la eliminación	elimination
el/la gobernante	ruler, leader
el grupo marginado	marginalized group
la independencia	independence
la integración	integration
el manifiesto	manifesto
la marginación	marginalization
la petición	request
el/la portavoz	spokesperson
el puesto de trabajo	job
la rueda de prensa	press conference
esperar	to hope; to wait for
estar adaptado/a	to be adapted
integrarse	to be integrated; to fit into
pedir (e:i)	to ask for
sufrir	to suffer
discapacitado/a	disabled
mental	mental
sordo/a	deaf

Marifé

con motivo de	on the occasion of
el atentado	attack; offense
el/la atleta	track-and-field athlete
el bronce	bronze
el/la cachorro/a	puppy
el casco viejo	historic neighborhood
el cupón	(lottery) ticket
el/la deportista	athlete
el/la educador(a)	trainer (of dogs)
la ilusión	hope; excitement
el/la jefe/a	boss
los Juegos Paralímpicos	Paralympic Games
la medalla	medal
la ONCE	Spanish National Organization of the Blind
el oro	gold
el/la perro/a guía	guide dog
el/la pintor(a)	painter
la plata	silver
la sigla	acronym
el socorro	help
el sorteo	lottery, drawing
el trato	interaction
educar	to train; to educate
hacer balance de	to take stock of
impedir (e:i)	to prevent; to stop
irse	to leave
pedir (e:i) permiso	to ask permission
ciego/a	blind
décimo/a	tenth
nacional	national
verdadero/a	real
a cambio	in return

Variación léxica

la barrera ⟷ el obstáculo

el/la educador(a) (de perros) ⟷ el/la adiestrador(a) ⟷ el/la entrenador(a)

los Juegos Paralímpicos ⟷ las Paralimpíadas (Amér. L.) ⟷ las Paralimpiadas

la marginación ⟷ la exclusión

el/la perro/a guía ⟷ el/la perro/a lazarillo

la rueda de prensa ⟷ la conferencia de prensa

Estrategias

① Ordenar la información

Lección 11A

Organizing information in order helps your reader better understand your message and improves communication.

○ Escriba las expresiones del recuadro en la postal de la derecha.

> **Por último**
> **En primer lugar**
> **Después**

> *¡Hola, familia!*
>
> *¿Cómo están? Hemos pasado unos días de vacaciones por el norte de España. (1)............................ pasamos unos días en Asturias y visitamos Oviedo. (2).................... fuimos a Bilbao y estuvimos en el Guggenheim, ¡es espectacular! (3)..................... pasamos dos noches en el Parador de Sos del Rey Católico y también hicimos senderismo en los Pirineos. ¡Se lo recomiendo!*
>
> *Un beso,*
>
> *Sara*

② Mostrar interés en la conversación

Lección 11B

Every language has certain expressions used to react or to keep a conversation going. These expressions will help you maintain the natural flow of conversation.

○ Reaccione.

"Este año vamos a Nicaragua de vacaciones."	"Quiero tener ocho hijos."	"He ganado 6 000 000 de euros en la lotería."
....	....	....

③ Cerrar una cita

Lección 12A

Use these expressions to confirm a date or appointment. They can soften the force of a statement and ease the flow of conversation.

○ Vuelva a escuchar el audio de la Actividad 11a de la Lección 12A y marque qué expresiones de cierre ha escuchado.

Entonces, ...	De acuerdo, nos vemos.	Vale, hasta la próxima.

④ Tomar la palabra

Lección 12B

When you want to interrupt someone or "take the floor," you will need to use the appropriate expressions in Spanish. Knowing these expressions will help you express yourself more naturally and effectively, and will ease communication. They will help you develop greater confidence in Spanish.

○ Inicie una conversación con su compañero/a sobre el tema 1. Interrúmpalo/la durante sus explicaciones y tome la palabra para preguntarle por el tema 2. Tome de nuevo la palabra e introduzca el tema 3.

> 1 Usted quiere saber el teléfono de un(a) compañero/a.
>
> 2 Quiere preguntarle a su compañero/a si conoce un restaurante argentino en su ciudad.
>
> 3 Desea saber de otros lugares donde se habla español en su ciudad.

Competencias

TRANSMITIR PALABRAS DE OTROS

1 Reescribir Vuelva a escribir estas oraciones siguiendo el modelo. No olvide usar las palabras entre paréntesis.

> Modelo: *¿Conocen un restaurante bueno? Me gusta la comida latina. (Ana / preguntar / decir)*
> *Ana ha preguntado si conocemos un restaurante bueno. Dice que le gusta la comida latina.*

1. Te recomiendo viajar a Puerto Rico. Es un lugar maravilloso.

   (María / recomendar / decir) ....

2. Si te quieres quedar en ese hotel, te recomiendo hacer la reserva con antelación.

   (Jorge / decir / deber) ....

3. ¿Dónde está el libro de quejas? Esta agencia de viajes es pésima.

   (Eduardo / preguntar / decir) ....

FORMULAR DESEOS, EXPRESAR VALORACIONES EN GRADO MÁXIMO Y EXPRESAR UN CONTRAARGUMENTO

2 Completar Complete las oraciones con palabras del recuadro. Exprese los adjetivos en grado máximo y los verbos en el condicional. Es posible usar algunas palabras más de una vez.

famoso/a
mucho/a
incómodo/a
fácil
gustar
difícil
grande
encantar
caro/a

1. ● Me .... vivir en una casa ....
   - A mí también, pero es .... limpiar un apartamento pequeño.

2. ● Me .... viajar por todo el mundo.
   - Sí, pero es ....

3. ● Me .... ser un(a) cantautor(a) ....
   - ¿A quién no? Pero es ....

4. ● Me .... vivir en las afueras.
   - Sí, pero es .... Debes viajar ....

DESCRIBIR EL CARÁCTER Y EL ASPECTO FÍSICO

3 Relacionar Relacione cada adjetivo con su opuesto. Luego use estos adjetivos y otros que aprendió en la **Lección 12A** para describir una de las personas de las fotos. Su compañero/a adivina quién es.

1. alto/a	a. moreno/a
2. de buen humor	b. bajo/a
3. largo/a	c. rizado/a
4. liso/a	d. pesimista
5. optimista	e. alegre
6. rubio/a	f. de mal humor
7. triste	g. corto/a

HABLAR DE COMPROMISOS FUTUROS

4 Futuro simple Complete la conversación con un verbo de la lista en la forma correcta del futuro simple.

buscar
dejar
llamar
organizar
pasar

● Gustavo, ¿cuándo (1)........................ más tiempo juntos? Viajas mucho por trabajo, incluso los fines de semana...

- Pronto, querida. Mi jefe me ha prometido que (2)........................ a otra persona para encargarse de algunos viajes. De esa manera, yo (3)........................ de trabajar tantas horas y (4)........................ mejor mi tiempo libre.

● ¿Y (5)........................ más a tus padres? Hace varias semanas que no hablas con ellos...

 Video

Las relaciones personales

Ya ha visto cómo el amor y las relaciones sentimentales son esenciales no solo en nuestra vida de cada día sino también para planear el futuro. En este episodio de **Flash Cultura** podrá ver cómo las personas se relacionan y disfrutan del tiempo libre en Madrid.

1 **Preguntas** Converse con un(a) compañero/a: Durante los fines de semana, ¿se reúne con sus amigos? ¿Le parece importante tener muchos amigos? ¿Cree que es posible enamorarse a primera vista?

2 **Mirar** Mire el video. Preste atención al entrevistador. ¿Cuál es el tema principal?

...grandes y chicos... van a la plaza a reunirse...

Las plazas son lo más romántico del mundo...

3 **Relacionar** Una las causas con las consecuencias.

1. Los españoles comen doce uvas el 31 de diciembre...	a. para amar a alguien hay que conocerlo.
2. Muchas crisis en las parejas se producen por...	b. conoces a mucha gente distinta.
3. El amor a primera vista es imposible porque...	c. para dar la bienvenida al Año Nuevo.
4. En Madrid hay un ritmo frenético y por eso...	d. culpa de los celos, sobre todo al comienzo.

4 **En la plaza** En parejas, imaginen que están en una plaza observando a la gente alrededor. Uno describe personajes conocidos y el otro adivina quién es.

> **Modelo:** • ¡Mira! Ese hombre es parecido a ese actor... rubio, alto...
> • ¿Quién...? ¿Chris Hemsworth?

 Practice more at **vhlcentral.com**.

Unidad 13

Nelson Morales y Edgar Hugo Torrico, bienvenidos a bordo

Cristina Rubio, asesora laboral

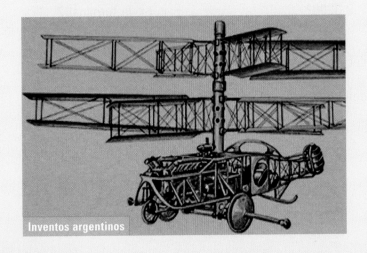

Inventos argentinos

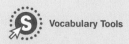
Vocabulary Tools

AVENTURAS COTIDIANAS

Señores pasajeros

¿Podría decirme cuál es el mostrador de facturación de Air Europa?

¿Puede decirme dónde es la entrega de equipaje?

¿Sabe si el avión de Aerolíneas Argentinas viene con retraso?

¿Le importaría confirmarme la sala de llegada del vuelo 1200 de Aeroméxico?

¿Sabe dónde está la puerta de embarque C-13?

¿Podría decirme si sale algún vuelo de Iberia a Santiago de Cuba?

Pedir y confirmar información

- ¿Podría decirme dónde está el mostrador de Iberia?
- ¿Le importaría confirmarme si ha llegado ya el vuelo...?

13A.1 ¿Sabe/Puede/Podría/ Le importaría decirme... + si/dónde/cuándo...?

Vocabulario

señores pasajeros *passengers/ladies and gentlemen*

el mostrador de facturación *check-in counter*

la entrega de equipaje *baggage claim*

con retraso *delayed*

¿Le importaría...? *Would you mind . . . ?*

la sala de llegada *arrival lounge/ area*

la puerta de embarque *boarding gate*

salir *to depart*

---

1 **Señores pasajeros** Lea las preguntas frecuentes de los viajeros e identifique los lugares del aeropuerto que se mencionan. Relacione después estos lugares con las imágenes.

1. *mostrador de facturación*
2. ....
3. ....
4. ....

2 **Preguntas y respuestas** Complete las preguntas con las palabras del recuadro. Luego, relaciónelas con las respuestas. Represente las conversaciones con un(a) compañero/a.

cuándo • cuál • dónde • quién • si

1. ¿Puede decirme .... es la terminal de Air Europa? ___
2. ¿Le importaría confirmarme .... ya ha llegado el vuelo IB 3200? ___
3. ¿Podría decirme .... están los carritos? ___
4. ¿Le importaría decirme .... es el responsable? ___
5. ¿Sabe .... llega el vuelo de Quito? ___

a. Sí, el señor Rodríguez, supervisor de facturación.
b. Sí, a las 17:00 h.
c. Sí, la terminal 2.
d. Sí, detrás de la cafetería.
e. Sí, acaba de llegar.

3 **Pedir** Pida información a su compañero/a sobre estos puntos.

| IB 3200 Frankfurt Salida 13:20 | | PUERTA DE EMBARQUE A-22 | |

4 Paneles informativos Escuche la información anunciada por los altavoces del aeropuerto y anótela en los paneles informativos. Pida confirmación a su compañero/a.

HORA	VUELO	ORIGEN	LLEGADA	SALA	OBSERVACIÓN
10:30	LH 2120		10:30	C	
15:15	VY	ROMA		C	RETRASO

HORA	VUELO	DESTINO	EMBARQUE	PUERTA	OBSERVACIÓN
9:30	EJ 3443	LAS PALMAS	9:00		
10:35	AE	CANCÚN	10:00	B 35	CANCELADO

5 ¿Avión o tren? En parejas, elijan una opción cada uno. Pregunte a su compañero/a por la información de su opción de viaje y después responda a las preguntas de su compañero/a.

ESTUDIANTE A

VUELO MADRID-BARCELONA (IBERIA)

Origen: Madrid-Barajas   **Destino:** Barcelona-El Prat
Duración: 1 hora, 10 minutos
Tarifas: desde 100 euros (ida y vuelta)
Horario:

lunes a viernes	06:30 a 22:45 h (cada 20 minutos)
sábados y domingos	08:00 a 22:45 h (menor frecuencia)

ESTUDIANTE B

AVE MADRID-BARCELONA (RENFE)

Origen: Madrid-Puerta de Atocha   **Destino:** Barcelona-Sants
Duración: 2 horas, 38 minutos
Tarifas: desde 100 euros (ida y vuelta)
Horario:

lunes a viernes	05:45 a 21:00 h (cada hora)
sábados y domingos	06:15 a 22:00 h (menor frecuencia)

MI EXPERIENCIA

6 Un viaje En parejas, imaginen que van a hacer un viaje. Elijan un medio de transporte y representen las conversaciones más frecuentes de un viaje.

GUIÓN DE TRABAJO

ANTES DE VIAJAR
¿Podría/Puede confirmarme...
    a qué hora sale el próximo vuelo/tren a...?
    a qué hora llega el próximo vuelo/tren de...?
    la hora de embarque/salida de...?

→ El próximo vuelo/tren sale/llega a las...

EN EL AEROPUERTO/ EN LA ESTACIÓN
¿Dónde es la entrega de equipaje, la facturación, el control de pasaportes/ equipaje, el cambio de dinero (divisas)?
¿Dónde está la puerta/el andén/la terminal...?

→ Vaya a...

Aeropuertos del mundo hispano

Algunos de los aeropuertos internacionales más frecuentados del mundo hispano son el Benito Juárez (MEX) en México, D.F.; El Dorado (BOG), Bogotá; Comodoro Arturo Merino Benítez (SCL), Santiago de Chile; Jorge Chávez (LIM), Lima; y Tocumen (PTY) en Ciudad de Panamá. En España son importantes los aeropuertos de Barajas (MAD) en Madrid y El Prat (BCN) en Barcelona.

Vocabulario

2
el carrito *baggage cart*
el/la responsable *person in charge*
la terminal, el/la supervisor(a)
4
el altavoz *loudspeaker*
la observación *remark*
el destino *destination*
el embarque *boarding*
procedente de *arriving from*
cancelado/a
5
la tarifa *fare*
la frecuencia
6
la hora de llegada *arrival time*
la hora de embarque *boarding time*
la hora de salida *departure time*
el control de pasaportes *passport control; immigration*
el control de equipaje *baggage screening*
el cambio de dinero *foreign currency exchange*
las divisas *foreign currency*
el andén *platform*
la confirmación

¡OJO!

Use **¿Dónde está?** to ask for the location of objects or places. Use **¿Dónde es?** to ask where an event or action occurs. **¿Dónde es el control de pasaportes? = ¿Dónde controlan los pasaportes?**

SAM: Actividades pp. 267–269

1

....

2

....

3

....

Rincones escondidos

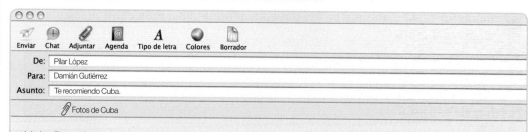

Enviar   Chat   Adjuntar   Agenda   Tipo de letra   Colores   Borrador

De: Pilar López
Para: Damián Gutiérrez
Asunto: Te recomiendo Cuba.

📎 Fotos de Cuba

¡Hola, Damián!
Sé que estás preparando un viaje y he pensado en escribirte para recomendarte un lugar: ¡Ve a Cuba! Hace una semana volví de allí y ¡ya tengo nostalgia! Es que fue un viaje increíble. Como el año pasado estuvimos en La Habana, esta vez visitamos otros rincones de Cuba y decidimos no organizar nada. No teníamos hotel y solo sabíamos la fecha del pasaje de vuelta. Primero volamos a la capital y allí alquilamos un carro para ir a Trinidad y a Santiago de Cuba.

Para volver tomamos el tren de Santiago a La Habana. Fue un viaje larguísimo. Estábamos a mitad de viaje y se averió el tren, pero nos pareció una experiencia maravillosa compartir 18 horas (avería incluida) con cubanos, ¡te lo recomiendo! Yo en tu lugar, no viajaría con un viaje organizado, e iría a otros lugares que no son tan turísticos, por ejemplo Trinidad. Este lugar nos trasladó al pasado; nos encantó su arquitectura colonial y había muchos carros de los años 50, preciosos. La ciudad de Santiago es más grande y más urbana, y tiene una catedral hermosa. Los días que pasamos en el Parque Baconao fueron maravillosos. ¡El paisaje me pareció espectacular! Había mar y montaña, y nos bañamos en la cascada El Saltón. Fue estupendo. Las playas cubanas son únicas; te las recomiendo.

Nos alojamos en casas particulares y no en hoteles. Los cubanos me parecieron muy hospitalarios. Yo que tú, no iría a hoteles tampoco. Comimos en muchos paladares (pequeños restaurantes en casas de cubanos). Me parecieron excelentes y nada caros; yo en tu lugar comería siempre en ellos. A propósito, la comida cubana es riquísima, te la recomiendo. En el viaje conocimos a muchos cubanos y sin duda, lo mejor de Cuba es su gente: ¡Son fantásticos! Bueno, llámame un día y te enseño más fotos.

Un beso, Pilar

Describir un viaje

- ¿Cómo te **fue** en Cuba?
- El vuelo **fue** muy largo, pero las vacaciones **fueron** fantásticas.

13A.2 Review: Preterite/Imperfect
Preterite to give opinions

Vocabulario
⑦

preparar un viaje *to organize a trip*
recomendar (e:ie) (un lugar) *to recommend (a place)*
el rincón *corner; spot*
averiarse *to break down*
el viaje organizado *package tour*
trasladar *to transport*
hermoso/a *lovely*
alojarse *to stay*
la casa particular *private home*
hospitalario/a *hospitable*
el/la cubano/a, excelente

⑦ **Fotos** Fíjese en las fotografías. ¿De dónde pueden ser? Lea el correo y escriba el nombre de los lugares que muestran las fotos.

⑧ **a. Escribir** ¿Qué cuenta Pilar sobre su viaje? ¿Qué experiencias vivieron ella y sus amigos y dónde estaban en esos momentos? Escriba un resumen.

b. Contestar ¿Cuáles fueron las etapas del viaje? ¿Qué medios de transporte utilizaron?

⑨ **a. El viaje de Pilar** ¿Cómo describe Pilar su viaje a Cuba? Complete las oraciones con palabras del recuadro.

> maravilloso/a • increíble • hospitalario/a
> excelente • estupendo/a • espectacular

1. El viaje a Cuba fue ....
2. El viaje en tren fue una experiencia ....
3. El baño en la cascada El Saltón fue ....
4. El paisaje de Cuba le pareció ....
5. Los cubanos le parecieron muy ....
6. Los paladares le parecieron ....

b. Responder ¿Qué tiene este viaje de particular? ¿Ha hecho usted un viaje similar? ¿Adónde? Cuénteselo a su compañero/a.

10 Relacionar Vuelva a leer el correo electrónico. ¿Qué le recomienda Pilar a Damián sobre estos temas? Relacione las columnas.

1. "Te lo recomiendo." ......
2. "Yo que tú, no iría a hoteles." ......
3. "Yo en tu lugar, comería siempre en ellos." ......

a. alojarse en casas particulares
b. comer en paladares
c. viajar en tren

11 Completar Complete las oraciones con las palabras y expresiones del recuadro.

> pediría • viajaría • te lo recomiendo • se la recomiendo

1. Yo en tu lugar, ... a México en enero.
2. Alojarse en hoteles de cinco estrellas es carísimo; no ....
3. Yo que tú .... una revista a la auxiliar de vuelo.
4. Esta aerolínea es muy buena; ....

12 Itinerarios Escriba el nombre de las ciudades que visitó Pilar. Después escuche el audio y escriba las ciudades que les recomienda la agencia a los novios. ¿Qué tipo de viaje le parece más atractivo? Recomiende su opción a su compañero/a.

La Habana • Matanzas • Varadero • Cienfuegos • Isla de la Juventud • Trinidad • Camagüey • Holguín • Santiago de Cuba

13 a. Expresiones Lea de nuevo el correo de Pilar. ¿Qué expresiones usa para dar una explicación?

b. Explicar Explique a su compañero/a el motivo de estas situaciones. Use las expresiones **como** y **es que**.

Modelo: *Como no oí el despertador, he perdido el tren.*

Situaciones
1. Ha perdido el vuelo.
2. No ha reservado los billetes de avión.
3. Ha pedido un cambio de asiento.
4. Han cancelado su vuelo.

Motivos
a. Sabe que no hay problemas de plazas.
b. Está nevando mucho.
c. No oyó el despertador.
d. Ahora está demasiado cerca del baño.

MI EXPERIENCIA

14 Las vacaciones Pregunte a su compañero/a cómo prefiere pasar las vacaciones.

GUIÓN DE TRABAJO

¿Qué tipo de viajes te gusta hacer?
¿Qué destinos prefieres?
¿Cómo fue el último viaje que hiciste?

→

Me gustaría hacer el mismo viaje.
¿Qué me recomiendas?
¿Por qué?

Me gusta...
Prefiero ir a la montaña/al mar...
En mi último viaje fui a...

Recomendar

- ¿Conoces Cuba?
- Te la recomiendo; yo que tú iría allí de vacaciones.
- ¿Alguna vez ha visitado las playas dominicanas?
- Sí, se las recomiendo. Son hermosas.

13A.3 (no) te lo recomiendo
yo que tú / yo en tu lugar + [*conditional*]

Vocabulario

⑪
el/la auxiliar de vuelo *flight attendant*

⑫
el viaje de novios *honeymoon*
proponer *to propose, to suggest*
apuntarse a *to sign up for*

⑬
perder (e:ie) un vuelo *to miss a flight*
reservar los billetes *to book the tickets*
el cambio de asiento *seat change*
la(s) plaza(s) *seat(s)*
demasiado *too*

Estrategia

Dar una explicación
Como ya conocía La Habana, esta vez fuimos a otras ciudades. **Es que** me gusta conocer nuevos lugares.

¡OJO!

The neutral terms usually used to refer to flight attendants in Spanish-speaking countries are **auxiliar de vuelo** or **tripulante de cabina de pasajeros** (**TCP**). These professionals are also known as **aeromozos/as** in most of Latin America. In Argentina and Spain, however, the most widespread term is **azafato/a**, a word of Arabic origin that was used to refer to some of the attendants of the Queen of Spain.

SAM: Actividades pp. 270–272

Nelson y Edgar, bienvenidos a bordo

Nelson Morales y Edgar Hugo Torrico, jefes de cabina de BoA, la aerolínea boliviana

Estamos con Nelson Morales y Edgar Hugo Torrico, dos jefes de cabina de Boliviana de Aviación (BoA). Hoy cumplen 10 años en la empresa...

NELSON *¡Exacto! Comenzamos como tripulantes de cabina de pasajeros el mismo día. Los dos estábamos muy nerviosos, pero nos dábamos ánimo y así nos hicimos amigos. Ahora tenemos diferentes trayectos, pero cuando hacemos escala en la misma ciudad intentamos almorzar o tomar un café juntos.*

¿Y por qué eligieron esta profesión?

EDGAR *Porque nos encanta. Es fantástico poder viajar por todo el mundo, conocer otras culturas... ¡Es una aventura diaria! Nelson y yo somos psicólogos, meseros, recepcionistas, enfermeros, bomberos, limpiadores... Nunca te aburres. ¡Se lo recomiendo a todo el mundo!*

Parece ser el trabajo ideal. ¿Tiene algún aspecto negativo?

NELSON *A veces debemos mostrar nuestra cara menos amable con peticiones como: "¿Podría regresar a su asiento?" o "¿Le importaría apagar su celular?" Es que una de las mayores responsabilidades para los tripulantes de cabina es la seguridad.*

EDGAR *Además, es una profesión sin horarios que da muchas satisfacciones, pero también exige sacrificios. Es que a veces estás de mal humor o extrañas a tu familia, y aún así debes sonreír.*

¿Y cómo es para sus familias tenerlos casi siempre lejos?

NELSON *Bueno, en mi caso es un poco más fácil porque soy soltero. Voy a visitar a mis padres y a mis hermanos cada vez que vuelo a Lima. Para Edgar es un poco más complicado...*

EDGAR *Así es. A veces estoy de viaje varias semanas y extraño mucho a mi señora y a mis hijas, que viven en La Paz. Pero las llamo por teléfono todos los días. Por suerte ellas comprenden que esta es mi vocación y me apoyan.*

Muchas gracias, caballeros. ¡Que tengan un feliz vuelo!

Desear buen viaje

¡Que tengan un feliz vuelo y que disfruten a bordo!

13A.4 que tengan/disfruten...

Vocabulario

15

a bordo *on board*

el/la jefe/a de cabina *purser*

cumplir *to reach; to fulfill*

dar ánimo *to offer encouragement*

el trayecto *route*

hacer escala *to stop over*

diario/a *daily*

el/la mesero/a (*Amér. L.*) *waiter/ waitress*

el asiento *seat*

la seguridad *safety*

exigir (j) sacrificios *to require sacrifices*

extrañar (*Amér. L.*) *to miss*

---

15 a. Nelson y Edgar Observe el título y la foto. ¿En qué consiste la profesión de Nelson y Edgar? Lea la entrevista. ¿Qué tienen en común los dos?

b. Auxiliares de vuelo Haga una lista de las tareas que tienen los auxiliares de vuelo. Relacione las tareas con las funciones que Edgar menciona. ¿Está de acuerdo con él?

16 a. Bienvenidos a bordo ¿Qué peticiones menciona Nelson en la entrevista? Relacione ahora estas peticiones con las imágenes.

Compruebe ☐   Apague ☐   Abróchese ☐

1	2	3
... el cinturón de seguridad.	... que el respaldo de su asiento esté en posición vertical y su mesa plegada.	... el celular y los aparatos electrónicos.

b. Oraciones Marque las oraciones que se pueden usar para desear un buen vuelo.

| ¡Bienvenidos! ☐ | ¡Les deseamos un feliz vuelo! ☐ |
| ¡Que tengan un buen viaje! ☐ | ¡Que tengan suerte! ☐ |

17 a. Leer Lea este artículo sobre la experiencia de viajar en un ómnibus de larga distancia en Argentina. ¿Alguna vez hizo un viaje largo en autobús? Comente sus experiencias con un(a) compañero/a.

UNA EXPERIENCIA DE LARGA DISTANCIA

Son las 19:45 en Buenos Aires. Es hora de subir al ómnibus de larga distancia para recorrer los 1300 kilómetros que me separan de Puerto Madryn, provincia de Chubut, en la Patagonia argentina. No me gusta mucho la idea de viajar durante 17 horas, pero un amigo me dijo que pasan rápido en un ómnibus cama. Una azafata amabilísima me ofrece unos chocolates, me pregunta si quiero beber vino, agua, jugo o alguna gaseosa, y me deja el menú. Decido que voy a cenar carne al horno con papas y una ensalada de fruta. Otras opciones eran un plato vegetariano o una cena *kosher*. Pienso que sería una buena idea lavarme las manos. Cuando regreso del baño, la mesa ya está lista. Disfruto de la exquisita cena mientras escucho música. Cuando termino, la azafata retira los platos. Luego me pasa un estuche con al menos diez DVD para que elija una película, y me ofrece un café. Le digo que así estoy bien y enciendo la pantalla. Cuando termina la película, me lavo los dientes, coloco mi asiento en posición horizontal, me abrigo con la frazada que me dieron y me quedo dormido.

Me despierto varias horas más tarde. Ya no hay tráfico ni luces brillantes. El paisaje es árido, casi desértico, y no veo ninguna ciudad en el horizonte. Aparece otra azafata que me pregunta si dormí bien y si quiero tomar el desayuno. Me ofrece té o café con leche, y unas galletas. ¡Qué suerte que elegí un ómnibus cama y no uno semi-cama, o uno tradicional! Estoy muy descansado. Enciendo el radio y escucho que afuera hace mucho frío. Busco mi computadora portátil y me conecto a Internet. Justo cuando respondo mi último correo, la azafata me dice que estamos llegando a destino. Guardo mis cosas, me pongo de pie y hago fila para bajar. La verdad es que mi amigo tenía razón, el viaje pasó rápido, ya estoy en Puerto Madryn. Tomo un taxi y me dirijo al hotel. Acaban de comenzar mis vacaciones.

b. Contestar Conteste las preguntas.

1. ¿Qué le preocupaba al autor acerca de su viaje?
2. ¿Qué servicios ofrecía el ómnibus?
3. ¿Qué diferencia hay entre un ómnibus cama y un ómnibus tradicional?

c. Preguntas ¿Le gustaría hacer un viaje en ómnibus cama? ¿Cuáles son sus ventajas?

18 Escribir Escriba un breve relato sobre un viaje imaginario muy largo en un ómnibus tradicional o semi-cama.

19 a. Aerolíneas de bandera ¿Sabe qué es una **aerolínea de bandera**? Lea el artículo.

En algunos países el estado es propietario, total o parcial, de una de las aerolíneas que funcionan en su territorio. Esas aerolíneas reciben el nombre de **abanderadas** o **de bandera**, y generalmente son las encargadas de todos los vuelos nacionales. Algunas de estas empresas han sido privatizadas, pero todavía representan a sus países. Entre las más conocidas del mundo hispanoamericano están Aerolíneas Argentinas, Cubana de Aviación e Iberia.

b. Buscar ¿Conoce otras aerolíneas de bandera? Busque en Internet los nombres de otras tres aerolíneas latinoamericanas. ¿Qué países representan?

 Practice more at vhlcentral.com.

Vocabulario cont.

sonreír (e:i) *to smile*
apoyar *to support*
el caballero *gentleman*
¡Que tengan un feliz vuelo! *Have a good flight!*
¡Que disfruten a bordo! *Enjoy your flight!*

16
comprobar (o:ue) *to check*
abrocharse *to fasten*
el cinturón de seguridad *seat belt*
el respaldo del asiento *seat back*
vertical *upright*
plegado/a *folded*

17
el ómnibus (*Arg.*) *bus*
(semi-)cama *(semi-)sleeper*
amabilísimo/a *very friendly*
la gaseosa (*Amér. L.*) *soft drink*
al horno *baked*
exquisito/a *delicious*
retirar *to remove*
el estuche *case*
la pantalla *screen*
abrigarse *to wrap up*
la frazada (*Amér. L.*) *blanket*
hacer fila *to get/wait in line*
árido/a

19
la aerolínea abanderada *national airline*
nacional *domestic*
privatizado/a

OPINIÓN

¿Cree que la calidad del servicio que ofrecen las aerolíneas refleja la cultura del país que representan? ¿Por qué?

SAM: Actividades pp. 273–276

20 **a. Avisos** Lea los avisos sobre tres rutas turísticas.

EL FIN DEL MUNDO

¿Le gustaría ver los mismos paisajes, escuchar los mismos sonidos y tener las mismas sensaciones que el famoso navegante Magallanes°? ¡Esta es su oportunidad! Puede hacerlo en un moderno catamarán, en un histórico barco de madera o en un romántico velero°. Descubrirá los misterios del canal Beagle, el archipiélago de las islas Bridges, el faro° del fin del mundo y una reserva natural con 3000 pingüinos. ¿Se lo va a perder?

UNA NOCHE BIEN "CHIVA"

¿Alguna vez has bailado en un autobús abierto, sin ventanillas y sin puertas? ¡Te lo recomendamos! Ven a Cartagena y da un paseo en una chiva° colombiana ambientada como discoteca, con luces, humo° y pista de baile°. Puedes tomar algo mientras escuchas música y recorres los barrios más divertidos de la ciudad. ¡Pasarás una noche única e inolvidable!

EL CAMINO DE SANTIAGO

Cada año, muchísimos peregrinos recorren a pie los caminos° de toda Europa para visitar los restos° del apóstol° Santiago. De todos los caminos, el más popular es el *Camino francés*. Te invitamos a recorrerlo este verano... ¡en bici! Partiremos de Roncesvalles y viajaremos por todo el norte de España hasta llegar a la maravillosa basílica°. Son 744 kilómetros de desafíos°, alegrías y muchísimo pedaleo°. ¡Acompáñanos!

Magallanes *Magellan* **velero** *sailing ship* **faro** *lighthouse* **chiva (Col.)** *country bus* **humo** *smoke* **pista de baile** *dance floor* **caminos** *paths* **restos** *remains* **apóstol** *apostle* **basílica** *basilica* **desafíos** *challenges* **pedaleo** *pedaling*

b. Recomendar Elija uno de los anuncios turísticos y escriba un correo electrónico a un amigo para recomendarle el viaje.

TAREA FINAL

El mejor destino para un viaje

Piense en sus viajes favoritos y escriba un breve relato.

Pongan en común sus relatos y en pequeños grupos elijan un lugar para recomendar al resto de la clase.

Piensen en el medio de transporte en el que van a hacer el viaje y en el itinerario que quieren proponer. Expliquen los motivos de su elección.

Compartan sus opiniones y decidan cuáles son los tres mejores destinos.

YO PUEDO...

- **Puedo pedir y confirmar información.**
  Busque una agencia de viajes especializada en viajes al Caribe. Infórmese si hay aeropuerto en un lugar que elija y confirme los datos que conoce.

- **Puedo describir un viaje.**
  Hable de un viaje muy especial y describa los distintos aspectos (alojamiento, comida, gente, etc.).

- **Puedo recomendar algo a alguien.**
  Recomiende a su compañero/a un lugar de vacaciones que usted conoce bien.

- **Puedo desear buen viaje.**
  Su profesor(a) vuela mañana; deséele un buen viaje.

GRAMÁTICA FUNCIONAL Tutorials

13A.1 Ask for and confirm information

¿Sabe + si/dónde/cuándo...?
¿Puede/Podría/Le importaría + [infinitive] + si/dónde/cuándo...? 5.13, 5.17.3, 12.8

- There are several ways to politely request and confirm information in Spanish.

> **¿Podría decirme cómo** llegar al control de pasaportes?
> *Could you tell me how to get to passport control?*

> **¿Sabes si** ya empezaron el embarque del vuelo 417?
> *Do you know if they've already started boarding flight 417?*

- To make a polite request for information, transform an information question using the constructions **¿Sabe(n)** (*Do you know*) + [question]?, **¿Puede(n) decirme** (*Can you tell me*) + [question]?, or **¿Le(s) importaría decirme** (*Would you mind telling me*) + [question]?

> **¿Dónde está el baño?**
> *Where is the bathroom?*
> { **¿Sabe** dónde está el baño?
> **¿Puede decirme** dónde está el baño?
> **¿Le importaría decirme** dónde está el baño?

- Remember to always use a written accent on question words such as **cómo, cuándo, dónde,** etc.

- To politely confirm information, transform a yes-or-no question using the constructions **¿Sabe(n) + si** (*if, whether*) + [question]?, **¿Puede(n) decirme + si** + [question]?, or **¿Le(s) importaría decirme + si** + [question]?

> **¿Llegó el vuelo 302?**
> *Did flight 302 arrive?*
> { **¿Sabe si** llegó el vuelo 302?
> **¿Puede decirme si** llegó el vuelo 302?
> **¿Le importaría decirme si** llegó el vuelo 302?

- In addition to **decir,** you can use other reporting verbs such as **confirmar** and **explicar** in this construction.

- To make a more formal request, use the conditional form **¿Podría(n)...?** (*Could you . . . ?*) instead of **¿Puede(n)...?** (*Can you . . . ?*).

13A.2 Describe a trip

Review of past tenses: use of the preterite to give opinions 5.2.3, 5.4.3, 5.6, 5.11.1

- Use the **pretérito indefinido** of the verbs and constructions **ser, parecer + [adjective],** and **gustar/encantar** in order to give opinions about a past experience.

> El viaje **fue** increíble.
> *The trip **was** incredible.*

> El hotel **nos pareció** muy bonito.
> *We thought that the hotel was very nice.*

> **Nos encantó** hacer una visita guiada de la ciudad.
> *We loved taking a guided tour of the city.*

¡Póngalo en práctica!

G1 **Conversación** Complete la conversación entre Paula y el responsable del quiosco de información.

> ¿(1)........................... (Poder, usted) confirmarme la hora de salida del vuelo 5544?

> Sí, a las 19:45 h.

> ¿(2)........................... (Saber, usted) cuál es la puerta de embarque?

> Sí, es la puerta 22.

> Gracias, y ¿puede decirme (3)........................... llegar hasta allí?

> Sí, tiene que seguir el pasillo a la derecha hasta el fondo.

> Le hago una última pregunta. ¿Le importaría decirme (4)........................... llega el vuelo de Ciudad de Guatemala?

> Sí. Tiene prevista su llegada a las 18:00 h.

G2 **Completar** Complete las oraciones con la forma correcta del verbo en el **pretérito indefinido** o el **pretérito imperfecto.**

- ¿Cómo te (1)............... (ir) en Perú, Antonio? ¿En qué parte del país (2)............... (estar)?
- En Cuzco, cerca de Machu Picchu. (3)............... (Ser) una experiencia estupenda. Las ruinas nos (4)............... (parecer) increíbles, pero el alojamiento no nos (5)............... (gustar) mucho. (6)............... (Estar) muy lejos del centro. Eso (7)............... (ser) lo único malo. Lo bueno es que (8)............... (haber) gente de todo el mundo.

S Practice more at **vhlcentral.com.**

13A.3 Make recommendations

(no) te lo recomiendo 6.8
yo que tú/yo en tu lugar + [*conditional*] 5.17.1, 5.17.3

- Use the e→ie stem-changing verb **recomendar** to give recommendations.

  > ¿Viajar a Costa Rica? **Te lo recomiendo.**
  > *Traveling to Costa Rica?* **I recommend it (to you).**

- Use the indirect object pronoun **te** followed by the neuter pronoun **lo** (*it*) to refer to general actions or ideas without relating them to a specific object or concrete example. When referring to a specific place or thing, use a direct object pronoun that agrees with this object (**lo, la, los, las**).

  > Las empanadas son riquísimas. Te **las** recomiendo.
  > *The empanadas are delicious. I recommend **them** (to you).*

- To make the same recommendation in a formal setting, say **Se lo/la/los/las recomiendo.**

- To say what you would do, use the construction **yo que tú/usted** or **yo en tu/su lugar** (*if I were you*) + [*conditional*].

  > **Yo que tú viajaría** a Buenos Aires.
  > *If I were you, I would travel to Buenos Aires.*

- The conditional (**condicional simple**) is a one-word tense equivalent to the English *would* + [*verb*].

  > Yo en su lugar **iría** en coche y **evitaría** el tren.
  > *If I were you,* **I would go** *by car and* **I'd avoid** *the train.*

- Form the conditional of regular verbs by adding the conditional endings to the infinitive. Note that all forms carry a written accent. The endings are the same for **-ar, -er,** and **-ir** verbs.

	VIAJAR	COMER	IR
(yo)	viajar**ía**	comer**ía**	ir**ía**
(tú)	viajar**ías**	comer**ías**	ir**ías**
(usted, él, ella)	viajar**ía**	comer**ía**	ir**ía**
(nosotros/as)	viajar**íamos**	comer**íamos**	ir**íamos**
(vosotros/as)	viajar**íais**	comer**íais**	ir**íais**
(ustedes, ellos/as)	viajar**ían**	comer**ían**	ir**ían**

13A.4 Wish someone a good trip

que tenga(n)/disfrute(n) 5.21.1, 14.26

- To tell someone to have a good trip, say **¡Buen viaje!** (*Have a good trip!/Bon voyage!*). If the person is traveling on an airplane, say **¡Feliz vuelo!**

- You can also use the following expressions: **¡Que tenga(n) un feliz vuelo!** and **¡Que disfrute(n) del viaje!**

¡Póngalo en práctica!

G3 **Pistas** Escriba la recomendación correcta según las pistas.

> Modelo: esta empresa / a usted
> *Se la recomiendo.*

1. esa playa / a ti
2. ese hotel / a usted
3. los plátanos fritos / a ti
4. las clases de salsa / a usted
5. este postre / a ti
6. esa excursión / a usted

G4 **Recomendaciones** Complete la conversación.

- Quiero viajar a las islas Canarias en agosto, ¿qué opinan?

- No te (1)...................... recomiendo; hay muchísimos turistas. Viaja en invierno; es la época ideal. Yo que (2).................... en agosto (3).................... (ir) a los Pirineos.

- ¡Ah! ¡El sur de Portugal! ¡Es espectacular! Te lo (4)...................... Yo en tu (5)...................., (6).................... (viajar) allí.

G5 **El condicional** Escriba la forma correcta del condicional.

1. yo, comprar	
2. Delfina, hablar	
3. nosotros, leer	
4. tú, descansar	
5. vosotros, estudiar	
6. los profesores, dar	
7. ustedes, alquilar	
8. yo, recomendar	

G6 **Oraciones** Complete las oraciones.

Señores pasajeros, gracias por volar con nosotros. En nombre de toda la tripulación, que (1)................ un feliz vuelo y (2)................ disfruten del viaje.

- Mañana salimos para el Caribe.

- (3)...

Practice more at **vhlcentral.com.**

VOCABULARIO 🔊 Ⓢ Vocabulary Tools

Señores pasajeros

¿Le importaría...?	Would you mind . . . ?
señores pasajeros	passengers/ladies and gentlemen
el altavoz	loudspeaker
el andén	platform
el cambio de dinero	foreign currency exchange
el carrito	baggage cart
la confirmación	confirmation
el control de equipaje	baggage screening
el control de pasaportes	passport control; immigration
el destino	destination
las divisas	foreign currency
el embarque	boarding
la entrega de equipaje	baggage claim
la frecuencia	frequency
la hora de embarque	boarding time
la hora de llegada	arrival time
la hora de salida	departure time
el mostrador de facturación	check-in counter
la observación	remark
la puerta de embarque	boarding gate
el/la responsable	person in charge
la sala de llegada	arrival lounge/area
el/la supervisor(a)	supervisor
la tarifa	fare
la terminal	terminal
salir	to depart
cancelado/a	cancelled
procedente de	arriving from
con retraso	delayed

Rincones escondidos

el/la auxiliar de vuelo	flight attendant
el cambio de asiento	seat change
la casa particular	private home
el/la cubano/a	Cuban person
la(s) plaza(s)	seat(s)
el viaje de novios	honeymoon
el viaje organizado	package tour
alojarse	to stay
apuntarse a	to sign up for
averiarse	to break down
perder (e:ie) un vuelo	to miss a flight
preparar un viaje	to organize a trip
proponer	to propose, to suggest
recomendar (e:ie) (un lugar)	to recommend (a place)
reservar los billetes	to book the tickets
trasladar	to transport
excelente	excellent
hermoso/a	lovely
hospitalario/a	hospitable
demasiado	too

Nelson y Edgar

a bordo	on board
¡Que disfruten a bordo!	Enjoy your flight!
¡Que tengan un feliz vuelo!	Have a good flight!
la aerolínea abanderada	national airline
el asiento	seat
el caballero	gentleman
el cinturón de seguridad	seat belt
el estuche	case

la frazada (Amér. L.)	blanket
la gaseosa (Amér. L.)	soft drink
el/la jefe/a de cabina	purser
el/la mesero/a (Amér. L.)	waiter/waitress
el ómnibus (Arg.)	bus
la pantalla	screen
el respaldo del asiento	seat back
la seguridad	safety
el trayecto	route
abrigarse	to wrap up
abrocharse	to fasten
apoyar	to support
comprobar (o:ue)	to check
cumplir	to reach; to fulfill
dar ánimo	to offer encouragement
exigir (j) sacrificios	to require sacrifices
extrañar (Amér. L.)	to miss
hacer escala	to stop over
hacer fila	to get/wait in line
retirar	to remove
sonreír (e:i)	to smile
amabilísimo/a	very friendly
árido/a	arid
(semi-)cama	(semi-)sleeper
diario/a	daily
exquisito/a	delicious
nacional	domestic
plegado/a	folded
privatizado/a	privatized
vertical	upright
al horno	baked

Variación léxica

el/la auxiliar de vuelo ⟷ **el/la azafato/a** (Arg., Esp.) ⟷ **el/la tripulante de cabina de pasajeros** (Amér. L.)

la entrega de equipaje ⟷ **la recogida de equipajes** (Esp.) ⟷ **el retiro de equipaje** (Arg.)

extrañar (Amér. L.) ⟷ **echar de menos** (Esp.)

la frazada (Amér. L.) ⟷ **la manta** (Esp.) ⟷ **la cobija** (Amér. L.)

hacer fila ⟷ **hacer cola**

nacional ⟷ **interno/a** ⟷ **de cabotaje** (Arg.)

el viaje de novios ⟷ **la luna de miel**

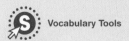

Vocabulary Tools

MUNDO TECNOLÓGICO

¿Imprescindibles?

@ Comopodiamossobrevivirsinellos.com

| INICIO | ACERCA DE... | CONTACTO | ARCHIVO | ENLACES | FOTOS | VIDEOS |

¿Cómo podíamos (sobre)vivir antes sin ellos?

☐ *iPod* Este pequeño aparato que se puede llevar en el bolsillo fue una revolución porque permitía escuchar música en todas partes, no ocupaba espacio y tenía mucha capacidad. Cambió nuestro modo de escuchar música. A pesar de todo, algunos nostálgicos prefieren el disco de vinilo o el CD porque permiten escuchar música en compañía y sin tanto aislamiento social. ¡Imprescindible en muchos momentos de placer!

☐ GPS Los primeros se construyeron en los años ochenta; sin embargo, no empezaron a fabricarse en serie en los coches hasta principios del siglo XXI. Llegas antes a tu destino y ya no tienes las típicas tensiones del viaje o de si vas a llegar o no. Aunque hay quienes prefieren no usarlos porque son una causa de distracción, sin duda son imprescindibles para muchos.

☐ Wi-Fi Aunque al principio no era fácil encontrar lugares desde donde conectarse a Internet sin cables, finalmente se transformó en moneda corriente en aeropuertos, hoteles, universidades, empresas y hogares. A pesar de ofrecer menor seguridad y velocidad, hoy es imprescindible porque es sinónimo de movilidad y libertad.

☐ Teléfono inteligente Al principio tenía menos capacidad y solo lo usábamos para hablar. Ahora puedes escuchar música, guardar canciones y fotos, enviar correos... A pesar de ser muy útil, tiene su lado malo. Ahora estamos siempre localizables. ¿Han mejorado realmente nuestras vidas? ¿Son tan imprescindibles un *iPhone* o un *Galaxy*?

Describir situaciones y causas en el pasado

- ¿Por qué **compraste** el GPS?
- **Porque** siempre me perdía.

13B.1 Review of past tenses
porque + [*imperfect*]

Vocabulario

①

imprescindible *indispensable*

sobrevivir *to survive*

el bolsillo *pocket*

ocupar espacio *to take up space*

tener capacidad *to have (storage) capacity*

a pesar de todo *in spite of everything*

el disco de vinilo *vinyl record*

el aislamiento *isolation*

fabricar en serie *to mass-produce*

---

1 **¿Imprescindibles?** Observe las imágenes. ¿Qué tecnologías muestran? Lea el blog y relacione las imágenes con las descripciones. ¿Cuál de estas u otras tecnologías es imprescindible para usted? ¿Cómo y por qué empezó a usarla?

2 **Describir** El dominio del inglés como lengua internacional de la ciencia, la tecnología y las comunicaciones lleva a la utilización de muchas palabras de ese idioma en español. Describa para qué sirven estas tecnologías.

- ⊙ red Wi-Fi
- ⊙ *iPhone*
- ⊙ *iPod*
- ⊙ navegador GPS

3 **Acontecimientos** Relacione estos acontecimientos con sus causas.

1. Mi empresa me dio un teléfono inteligente ......
2. Empecé a usar una red Wi-Fi ......
3. Pensé que el GPS era más seguro ......
4. Me pareció bien tener un *iPod* ......

a. porque no tenías que mirar un plano.
b. porque puedes guardar música y muchas cosas más.
c. porque podía estar conectado siempre, tanto en el jardín de casa como en un bar.
d. porque necesitaban poder localizarme siempre.

4 **Aparatos tecnológicos** Con su compañero/a, nombre otros dos aparatos tecnológicos sin los cuales no se puede (sobre)vivir en la actualidad. Expliquen su utilidad y describan cómo era la vida sin ellos en el pasado.

5 **a. Tecnología** Busque en el blog las ventajas y los inconvenientes de estas tecnologías.

	Ventajas	Inconvenientes
1. red Wi-Fi	*movilidad y libertad siempre*	*menor seguridad y velocidad*
2. teléfono inteligente	....	....
3. *iPod*	....	....
4. navegador GPS	....	....

b. Comparar Compare las ventajas y los inconvenientes y forme oraciones.

- red Wi-Fi: A pesar de ser...
- teléfono inteligente: Aunque...
- *iPod*: ...; sin embargo,...
- navegador GPS: A pesar de todo,...

6 **Relacionar ideas contrarias** Lea los intercambios sobre algunos avances tecnológicos. Dé su propio punto de vista relacionando las ideas contrarias con **aunque**, **sin embargo** y **a pesar de**. ¿Qué opina su compañero/a?

> Modelo: *Aunque es cierto que..., creo que... porque...*

Internet, los *iPod* y los reproductores de MP3 provocan el aislamiento social. De hecho, muchos jóvenes pasan horas y horas en su habitación frente a una computadora.	El acceso a redes sociales en Internet y en los celulares aumenta el número y la diversidad de contactos de la gente. La comunicación más habitual con familiares y amigos sigue siendo en persona.
Otro problema es la pobreza lingüística de los estudiantes. Acostumbrados a sintetizar los mensajes, usan un lenguaje con muchas abreviaturas, y sin comas, acentos ni vocales.	Cada uno sabe en qué contexto debe utilizar uno u otro código. En los SMS y en los correos electrónicos, este lenguaje permite ahorrar tiempo y dinero. Es una nueva forma de taquigrafía.

MI EXPERIENCIA

7 **Novedades** Hable con su compañero/a sobre la última novedad tecnológica que comenzó a usar. ¿Por qué la usa? Señale sus ventajas e inconvenientes.

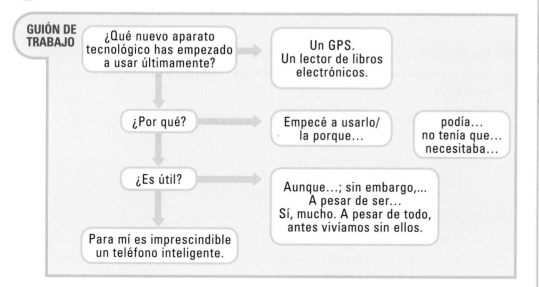

GUIÓN DE TRABAJO

¿Qué nuevo aparato tecnológico has empezado a usar últimamente? → Un GPS. Un lector de libros electrónicos.

¿Por qué? → Empecé a usarlo/la porque... · podía... no tenía que... necesitaba...

¿Es útil? → Aunque...; sin embargo,... A pesar de ser... Sí, mucho. A pesar de todo, antes vivíamos sin ellos.

Para mí es imprescindible un teléfono inteligente.

Relacionar ideas contrarias

- **A pesar de** no necesitar el GPS, lo compré. **Aunque** era un poco caro, valió la pena.
- Es un poco caro; **sin embargo**, es útil.

13B.2 **a pesar de, aunque, sin embargo**

Vocabulario *cont.*

aunque *although*

ser moneda corriente *to be common*

la velocidad *speed*

la movilidad *mobility*

la libertad *freedom*

el teléfono inteligente *smartphone*

guardar (canciones/fotos) *to save/ store (songs/photos)*

el lado malo *bad side*

estar localizable *to be reachable*

la revolución, la distracción
② _____

la red Wi-Fi *Wi-Fi network*

el navegador GPS *GPS*
③ _____

estar conectado/a *to be connected (to the Internet)*

localizar *to get hold of, to locate*
⑤ _____

el inconveniente *drawback*
⑥ _____

el reproductor de MP3 *MP3 player*

la red social *social network*

la pobreza *mediocrity*

estar acostumbrado/a a *to be used to*

la abreviatura *abbreviation*

la vocal *vowel*

el código *code*

la taquigrafía *shorthand*

sintetizar
⑦ _____

el lector de libros electrónicos *e-reader*

SAM: Actividades pp. 277–279

¿Un buen equipo?

contador

Ramón: Es serio y metódico. Su jefe está encantado con él, pero sus compañeros piensan que es un poco aburrido. Solo hay una cosa que no le gusta de su trabajo: las horas extras.

analista de marketing

Rosa: Dinámica e innovadora. A veces es demasiado impaciente, sobre todo con su jefe, que por cierto es su ex. Quiere abrir su propia empresa porque prefiere trabajar sola.

ejecutiva de ventas

Olga: No soporta la desorganización. Aunque es un poco tímida, le gusta trabajar en equipo, sobre todo con Rosa. Es muy ordenada y puntual.

director

Jaume: Es el ex de Rosa. Es un gran comunicador y muy bromista, aunque sus bromas solamente le parecen divertidas a él. Le encanta su trabajo. Sus empleados piensan que es un tirano.

Expresar posesión

● **Mis** compañeros de trabajo son estupendos, ¿y **los tuyos**?

■ **Los míos** también.

13B.3 Possessive adjectives and pronouns

Vocabulario

8

el/la contador(a) (*Amér. L.*) *accountant*

serio/a *reliable*

solo/solamente *only*

el/la analista de marketing *marketing analyst*

sobre todo *above all*

el/la ejecutivo/a de ventas *sales executive*

ordenado/a *organized*

ser un(a) gran comunicador(a) *to be a great communicator*

bromista *fond of joking*

el/la tirano/a *tyrant*

metódico/a, innovador/a, impaciente, puntual

9

discutir *to argue*

hacer horas extras *to do overtime*

comprensivo/a *understanding*

No te preocupes. *Don't worry.*

Te entiendo perfectamente. *I understand you perfectly.*

No pasa nada. *Everything is OK.*

estar motivado/a *to be motivated*

desagradable *unpleasant*

Siento verte así. *I'm sorry to see you like this.*

---

8 **Descripciones** Lea las descripciones y subraye los adjetivos que indican cómo son estas personas. ¿Cree que su perfil es adecuado a su puesto?

9 **a. Conversaciones** Escuche las conversaciones y complete la información. Lea de nuevo las descripciones si es necesario.

	¿Quién habla?	¿De qué hablan?
Conversación 1		
Conversación 2		

b. Opiniones ¿Coinciden las opiniones de los empleados y de su jefe? Vuelva a escuchar las conversaciones y elija la opción correcta en cada caso.

1
● ¿En **tu/tuya** empresa tenéis que hacer horas extras?
■ No, en **mi/mía** empresa no.
● Nuestro jefe es un tirano. El **vuestro/vuestra** es más comprensivo. Yo con **el mío/mi**, además, no me llevo bien.
■ Bueno, Rosa, no te preocupes.
● Quiero tener mi empresa, con mis ideas, no las **suyas/sus**.
■ Te entiendo perfectamente.

2
● ¡Hola, Jaume! ¿Cómo estás?
■ Bien, vengo de la oficina.
● ¿A estas horas? ¡Es tardísimo!
■ Sí, pero no pasa nada. **Mis/Mi** empleados están muy motivados y quieren hacer horas extras. Y tú, ¿qué tal en **tu/tuyo** nuevo trabajo?
● No muy bien, mis compañeros son un poco desagradables.
■ Siento verte así, no todas las empresas tienen tan buenos empleados como los **míos/mis**.

10 **Entrevista** Entreviste a un(a) compañero/a de su grupo, acerca de su familia y sus intereses. Luego comente los resultados con el grupo, siguiendo el modelo.

Modelo: ● *Mi hermana tiene catorce años, pero la suya tiene doce.* /
● *Su hermana tiene doce años, pero la mía tiene catorce.*

Cuestionario:

1. ¿Cuántos años tiene tu hermano/a?
2. ¿Cómo se llaman tus padres?
3. ¿Quién es la persona más bromista de tu familia?
4. ¿Cómo te llevas con tus vecinos?
5. ¿Cuál es tu clase más divertida?

11 Mejores amigos Piense en dos o tres características de su mejor amigo/a y compárelas con las de su compañero/a.

> Modelo: • *Mi mejor amigo/a es…* • *El/La mío/a…*

12 Expresiones Relacione estas expresiones del diálogo con la función que tienen.

> ¡Ánimo! • No te preocupes./No pasa nada.
> Siento verte así. • Te entiendo perfectamente.

Cuando quieres expresar…
1. que has vivido algo similar
2. que sientes la situación
3. calma o tranquilidad
4. energía o fuerza moral

13 a. Expresiones equivalentes Lea las descripciones de la página anterior y anote expresiones equivalentes a las siguientes.

únicamente: …………………… especialmente: ……………………

b. Diálogo Cree un diálogo a partir de una de estas situaciones. Su compañero/a intenta consolarlo y animarlo usando las expresiones anteriores.

Solo tienes una semana de vacaciones en marzo y tus amigos tienen dos.

Tiene un contrato de trabajo de solamente veinte horas, pero trabaja cuarenta horas.

No se lleva bien con su familia, sobre todo con su hermano pequeño.

14 a. El mundo académico En el mundo académico actual hay una mayor igualdad entre hombres y mujeres que en el pasado. El número de mujeres que obtienen un título universitario es igual o superior al de los hombres. ¿Cómo es la situación en las diferentes carreras que ofrece su universidad?

b. La mujer en el trabajo Lea la nota de la derecha sobre la presencia de la mujer en el mercado laboral. ¿Por qué cree que es así?

MI EXPERIENCIA

15 Carreras Piense en la carrera que está estudiando. Compárela con la carrera que sigue su compañero/a.

GUIÓN DE TRABAJO

¿Qué carrera estás estudiando? → Medicina/Derecho/Economía/…

¿Por qué elegiste esa carrera? → …, y sobre todo porque…

¿Qué empleo esperas conseguir con ese título? → Mi título me habilita para trabajar en/de… ¿Y el tuyo?

Consolar y animar

- Siento oír eso/verte así.
- Gracias.
- No te preocupes, no pasa nada.
- Estoy cansada de trabajar horas extras.
- ¡Ánimo! Te entiendo perfectamente porque me pasa algo similar.

13B.4 **siento + [infinitive]**
te entiendo, no pasa nada, no te preocupes, ¡Ánimo!

Vocabulario

(12)
Siento oír eso. *I'm sorry to hear that.*

(13)
únicamente *only*
el contrato de trabajo *employment contract*

(14)
el título *degree*
el puesto directivo *managerial position*

(15)
habilitar *to qualify*
la perspectiva *prospect*

Estrategia

Destacar una información
En mi empresa tenemos vacaciones solo/solamente en agosto.
Trabajo en equipo, sobre todo con Ana y Nacho.

La mujer en el trabajo

El 40 por ciento de los empleados mundiales son mujeres. Las áreas principales donde trabajan son la agricultura, la industria y el sector servicios. Sin embargo, aún hay discriminación, como menores salarios y falta de acceso a puestos directivos.

SAM: Actividades pp. 280–282

Cristina Rubio, asesora laboral

@ www.coachingporcristina.mx

En la empresa hay que tener psicología

A pesar de estar casi la mitad de nuestras vidas en el trabajo, no prestamos atención a los aspectos emocionales que condicionan nuestra actitud, nuestra motivación y nuestra forma de relacionarnos con los demás: identificar cuál es la tuya te puede ayudar a ser más eficaz.

Después de muchos años de experiencia como psicóloga, me especialicé en el área de *coaching* para empresas porque cuando era terapeuta encontraba muchos casos de conflicto y estrés emocional que tenían su origen en el trabajo y el ambiente laboral. Como en todos los ámbitos de nuestra vida, en la empresa "hay que tener psicología". ¿Qué significa esto? Comprender tus necesidades y las de los demás para saber manejarlas.

¿Cuál es la labor de *coaching*?

La labor de *coaching* se dirige a equipos que quieren ser eficaces, desarrollar habilidades concretas y conseguir sus objetivos. Los aspectos más humanos, como la calidad de las relaciones personales y el nivel de satisfacción personal del equipo, es decir, un buen ambiente laboral, son fundamentales para sentirnos realizados profesionalmente.

Un objetivo triple: persona, empresa y entorno afectivo.

El objetivo es triple. Por un lado, ayudo a las personas a sentirse realizadas a través del programa **"Tus emociones son las mías"**. La empatía es una de las bases fundamentales de la inteligencia emocional en la resolución de conflictos: solo comprendiendo las necesidades y, sobre todo, las motivaciones del otro, podemos buscar soluciones.

Por otro, asesoro a los departamentos de Recursos Humanos de las empresas para crear estructuras organizativas y equipos de trabajo eficaces con el programa **"Las alegrías de tus empleados son las tuyas"**, porque sólo un empleado feliz es un empleado motivado.

Y por último, con el programa **"La estabilidad de tu entorno es la tuya"**, contribuyo a la mejora de la interacción de los equipos de trabajo.

> **CRISTINA RUBIO**
> *Coaching* para empresas
> Boulevard Díaz Ordaz 140,
> Monterrey, 64650 (México)
> Licenciada en Psicología y Economía
> Máster en Gestión de Recursos Humanos

Estructurar la información

Por un lado, queremos ayudar a las personas; por otro, buscamos mejorar el rendimiento de las empresas.

13B.5 por un lado/una parte...
por otro/otra...

Vocabulario

16

el/la asesor(a) laboral *labor consultant*

casi *almost*

relacionarse *to interact*

eficaz *effective; efficient*

el ambiente laboral *work environment*

---

16 **a. Datos** Observe los datos de la tarjeta de nuestra protagonista. ¿A qué se dedica? ¿Cuál es su formación?

b. Servicios ¿Qué tipo de servicios cree que ofrece el *coaching* para empresas? Lea la página web de Cristina para comprobarlo. ¿Qué opina de estos servicios?

17 **a. Psicología en la empresa** ¿Cuáles son los programas que ofrece Cristina y cuál es su triple objetivo?

b. Estructurar la información ¿Qué aspectos pueden influir en el trabajo? Organice la información usando la construcción **Por un lado, ...; por otro,....**

18 **Expresión** ¿Qué cree que significa la expresión "hay que tener psicología"? Compare sus ideas con las de su compañero/a. ¿Cree que la psicología nos ayuda a ser más eficaces en el trabajo?

19 **Responder** Imagine un servicio de *coaching* para su universidad. ¿Qué tipo de persona lo dirige? ¿Qué objetivos tiene? ¿A través de qué medios se comunica con los estudiantes? ¿Aprovecha las nuevas tecnologías? ¿Cuáles?

20 **a. Leer** Lea estos anuncios que la bolsa de trabajo de su universidad ha enviado por correo electrónico. ¿Cuáles son algunas ventajas de hacer una pasantía de verano?

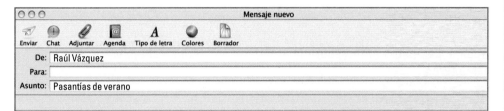

| | | | | | |

BOLSA DE EMPLEO

Para obtener más información sobre alguna de estas pasantías de verano o si necesita ayuda con el proceso de solicitud, no dude en escribirme.

Raúl Vázquez Peña
Orientador profesional

Buscamos estudiantes de las carreras de Recursos Humanos o Psicología (excluyente) para colaborar como auxiliares en la selección de personal. Las tareas principales serán: atención telefónica, lectura y clasificación de currículum vítae y asistencia a los entrevistadores. Se requiere una personalidad metódica, ordenada y analítica. Horario a convenir. Haz clic aquí para enviar tu solicitud.

Invitamos a estudiantes de Economía con un excelente desempeño° académico a trabajar en nuestro departamento de auditoría° interna. Los estudiantes seleccionados participarán en proyectos que requieren orientación a los resultados, trabajo bajo presión° y atención al detalle, así como capacidad para trabajar en equipo. Los pasantes trabajarán un promedio° de ocho horas diarias. ¡Te esperamos! Inscríbete con tu currículum vítae por Internet.

Ofrecemos pasantías para estudiantes universitarios interesados en trabajar con la comunidad latina. Los candidatos seleccionados darán clases de computación° en español. Deberán tener una actitud positiva, buenas habilidades interpersonales y el deseo de ayudar a la comunidad. Se requiere excelente dominio de computación y un buen nivel de español. De 16 a 20 horas a la semana. Envía tu carta de presentación y tu currículum vítae.

desempeño *performance* **auditoría** *auditing* **bajo presión** *under pressure* **promedio** *average* **computación** *computing*

b. Comentar Comente con su compañero/a cuál de estos trabajos le resulta más interesante. ¿Qué requisitos deben reunir los candidatos para ese puesto? ¿Cree que usted podría postularse? ¿Por qué?

21 **Escribir** Escriba un anuncio para una oferta de empleo. Describa las responsabilidades del puesto y el tipo de candidato que se busca (formación, personalidad, etc.).

22 **a. Palabras extranjeras** Lea el texto sobre el español de los negocios. ¿Qué palabras extranjeras se usan regularmente en inglés?

En el español de los negocios y la tecnología, a menudo se usan palabras que proceden de otros idiomas, especialmente del inglés, como *blog*, *web*, *link*, *online* o *coaching*, *mailing*, *marketing*, *master*, *freelance*... Algunas tienen una adaptación gráfica al español, como "máster" y otras tienen un equivalente muy usado, como "enlace" (*link*), "mercadeo" (*marketing*) o "autónomo" (*freelance*).

b. Más palabras ¿Conoce más palabras similares a estas en español? Compártalas con sus compañeros.

Practice more at **vhlcentral.com**.

Vocabulario *cont.*

comprender *to understand*
la necesidad *need*
manejar *to manage*
sentirse realizado/a *to feel fulfilled*
el entorno afectivo *emotional environment*
por un lado/por una parte *on the one hand*
por otro lado/por otra parte *on the other hand*
asesorar *to advise*
los Recursos Humanos (RR.HH.) *Human Resources (HR)*
el equipo de trabajo *work team*
la gestión *management*
el rendimiento *performance*
la actitud, la satisfacción personal, la empatía, la inteligencia emocional, la resolución de conflictos, la estabilidad
20
la bolsa de trabajo *job placement office*
la pasantía de verano *summer internship*
la solicitud *application*
No dude en... *Don't hesitate to . . .*
el/la orientador(a) profesional *career counselor*
excluyente *a must, required*
a convenir *to be agreed upon*
hacer clic *to click*
el/la pasante *intern*
el/la candidato/a *applicant*
el dominio *command*
la carta de presentación *cover letter*
reunir los requisitos *to meet the requirements*
postularse *to apply*

SAM: Actividades pp. 283–288

23 **a. Motivaciones** ¿Cuáles cree que son las principales motivaciones para permanecer en un empleo? Elija las tres más importantes para usted.

- ○ el dinero
- ○ la satisfacción con el trabajo
- ○ conseguir un ascenso°
- ○ la relación con jefes y/o compañeros
- ○ otros...

b. La satisfacción con el trabajo Lea estos datos sobre la satisfacción con el trabajo y coméntelos con sus compañeros.

La satisfacción con el trabajo: principal motivación para permanecer en un empleo

Según una encuesta que se realizó a 7508 trabajadores de América del Norte, Europa y Asia

En América del Norte, la satisfacción con el trabajo también es el factor que más anima a los trabajadores a querer permanecer en un empleo (33%), seguido de buenas condiciones laborales, como horarios flexibles, poco tiempo de viaje al trabajo, etc. (15%).

El dinero no es lo que más influye a la hora de dar un giro a la vida laboral. Aquellos que dijeron que, de poder elegir, no permanecerían en su trabajo actual es porque sienten que su carrera está estancada° (30%), no les gusta su trabajo ni desarrollan todo su potencial (25%), o no se llevan bien con su jefe (18%).

conseguir un ascenso *to get a promotion* **estancado/a** *stuck*

c. Opinar ¿Está de acuerdo con los resultados? Si no lo está, ¿cuáles cree que son las principales motivaciones entre sus amigos y familiares?

 T A R E A   F I N A L

Encuesta de ambiente laboral

Tome notas sobre los factores que favorecen la relación con los compañeros de trabajo y mejoran el ambiente laboral.

Compare sus notas con las de su compañero/a y elaboren preguntas a partir de sus notas. Elijan las mejores preguntas y anótenlas en una tarjeta.

Hagan una lluvia de ideas con la clase y coloquen todas las preguntas en un cartel. Hagan la encuesta a sus compañeros.

Y O   P U E D O . . .

- **Puedo describir situaciones en el pasado.**
  Cuente cómo se comunicaba la gente sin celular y sin computadora.

- **Puedo relacionar ideas contrarias.**
  Complete esta oración:
  La gente antes no tenía celular; ....,
  se comunicaba sin problemas.

- **Puedo expresar posesión.**
  Mi celular es pequeño, el .... (de Sara), no.

- **Puedo consolar y animar.**
  Diga todas las expresiones que sabe para expresar consuelo y dar ánimo.

- **Puedo estructurar la información.**
  ¿Qué piensa usted que se debe hacer cuando hay conflictos laborales?

  Por una parte...

GRAMÁTICA FUNCIONAL Ⓢ Tutorials

13B.1 Describe situations and causes in the past

Review of past tenses: **porque** + [*imperfect*]   5.2.3, 5.4.3, 5.6

- To describe situations and causes in the past, use the **pretérito imperfecto**. Use **porque** (*because*) to express a cause with the construction [*result*] + **porque** + [*cause (imperfect)*].

  > Empecé a usar un teléfono inteligente **porque podía** tenerlo todo en un solo aparato.
  > *I started to use a smartphone **because I was able to** have everything in just one device.*

- In order to begin a sentence by stating the cause, use **como** (*since/as*) + [*cause (imperfect)*], + [*result*].

  > **Como tenía** mucho sueño ayer por la tarde, dormí una siesta.
  > ***As I was** very sleepy yesterday afternoon, I took a nap.*

13B.2 Relate opposing ideas

a pesar de, aunque, sin embargo   12.11

- Use **aunque** (*although, even though*) to relate opposing ideas. Use the construction Aunque [*clause*], + [*clause*].

  > **Aunque** cuesta un poco más, la conexión rápida vale la pena.
  > ***Although** it costs a bit more, the fast connection is worth it.*

- **Aunque** can also be used in the middle of a sentence, in the construction [*clause*] + **aunque** [*clause*].

  > Ayer nos perdimos **aunque** usamos el nuevo GPS.
  > *Yesterday we got lost **even though** we used the new GPS.*

- Use a **pesar de** + [*infinitive/noun*] to express *despite* or *in spite of*.

  > **A pesar de tener** mucha música en mi *iPod*, siempre escucho las diez mismas canciones.
  > *In spite of having a lot of music on my iPod, I always listen to the same ten songs.*

- Use a **pesar de todo** (*in spite of everything*) before a clause to express an idea that opposes what was stated or implied earlier.

  > Internet genera inconvenientes de seguridad. También genera adicción. **A pesar de todo**, es una herramienta muy beneficiosa.
  > *The Internet creates problems of security. It's also addictive. **In spite of all that**, it is a very beneficial tool.*

- To express *however*, use **sin embargo** + [*clause*].

  > Los nuevos celulares son complicados. **Sin embargo**, nos permiten realizar muchas funciones.
  > *The new cell phones are complicated. **However**, they allow us to perform many functions.*

¡Póngalo en práctica!

G1 **Completar** Complete las oraciones con la forma correcta del verbo en el pretérito indefinido o el pretérito imperfecto.

1. Leila .... (estudiar) psicología en la universidad porque le .... (interesar) la mente humana.

2. Damián y Sergio .... (viajar) a España el verano pasado porque .... (tener) que hacer investigación para sus tesis doctorales.

3. Como siempre .... (nosotros, trabajar) hasta tarde, ... (nosotros, empezar) a pedir pizza con mucha frecuencia.

4. Carlos .... (comprar) un GPS porque no le .... (gustar) usar un plano.

G2 **Elegir** Elija el final más lógico para cada oración.

1. Aunque me gustaría comprar el nuevo *iPhone*, ...

2. A pesar de ser una herramienta útil, ...

3. Prefiero compartir las noticias importantes en persona; sin embargo, ...

4. La red Wi-Fi nos permite estar conectados sin cables, ...

   a. el GPS puede ser una distracción para el conductor.

   b. aunque a veces hay problemas de conectividad.

   c. el celular que tengo funciona perfectamente.

   d. las videoconferencias me permiten hablar con amigos que viven lejos.

G3 **A pesar de todo...** Complete las oraciones con las expresiones **aunque, a pesar de (todo)** y **sin embargo**.

1. .... los precios bajos, decidí no comprar una agenda electrónica porque prefiero usar una agenda de papel.

2. Con el celular estamos localizables las 24 horas del día, ... no siempre lo queremos.

3. Las computadoras portátiles son fáciles de transportar; ...., también son fáciles de romper.

4. La televisión genera muchas controversias. ...., puede utilizarse con fines educativos.

5. .... ampliar las conexiones, Internet también provoca aislamiento.

6. .... puedo hacer llamadas con mi celular, prefiero mandar mensajes de texto.

 Practice more at **vhlcentral.com**.

GRAMÁTICA FUNCIONAL

13B.3 Express possession

Possessive adjectives and pronouns **8.2**

- Use possessive adjectives with nouns to express possession. You learned possessive adjectives in **5B.2**.

    > **Mis** hermanos viven en Barcelona.
    > *My siblings live in Barcelona.*

- Use a possessive pronoun in place of [*possessive adjective*] + [*noun*] to express *mine, yours, his,* etc. Possessive pronouns agree in number and gender with the nouns they replace.

	singular		plural	
(yo)	el mío	la mía	los míos	las mías
(tú)	el tuyo	la tuya	los tuyos	las tuyas
(usted, él, ella)	el suyo	la suya	los suyos	las suyas
(nosotros/as)	el nuestro	la nuestra	los nuestros	las nuestras
(vosotros/as)	el vuestro	la vuestra	los vuestros	las vuestras
(ustedes, ellos/as)	el suyo	la suya	los suyos	las suyas

    > Mi celular ya no funciona bien. ¿Te gusta **el tuyo**?
    > *My cell phone does not work well anymore. Do you like **yours**?*

- Use the possessive pronoun with the corresponding definite article (**el, la, los, las**).

13B.4 Offer consolation and encouragement

siento + [*infinitive*], **te entiendo, ¡ánimo!** **5.13, 7.4, 14.26**

- To console someone, say **te entiendo** (*I understand [you]*), **no pasa nada** (*it's OK*), or **no te preocupes** (*don't worry*).

- Another way to console someone is with the construction **siento** + [*infinitive*] (*I am sorry . . .*).

    > Siento oír eso.   Siento verte tan triste.
    > *I'm sorry to hear that.*   *I'm sorry to see you're so sad.*

- Use **eso** (*that*) to refer to an unidentified or unspecified object, situation, or concept. You will learn more about **eso** and neuter demonstrative pronouns in **15B**.

- To offer encouragement or to cheer someone up, use expressions such as **¡Ánimo!** (*Cheer up!*), **¡Venga!** (*Come on!*), **¡Anímate!** (*Go for it!/Cheer up!*), or **¡Dale!** (*Come on!*). The use of these expressions varies according to country or region.

13B.5 Organize information

por un lado/una parte... por otro/otra **14.1**

- To structure an argument with more than one idea, use the construction **por un lado/una parte... por otro (lado)/otra (parte)** (*on the one hand . . . on the other*).

    > **Por un lado**, me gusta tu propuesta; **por otro**, me gustaría agregar un detalle más.
    > *On the one hand, I like your proposal; on the other, I would like to add one more detail.*

- Pay attention to agreement in this construction; always use the pairs **lado/otro** and **parte/otra**.

¡Póngalo en práctica!

G4 **Pronombre posesivo** Escriba el pronombre posesivo correspondiente.

    Modelo: mi tío ....*el mío*....

1. nuestro jefe ....
2. tus responsabilidades ....
3. su empresa ....
4. nuestros problemas ....
5. mis vacaciones ....

G5 **Pistas** Complete las oraciones con la forma apropiada del adjetivo o pronombre posesivo según las pistas.

1. Ese es Antonio; es el jefe de Susana, y también es .... (de ella) amigo.

2. ● Mis compañeros son estupendos.
   ¿Y .... (de ti)?
   ■ .... también.

3. ● Nuestra oficina está en el centro.
   ¿Y .... (de vosotros)?
   ■ .... también.

4. ● .... (de mí) hermana se llama Celia.
   ¿Y .... (de ti)?
   ■ .... se llama Beatriz.

G6 **Diálogos** Complete los diálogos con expresiones de consuelo y de ánimo.

● No estoy contento con mi trabajo.
■ No te (1)........................, seguro que encuentras una solución.

● He tenido un conflicto con mis compañeros de trabajo y estoy preocupado.
■ Te (2)........................, pero estas cosas pasan. Ya se va a resolver el problema.

● Tengo que dar una presentación mañana en el trabajo y estoy muy nerviosa.
■ (3)¡........................! Seguro que te sale bien.

● No voy a poder terminar este proyecto para mañana.
■ No (4)........................ nada, estamos todos atrasados.

G7 **Oraciones** Complete las oraciones.

1. Tener un buen clima laboral beneficia por un lado al trabajador, que se siente más cómodo y satisfecho, y .... a la empresa, porque aumenta la eficacia.

2. Hay muchos factores que contribuyen a un buen clima laboral. ...., es importante tener una buena relación con tus compañeros, y por otra, la satisfacción personal con tu trabajo.

Practice more at **vhlcentral.com**.

VOCABULARIO 🔊 Ⓢ Vocabulary Tools

¿Imprescindibles?

la abreviatura	abbreviation
el aislamiento	isolation
el bolsillo	pocket
el código	code
el disco de vinilo	vinyl record
la distracción	distraction
el inconveniente	drawback
el lado malo	bad side
el lector de libros electrónicos	e-reader
la libertad	freedom
la movilidad	mobility
el navegador GPS	GPS
la pobreza	mediocrity
la red social	social network
la red Wi-Fi	Wi-Fi network
el reproductor de MP3	MP3 player
la revolución	revolution
la taquigrafía	shorthand
el teléfono inteligente	smartphone
la velocidad	speed
la vocal	vowel
estar acostumbrado/a a	to be used to
estar conectado/a	to be connected (to the Internet)
estar localizable	to be reachable
fabricar en serie	to mass-produce
guardar (canciones/fotos)	to save/store (songs/photos)
localizar	to get hold of, to locate
ocupar espacio	to take up space
ser moneda corriente	to be common
sintetizar	to synthesize
sobrevivir	to survive
tener capacidad	to have (storage) capacity
imprescindible	indispensable
a pesar de todo	in spite of everything
aunque	although

¿Un buen equipo?

No pasa nada.	Everything is OK.
No te preocupes.	Don't worry.
Siento oír eso.	I'm sorry to hear that.
Siento verte así.	I'm sorry to see you like this.
Te entiendo perfectamente.	I understand you perfectly.
el/la analista de marketing	marketing analyst
el/la contador(a) (Amér. L.)	accountant
el contrato de trabajo	employment contract
el/la ejecutivo/a de ventas	sales executive
la perspectiva	prospect
el puesto directivo	managerial position
el/la tirano/a	tyrant
el título	degree
discutir	to argue
estar motivado/a	to be motivated
habilitar	to qualify
hacer horas extras	to do overtime
ser un(a) gran comunicador(a)	to be a great communicator
bromista	fond of joking
comprensivo/a	understanding
desagradable	unpleasant
impaciente	impatient
innovador(a)	innovative
metódico/a	methodical
ordenado/a	organized
puntual	punctual
serio/a	reliable
sobre todo	above all
solo/solamente	only
únicamente	only

Cristina Rubio

a convenir	to be agreed upon
No dude en...	Don't hesitate to. . .
la actitud	attitude
el ambiente laboral	work environment
el/la asesor(a) laboral	labor consultant
la bolsa de trabajo	job placement office
el/la candidato/a	applicant
la carta de presentación	cover letter
el dominio	command
la empatía	empathy
el entorno afectivo	emotional environment
el equipo de trabajo	work team
la estabilidad	stability
la gestión	management
la inteligencia emocional	emotional intelligence
la necesidad	need
el/la orientador(a) profesional	career counselor
el/la pasante	intern
la pasantía de verano	summer internship
los Recursos Humanos (RR.HH.)	Human Resources (HR)
el rendimiento	performance
la resolución de conflictos	conflict resolution
la satisfacción personal	personal satisfaction
la solicitud	application
asesorar	to advise
comprender	to understand
hacer clic	to click
manejar	to manage
postularse	to apply
relacionarse	to interact
reunir los requisitos	to meet the requirements
sentirse realizado/a	to feel fulfilled
eficaz	effective; efficient
excluyente	a must, required
casi	almost
por un lado/por una parte	on the one hand
por otro lado/por otra parte	on the other hand

Variación léxica

el/la contador(a) (Amér. L.) ⟷ el/la contable (Esp.)

hacer clic ⟷ pinchar (Esp.)

la pasantía ⟷ la práctica

la red Wi-Fi ⟷ la red inalámbrica

Juan José Millás es un escritor y periodista español nacido en Valencia en 1946. Empezó a estudiar Filosofía y Letras pero abandonó la universidad al tercer año y se dedicó a leer y escribir mientras trabajaba de diferentes cosas, entre ellas como administrativo en Iberia, la compañía aérea española. Es autor de muchas novelas y artículos periodísticos. Creó el *articuento*, un género literario a medio camino entre° el cuento y el artículo periodístico, en el que un hecho cotidiano puede convertirse en un evento fantástico que permite observar la realidad de forma crítica.

a medio camino entre *halfway between*

Vocabulario útil

la broma pesada *practical joke*
la casilla *box*
engañar *to fool*
la partida *departure*
la pesadilla *nightmare*
rellenar *to fill out*

FORMULARIOS

Juan José Millás

Al despertar, vi que la azafata había dejado sobre el brazo de mi asiento el formulario° que era preciso° rellenar para entrar en el país al que nos dirigíamos. El resto del pasaje dormía en medio de la penumbra°, pues era de noche y solo permanecían encendidas las luces que indicaban la situación de los baños y las que en los bajos de los asientos delimitaban el pasillo°. Comencé a rellenar el formulario y todo fue bien hasta que debajo de la línea en la que se solicitaba la fecha de nacimiento encontré otra donde había que anotar la de la muerte. Sobrecogido°, levanté el rostro y vi avanzar a una azafata en medio de aquella atmósfera espectral. Por favor, le dije en voz baja cuando llegó a mi altura, ¿qué hay que poner en esta casilla? ¿Usted qué cree?, respondió ella observándome con ironía, como si me estuviera haciendo el ingenuo°.

Suponiendo° entonces que me había sorprendido° la muerte mientras dormía, puse la fecha en la que había salido de Madrid, y en la que aún nos encontrábamos. Luego rellené el resto del formulario, tumbé° el respaldo del asiento, cerré los ojos y di un par de cabezadas°. Me despertó el ajetreo° de las azafatas, que comenzaban a servir el desayuno. Las ventanas estaban abiertas (había amanecido) y las luces encendidas. Vi el formulario, pero preferí (por miedo, supongo) no comprobar si lo de la casilla de la muerte había sido una alucinación. Llegué a destino, entregué el impreso en el control de policía, tomé un taxi, fui al hotel, hice en aquella ciudad lo que se esperaba de mí° y regresé a casa con regalos en la maleta. Mis rutinas son

(1) **Preguntas** Hable con un(a) compañero/a. ¿Cuál es la pregunta más extraña o difícil que tuvo que contestar? ¿Alguna vez confundió la realidad con un sueño (o una pesadilla)? ¿Qué opina de las bromas pesadas? ¿Lo engañaron alguna vez? ¿Se considera una persona realista o inclinada a la fantasía?

(2) **Elegir** Elija la opción correcta.

1. Cuando la azafata deja el formulario, el pasajero está ....
   a. dormido   b. despierto   c. distraído
2. Lo raro del formulario es ....
   a. todo   b. una pregunta   c. el color
3. Al leer el formulario, el pasajero queda ....
   a. indiferente   b. aterrorizado   c. sorprendido
4. La azafata responde al pasajero con ....
   a. amabilidad   b. ironía   c. confusión
5. Él supone que ....
   a. es una broma pesada   b. murió mientras dormía   c. está loco
6. Rellena la casilla con la fecha de ....
   a. su partida   b. su cumpleaños   c. su llegada
7. Al despertarse, el pasajero .... el formulario.
   a. relee   b. olvida   c. entrega
8. A partir de ese momento, sus rutinas ....
   a. son las mismas   b. son diferentes   c. desaparecen
9. Él tiene la sensación de que todo ....
   a. sigue igual   b. es diferente   c. fue un sueño

desde entonces las de siempre, mi relación con las personas y con el trabajo también. Todo sigue igual, pero de algún modo misterioso todo es diferente, como si, en vez de vivir, imitara° la vida que llevaba antes del viaje. No es desagradable, solo raro.

formulario *form* **era preciso** *it was necessary* **penumbra** *semi-darkness* **pasillo** *aisle* **Sobrecogido** *Startled* **como si me estuviera haciendo el ingenuo** *as though I were playing dumb* **Suponiendo** *Supposing* **me había sorprendido** *had surprised me* **tumbé** *I reclined* **di un par de cabezadas** *I had a nap* **ajetreo** *activity* **lo que se esperaba de mí** *what was expected of me* **como si... imitara** *as though . . . I were imitating*

► **Astronautas hispanos**

Arnaldo T. Méndez, piloto de la Fuerza Aérea Cubana, fue el primer latinoamericano en llegar al espacio. Fue seleccionado para el programa soviético Interkosmos y viajó en la nave rusa *Soyuz 38* con Yuri Romanenko en 1980.

Franklin R. Chang-Díaz, físico e ingeniero costarricense°, fue el primer astronauta latino de la NASA, con siete viajes al espacio, tres caminatas espaciales y más de 1601 horas fuera de la órbita terrestre. Cree que el ser humano vivirá en lugares como la Luna, los planetas o puntos del espacio entre la Tierra y su satélite, donde se podrían establecer colonias.

José Hernández es un californiano de ascendencia mexicana que decidió ser astronauta cuando escuchó la historia de Chang-Díaz: "Era alguien como yo, con los mismos problemas de manejo° del inglés, y si él pudo yo también lo haría", contó. En 2009 formó parte de la tripulación del transbordador espacial° *Discovery* en una misión de 14 días en la Estación Espacial Internacional (EEI).

costarricense *Costa Rican* **manejo** *use* **transbordador espacial** *space shuttle*

 3 a. **Representar** Una persona quiere comprar un pasaje a la Luna y el/la empleado/a de un agencia de turismo trata de explicar al cliente que no es posible, pero este insiste (puede ser una broma, una cámara oculta de un programa de televisión, etc.). En parejas, armen la conversación. Luego, representen la escena frente a la clase.

b. **Presentación** La AEXA (Agencia Espacial Mexicana) planea organizar viajes turísticos al espacio. En parejas, preparen una presentación del proyecto.

- Elijan el lugar del cosmos para promocionar y expliquen tiempo y condición del viaje.
- Presenten la nave y a los astronautas que la guían.
- Expliquen qué hace único este viaje (valoración de la experiencia, razones para hacerlo, etc.).
- Recomienden el viaje.

PROYECTO

 Informe Escriba un informe sobre el episodio del formulario en el vuelo de Madrid. Puede seguir esta estructura.

1. Descripción del incidente: contar qué pasó, cuándo y dónde.

2. Análisis del contexto: las circunstancias en las que se produjo.

3. Explicar la causa del evento: ¿por qué pasó? Si no se sabe, puede utilizar la frase: "Hasta el momento, se desconocen las causas del incidente."

4. Recomendación final: ¿qué se puede hacer para prevenir incidentes como este?

 Video

Inventos argentinos

Ya ha visto que en la vida moderna estamos rodeados de avances tecnológicos que nos resultan imprescindibles para viajar, trabajar y funcionar en las cosas de todos los días. En este episodio de **Flash Cultura** conocerá los inventos argentinos que cambiaron el mundo del siglo XX.

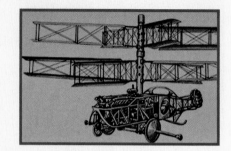

Estrategia

Asking questions

When watching a video, use questions to orient your viewing. Look at the title of the episode and think of questions you could ask using **qué, quién, dónde, cómo, cuándo, por qué,** etc. For example, since the title of this Flash Cultura is *Inventos argentinos,* you may ask from the start: **¿Cuáles son? ¿Quiénes los inventaron?**, etc. Write down your questions and check back afterward.

Vocabulario útil

la birome (*Arg.*) *ballpoint pen*
el dulce de leche (*Arg.*) *caramel spread*
en funcionamiento *running*
el frasco *bottle*
las huellas dactilares *fingerprints*
el invento *invention*
la jeringa descartable *disposable syringe*
la masa (cruda) *(raw) dough*
la pluma *fountain pen*
el/la porteño/a *person from Buenos Aires*
el relleno *filling*
la sangre *blood*
la tinta *ink*

Estrategia

Making excuses

In Spanish, when you need to make excuses or apologize, you might say: **Lo siento, Perdón, Discúlpame,** or **Te/Le pido disculpas/perdón.** If you were unaware of certain customs or prohibitions, you might say: **Yo no sabía/entendí/soy de aquí.**, or **No fue mi intención.**

1 **Preguntas** Converse con un(a) compañero/a. ¿Qué inventos del siglo XX conoce? ¿Cuál de los inventos modernos es el más importante para su vida? ¿Cuál le resulta imprescindible? ¿Qué cree que hace falta inventar en el mundo actual? ¿Le gustaría inventar algo?

2 **Mirar** Mire el video y haga las preguntas necesarias para reunir la información fundamental: qué es, para qué sirve, quién lo inventó, etc.

Buenos Aires sigue siendo la capital de un país de pioneros e innovadores.

El semáforo especial permite, mediante sonidos, avisarles a los ciegos o no videntes cuándo pueden cruzar la calle.

3 **Completar** Complete las oraciones sobre los inventos argentinos.

1. El colectivo para el transporte en la ciudad fue creado por dos .... a principios del siglo XX.
2. Un inmigrante húngaro llamado Biro inventó la ....
3. Las .... fueron idea de un policía argentino para identificar a las personas.
4. Hay inventos argentinos que salvan la vida de personas en todo el mundo como las transfusiones de ...., el *by-pass* y las ....
5. El tango y el .... son inventos esenciales para la cultura de los argentinos.

4 **Conversación** En parejas, escriban una conversación en la que opinan sobre los beneficios y perjuicios de ciertos inventos.

Modelo:
- *Aunque los colectivos son muy útiles para el transporte público, también contaminan el ambiente. Creo que sería mejor usar bicicletas.*
- *Es cierto. Sin embargo, los colectivos son más rápidos...*

 Practice more at vhlcentral.com.

Unidad 14

Acacio Maye Ocomo, una vida en el mar

Macarena Berlín, *Hablar por hablar*

La comida latina

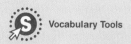
14A

UN IDIOMA COMÚN

Un mundo en movimiento

ESTA SEMANA Mis viajes a Guinea Ecuatorial

Mario Segura

Mi primera visita fue en el año 1995. Era mi quinto viaje por tierras africanas y tenía curiosidad por conocer un país hispanohablante en África. Pero ¿realmente era hispanohablante? Llegabas a un sitio y te decían *m'bolo* en fang, en otro *tuë a lövari*, en bubi, en el siguiente algo en ndowe, que son algunas de las otras lenguas que se hablan en este país, pero siempre me contestaban con "hola" y una sonrisa cuando los saludaba en español.

En mi segunda visita me quedé un mes y me fascinó su folclore y sus gentes. Casi siempre estaba en la calle, solía ir cada día al mercado y charlaba con los vendedores. La gente era siempre muy amable y me invitaba a comer en su casa. Su hospitalidad es un rasgo de identidad.

De vez en cuando tenía el placer de disfrutar de alguna de sus costumbres y ceremonias.

Los ecuatoguineanos combinan sus raíces africanas con la influencia española, y la tradición católica convive con muchas tradiciones espirituales como la danza *abira*, un ritual que celebran los curanderos para expulsar a los malos espíritus.

Adoro esta tierra, y ¡espero volver pronto!

Hablar de situaciones y acciones habituales en el pasado

En África **solía conocer** a personas interesantes. **De vez en cuando iba** a alguna expedición y...

14A.1 Use of the imperfect: **solía** + [*infinitive*] Time expressions

Vocabulario

(1)

un mundo en movimiento *a world in motion*

quinto/a *fifth*

africano/a *African*

hispanohablante *Spanish-speaking*

fascinar *to captivate*

casi siempre *almost always*

soler (o:ue) *to usually do something*

cada día *each day*

charlar *to chat*

el rasgo *characteristic*

de vez en cuando *from time to time*

ecuatoguineano/a *from Equatorial Guinea*

convivir con *to coexist with*

espiritual *spiritual*

el/la curandero/a *healer*

expulsar *to expel*

---

1 **a. Preguntar** ¿Qué sabe usted sobre Guinea Ecuatorial? Lea la crónica de Mario Segura, viajero en África. Haga preguntas a su compañero/a sobre estos temas que aparecen en el texto.

- los idiomas que se hablan en Guinea Ecuatorial
- la convivencia de culturas y religiones diferentes
- el carácter de la gente

b. Investigar ¿Qué otras preguntas tiene sobre Guinea Ecuatorial? Haga una lista de tres preguntas y busque sus respuestas en Internet. En grupos de cuatro, compartan sus averiguaciones.

2 **Contestar** ¿Qué solía hacer Mario durante su estancia en Guinea Ecuatorial? ¿Qué situaciones describe? ¿Cuál le parece a usted más interesante? ¿Por qué?

- (Casi) siempre...
- Cada día...
- De vez en cuando...

3 **Un viaje especial** Piense en un viaje especial y diferente que hizo, y explique a sus compañeros qué solía hacer.

Modelo: *Hace un tiempo viví diez meses en Sudamérica. Casi siempre me alojaba en posadas o en casas particulares. Solía hacer las compras en pequeños mercados.*

---

4 **a. Guinea Ecuatorial** Lea esta información sobre Guinea Ecuatorial y enumere los recursos económicos del país por orden de importancia.

- industria petrolera
- turismo
- recursos naturales

Antes del descubrimiento de petróleo en 1995, sus recursos naturales eran principalmente la madera, el uranio y el oro, pero no estaban explotados. Ahora es el tercer productor de petróleo del África subsahariana y su producto interior bruto per cápita es el más alto de África, aunque esta riqueza no ha llegado a todos los ecuatoguineanos.

El turismo es el otro gran potencial de este país en el corazón de África: sus playas, su clima tropical, su vegetación exuberante, su folclore, el calor de sus gentes y una atractiva mezcla de culturas, invitan a un viaje diferente.

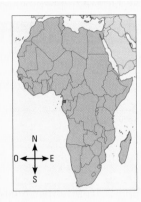

b. Puesto ¿Qué puesto ocupa Guinea Ecuatorial como productor de petróleo en el África subsahariana? ¿Y su producto interior bruto per cápita?

5 **Lenguas** Lea la nota sociocultural sobre las lenguas de Guinea Ecuatorial. ¿En su comunidad se hablan varios idiomas? ¿Cuáles, y en qué contexto?

6 **PIB de Bolivia y de España** Observe las gráficas sobre el PIB de Bolivia y de España. Luego conteste las preguntas y compare sus respuestas con las de su compañero/a.

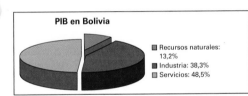

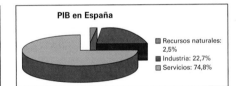

1. ¿Cuál es el segundo recurso económico de Bolivia? ¿Y el tercero?

2. ¿Qué diferencias hay entre el PIB en España y en Bolivia?

3. Los recursos naturales son importantes para el PIB de Bolivia. ¿Esto le parece algo positivo o negativo? ¿Por qué?

MI EXPERIENCIA

7 **Comentar** Cuando era pequeño/a, ¿estuvo en un país o región interesante? Describa qué solía hacer allí. ¿Qué le pareció destacable? Comente estos aspectos.

GUIÓN DE TRABAJO

Cuando era pequeño/a, solía ir a / me gustaba... → Cada día solía... Siempre/De vez en cuando... Me pareció interesante, en primer lugar..., en segundo lugar...

¿Y qué solías hacer allí? ¿Qué cosas hacías cada día? ¿Qué te pareció interesante?

Practice more at vhlcentral.com.

Lenguas de Guinea Ecuatorial

fa tela mulapu nkiel elotoo nkobo

Los ecuatoguineanos hablan sus lenguas maternas africanas, y el español se utiliza en el trabajo, en la escuela y en la administración. Guinea Ecuatorial es el único país del África subsahariana que tiene el español como lengua oficial, además del francés y del portugués.

SAM: Actividades pp. 289–291

Intercambios

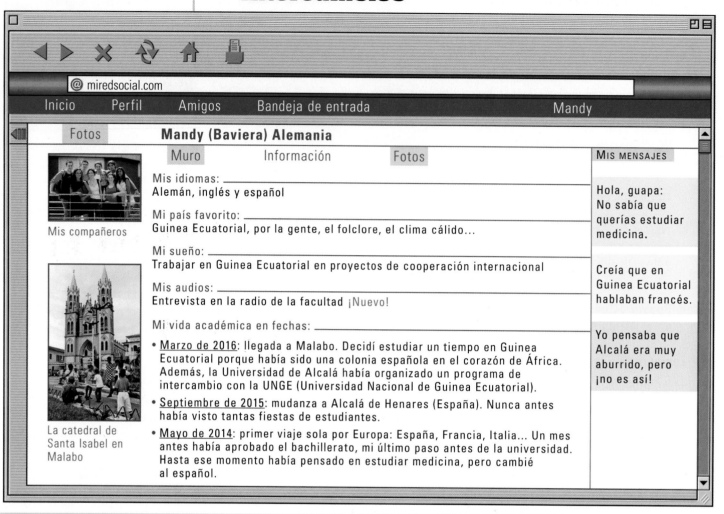

Hablar de acciones anteriores a una acción pasada

Antes de venir a España ya **había estudiado** español.

14A.3 Past perfect

Vocabulario

8

el perfil *profile*
la bandeja de entrada *inbox*
el programa de intercambio *exchange program*
la vida académica *academic life*
la mudanza *move*
aprobar (o:ue) *to pass*
el bachillerato *high school studies*
la colonia

9

el/la comerciante *storekeeper*
el/la tenista *tennis player*
la formación profesional *professional training*

---

(8) **Perfil** Fíjese en las fotos y en el perfil de esta estudiante de intercambio. ¿Utiliza usted alguna red social? ¿Qué había hecho Mandy antes de estos acontecimientos?

○ primer viaje por Europa ○ viaje a Alcalá ○ viaje a Guinea Ecuatorial

(9) **a. Completar** las oraciones con la forma correcta de cada verbo.

1. Antes de ir a Guinea Ecuatorial, Mandy ya .... (estudiar) español.

2. Tres semanas antes del examen, nosotros ya .... (leer) todos los libros.

3. Cuando viajasteis por Latinoamérica, ¿vosotros ya .... (aprobar) el bachillerato?

4. Antes de ser comerciante, yo .... (decidir) ser tenista.

5. Cuando llegamos a tu casa, tú ya .... (salir).

6. Antes de tomar clases de guitarra, ustedes .... (tomar) clases de piano.

b. Contar Lea estos acontecimientos y cuéntele a su compañero/a qué había hecho usted antes.

| ir a la universidad | viajar a un país hispanohablante | participar en un curso de español |

Modelo: *Antes de ir a la universidad, ya había aprendido idiomas.*

10 Comentar Vuelva a leer el perfil de Mandy. ¿Qué información era nueva para sus amigos de la red? ¿Aprendió algo usted? Comenten estos temas en parejas.

- la UNGE
- diferencias culturales
- Guinea Ecuatorial
- lenguas

11 a. Ordenar Escuche la entrevista que le hacen a Mandy y ordene los acontecimientos.

A. .... vivir en Alcalá de Henares ......1...... viajar por Europa

B. .... estudiar en Alemania .... estudiar en España

C. .... venir a España .... estudiar español

b. Fragmentos Escuche de nuevo. Fíjese en los recursos para pedir repetición y complete los fragmentos de la entrevista.

> - Cuéntanos, Mandy, ¿qué es lo que más te ha llamado la atención en Alcalá?
> - Sin duda, el volumen de las conversaciones.
> - ...., ¿el volumen?

> - Aunque no solo se habla español, también muchas otras lenguas como el fang, el bubi o el annobonés…
> - ¿ .... ? ¿Qué lenguas dices?

12 a. Leer Lea este texto sobre un programa de intercambio de estudiantes.

LA GENERACIÓN ERASMUS

ERASMUS se creó en 1987 para fomentar la integración de los jóvenes universitarios europeos, quienes pueden cursar materias de su carrera en otras universidades europeas y validarlas en la propia. Ya han participado 3 millones de jóvenes. Además, en 2004 se creó ERASMUS Mundus con el objetivo de integrar a jóvenes profesionales de todo el mundo. Estos programas de intercambio cultural no solo incentivan el perfeccionamiento académico y el estudio de idiomas, también buscan crear una sociedad global basada en el respeto y la tolerancia. Además, abren el mercado laboral y permiten el nacimiento de grandes amistades transfronterizas.

b. Contestar ¿En qué consiste el programa de becas ERASMUS? ¿Quiénes pueden participar?

c. Opinar ¿Qué opina acerca de este tipo de programas de intercambio? ¿Le gustaría presentar una solicitud para participar en alguno? ¿Por qué?

MI EXPERIENCIA

13 Antes ¿Qué cosas habían hecho ustedes antes de empezar la universidad? Hagan una lista y compárenlas. ¿Qué información les resulta sorprendente?

GUIÓN DE TRABAJO

¿Qué habías hecho antes de empezar la universidad? → Antes de empezar la universidad, yo... había estudiado... había vivido en... había viajado...

Perdona, no sabía que habías... ¿Cómo? Pensaba que...

Expresar desconocimiento

No sabía que en Guinea Ecuatorial se hablaba español.

Pensaba que había sido una colonia francesa.

14A.4 no sabía que, creía que, pensaba que...

Vocabulario

⑪

llamar la atención *to catch one's attention*

el volumen *volume*

¿Cómo? *What?; Excuse me?*

⑫

fomentar *to encourage*

cursar *to study*

incentivar *to encourage*

el perfeccionamiento *improvement*

transfronterizo/a *cross-border*

la beca ERASMUS *ERASMUS scholarship*

validar, el respeto, la tolerancia

Estrategia ············

Pedir repetición

- He aprendido ndowe.
- ¿Perdona?
- Ndowe: es una lengua bantú.
- Ban... ¿cómo?

¡OJO!

ERASMUS is an acronym of the program's official name in English: *European Region Action Scheme for the Mobility of University Students*, or **Plan de Acción de la Comunidad Europea para la Movilidad de Estudiantes Universitarios**.

SAM: Actividades pp. 292–294

Acacio Maye Ocomo, una vida en el mar

ORO NEGRO

Cuando el precio del barril de petróleo en la Bolsa de Nueva York llega a altos precios, es un buen día para Guinea Ecuatorial. El desarrollo del sector energético de este país es imparable. Tiene la renta per cápita más alta de África, pero la vida de la mayoría no ha mejorado.

Acacio Maye Ocomo trabaja como ingeniero en una de las plataformas petroleras más importantes del país en el golfo de Guinea. La demanda laboral en este sector ha crecido mucho.

"Si eres ecuatoguineano, es una buena alternativa para vivir bien aquí", explica Acacio. "Trabajo en el mar desde hace seis años. El primer año fue el más duro. Había vuelto a Guinea Ecuatorial después de estudiar ingeniería en España y fue muy difícil al principio. Si trabajas en una plataforma en el mar, pasas mucho tiempo solo. Al principio no tenía muchos días libres y solía quedarme en la plataforma, solía pasar el día en el exterior, leía y contemplaba los atardeceres en el mar.

En la plataforma convivíamos personas de los cinco continentes. Yo pensaba que no era posible entenderse con gente tan diferente, pero estaba equivocado. De vez en cuando podía haber algún malentendido, pero si la relación con tus compañeros es buena, son como una segunda familia. El tercer año cambié de compañía y, por tanto, de compañeros. Fue como volver a empezar. Ahora llevo en esta plataforma dos años, y he conocido a Nora, mi mujer. Trabaja como ingeniera también y es australiana. Nora y yo queremos formar una familia. Si seguimos aquí unos años más, ahorraremos para empezar en otra parte" nos cuenta Acacio, siempre con la sonrisa en los labios y muy esperanzado.

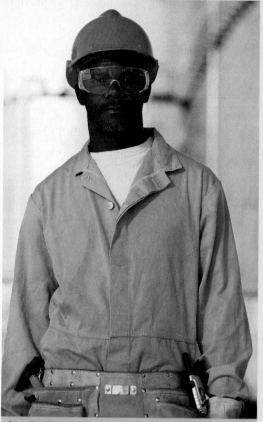

Acacio Maye Ocomo en la plataforma petrolera donde trabaja

Expresar condiciones posibles

Si quieres trabajar en Guinea Ecuatorial, **es** una alternativa segura.

Si repartimos los recursos, la situación **será** mejor para todos.

14A.5 **si** + [*present*], [*present/simple future*]

Vocabulario

14

el oro negro *black gold*

el barril de petróleo *oil barrel*

el desarrollo *development*

el sector energético *energy sector*

imparable *unstoppable*

la renta per cápita *per capita income*

la plataforma petrolera *oil rig*

la demanda laboral *labor demand*

el día libre *day off*

el atardecer *dusk*

equivocado/a *mistaken*

el malentendido *misunderstanding*

esperanzado/a *hopeful*

---

14 **Acacio Maye Ocomo** Lea el título de este artículo y observe la foto del protagonista. ¿Qué cree que es el "oro negro"? Después lea el reportaje y anote los datos más interesantes de la vida de este protagonista. Pregúntele a su compañero/a.

15 **El oro negro** Busque en el texto estos términos económicos y relaciónelos con su significado.

1. renta per cápita ......
2. sector energético ......
3. demanda laboral ......

a. necesidad de empleados
b. área económica relacionada con la producción de energía
c. renta nacional dividida por el número de habitantes de un país

16 **Contestar** ¿Qué solía hacer Acacio cuando empezó a trabajar en una plataforma? ¿Qué creía el protagonista antes de convivir con sus compañeros?

17 **Completar** Fíjese en estas oraciones que aparecen en el texto y complételas.

1. Si trabajas en una plataforma en el mar, ...
2. Si la relación con tus compañeros es buena, ...
3. Si seguimos aquí unos años más, ...

18 **Trabajos** Piense en situaciones posibles que pueden suceder en estos trabajos y compare sus ideas con las de su compañero/a.

○ pescador(a)   ○ domador(a) de leones   ○ astronauta

Modelo: *Si eres pescador...*

¿PROFESIONES COMUNES?

....

Estos oficios son únicos porque permiten un encuentro con la naturaleza y con nosotros mismos. Y si algo nos da tantas satisfacciones, el esfuerzo vale la pena.

"Todos los días debo levantarme tempranísimo y salir a trabajar. Paso mucho tiempo solo, y a veces hace frío o llueve, pero soy feliz. Este oficio es una tradición familiar y estoy orgulloso de formar parte de ella."

....

Son profesiones particulares, lugares a veces privilegiados donde vivir, en ocasiones fuera de la sociedad.

"Hace más de 10 años que me dedico a esto y me encanta, pero sé que es una profesión en extinción. La tecnología sustituye al hombre."

....

Hay profesiones que condicionan el lugar donde vives, profesiones que te alejan de la sociedad y de tu familia durante mucho tiempo y suponen grandes responsabilidades.

"Si preservamos nuestros espacios naturales, protegeremos el medio ambiente. Por eso no me molestan los sacrificios. Sé que estoy ayudando al planeta."

19 **a. ¿Profesiones comunes?** Lea estos fragmentos de un artículo sobre trabajos en lugares alejados de los centros urbanos. ¿A qué profesiones corresponden estos testimonios? Anote las profesiones en la imagen adecuada.

pescador(a) • farero/a • científico/a • guarda forestal

b. Lista ¿Qué profesión le parece más interesante? ¿Cuál le gustaría experimentar y por qué? Con su compañero/a, hagan una lista de otras profesiones y lugares poco comunes donde vivir o trabajar.

20 **c. Clasificar** Aquí tiene algunos datos sobre Guinea Ecuatorial. Clasifíquelos. ¿Recuerda alguno más? Compare sus respuestas con las de sus compañeros.

○ historia   ○ recursos   ○ geografía política   ○ población

- Guinea Ecuatorial es el tercer exportador de petróleo en el África subsahariana. ....
- Hay tres países en África con el nombre de Guinea: Guinea, Guinea Bissau y Guinea Ecuatorial. ....
- Se independizó en el año 1968 después de las primeras revueltas independentistas de 1967. ....
- Con unos 700 000 habitantes, es el único país hispanohablante con mayoría negra. La minoría blanca (1%) son los blancos europeos de ascendencia española. ....

Vocabulario

18
suceder *to happen*
el/la pescador(a) *fisherman/ fisherwoman*
el/la domador(a) de leones *lion tamer*
19
sustituir (y) *to replace*
el oficio *trade*
condicionar *to determine*
el/la farero/a *lighthouse keeper*
el/la guarda forestal *forest ranger*
la extinción
20
la revuelta *revolt*
la minoría *minority*
la ascendencia *ancestry*

OPINIÓN

¿Qué opina de la vida de nuestro protagonista?

¿Le gustaría vivir en una plataforma petrolera? ¿Por qué?

SAM: Actividades pp. 295–298

21 **a. Leer** Lea estos fragmentos del libro *Ekomo* (1985) de la escritora ecuatoguineana María Nsue. ¿Cuáles de estos temas trata la autora? ¿Con qué temas asocia usted África? ¿Y sus compañeros?

> folclore • tradición • modernidad • religión • naturaleza • magia • personalidad de un pueblo

Nfumbá'a, el africano de hoy, hombre del mañana, tras° estar dos lluvias en Europa dejó su tradición encerrada entre los libros; dejó allí su personalidad y sus creencias° africanas, y el ser° sin continente regresó a su pueblo con un disfraz° de europeo pero sin el europeo dentro. [...]

El poblado [...] estaba lleno de gente de las aldeas vecinas que habían acudido° al oír que aquella noche se iba a ejecutar nuestra danza. [...]

Las notas del tambor° llegaron a mis oídos. La danza daba comienzo. [...] Me convertí en los sonidos del tam-tam. Vibré°, vibré y vibré al son de sus sonidos. Mi espíritu se escapó del cuerpo y voló [...].

NSUE, María: *Ekomo*. Madrid, Ediciones Sial, 2008

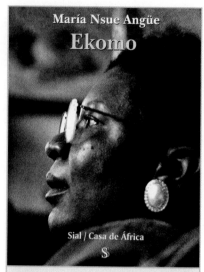

María Nsue Angüe
Ekomo

Sial / Casa de África

tras *after* **creencias** *beliefs* **el ser** *being* **disfraz** *disguise* **acudido** *attended* **tambor** *drum* **vibré** *I vibrated*

b. Responder ¿Qué cree que quiere decir la autora con estas frases?

- "el africano de hoy"
- "con un disfraz de europeo pero sin el europeo dentro"
- "tras estar dos lluvias en Europa"

c. María Nsue Lea los datos autobiográficos de la autora. ¿Qué relación encuentra con su obra?

María Nsue nació en 1945 en una familia de etnia fang. Emigró con sus padres a España cuando tenía ocho años, y allí realizó sus estudios y empezó su carrera literaria. Volvió a Guinea Ecuatorial y trabajó en el Ministerio de Educación y Cultura. Años después decidió instalarse en Madrid. *Ekomo* es la primera novela publicada por una mujer ecuatoguineana.

T A R E A   F I N A L

Intercambio cultural en red

Busque datos sobre un país o una región que le interese: lenguas, fiestas, cultura, tradiciones, etc. Escriba una historia en el pasado relacionada con alguno de estos temas.

Comparta su historia con sus compañeros y participen en una red de intercambio cultural para estudiantes. ¿Qué sabían o pensaban de estos temas?

Decidan qué quieren conseguir en esta red y en qué orden: intercambio de información cultural, música, chatear con otros estudiantes, etc.

Y O   P U E D O . . .

- Puedo hablar de situaciones y acciones habituales en el pasado.

  Piense en un momento de su vida en el pasado y en qué solía hacer.

- Puedo expresar orden y grado.

  Anote con letra estos números ordinales y complete la serie.
  1.° .... 2.° .... 3.° .... 4.° ....
  5.° .... , ...

- Puedo hablar de acciones anteriores a una acción pasada.

  Cuente qué idiomas había estudiado antes de aprender español.

- Puedo expresar desconocimiento.

  Diga qué cosas no sabía antes de estudiar esta lección.

- Puedo expresar condiciones posibles.

  Complete la oración.

  Si vives en un país extranjero...

GRAMÁTICA FUNCIONAL Ⓢ Tutorials

14A.1 Talk about past situations and habitual actions

Use of the imperfect: **solía** + [*infinitive*], (**casi**) **siempre, de vez en cuando, cada día** `5.4.3, 5.6, 5.15, 12.12`

- Use a form of the verb **soler** in the **pretérito imperfecto** to talk about habitual actions in the past. When used in the imperfect, **soler** + [*infinitive*] expresses the idea of *used to*.

  > **Solía comer** en ese restaurante cuando vivía en este barrio.
  > *I **used to eat** in that restaurant when I lived in this neighborhood.*

- [*Imperfect of* **soler**] + [*infinitive*] expresses the same idea as **normalmente** + [*imperfect*]; **solía estudiar** = **normalmente estudiaba** (*I usually studied*).

- Other expressions of frequency that often signal the use of the **pretérito imperfecto** include (**casi**) **siempre** [*(almost) always*], **de vez en cuando** (*from time to time*), and **cada día/mes** (*every day/month*).

  > Cuando vivía en Perú, solía dar un paseo **cada día** y **casi siempre** quedaba con mis amigos.
  > *When I lived in Peru, I used to take a walk **every day** and I **almost always** made plans to meet with my friends.*

  > **De vez en cuando** íbamos al cine.
  > ***Sometimes*** *we would go to the movies.*

- You have learned other uses of the **pretérito imperfecto** in 9A.1 and 13B.1 and you have seen the **pretérito imperfecto** compared with the **pretérito indefinido** in 9B.3 and 10B.1.

14A.2 Express order and degree

Ordinal numbers `13.2`

- Use ordinal numbers (**números ordinales**) to represent a position in a sequence. These numbers are equivalent to *first, second, third*, etc.

primer, primero/a (1.ᵉʳ/1.º/1.ª)	**sexto/a** (6.º/6.ª)
segundo/a (2.º/2.ª)	**séptimo/a** (7.º/7.ª)
tercer, tercero/a (3.ᵉʳ/3.º/3.ª)	**octavo/a** (8.º/8.ª)
cuarto/a (4.º/4.ª)	**noveno/a** (9.º/9.ª)
quinto/a (5.º/5.ª)	**décimo/a** (10.º/10.ª)

- Ordinal numbers are adjectives and must agree with the noun they modify.

  > Juan empezó a estudiar francés en el **sexto** grado.
  > *Juan began studying French in the **sixth** grade.*

- The shortened forms **primer** and **tercer** are used before masculine singular nouns. These forms are abbreviated as 1.ᵉʳ and 3.ᵉʳ, respectively.

  > Estaba nervioso el **primer** día de clase.
  > *He was nervous on the **first** day of class.*

- Use the abbreviated forms 1.ª, 2.ª, etc. when referring to the feminine forms.

¡Póngalo en práctica!

G1 **Párrafo** Complete el párrafo con los verbos en el pretérito imperfecto.

Cuando (1).................... (yo, ser) pequeña, (2).................... (yo, vivir) con mis padres en Guinea Ecuatorial. Ellos (3).................... (trabajar) en una empresa de exportación de madera. Nosotros (4).................... (tener) una casa en el centro de Malabo. (5).................... (Yo, soler) jugar con mis hermanos en la calle, pues siempre (6).................... (hacer) buen tiempo. La gente (7).................... (ser) muy amable y siempre (8).................... (ayudar) con las necesidades de sus vecinos.

G2 **Conversación** Complete la conversación de forma lógica.

- Cuando eras pequeño, ¿(1).................... ir a la piscina?
- Sí, iba (2)...................., excepto en diciembre.
- ¿Y por qué no ibas en diciembre?
- Porque mis hermanos y yo (3).................... pasar diciembre con los abuelos. ¿Y tú?
- Yo iba a la piscina sólo de (4).................... en (5).................... No me gusta nadar.
- ¿O sea que no hacías nada de deporte?
- En realidad, mis amigos y yo bajábamos a la plaza (6).................... día después de clases para jugar al fútbol.

G3 **Números ordinales** Complete las oraciones con los números ordinales.

1. España es el .... (1.ᵉʳ) productor de aceite de oliva del mundo.
2. Paco ha ganado el .... (3.ᵉʳ) premio en el concurso. Es la .... (1.ª) vez que gana y está muy contento.
3. Angola fue el .... (2.º) productor de petróleo de África en 2014.
4. Juana es la .... (5.ª) hermana de una familia de ocho.
5. Vivimos en el .... (9.º) piso del edificio.
6. Cuando terminamos el .... (7.º) grado, viajamos a Córdoba.

G4 **Escribir** Escriba la frase correspondiente según el modelo.

> Modelo: 3 / productor
> *el tercer productor*

1. 2 / clase	4. 1 / página
....	....
2. 7 / planta	5. 5 / país
....	....
3. 4 / lugar	6. 8 / viaje

 Practice more at **vhlcentral.com**.

GRAMÁTICA FUNCIONAL

14A.3 Talk about actions prior to a past action

The past perfect 5.5, 11.6

- To talk about actions that happened before another past action or event, use the past perfect (**pretérito pluscuamperfecto**). The **pretérito pluscuamperfecto** is formed with the imperfect of the verb **haber** + [*past participle*].

> Antes de vivir en Guinea Ecuatorial, Mariano ya **había viajado** por Europa.
> *Before living in Equatorial Guinea, Mariano **had** already **traveled** through Europe.*

	HABER	+ [*past participle*]
(yo)	había	
(tú)	habías	
(usted, él, ella)	había	hablado
(nosotros/as)	habíamos	comido
(vosotros/as)	habíais	vivido
(ustedes, ellos/as)	habían	

- The **pretérito pluscuamperfecto** is frequently used with the adverb **ya** (*already*) to emphasize that one action or event occurred prior to another.

14A.4 Express something unknown

Use of the imperfect: **no sabía que/creía que/pensaba que** 5.4.3

- Use the imperfect in constructions such as **no sabía que, creía que**, and **pensaba que** to express ignorance about a subject.

> **No sabía que había** intercambios entre universidades.
> *I didn't know that there were exchanges among universities.*

- The verb in the second clause of the sentence is also used in the imperfect.

> Yo creía que **vivías** en el centro.
> *I thought **you lived** downtown.*

14A.5 Express possible conditions

si + [*present*], [*present/simple future*] 12.9

- To express a possible situation in the present or the future, use the construction **si** + [*present*], [*present/simple future*].

> **Si viajas** al extranjero, **aprendes** la lengua y la cultura de otros países.
> *If you travel abroad, you learn the language and culture of other countries.*

- You can also switch the order of the clauses with no comma in between; just be sure that the condition (the *if*-clause) begins with **si**.

> Viajaremos a Costa Rica este verano **si ahorramos** suficiente dinero.
> *We'll travel to Costa Rica this summer if we save enough money.*

¡Póngalo en práctica!

G5 **Completar** Complete las oraciones con la forma correcta del pretérito pluscuamperfecto.

1. Antes de trabajar en la fábrica, Mariano .... (ser) camarero.
2. Cuando terminé la carrera de historia en 1999, ya .... (empezar) arqueología.
3. Antes de viajar a Guinea Ecuatorial, Flavia y Óscar ya .... (ir) a España.
4. Cuando vinimos a Guinea Ecuatorial, ya .... (estudiar) español.
5. Antes de ir a Nueva York, vosotros .... (vivir) en Los Ángeles.
6. Mariana ya me .... (decir) que no podía ir a la clase, pero me llamó de nuevo para avisarme.
7. Cuando llegamos a casa de Ana, ella ya .... (salir).
8. Antes de aceptar la oferta, Raúl .... (consultar) con varios expertos.

G6 **Pretérito imperfecto** Complete las oraciones con el pretérito imperfecto.

1. Los estudiantes no .... (saber) que el fang era una lengua bantú.
2. .... (Yo, pensar) que sabía español cuando viajé a España, pero aprendí muchas expresiones nuevas.
3. • ¿Sabíais que en Guinea Ecuatorial se hablaba español?
   ▪ No, nosotros .... (pensar) que se hablaba otro idioma.
4. Joaquín .... (creer) que ese libro iba a ser aburrido, pero le gustó mucho.

G7 **Si...** Complete las oraciones.

1. Si .... (tú, viajar) a Guinea Ecuatorial el año que viene, ... (tú, poder) practicar español.
2. Si .... (tú, trabajar) en el extranjero, ... (tú, conocer) a muchas personas interesantes.
3. Si .... (tú, aprender) la lengua del país, ... (tú, integrarse) sin problemas.
4. Si .... (yo, tener) vacaciones, te .... (yo, visitar) en julio.
5. Mi hermano .... (él, poder) ir también si .... (él, terminar) de escribir su tesis.

 Practice more at **vhlcentral.com**.

VOCABULARIO 🔊 Ⓢ Vocabulary Tools

Un mundo en movimiento

un mundo en movimiento	a world in motion
el África (f.) subsahariana	sub-Saharan Africa
la ceremonia	ceremony
la convivencia	coexistence
el/la curandero/a	healer
el folclore	folklore
la hospitalidad	hospitality
la industria de servicios	service industry
la industria petrolera	oil industry
la lengua materna	mother tongue
la lengua oficial	official language
la mezcla	mix
el petróleo	oil
el rasgo	characteristic
el recurso económico	economic resource
el recurso natural	natural resource
la riqueza	wealth
el ritual	ritual
el turismo	tourism
el uranio	uranium
charlar	to chat
convivir con	to coexist with
explotar	to exploit
expulsar	to expel
fascinar	to captivate
soler (o:ue)	to usually do something
africano/a	African
cuarto/a	fourth
destacable	noteworthy
ecuatoguineano/a	from Equatorial Guinea
espiritual	spiritual
hispanohablante	Spanish-speaking
primero/a	first
quinto/a	fifth
tercero/a	third
cada día	each day
casi siempre	almost always
de vez en cuando	from time to time

Intercambios

¿Cómo?	What?, Excuse me?
el bachillerato	high school studies
la bandeja de entrada	inbox
la beca ERASMUS	ERASMUS scholarship
la colonia	colony
el/la comerciante	storekeeper
la formación profesional	professional training
la mudanza	move
el perfeccionamiento	improvement
el perfil	profile
el programa de intercambio	exchange program
el respeto	respect
el/la tenista	tennis player
la tolerancia	tolerance
la vida académica	academic life
el volumen	volume
aprobar (o:ue)	to pass
cursar	to study
fomentar	to encourage
incentivar	to encourage
llamar la atención	to catch one's attention
validar	to validate
transfronterizo/a	cross-border

Acacio Maye Ocomo

la ascendencia	ancestry
el atardecer	dusk
el barril de petróleo	oil barrel
la demanda laboral	labor demand
el desarrollo	development
el día libre	day off
el/la domador(a) de leones	lion tamer
la extinción	extinction
el/la farero/a	lighthouse keeper
el/la guarda forestal	forest ranger
el malentendido	misunderstanding
la minoría	minority
el oficio	trade
el oro negro	black gold
el/la pescador(a)	fisherman/ fisherwoman
la plataforma petrolera	oil rig
la renta per cápita	per capita income
la revuelta	revolt
el sector energético	energy sector
condicionar	to determine
suceder	to happen
sustituir (y)	to replace
equivocado/a	mistaken
esperanzado/a	hopeful
imparable	unstoppable

Variación léxica

la convivencia ⟷ la coexistencia ⟷ la cohabitación

el día libre ⟷ el día de descanso ⟷ el día franco (Arg.)

el folclore ⟷ el folklore

fomentar ⟷ promover ⟷ incentivar

hispanohablante ⟷ hispanoparlante ⟷ de habla hispana

validar ⟷ homologar

PROGRAMAS DE SIEMPRE

La mejor década

@ www.lamejordecada.com

FORO LA MEJOR DÉCADA

El programa de televisión *La mejor década* nos recuerda la música que escuchábamos cuando éramos jóvenes, los actores que admirábamos cuando íbamos al cine o nuestros programas de televisión favoritos. ¿Qué recuerda usted, amigo internauta y telespectador, de las últimas tres décadas? Defienda en esta página web su década favorita.

Recuerdo que cuando pasaban la serie *Dallas* en la tele, no había nadie por la calle, y ¿quién no ha visto la película *E.T.*? Cuando tenía 16 años, me enamoré del cantante Prince y también escuchaba a The Police o Madonna (¡durante un año me estuve vistiendo como ella!). Sin duda, ¡es la década ganadora!

Ana 82

Cuando compré mi primer LP de U2 ¡no sabía nada de inglés!, pero me encantaba su música y todavía me gusta, hoy los he estado escuchando. En la tele veíamos *Friends*, ¡una serie muy divertida! Mi hermano estaba loco por *Los Simpson*. Y películas… ¡muchas! *La vida es bella* de Roberto Benigni, y más: *Thelma y Louise*, *Todo sobre mi madre* de Almodóvar, etc. Yo defiendo esta década.

Fibi

¡La primera década del siglo XXI, sin duda! Empezamos un nuevo milenio y eso es único. También se estrenó *Harry Potter*. Me aprendí de memoria todas las películas, ¡no podía dejar de verlas! Además, creo que todos quedamos fascinados con *Lost* (¡qué sorpresa el final!), nos volvimos investigadores con *CSI* y lloramos con las canciones del grupo musical Coldplay. Definitivamente: ¡la mejor década!

Y2K

Situar hechos pasados

Cuando era pequeña, no teníamos cable en casa…

Cuando instalaron el cable, ya no vivía con mis padres.

14B.1 **cuando** + [*imperfect*]/ [*preterite*]

Vocabulario

①

el/la telespectador(a) *television viewer*

la página web *Web page*

pasar la serie de televisión *to broadcast the television series*

la serie de televisión *television series*

ganador(a) *winning*

estrenarse *to premiere*

aprender de memoria *to memorize*

fascinado/a *fascinated*

llorar *to cry*

---

1 **La mejor década** Observe la página web del programa *La mejor década* y lea los mensajes del foro. ¿Qué décadas (los 80, 90 o 2000) recuerdan y defienden? Complete la ficha.

	Década	Película	Serie de televisión	Grupo musical
Ana 82				
Fibi				
Y2K				

2 **Foro** ¿Conoce usted las referencias de esas décadas que comentan en el foro? Participe en el foro con su recuerdo y después coméntelo con su compañero/a.

Modelo: • *Cuando tenía 13 años, a mí también me gustaba Coldplay.*
• *Yo compré todos sus CD y esta semana he visto un DVD de su último concierto.*

3 **Preguntar** Pida información a su compañero/a sobre estos temas.

¿Qué hacías…?   cuando tenías 15 años…

¿Qué te gustaba…?   cuando terminaste la escuela primaria…

¿Qué pasó…?   cuando…

(4) **Contestar** Conteste las preguntas. ¡Sea creativo/a!

Modelo: • *¿Qué escuchaba cuando iba al colegio?*
• *Cuando iba al colegio, estaba todo el día escuchando* Maná.

1. ¿Qué estaba haciendo tu hermana cuando llegamos?
....

2. ¿Qué serie de televisión estuviste mirando este último año?
....

3. ¿Qué estuvisteis estudiando en la clase de español?
....

4. ¿Qué estaban buscando nuestros compañeros en la biblioteca?
....

(5) **Aficionado** Fíjese en la foto y complete el comentario de este aficionado. ¿Ha visto usted un concierto de alguno de sus grupos favoritos? ¿Y su compañero/a?

Cuando U2 dio su último concierto en Barcelona, yo fui el primero de la fila. Al día siguiente, estuve en casa .... (escuchar) la radio y .... (mirar) la tele durante todo el día para revivir el maravilloso espectáculo. Aunque habíamos estado .... (esperar) durante horas, valió la pena.

(6) **Mafalda** Fíjese en la historieta. ¿Qué música le gusta a Mafalda? ¿Le parece necesario entender la letra de las canciones? ¿O piensa que es suficiente con disfrutar de la melodía? Coméntelo con su compañero/a.

© Joaquín Salvador Lavado (QUINO) Toda Mafalda — Ediciones de La Flor, 1993
entendés (voseo) *you understand* **perro** *dog* **guau** *woof*

 MI EXPERIENCIA

(7) **Un año** Elija con su compañero/a un año, descríbanlo y defiendan su opinión.

GUIÓN DE TRABAJO

En el año 2000, 2005, 2010, 2015, ¿cuántos años tenías?
¿qué música...?
¿qué película...?
¿qué programas...?
¿qué recuerdos...?
¿qué estabas haciendo...?

→ solía...
tenía...
escuchaba...
miraba...
En el año...
estaba...

 Practice more at **vhlcentral.com.**

Hablar de acciones pasadas en desarrollo

• ¿Qué hicieron ayer?
■ **Estuvimos durmiendo** la siesta toda la tarde.

14B.2 **estar** (*past tense*) + [*present participle*]

Vocabulario *cont.*

el grupo musical *music group*
el sitio web *Web site*
la década, admirar, instalar, el/la investigador(a)
(5)
el/la aficionado/a *fan*
revivir *to relive*
(6)
a mediados de los 60 *in the midsixties*
la clase media *middle class*
incansable *tireless*
plantearse preguntas *to question*
la historieta *comic strip*
brillante

Mafalda

Este simpático personaje del humorista Quino (Joaquín Salvador Lavado) es una niña muy inteligente que vive en Argentina a mediados de los 60 y principios de los 70. Forma parte de una típica familia de clase media y de un curioso grupo de amigos. Luchadora social incansable, siempre se plantea preguntas y hace comentarios brillantes sobre la actualidad de su país y del mundo. La historieta se publicó en los periódicos de 1964 a 1973 y ya ha sido traducida a 26 idiomas.

SAM: Actividades pp. 299–301

Cuéntame cómo pasó

Cuéntame cómo pasó

Es una serie de televisión española que durante muchos años ha sido y es líder de audiencia. Aunque se empezó a transmitir en 2001, la ficción se inicia en 1968 y muestra un retrato de la sociedad española a través de una familia de clase media, los Alcántara, que vive día a día la transformación de la España franquista en una democracia moderna. Los españoles recuerdan con esta serie lo del pluriempleo de sus padres, lo que representó la llegada de la tele al hogar, que se convirtió en un miembro más de la familia; lo de la emigración al resto de Europa; lo que contaban los abuelos; y más tarde la llegada de la democracia. En definitiva, representa la vida durante una transición democrática.

Antonio · Mercedes · Carlos · Herminia · Toni · Inés

Transmitir mensajes

Carlos: "Mañana voy a tu casa."

● Carlos me **comentó** ayer que hoy **venía** a mi casa.

14B.3 Indirect discourse: reporting verbs

Vocabulario

8

contar (o:ue) *to tell*

ser líder de audiencia *to be the highest rated*

el retrato *portrait*

día a día *day by day*

franquista *Francoist*

el pluriempleo *having more than one job, moonlighting*

la transición democrática *democratic transition*

la transformación, la democracia, la ficción

9

el capítulo *episode*

preguntar *to ask*

explicar *to explain*

comentar *to mention*

el sueldo *salary*

el/la publicista *publicist*

hondureño/a *Honduran*

---

8 a. Foto Observe la foto. ¿Qué tipo de familia representa? ¿De qué época? ¿Por qué aparece la tele en la foto familiar? Lea el texto y compruebe.

b. Personajes ¿Cómo cree que son los personajes de la serie? Coméntelo con su compañero/a.

9 a. Cuéntame cómo pasó Lea las descripciones de lo que dijeron los personajes en los primeros capítulos de la serie. ¿Quién dijo qué? Relacione las columnas.

1. Antonio preguntó a su familia por qué nunca cenaban todos juntos. → *¿Por qué nunca cenamos todos juntos?*

2. Toni le explicó a su hermana Inés que a sus padres los habían educado así, pero que ahora era diferente. — *Es necesario otro sueldo. Muchas chicas ya trabajan, es normal.*

3. Mercedes preguntó cuándo le habían dicho que traían la televisión. — *A papá y a mamá los educaron así, pero ahora es diferente.*

4. Inés le comentó a su madre que era necesario otro sueldo, que muchas chicas ya trabajaban y que era normal. — *¿Cuándo te han dicho que traen la televisión?*

b. Transformar Transforme las oraciones de estilo directo al estilo indirecto. Use los verbos **preguntar, decir** y **comentar.**

> **Modelo:** María: "Mi hermana quiere ser publicista."
> *María comentó que su hermana quería ser publicista.*

1. Pablo: "La semana pasada vi un musical muy divertido."
....

2. Cristina: "Tengo mucho sueño porque hoy me he levantado a las 6 de la mañana." ....

3. Teresa: "¿Qué solían hacer ustedes durante las vacaciones cuando eran niños?"
....

4. Marcelo: "La mamá de mi mejor amigo es guatemalteca y el papá es hondureño." ....

5. Analía: "¿Quieren cenar en casa? Mi marido va a preparar empanadas."
....

10 Representar Imagine con su compañero/a una conversación entre estos personajes de la serie sobre el tema propuesto. Represéntenla.

Mercedes empieza a trabajar.

Modelo: • **Mercedes**: *Antonio, quiero empezar a trabajar.*
        • **Antonio**: ...

En el anterior capítulo Mercedes le dijo a Antonio que quería empezar a trabajar y entonces Antonio le dijo que...

11 a. Temas Lea de nuevo el texto sobre la serie. ¿Qué temas trata?

Trata lo de... •
Trata lo que... •

- el pluriempleo.
- representó la llegada de la tele.
- la emigración al resto de Europa.
- contaban nuestros abuelos.

b. Responder ¿Era lo mismo en su país en esa época? ¿Qué vivieron sus padres y sus abuelos en esa época?

Modelo: *Mi madre cuenta que...*

12 Escuchar Escuche la publicidad de la serie en la radio. ¿Qué es lo de la hija de los Alcántara?

13 ¿Qué palabra? Escuche de nuevo el audio y señale qué palabra se usa para controlar el contacto en la conversación.

   ○ Mira...   ○ ¿Sabes?   ○ Ya...   ○ ¿Perdona?

14 Contestar ¿Hay alguna serie como *Cuéntame cómo pasó* en su país? ¿Cree que tendría éxito en otro país?

MI EXPERIENCIA

15 Mi serie de televisión favorita Seleccione su serie de televisión favorita (de ahora o de hace años) o una película para contársela a su compañero/a.

GUIÓN DE TRABAJO

Mi serie favorita es....
Cuando era pequeño/a, siempre miraba...
La mejor película que he visto es...

→

¿De qué trata?
¿Quiénes son los personajes?
¿Qué canal la emite?

Trata...
Los personajes...
En el último capítulo pasó...
Entonces el protagonista dijo/comentó/preguntó...

Los años 60

En España en los 60 tuvo lugar una gran transformación económica y social. La explosión turística, el éxodo rural y la emigración al resto de Europa, junto con las inversiones extranjeras, facilitaron la salida de la posguerra y la entrada en una sociedad de consumo. La ilusión de muchos era comprar un pequeño piso, un coche SEAT 600 y un televisor y tener unas pequeñas vacaciones en la costa.

Referirse a un tema

- ¿Sabes **lo que** dijo Toni ayer?
- Dijo que **lo de** casarse no tenía sentido.

14B.4 **lo que** + [*verb*], **lo de** + [*noun/infinitive*]

Estrategia

Controlar el contacto

- ¿Sigues la serie *Cuéntame*?
- No, no tengo tiempo, el trabajo, las clases... Me gusta más la radio, ¿sabes?

Vocabulario

10
anterior *previous*
el éxodo *exodus*
la inversión *investment*
la posguerra *postwar period*
la explosión

11
tratar *to be about*

15
emitir la serie *to broadcast the (television) series*

SAM: Actividades pp. 302–304

Macarena Berlín, *Hablar por hablar*

La periodista madrileña no quería dejar su programa de radio en Cadena Dial, pero en febrero de 2009, cuando le ofrecieron dirigir el programa de radio *Hablar por hablar* de la Cadena Ser —líder de la noche—, aceptó. Desde 1989, de lunes a viernes de 01:30 a 04:00 h, miles de personas escuchan cada noche las historias que otros oyentes cuentan a través de las líneas telefónicas del programa. Muchas veces la solución inmediata llega a través de otra llamada o por medio de los "chatines": redactores espontáneos que, a través de un chat, mandan sus comentarios a las historias. En Colombia, Radio Caracol, emisora hermana de la Cadena Ser, también emitió su *Hablar por hablar* de 2001 a 2014.

Macarena Berlín, locutora de radio

ENTREVISTA A MACARENA EN EL BLOG DE LOS CHATINES:

Macarena, cuando te acuestas cada día, ¿piensas en las personas que llaman al programa? [...]
Procuro desconectar antes de dormir, pero a veces es inevitable no recordar esa llamada que te ha tocado el corazón.

¿Echas de menos los programas que estabas haciendo?
Yo entiendo la vida como un camino con etapas. Cada aventura es una nueva y fascinante, así que no te permite extrañar la anterior.

¿Te ha costado adaptarte al horario de la noche?
Como ya llevaba unos años de noche, la verdad es que no.

¿Con qué tipo de periodismo identificas tu profesión?
Con el que no traspasa los límites del respeto.

¿Crees que el hilo conductor que mueve el programa es el morbo, el insomnio, la empatía o simplemente la curiosidad?
La empatía, seguro... todos hemos vivido conflictos alguna vez.

Expresar intenciones no realizadas

- ¿**Querías** cambiar de trabajo?
- Sí, **pensaba** cambiar de trabajo, **pero** me ofrecieron un nuevo proyecto y me quedé.

14B.5 **quería/pensaba +** [*infinitive*] **pero +** [*verb*]

Vocabulario

16

hablar por hablar *to talk for the sake of it*

la cadena de radio *radio network*

el/la oyente *listener*

a través de *through*

por medio de *by means of*

espontáneo/a *impromptu*

la emisora *radio station*

procurar *to try*

echar de menos (*Esp.*) *to miss*

costar (o:ue) *to be difficult*

traspasar *to go beyond*

el hilo *thread*

el morbo *morbid interest*

el insomnio

---

16 **a. Expresión** ¿Sabe lo que significa la expresión *hablar por hablar*? Después de conocer a nuestra protagonista y su programa, seleccione la definición adecuada. ¿Cree que es una expresión positiva? Coméntelo con sus compañeros.

- Decir algo sin fundamento.
- Hablar mucho.
- Hablar sin escuchar.

b. Contestar ¿Qué tipo de programa es *Hablar por hablar*? ¿De qué trata?

17 **Macarena Berlín** Lea la entrevista a Macarena Berlín. Marque verdadero (V) o falso (F).

	V	F
1. Macarena pensaba dirigir en 1989 *Hablar por hablar*, pero empezó en televisión.	☐	☐
2. La locutora dice que siempre extraña sus anteriores programas.	☐	☐
3. No fue difícil para Macarena adaptarse al horario de la noche.	☐	☐

18 **a. Motivos** Antes de escuchar la llamada titulada "Mercedes comienza a trabajar mañana después de 22 años", piense en los motivos de la llamada.

- ¿Cuál cree que es su testimonio?
- ¿Cree que Mercedes quería hacer algo en su pasado que al final no hizo?

b. La llamada Ahora escuche. ¿Por qué está Mercedes nerviosísima? ¿Cómo reacciona Macarena? ¿Qué dice Mercedes para comprobar que Macarena la escucha?

19 **Comentar** Mercedes no quería dejar su profesión, pero, por diferentes motivos, tuvo que hacerlo. ¿Hay algo que usted (no) quería o pensaba hacer en los últimos años pero (no) hizo? Coméntelo con su compañero/a.

Modelo: *Pensaba hacer un curso de..., pero...*

20 **Hablar por hablar** El programa *Hablar por hablar* tiene un blog que sirve de comunicación entre los oyentes, los "chatines" y Macarena. Lea lo que escribe esta persona y enumere los motivos por los que *Hablar por hablar* "engancha". ¿Se le ocurre alguno más?

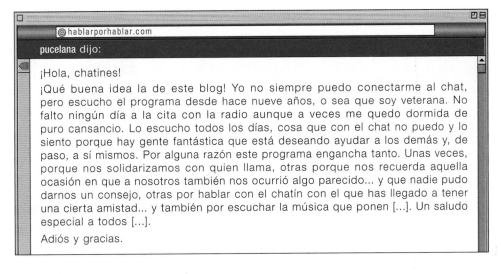

@ hablarporhablar.com

pucelana dijo:

¡Hola, chatines!

¡Qué buena idea la de este blog! Yo no siempre puedo conectarme al chat, pero escucho el programa desde hace nueve años, o sea que soy veterana. No falto ningún día a la cita con la radio aunque a veces me quedo dormida de puro cansancio. Lo escucho todos los días, cosa que con el chat no puedo y lo siento porque hay gente fantástica que está deseando ayudar a los demás y, de paso, a sí mismos. Por alguna razón este programa engancha tanto. Unas veces, porque nos solidarizamos con quien llama, otras porque nos recuerda aquella ocasión en que a nosotros también nos ocurrió algo parecido... y que nadie pudo darnos un consejo, otras por hablar con el chatín con el que has llegado a tener una cierta amistad... y también por escuchar la música que ponen [...]. Un saludo especial a todos [...].

Adiós y gracias.

- ○ Porque ....
- ○ Porque ....
- ○ Por ....
- ○ Por ....

21 **Escribir** Imagínese que usted es un "chatín" y escriba un comentario para Mercedes.

@ hablarporhablar.com

22 **Caracol** Lea este texto. ¿Por qué se emitió *Hablar por hablar* en Colombia? ¿Qué es lo que cambió de un programa a otro?

Colombia

Caracol Radio, una de las cadenas de radio más prestigiosas de América Latina, forma parte del Grupo Prisa Radio, el mismo grupo al que pertenece la Cadena Ser de España, y son "emisoras hermanas". Por eso, algunos programas tienen el mismo formato en los dos países, pero se producen con contenidos propios en cada país. Patricia Pardo fue "la Macarena colombiana": de lunes a jueves dirigió el programa *Hablar por hablar* de 23:00 a 2:00 de la mañana. En este espacio, los oyentes compartían sus historias, sus sueños, lo que les preocupaba o lo que les alegraba en la vida... y Patricia, sobre todo, los escuchaba. Todo con acento colombiano.

Vocabulario

20

enganchar *to get someone hooked*

la cita *appointment, date*

el cansancio *tiredness*

de paso *in the process*

solidarizarse (con) *to support someone*

la finalidad *purpose*

veterano/a

22

los contenidos *content*

el formato

23

el choque cultural *culture shock*

el reportaje *article*

el/la costarricense *person from Costa Rica*

chocar *to surprise; to collide*

OPINIÓN

¿Conoce algún programa como *Hablar por hablar*?

¿Qué finalidad tiene un programa así?

SAM: Actividades pp. 305–310

23 **a. Choque cultural** Lea el texto y complete el mapa de ideas en una hoja aparte.

@ choquecultural.com

INICIO   ACERCA DE...   CONTACTO   ARCHIVO   ENLACES   FOTOS   VIDEOS

Choque cultural

¡Hola a todos! Bienvenidos a *Choque cultural,* mi blog sobre viajes. Cada semana publicaré fotos, videos y reportajes de los diferentes lugares del mundo que he conocido. Quizás se pregunten quién soy y cómo es que he estado en tantos sitios. Me presentaré: Mi nombre es Rita y soy una guía de turismo costarricense. Gracias a mi trabajo he tenido la suerte de visitar muchísimos países y de conocer diferentes culturas, costumbres y tradiciones. Ahora quiero compartir con ustedes lo que más me gusta y lo que más me choca de todos esos destinos. Abróchense los cinturones y ¡buen viaje!

Montevideo, Uruguay

Cuzco, Perú

Chicago, Estados Unidos

Fez, Marruecos

Río de Janeiro, Brasil

(CHOQUE CULTURAL)

○ ¿Qué es? ○ ¿De qué trata? ○ ¿Quién lo escribe? ○ ¿Qué cree que es un choque cultural?

b. Fotos ¿Conoce alguna de las ciudades de las imágenes? Piense en un "choque cultural" que puede producirse para usted en alguno de estos sitios u otros y coméntelo con la clase.

c. Responder ¿Cree que Internet es un buen medio para conocer otras culturas? ¿Qué tipo de conocimiento cultural solo se puede aprender "en directo"?

TAREA FINAL

Las imágenes de una década

Decidan, en grupos pequeños, qué década quieren presentar y qué tipo de secciones va a tener la presentación: música, cine, series de televisión, anuncios, programas de radio, de deporte, etc.

Recojan imágenes, noticias y declaraciones de los personajes más significativos de esa década. Anoten también sus recuerdos sobre estos programas.

Seleccionen las declaraciones para transmitirlas a sus compañeros. Digan también qué les llamó la atención y por qué.

Desarrollen una presentación con las noticias, las imágenes y las declaraciones más representativas e interesantes.

YO PUEDO...

• Puedo situar hechos pasados.
¿Qué recuerdos tiene de su infancia? ¿Qué hacía cuando era joven?

• Puedo hablar de acciones pasadas en desarrollo.
Termine estas oraciones.
Ayer estaba vistiéndome cuando...
Durante todo el día he estado...

• Puedo transmitir mensajes.
Cuéntele a su compañero/a algo que le dijeron ayer.

• Puedo referirme a un tema.
Coméntele a su compañero/a algo referido a un tema de esta lección.

• Puedo expresar intenciones no realizadas.
¿Hay algo que quería hacer y no hizo, o algo que no iba a hacer y finalmente hizo?

GRAMÁTICA FUNCIONAL (S) Tutorials

14B.1 Situate past events

cuando + [*imperfect / preterite*]   5.2.3, 5.4.3, 5.6, 12.13

- Use **cuando** with either the **pretérito imperfecto** or the **pretérito indefinido** to describe when events occurred in the past. Use the **pretérito imperfecto** to refer to a habitual action or situation.

> **Cuando** Paula **trabajaba** en el restaurante, tomaba el autobús todos los días.
> *When Paula worked at the restaurant, she took the bus every day.*

- Always use the **pretérito imperfecto** to refer to age with **tener**.

> **Cuando tenía** 18 años, viajé a Europa por primera vez.
> *When I was 18 years old, I traveled to Europe for the first time.*

- Use **cuando** with the **pretérito indefinido** to refer to a specific, completed action.

> **Cuando terminé** la secundaria, mis padres me regalaron una cámara.
> *When I finished high school, my parents gave me a camera.*

14B.2 Talk about past actions in progress

estar (*past tense*) + [*present participle*];
Irregular present participles   5.14.2, 5.15

- Use a past form of the verb **estar** + [*present participle*] to describe an ongoing action in the past.

> Pedro **estaba cocinando** cuando escuchó la noticia por la radio.
> *Pedro was cooking when he heard the news on the radio.*

- You can use the **pretérito perfecto**, the **pretérito indefinido,** or the **pretérito imperfecto** in this construction. You learned the differences between these three tenses in **10B.1**.

- You learned the regular forms of the present participle (**el gerundio**) in **7A.3**. Remember that if the stem of an **-er** or **-ir** verb ends in a vowel, the present participle ends in **-yendo** (e.g., **traer→trayendo**).

- Stem-changing **-ir** verbs also undergo a change to form the present participle. Verbs with an **e→ie** or **e→i** stem change in the present tense undergo an **e→i** stem change to form the present participle. Verbs with an **o→ue** stem change in the present tense undergo an **o→u** stem change to form the present participle.

| e→i | prefer**ir**→prefir**iendo** | d**e**cir, v**e**nir, p**e**dir, v**e**stir... |
| o→u | dormir→durmiendo | p**o**der, m**o**rir... |

> Evo estaba **durmiendo** la siesta cuando llegamos a la casa.
> *Evo was taking a nap when we arrived at the house.*

¡Póngalo en práctica!

G1 **Cuando...** Complete las oraciones con el pretérito indefinido y/o el pretérito imperfecto.

1. Cuando .... (yo, ser) pequeño, siempre .... (yo, jugar) afuera con mis amigos después del colegio.

2. Anoche cuando tú y Gabriela .... (llegar) a la fiesta, los otros invitados ya .... (estar) ahí.

3. Cuando Miguel .... (estudiar) en la universidad, ... (vivir) en una residencia estudiantil.

4. Cuando .... (nosotros, tener) cinco años, ... (estrenarse) *Buscando a Nemo*.

5. Cuando .... (nacer) mi hermana menor, mis abuelos me .... (llevar) al hospital a conocerla.

6. Cuando Javier y Luis .... (empezar) a estudiar inglés en la academia, no .... (conocerse).

G2 **Pasado progresivo** Complete las oraciones con la forma correcta del pasado progresivo.

- Sr. Pérez, ¿(1)........................ (ir) a las reuniones de este mes?
- No, pero ayer (2)........................ (leer) las actas de todas las reuniones durante cuatro horas.

- ¿Qué hicieron tus hermanos ayer, Susana?
- Nada especial, (3)........................ (escuchar) la radio toda la tarde.

  Cuando Pepe (4)........................ (preparar) la comida, comenzó el programa.

  Últimamente yo (5)........................ (estudiar) en el café de la esquina.

  Anoche Julio y yo (6)........................ (mirar) el partido de fútbol hasta las once.

G3 **Contestar** Conteste las preguntas con la forma correcta del verbo entre paréntesis.

1. • ¿Qué estabas haciendo ayer a las ocho? (dormir)
   ■ ....

2. • ¿Qué estabais haciendo tú y tus amigas ayer a las siete? (vestirse)
   ■ .... para la fiesta.

3. • ¿Qué estaba haciendo Juan? (traer)
   ■ .... unos libros y se cayó.

4. • ¿Qué estuvieron haciendo tus primos ayer? (mirar)
   ■ .... la tele todo el día.

(S) Practice more at **vhlcentral.com.**

GRAMÁTICA FUNCIONAL

14B.3 Convey messages

Indirect discourse: reporting verbs 5.6, 12.10

- Use indirect discourse (**el estilo indirecto**) to report what another person has said. Reporting verbs, or verbs that are used to relate someone else's speech, include **decir**, **comentar**, **explicar**, and **preguntar**.

- In **11A.2**, you learned to use indirect discourse in the present tense. This chart shows the transformation of the main verb when using reporting verbs in the past tenses.

Direct discourse "...." →	Indirect discourse explicó/decía/comentó que...
presente	pretérito imperfecto
pretérito perfecto	pretérito pluscuamperfecto
pretérito imperfecto	pretérito imperfecto
pretérito indefinido	pretérito indefinido pretérito pluscuamperfecto

Gloria: "El mes pasado **fui** tres veces al cine."
Gloria me **comentó que** el mes pasado **fue/había ido** tres veces al cine.
Gloria: *"Last month I went to the movies three times."*
Gloria told me that she went/had gone to the movies three times last month.

14B.4 Refer to a topic

lo de + [*noun/infinitive*], **lo que** + [*verb*] 3.3.2, 5.13

- Use **lo de** + [*noun/infinitive*] or **lo que** + [*conjugated verb*] to refer to a topic in a general sense.

¿Sabes **lo que dijo** el ministro de Cultura? Dijo que **lo de ir** al cine gratis a partir de los 65 años no será posible.
*Do you know **what** the Minister of Culture **said**? He said that **the thing about going** to the movies for free if you are 65 or older is not going to be possible.*

14B.5 Express unfulfilled intentions

quería/pensaba + [*infinitive*], **pero** + [*verb*] 5.4.3, 12.8

- Use the **pretérito imperfecto** of **querer** or **pensar** + [*infinitive*] to express intentions that were not fulfilled.

Pensábamos organizar una fiesta sorpresa.
We were planning on organizing a surprise party.

- To express the condition or event that caused the plan to change, use **pero** + [*conjugated verb*].

Yo quería estudiar medicina, **pero** al final **hice** periodismo.
*I wanted to study medicine, **but** in the end I studied journalism.*

- Note that **poder** and **querer** have slightly different meanings in affirmative and negative statements in the preterite.

afirmativo	**pude**	*I succeeded*	**quise**	*I tried (to)*
negativo	**no pude**	*I failed (to)*	**no quise**	*I refused (to)*

¡Póngalo en práctica!

G4 **Transformar** Transforme las afirmaciones y preguntas al estilo indirecto.

Modelo: "Solía leer antes de acostarme."
Rosa dijo que *solía leer antes de acostarse.*

1. "¿Te acuerdas de las canciones de R.E.M.?"
   Andrés me preguntó si
   ....

2. "Antes había menos programas de televisión."
   Mi madre dijo que antes
   ....

3. "¿Cuándo te fuiste de vacaciones?"
   Mi jefe me preguntó cuándo
   ....

4. "Esta mañana he visto a un viejo amigo."
   Mi compañero de cuarto me comentó ayer que
   ....

5. "Me encanta la música hip-hop."
   Domingo me contó que
   ....

6. "Hemos viajado a Panamá cinco veces."
   Laura y Juan me comentaron que
   ....

G5 **Completar** Complete las oraciones con **lo que** o **lo de**.

- ¿Sabes (1).............. la hermana de Isa? Me han dicho que (2).............. nos contaba de su novio era mentira.
- Sí, y (3).............. irse a vivir a Jamaica también.

- ¿Piensas que es cierto (4).............. Felipe nos dijo ayer?
- ¿(5).............. la tormenta de granizo en verano? Sí, creo que sí.

G6 **Conversaciones** Complete las conversaciones con **pero** o la forma adecuada de **querer** o **pensar**.

- Dolores, ¿no (1)............................. (tú, querer) ir ayer a la exposición del Museo del Prado?
- Sí, (2)............................. (pensar) ir, (3)............................. al final no fui.

- Santiago y Víctor, ¿(4)............................. (pensar) trabajar en la biblioteca durante el verano?
- Sí, (5)............................. (querer) trabajar allí, (6)............................. no conseguimos el trabajo.

G7 **Reescribir** Reescriba las oraciones con **poder** o **querer**.

1. Me fue imposible abrir la puerta.
2. Le pidieron escribir una canción y dijo que no.
3. ¡Qué bien! Terminaste la investigación.

 Practice more at **vhlcentral.com**.

VOCABULARIO 🔊 Ⓢ Vocabulary Tools

La mejor década

a mediados de los 60	in the mid-sixties
el/la aficionado/a	fan
la clase media	middle class
la década	decade
el grupo musical	music group
la historieta	comic strip
el/la investigador(a)	investigator
la página web	Web page
la serie de televisión	television series
el sitio web	Web site
el/la telespectador(a)	television viewer
admirar	to admire
aprender de memoria	to memorize
estrenarse	to premiere
instalar	to install
llorar	to cry
pasar la serie de televisión	to broadcast the television series
plantearse preguntas	to question
revivir	to relive
brillante	brilliant
fascinado/a	fascinated
ganador(a)	winning
incansable	tireless

Cuéntame cómo pasó

el capítulo	episode
la democracia	democracy
el éxodo	exodus
la explosión	explosion
la ficción	fiction
la inversión	investment
el pluriempleo	having more than one job, moonlighting
la posguerra	postwar period
el/la publicista	publicist
el retrato	portrait
el sueldo	salary
la transformación	transformation
la transición democrática	democratic transition
comentar	to mention
contar (o:ue)	to tell
emitir la serie	to broadcast the (television) series
explicar	to explain
preguntar	to ask
ser líder de audiencia	to be the highest rated
tratar	to be about
anterior	previous
franquista	Francoist
hondureño/a	Honduran
día a día	day by day

Macarena Berlín

hablar por hablar	to talk for the sake of it
la cadena de radio	radio network
el cansancio	tiredness
el choque cultural	culture shock
la cita	appointment, date
los contenidos	content
el/la costarricense	person from Costa Rica
la emisora	radio station
la finalidad	purpose
el formato	format
el hilo	thread
el insomnio	insomnia
el morbo	morbid interest
el/la oyente	listener
el reportaje	article
chocar	to surprise; to collide
costar (o:ue)	to be difficult
echar de menos (Esp.)	to miss
enganchar	to get someone hooked
procurar	to try
solidarizarse (con)	to support someone
traspasar	to go beyond
espontáneo/a	impromptu
veterano/a	veteran
a través de	through
de paso	in the process
por medio de	by means of

Variación léxica

el capítulo ⟷ el episodio

fascinado/a ⟷ deslumbrado/a ⟷ encantado/a

pasar la serie de televisión ⟷ poner/echar la serie de televisión (Esp.)

el sueldo ⟷ la paga ⟷ el salario

el/la telespectador(a) ⟷ el/la televidente (Amér. L.)

Estrategias

1 Dar una explicación
Lección 13A

Explaining the reasoning behind a situation can help people understand you better. Expressions such as **es que** and **como** are used to introduce an explanation.

○ Busque la mejor explicación para estas situaciones y piense en otras.

Situación	Explicación

Situación

- Usted no ha hecho la tarea.
- Ha llegado tarde a la clase de español.
- Ha olvidado el cumpleaños de su mejor amigo/a.

Explicación

- Su perro está enfermo y ha tenido que ir al veterinario con él.
- En su oficina hay mucho trabajo. Ha tenido que hacer horas extras.
- No hay sitio en la calle para aparcar el coche.
- ¿...?

2 Destacar una información
Lección 13B

Emphasizing a particular piece of information with expressions such as **solo/solamente** or **sobre todo** will help you communicate more effectively.

○ Relacione estos elementos.

- En el trabajo, Paula se lleva mal con todos, pero... •
- Nunca tenemos vacaciones en invierno,... •
- Tengo un contrato de trabajo de... •
- No quiero trabajar por las mañanas,... •

solo/solamente
sobre todo

- • una semana en Navidad.
- • 20 horas.
- • con su jefe.
- • por mis estudios.

3 Pedir repetición
Lección 14A

It's important to be able to ask for repetition when you do not understand something. Use expressions such as **¿Perdona?/¿Perdone?** and **¿Cómo?** to ask for repetition.

○ Lea uno de estos textos a su compañero/a. Su compañero/a interrumpe cuando no entiende algo.

Estudiante A

Mi amigo Ndongo es ecuatoguineano. En su casa hablan el bubi, que es una de las lenguas que se hablan en Guinea Ecuatorial, además del español, que es una de las lenguas oficiales.

Estudiante B

Cuando llegué a casa de mi amiga, Petra me dijo *m'bolo*. Es el saludo fang, una de las lenguas que se hablan en Guinea Ecuatorial.

4 Controlar el contacto
Lección 14B

Use expressions such as **¿Sabes?/¿Sabe?** to check comprehension and ensure fluent conversation.

○ Complete este diálogo con la palabra adecuada.

- ¿Vas mucho al cine?
- Pues no, nunca tengo tiempo. Estudio dos carreras y encima trabajo, ... Prefiero comprarme las películas en DVD y así las veo cuando quiero.

mira | sí, ya...
¿sabes? | ¿perdona?

○ En parejas, preparen una conversación con otra de las expresiones para controlar el contacto.

Competencias

PEDIR Y CONFIRMAR INFORMACIÓN, DESCRIBIR UN VIAJE, RECOMENDAR

1 **En la agencia de viajes** Imagine que va a una agencia de viajes y su compañero/a es la persona que debe orientarlo/la. Escriban una conversación acerca de un viaje que hará a un lugar que su compañero/a ya ha visitado.

> Modelo: • Buenos días, ¿en qué puedo ayudarlo/la?
> • Buenos días. Me gustaría saber...

RELACIONAR IDEAS CONTRARIAS

2 **Las computadoras** Con su compañero/a, hable sobre las ventajas y los inconvenientes de usar una computadora portátil (*laptop*) y una computadora de escritorio (*desktop*). Usen las palabras del recuadro para relacionar las ideas contrarias.

> a pesar de • aunque • sin embargo

EXPRESAR POSESIÓN

3 **Completar** Complete la conversación con los adjetivos y pronombres posesivos correspondientes.

● ¿Te conté que estoy buscando empleo?

■ ¿Y (1)............. anterior trabajo? ¿No te gustaba?

● No era el trabajo en sí lo que me afectaba; era (2)............. jefe.

■ Por suerte, yo me llevo bien con el (3)............... ¿Qué pasó?

● Después de cinco años aconsejándole sobre todo, desde una buena escuela para (4)............. hijos hasta la corbata que debía llevar para (5)............. reuniones, he puesto punto final. (6)............. problemas se estaban convirtiendo en los (7)...............

HABLAR DE SITUACIONES HABITUALES EN EL PASADO, Y EXPRESAR DESCONOCIMIENTO Y CONDICIONES POSIBLES

4 **Elegir** Lucía escribió un testimonio acerca de su infancia, pero tiene algunas dudas con los tiempos verbales. ¿Puede ayudarla?

Cuando era pequeña, solía (1)**almorzar/almorzaba** en la casa de mi abuela después de la escuela. Me (2)**gustar/gustaba** acompañarla en la cocina cada día. Recuerdo que una vez (3)**preparaba/preparó** empanadas. Yo nunca las (4)**pruebo/había probado** y me encantaron. (5)**Pensaba/Pienso** que era una comida que mi abuela había inventado. No sabía que (6)**era/fue** un plato típico argentino. Algunos años más tarde (7)**encontraré/encontré** la receta en un blog de cocina. Las primeras no me (8)**salieron/salen** bien, pero la quinta docena que (9)**preparé/había preparado** fue exquisita. Si (10)**quisieron/quieren**, les enseño a hacerlas.

SITUAR HECHOS PASADOS, HABLAR DE ACCIONES PASADAS EN DESARROLLO, REFERIRSE A UN TEMA Y TRANSMITIR MENSAJES

5 **Estilo indirecto** Complete las oraciones y luego transmítalas en estilo indirecto.

> Modelo: "Cuando era pequeño, *iba* (ir) al parque todos los días."
> Pedro *dijo que cuando era pequeño, iba al parque todos los días.*

1. "Estoy cansada porque .... (estar) estudiando toda la semana."
Clara ....

2. "¿Ustedes cuándo .... (ir) a un partido de fútbol por última vez?"
Juan y Esteban ....

3. "Cuando tu mamá .... (tener) 10 años, no .... (haber) teléfonos inteligentes."
Tomás ....

4. "¿Sabéis lo que .... (comentar) la profesora el otro día?"
Yo ....

Video

La comida latina

Ya ha leído sobre cómo las distintas culturas influyen en las personas y se convierten en parte de su historia, sea en Guinea Ecuatorial o en España. Este episodio de **Flash Cultura** muestra uno de los aspectos esenciales de la cultura hispana: la comida, presente con sus platos tradicionales en la ciudad de Los Ángeles.

(1) **Preguntas** Hable con un(a) compañero/a. ¿Ha probado platos de distintos países? ¿Cuál es su favorito? ¿Qué piensa que debe ofrecer un restaurante de comida típica de su país en el extranjero?

(2) **Mirar** Mire el video. ¿Cuánto sabía sobre la comida latina antes de verlo? Y ahora, ¿qué cosas nuevas aprendió?

Vocabulario útil

abarcar *to encompass, to cover*
confeccionar *to make*
en cada esquina *on every corner*
molido/a *ground*
picado/a *chopped*
probar (o:ue) *to taste*
rallar *to grate*
la rebanada *slice*
sin remedio/no hay
   remedio *hopeless*
sabroso/a *tasty*

Hay quienes aseguran que el taco es la hamburguesa del siglo XXI.

En los últimos años... también hay más lugares donde podemos comprar productos hispanos.

(3) **Seleccionar** Complete las oraciones con la opción correcta.

1. Un taco americano lleva carne
   a. molida.   b. rallada.

2. El ingrediente fundamental de la comida mexicana es el
   a. aguacate.   b. chile.

3. El cortadito es la versión cubana del
   a. licor de café.   b. café espresso.

4. Inca Kola es una bebida de
   a. Perú.   b. México.

5. Para condimentar una comida latina se necesitan
   a. cocos.   b. especias.

(4) **Representar** Con un(a) compañero/a, represente una conversación en la que comenta las sorpresas que tuvo al visitar Los Ángeles.

> Modelo: • *Antes de ir a Los Ángeles, no había probado nunca los tamales. Son muy ricos.*
>   • *¿Hay tamales en Los Ángeles? Pensaba que era comida mexicana...*

 Practice more at **vhlcentral.com**.

Unidad 15

Evaristo Acebedo, Casa Vera

Marina Sánchez, un genio de los números

Las alpacas

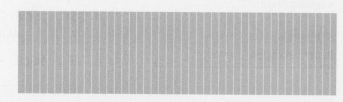

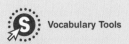
15A

DE LA MADRE TIERRA

¿Qué comeremos?

CACAO EN POLVO
CONSERVAR EN LUGAR FRESCO Y SECO
CONSUMIR PREFERENTEMENTE
ANTES DE: Ver zona superior
250 g

Ingredientes: frambuesas, azúcar, gelificante (pectina), acidulante (ácido cítrico), conservante (E-202).
Preparado con 45 g de frambuesas por 100 g
Contenido total de azúcares 50 g por 100 g

AZÚCAR MORENO DE CAÑA INTEGRAL
PROCEDENTE DE LA AGRICULTURA ECOLÓGICA
Valores nutricionales

Valores energéticos y nutricionales medios por 100g:

1700 kJ - 400 kcal	
Proteínas	0g
Hidratos de carbono	100g
Grasas/Lípidos	0g

Sin Gluten

Ingredientes: tomate, aceite de oliva virgen extra (6.1%), azúcar y sal.

SIN CONSERVANTES NI COLORANTES

Ideal para sus recetas vegetarianas

Expresar probabilidad

¿**Habrá** algún producto de alimentación 100% natural o **tendrán** todos conservantes?

15A.1 Review of simple future
Simple future: irregular forms

Vocabulario

①

la frambuesa *raspberry*

el conservante *preservative*

el cacao en polvo *cocoa powder*

seco/a *dry*

la agricultura ecológica *organic farming*

el hidrato de carbono *carbohydrate*

la grasa *fat*

el tomate frito *tomato sauce*

el aceite de oliva virgen extra *extra virgin olive oil*

endulzar *to sweeten*

cocido/a *cooked*

espolvorear *to sprinkle*

el ingrediente, la proteína, el gluten, el colorante, vegetariano/a

②

la etiqueta *label*

la conservación *preservation*

---

1 **Relacionar** Fíjese en la imagen y relacione los productos con las descripciones.

- Se usa sobre los platos de pasta. ☐
- Es fruta cocida en azúcar. ☐
- Sirve para endulzar el café. ☐
- Se espolvorea sobre el tiramisú. ☐

2 **Clasificar** Lea la información que ofrecen las etiquetas y clasifíquela. ¿Qué información le interesa a usted y por qué?

Composición	frambuesas,...
Conservación y consumo	conservar en lugar fresco y seco, ...
Información nutricional	proteínas,...
Origen	agricultura ecológica

3 **Escuchar** Escuche esta conversación entre dos clientes en un supermercado. Escriba el infinitivo que se usa en cada oración.

saber • querer • poner • venir
decir • haber • hacer • poder

1. ¿De dónde vendrán? (las frutas) ....
2. Lo pondrá en la etiqueta. (el origen) ....
3. ¿Podremos encontrar esta información? ....
4. ¿Quién lo sabrá? ....
5. ¿Cómo harán estos alimentos? ....
6. ¿Habrá algún dependiente? ....
7. ¿Querrán atendernos? ....
8. Me dirán que si... ....

4 **Completar** Complete el diálogo con el futuro simple de probabilidad.

- Invité a Carlos y a Graciela a cenar.
- Hay que preparar algo especial para Graciela, ¿no?

- Sí, pero no recuerdo qué. ¿............. (Ser) vegetariana?
- Sí, alguna vez me dijo que no come carne ni pescado.

- ¿............. (Poder) comer queso? Así le preparamos un suflé...
- Sí. ¿............. (Tener) problema si los demás comemos un asado?

5 **Sugerencias** Escuche la conversación de nuevo y anote las sugerencias sobre estos temas.

- ¿Tendrán gluten estas galletas?
- ¿Habrá algún dependiente por aquí?
- Yo creo que sí, pero...
- No sé, yo creo que...

6 **Escribir** Elija una situación y escriba un correo electrónico a la tienda de alimentación donde lo compró con sus dudas y sugerencias como consumidor.

Compra un producto fresco, pero no tiene etiqueta y no sabe si tiene algún conservante.

Es celíaco. Compra un producto que cree que no tiene gluten, pero en la etiqueta no encuentra ninguna información.

Compra un producto en un envase de plástico. Lleva el símbolo de envase reciclable, pero no sabe en qué contenedor reciclar el envase.

7 **a. Símbolos** ¿Qué cree que significan estos símbolos? Revise las etiquetas de los envases de la actividad 1 y relacione.

vegetariano [3] comercio justo [ ] producto ecológico [ ] envase reciclable [ ] sin gluten [ ]

b. Ordenar Ordene de mayor a menor importancia, para usted, la información que aportan estos símbolos y comente su opinión con su compañero/a.

MI EXPERIENCIA

8 **Dudas y sugerencias** Fíjese en los datos que aparecen en el envase de helado. Comparta con un(a) compañero/a sus dudas y sugerencias sobre este y otros productos.

GUIÓN DE TRABAJO

Composición
Información nutricional

Conservación y consumo
Origen

¿Será un producto bajo en calorías?
¿Qué fecha de caducidad tendrá?
¿Será ecológico?

Lo mejor es/sería...

Hacer sugerencias

- Lo mejor sería leer la etiqueta.
- Lo mejor es la confianza en el producto.

15A.2 **lo mejor es/sería** + [*infinitive/noun*]

Vocabulario *cont.*

la información nutricional
nutritional information

la composición
④ _____

la certeza *certainty*

el suflé
⑥ _____

el producto fresco *fresh food*

el envase de plástico *plastic container*

el envase reciclable *recyclable container*

el contenedor *(recycling) container*

celíaco/a
⑦ _____

el producto ecológico *organic product*
⑧ _____

la leche entera *whole milk*

la leche descremada en polvo *powdered skim milk*

el jarabe *syrup*

apto/a para *appropriate/safe for*

bajo/a en calorías *low-calorie*

la fecha de caducidad *expiration date*

artificial

INGREDIENTES: leche entera, azúcar, leche descremada en polvo, jarabe de glucosa, cacao en polvo, estabilizantes, emulsionantes, colorantes, aromatizantes artificiales.

SAM: Actividades pp. 311–313

Practice more at **vhlcentral.com**.

Mucho sabor

De: info@supermercadosveracruz.mx
Para: ana.rodriguez.pelaez@micorreo.mx
Asunto: Próxima apertura Supermercados Veracruz

SUPERMERCADOS VERACRUZ

¡Su mercado natural!

Estimado cliente:

SUPERMERCADOS VERACRUZ le ofrece la calidad de nuestros productos ecológicos, recogidos directamente de la tierra, sin conservantes ni colorantes, con todo su sabor y sus nutrientes. Queremos que nuestros productos le aporten todo lo mejor. Deseamos preservar el medio ambiente y que disfrute del sabor más auténtico de los alimentos. Queremos evitar el uso de pesticidas y ofrecer el alimento en su estado puro. Esperamos que asista a la apertura de nuestra nueva tienda y que disfrute de las promociones especiales. Ojalá que **SUPERMERCADOS VERACRUZ** cumpla con sus expectativas y mejore su alimentación y su salud.
Atentamente,
SUPERMERCADOS VERACRUZ, su mercado natural

Queremos potenciar el consumo de los alimentos naturales.
Queremos vender productos de calidad a buen precio.
Queremos cumplir con las necesidades y peticiones del consumidor.

Hablar de objetivos

Espero que nuestros productos **aporten** mucha calidad.

15A.3 **esperar/querer/desear que** + [*subjunctive*]
Present subjunctive: regular forms

Vocabulario

9

recogido/a *picked*
el sabor *flavor*
aportar *to provide*
evitar *to avoid*
asistir (a) *to attend*
la apertura *opening*
Ojalá *I/We wish*
cumplir con *to meet*
la expectativa *expectation*
potenciar *to foster*
el alimento natural *natural food*
el nutriente, preservar, el pesticida

---

9 **Correo** ¿Qué tipo de empresa envía este correo? ¿Qué la distingue de otras empresas? ¿Cuáles son sus objetivos en relación con estos temas?

- medio ambiente
- sabor de los alimentos
- apertura de tienda

Modelo: *Desean preservar el medio ambiente y quieren que sus productos le aporten al cliente todo lo mejor.*

10 **Supermercados Veracruz** Fíjese en la gráfica y complete las oraciones.

SUPERMERCADOS VERACRUZ
quiere/espera/desea

potenciar el consumo
vender productos de calidad
cumplir con las necesidades del consumidor

que EL CLIENTE/CONSUMIDOR...
......*consuma*...... (consumir) productos naturales.
.... (comprar) productos de calidad.
.... (ver) sus necesidades satisfechas.

11 **Objetivos** Añada más objetivos a este correo publicitario y haga una lista con su compañero/a. ¿Qué desean las empresas de sus clientes? ¿Y los clientes de las empresas?

Modelo: *Las empresas, por ejemplo las ecológicas, desean que sus clientes...*

12 a. Esperanzas En la cadena de consumo, el productor, la empresa y el consumidor tienen sus propios intereses. ¿A quién cree que pertenecen estas esperanzas?

> Ojalá que vendamos mucho.

> A ver si bajan los precios.

> A ver si llueve...

> Ojalá este año el tiempo mejore.

b. Mis esperanzas ¿Qué espera usted como consumidor(a) de los productores y de las empresas?

13 Desacuerdo Lea esta conversación. ¿Cómo se expresa el desacuerdo con una opinión?

> Queremos que las ventas aumenten con las exportaciones...

> Yo diría que lo mejor es vender y consumir en tu región. Es más barato para el cliente y mejor para la región.

14 a. Encuesta Complete la encuesta que su universidad hace a los estudiantes.

> **Queremos que nuestros servicios mejoren todo el tiempo. Por eso, son bienvenidas todas tus opiniones, quejas y sugerencias.**
>
> • Comida   • Ambiente   • Calidad de servicio   • Relación calidad/precio
>
> **Lo que más me gusta:** ....
> **Lo que menos me gusta:** ....

b. Comparar Compare sus respuestas con las de sus compañeros de grupo. Exprese y justifique su desacuerdo con las opiniones que son diferentes.

> Modelo: *Yo diría que las largas colas no son el principal problema...*

c. Soluciones Con el grupo, propongan soluciones para los aspectos negativos de la cafetería. Usen expresiones como **Ojalá...** o **A ver si...** Escríbanlas.

> Modelo: *A ver si ponen más empleados en las horas de más demanda.*

15 Opinar ¿Y usted qué diría? Exponga su opinión a la clase sobre las afirmaciones de la columna a la derecha y sus esperanzas al respecto.

> **MI EXPERIENCIA**

16 Cadena de consumo Representen a cada integrante de la cadena de consumo. Cada integrante define sus objetivos particulares.

GUIÓN DE TRABAJO		
¿Qué desean los productores?	→	Los productores deseamos que aumenten las exportaciones. Ojalá que...
¿Qué esperan las empresas?	→	Las empresas esperamos que se incrementen las ventas. A ver si...
¿Qué quieren los consumidores?	→	Los consumidores queremos que los alimentos cumplan con los estándares básicos de calidad y seguridad...

Practice more at **vhlcentral.com**.

Expresar esperanza

- ● ¡Ojalá que vendáis mucho!
- ■ A ver si es verdad.

15A.4 **ojalá (que)** + [*subjunctive*]
a ver si + [*indicative*]

Estrategia ·············

Suavizar una opinión
Yo diría que no tienes razón.

Vocabulario

10
consumir

12
bajar *to go down*

14
la cola *line*
la demanda

15
envasado/a *packaged*
el alimento transgénico *genetically modified food*
el reciclaje *recycling*

16
conquistar *to captivate*

> Los productos envasados son la mejor opción.

> Los alimentos transgénicos son malos para la salud.

> Las campañas de reciclaje no son necesarias.

SAM: Actividades pp. 314–316

Evaristo Acebedo, propietario de Casa Vera

Evaristo Acebedo, Casa Vera

Latino de honor

Evaristo Acebedo, un hombre muy conocido y querido por toda la comunidad latina de Miami, es, en este número de COMUNIDAD LATINA, nuestro LATINO DE HONOR. Evaristo dirige con éxito desde 1990 CASA VERA, una tienda dedicada a los productos de alimentación latinos.

Evaristo empezó su negocio importando y vendiendo productos típicos de su país de origen, Cuba, y de otros países del Caribe. De personalidad emprendedora, poco tiempo después de haber llegado a los Estados Unidos, vio la oportunidad en Miami y la aprovechó: "Decidí probar porque aquí la comunidad latina es muy importante. Hay mucha población cubana, dominicana... Es necesario conocer las características de la zona antes de abrir un negocio."

Sus productos tuvieron una excelente acogida, así que pronto amplió el negocio para ofrecer productos imprescindibles a la hora de preparar muchos de los platos de toda América Latina: harina de maíz, picantes y adobos, arroces para todos los gustos, crema de coco, frijoles, gandules, etc.

Hoy su tienda es un referente en Miami, no solo para los latinos. "Es importante que los estadounidenses descubran nuestros productos y que vean que hay más cosas que los tacos o el arroz con frijoles."

Pero no todo es negocio en su vida. Evaristo colabora también, junto con su esposa Lidia, de origen dominicano, en el proyecto solidario "Comida y amor", que reparte productos de alimentación y platos de comida a personas sin recursos: "Es necesario ser conscientes de que no todos tenemos los mismos medios económicos. No queremos que nadie pase hambre por aquí."

Expresar necesidad

Es necesario **importar** los productos más conocidos y **que** la gente **acceda** a ellos fácilmente.

Es importante **ser** solidarios y **que** la gente de pocos recursos no **pase** hambre.

15A.5 es necesario/importante + [*infinitive*]/**que** + [*subjunctive*]

Vocabulario

17

el número *issue*

aprovechar *to take advantage of*

abrir un negocio *to open a business*

la acogida *acceptance*

ampliar un negocio *to expand a business*

la harina de maíz *cornmeal*

los picantes *hot sauces*

el adobo *marinade*

el coco *coconut*

el gandul *pigeon pea*

sin recursos *in need*

los medios *means*

pasar hambre *to go hungry*

importar

---

17 **a. Evaristo Acebedo** Lea el artículo sobre Evaristo. ¿Qué tipo de publicación es *Comunidad latina*? ¿Dónde se publica y por qué? Destaque tres factores por los que los editores han considerado "Latino de honor" a este emprendedor cubano.

b. Latino de honor ¿Qué es Casa Vera? ¿Qué productos vende? ¿Cómo empezó y se desarrolló? ¿Conoce algún negocio similar en su ciudad?

c. Lista Haga una lista con su compañero/a donde expresen esperanzas positivas para Evaristo y su negocio.

Modelo: *Ojalá que...*

18 **a. Opinión** ¿Cuál es la opinión de Evaristo sobre las siguientes cuestiones? ¿Qué necesidades expresa?

| abrir un negocio | los estadounidenses | las personas sin recursos |

b. Negocios ¿Qué tipo de negocio le parece más interesante? ¿Cuáles de estas categorías cree que sería necesario o importante considerar antes de abrir ese negocio? ¿Por qué? Comparta sus opiniones con el resto de la clase.

Modelo: *Es necesario hacer una investigación de mercado y que nuestros potenciales consumidores nos cuenten acerca de sus gustos y preferencias.*

| investigación de mercado | público | ubicación | inversión inicial | productos de calidad |
| higiene | estrategias de *marketing* | servicio al cliente | paciencia y dedicación |

19 **a. Leer** Observe las imágenes y haga hipótesis sobre el contenido del texto. ¿Qué tienen en común los productos de las fotos? Después lea el texto y compruebe sus predicciones.

Chefs contra el hambre es un proyecto que pertenece a la "Iniciativa América Latina y Caribe sin Hambre" de la Organización para la Alimentación y la Agricultura (FAO, por sus siglas en inglés). El objetivo es reunir en un libro recetas que se pueden elaborar con los ingredientes más básicos y con utensilios de cocina sencillos. Se invita a los chefs y amantes de la cocina a compartir sus recetas. Quieren potenciar la elaboración de recetas ricas, nutritivas y económicas, además de enseñar a utilizar y enriquecer los alimentos. La iniciativa espera que los habitantes de los países con menor variedad de materias primas mejoren sus hábitos alimenticios y disfruten de los alimentos con un buen toque de sabor.

maíz

trigo

arroz

papas

b. Objetivos ¿Cuáles son los objetivos de esta iniciativa? ¿Quién participa y a quién va dirigida? ¿Cómo propone la FAO conseguir estos objetivos?

Modelo: *La "Iniciativa América Latina y Caribe sin Hambre" desea/espera/quiere...*

c. Buscar Busque en el texto palabras relacionadas con estos términos.

costumbre • sabroso • productos • preparar • plato

20 **Escribir** Piense en un alimento básico de su comunidad y escriba una receta que quiere compartir.

21 **a. Frutas y verduras** Algunas frutas y verduras reciben diferentes nombres en los países del mundo hispano. Busque las palabras del recuadro en un diccionario y escríbalas al lado de su sinónimo de la lista.

durazno • damasco • palta • alcaucil • ananá • frutilla

piña = ...
melocotón = ...
aguacate = ...
fresa = ...
alcachofa = ...
albaricoque = ...

b. Otros nombres ¿Encuentran otro nombre para alguna de estas frutas y verduras?

c. Más ejemplos Busque más ejemplos como los anteriores con su grupo y compártanlos con el resto de la clase.

Practice more at vhlcentral.com.

Vocabulario

18
el gusto *taste*
la investigación de mercado *market research*
la ubicación *location*
la paciencia *patience*
la higiene, la dedicación
19
reunir *to collect*
el recetario *recipe collection*
la elaboración *production*
nutritivo/a *nutritious*
la materia prima *raw material*
el toque *touch*
el trigo *wheat*
la costumbre *habit*
sabroso/a *tasty*
el utensilio
21
la piña *pineapple*
el melocotón *peach*
la fresa *strawberry*
la alcachofa *artichoke*
el albaricoque *apricot*

O P I N I Ó N

¿Cuáles son los productos de alimentación típicos de la gastronomía de su comunidad? ¿Es popular la gastronomía de su país o comunidad en el mundo? ¿Por qué?

SAM: Actividades pp. 317–320

22 **a. Describir** Mire las fotos y describa lo que ve. ¿Qué tipo de ceremonia cree que se está celebrando? Luego lea el texto sobre la Pachamama y compruebe sus respuestas.

La fiesta de la Pachamama

La adoración a la Pachamama, o Madre Tierra, es un legado° del imperio incaico° que sobrevive con fuerza entre los pueblos del noroeste de Argentina, el norte de Chile y las regiones andinas de Bolivia y Perú. Muchas son las ceremonias en honor de la Pachamama, pero el homenaje° principal se celebra durante el mes de agosto, en especial el primer día del mes. Aunque en otras épocas las ceremonias se hacían solamente en los hogares, estas han ganado protagonismo y ahora es común realizar una fiesta para toda la comunidad.

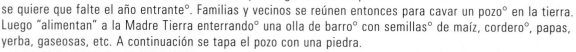

De acuerdo con el rito, es importante agradecer° a la Pachamama por los bienes° recibidos durante el año transcurrido° y entregarle todo lo que no se quiere que falte el año entrante°. Familias y vecinos se reúnen entonces para cavar un pozo° en la tierra. Luego "alimentan" a la Madre Tierra enterrando° una olla de barro° con semillas° de maíz, cordero°, papas, yerba, gaseosas, etc. A continuación se tapa el pozo con una piedra.

Nadie falta a esta cita. Mayores y niños de todas las edades se hacen presentes° en el lugar y continúan la celebración comiendo, bebiendo y festejando con música y coplas°. También es costumbre realizar una procesión y elegir a la representante de la Madre Tierra entre las ancianas° de mayor edad.

legado *legacy* **incaico** *Incan* **homenaje** *tribute* **agradecer** *to thank* **bienes** *goods* **transcurrido** *that passed* **entrante** *coming* **cavar un pozo** *dig a hole* **enterrando** *by burying* **olla de barro** *clay pot* **semillas** *seeds* **cordero** *lamb* **se hacen presentes** *participate* **coplas** *popular folk songs* **ancianas** *old women*

b. La fiesta de la Pachamama ¿Qué es la fiesta de la Pachamama? ¿Dónde y cuándo se celebra? ¿En qué consiste la celebración?

c. Contestar ¿Conoce alguna tradición similar en su comunidad?

d. Responder La fiesta de la Pachamama tiene su origen en el respeto por la tierra. Con sus compañeros, piense en otras maneras de respetar a nuestra Madre Tierra.

> Modelo: *Es necesario que aprendamos a no ensuciar ni contaminar la tierra con nuestras actividades.*

TAREA FINAL

Un negocio en el extranjero

Formen pequeños grupos y seleccionen los productos que quieren vender, el país y el lugar donde quieren abrir el negocio.

Piensen en las probabilidades de mercado, fijen los objetivos del proyecto, las esperanzas y las necesidades.

Expongan su proyecto al grupo y voten por el mejor proyecto o incluso una fusión de varios proyectos.

YO PUEDO...

- **Puedo expresar probabilidad.**
  Ha recibido una llamada de un número desconocido. Exprese probabilidad.

- **Puedo hacer sugerencias.**
  Sugiera una solución para la situación mencionada arriba.

- **Puedo hablar de objetivos.**
  Anote los objetivos que tiene usted para este curso.

- **Puedo expresar esperanza.**
  Exprese algo que espera que le suceda a uno de sus compañeros.

- **Puedo expresar necesidad.**
  ¿Qué es necesario para tener éxito en un negocio?

GRAMÁTICA FUNCIONAL Tutorials

15A.1 Express probability

Review of simple future; irregular simple future 5.16.2b, 5.16.2c

- Use the **futuro simple** to express conjecture or probability.

  ¿Qué hora **será**?
  I wonder what time it is.

  Serán las ocho.
  It is probably about eight.

- Note that this usage does not imply a future meaning. English words and expressions that convey this idea include *I wonder, I bet, may be, might,* and *probably.*

- Use the future of **estar** + [*present participle*] to make conjectures about what is happening at that moment.

  ¿De qué **estarán** hablando?
  What must they be talking about?

  Estarán planeando la fiesta sorpresa para Paula.
  I bet they're planning Paula's surprise party.

- You learned the regular forms of the **futuro simple** in 12B.1. Some common verbs have irregular stems.

decir	→	dir-	
haber	→	habr-	
hacer	→	har-	
poder	→	podr-	é
poner	→	pondr-	ás
querer	→	querr-	+ á
saber	→	sabr-	emos
salir	→	saldr-	éis
tener	→	tendr-	án
valer	→	valdr-	
venir	→	vendr-	

- Irregular future forms use the same set of endings as regular forms. Remember that all forms except for the **nosotros/as** form carry a written accent.

  El avión **saldrá** para San Salvador dentro de dos horas; **tendremos** que darnos prisa.
  *The airplane **will leave** for San Salvador in two hours; **we'll have** to hurry up.*

- The future form of **hay** (*there is/are*) is **habrá** (*there will be*).

  Dicen que mañana **habrá** una tormenta.
  *They say that **there will be** a storm tomorrow.*

15A.2 Make suggestions

lo mejor es/sería + [*infinitive/noun*] 3.3.1, 5.8.3, 5.13, 5.17.3

- Use **lo mejor es/sería** + [*infinitive/noun*] to make suggestions.

  Lo mejor es el pan casero.
  *Homemade bread **is the best**.*

  Lo mejor sería cultivar nuestros propios productos.
  *It **would be best** to grow our own produce.*

¡Póngalo en práctica!

G1 **Escribir** Escriba la forma correcta de cada verbo en el futuro simple.

1. tú, salir	
2. Gael, hacer	
3. nosotros, poder	
4. vosotros, saber	
5. ellas, querer	
6. yo, venir	
7. usted, poner	
8. Nina y Ramón, decir	

G2 **Conversación** Complete la conversación con el futuro simple.

¿Estos frijoles (1)............... (tener) conservantes?

No sé. ¿(2)............... (Estar) esa información en la etiqueta?

No, no dice nada en la etiqueta. ¿No (3)............... (haber) algún teléfono de información para preguntarlo?

G3 **Futuro simple** Complete las oraciones usando el futuro simple.

1. ¿De dónde .... (venir) estos tomates?
2. Esta salsa, ¿ .... (poder) usarse fría, o .... (tener, yo) que calentarla?
3. ¿ .... (querer) cenar todos en casa mañana?
4. ¿ .... (saber) Julia preparar los platos tradicionales que pensamos servir?

G4 **Diálogos** Complete los diálogos.

- Lo mejor de la tienda (1)............. el chocolate negro.
- Sí, (2)............. sería comprar varios paquetes.
- Lo (3)............. es tomar una bebida fría en la playa.
- Tienes razón, lo mejor (4)............. ir al supermercado antes de salir para la costa; así compramos algunas.
- (5)............. mejor es poder comer verduras locales.
- Sí, lo mejor (6)............. encontrar una granja dónde conseguirlas.

Practice more at vhlcentral.com.

esperar/querer/desear + **que** + [*subjunctive*];
Regular present subjunctive 5.20.1, 5.21.1

- Use the subjunctive (**el subjuntivo**) to express hopes and wishes with the verbs **esperar**, **querer**, and **desear**.

  Quiero que ustedes ayuden con los quehaceres domésticos.
  I want you to help with the household chores.

- Except for commands, all of the verb forms you have learned up until now have been in the indicative mood (**el indicativo**), which is used to state facts and express actions. The subjunctive is used to express will and influence, among many other uses that you will learn in subsequent lessons.

- To form the present subjunctive (**presente del subjuntivo**), start with the **yo** form of the present indicative, drop the **-o** ending, and replace it with the endings of the **presente del subjuntivo**.

	TRABAJAR	VENDER	ASISTIR
(yo)	trabaj**e**	vend**a**	asist**a**
(tú)	trabaj**es**	vend**as**	asist**as**
(usted, él, ella)	trabaj**e**	vend**a**	asist**a**
(nosotros/as)	trabaj**emos**	vend**amos**	asist**amos**
(vosotros/as)	trabaj**éis**	vend**áis**	asist**áis**
(ustedes, ellos/as)	trabaj**en**	vend**an**	asist**an**

- The endings of the **presente del subjuntivo** for **-ar** verbs (except for the **yo** form) are the same as the endings of **-er** verbs in the present indicative. Likewise, the endings of the present subjunctive for **-er** and **-ir** verbs are the same as the endings of **-ar** verbs in the present indicative, with the exception of the **yo** form.

$$-ar \rightarrow -e$$
$$-er/-ir \rightarrow -a$$

- The subjunctive is used in sentences with two subjects and two verbs. Sentences that use the subjunctive have a main clause and a subordinate clause.

  MAIN CLAUSE   SUBORDINATE CLAUSE

  Mi mamá quiere **que yo hable** con el supervisor.
  *My mom wants **me to speak** with the supervisor.*

- Use the infinitive in sentences with only one subject.

  Mi mamá quiere **hablar** con el supervisor.
  *My mom wants **to speak** with the supervisor.*

- Use the conjunction **que** (*that*) to connect the two clauses in the sentence.

  El gerente quiere **que** hablemos más con los clientes.
  The manager wants us to speak more with the clients.

- Note that the word *that* is often omitted in the English translation.

  Espero **que** nos lleven a un restaurante vegetariano.
  I hope (that) they take us to a vegetarian restaurant.

¡Póngalo en práctica!

G5 **Escoger** Empareje el comienzo de cada oración con el final correcto.

	1. Espero que tú	a. llame a todos los productores esta semana.
	2. Deseamos que vosotros	b. celebremos la Navidad en su casa.
	3. El gerente quiere que Marcos	c. colaboren en este proyecto.
	4. Mis abuelos quieren que mis hermanos y yo	d. te mejores pronto.
	5. La profesora quiere que ustedes	e. lo paséis bien en vuestras vacaciones.

G6 **Oraciones** Complete las oraciones con la forma correcta del verbo (infinitivo o presente del subjuntivo).

Quiero (1).................... (comunicarse) con nuestros clientes y que nuestros clientes (2).................... (valorar) nuestros productos.

Sí, las empresas esperamos (3).................... (promocionar) nuestros productos y que los clientes (4).................... (comprar) con frecuencia.

Los consumidores esperamos que los productores (5).................... (trabajar) bien y que las empresas (6).................... (vender) buenos productos.

Queremos que las empresas (7).................... (usar) más ingredientes naturales porque queremos que nuestros hijos (8).................... (comer) mejor.

El propietario del negocio desea (9).................... (anunciar) la apertura de su tienda en la calle Mayor el próximo 7 de octubre. Espera que todos (10).................... (pasar) por la tienda para ver las ofertas.

 Practice more at **vhlcentral.com.**

GRAMÁTICA FUNCIONAL

15A.4 Express hope

ojalá que + [*subjunctive*];
a ver si + [*indicative*] 5.21.1, 11.5

- Always use the **subjunctive** with the interjection **ojalá (que)**. **Ojalá (que)** means *I/We hope* or *I/We wish* and its form is invariable.

> **Ojalá (que) recibamos** buenas ofertas.　　**Espero que recibamos** buenas ofertas.
> *I hope (that) we receive good offers.*

> **Ojalá lleguemos** antes de las siete.
> *I hope we get there before seven.*

- Use the **indicative** with the construcion **a ver si** (*let's see if*). **A ver si** is used in colloquial language.

> **A ver si recibimos** buenas ofertas.
> *Let's see if we receive good offers.*

> **A ver si llegamos** antes de las siete.
> *Let's see if we get there before seven.*

15A.5 Express necessity

es necesario + [*infinitive*];
es necesario + **que** + [*subjunctive*] 5.8.4, 5.21.6

- Use **es necesario** (*it is necessary*) + [*infinitive*] to express necessity in a general sense.

> **Es necesario aumentar** nuestras ventas.
> *It is necessary to increase our sales.*

> **Es necesario bajar** los precios.
> *It is necessary to reduce prices.*

- Use **es necesario** + **que** + [*subjunctive*] to express what a specific person or group needs to do.

> **Es necesario que** nuestras ventas **aumenten.**
> *It is necessary that our sales increase.*

> **Es necesario que** las empresas de alimentos **bajen** los precios.
> *It is necessary that food companies reduce prices.*

- **Es necesario que** is an impersonal expression that always requires the use of the **subjunctive**. Other examples of impersonal expressions that are always used with the subjunctive include **es importante que, es esencial que,** and **es imprescindible que.**

> **Es importante que escuchemos** las opiniones de los demás.
> *It is important that we listen to the opinions of others.*

> **Es esencial que** las empresas **usen** ingredientes frescos.
> *It is essential that companies use fresh ingredients.*

> **Es imprescindible que trates** con respeto a los clientes.
> *It is essential that you treat clients with respect.*

¡Póngalo en práctica!

G7 Completar Complete las oraciones.

1. ¡.................... que vendamos todo el cacao!
2. A ver si .... (ser) verdad.
3. Ojalá me .... (llamar) del trabajo al que me postulé.
4. A ver si .... (nosotros, poder) terminar el proyecto a tiempo.
5. Ojalá que .... (nosotros, ganar) el partido mañana.
6. ¡Ojalá que .... (dejar) de llover!

G8 Conversaciones Complete las conversaciones usando el infinitivo o el presente del subjuntivo.

> Yo creo que es absolutamente necesario (1).................... (leer) con atención las etiquetas de los productos.

> Sí, pero es necesario también que las etiquetas (2).................... (transmitir) la información con claridad.

• • • • •

> Si quieres sacar una buena nota, es necesario (3).................... (dedicar) mucho tiempo al estudio.

> Claro que sí, pero también es importante que los estudiantes (4).................... (participar) mucho en la clase.

• • • • •

> Es importante que (5).................... (nosotros, comer) bien.

> También es importante (6).................... (hacer) ejercicio para sentirse bien.

S Practice more at **vhlcentral.com.**

SÍNTESIS

Mire las fotografías y escriba un diálogo corto para cada una, usando el vocabulario indicado.

1.

| ojalá | variado | compartir | compañeros de trabajo |

● _____

■ _____

● _____

■ _____

2.

| vendrán | alimentos | supermercado | consumir |

● _____

■ _____

● _____

■ _____

3.

| espero que | fruta | mercado | sabor |

● _____

■ _____

● _____

■ _____

4.

| a ver si | conservantes | fresco | gluten |

● _____

■ _____

● _____

■ _____

¿Qué comeremos?

el aceite de oliva virgen extra	extra virgin olive oil
la agricultura ecológica	organic farming
el cacao en polvo	cocoa powder
la certeza	certainty
el colorante	colorant, coloring
la composición	composition
la conservación	preservation
el conservante	preservative
el contenedor	(recycling) container
el envase de plástico	plastic container
el envase reciclable	recyclable container
la etiqueta	label
la fecha de caducidad	expiration date
la frambuesa	raspberry
el gluten	gluten
la grasa	fat
el hidrato de carbono	carbohydrate
la información nutricional	nutritional information
el ingrediente	ingredient
el jarabe	syrup
la leche descremada en polvo	powdered skim milk
la leche entera	whole milk
el producto ecológico	organic product
el producto fresco	fresh food
la proteína	protein
el suflé	soufflé
el tomate frito	tomato sauce
endulzar	to sweeten
espolvorear	to sprinkle
apto/a para	appropriate/safe for
artificial	artificial
bajo/a en calorías	low-calorie
celíaco/a	celiac
cocido/a	cooked
seco/a	dry
vegetariano/a	vegetarian

Mucho sabor

Ojalá	I/We wish
el alimento natural	natural food
el alimento transgénico	genetically modified food
la apertura	opening
la cola	line
la demanda	demand
la expectativa	expectation
el nutriente	nutrient
el pesticida	pesticide
el reciclaje	recycling
el sabor	flavor
aportar	to provide
asistir (a)	to attend
bajar	to go down
conquistar	to captivate
consumir	to consume
cumplir con	to meet
evitar	to avoid
potenciar	to foster
preservar	to preserve
envasado/a	packaged
recogido/a	picked

Evaristo Acebedo

la acogida	acceptance
el adobo	marinade
el albaricoque	apricot
la alcachofa	artichoke
el coco	coconut
la costumbre	habit
la dedicación	dedication
la elaboración	production
la fresa	strawberry
el gandul	pigeon pea
el gusto	taste
la harina de maíz	cornmeal
la higiene	hygiene
la investigación de mercado	market research
la materia prima	raw material
los medios	means
el melocotón	peach
el número	issue
la paciencia	patience
los picantes	hot sauces
la piña	pineapple
el recetario	recipe collection
el toque	touch
el trigo	wheat
la ubicación	location
el utensilio	utensil
abrir un negocio	to open a business
ampliar un negocio	to expand a business
aprovechar	to take advantage of
importar	to import
pasar hambre	to go hungry
reunir	to collect
nutritivo/a	nutritious
sabroso/a	tasty
sin recursos	in need

Variación léxica

el aguacate ⟷ la palta (C. S., Bol., Per.)

el albaricoque ⟷ el damasco (C. S.) ⟷ el chabacano (Méx.)

la alcachofa ⟷ el alcaucil (Arg., Uru.)

el azúcar moreno ⟷ el azúcar negro (Arg.) ⟷ la panela (Col.)

el durazno (Amér. L.) ⟷ el melocotón (Esp.)

la fecha de caducidad ⟷ la fecha de vencimiento

la fresa ⟷ la frutilla (C. S., Bol.)

el maíz ⟷ el choclo (Amér. S.) ⟷ el elote (Méx.)

la piña ⟷ el ananá (Arg., Uru.)

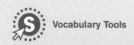
15B

REBELDES CON CAUSA

No me entienden

No entiendo a mis hijos...   ¿Te entendían tus padres a ti?
¿Cuántas veces has dicho o te han dicho que...?

1 ¡Me molesta que siempre tengan que decidir sobre todo lo que hago!

2 ¡No me gusta que salgas hasta tan tarde!

3 ¿Qué tenemos que hacer para que nos hagas caso con tus estudios?

4 ¡Mis padres no me entienden!

5 ¡No soporto que me digáis siempre lo que tengo que hacer!

6 ¡Es ridículo que te enojes! ¡Te lo decimos por tu bien y para que estés bien!

JORNADAS DE LA FAMILIA

Expresar disgusto y enfado

- A mí me **molesta** que mis padres **controlen** mi vida.
- Mis padres **no soportan que salga** siempre con mis amigos.

| 15B.1 | **no gustar / molestar / no soportar** + **que** + [*subjunctive*] |

Vocabulario

(1)

molestar *to bother*

hacer caso (a alguien) *to pay attention (to somebody)*

no soportar *to not stand*

por tu bien *for your own good*

la campaña de conciliación *conciliation campaign*

el disgusto *annoyance*

rebelde, ridículo/a, controlar, terrible

(2)

la norma *rule*

la falta de comunicación *lack of communication*

generacional

1 **Cartel** Fíjese en el cartel de esta campaña de conciliación. ¿Cuál es el tema? ¿Cuál cree que es el objetivo? ¿Qué tipo de institución cree que promueve esta campaña?

2 **Rebeldes con causa** Lea los comentarios en el cartel y marque los conflictos generacionales (entre padres e hijos) que se tratan.

☐ los estudios   ☐ las normas   ☐ las fiestas
☐ la hora de llegar a casa   ☐ la ropa   ☐ la falta de comunicación

3 **a. Disgusto y enfado** Busque en el cartel frases en las que se expresa disgusto y enfado. ¿Quién dice cada frase, los padres o los hijos?

b. Oraciones Elija un tema de la Actividad 2 y escriba otras oraciones frecuentes en los conflictos entre padres e hijos. Compare sus oraciones con las del grupo.

4 **Opinar** ¿Cree que estos u otros conflictos generacionales siempre han existido y existirán? ¿Qué puede significar la expresión "rebeldes con causa"? Coméntelo con su compañero/a.

en mi opinión • yo creo que • yo pienso que • es ridículo que

5 **Actividades extraescolares** Muchos padres inscriben a sus hijos en actividades extraescolares (deporte, música, etc.). Lea la opinión de una psicóloga escolar al respecto. ¿Coincide usted con esta opinión? ¿Y su compañero/a?

> *Los padres quieren que los hijos hagan actividades extraescolares para que tengan una formación completa. Hoy en día hay mucha oferta: deportes, música, idiomas, informática… pero son niños o adolescentes, y una parte muy importante de su formación debe ser el juego. Los chicos salen de la escuela a las cinco de la tarde, pero no llegan a casa hasta las siete u ocho. Solo tienen tiempo para hacer los deberes y cenar. Yo recomiendo reducir estas actividades a dos tardes por semana, y respetar los gustos del niño o adolescente para que se desarrolle de una manera más natural.*

6 **a. Leer** Muchas veces, padres e hijos tienen distintos puntos de vista sobre el mismo tema. Macarena quiere buscar trabajo cuando termine el instituto y Sandra, su mamá, quiere que vaya a la universidad. Lea los testimonios.

"Me molesta que mi mamá no acepte que ya soy mayor. Pretende decirme lo que tengo que hacer sin que yo opine. Dice que es por mi bien, pero en realidad quiere vivir mi vida. Yo quiero tomar mis propias decisiones, no soporto que me dé órdenes. En caso de que necesite ayuda, se la voy a pedir."

"Macarena piensa que es una mujer adulta, pero aún es una niña. No sé qué hacer para que me escuche. Yo le doy consejos para que no tenga los mismos problemas que yo tuve. Le permitiré que tome algunas decisiones por su cuenta con tal de que continúe sus estudios. Es ridículo que desperdicie su potencial."

b. Comentar ¿Qué le parece esta situación? ¿A usted le pasó algo parecido alguna vez? Comente sus experiencias con su compañero/a.

7 **Escribir** Con su compañero/a, escriban una posible conversación entre Sandra y Macarena. Asegúrense de usar todas las expresiones del recuadro.

> con tal (de) que • sin que • en caso (de) que
> no gustar • para que • molestar

8 **Responder** ¿Para qué creen ustedes que inscriben los padres a sus hijos en estas escuelas?

> bilingües | públicas/privadas | con comedor | con actividades extraescolares

MI EXPERIENCIA

9 **Conflictos** Comparta con su compañero/a qué conflictos puede haber entre padres e hijos.

GUIÓN DE TRABAJO

¿Qué problemas puede haber entre padres e hijos? → A los padres/hijos... no les gusta que... les molesta que...

¿Se le ocurre alguna solución? → Creo que.... con tal (de) que... en caso de que... sin que...

Expresar finalidad

• Te hemos inscrito en una academia **para que** aprendas...

■ Sí, y **para que** no nos digas que no te ayudamos con tus estudios.

15B.2 **para que** + [*subjunctive*]

Expresar condiciones

Con tal de que me llames al llegar, te dejo el coche.

15B.3 **con tal (de) que, en caso (de) que, sin que** + [*subjunctive*]

Vocabulario

5

inscribir (a alguien en algo) *to enroll (somebody in something)*

la actividad extraescolar *extracurricular activity*

hoy en día *nowadays*

los deberes *homework*

desarrollar *to develop*

la academia

6

el instituto *high school*

aceptar *to accept*

pretender *to try to*

aún *still, yet*

desperdiciar *to waste*

7

retrasarse *to be late*

8

la escuela bilingüe *bilingual school*

la escuela pública *public school*

la escuela privada *private school*

el comedor *dining hall*

SAM: Actividades pp. 321–323

Ⓢ Practice more at **vhlcentral.com**.

El proceso de independizarse

Para padres e hijos

Consultas

Comenzar la universidad es uno de los acontecimientos más esperados y temidos por todos: los gastos y también los miedos de padres e hijos ante el gran cambio hacen que recibamos muchas consultas. Hemos seleccionado algunas de las preocupaciones más frecuentes.

"Este año comienzo la universidad lejos de casa. Estoy muy contenta porque estudiaré una carrera que me interesa mucho y porque estaré con casi todos mis amigos. Pero me preocupa que mis padres no me dejen independizarme. ¡Mi mamá ya está pensando en visitarme todos los fines de semana!"

—**Micaela, Los Ángeles**

"Este año termino el colegio. Me gustaría estudiar música, pero temo que mis padres se opongan. Ellos quieren que sea médico, igual que mi padre y mi abuelo. El problema es que la medicina no me interesa para nada... No sé cómo decirles que me dejen decidir a mí sin herirlos."

—**Claudio, San Francisco**

"Tengo una hija adolescente que pronto viajará a otra ciudad para comenzar la universidad y me preocupa su adaptación. Me da miedo que no se alimente bien y que no descanse lo suficiente. No quiero sobreprotegerla, pero no creo que esté lista para organizarse sola. Estoy pensando en llamarla todos los días para asegurarme de que esté bien."

—**Susana, Sacramento**

"Mi esposa y yo siempre quisimos darle lo mejor a nuestro hijo. Estamos orgullosos: es un chico simpático, deportista y estudioso. Pero nos preocupa que cuando termine la escuela no podamos pagarle una educación universitaria. Daríamos todo con tal de que él pueda cumplir sus sueños, pero esto está fuera de nuestro alcance."

—**Pablo, San Diego**

Expresar temor y preocupación

● Me preocupa que **no tengamos** tiempo para nuestros hijos.

■ A mí me da miedo que los niños no **quieran** estudiar.

◆ Temo que mi hija no **pueda** estudiar por falta de dinero.

| 15B.4 | preocupar / dar miedo / temer + que + [*subjunctive*] |

Vocabulario

10

independizarse *to become independent*

el gasto *expense*

oponerse *to object*

herir (e:ie) *to hurt*

sobreproteger (j) *to overprotect*

cumplir sus sueños *to make his/her dreams come true*

estar fuera del (de nuestro) alcance *to be beyond one's (our) means*

---

10 **Padres e hijos** Fíjese en el título de la revista *Para padres e hijos*. ¿Qué implica ser padres hoy en día? ¿Qué diferencias hay entre ser padres de niños pequeños y ser padres de adolescentes?

11 **a. Consultas** Observe las fotos. ¿Qué le llama la atención? Lea el consultorio de la revista. ¿Qué les preocupa a los padres y a los adolescentes de la universidad? ¿Coinciden?

☐ gasto económico ☐ carrera universitaria ☐ integración
☐ transporte ☐ alimentación y descanso ☐ independencia

b. Contestar ¿Usted o algún amigo ha tenido las mismas preocupaciones o los mismos conflictos? ¿Qué solución encontró?

12 **a. Expresar temor y preocupación** Expresen sus preocupaciones y temores sobre los siguientes temas.

| Costo de la educación | Elección de la universidad | Elección de la carrera |

Modelo: *A mí me preocupa...*
A algunos padres les preocupa...

b. Me precupa... ¿Qué otros temas educativos le preocupan a usted?

13 a. Para padres e hijos Algunos de los participantes han dirigido sus dudas a un sociólogo del programa de radio *Para padres e hijos*. Escuche las consultas. ¿Qué les sorprende a los participantes? Marque verdadero (V) o falso (F).

V F

1. A Micaela no le sorprende la reacción de sus padres. ☐ ☐

2. Al sociólogo no le extraña que los padres de Micaela la quieran cuidar. ☐ ☐

3. Al sociólogo le parece raro que Susana esté preocupada por su hija. ☐ ☐

b. Me sorprende... ¿Qué le sorprende a usted de estas consultas?

14 Expresiones Vuelva a escuchar el audio y anote las expresiones que se usan para reforzar lo que dice el interlocutor. ¿Cuáles son? ¿Expresan acuerdo o desacuerdo?

15 a. Tabla de datos Observe la tabla de datos sobre las universidades públicas de Argentina, España y los Estados Unidos.

	¿Cuánto cuesta por año estudiar en una universidad pública?	¿Cuántos estudiantes hay por cada profesor?	¿Cuánto duran las carreras?	¿Cuál es el porcentaje de deserción universitaria?
Argentina	$0	19	5–6 años	60%
España	700–3700 €	12	4–5 años	25%
Estados Unidos	$ 9000– 50 000	14,1	4 años	35%

b. Expresar extrañeza Comente con su compañero/a los datos que le parecen raros o que le sorprenden.

> Modelo:
> • *A mí me sorprende que la universidad sea gratuita en Argentina.*
> • *Desde luego. Yo no lo sabía.*

16 Los sistemas de calificaciones Lea la nota sociocultural sobre los sistemas de calificaciones. ¿Cuál es el equivalente en su país?

🔲 **MI EXPERIENCIA**

17 Las universidades ¿Qué le preocupa o le parece raro de las universidades de su país? Coméntelo con su compañero/a.

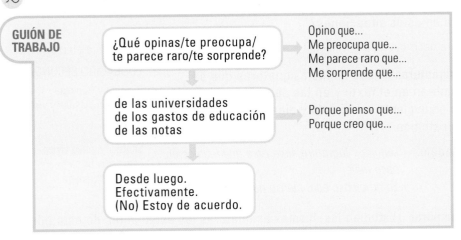

GUIÓN DE TRABAJO

¿Qué opinas/te preocupa/ te parece raro/te sorprende? →
Opino que...
Me preocupa que...
Me parece raro que...
Me sorprende que...

de las universidades
de los gastos de educación
de las notas →
Porque pienso que...
Porque creo que...

Desde luego.
Efectivamente.
(No) Estoy de acuerdo.

Ⓢ Practice more at **vhlcentral.com**.

Expresar extrañeza

• Me sorprende que los padres no **comprendan** a sus hijos.

■ A mí me parece raro que los padres no lo **intenten**.

15B.5 sorprender / extrañar / parecer raro + que + [*subjunctive*]

Estrategia ···········

Reforzar argumentos

• Me preocupa que no vengan.

■ Desde luego. Ya es tarde.

• Efectivamente.

Vocabulario

⑬
sorprender *to surprise*
extrañar *to surprise*
exagerar *to exaggerate*
parecer (zc) raro *to seem strange*
⑮
la deserción universitaria *college dropouts*
⑯
la calificación *grade*
la nota *grade*
el suspenso *failure*
el aplazo *failure*
la escala *scale*
⑰
efectivamente *indeed*

Las notas

En el mundo hispano, las calificaciones escolares en la secundaria suelen ser numéricas. En Argentina, Colombia, España y México, por ejemplo, 1–3 es suspenso o aplazo, 4–5 es regular, 6–7 es bueno, 8–9 es muy bueno, y 10 es sobresaliente o excelente. En otros países, la escala es diferente: En Cuba, Guatemala y Honduras, va del 1 al 100; en Ecuador y Venezuela, del 1 al 20; en Bolivia y Chile, del 1 al 7; y en Paraguay, del 1 al 5. En Puerto Rico, se califica con letras, de la A (excelente) a la F (aplazo).

SAM: Actividades pp. 324–326

Marina Sánchez, un genio de los números

Marina Sánchez es una de las finalistas de la Olimpiada Matemática de Centroamérica y El Caribe, en la que participan más de 40 estudiantes de secundaria o bachillerato de 15 países de la región. Todos ellos ganaron medallas en las olimpiadas nacionales de sus respectivos países. Marina es una de las representantes de la República Bolivariana de Venezuela y hemos hablado con ella.

Hola, Marina, ¿es la primera vez que te presentas a este concurso?
No, qué va. Ya me he presentado dos veces, pero esta es la primera vez que llego a la final.

¿Piensas que este tipo de concursos son solo para cerebritos?
No pienso eso, ¡qué va! Es una oportunidad para que nos interesemos más por las matemáticas. Me molesta que piensen que solo les interesa a los cerebritos.

¿Qué harás si ganas el concurso?
Bueno, mis padres me han dado permiso para que haga un viaje a España.

Supongo que las matemáticas son tu asignatura favorita, ¿no?
No son las matemáticas, sino la física. Aunque también me gustan mucho las ciencias sociales. Y bueno, el profe de Tecnología es muy chévere, y también me gusta esa asignatura. A veces es un poco aburrida, pero sirve para que comprendamos el mundo que nos rodea.

¿Y qué asignaturas te gustan menos?
Lengua y literatura, por ejemplo, no me gusta, pero bueno, por lo menos sirve para que leamos un poco más.

¿Y en tu tiempo libre? Imagino que no te dedicas a resolver ecuaciones y que prefieres salir con tus amigos, ¿no?
Desde luego, en mi tiempo libre prefiero divertirme con mis amigos.

¿Y qué te gustaría hacer en el futuro? ¿Piensas estudiar matemáticas en la universidad?
No, ¡para nada!, me gustaría estudiar alguna carrera técnica como informática o ingeniería.

Mañana es la final. ¿Estás nerviosa o te preocupa algo?
Me da miedo quedarme en blanco, pero no, no me preocupa mucho.

Marina Sánchez, estudiante

Enfatizar opiniones

- ¡Qué va! No pienso eso.
- No me gustan las matemáticas sino la física.
- ¿Qué dices? ¡Para nada!
- No me gusta la informática, pero me parece importante.

15B.6 ¡qué va!, no pienso eso, no... sino..., no... pero

Vocabulario

(18)
el/la cerebrito *nerd*
la asignatura *school subject*
las matemáticas *math*

18 a. Olimpiada ¿Qué cree que es una "olimpiada matemática"? ¿Cuántos años cree que tiene nuestra protagonista? Lea la entrevista y compruebe.

b. Marina Sánchez ¿Por qué participa Marina en esta olimpiada? ¿Qué le gusta, le molesta, le preocupa?

19 Opiniones ¿De qué manera enfatiza Marina sus opiniones? ¿Qué estructuras utiliza en estas situaciones?

- Para decir que una afirmación no es cierta. - Para dar la alternativa cierta.

20 a. Asignaturas Fíjese en las asignaturas que se nombran en el texto y en las de la lista. Piense en un equivalente en su país y diga para qué cree que se estudian.

Modelo: • *Lengua y literatura sirve para que leamos un poco más.*
• *Yo no pienso eso, pienso que sirve para...*

EDUCACIÓN SECUNDARIA

Biología y Geología
Educación plástica y visual
Música
Química
Educación ético-cívica
Educación física
Lengua extranjera

b. Comparar ¿Estudian las mismas asignaturas los estudiantes de esta edad en su país? Compare con sus compañeros.

21 **a. Maldita adolescente** Lea la carta que escribe Adriana, la protagonista de la novela *Maldita adolescente*. ¿A quién le dirige la carta? ¿Por qué está tan contenta?

Adriana escribe cartas a Nick, miembro de los *Backstreet Boys*, contándole todo lo que le pasa. *Maldita adolescente* es una novela que trata sobre la necesidad de sentirse querido y la importancia de buscar ilusiones nuevas cada día.

EVERYBODY

¡Bien, Nick, lo conseguí! Estoy tan contenta que no paro de bailar y cantar "Everybody". Mi hermano dice que estoy loca y que soy una maldita° adolescente, pero me da igual°, estoy eufórica. Me voy de compras con Sandra y con Carmen, a ver si tengo más suerte que con mi madre. Por fin ha accedido a darme la pasta° para que me compre yo la ropa, ¡lo que le ha costado! De verdad, no la entiendo. Se pasa el día° diciendo lo importante que es para una mujer ser independiente y tener su propio dinero y patatín y patatán°, y luego quiere controlar cada cosa que entra en mi

armario. Fue papá quien le dijo por teléfono que me diera la pasta ["dale el dinero"]. "¡A saber lo que se compra!", respondió ella. Pero papá le dijo que si era mayor para cuidar de mis hermanos, también lo era para elegir mi propia ropa. ¡Yabadabadúuu! ¡Papi for president! […]
- ¡Adriana!
- ¡Ya voooooooy!
Te dejo, Nick, me llama mi hermano. Seguro que mis amigas están abajo esperándome. […]

MENÉNDEZ, María: *Maldita adolescente*. Madrid, Ediciones SM, 2009.

maldita *darn* **me da igual** *I don't care* **pasta** *money* **Se pasa el día** *She spends all day* **patatín y patatán** *this and that*

b. Contestar ¿Tiene algún conflicto esta adolescente? ¿Con quién y por qué? ¿Hay algo que no entiende o le molesta?

c. Lenguaje coloquial Subraye las expresiones o palabras del texto que relaciona con un lenguaje coloquial. ¿Conoce otra forma de expresar lo mismo?

22 **Escribir** Escriba un breve texto sobre las aficiones, el carácter y los gustos de su grupo de amigos.

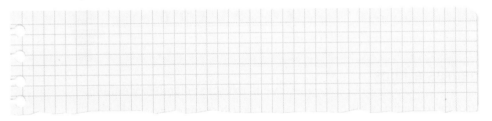

23 **Sistemas educativos** Lea la información sobre el sistema educativo español y compárelo con el de su país. ¿A qué edad empiezan los niños el colegio? ¿Piensa que esa es la edad apropiada? ¿Para qué edades es obligatoria la educación?

La educación infantil es voluntaria, aunque la mayoría de los padres llevan a sus hijos al colegio a los tres años. La escuela infantil ayuda a los padres en la educación de sus hijos y potencia sus capacidades y su relación con otros niños. La educación primaria y secundaria son obligatorias.

- Educación infantil (0–6 años)
- Educación primaria (6–12 años)
- Educación secundaria obligatoria (ESO) (12–16 años)
- Educación secundaria no obligatoria: Bachillerato (16–18 años) Ciclos formativos (16–18 años)
- Educación superior, universidad (18–21 años)

Vocabulario *cont.*

la física *physics*

las ciencias sociales *social studies*

Lengua y literatura *Language and Literature*

estudiar una carrera *to study for a degree*

quedarse en blanco *to draw a blank*

el genio, la ecuación

20

Educación plástica y visual *Art*

Educación ético-cívica *Civics*

Educación física *Physical Education*

la lengua extranjera *foreign language*

Geología

21

eufórico/a *euphoric*

OPINIÓN

¿Conoce otros concursos como las olimpiadas matemáticas? ¿Para qué sirven?

¿Marina le parece una adolescente "típica"?

SAM: Actividades pp. 327–332

24 **Esperanzas y miedos** Lea acerca de las esperanzas y los miedos de tres estudiantes. ¿Algo le sorprende? Comente con su compañero/a si han sentido lo mismo alguna vez.

"Hoy he recibido la carta de aceptación de mi futura universidad. ¡No puedo creerlo! Estoy muy ilusionada con la vida universitaria: el campus, los profesores, los otros estudiantes, las fiestas... Lo único que me preocupa es no poder conseguir empleo. Mis padres me ayudarán con la universidad, pero yo debo pagar los otros gastos."

"En unos meses terminaré la carrera de medicina y estoy muy orgulloso de mis logros°. Tuve algunas dificultades y en varias ocasiones pensé en dejar los estudios, pero ahora veo que mi esfuerzo valió la pena. Me preocupa que no pueda pagar mi préstamo estudiantil°... ¡es mucho dinero!"

"Estoy estudiando dirección de cine; es mi vocación. Cuando era pequeña, miraba las mismas películas muchas veces para intentar descubrir cómo las hacían. Me encanta esta carrera, pero sé que no será fácil encontrar empleo inmediatamente. Temo que deba regresar a casa de mis padres cuando termine la universidad."

logro *achievement* **préstamo estudiantil** *student loan*

 TAREA FINAL

Conversaciones entre padres e hijos

 Hagan dos grupos en clase. Uno son los padres y el otro, los hijos.

Preparen una lista de los conflictos que tienen con el otro grupo y expónganlos.

Elijan los temas más interesantes y representen conversaciones entre padres e hijos en la clase.

Voten y elijan la mejor representación.

YO PUEDO...

- Puedo expresar disgusto y enfado.
  Diga cuatro cosas que no soporta.

- Puedo expresar finalidad.
  ¿Para qué cree usted que los padres inscriben a sus hijos en actividades extraescolares?

- Puedo expresar temor y preocupación.
  ¿Cuáles cree usted que son las principales preocupaciones sobre la educación universitaria?

- Puedo expresar extrañeza.
  En esta unidad ha aprendido mucho sobre varios sistemas escolares. Diga qué le extraña o le parece raro de estos sistemas.

- Puedo enfatizar opiniones.
  ¿Piensa que el costo de la educación en su país es demasiado alto?

GRAMÁTICA FUNCIONAL Tutorials

15B.1 Express displeasure and annoyance

no gustar/molestar/no soportar + que + [*subjunctive*];
Irregular subjunctive forms 5.11.1, 5.20.2

- Use **no gustar** (*not to like*)/**molestar** (*to bother*) + **que** + [*subjunctive*] to express disapproval. **Gustar** and **molestar** are used with indirect object pronouns.

  No me gusta que la gente **hable** durante la película.
  *I don't like that people **talk** during the movie.*

- **No soportar** (*to be unable to stand*) + **que** + [*subjunctive*] is another verb of emotion that triggers the subjunctive in the subordinate clause.

  No soporto que mis padres me **pregunten** si tengo deberes o no.
  *I can't stand that my parents **ask** me whether I have homework or not.*

- In the examples above, the two clauses in each sentence have different subjects. If the subject of the two verbs in a sentence is the same, use the infinitive of the second verb.

  different subjects
  No soportamos que vivas tan lejos de casa.
  We can't stand that you live so far away from home.

  same subject
  No soporto vivir tan lejos de casa.
  I can't stand to live so far away from home.

- Use the subjunctive in the subordinate clause with expressions such as **es ridículo que** (*it is ridiculous that*) and **es terrible que** (*it is terrible that*). In **15A.5** you learned about other impersonal expressions that require the subjunctive in the subordinate clause.

  Es ridículo que tenga que estar en casa a las ocho de la noche.
  It is ridiculous that I have to be home by eight.

- As you learned in 15A.3, most forms of the present subjunctive are based on the **yo** form of the present indicative. If a verb has an irregular **yo** form in the present indicative, this spelling will be carried throughout all forms in the present subjunctive.

HACER (ha**go**)	→	ha**g**a, ha**g**as, ha**g**a, ha**g**amos, ha**g**áis, ha**g**an
TENER (ten**go**)	→	ten**g**a, ten**g**as, ten**g**a, ten**g**amos, ten**g**áis, ten**g**an
SALIR (sal**go**)	→	sal**g**a, sal**g**as, sal**g**a, sal**g**amos, sal**g**áis, sal**g**an
DECIR (di**go**)	→	di**g**a, di**g**as, di**g**a, di**g**amos, di**g**áis, di**g**an

  Quiero que me **digas** la verdad.
  *I want you to **tell** me the truth.*

¡Póngalo en práctica!

G1 **Escoger** Empareje el comienzo de cada oración con el final apropiado.

	1. A Julián no le gusta que sus compañeros de cuarto	a. salgas la noche antes de un examen.
	2. Marisa no soporta que su hermana	b. dejen la ropa tirada en el piso.
	3. Es ridículo que tú	c. diga que no somos responsables.
	4. Nos molesta que la gente	d. use su ropa sin pedirle permiso.
	5. Es terrible que vosotros	e. tengáis que volver a escribir las monografías.

G2 **¿Indicativo o subjuntivo?** Complete las oraciones con el indicativo o el subjuntivo de los verbos indicados.

1. No .... (soportar) que mis padres me .... (decir) lo que tengo que hacer.

2. No me .... (gustar) que .... (nosotros, tener) deberes para el fin de semana.

3. A los padres de Sara les .... (molestar) que ella .... (salir) durante la semana.

4. .... (Ser) ridículo que los estudiantes no .... (hacer) proyectos grupales más a menudo.

5. Me gusta que mis estudiantes .... (hacer) actividades extraescolares, pero no soporto que por culpa de estas actividades no .... (terminar) la tarea.

G3 **Escribir** Escriba oraciones sobre lo que a usted no le gusta. Siga el modelo.

  Modelo: no gustar / los niños / hacer tarea los fines de semana.
  No me gusta que los niños hagan tarea los fines de semana.

1. no soportar / mis padres / llamar todos los días
  ....

2. no gustar / mis compañeros / tener más tiempo libre que yo ....

3. molestar / mi vecino / hacer tanto ruido
  ....

4. no soportar / mi hermana / usar mi celular
  ....

 Practice more at **vhlcentral.com**.

15B.2 Express purpose

para que + [*subjunctive*] `5.21.2, 12.6`

- Use the subjunctive after **para que** (*so that*) to express purpose.

    Mis padres me inscriben en un programa **para que estudie** más.
    *My parents are enrolling me in a program **so that I study** more.*

    Te recomiendo este libro **para que aprendas** español.
    *I recommend this book **so that you learn** Spanish.*

- Note that the two verbs in the examples above have different subjects. If both verbs refer to the same person, use the construction **para** + [*infinitive*].

    Estudio español **para viajar**.
    *I am studying Spanish **in order to travel**.*

    Esteban trabaja los fines de semana **para pagar** sus estudios.
    *Esteban works on weekends **to pay for** his studies.*

15B.3 Express conditions

con tal (de) que, en caso (de) que, sin que `5.21.8`

- Always use the subjunctive with the conjunctions **con tal (de) que** (*provided that*) and **en caso (de) que** (*in case*). Note that the preposition **de** is optional in the first two conjunctions.

    Te dejo salir esta noche **con tal de que termines** toda la tarea.
    *I will let you go out tonight **provided that you finish** all your homework.*

    Te presto mi diccionario **en caso de que lo necesites**.
    *I'll lend you my dictionary **in case you need it**.*

- When the subject of the two verbs is the same, you can use **con tal de** and **en caso de** + [*infinitive*]. In this case **de** is required.

    Con tal de aprobar el examen, voy a estudiar toda la noche.
    ***In order to pass** the exam, I will study all night.*

    Cómprate un sándwich **en caso de tener hambre** esta tarde.
    *Buy yourself a sandwich **in case you get hungry** this afternoon.*

- Always use the subjunctive with the conjunction **sin que** (*without*).

    Siempre ayudo a mis padres **sin que me lo pidan**.
    *I always help my parents **without them asking** me to.*

- Use **sin** + [*infinitive*] when the subject of the two verbs is the same.

    Nunca tomo el coche **sin pedir** permiso antes.
    *I never take the car **without asking for** permission first.*

¡Póngalo en práctica!

G4 **¿Infinitivo o subjuntivo?** Complete las oraciones con el infinitivo o el presente del subjuntivo.

1. Inscribimos a nuestros hijos en una academia para que .... (ellos, recuperar) las asignaturas.

2. No, no te voy a comprar un celular para que .... (tú, hablar) todo el día con tus amigos.

3. Voy a estudiar para .... (yo, poder) viajar con todos mis compañeros a la playa al final del semestre.

4. Germán ha comprado una bicicleta para .... (Germán, llegar) más rápido a la universidad.

5. He decidido estudiar con mis amigos para que .... (nosotros, preparar) juntos el examen.

6. Mis padres me han regalado una computadora portátil para que .... (yo, tener) la posibilidad de trabajar en muchos sitios.

G5 **Conversación** Complete la conversación.

- Tu papá y yo te permitimos salir con tus amigos mañana por la noche con tal de que (1) .... (hacer) los quehaceres domésticos. También tienes que mantener tu celular encendido en caso de que (2) .... (nosotros, necesitar) llamarte.

■ Está bien, pero siempre permiten que salga Florencia sin que (3) .... (terminar) toda su tarea, y no me parece justo.

- Florencia ya terminó la secundaria, es una situación distinta. Terminaste la tarea para mañana, ¿no?

■ Bueno, tengo que estudiar un poco más para mi examen de biología.

- Entonces, te dejamos salir mañana con tal de que (4) .... (estudiar) para tu examen hoy por la noche. Y no te olvides de los quehaceres domésticos.

G6 **Emparejar** Empareje las frases para formar oraciones completas.

1. Te ayudo con tal de que ....

2. No me importa no salir con mis amigos hoy con tal de ....

3. Pedí una pizza en caso de ....

4. Voy a estudiar el subjuntivo en caso de que ....

a. aprobar el examen mañana.

b. tener hambre mientras estudio.

c. tú me ayudes mañana.

d. el profesor lo exija en el examen.

 S Practice more at **vhlcentral.com**.

GRAMÁTICA FUNCIONAL

preocupar/dar miedo/temer + que + [*subjunctive*];
Irregular subjunctive forms 5.11.1, 5.20.2, 5.21.1

- Use **preocupar** (*to worry*) and **dar miedo** (*to scare*) + **que** + [*subjunctive*] to express fear and concern. These expressions are used with indirect object pronouns.

(a mí)	me		
(a ti)	te		
(a usted/él/ella)	le	preocupa	**+ que +**
(a nosotros/as)	nos	da miedo	[*subjunctive*]
(a vosotros/as)	os		
(a ustedes, a ellos/as)	les		

> **Me preocupa que** mis hijos no **quieran** estudiar.
> *It worries me that my children do not **want** to study.*

> **Nos da miedo que** nuestros hijos **vivan** lejos de casa.
> *It scares us that our children **live** far from home.*

- If the other verb and **preocupar/dar miedo** refer to the same subject, use an infinitive after **preocupar/dar miedo.**

> **Me da miedo cambiar** de colegio.
> *It scares me to change schools.*

> **Nos preocupa no encontrar** trabajo.
> *It worries us that we may not find work.*

- Use the subjunctive with the verb of emotion **temer** (*to be afraid*) + **que** when **temer** and the verb that follows it have different subjects.

> **Temo que** mis compañeros no **colaboren** en el proyecto.
> *I am afraid that my classmates won't **collaborate** on the project.*

- Use the infinitive after **temer** if the subject is the same.

> **Temo no aprobar** el examen de Química.
> *I am afraid I **won't pass** the Chemistry exam.*

- In 15B.1, you learned the present subjunctive of several verbs with irregular **yo** forms. If an **-ar** or **-er** verb has a stem change in the present indicative, this change will be carried throughout the **subjunctive**, with the exception of the **nosotros/as** and **vosotros/as** forms.

PENSAR (p**ie**nso) →	p**ie**nse, p**ie**nses, p**ie**nse, pensemos, penséis, p**ie**nsen
PODER (p**ue**do) →	p**ue**da, p**ue**das, p**ue**da, podamos, podáis, p**ue**dan
QUERER (qu**ie**ro) →	qu**ie**ra, qu**ie**ras, qu**ie**ra, queramos, queráis, qu**ie**ran

- **-Ir** stem-changing verbs maintain the present indicative stem change, but they also show a second stem change in the **nosotros/as** and **vosotros/as** forms. This is the same stem change that occurs in the present participle.

| **PREFERIR** (pref**ie**ro) → | pref**ie**ra, pref**ie**ras, pref**ie**ra, pref**i**ramos, pref**i**ráis, pref**ie**ran |
| **DORMIR** (d**ue**rmo) → | d**ue**rma, d**ue**rmas, d**ue**rma, d**u**rmamos, d**u**rmáis, d**ue**rman |

¡Póngalo en práctica!

G7 **Presente de subjuntivo** Escriba la forma correcta del verbo en el presente del subjuntivo.

1. Alicia, sentir	
2. nosotros, dormir	
3. los aviones, volar	
4. yo, poder	
5. vosotros, servir	
6. tú, contar	
7. nosotros, perder	
8. la profesora, recomendar	

G8 **Completar** Complete las oraciones con la forma apropiada del verbo indicado.

Ema (1)........................ (temer) que a sus invitados no les (2)........................ (gustar) la comida que preparó.

A los profesores les (3)........................ (preocupar) que sus estudiantes no (4)........................ (leer) el material antes de ir a la clase.

¿Te (5)........................ (dar miedo) (6)........................ (empezar) la universidad?

A Consuelo le (7)........................ (preocupar) que sus amigos no (8)........................ (seguir) en contacto.

G9 **Significados** Elija la opción que tiene el mismo significado.

1. No sé si voy a aprobar el examen y esto me da miedo. ....
   a. Me da miedo que no apruebes el examen.
   b. Me da miedo no aprobar el examen.

2. Vas a volver tarde y eso me preocupa. ....
   a. Me preocupa que vuelvas tarde.
   b. Me preocupa volver tarde.

3. Quieres ir a acampar con tus amigos y eso nos preocupa. ....
   a. Nos preocupa que quieras ir a acampar con tus amigos.
   b. Nos preocupa acampar con tus amigos.

4. Nunca me dices adónde vas y eso me molesta. ....
   a. Me molesta decirte adónde voy.
   b. Me molesta que no me digas adónde vas.

 Practice more at **vhlcentral.com.**

15B.5 **Express surprise**

sorprender/extrañar/parecer raro + que + [*subjunctive*] 5.11.1, 5.21.1

- Use the subjunctive with the verbs **sorprender** (*to surprise*), **extrañar** (*to surprise*), and **parecer raro** (*to seem strange*) to express surprise. These verbs are used with indirect object pronouns.

  Me sorprende que prefieran un colegio privado.
  I am surprised that they prefer a private school.

  A Javier **le extraña que no quieras** venir a la fiesta.
  Javier is surprised that you don't want to come to the party.

- As with other verbs of emotion, use the subjunctive if the verbs in the sentence have different subjects. If both verbs have the same subject, use the infinitive for the second verb.

  Me parece raro usar uniforme.
  It seems strange to me to wear a uniform.

15B.6 **Emphasize opinions**

¡qué va!, no pienso eso; no... sino; pero vs. **sino** 7.4, 12.8, 14.26

- To stress your disagreement with a statement, say **no pienso eso, pienso que...** (*I don't think so, I think that . . .*).

- Use **¡qué va!** (*no way!/come on!*) to express disagreement about a stated idea. **¡Qué va!** is a very informal expression. Other similar expressions include **¿qué dices?** (*what are you talking about?*) and **para nada** (*not in the least; not at all*). Both expressions are used in informal conversations.

  - ¿Piensas que debería pedir disculpas?
  - No, **para nada**. Solo dijiste la verdad.

  - *Do you think that I should apologize?*
  - *No, **not at all**. You just told the truth.*

- Use **no... sino** (*no/not . . . but/but rather*) to present an alternative to an idea that has already been stated or implied.

  No hemos pedido carne, **sino** pescado.
  *We didn't order meat, **but** fish.*

- Although **pero** and **sino** both mean *but*, they are used in different situations. **Sino** is used when the first part of a sentence is negative and the second part contradicts it. **Sino** can often be translated as *but rather* or *on the contrary*. In all other cases, use **pero** to mean *but*.

  Manuel **no** viajará a la ciudad esta noche, **sino** que tomará el tren por la mañana.
  *Manuel will **not** travel to the city tonight, **but rather** will take the train in the morning.*

  Manuel quiere volver a la ciudad lo antes posible, **pero** prefiere dormir una noche más en el hotel.
  *Manuel wants to return to the city as soon as possible, **but** he prefers to sleep in the hotel one more night.*

¡Póngalo en práctica!

G10 **Conversaciones** Complete las conversaciones.

- Nos (1)......................... (extrañar) que los padres (2)......................... (aceptar) la nueva situación.
- Sí, a nosotros también nos (3)......................... (parecer) raro que los niños no (4)......................... (tener) clase por la tarde.

- ¿Te (5)......................... (sorprender) que algunos profesores (6)......................... (permitir) el uso de computadoras portátiles en la clase?
- No, ya no me (7)......................... (extrañar) (8)......................... (ver) el uso de tecnología en el aula.

G11 **Diálogos** Complete las conversaciones.

¿Crees que a los estudiantes no les interesan las asignaturas de ciencias (1)............. las de letras?

No, ¡qué (2).............! No (3)............. (pensar) eso. Pienso que depende de gustos.

• • • • •

Para ti, ¿es importante que los estudiantes (4)............. (tomar) clases en todas las disciplinas posibles antes de elegir una carrera universitaria?

No, para (5)............., no pienso (6)............. Creo que algunos estudiantes empiezan la universidad con una idea muy clara de la carrera que quieren elegir en sus estudios.

• • • • •

Creo que lo importante a la hora de buscar un trabajo no es la experiencia que uno tiene, (7)............. el interés que uno muestra en la entrevista.

¿Qué (8).............? En mi opinión, la experiencia es fundamental.

 Practice more at **vhlcentral.com**.

VOCABULARIO 🔊 Ⓢ Vocabulary Tools

No me entienden

hoy en día	nowadays
por tu bien	for your own good
la academia	academy
la actividad extraescolar	extracurricular activity
la campaña de conciliación	conciliation campaign
el comedor	dining hall
los deberes	homework
el disgusto	annoyance
la escuela bilingüe	bilingual school
la escuela privada	private school
la escuela pública	public school
la falta de comunicación	lack of communication
el instituto	high school
la norma	rule
aceptar	to accept
controlar	to control
desarrollar	to develop
desperdiciar	to waste
hacer caso (a alguien)	to pay attention (to somebody)
inscribir (a alguien en algo)	to enroll (somebody in something)
molestar	to bother
pretender	to try to
retrasarse	to be late
no soportar	to not stand
generacional	generational
rebelde	rebel
ridículo/a	ridiculous
terrible	terrible
aún	still, yet

El proceso de independizarse

estar fuera del (de nuestro) alcance	to be beyond one's (our) means
el aplazo	failure
la calificación	grade
la deserción universitaria	college dropouts
la escala	scale
el gasto	expense
la nota	grade
el suspenso	failure
cumplir (sus) sueños	to make his/her dreams come true
exagerar	to exaggerate
extrañar	to surprise
herir (e:ie)	to hurt
independizarse	to become independent
oponerse	to object
parecer (zc) raro	to seem strange
sobreproteger (j)	to overprotect
sorprender	to surprise
efectivamente	indeed

Marina Sánchez

quedarse en blanco	to draw a blank
la asignatura	school subject
el/la cerebrito	nerd
las ciencias sociales	social studies
la ecuación	equation
Educación ético-cívica	Civics
Educación física	Physical Education
Educación plástica y visual	Art
la física	physics
el genio	genius
Geología	Geology
la lengua extranjera	foreign language
Lengua y literatura	Language and Literature
las matemáticas	math
estudiar una carrera	to study for a degree
eufórico/a	euphoric

Variación léxica

la asignatura ⟷ la materia (Amér. L.)

el/la cerebrito (Amér. L.) ⟷ el empollón/la empollona (Esp.)

inscribir (a alguien en algo) ⟷ apuntar (a alguien en algo) (Esp.) ⟷ anotar (a alguien en algo) (Arg.)

LECTURA

El poeta chileno **Pablo Neruda** (1904–1973) siempre apreció la buena mesa, y prueba de eso son sus odas dedicadas a frutas y verduras, como *Oda a la cebolla, Oda a la alcachofa, Oda al tomate, Oda a la papa* y *Oda a la manzana.* En 1971, Neruda recibió el Premio Nobel de Literatura.

Vocabulario útil

agregar *to add*

apreciar *to value*

el asado *roast*

asesinar *to murder*

la buena mesa *fine dining*

la cebolla *onion*

desatarse *to go wild*

hervir (e:ie) *to boil*

el hueso *pit*

Estrategia ···········

Figurative language

Figurative language, which uses imagery, shouldn't be interpreted in a literal sense. The writer or speaker appeals to the reader's imagination with comparisons, describing something through metaphors (the implicit comparison between two objects that have something in common), personifications (which attribute human qualities to objects), hyperbole (strong exaggeration), etc. You can find figurative language in poems, songs, advertising, and even in everyday language.

Oda al tomate

Pablo Neruda

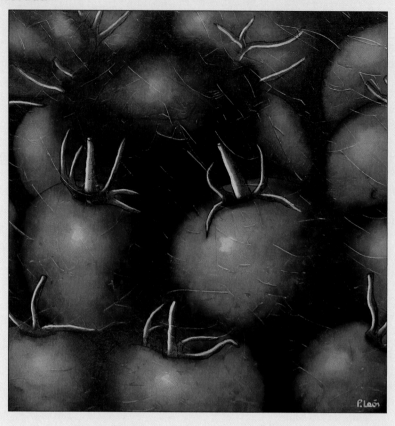

① **Alimentos** Converse con un(a) compañero/a.

1. ¿Qué comida no falta nunca en...?
   a. el Día de Acción de Gracias
   b. Navidad
   c. Halloween
   d. el Día de San Valentín

2. ¿Qué estado de los Estados Unidos se relaciona con estos alimentos?
   a. chile y frijoles
   b. manzanas
   c. queso
   d. maíz

3. Proponga un alimento que merece su mes/día nacional y cuándo sería.

② **Elegir** Después de leer el poema *Oda al tomate*, elija la opción que corresponde.

1. ¿Qué quiere decir "la calle se llenó de tomates"?
   a. Se cultivan tomates en la calle.
   b. Han comenzado a vender tomates en la calle.

2. ¿Qué significa "en diciembre se desata el tomate"?
   a. Diciembre es la estación del tomate.
   b. En diciembre los tomates se rompen.

3. ¿A qué se refiere el poeta con "debemos asesinarlo"?
   a. El tomate no es bueno para la salud y hay que evitarlo.
   b. Hay que cortar el tomate para comerlo.

4. Cuando el poeta dice "¡es hora!" se refiere a que...
   a. es el tiempo ideal para comprar tomates.
   b. es la hora de ir a comer.

La calle
se llenó de tomates,
mediodía,
verano,
la luz
se parte
en dos
mitades°
de tomate,
corre
por las calles
el jugo.
En diciembre
se desata
el tomate,
invade
las cocinas,
entra por los almuerzos
se sienta
reposado
en los aparadores°,
entre los vasos,

las mantequilleras,
los saleros azules.
Tiene
luz propia,
majestad benigna.
Debemos, por desgracia,
asesinarlo:
se hunde°
el cuchillo
en su pulpa viviente°,
es una roja
víscera,
un sol
fresco,
profundo,
inagotable°,
llena las ensaladas
de Chile,
se casa alegremente
con la clara cebolla,
y para celebrarlo
se deja
caer°

aceite,
hijo
esencial del olivo,
sobre sus hemisferios
  entreabiertos°,
agrega
la pimienta
su fragancia,
la sal su magnetismo:
son las bodas
del día,
el perejil°
levanta
banderines,
las papas
hierven vigorosamente,
el asado
golpea°
con su aroma
en la puerta,
es hora!
vamos!
y sobre

la mesa, en la cintura°
del verano,
el tomate,
astro° de tierra
estrella
repetida
y fecunda,
nos muestra
sus circunvoluciones°,
sus canales,
la insigne plenitud°
y la abundancia
sin hueso,
sin coraza°,
sin escamas° ni
  espinas°,
nos entrega
el regalo
de su color fogoso°
y la totalidad de
  su frescura°.

se parte... *splits in half* **aparadores** *sideboards* **se hunde** *sinks* **viviente** *living* **inagotable** *inexhaustible* **se deja caer** *is poured* **entreabiertos** *half-open* **perejil** *parsley* **golpea** *knocks* **cintura** *waist* **astro** *star* **circunvoluciones** *turns* **insigne plenitud** *distinguished fullness* **coraza** *shell* **escamas** *scales* **espinas** *bones* **fogoso** *passionate* **frescura** *freshness*

---

(3) **Comparar** En parejas, hagan comparaciones siguiendo estos pasos. Luego escriban oraciones completas y compártanlas con la clase.

1. Elija un objeto cualquiera.
2. Anote alguna característica de ese objeto.
3. Para cada característica, busque otro objeto que la comparta.

Objeto 1	Característica	Objeto 2
Luna	brillante	moneda

PROYECTO

 Una oda Escriba una oda a un objeto, animal, lugar o persona.

Paso 1: Decida cuál es el objeto que va a retratar en su oda y haga una lista de las palabras que pueden describirlo.

Paso 2: Escriba frases sobre las cualidades únicas del objeto que eligió.

Paso 3: Explique su preferencia e interés por ese objeto.

Paso 4: Revise todo lo que escribió: tache las repeticiones y desarrolle algunas comparaciones que hagan más vívida la descripción.

Paso 5: Elija las dos oraciones con más fuerza y ubique una al comienzo y la otra al final de su oda. Ordene las oraciones restantes como mejor le parezca. ¡Y no se preocupe por la rima!

Estrategia ··········

Odes

Have you ever read an ode before? An ode celebrates a person, a place, or a thing, usually identified in the title. Ancient Greeks and Romans wrote odes to praise athletes, champions, memorable places, victory at war, and celebrations, but modern odes have evolved to praise the most simple things in everyday life; some odes include a subtle sense of humor.

Video

Las alpacas

Ya ha aprendido sobre la producción de alimentos orgánicos y la educación de los niños. Este episodio de **Flash Cultura** muestra cómo en la región andina del Perú existe una industria ecológica que da trabajo a miles de personas: la cría de la alpaca, un animal que los incas consideraban digno de un rey.

1 Preguntas ¿Alguna vez tuvo una mascota o intentó cultivar alguna planta? ¿Existe algún conocimiento que se transmite de generación en generación en su familia?

2 Mirar Mire este episodio de **Flash Cultura** y preste atención a las distintas etapas y condiciones del proceso para la cría de alpacas. ¿Es diferente o parecido a lo que imaginaba?

La alpaca posee una de las fibras más finas del mundo.

Esta preciosa fibra cuenta con la gama de colores naturales más grande del mundo.

3 Escoger Relacione los elementos de las dos columnas para formar oraciones.

1. Algunas personas en Perú tienen alpacas para que ....
2. Para que las niñas puedan formar parte de sus comunidades, es necesario que ....
3. Lo mejor es esquilar a las alpacas ....
4. Es necesario girar la fibra para que ....

a. antes de la temporada de lluvia.
b. aprendan a tejer.
c. se transforme en una hebra de hilo.
d. les den buena suerte.

4 Diálogo Con un(a) compañero/a, invente un diálogo entre un(a) vendedor(a) de una tienda de mascotas y un(a) cliente que busca su mascota ideal.

Modelo:
• *No soporto los pelos largos y me molesta mucho que las mascotas tengan olor. ¿Habrá una mascota para mí?*
• *Lo mejor para usted sería una tortuga (turtle).*

 Practice more at **vhlcentral.com**.

Estrategia

Make predictions

Before watching this **Flash Cultura** episode, make some guesses about what you will learn about animals, farms, native cultures, climates, old traditions, etc. Then, watch the video and check your predictions. Don't worry if your predictions weren't accurate. The purpose of making predictions is to access prior knowledge in order to make it easier to take in new information.

Vocabulario útil

esquilar *to shear*
la gama *range*
la hebra de hilo *thread*
la joroba *hump*
la mascota *pet*
la manta *blanket*
tejer *to weave*
la temporada *season*

Estrategia

Word origin

In everyday Spanish there are many words from ancient languages spoken by native peoples of the Americas. For example, **alpaca** comes from Aymara, and **llama**, **vicuña**, and **guanaco** come from Quechua. Many words for food come from Quechua, Guaraní, and Nahuatl. Can you find some examples?

Unidad 16

Ingrid Betancourt, una luchadora

Estela y Mario, publicistas

Puerto Rico, ¿nación o estado?

16A

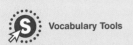 **Vocabulary Tools**

EMBAJADORES DE LA PAZ

Compromiso de todos

FORMULARIO DE ADHESIÓN
MARCHA MUNDIAL POR LA PAZ Y LA NO VIOLENCIA

La Marcha Mundial por la Paz y la No Violencia es una propuesta de movilización social en la que participan más de 100 países. La verdadera fuerza de esta marcha nace de la adhesión y del compromiso de todos.

Me adhiero a la MARCHA MUNDIAL POR LA PAZ Y LA NO VIOLENCIA porque:

1 Creo que las armas nucleares deben desaparecer en todo el mundo y que debemos reducir progresivamente las armas convencionales. 2 No creo que ningún ejército deba invadir otro territorio. 3 Me parece que el respeto de los derechos humanos y la firma de tratados de no agresión entre países son imprescindibles para la paz. 4 Dudo que las guerras sean el camino o den la solución para resolver conflictos. 5 Pienso que los gobiernos deben renunciar a la guerra como medio para resolverlos.

Y además porque rechazo toda forma de violencia.

Exponer una opinión

- Pienso que la paz mundial es posible.
- Pues yo no creo que sea fácil conseguirla.

16A.1	creer/pensar/parecer que + [indicative] no creer que + [subjunctive]

Vocabulario

①

el formulario *form*

la adhesión *support*

la no violencia *non-violence*

la movilización social *social mobilization*

la fuerza *strength, power*

adherirse (e:ie) *to join*

el arma nuclear *nuclear weapon*

el ejército *army*

los derechos humanos *human rights*

la firma *signing*

---

1 **Marcha Mundial** ¿Ha oído hablar de la Marcha Mundial por la Paz y la No Violencia? Lea la introducción de este formulario de adhesión y coméntelo con su compañero/a.

2 **Adhesión** Elabore una definición de la palabra "adhesión" con su compañero/a y compártala con la clase.

3 a. **Palabras** Fíjese en estas palabras y expresiones. ¿Qué cree que significan? Escriba una definición o explicación en español. ¿Qué relación tienen con la paz?

derechos humanos   *PAZ*   invasiones territoriales

violencia   armas nucleares

ejércitos   compromiso

guerras

b. **Opiniones** ¿Qué opiniones se exponen en la adhesión a la Marcha Mundial sobre los temas de la actividad anterior? ¿Qué opina usted? ¿Y su compañero/a?

Modelo: *Yo también pienso que... / No creo que...*

4 **Escepticismo** Fíjese en estos comentarios que muestran escepticismo sobre la Marcha Mundial. Encuentre en el formulario otra frase que expresa escepticismo.

> Dudo que los pacifistas consigan algo con la Marcha Mundial.

> Yo dudo que logremos la paz mientras haya dictadores en el mundo.

5 **a. Marcha por la paz** Complete los diálogos con la forma correcta de los verbos. Luego compruebe sus respuestas con las de su compañero/a.

- ¡Hola! Te invito a firmar este formulario de adhesión a la Marcha Mundial por la Paz y la No Violencia.

  ■ Seguro. ¿Dónde firmo? Pienso que (1)............. (ser) una causa maravillosa.

- Desde luego. Nosotros creemos que todos (2)............... (deber) unirnos para luchar por la paz.

  ■ ¿Todos? Dudo que todos (3)............. (querer) la paz.

- Pues pienso que (4)............. (hacer) falta convencerlos.

  ■ Creo que (5)............. (tener) razón.

✦ Buenos días, señora. La invito a firmar este formulario.

- ¿De qué se trata?

✦ Se trata de una marcha por la paz mundial. Pensamos que (6)............. (ser) importante que todos juntos reclamemos a los gobiernos el fin de las guerras.

- Pues yo no creo que eso (7)............. (ser) posible de un día para el otro. Pienso que a veces las guerras (8)............. (ayudar). No me parece que la paz se (9)............. (lograr) sólo con buenos deseos. Perdone, pero dudo que la marcha (10)............. (servir) de algo.

b. Opinar ¿Y usted qué opina de la marcha? ¿Está de acuerdo o en desacuerdo? Comente su opinión con su compañero/a.

6 **Cita** Lea esta cita del argentino Adolfo Pérez Esquivel. ¿Qué duda, piensa y no cree Pérez Esquivel?

"La paz no nos la van a regalar, incluso podemos decir que la paz no es ausencia de conflicto. La paz se logra sobre la base de entender lo vital de la unidad popular, del consenso y del respeto a la diversidad."

Adolfo Pérez Esquivel

7 **Premios Nobel** Comente con su compañero/a su opinión sobre el Premio Nobel de la Paz. ¿Cuál es su significado? ¿Le parece importante? ¿Por qué? La nota de la derecha hace referencia a tres ganadores de ese premio. ¿Los conoce?

⁂ MI EXPERIENCIA

8 **Exponer una opinión** Exponga su opinión o manifieste escepticismo ante la guerra u otros conflictos a partir de las citas de la derecha. Coméntelas con su compañero/a.

GUIÓN DE TRABAJO

¿Qué piensa/cree acerca de...?

OPINIÓN
(No) Creo que...
(No) Pienso que...
(No) Me parece que...

ESCEPTICISMO
Dudo que...

 Practice more at vhlcentral.com.

Mostrar escepticismo

Dudo que haya paz sin la unión y el apoyo de todas las naciones.

16A.2 **dudar que** + [*subjunctive*]

Vocabulario *cont.*

el tratado *treaty*

dudar *to doubt*

el gobierno *government*

renunciar (a) *to give up*

rechazar *to reject*

la marcha, reducir (zc), convencional, invadir, el territorio, la agresión
④

el/la pacifista, el/la dictador(a)
⑤

firmar *to sign*

hacer falta *to be necessary*

convencer (z) *to convince*

de un día para el otro *overnight*
⑥

sobre la base de *based upon*

la unidad popular *unity of the people*

el consenso
⑦

el/la escultor(a) *sculptor*

la justicia social *social justice*
⑧

el desastre, el pretexto

Premios Nobel

¿Qué tienen en común un arquitecto argentino, un político costarricense y una líder indígena guatemalteca? El Premio Nobel de la Paz. Adolfo Pérez Esquivel lo recibió en 1980 por su defensa de los derechos humanos. Óscar Arias Sánchez lo obtuvo en 1987 por su participación en los procesos de paz en América Central. Rigoberta Menchú fue premiada en 1992 por su lucha por los derechos de los indígenas.

"De la paz se debe esperar todo, de la guerra, nada más que desastre." (Simón Bolívar)

"El pretexto para todas las guerras: conseguir la paz." (Jacinto Benavente)

"La violencia es el miedo a los ideales de los demás." (Mahatma Gandhi)

SAM: Actividades pp. 333–335

Debate social

Colombia estará a la cabeza del turismo latinoamericano
Se pondrá en marcha un ambicioso plan para estimular la llegada de visitantes a los tres principales destinos turísticos de Colombia: Cartagena, Santa Marta y la isla de San Andrés.

La iniciativa "Mil grullas por la Paz" se celebrará como en años anteriores en Rosario (Argentina)
Esta original iniciativa intentará sensibilizar por la paz a la población en general y a los niños en particular. En cuanto a la proyección internacional, este año Chile también participará en la convocatoria.

La Secretaría de Inclusión de El Salvador propondrá nuevas políticas sociales y culturales
Con respecto a los grupos más desfavorecidos: niños, jóvenes y mujeres, anunció que habrá medidas especiales.

Perú tendrá un crecimiento del 7% anual durante los próximos 15 años
Un aprovechamiento más racional de sus enormes recursos naturales será la clave.

Transmitir información

- "Mañana **saldrá** la Marcha por la Paz."
- Ayer uno de los organizadores confirmó que la Marcha por la Paz **saldría** hoy.

16A.3 Indirect discourse (Future-Conditional)

Vocabulario

9

estar a la cabeza *to lead*
poner en marcha *to set in motion*
la grulla *crane*
sensibilizar *to raise awareness*
la convocatoria *call (to action)*
la secretaría *ministry, department*
desfavorecido/a *underprivileged*
anunciar *to announce*
la medida *measure*
el crecimiento *growth*
el aprovechamiento *exploitation*
enorme *huge*
la clave *key*
el titular *headline*
la sensibilización *increased awareness*
el debate, ambicioso/a, estimular, racional

9 **Relacionar** Fíjese en las imágenes y lea los titulares. Relaciónelos con estas palabras clave.

☐ sensibilización ☐ recursos naturales ☐ destinos turísticos ☐ plan social

10 **a. Escuchar** Escuche el programa de radio. ¿De qué país es? ¿Qué tipo de programa es?

b. Emparejar Escuche de nuevo a la locutora de radio que habla de estas noticias y emparéjelas con el titular de arriba al que se refiere.

- La Oficina de Prensa del Ministerio de Transporte de Colombia informó que se pondría en marcha... ☐
- El ministro de Economía peruano declaró que su país tendría... ☐
- La asociación argentina CHICOS confirmó que un año más el proyecto intentaría sensibilizar... y añadieron que Chile participaría... ☐
- El presidente de El Salvador anunció que la Secretaría de Inclusión propondría... ☐

11 **Transmitir información** Imagine que usted trabaja como locutor(a) en un programa de radio y debe transmitir estos titulares. Use los sustantivos del recuadro **A** y los verbos del recuadro **B** como ayuda.

"La marcha comenzará a las 10 de la mañana."
"Haremos una campaña electoral."
"Iniciaremos las negociaciones de paz."
"Aumentaremos los sueldos."
"Además, estaremos buscando voluntarios."

A	B
coordinadores	añadir
director(a)	declarar
gobierno	confirmar
ministros	anunciar
presidente/a	afirmar

12 Titulares ¿Qué titulares le gustaría leer en la prensa? Complete con su compañero/a los siguientes titulares con noticias futuras.

- Los líderes mundiales anunciaron que...
- El/La presidente/a de la multinacional... dijo que...
- El/La jefe/a de prensa de la ONG... confirmó que...

13 Planes Coméntele a su compañero/a sus planes en cuanto a estos temas. Después imagine que ha pasado un día y transmita a la clase la información que su compañero/a le dijo ayer.

| familia | trabajo | aficiones | cambios | iniciativas |

Modelo:
- *Continuaré con mi afición a la política.*
- *Iris me dijo ayer que continuaría con su afición a la política, y en cuanto al trabajo...*

14 a. Objetivos Lea con su compañero/a los objetivos que menciona uno de los coordinadores de la Campaña Mundial por la Educación. Luego túrnense para transformar las oraciones al estilo indirecto.

"Lograremos la enseñanza primaria universal y gratuita."
"Eliminaremos las desigualdades entre niños y niñas en la enseñanza."
"Reduciremos el analfabetismo de adultos en un 50%."
"Mejoraremos la calidad de la educación en todos los niveles."

Modelo: *El coordinador afirmó que lograrían la enseñanza primaria universal y gratuita.*

b. Historieta Lea la historieta de Mafalda. ¿Qué duda expresa su amigo Felipe sobre la educación?

NUESTRO DERECHO A LA EDUCACIÓN ES TAN INDISCUTIBLE......

...QUE NO HAY LA MÁS MÍNIMA ESPERANZA DE QUE ALGÚN ALMA CARITATIVA NOS LO QUITE!

© Joaquín Salvador Lavado (QUINO) Toda Mafalda — Ediciones de La Flor, 1993

Modelo: *Felipe duda que...*

MI EXPERIENCIA

15 Noticias Busque cinco noticias interesantes y coméntelas con su compañero/a.

GUIÓN DE TRABAJO

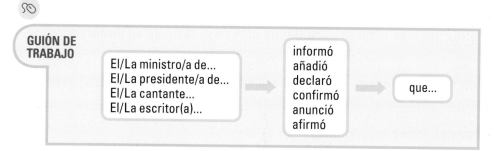

El/La ministro/a de...
El/La presidente/a de...
El/La cantante...
El/La escritor(a)...

→

informó
añadió
declaró
confirmó
anunció
afirmó

→

que...

Estrategia

Introducir un tema

En cuanto a la economía, el Ministerio anunció nuevas medidas.

Con respecto a las conversaciones de paz, hoy hubo grandes avances.

Vocabulario

10
la oficina de prensa *press office*
el ministerio *ministry, department*
informar *to inform*
declarar *to declare; to state*
el/la ministro/a,
el/la presidente/a

11
el/la locutor(a) *announcer*
afirmar *to assert*
la campaña electoral *electoral campaign*
el/la coordinador(a)

12
los líderes mundiales *world leaders*
en cuanto a *as for*
con respecto a *regarding*
la multinacional

13
la política *politics*

14
la desigualdad *inequality*
el analfabetismo *illiteracy*
el nivel *level*
caritativo/a *charitable*
indiscutible *indisputable*
eliminar

SAM: Actividades pp. 336-338

Ingrid Betancourt, una luchadora

Ingrid Betancourt, política colombiana

"Nuestro mundo debe cambiar y cada uno de nosotros debe romper la maldición de su propia indiferencia."

Ingrid Betancourt, política colombiana secuestrada durante más de seis años por las Fuerzas Armadas Revolucionarias de Colombia (FARC), recibió en 2008 el Premio Príncipe de Asturias de la Concordia.

En el discurso que pronunció en la ceremonia, afirmó que no se sentiría totalmente libre ni feliz mientras tenga compañeros presos en la selva.

Estos son algunos fragmentos de su discurso en la entrega del premio:

"Tengo la profunda convicción que cuando hablamos, estamos cambiando el mundo."

"Las guerrillas de Colombia deben oír desde aquí las voces de quienes reclamamos la libertad de todos los colombianos."

"Desde Asturias, hacemos un desgarrador llamado a nuestros pueblos hermanos en toda América Latina, para que impidan que el secuestro se generalice en nuestro continente. Pedimos que la droga que se produce en Colombia y en otras regiones no pueda transitar por los territorios de nuestras geografías, porque con la riqueza que genera se alimenta el terrorismo y se incrementa el secuestro. Pedimos que todos nuestros pueblos detengan el tráfico de armas porque esas mismas armas se utilizan en contra de nuestra población para quitar la vida y la libertad de nuestros seres queridos."

Pedir algo por una razón

Pedimos que los secuestrados queden libres porque la libertad es un derecho.

| 16A.4 | **pedir que** + [*subjunctive*] |
| | **porque** + [*indicative*] |

Vocabulario

(16)

el/la luchador(a) *fighter*

el/la político/a *politician*

el/la secuestrado/a *kidnapping victim*

las fuerzas armadas *armed forces*

la concordia *harmony*

el discurso *speech*

libre *free*

el/la preso/a *prisoner*

la selva *jungle*

desgarrador(a) *heartrending*

el secuestro *kidnapping*

la droga *drug(s)*

el tráfico de armas *arms trade*

quitar *to take away*

romper *to break*

la maldición *curse*

la convicción, la guerrilla, el terrorismo, la indiferencia

(18)

el/la embajador(a) de la paz *ambassador for peace*

---

16 **a. Protagonista** ¿Conoce a la protagonista? Comente con su compañero/a lo que sabe de ella.

b. Conflicto en Colombia ¿Conoce el conflicto que existe en Colombia? ¿Qué cree que puede ayudar a resolverlo?

c. Responder Lea la cita a pie de foto y la introducción al artículo. ¿Por qué cree que es una luchadora? ¿Por qué recibió el Premio Príncipe de Asturias de la Concordia?

17 **a. Ingrid Betancourt** En la ceremonia de entrega del Premio Príncipe de Asturias, Ingrid Betancourt dio un discurso. ¿Sobre qué habló? Lea los fragmentos del discurso y marque los temas.

| libertad | terrorismo | educación | derechos humanos |

| cambio climático | turismo en Colombia | inmigración |

| guerra | FARC | droga |

b. Peticiones ¿Qué pide Ingrid Betancourt sobre la droga y por qué? Imagine otras posibles peticiones de Betancourt en el resto de su discurso.

18 **Pedir algo** Imagine que usted es embajador(a) de la paz. ¿Qué pide? ¿Por qué? Comparta sus ideas con su compañero/a.

Modelo: *Pido que... porque...*

19 **a. Leer** Lea algunos datos adicionales de la biografía de Ingrid Betancourt.

1961	Nació el 25 de diciembre de 1961 en Bogotá. Hija del político Gabriel Betancourt, ministro de Educación, y de Yolanda Pulecio, política colombiana.
1983	Estudió Comercio Exterior y Relaciones Internacionales en el Instituto de Estudios Políticos de París. Ese mismo año se casó con el diplomático Fabrice Delloye (con quien tuvo dos hijos) y obtuvo la doble nacionalidad francesa y colombiana.
1989	Regresó a Colombia. Se afilió al Partido Liberal para denunciar la corrupción y el caciquismo.
1994	Hizo su primera campaña política.
1997	Se casó con el publicista Juan Carlos Lecompte.
1998	Fundó el Partido Verde Oxígeno, ecologista y progresista, y se presentó como candidata en las elecciones legislativas de Colombia.
1998–2001	Fue miembro del Senado de Colombia.
2001	Renunció a su cargo como senadora y se presentó como candidata a la presidencia.
2002	Durante la campaña electoral, ella y su asesora Clara Rojas visitaron una zona de actividad guerrillera, y las FARC las secuestraron.
2008	El ejército colombiano liberó a Ingrid Betancourt el 2 de julio.
2008	Recibió el Premio Príncipe de Asturias de la Concordia.

b. Fechas significativas Destaque tres fechas significativas para usted de la biografía y explique a su compañero/a por qué las eligió.

c. Opinar ¿Cree que Ingrid Betancourt podría ser "embajadora de la paz"? ¿Por qué?

Modelo: *A mí me parece...*

20 **Escribir** Escriba algunos datos significativos de la biografía de una persona conocida por sus acciones pacifistas o por la defensa de los derechos humanos. Después comparta su biografía con la clase y exponga su opinión.

21 **Diana** Escuche lo que narra Diana sobre los acentos y las expresiones en Colombia. Después, indique si las oraciones son verdaderas (V) o falsas (F).

	V	F
1. Diana dice que en su país las diferencias en los acentos y en las expresiones son muy marcadas.	☐	☐
2. Natalia, la prima de Diana, vive en Manizales.	☐	☐
3. En Colombia, encontrar a alguien "de chepa" es encontrarlo de casualidad.	☐	☐
4. A Natalia la invitaron a comer postre.	☐	☐
5. "Estar como un postre" significa ponerse lindo/a.	☐	☐
6. Diana piensa que Colombia es un país sin diversidad.	☐	☐

Vocabulario

19
el/la diplomático/a *diplomat*
afiliarse *to join*
el caciquismo *despotism*
el partido político *political party*
liberar *to set free*
las letras *literature*
denunciar, la corrupción, el/la candidato/a

20
pacífico/a *peaceful*
la defensa *defense*

21
la casualidad *chance*

22
el pueblo indígena *native people*
la lengua nativa *native language*
el/la mestizo/a *person of mixed race*
el/la gitano/a *gypsy*

Desde 1981, la Fundación Príncipe/Princesa de Asturias organiza cada año una ceremonia en Oviedo, España, para entregar los Premios Príncipe/Princesa de Asturias (el nombre cambió en 2014 con la proclamación del príncipe Felipe como rey de España; su hija Leonor asumió el título de princesa de Asturias). Es un reconocimiento a las personas, instituciones o grupos de trabajo que se hayan destacado en las siguientes categorías: Artes, Comunicación y Humanidades, Letras, Deportes, Ciencias Sociales, Investigación Científica y Técnica, Cooperación Internacional y Concordia.

22 **a. Colombia, Colombias** ¿Qué sabe de la diversidad cultural colombiana? Lea el texto. ¿Cómo interpreta el título "Colombia, Colombias"? ¿Qué información ofrecen estas imágenes? ¿Qué culturas conviven en Colombia?

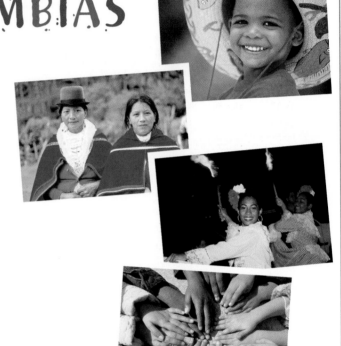

Colombia, COLOMBIAS

El Ministerio de Cultura de Colombia organiza todos los años muchos eventos este día, el 21 de mayo: Día de la Diversidad Cultural y Día Nacional de la Afrocolombianidad.

En Colombia conviven:

- 87 pueblos indígenas
- 65 lenguas nativas (wayuunaiki, lenguas makú, guahibo, etc.)
- más de 10 millones de afrocolombianos
- 30 millones de mestizos
- 25 000 raizales
- 12 000 gitanos
- gran número de inmigrantes de diferentes lugares (sirios, libaneses, japoneses, chinos y europeos, entre otros)

Colombia

21 de mayo Día Mundial de la Diversidad Cultural y Día Nacional de la Afrocolombianidad

b. Diversidad cultural ¿Qué diversidad cultural hay en su región? Comparta sus conocimientos con la clase.

TAREA FINAL

Manifiesto por...

Elijan el tema de su manifiesto (la paz, la educación, los derechos humanos...).

Redacten entre todos la introducción (motivo, quién firma el manifiesto, etc.).

En parejas, redacten dos o tres oraciones con sus opiniones.

Léanlas y hagan una lista común con toda la clase. Añadan sus peticiones en cuanto al tema de su manifiesto.

Elaboren una presentación con todas las frases. Añadan fotos o dibujos, y la firma de todos.

YO PUEDO...

- **Puedo exponer una opinión.**
  Opine con una oración afirmativa y otra negativa sobre un tema de actualidad.
  - *Creo que... No creo que...*

- **Puedo mostrar escepticismo.**
  Lea esta afirmación y exprese escepticismo.
  "El hombre podrá vivir en la Luna."

- **Puedo transmitir información.**
  Transmita estas afirmaciones que escuchó ayer.

  Meteorólogo: "El fin de semana hará muy buen tiempo."

  Profesor: "La próxima semana habrá un examen."

- **Puedo pedir algo por una razón.**
  Exprese una petición a la clase y diga por qué.

GRAMÁTICA FUNCIONAL (S) Tutorials

16A.1 **Express an opinion**

creer/pensar/parecer que + [*indicative*];
no creer que + [*subjunctive*] 5.21.4
Irregular subjunctive forms 5.20.2

- To express an opinion, use **creer/pensar/parecer que** + [*indicative*]. Use an indirect object pronoun with **parecer que**.

  Me parece que el desarme nuclear **es** importante para lograr la paz mundial.
  I think that nuclear disarmament is important in order to achieve world peace.

- Use the **subjunctive** with the constructions **no creer/no pensar/ no parecer que**. Statements with these constructions convey uncertainty or doubt.

  No creo que el desarme nuclear **sea** posible.
  I don't think that nuclear disarmament is possible.

- (**No**) **creer/pensar/parecer** + [*infinitive*] can be used if the verb that follows has the same subject.

  No creo que pueda ir a la fiesta mañana. Estoy enfermo.
  No creo poder ir a la fiesta mañana. Estoy enfermo.
  I don't think I can go to the party tomorrow. I'm sick.

- You have learned the formation of the regular present subjunctive forms, as well as the present subjunctive of stem-changing verbs and verbs with irregular **yo** forms. Some verbs are irregular in the present subjunctive.

DAR	ESTAR	SER	IR
dé	esté	sea	vaya
des	estés	seas	vayas
dé	esté	sea	vaya
demos	estemos	seamos	vayamos
deis	estéis	seáis	vayáis
den	estén	sean	vayan

No creo que el profesor nos **dé** más tiempo para escribir el trabajo.
I don't think that the professor will give us more time to write the paper.

16A.2 **Show skepticism**

dudar que + [*subjunctive*] 5.21.4

- To show skepticism, use **dudar que** + [*subjunctive*].

  Dudamos que nos **den** una oportunidad.
  We doubt that they will give us an opportunity.

- The construction **dudar de que** + [*subjunctive*] is also correct.

  Dudo de que Mario **quiera** venir.
  I doubt (that) Mario wants to come.

- If both **dudar** and the verb that follows have the same subject, you can use the construction **dudar** + [*infinitive*].

  Dudo que pueda ir. / Dudo poder ir.
  I doubt I can go.

¡Póngalo en práctica!

G1 **Conversaciones** Complete las conversaciones.

- Creo que te van a (1)............... (dar) el premio.
- ¿De verdad? No creo que me lo (2)............... (dar); hay mucha gente cualificada.

- Creo que iremos a la marcha por la paz mañana. ¿Piensan (3)............... (ir) ustedes?
- No, no creo que (4)............... (ir); no solemos ir a las marchas.

- Llamé a Juan Cruz, pero no contestó. No me parece que (5)............... (estar) en casa.
- Entonces creo que (6)............... (ir) a llamar a César para ver si me puede ayudar.

- No creo que (7)............... (nosotros, ir) a la fiesta mañana porque todavía estamos un poco resfriados.
- Creo que (8)............... (ustedes, deber) descansar.

- ¿Crees (9)............... (poder) terminar el proyecto escolar?
- Sí, pero no creo que Marta lo (10)............... (terminar).

G2 **Emparejar** Empareje el comienzo de la oración con el final apropiado.

1. No creo que nosotros	a. es importante eliminar la desigualdad social.
2. Rosa no cree	b. estén preparados para el debate.
3. A Leticia no le parece que	c. podamos ir al evento del candidato.
4. Creo que	d. poder ayudar con el discurso.
5. Cecilia no cree que sus compañeros	e. sea buena idea poner en marcha el plan.

G3 **Completar** Complete las conversaciones.

- ¿Dudas que la paz (1)............... (ser) posible?
- Sí, y Elena también duda que los gobiernos (2)............... (dar) la respuesta y (3)............... (estar) comprometidos con la paz.
- Yo también dudo que lo (4)............... (hacer).

- Dudo que la nueva iniciativa (5)............... (tener) resultados positivos. Hay mucha violencia en esta ciudad.
- Sí, todos dudamos que (6)............... (cambiar) la situación.

 Practice more at **vhlcentral.com**.

GRAMÁTICA FUNCIONAL

16A.3 Convey information

Indirect discourse: future-conditional 12.10
Simple future and conditional: irregular forms 5.16.2b, 5.17.2

- Use indirect discourse (**el estilo indirecto**) to report what another person has said. When the direct speech is given in the **futuro simple**, use the **condicional** in indirect speech.

> "**Estudiaremos** los resultados."
> Ayer nos informaron que **estudiarían** los resultados.

> "*We will study* the results."
> *Yesterday they informed us that **they would study** the results.*

- You have seen the use of indirect discourse in **11A.2** and **14B.3**, and you have learned the use of the reporting verbs **decir, comentar, explicar,** and **preguntar**. Other reporting verbs include **informar, declarar, añadir, confirmar, anunciar,** and **afirmar**.

- Several verbs have irregular forms in the **futuro simple** and the **condicional**. You learned the regular forms in **12B.1** and **13A.3**, and the irregular forms of the **futuro simple** in **15A.1**. The same verbs that have irregular forms in the **futuro simple** are also irregular in the **condicional**. The endings of irregular and regular verbs in the **condicional** are the same.

	Direct discourse	→		Indirect discourse
Infinitive	**Simple future**	**Reporting verb**		**Conditional**
haber	**habr**á	informó		**habr**ía
hacer	**har**á	declaró		**har**ía
poder	**podr**á	añadió	+ que	**podr**ía
salir	**saldr**á	confirmó		**saldr**ía
tener	**tendr**á	anunció		**tendr**ía
poner	**pondr**á	afirmó		**pondr**ía

> "Mañana **saldremos** para Montevideo."
> Gabriel me confirmó que **saldrían** para Montevideo al día siguiente.

> "*We will leave* for Montevideo tomorrow."
> *Gabriel confirmed to me that **they would leave** for Montevideo the following day.*

16A.4 Request something for a reason

pedir que + [*subjunctive*], **porque** + [*indicative*] 5.21.1, 12.6

- Use the subjunctive with **pedir** (*to ask [for]*) + **que** to make a request. To give a reason, use **porque** + [*indicative*].

> **Pedimos que** los gobiernos **renuncien** a la violencia **porque** no **es** la solución de ningún conflicto.
> *We ask that governments renounce violence because it is not the solution to any conflict.*

> Te **pido que escuches** lo que tengo que decir **porque es** importante estar bien informado.
> *I ask you to listen to what I have to say because it is important to be well informed.*

¡Póngalo en práctica!

G4 **Escribir** Escriba la forma correcta del verbo en el condicional.

1. Lourdes, hacer	
2. Néstor y yo, salir	
3. ustedes, poner	
4. vosotros, tener	
5. tú, poder	
6. una razón, haber	

G5 **Declaraciones** Transforme estas declaraciones al estilo indirecto.

1. "Este año no tendré vacaciones hasta septiembre."
   Mi padre nos confirmó que este año no
   ....

2. "Pondremos en marcha un plan contra la crisis."
   El ministro de Economía afirmó que
   ....

3. "Mañana haré una fiesta."
   Mi compañero de trabajo me dijo que hoy
   ....

4. "Podremos entregar la nueva propuesta antes del viernes."
   El gerente declaró que
   ....

5. "La universidad extenderá la convocatoria hasta el próximo viernes."
   La profesora anunció que la universidad
   ....

6. "Habrá otro debate la semana que viene."
   El locutor añadió que
   ....

G6 **Oraciones** Complete las oraciones.

Pedimos que nos (1)..................... (ellos, dar) una explicación porque no lo (2)..................... (nosotros, entender). Os pido que, por favor, (3)..................... (vosotros, ir) a la Marcha Mundial, (4)..................... es importante el compromiso de todos.

El profesor nos pide que (5)..................... (nosotros, preparar) unas preguntas para hacerle al candidato que viene a la clase mañana porque (6)..................... (él, querer) que todos participemos.

Clara me pide que la (7)..................... (yo, ayudar) con los titulares desde la oficina de prensa porque (8)..................... (ella, estar) muy ocupada hoy.

Compromiso de todos

la adhesión	support
la agresión	aggression
el arma nuclear	nuclear weapon
el consenso	consensus
los derechos humanos	human rights
el desastre	disaster
el/la dictador(a)	dictator
el ejército	army
el/la escultor(a)	sculptor
la firma	signing
el formulario	form
la fuerza	strength, power
el gobierno	government
la justicia social	social justice
la marcha	march
la movilización social	social mobilization
la no violencia	non-violence
el/la pacifista	pacifist
el pretexto	pretext
el territorio	territory
el tratado	treaty
la unidad popular	unity of the people
adherirse (e:ie)	to join
convencer (z)	to convince
dudar	to doubt
firmar	to sign
hacer falta	to be necessary
invadir	to invade
rechazar	to reject
reducir (zc)	to reduce
renunciar (a)	to give up
convencional	conventional
de un día para el otro	overnight
sobre la base de	based upon

Debate social

estar a la cabeza	to lead
poner en marcha	to set in motion
el analfabetismo	illiteracy
el aprovechamiento	exploitation
la campaña electoral	electoral campaign
la clave	key
la convocatoria	call (to action)
el/la coordinador(a)	coordinator
el crecimiento	growth
el debate	debate
la desigualdad	inequality
la grulla	crane
los líderes mundiales	world leaders
el/la locutor(a)	announcer
la medida	measure
el ministerio	ministry, department
el/la ministro/a	minister
la multinacional	multinational (firm)
el nivel	level
la oficina de prensa	press office
la política	politics
el/la presidente/a	president
la secretaría	ministry, department
la sensibilización	increased awareness
el titular	headline
afirmar	to assert
anunciar	to announce
declarar	to declare; to state
eliminar	to eliminate
estimular	to stimulate
informar	to inform
sensibilizar	to raise awareness
ambicioso/a	ambitious
caritativo/a	charitable
desfavorecido/a	underprivileged
enorme	huge
indiscutible	indisputable
racional	rational
en cuanto a	as for
con respecto a	regarding

Ingrid Betancourt

el caciquismo	despotism
el/la candidato/a	candidate
la casualidad	chance
la concordia	harmony
la convicción	conviction
la corrupción	corruption
la defensa	defense
el/la diplomático/a	diplomat
el discurso	speech
la droga	drug(s)
el/la embajador(a) de la paz	ambassador for peace
las fuerzas armadas	armed forces
el/la gitano/a	gypsy
la guerrilla	guerrilla
la indiferencia	indifference
la lengua nativa	native language
las letras	literature
el/la luchador(a)	fighter
la maldición	curse
el/la mestizo/a	person of mixed race
el partido político	political party
el/la político/a	politician
el/la preso/a	prisoner
el pueblo indígena	native people
el/la secuestrado/a	kidnapping victim
el secuestro	kidnapping
la selva	jungle
el terrorismo	terrorism
el tráfico de armas	arms trade
afiliarse	to join
denunciar	to denounce
liberar	to set free
quitar	to take away
romper	to break
desgarrador(a)	heartrending
libre	free
pacífico/a	peaceful

Variación léxica

la convicción ⟷ la certeza ⟷ el convencimiento

el pretexto ⟷ la excusa ⟷ la justificación

la selva ⟷ la jungla

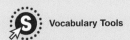
TÍPICOS TÓPICOS

Publicidad hasta en el café

No se lo tome solo.
¡TÓMESELO EN BUENA COMPAÑÍA!
CAFÉ ANTIGUA

Se lo garantizamos: nuestro café es 100 × 100 orgánico. Nuestros expertos se lo compran directamente a la población maya del departamento de Sacatepéquez, en Guatemala.

No se confunda, no ahorre en calidad. Exíjala. No lo olvide. Es mejor que consuma productos certificados. Invite a sus amigos: ¡saboréenlo y disfrútenlo juntos!

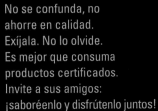

¡DESPERTAOS CON CHOCOLATE BUEN DÍA Y EMPEZAD EL DÍA CON ENERGÍA!

Consejos para papás y mamás:
Tomad Chocolate Buen Día a la taza o comedlo con pan. Dádselo a vuestros hijos en el desayuno o en la merienda y... ¡tomáoslo con ellos! ¡No os lo perdáis!

Animar a la acción y dar consejo

No lo olvide: Es mejor que consuma productos certificados.

Desayunad chocolate. Es pura energía.

16B.1 Affirmative and negative commands
es mejor que + [subjunctive]

Vocabulario

(1)

el tópico *cliché*
la publicidad *advertising*
en buena compañía *in good company*
confundirse *to become confused*
exigir (j) *to demand*
certificado/a *certified*
saborear *to savor*
la merienda *(afternoon) snack*
perdérselo (e:ie) *to miss out*

---

(1) **Publicidad** Observe la publicidad y complete el mapa de ideas asociado con el café.

gustos
solo o con leche

lugares

personas

estados de ánimo

expresiones, palabras...

otros

(2) **a. Frases que animan a la acción** Lea los anuncios y seleccione las frases que animan a la acción. ¿Qué le sugieren? ¿Le parecen anuncios eficaces?

Modelo: • *"No se lo tome solo." Me gusta porque...*
• *"Es mejor que..."*

b. Escribir Localice los verbos en imperativo de los anuncios, observe su formación y complete la tabla.

	Imperativo afirmativo (+)	Imperativo negativo (−)
tú	toma	no tomes
usted	tome	....
vosotros/as	....	....
ustedes	....	....

(3) **Preferencias** ¿Café, chocolate, té o alguna otra infusión? ¿Usted cómo se lo toma y cuándo? Pregunte a su compañero/a.

Modelo: *Yo prefiero café, y me lo tomo...*

(4) **Animar a la acción** Cree con su compañero/a otras oraciones y eslóganes que animen a tomar estos productos.

5 **Escuchar** Escuche los anuncios publicitarios y relacione cada uno con el eslogan correspondiente.

- Siéntate a nuestra mesa y siéntete como en casa. ☐
- No lo piense más: haga su diseño, díganoslo y se lo llevamos a casa. ☐
- Venid a la naturaleza, vividla. ☐

6 **a. Anuncios** Fíjese en estas oraciones de los anuncios presentados en esta lección. ¿A qué se refieren?

| Se lo garantizamos. | Dádselo en el desayuno. | Se lo llevamos a casa. | Exíjala. |

b. Relacionar Relacione las diferentes versiones (con y sin pronombres) de los mismos eslóganes.

1. Si encuentra algo más barato, le devolvemos la diferencia. ....
2. Hasta que no prueben estos yogures, no saben lo que se pierden. ....
3. Conozca la nueva fragancia. Le recomiendo la experiencia. ....
4. Subid vuestra mejor foto y ganad un crucero por el Caribe. ....

a. Subidla y ganáoslo.
b. Hasta que no los prueben, no lo saben.
c. Si lo encuentra más barato, se la devolvemos.
d. Conózcala. Se la recomiendo.

7 **Viñeta** Observe la viñeta cómica. ¿Es habitual una situación así en su cultura?

Yo te lo pago.

No, no, yo se lo pago.

A mí me lo podéis pagar los dos, no hay problema.

8 **a. El café** Lea la nota. ¿Es también para usted un ritual tomar café?

b. Productos Piense en un producto conocido por la clase y hable de él a sus compañeros sin decir el nombre. Sus compañeros adivinan qué es.

Modelo: *Antes de acostarme, la tomo tibia para dormir mejor. (la leche)*

👥 **MI EXPERIENCIA**

9 **Eslóganes** Cree eslóganes para animar a sus compañeros a adoptar hábitos de vida saludables. Comparen los eslóganes de toda la clase y elijan los más eficaces.

GUIÓN DE TRABAJO

¿Qué hábitos saludables puedo incorporar en mi vida diaria?

Compra frutas y verduras. Cómelas todos los días.

Es mejor que camines en vez de tomar el autobús.

Aprende a relajarte. No lo olvides: tu salud es lo primero.

Vocabulario

5

sentirse (e:ie) como en casa *to feel at home*

el pico *peak, mountain*

6

devolver (o:ue) *to return*

la diferencia *difference (in price)*

probar (o:ue) *to taste*

la fragancia *fragrance, perfume*

el crucero *cruise*

8

provenir de *to come from*

un tercio *a third*

Referirse a personas u objetos conocidos

- Le he comprado este paquete de café. ¿Dónde **se lo** dejo?
- Déje**melo** aquí mismo. Ahora **se lo** pago.

16B.2 **me, te, se... + lo/la...**

El café

Además de ser un producto de consumo básico, el café es casi un ritual en muchos países hispanos, donde la gente queda para tomarlo o invita a un café a sus amigos o familiares.

La mayor parte de la producción mundial de café proviene de Latinoamérica, especialmente de Brasil, Colombia, Guatemala, Honduras y México. Brasil es el principal productor mundial de café y el mayor exportador, con cerca de un tercio del mercado global.

SAM: Actividades pp. 343–345

Usos y costumbres

El Salvador

De los países de Centroamérica, El Salvador es el más pequeño y el más densamente poblado. La gente habla español y, en menor medida, el náhuatl. El plato típico es la pupusa, o tortilla de maíz que se come rellena con queso, frijoles fritos u otros ingredientes. La moneda es el dólar estadounidense, y se exportan café, azúcar y camarones. El 6 de agosto se celebra la tradicional "Bajada", que es la fiesta nacional más importante. Ese día la gente que vive al pie del volcán y en las poblaciones vecinas baja a la ciudad a venerar al patrono de la república y participar en la procesión por las calles de la capital.

Atracciones turísticas

- Con sus 300 kilómetros de costa a lo largo del océano Pacífico y sus altísimas olas, El Salvador es uno de los destinos favoritos en Latinoamérica para los surfistas.

- En el pueblo de Ilobasco se elaboran artesanías con arcilla y cerámica pintada a mano. Igual de famosas son las "sorpresas", o pequeñas piezas de cerámica en cuyo interior se representan escenas de la vida diaria.

- En el Parque Nacional Montecristo hay orquídeas, monos araña, pumas, quetzales y tucanes. Se le conoce también como El Trifinio porque está ubicado donde se unen las fronteras de Guatemala, Honduras y El Salvador.

Hablar sobre usos y costumbres

- En El Salvador, el 6 de agosto **se celebra** una de las fiestas nacionales más importantes. Ese día **los salvadoreños veneran** al santo patrono de la república.

- ¿Y qué hace la gente?

16B.3 **se** + [3rd-person verb]
la gente...
3rd-person plural verb

Vocabulario
⑩

densamente *densely*
poblado/a *populated*
relleno/a *stuffed, filled*
el camarón *shrimp*
el/la patrono/a *patron saint*
turístico/a *tourist*
la ola *wave*
el/la surfista *surfer*
la arcilla *clay*
el/la mono/a araña *spider monkey*
el tucán *toucan*
el uso *custom*
la procesión, venerar

⑩ **a. Leer** Lea el texto sobre El Salvador. ¿Dónde es posible encontrar este tipo de artículos?

b. Contestar ¿Por qué puede ser importante conocer los usos y costumbres de un país?

c. Relacionar Relacione estos términos con su significado.

1. densamente ......
2. náhuatl ......
3. procesión ......
4. surfista ......
5. ubicado ......

a. marcha de personas que realizan un recorrido religioso
b. situado
c. con muchos habitantes en poco espacio
d. persona que practica el surf
e. lengua indígena

⑪ **El Salvador** Busque en el texto esta clase de información sobre los usos y costumbres de El Salvador.

gastronomía   lenguas   fiestas

turismo   comercio

Modelo: *En El Salvador, la gente come... Se habla...*

⑫ **Lugares especiales** Elija dos lugares especiales para usted y anote sus usos y costumbres. Después comparta la información con sus compañeros sin decirles el nombre de los lugares. ¿Adivinaron de qué lugares se trataba?

LUGAR	Se habla...	Se come...	Se celebra...	Son...	La gente...

⑬ **a. Escribir** Escriba oraciones para comparar la información dada.

> **Modelo:** *mi ciudad / cara / la tuya*
> *Mi ciudad es igual de cara que la tuya.*

1. los hombres / comunicativos / las mujeres
2. el sedentarismo / peligroso / otros malos hábitos
3. ocultar la verdad / mentir
4. la verdura congelada / nutritiva / la verdura fresca / ¿?
5. todas las lenguas del mundo / complejas

b. Hacer comparaciones Con su compañero/a, elija uno de estos temas para continuar haciendo comparaciones.

> **Modelo:** *Mi celular tiene menos funciones que los nuevos teléfonos inteligentes, pero es igual de útil si tengo que hacer una llamada.*

(profesiones)   (nacionalidades o grupos étnicos)   (empresas o productos)

⑭ **Comparaciones** Fíjese en los datos y compare estos dos países centroamericanos.

Costa Rica	Nicaragua
• interesante +	• interesante +
• turístico + +	• turístico +
• extenso –	• extenso +
• poblado –	• poblado +
• bello +	• bello +
• hospitalario +	• hospitalario +

> **Modelo:** *Costa Rica es igual de interesante que Nicaragua.*
> *Costa Rica es más turístico que...*

⑮ **Generalizaciones** Piense en su país y los tópicos más frecuentes en relación con él. ¿Encuentra alguna generalización que desee atenuar?

(No todos los españoles duermen la siesta.)   (No todos los argentinos bailan el tango.)   (En México se comen tacos, pero eso no es todo.)

🔗 **MI EXPERIENCIA**

⑯ **Hablar sobre usos y costumbres** ¿Cuál es más atractiva: la vida en una ciudad cosmopolita o la vida en un pueblo de montaña? Compare con su compañero/a y describa los usos y costumbres de cada estilo de vida.

GUIÓN DE TRABAJO

(¿Crees que la vida en una ciudad es más atractiva que la vida en un pueblo?)
→
(No, es menos atractiva. En la ciudad, la gente vive... Se viaja... y se come... La gente que vive en la ciudad está acostumbrada a... ¿Tú qué opinas?)
←
(Para mí es igual de atractiva. Simplemente se trata de dos cosas diferentes.)

Hacer comparaciones

- ¿Es el país más interesante para visitar?
- No, es **igual de** interesante **que** todos. Todos los países son **igual de** interesantes. Para el verdadero viajero, la costa es **igual que** la sierra y el lago es **igual que** el volcán.

16B.4 **igual (de** + [*adjective*]**) + que**

Vocabulario

⑬
comunicativo/a *communicative*
el sedentarismo *sedentary lifestyle*
ocultar *to hide*
congelado/a *frozen*
complejo/a *complex*
anticuado/a, el grupo étnico
⑭
extenso/a *vast*
bello/a *beautiful*
homogéneo/a *homogeneous*
⑯
cosmopolita *cosmopolitan*

¡OJO!

Note that **igual** is invariable in the comparative structure **igual de** + [*adjective*] **+ que**. As with all adverbs, it does not agree in number with the preceding noun. Examples: **Su población es igual de homogénea que la de Honduras** and **Sus platos típicos son igual de deliciosos que los de otros países de Centroamérica.**

Estrategia

Atenuar las generalizaciones
No todos los argentinos son de Buenos Aires.
Centroamérica tiene unas playas maravillosas, pero eso no es todo.

SAM: Actividades pp. 346–348

🅢 Practice more at **vhlcentral.com**.

Estela y Mario, publicistas

MIRADOR: ESCUELA DE MARKETING Y PUBLICIDAD

MIRADOR: Estela y Mario, antiguos alumnos de nuestra escuela, ¿en qué están trabajando ahora mismo?

MARIO: *Estamos a punto de lanzar una campaña para dar a conocer una nueva bebida.*

ESTELA: *Es un encargo muy amplio que incluye el diseño de la botella, la etiqueta y la campaña de promoción propiamente dicha que vendrá después.*

MIRADOR: ¿Pueden anticiparnos algún detalle?

MARIO: *Se trata de una bebida muy especial y muy guatemalteca. No podemos decir más. El trabajo es muy lindo y el desafío es enorme, parecido al que hice en Managua, de donde soy oriundo, cuando me contrataron junto a otros publicistas para encontrar la marca país, o sea, el logo representativo del país.*

ESTELA: *De hecho, los objetivos son iguales que los de marca país. Buscamos representar a Guatemala de cara al turismo y la exportación.*

MARIO: *Estamos trabajando con los colores y sus símbolos: el amarillo para la autenticidad, el morado para el misticismo, el verde claro para la diversidad, el rojo para la evolución y el verde oscuro para la cercanía.*

MIRADOR: ¿Qué le dirían a los alumnos de nuestra escuela que están a punto de terminar sus estudios este año?

ESTELA: *No tengan miedo y sean honestos. La valentía y la honestidad son las fuerzas más poderosas de la tierra.*

Estela Salvador y Mario Martínez, redactores, publicistas y productores gráficos

---

Hablar sobre un suceso próximo

Estamos a punto de terminar el proyecto.

16B.5 **estar a punto de +** [*infinitive*]

Vocabulario

17

lanzar una campaña *to launch a campaign*

dar a conocer *to make known*

el encargo *assignment*

la campaña de promoción *promotional campaign*

propiamente dicho/a *per se*

oriundo/a *native*

morado/a *purple*

claro/a *light*

oscuro/a *dark*

la cercanía *proximity*

la valentía *courage*

anticipar, el logo, la autenticidad

---

17 **a. Publicistas** ¿Cómo se imagina usted la profesión de un publicista? ¿Qué habilidades se necesitan para esta profesión?

b. Entrevista Lea la entrevista a estos publicistas. ¿En qué consiste su proyecto? ¿Qué le parece la idea? Anote ideas sobre estos temas.

- elementos gráficos
- producto
- objetivos
- valores

18 **a. Estela y Mario** ¿En qué fase del proyecto están Estela y Mario? Señale verdadero (V) o falso (F).

	V	F
1. Estela y Mario están a punto de lanzar su campaña.	☐	☐
2. Están a punto de terminar la campaña de promoción.	☐	☐
3. Están a punto de empezar el diseño.	☐	☐

b. Sugerencias Dé sus propios consejos y sugerencias a Estela y a Mario acerca de la campaña en la que están trabajando. Use algunas de estas expresiones.

- Es mejor que...
- Tienen que...
- En su lugar, yo...
- Les recomiendo...
- Lo mejor es/sería...
- ¿Por qué no...?

Modelo: *Es mejor que la publicidad apele a las emociones del consumidor.*

19 **Hablar sobre un suceso próximo** Piense en un proyecto que está a punto de comenzar o finalizar, o en las decisiones que está a punto de tomar. Coménteselo al grupo.

20 **a. Productos** ¿Qué productos asocia con estos países? Luego lea el texto e identifique el producto y el país del que trata. ¿Coincide con las ideas que tenía? ¿Conocía este producto?

- Alemania
- Guatemala
- España
- México
- Italia
- China
- Cuba
- Colombia

En el marco de° la XI Feria Alimentaria de Guatemala, tuvo lugar la final del certamen para elegir la bebida nacional. El premio fue para "Xelateca", un cóctel destinado a representar al país dentro y fuera de sus fronteras.

El jurado tuvo en cuenta para su elección el costo de elaboración, sabor e ingredientes representativos de Guatemala, y los sorprendió el uso creativo de las frutas nativas y la amplia gama de sabores.

La bebida ganadora está compuesta por agua de guinda, jarabe de azúcar, jugo de limón y durazno. Su sabor evoca aromas de selvas, lagos y volcanes. Todo esto y mucho más en una botella.

María Urzua, ganadora del concurso junto a su bebida: "Xelateca"

El proyecto surge de la iniciativa de un creciente grupo de países de la región centroamericana, firmemente decididos a proyectar su imagen en el extranjero a través de símbolos e imágenes fácilmente reconocibles e identificables.

Queda ahora por delante un largo camino para dar a conocer al mercado estos nuevos productos, así como el de hacerse un hueco° en el imaginario colectivo°, al lado de la margarita, el mate, el pisco… ¡Salud!°

En el marco de *Within the framework of* **hacerse un hueco** *to make a place for itself* **el imaginario colectivo** *collective imagination* **¡Salud!** *Cheers!*

b. Ingredientes Subraye los ingredientes de esta bebida. ¿Le parece una bebida apetitosa? ¿Qué ingredientes son típicos de la ciudad o región?

21 **Escribir** Escriba tres eslóganes publicitarios para dar a conocer la bebida "Xelateca" y promocionar Guatemala. Luego compare con el grupo y elijan el mejor eslogan.

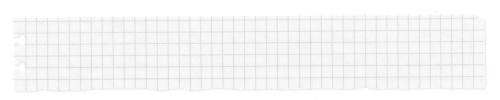

22 **a. Leer** Lea el texto. ¿Cuál es el origen de los nombres de los países que se mencionan?

¿De dónde provienen los nombres de los países latinoamericanos? A veces, el origen no es difícil de adivinar, como ocurre con Ecuador, cuyo nombre revela su posición geográfica. En otros casos, el nombre es una derivación de un apellido. Por ejemplo, Bolivia debe su denominación a Simón Bolívar, el libertador del país, mientras que Colombia lleva ese nombre en honor a quien descubrió América, Cristóbal Colón (*Colombo* en italiano). El origen de otros países es más difícil de deducir a simple vista. Guatemala proviene del náhuatl *quauhtlemallan*, que significa "bosque, lugar de muchos árboles". En el caso de Chile existen diferentes teorías; una de ellas es que el nombre viene del aimara *tili*, que significa "fin del mundo".

b. Nombres Investigue el origen del nombre de otro país latinoamericano. Explíquelo.

Vocabulario

18
apelar *to appeal*

20
feria *(trade) fair*
tener lugar *to be held*
el certamen *contest*
el cóctel *cocktail*
el jurado *panel of judges*
tener en cuenta *to take into account*
la gama *range*
compuesto/a por *made up of*
la guinda *wild cherry*
el durazno *peach*
el aroma *aroma, scent*
creciente *growing*
así como *as well as*

22
geográfico/a

23
el dinamismo

¡OJO!

To be made up of translates as **estar compuesto/a por** *or* **componerse de.** *Note the preposition used in each case, since they are not interchangeable. Examples:* **La mayor parte del cuerpo humano está compuesta por agua** *or* **La mayor parte del cuerpo humano se compone de agua.**

OPINIÓN

¿La publicidad nos aclara o nos confunde?

¿Cuál cree que sería el mejor símbolo para representar a su país?

SAM: Actividades pp. 349–354

23 **a. Eslóganes publicitarios** Lea el texto y estos eslóganes publicitarios de varios países latinoamericanos. ¿Qué elementos destaca cada país? Relacione estos conceptos con los eslóganes y coméntelo con el grupo.

> Igual que en el mundo de los negocios, los países compiten entre sí como productos y crean también su propio eslogan, que los caracteriza y diferencia para potenciar su imagen y atraer el turismo y las inversiones.

naturaleza • cultura • historia • comida • fiestas

CUBA
Explore nuestra riqueza cultural

COLOMBIA:
el riesgo es que te quieras quedar.

Honduras:
Un país pequeño, tres grandes mundos
Naturaleza tropical • Renacimiento maya • Creación caribeña

Nicaragua...
única... ¡original!

El Salvador
¡Impresionante!

Costa Rica
Sin ingredientes artificiales

Playas *hermosas.*
Fiestas *impresionantes.*
Frutas *exóticas.*
Así es PANAMÁ.

República Dominicana
Lo tiene todo

Bienvenido a
Guatemala,
corazón del mundo maya.

Argentina

b. Marca país Los países también crean su propio logo, la marca país, como esta de Argentina. Busque marcas o símbolos que identifican a otros países o sus distintas regiones y cuente al grupo qué conceptos transmiten y por qué son populares.

TAREA FINAL

Una campaña publicitaria

Seleccionen un país o una región y un producto que lo/la caracterice.

Piensen en los valores más positivos de ese país y producto, y compárenlos para seleccionar el más adecuado.

Diseñen un buen eslogan y seleccionen una o más imágenes representativas.

Elijan la mejor campaña para exponerla en el tablero de anuncios del departamento de español.

YO PUEDO...

- **Puedo animar a la acción.**
  Escriba tres eslóganes para animar a hacer más deporte.

- **Puedo referirme a personas u objetos conocidos.**
  El CD .... he dejado al lado de la computadora. No es necesario que .... lo devuelvas; es para ti, ... regalo. No .... des las gracias.

- **Puedo hablar sobre usos y costumbres.**
  Describa algún grupo profesional muy estereotipado para que sus compañeros puedan identificarlo.

- **Puedo hacer comparaciones.**
  Compare dos productos que ha visto en esta lección.

- **Puedo hablar sobre un suceso próximo.**
  Diga dos cosas que está a punto de hacer.

GRAMÁTICA FUNCIONAL Tutorials

16B.1 **Encourage and give advice**

Affirmative and negative commands   5.18, 5.19
es mejor que + [*subjunctive*]   5.8.3, 5.21.5

- Use the imperative (el **imperativo**) to give instructions and advice. Regular affirmative **tú** commands have the same form as the **usted/él/ella** form of the present indicative. Affirmative **usted** commands are the same as the present form of the subjunctive.

TOMAR	
(tú)	tom**a**
(usted)	tom**e**

- The affirmative **vosotros/as** command is formed by dropping the -r from the infinitive and adding a **-d**. Affirmative **ustedes** commands are the same as the present form of the subjunctive.

	TOMAR	BEBER	CONSUMIR
(vosotros/as)	toma**d**	bebe**d**	consumi**d**
(ustedes)	tom**en**	beb**an**	consum**an**

- With affirmative commands, attach the reflexive pronoun to the end of the verb. When the command has two or more syllables, add a written accent to maintain the original stress.

- In affirmative **vosotros/as** commands, the **-d** is dropped when the reflexive pronoun **os** is added to the end of the verb.

Levantaos.   **Callaos.**
Get up.   *Be quiet.*

- All other pronouns are added directly to the end of affirmative commands. Add a written accent if necessary to maintain the original pronunciation of the command.

Leedlo.   **Míreme.**
Read it.   *Look at me.*

- All forms of the negative imperative are the same as the conjugation of the present subjunctive.

	TOMAR	BEBER	CONSUMIR
(tú)	no tom**es**	no beb**as**	no consum**as**
(usted)	no tom**e**	no beb**a**	no consum**a**
(vosotros/as)	no tom**éis**	no beb**áis**	no consum**áis**
(ustedes)	no tom**en**	no beb**an**	no consum**an**

- Place object and reflexive pronouns before the verb with negative commands.

No se sienten allí, por favor.   **No le prestes** ese libro.
Do not sit there, please.   *Don't lend him that book.*

- Always use the subjunctive with the construction **es mejor que.**

Es mejor que leas las instrucciones.
It is better that you read the instructions.

¡Póngalo en práctica!

G1   **Imperativo** Complete la tabla con la forma correcta del imperativo.

	afirmativo	negativo
1. hablar, tú		no hables
2. poner, usted		
3. escribir, vosotros	escribid	
4. creer, ustedes		no crean
5. estudiar, tú	estudia	
6. bailar, ustedes		

G2   **Completar** Complete las oraciones.

No (1).................. (usted, comprar) el café allí. Lo venden muy caro. Es mejor que lo (2)................... (comprar) en otro sitio.

No te lo (3).................. (tú, pensar) dos veces. Decide tú y no se lo (4).................. (tú, decir) a nadie.

(5).................. (Vosotros, despertarse) con alegría y (6).................. (vosotros, comenzar) bien el día.

(7).................. (Ustedes, abrir) los libros y (8).................. (ustedes, leer) la primera página, por favor.

G3   **Reescribir** Reescriba las oraciones usando el imperativo con un pronombre.

Modelo: Quiero que termines la tarea.
           Termínala.

1. Quiero que preparen el almuerzo. ....
2. Es necesario que estudiéis las lecciones.
....
3. No quiero que comas los postres. ....
4. Te pido que te despiertes. ....
5. Es mejor que usted lea el capítulo. ....
6. No quiero que miréis las fotografías. ....

G4   **Contrarios** Escriba lo contrario de estas oraciones.

Modelo: Dale su diccionario.
           No le des su diccionario.

1. Regálale un libro. ....
2. Dime la verdad. ....
3. Sal de aquí. ....
4. No le hables. ....
5. Dame ese libro. ....
6. No le prestes tu carro. ....
7. No le tomes una foto. ....

S Practice more at **vhlcentral.com.**

GRAMÁTICA FUNCIONAL

16B.2 Refer to known people or objects

Double pronouns 5.18.6, 5.19.2, 6.3

- When using direct object pronouns with either indirect object pronouns or reflexive pronouns, always place the indirect object pronoun or reflexive pronoun first. Place both pronouns before the verb.

  ¿Te gusta el libro? **Te lo** compro.
  *Do you like the book? I will buy **it for you**.*

- In infinitive constructions and progressive tenses, the pronouns can be placed before the conjugated verb or attached to the end of the infinitive or present participle.

  Te lo quiero comprar. / Quiero comprár**telo**.
  *I want to buy **it for you**.*

  Me las está preparando. / Está preparándo**melas**.
  *He's making **them for me**.*

- When third-person indirect object pronouns (**le, les**) are combined with third-person direct object pronouns (**lo, la, los, las**), the indirect object pronoun is changed: **le/les → se**.

  A mi hermana le encanta el flan. **Se** lo voy a preparar mañana.
  *My sister loves flan. I am going to make it **for her** tomorrow.*

Mando	la carta	a mi amiga.	→	Se la mando.
	↓	↓		
	la	le	le + la →	se la

Order of pronouns:

1st: **me, te, le/se, nos, os, les/se** (indirect object and reflexive)

2nd: **lo, la, los, las** (direct object)

- In affirmative commands, the pronouns are attached to the end of the verb, as you have seen in **16B.1**. The same order of pronouns is maintained with commands, and **le/les** changes to **se** when used with a direct object pronoun.

  Mándaselo. / **Regáleselos.**
  Send it to him/her/them. / *Give them to him/her/them.*

- Add a written accent if needed in order to maintain the original pronunciation of the command.

- With the exception of the reflexive pronoun **os**, all pronouns can be directly added to affirmative **vosotros/as** commands. Remember that the **vosotros/as** command loses the final **-d** when used with the reflexive pronoun **os**, as you have seen in **16B.1**.

  Mandádmelos. / **Ponéoslas.**
  Send them to me. / *Put them on.*

- As you have seen in **16B.1**, pronouns must be placed before negative commands. The same order of pronouns is maintained, and **le/les** is changed to **se** if used with direct object pronouns.

  No me los mandes. / **No se lo digan.**
  Don't send them to me. / *Don't tell (it to) him/her/them.*

¡Póngalo en práctica!

G5 Conversaciones Complete las conversaciones.

> Me gustaría comprar este libro. ¿(1).......... (2).......... puede cobrar ya? Es que tengo mucha prisa.

> Aquí tiene, ¿quiere que (3).......... (4).......... envuelva?

> Sí, por favor, (5).......... (6).......... voy a regalar a mi hermano.

• • • • •

> A mi madre le encantaría esta cámara.

> ¡Cómprasela!

> Sí, tienes razón, (7).......... (8).......... voy a comprar.

• • • • •

> Necesito enviar estos paquetes a mis primos antes de sus cumpleaños.

> ¿Cómo (9).......... (10).......... quiere enviar?

> Por correo prioritario, por favor, así llegan más rápido.

G6 Transformar Transforme los mandatos afirmativos en mandatos negativos y viceversa.

Modelo: No se lo des.
Dáselo.

1. Coméoslos. ....
2. No se lo olvide. ....
3. No se los mandes. ....
4. Dádnoslos. ....
5. Regálesela. ....
6. Prepárenselo. ....
7. No me lo digan. ....
8. Recuérdamelo. ....

 Practice more at **vhlcentral.com**.

GRAMÁTICA FUNCIONAL

16B.3 Talk about habits and customs

se + [*3ʳᵈ-person verb form*]; **la gente**...; 3ʳᵈ-person
plural verb   3.4, 6.7

- Use the construction **se** + [*third-person verb*] to make
  impersonal statements.

    Se vive bien ahí.
    One lives well there. / People live well there.

- When the object of the verb is a person, use the preposition **a**
  and a third-person singular verb form.

    En Guatemala **se respeta** mucho a los ancianos.
    *In Guatemala, the elderly **are well respected**.*

- With things, the verb can be singular or plural. The verb must
  agree with the subject.

    Se usa el picante.
    *Hot sauce **is used**.*

    Se exportan muchas materias primas.
    *Many raw materials **are exported**.*

- Use **la gente** (*people*) to refer to a group of people in general
  terms. **La gente** is a singular noun that requires a singular
  article. Note that this noun also requires the third-person
  singular verb form.

    La gente es amable.   A **la gente** le gusta hablar.
    ***People** are friendly.*   ***People** like to talk.*

- You can also say **los/las** + [*plural noun*] to make generalizing
  statements. Use the third-person plural verb form with
  this construction.

    Los centroamericanos hablan varias lenguas.
    ***Central Americans** speak several languages.*

16B.4 Make comparisons

igual de/que   12.7

- Use **igual de** + [*adjective*] + **que** (*as ... as*) to make comparisons.

    Tu país es **igual de bello que** el mío.
    *Your country is **as beautiful as** mine.*

- You can also express this equivalence with **igual de** +
  [*plural adjective*].

    Estela y Mario son **igual de trabajadores**.
    *Estela and Mario are **equally hard-working**.*

- Use **igual que** (*the same as*) to compare two things without
  specifying the characteristic being compared.

    La costa es **igual de** turística **que** el interior.
    *The coast is **as touristy as** the interior.*

    La costa es **igual que** el interior.
    *The coast is **the same as** the interior.*

G7 Diálogo Complete la conversación.

> En muchos pueblos pequeños, la gente
> (1).......... (ser) muy simpática y (2)..........
> (estar) siempre dispuesta a ayudarte.

> Sí, (3)................. vive de otra manera
> en las áreas rurales, más relajada. En
> las ciudades modernas (4)................
> (vivir) muy deprisa. (5)................
> (Comer) rápido y la gente (6)................
> (tener) otro ritmo de vida. (7)................
> (Perder) muchas buenas costumbres.

> Sí, en los pueblos pequeños
> (8)................. no tiene tanta prisa.

G8 Costumbres Reescribe las oraciones usando **se**.

Modelo: Aquí la gente habla dos idiomas.
        Aquí se hablan dos idiomas.

1. Aquí la gente toma mucho café.
   ....

2. En Paraguay la gente habla guaraní.
   ....

3. En Uruguay la gente toma mate en todos lados.
   ....

4. En el Caribe la gente toma muchos jugos.
   ....

G9 Oraciones Complete las oraciones.

- Para mí, el café más barato es el más sabroso.

- No estoy de acuerdo. Todos los cafés son
  (1).............. de ricos. El más barato es igual
  (2).............. el más caro.

  Tu hermana es (3).............. de simpática
  (4).............. tú.

  La torta de chocolate que hace Guadalupe es igual
  (5).............. rica (6).............. la que hacía mi abuela.

  Mi primo y yo somos igual (7).............. inteligentes,
  pero no somos igual (8).............. trabajadores.

- ¡Esta película es igual (9).............. todas las
  comedias románticas!

- No es cierto. No es (10).............. de optimista y no
  tiene un final feliz.

S Practice more at **vhlcentral.com**.

GRAMÁTICA FUNCIONAL

16B.5 Talk about an imminent event

estar a punto de + [*infinitive*] 5.15

- Use the construction **estar a punto de** (*to be about to*) + [*infinitive*] to tell that an action is imminent.

  Estoy a punto de salir.   La peli **está a punto de empezar.**
  I am about to go out.   *The movie is about to begin.*

- Use **estar** in a past tense to indicate an event that was imminent in the past.

  Diego **estaba a punto de volver** a su casa cuando Gisela llegó al restaurante.
  Diego was about to return home when Gisela arrived at the restaurant.

¡Póngalo en práctica!

G10 **Sucesos próximos** Complete las conversaciones.

- Hola, ¿Marta?
- Hola, (1)............. (yo, estar) a punto de llamarte.
- Y yo estoy a (2)............. de llegar, por eso te llamo.

- (3)............. a punto (4)............. terminar esta novela. Me gusta muchísimo.
- Menos mal que me lo dices, (5)............. a punto de preguntarte si te gustó el final.

Practice more at **vhlcentral.com**.

SÍNTESIS

Mire las fotografías y escriba un diálogo corto para cada una, usando el vocabulario indicado.

1.

| igual de | la gente | se vive | bello |

- _____
- _____
- _____
- _____

2.

| se venden | está a punto de | turístico | costumbres |

- _____
- _____
- _____
- _____

3.

| no compres | marca | gente | se |

- _____
- _____
- _____
- _____

VOCABULARIO 🔊 Ⓢ Vocabulary Tools

Publicidad hasta en el café

en buena compañía	in good company
el crucero	cruise
la diferencia	difference (in price)
la fragancia	fragrance, perfume
la merienda	(afternoon) snack
el pico	peak, mountain
la publicidad	advertising
un tercio	a third
el tópico	cliché
confundirse	to become confused
devolver (o:ue)	to return
exigir (j)	to demand
perdérselo (e:ie)	to miss out
probar (o:ue)	to taste
provenir de	to come from
saborear	to savor
sentirse (e:ie) como en casa	to feel at home
certificado/a	certified

Usos y costumbres

la arcilla	clay
el camarón	shrimp
el grupo étnico	ethnic group
el/la mono/a araña	spider monkey
la ola	wave
el/la patrono/a	patron saint
la procesión	procession
el sedentarismo	sedentary lifestyle
el/la surfista	surfer
el tucán	toucan
el uso	custom
ocultar	to hide
venerar	to venerate
anticuado/a	antiquated
bello/a	beautiful
complejo/a	complex
comunicativo/a	communicative
congelado/a	frozen
cosmopolita	cosmopolitan
extenso/a	vast
homogéneo/a	homogeneous
poblado/a	populated
relleno/a	stuffed, filled
turístico/a	tourist
densamente	densely

Estela y Mario

propiamente dicho/a	per se
el aroma	aroma, scent
la autenticidad	authenticity
la campaña de promoción	promotional campaign
la cercanía	proximity
el certamen	contest
el cóctel	cocktail
el dinamismo	dynamism
el durazno	peach
el encargo	assignment
la feria	(trade) fair
la gama	range
la guinda	wild cherry
el jurado	panel of judges
el logo	logo
la valentía	courage
anticipar	to anticipate
apelar	to appeal
dar a conocer	to make known
lanzar una campaña	to launch a campaign
tener en cuenta	to take into account
tener lugar	to be held
claro/a	light
compuesto/a por	made up of
creciente	growing
geográfico/a	geographic
morado/a	purple
oriundo/a	native
oscuro/a	dark
así como	as well as

Variación léxica

celebrarse ⟷ tener lugar

el certamen ⟷ el concurso

extenso/a ⟷ vasto/a

oriundo/a ⟷ nativo/a

provenir ⟷ proceder

la publicidad ⟷ la propaganda

el/la surfista ⟷ el/la tablista (Per., Col.)

tener en cuenta ⟷ tomar en cuenta

AVANCE

Estrategias

(1) Suavizar una opinión

Use expressions of courtesy such as **Yo diría que...** (*I'd say that . . .*) to soften your opinions. This will allow you to give your opinion without forcing it on another person.

○ Lea los diálogos e introduzca la estrategia en las frases en las que considere necesario.

- • Yo siempre hago las compras en el supermercado. Es más cómodo.
- • Pero los productos no son tan frescos como en el mercado.

- • Hay que promocionar este producto con una idea ecológica.
- • ¿Un coche? ¿Y cómo vamos a hacerlo?

- • Las tiendas deben permanecer abiertas el mayor tiempo posible.
- • ¿Y abrir también los domingos? ¡Es demasiado!

(2) Reforzar argumentos

Expressions such as **efectivamente** (*indeed*) and **desde luego** (*of course*) will help you show that you are very much in agreement, and will show empathy toward the person you are speaking with.

○ Complete los diálogos empleando alguna de estas palabras o expresiones.

efectivamente • desde luego • pero • también • no

- • .... la paz se construye con el compromiso de todos nosotros.
- • Sí, ... también hay que tomar decisiones políticas.

- • La fecha de caducidad de esta mermelada es de la semana pasada.
- • Sí, yo .... lo he visto. ...., hay que leer las etiquetas con atención.

- • Si en casa no hay colaboración con la labor de la escuela, ... se va a conseguir nada.
- • Los padres tienen que apoyar a los profesores y no ir en su contra.

(3) Introducir un tema

Expressions such as **en cuanto a** (*as for*) and **con respecto a** (*regarding*) will help you control the direction of a conversation with naturalness and fluency.

○ Converse con sus compañeros con relación a los temas propuestos e introduzca sus ideas.

el costo de la educación   **el proceso de independizarse**   **los conflictos generacionales**

(4) Atenuar las generalizaciones

Use expressions such as **no todos los** + [*noun*] (*not all . . .*) or **eso no es todo** (*that's not all*) to refute a generalization or contradict stereotypes.

○ Observe las siguientes generalizaciones y busque argumentos para matizarlas.

- • Todos los productos envasados llevan fecha de caducidad.
- • Todos los adolescentes tienen problemas en su desarrollo.
- • Los anuncios siempre tratan de venderte algo.

Competencias

EXPRESAR PROBABILIDAD

1 **Reaccionar** Reaccione ante estas situaciones usando el futuro para expresar probabilidad.

Modelo: *Su compañero/a no vino al curso de español.*
(estar / enfermo) ....

1. No está seguro/a del origen de un producto.

   (ser / importado) ¿ .... ?

2. Suena el timbre de su casa a la medianoche.

   (quién / venir / a estas horas) ¿ .... ?

3. Le sorprende ver pocos clientes en un negocio céntrico.

   (por qué / haber / tan poca gente) ¿ .... ?

4. No encuentra el símbolo de "reciclable" en un envase.

   (poder / reciclarse) ¿ .... ?

5. Acaba de colgar con su madre y vuelve a sonar el teléfono.

   (qué / querer / ahora) ¿ .... ?

6. Lee la etiqueta de un alimento para saber su composición.

   (tener / conservantes) ¿ .... ?

EXPRESAR TEMOR, FINALIDAD, EXTRAÑEZA, DISGUSTO Y ENFADO

2 **Diálogo** Amanda quiere pasar las vacaciones con su novio y su madre no está de acuerdo. Escriba con su compañero/a un diálogo entre ellas. Usen todas las expresiones del recuadro.

importante	esperar	extrañar	necesario	soportar
molestar	querer	preocupar	dar miedo	sorprender

EXPONER UNA OPINIÓN, MOSTRAR ESCEPTICISMO, TRANSMITIR INFORMACIÓN

3 **Reportaje** Lea este reportaje sobre una marcha por la paz. Imagine que es un(a) periodista que debe transmitir la información pero que se opone a la manifestación.

> Esta tarde comenzará la marcha por la paz en Bogotá. Pediremos la libertad de los secuestrados y el cese de los enfrentamientos armados. Pensamos que la única manera de que el gobierno y las FARC se pongan de acuerdo es por medio del diálogo.

Modelo: *En cuanto a las noticias políticas, los organizadores confirmaron que la marcha comenzaría esta tarde. Pero yo no creo que...*

ANIMAR A LA ACCIÓN

4 **Mandatos** Escriba una oración imperativa con pronombre para cada una de estas sugerencias.

Modelo: *Tiene que acompañar sus recetas con aceite de oliva.*
Acompáñelas con aceite de oliva.

1. Tienen que comprar este libro de cocina pronto porque se agota.

2. No tiene que dejar de comer frutas y verduras.

3. Tienes que consumir productos frescos.

4. Tenéis que beber este jugo refrescante bien frío.

 Video

Puerto Rico, ¿nación o estado?

Vocabulario útil

la aduana *customs*
el buzón *mailbox*
la estadidad *statehood*
el partido *game*
la patria *homeland*
permanecer (zc) *to remain*
las relaciones exteriores *foreign relations*

Ya ha leído sobre la lucha por la libertad como derecho de todos los seres humanos y también sobre la búsqueda de identidad en países de habla hispana. Este episodio de **Flash Cultura** se ocupa de la importancia del debate político que toca estos dos temas en la isla de Puerto Rico.

1 **Preguntas** ¿Qué opina de la libertad y la igualdad como derechos? ¿Qué cosas son menos importantes y se pueden negociar? ¿Lee habitualmente los diarios para conocer la situación política de su país? ¿Conversa con sus amigos o familia sobre esos temas? ¿Le parece divertido discutir sobre política?

2 **Mirar** Mire el episodio de **Flash Cultura** y escuche lo que dicen los entrevistados; preste atención a cómo lo dicen, mientras imagina qué diría usted en esa situación.

El debate se ha convertido en el deporte nacional de Puerto Rico.

Creo que Puerto Rico necesita soberanía para tomar sus propias decisiones.

3 **Escoger** Ordene las características de Puerto Rico en la columna adecuada.

Como estado libre asociado	Como territorio de Estados Unidos

1. Se habla español.
2. La moneda es el dólar.
3. No hace falta visa para entrar a EE.UU.
4. No se vota para presidente de EE.UU.
5. Se pagan sólo impuestos locales.
6. Funciona el servicio de correos de EE.UU.
7. No se pagan impuestos federales.
8. Tiene un representante en el Congreso de EE.UU.

4 **Escribir** En parejas, escriban la conversación entre un(a) visitante que comenta sus impresiones sobre la ciudad y un lugareño/a que le explica la otra cara de las cosas.

Modelo: • *Me parece que aquí la gente está siempre feliz.*
• *No todos los habitantes son igual de felices.*

 Practice more at **vhlcentral.com**.

Unidad 17

Salvador Moncada, ciencia para la vida

Amanda y Rubén, la vida es un tango

Lo mejor de Argentina

17A

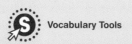
EL FUTURO POR DELANTE

Dentro de cien años...

Si observamos las nuevas tendencias, pensaremos en un futuro muy tecnológico. ¿Qué novedades vendrán? ¿Cuáles harán nuestra vida más fácil? ¿Cómo será nuestra vida dentro de 50 o 100 años? ¿Podemos saberlo con antelación? Son muchos los que se han hecho estas preguntas. En este número recordamos algunas de las más **famosas predicciones de las últimas décadas** y nos atrevemos con **predicciones de un futuro probable**.

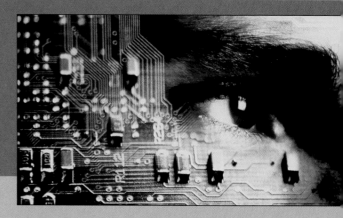

FAMOSAS PREDICCIONES DE LAS ÚLTIMAS DÉCADAS

- "La TV no llegará muy lejos. La gente no querrá mirar todas las noches una caja de madera."
  Darryl Zanuck, productor de la 20th Century Fox, 1946

- "Podremos enviar el correo por misil antes de llegar a la Luna."
  Arthur Summerfield, director general del Servicio Postal de EE.UU., 1959

- "No habrá necesidad de tener una computadora en cada casa."
  Ken Olsen, fundador de Digital Equipment Corporation, 1977

- "Dentro de dos años no sabremos qué es el spam."
  Bill Gates, Fundador de Microsoft, 2004

- "El *iPod* nunca tendrá éxito."
  Alan Sugar, fundador de Amstrad, 2005

PREDICCIONES DE UN FUTURO PROBABLE

- Tal vez las computadoras estén dentro de nuestro cuerpo.
- A lo mejor habrá una moneda electrónica común.
- Seguro que los libros serán electrónicos y no de papel.
- Puede que se hablen muy pocos idiomas, cuatro o cinco como mucho.
- Es muy probable que haya profesiones que se desarrollen a distancia, por ejemplo, la medicina.
- Quizá dentro de cien años nos comunicaremos con la mente.

Hacer predicciones

- ¿Cuáles **serán** las lenguas del futuro?
- **Dentro de** algún tiempo se **hablarán** menos lenguas.

17A.1 Simple future of irregular verbs
dentro de

Vocabulario

①

dentro de *in, within*
la tendencia *trend*
la novedad *innovation*
hacer la vida más fácil *to make life easier*
atreverse *to dare*
tal vez *maybe*
a lo mejor *maybe*
quizá(s) *perhaps*
el avance *breakthrough*
tecnológico/a, la predicción, probable

---

1 **a. Introducción** Lea la introducción de este artículo sobre avances tecnológicos. ¿Qué es una predicción?

b. Contestar Lea el texto "Famosas predicciones de las últimas décadas". ¿Conoce a las personas citadas? ¿Qué le parece curioso de estas predicciones? ¿Qué tienen en común?

2 **Dentro de** Fíjese en los dibujos y en los dos usos de **dentro de**. ¿Con cuál de las preposiciones que ya ha aprendido se puede reemplazar **dentro de**?

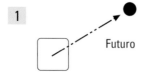

Futuro

(1) **Dentro de** cien años puede que las computadoras estén...

(2) ...**dentro de** nuestros cuerpos.

3 **Hacer predicciones** Seleccione tres de estos temas y haga sus predicciones. Compare sus predicciones con las de su compañero/a.

○ Medicina   ○ Comunicación   ○ Trabajo   ○ Lenguas   ○ Tecnología

Modelo: *Dentro de... años...*

4 **Responder** Lea el texto "Predicciones de un futuro probable". ¿En qué se diferencian las predicciones de ambos textos de la página anterior? ¿Qué predicciones le parecen más y menos probables? ¿Coincide con su compañero/a?

5 **a. Subjuntivo** Lea estas predicciones para dentro de diez años. Marque las oraciones en las que se usa el subjuntivo.

☐ Seguro que todos los objetos de uso diario serán desechables.

☐ Tal vez algunos seres humanos puedan vivir en Marte.

☐ Puede ser que dejemos de usar petróleo para producir energía.

☐ A lo mejor todos los alimentos serán transgénicos.

☐ Quizá se terminen todos los conflictos armados.

☐ Es posible que se encuentre la cura a todas las enfermedades.

☐ Es probable que todos podamos trabajar desde casa.

b. Clasificar Clasifique las expresiones de probabilidad anteriores.

Más probable	Menos probable

c. Expresar probabilidad ¿Qué piensa que es probable, posible o seguro que pase dentro de diez años? Comente sus predicciones con su compañero/a. ¿Están de acuerdo o en desacuerdo?

6 **Historieta** Observe la historieta de *Mafalda* sobre el futuro. ¿Cuáles son las predicciones de Felipe? ¿Qué le parece probable que suceda en un mundo gobernado por niños?

© Joaquín Salvador Lavado (QUINO) Toda Mafalda — Ediciones de La Flor, 1993

MI EXPERIENCIA

7 **Predicciones** Comparta con su compañero/a algunas predicciones para un futuro lejano.

GUIÓN DE TRABAJO

¿Cómo será el mundo dentro de 100/200/300 años?

Puede (ser) que...   Seguro que...
Es probable que...   Tal vez / Quizá...
Es posible que...   A lo mejor...

Expresar probabilidad

● Es muy probable que los médicos trabajen a distancia.

■ Sí, seguro que lo harán.

17A.2 **es probable que** + [*subjunctive*]
a lo mejor + [*indicative*]

Vocabulario

5

desechable *disposable*

Marte (*m.*) *Mars*

la cura *cure*

6

enterarse de *to find out (about)*

el cargo *position*

estar en manos de alguien *to be under someone's control*

¡Pero, hombre/mujer! *Come on!*

amargarle la vida a alguien *to make someone's life miserable*

¡OJO!

Although the meaning of the expression **a lo mejor** is similar to that of **tal vez** or **quizá**, this expression is always followed by verbs in the indicative mood.

SAM: Actividades pp. 355–357

Practice more at **vhlcentral.com**.

Ciencia con conciencia

XII Feria Internacional de Educación, Ciencia y Tecnología

Es obvio que todos nos beneficiamos de los avances de la ciencia. Sin embargo, no estamos seguros de que los investigadores reciban toda la ayuda que necesitan. Por eso, cada año organizamos en Lima, Perú, la Feria Internacional de Educación, Ciencia y Tecnología, CIENTEC. El objetivo de esta feria es crear un espacio para que los investigadores puedan tratar problemas y necesidades relacionados con su profesión. Queremos promover las actividades de investigación que respeten la naturaleza y que permitan a las generaciones futuras vivir en un mundo donde haya paz, equidad y un desarrollo sostenible.

Por otro lado, es evidente que detrás de cada gran científico hay un niño curioso. Sin embargo, no está demostrado que nuestros jóvenes reciban suficientes incentivos para formar parte del mundo científico. Por eso hemos creado dos programas dirigidos a ellos:

- Programa Internacional Minicientíficos: Queremos estimular el interés de los niños de 7 a 11 años por la ciencia y los experimentos. Por lo tanto, hemos creado una serie de actividades interactivas cuyo objetivo es el descubrimiento y la experimentación: talleres, cursos, excursiones, campamentos, concursos, etcétera.

- Programa Internacional Evaluador Joven: Intentamos promover el uso del método científico entre los estudiantes para complementar su formación, y fomentar la apreciación y comprensión de la ciencia. De este modo, estarán mejor preparados para responder a las necesidades del mundo actual.

Estamos seguros de que le gustará participar, así que lo invitamos a recorrer esta exposición interactiva y descubrir la ciencia con otros ojos. Lo esperamos del 15 al 19 de noviembre en el Club de la Unión, Plaza de Armas, Lima.

Expresar certeza y evidencia

- **Es evidente que** la energía solar **es** ecológica.
- Sí, pero **no está demostrado** que **sea** más económica.

17A.3 **no estar seguro/a de que** + [*subjunctive*]
estar seguro/a de que + [*indicative*]

Vocabulario

⑧

obvio/a *obvious*

el/la investigador(a) *researcher*

la equidad *fairness*

sostenible *sustainable*

evidente *obvious, clear*

demostrar (o:ue) *to prove*

el incentivo *encouragement*

el descubrimiento *discovery*

el método científico *scientific method*

descubrir *to discover*

la conciencia, el experimento, interactivo/a, la experimentación, la apreciación

---

⑧ **a. Título** Fíjese en el título "Ciencia con conciencia". ¿Qué le sugiere la relación entre las palabras **ciencia** y **conciencia**? ¿De qué cree que tratará el texto?

b. Leer Lea el folleto de la feria y busque en el texto expresiones equivalentes a estas.

- Es verdad/cierto que...
- No es verdad/cierto que...

c. Ciencia con conciencia Observe los ejemplos del texto y seleccione la opción correcta.

- Con **frases afirmativas** se usa **indicativo/subjuntivo.**
  Es obvio que todos nos **beneficiamos/beneficiemos** de los avances de la ciencia.
  Es evidente que detrás de cada gran científico **hay/haya** un niño curioso.
- Con **frases negativas** se usa **indicativo/subjuntivo.**
  No estamos seguros de que los investigadores **reciben/reciban** toda la ayuda que necesitan.
  No está demostrado que nuestros jóvenes **reciben/reciban** suficientes incentivos.

⑨ **Responder** ¿Alguna vez ha estado en una feria como la que se describe? ¿Le pareció interesante? ¿Por qué? ¿Qué opina de los programas para fomentar el interés de los niños y jóvenes por la ciencia? Coméntelo con la clase.

10 **Comentar** Algunos avances científicos están muy presentes en nuestra vida diaria y a veces hay debate sobre su utilidad y sus (des)ventajas. Comente con su compañero/a qué sabe sobre los avances representados en las fotos.

el teléfono
celular

+ cómodo, móvil, inmediato...

− ¿peligro para la salud?

los alimentos
transgénicos

+ abundantes, resistentes, baratos...

− ¿saludables?

la energía nuclear y la energía solar

+ sostenible, abundante, renovable...

− ¿ecológica? ¿económica?

Internet

+ universal, comunitario, rápido...

− ¿fiable, libre?
¿privacidad, seguridad?

11 **a. Conectores** Encuentre en el texto de la página anterior estos conectores y escriba las frases que unen.

... así (es) que...
... por lo tanto...

b. Anotar Anote alguna consecuencia de su conversación de la Actividad 10.

12 **Crear conciencia con ciencia** Lea la nota de la derecha. ¿Cuál es el objetivo del evento que se describe? Y usted, ¿cómo está presente la ciencia en su vida?

🗣 **MI EXPERIENCIA**

13 **Avances científicos** Seleccionen un avance científico importante y decisivo para todo el mundo. Describan por qué es importante y qué consecuencias tiene en sus vidas.

GUIÓN DE TRABAJO

¿Cuál crees que es el avance científico más importante? → Es evidente/obvio que...
Estoy seguro/a de que...

¿Qué consecuencias tuvo? → así que...
por eso...
por lo tanto...

Vocabulario

⑩
cómodo/a *convenient*
móvil *mobile*
abundante *plentiful*
resistente *strong, tough*
renovable *renewable*
comunitario/a *communal*
rápido/a *fast*
fiable *reliable*
la seguridad *security*
el/la alarmista *alarmist*
inmediato/a, ecológico/a, universal, la privacidad
⑪
así (es) que *so*
por lo tanto *therefore*
por eso *therefore*

Estrategia ············

Expresar consecuencia
No está claro que el teléfono celular sea seguro, pero no está demostrado que sea peligroso, **así (es) que / por lo tanto** no seas alarmista.

Crear conciencia con ciencia
Es el lema de la Feria Nacional Infantil y Juvenil de Experimentación Científica, organizada por el Consejo Hondureño de Ciencia, Tecnología e Innovación, que tiene como objetivo motivar vocaciones científicas y tecnológicas, y crear mayor interés y conciencia sobre la importancia de la ciencia en nuestra vida diaria.

SAM: Actividades pp. 358–360

Practice more at **vhlcentral.com**.

Salvador Moncada, ciencia para la vida

Quark

Número 12

Salvador Moncada, científico

Salvador Moncada (Tegucigalpa, 1944), investigador y científico hondureño. Ha dedicado gran parte de su carrera a la investigación farmacéutica. Ha patentado diez nuevos fármacos y ha publicado más de 700 artículos en diferentes revistas científicas de prestigio internacional. Es uno de los 25 científicos más citados del mundo.

Entrevista a Salvador Moncada

El científico e investigador Salvador Moncada nos habla del papel de la ciencia en la sociedad actual. A Salvador Moncada le preocupa la modernización de la ciencia.

☐ *"La inversión en ciencia y tecnología va a redundar a medio o largo plazo en beneficios para la sociedad, en creación de riqueza, de empleo, y en mejores condiciones de vida."*

El doctor Moncada se expresa abiertamente sobre la comunidad a la que pertenece y afirma que:

☐ *"Los científicos muchas veces no se llevan su tiempo para explicar a la sociedad qué es lo que están haciendo y por qué lo están haciendo."*

Sobre la aplicación de la ciencia en la vida, Moncada añade que:

☐ *"El científico debería estar interesado en las posibilidades de aplicación práctica de la ciencia y empezar a pensar 'Bueno, voy a hacer esto, pero ¿con qué fin?'. Estamos en un momento en que la cuestión está en saber cómo cerrar la brecha para lograr que el conocimiento básico se torne en conocimiento productivo."*

1 *"Los científicos también debemos tener una conciencia y una responsabilidad hacia lo que se está haciendo."*

2 *"La comunidad científica debería comunicar mucho más y participar mucho más en la discusión general de la sociedad de por qué se hace investigación."*

3 *"La comunidad científica debe vivir en sociedad."*

Vocabulario

14

redundar en *to benefit*

a corto/medio/largo plazo *in the short/medium/long term*

abiertamente *openly, frankly*

estar interesado/a en *to be interested in*

cerrar (e:ie) la brecha *to close the gap*

tornarse *to become*

farmacéutico/a *pharmaceutical*

patentar *to patent*

el fármaco *medicine*

citado/a *cited, quoted*

la modernización

15

la modernidad *modernity*

16

dominar *to dominate*

el campo científico *scientific field*

rezagado/a *lagging behind*

la infraestructura

Expresar continuidad

Sigue habiendo muy buenos científicos hispanos, pero muchos de ellos siguen sin volver a sus países.

17A.4 seguir + *[present participle]*
seguir sin + *[infinitive]*

---

14 **a. Protagonista** Observe el título de la página. ¿Quién cree que es nuestro protagonista y por qué cree usted que es el protagonista de esta lección?

b. Ciencia para la vida Lea los datos de su biografía y señale sobre qué aspectos informa.

☐ profesión ☐ país de origen ☐ premios ☐ domicilio
☐ carrera profesional ☐ edad ☐ campo de investigación ☐ los académicos

15 **a. Citas** Fíjese ahora en las citas del texto a la derecha. ¿Cuáles cree que son los principales temas de la entrevista? Lea después todo el texto e identifique a qué cita se refiere cada uno de estos tres temas.

☐ Comunidad científica ☐ Responsabilidad de los científicos ☐ Ciencia y sociedad

b. La entrevista ¿Con qué temas se relaciona la ciencia en esta entrevista? Busque información en el texto para justificar su respuesta.

☐ modernidad ☐ comunidad científica ☐ sociedad ☐ investigación
☐ cultura ☐ comunicación ☐ industria ☐ otros

16 **a. Salvador Moncada** Escuche este fragmento de una entrevista sobre Salvador Moncada y complete esta cita del investigador. ¿A qué región del mundo se refiere la conversación?

"Sigue .... científicos y sigue .... la infraestructura necesaria para mantener los científicos en sus países."

b. Expresar continuidad Reformule estas frases con las estructuras anteriores.

○ Antes no se invertía en ciencia. Ahora tampoco se invierte en ciencia.

....

○ Antes la ciencia estaba lejos de la sociedad. Ahora también.

....

17 **a. Leer** Lea este artículo. ¿Qué descubrimiento describe? ¿Qué aplicación tendrá en la vida diaria?

Las personas con diabetes podrán controlar los niveles de glucosa con un chip

El chip, en fase de investigación, medirá el nivel de azúcar en la sangre y mandará un aviso al teléfono celular del paciente y a su centro médico.

Las personas diabéticas podrán olvidarse de los pinchazos diarios para medir el nivel de azúcar y de inyectarse la dosis de insulina que necesitan.

Un gran equipo de investigadores de ocho países europeos está desarrollando un sensor subcutáneo (un chip instalado debajo de la piel) que controlará el nivel de azúcar de los pacientes. Cada 10 o 15 minutos podrá transmitir esos datos al teléfono celular del paciente y al centro médico, y podrá incluso suministrar la dosis necesaria de insulina en cada momento a través de unas bombas de insulina que el paciente llevará también dentro de su cuerpo.

El proyecto, denominado Paul Cezanne, está coordinado en España por el investigador del Instituto de Microelectrónica de Barcelona —Consejo Superior de Investigaciones Científicas (CSIC)—, Carlos Domínguez. Este profesor bilbaíno explica que el proyecto quiere "desarrollar un sensor lo más ajustado posible a las necesidades de los pacientes" para "mejorar su calidad de vida".

b. Diabetes Busque en el texto las palabras que se ajustan a cada definición.

1. Enfermedad que produce un exceso de glucosa en la sangre: ....
2. Persona que padece diabetes: ....
3. Azúcar presente en el organismo: ....
4. Hormona para tratar la diabetes: ....
5. Dar algo que se necesita: ....
6. Introducir en el cuerpo un líquido a través de una jeringa: ....

c. Lista Haga una lista de otros inventos (reales o imaginarios) que podrían mejorar la calidad de vida de las personas diabéticas.

18 **Escribir** Piense en un avance científico que haya cambiado su vida. ¿Tiene consecuencias negativas? ¿Cómo se podría perfeccionar?

19 **Foto** Observe la foto. ¿Para qué se usa este medicamento? Lea el texto y encuentre su relación con el doctor Moncada.

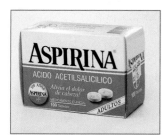

Las investigaciones sobre el ácido acetilsalicílico y el óxido nítrico han llevado al doctor Moncada a las puertas del Nobel en dos ocasiones porque revolucionaron el tratamiento de las enfermedades cardiovasculares. Fue en 1987 cuando Salvador Moncada publicó los resultados de sus investigaciones, que renovaron la utilidad de la aspirina para tratar las enfermedades cardiovasculares.

Vocabulario

17

controlar *to monitor*

la fase *stage*

medir (e:i) *to measure*

la sangre *blood*

el pinchazo *prick*

inyectarse *to give oneself an injection*

suministrar *to administer*

la bomba *pump*

denominarse *to be called*

bilbaíno/a *from Bilbao (Spain)*

lo más... posible *as... as possible*

ajustado/a a *adapted to*

la jeringa *syringe*

la diabetes, la glucosa, el chip, diabético/a, la dosis, la insulina, el organismo

19

el ácido *acid*

cardiovascular

20

conmemorar *to commemorate*

el sistema inmunológico *immune system*

el/la discípulo/a *disciple*

la humanidad *humankind*

la salsa golf *sauce similar to Thousand Island dressing*

la capa de ozono *ozone layer*

el metabolismo

OPINIÓN

¿La ciencia es una prioridad en nuestra sociedad?

¿Es el desarrollo científico un avance? ¿En qué sentido?

SAM: Actividades pp. 361–364

Practice more at **vhlcentral.com**.

20 **a. Científicos latinoamericanos** En los 115 años de historia del Premio Nobel, estos cuatro científicos latinoamericanos han sido premiados por sus aportes a las ciencias. ¿Los conoce?

Bernardo Alberto Houssay (1887–1971) recibió el Premio Nobel de Fisiología y Medicina en 1947 por sus estudios sobre el metabolismo del azúcar en el cuerpo y su relación con la diabetes. En honor de este gran médico argentino, el día de su nacimiento se conmemora el Día del Investigador Científico en su país.

César Milstein (1927–2002), biólogo argentino, recibió el Premio Nobel de Fisiología y Medicina en 1984 por sus investigaciones sobre el sistema inmunológico humano. Por motivos políticos, debió mudarse a Inglaterra en 1963, aunque viajaba a Argentina con frecuencia. En 2010 se estrenó un documental sobre su vida, filmado por Ana Fraile, su sobrina nieta: *Un fueguito: La historia de César Milstein.*

Luis Federico Leloir (1906–1987), discípulo de Houssay, recibió el Premio Nobel de Química en 1970 gracias a sus descubrimientos sobre la biosíntesis de los carbohidratos. Además de sus importantes descubrimientos científicos, este brillante investigador argentino hizo otro gran aporte a la humanidad: inventó la salsa golf.

Mario José Molina nació en 1943 y es un ingeniero químico mexicano. En 1995, se convirtió en el primer estudioso del medio ambiente en recibir el Premio Nobel de Química. Fue por sus investigaciones sobre la formación y la descomposición de la capa de ozono. ¿Un dato curioso? Cuando era pequeño, quería ser músico.

b. Comentar Comente con su compañero/a cuál de los descubrimientos de estos científicos le parece el más interesante. Describa por qué y qué consecuencias tiene para la humanidad.

c. Premios Nobel En total, diecisiete latinoamericanos han recibido el Premio Nobel. Busque información en español sobre uno de ellos y preséntela al resto de la clase.

TAREA FINAL

Una exposición científica

Elabore una lista de avances científicos con aplicación en la vida diaria.

Seleccionen los mejores, los más útiles y positivos.

Elaboren un cartel con fotos de estos avances y todas sus conclusiones para dar una presentación.

YO PUEDO...

- Puedo hacer predicciones.
  Escriba tres predicciones sobre el futuro con sus correspondientes plazos.

- Puedo expresar probabilidad.
  Exprese las probabilidades con relación a su propio futuro.

- Puedo expresar certeza y evidencia.
  Exprese sus certezas sobre esta oración:
  La energía solar es ecológica y económica.

- Puedo expresar continuidad.
  ¿Qué cosas sigue haciendo desde que empezó a estudiar español? ¿Qué cosas sigue sin hacer?

GRAMÁTICA FUNCIONAL Tutorials

17A.1 Make predictions

Simple future of irregular verbs 5.16.2b
dentro de 5.16.2d, 10.6, 12.13

- Use the **simple future** to make predictions about the future. You have learned regular and irregular forms of the **futuro simple** in 12B.1 and 15A.1.

  > En el año 2050, muchas personas **sabrán** hablar más de dos idiomas.
  > *In the year 2050, many people **will know how** to speak more than two languages.*

- As you are studying irregular forms of the **futuro simple**, it may help to group stems into three categories. Remember that these verbs undergo the same stem changes in the **condicional**.

PONER	pon**d**ré	
SALIR	sal**d**ré	
TENER	ten**d**ré	add a **d**
VENIR	ven**d**ré	
PODER	podré	
QUERER	querré	take away an **e**
SABER	sabré	
DECIR	**dir**é	stem change
HACER	**har**é	

- The future form of **hay** is **habrá**.

- Use **dentro de** (*in, within*) + [*length of time*] to talk about the future.

  > **Dentro de** cincuenta años, **habrá** muchos avances en la medicina.
  > *Within fifty year's time, **there will be** many advances in medicine.*

17A.2 Express probability

es probable que + [*subjunctive*] 5.8.5, 5.20.2, 5.21.7
a lo mejor + [*indicative*] 11.5

- Use the subjunctive with the expressions **es (poco/muy/bastante) probable/posible que** and **puede (ser) que** to express probability.

  > **Es muy probable que tengamos** más vacunas.
  > *It is very likely that we will have more vaccines.*

- Use **tal vez** (*maybe*) and **quizá(s)** (*perhaps*) with the indicative in order to indicate a greater degree of probability. These expressions may also be used with the subjunctive to indicate a lesser degree of probability.

  > **Tal vez vamos** al museo mañana.
  > **Tal vez vayamos** al museo mañana.
  > *Maybe we will go to the museum tomorrow.*

- Always use the indicative with **a lo mejor**.

  > **A lo mejor** los niños **empezarán** a estudiar lenguas extranjeras a una edad más temprana.
  > *Perhaps children **will begin** to study foreign languages at an earlier age.*

¡Póngalo en práctica!

G1 **Completar** Complete la conversación.

- (1)..................... 55 años, yo (2)..................... (tener) 75 años y (3)..................... (estar) jubilada.
- ¿Y crees que (4)..................... (nosotros, hacer) la misma vida que ahora?
- Creo que (5)..................... (nosotros, poder) viajar más y en todas las casas (6)..................... (haber) robots.
- Sí, a lo mejor (7)..................... (venir) otros avances técnicos y no (8)..................... (nosotros, tener) que trabajar tantas horas.

G2 **Dentro de cuánto** Son las ocho de la mañana. ¿Dentro de cuánto tiempo hará Mario estas cosas?

> Modelo: 12 h, ir a la tienda
> *Dentro de cuatro horas irá a la tienda.*

1. 14 h, estudiar francés

   ....

2. 16 h, llamar a Carlos

   ....

3. 19 h, salir con María

   ....

4. 21 h, hacer la tarea

   ....

5. 23 h, poner la tele

   ....

G3 **Conversaciones** Complete las conversaciones.

- A lo mejor (1)..................... (descubrirse) pronto un medicamento contra el cáncer.
- Sí, puede ser que lo (2)..................... (ver) nosotros mismos.

- Es muy posible que (3)..................... (ser) así, aunque quizá (4)..................... (pasar) algún tiempo todavía.
- Tal vez no (5)..................... (nosotros, tener) que esperar tanto tiempo. Es seguro que en el campo de la medicina (6)..................... (haber) avances importantes todos los años.

- El otro día la hermana de Federico nos habló del semestre que pasó en París. Quizás yo también (7)..................... (estudiar) en una universidad extranjera.
- Es seguro que muchos estudiantes (8)..................... (decidir) estudiar en otro país por un semestre. Es una oportunidad muy buena de aprender otras lenguas y conocer otras culturas.

S Practice more at **vhlcentral.com**.

GRAMÁTICA FUNCIONAL

- Always use the indicative with the impersonal expression **es seguro que**.

  > **Es seguro que** más personas tendrán acceso a Internet.
  > *It is a sure thing that more people will have Internet access.*

- The present subjunctive form of **hay** is **haya**.

  > Quizás **haya** menos conflictos internacionales en el futuro.
  > *Maybe there will be fewer international conflicts in the future.*

17A.3 Express certainty and evidence

(no) estar seguro/a de que, (no) es evidente que, (no) está claro/demostrado que + [*indicative/subjunctive*] 5.8.2, 5.8.6, 5.21.4b

- Use the indicative in affirmative sentences with the expressions **estar seguro/a de que** (*to be sure that*), **es evidente que** (*to be evident that*), and **está claro/demostrado que** (*it is clear/proven that*), as these expressions indicate certainty.

  > **Estamos** totalmente **seguros de que** dentro de cien años todos los libros **serán** digitales.
  > *We are completely sure that all books will be digital within a hundred years.*

- Use the subjunctive with these same expressions in negative statements, as they convey doubt.

  > **No está demostrado que** dentro de cien años **podamos** viajar a otros planetas.
  > *It is not proven that we will be able to travel to other planets within a hundred years.*

17A.4 Express continuity

seguir + [*present participle*]; **seguir sin** + [*infinitive*] 5.13, 5.15

- Use **seguir** + [*present participle*] to express continuity of an action.

  > **Siguen investigando** los efectos de la nueva medicina.
  > *They are still investigating the effects of the new medicine.*

  > Afirman que **sigue bajando** el riesgo de contraer gripe A.
  > *They state that the risk of contracting Type-A flu keeps declining.*

- Use **seguir sin** + [*infinitive*] to express the continuity of an unfulfilled action.

  > **Sigo sin visitar** la exposición.
  > *I still have not visited the exposition.*

  > Aunque me lo explicaron, **sigo sin entender** cómo funciona este experimento.
  > *Even though they explained it to me, I still don't understand how this experiment works.*

¡Póngalo en práctica!

G4 **Escribir** Escriba oraciones completas para hacer predicciones en el futuro.

1. quizá / Joaquín / hacerse médico
....

2. a lo mejor / nosotros / desarrolla / la vacuna
....

3. es posible que / el gobierno / aumentar / su apoyo
....

G5 **La tecnología** Complete las oraciones.

- Es evidente que los países (1)........................ (tener) que invertir en ciencia y tecnología.
- Sí, aunque no está claro que los descubrimientos (2)........................ (ser) propiedad exclusiva de un país.
- Está completamente demostrado que la tecnología (3)........................ (ayudar) a muchas personas, pero que también (4)........................ (poder) causar problemas.
- Sí, por ejemplo, está claro que Internet (5)........................ (ofrecer) muchos beneficios, pero no es evidente que (6)........................ (ser) la mejor forma de informarse ni de comunicarse.
- Desde luego. Estoy segura de que (7)........................ (haber) muchas cosas que se comunican mejor en persona.

G6 **Seguir** Complete las oraciones.

- La ciencia (1)........................ avanzando en la investigación, pero sigue sin (2)........................ (dar) una buena solución.
- En los próximos años los científicos (3)........................ intentándolo.
- El restaurante sigue (4)........................ (preparar) comida muy rica, pero todavía no tiene muchos clientes.
- ¿Sigue (5)........................ tener una página web? Los dueños tienen que (6)........................ pensando en cómo atraer a más clientes.

G7 **Y sigue sin llover** Complete las oraciones de forma lógica con el gerundio o con **sin** + [*infinitivo*].

1. ¡Qué problema! Sigo .... (entender) cómo funciona esta máquina.

2. Los científicos siguen .... (investigar) la causa de la explosión en el laboratorio.

3. El ingeniero sigue .... (esperar) los materiales. Aún no han llegado.

4. El director del laboratorio sigue .... (contratar) nuevos científicos. Quiere hacer todo el trabajo solo.

 Practice more at **vhlcentral.com**.

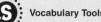
Dentro de cien años...

amargarle la vida a alguien	to make someone's life miserable
estar en manos de alguien	to be under someone's control
hacer la vida más fácil	to make life easier
¡Pero, hombre/mujer!	Come on!
el avance	breakthrough
el cargo	position
la cura	cure
Marte (m.)	Mars
la novedad	innovation
la predicción	prediction
la tendencia	trend
atreverse	to dare
enterarse de	to find out (about)
desechable	disposable
probable	probable
tecnológico/a	technological
a lo mejor	maybe
quizá(s)	perhaps
tal vez	maybe
dentro de	in, within

Ciencia con conciencia

el/la alarmista	alarmist
la apreciación	appreciation
la conciencia	conscience
el descubrimiento	discovery
la equidad	fairness
la experimentación	experimentation
el experimento	experiment
el incentivo	encouragement
el/la investigador(a)	researcher
el método científico	scientific method
la privacidad	privacy
la seguridad	security
demostrar (o:ue)	to prove
descubrir	to discover
abundante	plentiful
cómodo/a	convenient
comunitario/a	communal
ecológico/a	ecological
evidente	obvious, clear
fiable	reliable
inmediato/a	immediate
interactivo/a	interactive
móvil	mobile
obvio/a	obvious
rápido/a	fast
renovable	renewable
resistente	strong, tough
sostenible	sustainable
universal	universal
así (es) que	so
por eso	therefore
por lo tanto	therefore

Salvador Moncada

a corto/medio/largo plazo	in the short/medium/long term
lo más... posible	as... as possible
el ácido	acid
la bomba	pump
el campo científico	scientific field
la capa de ozono	ozone layer

el chip	chip
la diabetes	diabetes
el/la discípulo/a	disciple
la dosis	dose
el fármaco	medicine
la fase	stage
la glucosa	glucose
la humanidad	humankind
la infraestructura	infrastructure
la insulina	insulin
la jeringa	syringe
el metabolismo	metabolism
la modernidad	modernity
la modernización	modernization
el organismo	organism
el pinchazo	prick
la salsa golf	sauce similar to Thousand Island dressing
la sangre	blood
el sistema inmunológico	immune system
cerrar (e:ie) la brecha	to close the gap
conmemorar	to commemorate
controlar	to monitor
denominarse	to be called
dominar	to dominate
estar interesado/a en	to be interested in
inyectarse	to give oneself an injection
medir (e:i)	to measure
patentar	to patent
redundar en	to benefit
suministrar	to administer
tornarse	to become
ajustado/a a	adapted to
bilbaíno/a	from Bilbao (Spain)
cardiovascular	cardiovascular
citado/a	cited, quoted
diabético/a	diabetic
farmacéutico/a	pharmaceutical
rezagado/a	lagging behind
abiertamente	openly, frankly

Variación léxica

desechable ⟷ descartable (Arg.)

la fase ⟷ la etapa

la jeringa ⟷ la jeringuilla (Esp.)

medio plazo ⟷ mediano plazo (C.S.)

quizá ⟷ quizás

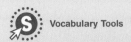
AFICIONES COMUNES

¿Bailas conmigo?

TRES PASOS

TRAE A OTRA PERSONA CONTIGO Y APRENDAN A BAILAR JUNTOS. ¡NO TE LO PIERDAS!

oferta del mes
2 × 1

Para todas las edades y niveles

"Desde que he aprendido en Tres pasos, ya no me aburre el baile. Ahora me divierte bailar y que mi mujer y yo bailemos juntos. Gracias al baile, nos entendemos mejor."
Luis

"Lo paso muy bien con mis compañeros de baile. Me río mucho con ellos y nos llevamos de maravilla. A través del baile también nos comunicamos."
Irene

"A mí me divierte mucho bailar con mi amiga, pero me aburre bailar un solo ritmo y que siempre hagamos los mismos pasos. Por eso vinimos a la escuela. Ven tú también a aprender con nosotros. En clase lo pasamos muy bien."
Miguel

CLASES DE BAILE DE SALÓN

sevillanas	tango	merengue	cumbia
vals	salsa	pasodoble	chachachá

Expresar diversión y aburrimiento

- Me divierte bailar contigo y me río mucho.
- Yo también lo paso muy bien, pero me aburre que siempre bailemos lo mismo.

17B.1 reírse, pasarlo bien divertir/aburrir + [*infinitive*]/ que + [*subjunctive*] conmigo, contigo...

Vocabulario

①

el paso (de baile) *(dance) step*

el baile de salón *ballroom dance*

las sevillanas *(pl.)* *popular dance originated in Seville*

el vals *waltz*

el pasodoble *Spanish march-like dance*

la cumbia *dance typical of the Caribbean coast of Colombia*

el chachachá *cha-cha*

divertir(se) (e:ie) *to amuse/to have fun*

aburrir(se) *to bore/to get bored*

---

1 **Folleto** Fíjese en el folleto de esta escuela de baile y relacione alguno de los bailes de la lista con las imágenes. ¿Conoce el resto de los bailes? ¿Qué representa el nombre de la escuela?

2 **a. ¿Bailas conmigo?** Lea los comentarios de los alumnos de la escuela y complete las oraciones.

REÍRSE		.... río.	CONmigo
PASARLO BIEN		.... paso bien.	CON.......

b. Diversión y aburrimiento ¿Qué le aburre a Miguel? ¿Qué le divierte a Luis?

Miguel:
"Me aburre ⟨ .... "
que .... "

Luis:
"Me divierte ⟨ .... "
que .... "

3 **a. Asociar** ¿Con qué asocia la palabra **bailar**? Complete el mapa de ideas y coméntelo con su compañero/a.

.... celebraciones

.... *bailar* ....

.... música

b. El baile ¿Es el baile una afición popular en su región? ¿Cuáles son los bailes más populares? Y a usted, ¿qué actividades le divierten y cuáles le aburren?

4 **Explicar** Fíjese en cómo influye el baile en las relaciones personales de estos alumnos. Lea las siguientes oraciones y explíquelas.

Modelo: *Luis entiende a...*

○ "Gracias al baile, nos entendemos mejor." **¿Quién entiende a quién?**

○ "A través del baile también nos comunicamos." **¿Quién se comunica con quién?**

5 **a. Tres pasos** Escuche a una pareja que va a la escuela Tres pasos. Marque verdadero (V) o falso (F). ¿Qué baile eligen finalmente?

V F

1. La pareja y la secretaria de la escuela se tutean. ☐ ☐
2. Los alumnos de los cursos se abrazan y se besan en clase. ☐ ☐
3. La pareja se entiende bien. ☐ ☐

b. Acciones recíprocas Fíjese en estas acciones recíprocas. Decida si cada una debe usar **nos, os** o **se**. Luego complete las oraciones.

1. Mi hermano y yo .... queremos mucho.
2. ¿......... entendéis tú y tus padres?
3. Peter y María .... comunican en inglés.
4. Los buenos amigos siempre .... ayudan en tiempos difíciles.
5. Mi abuela y yo .... llevamos bien.
6. Los estudiantes y el profesor .... saludan al comienzo de la clase.

6 **Expresar acciones recíprocas** Piense en qué situaciones realiza usted estas acciones recíprocas y compártalo con su compañero/a.

> escribirse • besarse • abrazarse • mirarse • saludarse
> quererse • contarse algo • comunicarse en español

Modelo: *Mi amiga alemana y yo nos escribimos una vez al mes.*

MI EXPERIENCIA

7 **Aficiones** Averigüe con qué aficiones o actividades lo pasa bien o se aburre su compañero/a y con quién se entiende mejor para hacerlas.

GUIÓN DE TRABAJO

¿Te diviert tocar un instrumento? → No, me aburre mucho tocar. Me aburre que sea necesario practicar tanto para tocar bien.

¿Con qué/quién lo pasas bien? → Me divierte... y me río mucho con...

¿Quién comparte esa afición contigo? → Mi pareja/mejor amiga/hermano... Nos entendemos/llevamos/ comunicamos muy bien.

Expresar acciones recíprocas

● **¿Se tutean** en la escuela de baile?

■ Sí, **nos tuteamos** todos.

17B.2 Reciprocal verbs

Vocabulario *cont.*

el ritmo *rhythm*
pasarlo bien *to have a good time*
reírse (e:i) *to laugh*
de maravilla *wonderfully*
el aburrimiento *boredom*
el merengue
⑤
tutearse *to use the* **tú** *form of address*
enfadarse *to get angry*
abrazarse *to hug each other*
besarse *to kiss each other*
enojarse *to get angry*
quererse (e:ie) *to love each other*
saludarse *to greet each other*
⑥
escribirse *to write to each other*
mirarse *to look at each other*
contarse (o:ue) *to tell each other*
⑦
cantar *to sing*

¡OJO!

The preposition **con** followed by **mí** or **ti** forms **conmigo** and **contigo**. This rule does not apply to the preposition **sin**. So you should say, for example, Vino conmigo; no quiso ir sin mí.

Bailes
Los bailes son la expresión de los gustos populares de sus países de origen. La salsa en Colombia, Cuba y Puerto Rico; la cumbia en Colombia; el merengue y la bachata en la República Dominicana; el tango en Argentina y Uruguay; y las sevillanas, el flamenco y el pasodoble en España.

SAM: Actividades pp. 365–367

Practice more at **vhlcentral.com.**

Buena comunicación

Compruebe el grado de afinidad que tiene con sus amigos, familiares, compañeros de trabajo...

GUSTOS

1. Le gusta que sus amigos, familiares...
- **a.** sean divertidos, cuenten chistes, se rían mucho.
- **b.** sean personas serias e intelectuales.
- **c.** expresen su estado de ánimo en cada momento.
- **d.** sean honestos y le digan siempre la verdad.

2. Le gusta que...
- **a.** tengan el mismo gusto por el arte, la literatura, etc.
- **b.** sean aficionados del mismo equipo de fútbol.
- **c.** miren los mismos programas de televisión.
- **d.** tengan gustos diferentes de los suyos.

INTERESES

3. Cuando sale a divertirse, no le interesa que sus amigos...
- **a.** le hablen de política.
- **b.** le hagan preguntas personales.
- **c.** le cuenten sus problemas.
- **d.** estén mirando el celular constantemente.

4. Le interesa que...
- **a.** le recomienden libros, música, películas...
- **b.** le cuenten dónde están las mejores ofertas.
- **c.** lo/la pongan al día sobre los últimos chismes.
- **d.** le propongan hacer viajes juntos.

PREFERENCIAS

5. En su cumpleaños prefiere que...
- **a.** le preparen alguna sorpresa.
- **b.** nadie lo recuerde.
- **c.** le hagan regalos prácticos, como ropa, algo para la cocina, etc.
- **d.** sus familiares salgan con usted a cenar.

6. Ante la opción de quedarse en casa un sábado, le gusta más que...
- **a.** le propongan ir a un centro comercial.
- **b.** lo/la inviten a un restaurante y a ver una película.
- **c.** le organicen una excursión.
- **d.** lo/la llamen para salir a pasear por la ciudad.

> **Resultados:** cuente el número de respuestas iguales.
> 6 respuestas = Son totalmente afines. 5 = Son muy afines. 4 = Son bastante afines. 3 = Comparten algunos intereses.
> 2 = No son muy afines. 1 = Tienen muy poco en común. 0 = No son nada afines.

Expresar gustos, intereses y preferencias

- En un restaurante, ¿le gusta que le recomienden un menú?
- No, prefiero que no me digan nada.

17B.3 **gustar/interesar** + **que** + [*subjunctive*]; **preferir** + **que** + [*subjunctive*]

Vocabulario

(8)

contar (o:ue) chistes *to tell jokes*
decir la verdad *to tell the truth*
poner (a alguien) al día *to update (someone)*
el chisme *piece of gossip*
la sorpresa *surprise*
ser afín *to have a lot in common*
la afinidad, intelectual, invitar

(10)

la cualidad *characteristic*

8 Test Haga el test y compare sus resultados con los de su compañero/a. ¿Tienen gustos, intereses y preferencias comunes?

9 Verbos Subraye las formas verbales de las respuestas del test. Después complete la tabla de verbos.

	indicativo	subjuntivo
CONTAR	(yo) cuento →	(yo) cuente
RECORDAR	recuerdo	....
RECOMENDAR	recomiendo	....
DECIR	digo	....
HACER	hago	....
PONER	pongo	....
PROPONER	propongo	....
SALIR	salgo	....

10 Cualidades Basándose en el test, describa con tres cualidades su personalidad. Sus compañeros adivinan cuáles son sus gustos, intereses y preferencias.

11 Opciones Añada otra opción para cada situación del test y comparta las opciones adicionales con un(a) compañero/a.

12 **a. Sobre fútbol** Ordene el diálogo de estas dos personas que hablan sobre el fútbol.

☐ A mí tampoco, no me gusta nada el fútbol.

☐ Pero como eres argentino seguro que te interesa más que gane River Plate.

☐ A mí no me interesa nada que gane o pierda un equipo de fútbol, ¿y a ti?

☐ No es verdad. No me interesa nada.

b. Reforzar una negación Observe cómo se refuerza una negación. Por cierto, ¿a usted le interesa el fútbol? ¿Hay algún deporte que no le gusta nada?

13 **Reacciones** Exprese la reacción de estas personas ante los sucesos que se mencionan.

> Modelo: *Mi amigo llegó una hora tarde.*
> (molesta) Me molesta que haya llegado una hora tarde.

1. *Te olvidaste de mi cumpleaños.*
   (decepciona) ....

2. *Mis padres postergaron su viaje.*
   (entristece) ....

3. *Mi novio leyó mi correo electrónico.*
   (molesta) ....

4. *Mis hermanos no llamaron desde que salieron esta mañana.*
   (preocupa) ....

14 **a. Viñeta** Fíjese en la viñeta cómica. ¿Tienen estas personas algún interés común? Coméntelo con su compañero/a. ¿Hay buena comunicación en esta familia?

ME GUSTA QUE TODA LA FAMILIA TENGA LOS MISMOS INTERESES.

b. Intereses Comente con su compañero/a qué intereses comparten ustedes con sus respectivas familias.

15 **Escribir** Escriba lo que le gusta, lo que le interesa y lo que prefiere en relación con estos temas. Añada otros temas si lo desea.

- los deportes
- los viajes
- la política

MI EXPERIENCIA

16 **Gustos, intereses y preferencias** Hable con su compañero/a y descubra sus gustos, intereses y preferencias sobre el aprendizaje del español.

GUIÓN DE TRABAJO

¿Cuáles son tus gustos, intereses y preferencias sobre la manera de aprender español?

¿Qué aspectos te preocupan sobre tu rendimiento en el curso al que estás asistiendo?

Me interesa más que me enseñen palabras argentinas (o cubanas, etc...).
Prefiero que me den deberes para hacer en casa.
Me gusta que el profesor nos recomiende música en español.

Me preocupa que todavía no haya aprendido a usar bien el subjuntivo.

Estrategia ···········

Reforzar una negación

- A Pepa no le gusta que le hagan regalos.
- Es verdad. No le gusta nada.

Reaccionar de forma negativa

Me molesta que me haya mentido.

Me preocupa que no hayas aprobado el examen.

Me decepciona que hayas reaccionado así.

Me entristece que hayan decidido no venir.

17B.4 **me molesta/preocupa/ decepciona/entristece + que + [subjunctive]**
Present perfect subjunctive

Vocabulario

13

mentir (e:ie) *to lie*

decepcionar *to disappoint*

entristecer (zc) *to sadden*

postergar *to postpone*

SAM: Actividades pp. 368–370

Amanda y Rubén, la vida es un tango

Amanda Roa y Rubén Sosa ganaron el concurso de tango para parejas maduras que se celebró en la Plaza Dorrego del barrio porteño de San Telmo, en Buenos Aires.

Amanda, ¿desde cuándo baila tango?

Empecé de joven. Recién llegada de Paraguay, conocí a Rubén y él me enseñó. Me divierte bailar, la paso bien y creo que no lo hago mal.

¿Y usted, Rubén, siempre bailó tango?

Era jovencito y la gente me decía: "Pibe, vos sos muy bueno en esto del tango, no podés seguir bailando gratarola", y así empecé. La pasé bien pero, realmente, nunca viví solo de bailar.

¿Cuántos años llevan casados?

(Amanda) Mirá, 15 años nomás. Pero nos conocemos desde hace 43 años. Rubén fue mi primer novio, pero nos separamos. Después de más de 20 años nos vimos un día casualmente cuando él iba manejando y yo, en colectivo.

Amanda y Rubén, en el último tango ganador del concurso

Como Rubén es muy buen bailarín, me enamoré otra vez al volver a ser su pareja de tango. Nos llevamos rebién y nos amamos profundamente.

¿Cuál es su tango favorito?

(Rubén) Volver, siempre volvemos al primer amor.

(Amanda) Sí, Volver, y me gusta más que lo cante una voz masculina. La versión de Carlos Gardel, por ejemplo, es buenísima.

Además del tango, ¿tienen otras aficiones comunes?

(Rubén) Sí, casi todas. Nos entendemos muy bien. Somos hinchas de Boca Juniors, y nos divierte mucho ir a la cancha. También somos buenos cocineros. Solemos organizar cenas con amigos; preferimos que vengan a casa y pasarla bien acá.

(Amanda) Rubén hace unos asados muy ricos y yo soy buena con las empanadas. Bueno, digamos que se pueden comer…

Gracias por atendernos y ¡felicitaciones a los dos!

Hablar de habilidades

- ¿Eres bueno para el baile?
- No lo hago mal. Soy bueno con los ritmos latinos. Además, tomo clases particulares con Verónica. Ella es muy buena profesora.

17B.5	**ser bueno/a en/para/con +** [*noun*] **ser + buen(a)/mal(a) +** [*noun*] **no lo hago (nada) mal**

Vocabulario

⑰

maduro/a *mature*

porteño/a *of/from the city of Buenos Aires*

recién *just*

pasarla bien (*Amér. L.*) *to have a good time*

ser bueno/a (en algo) *to be good (at something)*

ser malo/a (en algo) *to be bad (at something)*

el/la pibe/a (*Arg.*) *young boy/girl*

gratarola (*C. S.*) *for free*

nomás *only*

casualmente *by chance*

manejar (*Amér. L.*) *to drive*

el colectivo (*Arg.*) *bus*

---

17 **Foto** Mire a la pareja de la foto. ¿Qué están haciendo y dónde? ¿Cree que son solo pareja de baile o también en la vida real? Lea la entrevista y compruebe.

18 **Entrevista** ¿Cuál es el motivo de la entrevista? ¿Qué relación tiene esta pareja con el tango? ¿Desde cuándo?

19 **Amanda y Rubén** ¿Cuáles son las aficiones de Amanda y Rubén? ¿Qué dicen de sus habilidades?

- bailar: *Rubén dice que es muy bueno y Amanda dice que…*
- …

20 **Hablar de habilidades** ¿En qué es usted bueno/a? ¿Y su compañero/a?

Modelo: •*¿Eres bueno en la cocina?*
• *No lo hago nada mal.*

21 **Expresiones** Fíjese en estas palabras y expresiones típicas del habla argentina que aparecen en el texto. ¿Qué significan? Escriba un equivalente y diga si conoce otros ejemplos de argentinismos.

1. pasarla bien	7. nomás ....
2. pibe	8. manejando ....
3. vos sos	9. colectivo ....
4. podés	10. rebién ....
5. gratarola	11. acá ....
6. mirá	12. felicitaciones ....

22 **Parejas** ¿Conoce usted a parejas que comparten una misma pasión como el baile? ¿Son buenos en lo que hacen?

23 **a. Astor Piazzolla** ¿Sabe quién era Astor Piazzolla? ¿En qué cree que fue bueno? Lea el artículo y compruebe.

Astor Piazzolla (Mar del Plata, 1921; Buenos Aires; 1992), compositor y bandoneonista argentino, es uno de los músicos de tango más importantes.

En los años 50 y 60, Piazzolla introdujo una nueva forma de hacer tango. Por entonces, fue muy criticado por los tangueros clásicos. Para ellos, estas composiciones no eran tango. Piazzolla respondió con una nueva definición: "Es música contemporánea de Buenos Aires." Sus obras no se escuchaban en la radio, y los sellos discográficos no editaban su música.

Más tarde, lo reconocieron intelectuales y músicos de todo el mundo.

"Sí, es cierto, soy un enemigo del tango; pero del tango como ellos lo entienden. [...] Si todo ha cambiado, también debe cambiar la música de Buenos Aires."

PIAZZOLLA, Astor: *En Revista Antena Buenos Aires, 1954.*

En sus últimos diez años, escribió más de 300 tangos y unas 50 bandas sonoras de películas. Dio conciertos en Europa y América. Buenos Aires lo nombró "ciudadano ilustre".

Su música no se parece a ninguna otra: es, simplemente, Piazzolla.

b. Título ¿Qué título resume mejor la trayectoria de Astor Piazzolla? Proponga otro título adecuado.

"Piazzolla, único"   "Otra idea del tango"   "..."

c. Asociar Lea el texto y asocie la visión que Piazzolla tenía del tango con alguna de estas palabras. Explique el porqué de su elección a su compañero/a.

> innovación • cambio • adaptación • tradición • modernidad • respeto

24 **Escribir** Piense en un(a) artista que conoce y escriba un breve texto sobre sus habilidades.

25 **a. El lunfardo** ¿Sabe qué es el lunfardo? Compruebe en el texto.

El lunfardo es inseparable del tango. No se trata de un idioma, un dialecto ni una jerga, porque carece de gramática propia. El lunfardo es un conjunto de palabras (aproximadamente 5000) referidas a las distintas partes del cuerpo, la comida, la bebida, el dinero, la ropa, el delito, etc. Nace durante la segunda mitad del siglo XIX en Buenos Aires y Montevideo gracias a la inmigración italiana, aunque también tiene influencias de otros idiomas como el gallego, el francés, el portugués, el quechua y el guaraní, entre otros. Muchas palabras y expresiones del lunfardo ya son de uso habitual, por ejemplo: *morfar* (comer), *laburar* (trabajar), *mango* (dinero), *guita* (dinero). La cantidad y los términos de lunfardo que se utilizan dependen del hablante y de la persona con quien este se comunica, ya que muchas palabras del lunfardo son vistas como vulgares.

b. Palabras ¿Ha escuchado alguna de estas palabras en tangos o de personas argentinas? ¿Qué significa la oración "Laburo noche y día, pero no tengo un mango"?

Vocabulario *cont.*

rebién (*Arg.*) *very well*

ser hincha de *to be a supporter of*

la cancha (*Amér. L.*) *sports field*

la clase particular *private lesson*

23

el bandoneón *type of accordion*

el/la bandoneonista *bandoneón player*

criticar *to criticize*

el sello discográfico *record label*

editar *to release (music)*

más tarde *later*

la banda sonora *sound track*

el/la ciudadano/a ilustre *distinguished citizen*

el porqué *reason*

el/la enemigo/a

25

la jerga *slang, jargon*

carecer (de) *to lack*

el delito *crime*

26

la sabiduría *wisdom*

alejados/as entre sí *far from each other*

la estrofa *stanza*

la frente *forehead*

agarrar *to grab*

tener canas *to have gray hair*

apenado/a *sad*

el dialecto, diferenciarse de

O P I N I Ó N

¿Cree que bailar favorece la buena comunicación?

¿Hay edad para el baile, para aprender un idioma, para el amor...?

SAM: Actividades pp. 371–376

Practice more at **vhlcentral.com**.

26 **a. El tango** ¿Para qué es bueno el tango según Mario Benedetti?

"Es virtualmente imposible que, después de varios tangos, dos cuerpos no empiecen a conocerse. En esa sabiduría, en ese desarrollo del contacto se diferencia el tango de otros pasos de baile que mantienen a los bailarines alejados entre sí [...]. El abrazo del tango es sobre todo comunicación."

BENEDETTI, Mario: *La borra del café*. Madrid, Punto de Lectura, 2007.

b. Relacionar Lea ahora el fragmento del tango *Volver* y relacione las estrofas con las emociones e ideas siguientes: nostalgia, tristeza y paso del tiempo. Después relacione las palabras señaladas con su significado.

Volver,
con la frente **marchita**[1],
las nieves del tiempo
platearon[2] mi sien.
Sentir, que es un **soplo**[3] la vida,
que veinte años no es nada,
que **febril**[4] la mirada,
errante[5] en las sombras,
te busca y te nombra.
Vivir,
con el alma **aferrada**[6]
a un dulce recuerdo,
que lloro otra vez.

Música: Carlos Gardel
Versos: Alfredo Le Pera

☐ Espacio muy breve de tiempo.

☐ Que va de un lugar a otro.

☐ Sin vitalidad.

☐ Agarrada fuertemente.

☐ Tener canas en el pelo. Envejecer.

☐ Inquieta, apenada.

c. Otro tango Con su grupo, ahora busque en Internet los versos de otro tango, como *Mi Buenos Aires querido*, *El día que me quieras* o *Balada para un loco*. Compártalos con el resto de la clase. Comente con sus compañeros qué emociones le produjo escuchar esos versos.

TAREA FINAL

Test de afinidad

 En parejas, piensen en dos preguntas para conocer las aficiones de sus compañeros.

Hagan una lista común con las preguntas de todos.

Háganse el test unos a otros.

Hagan el balance de aficiones de la clase. ¿Comparten muchas?

YO PUEDO...

• **Puedo expresar diversión y aburrimiento.**

¿Qué le aburre y qué le divierte cuando está en una fiesta? ¿Con quién se ríe?

• **Puedo expresar acciones recíprocas.**

Cuente todo lo que hacen recíprocamente usted y su mejor amigo/a.

• **Puedo expresar gustos, intereses y preferencias.**

Nombre algo que le gusta, algo que le interesa y algo que prefiere de su clase de español.

• **Puedo hablar de habilidades.**

Piense en alguien cercano a usted. ¿En qué es bueno/a esta persona?

GRAMÁTICA FUNCIONAL Tutorials

17B.1 Express delight and boredom

reírse, pasarlo bien, divertir/aburrir + [*infinitive*]/**que** +
[*subjunctive*] 5.7.1, 5.21.1d, 6.4, 6.8 **conmigo, contigo** 6.6, 10.4

- Use the reflexive verb **reírse** (*to laugh*) to express delight.
  Reírse is an irregular verb.

REÍRSE

(yo)	me r**ío**	(nosotros/as)	nos re**ímos**
(tú)	te r**íes**	(vosotros/as)	os reís
(usted, él, ella)	se r**íe**	(ustedes, ellos/as)	se r**íen**

Me río mucho con mis amigos.
I laugh a lot with my friends.

- Use the expression **pasarlo bien** (*to have a good time*) to describe
  having fun. The expression **pasarla bien**, more common in Latin
  America than in Spain, is also correct.

  ¿Lo has pasado bien?
  Have you had a good time?

- Use [*indirect object pronoun*] + **divertir** (*to have fun, to enjoy*)/
  aburrir (*to bore, to get bored*) + **que** + [*subjunctive*] to express
  delight and boredom.

(a mí)	me		
(a ti)	te		
(a usted, él, ella)	le	divierte	+ que +
(a nosotros/as)	nos	aburre	[*subjunctive*]
(a vosotros/as)	os		
(a ustedes, ellos/as)	les		

A Mónica **le aburre que** su pareja siempre **baile** salsa.
It bores Mónica that her partner always dances salsa.

- As you have seen, the subjunctive is used with many expressions
  when a sentence has two verbs with different subjects. If the two
  verbs refer to the same person, use an infinitive after
  divertir/aburrir.

  Me divierte leer.   **Les aburre leer** el periódico.
  I enjoy reading.   *They get bored when they read the paper.*

¡OJO!

Divertir and **aburrir** can also be used reflexively.

No nado porque **me aburro**.   **Me divierto** cuando nado.
I don't swim because I get bored.   *I have fun when I swim.*

- When used with the preposition **con**, the pronouns **yo** and **tú**
  take the forms **conmigo** and **contigo**. In all other cases, subject
  pronouns are used with the preposition **con**.

  Lo paso muy bien **contigo**.
  I have a good time with you.

  Viviana se ríe mucho **con ellos**.
  Viviana laughs a lot with them.

¡Póngalo en práctica!

G1 **Mucha diversión** Complete las conversaciones.

> Anoche fui a un salón de baile y
> (1)............... (yo, pasarlo) fenomenal:
> bailé salsa, tango y (2)...............
> (yo, reírse) mucho con unos chicos
> muy graciosos.

> A mí, en cambio, no me divierte mucho
> (3)............... (bailar).

• • • • •

> ¿(4)................ (Divertir, tú) cocinar
> (5)................ (tú y yo)?

> Sí, pero me aburre que tú lo
> (6)................ (hacer) todo.

• • • • •

> Me divierte (7)................ (ir) al cine para
> ver comedias con mis amigos.

> A mí también me gustan las comedias,
> pero me divierte que mis amigos y yo
> (8)................ (alquilar) películas para
> verlas juntos en casa.

G2 **Unir** Una las frases para formar oraciones lógicas.

1. ¡Cállate! Me aburre ....

2. Me divierte mucho ....

3. Nos aburrimos mucho ....

4. A mi hermano y a mí nos divierte que ....

a. cuando vamos a la ópera.

b. que hables tanto.

c. ir al teatro.

d. papá se vista de Santa Claus.

G3 **Con mi hermano** Complete el párrafo con las
palabras y expresiones de la lista.

le aburre   conmigo   río   venga   me divierte

Me (1).................... mucho cuando mi
hermano se viste de payaso (*clown*). ¡Es tan
divertido! También (2)....................
mucho que (3).................... al parque
(4).................... Sé que a él
(5).................... ir al parque, pero
lo hace por mí.

17B.2 | **Express reciprocal actions**

Reciprocal verbs 5.7.2, 6.4

- Use reciprocal verbs (**verbos recíprocos**) to express a shared or reciprocal action between two or more people or things. Reciprocal verbs are conjugated only in plural forms and are accompanied by the plural reflexive pronouns (**nos, os, se**).

> Marisela y Jorge **se quieren** mucho.
> *Marisela and Jorge **love each other** a lot.*

> **Se hablan** todos los días y **se ven** cuatro veces por semana.
> *They **talk to each other** every day and they **see each other** four times a week.*

- The reflexive pronoun is understood as *(to) each other* or *(to) one another*. When a verb is reciprocal, you can add **el uno al otro/la una a la otra** (*each other*) or **mutuamente** (*mutually*) to make this idea explicit.

> Mi vecina y yo **nos saludamos** todos los días.
> *My neighbor and I **greet each other** every day.*

> **Os entendéis** muy bien el uno al otro.
> *You **understand each other** very well.*

- Examples of other reciprocal verbs include **abrazarse** (*to hug each other*), **amarse** (*to love each other*), **besarse** (*to kiss each other*), **encontrarse** (*to meet*), **escribirse** (*to write to each other*), **mirarse** (*to look at each other*), and **darse la mano** (*to shake hands*).

> Raúl y Maribel **se miraron** a los ojos.
> *Raúl and Maribel **looked each other** in the eye.*

- Use the verb **tutearse** to talk about the use of the familiar form **tú** in conversation. Synonymous expressions include **darse del tú** and **tratarse de tú**.

> Nos **tuteamos**.
> *We use the **tú** form with each other.*

¡OJO!

Context is important to distinguish reciprocal verbs from plural reflexive verbs. For example, note the difference in meaning between these two sentences.

Nos llamamos una vez por semana.
*We **call each other** once a week.*

Nos llamamos Armando y Estela.
*Our **names** are Armando and Estela.*

¡Póngalo en práctica!

G4 **Nos, os o se** Complete las oraciones.

- Vosotros, ¿cómo (1)............ saludáis en Argentina?
- (2)............ besamos también.

Mis padres (3)............ quieren (el uno al otro) como el primer día.

Mi amiga Marisa vive en Buenos Aires, pero (4)............ escribimos casi todos los días.

Los primos de Graciela (5)............ visitan (el uno al otro) con frecuencia.

Cristián y yo (6)............ encontramos en un café antes de la clase de historia para estudiar juntos.

G5 **Escribir** ¿Qué hacen las personas de las fotos?

1. .... 2. ....

3. .... 4. ....

G6 **Recíproco** Complete las oraciones con la forma correcta del verbo recíproco.

1. En el trabajo, mis compañeros y yo .... (tutearse).

2. Los primos de Gisela siempre .... (mandarse) tarjetas de cumpleaños.

3. Enrique y yo decidimos .... (encontrarse) en la entrada del museo para ver juntos la nueva exposición.

4. Vosotros .... (llamarse) casi todos los días, ¿no?

5. Camila y José Luis .... (amarse) mucho y se van a casar el año que viene.

6. Anoche en la fiesta de despedida, Paloma y Nicolás .... (abrazarse) antes de salir.

S Practice more at **vhlcentral.com.**

GRAMÁTICA FUNCIONAL

17B.3 Express tastes, interests, and preferences

gustar/interesar + **que** + [*subjunctive*]; **preferir** + **que** + [*subjunctive*];
Irregular subjunctive forms   5.11.1, 5.20, 5.21.1c

- Use **gustar/interesar** + **que** + [*subjunctive*] to express likes and interests when the verbs in the sentence have different subjects. Use these verbs with indirect object pronouns.

> **Me gusta que** mis amigos me **llamen** si van a llegar tarde.
> *I like my friends to call me if they are going to arrive late.*

- Use the infinitive with **gustar/interesar** if both verbs in the sentence refer to the same person.

> **No me gusta contar** mis historias de viajes.
> *I don't like to tell stories about my trips.*

- Use the construction **preferir** + **que** + [*subjunctive*] to talk about preferences.

> **Prefiero que vayamos** de compras más tarde.
> *I prefer that we go shopping later.*

> **Prefiero ir** al gimnasio después de la clase.
> *I prefer to go to the gym after class.*

- As you learned in 15B.4, **-ar** and **-er** verbs with a stem change in the **yo** form of the present indicative reflect the same stem change in the present subjunctive, except for the **nosotros/as** and **vosotros/as** forms.

CONTAR (cuento)	→	cuente, cuentes, cuente, contemos, contéis, cuenten (*similar verbs:* recordar, volver, poder)
RECOMENDAR (recomiendo)	→	recomiende, recomiendes, recomiende, recomendemos, recomendéis, recomienden (*similar verbs:* querer, preferir)

- As you learned in 15B.1, if the verb has an irregular **yo** form in the present, this spelling is used in all forms in the subjunctive.

PONER (pongo)	→	ponga, pongas, ponga, pongamos, pongáis, pongan (*similar verbs:* proponer, hacer)

17B.4 Express dislikes and reproach

molestar/preocupar + **que** + [*subjunctive*]; **decepcionar/ entristecer** + **que** + [*subjunctive*]   5.11.1, 5.21.1d
Present perfect subjunctive   5.22.1

- Use **molestar/preocupar** (*to bother/to worry*) to express dislikes and concerns. Use **decepcionar/entristecer** (*to disappoint/to sadden*) to express reproach or disappointment. These verbs are followed by **que** + [*subjunctive*] when the verbs in the sentence have different subjects. Use these verbs with indirect object pronouns, and use the infinitive when both verbs in the sentence refer to the same person.

> **Me molesta que** la gente **fume** cuando estoy comiendo.
> *It bothers me if people smoke when I am eating.*

> **Me decepciona que** no me **llames.**
> *It disappoints me that you don't call.*

> **Me preocupa tener** que leer tanto para mañana.
> *It worries me to have to read so much for tomorrow.*

¡Póngalo en práctica!

G7 **Completar** Complete las oraciones.

Me gusta que mis amigos (1)........................ (ser) divertidos y me gusta (2)........................ (yo, pasarlo) bien con ellos.

Me interesa que (3)........................ (nosotros, volver) a este lugar en algún momento.

Me gusta que mi familia y yo (4)........................ (poder) comunicarnos.

- ¿Os interesa que os (5)........................ (yo, proponer) otra opción?

- Sí, preferimos que nos (6)........................ (tú, hacer) otra propuesta mejor.

G8 **Oraciones** Complete las oraciones.

1. Eva........................ (preferir) que vosotros le........................ (recomendar) un restaurante menos caro.
2. A Juan Carlos le........................ (interesar) .... (alquilar) un apartamento en Barcelona durante el verano.
3. ¿Te........................ (gustar) que tus hermanos te........................ (llamar) por Skype?
4. No me........................ (gustar) que mis padres me........................ (decir) lo que debería hacer.

G9 **Elegir** Elija la opción correcta para completar cada oración.

1. Nos molesta que **llegar/llegues** a casa tan tarde.
2. Me preocupa no **poder/pueda** pagar la cuenta.
3. A mi madre le decepciona que mi hermano no **ser/sea** abogado.
4. Me entristece no **verte/te vea** más a menudo.
5. ¿No te molesta **salir/salgas** sin paraguas con este tiempo?
6. Nos preocupa que la abuela ya no **reírse/se ría** como antes.

 Practice more at vhlcentral.com.

GRAMÁTICA FUNCIONAL

- Use the present perfect subjunctive (**pretérito perfecto de subjuntivo**) in order to comment on past events. The **pretérito perfecto de subjuntivo** is used to refer to past events that in some way act upon the present.

> **Me decepciona** que no me **hayas llamado**.
> *It disappoints me that you haven't called.*

- The **pretérito perfecto de subjuntivo** is formed with the present subjunctive of the verb **haber** + [*past participle*]. The verb **haber** is irregular in the present subjunctive. You learned regular past participles in **6A.4** and irregular past participles in **7B.1**.

HABER

(yo)	**haya**	(nosotros/as)	**hayamos**
(tú)	**hayas**	(vosotros/as)	**hayáis**
(usted, él, ella)	**haya**	(ustedes, ellos/as)	**hayan**

> Me molesta que no me **hayáis ayudado** con la limpieza.
> *It bothers me that you **didn't help** me with the cleaning.*

17B.5   Talk about skills and abilities

ser bueno/a en/para/con + [*noun*]   5.8.7, 10.4, 10.12, 10.15
no lo hago (nada) mal   11.1   **ser buen(a)/mal(a)** + [*noun*]

- Use **ser bueno/a** or **malo/a** + **en/para/con** to talk about someone's or something's abilities. Use **en/para** + [*discipline*] and **con** + [*a specific thing*].

> Luisa **es muy buena en** matemáticas/**para** el diseño/**con** las cuentas.
> *Luisa **is very good at** math/at design/at calculations.*

- Use (**nada**) **mal** as an adverb of manner to describe something that someone does well.

> Me gusta jugar al tenis y no lo hago **nada mal**.
> *I like playing tennis and I play **pretty well**.*

- Use the construction **ser buen(a)/mal(a)** + [*noun*] to describe someone's skill in a specific role.

> Andrés **es buen pintor**.
> *Andrés **is a good painter**.*

- When **bueno/a** or **malo/a** is placed after the noun, the adjective emphasizes the good or bad qualities of the individual's personal characteristics, instead of highlighting the abilities of the person.

> Es **buena profesora**.
> *She is **a good teacher**. (She is good at her profession.)*

> Es una **profesora buena**.
> *She is **a good teacher**. (She is a teacher and a good person.)*

¡Póngalo en práctica!

G10   **Eventos pasados** Complete las oraciones con la forma correcta del verbo en el pretérito perfecto de subjuntivo.

1. No soporto que mis amigos no me .... (decir) si vienen a la fiesta o no.

2. A David le parece raro que Candelaria no lo .... (llamar).

3. Nos preocupa que no .... (tú, leer) el manual de instrucciones.

4. A los profesores les extraña que .... (nosotros, decidir) estudiar en la cafetería.

5. No creo que nuestro equipo .... (ganar).

6. Pía no está totalmente segura de que sus compañeros .... (ir) a la biblioteca.

G11   **Subjuntivo** Complete las oraciones. Use el pretérito perfecto de subjuntivo en la segunda cláusula.

1. Nos .... (decepcionar) que Teo y Lucas todavía no .... (llegar).

2. Me .... (entristecer) que mi hermano .... (olvidar) mi cumpleaños otra vez.

3. A Uriel le .... (molestar) que no .... (vosotros, hacer) la tarea para hoy.

G12   **Conversaciones** Complete las conversaciones.

> (1)........... (Yo, ser) bueno (2)........... la cocina, sobre todo (3)........... los postres, pero no sé bailar. ¿Y tú?

> A mí me gusta bailar. Sí, creo que (4)........... (ser) buena (5)........... el baile. No lo (6)........... (yo, hacer) mal. Y en la universidad, ¿cómo te va?

> En general, soy bueno (7)........... las ciencias, pero las humanidades me cuestan un poco más.

> Para mí es lo contrario: historia es mi materia preferida. Tengo un (8)........... profesor este semestre; explica muy bien el material.

Practice more at **vhlcentral.com**.

VOCABULARIO 🔊 Ⓢ Vocabulary Tools

¿Bailas conmigo?

el aburrimiento	boredom
el baile de salón	ballroom dance
el chachachá	cha-cha
la cumbia	dance typical of the Caribbean coast of Colombia
el merengue	merengue
el paso (de baile)	(dance) step
el pasodoble	typical Spanish march-like dance
el ritmo	rhythm
las sevillanas (pl.)	popular dance originated in Seville
el vals	waltz
abrazarse	to hug each other
aburrir	to bore
aburrirse	to get bored
besarse	to kiss each other
cantar	to sing
contarse (o:ue)	to tell each other
divertir (e:ie)	to amuse
divertirse (e:ie)	to have fun
enfadarse	to get angry
enojarse	to get angry
escribirse	to write to each other
mirarse	to look at each other
pasarlo bien	to have a good time
quererse (e:ie)	to love each other
reírse (e:i)	to laugh
saludarse	to greet each other
tutearse	to use the **tú** form of address
de maravilla	wonderfully

Buena comunicación

la afinidad	affinity
el chisme	piece of gossip
la cualidad	characteristic
la sorpresa	surprise
contar (o:ue) chistes	to tell jokes
decepcionar	to disappoint
decir la verdad	to tell the truth
entristecer (zc)	to sadden
invitar	to invite
mentir (e:ie)	to lie
poner (a alguien) al día	to update (someone)
postergar	to postpone
ser afín	to have a lot in common
intelectual	intellectual

Amanda y Rubén

la banda sonora	sound track
el bandoneón	type of accordion
el/la bandoneonista	**bandoneón** player
la cancha (Amér. L.)	sports field
el/la ciudadano/a ilustre	distinguished citizen
la clase particular	private lesson
el colectivo (Arg.)	bus
el delito	crime
el dialecto	dialect
el/la enemigo/a	enemy
la estrofa	stanza
la frente	forehead
la jerga	slang, jargon
el/la pibe/a (Arg.)	young boy/girl
el porqué	reason
la sabiduría	wisdom
el sello discográfico	record label
agarrar	to grab
carecer (de)	to lack
criticar	to criticize
diferenciarse de	to be different from
editar	to release (music)
manejar (Amér. L.)	to drive
pasarla bien (Amér. L.)	to have a good time
ser bueno/a (en algo)	to be good (at something)
ser hincha de	to be a supporter of
ser malo/a (en algo)	to be bad (at something)
tener canas	to have gray hair
alejados/as entre sí	far from each other
apenado/a	sad
maduro/a	mature
porteño/a	of/from the city of Buenos Aires
casualmente	by chance
gratarola (C. S.)	for free
más tarde	later
nomás	only
rebién (Arg.)	very well
recién	just

Variación léxica

el chisme ⟷ el cotilleo (Esp.)

muy bien ⟷ rebién (fam., Arg.)

nomás (Amér. L.) ⟷ no más ⟷ solamente

pasarlo bien/mal ⟷ pasarla bien/mal (Amér. L.) ⟷ pasárselo bien/mal (Esp.)

el/la pibe/a (Arg.) ⟷ el/la chamaco/a (Méx.) ⟷ el/la chaval(a) (Esp.)

El viaje

Cristina Fernández Cubas

La escritora española **Cristina Fernández Cubas** (1945–) estudió periodismo y derecho en Barcelona. Durante los últimos treinta años ha escrito cuentos, novelas y obras de teatro y ha viajado por todo el mundo. Vivió en ciudades como El Cairo, París, Berlín y Lima. Su obra ha sido traducida a diez idiomas y actualmente es un referente muy importante para los escritores de relatos breves.

Vocabulario útil

la abadesa *abbess*

alcanzar a ver *to catch a glimpse of*

la celosía *lattice*

el convento de clausura *cloistered convent*

el encierro *seclusion*

la fachada *façade*

habitualmente *normally, usually*

la monja *nun*

no le interesa lo más mínimo *he/she couldn't care less*

Estrategia ⋯⋯⋯⋯

Visualizing

When reading a text, pay attention to the details and descriptions: use your five senses to create images in your mind reflecting the ideas in the text. These images will help you go deeper into the text and make the world of the story come alive in your mind while you are reading, much as if you were watching a movie. Imagine what characters look like, how they walk and talk, where the story takes place, what time of the day it is, etc.

Un día la madre de una amiga me contó una curiosa anécdota.

Estábamos en su casa, en el barrio antiguo de Palma de Mallorca, y desde el balcón interior, que daba a° un pequeño jardín, se alcanzaba a ver la fachada del vecino convento de clausura. La madre de mi amiga solía visitar a la abadesa; le llevaba helados para la comunidad y conversaban durante horas a través de la celosía. Estábamos ya en una época en que las reglas de clausura eran menos estrictas de lo que fueron antaño°, y nada impedía a la abadesa, si así lo hubiera deseado°, que interrumpiera en más de una ocasión su encierro y saliera al mundo.

① **Conversar** Converse con un(a) compañero/a: Imagine que no puede salir de su casa. ¿Qué haría? ¿Cómo conocería el mundo exterior? ¿Alguna vez estuvo de visita en un convento o monasterio? ¿Cuál sería para usted el viaje más largo?

② **Emparejar** Empareje elementos de las columnas para formar oraciones y completar el relato.

1. La autora escuchó esta historia de boca ……..
2. Desde el balcón de su casa se alcanza a ver ……..
3. La mujer habitualmente llevaba ……..
4. A través de la celosía, ……..
5. Hacía casi treinta años que ……..
6. Una mañana, la abadesa ……..
7. Ella pidió permiso para ……..
8. Después de observar en silencio, dijo que ……..
9. Con mucha alegría, la abadesa ……..
10. Supuestamente, la abadesa no ……..

a. esta mujer conversaba horas con la abadesa.
b. se presentó en la puerta de la casa de su vecina.
c. se despidió y salió.
d. ha vuelto a salir del encierro de su convento.
e. de la madre de una amiga que vive en Palma.
f. la fachada de un convento de clausura.
g. el convento se veía muy bonito.
h. helados a la comunidad de monjas.
i. la abadesa no salía de su encierro.
j. contemplar su convento desde el balcón.

Pero ella se negaba en redondo°. Llevaba casi treinta años entre aquellas cuatro paredes y las llamadas del exterior no le interesaban lo más mínimo.

Por eso la señora de la casa creyó que estaba soñando° cuando una mañana sonó el timbre° y una silueta oscura se dibujó° al trasluz° en el marco de la puerta°. "Si no le importa", dijo la abadesa tras los saludos de rigor°, "me gustaría ver el convento desde fuera". Y después, en el mismo balcón en el que fue narrada la historia se quedó unos minutos en silencio. "Es muy bonito", concluyó. Y, con la misma alegría con la que había llamado a la puerta, se despidió y regresó al convento.

Creo que no ha vuelto a salir, pero eso ahora no importa. El viaje de la abadesa me sigue pareciendo, como entonces, uno de los viajes más largos de todos los viajes largos de los que tengo noticias.

daba a *looked onto* **antaño** *in the past* **si así...** *if she had wanted to* **se negaba en redondo** *refused point blank* **soñando** *dreaming* **timbre** *doorbell* **se dibujó** *was outlined* **al trasluz** *against the light* **marco de la puerta** *door frame* **los saludos de rigor** *the usual greetings*

---

(3) **Responder** Converse con un(a) compañero/a.

1. ¿Qué cree que pensaron los vecinos al ver a la abadesa por la calle? ¿Y las otras monjas del convento: le reprocharon su salida o quisieron imitarla? ¿Les pareció divertido o escandaloso?

2. Imagine un final diferente: cuando la abadesa ve el convento desde el balcón, toma una decisión importante: ¿cuál es y qué hace después?

PROYECTO

Un relato Busque algún monumento importante de un país hispanohablante e investigue los datos principales sobre su historia:

- ubicación geográfica
- época de construcción
- motivo por el cual se construyó
- significado

Luego escriba su descripción en un relato: puede ser desde el punto de vista de alguien que lo ve por primera vez, o de un(a) enamorado/a que espera a su novio/a allí, etc. Siga estos pasos:

1. Describa físicamente el monumento y su reacción personal al conocerlo.

2. Visualice sus sensaciones y sus emociones (miedo, sorpresa, etc.) y anótelas.

3. Para que el lector pueda relacionarse con el relato, identifique el tema del monumento y subraye por qué es importante.

4. Elija el punto de vista más adecuado para su historia (primera o tercera persona) y escríbala.

Estrategia ··········

Narrative writing

"A story should have a beginning, a middle, and an end... but not necessarily in that order." This deceptively simple quote from film director Jean-Luc Godard has long helped writers approach the task of narration. Keep this concept in mind as you plan your writing. Notice, for example, in *El viaje*, that the beginning of the narrative—a visit with a friend's mother—occurs at a point in time after the actions of the plot—the abbess's visit—have already ended.

Lo mejor de Argentina

Ya ha leído sobre cómo las pasiones son el motor de la vida: puede ser una pasión por buscar la verdad o por disfrutar de las cosas que nos hacen felices. En este episodio de **Flash Cultura** descubrirá algunas de las pasiones esenciales de los argentinos.

1 **Preguntas** ¿Qué le apasiona? (actividades, ideas...) ¿A qué no renunciaría nunca? ¿Le gustan las cosas exóticas o prefiere las tradicionales? ¿Qué tradiciones conserva? ¿Se siente más atraído/a por el pasado, el presente o el futuro?

2 **Mirar** Mientras mira el episodio de **Flash Cultura**, tenga en mente: ¿Qué sabe sobre el tango, el mate, el asado? ¿Qué idea tiene de los argentinos?

...en el corazón del barrio de San Telmo... se puede disfrutar de una de las cosas que más les gustan a los argentinos: el tango.

...a nadie se le ocurriría tomar café de la taza de otra persona... ¡pero el mate es para compartir!

3 **Oraciones** Indique si estas oraciones son verdaderas o falsas. Después, con un(a) compañero/a, corrija las falsas.

1. En Buenos Aires existen muchos cafés.
2. El Tortoni está en las afueras de la ciudad.
3. Borges prefería tomar submarinos.
4. Carlos Gardel fue un famoso escritor.
5. El bandoneón es un instrumento importante para el tango.
6. El asado necesita de mucho tiempo para cocinarse.
7. El mate se hace con café.
8. En Argentina se come mucha carne.

4 **Diálogo** En parejas, escriban un diálogo entre una persona que le quiere hacer un regalo a su novio/a y un(a) amigo/a que le da consejos.

Modelo: • Estoy seguro de que un CD de tango es un buen regalo.
• Pero a ella no le gusta nada bailar...

Estrategia
Using prior knowledge

Before, during, and after watching a video, consider what you already know about that particular topic. This will improve your comprehension. Before watching this **Flash Cultura** episode, think: What do you know about Argentina? (What have you read or heard about it, have you been there, etc.?)

Vocabulario útil

ajetreado/a *hectic*
a las apuradas *in a hurry*
chupar *to suck*
la parrilla *grill*
reconocido/a *renowned*

Estrategia
Understanding cultural rituals

In Argentina, Uruguay, or Paraguay, sharing **mate** is a symbol of interpersonal relationships. **Mate** is traditionally drunk in family gatherings or with friends and is part of everyday life; discussions, love quarrels, and confessions are sealed with a **mate**. To be invited to share **mate** is an invitation to friendship, so beware! Rejecting it or making faces at the prospect of sharing the **bombilla** with other people might be offensive. What other customs and rituals have you learned about that at first struck you as odd?

Unidad 18

Rafa Nadal, un número uno

Marián Rico, ¡pura vida!

Palacios del arte

AVANCE

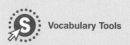
NUEVOS RETOS

Al límite

Retos deportivos

¿Quién es para usted el deportista que ha superado el reto deportivo más difícil?

Iván Vallejo decidió ser montañista a los 8 años.

Iván Vallejo es un montañista ecuatoriano al que admiro mucho. Es un gran deportista para quien es necesario superarse día a día. Es el primer sudamericano que logró escalar todos los ochomiles (las 14 montañas más altas del mundo) sin auxilio de oxígeno. Además, es ingeniero químico y da conferencias sobre la realización de metas. ¡Es increíble todo lo que hace!

Esteban Rodríguez, Mendoza

Yo estoy impresionada con Andoni Rodelgo y Alice Goffart. Son dos deportistas para los que las adversidades no existen. Hace un tiempo, dieron la vuelta al mundo en bicicleta. Recorrieron aproximadamente 44 000 kilómetros en tres años, tres meses y tres días. Ahora repiten la experiencia con su hija, Maia, y su hijo, Unai. ¡Es increíble la energía que tienen! Nada es imposible para ellos.

Julia Fernández, Quito

Andoni y Alice han recorrido cinco continentes con sus bicicletas.

Identificar

Es un montañista ecuatoriano **que** ha superado muchos retos y **para el que** no existen retos imposibles.
Son deportistas **a los que** admiro.

18A.1 [preposition] + **quien/el, la, los, las + que**

Vocabulario

①

el reto deportivo *sports challenge*

el/la deportista *sportsman, sportswoman*

superar retos *to overcome challenges*

el/la montañista *mountain climber*

superarse *to outdo oneself*

sudamericano/a *South American*

escalar *to climb (a mountain)*

el auxilio *help*

la meta *goal*

estar impresionado/a *to be impressed*

la adversidad *setback*

1 **Retos deportivos** Observe las fotos de estos deportistas. ¿Qué deportes practican? Relacione después los nombres de los deportes y los deportistas.

tenis	atletismo	gimnasia	natación
ciclismo	Fórmula 1	maratón	montañismo

1. atleta: _____atletismo_____
2. nadador(a): _____
3. piloto: _____
4. montañista: _____
5. corredor(a): _____
6. ciclista: _____
7. tenista: _____
8. gimnasta: _____

2 **Resumir** Lea el artículo de la revista de deporte y resuma los datos más sorprendentes acerca de estos deportistas.

> **Modelo:** *Iván Vallejo es un montañista que... para quien...*

3 **Completar** Complete las oraciones con las expresiones del recuadro.

> del que • para el que • que • con los que • a quien

1. Es el atleta _____ ha batido el récord en los 110 metros.
2. ¡No sabes todos los desafíos _____ se enfrentaron estos ciclistas!
3. Hoy he conocido al deportista guatemalteco _____ todos hablan.
4. Es un montañista _____ no hay retos imposibles.
5. Es una deportista formidable y una persona _____ admiro mucho.

④ **Preguntar** Mire las fotos y lea las informaciones. Haga preguntas a su compañero/a como en el ejemplo.

Fátima del Ángel Palacios

Ricardo Abad

Juan Carlos Sagastume

Fátima del Ángel se convirtió en la primera latinoamericana en llegar al Polo Norte.

Corrió 500 maratones (21 000 km) en 500 días.

Cruzó el océano Atlántico en un bote de remos: 5280 km en 64 días, 13 horas y 17 minutos.

Modelo: *¿Quién es el que corrió 500 maratones en 500 días?*

⑤ **Opiniones** Complete las opiniones de los lectores. Luego, elija al deportista de la lección que más le impresiona a usted y explique a su compañero/a por qué.

1. Esteban admira mucho a Iván porque...

2. Julia está impresionada con Andoni y Alice porque...

3. Yo admiro a... porque...

⑥ **Logros** Escuche las llamadas de otros lectores de la revista y complete las oraciones.

1. Joaquín .... Fátima del Ángel por .... al Polo Norte y al desierto del Sahara.

2. Amélie piensa que .... Andoni y Alice .... algo así.

3. María Elena .... Juan Carlos por todos sus logros.

⑦ **Admirables** Lea las oraciones y elija la forma correcta de cada verbo.

1. Es sorprendente que Ricardo **corra/haya corrido** 21 000 km en dieciséis meses.

2. Es increíble que Juan Carlos **pueda/haya podido** superar todos esos retos y que además **tenga/haya tenido** su propia empresa.

3. Es impresionante que Andoni y Alice **decidan/hayan decidido** viajar en bicicleta con sus hijos.

4. Me parece admirable que Fátima del Ángel **sea/haya sido** una deportista tan completa.

 **MI EXPERIENCIA**

⑧ **Héroes deportivos** Piense en un(a) deportista o equipo que ha superado algún reto especial y explique a su compañero/a quién es, qué ha hecho y por qué lo/la admira.

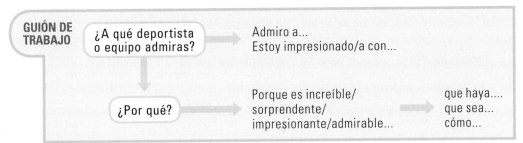

GUIÓN DE TRABAJO

¿A qué deportista o equipo admiras? → Admiro a... Estoy impresionado/a con...

¿Por qué? → Porque es increíble/ sorprendente/ impresionante/admirable... → que haya.... que sea... cómo...

 Practice more at **vhlcentral.com**.

Expresar admiración

● Admiro a Rafa Nadal. Estoy impresionado con su juego. ¡Es increíble cómo juega!

■ Yo admiro a Ricardo Abad. ¡Es sorprendente que haya corrido 21 000 km en 500 días!

| 18A.2 | admirar a
estar impresionado/a con
es increíble cómo
es increíble/sorprendente/
impresionante/admirable
que + [*subjunctive*] |

Vocabulario *cont.*

dar la vuelta al mundo *to go around the world*

el atletismo *track and field*

la gimnasia *gymnastics*

el ciclismo *cycling*

el montañismo *mountain climbing*

el/la nadador(a) *swimmer*

el/la piloto *race car driver*

el/la corredor(a) *runner*

el oxígeno, la Fórmula 1, el maratón, el/la ciclista, el/la gimnasta
②

sorprendente *surprising*
③

batir un récord *to break a record*

enfrentarse a/con *to face*
④

el Polo Norte *North Pole*

cruzar *to cross*

el océano *ocean*

el bote de remos *rowboat*

ascender (e:ie) *to climb*

¿Alpinismo o andinismo?

El montañismo de altura recibe nombres específicos según el lugar en que se practica. Por eso, se llama *alpinismo* en los Alpes y *andinismo* en los Andes. La principal diferencia entre los *alpinistas* y los *andinistas* es el número de metros sobre el nivel del mar que deben ascender: hasta 5000 en Europa y de 5000 a 7000 en América.

SAM: Actividades pp. 377–379

Nuevos aires

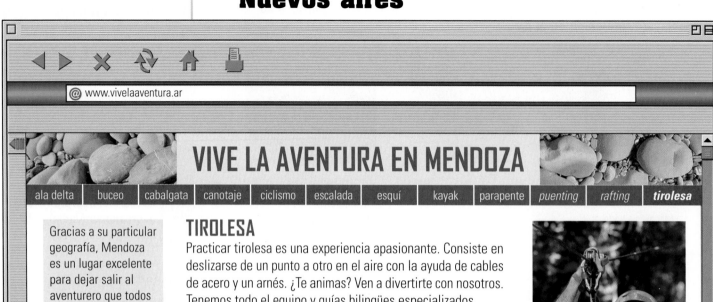

VIVE LA AVENTURA EN MENDOZA

| ala delta | buceo | cabalgata | canotaje | ciclismo | escalada | esquí | kayak | parapente | *puenting* | *rafting* | **tirolesa** |

Gracias a su particular geografía, Mendoza es un lugar excelente para dejar salir al aventurero que todos llevamos dentro. ¡Después de que practiques un deporte de aventura, serás otro! Las opciones son infinitas.

TIROLESA

Practicar tirolesa es una experiencia apasionante. Consiste en deslizarse de un punto a otro en el aire con la ayuda de cables de acero y un arnés. ¿Te animas? Ven a divertirte con nosotros. Tenemos todo el equipo y guías bilingües especializados.

Información importante:

- El plazo de inscripción es del 1 al 10 de cada mes. Puedes reservar tu lugar en línea en cualquier momento.
- Salida en colectivo a las 8:00 h (hay que presentarse 15 minutos antes de que salga el colectivo).
- Llegada a Potrerillos a las 10:00 h.
- Después de que tengamos una charla de seguridad, comienza la aventura. El recorrido es de 1400 metros y se divide en 6 etapas.
- La actividad termina a las 13:00 h. Almorzaremos asado y daremos un paseo.
- Regresaremos a las 17:00 h, después de una ronda de mate.

Relacionar acontecimientos

Tenemos que presentarnos 15 minutos **antes de que salga** el autobús.

La aventura comenzará **después de que tengamos** una charla de seguridad.

18A.3 **antes/después de que** + [*subjunctive*]

Vocabulario

⑨

el/la aventurero/a *adventurer*

el ala delta (*f.*) *hang glider*

la cabalgata *horseback riding*

el canotaje *canoeing*

la escalada *climbing*

el parapente *paragliding*

el *puenting* *bungee jumping*

la tirolesa *zip-lining*

deslizarse *to glide*

el acero *steel*

---

9 a. **Actividades deportivas** Observe la página web de una empresa que organiza actividades deportivas en Mendoza, Argentina. ¿Quién organiza en su pueblo o ciudad ese tipo de actividades?

- ☐ los clubes privados
- ☐ el ayuntamiento
- ☐ la universidad
- ☐ otros...

b. **Responder** ¿En qué tipo de deportes se especializa esta empresa? ¿Le gustaría practicar alguno?

10 **Aventura de Mendoza** Fíjese en la información sobre los horarios y marque la opción correcta.

1. La actividad comienza **antes/después** de que se sirva el asado.
2. Hay que inscribirse para practicar tirolesa **antes/después** del día 10 de cada mes.
3. **Antes/Después** de dar un paseo, tomarán mate.
4. Tendrán la charla de seguridad **antes/después** de la llegada a Potrerillos.

11 **Preguntar** Haga preguntas a su compañero/a sobre las actividades.

Modelo: • *¿Cuándo hay que presentarse en el colectivo?*
• *Quince minutos antes de que salga el colectivo.*

12 Relacionar acontecimientos ¿Qué va a hacer después de la clase de español? ¿Y antes de que termine? Con sus compañeros, forme oraciones que relacionen acontecimientos.

> Modelo: • *Antes de que termine la clase, haremos esta actividad.*
> • *Después de que entreguemos el ejercicio, el/la profesor(a)...*

13 a. Objetos Mire las fotos. ¿Qué objetos reconoce? Relacione con flechas.

| brújula | botas de trekking | mochila | casco |

| tienda de campaña | guantes | gafas | bastones |

b. Publicidad Lea la publicidad de esta tienda. ¿Por qué se repiten las palabras señaladas?

> Practicar deportes de aventura no es fácil. Necesitas **horas y horas** de entrenamiento y un buen equipo. Tú pon la dedicación, nosotros ponemos todo lo demás.

14 a. Deportes Relacione estos eslóganes con las imágenes y anote el nombre de los deportes.

"Vuela y vuela como un pájaro" ☐ ....

"Metros y metros de montaña para ti" ☐ ....

"Más y más océano frente a tus ojos" ☐ ....

b. Eslogan En parejas, decidan cuál es la actividad deportiva más interesante de la lección y creen un eslogan publicitario.

MI EXPERIENCIA

15 Programa de actividades Elija una actividad y escriba un breve programa o calendario. Informe a su compañero/a y pregúntense por los programas.

| GUIÓN DE TRABAJO | ¿Cuál es el plazo de inscripción? ¿Cómo se forman los grupos? | → | Antes de (que)... Después de que sepamos el número de personas inscritas... |
| | ¿Qué equipo necesito? ¿Qué entrenamiento previo necesito? | → | Para este deporte necesitas... El entrenamiento que necesitas... |

 Practice more at **vhlcentral.com**.

Vocabulario *cont.*

el arnés *harness*
el equipo *equipment*
el plazo de inscripción *enrollment period*
antes de que *before*
después de que *after*
infinito/a, el *rafting*

13

la brújula *compass*
el casco *helmet*
la tienda de campaña *tent*
los guantes *gloves*
el bastón *pole*
descender (e:ie) *to descend*
la pendiente *slope*

Estrategia ·············

Intensificar
Nadó **kilómetros y kilómetros** completamente solo.

Nuevos deportes

El ser humano siempre intenta superar retos. Por eso, no es extraño que surjan nuevos deportes extremos como el surf volcánico. Este deporte se practica en el Cerro Negro, un volcán de 730 metros de alto que está ubicado en Nicaragua. Desde 2005, unos 10 000 surfistas han descendido con sus tablas por una pendiente de 500 metros a una velocidad de hasta 97 km por hora.

SAM: Actividades pp. 380–382

Rafa Nadal, un número uno

¿Cómo es Rafael Nadal antes de salir a la cancha y después de que millones de personas sigan sus partidos?

El deportista más joven que ha recibido el Premio Príncipe de Asturias y el ídolo de millones de aficionados por su carisma y su valía personal, nació el 3 de junio de 1986 en Manacor, Mallorca. De pequeño era uno de esos niños que decía "Cuando sea mayor, seré futbolista". Sin embargo, su tío y entrenador Toni Nadal vio que Rafa tenía buenas cualidades físicas para el tenis. Para Rafa Nadal, los entrenamientos con su tío han sido decisivos. "Me exige mucho, supongo que por ser de mi familia. Él me ha enseñado a ser deportista, y sobre todo a ser mejor persona."

Dice mucho sobre su carácter esta anécdota que cuenta su tío de un torneo en el que Rafa, que tenía siete años entonces, jugaba contra un tenista de catorce. Toni le dijo a su sobrino: "Si veo que te da una paliza descomunal, tú no te preocupes, que yo haré llover y pararemos el partido". El cielo estaba nublado y el partido empezó. Rafael perdía 3-0, pero con siete años Rafael ya era muy luchador y tenía una confianza verdaderamente ciega en sí mismo; así que empezó a remontar el partido.

Rafa Nadal, en la final del Abierto de Australia

En ese momento empezó a llover y se paró el partido. Después de cinco minutos, Rafael se acercó a su tío y le dijo: "Toni, puedes parar la lluvia cuando quieras, ¡creo que puedo ganar!"

Hablar de retos futuros

Cuando sea mayor, seré futbolista.

18A.4 cuando + [subjunctive]

Vocabulario

(16)

la cancha *court*
el partido *match*
la valía *worth*
el/la entrenador(a) *coach*
el entrenamiento *training*
el torneo *tournament*
la paliza *thrashing*
descomunal *massive*
la confianza *confidence*
remontar *to surmount*
ganar torneos *to win tournaments*
el ídolo, el carisma

(18)

estar seguro/a de sí mismo/a *to be self-confident*

---

16 Protagonista Mire la imagen. ¿Qué sabe sobre el protagonista de esta unidad?

(ganar torneos)   (Mallorca (España))   (...............................)

Modelo: *Rafa Nadal es un tenista que....*

17 a. Contestar Lea el artículo sobre Rafael Nadal. ¿Qué relación profesional tiene con su tío Toni? ¿Por qué Toni es tan importante para el deportista?

b. Retos ¿Qué decía Rafael cuando era pequeño? ¿Quería ser tenista? ¿Qué retos tenía para el futuro? ¿Y usted qué decía cuando era pequeño/a?

Modelo: *Cuando sea mayor...*

18 a. Anécdota ¿Qué nos dice la anécdota de Rafa y su tío sobre la personalidad de este deportista? Busque expresiones equivalentes a estas.

seguro de sí mismo • bueno para el tenis • constante

b. Frases ¿Qué diferencia hay entre estas frases? ¿Cuál de ellas le parece indicada para Rafael Nadal?

○ *Si llego* a número uno...   ○ *Cuando llegue* a número uno...

19 Hablar de retos futuros Expresen retos futuros en relación a estos temas con mayor o menor optimismo.

(conseguir el trabajo de mis sueños)   (dar la vuelta al mundo)   (tener más tiempo libre)

Muy optimista: *Cuando termine...*   No tan optimista: *Si termino...*

20 **a. Juegos Panamericanos** Lea el texto sobre los Juegos Panamericanos. Luego haga una lista de los datos que más le llaman la atención.

LOS JUEGOS PANAMERICANOS

Los Juegos Panamericanos están entre los acontecimientos deportivos más importantes del mundo. La Organización Deportiva Panamericana (ODEPA) los lleva a cabo cada cuatro años, siempre un año  antes de los Juegos Olímpicos de Verano. Allí compiten miles de atletas de 42 naciones de América del Norte, América Central, Sudamérica y el Caribe.

Los primeros Juegos Panamericanos se celebraron en Buenos Aires en 1951. Originariamente iban a realizarse en el año 1942, pero se pospusieron por la Segunda Guerra Mundial. Desde entonces, se han celebrado ininterrumpidamente.

Además de promover el desarrollo deportivo, el objetivo de estos juegos es fortalecer la unión y la amistad entre los pueblos. Por eso, el lema de la ODEPA, "América, Espíritu, Sport, Fraternité", incorpora cuatro de los idiomas más usados en las Américas: español, portugués, inglés y francés. Además, en su emblema se ven cinco círculos de colores (azul, rojo, blanco, amarillo y verde). Al menos uno de esos colores aparece en cada bandera nacional de los países participantes.

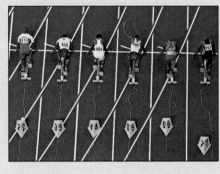

b. Expresión ¿Qué cree que significa la expresión "llevar a cabo" en el texto? Piense en otros tres casos en los que se podría usar esta expresión.

21 **Escribir** ¿Qué acontecimiento deportivo le resulta especialmente interesante? Escriba una crónica breve.

22 **Leyendas del deporte** ¿Conoce a estas leyendas del deporte? ¿Con qué deporte los asocia?

beisbolista ☐   boxeador ☐   lanzadora de disco ☐
tenista ☐   nadadora de sincronizada ☐

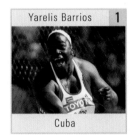

Yarelis Barrios **1**
Cuba

Pedro Martínez **2**
República Dominicana

Oscar de la Hoya **3**
EE.UU.

Juan Martín del Potro **4**
Argentina

Gemma Mengual **5**
España

Practice more at **vhlcentral.com.**

Vocabulario

20

los Juegos Panamericanos *Pan-American Games*

llevar a cabo *to carry out*

competir (e:i) *to compete*

la Segunda Guerra Mundial *World War II*

ininterrumpidamente *uninterruptedly*

fortalecer (zc) *to strengthen*

incorporar *to include*

posponer, el círculo, el emblema

22

la leyenda *legend*

el/la beisbolista *baseball player*

el béisbol *baseball*

el/la boxeador(a) *boxer*

el/la lanzador(a) de disco *discus thrower*

el/la nadador(a) de sincronizada *synchronized swimmer*

23

hípico/a *equestrian*

la pelota *ball*

el asa (f.) *handle*

el aro *hoop*

el/la contrincante *opponent*

el/la pato/a *duck*

lanzar *to throw*

la pólvora *gunpowder*

atrapar *to catch*

el frontón *jai-alai court*

la raqueta

OPINIÓN

¿Cuáles son, en su opinión, las cualidades que debe tener un deportista para triunfar?

SAM: Actividades pp. 383–386

23 a. Leer ¿Qué deportes asocia con Argentina, Colombia y España? Si su respuesta es "fútbol" o "béisbol", lo invitamos a conocer deportes tradicionales de esos tres países hispanohablantes.

El *pato* es un deporte hípico que se ha practicado en Argentina por 400 años. Los jugadores de un equipo deben pasarse una pelota con asas unos a otros hasta lograr introducirla en el aro de sus contrincantes. El nombre del deporte se debe a que, en un principio, los gauchos argentinos usaban un pato vivo en lugar de una pelota.

El *tejo* es el deporte nacional de Colombia. Es un deporte muy antiguo, ya que lo practicaban los indígenas antes de la llegada de Colón. En la actualidad, los jugadores deben lanzar un disco (tejo) e introducirlo en un círculo metálico (bosín) en cuyos bordes se colocan "mechas" (pequeñas bolsas con pólvora). Gana el jugador que hace explotar más mechas.

El *jai alai*, o cesta punta, es un deporte de origen vasco parecido al *squash*. En lugar de raqueta, los jugadores usan una cesta para atrapar la pelota y lanzarla contra un frontón. Para practicarlo, es conveniente usar casco: ¡la pelota puede alcanzar una velocidad de hasta 250 kilómetros por hora!

b. Deportes ¿Qué deportes asocia con su ciudad/estado/región? ¿Por qué? ¿Alguna vez ha visto cómo se juegan? Comente su experiencia con sus compañeros.

 TAREA FINAL

Revista deportiva

En parejas, elijan un deporte y busquen información sobre deportistas y eventos deportivos relacionados, récords, etc.

Escriban un artículo o crónica deportiva breve con la información que han seleccionado. Incluyan imágenes.

Compartan y clasifiquen los artículos y elaboren entre todos una revista deportiva.

YO PUEDO...

- **Puedo identificar.**
  Identifique a un(a) deportista que admira.

- **Puedo expresar admiración.**
  Explique por qué admira a este/a u otros deportistas.

- **Puedo relacionar acontecimientos.**
  Después de que .... (pasar) el verano, jugaremos al tenis en cancha cubierta.

- **Puedo hablar de retos futuros.**
  Cuando .... (ir de vacaciones) ,
  ....

GRAMÁTICA FUNCIONAL Tutorials

18A.1 Identify someone or something

[*preposition*] + quien / el, la, los, las + que `3.1.2, 6.9`

• Use a preposition followed by the relative pronouns (**pronombres relativos**) **quien** (*who; whom; that*) or **el, la, los, las + que** (*that; which; who*) to identify someone or something already mentioned in the sentence.

> Nadia es la amiga **con quien/con la que** hice tirolesa.
> *Nadia is the friend **with whom** I went zip-lining.*

• Use **que** by itself when no preposition is present.

> Es un deportista **que** ha corrido 150 maratones.
> *He is an athlete **who** has run 150 marathons.*

• **Que** and **quien** both introduce a clause that refers to an antecedent (something or someone already mentioned in the sentence).

• The antecedent of the pronoun **que** can be a person or thing, while the antecedent of **quien** can only be a person. Use **quien** after a preposition or the personal **a**.

> Es un deportista **a quien** admiro.
> Es un deportista **que** admiro.
> *He is an athlete **whom** I admire.*

• The construction [*preposition*] + **el, la, los, las + que** may also be used in place of [*preposition*] + **quien**. The definite article must match the antecedent in both gender and number.

> Son **las tenistas a las que** más me gusta ver jugar.
> Son **las tenistas a quienes** más me gusta ver jugar.
> *They are **the tennis players that** I like best to watch play.*

> Es **un alpinista para el que** no hay retos imposibles.
> Es **un alpinista para quien** no hay retos imposibles.
> *He is **a mountain climber for whom** there are no impossible challenges.*

• Note that **que** and **quien** do not carry a written accent in these constructions.

¡OJO! In English, relative pronouns are sometimes optional. In Spanish, relative pronouns are never omitted.

> Es la deportista **que** más me gusta.
> *She is the athlete **(that)** I like best.*

¡Póngalo en práctica!

G1 **Que o quien** Complete las oraciones con el pronombre relativo correcto: **que** o **quien**.

1. La escaladora vasca Edurne Pasaban es la única .... ha alcanzado todos los ochomiles.
2. Rafael Nadal es uno de los deportistas a .... más admiran los españoles.
3. Manu Ginóbili es un jugador de básquetbol argentino .... juega en la NBA.
4. Diego Forlán es un jugador de fútbol uruguayo para el .... ganar el Balón de Oro en el Mundial de Sudáfrica 2010 no fue imposible.
5. Antonio Abertondo es un nadador .... cruzó el Canal de la Mancha.
6. Miguel Indurain es un ciclista .... ha ganado carreras en varios países.

G2 **Oraciones completas** Empareje las frases para formar oraciones completas.

1. El jugador		4. Las deportistas	
2. El equipo		5. La deportista	
3. Los entrenadores			

a. que toman más riesgos son los que ganan más torneos.
b. al que le dieron el premio fue contratado por un equipo europeo.
c. a quienes eligieron para el equipo fueron las que entrenaron todo el invierno.
d. que perdió ante el Barça es el segundo en la liga.
e. a la que le interesa el periodismo tiene oportunidades de trabajo después de los Juegos Olímpicos.

G3 **Combinar** Combine las oraciones usando pronombres relativos.

> Modelo: El jugador tiene solo dieciocho años.
> El jugador marcó el último gol.
> *El jugador que tiene solo dieciocho años marcó el último gol.*

1. A la montañista le gusta superar retos. La montañista ascendió el Aconcagua.
2. El ciclismo es un deporte divertido. El ciclismo atrae a deportistas de todas las edades.
3. La brújula está en la mochila. La mochila está en la tienda de campaña.
4. Gabriel es un nadador. Para Gabriel, es muy importante intentar batir un récord.

 Practice more at **vhlcentral.com**.

GRAMÁTICA FUNCIONAL

admirar a, estar impresionado/a con 5.8.2
es increíble cómo/que + [*verb*] 5.8.8
Use of present perfect subjunctive 5.22.2

- Use the verb **admirar** (*to admire*) to express admiration for a person. Remember to use the personal **a**.

  ¿A qué deportista **admiras**?
  What athlete do you admire?

  Admiro a Iván Vallejo.
  I admire Iván Vallejo.

- Use the construction **estar impresionado/a con** (*to be impressed with/by*) to show admiration for someone or something.

  Estoy impresionada con su valentía.
  I am impressed with his courage.

- Use the construction **es increíble cómo** (*it is incredible how*) + [*verb*] to express admiration for an action or event. This construction does not use the subjunctive.

  Es increíble cómo escala Iván Vallejo.
  It is incredible how Iván Vallejo climbs.

  Es increíble cómo anotó ese gol.
  It's amazing how he scored that goal.

- Remember to use a written accent on **cómo** in this construction.

- Use the **presente de subjuntivo** with the construction **es increíble/impresionante/sorprendente** (*to be incredible/impressive/surprising*) + **que** to express astonishment about an event in the present.

  Es impresionante que juegue tan bien.
  It is amazing that he plays so well.

  Es sorprendente que el béisbol **sea** tan popular en Japón.
  It's surprising that baseball is so popular in Japan.

- Use the **pretérito perfecto de subjuntivo** with the construction **es increíble/impresionante/sorprendente** + **que** to express astonishment about a past event.

  Es impresionante que hayan escalado tantas montañas altas.
  It is impressive that they have climbed so many tall mountains.

  Es increíble que haya participado en tres Juegos Olímpicos.
  It's incredible that she has participated in three Olympic Games.

¡Póngalo en práctica!

G4 **Completar** Complete las oraciones.

1. ¡Es increíble .... entrenan los deportistas de élite!

2. Estoy impresionada .... el nuevo equipo de mi ciudad.

3. .... (yo, admirar) a Lionel Messi porque es un gran futbolista y un buen deportista.

4. Admiro mucho .... esta deportista.

5. Es increíble cómo .... (dedicar) su vida al deporte.

6. Estoy impresionado .... ella.

7. Es sorprendente que ella .... (poder) ganar la medalla de oro cuando solo tenía veinte años.

8. Es increíble que los atletas olímpicos .... (dedicar) tantos años de su infancia a entrenar.

G5 **En otras palabras** Complete las oraciones para que transmitan las mismas ideas que las originales.

1. Admiro a la escaladora española.
   Estoy impresionado ....

2. Es increíble cómo el equipo ha ganado tantos torneos.
   Es increíble que el equipo ....

3. Es impresionante cómo los deportistas profesionales siempre tratan de superarse.
   Es impresionante que los deportistas profesionales siempre ....

4. Estamos impresionados con este boxeador.
   Admiramos ....

5. Es increíble que Carolina y Héctor vayan al gimnasio todos los días.
   Es increíble cómo Carolina y Héctor ....

G6 **Emparejar** Empareje las oraciones para formar mini-conversaciones.

- 1. Admiro mucho al jugador nuevo en el equipo de fútbol. ....

- 2. ¿Qué pensáis del torneo? ....

- 3. Es sorprendente que el nadador haya podido cruzar el río en tan poco tiempo. ....

- 4. Es increíble que Ricardo y Luisa hayan decidido hacer *puenting*. ....

- 5. Es impresionante que haya tantas personas interesadas en correr maratones en los últimos años. ....

- a. Me dijeron que querían superar este reto tan difícil.

- b. Sí, parece que es una meta personal de muchas personas correr uno.

- c. Estamos impresionados con todos los equipos este año.

- d. Tienes razón. Creo que batió un récord.

- e. Sí, es increíble cómo juega. Yo también lo admiro.

 Practice more at vhlcentral.com.

GRAMÁTICA FUNCIONAL

18A.3 Relate events to one another

antes/después de que + [*subjunctive*] 5.13, 5.21.3a, 12.13
Spelling changes in the present subjunctive 5.20.2

- Use **antes de que** (*before*) and **después de que** (*after*) to relate events in time. Use these constructions in sentences that have verbs with different subjects. Always use the subjunctive after **antes de que**.

  Antes de que vayamos al partido, quiero pasar por la casa de un amigo.
  Before we go to the game, I want to stop by my friend's house.

- Use the subjunctive after **después de que** to relate anticipated events in the future.

  Después de que lleguen todos, vamos a ir al estadio.
  After everyone arrives, we are going to go to the stadium.

- If both events occurred in the past, use **después de que** + [*indicative*].

  Después de que terminó el torneo, volvimos a la universidad en autobús.
  After the tournament ended, we returned to the university by bus.

- If the sentence has only one subject, use **antes/después de** + [*noun/infinitive*] to compare two events in time.

  Antes de hacer montañismo, tenemos que conseguir el equipo adecuado.
  Before doing mountaineering, we have to get the proper equipment.

  Después del campeonato, Gonzalo dejó de entrenar los fines de semana.
  After the championship, Gonzalo stopped training on the weekends.

- Verbs that end in **-car**, **-gar**, and **-zar** have spelling changes in all forms of the present subjunctive in order to maintain the original pronunciation of the verb stem.

PRACTI_C_AR (c→qu) →	practi**qu**e, practi**qu**es, practi**qu**e, practi**qu**emos, practi**qu**éis, practi**qu**en
ENTRE_G_AR (g→gu) →	entre**gu**e, entre**gu**es, entre**gu**e, entre**gu**emos, entre**gu**éis, entre**gu**en
EMPE_Z_AR (z→c) →	empie**c**e, empie**c**es, empie**c**e, empe**c**emos, empe**c**éis, empie**c**en

No podéis inscribiros después de que **empiece** el torneo.
*You can't register after the tournament **begins**.*

Es importante que **practiques** antes de que comience el campeonato.
*It's important that **you practice** before the championship begins.*

¡Póngalo en práctica!

G7 **Antes o después** Complete las oraciones.

1. Los atletas tienen que prepararse antes de que las olimpiadas .... (empezar).
2. Después de que .... (terminar) las competiciones, los atletas seguirán con sus entrenamientos.
3. Tienes que inscribirte antes de que .... (llegar) el día del torneo.
4. Después de que .... (vosotros, practicar) montañismo, vamos a empezar a entrenar para el triatlón.
5. Antes de que .... (ustedes, probar) el montañismo, tienen que informarse de las mejores rutas.
6. Después de que .... (nosotros, volver) del campeonato, nuestro entrenador nos habló de cómo mejorar nuestro rendimiento.
7. Antes de que .... (comenzar) el verano, los atletas aprovechan los días menos calurosos de la primavera para entrenar más horas.
8. Después de que .... (nosotros, entrenar) por tres horas, empezó a llover.

G8 **Las mismas ideas** Complete la tercera oración para que trasmita las mismas ideas.

> **Modelo:** Voy al gimnasio a las 8:00 de la mañana. La clase de español empieza a las 10:30.
>
> Antes de que *empiece la clase de español, voy al gimnasio.*

1. El instructor va a llegar pronto. Después, vamos a hacer *rafting*.
   Después de que ....
   ....
2. Arturo y Paula encontraron un sitio en el camping a las 4:00 de la tarde. A las 4:15, armaron su tienda de campaña.
   Después de ....
   ....
3. Rosario habló con la otra entrenadora a las 3:30 de la tarde. El equipo empezó a entrenar a las 4:00.
   Después de que ....
   ....
4. Roberto sale a correr a las 7:00 de la mañana. El periódico llega a su puerta a las 6:00 de la mañana.
   Antes de que ....
   ....
5. El plazo de inscripción cierra el 25 de octubre. Después de esa fecha, tenéis que pedir un permiso especial para poder participar.
   Después de que ....
   ....

 Practice more at vhlcentral.com.

GRAMÁTICA FUNCIONAL

cuando + [*subjunctive*]   5.21.3b, 12.12

- Use the subjunctive with **cuando** to refer to a pending action or event in the future. Use the present subjunctive in the clause that follows **cuando** to refer to any action that has not yet occurred.

  > **Cuando me jubile**, viajaré más.
  > *When I retire, I will travel more.*

  > Cuando era pequeña, siempre decía: "**Cuando sea** mayor, seré futbolista."
  > *When I was young, I always said: "When I am older, I will be a soccer player."*

- Use **cuando** + [*present indicative*] to talk about a habitual action in the present.

  > **Cuando viajo**, me gusta escribir en mi diario.
  > *When I travel, I like to write in my diary.*

- Use **cuando** + [*preterite*] to refer to a completed action in the past.

  > **Cuando llegamos** al hotel, estábamos muy cansados.
  > *When we arrived at the hotel, we were very tired.*

- Use **cuando** + [*imperfect*] to talk about a habitual past action. In **14B.1**, you learned to use **cuando** with either the preterite or the imperfect to situate past events.

  > **Cuando era** pequeño, mi familia vivía en las afueras de la ciudad.
  > *When I was young, my family lived outside the city.*

¡Póngalo en práctica!

G9 **Cuando...** Complete las oraciones.

1. Iremos a ver un partido de tenis cuando .... (vosotros, querer).

2. Cuando .... (yo, tener) tiempo, escribiré un blog sobre deporte.

3. Cuando mi hermana .... (estar) cansada durante la tarde, le gusta dormir la siesta.

4. Cuando Benjamín .... (jugar) al fútbol en la secundaria, su posición preferida era de mediocampista.

5. Me gustaría trabajar en un canal de televisión cuando .... (terminar) mis estudios.

6. Cuando .... (nosotros, llegar) a la fiesta de cumpleaños, ya habían servido la tarta.

7. Te llamaré cuando .... (yo, llegar) a casa.

8. Cuando .... (empezar) el partido, voy a tomar un descanso del estudio.

9. Cuando .... (ser) pequeño, David jugaba al fútbol todos los días.

10. Nos gustaría conocer Chichén Itzá cuando .... (ir) a México.

Practice more at **vhlcentral.com**.

SÍNTESIS

Mire las fotografías y escriba un diálogo o párrafo corto para cada una, usando el vocabulario indicado.

1.

| el reto | es increíble cómo | el montañismo | antes (de) que |

- _____
- _____
- _____
- _____

2.

| el futbolista | cuando sea | entrenar | estoy impresionado/a con |

- _____
- _____
- _____
- _____

Al límite

la adversidad	setback
el atletismo	track and field
el auxilio	help
el bote de remos	rowboat
el ciclismo	cycling
el/la ciclista	cyclist
el/la corredor(a)	runner
el/la deportista	sportsman, sportswoman
la Fórmula 1	Formula 1
la gimnasia	gymnastics
el/la gimnasta	gymnast
el maratón	marathon
la meta	goal
el montañismo	mountain climbing
el/la montañista	mountain climber
el/la nadador(a)	swimmer
el océano	ocean
el oxígeno	oxygen
el/la piloto	race car driver
el Polo Norte	North Pole
el reto deportivo	sports challenge
ascender (e:ie)	to climb
batir un récord	to break a record
cruzar	to cross
dar la vuelta al mundo	to go around the world
enfrentarse a/con	to face
escalar	to climb (a mountain)
estar impresionado/a	to be impressed
superar retos	to overcome challenges
superarse	to outdo oneself
sorprendente	surprising
sudamericano/a	South American

Nuevos aires

el acero	steel
el ala delta (f.)	hang glider
el arnés	harness
el/la aventurero/a	adventurer
el bastón	pole
la brújula	compass
la cabalgata	horseback riding
el canotaje	canoeing
el casco	helmet
el equipo	equipment
la escalada	climbing
los guantes	gloves
el parapente	paragliding
la pendiente	slope
el plazo de inscripción	enrollment period
el *puenting*	bungee jumping
el *rafting*	rafting
la tienda de campaña	tent
la tirolesa	zip-lining
descender (e:ie)	to descend
deslizarse	to glide
infinito/a	infinite
antes de que	before
después de que	after

Rafa Nadal

el aro	hoop
el asa (f.)	handle
el béisbol	baseball
el/la beisbolista	baseball player
el/la boxeador(a)	boxer
la cancha	court
el carisma	charisma
el círculo	circle
la confianza	confidence
el/la contrincante	opponent
el emblema	emblem
el/la entrenador(a)	coach
el entrenamiento	training
el frontón	jai-alai court
el ídolo	idol
los Juegos Panamericanos	Pan-American Games
el/la lanzador(a) de disco	discus thrower
la leyenda	legend
el/la nadador(a) de sincronizada	synchronized swimmer
la paliza	thrashing
el partido	match
el/la pato/a	duck
la pelota	ball
la pólvora	gunpowder
la raqueta	racket
la Segunda Guerra Mundial	World War II
el torneo	tournament
la valía	worth
atrapar	to catch
competir (e:i)	to compete
estar seguro/a de sí mismo/a	to be self-confident
fortalecer (zc)	to strengthen
ganar torneos	to win tournaments
incorporar	to include
lanzar	to throw
llevar a cabo	to carry out
posponer	to postpone
remontar	to surmount
descomunal	massive
hípico/a	equestrian
ininterrumpidamente	uninterruptedly

Variación léxica

la adversidad ⟷ el percance ⟷ el contratiempo ⟷ el revés

la cancha ⟷ la pista (*Esp.*)

el/la contrincante ⟷ el/la oponente ⟷ el/la adversario/a ⟷ el rival

hípico/a ⟷ ecuestre

el/la montañista ⟷ el/la montañero/a

el *rafting* ⟷ el balsismo

la tienda de campaña ⟷ la carpa (*Amér. L.*)

la tirolesa ⟷ el canopy

MEJOR IMPOSIBLE

Acontecimientos de la vida

Nos da pena que deje la empresa, pero nos alegramos de que pueda disfrutar de su jubilación con salud.

¡FELICIDADES!

1

Nos alegramos de que celebren 25 años de casados. ¡Felicitaciones!

¡Que cumplan juntos muchos más!

2

¡FELIZ DÍA, MAMÁ!

GRACIAS...

Porque te alegras de que la vida me sonría.

Porque te da pena que sufra.

Porque te pones contenta si estoy cerca.

Porque te pones triste al marcharme.

Porque escuchas mis sentimientos, por tu amor sin condiciones.

3

Feliz Año Nuevo

Me alegro de que empecemos juntos este nuevo año.

4

¡Seguro que será el mejor!

Expresar sentimientos

- Me puse triste cuando te marchaste y hoy me alegro de que estés aquí.
- Me da pena que no vengan.

18B.1 alegrarse de que + [*subjunctive*]; ponerse triste + cuando/si + [*indicative*]/al + [*infinitive*]

Vocabulario

① ————

dar pena *to sadden*

la jubilación *retirement*

ponerse contento/a *to become happy*

ponerse triste *to become sad*

marcharse *to go away*

el Día de la Madre *Mother's Day*

cumplir años de casados *to have one's wedding anniversary*

el Año Nuevo *New Year*

las bodas de plata *silver wedding anniversary*

② ————

cumplir años *to have one's birthday*

acordarse (o:ue) de *to remember*

---

① **a. Tarjetas** Lea las tarjetas de felicitación y hable con su compañero/a.

Tarjeta 1: ¿Quiénes se alegran? ¿De qué se alegran?

Tarjeta 2: ¿Qué acontecimiento celebran?

Tarjeta 3: ¿Cuándo se ponen tristes las madres? ¿Cuándo se ponen contentas?

Tarjeta 4: ¿Qué empiezan juntos? ¿De qué se alegra?

b. Expresar sentimientos ¿Qué sentimientos le producen a usted normalmente estos acontecimientos?

Modelo: *Me alegro de que un matrimonio celebre sus bodas de plata.*

② **Diálogo** Complete el diálogo con la forma correcta de los verbos del recuadro.

| tener estar pensar ponerse acordarse |

MARTÍN: ¡Hola, Paola! ¡Feliz cumpleaños!

PAOLA: Ah, bueno. Gracias.

MARTÍN: ¿No te alegra cumplir años?

PAOLA: No. ¡.................. triste cuando .... que soy un año más vieja!

MARTÍN: Bueno, alégrate de que .... sana, ... un buen trabajo y tu familia esté bien. ¡Alégrate también de que .... de que hoy es tu cumpleaños!

③ **Ocasiones** ¿Escribe usted este tipo de felicitaciones? ¿En qué otras ocasiones felicita a sus familiares, compañeros o amigos?

4 **Felicitaciones** Escuche estas felicitaciones y anote el número de la conversación correspondiente en la imagen.

5 **Tipos de felicitaciones** Marque cómo se felicita en cada ocasión.

	¡Felicitaciones! ¡Felicidades! ¡Enhorabuena!	¡Feliz cumpleaños!	¡Feliz Día de...!	¡Feliz Navidad! ¡Felices fiestas!
aniversario (boda, negocio)				
boda				
conseguir algo: trabajo, premio				
cumpleaños				
Día del Padre/de la Madre/ de San Valentín				
graduación				
nacimiento				
Navidad				
quince años				

6 **Viñeta** Lea la viñeta cómica. ¿Entiende el chiste? Coméntelo con su compañero/a. ¿Cómo se felicita el cumpleaños en su lengua?

7 **Preguntar** ¿Qué cree que puede celebrar su compañero/a pronto? Investigue a través de preguntas y felicítelo/a.

Modelo: *¿Tu cumpleaños es este mes?*

🎭 **MI EXPERIENCIA**

8 **Sentimientos** ¿Qué le produce a su compañero/a sentimientos de alegría? ¿Y de tristeza?

GUIÓN DE TRABAJO

¿Qué te alegra? ¿Qué te pone contento/a? ➡ Me alegro de que... Me pongo contento/a cuando/si... ➡ los logros personales, los cumpleaños, las celebraciones, el inicio/fin de las vacaciones, el inicio/fin del curso, el invierno, el verano, las despedidas

¿Qué te da pena? ¿Qué te pone triste? ➡ Me da pena que... Me pongo triste cuando/si...

Felicitar y expresar deseos

• ¡Felicidades! ¡Que seas muy feliz!

■ ¡Gracias, igualmente!

18B.2 **felicidades, feliz** + [*noun*] **que** + [*subjunctive*]

Vocabulario

5
la fiesta de quince años
fifteenth birthday party
la graduación

¡OJO!

¡Felicitaciones!, ¡Felicidades!, and ¡Enhorabuena! are synonyms. However, there are slight differences in meaning: **felicitaciones** and **enhorabuena** are more often used to commemorate an achievement, whereas **felicidades** has a more general meaning and does not imply a particular achievement on the part of the recipient. Note that **enhorabuena** is more frequently used in Spain and **felicitaciones** is commonly used in Latin America.

SAM: Actividades pp. 387–389

Ⓢ Practice more at **vhlcentral.com**.

Celebraciones a la carta

eventoscostarica.cr

Eventos Costa Rica

- **Inicio**
- **Eventos**
  - Bodas
  - Quince años
  - Despedidas de soltero/a
  - Bautizos
  - Aniversarios
  - Cumpleaños
  - Graduaciones
  - Jubilaciones
  - Fiestas de empresas
- **Menús**
- **Galería de fotos**
- **Contacto**

¡Es una excelente idea que nosotros le planifiquemos y organicemos su celebración como usted la ha soñado!

Realizamos toda clase de eventos especiales: su boda, la fiesta de cumpleaños de su esposo/a, los quince años de su hija, el bautizo del bebé, la graduación de sus hijos, la despedida de soltera de su mejor amiga… ¿No es una buena idea que usted disfrute de cada uno de estos momentos al máximo? Para ello nosotros nos ocupamos de todos los detalles.

Disponemos de salones con una decoración exquisita, terraza al aire libre con vista panorámica y piscina. Nuestra experiencia y profesionalidad le garantiza que es una excelente idea dejarlo todo en nuestras manos. Sus invitados se sentirán cómodos, se divertirán, comerán rico y se llevarán un hermoso recuerdo de ese día. Nuestro servicio puede incluir: coordinadores, maestros de ceremonias, decoración especial, música, limusina, *catering* de calidad, pasteles y mucho más; en definitiva, todo lo que necesita.

En resumen, si quiere disfrutar de un evento bien organizado, en un lugar mágico, contáctenos y solicite ya su cotización sin compromiso. Estamos al alcance de su teléfono o computadora, y nos ponemos a sus órdenes.

¡Si tiene un sueño, hágalo realidad con nosotros!

Evaluar ideas

- ¿Es una buena idea celebrar mi cumpleaños?
- Sí, es una **excelente idea** que **puedas** disfrutar de tu día.

18B.3 (no) es (una) buena idea + [*infinitive*]/**que** + [*subjunctive*]

Vocabulario

(9)

la despedida de soltero/a *bachelor(ette) party*

planificar *to plan*

ocuparse de los detalles *to take care of the details*

el salón de fiestas *function hall*

disponer de *to have (at one's disposal)*

el/la invitado/a *guest*

el/la maestro/a de ceremonias *master of ceremonies*

el pastel *cake*

en definitiva *all in all*

---

9 a. Celebraciones La palabra "evento" se usa para referirse a una fiesta o celebración. ¿Cuántas celebraciones se le ocurren en un minuto? Anótelas y compare con su compañero/a. ¿Están todas las que aparecen en esta página web?

b. Eventos Costa Rica Lea el texto y marque verdadero (V) o falso (F).

	V	F
1. Eventos Costa Rica es un salón de fiestas.	☐	☐
2. Todas las celebraciones se realizan en una terraza con piscina.	☐	☐
3. Eventos Costa Rica solo organiza celebraciones familiares.	☐	☐
4. El pedido de cotización no genera ninguna obligación.	☐	☐
5. Eventos Costa Rica ofrece servicio de transporte para los invitados.	☐	☐

10 a. Relacionar Relacione las columnas.

¿Es buena idea... •
• me organicen la despedida de soltera? ¡Nos vamos a reír mucho!

¿No es una excelente idea que mis amigas... •
• organizar una fiesta de graduación?

b. Propuestas Elija un evento y anote sus propuestas para celebrarlo. Evalúe las propuestas de su compañero/a.

11 Responder ¿Cómo valora usted este tipo de empresas? ¿Ha celebrado o ha asistido a algún evento organizado por una empresa como Eventos Costa Rica?

12 **Sugerencias** ¿Qué nos sugiere Eventos Costa Rica si queremos celebrar un evento?

> Si quiere disfrutar de un evento bien organizado,... ⟶ ....

> Si tiene un sueño,... ⟶ ....

13 **a. Condiciones** Piense en posibles condiciones para estas oraciones.

1. Si _vas a casarte_, vístete como una reina.
2. Si quieres una boda especial, ...
3. Si .... celebrar la mejor fiesta de quince años, ...
4. Si quiere sorprender a sus invitados, ...
5. Si .... despedida de soltero/a, ...

b. Problemas Usted quiere hacer una fiesta de cumpleaños e invitar a mucha gente. Piense en los problemas que pueden surgir. Cuénteselos a su compañero/a para que le dé una solución.

> Modelo: • No tengo mucho espacio en casa.
> • Si no tienes mucho espacio, celébralo en un restaurante.

14 **Resumir** Lea de nuevo el texto de presentación de Eventos Costa Rica y resuma el contenido en dos ideas principales.

• En resumen, esta empresa...
• En definitiva, ...

15 **Diada de Sant Jordi** Lea la nota sobre la Diada de Sant Jordi. En su país, ¿hay alguna celebración como la que se describe? Escriba un pequeño reportaje sobre ella.

MI EXPERIENCIA

16 **Celebraciones favoritas** Pregúntele a su compañero/a cuál es la celebración que más le gusta. ¿Qué valora a la hora de prepararla y celebrarla? ¿Qué condiciones pueden favorecer la celebración? En resumen, ¿qué es lo principal?

GUIÓN DE TRABAJO

¿Cuál es la celebración que más te gusta? ⟶	La celebración que más me gusta es... Las celebraciones que más me gustan son... ⟶	la Navidad las bodas los cumpleaños las fiestas de la empresa San Valentín otras
¿Qué te parece importante para prepararla? ⟶	Es una buena idea... No es mala idea... Si (no) tengo dinero...	

> En resumen...
> En definitiva...

Expresar condiciones posibles

Si puede, llámeme.

18B.4 si + [present], [imperative]

Vocabulario cont.

en resumen *in short*
la cotización *estimate*
ocurrirse *to think of*
el evento, la celebración, la limusina, mágico/a

15
rescatar *to rescue*
matar *to kill*
la espada *sword*
derramarse *to spill*
devorar, la rosa

Estrategia

Resumir ideas principales

• En resumen, si usted quiere sorprender a sus invitados, contáctenos.

■ Sí, en definitiva, somos su mejor opción.

Diada de Sant Jordi

El 23 de abril se celebra el Día del Libro para conmemorar la muerte de Miguel de Cervantes, William Shakespeare e Inca Garcilaso de la Vega. Ese día también se recuerda a San Jorge, patrono de Cataluña. Según la leyenda, un dragón iba a devorar a una princesa, pero San Jorge la rescató y mató al dragón con su espada. Donde se derramó la sangre del dragón, creció un rosal de rosas rojas. Por eso, todos los años, los catalanes intercambian rosas y libros en la **Diada de Sant Jordi** (*Día de San Jorge* en catalán).

SAM: Actividades pp. 390–392

Marián Rico, ¡pura vida!

Marián Rico, florista de Costa Rica

Dígaselo con flores

Marián Rico

¡Vuelva a vernos pronto!

Calle Llorente de Tibás 2, San José

Marián Rico es una joven tica que trabaja como florista en San José. Su país es uno de los grandes exportadores de flores, especialmente a los EE.UU. Hoy vuelve a trabajar después de la cita anual con Iberiada, un evento que durante una semana reúne a floristas de diferentes países de América Latina y de España.

Marián, ¿fue interesante el encuentro?

Sí, fue muy interesante. Este tipo de encuentros nos permite conocer tendencias y volver a ver a compañeros floristas. Es una excelente idea que se organicen estos eventos.

Veo que le gusta su trabajo de florista, ¿le va bien?

¡Pura vida! Me alegro de que mi gran pasión sea mi trabajo.

¿Venden flores solo en San José?

No, no, acá hacemos arreglos florales para entregar en cualquier parte del país. También trabajamos mucho con empresas que organizan todo tipo de eventos y celebraciones.

¿Qué flores se venden más y en qué fechas?

Nuestra flor nacional, la orquídea; también los arreglos de rosas y flores variadas. Depende de la estación; por ejemplo, los claveles o los tulipanes ahora vuelven a venir... Hay muchas ocasiones para regalar flores, pero el día que más flores se venden es el 14 de febrero, Día de San Valentín. También el Día de la Madre (15 de agosto) o en Navidad.

Dicen que las flores hablan...

Sí, las flores tienen un lenguaje propio, muestran nuestros sentimientos de alegría, amor, amistad o incluso tristeza. Si quiere felicitar a una persona o mostrarle su afecto, ¡dígaselo con flores!

Muchas gracias, Marián.

Con gusto. Vuelva a visitarme cuando quiera.

Indicar acciones que se repiten

Las rosas rojas son la mejor opción para **volver a enamorar** a tu pareja.

18B.5 **volver a** + [*infinitive*]

Vocabulario

(17)

¡Pura vida! (*C. R.*) *Great!*

el/la tico/a (*fam.*) *Costa Rican*

el/la exportador(a) *exporter*

el arreglo floral *flower arrangement*

el clavel *carnation*

el tulipán *tulip*

mostrar (o:ue) afecto *to show affection*

Con gusto. *You're welcome.*

el/la florista

(19)

la tarjeta de visita *business card*

---

17 **a. Marián Rico** Mire la foto de Marián Rico. ¿A qué se dedica? ¿Qué está haciendo en la imagen? Lea la entrevista. ¿De qué habla Marián? Ordene los temas según aparecen.

☐ sentimientos que expresan las flores

☐ fechas de mayor venta

☐ flores más vendidas

☐ congreso de Iberiada

☐ lugares donde envían flores

b. Expresión ¿Ha escuchado alguna vez la expresión **¡Pura vida!**? Localícela en el texto. ¿Qué cree que significa?

18 **a. Contestar** ¿Qué piensa Marián sobre las flores? ¿Por qué dice *Dígaselo con flores*?

b. Las ventas ¿Qué flores se venden más y cuándo? Complete la oración.

"Ahora los claveles o los tulipanes ...."

c. Volver a... Busque en el texto la estructura **volver a**... ¿Qué significa?

○ siempre   ○ otra vez   ○ nunca más

19 **a. Tarjeta de visita** ¿A quién va dirigida la frase *Vuelva a vernos pronto* de la tarjeta de visita de la tienda? ¿Qué mensaje transmite?

b. Indicar acciones que se repiten ¿Qué quiere volver a hacer usted pronto? ¿Y su compañero/a?

20 **a. Flores nacionales** Lea este texto. ¿Por qué los países eligen una "flor nacional"? ¿Cuáles son algunos de los motivos por los que se elige una flor en particular?

Los países tienen diferentes símbolos que representan su identidad: banderas, escudos, himnos, etc. Muchos países de América Latina también tienen una "flor nacional".

La orquídea guaria morada es la flor nacional y la más cultivada de Costa Rica. Los indios y los primeros colonizadores la apreciaban, y a las mujeres indígenas les gustaba adornarse la cabeza con sus grandes flores moradas.

La flor que actualmente representa a la República Dominicana es la rosa de Bayahibe, pero no siempre fue así. En 1957, el estado dominicano eligió la caoba como flor y árbol nacional. Sin embargo, muchos dominicanos no estaban de acuerdo con esa decisión. Por eso, en 2011 se estableció que la rosa de Bayahibe sería la flor nacional.

Argentina y Uruguay tienen la misma flor nacional: el ceibo. En el caso de Argentina, la decisión se tomó en el año 1942 después de una serie de encuestas entre los habitantes. Debido a la diversidad de climas y relieves, era imposible encontrar una flor que se pudiera cultivar en todo el territorio. Los uruguayos, en cambio, optaron por esa flor debido a que crece naturalmente en todos sus departamentos.

b. La flor oficial Hable con sus compañeros sobre la flor de su estado o región. Si ya hay una flor, ¿está usted de acuerdo con la elección? Si no, ¿qué opción propondría?

21 **Mi flor preferida** Elija la flor que más le gusta y descríbala. Exprese los sentimientos que le produce. ¿Le gusta regalarlas o que se las regalen? ¿En qué ocasiones?

Mi flor preferida es...

22 **Lenguaje de las flores** ¿Ha oído hablar del "lenguaje de las flores"? Lea el texto. ¿Qué flor le parece más apropiada para regalar a una madre? ¿Y a su pareja? ¿Por qué?

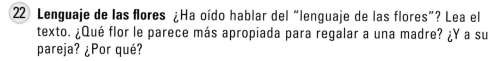

Las flores tienen un lenguaje propio. Cada tipo de flor tiene un significado y su color puede expresar diferentes sentimientos. Por ejemplo, las margaritas blancas representan la inocencia y la pureza. Las amarillas, en cambio, son una sutil declaración de amor. En el caso de las rosas, el color rosado claro simboliza admiración y simpatía, mientras que el amarillo indica alegría y agradecimiento.

Vocabulario

20

el escudo *coat of arms*
el himno *anthem*
el/la colonizador(a) *colonizer*
apreciar *to appreciate*
adornar(se) *to decorate*
la caoba *mahogany tree*
el ceibo *coral tree*
la encuesta *survey*
el relieve *terrain*
la identidad, optar

22

expresar un sentimiento *to express a feeling*
la margarita *daisy*
la pureza *purity*
sutil *subtle*
la declaración de amor *declaration of love*
rosado/a *pink*
la simpatía *affection*
la inocencia, simbolizar

O P I N I Ó N

¿Compra habitualmente flores? ¿Por qué?

Si regala flores, ¿en qué ocasiones lo hace?

SAM: Actividades pp. 393–398

23 **a. Costumbres del Año Nuevo** El Año Nuevo se celebra con costumbres diferentes según las culturas. Fíjese en las fotos. ¿Qué elementos le llaman la atención? ¿Qué pueden representar? Lea el texto y compruebe sus predicciones.

Para cenar, los venezolanos hacen **hallacas**, que son pasteles de maíz rellenos. Muchos latinoamericanos comen carne de cerdo° para tener abundancia durante el nuevo año. En Argentina quedan muchas tradiciones europeas; por eso, a pesar del calor, comen nueces°, turrones° y platos más propios de invierno. En Chile comen lentejas.

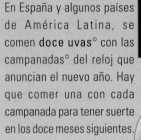

En España y algunos países de América Latina, se comen **doce uvas**° con las campanadas° del reloj que anuncian el nuevo año. Hay que comer una con cada campanada para tener suerte en los doce meses siguientes.

¡FELIZ AÑO NUEVO!

En Costa Rica, encontrar en Año Nuevo una pequeña **flor silvestre**° llamada Santa Lucía, significa suerte. Si se mete en el billetero°, no faltará dinero.

En Ecuador, Colombia, México, Venezuela, Argentina y otros países de América Latina, para recibir el Año Nuevo se quema° el "**Año Viejo**" (un muñeco de cartón°, telas…).

carne de cerdo *pork* **nueces** *walnuts* **turrones** *nougat candy* **flor silvestre** *wildflower*
billetero *wallet* **uvas** *grapes* **campanadas** *peals of a bell* **se quema** *is burned*
muñeco de cartón *cardboard dummy*

b. El Año Nuevo ¿Cómo se celebra el Año Nuevo en su cultura? ¿Existe algún ritual? ¿Hay una comida típica o tradición especial? Piense en otras celebraciones importantes y comparta con la clase.

TAREA FINAL

Organizar una celebración

Piensen en ocasiones (día del español, fin de curso, graduación, cumpleaños del/de la profesor(a)…) para organizar una celebración y hagan una lista.

Decidan entre todas las propuestas cuál van a celebrar.

Evalúen ideas de organización (*es una buena idea que cada pareja se ocupe de...*) y repartan tareas. Señalen condiciones para la realización de las tareas.

Si necesitan una tarjeta de felicitación, háganla.

Si ya tienen todo organizado, ¡celebren su fiesta!

YO PUEDO...

- Puedo expresar sentimientos.

  Diga qué le da pena y de qué se alegra en estos momentos: ¿Cuándo se pone más contento/a, al empezar o al terminar un proyecto?

- Puedo felicitar.

  Hoy es el Día del Estudiante de Español. Felicite a su compañero/a.

- Puedo evaluar ideas.

  Piense en alguna de las ideas que ha escuchado referidas a la celebración de eventos y evalúela.

- Puedo expresar condiciones posibles.

  Complete la oración.
  Si quieres aprender español, ...

- Puedo indicar acciones que se repiten.

  Describa dos cosas que hace todos los años en septiembre o en diciembre.

GRAMÁTICA FUNCIONAL 🅢 Tutorials

Express feelings

alegrarse de/dar pena + **que** + [*subjunctive*] 5.7.1, 5.21.1d, 6.4
ponerse triste 5.7.3, 6.4
cuando/si + [*indicative*]/**al** + [*infinitive*] 5.13, 12.13

- Use **alegrarse de** + **que** + [*subjunctive*] to express what makes someone happy. **Alegrarse** is a reflexive verb.

  Nos alegramos de que hayas venido.
  We are happy that you came.

  Se alegra de que puedas venir a visitarlo.
  He is glad you can come to visit him.

- Use [*indirect object pronoun*] + **da pena que** + [*subjunctive*] to express sadness.

  Nos da pena que te vayas.
  It saddens us that you are leaving.

  Le da pena que no puedas venir a visitarlo.
  He is sad you can't come to visit him.

- Use the subjunctive with these two constructions when the two verbs in a sentence refer to different people. As you have seen in previous lessons, if both verbs refer to the same person, use an infinitive after **alegrarse de** or **dar pena**.

  Me alegro de estar aquí.
  I am happy to be here.

  Me da pena no poder ir.
  I'm sad I can't go.

- Use the reflexive verb **ponerse** (*to become*) with an adjective (**triste, alegre**) to express a change in a subject's mood that is usually considered to be temporary.

  Me puse muy triste cuando recibí la noticia.
  I became very sad when I got the news.

  Mi abuela **se pone alegre** cuando vamos a visitarla.
  *My grandmother is **happy** when we go visit her.*

- Use **al** + [*infinitive*] to refer to a specific moment when something happens or happened.

  Mi perro se pone muy contento **al verme.**
  *My dog becomes happy **upon seeing** me **(when/if he sees** me).*

- Express a similar idea with **cuando/si** + [*indicative*].

  Mi perro se pone muy contento **cuando** me **ve.**
  *My dog becomes happy **when** he **sees** me.*

  Se pone muy triste **si** me **voy.**
  *He gets very sad **if** I **leave.***

¡Póngalo en práctica!

G1 **Completar** Complete las oraciones.

1. Dafne .... (alegrarse) de que su abuela .... (sentirse) mejor.

2. A Alejandro .... (dar pena) que no .... (poder, nosotros) ir a su fiesta de jubilación.

3. Mis primos siempre .... (ponerse contento) cuando .... (ir, nosotros) a la casa de sus padres para cenar.

4. Anoche .... (ponerse, tú) triste al .... (oír) la canción que te hizo pensar en tu ex novio.

G2 **Conversaciones** Complete las conversaciones.

- ¿Te alegras de que nos (1)..................... (ver) pronto?

- Sí, ayer me puse muy contento cuando mi madre me (2)..................... (decir) que vendrías a la boda.

- ¿No os da pena que (3)..................... (terminar) el verano?

- Sí, yo me pongo triste al (4)..................... (pensar) que pronto vendrá el otoño.

- Me alegro de que (5)..................... (poder) venir a la fiesta.

- ¡Muchas gracias por habernos invitado! Lo pasamos muy bien y nos da pena (6)..................... que irnos temprano.

- Al (7)..................... (llegar) al apartamento, me puse contenta porque la cena estaba preparada.

- Me alegro de que (8)..................... (llevarse) bien con tu compañera de cuarto. ¡Qué simpática que es!

G3 **Oraciones completas** Empareje el comienzo de la oración con el final apropiado.

1. Siempre me pongo muy contento	
2. Candela se puso un poco triste	
3. Verónica y Paula se alegran de que	
4. Me da pena que	
5. Mis compañeros de piso se pusieron muy contentos	

a. al terminar la novela porque le había gustado mucho.

b. cuando hablo con un viejo amigo.

c. no me hayan invitado a la fiesta.

d. a su jefa le haya gustado su propuesta.

e. cuando vieron que había limpiado la cocina.

18B.2 Offer congratulations and best wishes

felicidades, enhorabuena, feliz + [*noun*],
que + [*subjunctive*]   5.21.1, 14.26

- Say **felicidades**, **felicitaciones**, or **enhorabuena** to congratulate someone. All three expressions can mean *congratulations*, but **felicitaciones** is used more frequently in Latin America and **enhorabuena** is more common in Spain.

    ¡**Felicitaciones** por tu graduación!
    Congratulations on your graduation!

    ¡**Enhorabuena** por el premio!
    Congratulations on the prize!

- **Felicitaciones** and **enhorabuena** are more often used to congratulate someone on a more significant, unique accomplishment, while the more general **felicidades** can be used to mean *congratulations, happy birthday,* and *happy holidays.*

- Use the construction **feliz** + [*noun*] for well-wishes, as in ¡**Feliz cumpleaños!** (*Happy birthday!*) and ¡**Feliz Día de la Madre!** (*Happy Mother's Day!*). Use **felices** with plural nouns.

    ¡**Feliz Año Nuevo!**   ¡**Felices fiestas!**
    Happy New Year!   *Happy holidays!*

- Say **igualmente** (*likewise; the same to you*) to return the greeting.

    Gracias, **igualmente**. ¡**Felices fiestas!**
    *Thanks, **the same to you. Happy holidays!***

- Use the subjunctive in set phrases that take **que** + [*subjunctive*].

    ¡**Que** lo **pasen** bien!   ¡**Que vuelvan** pronto!
    Have a good time!   ***Come back** soon!*

18B.3 Evaluate ideas

(no) es (una) buena idea + [*infinitive*] / **que** + [*subjunctive*]
5.8.9, 5.13, 5.21.5

- Use **(no) es (una) buena idea** + [*infinitive*] / **que** + [*subjunctive*] to assess an idea. Use the infinitive to assess an idea in general terms or **que** + [*subjunctive*] when there is a specified subject. Note that other adjectives can be substituted for **buena**.

    Es buena idea celebrar los cumpleaños infantiles en un parque.
    It is a good idea to celebrate children's birthdays at a park.

    No **es una buena idea** que siempre **llegues** tarde al trabajo.
    *It's not a good idea for you **to** always **arrive** late to work.*

- As in English, use the negative question in order to ask another person to confirm your idea.

    ¿**No es una excelente idea que pasemos** la Nochevieja en Buenos Aires?
    Isn't it an excellent idea for us to spend New Year's Eve in Buenos Aires?

¡Póngalo en práctica!

G4 **Diálogos** Complete los diálogos.

- ¡(1).. Navidad!
- Gracias, (2)............................; y si no nos vemos en los próximos días, ¡Feliz Año Nuevo!

- Empiezo un nuevo trabajo mañana.
- ¡(3).. ! ¡Te deseo mucha suerte!

- ¡(4).. cumpleaños!
  ¡(5).. cumplas muchos más!
- ¡Muchas gracias!

- Hoy es nuestro aniversario.
- ¡(6).. !

- ¡(7).. Día de San Valentín!
- Gracias, (8)..

G5 **Emparejar** Empareje las dos partes de estas conversaciones.

- 1. ¡Feliz Año Nuevo! ....
- 2. Mañana celebro mi jubilación. ....
- 3. ¡Feliz cumpleaños! ....
- 4. La semana que viene mi esposa y yo celebramos nuestras bodas de plata. ....
- 5. El viernes salimos para la costa. ....

- a. ¡Felicitaciones! Sé que usted trabajó muchos años en la empresa.
- b. ¡Felicidades!
- c. ¡Que lo pasen muy bien!
- d. ¡Igualmente!
- e. Muchas gracias. ¿Te puedes creer que ya cumplo veinte años?

G6 **¿Te parece una buena idea?** Complete las oraciones.

- ¿Qué opinas? ¿No es una buena idea (1)..................... (hacer) una fiesta y (2)..................... (celebrar) juntos nuestros cumpleaños?

- No, es mejor idea que cada uno (3)..................... (hacer) su propia fiesta y así nos divertimos dos días.

- ¿Es buena idea que (4)..................... (nosotros, salir) temprano para la playa mañana?

- Creo que sí, pero no es buena idea (5)..................... (salir) muy tarde.

- ¿No es buena idea que (6)..................... (nosotros, organizar) una fiesta de Año Nuevo?

- No sé, es mucho trabajo planificar una fiesta de ese tipo. En mi opinión, es mejor idea (7)..................... (ir) con todos nuestros amigos a la plaza y (8)..................... (celebrar) juntos.

 Practice more at **vhlcentral.com**.

GRAMÁTICA FUNCIONAL

18B.4 **Express possible conditions**

si + [*present indicative*], [*imperative*]   5.18.1, 12.9

- Use the construction **si** + [*present indicative*], [*imperative*] to make a suggestion or give a command with a condition.

  > Si me **quieres** localizar la semana que viene, **llámame** al celular porque estaré de viaje.
  > *If you want to reach me next week, call me on my cell phone because I will be on a trip.*

- If the sentence starts with **si** + [*verb*], use a comma after the verb. If the **si** clause comes at the end of the sentence, you don't need a comma.

  > Si me necesitas, llámame.
  > *If you need me, call me.*

  > Llámame si me necesitas.
  > *Call me if you need me.*

- Remember to use the correct imperative form (**tú**, **usted**, **vosotros/as**, or **ustedes**) for the person or group you are addressing.

  > Si quieren viajar a Buenos Aires para Año Nuevo, **hagan** la reserva ya.
  > *If you want to travel to Buenos Aires for New Year's, make your reservations now.*

  > No **invitéis** a mucha gente si no queréis molestar a los vecinos.
  > *Don't invite a lot of people if you don't want to bother the neighbors.*

- Remember that indirect object, direct object, and reflexive pronouns may also be used with command forms. You learned how to use direct object pronouns with either indirect object pronouns or reflexive pronouns in **16B.2**.

  > Si **vienes** a mi boda, **confírmamelo** con antelación.
  > *If you are coming to my wedding, let me know (it) in advance.*

  > Si van a armar una fiesta sorpresa, **no se lo digan** a Eduardo.
  > *If you're going to throw a surprise party, don't tell Eduardo.*

- You have already learned other constructions with **si** clauses. In **8A.3**, you learned to propose plans with **si** + [*present indicative*], [*present indicative*].

  > Si **quieres**, **podemos** ir al cine más tarde.
  > *If you want, we can go to the movies later.*

- In **14A.5**, you learned to express a possible situation in the present or the future with the construction **si** + [*present*], [*present/simple future*].

  > Si **estudias** español, **tendrás** muchas oportunidades laborales.
  > *If you study Spanish, you will have many job opportunities.*

G7 **Condiciones** Complete las oraciones.

Si (1)............................. (vosotros, ir) a la fiesta de cumpleaños del hijo de Ana y Pedro, (2)............................. (a nosotros, decir, lo) para que vayamos juntos.

Sr. Montejo, si (3)........................... (haber) reunión el jueves, por favor, (4)..................................... (mandar a mí) un mensaje.

Si (5)............................. (ustedes, pensar) salir hasta tarde, (6).. (llamar a mí).

Si te (7).............................. (gustar) el vestido, (8)........................... (comprarlo).

G8 **Si sales, ven a mi casa** Complete las oraciones con el imperativo.

1. Si tienes tiempo después de clase, ... (llamar a mí).

2. Si terminas el arreglo floral en una hora, ... (llevar, lo) a la iglesia.

3. Si usted consigue pasajes a un buen precio, ... (pasar) el Año Nuevo en Barcelona.

4. Si ustedes terminan su tarea a tiempo, ... (salir) con sus amigos.

5. Si no llueve, ... (celebrar) vuestra graduación con un evento al aire libre.

6. Si usted va a la casa de sus abuelos en Navidad, ... (saludar, ellos) de mi parte.

G9 **Si...** Empareje el comienzo de cada oración con el final apropiado.

1. Si conocen una buena panadería para conseguir un pastel de cumpleaños,	
2. Si se te ocurren más ideas para la despedida de soltera de Isabel,	
3. Si decidís pasar las fiestas en la costa,	
4. Si ves a Matías,	
5. Si no le gusta el arreglo floral,	

a. llámame porque me estoy ocupando de los detalles.

b. dile que la fiesta de 15 años de su prima es el próximo sábado.

c. llámenos enseguida y se lo podemos cambiar.

d. por favor, denme la dirección.

e. llamadnos, así nos vemos.

 Practice more at vhlcentral.com.

GRAMÁTICA FUNCIONAL

volver a + [*infinitive*] 5.15

- Use the construction **volver a** + [*infinitive*] to express the repetition of an action.

> Siempre es bonito **volver a ver** a los amigos de la infancia.
> *It is always nice **to see** childhood friends **again**.*

- The verb **volver** can be used in different tenses in this construction.

> ¿Cuándo **volverás a ofrecer** el curso de español?
> *When **will you offer** the Spanish course **again**?*

- Other constructions that express repeated actions include **otra vez**, **de nuevo**, **nuevamente**, and **una vez más**.

> ¡Qué alegría verte **de nuevo**!
> *It's so great to see you **again**!*

¡Póngalo en práctica!

G10 **Acciones que se repiten** Complete las oraciones.

- ¿Cómo puedo volver a (1)....................... (ver) a tu compañera de cuarto?

- Un día, cuando (2)....................... (nosotras, volver) a salir juntas, te aviso.

Ayer (3)....................... (yo, volver) a escuchar un CD de mi grupo preferido.

Ezequiel siempre (4)....................... (volver) a contar los mismos chistes.

¡Cuidado! No quiero que (5)....................... (tú, volver) a caerte.

(6)....................... (Yo, volver) a pensar en mi infancia cuando oigo esa canción.

 Practice more at **vhlcentral.com**.

S Í N T E S I S

Mire las fotografías y escriba un diálogo o párrafo corto para cada una, usando el vocabulario indicado.

1.

| pastel | cumplir | felicidades | alegrarse de |

- _____
- _____
- _____
- _____

2.

| feliz | acordarse | florista | simbolizar |

- _____
- _____
- _____
- _____

3.

| aniversario | volver a | cuando | si |

- _____
- _____
- _____
- _____

VOCABULARIO 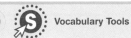 Vocabulary Tools

Acontecimientos de la vida

el Año Nuevo	New Year
las bodas de plata	silver wedding anniversary
el Día de la Madre	Mother's Day
la fiesta de quince años	fifteenth birthday party
la graduación	graduation
la jubilación	retirement
acordarse (o:ue) de	to remember
cumplir años	to have one's birthday
cumplir años de casados	to have one's wedding anniversary
dar pena	to sadden
marcharse	to go away
ponerse contento/a	to become happy
ponerse triste	to become sad

Celebraciones a la carta

en definitiva	all in all
en resumen	in short
la celebración	celebration
la cotización	estimate
la despedida de soltero/a	bachelor(ette) party
la espada	sword
el evento	event
el/la invitado/a	guest
la limusina	limousine
el/la maestro/a de ceremonias	master of ceremonies
el pastel	cake
la rosa	rose
el salón de fiestas	function hall
derramarse	to spill
devorar	to devour
disponer de	to have (at one's disposal)
matar	to kill
ocuparse de los detalles	to take care of the details
ocurrirse	to think of
planificar	to plan
rescatar	to rescue
mágico/a	magic

Marián Rico

Con gusto.	You're welcome.
¡Pura vida! (C.R.)	Great!
el arreglo floral	flower arrangement
la caoba	mahogany tree
el ceibo	coral tree
el clavel	carnation
el/la colonizador(a)	colonizer
la declaración de amor	declaration of love
la encuesta	survey
el escudo	coat of arms
el/la exportador(a)	exporter
el/la florista	florist
el himno	anthem
la identidad	identity
la inocencia	innocence
la margarita	daisy
la pureza	purity
el relieve	terrain
la simpatía	affection
la tarjeta de visita	business card
el/la tico/a (fam.)	Costa Rican
el tulipán	tulip
adornar(se)	to decorate
apreciar	to appreciate
expresar un sentimiento	to express a feeling
mostrar (o:ue) afecto	to show affection
optar	to opt
simbolizar	to symbolize
rosado/a	pink
sutil	subtle

Variación léxica

el billetero ⟷ la billetera ⟷ la cartera

la cotización ⟷ el presupuesto

dar pena ⟷ apenar

ponerse triste ⟷ entristecerse (zc)

el/la tico/a (fam.) ⟷ el/la costarricense

Estrategias

1 Expresar consecuencia
Lección 17A

Expressions that show consequence, such as **así (es) que** (*so*) or **por lo tanto** (*therefore*), help you bring ideas together and express a natural conclusion to an intervention.

○ Termine estas oraciones con una consecuencia.

"En el futuro, todos los profesionales podrán trabajar desde casa, ...
...."

"Es muy probable que los robots hagan el trabajo de muchas personas, ...
...."

"Está claro que el idioma español se habla cada día más, ...
...."

2 Reforzar una negación
Lección 17B

Unlike in English, multiple negative words can, and should, be used together in Spanish to reinforce the negation (**no... nada**). Using negative expressions correctly will help you express yourself with greater fluency.

○ Refuerce la negación de estas oraciones, así como lo haría un hispanohablante. Piense en otras situaciones y emplee este recurso.

| A los niños no les gusta que les prohíban ver la tele. | .... |
| No les divierte ver las películas de mayores. | .... |

3 Intensificar
Lección 18A

Spanish uses repeated words in order to add intensity and subjectiveness to speech.

○ Piense que ha realizado estas acciones y reformule las frases añadiendo intensidad a la acción.

caminar 20 horas	hacer frío durante todo el invierno	escribir cien páginas cada día
....	....	....
....	....	....

4 Resumir ideas principales
Lección 18B

In a conversation, it can be helpful to sum up the main ideas and call attention to the most important concepts. To do so, use expressions such as **en resumen** (*in short*) or **en definitiva** (*all in all*). Sometimes what follows is not just a summary, but also a personal conclusion or assessment.

○ Resuma lo que dice esta persona.

| El sábado es la boda de Juan y Ana, pero ese día tengo otra fiesta, no tengo mucha relación con ellos y... | .... |

Competencias

HACER PREDICCIONES, EXPRESAR PROBABILIDAD, EXPRESAR CONTINUIDAD

1 **Predicciones** Haga predicciones sobre un futuro cercano. Su compañero/a deberá expresar la probabilidad de que eso suceda.

Modelo: • *Dentro de cinco años habrá una moneda única en todo el mundo.*
• *Me parece poco probable que sea así. Es seguro que seguirá habiendo...*

EXPRESAR ACCIONES RECÍPROCAS

2 **Fotos** Describa las acciones que muestran las fotos. Use **nos, os** o **se**.

(Daniel y Virginia / besarse)   (Andrea y yo / abrazarse)   (vosotros / saludarse)

REACCIONAR DE FORMA NEGATIVA, EXPRESAR SENTIMIENTOS

3 **Comentarios** Alicia ha estado muy ocupada últimamente y no ha tenido tiempo para sus familiares y amigos. Complete los comentarios de algunos de ellos.

1. Me molesta que no .... (darse cuenta) de que me corté el pelo.

2. Me entristece que no .... (acordarse) de mi cumpleaños.

3. Me decepciona que .... (olvidarse) de ir a nuestra clase de baile.

IDENTIFICAR, EXPRESAR ADMIRACIÓN, RELACIONAR ACONTECIMIENTOS, HABLAR DE RETOS FUTUROS, FELICITAR

4 **Completar** Complete esta conversación con la forma correcta de los verbos.

VICENTE: ¿Sabes lo que me (1)................ (decir) mi nieto? Que cuando (2)................ (ser) mayor, (3)................ (ser) un aventurero como Iván Vallejo.

CAMILA: ¿Cómo quién?

VICENTE: Iván Vallejo. Es un montañista ecuatoriano al que (4)................ (admirar) mucho.

CAMILA: ¿Y por qué?

VICENTE: Porque (5)................ (estar) impresionado con sus logros. La verdad, ¡(6)................ (ser) increíble que (7)................ (escalar) tantas montañas!

CAMILA: Ya veo. ¿Y cuándo te lo (8)................ (decir)?

VICENTE: Ayer, después de (9)................ (ver) un documental sobre la vida del deportista.

CAMILA: ¡Felicitaciones! (10)................ (Tener) un nieto muy decidido.

Video

Palacios del arte

Ya ha visto que la vida está llena de ocasiones para celebrar: triunfos en el deporte, logros en el trabajo, eventos familiares, un nuevo año o simplemente el amor y la amistad. Este episodio de **Flash Cultura** prueba que el arte imita a la vida y muestra cómo lo hace grandiosamente en los famosos museos del Triángulo Dorado de Madrid.

1 **El arte** ¿Prefiere el arte antiguo o el moderno? ¿Cree que el arte es aburrido mientras que el espectáculo es divertido? ¿Admira a algún artista? ¿Opina que las tendencias, en el arte como en la moda, vuelven a repetirse?

2 **Mirar** Mire el episodio de **Flash Cultura**. ¿Qué generalizaciones puede hacer sobre el tema? ¿Qué idea o reflexión se le ocurre? ¿Cuál es su opinión?

Los grises, los negros dan una sensación de horror...

Vocabulario útil

alargado/a *elongated*
alucinante *amazing*
ceder *to hand over*
el lienzo *canvas*
la muestra *exhibition*
la planta *floor (of a building)*
polémico/a *controversial*
el primer plano *foreground*
el tamaño *size*

Otra corta caminata y llegamos al Museo Thyssen. Las pinturas de este museo provienen de una extraordinaria colección privada...

3 **Palacios del arte** Complete estas oraciones con la opción correcta.

1. El Paseo del Prado es una
   a. plaza.   b. calle.   c. galería.
2. Uno de los pintores españoles más famosos es
   a. Diego de la Vega.   b. Darío Blasco.   c. Diego Velázquez.
3. De la modelo del cuadro *La maja vestida* de Goya se desconoce
   a. la nacionalidad.   b. la edad.   c. la identidad.
4. El Museo Reina Sofía fue construido como
   a. hospital.   b. palacio.   c. hotel.
5. El *Guernica* de Picasso es un cuadro muy
   a. antiguo.   b. grande.   c. colorido.

Estrategia

Using the verb *dar*

Dar is one of the most versatile verbs in Spanish and it is used in a number of expressions, such as **darse cuenta** (*to realize*) or **dar por sentado** (*to take for granted*). One of the meanings of **dar** is *to cause* or *produce*: **me da asco** (*it makes me sick*), **me da miedo** (*it scares me*). There are hundreds of feelings you can express in Spanish with **dar**. Try it with **envidia, rabia, confianza, frío, vergüenza, alegría.**

4 **Conversar** Con un(a) compañero/a, converse sobre las tres cosas/lugares/personas que más admira. Comente por qué son importantes para usted.

Modelo: • *Una persona a la que admiro mucho es... /Antes de morirme quiero ver el cuadro de...*
   • *Es increíble cómo puede... Me alegro de que vuelva a...*

 Practice more at **vhlcentral.com**.

Apéndice

Verb Conjugation Tables

This list includes the infinitive of verbs introduced as active vocabulary in **PROTAGONISTAS**, as well as other common verbs. Each verb is followed by a model verb conjugated in the same pattern. The number in parentheses indicates where in the verb tables, pages **A4–A11**, you can find the conjugated forms of the model verb. Many of these verbs can be used reflexively. To check the verb conjugation, use the tables on pages **A4–A11**. For placement of reflexive pronouns, see page **A12**.

abandonar like hablar (1)
abonar like hablar (1)
abrazarse like cruzar (37)
abrigarse like llegar (41)
abrir like vivir (3) *except* **p. p.** is abierto
abrocharse like hablar (1)
aburrirse like vivir (3)
acariciar like hablar (1)
aceptar like hablar (1)
acompañar like hablar (1)
aconsejar like hablar (1)
acordarse (o:ue) like contar (24)
acostarse (o:ue) like contar (24)
actualizar like cruzar (37)
actuar like graduar (40)
adaptar like hablar (1)
adivinar like hablar (1)
admirar like hablar (1)
adoptar like hablar (1)
adornar like hablar (1)
afectar like hablar (1)
afiliarse like hablar (1)
afirmar like hablar (1)
agarrar like hablar (1)
agrupar like hablar (1)
ahorrar like hablar (1)
albergar like llegar (41)
alegrarse like hablar (1)
almorzar (o:ue) like contar (24) *except* **(z:c)** before **e**
alojarse like hablar (1)
amargar like llegar (41)
ampliar like hablar (1)
añadir like vivir (3)
anotar like hablar (1)
anticipar like hablar (1)
anunciar like hablar (1)
apagar like llegar (41)
apelar like hablar (1)
aportar like hablar (1)
apoyar like hablar (1)
apreciar like hablar (1)
aprender like comer (2)
aprobar (o:ue) like contar (24)
aprovechar like hablar (1)
apuntarse like hablar (1)
arreglar like hablar (1)
ascender (e:ie) like entender (27)
asesorar like hablar (1)
asistir like vivir (3)
asumir like vivir (3)
asustar like hablar (1)
atender (e:ie) like entender (27)
atrapar like hablar (1)

atreverse like comer (2)
averiarse like enviar (39)
averiguar like hablar (1) *except* **(u:ü)** before **e**
ayudar like hablar (1)
bailar like hablar (1)
bajar like hablar (1)
bañarse like hablar (1)
batir like vivir (3)
beber like comer (2)
besar like hablar (1)
buscar like tocar (43)
calcular like hablar (1)
cambiar like hablar (1)
caminar like hablar (1)
cansarse like hablar (1)
cantar like hablar (1)
cargar like llegar (41)
casarse like hablar (1)
celebrar like hablar (1)
cenar like hablar (1)
cerrar (e:ie) like pensar (30)
charlar like hablar (1)
chatear like hablar (1)
chocar like tocar (43)
clasificar like tocar (43)
clavar like hablar (1)
cocinar like hablar (1)
colaborar like hablar (1)
coleccionar like hablar (1)
colocar like tocar (43)
comentar like hablar (1)
comenzar (e:ie) like empezar (26)
comer (2)
compaginar like hablar (1)
comparar like hablar (1)
compartir like vivir (3)
competir (e:i) like pedir (29)
completar like hablar (1)
componer like poner (15)
comprar like hablar (1)
comprender like comer (2)
comprobar (o:ue) like contar (24)
conciliar like hablar (1)
condicionar like hablar (1)
conducir (zc) (6)
confirmar like hablar (1)
confundirse like vivir (3)
conjugar like llegar (41)
conmemorar like hablar (1)
conocer (zc) (35)
conquistar like hablar (1)
conseguir (e:i) like seguir (32)
conservar like hablar (1)
construir (y) like destruir (38)
consumir like vivir (3)

contar (o:ue) (24)
contestar like hablar (1)
controlar like hablar (1)
convencer (z) like vencer (44)
convenir like venir (22)
convertir (e:ie) like sentir (33)
convivir like vivir (3)
correr like comer (2)
costar (o:ue) like contar (24)
crecer (zc) like conocer (35)
creer (36)
criticar like tocar (43)
cruzar (37)
cuidar like hablar (1)
cultivar like hablar (1)
cumplir like vivir (3)
cursar like hablar (1)
dar (7)
decepcionar like hablar (1)
decidir like vivir (3)
decir (8)
declarar like hablar (1)
dedicar like tocar (43)
defender (e:ie) like entender (27)
dejar like hablar (1)
demostrar (o:ue) like contar (24)
denominarse like hablar (1)
denunciar like hablar (1)
depender like comer (2)
derramar like hablar (1)
derribar like hablar (1)
desaparecer (zc) like conocer (35)
desarrollar like hablar (1)
desayunar like hablar (1)
descansar like hablar (1)
descender (e:ie) like entender (27)
desconectarse like hablar (1)
describir like vivir (3)
descubrir like vivir (3) *except* **p. p.** is **descubierto**
desear like hablar (1)
deslizar like cruzar (37)
desperdiciar like hablar (1)
despertar (e:ie) like pensar (30)
despertarse (e:ie) like pensar (30)
devolver (o:ue) like volver (34)
devorar like hablar (1)
dibujar like hablar (1)
diferenciarse like hablar (1)
dirigir (j) like proteger (42)
discutir like vivir (3)
diseñar like hablar (1)
disfrutar like hablar (1)

divertirse (e:ie) like sentir (33)
divorciarse like hablar (1)
doler (o:ue) like volver (34)
dominar like hablar (1)
dormir (o:ue) (25)
ducharse like hablar (1)
dudar like hablar (1)
echar like hablar (1)
editar like hablar (1)
educar like tocar (43)
egresar like hablar (1)
elaborar like hablar (1)
elegir (j) (e:i) like pedir (29) *except* **(g:j)** before **a** and **o**
eliminar like hablar (1)
emitir like vivir (3)
empezar (e:ie) (26)
enamorarse like hablar (1)
encantar like hablar (1)
encender (e:ie) like entender (27)
encontrar (o:ue) like contar (24)
encontrarse (o:ue) like contar (24)
endulzar like cruzar (37)
enfadarse like hablar (1)
enfrentarse like hablar (1)
enganchar like hablar (1)
enojarse like hablar (1)
enseñar like hablar (1)
entender (e:ie) (27)
enterarse like hablar (1)
entrar like hablar (1)
entretenerse like tener (20)
entristecer (zc) like conocer (35)
enviar (39)
escalar like hablar (1)
escenificar like tocar (43)
escribir like vivir (3) *except* **p. p.** is **escrito**
escuchar like hablar (1)
esperar like hablar (1)
espolvorear like hablar (1)
establecer (zc) like conocer (35)
estar (9)
estimular like hablar (1)
estrenar like hablar (1)
estudiar like hablar (1)
evitar like hablar (1)
exagerar like hablar (1)
exigir (j) like proteger (42)
exiliarse like hablar (1)
explicar like tocar (43)
explorar like hablar (1)
exponer like poner (15)
exportar like hablar (1)

expresar like hablar (1)
expulsar like hablar (1)
extrañar like hablar (1)
fabricar like tocar (43)
faltar like hablar (1)
fascinar like hablar (1)
favorecer (zc) like conocer (35)
fijarse like hablar (1)
financiar like hablar (1)
firmar like hablar (1)
flexibilizar like cruzar (37)
fomentar like hablar (1)
formar like hablar (1)
fortalecer (zc) like conocer (35)
fumar like hablar (1)
funcionar like hablar (1)
ganar like hablar (1)
garantizar like cruzar (37)
girar like hablar (1)
graduarse (40)
guardar like hablar (1)
gustar like hablar (1)
haber (10)
habilitar like hablar (1)
hablar (1)
hacer (11)
heredar like hablar (1)
herir (e:ie) like sentir (33)
imaginar like hablar (1)
impedir (e:i) like pedir (29)
importar like hablar (1)
imprimir like vivir (3) *except*
  p. p. is **impreso** or **imprimido**
inaugurar like hablar (1)
incentivar like hablar (1)
incluir (y) like destruir (38)
incorporar like hablar (1)
independizarse like cruzar (37)
informar like hablar (1)
inscribir like vivir (3)
instalar like hablar (1)
integrarse like hablar (1)
intercambiar like hablar (1)
interesar like hablar (1)
interpretar like hablar (1)
invadir like vivir (3)
invitar like hablar (1)
inyectar like hablar (1)
ir (12)
jugar (u:ue) (28)
lanzar like cruzar (37)
lavar like hablar (1)
leer like creer (36)
levantarse like hablar (1)
liberar like hablar (1)
limitar like hablar (1)
limpiar like hablar (1)
llamar like hablar (1)
llamarse like hablar (1)
llegar (41)
llevar like hablar (1)
llorar like hablar (1)
llover (o:ue) like volver (34)
localizar like cruzar (37)
lograr like hablar (1)

madrugar like llegar (41)
mandar like hablar (1)
manejar like hablar (1)
mantener like tener (20)
maquillarse like hablar (1)
marcar like tocar (43)
marcharse like hablar (1)
matar like hablar (1)
medir (e:i) like pedir (29)
mejorar like hablar (1)
mencionar like hablar (1)
meter like comer (2)
mirar like hablar (1)
molestar like hablar (1)
montar like hablar (1)
morir (o:ue) like dormir (25)
  except **p. p.** is **muerto**
mostrar (o:ue) like contar (24)
mudarse like hablar (1)
nacer (zc) like conocer (35)
nadar like hablar (1)
navegar like llegar (41)
nevar (e:ie) like pensar (30)
nombrar like hablar (1)
observar like hablar (1)
obtener like tener (20)
ocultar like hablar (1)
ocupar like hablar (1)
ocurrir like vivir (3)
ofrecer (zc) like conocer (35)
oír (13)
olvidar like hablar (1)
oponerse like poner (15)
optar like hablar (1)
ordenar like hablar (1)
organizar like cruzar (37)
parar like hablar (1)
parecer (zc) like conocer (35)
participar like hablar (1)
pasar like hablar (1)
pasear like hablar (1)
patentar like hablar (1)
pedir (e:i) (29)
pelar like hablar (1)
pensar (e:ie) (30)
perder (e:ie) like entender (27)
perdonar like hablar (1)
permitir like vivir (3)
pertenecer (zc) like conocer (35)
pintar like hablar (1)
planificar like tocar (43)
plantearse like hablar (1)
poder (o:ue) (14)
poner (15)
posponer like poner (15)
postergar like llegar (41)
postular like hablar (1)
potenciar like hablar (1)
practicar like tocar (43)
preguntar like hablar (1)
preocupar like hablar (1)
preparar like hablar (1)
presentar like hablar (1)
preservar like hablar (1)
prestar like hablar (1)

pretender like comer (2)
probar (o:ue) like contar (24)
procurar like hablar (1)
programar like hablar (1)
pronunciar like hablar (1)
proponer like poner (15)
proteger (j) (42)
protestar like hablar (1)
provenir like venir (22)
quedar like hablar (1)
quemar like hablar (1)
querer (e:ie) (16)
quererse (e:ie) (16)
realizar like cruzar (37)
rechazar like cruzar (37)
recibir like vivir (3)
reciclar like hablar (1)
recoger (j) like proteger (42)
recomendar (e:ie) like pensar (30)
recordar (o:ue) like contar (24)
recorrer like comer (2)
redactar like hablar (1)
reducir (zc) like conducir (6)
redundar like hablar (1)
reencontrar (o:ue) like contar (24)
reformular like hablar (1)
regalar like hablar (1)
regatear like hablar (1)
regresar like hablar (1)
reír (31)
relacionar like hablar (1)
rellenar like hablar (1)
remontar like hablar (1)
rendir (e:i) like pedir (29)
renunciar like hablar (1)
repartir like vivir (3)
repetir (e:i) like pedir (29)
representar like hablar (1)
rescatar like hablar (1)
reservar like hablar (1)
respetar like hablar (1)
respirar like hablar (1)
responder like comer (2)
restaurar like hablar (1)
resumir like vivir (3)
retirar like hablar (1)
reunir like vivir (3) *except* **reú-** in
  the present (all sing. forms and
  3ʳᵈ person pl.)
revisar like hablar (1)
revivir like vivir (3)
rodar (o:ue) like contar (24)
rodear like hablar (1)
romper like comer (2) *except*
  p. p. is **roto**
saber (17)
saborear like hablar (1)
salir (18)
saludar like hablar (1)
salvar like hablar (1)
seguir (g) (e:i) (32)
seleccionar like hablar (1)
señalar like hablar (1)

sensibilizar like cruzar (37)
sentir (e:ie) (33)
separarse like hablar (1)
ser (19)
servir (e:i) like pedir (29)
significar like tocar (43)
simbolizar like cruzar (37)
sintetizar like cruzar (37)
sobreproteger (j) like proteger (42)
sobrevivir like vivir (3)
soler (o:ue) like poder (14)
solicitar like hablar (1)
solidarizarse like cruzar (37)
solucionar like hablar (1)
sonreír like reír (31)
soportar like hablar (1)
sorprender like comer (2)
subir like vivir (3)
subrayar like hablar (1)
suceder like comer (2)
sufrir like vivir (3)
sujetar like hablar (1)
suministrar like hablar (1)
superar like hablar (1)
surgir (j) like proteger (42)
sustituir (y) like destruir (38)
tachar like hablar (1)
tapear like hablar (1)
tener (20)
terminar like hablar (1)
tocar (43)
tomar like hablar (1)
tornarse like hablar (1)
trabajar like hablar (1)
traducir (zc) like conducir (6)
traer (21)
transformar like hablar (1)
transportar like hablar (1)
trasladar like hablar (1)
traspasar like hablar (1)
tratar like hablar (1)
trotar like hablar (1)
tutearse like hablar (1)
usar like hablar (1)
utilizar like cruzar (37)
vacunar like hablar (1)
valer like salir (18) *except*
  -er verb and **tú** imperative is **vale**
validar like hablar (1)
vender like comer (2)
venerar like hablar (1)
venir (22)
ver (23)
vestirse (e:i) like pedir (29)
viajar like hablar (1)
visitar like hablar (1)
vivir (3)
volar (o:ue) like contar (24)
volver (o:ue) (34)
votar like hablar (1)

Verb Conjugation Tables

Regular verbs: simple tenses

1 — hablar
Participles: hablando, hablado

	INDICATIVE					SUBJUNCTIVE		IMPERATIVE
	Present	Imperfect	Preterite	Future	Conditional	Present	Past	
	hablo	hablaba	hablé	hablaré	hablaría	hable	hablara	
	hablas	hablabas	hablaste	hablarás	hablarías	hables	hablaras	habla tú (no hables)
	habla	hablaba	habló	hablará	hablaría	hable	hablara	hable Ud.
	hablamos	hablábamos	hablamos	hablaremos	hablaríamos	hablemos	habláramos	hablemos
	habláis	hablabais	hablasteis	hablaréis	hablaríais	habléis	hablarais	hablad (no habléis)
	hablan	hablaban	hablaron	hablarán	hablarían	hablen	hablaran	hablen Uds.

2 — comer
Participles: comiendo, comido

	INDICATIVE					SUBJUNCTIVE		IMPERATIVE
	Present	Imperfect	Preterite	Future	Conditional	Present	Past	
	como	comía	comí	comeré	comería	coma	comiera	
	comes	comías	comiste	comerás	comerías	comas	comieras	come tú (no comas)
	come	comía	comió	comerá	comería	coma	comiera	coma Ud.
	comemos	comíamos	comimos	comeremos	comeríamos	comamos	comiéramos	comamos
	coméis	comíais	comisteis	comeréis	comeríais	comáis	comierais	comed (no comáis)
	comen	comían	comieron	comerán	comerían	coman	comieran	coman Uds.

3 — vivir
Participles: viviendo, vivido

	INDICATIVE					SUBJUNCTIVE		IMPERATIVE
	Present	Imperfect	Preterite	Future	Conditional	Present	Past	
	vivo	vivía	viví	viviré	viviría	viva	viviera	
	vives	vivías	viviste	vivirás	vivirías	vivas	vivieras	vive tú (no vivas)
	vive	vivía	vivió	vivirá	viviría	viva	viviera	viva Ud.
	vivimos	vivíamos	vivimos	viviremos	viviríamos	vivamos	viviéramos	vivamos
	vivís	vivíais	vivisteis	viviréis	viviríais	viváis	vivierais	vivid (no viváis)
	viven	vivían	vivieron	vivirán	vivirían	vivan	vivieran	vivan Uds.

All verbs: compound tenses

PERFECT TENSES

INDICATIVE

Present Perfect		Past Perfect		Future Perfect		Conditional Perfect	
he	hablado	había	hablado	habré	hablado	habría	hablado
has	comido	habías	comido	habrás	comido	habrías	comido
ha	vivido	había	vivido	habrá	vivido	habría	vivido
hemos		habíamos		habremos		habríamos	
habéis		habíais		habréis		habríais	
han		habían		habrán		habrían	

SUBJUNCTIVE

Present Perfect		Past Perfect	
haya	hablado	hubiera	hablado
hayas	comido	hubiera	comido
haya	vivido	hubiera	vivido
hayamos		hubiéramos	
hayáis		hubierais	
hayan		hubieran	

PROGRESSIVE TENSES

INDICATIVE				SUBJUNCTIVE	
Present Progressive	Past Progressive	Future Progressive	Conditional Progressive	Present Progressive	Past Progressive
estoy	estaba	estaré	estaría	esté	estuviera
estás	estabas	estarás	estarías	estés	estuvieras
está *hablando*	estaba *hablando*	estará *hablando*	estaría *hablando*	esté *hablando*	estuviera *hablando*
estamos *comiendo*	estábamos *comiendo*	estaremos *comiendo*	estaríamos *comiendo*	estemos *comiendo*	estuviéramos *comiendo*
estáis *viviendo*	estabais *viviendo*	estaréis *viviendo*	estaríais *viviendo*	estéis *viviendo*	estuvierais *viviendo*
están	estaban	estarán	estarían	estén	estuvieran

Irregular verbs

Infinitive	INDICATIVE					SUBJUNCTIVE		IMPERATIVE
	Present	Imperfect	Preterite	Future	Conditional	Present	Past	
4 caber	**quepo**	cabía	**cupe**	**cabré**	**cabría**	**quepa**	**cupiera**	
	cabes	cabías	**cupiste**	**cabrás**	**cabrías**	**quepas**	**cupieras**	cabe tú (no **quepas**)
Participles:	cabe	cabía	**cupo**	**cabrá**	**cabría**	**quepa**	**cupiera**	**quepa** Ud.
cabiendo	cabemos	cabíamos	**cupimos**	**cabremos**	**cabríamos**	**quepamos**	**cupiéramos**	**quepamos**
cabido	cabéis	cabíais	**cupisteis**	**cabréis**	**cabríais**	**quepáis**	**cupierais**	cabed (no **quepáis**)
	caben	cabían	**cupieron**	**cabrán**	**cabrían**	**quepan**	**cupieran**	**quepan** Uds.
5 caer	**caigo**	caía	caí	caeré	caería	**caiga**	**cayera**	
	caes	caías	**caíste**	caerás	caerías	**caigas**	**cayeras**	cae tú (no **caigas**)
Participles:	cae	caía	**cayó**	caerá	caería	**caiga**	**cayera**	**caiga** Ud. (no **caiga**)
cayendo	caemos	caíamos	**caímos**	caeremos	caeríamos	**caigamos**	**cayéramos**	**caigamos**
caído	caéis	caíais	**caísteis**	caeréis	caeríais	**caigáis**	**cayerais**	caed (no **caigáis**)
	caen	caían	**cayeron**	caerán	caerían	**caigan**	**cayeran**	**caigan** Uds.
6 conducir (c:zc)	**conduzco**	conducía	**conduje**	conduciré	conduciría	**conduzca**	**condujera**	
	conduces	conducías	**condujiste**	conducirás	conducirías	**conduzcas**	**condujeras**	conduce tú (no **conduzcas**)
Participles:	conduce	conducía	**condujo**	conducirá	conduciría	**conduzca**	**condujera**	**conduzca** Ud. (no **conduzca**)
conduciendo	conducimos	conducíamos	**condujimos**	conduciremos	conduciríamos	**conduzcamos**	**condujéramos**	**conduzcamos**
conducido	conducís	conducíais	**condujisteis**	conduciréis	conduciríais	**conduzcáis**	**condujerais**	conducid (no **conduzcáis**)
	conducen	conducían	**condujeron**	conducirán	conducirían	**conduzcan**	**condujeran**	**conduzcan** Uds.

Infinitive	INDICATIVE					SUBJUNCTIVE		IMPERATIVE
	Present	Imperfect	Preterite	Future	Conditional	Present	Past	
7 dar	doy	daba	di	daré	daría	dé	diera	
Participles:	das	dabas	diste	darás	darías	des	dieras	da tú (no des)
dando	da	daba	dio	dará	daría	dé	diera	dé Ud.
dado	damos	dábamos	dimos	daremos	daríamos	demos	diéramos	demos
	dais	dabais	disteis	daréis	daríais	deis	dierais	dad (no deis)
	dan	daban	dieron	darán	darían	den	dieran	den Uds.
8 decir	digo	decía	dije	diré	diría	diga	dijera	
Participles:	dices	decías	dijiste	dirás	dirías	digas	dijeras	di tú (no digas)
diciendo	dice	decía	dijo	dirá	diría	diga	dijera	diga Ud.
dicho	decimos	decíamos	dijimos	diremos	diríamos	digamos	dijéramos	digamos
	decís	decíais	dijisteis	diréis	diríais	digáis	dijerais	decid (no digáis)
	dicen	decían	dijeron	dirán	dirían	digan	dijeran	digan Uds.
9 estar	estoy	estaba	estuve	estaré	estaría	esté	estuviera	
Participles:	estás	estabas	estuviste	estarás	estarías	estés	estuvieras	está tú (no estés)
estando	está	estaba	estuvo	estará	estaría	esté	estuviera	esté Ud.
estado	estamos	estábamos	estuvimos	estaremos	estaríamos	estemos	estuviéramos	estemos
	estáis	estabais	estuvisteis	estaréis	estaríais	estéis	estuvierais	estad (no estéis)
	están	estaban	estuvieron	estarán	estarían	estén	estuvieran	estén Uds.
10 haber	he	había	hube	habré	habría	haya	hubiera	
Participles:	has	habías	hubiste	habrás	habrías	hayas	hubieras	
habiendo	ha	había	hubo	habrá	habría	haya	hubiera	
habido	hemos	habíamos	hubimos	habremos	habríamos	hayamos	hubiéramos	
	habéis	habíais	hubisteis	habréis	habríais	hayáis	hubierais	
	han	habían	hubieron	habrán	habrían	hayan	hubieran	
11 hacer	hago	hacía	hice	haré	haría	haga	hiciera	
Participles:	haces	hacías	hiciste	harás	harías	hagas	hicieras	haz tú (no hagas)
haciendo	hace	hacía	hizo	hará	haría	haga	hiciera	haga Ud.
hecho	hacemos	hacíamos	hicimos	haremos	haríamos	hagamos	hiciéramos	hagamos
	hacéis	hacíais	hicisteis	haréis	haríais	hagáis	hicierais	haced (no hagáis)
	hacen	hacían	hicieron	harán	harían	hagan	hicieran	hagan Uds.
12 ir	voy	iba	fui	iré	iría	vaya	fuera	
Participles:	vas	ibas	fuiste	irás	irías	vayas	fueras	ve tú (no vayas)
yendo	va	iba	fue	irá	iría	vaya	fuera	vaya Ud.
ido	vamos	íbamos	fuimos	iremos	iríamos	vayamos	fuéramos	vamos (no vayamos)
	vais	ibais	fuisteis	iréis	iríais	vayáis	fuerais	id (no vayáis)
	van	iban	fueron	irán	irían	vayan	fueran	vayan Uds.
13 oír (y)	oigo	oía	oí	oiré	oiría	oiga	oyera	
Participles:	oyes	oías	oíste	oirás	oirías	oigas	oyeras	oye tú (no oigas)
oyendo	oye	oía	oyó	oirá	oiría	oiga	oyera	oiga Ud.
oído	oímos	oíamos	oímos	oiremos	oiríamos	oigamos	oyéramos	oigamos
	oís	oíais	oísteis	oiréis	oiríais	oigáis	oyerais	oíd (no oigáis)
	oyen	oían	oyeron	oirán	oirían	oigan	oyeran	oigan Uds.

INDICATIVE / SUBJUNCTIVE / IMPERATIVE

14 poder (o:ue) — Participles: **pudiendo**, podido

	Present	Imperfect	Preterite	Future	Conditional	Subj. Present	Subj. Past	Imperative
	puedo	podía	**pude**	**podré**	**podría**	**pueda**	**pudiera**	
	puedes	podías	**pudiste**	**podrás**	**podrías**	**puedas**	**pudieras**	**puede** tú (no **puedas**)
	puede	podía	**pudo**	**podrá**	**podría**	**pueda**	**pudiera**	**pueda** Ud.
	podemos	podíamos	**pudimos**	**podremos**	**podríamos**	podamos	**pudiéramos**	podamos
	podéis	podíais	**pudisteis**	**podréis**	**podríais**	podáis	**pudierais**	poded (no podáis)
	pueden	podían	**pudieron**	**podrán**	**podrían**	**puedan**	**pudieran**	**puedan** Uds.

15 poner — Participles: poniendo, **puesto**

	Present	Imperfect	Preterite	Future	Conditional	Subj. Present	Subj. Past	Imperative
	pongo	ponía	**puse**	**pondré**	**pondría**	**ponga**	**pusiera**	
	pones	ponías	**pusiste**	**pondrás**	**pondrías**	**pongas**	**pusieras**	**pon** tú (no **pongas**)
	pone	ponía	**puso**	**pondrá**	**pondría**	**ponga**	**pusiera**	**ponga** Ud.
	ponemos	poníamos	**pusimos**	**pondremos**	**pondríamos**	**pongamos**	**pusiéramos**	**pongamos**
	ponéis	poníais	**pusisteis**	**pondréis**	**pondríais**	**pongáis**	**pusierais**	poned (no **pongáis**)
	ponen	ponían	**pusieron**	**pondrán**	**pondrían**	**pongan**	**pusieran**	**pongan** Uds.

16 querer (e:ie) — Participles: queriendo, querido

	Present	Imperfect	Preterite	Future	Conditional	Subj. Present	Subj. Past	Imperative
	quiero	quería	**quise**	**querré**	**querría**	**quiera**	**quisiera**	
	quieres	querías	**quisiste**	**querrás**	**querrías**	**quieras**	**quisieras**	**quiere** tú (no **quieras**)
	quiere	quería	**quiso**	**querrá**	**querría**	**quiera**	**quisiera**	**quiera** Ud.
	queremos	queríamos	**quisimos**	**querremos**	**querríamos**	queramos	**quisiéramos**	queramos
	queréis	queríais	**quisisteis**	**querréis**	**querríais**	queráis	**quisierais**	quered (no queráis)
	quieren	querían	**quisieron**	**querrán**	**querrían**	**quieran**	**quisieran**	**quieran** Uds.

17 saber — Participles: sabiendo, sabido

	Present	Imperfect	Preterite	Future	Conditional	Subj. Present	Subj. Past	Imperative
	sé	sabía	**supe**	**sabré**	**sabría**	**sepa**	**supiera**	
	sabes	sabías	**supiste**	**sabrás**	**sabrías**	**sepas**	**supieras**	sabe tú (no **sepas**)
	sabe	sabía	**supo**	**sabrá**	**sabría**	**sepa**	**supiera**	**sepa** Ud.
	sabemos	sabíamos	**supimos**	**sabremos**	**sabríamos**	**sepamos**	**supiéramos**	**sepamos**
	sabéis	sabíais	**supisteis**	**sabréis**	**sabríais**	**sepáis**	**supierais**	sabed (no **sepáis**)
	saben	sabían	**supieron**	**sabrán**	**sabrían**	**sepan**	**supieran**	**sepan** Uds.

18 salir — Participles: saliendo, salido

	Present	Imperfect	Preterite	Future	Conditional	Subj. Present	Subj. Past	Imperative
	salgo	salía	salí	**saldré**	**saldría**	**salga**	saliera	
	sales	salías	saliste	**saldrás**	**saldrías**	**salgas**	salieras	**sal** tú (no **salgas**)
	sale	salía	salió	**saldrá**	**saldría**	**salga**	saliera	**salga** Ud.
	salimos	salíamos	salimos	**saldremos**	**saldríamos**	**salgamos**	saliéramos	**salgamos**
	salís	salíais	salisteis	**saldréis**	**saldríais**	**salgáis**	salierais	salid (no **salgáis**)
	salen	salían	salieron	**saldrán**	**saldrían**	**salgan**	salieran	**salgan** Uds.

19 ser — Participles: siendo, sido

	Present	Imperfect	Preterite	Future	Conditional	Subj. Present	Subj. Past	Imperative
	soy	**era**	**fui**	seré	sería	sea	fuera	
	eres	**eras**	**fuiste**	serás	serías	seas	fueras	**sé** tú (no **seas**)
	es	**era**	**fue**	será	sería	sea	fuera	sea Ud.
	somos	**éramos**	**fuimos**	seremos	seríamos	seamos	fuéramos	seamos
	sois	**erais**	**fuisteis**	seréis	seríais	seáis	fuerais	sed (no **seáis**)
	son	**eran**	**fueron**	serán	serían	sean	fueran	sean Uds.

20 tener — Participles: teniendo, tenido

	Present	Imperfect	Preterite	Future	Conditional	Subj. Present	Subj. Past	Imperative
	tengo	tenía	**tuve**	**tendré**	**tendría**	**tenga**	**tuviera**	
	tienes	tenías	**tuviste**	**tendrás**	**tendrías**	**tengas**	**tuvieras**	**ten** tú (no **tengas**)
	tiene	tenía	**tuvo**	**tendrá**	**tendría**	**tenga**	**tuviera**	**tenga** Ud.
	tenemos	teníamos	**tuvimos**	**tendremos**	**tendríamos**	**tengamos**	**tuviéramos**	**tengamos**
	tenéis	teníais	**tuvisteis**	**tendréis**	**tendríais**	**tengáis**	**tuvierais**	tened (no **tengáis**)
	tienen	tenían	**tuvieron**	**tendrán**	**tendrían**	**tengan**	**tuvieran**	**tengan** Uds.

21

Infinitive	INDICATIVE					SUBJUNCTIVE		IMPERATIVE
	Present	Imperfect	Preterite	Future	Conditional	Present	Past	
traer	traigo	traía	traje	traeré	traería	traiga	trajera	
	traes	traías	trajiste	traerás	traerías	traigas	trajeras	trae tú (no traigas)
	trae	traía	trajo	traerá	traería	traiga	trajera	traiga Ud.
Participles:	traemos	traíamos	trajimos	traeremos	traeríamos	traigamos	trajéramos	traigamos
trayendo	traéis	traíais	trajisteis	traeréis	traeríais	traigáis	trajerais	traed (no traigáis)
traído	traen	traían	trajeron	traerán	traerían	traigan	trajeran	traigan Uds.

22

Infinitive	INDICATIVE					SUBJUNCTIVE		IMPERATIVE
	Present	Imperfect	Preterite	Future	Conditional	Present	Past	
venir	vengo	venía	vine	vendré	vendría	venga	viniera	
	vienes	venías	viniste	vendrás	vendrías	vengas	vinieras	ven tú (no vengas)
	viene	venía	vino	vendrá	vendría	venga	viniera	venga Ud.
Participles:	venimos	veníamos	vinimos	vendremos	vendríamos	vengamos	viniéramos	vengamos
viniendo	venís	veníais	vinisteis	vendréis	vendríais	vengáis	vinierais	venid (no vengáis)
venido	vienen	venían	vinieron	vendrán	vendrían	vengan	vinieran	vengan Uds.

23

Infinitive	INDICATIVE					SUBJUNCTIVE		IMPERATIVE
	Present	Imperfect	Preterite	Future	Conditional	Present	Past	
ver	veo	veía	vi	veré	vería	vea	viera	
	ves	veías	viste	verás	verías	veas	vieras	ve tú (no veas)
	ve	veía	vio	verá	vería	vea	viera	vea Ud.
Participles:	vemos	veíamos	vimos	veremos	veríamos	veamos	viéramos	veamos
viendo	veis	veíais	visteis	veréis	veríais	veáis	vierais	ved (no veáis)
visto	ven	veían	vieron	verán	verían	vean	vieran	vean Uds.

Stem-changing verbs

24

Infinitive	INDICATIVE					SUBJUNCTIVE		IMPERATIVE
	Present	Imperfect	Preterite	Future	Conditional	Present	Past	
contar (o:ue)	cuento	contaba	conté	contaré	contaría	cuente	contara	
	cuentas	contabas	contaste	contarás	contarías	cuentes	contaras	cuenta tú (no cuentes)
	cuenta	contaba	contó	contará	contaría	cuente	contara	cuente Ud.
Participles:	contamos	contábamos	contamos	contaremos	contaríamos	contemos	contáramos	contemos
contando	contáis	contabais	contasteis	contaréis	contaríais	contéis	contarais	contad (no contéis)
contado	cuentan	contaban	contaron	contarán	contarían	cuenten	contaran	cuenten Uds.

25

Infinitive	INDICATIVE					SUBJUNCTIVE		IMPERATIVE
	Present	Imperfect	Preterite	Future	Conditional	Present	Past	
dormir (o:ue)	duermo	dormía	dormí	dormiré	dormiría	duerma	durmiera	
	duermes	dormías	dormiste	dormirás	dormirías	duermas	durmieras	duerme tú (no duermas)
	duerme	dormía	durmió	dormirá	dormiría	duerma	durmiera	duerma Ud.
Participles:	dormimos	dormíamos	dormimos	dormiremos	dormiríamos	durmamos	durmiéramos	durmamos
durmiendo	dormís	dormíais	dormisteis	dormiréis	dormiríais	durmáis	durmierais	dormid (no durmáis)
dormido	duermen	dormían	durmieron	dormirán	dormirían	duerman	durmieran	duerman Uds.

26

Infinitive	INDICATIVE					SUBJUNCTIVE		IMPERATIVE
	Present	Imperfect	Preterite	Future	Conditional	Present	Past	
empezar	empiezo	empezaba	empecé	empezaré	empezaría	empiece	empezara	
(e:ie) (z:c)	empiezas	empezabas	empezaste	empezarás	empezarías	empieces	empezaras	empieza tú (no empieces)
	empieza	empezaba	empezó	empezará	empezaría	empiece	empezara	empiece Ud.
Participles:	empezamos	empezábamos	empezamos	empezaremos	empezaríamos	empecemos	empezáramos	empecemos
empezando	empezáis	empezabais	empezasteis	empezaréis	empezaríais	empecéis	empezarais	empezad (no empecéis)
empezado	empiezan	empezaban	empezaron	empezarán	empezarían	empiecen	empezaran	empiecen Uds.

Infinitive	Present	Imperfect	Preterite	Future	Conditional	Subjunctive Present	Subjunctive Past	Imperative
27 entender (e:ie) Participles: entendiendo podido	entiendo / entiendes / entiende / entendemos / entendéis / entienden	entendía / entendías / entendía / entendíamos / entendíais / entendían	entendí / entendiste / entendió / entendimos / entendisteis / entendieron	entenderé / entenderás / entenderá / entenderemos / entenderéis / entenderán	entendería / entenderías / entendería / entenderíamos / entenderíais / entenderían	entienda / entiendas / entienda / entendamos / entendáis / entiendan	entendiera / entendieras / entendiera / entendiéramos / entendierais / entendieran	entiende tú (no entiendas) / entienda Ud. / entendamos / entended (no entendáis) / entiendan Uds.
28 jugar (u:ue) (g:gu) Participles: jugando jugado	juego / juegas / juega / jugamos / jugáis / juegan	jugaba / jugabas / jugaba / jugábamos / jugabais / jugaban	jugué / jugaste / jugó / jugamos / jugasteis / jugaron	jugaré / jugarás / jugará / jugaremos / jugaréis / jugarán	jugaría / jugarías / jugaría / jugaríamos / jugaríais / jugarían	juegue / juegues / juegue / juguemos / juguéis / jueguen	jugara / jugaras / jugara / jugáramos / jugarais / jugaran	juega tú (no juegues) / juegue Ud. / juguemos / jugad (no juguéis) / jueguen Uds.
29 pedir (e:i) Participles: pidiendo pedido	pido / pides / pide / pedimos / pedís / piden	pedía / pedías / pedía / pedíamos / pedíais / pedían	pedí / pediste / pidió / pedimos / pedisteis / pidieron	pediré / pedirás / pedirá / pediremos / pediréis / pedirán	pediría / pedirías / pediría / pediríamos / pediríais / pedirían	pida / pidas / pida / pidamos / pidáis / pidan	pidiera / pidieras / pidiera / pidiéramos / pidierais / pidieran	pide tú (no pidas) / pida Ud. / pidamos / pedid (no pidáis) / pidan Uds.
30 pensar (e:ie) Participles: pensando pensado	pienso / piensas / piensa / pensamos / pensáis / piensan	pensaba / pensabas / pensaba / pensábamos / pensabais / pensaban	pensé / pensaste / pensó / pensamos / pensasteis / pensaron	pensaré / pensarás / pensará / pensaremos / pensaréis / pensarán	pensaría / pensarías / pensaría / pensaríamos / pensaríais / pensarían	piense / pienses / piense / pensemos / penséis / piensen	pensara / pensaras / pensara / pensáramos / pensarais / pensaran	piensa tú (no pienses) / piense Ud. / pensemos / pensad (no penséis) / piensen Uds.
31 reír (e:i) Participles: riendo reído	río / ríes / ríe / reímos / reís / ríen	reía / reías / reía / reíamos / reíais / reían	reí / reíste / rio / reímos / reísteis / rieron	reiré / reirás / reirá / reiremos / reiréis / reirán	reiría / reirías / reiría / reiríamos / reiríais / reirían	ría / rías / ría / riamos / riáis / rían	riera / rieras / riera / riéramos / rierais / rieran	ríe tú (no rías) / ría Ud. / riamos / reíd (no riáis) / rían Uds.
32 seguir (e:i) (gu:g) Participles: siguiendo seguido	sigo / sigues / sigue / seguimos / seguís / siguen	seguía / seguías / seguía / seguíamos / seguíais / seguían	seguí / seguiste / siguió / seguimos / seguisteis / siguieron	seguiré / seguirás / seguirá / seguiremos / seguiréis / seguirán	seguiría / seguirías / seguiría / seguiríamos / seguiríais / seguirían	siga / sigas / siga / sigamos / sigáis / sigan	siguiera / siguieras / siguiera / siguiéramos / siguierais / siguieran	sigue tú (no sigas) / siga Ud. / sigamos / seguid (no sigáis) / sigan Uds.
33 sentir (e:ie) Participles: sintiendo sentido	siento / sientes / siente / sentimos / sentís / sienten	sentía / sentías / sentía / sentíamos / sentíais / sentían	sentí / sentiste / sintió / sentimos / sentisteis / sintieron	sentiré / sentirás / sentirá / sentiremos / sentiréis / sentirán	sentiría / sentirías / sentiría / sentiríamos / sentiríais / sentirían	sienta / sientas / sienta / sintamos / sintáis / sientan	sintiera / sintieras / sintiera / sintiéramos / sintierais / sintieran	siente tú (no sientas) / sienta Ud. / sintamos / sentid (no sintáis) / sientan Uds.

34 volver (o:ue)

Participles: volviendo, **vuelto**

Infinitive	INDICATIVE					SUBJUNCTIVE		IMPERATIVE
	Present	Imperfect	Preterite	Future	Conditional	Present	Past	
	vuelvo	volvía	volví	volveré	volvería	**vuelva**	volviera	
	vuelves	volvías	volviste	volverás	volverías	**vuelvas**	volvieras	**vuelve** tú (no **vuelvas**)
	vuelve	volvía	volvió	volverá	volvería	**vuelva**	volviera	**vuelva** Ud.
	volvemos	volvíamos	volvimos	volveremos	volveríamos	volvamos	volviéramos	volvamos
	volvéis	volvíais	volvisteis	volveréis	volveríais	volváis	volvierais	volved (no volváis)
	vuelven	volvían	volvieron	volverán	volverían	**vuelvan**	volvieran	**vuelvan** Uds.

Verbs with spelling changes only

35 conocer (c:zc)

Participles: conociendo, conocido

Infinitive	INDICATIVE					SUBJUNCTIVE		IMPERATIVE
	Present	Imperfect	Preterite	Future	Conditional	Present	Past	
	conozco	conocía	conocí	conoceré	conocería	**conozca**	conociera	
	conoces	conocías	conociste	conocerás	conocerías	**conozcas**	conocieras	conoce tú (no **conozcas**)
	conoce	conocía	conoció	conocerá	conocería	**conozca**	conociera	**conozca** Ud.
	conocemos	conocíamos	conocimos	conoceremos	conoceríamos	**conozcamos**	conociéramos	**conozcamos**
	conocéis	conocíais	conocisteis	conoceréis	conoceríais	**conozcáis**	conocierais	conoced (no **conozcáis**)
	conocen	conocían	conocieron	conocerán	conocerían	**conozcan**	conocieran	**conozcan** Uds.

36 creer (y)

Participles: **creyendo**, **creído**

Infinitive	INDICATIVE					SUBJUNCTIVE		IMPERATIVE
	Present	Imperfect	Preterite	Future	Conditional	Present	Past	
	creo	creía	creí	creeré	creería	crea	**creyera**	
	crees	creías	**creíste**	creerás	creerías	creas	**creyeras**	cree tú (no creas)
	cree	creía	**creyó**	creerá	creería	crea	**creyera**	crea Ud.
	creemos	creíamos	**creímos**	creeremos	creeríamos	creamos	**creyéramos**	creamos
	creéis	creíais	**creísteis**	creeréis	creeríais	creáis	**creyerais**	creed (no creáis)
	creen	creían	**creyeron**	creerán	creerían	crean	**creyeran**	crean Uds.

37 cruzar (z:c)

Participles: cruzando, cruzado

Infinitive	INDICATIVE					SUBJUNCTIVE		IMPERATIVE
	Present	Imperfect	Preterite	Future	Conditional	Present	Past	
	cruzo	cruzaba	**crucé**	cruzaré	cruzaría	**cruce**	cruzara	
	cruzas	cruzabas	cruzaste	cruzarás	cruzarías	**cruces**	cruzaras	cruza tú (no **cruces**)
	cruza	cruzaba	cruzó	cruzará	cruzaría	**cruce**	cruzara	**cruce** Ud.
	cruzamos	cruzábamos	cruzamos	cruzaremos	cruzaríamos	**crucemos**	cruzáramos	**crucemos**
	cruzáis	cruzabais	cruzasteis	cruzaréis	cruzaríais	**crucéis**	cruzarais	cruzad (no **crucéis**)
	cruzan	cruzaban	cruzaron	cruzarán	cruzarían	**crucen**	cruzaran	**crucen** Uds.

38 destruir (y)

Participles: **destruyendo**, destruido

Infinitive	INDICATIVE					SUBJUNCTIVE		IMPERATIVE
	Present	Imperfect	Preterite	Future	Conditional	Present	Past	
	destruyo	destruía	destruí	destruiré	destruiría	**destruya**	**destruyera**	
	destruyes	destruías	destruiste	destruirás	destruirías	**destruyas**	**destruyeras**	**destruye** tú (no **destruyas**)
	destruye	destruía	**destruyó**	destruirá	destruiría	**destruya**	**destruyera**	**destruya** Ud.
	destruimos	destruíamos	destruimos	destruiremos	destruiríamos	**destruyamos**	**destruyéramos**	**destruyamos**
	destruis	destruíais	destruisteis	destruiréis	destruiríais	**destruyáis**	**destruyerais**	destruid (no **destruyáis**)
	destruyen	destruían	**destruyeron**	destruirán	destruirían	**destruyan**	**destruyeran**	**destruyan** Uds.

39 enviar

Participles: enviando, enviado

Infinitive	INDICATIVE					SUBJUNCTIVE		IMPERATIVE
	Present	Imperfect	Preterite	Future	Conditional	Present	Past	
	envío	enviaba	envié	enviaré	enviaría	**envíe**	enviara	
	envías	enviabas	enviaste	enviarás	enviarías	**envíes**	enviaras	**envía** tú (no **envíes**)
	envía	enviaba	envió	enviará	enviaría	**envíe**	enviara	**envíe** Ud.
	enviamos	enviábamos	enviamos	enviaremos	enviaríamos	enviemos	enviáramos	enviemos
	enviáis	enviabais	enviasteis	enviaréis	enviaríais	enviéis	enviarais	enviad (no enviéis)
	envían	enviaban	enviaron	enviarán	enviarían	**envíen**	enviaran	**envíen** Uds.

40 graduar
Participles: graduando, graduado

	Present	Imperfect	Preterite	Future	Conditional	Subjunctive Present	Subjunctive Past	Imperative
	gradúo	graduaba	gradué	graduaré	graduaría	gradúe	graduara	
	gradúas	graduabas	graduaste	graduarás	graduarías	gradúes	graduaras	gradúa tú (no gradúes)
	gradúa	graduaba	graduó	graduará	graduaría	gradúe	graduara	gradúe Ud.
	graduamos	graduábamos	graduamos	graduaremos	graduaríamos	graduemos	graduáramos	graduemos
	graduáis	graduabais	graduasteis	graduaréis	graduaríais	graduéis	graduarais	graduad (no graduéis)
	gradúan	graduaban	graduaron	graduarán	graduarían	gradúen	graduaran	gradúen Uds.

41 llegar (g:gu)
Participles: llegando, llegado

	Present	Imperfect	Preterite	Future	Conditional	Subjunctive Present	Subjunctive Past	Imperative
	llego	llegaba	llegué	llegaré	llegaría	llegue	llegara	
	llegas	llegabas	llegaste	llegarás	llegarías	llegues	llegaras	llega tú (no llegues)
	llega	llegaba	llegó	llegará	llegaría	llegue	llegara	llegue Ud.
	llegamos	llegábamos	llegamos	llegaremos	llegaríamos	lleguemos	llegáramos	lleguemos
	llegáis	llegabais	llegasteis	llegaréis	llegaríais	lleguéis	llegarais	llegad (no lleguéis)
	llegan	llegaban	llegaron	llegarán	llegarían	lleguen	llegaran	lleguen Uds.

42 proteger (g:j)
Participles: protegiendo, protegido

	Present	Imperfect	Preterite	Future	Conditional	Subjunctive Present	Subjunctive Past	Imperative
	protejo	protegía	protegí	protegeré	protegería	proteja	protegiera	
	proteges	protegías	protegiste	protegerás	protegerías	protejas	protegieras	protege tú (no protejas)
	protege	protegía	protegió	protegerá	protegería	proteja	protegiera	proteja Ud.
	protegemos	protegíamos	protegimos	protegeremos	protegeríamos	protejamos	protegiéramos	protejamos
	protegéis	protegíais	protegisteis	protegeréis	protegeríais	protejáis	protegierais	proteged (no protejáis)
	protegen	protegían	protegieron	protegerán	protegerían	protejan	protegieran	protejan Uds.

43 tocar (c:qu)
Participles: tocando, tocado

	Present	Imperfect	Preterite	Future	Conditional	Subjunctive Present	Subjunctive Past	Imperative
	toco	tocaba	toqué	tocaré	tocaría	toque	tocara	
	tocas	tocabas	tocaste	tocarás	tocarías	toques	tocaras	toca tú (no toques)
	toca	tocaba	tocó	tocará	tocaría	toque	tocara	toque Ud.
	tocamos	tocábamos	tocamos	tocaremos	tocaríamos	toquemos	tocáramos	toquemos
	tocáis	tocabais	tocasteis	tocaréis	tocaríais	toquéis	tocarais	tocad (no toquéis)
	tocan	tocaban	tocaron	tocarán	tocarían	toquen	tocaran	toquen Uds.

44 vencer (c:z)
Participles: venciendo, vencido

	Present	Imperfect	Preterite	Future	Conditional	Subjunctive Present	Subjunctive Past	Imperative
	venzo	vencía	vencí	venceré	vencería	venza	venciera	
	vences	vencías	venciste	vencerás	vencerías	venzas	vencieras	vence tú (no venzas)
	vence	vencía	venció	vencerá	vencería	venza	venciera	venza Ud.
	vencemos	vencíamos	vencimos	venceremos	venceríamos	venzamos	venciéramos	venzamos
	vencéis	vencíais	vencisteis	venceréis	venceríais	venzáis	vencierais	venced (no venzáis)
	vencen	vencían	vencieron	vencerán	vencerían	venzan	vencieran	venzan Uds.

45 esparcir (c:z)
Participles: esparciendo, esparcido

	Present	Imperfect	Preterite	Future	Conditional	Subjunctive Present	Subjunctive Past	Imperative
	esparzo	esparcía	esparcí	esparciré	esparciría	esparza	esparciera	
	esparces	esparcías	esparciste	esparcirás	esparcirías	esparzas	esparcieras	esparce tú (no esparzas)
	esparce	esparcía	esparció	esparcirá	esparciría	esparza	esparciera	esparza Ud.
	esparcimos	esparcíamos	esparcimos	esparciremos	esparciríamos	esparzamos	esparciéramos	esparzamos
	esparcís	esparcíais	esparcisteis	esparciréis	esparciríais	esparzáis	esparcierais	esparcid (no esparzáis)
	esparcen	esparcían	esparcieron	esparcirán	esparcirían	esparzan	esparcieran	esparzan Uds.

46 extinguir (gu:g)
Participles: extinguiendo, extinguido o extinto

	Present	Imperfect	Preterite	Future	Conditional	Subjunctive Present	Subjunctive Past	Imperative
	extingo	extinguía	extinguí	extinguiré	extinguiría	extinga	extinguiera	
	extingues	extinguías	extinguiste	extinguirás	extinguirías	extingas	extinguieras	extingue tú (no extingas)
	extingue	extinguía	extinguió	extinguirá	extinguiría	extinga	extinguiera	extinga Ud.
	extinguimos	extinguíamos	extinguimos	extinguiremos	extinguiríamos	extingamos	extinguiéramos	extingamos
	extinguís	extinguíais	extinguisteis	extinguiréis	extinguiríais	extingáis	extinguierais	extinguid (no extingáis)
	extinguen	extinguían	extinguieron	extinguirán	extinguirían	extingan	extinguieran	extingan Uds.

Reflexive verbs: simple tenses

○ In all simple indicative and subjunctive tenses, the reflexive pronoun is placed before the conjugated verb. In the imperative, the reflexive pronoun is attached to the verb in affirmative commands, but precedes the verb in negative commands.

Infinitive	SIMPLE INDICATIVE TENSES	SIMPLE SUBJUNCTIVE TENSES	IMPERATIVE
casarse	**me** caso **te** casas **se** casa **nos** casamos **os** casáis **se** casan	**me** case **te** cases **se** case **nos** casemos **os** caséis **se** casen	 cása**te** tú (no **te** cases) cáse**se** Ud. (no **se** case) casé**monos** (no **nos** casemos) casa**os** (no **os** caséis) cáen**se** Uds. (no **se** casen)

Reflexive verbs: compound tenses

○ In all compound tenses, the reflexive pronoun is placed before the conjugated verb.

Infinitive	COMPOUND INDICATIVE TENSES	COMPOUND SUBJUNCTIVE TENSES
casarse	**me** he casado **te** has casado **se** ha casado **nos** hemos casado **os** habéis casado **se** han casado	**me** haya casado **te** hayas casado **se** haya casado **nos** hayamos casado **os** hayáis casado **se** hayan casado

Glossary of Grammatical Terms

ADJECTIVE A word that modifies, or describes, a noun or pronoun.

muchos libros	un hombre **rico**
many books	*a* **rich** *man*

Demonstrative adjective An adjective that specifies which noun a speaker is referring to.

esta fiesta	**ese** chico
this party	*that* boy
aquellas flores	
those flowers	

Possessive adjective An adjective that indicates ownership or possession.

su mejor vestido	Este es **mi** hermano.
her best dress	*This is* **my** *brother.*

Stressed possessive adjective A possessive adjective that emphasizes the owner or possessor.

un libro **mío**	una amiga **tuya**
a book **of mine**	*a friend* **of yours**

ADVERB A word that modifies, or describes, a verb, an adjective, or another adverb.

Pancho escribe **rápidamente**.
Pancho writes **quickly**.

Este cuadro es **muy** bonito.
This picture is **very** *pretty.*

ANTECEDENT The noun to which a pronoun or dependent clause refers.

El **libro** que compré es interesante.
The book that I bought is interesting.

Le presté cinco dólares a **Diego**.
I loaned Diego five dollars.

ARTICLE A word that points out a noun in either a specific or a non-specific way.

Definite article An article that points out a noun in a specific way.

el libro	**la** maleta
the book	*the* suitcase
los diccionarios	**las** palabras
the dictionaries	*the* words

Indefinite article An article that points out a noun in a general, non-specific way.

un lápiz	**una** computadora
a pencil	*a* computer
unos pájaros	**unas** escuelas
some birds	*some* schools

CLAUSE A group of words that contains both a conjugated verb and a subject, either expressed or implied.

Main (or Independent) clause A clause that can stand alone as a complete sentence.

Pienso ir a cenar pronto.
I plan to go to dinner soon.

Subordinate (or Dependent) clause A clause that does not express a complete thought and therefore cannot stand alone as a sentence.

Trabajo en la cafetería **porque necesito dinero para la escuela**.
I work in the cafeteria **because I need money for school**.

Adjective clause A dependent clause that functions to modify or describe the noun or direct object in the main clause. When the antecedent is uncertain or indefinite, the verb in the adjective clause is in the subjunctive.

Queremos contratar al candidato **que mandó su currículum ayer**.
We want to hire the applicant **who sent his résumé yesterday**.

¿Conoce un buen restaurante **que esté cerca del teatro**?
Do you know of a good restaurant **that's near the theater**?

Adverbial clause A dependent clause that functions to modify or describe a verb, an adjective, or another adverb. When the adverbial clause describes an action that has not yet happened or is uncertain, the verb in the adverbial clause is usually in the subjunctive.

Llamé a mi mamá **cuando me dieron la noticia**.
I called my mom **when they gave me the news**.

El ejército está preparado **en caso de que haya un ataque**.
The army is prepared **in case there is an attack**.

Noun clause A dependent clause that functions as a noun, often as the object of the main clause. When the main clause expresses will, emotion, doubt, or uncertainty, the verb in the noun clause is in the subjunctive.

José sabe **que mañana habrá un examen**.
José knows **that tomorrow there will be an exam**.

Luisa dudaba **que la acompañáramos**.
Luisa doubted **that we would go with her**.

COMPARATIVE A grammatical construction used with nouns, adjectives, verbs, or adverbs to compare people, objects, actions, or characteristics.

Tus clases son **menos interesantes** que las mías.
*Your classes are **less interesting** than mine.*

Como **más frutas** que verduras.
*I eat **more fruits** than vegetables.*

CONJUGATION A set of the forms of a verb for a specific tense or mood, or the process by which these verb forms are presented.

PRETERITE CONJUGATION OF **CANTAR**:

cant**é**	cant**amos**
cant**aste**	cant**asteis**
cant**ó**	cant**aron**

CONJUNCTION A word used to connect words, clauses, or phrases.

Susana es de Cuba **y** Pedro es de España.
*Susana is from Cuba **and** Pedro is from Spain.*

No quiero estudiar, **pero** tengo que hacerlo.
*I don't want to study, **but** I have to.*

CONTRACTION The joining of two words into one. The only contractions in Spanish are **al** and **del**.

Mi hermano fue **al** concierto ayer.
*My brother went **to the** concert yesterday.*

Saqué dinero **del** banco.
*I took out money **from the** bank.*

DIRECT OBJECT A noun or pronoun that directly receives the action of the verb.

Tomás lee **el libro.**   **La** pagó ayer.
*Tomás reads **the book**.   She paid **it** yesterday.*

GENDER The grammatical categorizing of certain kinds of words, such as nouns and pronouns, as masculine, feminine, or neuter.

MASCULINE
articles **el, un**
pronouns **él, lo, mío, este, ese, aquel**
adjective **simpático**

FEMININE
articles **la, una**
pronouns **ella, la, mía, esta, esa, aquella**
adjective **simpática**

IMPERSONAL EXPRESSION A third-person expression with no expressed or specific subject.

Es muy importante.   **Llueve** mucho.
It's very important.   *It's raining hard.*

Aquí **se habla** español.
*Spanish **is spoken** here.*

INDIRECT OBJECT A noun or pronoun that receives the action of the verb indirectly; the object, often a living being, to or for whom an action is performed.

Eduardo **le** dio un libro **a Linda.**
*Eduardo gave a book **to Linda**.*

La profesora **me** puso una C en el examen.
*The professor gave **me** a C on the test.*

INFINITIVE The basic form of a verb. Infinitives in Spanish end in **-ar**, **-er**, or **-ir**.

hablar	**correr**	**abrir**
to speak	*to run*	*to open*

INTERROGATIVE A word used to ask a question.

¿Quién habla?   **¿Cuántos** compraste?
***Who** is speaking?*   ***How many** did you buy?*

¿Qué piensas hacer hoy?
***What** do you plan to do today?*

MOOD A grammatical distinction of verbs that indicates whether the verb is intended to make a statement or command, or to express doubt, emotion, or condition contrary to fact.

Imperative mood Verb forms used to give commands.

Di la verdad.   **Caminen** ustedes conmigo.
***Tell** the truth.*   ***Walk** with me.*

¡Comamos ahora!   **¡No** lo **hagas!**
***Let's eat** now!*   ***Don't do** it!*

Indicative mood Verb forms used to state facts, actions, and states considered to be real.

Sé que **tienes** el dinero.
***I know** that **you have** the money.*

Subjunctive mood Verb forms used principally in subordinate (dependent) clauses to express wishes, desires, emotions, doubts, and certain conditions, such as contrary-to-fact situations.

Prefieren que **hables** en español.
*They prefer that **you speak** in Spanish.*

NOUN A word that identifies people, animals, places, things, and ideas.

hombre	**gato**
man	*cat*
México	**casa**
Mexico	*house*
libertad	**libro**
freedom	*book*

NUMBER A grammatical term that refers to singular or plural. Nouns in Spanish and English have number. Other parts of a sentence, such as adjectives, articles, and verbs, also have number in Spanish.

SINGULAR	PLURAL
una cosa	**unas** cosa**s**
a thing	*some things*
el profesor	**los** profesor**es**
the professor	*the professors*

PASSIVE VOICE A sentence construction in which the recipient of the action becomes the subject of the sentence. Passive statements emphasize the thing that was done or the person that was acted upon. They follow the pattern [*recipient*] + **ser** + [*past participle*] + **por** + [*agent*].

ACTIVE VOICE:
Juan **entregó** la tarea.
*Juan **turned in** the assignment.*

PASSIVE VOICE:
La tarea **fue entregada por** Juan.
*The assignment **was turned in by** Juan.*

PAST PARTICIPLE A past form of the verb used in compound tenses. The past participle may also be used as an adjective, but it must then agree in number and gender with the word it modifies.

Han **buscado** por todas partes.
*They have **searched** everywhere.*

Yo no había **estudiado** para el examen.
*I hadn't **studied** for the exam.*

Hay una ventana **abierta** en la sala.
*There is an **open** window in the living room.*

PERSON The form of the verb or pronoun that indicates the speaker, the one spoken to, or the one spoken about. In Spanish, as in English, there are three persons: first, second, and third.

PERSON	SINGULAR	PLURAL
1st	**yo** *I*	**nosotros/as** *we*
2nd	**tú, usted** *you*	**vosotros/as,**
		ustedes *you*
3rd	**él, ella** *he, she*	**ellos, ellas** *they*

PREPOSITION A word or words that describe(s) the relationship, most often in time or space, between two other words.

Anita es **de** California.
*Anita is **from** California.*

La chaqueta está **en** el carro.
*The jacket is **in** the car.*

PRESENT PARTICIPLE In English, a verb form that ends in *-ing*. In Spanish, the present participle ends in **-ndo**, and is often used with **estar** to form a progressive tense.

Está **hablando** por teléfono ahora mismo.
*He is **talking** on the phone right now.*

PRONOUN A word that takes the place of one or more nouns.

Demonstrative pronoun A pronoun that takes the place of a specific noun.

Quiero **esta**.
*I want **this one**.*

¿Vas a comprar **ese**?
*Are you going to buy **that one**?*

Juan prefirió **aquellos**.
*Juan preferred **those** (over there).*

Object pronoun A pronoun that functions as a direct or indirect object of the verb.

Te digo la verdad.
*I'm telling **you** the truth.*

Me lo trajo Juan.
*Juan brought **it to me**.*

Possessive pronoun A pronoun that functions to show ownership or possession. Possessive pronouns are preceded by a definite article and agree in gender and number with the nouns they replace.

Perdí mi libro. ¿Me prestas **el tuyo**?
*I lost my book. Will you loan me **yours**?*

Las clases suyas son aburridas, pero **las nuestras** son buenísimas.
*Their classes are boring, but **ours** are great.*

Prepositional pronoun A pronoun that functions as the object of a preposition. Except for **mí, ti,** and **sí**, these pronouns are the same as subject pronouns. The adjective **mismo/a** may be added to express *myself, himself*, etc. After the preposition **con**, the forms **conmigo, contigo,** and **consigo** are used.

¿Es **para mí**?	Juan habló **de ella**.
*Is this **for me**?*	*Juan spoke **about her**.*
Iré **contigo**.	Se lo regaló **a sí mismo**.
*I will go **with you**.*	*He gave it **to himself**.*

Reflexive pronoun A pronoun that indicates that the action of a verb is performed by the subject on itself. These pronouns are often expressed in English with *-self: myself, yourself*, etc.

Yo **me bañé**.	Elena **se acostó**.
*I **took a bath**.*	*Elena **went to bed**.*

Relative pronoun A pronoun that connects a subordinate clause to a main clause.

El edificio **en el cual** vivimos es antiguo.
*The building **that** we live in is old.*

La mujer **de quien** te hablé acaba de renunciar.
*The woman **(whom)** I told you about just quit.*

Subject pronoun A pronoun that replaces the name or title of a person or thing, and acts as the subject of a verb.

Tú debes estudiar más.
***You** should study more.*

Él llegó primero.
***He** arrived first.*

SUBJECT A noun or pronoun that performs the action of a verb and is often implied by the verb.

María va al supermercado.
***María** goes to the supermarket.*

(Ellos) Trabajan mucho.
***They** work hard.*

Esos libros son muy caros.
***Those books** are very expensive.*

SUPERLATIVE A grammatical construction used to describe the most or the least of a quality when comparing a group of people, places, or objects.

Tina es **la menos simpática** de las chicas.
*Tina is **the least pleasant** of the girls.*

Tu coche es **el más rápido** de todos.
*Your car is **the fastest** one of all.*

Los restaurantes en Calle Ocho son **los mejores** de todo Miami.
*The restaurants on Calle Ocho are **the best** in all of Miami.*

Absolute superlatives Adjectives or adverbs combined with forms of the suffix **-ísimo/a** in order to express the idea of *extremely* or *very*.

¡Lo hice **rapidísimo**!
*I did it **so fast**!*

Ella es **jovencísima**.
*She is **very, very young**.*

TENSE A set of verb forms that indicates the time of an action or state: past, present, or future.

Compound tense A two-word tense made up of an auxiliary verb and a present or past participle.

En este momento, **estoy estudiando**.
*At this time, **I am studying**.*

El paquete no **ha llegado** todavía.
*The package **has** not **arrived** yet.*

Simple tense A tense expressed by a single verb form.

María **estaba** mal anoche.
*María **was** ill last night.*

Juana **hablará** con su mamá mañana.
*Juana **will speak** with her mom tomorrow.*

VERB A word that expresses actions or states of being.

Auxiliary verb A verb used with a present or past participle to form a compound tense. **Haber** is the most commonly used auxiliary verb in Spanish.

Los chicos **han** visto los elefantes.
*The children **have** seen the elephants.*

Espero que **hayas** comido.
*I hope you **have** eaten.*

Reflexive verb A verb that describes an action performed by the subject on itself and is always used with a reflexive pronoun.

Me compré un carro nuevo.
***I bought myself** a new car.*

Pedro y Adela **se levantan** muy temprano.
*Pedro and Adela **get (themselves) up** very early.*

Spelling-change verb A verb that undergoes a predictable change in spelling, in order to reflect its actual pronunciation in the various conjugations.

practicar	c→qu	practico	practiqué
dirigir	g→j	dirigí	dirijo
almorzar	z→c	almorzó	almorcé

Stem-changing verb A verb whose stem vowel undergoes one or more predictable changes in the various conjugations.

entender	(e:ie)	entiendo
pedir	(e:i)	piden
dormir	(o:ue, u)	duermo, durmieron

Grammar Reference

This grammar reference organizes all of the grammatical structures presented in **PROTAGONISTAS** by part of speech. The lozenges next to each topic show you which lessons teach these structures in their communicative context.

Table of Contents

1 Pronunciation, Intonation, and Spelling (Pronunciación, entonación y ortografía)

1.1 The alphabet (El alfabeto) U0

- The Spanish alphabet is comprised of 27 letters and contains a special letter: **ñ**, which comes after **n**. The letter combinations **ch** and **ll** are no longer considered letters.

letter	name of letter	sound (international phonetic alphabet)	sound (in relation to English)	examples
a	a	[a]	• like the *a* in *father*, but shorter	**A**na, t**a**p**a**s, **a**diós
b	be	[b] [β]	• like the English hard *b* when at the beginning of a word • like a soft *b* with no equivalent in English in all other positions	**B**arcelona, **b**eso L2A, L5A Ro**b**erto, escri**b**ir
c	ce	[k] [θ] [Esp.]* [s] [Amér. L.]*	• before **a**, **o**, or **u**, like the *c* in *car* • in parts of Spain, like the *th* in *think* when before **e** or **i** • in Latin America, like the *s* in *sit* when before **e** or **i**	**C**arlos, **c**osa, **c**urso L1A, L4B **c**inco, Bar**c**elona L1A, L5B ha**c**er, **c**o**c**ina
ch	che	[tʃ]	• like the *ch* in *chair*	o**ch**o, no**ch**e, **Ch**ile L3A
d	de	[d] [ð]	• when at the beginning of a word, similar to the *d* in *dog*, but softer • in all other positions, a softer sound similar to the English *th* in *there*	**d**ónde, **d**ormir ma**d**re, Ma**d**rid, ciu**d**a**d** L6B
e	e	[ɛ]	• like the *e* in *they*, but shorter	P**e**dro, **e**spañol
f	efe	[f]	• like the English *f*	ca**f**é, **F**élix, ga**f**as
g	ge	[g] [x]	• like the *g* in *girl* • before **e** or **i**, similar to the English *h*	**g**amba, ten**g**o, **g**ustar L1A, L3B Mi**g**uel, **G**uernica a**g**enda, **g**imnasia L1A, L3B
h	hache		• The Spanish **h** is always silent.	**h**otel, **h**ola
i	i	[i]	• like the *ee* in *beet*, but shorter	h**i**jo, Fr**i**da
j	jota	[x]	• similar to the *h* in *his*	**j**ulio, ro**j**o L3B relo**j** L6B
k	ka (ca)	[k]	• like the *k* in *key*; this letter is rarely used in Spanish	**k**ilo, **k**ilómetro L4B
l	ele	[l]	• like the *l* in *lake*	**l**ámpara, hospita**l**
ll	elle	[j] [Amér. L.]* [ʒ] [R. P.] [ʎ] [Esp.]*	• like the *y* in *yes* • in Argentina and Uruguay, like the *sh* in *shoe* • in some areas of Spain, like a continuous *lj* sound	Sevi**ll**a, **ll**amada L3A
m	eme	[m]	• like the *m* in *home*	**M**aría, A**m**érica
n	ene	[n]	• like the *n* in *nice*	bue**n**o, A**n**a

letter	name of letter	sound (international phonetic alphabet)	sound (in relation to English)	examples
ñ	eñe	[ɲ]	• much like the *ny* in *canyon*	ma**ñ**ana, Espa**ñ**a L3A
o	o	[o]	• like the *o* in *tone*, but shorter	d**ó**nde, h**o**la
p	pe	[p]	• like the *p* in *top*, but softer; no air is expelled from the mouth	**p**aella, Es**p**aña, **p**laya L5A, L6A
q	cu	[k]	• like the *k* in *key; q* is always followed by *u* in Spanish	**qu**erer, pe**qu**eño L4B
r	ere	[r]	• a sound similiar to the *dd* in *ladder* when in the middle or at the end of a word, but the tongue touches the roof of the mouth behind the teeth	ba**r**, me**r**cado, ca**r**ácte**r** L4A
	erre	[rr]	• when at the beginning of a word, after the consonants **l**, **n**, and **s**, or in the combination **rr**, a strong trilled sound that does not exist in English	ba**rr**io, **r**astro, **r**estaurante L4A
s	ese	[s]	• like the *s* in *summer*	que**s**o, **S**evilla, e**s**e
t	te	[t]	• shorter than the English *t;* no air is expelled from the mouth	**t**iempo, Mar**t**a L6A
u	u	[u]	• like the *oo* in *room*, but shorter	**u**no, Per**ú**
v	ve (uve)	[b] [β]	• like the English hard *b* when at the beginning of a word • a soft *b* with no equivalent in English in all other positions	**v**iaje, **v**ino L2A, L5A Ja**v**ier, por fa**v**or
w	doble ve (uve doble)	[w]	• like the *w* in *web* or the Spanish *b/v*; this letter is found only in foreign words	**w**eb cam
x	equis	[ks] [s]*	• pronounced like an English *x* • in some Spanish-speaking areas, like an aspirated *s*; in others, like a weak *h*	ta**x**i, e**x**acto e**x**plicar, e**x**tranjero
y	i griega (ye)	[i] [j]* [ʒ] [R. P.]*	• when at the end of a word, like the *ee* in *beet*, but shorter • when at the beginning or in the middle of a word, like the *y* in *yes* • in Argentina and Uruguay, like the *sh* in *shoe* when at the beginning or in the middle of a word	ha**y**, vo**y**, so**y**, **y** **y**o, ma**y**o
z	zeta (ceta)	[θ] [Esp.]* [s] [Amér. L.]*	• in parts of Spain, pronounced like the *th* in *think* • in Latin America, pronounced like the *s* in *sit*	**Z**aragoza L5B Vene**z**uela, a**z**úcar

*As noted, the pronunciation of **c**, **z**, **ll**, and **y** varies between Latin America (**Amér. L.**), the **Rioplatense** region (**R. P.**), and parts of Spain (**Esp.**); the pronunciation of **x** also varies in some Spanish-speaking countries.

1.2 Spoken stress and written accents (**Entonación y acento ortográfico**) `L2B`

- The next-to-last syllable is stressed in most Spanish words.

    postre, **chu**rro, pa**ta**ta, **ta**pa

- Words ending in a consonant (all but **n** and **s**) are stressed on the last syllable.

    cami**nar**, re**loj**, ver**dad**

- When a word does not follow these rules, the stressed syllable carries a written accent mark.

    ja**món**, al**bón**digas, a**zú**car

- A written accent mark is also used to differentiate between monosyllabic words that are spelled the same but have different meanings.

    el **él**   **té** te
    the he   *tea you*

- All interrogative words are written with an accent.

    ¿cu**á**ndo? ¿c**ó**mo? ¿qui**é**n? ¿qu**é**? ¿d**ó**nde?

1.3 Linking

- The sound and rhythm of spoken Spanish are influenced by linking, in which two syllables are merged into one. This phenomenon mainly occurs when a word that ends in a vowel is followed by a word that begins with a vowel.

    Me llamo͜ Eladio. Soy de͜ Argentina. Vivo͜ en Córdoba.

- When identical vowel sounds appear together, they are pronounced like one long vowel.

    mi͜ hijo   una clase͜ excelente

- Two identical consonants together sound like a single consonant.

    con͜ Natalia   sus͜ sobrinos   las͜ sillas

- Also, a consonant at the end of a word is linked with the vowel at the beginning of the next word.

    es͜ ingeniera   mis͜ abuelos   sus͜ hijos

1.4 Upper and lower case letters (**Mayúsculas y minúsculas**)

- In Spanish, upper case letters are used less often than in English. Upper case letters are used for proper nouns naming people, countries, cities, and provinces, as well as for the first word in a sentence.

    Es **C**armen **A**breu, de la **R**epública **D**ominicana.

    ¡**H**ola! **M**e llamo **S**alma **H**ayek.

- Unlike in English, upper case letters are not used in Spanish for days of the week, months, or adjectives of nationality and religion. `L1B, L3A`

    Alejandra, mi amiga **boliviana**, llega el primer **miércoles** de **junio**.
    *Alejandra, my **Bolivian** friend, arrives on the first **Wednesday** in **June**.*

1.5 Question marks and exclamation points
(**Signos de interrogación y exclamación**) `U0`

- Question marks (¿ ?) and exclamation points (¡ !) precede and follow questions and exclamations, respectively.

    ¿Cómo se escribe?   ¡Buenos días!   ¡Hola!, ¿qué tal?

2 Nouns (Sustantivos) `L1A`

2.1 Gender (El género) `L1A, L3A`

- Spanish nouns have gender and are considered either masculine or feminine. Often the ending of the word indicates its gender.

masculine		feminine	
-o	banc**o**, muse**o**, puebl**o**	**-a**	comid**a**, isl**a**, paell**a**
-r	amo**r**, ba**r**, ma**r**	**-ión**	canc**ión**, profes**ión**
-l	hospita**l**, hote**l**, so**l**	**-ad, -ud**	ciud**ad**, sal**ud**

- Nouns ending in **-e** can be either masculine or feminine.

masculine		feminine	
-e	nombr**e**, restaurant**e**, tomat**e**	**-e**	clas**e**, madr**e**, noch**e**

- Some important exceptions:

masculine	feminine
(el) dí**a**, map**a**, sof**á**, clim**a**, idiom**a**, problem**a**, av**ión**, cam**ión**	(la) flo**r**, man**o**, radi**o**

- Other important distinctions:

masculine		feminine	
Days of the week	el martes, el lunes	Letters	la b, la a
Numbers	el uno, el dos	Telling time	la una, las dos
Place names that do not end in **-a***	Quito es muy bonit**o**. Perú es montaños**o**. **El** Amazonas es enorme.	Place names that end in an unaccented **-a**	Barcelona es muy bonit**a**. España es montaños**a**.

*Note that it is appropriate to use the feminine article with any city name.

- Names of professions: `L1B`

masculine		feminine	
-o	médic**o**, ingenier**o**	**-a**	médic**a**, ingenier**a**
-ero	camar**ero**, panad**ero**	**-era**	camar**era**, panad**era**
-or	profes**or**, pint**or**	**-ora**	profes**ora**, pint**ora**
-ista	dent**ista**, period**ista**	**-ista**	dent**ista**, period**ista**
-nte	estudia**nte**, canta**nte**	**-nte**	estudia**nte**, canta**nte**

- Note that many professions ending in **-ista** or **-nte** can refer to both men and women. In these cases, the article also agrees with the person's gender, e.g., **el** estudiante, **la** dentista. Some nouns ending in **-nte**, such as **dependiente/a** and **presidente/a**, do have a distinct feminine form.

2.2 Formation of the plural (**El plural**) `L1B, L2A`

singular		plural	
Ending in a vowel	casa, coche, camarero	**+ -s**	casa**s**, coche**s**, camarero**s**
Ending in a consonant	hospita**l**, me**s**, profeso**r**, tre**n**	**+ -es**	hospital**es**, mes**es**, profesor**es**, tren**es**
Ending in **-s** (after an unstressed vowel)	(el) lunes, (la) crisis	No change	(los) lunes, (las) crisis

• When the final syllable of a noun carries a written accent in the singular form, the written accent is dropped in the plural.

> **la nación**   **las naciones**
> *the nation*   *the nations*

• When a singular noun ends in **-z**, change the **z** to **c** before adding **-es**.

> **el lápiz**   **los lápices**
> *the pencil*   *the pencils*

3 Articles (Los artículos) `L1A`

3.1 Definite articles (**Los artículos determinados**) `L2A`

• Definite articles, equivalent to *the* in English, identify specific nouns.

	singular	plural
masculine	**el** carro	**los** carros
feminine	**la** plaza	**las** plazas

• The masculine definite article **el** is used with the singular form of feminine nouns that begin with a stressed **a**, such as **agua**, **alma**, or **área**. Feminine adjectives are still used with these words, and plural forms of these nouns take feminine articles.

> **el** aula   **un** aula   **las** aulas   **el** agua fría
> *the classroom*   *a classroom*   *the classrooms*   *the cold water*

3.1.1 el/la de + [*noun*]; el/la que + [*verb*] `L9B`

• Use the construction **el/la** + [*noun*] + **de** + [*noun*] or **el/la** + [*noun*] + **que** + [*verb*] to refer to a person based on another point of reference.

> **El (señor) de** la frutería se llama Antonio.
> **The man from** the fruit stand is named Antonio.

> Magdalena es **la (señora) que** tiene el estanco.
> Magdalena is **the woman who** has the tobacconist shop.

• The noun between the article and **de/que** can be omitted. Remember to use the contraction **del** when **de** appears before the masculine definite article **el**.

> **La del** quiosco es mi amiga Juana.
> **The girl (The one)** from the kiosk is my friend Juana.

> **Los de** la panadería son ecuatorianos.
> **The people** from the bakery are Ecuadorean.

> **El que** vive en esa casa es Pedro.
> **The one who** lives in that house is Pedro.

3.1.2 [*preposition*] + [*definite article*] + **que**   L18A

- In a relative clause (**cláusula relativa**), the construction [*definite article*] + **que** refers to the noun that is the object of the clause. The article must match the corresponding noun in gender and number.

> Es **una deportista a la que** admiro.
> *She is **an athlete whom** I admire.*

> Son **profesionales para los que** no hay retos imposibles.
> *They are **professionals for whom** there are no impossible challenges.*

3.2 Indefinite articles (**Los artículos indeterminados**)   L1A, L2A

- Indefinite articles, equivalent to *a*, *an*, *one*, or *some* in English, identify unspecified nouns.

	singular	plural
masculine	**un** pueblo	**unos** pueblos
feminine	**una** montaña	**unas** montañas

 The plural forms of the indefinite article, **unos** and **unas**, are used to indicate approximate amounts.

> Medellín tiene **unos** barrios bonitos.
> *Medellín has **some** pretty neighborhoods.*

> Tengo **unas** postales de Santiago de Chile.
> *I have **some** postcards from Santiago, Chile.*

- Note the difference in meaning when the indefinite article is omitted.

> Medellín tiene barrios bonitos.
> *Medellín has pretty neighborhoods.*

3.3 The neuter article **lo** (**El artículo neutro *lo***)

3.3.1 lo + [*adjective*]   L12B, L15A

- Use the neuter article **lo** to form a noun phrase from an adjective.

> **Lo bueno** es que gano mucho; **lo malo** es que siempre estoy de viaje.
> ***The good thing** is that I earn a lot; **the bad thing** is that I am always traveling.*

> Para mí, **lo más importante** es la familia.
> *For me, **the most important thing** is family.*

> **Lo mejor** sería consumir productos ecológicos.
> ***The best thing** would be to eat organic products.*

3.3.2 lo de + [*noun/infinitive*]; **lo que** + [*verb*]   L14B

- To refer to a topic that has already been alluded to, use **lo de** + [*noun/infinitive*] or **lo que** + [*verb*].

> El último capítulo trataba sobre **lo de** la hija de los Alcántara... **lo de** irse a Londres con su novio.
> *The last episode was about **the thing with** the Alcántaras' daughter . . . **the thing about** going to London with her boyfriend.*

> ¿Es verdad **lo que** me contaste ayer?
> *Is **what** you told me yesterday true?*

3.4 Generalizing (**Generalizar**)   L16B

- When referring to a group of people in general terms, use **la gente** (*people*). **La gente** is a singular noun and requires a singular article. Note that this noun also requires the third-person singular verb form.

> **La gente es** muy amable.
> ***People are** really nice.*

- Another way to refer to a group of people in general terms is **la mayoría** (*the majority; most people*). When **la mayoría** is followed by **de** + [*plural noun*], the verb can agree with **mayoría** (singular) or with the other noun (plural).

  La mayoría de los estudiantes **habla(n)** un poco de español.
  ***Most** students **speak** a little Spanish.*

- The plural verb must be used with the verbs **ser, estar,** and **parecer**.

  La mayoría de los profesores **son** latinoamericanos.
  ***The majority** of the professors **are** Latin American.*

- You can also use **los/las** + [*plural noun*] to make generalizing statements. Use the third-person plural verb form with this construction.

  Los actores son personas abiertas.
  ***Actors are** outgoing people.*

4 Adjectives (Los adjetivos) L1B, L2A

- An adjective always agrees with the corresponding noun in both gender and number, even when the noun and the adjective are found in separate sentences.

  Granada es un**a** ciudad fantástic**a**. Está llen**a** de impresionantes monumentos históricos.
  Granada is a fantastic city. It is full of impressive historic monuments.

4.1 Gender (**El género**) L2A, L12A

- As with nouns, the gender of adjectives is often signaled by the final letter. Some adjectives have distinct masculine and feminine forms; most adjectives ending in -**e**, -**ista**, or a consonant use the same form for masculine and feminine.

masculine		feminine	
-**o**	divertid**o**, content**o**	-**a**	divertid**a**, content**a**
-**e**	responsabl**e**, trist**e**	-**e**	responsabl**e**, trist**e**
-*consonant*	feli**z**	-*consonant*	feli**z**
-**ista**	optim**ista**	-**ista**	optim**ista**

- You have seen that the ending -**ista** is used in certain nouns (**taxista, periodista**). In adjectives, this ending remains unchanged when describing both masculine and feminine nouns.

  Clara es siempre muy optim**ista**.
  Clara is always very optimistic.

  Su novio Pedro es pesim**ista**.
  Her boyfriend Pedro is pessimistic.

⚠ Adjectives that describe colors and end in -**o** change to the ending -**a** in the feminine form: blanc**o/a**, negr**o/a**, etc. As with all adjectives, adjectives of color that end in -**e** or a consonant, such as **verde, azul, marrón,** and **gris,** can be masculine or feminine. In addition, some nouns, such as **café, rosa,** and **naranja,** can be used as invariable adjectives. L3B

⚠ Note that the adjectives **otro/a** and **medio/a** are used without an indefinite article.

  Otra botella de agua, por favor. L2B
  ***Another** bottle of water, please.*

  ¿Me da **medio** kilo de tomates? L4A
  *Would you give me a **half** kilogram of tomatoes?*

- Nationalities `L1B`

masculine		feminine	
-o	italian**o**	**-a**	italian**a**
-consonant	alem**án** español	*-consonant* + **a**	aleman**a** español**a**

⚠ Note that the written accent on the final syllable of adjectives of nationality such as **alemán** or **inglés** is dropped when **-a** is added to form the feminine: **alemana, inglesa**.

⚠ For adjectives of nationality that end in an accented **í**, such as **paquistaní** or **marroquí**, form the plural by adding **-es**: **paquistaníes, marroquíes**.

4.2 The plural (**El plural**) `L2A`

singular			plural
Ending in a vowel	simpátic**o**, típic**a**, important**e**	+ **s**	simpático**s**, típica**s**, importante**s**
Ending in a consonant	internaciona**l**, popula**r**	+ **es**	internacional**es**, popular**es**

4.3 Position of adjectives (**Posición de los adjetivos**) `U0, L1B`

- In Spanish, the adjective is usually placed after the noun it modifies.

  La medicina es una profesión **interesante**.
  *Medicine is an **interesting** profession.*

- Adjectives used in greetings are placed in front of the noun.

  Buenos días, **buenas** tardes, **buenas** noches.
  ***Good** morning, **good** afternoon, **good** night.*

4.4 The comparative and the superlative (**El comparativo y el superlativo**)

4.4.1 Regular forms (Las formas regulares) `L6A, L9A`

- Form regular comparatives and superlatives using **más** (*more*) and **menos** (*less*).

	comparative	superlative
interesante(s)	**más interesante(s)**	**el/la más interesante** **los/las más interesantes**
	menos interesante(s)	**el/la menos interesante** **los/las menos interesantes**
divertido/a(s)	**más divertido/a(s)**	**el más divertido** **la más divertida** **los más divertidos** **las más divertidas**
	menos divertido/a(s)	**el menos divertido** **la menos divertida** **los menos divertidos** **las menos divertidas**

Para mí, **los** programas **más divertidos** son los concursos. **Los menos divertidos** son las noticias.
*In my opinion, game shows are **the most entertaining** TV programs. **The least entertaining ones** are the news broadcasts.*

4.4.2 Irregular forms (Las formas irregulares) L6A, L9A

	comparative	superlative
bueno/a	**mejor**	**el/la mejor**
malo/a	**peor**	**el/la peor**
grande	**mayor**	**el/la mayor**
pequeño/a	**menor**	**el/la menor**
joven	**menor**	**el/la menor**
viejo/a	**mayor**	**el/la mayor**

El perro es **el mejor** amigo del hombre.
*Dog is man's **best** friend.*

Para mí, el lunes es **el peor** día de la semana.
*In my opinion, Monday is **the worst** day of the week.*

- Use the regular forms for **grande** and **pequeño/a** to refer to size; the irregular forms are used to refer to age.

4.4.3 Comparisons of equality (El comparativo de igualdad) L8B

- Comparisons of equality are formed with the construction **tan/tanto... como...**
- **Tan** precedes adjectives and adverbs and always remains unchanged.

Aquí la vida no es **tan** fácil **como** en Europa.
*Life here is not **as** easy **as** in Europe.*

Viajar en el tren de alta velocidad es casi **tan** rápido **como** viajar en avión.
*Traveling on the high-speed train is almost **as** fast **as** traveling by plane.*

- **Tanto** can be used alone or in front of a noun, in which case it needs to agree in both gender and number.

¡Esa canción me gusta **tanto**!   Aquí hay **tantas** panaderías **como** en mi barrio.
*I like that song **so much**!*   *There are **as many** bakeries here **as** in my neighborhood.*

- Comparisons of equality with verbs are formed by placing **tanto como** after the verb. Note that in this construction **tanto** does not change in number or gender.

Mi hermana ya gana **tanto como** yo.
*My sister already earns **as much as** I do.*

4.5 The absolute superlative (**El superlativo absoluto**) L11B

- The absolute superlative describes a quality without making reference to other people or things. It is equivalent to *extremely*, *super*, or *very*.
- To form the absolute superlative, drop the final vowel of the adjective (if there is one) and add **-ísimo/a(s)**. The ending always carries a written accent mark.

pequeño/a(s)	pequeñísimo/a(s)
caro/a(s)	carísimo/a(s)
grande(s)	grandísimo/a(s)
fácil(es)	facilísimo/a(s)

- Note these spelling changes that are necessary to preserve the original pronunciation of the adjective.

rico → ri**qu**ísimo

largo → lar**gu**ísimo

feliz → feli**c**ísimo

- In colloquial language, other superlative constructions are used, such as **muy muy** and the prefix **super-**.

> Esta película es **muy muy buena**.
> *This movie is **really good**.*

> Este sofá es **supercómodo**.
> *This sofa is **super comfortable**.*

4.6 Shortened adjectives (**El adjetivo apocopado**) `L12B`

- The adjectives **bueno** and **grande** are shortened to **buen** and **gran** before a masculine singular noun (**grande** is also shortened before a feminine singular noun). Note that the adjective is not shortened when used with feminine or plural nouns or when used after the noun.

¡**Buen** viaje! (*masc. sing.*) *Have a **good** trip!*	un **gran** libro *a **great** book*
¡**Buena** suerte! (*fem. sing.*) ***Good** luck!*	un libro **grande** *a **big** book*

 Note that there are slight differences in meaning when the adjective is placed before or after the noun.

5 Verbs (Los verbos)

- Spanish verbs are classified into three groups, according to their endings:

  -**ar** verbs: hablar, trabajar, tomar...

  -**er** verbs: aprender, beber, comer...

  -**ir** verbs: vivir, escribir, compartir...

5.1 The present (**El presente**)

5.1.1 Regular forms (Formas regulares) `L1B, L2A, L2B, L3B`

	-**ar** verbs (**trabajar**)	-**er** verbs (**aprender**)	-**ir** verbs (**vivir**)
(yo)	trabaj**o**	aprend**o**	viv**o**
(tú)	trabaj**as**	aprend**es**	viv**es**
(usted, él, ella)	trabaj**a**	aprend**e**	viv**e**
(nosotros/as)	trabaj**amos**	aprend**emos**	viv**imos**
(vosotros/as)	trabaj**áis**	aprend**éis**	viv**ís**
(ustedes, ellos/as)	trabaj**an**	aprend**en**	viv**en**

- Stem-changing verbs (**Verbos con cambio en la raíz**) `L2B, L3B, L4A, L4B, 10B, L11A, L12A, L12B`

	e > ie (**querer**)	o > ue (**poder**)	e > i (**servir**)
(yo)	qu**ie**ro	p**ue**do	s**i**rvo
(tú)	qu**ie**res	p**ue**des	s**i**rves
(usted, él, ella)	qu**ie**re	p**ue**de	s**i**rve
(nosotros/as)	queremos	podemos	servimos
(vosotros/as)	queréis	podéis	servís
(ustedes, ellos/as)	qu**ie**ren	p**ue**den	s**i**rven

 The **nosotros/as** and **vosotros/as** forms of these verbs do not have changes in the stem vowel.

> Yo qu**ie**ro ir al cine, pero vosotras qu**e**réis salir a cenar.
> *I want to go to the movies, but you want to go out to dinner.*

 Some verbs have a spelling change in the **yo** form in order to maintain the original pronunciation of the verb stem, e.g., **g → j**: **recoger** (**recojo**) or **gu → g**: **seguir** (**sigo**).

5.1.2 Irregular forms (Formas irregulares) `L3B, L4A, L6B, L11A, L11B`

- Certain verbs undergo changes in the first-person singular form (**Cambios en la primera persona del singular**).

  The following verbs are irregular in the first-person singular form (**yo**).

	infinitive	first-person singular (present)	
-g-	hacer poner salir	ha**g**o pon**g**o sal**g**o	`L3A, L4A`
-y	dar estar	do**y** esto**y**	
-zc-	conocer	cono**zc**o	`L5B, L7A`
	saber	**sé**	`L6B`
	ver	**veo**	

- Stem-changing verbs with irregular **yo** forms (**Verbos mixtos**) `L2A, 11A, L12A`

  These stem-changing verbs are also irregular in the **yo** form.

	tener	venir	decir
(yo)	ten**g**o	ven**g**o	di**g**o
(tú)	tie**n**es	vie**n**es	dices
(usted, él, ella)	tie**n**e	vie**n**e	dice
(nosotros/as)	tenemos	venimos	decimos
(vosotros/as)	tenéis	venís	decís
(ustedes, ellos/as)	tie**n**en	vie**n**en	dicen

- Fully irregular verbs (**Verbos totalmente irregulares**) `L1A, L1B, L3A, L3B, L6B, L12A`

	ser	ir	haber
(yo)	soy	voy	he
(tú)	eres	vas	has
(usted, él, ella)	es	va	ha
(nosotros/as)	somos	vamos	hemos
(vosotros/as)	sois	vais	habéis
(ustedes, ellos/as)	son	van	han

 In the present tense, the verb **haber** is principally used in the form **hay**, which is impersonal and invariable. Use **hay** to express both *there is* and *there are* in Spanish. The conjugated present-tense forms of **haber** are used only as auxiliary verbs, such as in the formation of the present perfect: **He trabajado.** `L3A`

5.2 The preterite (El pretérito indefinido) `L5A, L5B, L8B, L9B, L10B`

5.2.1 Regular forms (Las formas regulares) `L5A`

	-ar verbs (terminar)	-er verbs (nacer)	-ir verbs (vivir)
(yo)	terminé	nací	viví
(tú)	terminaste	naciste	viviste
(usted, él, ella)	terminó	nació	vivió
(nosotros/as)	terminamos	nacimos	vivimos
(vosotros/as)	terminasteis	nacisteis	vivisteis
(ustedes, ellos/as)	terminaron	nacieron	vivieron

- ¿Cuándo **terminaste** los estudios?
- *When **did you finish** your studies?*

- ¿Dónde **naciste**?
- *Where **were you born**?*

■ **Terminé** en 1999.
■ *I **finished** in 1999.*

■ **Nací** en Montevideo y **viví** allí veinte años.
■ *I **was born** in Montevideo and **I lived** there for twenty years.*

 The endings of **-er** and **-ir** verbs are identical in the preterite.

In **-ar** and **-ir** verbs, the conjugations of the first-person plural (**nosotros/as**) are identical in the present and in the preterite: **hablamos** (present) - **hablamos** (preterite); **abrimos** (present) - **abrimos** (preterite).

In the preterite, the spoken stress always falls on the first vowel of the the verb ending. In the regular forms of this tense, the root does not carry the stressed syllable. This pronunciation pattern is characteristic of the preterite: **hablé, hablaste, habló, hablamos, hablasteis, hablaron; vendí, vendiste, vendió, vendimos, vendisteis, vendieron; abrí, abriste, abrió, abrimos, abristeis, abrieron.**

5.2.2 Irregular forms (Las formas irregulares) `L5B, L8B`

	ser	ir	dar
(yo)	fui	fui	di
(tú)	fuiste	fuiste	diste
(usted, él, ella)	fue	fue	dio
(nosotros/as)	fuimos	fuimos	dimos
(vosotros/as)	fuisteis	fuisteis	disteis
(ustedes, ellos/as)	fueron	fueron	dieron

 The forms of the verbs **ser** and **ir** are identical in the preterite. Use context to determine their meaning.

Camila **fue** a la fiesta anoche.
*Camila **went** to the party last night.*

Jorge **fue** periodista del diario universitario por varios años.
*Jorge **was** a reporter for the university newspaper for several years.*

- The endings for **dar** in the preterite are the same as the regular preterite endings for **-er** and **-ir** verbs, but there are no written accent marks. The preterite of the verb **ver** follows a similiar pattern (**vi, viste, vio**, etc.).

- A number of other verbs have irregular forms in the preterite. These verbs can be divided into three categories (**u**-stem, **i**-stem, and **j**-stem), according to the stem change that the verb undergoes in the preterite.

	tener (u-stem)	venir (i-stem)	decir (j-stem)
(yo)	tuv**e**	vin**e**	dij**e**
(tú)	tuv**iste**	vin**iste**	dij**iste**
(usted, él, ella)	tuv**o**	vin**o**	dij**o**
(nosotros/as)	tuv**imos**	vin**imos**	dij**imos**
(vosotros/as)	tuv**isteis**	vin**isteis**	dij**isteis**
(ustedes, ellos/as)	tuv**ieron**	vin**ieron**	dij**eron**

 The endings of these verbs are the regular preterite endings of **-er** and **-ir** verbs, except for the **yo** and **usted** forms. Note that these two endings do not have written accents.

- These verbs are irregular in the preterite and undergo similar stem changes to **tener, venir,** and **decir**.

infinitive	u-stem	preterite forms
poder	pud-	pude, pudiste, pudo, pudimos, pudisteis, pudieron
poner	pus-	puse, pusiste, puso, pusimos, pusisteis, pusieron
saber	sup-	supe, supiste, supo, supimos, supisteis, supieron
estar	estuv-	estuve, estuviste, estuvo, estuvimos, estuvisteis, estuvieron

infinitive	i-stem	preterite forms
querer	quis-	quise, quisiste, quiso, quisimos, quisisteis, quisieron
hacer	hic-	hice, hiciste, hizo, hicimos, hicisteis, hicieron

 Note that the third-person singular preterite form of **hacer** undergoes a **c→z** spelling change: **hizo**.

- Preterite verbs with **j**-stems, like **decir**, omit the letter **i** in the ending of the **ustedes/ellos/ellas** form.

infinitive	j-stem	preterite forms
traer	traj-	traje, trajiste, trajo, trajimos, trajisteis, tra**j**eron
conducir	conduj-	conduje, condujiste, condujo, condujimos, condujisteis, condu**j**eron
traducir	traduj-	traduje, tradujiste, tradujo, tradujimos, tradujisteis, tradu**j**eron

Todos **trajeron** comida o bebidas a la fiesta.
*Everyone **brought** food or drinks to the party.*

 Most verbs that end in **-cir** follow the pattern of **j**-stem verbs in the preterite. For example, **producir → produje, produjiste,** etc.

 In the first- and third-person singular forms of irregular verbs in the preterite, the stress falls on the root and not the ending: hice, hizo, vine, vino, quise...

- The preterite form of **hay** (*inf.* **haber**) is **hubo** (*there was; there were*).

    Hubo una tormenta muy fuerte el sábado por la noche.
    ***There was** a very strong storm on Saturday night.*

- *See the verb tables on pp. A4–A11 for the full conjugations of irregular verb patterns.*

5.2.3 Use of the preterite (El uso del pretérito indefinido) `L5A, L5B, L8B, L9B, L10B, L13A, L13B, L14B`

- The preterite is used to talk about finished actions and events in the past.

    El mes pasado **viajé** a Puerto Rico. Ahí **conocí** a mucha gente y **me divertí** mucho.
    *Last month **I traveled** to Puerto Rico. **I met** a lot of people there and **I had** a lot of **fun**.*

- The preterite is often used with time expressions that specify the moment in the past: **anoche, ayer, el otro día, la semana pasada, el mes pasado, hace dos años, el año pasado, en 1990,** etc.

El 28 de junio de 1987, Manuela terminó la universidad.
*Manuela graduated from college **on June 28, 1987**.*

En 1993, celebró su boda.
In 1993, she got married.

Hace un mes, Manuela y Carolina abrieron la tienda.
*Manuela and Carolina opened the shop **a month ago**.*

- The preterite is also used in order to comment on or evaluate an experience in the past.

Mi viaje a la Patagonia **fue** increíble. Me **gustó** mucho el paisaje y la gente me **pareció** muy amable.
*My trip to Patagonia **was** incredible. I really **liked** the scenery and the people **seemed** really friendly.*

5.3 The present perfect (**El pretérito perfecto**) `L6A, L7B, L10B`

- The present perfect is formed with the present of the verb **haber** and the past participle of the main verb.

	haber	+ [*past participle*]
(yo)	he	
(tú)	has	hablado
(usted, él, ella)	ha	comido
(nosotros/as)	hemos	dormido
(vosotros/as)	habéis	
(ustedes, ellos/as)	han	

¿**Has viajado** a Europa alguna vez?
***Have you** ever **traveled** to Europe?*

- ¿**Has tomado** ya un café?
- No, todavía no.
- *Have you had a cup of coffee yet?*
- *No, not yet.*

5.3.1 The past participle (El participio pasado)

- **-ar** verbs: **-ado**	**hablar** → **hablado** **trabajar** → **trabajado** **estudiar** → **estudiado** **estar** → **estado**	**Has trabajado** mucho. *You have worked a lot.*

- **-er** and **-ir** verbs: **-ido**	**comer** → **comido** **vender** → **vendido** **dormir** → **dormido** **ir** → **ido**	**He vendido** mi coche. *I have sold my car.*

⚠️ The past participles of **-er** and **-ir** verbs whose stems end in **-a, -e,** or **-o** have an accent mark on the **i** of the **-ido** ending.

infinitive	past participle
caer	caído
creer	creído
leer	leído
oír	oído
reír	reído
traer	traído

5.3.2 Irregular past participles (Los participios pasados irregulares) L7B

infinitive	past participle
abrir	abierto
cubrir	cubierto
decir	dicho
escribir	escrito
hacer	hecho
morir	muerto
poner	puesto
romper	roto
ver	visto
volver	vuelto

- ¿Qué **has hecho** esta tarde?
  *What **have you done** this afternoon?*

- **He escrito** un ensayo para la clase de sociología y **he visto** a mis padres.
  *I **wrote** en essay for sociology class and **I saw** my parents.*

5.3.3 Placement of direct object pronouns
(La posición de los pronombres de objeto directo) L7B

- The present perfect is composed of the verb **haber** + [*past participle*]. These two components always appear together and cannot be separated by another word. When an object pronoun is used, it is placed before the conjugated form of **haber**.

  - ¿**Has puesto** la mesa?
  - Sí, **la he puesto**.
  - *Have you set the table?*
  - *Yes, I have set it.*

  - ¿**Habéis visto** a Juan?
  - No, no **lo hemos visto** todavía.
  - *Have you seen Juan?*
  - *No, we have not seen him yet.*

5.3.4 Use of the present perfect (El uso del pretérito perfecto) L6A, L10B

- The present perfect is used to refer to past events that in some way act upon the present, either because the consequences of the past action affect the present or because the past action has taken place within a time period that has not ended.

  ¿**Has llamado** a Carla?
  Have you called Carla?

- The present perfect is frequently used with the adverb **ya** (*already*).

  ¿**Ya han terminado** la tarea?
  Have you already finished the homework?

 In some Latin American countries, the present perfect is seldom used, and the preterite is used instead. In Spain, the present perfect is frequently used to refer to events in the recent past.

5.4 The imperfect (El pretérito imperfecto) `L9A`

5.4.1 Regular forms (Las formas regulares)

	-ar verbs	-er verbs	-ir verbs
	HABL**AR**	TEN**ER**	VIV**IR**
(yo)	habl**aba**	ten**ía**	viv**ía**
(tú)	habl**abas**	ten**ías**	viv**ías**
(usted, él, ella)	habl**aba**	ten**ía**	viv**ía**
(nosotros/as)	habl**ábamos**	ten**íamos**	viv**íamos**
(vosotros/as)	habl**abais**	ten**íais**	viv**íais**
(ustedes, ellos/as)	habl**aban**	ten**ían**	viv**ían**

De niño, **vivía** en Córdoba con mis abuelos.
*As a child, **I lived** in Córdoba with my grandparents.*

Teníamos una casa muy bonita.
***We had** a very nice house.*

⚠ The first- and third-person singular forms are the same in all conjugations of the imperfect.

⚠ Additionally, the endings of **-er** and **-ir** verbs in the imperfect are the same.

5.4.2 Irregular forms (Las formas irregulares) `L9A`

	ser	ir	ver
(yo)	**era**	**iba**	**veía**
(tú)	**eras**	**ibas**	**veías**
(usted, él, ella)	**era**	**iba**	**veía**
(nosotros/as)	**éramos**	**íbamos**	**veíamos**
(vosotros/as)	**erais**	**ibais**	**veíais**
(ustedes, ellos/as)	**eran**	**iban**	**veían**

Cuando **era** más joven, **iba** a conciertos de rock.
*When **I was** younger, **I used to go** to rock concerts.*

5.4.3 Use of the imperfect (El uso del pretérito imperfecto) `L9A, L9B, L10B, L13A, L13B, L14A, L14B`

The imperfect is used to:

- speak about habitual or repeated actions in the past

  Cuando **estudiaba, compartía** un apartamento con dos compañeros. **Estaba** siempre con ellos y **teníamos** un grupo de música.
  *When **I was** a student, **I shared** an apartment with two roommates. **I was** with them all the time and **we had** a band.*

- describe situations or contexts in the past

  Era de noche, **hacía** mucho calor y yo **no podía** dormir.
  ***It was** night, **it was** very hot, and **I couldn't** sleep.*

- describe the context and the circumstances of a past event

  Esta mañana **estaba** en casa; por eso he recibido la noticia.
  ***I was** at home this morning, so I received the news.*

  En 2008 voté por primera vez. **Tenía** 18 años.
  *In 2008 I voted for the first time. **I was** 18 years old.*

  Estábamos en Mallorca cuando llegó la noticia.
  ***We were** in Mallorca when the news arrived.*

- compare the past and the present

    Yo antes **era** muy inseguro. Ahora sé lo que quiero.
    *I **used to be** very insecure. Now I know what I want.*

    Hace 10 años **vivía** todavía en casa de mis padres. Hoy vivo con mi esposa.
    *Ten years ago I still **lived** with my parents. Now I live with my wife.*

- express ignorance on a subject

    No **sabía** que en Guinea Ecuatorial hablaban español. **Pensaba** que se hablaban otros idiomas.
    *I **didn't know** that they spoke Spanish in Equatorial Guinea. I **thought** that they spoke other languages.*

- express intentions that were not realized

    Yo **quería** estudiar sociología, pero al final estudié derecho.
    *I **wanted** to study sociology, but I ended up studying law.*

5.5 The past perfect (**El pretérito pluscuamperfecto**) L14A

5.5.1 Conjugation (Conjugación)

- The past perfect is formed with the imperfect of the verb **haber** and the past participle of the main verb.

	haber	**+ [*past participle*]**
(yo)	había	
(tú)	habías	
(usted, él, ella)	había	hablado
(nosotros/as)	habíamos	tenido
(vosotros/as)	habíais	vivido
(ustedes, ellos/as)	habían	

5.5.2 Use of the past perfect (El uso del pretérito pluscuamperfecto)

- The past perfect is used to express a past action that occurred before a previous past action.

    Cuando llegué, el tren ya **había salido**.
    *When I arrived, the train **had** already **left**.*

5.6 Contrasting past verb tenses (**Contraste de los tiempos del pasado**)
L9B, L10B, L13A, L13B, L14A, L14B

- Present perfect (**El pretérito perfecto**)

    Use the present perfect to speak about past events that influence the present. When this tense is used, either the consequences of the past event reach into the present, or the time expression refers to a period of time that is not yet over.

    ¿**Has estado** en Costa Rica alguna vez?
    ***Have you** ever **been** to Costa Rica?*

    No, **todavía no he estado**.
    *No, I **haven't been there yet**.*

    Hoy **he aprendido** muchas cosas.
    *I **have learned** many things today.*

- Preterite (**El pretérito indefinido**)

  Use the preterite to narrate past actions that belong to a period of time that is over. When narrating past events, time expressions such as **de repente** and **(y) entonces** can signal the use of the preterite.

  > **Fui** a México hace dos años.
  > *I **went** to Mexico two years ago.*

  > **Apagaron** las luces del teatro, y entonces **empezó** la función.
  > *The lights in the theater **were shut off**, and then the show **began**.*

- The use of the present perfect and the preterite also depends on factors such as the point of view of the speaker and the differences between different Spanish-speaking countries. In most countries in Latin America, the use of the present perfect is limited and the preterite is preferred.

  > Este año **estuve** en España. (*Latin American Spanish*)
  > Este año **he estado** en España. *(Iberian Spanish)*
  > *I **was** in Spain this year. / I **have been** to Spain this year.*

- Imperfect (**El pretérito imperfecto**)

  Use the imperfect to describe past situations and causes that establish the background details to the main action. This tense is often used along with other past tenses.

  > Como **llovía** mucho, no salimos.
  > *Because **it was raining** a lot, we didn't go out.*

  > Ayer no fui a trabajar porque **estaba** enferma.
  > *I didn't go to work yesterday because **I was** sick.*

- Past perfect (**El pretérito pluscuamperfecto**)

  This tense expresses an action in the past that occurred before another past action.

  > Antes de aprender español, **había estudiado** francés.
  > *Before learning Spanish, **I had studied** French.*

5.7 Reflexive verbs (**Verbos reflexivos**)

5.7.1 Reflexive pronouns (Pronombres reflexivos)   U0, L7A, L10B, L11A, L12A, L17B, L18B

- A reflexive verb is made up of a form of the verb and the reflexive pronoun.

	llamarse
(yo)	**me** llamo
(tú)	**te** llamas
(usted, él, ella)	**se** llama
(nosotros/as)	**nos** llamamos
(vosotros/as)	**os** llamáis
(ustedes, ellos/as)	**se** llaman

- With a reflexive verb, the subject both performs and receives the action of the verb.

  Me lavo la cara.　　　　　　　　　**Nos despertamos** a las siete y media.
  *I **wash** my face.*　　　　　　　　　*We **wake up** at seven-thirty.*

- Note the difference in meaning when the verb is not reflexive.

  Siempre **lavo los platos** después de cenar.　　　Claudia **despierta a su hermano** por la mañana.
  *I always **wash the dishes** after dinner.*　　　　*Claudia **wakes up her brother** in the morning.*

Note that the definite article is generally used to refer to parts of the body or clothing in conjunction with reflexive verbs.

> Te pones **el** abrigo.
> *You put on **your** coat.*

> Ella se lava **las** manos.
> *She washes **her** hands.*

 Reflexive verbs in Spanish do not always translate to a reflexive meaning in English.

- ¿Cómo **te sientes**?
- **Me siento** mejor, gracias.
- **Me alegro.**

- *How **do you feel**?*
- *I **feel** better, thank you.*
- *I **am glad.***

- Reflexive verbs are frequently used to talk about relationships and emotions.

> **Me separé** de mi ex, pero **nos llevamos** bien.
> ***I broke up** with my ex, but **we get along** well.*

> Mi hijo **se parece** mucho a los dos.
> *My son **looks** a lot **like** both of us.*

> **Me alegro** de que te jubiles, aunque **nos lo hemos pasado** muy bien contigo.
> ***I am happy** that you are retiring, although **we have had a good time** with you.*

> **Se ríe** mucho con sus compañeros de baile. Les divierte bailar.
> ***She laughs** a lot with her dance partners. They have a good time dancing.*

5.7.2. Reciprocal verbs (Verbos recíprocos) `L17B`

- Reciprocal verbs are conjugated only in plural forms and are accompanied by the plural reflexive pronouns (**nos, os, se**). These verbs express a shared or reciprocal action between two or more people or things. When a verb is reciprocal, the phrase **el uno al otro/a la otra** can be added to the sentence, and the pronoun is understood as *(to) each other* or *(to) one another*.

> María y Carlos **se abrazan.** (María abraza a Carlos y Carlos abraza a María.)
> *María and Carlos **hug each other.** (María hugs Carlos and Carlos hugs María.)*

> Mi hermana y yo **nos llamamos** todos los días.
> *My sister and I **call each other** every day.*

5.7.3 Pronominal verb of change: *ponerse* (Verbo pronominal de cambio) `L18B`

- The pronominal verb **ponerse** is conjugated with the reflexive pronouns **me, te, se, nos, os,** and **se** and can be followed by an adverb (**muy, un poco**) and/or an adjective (**triste, alegre**). **Ponerse** expresses a change in a subject's mood that is usually considered to be temporary. When used with an adjective, the verb is often translated into English as *to become.*

> Mi madre **se puso** muy contenta al verme.
> *My mother **became** very happy when she saw me.*

> **Nos ponemos** un poco tristes cuando nos despedimos.
> ***We get** a little sad when we say goodbye to each other.*

5.8 ser/estar

5.8.1 Comparison of uses `L1A, L1B, L2A, L2B, L3A, L3B, L5B`

ser	estar
Used to identify: `L1A`	**Used to identify:**
• names and identity **Soy** Eva. *I am Eva. (My name is Eva.)*	• geographical and relative location `L2A, L3B` ¿Dónde **está** Sevilla? *Where is Seville?*
• nationality `L1B` **Soy** polaca. **Soy** de Varsovia. *I am Polish. I am from Warsaw.*	Sevilla **está** en el sur de España. *Seville is in the south of Spain.*
• profession `L1B` Antonio **es** arquitecto. *Antonio is an architect.* María **es** médica. *María is a doctor.*	Los CD **están** a la derecha del despertador. *The CDs are to the right of the alarm clock.* • marital status `L5B` ¿**Está** usted casada? ***Are you** married?*
• characteristics of people and things (descriptions) `L1B, L2A` Sevilla **es** una ciudad muy bonita. *Seville is a very pretty city.* Sevilla **es** la capital de Andalucía. *Seville is the capital of Andalucía.*	No, **estoy** soltera. *No, I am single.* • tastes of food and drinks `L2B` El pulpo **está** muy rico. *The octopus is very good.*
• time `L3A` ¿Qué hora **es**? **Son** las tres de la tarde. *What time is it? It is 3 o'clock in the afternoon.*	

5.8.2 ser/estar + [*adjective*] `L1B, L4B, L10A, L11A, L12A`

ser + [*adjective*]	estar + [*adjective*]
• expresses characteristics Emilio **es** una persona **optimista**. *Emilio is an optimistic person.* Carmen **es** un poco **tímida**. *Carmen is a bit shy.* **Son** muy **simpáticos**. ***They are** very **nice**.*	• expresses physical or mental states **Estamos contentos** con la casa nueva. ***We are happy** with the new house.* Ángel **está** muy **enamorado** de ella. *Ángel **is** quite **in love** with her.* Mi padre **está enfermo. Está resfriado**. *My father **is sick. He has a cold**.*

- With negative adjectives, **un poco** can soften the negative impact.

  Pedro es muy amable, pero **un poco** pesimista.
  *Pedro is very friendly, but he is **a bit** pessimistic.*

- **Estar** + [*adjective*] is normally used to express a temporary state experienced by the subject of the sentence, while **ser** + [*adjective*] is normally used to express an inherent characteristic. `L11A`

  La paella **es** un plato **típico** de Valencia. La paella que han servido hoy **está** muy **rica**.
  *Paella **is** a **typical** Valencian dish. The paella they served today **is** very **tasty**.*

- Use the construction **estar impresionado/a con** + [*noun*] to express admiration. `L18A`

  Estoy impresionado con las aventuras de esta alpinista.
  I am impressed by the adventures of this mountain climber.

- **Estar seguro/a de que** and **está demostrado que** are used to express certainty and evidence in affirmative statements. Use these constructions in negative sentences with the subjunctive. (See **5.21**) **L17A**

> **Estoy** (completamente) **seguro de que** esta técnica **ayuda** a las personas.
> *I am (completely) **sure that** this technique **helps** people.*

> **Está demostrado que** esta técnica **ayuda** a las personas.
> *It **has been shown that** this technique **helps** people.*

> **No estamos seguros de que** los avances de la ciencia **representen** una mejora.
> *We are **not sure that** scientific advances **have made** improvements.*

> **No está demostrado que sea** un invento original.
> *It **has not been shown to be** an original invention.*

5.8.3 es mejor que + [*subjunctive*], lo mejor es/sería + [*infinitive/noun*] L15A, L16B

- Use the verb **ser** with these constructions to make suggestions. (See **5.21**)

> **Lo mejor es** consumir productos frescos.
> *It is **best** to eat fresh produce.*

> **Es mejor que leas** la etiqueta.
> *It is **better that you read** the label.*

> **Lo mejor son** las marcas conocidas.
> *The most well-known brands **are the best**.*

- When used with a noun, the verb agrees in number.

> Lo mejor **es el precio**.
> *The best thing **is the price**.*

> Lo mejor **son los conservantes naturales**.
> *Natural preservatives **are** the best.*

- Use **ser** in the conditional to make polite suggestions.

> Lo mejor **sería** usar envases reciclables.
> *It **would be** best to use recyclable containers.*

> Lo mejor **sería** un modelo de etiqueta único.
> *A unique label **would be** best.*

5.8.4 es necesario + [*infinitive*] / que + [*subjunctive*] L15A

- Use the infinitive when describing necessity in a general or global sense.

> **Es necesario conocer** los productos típicos de cada país.
> *It is **necessary to become familiar with** each country's typical products.*

- Use the subjunctive when describing what a specific person or group needs to do. (See **5.21**)

> **Es necesario que** ustedes **conozcan** nuestros productos.
> *It is **necessary** for you **to become familiar with** our products.*

5.8.5 es probable/posible que + [*subjunctive*] L17A

- Probability can be gauged through the use of adverbs of degree, such as **muy, poco**, and **bastante**. (See **5.21**)

> **Es poco** probable que desaparezcan los libros.
> *It is **hardly** probable that books will disappear.*

> **Es bastante** posible que sea verdad.
> *It is **fairly** possible that it is true.*

> **Es muy** probable que tengas razón.
> *It is **very** probable that you are right.*

5.8.6 (no) es evidente que + [*indicative/subjunctive*] `L17A`

- Use the indicative to express certainty and evidence, and the subjunctive to express lack of certainty and evidence. (See **5.21**)

    Es evidente que **hay** una solución.
    It is clear that there is a solution.

    No es evidente que los móviles **sean** malos para la salud.
    It is not clear that cell phones are bad for your health.

5.8.7 ser bueno/a, malo/a en/para/con + [*noun*] `L17B`

- Express someone's or something's ability with **ser + bueno/a, malo/a + en/para/con**. Use **en/para** + [*discipline*] and **con** + [*a specific thing*].

    Es muy **buena para** la música y bastante **mala en** matemáticas.
    She is very good at music and pretty bad at math.

    Sí, **es malo para** las relaciones públicas, pero **es bueno con** las cuentas.
    Yes, he is bad at public relations, but he is good at calculations.

5.8.8 es increíble cómo + [*verb in the indicative*] `L18A`

- Use this construction to express admiration.

    Es increíble cómo recorrió en bicicleta tantos lugares de Sudamérica.
    It's incredible how she traveled through so many places in South America by bicycle.

5.8.9 (no) es (una) buena idea + [*infinitive*] / que + [*subjunctive*] `L18B`

- Use this construction to assess an idea in general terms (with the infinitive) or a concrete way (with the subjunctive). (See **5.21**)

    No es una buena idea contratar una empresa de eventos.
    It is not a good idea to hire an event-planning service.

    Es una excelente idea que celebres tu cumpleaños en la piscina.
    It is an excellent idea for you to celebrate your birthday at the pool.

5.9 hay/estar `L2A, L3B, L4B`

hay	estar
• Expresses the existence of something. **Hay** is a form of the verb **haber**. This form is used in the present and it is invariable.	• Expresses the location or position of an object or person. Lupe **está** en México. `L2A` *Lupe is in Mexico.*
¿Qué **hay** en esta calle? `L3B` *What is there on this street?*	¿Dónde **está** el hotel? **Está** en el centro. *Where is the hotel? It is downtown.*
Hay una librería y una zapatería. *There is a bookstore and a shoestore.*	
Hay can be followed by:	**Estar** can be used with:
• a noun without an article `L3B` En mi barrio **no hay** parque. *There isn't a park in my neighborhood.*	• [*definite article*] + [*singular noun*] `L3B` ¿Dónde **está** el bolígrafo? Está en la mesa. *Where is the pen? It is on the table.*
• [*indefinite article*] + [*noun*] `L3B` Cerca de mi apartamento **hay** un colegio. *There is a school near my apartment.*	• [*preposition*] + [*noun*] `L4B` El metro **está** a cinco minutos. *The subway is five minutes away.*
• plural noun with no article En el barrio **hay** bares y tiendas. `L3B` *There are bars and shops in the neighborhood.*	• [*definite article*] + [*plural noun*] Los estudiantes **están** en el bar. *The students are at the bar.*
• [*number*] + [*noun*] En este barrio **hay** dos mercados. `L3B` *There are two markets in this neighborhood.*	• proper nouns El Rastro **está** en Madrid. `L3B` *El Rastro is in Madrid.*

5.10 Verbs used with an infinitive (**Verbos con infinitivo**)

- Many verbs are regularly used in combination with other verbs. In these constructions, the second verb is used in the infinitive.

ir a L6A	¿Qué **vas a hacer** este verano? *What are you **going to do** this summer?*
poder L3B, L7B	**No podemos jugar.** ***We can't play.***
saber L8A	Irene ya **sabe nadar**. *Irene already **knows how to swim**.*
empezar a L9B	**Empecé a trabajar** en Caracas. ***I started working** in Caracas.*
tener que L6A, L10A	Juan **tiene que estudiar**. *Juan **has to study**.*
hay que L10A	**Hay que solucionar** muchos problemas. ***We need to fix** a lot of problems.*
recomendar L11A	**Te recomiendo ir** a un buen hotel. ***I recommend that you go** to a good hotel.*
alegrarse de L11A	**Me alegro** mucho **de oírte**. *I am very **happy to hear from you**.*
querer L3B, L8B, L12B	**Quiero ir** de vacaciones a Costa Rica. ***I want to go** on vacation to Costa Rica.*
esperar L12B	**Esperamos tener** muchos invitados. ***We hope to have** many guests.*
desear L12B	**Deseo tener** un trabajo interesante. ***I want to have** an interesting job.*

 Saber de + [*noun*] means to know about something or to possess certain knowledge. L8A

Ella **sabe** mucho **de** computadoras.
*She **knows** a lot **about** computers.*

 Empezar a indicates the beginning of an action or an event. L9B

Todos los días **empiezo a** trabajar a las 8:00 de la mañana.
*Every day **I start** working at 8:00 in the morning.*

Este año **empiezo a** estudiar japonés.
*This year **I will start to** study Japanese.*

Esta semana **empezamos a** pintar la casa.
*This week **we start** painting the house.*

- The preterite of **empezar** is generally used to talk about past actions or events.

En 2005 **empecé a** estudiar.
I started studying in 2005.

 Quería, the imperfect form of **querer**, is a polite way to express a request. L3B

Quería un perfume.
I'd like a perfume.

Quería información sobre los precios de habitaciones en agosto. L6B
I'd like information about the prices of rooms in August.

5.11 **Gustar** and similar verbs (**Gustar y verbos semejantes**)

- Use **gustar** with indirect object pronouns (**me, te, le, nos, os, les**).

  Gustar must agree with the subject of the sentence. When the subject is an infinitive, use the third-person singular form, **gusta**. `L4A`

  Me gusta la ciudad.
  I like the city.

  No **me gustan** los edificios modernos.
  I don't like modern buildings.

  Nos gusta leer el periódico por la mañana.
  We like to read the newspaper in the morning.

⚠ Although constructions with **gustar** are roughly equivalent to the English expression *to like*, note that the object that is liked is the subject of the Spanish sentence with **gustar** and the person who likes the object is expressed through the indirect object pronoun.

- Use **mucho** with **gustar** to express different degrees of preference.

  ¿**Te gusta** tu barrio?　　　　　　　　　Sí, **me gusta** mucho.
  Do you like your neighborhood?　　　　*Yes, I like it a lot.*

- Use **me gustaría** + [*infinitive*] to express a desire or request information. **Gustaría** is the conditional form of **gustar**. `L6B`

  Me gustaría ir a Cuba de vacaciones.　　Hola, buenos días. **Me gustaría reservar** una habitación.
  I would like to go to Cuba on vacation.　*Hello, good morning. I would like to reserve a room.*

5.11.1 Verbs with indirect object pronouns (Verbos con pronombres de objeto indirecto)
`L7A, L11A, L13A, L15B, L17B, L18B`

- Verbs such as **encantar**, **molestar**, **interesar**, and **preocupar** express pleasure or displeasure, surprise, concern, or other feelings. These verbs are frequently used with indirect object pronouns in similar constructions to **gustar**. The verb **dar** can also be used with indirect object pronouns in certain constructions. When used with indirect object pronouns, these verbs are conjugated in the third-person singular or plural forms, depending on the subject.

(A mí)	**me**	gusta(n)	
(A ti)	**te**	molesta(n)	
(A usted, a él, a ella)	**le**	da(n) miedo/pena	[*infinitive*]
(A nosotros/as)	**nos**	divierte(n)	[*singular or plural noun*]
(A vosotros/as)	**os**	aburre(n)	**que** + [*subjunctive*]
(A ustedes, a ellos/as)	**les**	parece(n)	

A mis hijos **les encantan** los videojuegos.　　¿**Os interesa** estar en forma?
*My children **love** video games.*　　　　　　*Are you interested in getting in shape?*

No **me interesa** la política.　　　　　　　　**Me preocupa** mucho la economía actual.
*Politics **do not interest me**.*　　　　　　　*The current economy **worries me**.*

- Use **a mí, a ti**, etc., for emphasis or clarification.

  ¿Qué **te parece** el hotel **a ti**?　　　　**A mí me parece** horrible.
  *What **do you think** of the hotel?*　　　*I think it is horrible.*

- If a subordinate clause has a different subject than the sentence's main clause, use the subjunctive in the subordinate clause. (See **5.21**)

  Me molesta que la gente **llegue** tarde a clase.
  ***It bothers me that** people **arrive** late to class.*

5.11.2 doler `L10A`

- The verb **doler** is conjugated in the third person. Use **doler** in the singular or plural form in order to agree with the subject, the part of the body that hurts. As with the previous list of verbs (**5.11.1**), use **doler** with indirect object pronouns.

  (A mí) **me duele** la cabeza.
  *My head **hurts**.*

  (A mí) **me duelen** los pies.
  *My feet **hurt**.*

  (A ella) **le duele** la garganta.
  *Her throat **hurts**.*

5.12 Third-person verb forms (**Verbos en tercera persona**)

5.12.1 se + [*third-person verb form*] `L7B`

- Use **se puede** + [*infinitive*] to express what can or cannot be done, or what is or is not permitted.

  En un pueblo **se puede** jugar en la calle.
  *In a small town, **one can** play in the street.*

  Aquí **no se puede** fumar.
  *Smoking **is not permitted** here.*

- Use **se dice** to ask for or give a translation.

  - ¿Cómo **se dice** "hello" en español?
  - **Se dice** "hola".
  - *How do you say "hello" in Spanish?*
  - ***You say**, "hola."*

- Use **se escribe** to ask for or provide a spelling.

  "Hola" **se escribe** con *hache*.
  *"Hola" **is written** with an* h.

- Use **se habla(n)** to ask or tell what languages are spoken in a certain place. `L1B`

  En México **se habla** español.
  *Spanish **is spoken** in Mexico.*

5.12.2 Impersonal third-person verb forms used in weather expressions
(**Verbos impersonales de fenómenos meteorológicos en tercera persona**) `L10A`

- Use the verbs **llover** (*to rain*) and **nevar** (*to snow*) in the third-person singular.

  Hoy **llueve** mucho.   Siempre **nieva** en enero.
  ***It's raining** a lot today.*   ***It** always **snows** in January.*

- Use the third-person singular form of **hacer** in many common expressions about the weather.

Hace sol.	**Hace** mal tiempo.	**Hace** calor.
It is sunny.	*The weather is bad.*	*It's hot.*
Hace buen tiempo.	**Hace** frío.	**Hace** 30 °C.
The weather is good.	*It's cold.*	*It's 30° C.*

5.12.3 ser `L12A`

- The verb **ser** is used in the third person in many impersonal constructions, such as **es importante** + [*noun/infinitive*].

  Es importante tener buenos amigos.   **Es importante la amistad.**
  It is important to have good friends.   *Friendship is important.*

- Other adjectives that can be used in this construction include **interesante**, **imprescindible**, **difícil**, **fácil**, etc.

5.12.4 hace `L5A, L8B`

- Use the third-person singular form of **hacer**, **hace**, to express *ago*.

  Hace dos años, abrí la tienda.
  *I opened the store two years **ago**.*

5.13 The infinitive (**El infinitivo**)

- Use **podría/puede** + [*infinitive*] in polite requests. `L13A`

  ¿Podría confirmarme la hora de llegada de este tren, por favor?
  *Could you confirm the arrival time of this train **for me**, please?*

- Alternatively, make polite requests using the construction **le importaría** + [*infinitive*].

  ¿Le importaría decirme dónde está la Terminal 2?
  ***Would you mind telling me** where Terminal 2 is?*

- **Sentir** + [*infinitive*] is used to offer consolation. `L13B`

  Siento oír eso.
  ***I am sorry to hear** that.*

- Use **lo de** + [*infinitive*] to refer to a topic or matter that has been mentioned previously. (See **3.3**) `L14B`

  ¿Te han comentado **lo de quedar** mañana?
  *Have they told you **about getting together** tomorrow?*

- Use **es mejor** + [*infinitive*] or **lo mejor es/sería** + [*infinitive*] to make suggestions. (See **5.8.3** and **5.21**) `L15A`

  Lo mejor es consumir de forma responsable.
  ***It is best to consume** in a responsible way.*

  Lo mejor sería tener buena información.
  ***It would be best to have** good information.*

- Use **seguir sin** + [*infinitive*] to express the continuity of an unrealized action. (See **5.15**) `L17A`

  Siguen sin descubrir ningún remedio eficaz.
  ***They still have not discovered** an effective remedy.*

- Use **antes/después de** + [*noun/infinitive*] to compare two events temporally. (See **5.21**) `L18A`

  Antes de convertirse en deportista, trabajaba como mecánico.
  ***Before becoming** an athlete, he worked as a mechanic.*

  Después de ganar la medalla de oro, se jubiló.
  ***After winning** the gold medal, he retired.*

  Después de la medalla de oro, se jubiló.
  ***After the** gold medal, he retired.*

- Use **(no) es (una) buena/mala/excelente idea** + [*infinitive*] to assess an idea. (See **5.21**) `L18B`

  Es una buena idea enviar tarjetas de invitación.
  ***It is a good idea to send** invitations.*

- Use **al** + [*infinitive*] to relate two simultaneous events. This structure is equivalent to **cuando** + [*conjugated verb in the indicative*].   `L18B`

    Se puso triste **al terminar** la fiesta. (Se puso triste **cuando terminó** la fiesta.)
    *He became sad **when** the party **ended**.*

    Al enterarse de la noticia, se puso triste.
    ***Upon hearing** the news, he became sad.*

5.14 The present participle (**El gerundio**)   `L7A, L14B`

5.14.1 estar + [*present participle*]

- Form the present progressive with a present-tense form of the verb **estar** followed by the present participle. Regular verbs form the present participle with these endings:

-ar →	**-ando**
-er →	**-iendo**
-ir →	**-iendo**

	estar	+ *present participle*
(yo)	estoy	
(tú)	estás	
(usted, él, ella)	está	habl**ando**
(nosotros/as)	estamos	aprend**iendo**
(vosotros/as)	estáis	escrib**iendo**
(ustedes, ellos/as)	están	

- Use the construction **estar** + [*present participle*] to describe actions and events that are in progress, or to express the development of an action.

    - ¿Qué haces? / ¿Qué **estás haciendo**?
    - **Estoy jugando** con mi hijo.
    - *What **are you doing**?*
    - ***I am playing** with my son.*

    - ¿Qué hacen las chicas?
    - **Están haciendo** deporte.
    - *What are the girls doing?*
    - *They **are exercising**.*

- Use a past-tense form of **estar** with the present participle to talk about actions that were in progress in the past.

    Estuvo llamando toda la mañana.
    ***She was calling** all morning.*

- This structure is also used to describe actions that began in the past and continue in the present.

    Últimamente **estoy estudiando** idiomas.
    *Lately **I've been studying** languages.*

    Hemos estado comprando los regalos de Navidad.
    ***We have been buying** Christmas presents.*

- In colloquial language, the present participle can be used without **estar** as a short answer.   `L14B`

    - ¿Qué hiciste el fin de semana?
    - Nada especial, en casa **leyendo** y **viendo** la tele.

    - *What did you do this weekend?*
    - *Nothing special, at home **reading** and **watching** TV.*

5.14.2 Irregular forms of the present participle (Las formas irregulares del gerundio) `L14B`

- There is a group of verbs with irregular present participles. They are **-ir** verbs with an **e** or an **o** in the root, which change to **i** and **u**, respectively. This group also includes the verb **poder**, whose present participle is **pudiendo**.

	present participle
e-ir: PREFERIR (e → i)	prefiriendo
o-ir: DORMIR (o → u)	durmiendo

- When the stem of an **-er** or **-ir** verb ends in a vowel, the present participle ends in **-yendo**.

infinitive	present participle
ir	**y**endo
leer	le**y**endo
oír	o**y**endo

* For more irregular present participles, see the verb tables on pages A4–A11.

5.15 Verbal periphrases (**Perífrasis verbales**)

- Verbal periphrases are constructions consisting of a verb followed by an infinitive, present participle, or past participle.

- **Soler** + [*infinitive*] is used to express habitual actions. `L14A`

  Suelo trabajar por la noche. (**Normalmente trabajo** por la noche.)
  I usually work at night.

- Use **estar** + [*present participle*] to express the development of an action. `L14B`

  Ayer **estuve leyendo** toda la tarde.
  I was reading all afternoon yesterday.

- Use **estar a punto de** + [*infinitive*] to express that an action is imminent. `L16B`

  Estamos a punto de cenar.
  We are about to have dinner.

- Use **seguir** + [*present participle*] to express a continuous action. `L17A`

  Hace un mes empecé a buscar trabajo y **sigo buscando** trabajo en mi especialidad.
  *I started to look for work a month ago and **I am still looking for** a job in my specialty.*

- Use **seguir sin** + [*infinitive*] to express the continuity of an unrealized action. `L17A`

  Sigo sin trabajar en mi especialidad.
  I am still not working in my specialty.

- Use **volver a** + [*infinitive*] to express the repetition of an action. `L18B`

  Nací en Buenos Aires, pasé mi juventud en Bariloche y de mayor **volví a vivir** en la capital.
  *I was born in Buenos Aires, I grew up in Bariloche, and when I was older **I lived** in the capital **again**.*

5.16 The future (**El futuro**)

5.16.1 ir a + [*infinitive*] (El futuro próximo) `L6B`

	ir	+ a + [*infinitive*]
(yo)	voy	
(tú)	vas	
(usted, él, ella)	va	a estudiar
(nosotros/as)	vamos	a volver
(vosotros/as)	vais	a dormir
(ustedes, ellos/as)	van	

- This construction is generally used with time expressions that indicate that an event will occur in the immediate future, such as **esta tarde, este año, el próximo año, la semana que viene,** etc.

> ¿Qué **vas a hacer** estas vacaciones?
> *What **are you going to do** during vacation?*

> **Voy a viajar.** Todavía no sé si **voy a ir** a Caracas.
> *I am going to travel.* I still don't know if *I am going to go to Caracas.*

> El próximo mes **voy a hacer** un viaje a Ecuador.
> *Next month **I am going to take** a trip to Ecuador.*

5.16.2 The simple future (El futuro simple)

5.16.2a Regular forms (**Las formas regulares**) `L12B`

	-ar verbs	-er verbs	-ir verbs
	HABL**AR**	APREND**ER**	ABR**IR**
(yo)	hablar**é**	aprender**é**	abrir**é**
(tú)	hablar**ás**	aprender**ás**	abrir**ás**
(usted, él, ella)	hablar**á**	aprender**á**	abrir**á**
(nosotros/as)	hablar**emos**	aprender**emos**	abrir**emos**
(vosotros/as)	hablar**éis**	aprender**éis**	abrir**éis**
(ustedes, ellos/as)	hablar**án**	aprender**án**	abrir**án**

- The endings of the simple future tense are added to the infinitive of the verb. The endings are the same for **-ar, -er,** and **-ir** verbs.

> Paula **llamará** más a su familia.
> *Paula **will call** her family more.*

> **Volverá** a casa en enero.
> ***She will return** home in January.*

> A partir de ahora **estaremos** más a menudo en contacto.
> *From now on **we will be** in contact more often.*

- The simple future expresses actions and events in the future, such as anticipated plans or objectives.

> Médicos Sin Fronteras **abrirá** más hospitales de emergencia en África.
> *Doctors Without Borders **will open** more emergency hospitals in Africa.*

> Aldeas Infantiles SOS **dará** información profesional a más jóvenes en Sudamérica.
> *SOS Children's Villages **will provide** professional information to more young people in South America.*

5.16.2b Irregular forms (**Las formas irregulares**) `L15A, L16A, L17A`

infinitive	stem	future forms
decir	dir-	diré, dirás, dirá, diremos, diréis, dirán
hacer	har-	haré, harás, hará, haremos, haréis, harán
poner	pondr-	pondré, pondrás, pondrá, pondremos, pondréis, pondrán
salir	saldr-	saldré, saldrás, saldrá, saldremos, saldréis, saldrán
tener	tendr-	tendré, tendrás, tendrá, tendremos, tendréis, tendrán
venir	vendr-	vendré, vendrás, vendrá, vendremos, vendréis, vendrán
haber	habr-	habré, habrás, habrá, habremos, habréis, habrán
poder	podr-	podré, podrás, podrá, podremos, podréis, podrán
querer	querr-	querré, querrás, querrá, querremos, querréis, querrán
saber	sabr-	sabré, sabrás, sabrá, sabremos, sabréis, sabrán

5.16.2c Use of the simple future (**El uso del futuro simple**) `L15A, L17A`

Use the simple future:

• to express commitments or planned objectives

> Este año **estudiaré** español.
> *This year **I will study** Spanish.*

• to express probability or supposition about the present

> Estas galletas **tendrán** muchos conservantes.
> *These cookies **must have** a lot of preservatives.*

> ¿**Vendrán** de España estas naranjas?
> ***I wonder if** these oranges **come** from Spain.*

• to make predictions about the future

> Dentro de poco tiempo, todos los libros **serán** digitales.
> *In a very short time, all books **will come** in digital form.*

> En el futuro, **habrá** menos lenguas que ahora.
> *In the future **there will be** fewer languages than there are now.*

5.16.2d Time expressions (**Marcadores temporales**) `L17A`

• Use **dentro de** followed by a period of time to refer to the future.

> **Dentro de 50 años**, los seres humanos vivirán en la Luna.
> ***In 50 years' time**, humans will live on the Moon.*

> **Dentro de muy poco**, todos tendremos algún libro electrónico.
> ***Within a short period of time**, we will all have some kind of e-book.*

5.17 Simple conditional (**Condicional simple**) `L13A, L16A`

• The simple conditional is formed by adding the conditional endings to the infinitive. The endings are the same for **-ar**, **-er**, and **-ir** verbs.

5.17.1 Regular forms (Las formas regulares)

	-ar verbs	**-er** verbs	**-ir** verbs
	GAN**AR**	V**ER**	SERV**IR**
(yo)	ganar**ía**	ver**ía**	servir**ía**
(tú)	ganar**ías**	ver**ías**	servir**ías**
(usted, él, ella)	ganar**ía**	ver**ía**	servir**ía**
(nosotros/as)	ganar**íamos**	ver**íamos**	servir**íamos**
(vosotros/as)	ganar**íais**	ver**íais**	servir**íais**
(ustedes, ellos/as)	ganar**ían**	ver**ían**	servir**ían**

⚠ Note that the conditional endings are the same as the imperfect endings for **-er** and **-ir** verbs.

5.17.2 Irregular forms (Las formas irregulares) `L13A, L16A`

- The verbs that have irregular forms in the conditional are the same verbs that have irregular forms in the future tense, and the same irregular stems are used. (See **5.16.2b**) To form the conditional of these verbs, add the endings used with regular verbs to the irregular stems.

infinitive	stem	conditional forms
decir	dir-	diría, dirías, diría, diríamos, diríais, dirían
hacer	har-	haría, harías, haría, haríamos, haríais, harían
poner	pondr-	pondría, pondrías, pondría, pondríamos, pondríais, pondrían
salir	saldr-	saldría, saldrías, saldría, saldríamos, saldríais, saldrían
tener	tendr-	tendría, tendrías, tendría, tendríamos, tendríais, tendrían
venir	vendr-	vendría, vendrías, vendría, vendríamos, vendríais, vendrían
haber	habr-	habría, habrías, habría, habríamos, habríais, habrían
poder	podr-	podría, podrías, podría, podríamos, podríais, podrían
querer	querr-	querría, querrías, querría, querríamos, querríais, querrían
saber	sabr-	sabría, sabrías, sabría, sabríamos, sabríais, sabrían

5.17.3 Use of the simple conditional (El uso del condicional simple) `L10A, L11B, L13A`

- Use **poder** and **importar** in the second- or third-person conditional to ask for information in a polite way.

> ¿**Podrías** decirme qué hora es?
> *Could you tell me what time it is?*

> ¿**Le importaría** confirmarme la salida de mi vuelo?
> *Would you mind confirming the departure of my flight for me?*

- Use the conditional form **debería** to ask for or give advice.

  - No puedo dormir. ¿Qué **debería** hacer?
  - **Deberías** trabajar menos y descansar más.
  - *I can't sleep. What **should I** do?*
  - *You should work less and rest more.*

- Use the expressions **yo que tú / yo en tu lugar** with the conditional to make recommendations.

  Yo que tú, viajaría a Cuba.   **Yo en tu lugar** alquilaría un coche.
  If I were you, I would travel to Cuba.   *If I were you, I would rent a car.*

- Use the conditional constructions [*indirect object pronoun*] + **gustaría/encantaría** + [*infinitive*] to express desires.

(a mí)	me	
(a ti)	te	
(a usted, a él, a ella)	le	gustaría/encantaría + [*infinitive*]
(a nosotros/as)	nos	
(a vosotros/as)	os	
(a ustedes, a ellos/as)	les	

  - ¿Dónde **te gustaría vivir**?   - *Where **would you like to live**?*
  - **Me encantaría vivir** en Andalucía.   - *I **would love to live** in Andalucía.*

- Use the conditional to make suggestions with the construction **lo mejor +** [*conditional*]. `L15A`

  Lo mejor sería consumir productos frescos.
  *It **would be best** to consume fresh products.*

5.18 Affirmative commands (El imperativo afirmativo)

5.18.1 Use of the imperative (El uso del imperativo) L8A, L9B, L10A, L11A, L16B, L18B

- Use the imperative to give instructions.

    Añade miel a la receta.
    Add honey to the recipe.

- Use the imperative to give commands or advice.

    ¡**Empezad** el día con nuestro chocolate Buen día!
    Start the day with our Buen día hot chocolate!

    Si quieres quedar, **llámame** esta semana.
    *If you want to make plans, **call me** this week.*

5.18.2 Regular forms (Las formas regulares)

5.18.2a Singular commands (Mandatos singulares) L8A, L9B

	-ar verbs	-er verbs	-ir verbs
	TOM**AR**	COM**ER**	ABR**IR**
(tú)	tom**a**	com**e**	abr**e**
(usted)	tom**e**	com**a**	abr**a**

    Toma la primera calle a la derecha.
    Take the first street on the right.

    Gire a la izquierda.
    Turn left.

- Affirmative **tú** commands (familiar commands) usually have the same form as the third-person singular form of the present indicative. Affirmative **usted** commands (formal commands) are the same as the third-person singular form of the present subjunctive. (See **5.20**) **Usted** commands are formed by dropping the final **-o** of the **yo** form of the present indicative. For **-ar** verbs, add **-e**; for **-er** and **-ir** verbs, add **-a**.

- The imperative undergoes the same stem changes as verbs in the present tense.

	seguir	cerrar	contar
(tú)	s**i**gue	c**i**erra	c**ue**nta
(usted)	s**i**ga	c**i**erre	c**ue**nte

    Sigue todo recto.
    Continue straight ahead.

    Cierra la ventana, por favor.
    Close the window, please.

5.18.2b Plural commands (Mandatos plurales) L16B, L18B

- The affirmative **vosotros/as** command is formed by dropping the **r** from the infinitive and adding a **-d**.

	-ar verbs	-er verbs	-ir verbs
	AHORR**AR**	BEB**ER**	CONSUM**IR**
(vosotros/as)	ahorra**d**	bebe**d**	consumi**d**

- The **ustedes** command is formed by dropping the final **-o** of the **yo** form in the present tense and adding the appropriate ending. For **-ar** verbs, add **-en**; for **-er** and **-ir** verbs, add **-an**.

	-ar verbs	-er verbs	-ir verbs
	AHORR**AR**	BEB**ER**	CONSUM**IR**
(ustedes)	ahorr**en**	beb**an**	consum**an**

- Stem-changing verbs include the stem change in the **ustedes** command.

	seguir	cerrar	contar
(ustedes)	s**i**gan	c**ie**rren	c**ue**nten

5.18.3 Irregular forms (Las formas irregulares)

5.18.3a Singular commands (**Mandatos singulares**) L9B, L11A

- Irregular affirmative **tú** commands:

	decir	hacer	ir	poner	salir	ser	tener	venir
(tú)	di	haz	ve	pon	sal	sé	ten	ven

Ve a la playa, **haz** excursiones y **ven** a visitarme.
*Go to the beach, **do** some day trips, and **come** visit me.*

- Irregular **usted** commands:

	dar	estar	ir	saber	ser
(usted)	dé	esté	vaya	sepa	sea

Sea puntual, por favor.
Be punctual, please.

- Verbs ending in **-car**, **-gar**, and **-zar** have a spelling change in the formal command forms.

sa**car**	c → qu	sa**que**(n)
ju**gar**	g → gu	jue**gue**(n)
almor**zar**	z → c	almuer**ce**(n)

5.18.3b Plural commands (**Mandatos plurales**)

- **Vosotros** commands have no irregular forms.

- The same verbs that have irregular **usted** commands have irregular **ustedes** commands. L16B

	dar	estar	ir	saber	ser
(ustedes)	den	estén	vayan	sepan	sean

5.18.4 Commands with reflexive verbs (El imperativo de los verbos reflexivos) `L10A`

5.18.4a Singular commands (**Mandatos singulares**) `L10A`

- With affirmative commands, attach the reflexive pronoun to the end of the verb.

	ducharse	levantarse	acostarse
(tú)	dúcha**te**	levánta**te**	acuésta**te**
(usted)	dúche**se**	levánte**se**	acuéste**se**

> **Acuéstate** pronto.
> *Go to bed soon.*

⚠ When a reflexive pronoun is attached to an affirmative command that has two or more syllables, an accent mark is added to maintain the original stress.

5.18.4b Plural commands (**Mandatos plurales**) `L16B`

- In affirmative **vosotros/as** commands, the **-d** is dropped when the reflexive pronoun **os** is added to the end of the verb.

> Poned + **os** → **Poneos** los abrigos.
> **Put on** *your coats.*

- In affirmative **ustedes** commands, attach the reflexive pronoun to the end of the imperative form of the verb. As in singular commands, a written accent is added to maintain the original pronunciation of the verb.

> **Lávense** las manos antes de cenar.
> **Wash** *your hands before dinner.*

5.18.5 The imperative with direct object pronouns
(El imperativo con pronombres de objeto directo)

5.18.5a Singular commands (**Mandatos singulares**) `L10A`

- As with all pronouns, direct object pronouns (**lo, la, los, las**) are attached to the end of affirmative commands.

	tomar	comer	poner	hacer
(tú)	tóma**lo**	cóme**la**	pon**lo**	haz**la**
(usted)	tóme**los**	cóma**las**	pónga**los**	hága**las**

> ● Es bueno comer fruta, ¿no?
> ▪ Sí, sí, **cómela** varias veces al día.
> ● *It is good to eat fruit, isn't it?*
> ▪ *Yes, yes, **eat it** several times a day.*

⚠ A written accent is placed on the verb in order to maintain the original stress after the pronoun is attached.

5.18.5b Plural commands (**Mandatos plurales**) `L16B`

- In affirmative **vosotros/as** commands, attach direct object pronouns directly to the imperative form. The final **-d** is not dropped.

> **Leedlo**.   **Probadlas.**
> *Read it.*   *Try them.*

- Direct object pronouns are also attached to affirmative **ustedes** commands.

> **Pónganlo** sobre la mesa.
> **Put it** *on the table.*

5.18.6 The imperative with direct and indirect object pronouns (El imperativo con pronombres de objeto directo e indirecto) `L16B`

- In affirmative commands, the pronouns are attached to the end of the verb. When both direct and indirect object pronouns are used, the indirect object pronoun is always placed before the direct object pronoun. Remember that **le/les** changes to **se** if it precedes **lo/la/los/las**. A written accent is added in order to preserve the original pronunciation of the verb.

5.18.6a Singular commands (**Mandatos singulares**)

	dar	escribir
(tú)	dá**melo**	escríbe**melo**
(usted)	dé**melo**	escríba**melo**

Dámelo.
Give it to me.

5.18.6b Plural commands (**Mandatos plurales**)

	dar	escribir
(vosotros/as)	dád**melo**	escribíd**melo**
(ustedes)	dén**melo**	escríban**melo**

Escribídmelo.
Write it for me.

5.19 Negative commands (El imperativo negativo)

5.19.1 Formation of the negative imperative `L16B, L18B`

- All forms of the negative imperative are the same as the forms of the present subjunctive.

	NEGATIVE IMPERATIVE		
	-ar verbs	**-er** verbs	**-ir** verbs
	OLVID**AR**	CRE**ER**	CONSUM**IR**
(tú)	no olvid**es**	no cre**as**	no consum**as**
(usted)	no olvid**e**	no cre**a**	no consum**a**
(vosotros/as)	no olvid**éis**	no cre**áis**	no consum**áis**
(ustedes)	no olvid**en**	no cre**an**	no consum**an**

No olvidéis la tarea para mañana.
Don't forget the homework for tomorrow.

5.19.2 Use of the negative imperative with pronouns `L16B`

- Object and reflexive pronouns must be placed in front of the verb when used with negative commands.

No la olvidéis.
Don't forget it.

- If indirect and direct object pronouns are used together, place the indirect object pronoun in front of the direct object pronoun. Note that **le/les** must be changed to **se** if used before **lo/la/los/las**.

No se lo digan (a ellos).
Don't tell (it to) them.

5.20 Present subjunctive (**Presente del subjuntivo**) `L15A, L15B, L16A, L17A, L17B, L18A, L18B`

5.20.1 Regular forms (Las formas regulares)

	-ar verbs	**-er** verbs	**-ir** verbs
	TRABAJ**AR**	VEND**ER**	VIV**IR**
(yo)	trabaj**e**	vend**a**	viv**a**
(tú)	trabaj**es**	vend**as**	viv**as**
(usted, él, ella)	trabaj**e**	vend**a**	viv**a**
(nosotros/as)	trabaj**emos**	vend**amos**	viv**amos**
(vosotros/as)	trabaj**éis**	vend**áis**	viv**áis**
(ustedes, ellos/as)	trabaj**en**	vend**an**	viv**an**

- The endings of the present subjunctive for **-ar** verbs (except for the **yo** form) are the same as the endings of **-er** and **-ir** verbs in the present indicative. Likewise, the present subjunctive endings for **-er** and **-ir** verbs are the same as the endings of **-ar** verbs in the present indicative, with the exception of the **yo** form.

-ar ➜ **-e**
-er, -ir ➜ **-a**

 Note that in the present subjunctive, the **yo** form of regular verbs is the same as the third-person singular form (**usted, él, ella**).

5.20.2 Irregular forms (Las formas irregulares) `L15B, L16A, L17A, L17B, L18A`

- Verbs with an irregular **yo** form in the present indicative show the same irregularity in all forms of the present subjunctive. **-ar** and **-er** verbs that undergo a stem change in the **yo** form of the present indicative maintain the same stem change in the present subjunctive (e➜ie: qu**ie**ro, o➜ue: c**ue**nto), with the exception of the **nosotros/as** and **vosotros/as** forms. In addition, verbs ending in **-car, -gar,** and **-zar** have a spelling change in all forms of the present subjunctive in order to maintain the original pronunciation.

	hacer (-go)	**pensar** (e:ie)	**contar** (o:ue)	**educar** (c:qu)	**entregar** (g:gu)	**comenzar** (e:ie) (z:c)
(yo)	ha**ga**	p**ie**nse	c**ue**nte	edu**que**	entre**gue**	com**ie**nce
(tú)	ha**ga**s	p**ie**nses	c**ue**ntes	edu**que**s	entre**gue**s	com**ie**nces
(usted, él, ella)	ha**ga**	p**ie**nse	c**ue**nte	edu**que**	entre**gue**	com**ie**nce
(nosotros/as)	ha**ga**mos	pensemos	contemos	edu**que**mos	entre**gue**mos	comencemos
(vosotros/as)	ha**gá**is	penséis	contéis	edu**qué**is	entre**gué**is	comencéis
(ustedes, ellos/as)	ha**ga**n	p**ie**nsen	c**ue**nten	edu**que**n	entre**gue**n	com**ie**ncen

- **-ir** stem-changing verbs undergo the same stem changes in the subjunctive as they do in the present indicative, but the **nosotros/as** and **vosotros/as** forms also have a stem change. The unstressed **e** changes to **i**, while the unstressed **o** changes to **u**.

	pedir (e:i)	**sentir** (e:ie)	**dormir** (o:ue)
(yo)	p**i**da	s**ie**nta	d**ue**rma
(tú)	p**i**das	s**ie**ntas	d**ue**rmas
(usted, él, ella)	p**i**da	s**ie**nta	d**ue**rma
(nosotros/as)	p**i**damos	s**i**ntamos	d**u**rmamos
(vosotros/as)	p**i**dáis	s**i**ntáis	d**u**rmáis
(ustedes, ellos/as)	p**i**dan	s**ie**ntan	d**ue**rman

- These verbs have irregular forms in the present subjunctive.

	dar	estar	ir	saber	ser
(yo)	dé	esté	vaya	sepa	sea
(tú)	des	estés	vayas	sepas	seas
(usted, él, ella)	dé	esté	vaya	sepa	sea
(nosotros/as)	demos	estemos	vayamos	sepamos	seamos
(vosotros/as)	deis	estéis	vayáis	sepáis	seáis
(ustedes, ellos/as)	den	estén	vayan	sepan	sean

- The present subjunctive of the impersonal verb **haber** is **haya**.

- See the verb tables on pages A4–A11 for more irregular verbs.

5.21 Use of the subjunctive (El uso del subjuntivo)

5.21.1 Use of the subjunctive to express desires, requests, interests, and feelings (Para expresar deseos, peticiones, intereses y sentimientos)

- The subjunctive is used in sentences with two subjects and two verbs. `L15B`

   (Yo) quiero que **(tú)** salgas.
   *I want **you** to leave.*

- Use the infinitive when two verbs in a sentence refer to the same subject.

   (Yo) quiero salir.
   I want to leave.

a) With verbs such as **desear, querer,** and **esperar** `L15A`

   Deseo que Fernando **asista** a la reunión.
   *I want Fernando **to attend** the meeting.*

   Queremos que todos **trabajen** contentos.
   ***We want** everyone **to work** happily.*

   ¿Espera usted que los productos **se vendan** en países extranjeros?
   ***Do you hope that** the products **will be sold** in foreign countries?*

- Use the subjunctive in set phrases that take **que** + [*subjunctive*]. `L13A, L18B`

   ¡Que tengan un buen viaje!
   ***Have** a good trip!*

   ¡Que te mejores!
   *(I hope you) **Feel better**!*

- The subjunctive is always used with the interjection **ojalá (que)**.
   Ojalá (que) means *I hope* or *I wish*. `L15A`

   ¡Ojalá (que) tenga éxito su negocio!
   *I hope (that) your business **is** successful!*

b) With the verb **pedir** `L16A`

Ingrid Betancourt **pide que haya** paz en Colombia y en toda América Latina.
*Ingrid Betancourt **asks for** peace in Colombia and in all of Latin America.*

c) With verbs such as **gustar, interesar,** and **preferir** `L17B`

(A mí) **no me interesa que** la gente me **cuente** su vida.
I am not interested in people telling me about their lives.

Prefiero que me **inviten** a una excursión que a cenar.
I prefer that people invite me on a trip rather than out to dinner.

d) To express feelings `L15B`

• Express displeasure and annoyance using verbs and expressions such as **molestar**, **no gustar**, or **no soportar**. `L15B, L17B`

A Juliana **no le gusta que** le **digan** lo que tiene que hacer.
Juliana does not like being told what to do.

A mi hijo **le molesta que** el profesor le **haga** repetir los ejercicios.
It bothers my son that the teacher makes him repeat exercises.

No soporto que mis alumnos no **escuchen** en clase.
I can't stand the fact that my students don't listen in class.

• Express fear and concern using verbs such as **preocupar** and **dar miedo**. `L15B`

Me preocupa que la educación en ese colegio no **sea** buena.
It concerns me that the education at that school is not good.

Nos da miedo que vuelva a casa tarde.
We're afraid that he will return home late.

• Express surprise using verbs and expressions such as **sorprender**, **extrañar**, and **parecer raro**. `L15B`

Me sorprende que no te **guste** este colegio.
I am surprised that you don't like this school.

A Miguel **le extraña que** tantos padres **lleven** a sus hijos a ese colegio.
Miguel is surprised that so many parents send their children to that school.

Nos parece raro que un pueblo tan grande **tenga** solo un colegio.
It seems strange to us that a town of that size has only one school.

• Express disappointment using verbs such as **decepcionar** and **entristecer**. `L17B`

Nos decepciona que no **estudies** los fines de semana.
It disappoints us that you don't study on the weekends.

Me entristece que no **llames** con frecuencia.
It saddens me that you don't call often.

• Express happiness and sadness using expressions such as **alegrarse de** and **dar pena**. `L18B`

Me alegro de que te jubiles con salud.
I am glad that you are retiring in good health.

Nos da pena que te vayas.
It makes us sad to see you go.

• Express delight and boredom using verbs such as **divertir** and **aburrir**. `L17B`

Le divierte mucho **que haya** baile todos los sábados.
He enjoys the fact that there is a dance every Saturday.

Me aburre que siempre **escuchemos** la misma música.
It bores me that we always listen to the same music.

5.21.2 Use of the subjunctive to express purpose (Para expresar finalidad) `L15B`

- Use the subjunctive with **para que** if the sentence has clauses with different subjects.

    Mis hijos quieren un teléfono celular **para que** sus amigos los **puedan** llamar durante el día.
    *My children want a cell phone **so that** their friends **can** call them during the day.*

**5.21.3 Use of the subjunctive to compare two events temporally
(Para relacionar temporalmente dos hechos)**

a) With the phrases **antes de que / después de que** `L18A`

- Use the subjunctive if the sentence has clauses with different subjects.

    Tenemos que prepararlo todo **antes de que vengan** los invitados.
    *We have to prepare everything **before** the guests **arrive**.*

    Podemos quedar para cenar **después de que termine el partido**.
    *We can arrange to have dinner **after the game ends**.*

b) To compare two events temporally with **cuando** `L18A`

- Use the indicative if the clause that follows **cuando** refers to habitual actions in the present or completed actions in the past.

    Cuando era joven, me gustaba mucho salir por la noche.
    When I was young, I really enjoyed going out at night.*

    Estábamos mirando el noticiero **cuando** mi tío **llamó**.
    *We were watching the newscast **when** my uncle **called**.*

- Use the subjunctive to refer to a pending action in the future with **cuando**.

    Cuando llegue a la cima de la montaña, pensaré en vosotros.
    When I arrive at the top of the mountain, I will think of you.*

**5.21.4 Use of the subjunctive to express opinion, certainty, evidence, or skepticism
(Para expresar opinión, certeza, evidencia y escepticismo)**

- The indicative is used in statements that express certainty or belief.

    Creo que Pablo **viene** mañana.
    I think that Pablo **is coming** tomorrow.*

- The subjunctive is used in statements that convey uncertainty or doubt.

    No creo que Pablo **venga** mañana.
    I don't think that Pablo **is coming** tomorrow.*

- The subjunctive is not used in simple sentences (with one conjugated verb).

    Pablo **viene** mañana.
    *Pablo **is coming** tomorrow.*

    Pablo **no viene** mañana.
    *Pablo **is not coming** tomorrow.*

a) With verbs such as **creer, pensar,** or **parecer** `L16A`

    No creo que la paz **se logre** sin trabajo.
    I don't think that peace **can be achieved** without effort.*

    No nos parece que la guerra **sea** una solución.
    We don't think that war **is** a solution.*

    No pienso que eso **sea** imposible.
    I don't think that it **is** impossible.*

b) No estar (totalmente/muy) seguro de/claro/demostrado que; no ser evidente/obvio que; dudar que `L16A, L17A`

> **No estoy totalmente seguro de que** mi empresa **invierta** dinero en ese proyecto.
> *I am not totally sure that my company will invest money in that project.*

> **No está demostrado que** las computadoras **sean** perjudiciales para la salud.
> *It is not proven that computers are dangerous to your health.*

> **No es evidente que** la enfermedad **se transmita**.
> *It is not clear that the disease is transmitted.*

c) Use the subjunctive with the expression **dudar que**. `L16A`

> **Dudo que** la paz **sea** una realidad sin el compromiso de todos.
> *I doubt that peace can be a reality without the commitment of everyone.*

5.21.5 Use of the subjunctive to express assessments (Para expresar valoraciones): (no) es (una) buena/mala idea que and es mejor que `L16B, L18B`

- Use these expressions with the subjunctive to assess an idea in a specific or concrete way.

- Use these expressions with an infinitive to assess an idea in general terms.

> En general **es una buena idea ir de vacaciones** a la playa, pero creo que esta vez **es mejor que vayamos a la montaña**.
> *Generally, it is a good idea to vacation at the beach, but I think that this time it is better that we go to the mountains.*

5.21.6 Use of the subjunctive to express necessity (Para expresar necesidad) `L15A`

- Use the subjunctive to express necessity or influence in a specific or concrete way.

> **Es necesario que tu empresa lance** una campaña publicitaria.
> *It is necessary that your company launch a publicity campaign.*

- Use the infinitive to express necessity or influence in general terms.

> Para vender, **es necesario conocer** el mercado.
> *In order to sell, it is necessary to be familiar with the market.*

5.21.7 Use of the subjunctive to express probability (Para expresar probabilidad) `L17A`

- The subjunctive is always used with these expressions: **es (poco/muy/bastante) probable/posible que; puede (ser) que.**

> **Es poco probable que haya** vida en otros planetas.
> *It is not very likely that there is life on other planets.*

> **Puede (ser) que** algún día **descubran** una vacuna contra el cáncer.
> *It is possible that one day they will discover a vaccine for cancer.*

- **Tal vez** and **quizá(s)** can be used with the indicative in order to indicate a greater degree of probability or with the subjunctive to indicate greater uncertainty. The forms **quizá** and **quizás** are both correct.

> **Tal vez son** hermanos. (more probable)
> **Tal vez sean** hermanos. (less probable)
> *Maybe they are brothers/siblings.*

> **Quizás hay** una solución. (more probable)
> **Quizás haya** una solución. (less probable)
> *Perhaps there is a solution.*

- **A lo mejor** is always used with the indicative.

> **A lo mejor** en el futuro se hablan solo dos o tres lenguas.
> *In the future perhaps only two or three languages will be spoken.*

5.21.8 Use of the subjunctive to express conditions (Para expresar condiciones) `L15B`

- Use the subjunctive with the conjunctions **con tal (de) que, en caso (de) que,** and **sin que**. Note that the use of the preposition **de** is optional in the first two conjunctions.

  Te permito salir con tus amigos **con tal de que** me **ayudes** con la cena.
  *I will let you go out with your friends **provided that you help** me with dinner.*

  Voy a llevar mi celular **en caso de que** mis padres **necesiten** llamarme.
  *I am going to take my cell phone **in case** my parents **need** to call me.*

  Quiero planear una fiesta sorpresa **sin que** mi amiga **se entere**.
  *I want to plan a surprise party **without** my friend **finding out**.*

5.22 Present perfect subjunctive (**Pretérito perfecto de subjuntivo**)

5.22.1 Conjugation (Conjugación) `L17B`

- The present perfect subjunctive is composed of the present subjunctive of the verb **haber** + [*past participle*]. The verb **haber** is irregular in the present subjunctive. As in the indicative mood, the past participle does not change in form depending on the subject; only the form of **haber** changes.

	haber	+ [*past participle*]
(yo)	**haya**	
(tú)	**hayas**	
(usted, él, ella)	**haya**	hablado
(nosotros/as)	**hayamos**	tenido
(vosotros/as)	**hayáis**	vivido
(ustedes, ellos/as)	**hayan**	

5.22.2 Use of the present perfect subjunctive (El uso del pretérito perfecto de subjuntivo) `L18A`

- As in the indicative mood, the present perfect subjunctive is used to refer to past events that in some way relate to or influence the present. The present perfect subjunctive is often used when expressing present reactions to past events.

  Me sorprende que **hayas tenido** dificultades en la clase de historia.
  *It surprises me that **you have had/you had** difficulties in history class.*

- Use the present perfect subjunctive in a dependent clause when the verb in the main clause is in the present and the dependent clause refers to an action or state in the past.

6 Pronouns (Los pronombres)

6.1 Subject pronouns (**Los pronombres de sujeto**) `L1A, L1B`

- Subject pronouns replace the name or title of a person who acts as the subject of a verb. Note that, unlike in English, subject pronouns are often omitted in Spanish, because verb conjugations generally indicate the subject of the verb.

	singular		plural	
first person	**yo**	*I*	**nosotros**	*we* (m., m. + f.)
			nosotras	*we* (f.)
second person	**tú**	*you* (fam.)	**vosotros**	*you* (m., m. + f.; fam.)
			vosotras	*you* (f., fam.)
	usted	*you* (form.)	**ustedes**	*you* (form./fam.)
third person	**él**	*he*	**ellos**	*they* (m., m. + f.)
	ella	*she*	**ellas**	*they* (f.)

When referring to a group of mixed gender, use the masculine plural forms **nosotros, vosotros,** and **ellos**. Use the feminine forms **nosotras, vosotras,** and **ellas** only when all members of the group are female.

 Personal pronouns are used for emphasis or to contrast one person with another. They are also sometimes used in a short answer that does not contain a verb.

- Buenos días, ¿qué desean?
- **Yo**, un café con leche.
- ¿Y **usted**?
- **Yo**, un té.

- *Good morning, what would you like?*
- *For me, a coffee with milk.*
- *And you?*
- *For me, a cup of tea.*

 In Latin America, **ustedes** is used in place of **vosotros/as** to address a group in an informal setting. In addition, some regions of Latin America, particularly Argentina and Uruguay, use **vos** instead of **tú**.

6.2 Object pronouns (**Los pronombres de objeto**) `L3B, L4A`

- Spanish has both stressed and unstressed object pronouns. Unstressed object pronouns are used along with a verb and may be accompanied by a stressed object pronoun for emphasis. Stressed object pronouns are used with a preposition. Unstressed object pronouns are divided into direct and indirect object pronouns.

6.2.1 Direct object pronouns (Los pronombres de objeto directo) `L3B, L12A`

- Direct object pronouns replace direct object nouns, which directly receive the action of the verb. Third-person direct object pronouns are used when the direct object noun has already been mentioned.

singular		plural	
me	*me*	**nos**	*us*
te	*you* (fam.)	**os**	*you* (fam.)
lo	*you* (m., form.); *him; it* (m.)	**los**	*you* (m., m. + f.; form./fam.); *them* (m., m. + f.)
la	*you* (f., form.); *her, it* (f.)	**las**	*you* (f., form./fam.); *them* (f.)

Quería esa camisa. ¿**La** puedo ver?
*I would like that shirt. Can I see **it**?*

Queríamos esos zapatos. ¿**Los** podemos ver?
*We would like those shoes. Can we see **them**?*

Debo llamar a mi tía porque hoy es su cumpleaños. Voy a llamar**la**.
*I should call my aunt because today is her birthday. I am going to call **her**.*

 The **personal a** is used when the direct object is a person. It is not needed when the direct object pronoun is used.

Vi **a** Susi.   *I saw Susi.*
La vi.   *I saw her.*

6.2.2 Indirect object pronouns (Los pronombres de objeto indirecto) `L4A`

- An indirect object is a noun or pronoun that answers the question *to whom* or *for whom* an action is done. An indirect object pronoun and the noun to which it refers are frequently used in the same sentence in order to emphasize and clarify to whom the pronoun refers.

singular		plural	
me	*(to, for) me*	**nos**	*(to, for) us*
te	*(to, for) you* (fam.)	**os**	*(to, for) you* (fam.)
le	*(to, for) you* (form.); *(to, for) him, her*	**les**	*(to, for) you* (form./fam.); *(to, for) them*

Juan **me** presta su libro de texto.
*Juan lends **me** his textbook.*

Le doy la tarjeta a mi abuela.
I give the card to my grandmother.

6.2.3 Stressed object pronouns (Los pronombres tónicos de objeto) `L4A`

- Stressed object pronouns, or prepositional pronouns, have the same forms as the subject pronouns, except for **mí** and **ti**. These pronouns act as the object of a preposition and are often used with the preposition **a** to clarify the person or group that is receiving the action of the verb. They can also be used with other prepositions.

a mí	**a él**	**a vosotros/as**
a ti	**a ella**	**a ustedes**
a usted	**a nosotros/as**	**a ellos/as**

 Note that **mí** carries a written accent in order to differentiate it from the possessive adjective **mi**.

- ¿Os gusta el teatro?
- **A mí** me encanta.
- **A mí** no me gusta mucho.

- Do you like the theater?
- I love it.
- I don't like it very much.

Enrique se sienta **delante de mí** en la clase de biología.
*Enrique sits **in front of me** in biology class.*

 Unstressed object pronouns are used with a verb (**me** gusta, **nos** gusta, **me** toca...), but stressed object pronouns may be used alone.

- El barrio me gusta, ¿y **a ti**?
- **A mí** no me gusta mucho.

- I like the neighborhood, and **you**?
- I don't like it very much.

 Often an indirect or direct object appears at the beginning of a sentence and is then repeated, immediately before the verb, in the form of an unstressed pronoun.

A Rosa le gusta vivir en el centro.
***Rosa** likes living downtown.*

¿**A ti te** gustan los mercados tradicionales?
*Do **you** like traditional markets?*

 Tocar is used with indirect object pronouns to indicate whose turn is next.

- ¿**A quién le** toca?
- **Me** toca **a mí**.

- **Whose** turn is it?
- It is **my** turn.

6.2.4 Placement of object pronouns (La posición de los pronombres de objeto)
`L7B, L8B, L10A, L11A, L16B`

- Object pronouns are always placed before the conjugated verb.

- ¿**Me** ayudas?
- Claro que **te** ayudo.

- Will you help **me**?
- Of course I'll help **you**.

Le recomiendo este hotel.
*I recommend this hotel **to you**.*

- When a conjugated verb is followed by an infinitive or the present participle, the object pronoun may be placed before the conjugated verb or attached to the infinitive or present participle. If the pronoun is attached to a present participle, add an accent mark to maintain the original stress.

¿**Te** puedo ayudar? / ¿Puedo ayudar**te**?
*Can I help **you**?*

Te estoy escribiendo un mensaje. / Estoy escribiéndo**te** un mensaje.
*I am writing a message **to you**.*

Object pronouns are also attached to affirmative commands. Sometimes an accent mark is needed to maintain the original stress.

Lláma**me**.	Avíse**nos**.
*Call **me**.*	*Let **us** know.*

6.3 Using direct and indirect pronouns together (**La posición y combinación de los pronombres de objeto directo e indirecto**) `L16B`

- The indirect object pronoun (**me, te, le, nos, os, les**) or reflexive pronoun (**me, te, se, nos, os**) is placed before a direct object pronoun. When third-person indirect object pronouns (**le, les**) are combined with third-person direct object pronouns (**lo, la, los, las**), the indirect object pronoun changes to **se**. Both object pronouns can be added to the end of an infinitive or present participle, in which case a written accent is added to maintain the original stress.

  Quiero mandar**le** esta postal a Marina. **Se la** quiero **mandar**. / Quiero **mandársela**.
  *I want to send this postcard **to Marina**. I want to **send it to her**.*

  Voy a dar**te** mi libro. **Te lo** voy a **dar**. / Voy a **dártelo**.
  *I am going to give **you** my book. I am going to **give it to you**.*

6.4 Reflexive and reciprocal constructions (**Estructuras reflexivas y recíprocas**) `L17B, L18B`

- Reflexive verbs are used with the reflexive pronouns **me, te, se, nos, os,** and **se**.

  Me río mucho contigo.
  *I **laugh** a lot with you.*

  Nos pusimos muy contentos con la noticia.
  ***It made us** very happy to hear the news.*

- Reciprocal actions are expressed using the plural reflexive pronouns **nos, os,** and **se**.

  Mi hermano y yo **nos queremos** mucho.
  *My brother and I **love each other** a lot.*

  Diego y Jimena **se abrazan**.
  *Diego and Jimena **hug each other**.*

6.5 Indefinite pronouns and adjectives (**Los adjetivos y pronombres indefinidos**) `L2B, L3A, L8A, L9A`

- **algo/nada** `L2B , 8A`

  - ¿Desea **algo** más?
  - No, gracias, **nada** más.

  - *Would you like **anything** else?*
  - *No, thank you, **nothing** else.*

- **otro/a** `L2B`

  Camarero, por favor, **otra** botella de agua.
  *Waiter, **another** bottle of water, please.*

⚠ Do not use an indefinite article with **otro/a**.

  Otro café, por favor.
  ***Another** coffee, please.*

- **todo/a(s)** `L3A`

todo el día	**todos** los días	**todos** los viernes
***all** day long*	***every** day*	***every** Friday*

- **alguien/nadie** `L8A`

  - ¿Hay **alguien** en la oficina?
  - No, en este momento **no** hay **nadie**.

  - *Is **anyone** in the office?*
  - *No, at this moment there isn't **anyone** / **no one** is there.*

- **alguno/a; algún/ninguno/a; ningún** `L9A`

  - ¿Hay **algún** documental en la tele?
  - Sí, creo que hay **alguno**.
  - No, **no** hay **ninguno**.

  - *Are there **any** documentaries on television?*
  - *Yes, I think there is **one**.*
  - *No, there aren't **any**.*

⚠ **Alguno/a** and **ninguno/a** can be used with or without nouns. In front of a masculine singular noun, drop the final **-o**.

  - ¿No hay **ningún** debate esta noche?
  - No, no hay **ninguno**.
  - Sí, creo que hay **alguno**.

  - *Aren't there **any** debates tonight?*
  - *No, there aren't **any**.*
  - *Yes, I think there is **one**.*

6.6 Pronouns and the preposition **con** (**Pronombres y la preposición** *con*) `L17B`

- Use subject pronouns with the preposition **con**, except **yo** and **tú**, which take the forms **conmigo** and **contigo**.

  Lola no quiere bailar **conmigo** ni **contigo**; solo baila **con él**.
  *Lola does not want to dance **with me** or **with you**; she only dances **with him**.*

  - ¿Vienes **conmigo** al cine mañana?
  - No, lo siento, he quedado **con mis amigos**.

  - *Are you coming **with me** to the movies tomorrow?*
  - *No, I'm sorry, I made plans **with my friends**.*

6.7 Impersonal contructions with **se** + [*third-person verb form*] (**Construcciones impersonales**) `L16B`

- The construction **se** + [*third-person verb form*] is used in impersonal statements equivalent to the English passive voice. As always, the verb must agree with the subject (singular or plural).

  En Argentina **se celebra** la Navidad en verano.
  En Argentina **se celebran** las Navidades en verano.
  *Christmas **is celebrated** in the summer in Argentina.*

- **Se** + [*third-person singular verb form*] is also used to express an unspecified or general subject, often expressed as *one*, *people*, *they*, or *you* in English.

  En este restaurante **se come** bien.
  *In this restaurant, **one eats/you eat** well.*

- The third-person plural verb form can also be used to make general statements.

  Los españoles no siempre **duermen** la siesta.
  *Spaniards do not always **take** an afternoon nap.*

6.8 The neuter pronoun **lo** (**El pronombre neutro** *lo*) `L13A, L16B, L17B`

- The pronoun **lo** is used to refer to actions or ideas in general, without being related to a specific object or concrete example. It forms part of some expressions, such as **pasarlo bien/mal** (*to have a good/bad time*).

  Yo suelo viajar sola. Te **lo** recomiendo.
  *I often travel alone. I recommend **it** to you.*

  Nos vemos mañana a las 22:30 h, no **lo** olvide.
  *See you tomorrow at 10:30 p.m., don't forget **(it)**.*

  Ayer estuvimos bailando y **lo** pasamos muy bien.
  We were dancing yesterday and we had a good time.

6.9 Relative pronouns (**Los pronombres relativos**) `L18A`

- Relative pronouns **que** (*that; which; who*) and **quien** (*who; whom; that*) introduce a relative clause that refers to an antecedent, i.e., something or someone already mentioned in the sentence. The antecedent of the pronoun **que** can be a person or thing, while the antecedent of **quien** can only be a person. **Quien** is often used after a preposition or the personal **a**.

> Es un <u>deportista</u> **que** ha ganado muchos campeonatos.
> *He is an <u>athlete</u> **who** has won many championships.*

> Es un <u>deporte</u> **que** tiene muchos aficionados.
> *It is a <u>sport</u> **that** has many fans.*

> Es un <u>deportista</u> **a quien** admiro.
> *He is an <u>athlete</u> **whom** I admire.*

7 Demonstratives (Demostrativos)

7.1 Demonstrative adjectives (**Los adjetivos demostrativos**) `L3B`

- Demonstrative adjectives precede the nouns they modify and agree with them in both gender and number. They designate objects or people situated at varied distances from the speaker.

singular		plural		
masculine	feminine	masculine	feminine	
este	esta	estos	estas	*this; these*
ese	esa	esos	esas	*that; those*
aquel	aquella	aquellos	aquellas	*that; those (over there)*

- ¿**Este** libro de **aquí** es de arte?
- No, **ese** libro de **ahí** es de arte.

- *Is **this** book **here** about art?*
- *No, **that** book **there** is about art.*

7.2 Demonstrative pronouns (**Los pronombres demostrativos**) `L3B`

- Demonstrative pronouns are identical to their corresponding demonstrative adjectives.

- ¿Piensas que este vestido es el mejor?
- No, prefiero **ese**.

- *Do you think that this dress is the best?*
- *No, I prefer **that one**.*

⚠️ Demonstrative pronouns have traditionally carried an accent mark to distinguish them from demonstrative adjectives.

7.3 Use of demonstrative adjectives and pronouns (**Uso de los adjetivos y pronombres demostrativos**)

- The use of each category of demonstrative adjectives and pronouns is determined by the distance between the speaker or the listener and the person or thing referenced by the speaker.

> **este** (*this*): close to the speaker
> **ese** (*that*): can be close to the listener, farther from the speaker
> **aquel** (*that . . . over there*): far from both the speaker and the listener

7.4 Neuter demonstrative pronouns (**Los pronombres demostrativos neutros**)
`L13B, L15B`

- The three neuter demonstrative pronouns, **esto, eso,** and **aquello**, are used to refer to unidentified or unspecified things, situations, and concepts.

> Siento oír **eso**.
> *I am sorry to hear **that**.*

> ¿Y **esto** te parece bien?
> *And **this** seems OK to you?*

8 Possessive adjectives and pronouns (Los adjetivos y pronombres posesivos)

8.1 Possessive adjectives (**Los adjetivos posesivos**) `L2A, L5B`

singular	plural	
mi	mis	*my*
tu	tus	*your* (fam.)
su	sus	*your* (form.), *his, her, its*
nuestro/a	nuestros/as	*our*
vuestro/a	vuestros/as	*your* (fam.)
su	sus	*your* (form.), *their*

- Possessive adjectives indicate possession and they agree in number (**nuestro/a** and **vuestro/a** also agree in gender) with the nouns that they modify, i.e., the person or object that is possessed.

mi barrio	**mi** ciudad	**mis** libros	**mis** clases
my neighborhood	*my city*	*my books*	*my classes*

¿Dónde viven **vuestros** hermanos?
*Where do **your** siblings live?*

⚠ **Su** and **sus** have multiple meanings (*your, his, her, its, their*). To avoid confusion, you can use the construction [*article*] + [*noun*] + **de** + [*subject pronoun/name*].

su abuelo — ***his/her/your/their** grandfather*

el abuelo de **él/ella**	*his/her grandfather*
el abuelo de **usted/ustedes**	*your grandfather*
el abuelo de **ellos/ellas**	*their grandfather*
el abuelo de **Ernesto**	*Ernesto's grandfather*

8.2 Possessive pronouns (**Los pronombres posesivos**) `L13B`

singular		plural		
masculine	feminine	masculine	feminine	
mío	mía	míos	mías	*my, (of) mine*
tuyo	tuya	tuyos	tuyas	*your, (of) yours*
suyo	suya	suyos	suyas	*your, (of) yours; his, (of) his; her, (of) hers; its*
nuestro	nuestra	nuestros	nuestras	*our, (of) ours*
vuestro	vuestra	vuestros	vuestras	*your, (of) yours*
suyo	suya	suyos	suyas	*your, (of) yours; their, (of) theirs*

- Possessive pronouns agree in both gender and number with the thing that is possessed.

- The possessive pronoun is used with an article in order to take the place of a noun that has already been mentioned.

  - Mi empresa es muy grande, ¿y **la tuya**?
  - **La mía** no.

  - *My company is very big, and **yours**?*
  - ***Mine** isn't.*

- The possessive pronoun can be used without an article in order to state the identity of the owner.

  - ¿De quién es este libro?
  - Es **mío**.

  - *Whose book is this?*
  - *It is **mine**.*

⚠ Note that these words can also be used as adjectives when placed after the corresponding nouns.
Ex. **ese libro mío** (*that book of mine*).

9 Interrogative Words (Las palabras interrogativas)

- In Spanish, all interrogative words carry a written accent.

¿Cómo?	**¿Cómo** se escribe "hola"? `U0, L1A` *How do you spell "hola"?*
¿Quién(es)?	**¿Quién** es? `L1A` *Who is it?* **¿Quiénes** vinieron a la fiesta? *Who came to the party?*
¿Dónde?	**¿Dónde** está Granada? `L2A` *Where is Granada?*
¿Adónde?	**¿Adónde** fuiste el año pasado? *Where did you go last year?*
¿De dónde?	**¿De dónde** es usted? `L1A` *Where are you from?*
¿Cuánto/a?	**¿Cuánto** es? `L2B` *How much is it?*
¿Cuántos/as?	**¿Cuántos** dormitorios tiene tu apartamento? `L4B` *How many bedrooms does your apartment have?*
¿Por qué?	**¿Por qué** no trabajas menos? `L6A` *Why don't you work less?*
¿Qué + [*verb*]?	**¿Qué** significa "carne"? `U0, L2B` *What does "carne" mean?* **¿Qué** es eso? `L1A` *What is that?*
¿Qué + [*noun*]?	**¿Qué** hora es? `L3A` *What time is it?* **¿Qué** apartamentos te gustan? `L4B` *Which apartments do you like?*
¿Cuál(es)?	**¿Cuál** es de alquiler? `L4B` *Which (one) is for rent?* **¿Cuáles** tienen piscina? *Which (ones) have a pool?*
¿Qué tal?	**¿Qué tal?** `U0` *How are you?* (informal)
¿Cuándo?	**¿Cuándo** naciste tú? `L5A` *When were you born?*

10 Prepositions (Las preposiciones)

10.1 a

• time indications	• ¿**A** qué hora vas a la biblioteca? `L3A` ▪ **A** las siete. • *What time are you going to the library?* ▪ ***At** seven o'clock.* La biblioteca abre de diez **a** ocho. `L5A` *The library is open from ten **to** eight.*
• place indications, directions	• ¿**A**dónde vas? ▪ Voy **al** trabajo. `L3A, L6B` • *Where are you going?* ▪ *I am going **to** work.*
• distance, location	Está **a** 100 kilómetros de aquí. `L2A` *It is 100 kilometers from here.* • ¿Quería ver el pañuelo **a la derecha del** marco? `L3A` ▪ No, no. Me interesa el que está **a la izquierda del** marco, **al lado de** la lámpara. • *Did you want to see the scarf **to the right** of the picture frame?* ▪ *No, no. I'm interested in the one **to the left** of the frame, **next to** the lamp.*
• with a direct object (people)	• ¿Conoces **a** Laura? `L5B, L7B` ▪ No, no la conozco. • *Do you know Laura?* ▪ *No, I don't know her.*
• indirect object	**A** María no le gusta el barrio. `L4A, L7A, L12A` *María does not like the neighborhood.*

⚠ Remember to use the contraction **al** when **a** is followed by the masculine singular article **el**: **a + el = al.**

10.2 a partir de

A partir de ahora practicaré más deporte. `L12B`
***From** now **on** I will play more sports.*

A partir de mañana dejaré de trabajar tanto.
***Starting** tomorrow, I will stop working so much.*

10.3 antes de

Antes de retirarse, Indurain ganó el Tour de Francia cinco veces. `L10B`
***Before** retiring, Indurain won the Tour de France five times.*

10.4 con `U0, L8A, L17B`

• When used with the preposition **con** (*with*), the pronouns **yo** and **tú** take the forms **conmigo** and **contigo**. In all other cases, use subject pronouns with the preposition **con**.

¿Quieres que vaya **contigo** al médico?
*Do you want me to go **with you** to the doctor?*

• **Con** is also used in the construction **ser bueno/malo con** (*to be good/bad at*) + [*a specific thing*] to express ability.

Verónica es muy buena **con** la videoconsola.
*Verónica is very good **at** the video game console.*

10.5 de

• time indications	Son las cinco **de** la tarde. `L3A` *It is five o'clock **in** the afternoon.* David nació el 14 **de** febrero **de** 1995. `L5A` *David was born on February 14th, 1995.* 15 **de** mayo **de** 2005 *May 15, 2005* El museo abre **de** diez a ocho. `L3A` *The museum is open **from** ten to eight.* **De** 2003 a 2004 viajé por Asia. `L5A` ***From** 2003 to 2004, I traveled throughout Asia.*
• place indications: origin	Ana es **de** Bogotá. `L1A` *Ana is **from** Bogotá.* Vamos **de** Madrid a San Sebastián. `L6B` *We are going **from** Madrid to San Sebastián.*
• place indications: in prepositional phrases	Sevilla está cerca **de** Córdoba. `L2A` *Sevilla is close to Córdoba.* El bolígrafo está debajo **del** sofá. `L3B` *The pen is under the sofa.*
• to order food at a restaurant	**De** primero, las lentejas con chorizo. ***As** a first course, lentils with chorizo.* `L2B`
• indicating quantity	Un kilo **de** queso, por favor. `L4A` *A kilogram **of** cheese, please.*
• to indicate possession or belonging	los días **de** la semana `L3A` *the days **of** the week* Dolores es la madre **de** Manuel. `L5B` *Dolores is Manuel's mother.*
• **ser** + **de** to describe material	La mesa es **de** vidrio. `L8A` *The table is made (out) **of** glass.* Los pañuelos son **de** papel. *The handkerchiefs are made (out) **of** paper.*

10.6 dentro de   `L17A`

- Use **dentro de** + [*length of time*] to talk about the future.

  Dentro de unos años no habrá teléfonos fijos.
  ***Within/In** a few years there will be no home phone lines.*

- **Dentro de** may also be used to refer to location in space. When used with this meaning, **dentro de** is translated in English as *in* or *inside*.

  Dentro de la mochila está el libro.
  *The book is **inside** the backpack.*

10.7 desde

• time indications: a certain moment	• ¿**Desde** cuándo conoces a Eva? `L5B, L8B` ▪ **Desde** 1992. • _How long have you known Eva?_ ▪ _**Since** 1992._ Tengo vacaciones **desde** el 15 de agosto hasta el 10 de septiembre. _I have vacation **from** August 15th to September 10th._

10.8 desde hace

• time indications: interval	• ¿Desde cuándo vivís en Cádiz? ▪ **Desde hace** tres años. `L5B` • _How long have you lived in Cádiz?_ ▪ _**For** three years._

10.9 desde que + [_verb_]

Desde que me jubilé, vivo en Sevilla. `L8B`
**Since** I retired, I live in Seville.

10.10 después de

El Muro de Berlín se derribó 31 años **después de** su construcción. `L10B`
The Berlin Wall was brought down 31 years **after** its construction.

10.11 durante `L8B`

Viví en Bogotá **durante** cinco años.
I lived in Bogotá **for** five years.

10.12 en

• time indications	**En** julio Manuela abrió la tienda. `L5A` _Manuela opened the store **in** July._
• place indications	Granada está **en** el sur de España. `L1B, L2A, L3B` _Granada is **in** the south of Spain._ Normalmente desayuno **en** casa. _I usually have breakfast **at** home._
• means of transportation	Voy a París **en** tren. `L6B` _I go to Paris **by** train._
• in the construction **ser bueno/malo en** + [_discipline_], to express ability	No soy bueno **en** deportes. `L17B` _I am not good **at** sports._

10.13 entre

• place indications	El bolígrafo está **entre** el libro y el teléfono. `L2A` _The pen is **between** the book and the phone._

⚠ The preposition **entre** can mean both _between_ and _among._

Entre todas las personas aquí presentes, nadie estuvo en Asia.

**Among** all the people here, no one has been to Asia.

10.14 hasta

• time expressions	**Hasta** hoy no he tenido tiempo para escribirte. `L8B` *I haven't had time to write to you **until** today.* Desde 1990 **hasta** 2005, Emilio vivió en Buenos Aires. *From 1990 **to** 2005, Emilio lived in Buenos Aires.*
• expression of farewell	¡**Hasta** luego! `U0` *See you later!*

10.15 para `L4B, L8A, L10B, L17B`

• the recipient of something *(for)*	La postal es **para** ti. *The postcard is **for** you.*
• purpose: + [*infinitive*] *(in order to)*	Estudio español **para** viajar a Uruguay. *I am studying Spanish **in order to** travel to Uruguay.*
• purpose: + [*noun*] *(for, used for)*	Este libro es **para** la clase de ciencia. *This book is **for** science class.*
• destination *(toward, in the direction of)*	Mañana salimos **para** Buenos Aires. *We are leaving **for** Buenos Aires tomorrow.*
• deadline *(by, for)*	Tengo que terminar este proyecto **para** el jueves. *I have to finish this project **by** Thursday.*
• comparison with others or an opinion *(for, considering)*	**Para** ser extranjero, habla muy bien el inglés. ***For** a foreigner, he speaks English very well.* **Para** mí, eso es positivo. ***For** me, that is a positive thing.*
• in the employ of *(for)*	Marcos trabaja **para** el gobierno. *Marcos works **for** the government.*
• in the construction **ser bueno/malo para** + [*discipline*] *(at)*	Soy muy bueno **para** las matemáticas. *I am very good **at** math.*

10.16 por `L3A, L6B`

• duration of an action *(for, during, in)*	**Por** la tarde no trabajo; **por** la mañana, sí. *I don't work **in** the afternoon, but I do **in** the morning.* Fuimos de vacaciones **por** un mes. *We went on vacation **for** a month.*
• general location, direction *(around, through, along, by)*	Vamos a Barcelona y pasamos **por** Tarragona. *We are going to Barcelona and we will pass **through** Tarragona.* Caminamos **por** el río. *We walked **along** the river.*
• means by which something is done *(by, by way of, by means of)*	Compramos productos **por** Internet. *We buy products online.* Ayer hablé con mi hermano **por** teléfono. *Yesterday I spoke with my brother **by** (on the) phone.*

por *cont.*	
• reason or motive for an action *(because of, on account of, on behalf of)*	Lo hice **por** ti. *I did it **for** you (for your sake).*
	Joaquín está nervioso **por** el examen. *Joaquín is nervous **because of** the exam.*
• object of a search *(for, in search of)*	Tuve que volver a casa **por** mi billetera. *I had to return home **for** my wallet.*
• exchange or substitution *(for, in exchange for)*	Le pagué 50 dólares **por** la mesa. *I paid him $50 **for** the table.*
	Muchas gracias **por** tu ayuda. *Thank you very much **for** your help.*
• unit of measurement *(per, by)*	Matías manejaba a 100 kilómetros **por** hora. *Matías was driving at 100 kilometers **per** hour.*

10.17 Prepositions of place (**Las preposiciones de lugar**)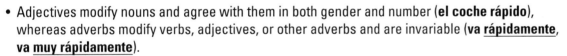

a la derecha de	*to the right of*	**debajo de**	*underneath*	**encima de**	*on top of*
a la izquierda de	*to the left of*	**delante de**	*in front of*	**enfrente de**	*across from*
al final de	*at the end of*	**detrás de**	*behind*	**entre**	*between*
al lado de	*next to*	**en**	*in*	**sobre**	*on, over*

- • Perdone, ¿hay un café por aquí?
- ▪ **Al final de** esta calle, **al lado del** gimnasio, hay un café.

- • *Excuse me, is there a café around here?*
- ▪ ***At the end of** this street, **next to** the gym there is a café.*

11 Adverbs (Los adverbios) L7A

- • Adjectives modify nouns and agree with them in both gender and number (**el coche rápido**), whereas adverbs modify verbs, adjectives, or other adverbs and are invariable (**va <u>rápidamente</u>**, **va <u>muy rápidamente</u>**).

- • One group of adverbs is formed by adding **-mente** to the feminine form of the corresponding adjective, much like the English ending *-ly*.

adjective	adverb
actual	actualmente
último/a	últimamente
activo/a	activamente
especial	especialmente
general	generalmente

Actualmente estoy escribiendo un libro.
Currently, I am writing a book.

Últimamente a Javier le interesa la política internacional.
Lately Javier is interested in international politics.

Generalmente la gente se habla de *tú*, **especialmente** los compañeros de trabajo.
*Generally people address each other as *tú*, **especially** co-workers.*

11.1 Adverbs of manner (**Adverbios de modo**) L11A, L12A, L17B

- Some adverbs have their own forms. These are some common adverbs.

así	*like this; so*
bien	*well*
despacio	*slowly*
fatal	*terribly* (informal)
mal	*badly*
mejor	*better*
nada mal	*not bad at all* (informal)
peor	*worse*
regular	*so-so*

Hablo **bien** inglés, pero hablo muy **mal** francés.
*I speak English **well**, but I speak French very **badly**.*

¿Es correcto **así**?
*Is it correct **like this**?*

Hable más **despacio**, por favor.
*Speak more **slowly**, please.*

- Lorenzo hace **muy bien** el asado.
- Sí, no lo hace **nada mal**.

- *Lorenzo prepares barbecue **very well**.*
- *Yes, he doesn't do **a bad job at all**.*

11.2 Adverbs of affirmation and negation (**Adverbios de afirmación y negación**)
L6A, L8A, L10B, L11B

- Adverbs of affirmation

sí	*yes*
claro	*clearly*
también	*too, also, as well*

- Yo estoy de acuerdo. ¿Y tú?
- Yo **también**.

- *I agree. Do you?*
- *I do, **too**.*

- Adverbs of negation

no	*no; not*
nunca	*never*
tampoco	*neither, not . . . either*
ya no	*no longer, (not) anymore*

- No estoy de acuerdo.
- Yo **tampoco**.

- *I don't agree.*
- *I don't **either**.*

- ¿**Ya no** trabajas?
- No, dejé de trabajar el año pasado.

- *You don't work **anymore**?*
- *No, I stopped working last year.*

11.3 Adverbs of inclusion (**Adverbios de inclusión**) `L11B`

además	*furthermore; besides; as well*
sobre todo	*above all*

El apartmento es bonito y **además** tiene mucha luz.
*The apartment is pretty and it has a lot of light **as well**.*

11.4 Adverbs of quantity (**Adverbios de cantidad**) `L2A, L2B, L6A, L8A`

algo	*somewhat*
aproximadamente	*approximately*
bastante	*enough; rather*
mucho	*a lot*
muy	*very*
nada	*not at all*
poco	*little; not much; not very*
un poco	*a little (bit)*

Me gusta **mucho**.
*I like it **a lot**.*

Ávila está **bastante** cerca.
*Ávila is **rather** close.*

Esos muebles son **poco** funcionales.
*That furniture is **not very** functional.*

El sofá es **muy** cómodo.
*The sofa is **very** comfortable.*

El pulpo está **un poco** salado, pero muy rico.
*The octopus is **a little** salty, but very good.*

No estoy **nada** de acuerdo.
*I don't agree **at all**.*

11.5 Adverbial phrases and adverbs of doubt
(**Locuciones adverbiales y adverbios de duda**) `L7B, L15A, L17A`

a lo mejor	*maybe, perhaps*
a ver si	*let's see if*
quizá(s)	*maybe, perhaps*
tal vez	*maybe, perhaps*

A lo mejor el nuevo producto tiene éxito en el mercado.
***Maybe** the new product will be successful in the market.*

A ver si el año que viene tenemos mejor tiempo.
***Let's see if** we have better weather next year.*

Quizá(s) Clara no ha llegado todavía.
***Perhaps** Clara hasn't arrived yet.*

Tal vez la ciencia encuentre pronto una respuesta.
***Maybe** science will find an answer soon.*

11.6 Adverbs of time (**Adverbios de tiempo**) L5A, L6A, L9B, L14A, L18A

ahora	*now*
anoche	*last night*
anteayer	*the day before yesterday*
antes	*before, earlier*
ayer	*yesterday*
de repente	*suddenly*
después	*after; then; afterward*
entonces	*then*
hoy	*today*
luego	*later (on); afterward; next; then*
mañana	*tomorrow*
primero	*first*
tarde	*late*
todavía	*still; yet* (in negative phrases)
ya	*already* (in affirmative phrases and questions); *anymore* (in negative phrases)

Antes practicaba karate; **ahora** practico baloncesto.
Before, I practiced karate; now I play basketball.

Anoche salí con amigos.
Last night I went out with friends.

Ayer fuimos al cine.
Yesterday we went to the movies.

Estábamos en la cocina cuando **de repente** se apagó la luz.
We were in the kitchen when the light suddenly went out.

Hoy vamos al concierto.
Today we are going to the concert.

Mañana ellos van al cine.
They are going to the movies tomorrow.

Inés viene **más tarde**.
Inés is coming later.

Primero trabajé en Berlín, **luego** volví a España y **después** trabajé en una organización no gubernamental.
First I worked in Berlin, afterward I returned to Spain, and then I worked in a non-governmental organization.

- ¿**Ya** has hecho los deberes?
- No, **todavía** no los he hecho.

- *Have you done the homework already?*
- *No, I haven't done it yet.*

11.7 Adverbs of place (**Adverbios de lugar**) L2A, L3B

cerca	*near, close*	**a la derecha**	*to/on the right*
lejos	*far*	**debajo**	*underneath*
aquí	*here*	**al lado**	*nearby*
ahí	*there*	**detrás**	*behind*
allí	*there; over there*	**delante**	*in front*
a la izquierda	*to/on the left*	**encima**	*on top*

- ¿La casa de Pedro está **cerca**?
- Sí, está **aquí al lado**.

- *Is Pedro's house **close**?*
- *Yes, it's **right near here**.*

11.8 Adverbs and expressions of frequency
(**Adverbios y expresiones de frecuencia**) L2B, L6A

a veces	*sometimes*
bastante	*enough; rather; quite; quite a lot*
casi nunca	*almost never*
mucho	*a lot*
nada	*(not) at all*
normalmente	*normally; usually*
nunca	*never*
siempre	*always*
una vez al mes	*once a month*

Siempre desayuno en casa.
*I **always** have breakfast at home.*

A veces cenamos afuera.
Sometimes we go out to dinner.

Normalmente como un menú del día en un restaurante.
*I **usually** order the set menu in a restaurant.*

- Yo voy **mucho** al cine, ¿y tú?
- Voy **bastante**.

- *I go to the movies **a lot**, and you?*
- *I go **quite a lot**.*

- ¿Vais **mucho** de viaje?
- No **mucho**, **una vez al mes**.

- *Do you go on trips **a lot**?*
- *Not **a lot**, **once a month**.*

Nunca voy al cine.
*I **never** go to the movies.*

Casi nunca veo la televisión.
*I **almost never** watch television.*

No duermo **nada** últimamente. Estoy un poco preocupado.
*I don't sleep **at all** lately. I am a little worried.*

11.9 Adverbs of exclusion (**Adverbios de exclusión**) `L13B`

solo	only
solamente	*only*

Solo uno de los países hispanohablantes está en África.
Only one Spanish-speaking country is in Africa.

⚠ The word **solo** is both a masculine singular adjective meaning *alone* or *lonely* and an adverb meaning *only*. In cases where the meaning of the word **solo** could be ambiguous, add a written accent to the adverb, **sólo**.

Marcos va **solo** al cine.
*Marcos goes to the movies **alone**.*

Marcos va **sólo** al cine.
*Marcos **only** goes to the movies.*

12 The Sentence (La oración)

12.1 The affirmative sentence (**La oración afirmativa**) `L1A`

subject	+ verb	+ complement
Pedro	es	de Málaga.
Pedro	*is*	*from Málaga.*

⚠ In Spanish, subject pronouns are rarely used because the verb conjugation reveals the subject.

- ¿De dónde eres?
- Soy de Caracas.

- *Where are **you** from?*
- *I am from Caracas.*

12.2 The negative sentence (**La oración negativa**) `L1A, L6A`

- In a negative sentence, place **no** before the verb.

No entiendo.
*I do **not** understand.*

Analía **no** es de España.
*Analía is **not** from Spain.*

- ¿Eres de León?
- **No**, **no** soy de León; soy de Toledo.

- *Are you from León?*
- ***No**, I am **not** from León. I am from Toledo.*

12.3 The double negative (**La doble negación**) `L6A, L8A`

- If **nada**, **nadie**, **nunca**, or **ni... ni** is used after the verb, place **no** before the verb.

⚠ Note that, unlike in English, all indefinite words in a negative sentence must be negative.

No hemos visto **nada**.
*We have **not** seen **anything**.*

No oigo a **nadie**.
*I do **not** hear **anyone**.*

No he estado **nunca** en Dinamarca.
*I have **never** been in Denmark.*

No me gusta **ni** el cine **ni** el teatro.
*I don't like the movies **or** the theater.*

- The first **ni** may be omitted.

- Yo estudio francés y bailo tango. ¿Y tú?
- Yo **no** estudio francés **ni** bailo tango, pero leo mucho.

- *I study French and dance tango. What about you?*
- *I don't study French **or** dance tango, but I read a lot.*

12.4 The interrogative sentence (**La oración interrogativa**) `U0, L1A`

- The syntax of an interrogative sentence without an interrogative word is the same as an affirmative sentence. They can only be distinguished by the intonation and punctuation.

Eres de Venezuela.
You are from Venezuela.

¿Eres de Venezuela?
Are you from Venezuela?

- If an interrogative word is used, place the verb before the subject.

¿De dónde es Andrea?
Where is Andrea from?

¿Cómo se llama usted?
What is your name?

12.5 The exclamatory sentence (**La oración exclamativa**) `L11A`

¡**Qué** + [*noun*]!	¡Qué casualidad! *What a coincidence!*
¡**Qué** + [*adjective*]!	¡Qué interesante! *How interesting!*
¡**Qué** + [*adverb*]!	¡Qué bien! *Great!*

12.6 Clauses of purpose and cause (**La cláusula de propósito y la cláusula causal**)

- **The causal conjunction** `L6B, L16A`
These conjunctions specify the cause of an action.

Voy a Caracas **porque** tengo amigos allí.
*I am going to Caracas **because** I have friends there.*

- **The conjunction of purpose** `L4B`

- Use **para** + [*infinitive*] to express purpose.

Saber lenguas es bueno **para viajar**.
*Knowing languages is good **for traveling**.*

- Use **servir para** + [*infinitive*] to describe the function of an object.

- ¿**Para qué sirve** este aparato?
- Es muy práctico; **sirve para hacer** pan en casa.

- *What is this machine **for**?*
- *It is very practical; **it is for making** bread at home.*

- Use **para que** + [*subjunctive*] to express purpose or intention in sentences with two verbs with `15B` different subjects.

Te voy a dar unos ejercicios **para que aprendas** las formas del subjuntivo.
*I'm going to give you some exercises **so that you learn** the forms of the subjunctive.*

12.7 The comparative sentence (**La oración comparativa**) `L3A, L6A, L8B, L16B`

igual de + [*adjective*] + **que**	*as . . . as*
igual que	*the same as*
más + [*adjective/adverb/noun*] + **que**	*more/(-er) . . . than*
menos + [*adjective/adverb/noun*] + **que**	*less/(-er) . . . than*
tan + [*adjective/adverb*] + **como**	*as . . . as*
tanto/a(s) + [*noun*] + **como**	*as much/many . . . as*
[*verb*] + **tanto como**	*as much as*

Mi país es **igual de bello que** el tuyo.	Leo **más** rápido **que** mi hermano.
My country is **as beautiful as** yours.	I read **faster than** my brother.
Mi acento es **igual que** el tuyo.	Mi jefa no es **tan** amable **como** la vuestra.
My accent is **the same as** yours.	My boss is not **as** friendly **as** yours.
Trabajas **más** horas **que** yo.	Tengo **tantos** libros **como** tú.
You work **more** hours **than** I (do).	I have **as many** books **as** you (do).
Este restaurante es **menos** caro **que** aquel.	Ella no habla **tanto como** él.
This restaurant is **less** expensive **than** that one.	She does not talk **as much as** he (does).

⚠ When using **más/menos** with a number, use the preposition **de** instead of **que** to make the comparison. `L3A`

> Mi compañera de cuarto tiene **más de** cien libros.
> My roommate has **more than** one hundred books.

12.8 Conjunctions (**Las conjunciones**) `L10B, L11B, L12B, L13A, L14B, L15B`

- Conjunctions are words used to connect words, clauses, or phrases.

Coordinating conjunctions	
y	Juan está enfermo **y** no puede ir a trabajar. Juan is sick **and** cannot go to work.
pero	Es difícil, **pero** no imposible. It is difficult, **but** not impossible.
no... sino	**No** me llamo Carlos, **sino** Tomás. My name is not Carlos, **but** (rather) Tomás.
Subordinating conjunctions	
que	Creo **que** esta es una buena oportunidad. I think **that** this is a good opportunity. ○ ¿Crees **que** es difícil vivir en otro país? ■ Creo **que** sí. ○ Do you think (**that**) it is difficult to live in another country? ■ I think so.
si + [indirect question]	¿Podría decirme **si** está abierta la farmacia? Could you tell me **whether** the pharmacy is open?
Subordinating adverbial conjunctions	
por eso	Quiero un trabajo digno; **por eso** hago una petición formal. I want a decent job; **that's why** I am making a formal request.

- The conjunction **si** introduces an interrogative phrase.

- A phrase introduced by **sino** presents information that opposes the information in the previous phrase.

- In Spanish, the verbs **creer**, **opinar**, and **pensar** are often used with the conjunction **que**.

12.9 The conditional sentence (**La oración condicional**) `L8A, L14A, L18B`

Possible conditions:

- **si** + [*present indicative*], [*present indicative*]

    Si conoces la lengua de un país, **es** más fácil integrarse.
    If you know a country's language, it is easier to become integrated.

- **si** + [*present indicative*], [*simple future*]

    Si vienes a mi país, **conocerás** muchos sitios interesantes.
    If you come to my country, you will see many interesting places.

- **si** + [*present indicative*], [*imperative*]

    Si tiene tiempo, **llámenos**.
    If you have time, call us.

12.10 Indirect discourse (**Estilo indirecto**) `L11A, L14B, L16A`

- Indirect discourse, or reported speech, refers to a sentence that reports what another person has said. The following verbs are often used to relate someone else's statement or question: **decir, comentar, explicar, preguntar, añadir, informar, declarar, confirmar, anunciar**, and **afirmar**.

    Dice que quiere una habitación doble.
    She says she wants a double room.

    Preguntó si la habitación tenía balcón.
    She asked if the room had a balcony.

- If the main clause of a sentence using reported speech is conjugated in the present or the present perfect, the verb in the subordinate clause is conjugated in the present.

Direct speech	Reported speech: Present	Reported speech: Present perfect
"El hotel no **está** muy lejos." *"The hotel is not very far."*	Ramón **dice que** el hotel no **está** muy lejos. *Ramón says that the hotel is not very far.*	Ramón **ha dicho que** el hotel no **está** muy lejos. *Ramón has said that the hotel is not very far.*
"¿Para cuándo **quiere** la reserva?" *"When do you want the reservation for?"*	Ella **pregunta para cuándo quiero** la reserva. *She asks/is asking when I want the reservation for.*	Ella **ha preguntado para cuándo quiero** la reserva. *She asked when I want the reservation for.*
"¿**Podéis** viajar en octubre?" *"Can you travel in October?"*	Manuela **pregunta si podemos** viajar en octubre. *Manuela asks/is asking if we can travel in October.*	Manuela **ha preguntado si podemos** viajar en octubre. *Manuela asked if we can travel in October.*

• If the verb reporting the message is in the past tense, follow these tense correlations.

Direct speech	Reported speech
Present "¿**Conoces** a Manu Chao?" *"Do you know Manu Chao?"*	**Imperfect** Margarita me preguntó si **conocía** a Manu Chao. *Margarita asked me if I knew Manu Chao.*
Present perfect "**He estado** en Mallorca." *"I have been to Mallorca."*	**Past perfect** María me dijo que **había estado** en Mallorca. *María told me that she had been to Mallorca.*
Imperfect "La situación económica **era** muy grave." *"The economic situation was very serious."*	**Imperfect** La gente comentaba que la situación económica **era** muy grave. *People commented that the economic situation was very serious.*
Preterite "Yo también **viví** en Hamburgo." *"I also lived in Hamburg."*	**Preterite/Past perfect** Peter me confirmó que él también **vivió/había vivido** en Hamburgo. *Peter confirmed to me that he also lived/had lived in Hamburg.*
Simple future "**Saldremos** mañana a las 20:00 h." *"We will leave tomorrow at 8:00 p.m."*	**Conditional** Ayer nos informaron que **saldríamos** hoy a las 20:00 h. *Yesterday they informed us that we would leave today at 8:00 p.m.*

12.11 Conjunctions of concession (**Conjunciones concesivas**) `L13B`

• **aunque** [*clause*] + [*clause*] / [*clause*] + **aunque** [*clause*]

Aunque no tenía celular, era muy fácil contactar con él.
Even though he did not have a cell phone, it was very easy to contact him.

Era muy fácil contactar con él **aunque** no tenía celular.
It was very easy to contact him, even though he did not have a cell phone.

• **a pesar de todo**

Sabía que era necesario tener celular. **A pesar de todo,** no se lo compró nunca.
He knew that it was necessary to have a cell phone. In spite of/Despite everything, he never bought himself one.

• **a pesar de** + [*infinitive/noun*]

A pesar de los avances tecnológicos, yo prefiero los medios tradicionales de comunicación.
In spite of/Despite advances in technology, I prefer traditional means of communication.

No me gusta el celular **a pesar de ser** útil para algunas cosas.
I don't like cell phones, even though they are useful for some things.

• [*clause*] + **sin embargo** + [*clause*]

No uso mucho la computadora; **sin embargo,** me gusta mucho navegar por Internet.
I don't use the computer much; however, I really like to surf the Web.

12.12 Expressions of frequency (**Expresiones de frecuencia**) `L6A, L14A, L14B`

- Expressions of frequency are often used with the imperfect in order to speak about habitual actions and situations in the past. `L14A`

(casi) siempre	(almost) always
de vez en cuando	from time to time
cada día/mes	every day/month

Cuando estaba estudiando, Federico **siempre se acostaba** tarde.
*When he was studying, Federico **always went to bed** late.*

Cuando Natalia estuvo trabajando en aquella empresa, **se levantaba cada día** a las cinco.
*When Natalia was working at that company, **she got up every day** at five o'clock.*

Cuando era pequeña, **de vez en cuando iba** al cine con mi hermana mayor.
*When I was young, **I went** to the movies with my older sister **from time to time**.*

12.13 Expressions of time (**Expresiones de tiempo**) `L14B`

- **cuando** + [*imperfect/preterite*] `L14B`

  Cuando iba a la escuela, no me gustaba aprender idiomas.
  ***When I went** to school, I didn't like learning languages.*

  Cuando terminé mis estudios, empecé a trabajar aquí.
  ***When I finished** my studies, I started working here (at that moment).*

- Use **al** + [*infinitive*] to refer to a specific moment in time. `L18B`

  Me quito los zapatos **al volver** (cuando vuelvo) a casa.
  *I take off my shoes **upon returning** (when I return) home.*

- **antes/después de** + [*infinitive/noun*] `L10B`

  Antes de las Olimpiadas, muchas personas no sabían dónde estaba Barcelona.
  ***Before the Olympic Games**, many people did not know where Barcelona was.*

  Después de pasar mis primeras vacaciones en España, decidí aprender español.
  ***After spending** my first vacation in Spain, I decided to study Spanish.*

- **antes de que / después de que** + [*subjunctive*] `L18A`

  Antes de que pase el verano, iré de vacaciones.
  ***Before** the summer **ends**, I will go on vacation.*

- **cuando** + [*subjunctive*] (to refer to the future) `L18A`

  Cuando termine la película, llamaré a mi madre.
  ***When** the movie **finishes**, I will call my mother.*

- **dentro de** + [*length of time*] (to refer to the future) `L17A`

  Dentro de un mes dejaré de trabajar.
  ***Within one month's time**, I will stop working.*

13 Numbers and Quantifiers (Los adjetivos numerales y los cuantificadores)

13.1 Cardinal numbers (Los números cardinales) `L1A, L1B, L2A, L4B`

`L1A, L1B`

0 cero	10 diez	20 veinte	30 treinta
1 uno	11 once	21 veintiuno	31 treinta y uno
2 dos	12 doce	22 veintidós	32 treinta y dos
3 tres	13 trece	23 veintitrés	33 treinta y tres
4 cuatro	14 catorce	24 veinticuatro	34 treinta y cuatro
5 cinco	15 quince	25 veinticinco	[...]
6 seis	16 dieciséis	26 veintiséis	40 cuarenta
7 siete	17 diecisiete	27 veintisiete	50 cincuenta
8 ocho	18 dieciocho	28 veintiocho	60 sesenta
9 nueve	19 diecinueve	29 veintinueve	70 setenta
			80 ochenta
			90 noventa

`L2A, L4B`

100 cien	500 quinientos/as	2000 dos mil
101 ciento uno	600 seiscientos/as	10 000 diez mil
153 ciento cincuenta y tres	700 setecientos/as	20 000 veinte mil
200 doscientos/as	800 ochocientos/as	100 000 cien mil
201 doscientos/as uno/a	900 novecientos/as	200 000 doscientos/as mil
299 doscientos/as noventa y nueve	1000 mil	1 000 000 un millón
300 trescientos/as	1001 mil uno/a	2 000 000 dos millones
400 cuatrocientos/as	1549 mil quinientos/as cuarenta y nueve	

 For numbers that end in **-uno**, use **-un** before masculine nouns and **-una** before feminine nouns.

 Numbers between 200 and 900 also have feminine forms to agree with feminine plural nouns: doscient**os** coch**es**, doscient**as** cas**as**.

 Mil is invariable: **mil** coches, **mil** casas.

 Only the last two digits (tens and ones) are joined by **y**: mil treinta **y** seis (1036). In the numbers 16–19 and 21–29, the digits are joined as one word by **i**: dieciocho (18), veinticuatro (24).

 The term **cien** is used in counting and when not followed by a lesser number. When it is followed by a lesser number, **ciento** is used: **ciento veinticinco** (125).

13.2 Ordinal numbers (**Los números ordinales**) `L5A, L14A`

- Ordinal numbers are used to indicate the order or sequence.

    Ella conoció a su mejor amiga en el **primer** grado.
    *She met her best friend in **first** grade.*

- They are also used to give order to an argument.

    En **primer** lugar, en **segundo** lugar... por último.
    *In the **first** place, in the **second** place . . . lastly.*

1.° primero/a, primer	*first*
2.° segundo/a	*second*
3.° tercero/a, tercer	*third*
4.° cuarto/a	*fourth*
5.° quinto/a	*fifth*
6.° sexto/a	*sixth*
7.° séptimo/a	*seventh*
8.° octavo/a	*eighth*
9.° noveno/a	*ninth*
10.° décimo/a	*tenth*

- **Primero** and **tercero** have shortened forms when they are used before masculine singular nouns: **primer** and **tercer**.

    Juan es el **primer** hijo de Manolita y el **tercer** nieto de sus abuelos.
    *Juan is Manolita's **first** son and his grandparents' **third** grandchild.*

13.3 Other quantifiers (**Otros cuantificadores**) `L3A`

- Quantifiers are words that indicate quantity.

    Todos/as los/las alumnos/as hablan español.
    ***All the** students speak Spanish.*

    Casi todos/as practican en casa.
    ***Almost all (of them)** practice at home.*

    La mayoría (**de** los alumnos) conoce algún país hispanohablante.
    ***The majority (of** the students) have been to a Spanish-speaking country.*

    Varios/as son amigos/as.
    ***Several (of them)** are friends.*

    Solo uno/a ha estado en Chile.
    ***Only one** has been to Chile.*

    Cada persona conoce sus preferencias.
    ***Each person** knows his or her preferences.*

- When **la mayoría** is followed by **de** + [*plural noun*], the verb can agree with **mayoría** (singular) or with the other noun (plural).

    La mayoría de los estudiantes estudia(n) español.
    ***The majority of the students** study Spanish.*

- The plural form must be used with the verbs **ser**, **estar**, and **parecer**.

    La mayoría de los profesores **son** latinoamericanos.
    ***The majority** of the professors **are** Latin American.*

14 Strategies For Improving Communication (Estrategias para mejorar la comunicación)

14.1 Discourse connectors (Conectores del discurso) `L13B`

- Expressions such as **por un lado... por otro** and **por una parte... por otra** help to structure discourse.

  Son muchas cosas. **Por un lado** el trabajo, los alumnos; **por otro**, la familia, los niños, la casa...
  *There are many things. **On the one hand**, work, the students; **on the other,** family, the children, the house . . .*

14.2 Giving examples (Dar ejemplos) `L7A`

- **por ejemplo**

  Me interesan mucho las ciudades peruanas, **por ejemplo**, Lima, Cuzco...
  *Peruvian cities interest me very much. **For example**, Lima, Cuzco . . .*

14.3 Generalizing and clarifying (Generalizar y matizar) `L7B`

generalmente en general especialmente	**Generalmente/En general** la gente no come muchas verduras, **especialmente** la gente joven. *Generally/In general people do not eat a lot of vegetables, **especially** young people.*

14.4 Introducing an explanation and encouraging (Introducir una explicación y animar) `L8A`

mira	∘ ¿Me puedes ayudar, por favor? ▪ **Mira**, ahora no tengo tiempo, pero más tarde sí. ∘ *Can you help me, please?* ▪ ***Look**, I don't have time now, but I can later on.*
venga	∘ Estoy muy cansado. ▪ **¡Venga!** ¡Ya casi hemos llegado! ∘ *I am very tired.* ▪ ***Come on**! We are almost there!*

 Venga is primarily used in Spain. Other expressions such as **vamos** or **dale** can be used in similar contexts.

14.5 Reformulating ideas (Reformular) `L8B`

o sea es decir	¿Usted no puede encontrar otro momento para hablar conmigo sobre mi trabajo? **O sea**, me gustaría hacerle unas preguntas. **Es decir**, quería preguntarle si me podría dar unos consejos sobre mi trabajo. *You don't have any other time to talk to me about my paper? **I mean,** I would like to ask you some questions. **That is**, I wanted to ask you if you could give me some advice about my paper.*

14.6 Buying time while one is thinking (**Ganar tiempo mientras pensamos**) L9A

pues no sé... bueno...	• ¿A qué hora cierra el supermercado? ▪ **Pues no sé... bueno...** creo que a las nueve. • *What time does the supermarket close?* ▪ *Well, I don't know . . . well . . . I think at nine o'clock.*
pues... a ver...	• ¿Qué ciudad es la capital de Chile? ▪ Mmmm... **a ver, pues...** ¡Santiago! • *What city is the capital of Chile?* ▪ *Mmmm . . . let's see, um . . . Santiago!*
¿cómo era?	• ¿Conoces esa canción que te digo? ▪ Pues sí, **a ver... ¿cómo era?** • *Do you know that song I'm talking about?* ▪ *Well yes, let's see . . . how did it go?*
entonces es que	• **Bueno, entonces,** vamos al cine mañana, ¿no? ▪ No puedo, **es que** tengo mucha tarea. • *Well, then, we are going to the movies tomorrow, right?* ▪ *I can't, the thing is, I have a lot of homework.*

• These interjections fall into different grammatical categories (conjunctions, adjectives, adverbs) and they are always invariable. They are used to join ideas and to fill gaps in communication. Other expressions include ¡**Anda ya**! (*Come on!/Oh my!*) and ¿**De verdad**? (*Really?*).

14.7 Calling someone's attention (**Llamar la atención**) L9B

perdona	**Perdona**, ¿sabes dónde hay una farmacia? *Excuse me, do you know where there is a pharmacy?*
perdone	**Perdone**, ¿puede ayudarme? Me he perdido. *Excuse me, can you help me? I am lost.*

⚠ **Perdona** is the familiar (**tú**) command and **perdone** is the formal (**usted**) command.

14.8 Asking for repetition (**Pedir repetición**) L14A

perdona	• Yo viví un tiempo en Guinea Ecuatorial. ▪ ¿**Perdona**? • *I lived in Equatorial Guinea for a while.* ▪ *Pardon me?*
¿cómo?	• La capital de Guinea Ecuatorial es Malabo. ▪ ¿**Cómo**? • *The capital of Equatorial Guinea is Malabo.* ▪ *Sorry?*

14.9 Adding information in a conversation (**Añadir información en una conversación**)

`L10A`

por cierto	**Por cierto**, la semana pasada vi a María. *By the way, I saw María last week.*
a propósito	**A propósito**, ¿desde cuándo no hablas con ella? *Incidentally, how long has it been since you have spoken with her?*

14.10 Minimizing disagreement (**Minimizar el desacuerdo**) `L10B`

pero (depende)	Es verdad que es difícil estar lejos de casa, **pero depende**... siempre se puede volver. *It is true that it is hard to be away from home, **but it depends**... you can always go back.*
pero (bueno)	El trabajo es difícil, **pero bueno**, a mí me gusta. *The job is difficult, **but you know**, I like it.*
claro que... pero	**Claro que** cambiar de trabajo es una buena idea, **pero** la situación es difícil. *Of course changing jobs is a good idea, **but** the situation is difficult.*

14.11 Softening an opinion (**Suavizar una opinión**) `L15A`

yo diría que	**Yo diría que** hay que consumir más frutas y verduras. *I would say that you should eat more fruits and vegetables.*

14.12 Putting information in order (**Ordenar la información**) `L5A, L11A`

en primer lugar después por último	**En primer lugar**, el apartamento es pequeño, **después**, es muy oscuro y, **por último**, no tiene muebles. *First of all, the apartment is small, **next**, it is very dark, and **lastly**, it does not have any furniture.*

14.13 Showing interest in the conversation (**Mostrar interés en la conversación**) `L11B`

sí, la verdad que sí	• Los alquileres en Barcelona son muy caros. ▪ **Sí, la verdad que sí.** • *Rents in Barcelona are very expensive.* ▪ ***Yes, you're right.***
¿sí?, ¿en serio?	• Álvaro se casa en mayo. ▪ **¿Sí?, ¿en serio?** • *Álvaro is getting married in May.* ▪ ***Really? Seriously?***

14.14 Confirming a plan (**Cerrar una cita**) `L8A, L12A`

entonces **de acuerdo** **nos vemos**	• **Entonces** vamos al cine el lunes a las siete, ¿no? ▪ Sí. • **De acuerdo**. **¡Nos vemos!** • *So we are going to the movies on Monday at seven o'clock, right?* ▪ *Yes.* • *OK. See you (then)!*

14.15 Taking the floor (**Tomar la palabra**) `L12B`

Perdón, quería decir que... **Sí, y además** **Una cosa más**	• **Perdón, quería decir que** los apartamentos en este edificio son muy caros. ▪ **Sí, y además** son muy pequeños. ✦ **Una cosa más**: no hay espacio suficiente para una pareja con hijos. • *Pardon me, I meant to say that the apartments in this building are very expensive.* ▪ *Yes, and furthermore they are very small.* ✦ *One more thing: there is not enough space for a couple with children.*

14.16 Giving an explanation (**Dar una explicación**) `L13A`

como	**Como** mi esposo conoce mis gustos, nos compró pasajes a Costa Rica para nuestras vacaciones. *As/Since my husband knows my preferences, he bought us tickets to Costa Rica for our vacation.*
es que	**Es que** me encanta este país. *It's just that (the reason is that) I love this country.*

14.17 Emphasizing a piece of information (**Destacar una información**) `L13B`

solo/solamente	Aunque a Isabel le encanta la música, **solo/solamente** ha asistido a dos conciertos. *Although Isabel loves music, she has **only** attended two concerts.*
sobre todo	A María José le gustan mucho los deportes, **sobre todo** los de aventura. *María José likes sports, **above all** adventure sports.*

14.18 Maintaining contact (**Controlar el contacto**) `L14B`

¿sabes?	Ella necesita más ayuda, **¿sabes?** *She needs more help, **you know?***

14.19 Reinforcing arguments (**Reforzar argumentos**) `L15B`

desde luego	**Desde luego**, ser adolescente no es fácil. ***Of course**, being an adolescent is not easy.*
efectivamente	**Efectivamente**, no lo es. ***Indeed**, it is not.*

14.20 Bringing up a topic (**Introducir un tema**) `L16A`

en cuanto a	**En cuanto a** la marcha por la paz, no hay novedades. ***With respect to** the peace march, there are no new developments.*

14.21 Diminishing generalizations (**Atenuar las generalizaciones**) `L16B`

no todos los...	**No todos los** caribeños viven cerca de la playa. ***Not all** inhabitants of the Caribbean live close to the beach.*
Eso no es todo.	Y **eso no es todo**. Hay muchos otros estereotipos que tampoco son ciertos. *And **that's not all**. There are many other stereotypes that aren't true either.*

14.22 Expressing consequences (**Expresar consecuencias**) `L17A`

así (es) que	La ciencia tiene soluciones, **así (es) que** vamos a esperar. *Science has solutions, **so** we are going to wait.*
por lo tanto	Los estudios no son concluyentes. **Por lo tanto**, no hay razón de alarma. *The studies are not conclusive. **Therefore**, there is no reason for alarm.*

14.23 Reinforcing a negation (**Reforzar una negación**) `L17B`

no... nada	A Ricardo **no** le gusta **nada** que le llamen por la mañana temprano. *Ricardo does **not** like it **at all** when people call him early in the morning.*

14.24 Intensifying meaning (**Intensificar**) `L18A`

repeating the word and using the conjunction y	Este deportista ha ganado **premios y premios**. *This athlete has won **prizes upon prizes**.*

14.25 Summarizing main ideas (**Resumir ideas principales**) `L18B`

en resumen	**En resumen**, no tienen fecha para la celebración. *In short, they do not have a date for the celebration.*
en definitiva	Sí, **en definitiva**, ese es el problema. *Yes, in short, that is the problem.*

14.26 Fixed expressions (**Expresiones lexicalizadas**)

- To express disagreement in a colloquial manner: **¡Qué va!** `L15B`
  - ¿Tienes mucha tarea?
  - **¡Qué va!** Solo de matemáticas.

  - *Do you have a lot of homework?*
  - *No, not really. Only math.*

- To express wishes: `L13A, L18B`

  Que te mejores pronto.   **Que tengan un buen viaje.**   **Que sean felices.**
  Feel better soon.   *Have a nice trip.*   *May you be happy.*

- To console: `L13B`

  Te entiendo.   **No pasa nada.**   **No te preocupes.**
  I understand.   *(There's) No problem.*   *Don't worry.*

Glossary

This glossary contains the active vocabulary words and expressions taught in each lesson of **PROTAGONISTAS**, as well as other useful vocabulary. A numeral following an entry indicates the lesson where the word or expression is introduced.

Note on alphabetization
For purposes of alphabetization, ñ follows **n**. Therefore, in this glossary you will find that **añadir**, for example, appears after **anuncio**.

Abbreviations used in this glossary

adj.	adjective	*f.*	feminine	*pl.*	plural
adv.	adverb	*fam.*	familiar	*prep.*	preposition
art.	article	*form.*	formal	*pron.*	pronoun
conj.	conjunction	*interrog.*	interrogative	*sing.*	singular
contrac.	contraction	*loc.*	phrase	*v.*	verb
exp.	expression	*m.*	masculine		

Español-Inglés

A

a *prep.* at; to; **¿A qué hora...?** *exp.* At what time...? **3A; a bordo** *loc. adv.* on board **13A; a cambio** *loc. adv.* in return **12B; a cambio de** *loc. adv.* in exchange for **8A; a convenir** *exp.* to be agreed upon **13B; a favor de** *loc. adv.* in favor of **12B; a finales del siglo XIX** *loc. adv.* toward the end of the 19th century **8B; a la derecha** *loc. adv.* (to the) right **9B; a la derecha de** *loc. adv.* to the right of **3B; a la izquierda** *loc. adv.* (to the) left **9B; a la izquierda de** *loc. adv.* to the left of **3B; a la venta** *loc. adv.* for sale **4B; a largo plazo** *loc. adv.* in the long term **9A; a mediados de los 60** *loc. adv.* in the mid sixties **14B; a partir de** *loc. prep.* from, starting **12B; a pesar de** *loc. prep.* despite **6B; a pesar de que** *conj.* in spite of the fact that **7A; a pesar de todo** *exp.* in spite of everything **13B; a principios del siglo XX** *loc. adv.* at the beginning of the 20th century **8B; a propósito** *exp.* incidentally; by the way **10A; a tiempo** *loc. adv.* in/on time **7B; a través de** *loc. prep.* through **14B; a tu servicio** *loc. adv.* at your service **7B; a veces** *loc. adv.* sometimes **2B; a ver** *exp.* let's see... **6A; amor a distancia** *m.* long-distance love **6B; dedicarse a (hacer) algo** *v.* to do something (for a living) **7A; desde/de... hasta/a...** *loc. prep.* from... until/to **8B; día a día** *m.* daily life **7A; día a día** *loc. adv.* day by day **14B; estar a... kilómetros de...** *exp.* to be... kilometers from... **2A; estar dirigido/a a** *v.* to be aimed at **6A; gracias a...** *loc. prep.* thanks to... **5B; ir a trabajar** *v.* to go to work **3A; jugar a la lotería** *v.* to play the lottery **9B; llegar a casa** *v.* to arrive home **3A; llevar a cabo** *v.* to carry out **18A; llevar a los niños al colegio** *v.* to take the kids to school **3A; Me toca a mí.** *exp.* It's my turn. **4A; parecerse a alguien** *v.* to look like somebody **12A; paseo a

caballo *m.* horseback ride **6B; reparto a domicilio** *m.* home delivery **7B; ser sensible a** *v.* to be sensitive to **10A; una vez a la semana** *loc. adv.* once a week **6A**
abanderado/a: aerolínea abanderada *f.* national airline **13A**
abandonar *v.* to leave; to give up **7B**
abanico *m.* (hand-held) fan **3B**
abiertamente *adv.* openly, frankly **17A**
abierto/a *adj.* open **3A**
abogado/a *m./f.* lawyer **1B**
abonar *v.* to fertilize **8A**
abrazarse *v.* to hug each other **17B**
abrazo *m.* hug **2A**
abreviatura *f.* abbreviation **13B**
abrigarse *v.* to wrap up **13A**
abril *m.* April **1B; el 13 de abril** *m.* April 13 **3A**
abrir *v.* open **3A; abrir un negocio** *v.* to open a business **15A**
abrocharse *v.* to fasten **13A**
abuela *f.* grandmother **5B**
abuelo *m.* grandfather **5B**
abuelos *m.* grandparents **5B**
abundante *adj.* plentiful **17A**
aburrido/a *adj.* boring **1B**
aburrimiento *m.* boredom **17B**
aburrir *v.* to bore **17B**
aburrirse *v.* to get bored **17B**
acá *adv.* here **6B**
academia *f.* academy **15B**
académico/a: vida académica *f.* academic life **14A**
acariciar *v.* to caress **9A**
aceite *m.* oil **8A; aceite de oliva** *m.* olive oil **2B; aceite de oliva virgen extra** *m.* extra virgin olive oil **15A**
aceituna *f.* olive **2B**
acento: con acento *loc. adv.* with an accent **0**
aceptación *f.* acceptance **12B**
aceptar *v.* to accept **15B**
acero *m.* steel **18A; cable de acero** *m.* steel cable **18A**
ácido *m.* acid **17A**
acogida *f.* acceptance **15A**
acompañado/a: sentirse acompañado/a *v.* to feel accompanied **9A**
acompañar *v.* to keep company **9A**
acondicionado/a *adj.* equipped **6B; aire

acondicionado *m.* air conditioning **11A**
aconsejar *v.* to advise **6A**
acontecimiento *m.* event **5A**
acordarse de *v.* to remember **18B**
acostarse *v.* to go to bed **7A**
acostumbrado/a: estar acostumbrado/a a *v.* to be used to **13B**
actitud *f.* attitude **13B**
actividad *f.* activity **0; actividad extraescolar** *f.* extracurricular activity **15B; actividad laboral** *f.* job **7B**
activo/a *adj.* active **5A**
acto: acto de fe *m.* matter of faith **8A**
actor *m.* actor **1A**
actriz *f.* actress **1A**
actuación *f.* acting **5A**
actualidad: en la actualidad *loc. adv.* today; nowadays **8B**
actualizar *v.* to update **7B**
actualmente *adv.* currently, **7A**
actuar *v.* to act **5A**
acuerdo: estar de acuerdo *v.* to agree **5B**
adaptado/a: estar adaptado/a *v.* to be adapted **12B**
adaptarse *v.* to adapt **10A**
adecuado/a *adj.* appropriate; suitable **5B**
además *adv.* in addition **2A**
adherirse *v.* to join **16A**
adhesión *f.* support **16A**
Adiós. *exp.* Goodbye. **0**
adivinar *v.* to guess **0**
administración *f.* administration **8A**
administrativo/a *adj.* administrative **7B**
admirar *v.* to admire **14B**
adobo *m.* marinade **15A**
adolescente *m. y f.* adolescent, teenager **9A**
adopción *f.* adoption **5B**
adoptar *v.* to adopt **5B**
adornar(se) *v.* to decorate **18B**
adversidad *f.* setback **18A**
aéreo/a: compañía aérea *f.* airline **11A**
aerolínea *f.* airline **13A; aerolínea abanderada** *f.* national airline **13A**
aeropuerto *m.* airport **0**
afectar *v.* to affect **10A; afectivo/a: entorno afectivo** *m.* emotional environment **13B**
afecto *m.* affection **12A; mostrar afecto** *v.* to show affection **18B**

afición *f.* hobby **11B**
aficionado/a *adj.* amateur **11B**
aficionado/a *m./f.* fan **14B**
afiliarse *v.* to join **16A**
afín: ser afín *v.* to have a lot in common **17B**
afinidad *f.* affinity **17B**
afirmar *v.* to assert **16A**
África *f.* Africa **14A; el África subsahariana** *f.* sub-Saharan Africa **14A**
africano/a *adj.* African **14A**
afuera: vivir afuera *v.* to live abroad **10B**
afueras *f.* outskirts **11B**
agarrar *v.* to grab **17B**
agasajado/a *m./f.* guest of honor **18B**
agencia *f.* agency **4B; agencia de lotería** *f.* lottery ticket booth **9B; agencia de viajes** *f.* travel agency **4B**
agenda: agenda semanal *f.* (weekly) planner **3A**
agosto *m.* August **3A**
agradable *adj.* pleasant **2A**
agresión *f.* aggression **16A**
agricultor(a) *m./f.* farmer **7B**
agricultura *f.* agriculture **15A; agricultura ecológica** *f.* organic farming **15A**
agromercado *m.* produce market **4A**
agrónomo/a: (ingeniero/a) agrónomo/a *m./f.* agronomist **7A**
agrupar *v.* to group, to organize **0**
aguacate *m.* avocado **12A**
ahorrar *v.* to save **12B**
ahorros *m.* savings **8B**
aimara *m.* Aymara **12A**
aire *m.* air **7B; aire acondicionado** *m.* air conditioning **11A; al aire libre** *loc. adv.* outdoors **3A; cambio de aires** *m.* change of scenery **11A**
aislamiento *m.* isolation **13B**
ajo *m.* garlic **8A**
ajustado/a a *adj.* adapted to **17A**
al *contrac.* (contraction of **a + el**); **al aire libre** *loc. adv.* outdoors **3A; al horno** *loc. adj.* baked **13A; al lado de** *loc. adv.* next to **3B; al mismo tiempo** *loc. adv.* at the same time **7A; al parecer** *loc. adv.* apparently **8B; dos veces al mes** *loc. adv.* twice a month **6A; llevar a los niños al colegio** *v.* to take the kids to school **3A; poner al día** *v.* to bring up to date **7B; tres veces al año** *loc. adv.* three times a year **3A**
ala: ala delta *f.* hang glider **18A**
alarmista *m. y f.* alarmist **17A**
albaricoque *m.* apricot **15A**
alberca *f.* pool **5B**
albergar *v.* to accommodate **11A**
albergue *m.* hostel **6B**
albóndiga *f.* meatball **2B**
álbum *m.* album **5B**
alcachofa *f.* artichoke **15A**
alcance: estar fuera del (de nuestro) alcance *exp.* to be beyond one's (our) means **15B**
aldea *f.* village **9A**
alegrarse (de) *v.* to be glad (that) **11A**
alegre *adj.* bright **4B; happy 5B**
alejado/a: alejados entre sí *loc. adv.* far from each other **17B**
alemán *m.* German **1B**
alemán/alemana *adj.* German **1B**
alergia *f.* allergy **10A**

alfombra *f.* rug **4B**
algo *pron.* something **2B; ¿Algo más?** *exp.* Anything else? **2B; dedicarse a (hacer) algo** *v.* to do something (for a living) **7A; estar haciendo algo** *v.* to be doing something **7A; hacer algo en casa** *v.* to do something at home **3A**
algodón *m.* cotton **9A**
alguien *pron.* someone **5B**
algún *adj.* some, any **9A**
alguno/a *adj.* some, any **9A**
algunos/as *adj.* some **5A**
alimentación: tienda de alimentación *f.* grocery store **4A; producto de alimentación** *m.* food product **15A**
alimento *m.* food **2B; alimento natural** *m.* natural food **15A; alimento transgénico** *m.* genetically modified food **15A**
allá *adv.* there **6B**
allí *adv.* there **2A**
alma *f.* soul **6A**
almorzar *v.* to eat lunch **2B**
alojamiento *m.* lodging **6B**
alojarse *v.* to stay **13A**
alquiler *m.* rental; rent **4B; de alquiler** *adj.* rental **11B**
alrededor *adv.* around **8A**
altavoz *m.* loudspeaker **13A**
altísimo/a *adj.* excessive, very high **11B**
alto/a *adj.* high; tall **8A; temporada alta** *f.* high season **4B**
alumno/a *m./f.* student **0**
amabilísimo/a *adj.* very friendly **13A**
amargar: amargarle la vida a alguien *exp.* to make someone's life miserable **17A**
amargo/a *adj.* bitter; painful **10B**
amarillo/a *adj.* yellow **3B; fiebre amarilla** *f.* yellow fever **10A**
Amazonas *m.* Amazon River **5A**
ambicioso/a *adj.* ambitious **16A**
ambiente *m.* atmosphere **2A; ambiente laboral** *m.* work environment **13B; medio ambiente** *m.* environment **4B**
ámbito: en el ámbito familiar *m.* among family **12A**
amistad *f.* friendship **5B**
amo/a de casa *m./f.* homemaker **1B**
amor *m.* love **6B; amor a distancia** *m.* long-distance love **6B; amor correspondido** *m.* requited love **12A; amor no correspondido** *m.* unrequited love **12A; declaración de amor** *f.* declaration of love **18B**
ampliar: ampliar un negocio *v.* to expand a business **15A**
amueblado/a *adj.* furnished **4B**
analfabetismo *m.* illiteracy **16A**
analgésico *m.* painkiller **10A**
analista: analista de *marketing* *m. y f.* marketing analyst **13B**
ananá *m.* pineapple **15A**
anaranjado/a *adj.* orange **3B**
ancho/a *adj.* wide **4B**
andar: ¡Anda ya! *exp.* Come on! **9B**
andén *m.* platform **13A**
anécdota *f.* anecdote **9B**
animal *m.* animal **7B**
anímico/a: estado anímico *m.* state of mind **10A**

ánimo: estado de ánimo *m.* state of mind, mood **12A; dar ánimo** *v.* to offer encouragement **13A**
aniversario *m.* anniversary **5A**
anoche *adv.* last night **5A**
anotar *v.* to write down **0**
antelación: con antelación *loc. adv.* in advance **11A**
anterior *adj.* previous **14B**
antes *adv.* before **9A; antes de que** *conj.* before **18A**
antibiótico *m.* antibiotic **10A**
anticipar *v.* to anticipate **16B**
anticuado/a *adj.* antiquated **16B**
antigüedad *f.* antique **4A**
antiguo/a *adj.* old **2A**
anunciar *v.* to announce **16A**
anuncio *m.* ad **4B**
añadir *v.* to add **4A**
año *m.* year **2B; Año Nuevo** *m.* New Year **18B; cumplir 15 años** *v.* to turn 15 years old **5A; cumplir años** *v.* to have one's birthday **18B; cumplir años de casados** *v.* to have one's wedding anniversary **18B; este año** *loc. adv.* this year **6A; fiesta de quince años** *f.* fifteenth birthday party **18B; los años 60** *m.* the sixties **8B; tres veces al año** *loc. adv.* three times a year **3A; una persona de 80 años** *f.* an 80-year-old person **3A**
apagado/a: luz apagada *f.* lights off **6A**
apagar *v.* to put out **7A**
aparato *m.* device **4B**
aparcamiento *m.* parking lot **11A**
apartamento *m.* apartment **4B**
apelar *v.* to appeal **16B**
apellido *m.* last name **1B; doble apellido** *m.* two last names **12A**
apenado/a *adj.* sad **17B**
apertura *f.* opening **15A**
aplazo *m.* failure **15B**
aportar *v.* to provide **15A**
apoyar *v.* to support **13A**
apreciación *f.* appreciation **17A**
apreciar *v.* to appreciate **18B**
aprender *v.* to learn **3A; aprender de memoria** *v.* to memorize **14B; aprender español** *v.* to learn Spanish **3A**
aprobar *v.* to pass **14A**
aprovechamiento *m.* exploitation **16A**
aprovechar *v.* to take advantage of **15A**
aproximadamente *adv.* approximately **3A**
apto/a para *adj.* appropriate/safe for **15A**
apuntarse a *v.* to sign up for **13A**
araña *f.* spider; **mono/a araña** *m./f.* spider monkey **16B**
árbol *m.* tree; **árbol genealógico** *m.* family tree **5B**
archivo *m.* file **7B**
arcilla *f.* clay **16B**
Argentina *f.* Argentina **0**
argentino/a *adj.* Argentine
árido/a *adj.* arid **13B**
arma *f.* weapon; **arma nuclear** *f.* nuclear weapon **16A; tráfico de armas** *m.* arms trade **16A**
armado/a: fuerzas armadas *f.* armed forces **16A**
armario *m.* closet **4B**

arnés *m.* harness **18A**
aro *m.* hoop **18A**
aroma *m.* aroma, scent **16B**
arquitecto/a *m./f.* architect **1A**
arquitectura *f.* architecture **8A**
arreglar *v.* to repair **7B**
arreglo: arreglo floral *m.* flower arrangement **18B**
arroz *m.* rice **2B; arroz con verduras** *m.* rice with vegetables **2B**
arte *m.* art **3B; obra de arte** *f.* work of art **8A**
artesanía *f.* crafts **3B**
artificial *adj.* artificial **15A**
asa *f.* handle **18A**
asado *m.* barbecue **1A**
ascendencia *f.* ancestry **14A**
ascender *v.* to climb **18A**
asequible *adj.* affordable **6B**
asesor(a) *m./f.* advisor **11B; asesor(a) laboral** *m./f.* labor consultant **13B**
asesorar *v.* to advise **13B**
así *adv.* like this, this way; **así (es) que** *conj.* so **17A; así como** *conj.* as well as **16B; Siento verte así.** *exp.* I'm sorry to see you like this. **13B**
asiento *m.* seat **13A; cambio de asiento** *m.* seat change **13A; respaldo del asiento** *m.* seat back **13A**
asignatura *f.* school subject **15B**
asistencia: asistencia sanitaria *f.* health care **10A**
asistir (a) *v.* to attend **15A**
asociación *f.* association **12A**
aspecto *m.* aspect **7B; aspecto físico** *m.* physical appearance **12A**
aspirina *f.* aspirin **10A**
asumir *v.* to assume, to take **12B**
asustado/a *adj.* frightened **12A**
asustar *v.* to frighten **7A**
atardecer *m.* dusk **14A**
atención *f.* attention; **llamar la atención** *v.* to catch one's attention **14A; poner atención (a)** *v.* pay attention (to) **0**
atender *v.* to attend to **7A**
atender to see (a patient), to examine **10A**
atentado *m.* attack; offense **12B**
Atentamente, *exp.* Sincerely, **6B**
atleta *m. y f.* track-and-field athlete **12B**
atletismo *m.* track and field **18A**
atractivo/a *adj.* attractive **12A**
atractivos *m.* attractions **4B**
atrapar *v.* to catch **18A**
atreverse *v.* to dare **17A**
audiencia *f.* audience; **ser líder de audiencia** *v.* to be the highest rated **14B**
aún *adv.* still, yet **15B**
aunque *conj.* although **13B**
ausencia *f.* absence **11A**
autenticidad *f.* authenticity **16B**
auténtico/a *adj.* authentic **4A**
auto *m.* car **6B**
autoayuda *f.* self-help **6A**
autobús *m.* bus **4B**
autosuficiente *adj.* self-sufficient **7B**
auxiliar *m. y f.* assistant **7B; auxiliar de vuelo** *m. y f.* flight attendant **13A**
auxilio *m.* help **18A**
avance *m.* breakthrough **17A**
avenida *f.* avenue **2A**

aventura *f.* adventure **5B**
aventurero/a *m. y f.* adventurer **18A;** *adj.* adventurous **9A**
averiarse *v.* to break down **13A**
averiguar *v.* to find out **0**
avión *m.* plane **6B; pasaje de avión** *m.* plane ticket **6B**
ayer *adv.* yesterday **5A**
ayuda *f.* help **5B; pedir ayuda** *v.* to ask for help **5B**
ayudar *v.* to help **5B**
ayuntamiento *m.* city hall **2A**
azteca *adj.* Aztec **12A**
azúcar *m.* sugar **0**
azul *adj.* blue **3B**

B

bacalao: bacalao en salsa *m.* cod with sauce **2B**
bachillerato *m.* high school studies **14A**
bailaor(a) *m./f.* flamenco dancer **7A**
bailar *v.* to dance **6A**
bailarín *m.* dancer **7A**
bailarina *f.* dancer **7A**
baile *m.* dance; ball **5A; baile de salón** *m.* ballroom dance **17B; baile flamenco** *m.* flamenco dance **7A; paso de baile** *m.* step **17B**
baja: baja por maternidad *f.* maternity leave **7B**
bajar *v.* to go down **15A**
bajo/a *adj.* low **4A;** short **12A; bajo/a en calorías** *adj.* low-calorie **15A**
balance: hacer balance de *v.* to take stock of **12B**
balcón *m.* balcony **4B**
baleares: Islas Baleares *f.* Balearic Islands **4B**
banana *f.* banana **15A**
bancario/a: transferencia bancaria *f.* bank transfer **7B**
banco *m.* bank; bench **0**
banda: banda sonora *f.* sound track **17B**
bandeja *f.* tray; **bandeja de entrada** *f.* inbox **14A**
bandera *f.* flag **8B**
bandoneón *m.* type of accordion **17B**
bandoneonista *m. y f.* bandoneón player **17B**
banquete *m.* reception **5A**
bañarse *v.* to swim **10A**
baño *m.* bathroom **4B; darse un baño** *v.* to take a bath **10A**
bar *m.* bar; café **0**
barato/a *adj.* cheap **4B**
barba *f.* beard **12A**
bárbaro *adj.* great **11B**
barco *m.* boat, ship; **en barco** *loc. adv.* by boat **5A**
barrera *f.* barrier **12B**
barril: barril de petróleo *m.* oil barrel **14A**
barrio *m.* neighborhood **1A**
base: sobre la base de *loc. prep.* based upon **16A**
bastante *adv.* quite a lot **5B**
bastón *m.* pole **18A**
basura *f.* garbage **8A; comida basura** *f.* junk food **10A**
bata *f.* robe **5A**

batería *f.* battery **7B**
batir *v.* to beat **8A; batir un récord** *v.* to break a record **18A**
bautizo *m.* baptism **5B**
bazar *m.* bazaar **8B**
beber *v.* to drink **2B**
bebida *f.* beverage **2B**
beca *f.* scholarship; grant **8B; beca (escolar)** *f.* scholarship **12B; beca ERASMUS** *f.* ERASMUS scholarship **14A**
béisbol *m.* baseball **18A**
beisbolista *m./f.* baseball player **18A**
Bélgica *f.* Belgium **10B**
belleza *f.* beauty **4B**
bello/a *adj.* beautiful **16B**
Berlín: Muro de Berlín *m.* Berlin Wall **10B**
besarse *v.* to kiss each other **17B**
beso *m.* kiss **2A**
biblioteca *f.* library **1A; biblioteca ambulante** *f.* traveling library **9A**
bici *f.* bike (bicycle) **6B**
bicicleta *f.* bike (bicycle) **6B**
bien *adv.* well **1A; bien comunicado/a** *loc. adj.* easily accessible **4B; Estoy bien.** *exp.* I'm OK. **7B; llevarse bien/mal** *v.* to get along/not to get along **12A; o bien** *exp.* or otherwise **12A; pasarla bien** *v.* to have a good time **17B; pasarlo bien** *v.* to have a good time **17B; por tu bien** *exp.* for your own good **15B**
bienestar *m.* well-being **6A**
bienvenida *f.* welcome **11A; dar la bienvenida** *v.* to welcome **11A**
Bienvenido/a(s) *exp.* Welcome! **11A**
bigote *m.* mustache **12A**
bilbaíno/a *adj.* from Bilbao **17A**
bilingüe *adj.* bilingual **18A; escuela bilingüe** *f.* bilingual school **15B**
billete *m.* ticket **6B; comprar (billetes de) lotería** *v.* to buy lottery tickets **9B; reservar los billetes** *v.* to book the tickets **13A**
billetero *m.* wallet **18B**
biografía *f.* biography **5A**
biología *f.* biology **1B**
biólogo/a biologist; **biólogo/a marino/a** *m./f.* marine biologist **11B**
blanco/a *adj.* white **3B; quedarse en blanco** *exp.* to draw a blank **15B**
blando/a *adj.* soft **9A**
blog *m.* blog **3A**
bloqueado/a *adj.* locked; blocked **7B**
boca *f.* mouth **9A**
boda *f.* wedding **5A; bodas de plata** *f.* silver wedding anniversary **18B**
bolígrafo *m.* ballpoint pen **3B**
Bolivia *f.* Bolivia **0**
bollería *f.* pastries **2B**
bolsa *f.* bag; sack **4A; bolsa de comercio** *f.* stock exchange **3A; bolsa de trabajo** *f.* job placement office **13B**
bolsillo *m.* pocket **13B**
bolso *m.* bag **3B**
bomba *f.* pump **17A**
bombero/a *m./f.* firefighter **7A**
bonito/a *adj.* pretty **2A**
bordo: a bordo *loc. adv.* on board **13A; ¡Que disfruten a bordo!** *exp.* Enjoy your flight! **13A**

boricua *adj.* Puerto Rican **11A**
bosque *m.* forest **5A; bosque virgen** *m.* virgin forest **6B**
bota *f.* boot **3B**
bote: bote de remos *m.* rowboat **18A**
botella *f.* bottle **2B**
botiquín *m.* first-aid kit **10A**
botón *m.* button **4B**
boxeador(a) *m./f.* boxer **18A**
Brasil *m.* Brazil **1A**
brazo *m.* arm **10A; del brazo** *loc. adv.* arm in arm **5A**
brecha: cerrar la brecha *v.* to close the gap **17A**
bricolage *m.* do-it-yourself **8A**
brillante *adj.* bright **9A;** brilliant **14B**
brócoli *m.* broccoli **15A**
bromista *adj.* fond of joking **13B**
bronce *m.* bronze **12B**
brújula *f.* compass **18A**
bruto/a: producto interior bruto (PIB) *m.* gross domestic product (GDP) **11A**
bueno *exp.* well… **2A; ¿Bueno?** *exp.* Hello? **6B**
bueno/a *adj.* good; **¡Buen provecho!** *exp.* Enjoy your meal. **8A; buen tiempo** *m.* good weather **2A; Buenas noches.** *exp.* Good evening/night. **0; Buenas tardes.** *exp.* Good afternoon. **0; Buenas.** *exp.* Hi. **0; Buenos días.** *exp.* Good morning. **0; de buen humor** *loc. adv.* in a good mood **12A; en buena compañía** *loc. adv.* in good company **16B; hacer buen tiempo** *v.* there is good weather **10A; lo bueno** *m.* the good thing **12B; ser bueno/a (en algo)** *v.* to be good (at something) **17B**
burro/a *m.* donkey **0**
buscar *v.* to look for **1B**

C

cabalgata *f.* horse back riding **18A**
caballero *m.* gentleman **13A**
caballo *m.* horse **6B; paseo a caballo** *m.* horseback ride **6B**
cabaña *f.* cabin **6B**
cabeza *f.* head **10A; estar a la cabeza** *exp.* to lead **16A**
cabina: jefe/a de cabina *m./f.* purser **13A**
cable *m.* cable, wire; **cable de acero** *m.* steel cable **18A**
cabo: llevar a cabo *v.* to carry out **18A**
cacahuate *m.* peanut **12A**
cacao: cacao en polvo *m.* cocoa powder **15A**
cachorro/a *m./f.* puppy **12B**
caciquismo *m.* despotism **16A**
cada *adj.* each; **cada día** *loc. adv.* each day **14A**
cadena *f.* chain; network; **cadena de radio** *f.* radio network **14B**
caducidad: fecha de caducidad *f.* expiration date **15A**
café *m.* coffee **0; café solo** *m.* black coffee **2B**
cafeína *f.* caffeine **2B**
cafetería *f.* café; cafeteria **1B**
caja *f.* box **8A**

cajero/a *m./f.* cashier **1B**
cajón *m.* drawer **8A**
calamares *m.* calamari, squid **2B**
calcular *v.* to calculate **0**
calendario *m.* calendar, schedule **3A**
calidad *f.* quality; **calidad de vida** *f.* quality of life **2A**
calificación *f.* grade **15B**
callado/a *adj.* silent; **estar callado/a** *v.* to be silent **9A**
calle *f.* street **2A**
calor *m.* heat **2A; hacer calor** *v.* to be hot out **10A; tener calor** *v.* to be hot **10A**
calorías *f. pl.* calories; **bajo/a en calorías** *adj.* low-calorie **15A**
calzado *m.* shoes **10A**
cama *f.* bed **4B; (semi-)cama** *adj.* (semi-) sleeper **13A; cama de matrimonio** *f.* double bed **4B; hacer la cama** *v.* to make the bed **3A**
cámara *f.* camera; **cámara web** *f.* webcam **6B**
camarero/a *m./f.* waiter/waitress **2B**
camarógrafo/a *m./f.* cameraperson **9A**
camarón *m.* shrimp **16B**
cambiar *v.* to change **7B; cambiar de casa** *v.* to move **5A; cambiar de trabajo** *v.* to change jobs **7B; cambiar de vida** *v.* to change one's life **7B**
cambio *m.* change; **a cambio** *loc. adv.* in return **12B; a cambio de** *loc. adv.* in exchange for **8A; cambio de aires** *m.* change of scenery **11A; cambio de asiento** *m.* seat change **13A; cambio de dinero** *m.* foreign currency exchange **13A**
caminar *v.* to walk **5B; caminar sin rumbo fijo** *v.* to wander aimlessly **17B**
camión *m.* truck **7A**
camionero/a *m./f.* truck driver **7A**
camisa *f.* shirt **3B**
camiseta *f.* T-shirt **3B**
campamento *m.* campsite **6B**
campana *f.* bell **18B**
campanada *f.* peal of a bell **18B**
campaña *f.* campaign **12B; campaña de conciliación** *f.* conciliation campaign **15B; campaña de promoción** *f.* promotional campaign **16B; campaña electoral** *f.* electoral campaign **16A; lanzar una campaña** *v.* to launch a campaign **16B; tienda de campaña** *f.* tent **18A**
campesino/a *m./f.* rural worker **9A**
camping *m.* campsite **6B**
campo *m.* country(side) **3A; campo científico** *m.* scientific field **17A**
Canadá *m.* Canada **0**
canadiense *adj.* Canadian **1B**
canal *m.* channel **9A**
canas: tener canas *v.* to have gray hair **17B**
cancelado/a *adj.* cancelled **13A**
cancha *f.* court **18A;** sports field **17B**
canción *f.* song **7A**
candidato/a *m./f.* applicant **13B;** candidate **16A**
canotaje *m.* canoeing **18A**
cansado/a *adj.* tired **6A**

cansancio *m.* tiredness **14B**
cansarse de (algo) *v.* to get tired/bored of (something) **9B**
cantante *m. y f.* singer **5A**
cantar *v.* to sing **17B**
cantautor(a) *m./f.* singer-songwriter **7A**
cantidad *f.* quantity **4A**
caoba *f.* mahogany tree **18B**
capa: capa de ozono *f.* ozone layer **17A**
capacidad: tener capacidad *v.* to have (storage) capacity **13B**
capital *f.* capital **2A**
capítulo *m.* episode **14B**
cara *f.* face **5A**
caracol *m.* snail **2B**
carácter *m.* atmosphere **4A;** character, personality **12A**
caravana: caravana de coches *f.* motorcade **5A**
carbono: hidrato de carbono *m.* carbohydrate **15A**
cardiovascular *adj.* cardiovascular **17A**
carecer (de) *v.* to lack **17B**
cargar *v.* to load; to carry **9A**
cargo *m.* position **17A**
Caribe: mar Caribe *m.* Caribbean Sea **4B**
caribeño/a *adj.* Caribbean **4B**
cariñoso/a *adj.* affectionate **12A**
carisma *m.* charisma **18A**
caritativo/a *adj.* charitable **16A**
carmelita *adj.* Carmelite **11A**
carne *f.* meat **2B; carne de cerdo** *f.* pork **18B**
caro/a *adj.* expensive **3B**
carpa *f.* tent **9A**
carpintería *f.* carpentry **8A**
carpintero/a *m./f.* carpenter **12B**
carrera *f.* major **1B;** career **5A; estudiar una carrera** *v.* to study for a degree **15B**
carrito *m.* baggage cart **13A**
carro *m.* car **5A**
carta *f.* letter; **carta al director** *f.* letter to the editor **2A; carta de presentación** *f.* cover letter **13B**
cartel *m.* poster **0**
casa *f.* house **4B; cambiar de casa** *v.* to move **5A; casa particular** *f.* private home **13A; en casa** *loc. adv.* at home **2B; ensalada de la casa** *f.* house salad **2B; hacer algo en casa** *v.* to do something at home **3A; llegar a casa** *v.* to arrive home **3A; sentirse como en casa** *v.* to feel at home **16B**
casado/a *adj.* married **5B; cumplir años de casados** *v.* to have one's wedding anniversary **18B**
casarse *v.* to get married **8B**
cascada *f.* waterfall **6B**
casco *m.* helmet **18A; casco viejo** *m.* historic neighborhood **12B**
casi *adv.* almost **13B; casi nunca** *loc. adv.* hardly ever **6A; casi siempre** *loc. adv.* almost always **14A**
casilla *f.* (check) box **0**
caso: hacer caso (a alguien) *v.* to pay attention (to somebody) **15B**
castaño/a *adj.* brown **12A**
castillo *m.* castle **6B**
casualidad *f.* chance **16A**

casualmente *adv.* by chance **17B**
catalán *m.* Catalan **1B**
catedral *f.* cathedral **2A**
católico/a *adj.* Catholic **5A**
ceibo *m.* coral tree **18B**
celebración *f.* celebration **18B**
celebrar *v.* to celebrate **5A**
celebrarse *v.* to be held **4A**
celeste *adj.* light blue **9A**
celíaco/a *adj.* celiac **15A**
celular: (teléfono) celular *m.* cell phone **1B**
cenar *v.* to eat supper **2B**
central *f.* main office **2A**
céntrico/a *adj.* in the center of town **7B**
centro *m.* center, downtown **1A; centro comercial** *m.* shopping mall **2A**
cerámica: hacer cerámica *f.* to make pottery **6A**
cerca de *prep.* near **2A**
cercanía *f.* proximity **16B**
cerdo *m.* pig; **carne de cerdo** *f.* pork **18B**
cereales *m. pl.* cereal **2B**
cerebrito *m./f.* nerd **15B**
ceremonia *f.* ceremony **14A; maestro/a de ceremonias** *m./f.* master of ceremonies **18B**
cerilla *f.* match **8A**
cerrar *v.* to close; **cerrar la brecha** *v.* to close the gap **17A**
certamen *m.* contest **16B**
certeza *f.* certainty **15A**
certificado/a *adj.* certified **16B**
cerveza *f.* beer **2B**
cesta *f.* basket **7B**
ceviche *m.* marinated seafood dish **1A**
chachachá *m.* cha-cha **17B**
chamaco/a *m./f.* kid, youngster **12A**
chamaquito/a (dim. de chamaco/a) *m./f.* kid, youngster **12A**
chaqueta *f.* jacket **3B**
charla *f.* chat **9A**
charlar *v.* to chat **14A**
chat *m.* chat room **3A**
chatear *v.* to chat (on the Internet) **6B**
Chau. *exp.* Bye. **0**
cheque *m.* check; **cheque-regalo** *m.* gift voucher **3B**
chicle *m.* chewing gum **9B**
chico/a *adj.* small **11B**
Chile *m.* Chile **0**
chimenea *f.* chimney **8B**
chino *m.* Chinese **1B**
chino/a *adj.* Chinese **1B**
chip *m.* chip **17A**
chisme *m.* piece of gossip **17B**
chiste *m.* joke **5B; contar chistes** *v.* to tell jokes **17B**
chocar *v.* to surprise; to collide **14B**
choclo *m.* corn **15A**
chocolate *m.* chocolate **0**
choque *m.* collision; **choque cultural** *m.* culture shock **14B**
chorizo *m.* sausage, chorizo **2B**
churros *m.* churros **2B**
cibercafé *m.* Internet café **4A**
ciclismo *m.* cycling **18A**
ciclista *m. y f.* cyclist **18A**
ciego/a *adj.* blind **12B**
cien: cien por ciento *exp.* one hundred percent **12A**

ciencia *f.* science **6A; ciencias políticas** *f.* political science **1B; ciencias sociales** *f.* social studies **15B**
científico/a *adj.* scientific; **campo científico** *m.* scientific field **17A; método científico** *m.* scientific method **17A**
ciento: cien por ciento *exp.* one hundred percent **12A**
cierto/a *adj.* right, true; **por cierto** *exp.* by the way **10A**
cine *m.* movie theater **3A**
cinturón *m.* belt **8A; cinturón de seguridad** *m.* seat belt **13A**
circulación *f.* circulation **10A**
círculo *m.* circle **18A**
cita *f.* appointment, date **14B**
citado/a *adj.* cited, quoted **17A**
ciudad *f.* city **0; Ciudad de Guatemala** *f.* Guatemala City **0; Ciudad de Panamá** *f.* Panama City **0**
ciudadano/a *m./f.* citizen **8B; ciudadano/a ilustre** *m./f.* distinguished citizen **17B**
cívico/a: Educación ético-cívica *f.* Civics **15B**
civil: estado civil *m.* marital status **5B; guerra civil** *f.* civil war **8B**
civilización *f.* civilization **11B**
claro *exp.* of course **1B**
claro/a *adj.* light **16B**
clase *f.* class **1B; (el resto de) la clase** *f.* (the rest of) the class **0; clase de música** *f.* music class **3A; clase media** *f.* middle class **14B; clase particular** *f.* private lesson **17B; dar clases (de algo)** *v.* to give [subject] classes **8A; fuera de clase** *loc. adv.* outside of class **3A; tener clase** *v.* to have class **3A**
clásico *m.* classic **9A**
clásico/a *adj.* classic **4B**
clasificar *v.* to classify **0**
clavar *v.* to nail down **8A**
clave *f.* key **6A; lugar clave** *m.* landmark **4A**
clavel *m.* carnation **18B**
clavo *m.* nail **8A**
clic: hacer clic *v.* to click **13B**
cliente *m. y f.* client **2A**
clima *m.* climate **2A**
clínica *f.* clinic **10A**
coche *m.* car **3A; caravana de coches** *f.* motorcade **5A; ir en coche** *v.* to go by car **3A**
cocido/a *adj.* cooked **15A**
cocina *f.* cooking **8A; kitchen **4B; receta (de cocina)** *f.* recipe **8A**
cocinar *v.* to cook **3A**
coco *m.* coconut **15A**
cóctel *m.* cocktail **16B**
código *m.* code **13B**
col *f.* cabbage **15A**
cola *f.* line (waiting) **15A; piano de cola** *m.* grand piano **10B**
colaborar *v.* to collaborate **10B;** to participate **3A**
colección *f.* collection **3B**
coleccionar *v.* to collect **9B**
colectivo *m.* bus **17B**
colectivo/a *adj.* collective **8A**
colega *m. y f.* colleague **7B**
colegio *m.* school **3A; llevar a los niños al colegio** *v.* to take the kids to school **3A**

colocar *v.* to place **9B**
Colombia *f.* Colombia **0**
colombiano/a *adj.* Colombian **3B**
colonia *f.* colony **14A**
colonial: zona colonial *f.* colonial area **3A**
colonizador(a) *m./f.* colonizer **18B**
color *m.* color **3B; ¿De qué color?** *exp.* What color? **3B**
colorante *m.* colorant, coloring **15A**
comedor *m.* dining hall **15B;** dining room **4B; salón-comedor** *m.* living room-dining room **4B**
comentar *v.* to discuss **0;** to mention **14B**
comenzar *v.* to start **8B**
comer *v.* to eat **2B**
comercial: centro comercial *m.* shopping mall **2A**
comerciante *m./f.* storekeeper **14A**
comercio *m.* commerce **8B; bolsa de comercio** *f.* stock exchange **3A; comercio justo** *m.* fair trade **3B**
cómics *m.* comics **7A**
comida *f.* food **1A; comida basura** *f.* junk food **10A**
como *conj.* as, like; **así como** *conj.* as well as **16B; sentirse como en casa** *v.* to feel at home **16B; tan/tanto… como** *conj.* as much/many… as **8B; tanto … como** *conj.* both … and **7A; trabajar como** *v.* to work as **11B**
cómo *interrog.* how **0; ¿Cómo?** *exp.* What?, Excuse me? **14A; ¿Cómo es…?** *exp.* What is… like? **2A; ¿Cómo se dice…?** *exp.* How do you say…? **6B; ¿Cómo se escribe…?** *exp.* How do you spell…? **0; ¿Cómo vas?** *exp.* How are you going there? **6B**
comodidades *f. pl.* comforts **7B**
cómodo/a *adj.* comfortable **2A;** convenient **17A**
compaginar *v.* to combine **7A**
compañero/a *m./f.* partner **2B; compañero/a de trabajo** *m./f.* coworker **5B**
compañía *f.* company; **(hacer) compañía** *v.* (to keep) company **7A; compañía aérea** *f.* airline **11A; en buena compañía** *loc. adv.* in good company **16B**
comparar *v.* to compare **0**
compartido/a *adj.* shared; **custodia compartida** *f.* joint custody **12A**
compartir *v.* to share **5A**
compatible *adj.* compatible **5B**
compatriota *m. y f.* countryman/countrywoman **10B**
competencia *f.* competence; ability **0**
competir *v.* to compete **18A**
complejo/a *adj.* complex **16B**
complementos *m.* accessories **3B**
completar *v.* to complete **0**
completo/a *adj.* complete **9A**
componer *v.* to compose **7A**
composición *f.* composition **15A**
comprar *v.* to buy **3B; comprar (billetes de) lotería** *v.* to buy lottery tickets **9B**
compras: hacer las compras *v.* to do the shopping **3A; lista de compras** *f.* shopping list **4A**
comprender *v.* to understand **13B**
comprensivo/a *adj.* understanding **13B**

comprobar *v.* to check **13A**

compromiso *m.* commitment **5A**

compuesto/a por *adj.* made up of **16B**

computadora *f.* computer **4B**

común *adj.* common, ordinary; **punto común** *m.* point in common **5B**

comunicación *f.* communication **3B**; **falta de comunicación** *f.* lack of communication **15B**; **medios de comunicación** *m.* media **9A**

comunicado/a: bien comunicado/a *loc. adj.* easily accessible **4B**

comunicador(a) *m./f.* communicator **13B**

comunicativo/a *adj.* communicative **16B**

comunidad *f.* community **1A**; **comunidad inmigrante** *f.* immigrant community **8B**

comunitario/a *adj.* communal **17A**

con *prep.* with; **¿Con qué frecuencia?** *exp.* How often? **3A**; **arroz con verduras** *m.* rice with vegetables **2B**; **con acento** *loc. adv.* with an accent **0**; **con antelación** *loc. adv.* in advance **11A**; **con encanto** *loc. adj.* charming **6B**; **Con gusto.** *exp.* You're welcome. **18B**; **con motivo de** *exp.* on the occasion of **12B**; **con respecto a** *loc. prep.* regarding **16A**; **con retraso** *loc. adv.* delayed **13A**; **con tarjeta** *loc. adv.* with a credit card **3B**; **contar con** *v.* to include **9A**; **salir (con amigos)** *v.* to go out (with friends) **3A**

conciencia *f.* conscience **17A**

concierto *m.* concert **1A**; **dar un concierto** *v.* to give a concert **7A**

conciliación: campaña de conciliación *f.* conciliation campaign **15B**

conciliar *v.* to reconcile **6A**

concordia *f.* harmony **16A**

concretamente *adv.* specifically **7B**

concreto/a: en concreto *loc. adv.* in particular **7B**

condicionar *v.* to determine **14A**

conducir *v.* to drive **7A**

conectado/a *adj.* connected (to the Internet) **13B**

conexión: estar en conexión *v.* to be connected **6A**

confianza *f.* confidence **18A**; **tener confianza en** *v.* to trust in **5B**

confirmación *f.* confirmation **13A**

confirmar *v.* to confirm **6B**

confitería *f.* café **4A**

conflicto *m.* conflict **7A**; **conflicto generacional** *m.* generational conflict **15B**; **resolución de conflictos** *f.* conflict resolution **13B**

confundirse *v.* to become confused **16B**

congelado/a *adj.* frozen **16B**

congreso *m.* conference **12B**

conjugar *v.* to conjugate **0**

conmemorar *v.* to commemorate **17A**

conocer *v.* to meet; to know (people) **5A**; **dar a conocer** *v.* to make known **16B**

conocido/a *adj.* known; **más conocido/a** *adj.* best-known **4A**

conquistar *v.* to captivate **15A**

consciente: hacer consciente *v.* to make aware **3B**

consecuencia *f.* consequence **12B**

conseguir *v.* to get; to obtain **4A**

consejo *m.* piece of advice **6A**

consenso *m.* consensus **16A**

conservación *f.* preservation **15A**

conservante *m.* preservative **15A**

conservar *v.* to keep **8A**

construir *v.* to build; to create **0**

consulta: hacer una consulta *v.* to ask somebody's advice **12A**

consultas *f.* questions **6B**

consultorio *m.* advice column **12A**; doctor's office **10A**

consumidor(a) *m./f.* consumer **3B**

consumir *v.* to consume **15A**

consumo *m.* consumption **3B**

contacto *m.* touch, contact **17B**; **estar en contacto** *v.* to be in touch **12B**

contador(a) *m./f.* accountant **13B**

contar *v.* to tell **14B**; **contar chistes** *v.* to tell jokes **17B**; **contar con** *v.* to include **9A**

contarse *v.* to tell each other **17B**

contemporáneo/a *adj.* contemporary **3B**

contenedor *m.* recycling container **15A**

contenidos *m. pl.* content **14B**

contento/a *adj.* happy **11A**; **ponerse contento/a** *v.* to become happy **18B**

contestar *v.* to answer **0**

contigo *prep.* + *pron.* with you **5A**

continente *m.* continent **11B**

contrato *m.* contract; **contrato de trabajo** *m.* employment contract **13B**

contrincante *m. y f.* opponent **18A**

control *m.* control; **control de equipaje** *m.* baggage screening **13A**; **control de pasaportes** *m.* passport control; immigration **13A**

controlar *v.* to monitor **17A**; to control **15B**

convencer *v.* to convince **16A**

convencional *adj.* conventional **16A**

convenir: a convenir *loc. adv.* to be agreed upon **13B**

convento *m.* convent **6B**

conversación *f.* conversation **1B**

convertirse (en) *v.* to become **7A**

convicción *f.* conviction **16A**

convivencia *f.* coexistence **14A**

convivir con *v.* to coexist with **14A**

convocatoria *f.* call (to action) **16A**

coordinador(a) *m./f.* coordinator **16A**

copiadora *f.* photocopier **7B**

corazón *m.* heart **2A**; **revista del corazón** *f.* gossip magazine **9B**

corbata *f.* tie **3B**

coreano *m.* Korean **1B**

coreano/a *adj.* Korean **1B**

correcto/a *adj.* correct **0**

corredor(a) *m./f.* runner **18A**

correo *m.* mail; **correo electrónico** *m.* e-mail **4B**

correr *v.* to run; **correr un maratón** *v.* to run a marathon **18A**

correspondido/a: amor (no) correspondido *m.* (un)requited love **12A**

corriente: ser moneda corriente *v.* to be common **13B**

corrupción *f.* corruption **16A**

corto/a *adj.* short **12A**; **a corto plazo** *loc. adv.* in the short term **17A**

cosa *f.* thing **4A**

cosmopolita *adj.* cosmopolitan **16B**

costa *f.* coast **4B**

Costa Rica *f.* Costa Rica **0**

costar *v.* to be difficult **14B**; to cost **4A**; **¿Cuánto cuesta(n)…?** *exp.* How much does/do… cost? **4A**

costarricense *m. y f.* Costa Rican **14B**

costumbre *f.* habit **15A**

cotización *f.* estimate **18B**

crecer *v.* to grow **7B**; to grow up **9B**

creciente *adj.* growing **16B**

crecimiento *m.* growth **16A**

crédito *m.* credit, loan; **pedir un crédito** *v.* to ask for a loan **5B**

creer *v.* to believe; **Creo que sí/no.** *exp.* I think so/not. **7B**

crema *f.* cream; **crema de leche** *f.* cream **15A**; **crema solar protectora** *f.* sunscreen **10A**

crisis *f.* crisis **12B**

criticar *v.* to criticize **17B**

crítico/a *m./f.* critic; **crítico/a literario/a** *m./f.* literary critic **10B**

cromo (de fútbol) *m.* (soccer) trading card **9B**

cronológicamente *adv.* chronologically **5B**

cruasán *m.* croissant **2B**

crucero *m.* cruise **16B**

cruzar *v.* to cross **18A**

cuadrado/a *adj.* square; **metros cuadrados (m²)** *m.* square meters **4B**

cuál *interrog.* what, which; **¿Cuál es tu número de teléfono?** *exp.* What is your phone number? **1B**; **¿cuál(es)?** *interrog.* which one(s)? **4B**

cualidad *f.* characteristic **17B**

cuando *conj.* when

cuándo *interrog.* When…? **0**

cuanto: en cuanto a *conj.* as for **16A**

cuánto/a *interrog.* how much; **¿Cuánto cuesta(n)…?** *exp.* How much does/do … cost? **4A**; **¿Cúanto es?** *exp.* How much is it? **2B**; **¿Cuánto tiempo (hace)…?** *exp.* How long have/has? **8B**; **cuántos/as** *interrog.* how many **4B**

cuarto/a *adj.* fourth **14A**

cuate/a (fam.) *m./f.* friend, pal **12A**

Cuba *f.* Cuba **0**

cubano/a *m./f.* Cuban person **13A**

cuenta *f.* bill **2B**; **tener en cuenta** *v.* to take into account **16B**

cuento *m.* short story **9B**

cuero *m.* leather **8A**

cuerpo *m.* body **6A**

cuestionario *m.* questionnaire **6A**

cuidar a/de *v.* to take care of **5B**

cultivar *v.* to grow; to cultivate **7B**

culto/a *adj.* educated **12A**

culto: lugar de culto *m.* place of worship **8A**

cultural *adj.* cultural **6A**; **choque cultural** *m.* culture shock **14B**

cumbia *f.* dance typical of the Caribbean coast of Colombia **17B**

cumpleaños (invar.) *m.* birthday **5A**

cumplir *v.* to reach; to fulfill **13A**; **cumplir (sus) sueños** *v.* to make (his/her) dreams come true **15B**; **cumplir 15 años** *v.* to turn 15 years old **5A**; **cumplir años** *v.* to have one's birthday **18B**; **cumplir años de casados** *v.* to have one's wedding anniversary **18B**; **cumplir con** *v.* to meet **15A**

cupón *m.* (lottery) ticket **12B**

cura *f.* cure **17A**
curandero/a *m./f.* healer **14A**
curioso/a *adj.* curious; **objeto curioso** *m.* curiosity; knickknack **4A**
currículum (vítae) *m.* résumé **11B**
cursar *v.* to study **14A**
curso *m.* class, course **3A**
custodia: custodia compartida *f.* joint custody **12A**
cuyo/a *adj.* whose **10B**

D

dado: tiren el dado *exp.* roll the die **10A**
dar *v.* to give **4A**; **¡Dale!** *exp.* Come on! **8A**; **dar a conocer** *v.* to make known **16B**; **dar ánimo** *v.* to offer encouragement **13A**; **dar clases (de algo)** *v.* to give [subject] classes **8A**; **dar la bienvenida** *v.* to welcome **11A**; **dar la vuelta** *v.* to flip; to turn over **8A**; **dar la vuelta al mundo** *v.* to go around the world **18A**; **dar pena** *v.* to sadden **18B**; **dar un concierto** *v.* to give a concert **7A**; **dar un ejemplo** *v.* to give an example **7A**; **dar un paseo** *v.* to take a walk **6A**; **darse un baño** *v.* to take a bath **10A**; **Me da...** *exp.* Give me... **4A**
datos *m. pl.* data, information **0**
de *prep.* of; **¿De qué color?** *exp.* What color? **3B**; **¿De qué talla?** *exp.* What size? **3B**; **¿De verdad?** *exp.* Really? **9B**; **a cambio de** *loc. adv.* in exchange for **8A**; **a favor de** *loc. adv.* in favor of **12B**; **a la derecha de** *loc. adv.* to the right of **3B**; **a la izquierda de** *loc. adv.* to the left of **3B**; **a partir de** *loc. prep.* from, starting **12B**; **al lado de** *loc. adv.* next to **3B**; **alegrarse de** *v.* to be glad that **18B**; **antes de que** *conj.* before **18A**; **aprender de memoria** *v.* to memorize **14B**; **cambiar de trabajo** *v.* to change jobs **7B**; **cambiar de vida** *v.* to change one's life **7B**; **con motivo de** *exp.* on the occasion of **12B**; **de... a...** *loc. adv.* from... until/to **8B**; **de alquiler** *adj.* rental **11B**; **de buen/mal humor** *loc. adv.* in a good/bad mood **12A**; **de hecho** *exp.* in fact **7A**; **de la mañana** *loc. adv.* a.m.; in the morning **3A**; **de la noche** *loc. adv.* p.m.; at night **3A**; **de la tarde** *loc. adv.* p.m.; in the afternoon **3A**; **de maravilla** *loc. adv.* wonderfully **17B**; **de nuevo** *loc. adv.* again **0**; **de paso** *loc. adv.* in the process **14B**; **de repente** *loc. adv.* suddenly **9B**; **de vez en cuando** *loc. adv.* from time to time **14A**; **debajo de** *loc. prep.* under **3B**; **dejar de fumar** *v.* to quit smoking **12B**; **delante de** *loc. prep.* in front of **3B**; **dentro de** *loc. prep.* in, within **17A**; **depender (de)** *v.* to depend (on) **10A**; **después de que** *conj.* after **18A**; **detrás de** *loc. prep.* behind **3B**; **día de la semana** *m.* day of the week **3A**; **el resto de** *m.* the rest of **12B**; **en vías de desarrollo** *adj.* developing **3B**; **encima de** *loc. prep.* on (top of) **3B**; **estar a... kilómetros de...** *exp.* to be... kilometers from... **2A**; **estar de acuerdo** *v.* to agree **5B**; **estar de vacaciones** *v.* to be on vacation **7B**; **estar de viaje** *v.* to be away **7A**; **estar**

fuera del (de nuestro) alcance *exp.* to be beyond one's (our) means **15B**; **estar seguro/a de sí mismo/a** *v.* to be self-confident **18A**; **hablarse de tú/ usted** *v.* to address somebody as **tú/ usted 7B**; **horario de trabajo** *m.* work schedule **3A**; **mayor de** *adj.* older than **9A**; **por medio de** *loc. prep.* by means of **14B**; **procedente de** *loc. adv.* arriving from **13A**; **rodeado/a de** *loc. adv.* surrounded by **6B**; **salir de** *v.* to leave **3A**; **sobre la base de** *loc. prep.* based upon **16A**; **Yo soy de Madrid.** *exp.* I'm from Madrid. **1A**
debajo: debajo de *loc. prep.* under **3B**
debate *m.* debate **16A**
deberes *m. pl.* homework **15B**
década *f.* decade **14B**
decepción *f.* disappointment **10B**
decepcionar *v.* to disappoint **17B**
decidir *v.* to decide **6A**
décimo/a *adj.* tenth **12B**
decir *v.* to say, to tell **7A**; **¡No me digas!** *exp.* You don't say! **9B**; **¿Cómo se dice...?** *exp.* How do you say...? **0**; **¿Diga?** *exp.* Hello? **6B**; **¿Dígame?** *exp.* Hello? **6B**; **decir la verdad** *v.* to tell the truth **17B**; **es decir** *exp.* in other words **8B**; **quería decir** *exp.* I meant... **12B**
decisivo/a *adj.* decisive **10B**
declaración: declaración de amor *f.* declaration of love **18B**
declarar *v.* to declare; to state **16A**
decoración *f.* decoration **3B**
decorador(a) *m./f.* decorator **11B**
dedicación *f.* dedication **15A**
dedicar *v.* to dedicate **6A**
dedicarse: dedicarse a (hacer) algo *v.* to do something (for a living) **7A**; **¿A qué te dedicas?** *exp.* What do you do (for work)? **1B**
defender *v.* to defend **12B**
defensa *f.* defense **16A**
definitiva/a: en definitiva *loc. adv.* all in all **18B**
dejar *v.* to quit; to give up **5A**; to leave behind **7B**; **dejar de** *v.* to stop **10B**; **dejar de fumar** *v.* to quit smoking **12B**
del *contrac.* of the **3B**; **a finales del siglo XIX** *loc. adv.* toward the end of the 19th century **8B**; **del brazo** *loc. adv.* arm in arm **5A**; **menú del día** *m.* fixed-price menu **2B**
delante: delante de *loc. prep.* in front of **3B**
delfín *m.* dolphin **5A**
delito *m.* crime **17B**
delta: ala delta *f.* hang glider **18A**
demanda *f.* demand **15A**; **demanda laboral** *f.* labor demand **14A**
demasiado *adv.* too **13A**
democracia *f.* democracy **14B**
democrático/a *adj.* democratic **10B**; **transición democrática** *f.* democratic transition **14B**
demostrar *v.* to prove **17A**
denominarse *v.* to be called **17A**
densamente *adv.* densely **16B**
dentista *m. y f.* dentist **10A**
dentro: dentro de *loc. prep.* in, within **17A**
denunciar *v.* to denounce **16A**

depender (de) *v.* to depend (on) **10A**
deporte *m.* sport(s) **3A**; **hacer deporte** *v.* to exercise **3A**; **zapatillas (de deporte)** *f.* running shoes; sneakers **3B**
deportista *m. y f.* athlete **12B**; sportsman/ sportswoman **18A**
deportivo/a *adj.* sporting **6A**; **reto deportivo** *m.* sports challenge **18A**
derecha *f.* right; **a la derecha** *loc. adv.* (to the) right **9B**; **a la derecha de** *loc. adv.* to the right of **3B**
derecho *m.* right **3B**; **derechos humanos** *m.* human rights **16A**
derramarse *v.* to spill **18B**
derribar *v.* to knock down, to demolish **10B**
desacuerdo *m.* disagreement **10B**; **estar en desacuerdo** *v.* to disagree **5B**
desagradable *adj.* unpleasant **13B**
desaparecer *v.* to disappear **10B**
desarrollar *v.* to develop **15B**
desarrollo *m.* development **14A**; **en vías de desarrollo** *adj.* developing **3B**
desastre *m.* disaster **16A**
desayunar *v.* to eat breakfast **2B**
desayuno *m.* breakfast **2B**
descafeinado *m.* decaf coffee **2B**
descansar *v.* to rest **5B**
descanso *m.* rest **3A**
descender *v.* to descend **18A**
descomunal *adj.* massive **18A**
desconectarse *v.* to disconnect (oneself) **7B**
descremado/a: leche descremada en polvo *f.* powdered skim milk **15A**
describir *v.* to describe **0**
descubrimiento *m.* discovery **17A**
descubrir *v.* to discover **17A**
descuento *m.* discount **6A**
desde *prep.* since; from **2A**; **desde entonces** *loc. adv.* since then **7A**; **desde hace** *loc. prep.* for (and until now) **5B**; **desde niño(s)/a(s)** *loc. adv.* since childhood **8B**; **desde pequeño/a** *loc. adv.* since childhood **5B**; **desde que** *conj.* since **8B**; **desde... hasta...** *loc. prep.* from... until/to **8B**
desear *v.* to wish **11A**; **¿Qué desean tomar?** *exp.* What would you like (to have)? **2B**
desechable *adj.* disposable **17A**
deserción: deserción universitaria *f.* college dropouts **15B**
desértico/a *adj.* desert-like **5A**
desfavorecido/a *adj.* underprivileged **16A**
desgarrador(a) *adj.* heartrending **16A**
desigualdad *f.* inequality **16A**
desinfectante *m.* disinfectant **10A**
deslizarse *v.* to glide **18A**
desocupado/a *adj.* unemployed **11B**
despacio *adv.* slowly **10A**; **Más despacio, por favor.** *exp.* Slower, please. **0**
despedida *f.* farewell **0**; **despedida de soltero/a** *f.* bachelor(ette) party **18B**
desperdiciar *v.* to waste **15B**
despertador *m.* alarm clock **3B**
despertar *v.* to wake up, to awaken; **despertar la inquietud** *v.* to stir up interest **9A**
despertarse *v.* to wake up **7A**
después *adv.* after **0**; **después de que** *conj.* after **18A**
destacable *adj.* noteworthy **14A**

destacado/a *adj.* notable **5A**

destino *m.* destination **13A; destinos turísticos** *m.* tourist destinations **4B**

desventaja *f.* disadvantage **9B**

detalle *m.* detail; **ocuparse de los detalles** *v.* to take care of the details **18B**

detrás: detrás de *loc. prep.* behind **3B**

devolución *f.* return **9A**

devolver *v.* to return **16B**

devorar *v.* to devour **18B**

día *m.* day; **Buenos días.** *exp.* Good morning. **0; cada día** *loc. adv.* each day **14A; de un día para el otro** *loc. adv.* overnight **16A; día a día** *m.* daily life **7A; día a día** *loc. adv.* day by day **14B; Día de la Madre** *m.* Mother's Day **18B; día de la semana** *m.* day of the week **3A; día festivo** *m.* holiday **3A; día libre** *m.* day off **14A; el otro día** *loc. adv.* the other day **9B; hoy en día** *loc. adv.* nowadays **15B; menú del día** *m.* fixed-price menu **2B; poner (a alguien) al día** *v.* to update **17B; poner al día** *v.* to bring up to date **7B; todo el día** *loc. adv.* all day **6A; todos los días** *loc. adv.* every day **3A**

diabetes *f.* diabetes **17A**

diabético/a *adj.* diabetic **17A**

dialecto *m.* dialect **17B**

diálogo *m.* dialogue **0**

diario *m.* diary; journal **5A**

diario/a *adj.* daily **13A; rutina diaria** *f.* daily routine **3A**

diarrea *f.* diarrhea **10A**

dibujar *v.* to draw **0**

dibujo *m.* drawing **3B**

dicho/a: propiamente dicho *exp.* per se **16B**

diciembre *m.* December **3A**

dictador(a) *m./f.* dictator **16A**

dictadura *f.* dictatorship **10B**

dieta *f.* diet **7B**

diferencia *f.* difference (in price) **16B**

diferenciarse de *v.* to be different from **17B**

diferente *adj.* different **2A**

difícil *adj.* difficult **7A**

dificultad *f.* difficulty **6B**

digital *adj.* digital **9B**

digno/a *adj.* decent **3B**

diminutivo *m.* diminutive, nickname **12A**

dinamismo *m.* dynamism **16B**

dinero *m.* money **6B; cambio de dinero** *m.* foreign currency exchange **13A**

Dios *m.* God **8A**

diplomático/a *m./f.* diplomat **16A**

dirección *f.* address

directivo/a *m./f.* manager **8B; puesto directivo** *m.* managerial position **13B**

directo/a: en directo *loc. adv.* live **4A**

director(a) *m./f.* director **1A; carta al director** *f.* letter to the editor **2A**

dirigido/a: estar dirigido/a a *v.* to be aimed at **6A**

dirigir *v.* to run; to manage **6A**

discapacidad *f.* disability **12B**

discapacitado/a *adj.* disabled **12B**

discípulo/a *m./f.* disciple **17A**

disco *m.* album **7A; disco de vinilo** *m.* vinyl record **13B; tienda de discos** *f.* music store **3B**

disco: lanzador(a) de disco *m./f.* discus thrower **18A**

discográfico/a: sello discográfico *m.* record label **17B**

discoteca *f.* disco, nightclub **2A**

discurso *m.* speech **16A**

discutir *v.* to argue **13B**

diseñador(a) *m./f.* designer **3B; diseñador(a) (de moda)** *m./f.* (fashion) designer **11B**

diseñar *v.* to design **0**

diseño *m.* design **4B; diseño gráfico** *m.* graphic design **7A**

disfrutar *v.* to enjoy **4A; ¡Que disfruten a bordo!** *exp.* Enjoy your flight! **13A**

disgusto *m.* annoyance **15B**

dispensador *m.* dispenser **9B**

disponer *v.* to have (at one's disposal) **18B**

distancia *f.* distance **2A; amor a distancia** *m.* long-distance love **6B**

distinto/a *adj.* different **4A**

distracción *f.* distraction **13B**

diversidad *f.* diversity **7A**

diversión *f.* fun **6A**

diverso/a *adj.* various **5B**

divertido/a *adj.* fun **1B**

divertir *v.* to amuse **17B**

divertirse *v.* to have fun **17B**

divisas *f. pl.* foreign currency **13A**

divorciado/a *adj.* divorced **5B**

divorciarse *v.* to get divorced **12A**

divorcio *m.* divorce **12A**

DNI (Documento Nacional de Identidad) *m.* national identity card **3A**

doble *m.* double **2B; doble apellido** *m.* two last names **12A; habitación doble** *f.* double room **6B**

docena *f.* dozen **4A; media docena** *f.* half a dozen **4A**

doctor(a) *m./f.* doctor **10A**

documental *m.* documentary **9A**

dolencia *f.* ailment **10A**

doler *v.* to hurt **10A**

dolor *m.* pain **10A**

domador(a): domador(a) de leones *m./f.* lion tamer **14A**

doméstico/a *adj.* home; **objetos domésticos** *m.* furnishings **4B; servicio doméstico** *m.* domestic service **8B**

domicilio *m.* home address **2A; reparto a domicilio** *m.* home delivery **7B**

dominar *v.* to dominate **17A**

domingo *m.* Sunday **3A**

dominical: suplemento dominical *m.* Sunday supplement **9B**

dominio *m.* command **13B**

donación *f.* donation **9A**

dónde *interrog.* where **2A; ¿De dónde eres?** *exp.* Where are you from? **1A; ¿De dónde es usted?** *exp.* Where are you from? **1A; ¿Dónde está...?** *exp.* Where is...? **2A**

dorada *f.* sea bream (type of fish) **2B**

dormir *v.* to sleep; **dormir la siesta** *v.* to take a nap **6A**

dormitorio *m.* bedroom **4B**

dos *adj.* two; **dos veces al mes** *loc. adv.* twice a month **6A; hace dos meses** *loc. adv.* two months ago **5A; los/las dos** *pron.* both **6B**

dosis *f.* dose **17A**

droga *f.* drug(s) **16A**

ducharse *v.* to shower **7A**

dudar *v.* to doubt **16A; No dude en...** *exp.* Don't hesitate to... **13B**

dueño/a *m./f.* owner **8B**

dulce *m.* candy, sweet **2B**

dulce *adj.* sweet **2B**

duración *f.* duration **6B**

durazno *m.* peach **16B**

duro/a *adj.* hard; tough **7B**

DVD *m.* DVD **9B; película en DVD** *f.* movie on DVD **4B**

E

e *conj.* and (before i or hi + consonant) **1B**

echar: echar de menos *v.* to miss **14B**

ecológico/a *adj.* ecological **17A;** organic **7B; agricultura ecológica** *f.* organic farming **15A; producto ecológico** *m.* organic product **15A**

economía *f.* economics **1B**

económico/a *adj.* affordable **2B; prensa económica** *f.* financial press **3A; recurso económico** *m.* economic resource **14A**

ecoturismo *m.* ecotourism **11A**

ecuación *f.* equation **15B**

Ecuador *m.* Ecuador **0**

ecuatoguineano/a *adj.* from Equatorial Guinea **14A**

edad *f.* age **4A**

edición: edición especial *f.* special edition **3B**

edificio *m.* building **2A**

editar *v.* to edit; to release **7A;** to release (music) **17B**

educación *f.* education **8A; Educación ético-cívica** *f.* Civics **15B; Educación física** *f.* Physical Education **15B; Educación plástica y visual** *f.* Art **15B**

educador(a) *m./f.* trainer (of dogs) **12B**

educar *v.* to train; to educate **12B**

efectivamente *adv.* indeed **15B**

efectivo: en efectivo *loc. adv.* in cash **3B**

efecto *m.* effect **6A**

eficaz *adj.* effective; efficient **13B**

egresar *v.* to graduate **9A**

ejecutivo/a: ejecutivo/a de ventas *m./f.* sales executive **13B**

ejemplo *m.* example **0; dar un ejemplo** *v.* to give an example **7A**

ejercicio *m.* exercise **10A; hacer ejercicio** *v.* to exercise; to work out **6A**

ejército *m.* army **16A**

el *art.* the (*m., sing.*) **2A**

él *pron.* he **1A; Él es...** *exp.* He is... **0**

El Salvador *m.* El Salvador **0**

el/la turista *m. y f.* tourist **1B**

elaboración *f.* production **15A**

elaborar *v.* to create, to make **0**

elástico/a: goma elástica *f.* rubber band **8A**

elecciones *f.* elections **10B**

electoral: campaña electoral *f.* electoral campaign **16A**

electricidad *f.* electricity **8A**

electrodoméstico *m.* appliance **8A**

electrónico/a *adj.* electronic; **correo electrónico** *m.* e-mail **4B; lector de libros electrónicos** *m.* e-reader **13B**

elegante *adj.* elegant **4B**

elegir *v.* to choose **7A**; **¿Qué … eliges?** *exp.* Which… do you choose? **1A**

eliminación *f.* elimination **12B**

eliminar *v.* to eliminate **16A**

ella *pron.* she **1A**; **Ella es…** *exp.* She is… **0**

ellos/as *pron.* they **1B**

embajada *f.* embassy **10A**

embajador(a): embajador(a) de la paz *m./f.* ambassador for peace **16A**

embargo: sin embargo *conj.* however **5A**

embarque *m.* boarding **13A; hora de embarque** *f.* boarding time **13A; puerta de embarque** *f.* boarding gate **13A**

emblema *m.* emblem **18A**

emergencia *f.* emergency **12B**

emigración *f.* emigration **8B**

emigrante *m. y f.* emigrant **8B**

emisora *f.* radio station **14B**

emitir: emitir la serie *v.* to broadcast the (TV) series **14B**

emocionado/a *adj.* excited **10B**

emocionante *adj.* exciting, moving **10B**

empanada *f.* empanada **17B**

empatía *f.* empathy **13B**

empezar *v.* to start **5A**

empleado/a *m./f.* employee **3A**

empleo *m.* employment **11B**

emprendedor(a) *adj.* enterprising **8B**

empresa *f.* company **6A**

empresario/a *m./f.* businessperson **8B; mujer empresaria** *f.* businesswoman **5A**

en *prep.* in; **bacalao en salsa** *m.* cod with sauce **2B; convertirse en** *v.* to become **7A; de vez en cuando** *loc. adv.* from time to time **14A; en barco** *loc. adv.* by boat **5A; en casa** *loc. adv.* at home **2B; en concreto** *loc. adv.* in particular **7B; en cuanto a** *loc. prep.* as for **16A; en definitiva** *loc. adv.* all in all **18B; en directo** *loc. adv.* live **4A; en efectivo** *loc. adv.* in cash **3B; en el ámbito familiar** *exp.* among family **12A; en equipo** *loc. adv.* as a team **7A; en especial** *loc. adv.* especially **7B; en general** *loc. adv.* generally **4A; en la actualidad** *loc. adv.* today; nowadays **8B; en línea** *loc. adv.* online **9B; En mi opinión, …** *exp.* In my opinion, … **10B; En parejas/ grupos** *loc. adv.* In pairs/groups **0; en regla** *loc. adv.* in order; valid **11A; en resumen** *loc. adv.* in short **18B; en vías de desarrollo** *adj.* developing **3B; entrar en** *v.* to enter **3A; especializado/a en** *adj.* specializing in **2B; estar en conexión** *v.* to be connected **6A; estar en contacto** *v.* to be in touch **12B; estar en desacuerdo** *v.* to disagree **5B; estar en forma** *v.* to be fit, in (good) shape **7A; estar en manos de alguien** *exp.* to be under someone's control **17A; estar en obras** *v.* to be under construction **11A; estar en paz** *v.* to be at peace **10B; estar interesado/a en** *v.* to be interested in **17A; hacer algo en casa** *v.* to do something at home **3A; hoy en día** *loc. adv.* nowadays **15B; ir en coche** *v.* to go by car **3A; ir en…** *v.* to go by (means of transportation) **6B; No dude en…** *exp.* Don't hesitate to… **13B; participar en** *v.* to participate in **3A; película en DVD** *f.*

movie on DVD **4B; quedarse en blanco** *exp.* to draw a blank **15B; tener confianza en** *v.* to trust in **5B**

enamorado/a (de) *adj.* in love with **2A; estar enamorado/a (de)** *v.* to be in love (with) **12A**

enamorarse *v.* to fall in love **12A**

encantado/a *adj.* delighted **11A; Encantado/a.** *exp.* Pleased to meet you. **0**

encantar *v.* to love; to get a kick out of **5B**

encanto *m.* charm **11A; con encanto** *loc. adj.* charming **6B**

encargo *m.* job, assignment **16B**

encender *v.* to turn on **4B**

encima: encima de *loc. prep.* on (top of) **3B**

encontrar *v.* to find **4A**

encontrarse *v.* to feel **10A**

encuentro *m.* encounter **10B; punto de encuentro** *m.* meeting point **9A**

encuesta *f.* survey **18B**

endulzar *v.* to sweeten **15A**

enemigo/a *m./f.* enemy **17B**

energético/a: sector energético *m.* energy sector **14A**

energía *f.* energy **7A**

enero *m.* January **5A**

enfadado/a *adj.* angry **12A**

enfadarse *v.* to get angry **17B**

enfermedad *f.* illness; disease **10A**

enfermero/a *m./f.* nurse **12B**

enfermo/a *adj.* sick **5B**

enfrentarse a/con *v.* to face **18A**

enganchar *v.* to get someone hooked **14B**

enojarse *v.* to get angry **17B**

enorme *adj.* huge **16A**

ensalada *f.* salad; **ensalada de la casa** *f.* house salad **2B**

ensayo *m.* rehearsal **7A**

enseñanza *f.* teaching **7A**

enseñar *v.* to show; to teach **5B**

entender *v.* to understand; **No entiendo.** *exp.* I don't understand. **0; Te entiendo perfectamente.** *exp.* I understand you perfectly. **13B**

enterarse de *v.* to find out (about) **17A**

entero/a: leche entera *f.* whole milk **15A**

entonces *adv.* then **7A; desde entonces** *loc. adv.* since then **7A**

entorno *m.* environment, surroundings **11A; entorno afectivo** *m.* emotional environment **13B**

entrada *f.* arrival (time) **6A; ticket **7B; bandeja de entrada** *f.* inbox **14A**

entrar en *v.* to enter **3A**

entre *prep.* between **2A; alejados entre sí** *loc. adv.* far from each other **17B**

entrega *f.* delivery **7B; entrega de equipaje** *f.* baggage claim **13A**

entrenador(a) *m./f.* coach **18A**

entrenamiento *m.* training **18A**

entretenerse *v.* to amuse oneself **9A**

entretenimiento *m.* entertainment **8B**

entrevista *f.* interview **3A**

entristecer *v.* to sadden **17B**

entusiasmo *m.* enthusiasm **10B**

envasado/a *adj.* packaged **15A**

envase *m.* container; **envase de plástico** *m.* plastic container **15A; envase reciclable** *m.* recyclable container **15A**

enviar *v.* to send **7B**

época *f.* time of year **6B**; time, period **9A**

equidad *f.* fairness **17A**

equilibrado/a *adj.* balanced **7B**

equilibrio *m.* balance **6A**

equipaje *m.* baggage **11A; control de equipaje** *m.* baggage screening **13A; entrega de equipaje** *f.* baggage claim **13A**

equipo *m.* equipment **18A**; *m.* team; **en equipo** *loc. adv.* as a team **7A; equipo de trabajo** *m.* work team **13B**

equivocado/a *adj.* mistaken **14A**

ERASMUS: beca ERASMUS *f.* ERASMUS scholarship **14A**

error *m.* error **11A**

escala *f.* scale **15B; hacer escala** *v.* to stop over **13A**

escalada *f.* climbing **18A**

escalar *v.* to climb (a mountain) **18A**

escaparate *m.* shop window **3B**

escenificar *v.* to role-play **0**

escocés/escocesa *adj.* Scottish **7B**

escondido/a *adj.* hidden **6B**

escribir *v.* to write **0; ¿Cómo se escribe…?** *exp.* How do you spell…? **0**

escribirse *v.* to write to each other **17B**

escritor(a) *m./f.* writer **1A**

escuchar *v.* to listen **0; escuchar la radio** *v.* to listen to the radio **2A**

escudo *m.* coat of arms **18B**

escuela *f.* school **3B; escuela bilingüe** *f.* bilingual school **15B; escuela primaria** *f.* elementary school **9A; escuela privada** *f.* private school **15B; escuela pública** *f.* public school **15B**

escultor(a) *m./f.* sculptor **16A**

ese/a *adj., pron.* that

esfuerzo *m.* effort **8A**

eslogan *m.* slogan **11A**

eso *pron.* that; **por eso** *conj.* therefore **17A; Siento oír eso.** *exp.* I'm sorry to hear that. **13B**

esos/as *adj., pron.* those

espacio *m.* space, room; **ocupar espacio** *v.* to take up space **13B**

espada *f.* sword **18B**

espalda *f.* back **10A**

España *f.* Spain **0**

español *m.* Spanish **1B; aprender español** *v.* to learn Spanish **3A**

español/a *adj.* Spanish

especial *adj.* special **2B; edición especial** *f.* special edition **3B; en especial** *loc. adv.* especially **7B**

especialista *m. y f.* specialist **10A**

especializado/a en *adj.* specializing in **2B**

especialmente *adv.* specially **7A**

espectacular *adj.* spectacular **11B**

espectáculo *m.* show **4A**

espejo *m.* mirror **9A**

esperanza *f.* hope **10B**

esperanzado/a *adj.* hopeful **14A**

esperar *v.* to hope; to wait for **12B**

espíritu *m.* spirit **6A**

espiritual *adj.* spiritual **14A**

espolvorear *v.* to sprinkle **15A**

espontáneo/a *adj.* impromptu **14B**

esposo/a *f.* husband/wife **5B; ex esposo/a** *m./f.* ex-husband/wife **12A**

esquí *m.* skiing **1A**
estabilidad *f.* stability **13B**
estable *adj.* stable **12B**
establecer *v.* to establish **6A**
establecimiento *m.* store;
establishment **9B**
estación *f.* station **4A; estación (del año)** *f.*
season **10A**
estado *m.* state **5B; estado anímico** *m.*
state of mind **10A; estado civil** *m.*
marital status **5B; estado de ánimo** *m.*
state of mind, mood **12A; estado físico**
m. physical condition **10A; golpe de
estado** *m.* coup d'état **10B**
Estados Unidos (EE.UU.) *m.* United States
(U.S.A.) **0**
estadounidense *adj.* American **1B**
estancia *f.* ranch **3A;** stay **11A;**
¡Feliz estancia! *exp.* Have a nice
stay! **11A**
estanco *m.* tobacconist's shop **9B**
estándar *adj.* standard **7B**
estar *v.* to be; **¿dónde está...?** *exp.* where
is...? **2A; ¿Está Carmen?** *exp.* Is Carmen
there? **6B; ¿Qué tal está(n)...?** *exp.* How
is/are...? **2B; estar a la cabeza** *exp.* to
lead **16A; estar a... kilómetros de...** *exp.*
to be... kilometers from... **2A; estar
acostumbrado/a a** *v.* to be used to **13B;
estar adaptado/a** *v.* to be adapted **12B;
estar callado/a** *v.* to be silent **9A; estar
conectado/a** *v.* to be connected (to
the Internet) **13B; estar de acuerdo** *v.*
to agree **5B; estar de vacaciones** *v.* to
be on vacation **7B; estar de viaje** *v.* to
be away **7A; estar dirigido/a a** *v.* to be
aimed at **6A; estar en conexión** *v.* to be
connected **6A; estar en contacto** *v.* to
be in touch **12B; estar en desacuerdo**
v. to disagree **5B; estar en forma** *v.* to be
fit, in (good) shape **7A; estar en manos
de alguien** *exp.* to be under someone's
control **17A; estar en obras** *v.* to be
under construction **11A; estar en paz** *v.*
to be at peace **10B; estar enamorado/a
(de)** *v.* to be in love (with) **12A; estar
encantado/a** *v.* to be delighted **11A;
estar fuera del (de nuestro) alcance** *exp.*
to be beyond one's (our) means **15B;
estar haciendo algo** *v.* to be doing
something **7A; estar ilusionado/a** *v.* to
be excited **12A; estar impresionado/a** *v.*
to be impressed **18A; estar interesado/a
en** *v.* to be interested in **17A; estar
localizable** *v.* to be reachable **13B; estar
motivado/a** *v.* to be motivated **13B;
estar resfriado/a** *v.* to have a cold **10A;
estar seguro/a de sí mismo/a** *v.* to be
self-confident **18A; Estoy bien.** *exp.* I'm
OK. **7B**
este *m.* east **2A**
este/a *adj., pron.* this; **esta semana** *loc.*
adv. this week **6A; este año** *loc. adv.*
this year **6A; este mes** *loc. adv.* this
month **6A**
estilo *m.* style **4B**
estimado/a *adj.* dear **6B; Estimados
señores:** *exp.* Dear sirs: **6B**
estimulante *adj.* stimulating **6A**
estimular *v.* to stimulate **16A**

estómago *m.* stomach **10A**
estos/as *adj., pron.* these
estrategia *f.* strategy **0**
estrella *f.* star **5A; hotel de cuatro estrellas**
m. four-star hotel **11A**
estrenarse *v.* to premiere **14B**
estrés *m.* stress **3A**
estresante *adj.* stressful **1B**
estrofa *f.* stanza **17B**
estuche *m.* case **13A**
estudiante *m./f.* student; **residencia de
estudiantes** *m.* dorm **12A**
estudiar *v.* to study **1B; estudiar una
carrera** *v.* to study for a degree **15B**
estudio *m.* studio apartment **4B**
estudios *m. pl.* studies **5A**
estupendo/a *adj.* wonderful **6B**
etapa *f.* stage **9A**
ético/a: Educación ético-cívica *f.* Civics **15B**
etiqueta *f.* label **15A**
étnico/a: grupo étnico *m.* ethnic group **16B**
eufórico/a *adj.* euphoric **15B**
euro *m.* euro; **Son 9 euros.** *exp.* It's 9
euros. **2B**
europeo/a *adj.* European **6A; Unión
Europea** *f.* European Union **10B**
euskera *m.* Basque (language) **1B**
evaluador(a) *m./f.* critic, appraiser **17A**
evento *m.* event **18B**
evidente *adj.* obvious, clear **17A**
evitar *v.* to avoid **15A**
evolución *f.* evolution **16B**
ex *pref.* former, ex; **ex esposo/a** *m.*
ex-husband/wife **12A**
exacto/a *adj.* exact **6A**
exagerar *v.* to exaggerate **15B**
excelente *adj.* excellent **13A**
excluyente *adj.* a must, required **13B**
excursión *f.* excursion **6A**
exigir *v.* to demand **16B; exigir sacrificios**
v. to require sacrifices **13A**
exiliarse *v.* to go into exile **10B**
exilio *m.* exile **8B**
exitoso/a *adj.* successful **5A**
éxodo *m.* exodus **14B**
exótico/a *adj.* exotic **4A**
expectativa *f.* expectation **15A**
experiencia *f.* experience **4B;
experiencia profesional** *f.* professional
experience **11B**
experimentación *f.* experimentation **17A**
experimento *m.* experiment **17A**
explicar *v.* to explain **14B**
explorar *v.* to explore **11B**
explosión *f.* explosion **14B**
explotar *v.* to exploit **14A**
exponer *v.* to display, to post **0**
exportador(a) *m./f.* exporter **18B**
exportar *v.* to export **7B**
exposición *f.* exhibition **6A**
expresar: expresar un sentimiento *v.* to
express a feeling **18B**
expulsar *v.* to expel **14A**
exquisito/a *adj.* delicious **13A**
extensión *f.* area **6B**
extenso/a *adj.* vast **16B**
extinción *f.* extinction **14A**
extra *adj.* extra; **aceite de oliva virgen
extra** *m.* extra virgin olive oil **15A; hacer
horas extras** *v.* to do overtime **13B**

extraescolar: actividad extraescolar *f.*
extracurricular activity **15B**
extranjero/a *adj.* foreign **2A; lengua
extranjera** *f.* foreign language **15B**
extrañar *v.* to miss **13A;** to surprise **15B**
extraordinario/a *adj.* extraordinary **11B**

F

fábrica *f.* factory **8B**
fabricar *v.* to manufacture; **fabricar en
serie** *v.* to mass-produce **13B**
fácil *adj.* easy **6B; hacer la vida más fácil**
exp. to make life easier **17A**
factor *m.* factor **6A**
facturación *f.* check-in counter **11A;
mostrador de facturación** *f.* check-in
counter **13A**
falda *f.* skirt **3B**
falso/a: ¿Verdadero o falso? *exp.* True or
false? **0**
falta *f.* lack **11B; falta de comunicación** *f.*
lack of communication **15B; hacer falta**
v. to be necessary **16A**
faltar *v.* to miss, to lack; **que faltan** *adj.*
missing **0**
familia *f.* family **2A; la Familia Real** *f.* the
royal family **4B; médico/a de familia**
m./f. family doctor **10A**
familiar *m.* relative **5B; en el ámbito
familiar** *exp.* among family **12A**
famoso/a *adj.* famous **2A**
fantástico/a *adj.* fantastic **2A**
farero/a *m./f.* lighthouse keeper **14A**
farmacéutico/a *adj.* pharmaceutical **17A**
fármaco *m.* medicine **17A**
fascinado/a *adj.* fascinated **14B**
fascinar *v.* to captivate **14A**
fase *f.* stage **17A**
fauna *f.* fauna; **observación de flora y fauna**
f. wildlife viewing **6B**
favor *m.* favor; **a favor de** *loc. adv.* in favor
of **12B; Más despacio, por favor.** *exp.*
Slower, please. **0; por favor** *exp.* please **2B**
favorecer *v.* to favor **11A**
favorito/a *m./f.* favorite **9B**
fax *m.* fax **7B**
fe *f.* faith; **acto de fe** *m.* matter of faith **8A**
febrero *m.* February **5A**
fecha *f.* date **5A; fecha de caducidad** *f.*
expiration date **15A**
Felicidades *exp.* Congratulations **5A**
felicitación: tarjeta de felicitación *f.*
greeting card **5A**
Felicitaciones *exp.* Congratulations **6A**
feliz *adj.* happy **5A; ¡Feliz estancia!** *exp.*
Have a nice stay! **11A; ¡Que tengan un
feliz vuelo!** *exp.* Have a good flight! **13A**
femenino/a *adj.* feminine **0**
feo/a *adj.* ugly **3B**
feria *f.* (trade) fair **16B**
ferry: tomar el ferry *v.* to take the ferry **3A**
festivo/a: día festivo *m.* holiday **3A**
fiable *adj.* reliable **17A**
fibra *f.* fiber **10A**
ficción *f.* fiction **14B**
fiebre *f.* fever **10A; fiebre amarilla** *f.* yellow
fever **10A**
fiesta *f.* festival **2A; fiesta de quince años**
f. fifteenth birthday party **18B; fiesta**

popular *f.* festival **6A; salón de fiestas** *m.* function hall **18B**

fijarse en *v.* to look at **0**

fijo/a: caminar sin rumbo fijo *v.* to wander aimlessly **17B**

fila: hacer fila *v.* to get/wait in line **13A**

Filadelfia *f.* Philadelphia **1A**

filete: filete de ternera *m.* fillet of veal **2B**

filosofía *f.* philosophy **5A; Filosofía y Letras** *f.* Arts **5A**

fin *m.* end; **fin de semana** *m.* weekend **2B; los fines de semana** *loc. adv.* (on) weekends **5B; por fin** *exp.* at last **10A**

final *m.* end, ending **0; a finales del siglo XIX** *loc. adv.* toward the end of the 19th century **8B**

finalidad *f.* purpose **14B**

finalista *m. y f.* finalist **9B**

financiar *v.* to finance **4B**

financiero/a *adj.* financial **11B**

finanzas *f., pl.* finance; **mundo de las finanzas** *m.* world of finance **3A**

finca *f.* farm **8B**

fiordo *m.* fjord **6B**

firma *f.* signing **16A**

firmar *v.* to sign **16A**

física *f.* physics **15B**

físico/a *adj.* physical **6A; aspecto físico** *m.* physical appearance **12A; Educación física** *f.* Physical Education **15B; estado físico** *m.* physical condition **10A**

flamenco/a: baile flamenco *m.* flamenco dance **7A**

flan *m.* flan (custard) **2B**

flexibilidad: flexibilidad horaria *f.* schedule flexibility **6A**

flexibilizar *v.* to make flexible **6A**

flexible: jornada flexible *f.* flexible workday **6A**

flor *f.* flower; **ramo de flores** *m.* bunch of flowers **18B**

flora: observación de flora y fauna *f.* wildlife viewing **6B**

floral: arreglo floral *m.* flower arrangement **18B**

florista *m. y f.* florist **18B**

floristería *f.* florist (shop) **9B**

flotante *adj.* floating **9A**

fluorescente *adj.* fluorescent **11A**

folclore *m.* folklore **14A**

folleto *m.* brochure **0**

fomentar *v.* to encourage **14A**

forestal: guarda forestal *m. y f.* forest ranger **14A**

forma *f.* shape; **estar en forma** *v.* to be fit, in (good) shape **7A**

formación *f.* education **6A; formación profesional** *f.* professional training **14A**

formar *v.* to create, to form **0**

formato *m.* format **14B**

Fórmula 1 *f.* Formula 1 **18A**

formulario *m.* form **16A**

foro *m.* forum **1B**

fortalecer *v.* to strengthen **18A**

fortaleza *f.* fortress **11A**

fortuna: hacer fortuna *v.* to make a fortune **8B**

foto *f.* photo **0; pie de foto** *m.* caption **5A; tomar fotos** *v.* to take pictures **6B**

fotocopiadora *f.* photocopier **7B**

fotografía *f.* photograph **1B**

fotográfico/a *adj.* photographic **11B**

fotógrafo/a *m./f.* photographer **11B**

fotonovela *f.* photo story **12A**

fragancia *f.* fragrance, perfume **16B**

frambuesa *f.* raspberry **15A**

francés *m.* French **1B**

francés/francesa *adj.* French **1B**

franquista *adj.* Francoist **14B**

frasco *m.* jar **8A**

frase *f.* phrase **0**

frazada *f.* blanket **13A**

frecuencia *f.* frequency **13A; ¿Con qué frecuencia?** *exp.* How often? **3A**

frecuente *adj.* common **2B**

frente *f.* forehead **17B**

fresa *f.* strawberry **15A**

fresco/a *adj.* fresh; **producto fresco** *m.* fresh food **15A**

frigorífico *m.* refrigerator **7B**

frijol *m.* bean **4A**

frío *m.* cold **2A; hacer frío** *v.* to be cold out **10A; tener frío** *v.* to be cold **10A**

frito/a *adj.* fried; **patatas fritas** *f.* potato chips **4A; tomate frito** *m.* tomato sauce **15A**

frontera *f.* border **7A**

frontón *m.* jai-alai court **18A**

frustrante *adj.* frustrating **12B**

fruta *f.* fruit **2B**

frutería *f.* fruit shop **9B**

frutero/a *m./f.* fruit seller **9B**

fuego *m.* heat; fire **8A**

fuera *adv.* out **2B; estar fuera del (de nuestro) alcance** *exp.* to be beyond one's (our) means **15B; fuera de clase** *loc. adv.* outside of class **3A**

fuerte *m.* fort **11A**

fuerza *f.* strength, power **16A; fuerzas armadas** *f.* armed forces **16A**

fumar *v.* to smoke; **dejar de fumar** *v.* to quit smoking **12B**

función *f.* function **4B**

funcional *adj.* functional **4B**

funcionar *v.* to function, to work **7B**

fundador(a) *m./f.* founder **4B**

fútbol *m.* soccer **1A**

futuro *m.* future **8B**

futuro/a *adj.* future **12B**

G

gafas *f.* glasses **3B; gafas de sol** *f.* sunglasses **3B**

gallego *m.* Galician (language) **1B**

galleta *f.* cookie **2B**

gama *f.* range **16B**

gamba *f.* shrimp **2B**

ganador(a) *adj.* winning **14B**

ganar *v.* to earn **11B;** to win **5A; ganar torneos** *v.* to win tournaments **18A**

gandul *m.* pigeon pea **15A**

garaje *m.* garage **4B**

garantía *f.* guarantee **11A**

garantizar *v.* to guarantee **3B**

garganta *f.* throat **10A**

gaseosa *f.* soft drink **13A**

gasto *m.* expense **15B**

gastronomía *f.* gastronomy; cuisine **4B**

gastronómico/a *adj.* culinary, gastronomic **2B**

genealógico/a: árbol genealógico *m.* family tree **5B**

generación *f.* generation **10B**

generacional *adj.* generational **15B**

general: en general *loc. adv.* generally **4A**

generalmente *adv.* generally **7B**

genético/a: manipulación genética *f.* genetic modification **7B**

genial *adj.* great **6B**

genio *m.* genius **15B**

gente *f.* people **2A; hablar con la gente** *v.* to talk to people **2A; mi gente** *exp.* my folks **5B**

geográfico/a *adj.* geographic **16B**

Geología *f.* Geology **15B**

gestión *f.* management **13B**

gimnasia *f.* gymnastics **18A; hacer gimnasia** *v.* to exercise **10A**

gimnasio *m.* gym **3A**

gimnasta *m. y f.* gymnast **18A**

girar *v.* to turn **9B**

gitano/a *m./f.* gypsy **16A**

glaciar *m.* glacier **11B**

glucosa *f.* glucose **17A**

gluten *m.* gluten **15A**

gobernante *m./f.* ruler, leader **12B**

gobierno *m.* government **16A**

golf *m.* golf **1A; salsa golf** *f.* sauce similar to Thousand Island dressing **17A**

golpe *m.* blow; **golpe de estado** *m.* coup d'état **10B**

goma *f.* rubber; **goma elástica** *f.* rubber band **8A**

gordo *m.* jackpot; first prize **9B**

gordo/a *adj.* fat **9B**

gorro *m.* cap **10A**

gota *f.* drop **2B**

GPS: navegador GPS *m.* GPS **13B**

gracias *f. pl.* thanks; **¡Gracias!** *exp.* Thank You! **0; gracias a...** *loc. prep.* thanks to... **5B; Nada más, gracias.** *exp.* Nothing else, thanks. **2B**

gracioso/a *adj.* funny **9A**

graduación *f.* graduation **18B**

graduarse *v.* to graduate **12A**

gráfico/a: diseño gráfico *m.* graphic design **7A**

grande *adj.* big **4B; gran** *adj.* great **5B; ser un(a) gran comunicador(a)** *v.* to be a great communicator **13B**

grasa *f.* fat **15A**

gratarola *adv.* for free **17B**

gratificante *adj.* rewarding **11A**

gratuito/a *adj.* free (of charge) **9B**

gris *adj.* gray **3B**

grulla *f.* crane **16A**

grupo *m.* group; **En parejas/grupos** *loc. adv.* In pairs/groups **0; grupo étnico** *m.* ethnic group **16B; grupo marginado** *m.* marginalized group **12B; grupo musical** *m.* music group **14B**

guacamole *m.* guacamole **1A**

guantes *m.* gloves **18A**

guapo/a *adj.* good-looking **9A**

guaraní *m.* Guarani **1B**

guarda: guarda forestal *m. y f.* forest ranger **14A**

guardar *v.* to save **7B; guardar (canciones/fotos)** *v.* to save/store (songs/photos) **13B**

guardería *f.* day care **5B**
Guatemala *f.* Guatemala **0**
guatemalteco/a *m./f.* Guatemalan **2A**
gubernamental: ONG (organización no gubernamental) *f.* NGO (non-governmental organization) **5A**
guerra *f.* war **8B; guerra civil** *f.* civil war **8B; Segunda Guerra Mundial** *f.* World War II **18A**
guerrilla *f.* guerrilla **16A**
guía *f.* guide(book) **1B; el/la guía turístico/a** *m. y f.* (tour) guide **1B; perro/a guía** *m. y f.* guide dog **12B**
guinda *f.* wild cherry **16B**
Guinea Ecuatorial *f.* Equatorial Guinea **0**
guitarra *f.* guitar **8A**
guitarrista *m. y f.* guitarist **7A**
gustar *v.* to like **4A**
gusto *m.* taste **15A; Con gusto.** *exp.* You're welcome. **18B; Mucho gusto.** *exp.* Pleased to meet you. **0**

H

habano: puro habano *m.* Cuban cigar **3B**
haber: ¡No hay problema! *exp.* No problem! **7B**
habilidad *f.* ability **8A**
habilitar *v.* to qualify **13B**
habitación *f.* room **4B; habitación doble** *f.* double room **6B; habitación individual** *f.* single room **6B**
habitante *m. y f.* inhabitant **2A**
hábito *m.* habit **7A**
hablar *v.* to speak **1B; ¿Qué lenguas hablas?** *exp.* What languages do you speak? **1B; hablar con la gente** *v.* to talk to people **2A; hablar por hablar** *v.* to talk for the sake of it **14B; se habla(n)** *v.* is/are spoken **1B**
hablarse: hablarse de tú/usted *v.* to address somebody as tú/usted **7B**
hace *v.* ago **5A: hace dos meses** *loc. adv.* two months ago **5A**
hacer *v.* to do, to make **3A; ¿Cuánto tiempo (hace)…?** *exp.* How long have/has? **8B; ¿Qué tiempo hace?** *exp.* What's the weather like? **10A; dedicarse a (hacer) algo** *v.* to do something (for a living) **7A; desde hace** *loc. prep.* for (and until now) **5B; estar haciendo algo** *v.* to be doing something **7A; hace 30 ºC de temperatura** *v.* the temperature is 30º C **10A; hace buen/mal tiempo** *v.* there is good/bad weather **10A; hace dos meses** *loc. adv.* two months ago **5A; hacer algo en casa** *v.* to do something at home **3A; hacer balance de** *v.* to take stock of **12B; hacer caso (a alguien)** *v.* to pay attention (to somebody) **15B; hacer cerámica** *v.* to make pottery **6A; hacer clic** *v.* to click **13B; hacer compañía** *v.* to keep company **7A; hacer consciente** *v.* to make aware **3B; hacer deporte** *v.* to exercise **3A; hacer escala** *v.* to stop over **13A; hacer falta** *v.* to be necessary **16A; hacer fila** *v.* to get/wait in line **13A; hacer fortuna** *v.* to make a fortune **8B; hacer frío/calor** *v.* to be cold/hot out **10A; hacer gimnasia** *v.* to

exercise **10A; hacer horas extras** *v.* to do overtime **13B; hacer la cama** *v.* to make the bed **3A; hacer la vida más fácil** *exp.* to make life easier **17A; hacer las compras** *v.* to do the shopping **3A; hacer las maletas** *v.* to pack **8B; hacer realidad** *v.* to make something happen **8B; hacer sol** *v.* to be sunny **10A; hacer una consulta** *v.* to ask somebody's advice **12A**
hacerse *v.* to become **8B; hacerse vegetariano/a** *v.* to become a vegetarian **7B**
hambre: tener hambre *v.* to be hungry; **pasar hambre** *v.* to go hungry **15A**
harina *f.* flour **15A; harina de maíz** *f.* cornmeal **15A**
hasta *prep.* until; **desde… hasta…** *loc. prep.* from… until/to **8B; Hasta la vista.** *exp.* See you later. **0; Hasta mañana.** *exp.* See you tomorrow. **0**
hebreo *m.* Hebrew **7A**
hecho *m.* event **10B; de hecho** *exp.* in fact **7A**
hectárea *f.* hectare **6B**
helado *m.* ice cream **2B**
hepatitis *f.* hepatitis **10A**
heredar *v.* to inherit **9B**
herida *f.* injury; wound **10A**
herir *v.* to hurt **15B**
hermano/a *m./f.* brother/sister **5A**
hermanos *m.* siblings **5B**
hermoso/a *adj.* lovely **13A**
hielo *m.* ice **2B; manto de hielo** *m.* ice sheet **11B**
hierba *f.* herb **6A**
higiene *f.* hygiene **15A**
hijo/a *m./f.* son/daughter **5A; tener un hijo** *v.* to have a child **8B**
hilo *m.* thread **14B**
himno *m.* anthem **18B**
hincha *m./f.* supporter, fan; **ser hincha de** *v.* to be a supporter of **17B**
hip-hop *m.* hip-hop **1A**
hípico/a *adj.* equestrian **18A**
hispanohablante *adj.* Spanish-speaking **14A**
historia *f.* history **1B; story 5A**
histórico/a *adj.* historic **6B**
historieta *f.* comic strip **14B**
hogar *m.* home **8A**
hoja *f.* sheet; leaf **0, 8A**
Hola *exp.* Hi. **0; ¿Hola?** *exp.* Hello? **6B**
hombre *m.* man **3B; ¡Pero, hombre!** *exp.* Come on! **17A; el hombre de mi vida** *exp.* the man of my dreams **12A**
homogéneo/a *adj.* homogeneous **16B**
Honduras *f.* Honduras **0**
hondureño/a *adj.* Honduran **14B**
hongo *m.* mushroom **11A**
hora ¿A qué hora…? *exp.* At what time…? **3A; ¿Qué hora es?** *exp.* What time is it? **3A; hacer horas extras** *v.* to do overtime **13B; hora de embarque** *f.* boarding time **13A; hora de llegada** *f.* arrival time **13A; hora de salida** *f.* departure time **13A**
horario/a: flexibilidad horaria *f.* schedule flexibility **6A**
horario *m.* schedule **3A; horario de trabajo** *m.* work schedule **3A**
horizonte *m.* horizon **8B**

horno *m.* oven; **al horno** *adj.* baked **13A**
horrible *adj.* horrible **2A**
hortaliza *f.* vegetable **7B**
hospital *m.* hospital **1B**
hospitalario/a *adj.* hospitable **13A**
hospitalidad *f.* hospitality **14A**
hostal *m.* hostel **11A**
hotel *m.* hotel **0; hotel de cuatro estrellas** *m.* four-star hotel **11A**
hotelero/a *m./f.* hotel manager **4B**
hour *f.* hour
hoy *adv.* today **6A; hoy en día** *loc. adv.* nowadays **15B**
hueso *m.* bone **9A**
huevo *m.* egg **2B**
humanidad *f.* humankind **17A; Patrimonio de la Humanidad** *m.* World Heritage (Site) **8A**
humano/a: derechos humanos *m.* human rights **16A; Recursos Humanos (RR.HH.)** *m.* Human Resources (HR) **13B; ser humano** *m.* human being **8A**
humor: de buen/mal humor *loc. adv.* in a good/bad mood **12A**

I

ida: ida y vuelta *exp.* round-trip **6B**
idea *f.* idea **4B**
ideal *adj.* ideal **2A; vivienda ideal** *f.* ideal home **4B**
identidad *f.* identity **18B; DNI (Documento Nacional de Identidad)** *m.* national identity card **3A**
idioma *m.* language **1B**
ídolo *m.* idol **18A**
iglesia *f.* church **2A**
igualdad *f.* equality **8B**
ilimitado/a *adj.* unlimited **8A**
ilusión *f.* hope; excitement **12B**
ilusionado/a *adj.* excited **12A; estar ilusionado/a** *v.* to be excited **12A**
ilustre: ciudadano/a ilustre *m./f.* distinguished citizen **17B**
imagen *f.* picture, image **1A**
imaginar *v.* to imagine **5B; imaginarse que…** *v.* to imagine that… **0**
impaciente *adj.* impatient **13B**
imparable *adj.* unstoppable **14A**
impedir *v.* to prevent; to stop **12B**
impermeable *m.* raincoat **10A**
importante *adj.* important **2A**
importar *v.* to import **15A; ¿Le importaría…?** *exp.* Would you mind…? **13A**
imprescindible *adj.* indispensable **13B**
impresionado/a *adj.* impressed **18A; estar impresionado/a** *v.* to be impressed **18A**
impresionante *adj.* impressive **5A**
impresora *f.* printer **7B**
imprimir *v.* to print **7B**
impuesto *m.* tax **4B**
inauguración *f.* housewarming **12A**
inaugurar *v.* to open; to inaugurate **12A**
incansable *adj.* tireless **14B**
incendio *m.* fire **7A**
incentivar *v.* to encourage **14A**
incentivo *m.* encouragement **17A**
incluido/a: IVA incluido *loc. adv.* tax included **2B**
incluir *v.* to include **11A**

incomodísimo/a *adj.* extremely uncomfortable **11B**
inconveniente *m.* drawback **13B**
incorporar *v.* to include **18A**
incorrecto/a *adj.* incorrect **0**
increíble *adj.* incredible **5B**; **¡Increíble!** *exp.* Unbelievable! **9B**
independencia *f.* independence **12B**
independiente *adj.* independent **12A**
independizarse *v.* to become independent **15B**
India *f.* India **6A**
indiferencia *f.* indifference **16A**
indígena *adj.* indigenous, native **1B**; **pueblo indígena** *m.* native people **16A**
indio/a *adj.* Indian **4A**
indiscutible *adj.* indisputable **16A**
individual: habitación individual *f.* single room **6B**
industria *f.* industry; **industria de servicios** *f.* service industry **14A**; **industria petrolera** *f.* oil industry **14A**
industrial *adj.* industrial **8B**
infancia *f.* childhood **9A**
infantil: moda infantil *f.* children's fashion **3B**
infección *f.* infection **10A**
infinito/a *adj.* infinite **18A**
influyente *adj.* influential **7A**
información *f.* information; **información nutricional** *f.* nutritional information **15A**
informado/a *adj.* informed **9B**
informar *v.* to inform **16A**
informática *f.* computer science **1B**
informático/a: técnico/a informático/a *m./f.* computer technician **1B**
informativo *m.* news (program) **9A**
infraestructura *f.* infrastructure **17A**
infusión *f.* infusion **6A**
ingeniería *f.* engineering **8A**
ingeniero/a *m./f.* engineer **1B**; **(ingeniero/a) agrónomo/a** *m./f.* agronomist **7A**
inglés *m.* English **1B**
inglés/inglesa *adj.* English **1B**
ingrediente *m.* ingredient **15A**
ingresos *m. pl.* income **11A**
inhóspito/a *adj.* inhospitable **11B**
ininterrumpidamente *adv.* uninterruptedly **18A**
inmediato/a *adj.* immediate **17A**
inmensidad *f.* immensity **11B**
inmigrante *m. y f.* immigrant **5B**; **comunidad inmigrante** *f.* immigrant community **8B**
inmobiliaria *f.* real-estate agency **4B**
inmunológico/a: sistema inmunológico *m.* immune system **17A**
innovador(a) *adj.* innovative **13B**
inocencia *f.* innocence **18B**
inolvidable *adj.* unforgettable **5B**
inquietud *f.* interest **9A**; **despertar la inquietud** *v.* to stir up interest **9A**
inscribir (a alguien en algo) *v.* to enroll (somebody in something) **15B**
inscripción: plazo de inscripción *m.* enrollment period **18A**
insomnio *m.* insomnia **14B**
insoportable *adj.* unbearable **2A**
instalación *f.* facility **11A**

instalar *v.* to install **14B**
instituto *m.* high school **15B**
insulina *f.* insulin **17A**
integración *f.* integration **12B**
integrarse *v.* to be integrated; to fit into **12B**
intelectual *adj.* intellectual **17B**
inteligencia: inteligencia emocional *f.* emotional intelligence **13B**
inteligente *adj.* intelligent **12A**; **teléfono inteligente** *m.* smartphone **13B**
intenso/a *adj.* intense **3A**
interactivo/a *adj.* interactive **17A**
intercambiar *v.* to exchange **8A**
intercambio *m.* exchange **1B**; **programa de intercambio** *m.* exchange program **14A**
interés *m.* interest **1A**
interesado/a: estar interesado/a en *v.* to be interested in **17A**
interesante *adj.* interesting **1B**; **¡Qué interesante!** *exp.* How interesting! **1B**
interesar *v.* to be of interest **7A**
interior: producto interior bruto (PIB) *m.* gross domestic product (GDP) **11A**
internacional *adj.* international **1B**; **Relaciones Internacionales** *f.* International Relations **11B**; **Salón Internacional de la Moda** *m.* International Fashion Fair **3B**
internauta *m. y f.* Internet user **6A**
Internet: navegar por Internet *v.* to surf the Internet **6A**
interpretación *f.* performance **5A**
interpretar *v.* to perform **7A**
invadir *v.* to invade **16A**
inversión *f.* investment **14B**
investigación *f.* research **8B**; **investigación de mercado** *f.* market research **15A**
investigador(a) *m./f.* investigator **14B**; researcher **17A**
invierno *m.* winter **2A**
invitado/a *m./f.* guest **18B**
invitar *v.* to invite **17B**
inyectarse *v.* to give oneself an injection **17A**
ir *v.* to go; **¿Cómo vas?** *exp.* How are you going there? **6B**; **ir a trabajar** *v.* to go to work **3A**; **ir en coche** *v.* to go by car **3A**; **ir en...** *v.* to go by (means of transportation) **6B**; **ir mal** *v.* to go wrong **7B**
irse *v.* to leave **12B**
isla *f.* island **1A**; **Islas Baleares** *f.* Balearic Islands **4B**
italiano *m.* Italian **1B**
italiano/a *adj.* Italian **1B**
IVA: IVA incluido *loc. adv.* tax included **2B**
izquierda *f.* left; **a la izquierda** *loc. adv.* (to the) left **9B**; **a la izquierda de** *loc. adv.* to the left of **3B**

J

jabón *m.* soap **8A**
jamón *m.* ham **0**; **jamón serrano** *m.* Serrano ham **2B**
janguear (fam.) *v.* to hang out **11A**
japonés *m.* Japanese **1B**
jarabe *m.* syrup **15A**
jardín *m.* yard **4B**

jardinería *f.* gardening **8A**
jazz *m.* jazz **7A**
jeans *m.* jeans **3B**
jefe/a *m./f.* boss **12B**; **jefe/a de cabina** *m./f.* purser **13A**
jerga *f.* slang, jargon **17B**
jeringa *f.* syringe **17A**
jornada: jornada flexible *f.* flexible workday **6A**
joven (pl. jóvenes) *adj.* young **2A**; **el/ la joven hecho/a y derecho/a** *exp.* all grown-up **9A**
jóvenes *m.* young people **2A**
jubilación *f.* retirement **18B**
jubilado/a *adj.* retired **5B**
judío/a *m./f.* Jew **7A**
juego *m.* game **0**; **Juegos Panamericanos** *m.* Pan-American Games **18A**; **Juegos Paralímpicos** *m.* Paralympic Games **12B**
jueves *m.* Thursday **3A**
jugar *v.* to play **7A**; **jugar a la lotería** *v.* to play the lottery **9B**
jugo *m.* juice; **jugo de naranja** *m.* orange juice **2B**
juguete *m.* toy **8B**
juguetería *f.* toy store **9B**
julio *m.* July **3A**
jungla *f.* jungle **5A**
junio *m.* June **5A**
juntos/as *adj.* together **5A**
jurado *m.* panel of judges **16B**
justicia: justicia social *f.* social justice **16A**
justo/a: comercio justo *m.* fair trade **3B**
juvenil *adj.* for young people **7A**
juventud *f.* youth **9A**

K

karate *m.* karate **3A**
kayak *m.* kayak **6B**
kilo *m.* kilogram **4A**; **medio kilo** *m.* half a kilogram **4A**
kilómetro *m.* kilometer **2A**; **estar a... kilómetro(s) de...** *exp.* to be... kilometers from... **2A**
kínder *m.* kindergarten **5B**

L

la *art.* the (*f., sing.*) **2A**
La Habana *f.* Havana **0**
labor *f.* work, task **12B**
laboral *adj.* working **7B**; **actividad laboral** *f.* job **7B**; **ambiente laboral** *m.* work environment **13B**; **asesor(a) laboral** *m./f.* labor consultant **13B**; **demanda laboral** *f.* labor demand **14A**
lado *m.* side; **al lado de** *m.* next to **3B**; **lado malo** *m.* bad side **13B**; **por otro lado** *loc. adv.* on the other hand **13B**; **por un lado** *loc. adv.* on the one hand **13B**
lago *m.* lake **6B**
lámpara *f.* lamp **3B**
lancha *f.* boat **9A**
lanzador(a) de disco *m./f.* discus thrower **18A**
lanzar *v.* to throw **18A**; **lanzar una campaña** *v.* to launch a campaign **16B**
largo/a *adj.* long **12A**; **a largo plazo** *loc. adv.* in the long term **9A**

las *art.* the (*f., pl.*) **2A**
latino/a: referente latino *m.* Hispanic icon **1A**
lavar *v.* to wash; **lavar los platos** *v.* to do the dishes **5A**
leche *f.* milk **0**; **crema de leche** *f.* cream **15A**; **leche descremada en polvo** *f.* powdered skim milk **15A**; **leche entera** *f.* whole milk **15A**
lector(a): lector de libros electrónicos *m.* e-reader **13B**
lectura *f.* reading **0**
leer *v.* to read **0**
legumbres *f.* legumes **2B**
lejos de *prep.* far from **2A**
lema *m.* motto **3B**
lengua *f.* tongue, language; **lengua extranjera** *f.* foreign language **15B**; **lengua materna** *f.* mother tongue **14A**; **lengua nativa** *f.* native language **16A**; **lengua oficial** *f.* official language **14A**; **Lengua y literatura** *f.* Language and Literature **15B**; **¿Qué lenguas hablas?** *exp.* What languages do you speak? **1B**
lenteja *f.* lentil **2B**; **lentejas con chorizo** *f.* lentils with chorizo sausage **2B**
lento/a *adj.* slow **7B**
león/leona *m./f.* lion/lioness; **domador(a) de leones** *m./f.* lion tamer **14A**
letra *f.* letter; lyrics **7A**
letras *f. pl.* literature **16A**
levantarse *v.* to get up **7A**
leyenda *f.* legend **18A**
liberar *v.* to set free **16A**
libertad *f.* freedom **13B**
libre *adj.* free **16A**; **al aire libre** *loc. adv.* outdoors **3A**; **día libre** *m.* day off **14A**; **tiempo libre** *m.* free time **5B**
librería *f.* bookstore **3B**
libro *m.* book **0**; **lector de libros electrónicos** *m.* e-reader **13B**; **libro de quejas** *m.* complaint form **11A**
licencia *f.* license **2A**; **licencia por maternidad** *f.* maternity leave **7B**
líder *m. y f.* leader; **líderes mundiales** *m. y f.* world leaders **16A**; **ser líder de audiencia** *v.* to be the highest rated **14B**
limitar *v.* to limit **6A**
limpiar *v.* to clean **3A**
limusina *f.* limousine **18B**
lindo/a *adj.* lovely **11B**
línea *f.* line **4A**; **en línea** *loc. adv.* online **9B**
liso/a *adj.* straight **12A**
lista *f.* list **0**; **lista de compras** *f.* shopping list **4A**
literario/a: crítico/a literario/a *m./f.* literary critic **10B**
literatura *f.* literature **1B**; **Lengua y literatura** *f.* Language and Literature **15B**
llamada *f.* call **3A**; **llamada de teléfono** *f.* phone call **3A**
llamar *v.* to call; **llamar la atención** *v.* to catch one's attention **14A**
llamar(se) *v.* to be named **0**; **(Él/Ella) se llama…** *exp.* His/Her name is… **0**; **¿Cómo se llama?** *exp.* What is your name? **0**; **¿Cómo te llamas?** *exp.* What is your name? **0**; **Yo me llamo…** *exp.* My

name is… **0**
llegada *f.* arrival **11A**; **hora de llegada** *f.* arrival time **13A**; **sala de llegada** *f.* arrival lounge/area **13A**
llegar *v.* to arrive **3A**; **llegar a casa** *v.* to arrive home **3A**
llevar *v.* to take **5B**; *v.* to wear **3B**; **llevar a cabo** *v.* to carry out **18A**; **llevar a los niños al colegio** *v.* to take the kids to school **3A**; **llevar un negocio** *v.* to run a business **9B**; **llevar una vida…** *v.* to lead a… life **10A**; **llevarse bien/mal** *v.* to get along/not to get along **12A**
llorar *v.* to cry **14B**
llover *v.* to rain **10A**
lluvia *f.* rain **6A**
lo *art.*; **lo malo/bueno** *m.* the bad/good thing **12B**; **lo más… posible** *m.* as… as possible **17A**; **lo mejor** *m.* the best (thing) **4B**; **Lo siento.** *exp.* I'm sorry. **3B**
localizable: estar localizable *v.* to be reachable **13B**
localizar *v.* to find, to locate **0**; to get hold of, to locate **13B**
loco/a *adj.* crazy **7B**
locutor(a) *m./f.* announcer **16A**
locutorio *m.* call center; Internet café **8B**
logo *m.* logo **16B**
lograr *v.* to achieve **5B**
Londres London **1A**
los *art.* the (*m. pl.*) **2A**; **los/las dos** *pron.* both **6B**
Los Ángeles *m.* Los Angeles **1A**
lotería *f.* lottery; **agencia de lotería** *f.* lottery ticket booth **9B**; **comprar (billetes de) lotería** *v.* to buy lottery tickets **9B**; **jugar a la lotería** *v.* to play the lottery **9B**; **vendedor(a) de lotería** *m./f.* lottery ticket seller **9B**
luchador(a) *adj.*; *m./f.* fighter **5A**; **16A**
luego *adv.* later, then **0**; **Hasta luego.** *exp.* See you later. **0**
lugar *m.* place **2A**; **lugar clave** *m.* landmark **4A**; **lugar de culto** *m.* place of worship **8A**; **lugar de nacimiento** *m.* birthplace **11B**; **tener lugar** *v.* to be held **16B**
lujoso/a *adj.* luxurious **11A**
lunes *m.* Monday **3A**
lunfardo *m.* Buenos Aires slang **17B**
luz *f.* light; **luz apagada** *f.* lights off **6A**

M

maceta *f.* flowerpot **8A**
madera *f.* wood **8A**
madre *f.* mother; **Día de la Madre** *m.* Mother's Day **18B**; **madre trabajadora** *f.* working mother **7B**
madrugar *v.* to get up early **7A**
maduro/a *adj.* mature **17B**
maestro/a *m./f.* master; teacher **6A**; **maestro/a de ceremonias** *m./f.* master of ceremonies **18B**
magacín *m.* news and talk show **9A**
mágico/a *adj.* magic **18B**
maíz *m.* corn **2B**; **harina de maíz** *f.* cornmeal **15A**
mal *adv.* badly; **ir mal** *v.* to go wrong **7B**;

llevarse bien/mal *v.* to get along/not to get along **12A**; **menos mal** *exp.* thank goodness **10A**
maldición *f.* curse **16A**
malentendido *m.* misunderstanding **14A**
maleta *f.* suitcase **8B**; **hacer las maletas** *v.* to pack **8B**
mallorca *f.* Puerto Rican pastry **1A**
malo/a *adj.* bad; **de mal humor** *loc. adv.* in a bad mood **12A**; **hacer mal tiempo** *exp.* there is bad weather **10A**; **lado malo** *m.* bad side **13B**; **lo malo** *m.* the bad thing **12B**; **ser malo/a (en algo)** *exp.* to be bad (at something) **17B**
mamá *f.* mom **5B**
manazas *m. y f.* clumsy person **8A**
mandar *v.* to send **7B**
manejar *v.* to manage **13B**; to drive **17B**
manera *f.* way **5A**
manifiesto *m.* manifesto **12B**
manipulación: manipulación genética *f.* genetic modification **7B**
manitas *m. y f.* handyperson **8A**
mano *f.* hand **8A**; **estar en manos de alguien** *v.* to be under someone's control **17A**; **manos a la obra** *exp.* (Let's) Get to work! **8A**
mantener *v.* to keep **5B**
mantenimiento *m.* maintenance **4B**
mantequilla *f.* butter **2B**
manto: manto de hielo *m.* ice sheet **11B**
manzana *f.* apple **4A**
manzanilla *f.* chamomile tea **10A**
mañana *adv.* tomorrow **0**; **de la mañana** *loc. adv.* a.m.; in the morning **3A**; **Hasta mañana.** *exp.* See you tomorrow. **0**; **pasado mañana** *loc. adv.* the day after tomorrow **11B**; **por la mañana** *loc. adv.* in the morning **3A**
mapa *m.* map **4B**
maquillarse *v.* to put makeup on **7A**
mar *m.* sea; **mar Caribe** *m.* Caribbean Sea **4B**
maratón *m.* marathon **18A**; **correr un maratón** *v.* to run a marathon **18A**
maravilla: de maravilla *loc. adv.* wonderfully **17B**
maravilloso/a *adj.* wonderful **5A**
marca *f.* brand **3B**
marcar *v.* to check off, to mark **0**
marcha *f.* march **16A**; **poner en marcha** *exp.* to set in motion **16A**
marcharse *v.* to go away **18B**
marco *m.* picture frame **3B**
margarita *f.* daisy **18B**
marginación *f.* marginalization **12B**
marginado/a: grupo marginado *m.* marginalized group **12B**
marido *m.* husband **5B**
marino/a: biólogo/a marino/a *m./f.* marine biologist **11B**
marketing: analista de marketing *m. y f.* marketing analyst **13B**
marrón *adj.* brown **3B**
marroquí *adj.* Moroccan **4A**
Marte *m.* Mars **17A**
martes *m.* Tuesday **3A**
marzo *m.* March **5A**
más *adv.*, more; **¿Algo más?** *exp.* Anything else? **2B**; **el/la más** *m./f.* the most **9A**;

hacer la vida más fácil *exp.* to make life easier **17A**; **lo más… posible** *m.* as… as possible **17A**; **más conocido/a** *adj.* best-known **4A**; **más que** *adj.* more than **3A**; **más tarde** *loc. adv.* later **17B**; **Nada más, gracias.** *exp.* Nothing else, thanks. **2B**

masculino/a *adj.* masculine **0**

masía (Cataluña) *f.* country house **7B**

matar *v.* to kill **18B**

mate *m.* mate **6A**

mate: yerba mate *f.* mate (infusion) **3B**

matemáticas *f.* math **15B**

materia: materia prima *f.* raw material **15A**

material *m.* material **8A**

maternidad *f.* maternity; **baja por maternidad** *f.* maternity leave **7B**; **licencia por maternidad** *f.* maternity leave **7B**

materno/a: lengua materna *f.* mother tongue **14A**

matrimonio *m.* marriage **5B**; married couple **11B**; **cama de matrimonio** *f.* double bed **4B**

mayo *m.* May **2A**

mayor *adj.* older **9A**; **las personas mayores** *f. pl.* the elderly **6A**

mayoría *f.* most, majority **5B**

me *pron.* me, to me; **¡No me digas!** *exp.* You don't say! **9B**; **Me da/pone…** *exp.* Give me… **4A**; **Me toca a mí.** *exp.* It's my turn. **4A**; **Yo me llamo…** *exp.* My name is… **0**

mecánica *f.* mechanics **8A**

mecánico/a *adj.*; *m./f.* mechanic **7B**; **taller (mecánico)** *m.* repair shop **7B**

medalla *f.* medal **12B**

mediados: a mediados de los 60 *loc. adv.* in the mid sixties **14B**

medicación *f.* medication **10A**

medicamento *m.* medicine **10A**

medicina *f.* medicine **10A**

médico/a *m./f.* doctor **1B**; **médico/a de familia** *m./f.* family doctor **10A**

medida *f.* measure **16A**

medio *m.* means; **medio ambiente** *m.* environment **4B**; **medio de transporte** *m.* means of transportation **4A**; **medio de vida** *m.* way of life **11B**; **medios** *m.* means **15A**; **medios de comunicación** *m.* media **9A**; **por medio de** *loc. prep.* by means of **14B**

medio/a *adj.* mean, average; half; **a medio plazo** *loc. adv.* in the medium term **17A**; **clase media** *f.* middle class **14B**; **media docena** *f.* half a dozen **4A**; **medio kilo** *m.* half a kilogram **4A**

medir *v.* to measure **17A**

meditación *f.* meditation **6A**

mejor *adv.* better **6A**; **a lo mejor** *loc. adv.* maybe **17A**; **el/la mejor** *m./f.* the best **9A**; **lo mejor** *m.* the best (thing) **4B**

mejorar *v.* to improve **6A**

melocotón *m.* peach **15A**

memoria *f.* memory **10B**; **aprender de memoria** *f.* to memorize **14B**

memorias *f. pl.* memoirs **5B**

mencionar *v.* to mention **0**

menos *adv.* less **6A**; **echar de menos** *v.* to miss **14B**; **el/la menos** *m./f.* the least **9A**; **menos mal** *exp.* thank goodness **10A**;

menos que *adj.* less than **3A**

mensajería *f.* messenger company **7B**

mental *adj.* mental **12B**

mente *f.* mind **6A**

mentir *v.* to lie **17B**

menú: menú del día *m.* fixed-price menu **2B**

mercado *m.* market **0**; **investigación de mercado** *f.* market research **15A**

merengue *m.* merengue **17B**

merienda *f.* (afternoon) snack **16B**

mermelada *f.* jam, marmalade **2B**

mes *m.* month; **dos veces al mes** *loc. adv.* twice a month **6A**; **el mes pasado** *loc. adv.* last month **5A**; **el próximo mes** *loc. adv.* next month **5B**; **este mes** *loc. adv.* this month **6A**; **hace dos meses** *loc. adv.* two months ago **5A**

mesa *f.* table **3B**

mesero/a *m./f.* waiter/waitress **13A**

mestizo/a *m./f.* person of mixed race **16A**

meta *f.* goal **18A**

metabolismo *m.* metabolism **17A**

metal *m.* metal **8A**

meter *v.* to put **8A**

metódico/a *adj.* methodical **13B**

método: método científico *m.* scientific method **17A**

metro *m.* meter; subway **0**; **metros cuadrados (m²)** *m.* square meters **4B**

mexicano/a *adj.* Mexican **2B**

México *m.* Mexico **0**; **México, D.F.** *m.* Mexico City **0**

mezcla *f.* mix **14A**

mi *adj.* my **2A**

miedo *m.* fear **10B**

miel *f.* honey **7B**

miembro *m.* member **5B**

miércoles *m.* Wednesday **3A**

migración *f.* migration **8B**

migrante: población migrante *m.* migrant population **8B**

milenio *m.* millennium **10B**

miles *m.* thousands **6B**

millón *m.* million **8B**

minipiso *m.* tiny apartment **11B**

ministerio *m.* ministry, department **16A**

ministro/a *m./f.* minister **16A**

minoría *f.* minority **14A**

minuto *m.* minute **1A**; **último minuto** *m.* last minute **12B**

mirar *v.* to look at; to watch **6A**; **Mira…** *v.* Look… **8A**

mirarse *v.* to look at each other **17B**

misa *f.* Mass **5A**

misil *m.* missile **17A**

misión *f.* mission **10A**

mismo/a *adj.* same; **al mismo tiempo** *loc. adv.* at the same time **7A**; **estar seguro/a de sí mismo/a** *v.* to be self-confident **18A**; **tiempo para uno/a mismo/a** *m.* time for oneself **3A**

misticismo *m.* mysticism **16B**

mochila *f.* backpack **9A**

moda *f.* fashion **3B**; **diseñador(a) (de moda)** *m./f.* (fashion) designer **11B**; **moda infantil** *f.* children's fashion **3B**; **Salón Internacional de la Moda** *m.* International Fashion Fair **3B**

modelo *m. y f.* (fashion) model **3B**; *m.* model **0**

moderado/a *adj.* moderate **6B**

modernidad *f.* modernity **17A**

modernización *f.* modernization **17A**

moderno/a *adj.* modern **2A**

molestar *v.* to bother **15B**

momento *m.* moment **5A**

moneda *f.* coin **0**; currency **10B**; **ser moneda corriente** *exp.* to be common **13B**

mono/a *m./f.* monkey; **mono/a araña** *m./f.* spider monkey **16B**

montaña *f.* mountain **3A**

montañismo *m.* mountain climbing **18A**

montañista *m. y f.* mountain climber **18A**

montar *v.* to assemble **8A**; to ride **9A**

monumento *m.* monument **1A**

morado/a *adj.* purple **16B**

morbo *m.* morbid interest **14B**

moreno/a *adj.* dark-haired **12A**

morir *v.* to die **10B**

mosquito *m.* mosquito **10A**

mostrador: mostrador de facturación *m.* check-in counter **13A**

mostrar *v.* to show **0**; **mostrar afecto** *v.* to show affection **18B**

motivado/a: estar motivado/a *v.* to be motivated **13B**

motivo: con motivo de *exp.* on the occasion of **12B**

móvil *adj.* mobile **17A**

movilidad *f.* mobility **13B**

movilización: movilización social *f.* social mobilization **16A**

movimiento: un mundo en movimiento *exp.* a world in motion **14A**

MP3: reproductor de MP3 *m.* MP3 player **13B**

mucho *adv.* a lot **6A**

mucho/a *adj.* a lot, much **2A**

mudanza *f.* move **14A**

mudarse *v.* to move (from home) **7B**

mueble *m.* piece of furniture **8A**

muela *f.* molar **10A**

muerte *f.* death **10B**

mujer *f.* woman; wife **3A**; **¡Pero, mujer!** *exp.* Come on! **17A**; **la mujer de mi vida** *exp.* the woman of my dreams **12A**; **mujer empresaria** *f.* businesswoman **5A**

multimedia (invar.) *adj.* multimedia **9B**

multinacional *f.* multinational (firm) **16A**

mundial *adj.* global; worldwide **7B**; **líderes mundiales** *m. y f.* world leaders **16A**; **Patrimonio Mundial** *m.* World Heritage **11B**; **Segunda Guerra Mundial** *f.* World War II **18A**

mundo *m.* world **4A**; **dar la vuelta al mundo** *v.* to go around the world **18A**; **mundo de las finanzas** *m.* world of finance **3A**; **un mundo en movimiento** *exp.* a world in motion **14A**

muñeco *m.* figure **18B**

muro *m.* wall; **Muro de Berlín** *m.* Berlin Wall **10B**

museo *m.* museum **0**

música *f.* music **1A**; **clase de música** *f.* music class **3A**

musical *adj.* musical; **grupo musical** *m.* music group **14B**

músico/a *m./f.* musician **3A**

muy *adv.* very **2A**; **muy bien** *adv.* very well **1A**

N

nacer *v.* to be born **5A**

nacimiento *m.* birth **5B; lugar de nacimiento** *m.* birthplace **11B**

nacional *adj.* domestic **13A;** national **12B; DNI (Documento Nacional de Identidad)** *m.* national identity card **3A; parador nacional** *m.* state-run hotel in Spanish historic building **6B**

nacionalidad *f.* nationality **1B**

nada *adv.* at all **8A; Nada más, gracias.** *exp.* Nothing else, thanks. **2B; No pasa nada.** *exp.* Everything is OK. **13B**

nadador(a) *m./f.* swimmer **18A; el/la nadador(a) de sincronizada** *m./f.* synchronized swimmer **18A**

nadar *v.* to swim **5A**

nadie *pron.* nobody **8A**

nado *m.* swimming; **nado sincronizado** *m.* synchronized swimming **18A**

náhuatl *m.* Nahuatl **12A**

naranja *f.* orange **2B; jugo de naranja** *m.* orange juice **2B; zumo de naranja** *m.* orange juice **2B**

nariz *f.* nose **9A**

narrativa *f.* fiction **10B**

nasal *adj.* nasal **10B**

natación *f.* swimming **10A**

nativo/a *adj.* native; **lengua nativa** *f.* native language **16A**

natural *adj.* fresh **2B; alimento natural** *m.* natural food **15A; recurso natural** *m.* natural resource **14A**

naturaleza *f.* nature **4B**

navegador: navegador GPS *m.* GPS **13B**

navegar *v.* to sail; **navegar por Internet** *v.* to surf the Internet **6A**

Navidad *f.* Christmas **5B**

necesidad *f.* need **13B**

negativo/a *adj.* negative **2B**

negocio *m.* business **7B; abrir un negocio** *v.* to open a business **15A; ampliar un negocio** *v.* to expand a business **15A; viaje de negocios** *m.* business trip **3A**

negro/a *adj.* black **3B; oro negro** *m.* black gold **14A**

nervioso/a *adj.* nervous **10A**

nevar *v.* to snow **10A**

Nicaragua *f.* Nicaragua **0**

nieto/a *m./f.* grandson/granddaughter **5B**

nietos *m.* grandchildren **5B**

ningún *adj.* no, not any **9A**

ninguno/a *adj.* no, not any, none **9A**

niño/a *m./f.* boy/girl **3A; desde niño(s)/a(s)** *loc. adv.* since childhood **8B; llevar a los niños al colegio** *v.* to take the kids to school **3A**

nivel *m.* level **16A**

no *adv.* no, not **1A; ¡No hay problema!** *exp.* No problem! **7B; ¡No me digas!** *exp.* You don't say! **9B; ¿Por qué no…?** *exp.* Why don't you…? **6A; amor (no) correspondido** *m.* (un)requited love **12A; Creo que no.** *exp.* I think not. **7B; No pasa nada.** *exp.* Everything is OK. **13B; no puede olvidarse** *v.* cannot be forgotten **10B; No se pierda…** *exp.* Don't miss… **11B; No se puede…** *exp.* You/

One can't… **7B; No te preocupes.** *exp.* Don't worry. **13B; todavía no** *loc. adv.* not yet **6A; no soportar** *v.* not to be able to stand **15B; no violencia** *f.* non-violence **16A**

n.º (número) *m.* number **2A**

Nobel: Premio Nobel *m.* Nobel Prize **10B**

noche *f.* night; **Buenas noches.** *exp.* Good evening/night. **0; de la noche** *loc. adv.* p.m.; at night **3A; pasar la noche** *v.* to spend the night **6B; por la noche** *loc. adv.* in the evening; at night **3A**

nocturno/a: vigilante nocturno/a *m./f.* night security guard **3A**

nomás *adv.* only **17B**

nombrar *v.* to name **0**

nombre *m.* name **0; nombre de pila** *m.* first name **12A**

norma *f.* rule **15B**

normalmente *adv.* normally **2B**

norte *m.* north **2A**

nos *pron.* us; **¡Nos vemos!** *exp.* See you! **0**

nosotros/as *pron.* we **1B**

nostalgia *f.* homesickness, nostalgia **10B**

nota *f.* grade **15B;** note **4A; nota de prensa** *f.* press release **10B**

noticia *f.* news **4A**

novedad *f.* innovation **17A**

noviembre *m.* November **5A**

novio/a *m./f.* boyfriend/girlfriend **5A;** groom/bride **5A; novios** *m.* sweethearts **6B; viaje de novios** *m.* honeymoon **13A**

nublado/a *adj.* cloudy **10A**

nuclear: arma nuclear *f.* nuclear weapon **16A**

Nueva Orleans *f.* New Orleans **1A**

Nueva York *f.* New York **1A**

nuevo/a: Año Nuevo *m.* New Year **18B**

nuez *f.* nut **18B**

número *m.* issue **15A;** number **0; ¿Cuál es tu número de teléfono?** *exp.* What is your phone number? **1B; nº** *m.* number **2A**

nunca *adv.* never **6A; casi nunca** *loc. adv.* hardly ever **6A**

nutricional: información nutricional *f.* nutritional information **15A**

nutriente *m.* nutrient **15A**

nutritivo/a *adj.* nutritious **15A**

O

o *conj.* or; **o bien** *exp.* or otherwise **12A; o sea** *exp.* that is **8B**

objetivo *m.* goal; objective **3B**

objeto *m.* object **3B; objeto curioso** *m.* curiosity; knickknack **4A; objetos domésticos** *m.* furnishings **4B**

obligación *f.* obligation **5B**

obra *f.* work (of art), piece; **manos a la obra** *exp.* (Let's) Get to work! **8A; obra de arte** *f.* work of art **8A**

obras *f. pl.* construction **2A; estar en obras** *v.* to be under construction **11A**

obrero/a *m./f.* worker **8B**

observación *f.* remark **13A; observación de flora y fauna** *f.* wildlife viewing **6B**

observar *v.* to observe **0**

obtener *v.* to get, to obtain **0**

obvio *adj.* obvious **17A**

océano *m.* ocean **18A**

ocio *m.* leisure **6A**

ocultar *v.* to hide **16B**

ocupado/a *adj.* busy **2A**

ocupar *v.* to spend; to take up **5B; ocupar espacio** *v.* to take up space **13B**

ocuparse: ocuparse de los detalles *v.* to take care of the details **18B**

ocurrirse *v.* to think of **18B**

oeste *m.* west **2A**

oficial *adj.* official; **lengua oficial** *f.* official language **14A**

oficina *f.* office **6A; oficina de prensa** *f.* press office **16A**

oficio *m.* trade **14A**

ofrecer *v.* to offer **4B**

oído *m.* ear **10A; ser todo oídos** *exp.* to be all ears **9A**

oír: Siento oír eso. *exp.* I'm sorry to hear that. **13B**

Ojalá. *exp.* I/We wish. **15A**

ojo *m.* eye **9A; ¡Ojo!** *exp.* Be careful! **0**

ola *f.* wave **16B**

oliva: aceite de oliva virgen extra *m.* extra virgin olive oil **15A; aceite de oliva** *m.* olive oil **2B**

olvidar *v.* to forget **5B; no puede olvidarse** *exp.* cannot be forgotten **10B**

ómnibus *m.* bus **13A**

ONCE *f.* Spanish National Organization of the Blind **12B**

ONG (organización no gubernamental) *f.* NGO (non-governmental organization) **5A**

opinión *f.* opinion; **En mi opinión, …** *exp.* In my opinion, … **10B**

oponerse *v.* to object **15B**

oportunidad *f.* opportunity **8B**

optar *v.* to opt **18B**

optimismo *m.* optimism **10B**

optimista *adj.* optimistic **12A**

oración *f.* sentence **0**

ordenado/a *adj.* organized **13B**

ordenador *m.* computer **7B**

ordenar *v.* to put in order **0**

orgánico/a *adj.* organic **7B**

organismo *m.* organism **17A**

organización *f.* organization **3B; ONG (organización no gubernamental)** *f.* NGO (non-governmental organization) **5A**

organizado/a: viaje organizado *m.* package tour **13A**

organizar *v.* to organize **6A**

orgulloso/a *adj.* proud **2A**

orientador(a): orientador(a) profesional *m./f.* career counselor **13B**

oriental *adj.* oriental **6A**

origen *m.* origin **1A**

original *adj.* original **3B**

orilla *f.* shore **6B**

oriundo/a *adj.* native **16B**

oro *m.* gold **12B; oro negro** *m.* black gold **14A**

orquídea *f.* orchid **11A**

oscuro/a *adj.* dark **16B**

otoño *m.* fall **10A**

otro/a *adj.* other; **de un día para el otro** *loc. adv.* overnight **16A; otra vez** *loc. adv.* again **0; por otro lado/por otra parte** *loc. adv.* on the other hand **13B**

Ottawa *f.* Ottawa **1A**
oxígeno *m.* oxygen **18A**
oyente *m. y f.* listener **14B**
ozono: capa de ozono *f.* ozone layer **17A**

paciencia *f.* patience **15A**
paciente *m. y f.* patient **10A**
pacífico/a *adj.* peaceful **16A**
pacifista *m. y f.* pacifist **16A**
padres *m.* parents **5B**
paella *f.* Spanish rice dish **1A**
página *f.* page **0; página web** *f.* Web page **14B**
pago *m.* payment **7B**
país *m.* country **0; país receptor** *m.* host country **8B; País Vasco** *m.* Basque Country **1B**
paisaje *m.* landscape **6B**
palabra *f.* word **0**
paliza *f.* thrashing **18A**
paludismo *m.* malaria **10A**
pan *m.* bread **2B**
panadería *f.* bakery **8B**
Panamá *m.* Panama **0**
panameño/a *m./f.* Panamanian **2A**
panamericano/a: Juegos Panamericanos *m.* Pan-American Games **18A**
panorámico/a *adj.* panoramic **18B**
pantalla *f.* screen **13A**
pantalones *m.* pants **3B**
pañuelo *m.* scarf; handkerchief **3B**
papa *f.* potato **2B**
papá *m.* dad **5B**
papel *m.* paper; **papel de** *m.* role of **5B**
papelería *f.* stationery store **9B**
paquete *m.* package **4A**
paquistaní *adj.* Pakistani **4A**
par *m.* pair **5A**
para *prep.* for; **¿Para qué sirve?** *exp.* What is it used for? **4B; apto/a para** *adj.* appropriate/safe for **15A; de un día para el otro** *loc. adv.* overnight **16A; para siempre** *loc. adv.* forever **8B; servir para...** *v.* to be good for... **4B; tiempo para uno/a mismo/a** *m.* time for oneself **3A**
parador: parador nacional *m.* state-run hotel in Spanish historic building **6B; Parador de Turismo de España** *m.* state-run hotel in Spanish historic building **11A**
paraguas *m.* umbrella **3B**
Paraguay *m.* Paraguay **0**
paraíso *m.* paradise **4B**
paralímpico/a: Juegos Paralímpicos *m.* Paralympic Games **12B**
parapente *m.* paragliding **18A**
parar *v.* to stop **3A**
parásito *m.* parasite **8A**
parecer *v.* to seem **5B; al parecer** *loc. adv.* apparently **8B; parecer raro** *v.* to seem strange **15B**
parecerse: parecerse a alguien *v.* to look like somebody **12A**
parecido *m.* resemblance **12A**
pareja *f.* couple; partner **5B; En parejas** *loc. adv.* In pairs **0**

parque *m.* park **2A**
párrafo *m.* paragraph **0**
parte: por otra parte *loc. adv.* on the other hand **13B**
participar en *v.* to participate in **3A**
particular *adj.* particular; private; **casa particular** *f.* private home **13A; clase particular** *f.* private lesson **17B**
partido *m.* match **18A; partido político** *m.* political party **16A**
partir: a partir de *loc. prep.* from, starting **12B**
pasado/a *adj.* last **5A; el mes pasado** *loc. adv.* last month **5A; la semana pasada** *loc. adv.* last week **5A; pasado mañana** *loc. adv.* the day after tomorrow **11B**
pasaje *m.* ticket; **pasaje de avión** *m.* plane ticket **6B**
pasajero/a *m./f.* passenger; **señores pasajeros** *exp.* ladies and gentlemen, passengers **13A**
pasante *m. y f.* intern **13B**
pasantía *f.* internship; **pasantía de verano** *f.* summer internship **13B**
pasaporte *m.* passport; **control de pasaportes** *m.* passport control; immigration **13A**
pasar *v.* to happen **8B; ¿Qué pasa?** *exp.* What's up? **0; No pasa nada.** *exp.* Everything is OK. **13B; pasar hambre** *v.* to go hungry **15A; pasar la noche** *v.* to spend the night **6B; pasar la serie de televisión** *v.* to broadcast the television series **14B; pasar las vacaciones** *v.* to spend one's vacation **4B; pasar por** *v.* to go via **6B; pasarlo/la bien** *v.* to have a good time **17B**
pasatiempo *m.* pastime **7A**
pasear *v.* to go for a walk **3A**
paseo *m.* walkway **2A; dar un paseo** *v.* to take a walk **6A; paseo a caballo** *m.* horseback ride **6B**
pasivo/a *adj.* passive **6A**
paso *m.* step; **de paso** *loc. adv.* in the process **14B; paso de baile** *m.* dance step **17B**
pasodoble *m.* typical Spanish march-like dance **17B**
pasta *f.* pasta **2B**
pastel *m.* cake **18B**
pata *f.* paw **5A**
Patagonia *f.* Patagonia **6B**
patata *f.* potato **2B; patatas fritas** *f.* potato chips **4A**
patentar *v.* to patent **17A**
pato/a *m./f.* duck **18A**
patrimonio *m.* heritage; **Patrimonio de la Humanidad** *m.* World Heritage (Site) **8A; Patrimonio Mundial** *m.* World Heritage **11B**
patrono/a *m./f.* patron saint **16B**
paz *f.* peace **2A; embajador(a) de la paz** *m./f.* ambassador for peace **16A; estar en paz** *v.* to be at peace **10B**
pedido *m.* order; request **7B**
pedir *v.* to ask for **12B; pedir ayuda** *v.* to ask for help **5B; pedir permiso** *v.* to ask permission **12B; pedir un crédito** *v.* to ask for a loan **5B**
peine *m.* comb **8A**

Pekín *m.* Beijing **1B**
pelar *v.* to peel **8A**
película *f.* movie **1A; película en DVD** *f.* movie on DVD **4B; ver películas** *v.* to watch movies **3A**
peligroso/a *adj.* dangerous **10A**
pelirrojo/a *adj.* red-haired **12A**
pelo *m.* hair **9A**
pelota *f.* ball **18A**
peludo/a *adj.* shaggy **9A**
peluquería *f.* hair salon **8B**
pena *f.* sadness; shame; **dar pena** *v.* to sadden **18B; valer la pena** *v.* to be worth it **11B**
pendiente *f.* slope **18A**
pensar (de) *v.* to think (of) **4A**
pepino *m.* cucumber **8A**
pequeñísimo/a *adj.* tiny **11B**
pequeño/a *adj.* small **4B; desde pequeño/a** *loc. adv.* since childhood **5B**
per cápita: renta per cápita *f.* per capita income **14A**
perder *v.* to lose **7B; perder un vuelo** *v.* to miss a flight **13A**
perderse *v.* to miss **16B; No se pierda...** *v.* Don't miss... **11B**
perdonar: Perdona, ... *exp.* Excuse me, ... **5A; perdone (form.)** *exp.* excuse me **9B**
peregrino/a *m./f.* pilgrim **11A**
perfeccionamiento *m.* improvement **14A**
perfectamente: Te entiendo perfectamente. *exp.* I understand you perfectly. **13B**
perfecto/a *adj.* perfect **2A**
perfil *m.* profile **14A**
perfume *m.* perfume **3B**
perfumería *f.* perfume/cosmetics shop **3B**
periferia *f.* suburbs **2A**
periódico *m.* newspaper **7A**
periodista *m. y f.* journalist **10B**
permiso *m.* permission; **pedir permiso** *v.* to ask permission **12B**
permitir *v.* to allow **6B**
pero *conj.* but **2A; ¡Pero, hombre/mujer!** *exp.* Come on! **17A**
perro/a *m./f.* dog; **perro/a guía** *m./f.* guide dog **12B**
persona *f.* person **1B; las personas mayores** *f.* the elderly **6A; una persona de 80 años** *f.* an 80-year-old person **3A**
personaje *m.* character, important figure **1A**
personal *adj.* personal **3B; satisfacción personal** *f.* personal satisfaction **13B;** *m.* staff **11A**
personalizado/a *adj.* personalized **11A**
perspectiva *f.* prospect **13B**
pertenecer *v.* to belong **3B**
Perú *m.* Peru **0**
pesar: a pesar de todo *loc. adv.* in spite of everything **13B**
pescado *m.* fish **2B; sopa de pescado** *f.* fish soup **2B**
pescador(a) *m./f.* fisherman/fisherwoman **14A**
pesimista *adj.* pessimistic **12A**
pésimo/a *adj.* dreadful **11A**
pesticida *m.* pesticide **15A**
petición *f.* request **12B**
petrificado/a *adj.* petrified **11B**

petróleo *m.* oil **14A**; **barril de petróleo** *m.* oil barrel **14A**

petrolero/a *adj.* oil; **industria petrolera** *f.* oil industry **14A**; **plataforma petrolera** *f.* oil rig **14A**

piano *m.* piano **8A**; **piano de cola** *m.* grand piano **10B**

PIB (producto interior bruto) *m.* GDP (Gross Domestic Product) **11A**

pibe/a *m./f.* young boy/girl **17B**

picante *adj.* spicy **2B**; **picantes** *m.* hot sauces **15A**

picazón *f.* itch **10A**

pico *m.* peak, mountain **16B**

pie *m.* foot **10A**; **pie de foto** *m.* caption **5A**

piel *f.* skin **10A**

pierna *f.* leg **10A**

pila: nombre de pila *m.* first name **12A**

piloto *m. y f.* race car driver **18A**

pimiento *m.* (bell) pepper **2B**

pinchazo *m.* prick **17A**

pintar *v.* to paint **6A**

pintor(a) *m./f.* painter **12B**

pintura *f.* painting **3A**

piña *f.* pineapple **15A**

pirámide *f.* pyramid **2A**

piscina *f.* swimming pool **3A**

piso *m.* floor, story **8A**

placer *m.* pleasure **5B**

planificar *v.* to plan **18B**

plano *m.* plan **8A**

planta *f.* plant **8A**

plantearse: plantearse preguntas *v.* to question **14B**

plástico *m.* plastic **8A**

plástico/a *adj.* plastic; **Educación plástica y visual** *f.* Art **15B**; **envase de plástico** *m.* plastic container **15A**

plata *f.* silver **12B**; money **11B**; **bodas de plata** *f.* silver wedding anniversary **18B**

plataforma: plataforma petrolera *f.* oil rig **14A**

plato *m.* dish; plate **8A**; **lavar los platos** *v.* to do the dishes **5A**; **plato principal** *m.* main course **2B**; **primer plato** *m.* first course **2B**

playa *f.* beach **1A**

plaza *f.* seat **13A**; square **1B**

plazo *m.* term, period; **a corto/medio/largo plazo** *loc. adv.* in the short/medium/long term **17A**; **a largo plazo** *loc. adv.* in the long term **9A**; **plazo de inscripción** *m.* enrollment period **18A**

plegado/a *adj.* folded **13A**

pluriempleo *m.* having more than one job, moonlighting **14B**

población *f.* population **2A**; **población migrante** *f.* migrant population **8B**

poblado/a *adj.* populated **16B**

pobreza *f.* mediocrity **13B**

poco/a *adj.* little **2B**

poco: un poco *loc. adv.* a little **2B**

pocos/as *adj.* few **2A**

poder *v.* to be able to; **¿Los puedo ver?** *exp.* Can I see them? **3B**; **no puede olvidarse** *v.* cannot be forgotten **10B**; **Yo puedo…** *v.* I can… **0**

poderse: No se puede… *v.* You/One can't… **7B**

poema *m.* poem **10B**

poeta *m./f.* poet **10B**

poetisa *f.* poet **10B**

policía *f.* police **0**

polideportivo *m.* sports center **2A**

políglota *adj.* multilingual **1B**

política *f.* policy **6A**; politics **16A**; **ciencias políticas** *f.* political science **1B**

político/a *m./f.* politician **16A**

político/a: partido político *m.* political party **16A**

Polo Norte *m.* North Pole **18A**

polvo *m.* powder; **cacao en polvo** *m.* cocoa powder **15A**; **leche descremada en polvo** *f.* powdered skim milk **15A**

pólvora *f.* gunpowder **18A**

poner *v.* to put **4A**; **Me pone…** *exp.* Give me… **4A**; **poner (a alguien) al día** *v.* to update (someone) **17B**; **poner al día** *v.* to bring up to date **7B**; **poner atención (a)** *v.* to pay attention (to) **0**; **poner en marcha** *exp.* to set in motion **16A**

ponerse: ponerse contento/a *v.* to become happy **18B**; **ponerse triste** *v.* to become sad **18B**

popular *adj.* popular **2B**; **fiesta popular** *f.* festival **6A**; **unidad popular** *f.* unity of the people **16A**

por *prep.* for, by; **¿Por qué no…?** *exp.* Why don't you? **6A**; **¿Por qué…?** *interrog.* Why…? **6A**; **baja por maternidad** *f.* maternity leave **7B**; **cien por ciento** *exp.* one hundred percent **12A**; **hablar por hablar** *v.* to talk for the sake of it **14B**; **licencia por maternidad** *f.* maternity leave **7B**; **Más despacio, por favor.** *exp.* Slower, please. **0**; **navegar por Internet** *v.* to surf the Internet **6A**; **pasar por** *v.* to go via **6B**; **por tu bien** *exp.* for your own good **15B**; **por cierto** *exp.* by the way, incidentally **10A**; **por eso** *conj.* therefore **17A**; **por favor** *exp.* please **2B**; **por fin** *exp.* at last **10A**; **por la mañana** *loc. adv.* in the morning **3A**; **por la noche** *loc. adv.* in the evening; at night **3A**; **por la tarde** *loc. adv.* in the afternoon **3A**; **por lo tanto** *conj.* therefore **17A**; **por medio de** *loc. prep.* by means of **14B**; **por otro lado/por otra parte** *loc. adv.* on the other hand **13B**; **por un lado/por una parte** *loc. adv.* on the one hand **13B**; **por vocación** *loc. adv.* by vocation **7A**

porción *f.* serving **15A**

porqué *m.* reason **17B**

portada *f.* cover **3B**

portavoz *m. y f.* spokesperson **12B**

porteño/a *adj.* of/from the city of Buenos Aires **17B**

Portugal *m.* Portugal **1A**

portugués *m.* Portuguese **1B**

portugués/portuguesa *adj.* Portuguese **1B**

posada *f.* inn **11B**

posguerra *f.* postwar period **14B**

posibilidad *f.* possibility **6A**

posible *adj.* possible **4A**; **lo más… posible** *m.* as… as possible **17A**

positivo/a *adj.* positive **2B**

posponer *v.* to postpone **18A**

postal *f.* postcard **9B**

póster *m.* poster **4A**

postergar *v.* to postpone **17B**

postre *m.* dessert **2B**

postularse *v.* to apply **13B**

potenciar *v.* to foster **15A**

practicar *v.* to practice **0**; **practicar tirolesa** *v.* to go zip-lining **18A**

práctico/a *adj.* practical **3B**

prado *m.* meadow **9A**

precio *m.* price **4A**

precioso/a *adj.* lovely **2A**

predicción *f.* prediction **17A**

preferido/a *adj.* favorite **3B**

pregunta *f.* question **0**; **plantearse preguntas** *v.* to question **14B**

preguntar *v.* to ask **14B**

premio *m.* award; prize **2B**; **Premio Nobel** *m.* Nobel Prize **10B**

prenda *f.* garment **3B**

prensa *f.* press **9B**; **nota de prensa** *f.* press release **10B**; **oficina de prensa** *f.* press office **16A**; **prensa económica** *f.* financial press **3A**; **prensa rosa** *f.* gossip press **9B**; **rueda de prensa** *f.* press conference **12B**

preocupación *f.* worry; concern **7A**

preocupado/a *adj.* worried **12A**

preocupar *v.* to worry; to concern **7A**; **No te preocupes.** *exp.* Don't worry. **13B**

preparar *v.* to prepare **7A**; **preparar un viaje** *v.* to organize a trip **13A**

presencia *f.* presence **8B**

presentación: carta de presentación *f.* cover letter **13B**

presentar *v.* to introduce, to present **0**

preservar *v.* to preserve **15A**

presidente/a *m./f.* president **16A**

presión *f.* pressure **4B**

preso/a *m./f.* prisoner **16A**

prestar *v.* to lend **9A**

prestigioso/a *adj.* prestigious **10A**

pretender *v.* to try to **15B**

pretexto *m.* pretext **16A**

prevención *f.* prevention **10A**

primario/a: escuela primaria *f.* elementary school **9A**

primavera *f.* spring **10A**

primero/a *adj.* first **14A**; **primer +** *m.*: **primer plato** *m.* first course **2B**

primo/a *m./f.* cousin **5B**

primogénito/a *m./f.* firstborn **12A**

principal *adj.* main **4B**; **plato principal** *m.* main course **2B**

príncipe *m.* prince; **Puerto Príncipe** *m.* Port-au-Prince **12B**

principio: a principios del siglo XX *loc. adv.* at the beginning of the 20th century **8B**

privacidad *f.* privacy **17A**

privado/a *adj.* private **4B**; **escuela privada** *f.* private school **15B**

privatizado/a *adj.* privatized **13A**

privilegiado/a *m./f.* privileged person **2A**

probabilidad *f.* probability **15A**

probable *adj.* probable **17A**

probablemente *adv.* probably **4A**

probar *v.* to taste **16B**; **probar suerte** *v.* to try one's luck **5A**

problema *m.* problem **2A**; **¡No hay**

problema! *exp.* No problem! **7B**
procedencia *f.* origin **8B**
procedente: procedente de *adj.* arriving from **13A**
procesión *f.* procession **16B**
procurar *v.* to try to **14B**
productividad *f.* productivity **6A**
producto *m.* product **3B**; **producto de alimentación** *m.* food product **15A**; **producto ecológico** *m.* organic product **15A**; **producto fresco** *m.* fresh food **15A**; **producto interior bruto (PIB)** *m.* gross domestic product (GDP) **11A**
productor(a) *m./f.* producer **3B**
profesión *f.* profession **1B**
profesional *m. y f.* professional **3A**
profesional *adj.* professional **2B**; **experiencia profesional** *f.* professional experience **11B**; **formación profesional** *f.* professional training **14A**; **orientador(a) profesional** *m./f.* career counselor **13B**
profesionalidad *f.* professionalism **2B**
profesor(a) *m./f.* teacher **1B**
programa *m.* program **9A**; **programa de intercambio** *m.* exchange program **14A**; **programa de radio** *m.* radio program **3A**
programar *v.* to plan **3A**
promoción *f.* graduating class **9A**; promotion **9B**; **campaña de promoción** *f.* promotional campaign **16B**
pronóstico *m.* weather forecast **9A**
pronto *adv.* soon **0**; **Hasta pronto.** *exp.* See you soon. **0**
pronunciar *v.* to pronounce **0**
propiamente: propiamente dicho *exp.* per se **16B**
propiedad *f.* property **6A**
propietario/a *m./f.* owner **8B**
proponer *v.* to propose, to suggest **13A**
propósito: a propósito *exp.* incidentally; by the way **10A**
Protagonistas *m. y f.* Protagonists **0**
protector(a): crema solar protectora *f.* sunscreen **10A**
proteger *v.* to protect **3B**
proteína *f.* protein **15A**
protesta *f.* complaint **11A**
protestar *v.* to complain **11A**
provecho: ¡Buen provecho! *exp.* Enjoy your meal. **8A**
provenir de *v.* to come from **16B**
provincia *f.* province **7B**
próximo/a: el próximo mes *loc. adv.* next month **5B**
proyecto *m.* project **4B**
prueba *f.* test **0**
psicología *f.* psychology **6A**
psicólogo/a *m./f.* psychologist **1B**
publicidad *f.* advertisement **6B**; *f.* advertising **16B**
publicista *m. y f.* publicist **14B**
público/a: escuela pública *f.* public school **15B**
pueblo *m.* town **1A**; **pueblo indígena** *m.* native people **16A**
puente *m.* long weekend **6B**
puenting *m.* bungee jumping **18A**
puerta *f.* door; **puerta de embarque** *f.* boarding gate **13A**

Puerto Príncipe *m.* Port-au-Prince **12B**
Puerto Rico *m.* Puerto Rico **0**
puertorriqueño/a *adj.* Puerto Rican **1A**
pues *exp.* well **6A**
puesto *m.* job; position **4B**; stand (in a market) **4A**; **puesto de trabajo** *m.* job **12B**; **puesto directivo** *m.* managerial position **13B**
pulpo *m.* octopus **2B**
pulsera: reloj de pulsera *m.* wristwatch **3B**
punto *m.* point; **punto en común** *m.* point in common **5B**; **punto de encuentro** *m.* meeting point **9A**
puntuación *f.* score, evaluation **11A**
puntual *adj.* punctual **13B**
puntualidad *f.* punctuality **11A**
pupusa *f.* Salvadoran filled tortilla **8B**
pupusería *f.* store where pupusas are sold **8B**
pureza *f.* purity **18B**
puro/a *adj.* pure **7B**; **¡Pura vida!** *exp.* Great! **18B**; **puro habano** *m.* Cuban cigar **3B**

Q

que *rel. pron.* that; **¡Que disfruten a bordo!** *exp.* Enjoy your flight! **13A**; **¡Que tengan un feliz vuelo!** *exp.* Have a good flight! **13A**; **antes de que** *conj.* before **18A**; **así (es) que** *conj.* so **17A**; **Creo que sí/no.** *exp.* I think so/not. **7B**; **desde que** *conj.* since **8B**; **después de que** *conj.* after **18A**; **más que** *adj.* more than **3A**; **menos que** *adj.* less than **3A**; **tener que** *v.* to have to **6A**
qué *interrog.* what; **¡Qué interesante!** *exp.* How interesting! **1B**; **¡Qué tiempos aquellos!** *exp.* Those were the days! **5B**; **¿A qué hora…?** *exp.* At what time…? **3A**; **¿Con qué frecuencia?** *exp.* How often? **3A**; **¿De qué color?** *exp.* What color? **3B**; **¿De qué talla?** *exp.* What size? **3B**; **¿Para qué sirve?** *exp.* What is it used for? **4B**; **¿Qué … eliges?** *exp.* Which… do you choose? **1A**; **¿Qué desean tomar?** *exp.* What would you like (to have)? **2B**; **¿Qué es?** *exp.* What is it? **1A**; **¿Qué hora es?** *exp.* What time is it? **3A**; **¿Qué tal está(n)…?** *exp.* How is/are…? **2B**; **¿Qué te/le pasa?** (*fam./form.*) *exp.* What's wrong? **10A**; **¿Qué tiempo hace?** *exp.* What's the weather like? **10A**
quechua *m.* Quechua **1B**
quedar *v.* to (arrange to) meet **8A**
quedarse *v.* to stay **8B**; **quedarse en blanco** *exp.* to draw a blank **15B**
queja *f.* complaint **11A**; **libro de quejas** *m.* complaint form **11A**
quemar *v.* to burn **18B**
querer *v.* to want **3B**; **querer a alguien** *v.* to love someone **12A**; **quería decir** *exp.* I meant… **12B**
quererse *v.* to love each other **17B**
queso *m.* cheese **2B**
quién *interrog.* who **1A**; **¿Quién es?** *exp.* Who is it? **1A**
química *f.* chemistry **1B**
químico/a *m./f.* chemist **8B**
quince: fiesta de quince años *f.* fifteenth birthday party **18B**

quinceañera *f.* fifteen-year-old girl **5A**
quinto/a *adj.* fifth **14A**
quiosco *m.* kiosk **9B**
quiosquero/a *m./f.* kiosk attendant **9B**
quitar *v.* to take away **16A**
quizá(s) *adv.* perhaps **17A**

R

ración *f.* portion **2B**
racional *adj.* rational **16A**
radio *f.* radio **4B**; **cadena de radio** *f.* radio network **14B**; **escuchar la radio** *v.* to listen to the radio **2A**; **programa de radio** *m.* radio program **3A**
rafting *m.* rafting **18A**
ramo *m.* bouquet **9B**; **ramo de flores** *m.* bunch of flowers **18B**
rápido/a *adj.* fast **17A**
raqueta *f.* racket **18A**
raro/a *adj.* strange, odd; **parecer raro** *v.* to seem strange **15B**
rasgo *m.* characteristic **14A**
ratón *m.* mouse **7B**
razón *f.* reason; **tener razón** *v.* to be right **10B**
real: la Familia Real *f.* the royal family **4B**
realidad *f.* reality; **hacer realidad** *v.* to make something happen **8B**
realista *adj.* realistic **12A**
realizado/a: sentirse realizado/a *v.* to feel fulfilled **13B**
realizar *v.* to do; to perform **5A**
rebaja *f.* discount **3B**
rebelde *adj.* rebel **15B**
rebién *adv.* very well **17B**
recepción *f.* pickup **11A**
receptor(a): país receptor *m.* host country **8B**
receta (de cocina) *f.* recipe **8A**
recetario *m.* recipe collection **15A**
rechazar *v.* to reject **16A**
recibir *v.* receive **2B**
reciclable: envase reciclable *m.* recyclable container **15A**
reciclado/a *adj.* recycled **8A**
reciclaje *m.* recycling **15A**
reciclar(se) *v.* to recycle (oneself) **11B**
recién *adv.* just **17B**
recoger *v.* to pick up **5B**
recogido/a *adj.* picked **15A**
recomendación *f.* recommendation **6A**
recomendado/a *adj.* recommended **4A**
recomendar (un lugar) *v.* to recommend (a place) **13A**
recompensa *f.* reward **8B**
récord: batir un récord *v.* to break a record **18A**
recordar *v.* to remember **5A**
recorrer *v.* to travel **5A**
recto *adv.* straight **9B**
recuadro *m.* box **0**
recuerdo *m.* memory; souvenir **5B**
recurso *m.* resource, means **12B**; **recurso económico** *m.* economic resource **14A**; **Recursos Humanos (RR.HH.)** *m.* Human Resources (HR) **13B**; **recurso natural** *m.* natural resource **14A**; **sin recursos** *loc. adj.* in need **15A**
Recursos Humanos (RR.HH.) *m., pl.* Human Resources (HR) **13B**
red *f.* network **9A**; **red social** *f.* social

network **13B**; **red Wi-Fi** *f.* Wi-Fi
network **13B**

redactar *v.* to write **0**

reducir *v.* to reduce **16A**

redundar en *v.* to benefit **17A**

reencontrar *v.* to meet again **9A**

reencuentro *m.* reunion **6B**

referente: referente latino *m.* Hispanic
icon **1A**

reformular *v.* to restate **8B**

refresco *m.* soft drink **4A**

refrigerador *m.* refrigerator **8A**

regalarse *v.* to give oneself **6B**

regalo *m.* present **3B**; **cheque-regalo** *m.*
gift voucher **3B**; **tienda de regalos** *f.* gift
shop **3B**

regatear *v.* to bargain **4A**

regiomontano/a *adj.* born in
Monterrey **12A**

regla: en regla *loc. adv.* in order;
valid **11A**

regresar *v.* to return **8B**

regular *adv.* so-so **8A**

Reino Unido *m.* United Kingdom **8B**

reír *v.* to laugh **6A**

reírse *v.* to laugh **17B**

relación *f.* relationship **5B**; **Relaciones
Internacionales** *f.* International
Relations **11B**

relacionar *v.* to match, to relate **0**

relacionarse *v.* to interact **13B**; to run in
the same circles **10B**

relajación *f.* relaxation **6A**

relajado/a *adj.* relaxed **3A**

relajante *adj.* relaxing **6A**

relieve *m.* terrain **18B**

religión *f.* religion **8A**

religioso/a *adj.* religious **8A**

rellenar *v.* to fill in **0**

relleno/a *adj.* stuffed, filled (with food) **16B**

reloj *m.* clock; watch **3A**; **reloj (de pulsera)**
m. (wrist)watch **3B**

remedio *m.* remedy **10A**

remo: bote de remos *m.* rowboat **18A**

remolacha *f.* beet **15A**

remontar *v.* to surmount **18A**

rendimiento *m.* performance **13B**

rendir *v.* to perform **6A**

renovable *adj.* renewable **17A**

renta: renta per cápita *f.* per capita
income **14A**

renunciar a *v.* to give up **16A**

repartir *v.* to deliver **7B**

repartir *v.* to distribute **12B**

reparto: reparto a domicilio *m.* home
delivery **7B**

repelente *m.* repellent **10A**

repetir *v.* to repeat **0**

reportaje *m.* article **14B**

reportero/a *m./f.* reporter **7B**

representante *m. y f.* representative **10B**

representar *v.* to represent **10B**; to
role-play **0**

reproductor(a): reproductor de MP3 *m.*
MP3 player **13B**

República Dominicana *f.* Dominican
Republic **0**

requisito: reunir los requisitos *v.* to meet
the requirements **13B**

rescatar *v.* to rescue **18B**

reseña *f.* summary; review **9A**

reserva *f.* reservation **6B**

reservar *v.* to set aside **6A**; to reserve, to
book **6B**; **reservar los billetes** *v.* to book
the tickets **13A**

resfriado/a: estar resfriado/a *v.* to have a
cold **10A**

residencia: residencia de estudiantes *f.*
dorm **12A**

resistente *adj.* strong, tough **17A**

resolución: resolución de conflictos *f.*
conflict resolution **13B**

respaldo: respaldo del asiento *m.* seat
back **13A**

respecto: con respecto a *loc. prep.*
regarding **16A**

respetar *v.* to respect **8A**

respeto *m.* respect **14A**

respetuoso/a *adj.* respectful **12A**

respirar *v.* to breathe **7B**

responder *v.* to answer **0**

responsabilidad *f.* responsibility **9A**

responsable *m. y f.* person in charge **13A**

responsable *adj.* responsible **3B**

respuesta *f.* answer **0**

restaurante *m.* restaurant **0**

restaurar *v.* to restore **11A**

resto *m.* rest; **el resto de** *m.* the rest
of **12B**; **el resto de la clase** *m.* the rest
of the class **0**

resultado *m.* result **12B**

resumen *m.* summary; **en resumen** *exp.* in
short **18B**

resumir *v.* to summarize **0**

retirar *v.* to remove **13B**

reto *m.* challenge; **reto deportivo** *m.* sports
challenge **18A**; **superar retos** *v.* to
overcome challenges **18A**

retrasarse *v.* to be late **15B**

retraso *m.* delay **11A**; **con retraso** *loc. adv.*
delayed **13A**

retrato *m.* portrait **14B**

reunión *f.* meeting **7B**

reunir *v.* to collect **15A**

reunir *v.* to gather **0**; **reunir los requisitos** *v.*
to meet the requirements **13B**

reunir(se) *v.* to meet; to gather **6A**

revisar *v.* to review **0**

revista *f.* magazine **9B**; **revista del corazón**
f. gossip magazine **9B**

revivir *v.* to relive **14B**

revolución *f.* revolution **13B**

revuelta *f.* revolt **14A**

rezagado/a *adj.* lagging behind **17A**

rico/a *adj.* rich **7A**; tasty **2B**

ridículo/a *adj.* ridiculous **15B**

riesgo *m.* risk **7A**

rincón *m.* spot, place **11A**

río *m.* river **3A**

riqueza *f.* richness **11B**; wealth **14A**

ritmo *m.* rhythm **17B**; **ritmo de vida** *m.*
pace of life **3A**

rito *m.* ritual **6A**

ritual *m.* ritual **14A**

rizado/a *adj.* curly **12A**

rodar *v.* to shoot, to film **9B**

rodeado/a de *loc. adv.* surrounded by **6B**

rodear *v.* to circle **0**

rojo/a *adj.* red **3B**

romanticismo *m.* romanticism **12A**

romántico/a *adj.* romantic **2A**

romper *v.* to break **16A**

ropa *f.* clothes, clothing; **tienda de ropa** *f.*
clothing store **3B**

rosa *f.* rose **18B**; **prensa rosa** *f.* gossip
press **9B**

rosado/a *adj.* pink **18B**

rosca: tapa de rosca *f.* screw top **8A**

rubio/a *adj.* blond(e) **12A**

rueda: rueda de prensa *f.* press
conference **12B**

ruido *m.* noise **2A**

ruinas *f.* ruins **2A**

rumbo: caminar sin rumbo fijo *v.* to wander
aimlessly **17B**

rural *adj.* rural **11A**

ruta *f.* route **6B**

rutina *f.* routine **7A**; **rutina diaria** *f.* daily
routine **3A**

S

sábado *m.* Saturday **3A**

saber *v.* to know; **saber (algo) (de)** *v.* to
know (something) (about) **8A**

sabiduría *f.* wisdom **17B**

sabor *m.* flavor **15A**

saborear *v.* to savor **16B**

sabroso/a *adj.* tasty **15A**

sacrificio: exigir sacrificios *v.* to require
sacrifices **13A**

sal *f.* salt **8A**

sala *f.* ward **10A**; **sala de llegada** *f.* arrival
lounge/area **13A**

salado/a *adj.* salty **2B**

salchicha *f.* sausage **4A**

Sale *exp.* Come on! **8A**

salida *f.* departure **6A**; **hora de salida** *f.*
departure time **13A**

salir *v.* to depart **13A**; **salir (con amigos)** *v.*
to go out (with friends) **3A**; **salir de** *v.* to
leave **3A**

salón *m.* living room **4B**; **baile de salón** *m.*
ballroom dance **17B**; **salón de fiestas** *m.*
function hall **18B**; **Salón Internacional
de la Moda** *m.* International Fashion
Fair **3B**; **salón-comedor** *m.* living room-
dining room **4B**

salsa *f.* salsa **1A**; **bacalao en salsa**
m. cod with sauce **2B**; **salsa golf** *f.*
sauce similar to Thousand Island
dressing **17A**

salud *f.* health **7A**

saludarse *v.* to greet each other **17B**

saludo *m.* greeting **0**

salvadoreño/a *adj.* Salvadoran **8B**

salvar *v.* to save **9B**

salvavidas (*invar.***)** *m. y f.* lifeguard **10A**

sándwich *m.* sandwich **2B**

sangre *f.* blood **17A**

sanitario/a: asistencia sanitaria *f.* health
care **10A**

sanjuanero/a *adj.* from San Juan **11A**

sano/a *adj.* healthy **5B**

sartén *f.* frying pan **8A**

satisfacción *f.* satisfaction **11A**;
satisfacción personal *f.* personal
satisfaction **13B**

sección *f.* section **8B**

seco/a *adj.* dry **15A**

secretaría *f.* ministry, department **16A**
secretario/a *m./f.* secretary **1B**
sector *m.* sector **8B; sector energético** *m.* energy sector **14A**
secuestrado/a *m./f.* kidnap victim **16A**
secuestro *m.* kidnap victim **16A**
sede *f.* headquarters **9A**
sedentarismo *m.* sedentary lifestyle **16B**
seguir *v.* to continue, to keep going **9B;** to go on, to keep (on) **11B**
Segunda Guerra Mundial *f.* World War II **18A**
seguridad *f.* safety **13A;** security **17A; cinturón de seguridad** *m.* seat belt **13A**
seguro/a *adj.* sure, safe; **estar seguro/a de sí mismo/a** *v.* to be self-confident **18A; Seguro que…** *exp.* I'm sure (that)… **9A**
seleccionar *v.* to select **0**
sello *m.* stamp; **sello discográfico** *m.* record label **17B**
selva *f.* jungle **16A**
semana *f.* week **2B; día de la semana** *m.* day of the week **3A; esta semana** *loc. adv.* this week **6A; fin de semana** *m.* weekend **2B; la semana pasada** *loc. adv.* last week **5A; los fines de semana** *loc. adv.* (on) weekends **5B; Semana Santa** *f.* Easter; Holy Week **5A; una vez a la semana** *loc. adv.* once a week **6A**
semanal: agenda semanal *f.* (weekly) planner **3A**
semi: semi-cama *adj.* semi-sleeper **13A**
senderismo *m.* hiking **11B**
sensibilización *f.* increased awareness **16A**
sensibilizar *v.* to raise awareness **16A**
sensible *adj.* sensitive; **ser sensible a** *v.* to be sensitive to **10A**
sentimiento *m.* feeling; **expresar un sentimiento** *v.* to express a feeling **18B**
sentir *v.* to be sorry; **Lo siento.** *exp.* I'm sorry. **3B; Siento oír eso.** *exp.* I'm sorry to hear that. **13B; Siento verte así.** *exp.* I'm sorry to see you like this. **13B**
sentirse *v.* to feel; **sentirse acompañado/a** *v.* to feel accompanied **9A; sentirse como en casa** *v.* to feel at home **16B; sentirse realizado/a** *v.* to feel fulfilled **13B**
señalar *v.* to indicate **0**
señor(a) *m./f.* sir/madam **6B; Estimados señores:** *exp.* Dear sirs: **6B**
señora *f.* Mrs. **2A**
señorita *f.* young lady; Miss **0**
separado/a *adj.* separated **12A**
separarse *v.* to split up, to separate **12A**
septiembre *m.* September **5A**
ser *v.* to be **1A; ¿Cómo es…?** *exp.* What is… like? **2A; ¿Cuánto es?** *exp.* How much is it? **2B; ¿Qué es?** *exp.* What is it? **1A; ¿Qué hora es?** *exp.* What time is it? **3A; ¿Quién es?** *exp.* Who is it? **1A; es posible** *exp.* it's possible **4A; o sea** *exp.* that is **8B; ser afín** *v.* to have a lot in common **17B; ser bueno/a (en algo)** *v.* to be good (at something) **17B; ser hincha de** *v.* to be a supporter of **17B; ser humano** *m.* human being **8A; ser líder de audiencia** *v.* to be the highest rated **14B; ser malo/a (en algo)** *v.* to be bad (at something) **17B; ser moneda**

corriente *exp.* to be common **13B; ser sensible a** *v.* to be sensitive to **10A; ser todo oídos** *exp.* to be all ears **9A; ser un(a) gran comunicador(a)** *v.* to be a great communicator **13B; ser verdad** *v.* to be true **10B; Son 9 euros.** *exp.* It's 9 euros. **2B; Yo soy de Madrid.** *exp.* I'm from Madrid. **1A; Yo soy…** *exp.* I am… **0**
serie *f.* series; **emitir la serie** *v.* to broadcast the TV series **14B; fabricar en serie** *v.* to mass-produce **13B; pasar la serie de televisión** *v.* to broadcast the television series **14B; serie de televisión** *f.* television series **14B**
serio/a *adj.* serious **12A;** reliable **13B**
serrano/a: jamón serrano *m.* Serrano ham **2B**
servicio *m.* service; **a tu servicio** *loc. adv.* at your service **7B; servicio doméstico** *m.* domestic service **8B; Servicios Sociales** *m.* Social Services **5B; industria de servicios** *f.* service industry **14A**
servir para *v.* to be good for… **4B; ¿Para qué sirve?** *exp.* What is it used for? **4B**
sevillanas *f.* popular dance originated in Seville **17B**
sí *adv.* yes **1A; alejados entre sí** *loc. adv.* far from each other **17B; Creo que sí.** *exp.* I think so. **7B; estar seguro/a de sí mismo/a** *v.* to be self-confident **18A**
siempre *adv.* always **2B; casi siempre** *loc. adv.* almost always **14A; para siempre** *loc. adv.* forever **8B**
siesta *f.* nap **6A; dormir la siesta** *v.* to take a nap **6A**
sigla *f.* acronym **12B**
siglo *m.* century; **a finales del siglo XIX** *loc. adv.* toward the end of the 19th century **8B; a principios del siglo XX** *loc. adv.* at the beginning of the 20th century **8B**
significar *v.* to mean; **¿Qué significa…?** *exp.* What does… mean? **0**
siguiente *adj.* following/next… **0**
silencio *m.* silence **6A**
silla *f.* chair **4B**
sillón *m.* armchair **4B**
silvestre *adj.* wild **18B**
simbolizar *v.* to symbolize **18B**
símbolo *m.* symbol **8A**
simpatía *f.* friendliness **2B;** affection **18B**
simpático/a *adj.* nice **2A**
sin *prep.* without; **caminar sin rumbo fijo** *v.* to wander aimlessly **17B; sin embargo** *conj.* however **5A; sin recursos** *adj.* in need **15A**
sincronizada: el/la nadador(a) de sincronizada *m./f.* synchronized swimmer **18A**
sintetizar *v.* to synthesize **13B**
síntoma *m.* symptom **10A**
sistema *m.* system; **sistema inmunológico** *m.* immune system **17A**
sitio *m.* place **11B;** *m.* room; space **9B; sitio web** *m.* Web site **14B**
sobre *prep.* on, about; **sobre la base de** *loc. prep.* based upon **16A; sobre todo** *loc. adv.* above all **13B**
sobreproteger *v.* to overprotect **15B**
sobrevivir *v.* to survive **13B**

sobrino/a *m./f.* nephew/niece **18A**
social *adj.* social **6A; ciencias sociales** *f.* social studies **15B; justicia social** *f.* social justice **16A; movilización social** *f.* social mobilization **16A; red social** *f.* social network **13B; Servicios Sociales** *m.* Social Services **5B**
sociedad *f.* society **9A**
socorro *m.* help **12B**
sofá *m.* sofa **4B**
sol *m.* sun **4B; gafas de sol** *f.* sunglasses **3B; hacer sol** *v.* to be sunny **10A; tomar el sol** *v.* to sunbathe **10A**
solar: crema solar protectora *f.* sunscreen **10A**
soler *v.* to usually do something **14A**
solicitar *v.* to request **4A**
solicitud *f.* application **13B**
solidarizarse (con) *v.* to support someone **14B**
solo/a *adj.* alone **7A; café solo** *m.* black coffee **2B**
solo/solamente *adv.* only **13B**
soltero/a *adj.* single **5B; despedida de soltero/a** *f.* bachelor(ette) party **18B**
solucionar *v.* to solve **10A**
soneto *m.* sonnet **10B**
sonoro/a: banda sonora *f.* sound track **17B**
sonreír *v.* to smile **13A**
sonrisa *f.* smile **10A**
sopa *f.* soup; **sopa de pescado** *f.* fish soup **2B**
sordo/a *adj.* deaf **12B**
sorprendente *adj.* surprising **18A**
sorprender *v.* to surprise **15B**
sorpresa *f.* surprise **17B**
sorteo *m.* drawing **9B;** *m.* lottery **12B**
soso/a *adj.* bland, lacking salt **2B**
sostenible *adj.* sustainable **17A**
souvenir *m.* souvenir **4A**
Sr./Sra. *m./f.* Mr./Mrs. **2A**
su *adj.* your/his/her/its **2A**
subir *v.* to climb **5A**
submarinismo *m.* scuba diving **11B**
subrayar *v.* to underline **0**
subsahariana: el África subsahariana *f.* sub-Saharan Africa **14A**
subte *m.* subway **4A**
subterráneo *m.* subway **4A**
suceder *v.* to happen **14A**
sudamericano/a *adj.* South American **18A**
sueldo *m.* salary **14B;** wage(s) **3B**
sueño *m.* dream **8B; cumplir (sus) sueños** *v.* to make (his/her) dreams come true **15B**
suerte *f.* (good) luck **8B; probar suerte** *v.* to try one's luck **5A**
suéter *m.* sweater **3B**
suficiente *adj.* enough **6A**
suflé *m.* soufflé **15A**
sufrir *v.* to suffer **12B**
sujetar *v.* to hold **8A**
sumario *m.* table of contents **1B**
suministrar *v.* to administer **17A**
superar: superar retos *v.* to overcome challenges **18A**
superarse *v.* to outdo oneself **18A**
superdifícil *adj.* extremely difficult **11B**
superficie *f.* area **2A**
supervisor(a) *m./f.* supervisor **13A**
suplemento: suplemento dominical *m.*

Sunday supplement **9B**
sur *m.* south **2A**
surfista *m. y f.* surfer **16B**
surgir *v.* to come up **15A**
suspenso *m.* failure **15B**
sustituir *v.* to replace **14A**
sutil *adj.* subtle **18B**

T

tabla *f.* chart, table **0**
tachar *v.* to cross out **0**
taco *m.* taco **2B**
taichí *m.* tai chi **8A**
tailandés *m.* Thai **7A**
Tailandia Thailand **7A**
talento *m.* talent **11B**
talla *f.* size **3B**; **¿De qué talla?** *exp.* What
    size? **3B**
taller *m.* workshop; **taller mecánico** *m.*
    repair shop **7B**
también *adv.* too **1B**
tampoco *adv.* not . . . either, neither **10B**
tan *adv.* so; **tan... como** *conj.* as … as **8B**
tanto *adv.* so much
tanto/a *adj.* so much
tantos/as *adj.* as many **8B**
tanto: tanto… como *conj.* as much/many…
    as **8B**; **tanto … como** *conj.* both …
    and **7A**
tapa *f.* tapa **2B**; **tapa de rosca** *f.* screw top **8A**
tapear *v.* to eat tapas **2B**
tapiz (pl. tapices) *m.* tapestry **3B**
taquigrafía *f.* shorthand **13B**
tarde *f.* afternoon; *adv.* late **7A**; **Buenas
    tardes.** *exp.* Good afternoon. **0**; **de la
    tarde** *loc. adv.* p.m.; in the afternoon **3A**;
    más tarde *loc. adv.* later **17B**; **por la tarde**
    loc. adv. in the afternoon **3A**
tarea *f.* homework **0**
tarifa *f.* fare **13A**
tarjeta *f.* card; **con tarjeta** *loc. adv.* with a
    credit card **3B**; **tarjeta de felicitación**
    f. greeting card **5A**; **tarjeta de visita** *f.*
    business card **18B**
taxi *m.* taxi **0**
taza *f.* cup **2B**
te *pron.* you, to you
té *m.* tea **2B**
teatro *m.* theater **1A**
técnico/a: técnico/a informático/a *m./f.*
    computer technician **1B**
tecnología *f.* technology **8A**
tecnológico/a *adj.* technological **17A**
tela *f.* (piece of) cloth; fabric **8A**
tele *f.* television **3A**
telefonía *f.* phone service **9B**
teléfono *m.* phone; **¿Cuál es tu número
    de teléfono?** *exp.* What is your phone
    number? **1B**; **llamada de teléfono** *f.*
    (phone) call **3A**; **teléfono celular** *m.*
    cell phone **1B**; **teléfono inteligente** *m.*
    smartphone **13B**
telenovela *f.* soap opera **5A**
telespectador(a) *m./f.* television viewer **14B**
televidente *m.* TV viewer **9A**
televisión *f.* television **3A**; **pasar la serie de
    televisión** *v.* to broadcast the television
    series **14B**; **serie de televisión** *f.*
    television series **14B**

televisor *m.* television (set) **4B**
temperatura *f.* temperature **10A**; **hace 30 ºC
    de temperatura** *v.* the temperature is
    30º C **10A**
temporada: temporada alta *f.* high season **4B**
temporalmente *adv.* temporarily **8B**
temprano *adv.* early **7A**
tendencia *f.* trend **17A**
tener *v.* to have **2A**; **¡Que tengan un feliz
    vuelo!** *exp.* Have a good flight! **13A**;
    tener canas *v.* to have gray hair **17B**;
    tener capacidad *v.* to have (storage)
    capacity **13B**; **tener clase** *v.* to have
    class **3A**; **tener confianza en** *v.* to trust
    in **5B**; **tener en cuenta** *v.* to take into
    account **16B**; **tener frío/calor** *v.* to
    be cold/hot **10A**; **tener lugar** *v.* to be
    held **16B**; **tener que** *v.* to have to **6A**;
    tener razón *v.* to be right **10B**; **tener un
    hijo** *v.* to have a child **8B**
tenis *m.* tennis **1A**
tenista *m. y f.* tennis player **14A**
tenso/a *adj.* tense **10A**
terapia *f.* therapy **3A**
tercero/a *adj.* third **14A**
tercio *m.* a third **16B**
termas *f.* hot springs **6B**
terminación *f.* ending **0**
terminal *f.* terminal **13A**
terminar *v.* to end **3A**
ternera: filete de ternera *m.* fillet of
    veal **2B**
terraza *f.* balcony **4B**
terrible *adj.* terrible **15B**
territorio *m.* territory **16A**
terrorismo *m.* terrorism **16A**
tertulia *f.* roundtable; talk show **9A**
tesoro *m.* treasure **10A**
test *m.* test **1A**
testigo *m. y f.* witness **10B**
testimonio *m.* testimony **8B**
tetería *f.* tearoom **8B**
texto *m.* reading, textbook **0**
tía *f.* aunt **5B**
tico/a (fam.) *adj.*; *m./f.* Costa Rican **18B**
tiempo *m.* time **3A**; weather **10A**; **¡Qué
    tiempos aquellos!** *exp.* Those were the
    days! **5B**; **¿Cuánto tiempo (hace)…?**
    exp. How long have/has? **8B**; **¿Qué
    tiempo hace?** *exp.* What's the weather
    like? **10A**; **a tiempo** *loc. adv.* in/on
    time **7B**; **al mismo tiempo** *loc. adv.* at
    the same time **7A**; **buen tiempo** *m.* good
    weather **2A**; **hacer buen/mal tiempo** *v.*
    there is good/bad weather **10A**; **tiempo
    libre** *m.* free time **5B**; **tiempo para uno/a
    mismo/a** *m.* time for oneself **3A**
tienda *f.* store **2A**; **tienda de alimentación**
    f. grocery store **4A**; **tienda de campaña**
    f. tent **18A**; **tienda de discos** *f.* music
    store **3B**; **tienda de regalos** *f.* gift shop **3B**;
    tienda de ropa *f.* clothing store **3B**
tierno/a *adj.* affectionate **9A**
tierra *f.* land, dirt **9A**
tímido/a *adj.* shy **12A**
tío *m.* uncle **5B**
típico/a *adj.* typical **2A**
tipo *m.* type **12A**
tirano/a *m./f.* tyrant **13B**
tiren el dado *exp.* roll the die **10A**

tirolesa *f.* zip-lining **18A**; **practicar tirolesa**
    v. to go zip-lining **18A**
titular *m.* headline **16A**
título *m.* degree **13B**
tocar *v.* to touch; **¿A quién le toca?** *exp.*
    Whose turn is it? **4A**; **Me toca a mí.** *exp.*
    It's my turn. **4A**; **tocar (un instrumento)**
    v. to play (an instrument) **8A**
tocayo/a *m./f.* namesake **12A**
todavía *adv.* still; **todavía no** *loc. adv.* not
    yet **6A**
todo *pron.* all, everything **2A**; **a pesar de
    todo** *loc. adv.* in spite of everything **13B**;
    sobre todo *loc. adv.* above all **13B**
todo/a *adj.* all; **todo el día** *loc. adv.* all
    day **6A**; **todos los días** *loc. adv.* every
    day **3A**; **todo recto** *loc. adv.* straight
    ahead
Toledo *m.* Toledo **1A**
tolerancia *f.* tolerance **14A**
tomar *v.* to take **9B**; **¿Qué desean tomar?**
    exp. What would you like (to have)? **2B**;
    tomar el ferry *v.* to take the ferry **3A**;
    tomar el sol *v.* to sunbathe **10A**; **tomar
    fotos** *v.* to take pictures **6B**
tomate *m.* tomato **4A**; **tomate frito** *m.*
    tomato sauce **15A**
tópico *m.* topic; cliché **16B**
toque *m.* touch **15A**
tormenta *f.* storm **10B**
tornarse *v.* to become **17A**
torneo *m.* tournament **10B**; **ganar torneos**
    v. to win tournaments **18A**
tortilla *f.* (Mexican) tortilla; **tortilla
    española** *f.* Spanish potato omelet **2B**
tostada *f.* toast **2B**
trabajador(a) *m./f.* worker **3A**; **madre
    trabajadora** *f.* working mother **7B**
trabajar *v.* to work **1B**; **ir a trabajar** *v.* to go to
    work **3A**; **trabajar como** *v.* to work as **11B**
trabajo *m.* job **1B**; **bolsa de trabajo** *m.*
    job placement office **13B**; **cambiar
    de trabajo** *m.* to change jobs **7B**;
    compañero/a de trabajo *m.* coworker **5B**;
    contrato de trabajo *m.* employment
    contract **13B**; **equipo de trabajo** *m.*
    work team **13B**; **horario de trabajo** *m.*
    work schedule **3A**; **puesto de trabajo** *m.*
    job **12B**; **trabajo voluntario** *m.* volunteer
    work **7A**
trabalenguas *m.* tongue twister **6A**
tradición *f.* tradition **2B**
tradicional *adj.* traditional **4A**
traducir *v.* to translate **7A**
traer *v.* to bring **7B**
tráfico *m.* traffic **2A**; **tráfico de armas** *m.*
    arms trade **16A**
traje *m.* suit **3B**
tranquilidad *f.* peace, tranquility **2A**
tranquilo/a *adj.* calm, quiet **2A**
transferencia: transferencia bancaria *f.*
    bank transfer **7B**
transformación *f.* transformation **14B**
transformar *v.* to transform **0**
transfronterizo/a *adj.* cross-border **14A**
transgénico/a: alimento transgénico *m.*
    genetically modified food **15A**
transición: transición democrática *f.*
    democratic transition **14B**
transparente *adj.* transparent **9A**

transportar *v.* to transport **7A**
transporte *m.* transportation;
  medio de transporte *m.* means of
  transportation **4A**
trasladar *v.* to transport **13A**
traspasar *v.* to go beyond **14B**
tratado *m.* treaty **16A**
tratamiento *m.* treatment **12B**
tratar *v.* to be about **14B**
trato *m.* interaction **12B**
trayecto *m.* route **13A**
trekking *m.* hiking **6B**
tren *m.* train **6B**
tres *adj.* three; **tres veces al año** *loc. adv.*
  three times a year **3A**
trigo *m.* wheat **15A**
triste *adj.* sad **12A; ponerse triste** *v.* to
  become sad **18B**
tristeza *f.* sadness **10B**
trompeta *f.* trumpet **7A**
trotamundos *m. y f.* globetrotter **9A**
trotar *v.* to trot **9A**
trovador(a) *m./f.* troubadour **7A**
truco *m.* trick **8A**
tu *adj.* your; **a tu servicio** *loc. adv.* at your
  service **7B**
tú *pron.* you (*sing. fam.*) **1A; ¿Y tú?** *exp.*
  And you? **1A; hablarse de tú** *v.* to
  address somebody as **tú 7B**
tucán *m.* toucan **16B**
tulipán tulip **18B**
turismo *m.* tourism **14A**
turista *m./f.* tourist **1B**
turístico/a *adj.* tourist **16B; destinos
  turísticos** *m.* tourist destinations **4B; el/
  la guía turístico/a** *m./f.* tour guide **1B**
turrón *m.* nougat candy **18B**
tutearse *v.* to use the **tú** form of address **17B**
tuteo *m.* use of **tú 7B**
TV *f.* TV **9A**

u *conj.* or (before a word beginning with **o**
  or **ho**) **11B**
ubicación *f.* location **15A**
ubicado/a *adj.* located **11A**
últimamente *adv.* lately **7A**
último/a *adj.* last **5B; último minuto** *m.* last
  minute **12B**
un(a) *art.* a, an **1A; por un lado/por una
  parte** *loc. adv.* on the one hand **13B; un
  poco** *loc. adv.* a little **2B; una vez a la
  semana** *loc. adv.* once a week **6A**
únicamente *adv.* only **13B**
único/a *adj.* unique **2A**
unidad *f.* unit, unity; **unidad popular** *f.*
  unity of the people **16A**
unión: Unión Europea *f.* European Union **10B**
universal *adj.* universal **17A**
universidad *f.* university **2A**
universitario/a *adj.; m./f.* college
  student **2A; deserción universitaria** *f.*
  college dropouts **15B**
universo *m.* universe **9B**
uno/a *adj. y pron.* one; **tiempo para uno/a
  mismo/a** *m.* time for oneself **3A**
uranio *m.* uranium **14A**
Uruguay *m.* Uruguay **0**
uruguayo/a *adj.* Uruguayan **7A**

usar *v.* to use **0**
uso *m.* custom **16B**
usted *pron.* you (*sing. form.*) **1A; ¿De dónde
  es usted?** *exp.* Where are you from? **1A;
  ¿Y usted?** *exp.* And you? **0; hablarse
  de usted** *v.* to address somebody as
  usted 7B
ustedes *pron.* you (*pl.*) **1A**
utensilio *m.* utensil **15A**
útil *adj.* useful **9A**
utilizar *v.* to use **0**
uva *f.* grape **18B**

vaca *f.* cow **0**
vacaciones *f. pl.* vacation **3A; estar de
  vacaciones** *v.* to be on vacation **7B;
  pasar las vacaciones** *v.* to spend one's
  vacation **4B**
vacío/a *adj.* empty **4B**
vacuna *f.* vaccine **12B**
vacunar *v.* to vaccinate **10A**
Vale *exp.* OK **2B**
valentía *f.* courage **16B**
valer: valer la pena *v.* to be
  worth it **11B**
valerse *v.* to be self-sufficient **5B**
valía *f.* worth **18A**
validar *v.* to validate **14A**
valle *m.* valley **11B**
vals *m.* waltz **17B**
variado/a *adj.* assorted **7B**
variedad *f.* variety **7A**
vasco/a *adj.* Basque **18A**
vecino/a *m./f.* neighbor **4A**
vegetación *f.* vegetation **6B**
vegetariano/a *adj.* vegetarian **15A;
  hacerse vegetariano/a** *v.* to become a
  vegetarian **7B**
vela *f.* candle **5A**
velocidad *f.* speed **13B**
vendedor(a) *m./f.* salesperson; **vendedor(a)
  de lotería** *m./f.* lottery ticket seller **9B**
vender *v.* to sell **8B**
venerar *v.* to venerate **16B**
Venezuela *f.* Venezuela **0**
Venga *exp.* Come on! **8A**
venir *v.* to come **3B**
venta *f.* sale **4B; a la venta** *loc. adv.* for
  sale **4B; ejecutivo/a de ventas** *m./f.* sales
  executive **13B**
ventaja *f.* advantage **9B**
ver *v.* to see **3B; ¿Los puedo ver?** *exp.* Can
  I see them? **3B; a ver** *exp.* let's see... **6A;
  Siento verte así.** *exp.* I'm sorry to see you
  like this. **13B; ver películas** *v.* to watch
  movies **3A**
verano *m.* summer **2A; pasantía de verano**
  f. summer internship **13B**
verdad: ¿De verdad? *exp.* Really? **9B;
  ¿verdad?** *exp.* right? **4A; decir la verdad**
  v. to tell the truth **17B; ..., la verdad** *exp.*
  to tell the truth **2A; ser verdad** *v.* to be
  true **10B**
verdadero/a *adj.* real **12B; ¿Verdadero o
  falso?** *exp.* True or false? **0**
verde *adj.* green **3B**
verduras *f.* vegetables **2B; arroz con
  verduras** *m.* rice with vegetables **2B**

vereda *f.* rural neighborhood **9A**
verse: ¡Nos vemos! *exp.* See you! **0**
versión *f.* version **9B**
vertical *adj.* upright **13A**
vestido *m.* dress **3B**
vestirse *v.* to get dressed **7A**
veterano/a *adj.* veteran **14B**
veterinario/a *m./f.* veterinarian **3A**
vez *f.* time **3A; a veces** *loc. adv.*
  sometimes **2B; de nuevo; otra vez** *loc.
  adv.* again **0; de vez en cuando** *loc. adv.*
  from time to time **14A; dos veces
  al mes** *loc. adv.* twice a month **6A; tal
  vez** *loc. adv.* maybe **17A; tres veces
  al año** *loc. adv.* three times a year **3A;
  una vez a la semana** *loc. adv.* once a
  week **6A**
vía: en vías de desarrollo *adj.*
  developing **3B**
viajar *v.* to travel **3A**
viaje *m.* trip **3B; agencia de viajes** *f.*
  travel agency **4B; estar de viaje** *v.* to
  be away **7A; preparar un viaje** *v.* to
  organize a trip **13A; viaje de negocios**
  m. business trip **3A; viaje de novios** *m.*
  honeymoon **13A; viaje organizado** *m.*
  package tour **13A**
viajero/a *m./f.* traveler **11A**
vida *f.* life; **¡Pura vida!** *exp.* Great! **18B;
  amargarle la vida a alguien** *exp.* to make
  someone's life miserable **17A; calidad de
  vida** *f.* quality of life **2A; cambiar de vida**
  v. to change one's life **7B; el hombre/la
  mujer de mi vida** *exp.* the man/woman of
  my dreams **12A; hacer la vida más fácil**
  exp. to make life easier **17A; llevar una
  vida...** *v.* to lead a... life **10A; medio de
  vida** *m.* way of life **11B; ritmo de vida**
  m. pace of life **3A; vida académica** *f.*
  academic life **14A**
vidrio *m.* (pane of) glass **8A**
viejo/a *adj.* old **5B; casco viejo** *m.* historic
  neighborhood **12B**
viernes *m.* Friday **3A**
vigilante: vigilante nocturno/a *m. y f.* night
  security guard **3A**
vinilo: disco de vinilo *m.* vinyl record **13B**
vino *m.* wine **2B**
viñeta (cómica) *f.* cartoon panel **0**
violencia: no violencia *f.* non-violence **16A**
virgen *adj.* virgin; **aceite de oliva virgen
  extra** *m.* extra virgin olive oil **15A;
  bosque virgen** *m.* virgin forest **6B**
visita: tarjeta de visita *f.* business card **18B**
visitante *m. y f.* visitor **8B**
visitar *v.* to visit **4A**
vista *f.* view **11A; Hasta la vista.** *exp.* See
  you later. **0**
visual: Educación plástica y visual *f.*
  Art **15B**
vital *adj.* vital **7A**
Viva *exp.* Long live... **2A**
vivienda *f.* home; housing **11B; vivienda
  ideal** *f.* ideal home **4B**
vivir *v.* to live **2A; vivir afuera** *v.* to live
  abroad **10B**
vocación *f.* vocation **7A; por vocación** *loc.
  adv.* by vocation **7A**
vocal *f.* vowel **13B**
volar *v.* to fly **5A**

volcán *m.* volcano **6B**
volumen *m.* volume **14A**
voluntario/a *m./f.* volunteer **12B; trabajo
 voluntario** *m.* volunteer work **7A**
volver *v.* to return **6B; volver a** *v.*
 to do … again **11B**
vosotros/as *pron.* you (*pl. fam.*) **1B**
votar *v.* to vote **10B**
voz (pl. voces) *f.* voice **6A**
vuelo *m.* flight **6B; ¡Que tengan un feliz
 vuelo!** *exp.* Have a good flight! **13A;
 auxiliar de vuelo** *m. y f.* flight
 attendant **13A; perder un vuelo** *v.* to miss
 a flight **13A**
vuelta *f.* turn; **dar la vuelta** *v.* to flip; to
 turn over **8A; dar la vuelta al mundo** *v.*
 to go around the world **18A; ida y vuelta**
 exp. round-trip **6B**

W

web *f.* web; **cámara web** *f.* webcam **6B;
 página web** *f.* Web page **14B; sitio web**
 m. Web site **14B**
Wi-Fi: red Wi-Fi *f.* Wi-Fi network **13B**

Y

y *conj.* and **0; ida y vuelta** *exp.* round-
 trip **6B; observación de flora y fauna** *f.*
 wildlife viewing **6B**
ya *adv.* already **6A; ¡Anda ya!** *exp.* Come
 on! **9B**
yerba: yerba mate *f.* mate (infusion) **3B**
yo *pron.* I **1A; Yo soy…** *exp.* I am… **0**
yoga *m.* yoga **3A**
yogur *m.* yogurt **2B**
yuca *f.* yucca **4A**

Z

zapatería *f.* shoe store **3B**
zapatillas (de deporte) *f.* running shoes;
 sneakers **3B**
zapato *m.* shoe **3B**
zona *f.* region **5A; zona colonial** *f.* colonial
 area **3A**
zumo *m.* juice **2B; zumo de naranja** *m.*
 orange juice **2B**

English-Spanish

A

a un(a) *art.* **1A: 11A: a little** un poco *loc. adv.* **2B: a lot** mucho *adv.* **2A: half a dozen** media docena *f.* **4A: half a kilogram** medio kilo *m.* **4A: once a week** una vez a la semana *loc. adv.* **6A: quite a lot** bastante *adv.* **5B: three times a year** tres veces al año *loc. adv.* **3A: twice a month** dos veces al mes *loc. adv.* **6A**

a.m. de la mañana *loc. adv.* **3A**

abbreviation abreviatura *f.* **13B**

ability competencia *f.* **2: habilidad** *f.* **8A**

about sobre *prep.* : **to be about** tratar *v.* **14B: to know (something) (about)** saber (algo) (de) *v.* **8A**

above: above all sobre todo *loc. adv.* **13B**

abroad: to live abroad vivir afuera *v.* **10B**

absence ausencia *f.* **11A**

academic: academic life vida académica *f.* **14A**

academy academia *f.* **15B**

accent acento *m.* **0: with an accent** con acento *loc. adv.* **0**

accept aceptar *v.* **15B**

acceptance aceptación *f.* **12B: acogida** *f.* **15A**

accessible: easily accessible bien comunicado/a *loc. adj.* **4B**

accessories complementos *m. pl.* **3B**

accommodate albergar *v.* **11A**

accompanied: to feel accompanied sentirse acompañado/a *v.* **9A**

accordion (type of) bandoneón *m.* **17B**

account cuenta *f.* : **to take into account** tener en cuenta *v.* **16B**

accountant contador(a) *m./f.* **13B**

achieve lograr *v.* **5B**

acid ácido *m.* **17A**

acronym sigla *f.* **12B**

act actuar *v.* **5A: acting** actuación *f.* **5A**

active activo/a *adj.* **5A**

activity actividad *f.* **0: extracurricular activity** actividad extraescolar *f.* **15B**

actor actor *m.* **1A**

actress actriz *f.* **1A**

ad anuncio *m.* **4B**

adapt adaptarse *v.* **10A**

adapted adaptado/a *adj.* **12B: adapted to** ajustado/a a *adj.* **17A**

add añadir *v.* **4A**

address dirección *f.* : **home address** domicilio *m.* **2A: to address somebody as tú** hablarse de tú *v.* **7B: to use the tú form of address** tutearse *v.* **17B: to address somebody as usted** hablarse de usted *v.* **7B**

adjusted ajustado/a *adj.* **17A**

administer suministrar *v.* **17A**

administration administración *f.* **8A**

administrative administrativo/a *adj.* **7B**

admire admirar *v.* **14B**

adolescent adolescente *m. y f.* **9A**

adopt adoptar *v.* **5B**

adoption adopción *f.* **5B**

advance: in advance con antelación *loc. adv.* **11A**

advantage ventaja *f.* **9B: to take advantage of** aprovechar *v.* **15A**

adventure aventura *f.* **5B**

adventurer aventurero/a *m. y f.* **18A**

adventurous aventurero/a *adj.* **9A**

advertisement publicidad *f.* **6B: anuncio** *m.* **4B**

advertising publicidad *f.* **16B**

advice consejos *m. pl.* **6A: advice column** consultorio *m.* **10A: to ask somebody's advice** hacer una consulta *v.* **12A**

advise aconsejar *v.* **6A: asesorar** *v.* **13B**

advisor asesor(a) *m./f.* **11B**

affect afectar *v.* **10A**

affection afecto *m.* **12A: simpatía** *f.* **18B: to show affection** mostrar afecto *v.* **18B**

affectionate cariñoso/a *adj.* **12A: tierno/a** *adj.* **9A**

affinity afinidad *f.* **17B**

affordable asequible *adj.* **6B: económico/a** *adj.* **2B**

Africa África *f.* **14A: sub-Saharan Africa** África subsahariana *f.* **14A**

African africano/a *adj.* **14A**

after después *adv.* **0: después de que** *conj.* **18A: the day after tomorrow** pasado mañana *loc. adv.* **11B**

afternoon tarde *f.* **0: Good afternoon.** Buenas tardes. *exp.* **0: in the afternoon** de la tarde *loc. adv.* **3A: in the afternoon** por la tarde *loc. adv.* **3A**

again de nuevo; otra vez *loc. adv.* **0: to do . . . again** volver a *v.* **11B: to meet again** reencontrar *v.* **9A**

age edad *f.* **4A**

agency agencia *f.* **4B: real-estate agency** inmobiliaria *f.* **4B: travel agency** agencia de viajes *f.* **4B**

aggression agresión *f.* **16A**

ago hace *v.* **5A: two months ago** hace dos meses *loc. adv.* **5A**

agree estar de acuerdo *v.* **5B: to be agreed upon** a convenir *loc. adv.* **13B**

agriculture agricultura *f.* **15A**

agronomist (ingeniero/a) agrónomo/a *m./f.* **7A**

ahead: straight ahead todo recto *loc. adv.*

ailment dolencia *f.* **10A**

aimed: to be aimed at estar dirigido/a a *v.* **6A**

air aire *m.* **7B: air conditioning** aire acondicionado *m.* **11A**

airline compañía aérea *f.* **11A: aerolínea** *f.* **13A: national airline** aerolínea abanderada *f.* **13A**

airport aeropuerto *m.* **0**

alarm clock despertador *m.* **3B**

alarmist alarmista *m. y f.* **17A**

album álbum *m.* **5B: disco** *m.* **7A**

all todo *pron.* **2A: above all** sobre todo *loc. adv.* **13B: all day** todo el día *loc. adv.* **6A: all grown-up** joven hecho/a y derecho/a *exp.* **9A: all in all** en definitiva *loc. adv.* **18B: at all** nada *adv.* **8A: in spite of everything** a pesar de todo *loc. adv.* **13B: to be all ears** ser todo oídos *exp.* **9A**

allergy alergia *f.* **10A**

allow permitir *v.* **6B**

almost casi *adj.* **13B: almost always** casi siempre *loc. adv.* **14A**

alone solo/a *adj.* **7A**

along: to get along/not to get along llevarse bien/mal *v.* **12A**

already ya *adv.* **6A**

although aunque *conj.* **13B**

always siempre *adv.* **2B: almost always** casi siempre *loc. adv.* **14A**

amateur aficionado/a *adj.* **11B**

Amazon River Amazonas *m.* **5A**

ambassador embajador(a) *m./f.* **16A: ambassador for peace** embajador(a) de la paz *m./f.* **16A**

ambitious ambicioso/a *adj.* **16A**

American estadounidense *adj.* **1B: South American** sudamericano/a *adj.* **18A**

among entre *prep.* **2A: among family** en el ámbito familiar *m.* **12A**

amuse divertir *v.* **17B: to amuse oneself** entretenerse *v.* **9A**

an un(a) *art.* **1A**

analyst: marketing analyst analista de marketing *m. y f.* **13B**

ancestry ascendencia *f.* **14A**

and y *conj.* **0: e** (before **i** or **hi** + consonant) *conj.* **1B: both ... and** tanto ... como *conj.* **7A**

anecdote anécdota *f.* **9B**

angry enfadado/a *adj.* **12A: to get angry** enfadarse *v.*, enojarse *v.* **17B**

animal animal *m.* **7B**

anniversary aniversario *m.* **5A: silver wedding anniversary** bodas de plata *f. pl.* **18B: to have one's wedding anniversary** cumplir años de casados *v.* **18B**

announce anunciar *v.* **16A**

announcer locutor(a) *m./f.* **16A**

annoyance disgusto *m.* **15B**

answer respuesta *f.* **0: contestar** *v.* **0: responder** *v.* **0**

anthem himno *m.* **18B**

antibiotic antibiótico *m.* **10A**

anticipate anticipar *v.* **16B**

antiquated anticuado/a *adj.* **16B**

antique antigüedad *f.* **4A**

any algún *adj.* **9A: alguno/a** *adj.* **9A**

anybody alguien *pron.*, **(in negative statements)** nadie *pron.* **8A**

anything algo *pron.* **2B: Anything else?** ¿Algo más? *exp.* **2B**

apartment apartamento *m.* **4B: tiny apartment** minipiso *m.* **11B**

apparently al parecer *loc. adv.* **8B**

appeal apelar *v.* **16B**

appearance: physical appearance aspecto físico *m.* **12A**

apple manzana *f.* **4A**

appliance electrodoméstico *m.* **8A**

applicant candidato/a *m./f.* **13B**

application solicitud *f.* **13B**

apply postularse *v.* **13B**

appointment cita *f.* **14B**

appraiser evaluador(a) *m./f.* **17A**

appreciate apreciar *v.* **18B**

appreciation apreciación *f.* **17A**

appropriate adecuado/a *adj.* **5B: apto/a** *adj.* **15A**

approximately aproximadamente *adv.* **3A**

apricot albaricoque *m.* **15A**

April abril *m.* **1B: April 13** el 13 de abril *m.* **3A**

architect arquitecto/a *m./f.* **1A**

architecture arquitectura *f.* **8A**

area extensión *f.* **6B:** superficie *f.* **2A:** área *f.* **: the colonial area** zona colonial *f.* **3A**

Argentina Argentina *f.* **0**

Argentine argentino/a *adj.*

argue discutir *v.* **13B**

arid árido/a *adj.* **13A**

arm brazo *m.* **10A: arm in arm** del brazo *loc. adv.* **5A**

armchair sillón *m.* **4B**

armed forces fuerzas armadas *f.* **16A**

arms armas *f. pl.* **16A: arms trade** tráfico de armas *m.* **16A: coat of arms** escudo *m.* **18B**

army ejército *m.* **16A**

aroma aroma *m.* **16B**

around alrededor *adv.* **8A: to go around the world** dar la vuelta al mundo *v.* **18A**

arrange (to meet) quedar *v.* **8A**

arrangement: flower arrangement arreglo floral *m.* **18B**

arrival llegada *f.* **6A: arrival lounge** sala de llegada *f.* **13A: arrival time** hora de llegada *f.* **13A**

arrive llegar *v.* **3A: to arrive home** llegar a casa *v.* **3A: arriving from** procedente de *adj.* **13A**

Art Educación plástica y visual *f.* **15B**

art arte *m.* **3B: work of art** obra de arte *f.* **8A**

article reportaje *m.* **14B**

Arts Filosofía y letras *f.* **5A**

artichoke alcachofa *f.* **15A**

artificial artificial *adj.* **15A**

as: as a team en equipo *loc. adv.* **7A: as many** tantos/as *adv.* **8B: as much/many… as** tan/tanto… como *conj.* **8B: as well as** así como *conj.* **16B: as… as possible** lo más… posible *m.* **17A: to work as** trabajar como *v.* **11B: as for** en cuanto a *loc. prep.* **16A**

aside: to set aside reservar *v.* **6A**

ask preguntar *v.* **0: to ask for** pedir *v.* **12B: to ask for a loan** pedir un crédito *v.* **5B: to ask for help** pedir ayuda *v.* **5B: to ask permission** pedir permiso *v.* **12B: to ask somebody's advice** hacer una consulta *v.* **12A**

aspect aspecto *m.* **7B**

aspirin aspirina *f.* **10A**

assemble montar *v.* **8A**

assert afirmar *v.* **16A**

assignment encargo *m.* **16B**

assistant auxiliar *m. y f.* **7B**

association asociación *f.* **12A**

assorted variado/a *adj.* **7B**

assume asumir *v.* **12B**

at en *prep.* **2B: at all** nada *adv.* **8A: at home** en casa *loc. adv.* **2B: at last** por fin *exp.* **10A: at night** de la noche *loc. adv.* **3A: at night** por la noche *loc. adv.* **3A: at the beginning of the 20th century** a principios del siglo XX *loc. adv.* **8B: at the same time** al mismo tiempo *loc. adv.* **7A: At what time…?** ¿A qué hora…? *exp.* **3A: at your service** a tu /su servicio *loc. adv.* **7B: to be aimed at** estar dirigido/a a *v.* **6A: to be at peace** estar en paz *v.* **10B**

athlete deportista *m. y f.* **12B: track-and-field athlete** atleta *m. y f.* **12B**

atmosphere ambiente *m.* **2A:** carácter *m.* **4A**

attack atentado *m.* **12B**

attend asistir (a) *v.* **15A: attend to** atender *v.* **7A**

attendant: flight attendant auxiliar de vuelo *m. y f.* **13A: kiosk attendant** quiosquero/a *m./f.* **9B**

attention atención *f.* **0: pay attention to** poner atención a *v.* **0: to catch one's attention** llamar la atención *v.* **14A: to pay attention (to somebody)** hacer caso (a alguien) *v.* **15B**

attitude actitud *f.* **13B**

attraction atractivo *m.* **4B**

attractive atractivo/a *adj.* **12A**

August agosto *m.* **3A**

aunt tía *f.* **5B**

authentic auténtico/a *adj.* **4A**

authenticity autenticidad *f.* **16B**

avenue avenida *f.* **2A**

avocado aguacate *m.* **12A**

avoid evitar *v.* **15A**

award premio *m.* **2B**

aware consciente *adj.* **3B: to make aware** hacer consciente *v.* **3B**

awareness: increased awareness sensibilización *f.* **16A: to raise awareness** sensibilizar *v.* **16A**

away: to be away estar de viaje *v.* **7A**

Aymara aimara *m.* **12A**

Aztec azteca *adj.* **12A**

B

bachelor(ette): bachelor(ette) party despedida de soltero/a *f.* **18B**

back espalda *f.* **10A: seat back** respaldo del asiento *m.* **13A**

backpack mochila *f.* **9A**

bad malo/a *m.* **10A: bad side** lado malo *m.* **13B: in a bad mood** de mal humor *loc. adv.* **12A: the bad thing** lo malo *m.* **12B: there is bad weather** hacer mal tiempo *v.* **10A: to be bad (at something)** ser malo/a (en algo) *exp.* **17B**

bag bolsa *f.* **4A:** bolso *m.* **3B**

baggage equipaje *m.* **11A: baggage cart** carrito *m.* **13A: baggage claim** entrega de equipaje *f.* **13A: baggage screening** control de equipaje *m.* **13A**

baked al horno *loc. adj.* **13A**

bakery panadería *f.* **8B**

balance equilibrio *m.* **6A**

balanced equilibrado/a *adj.* **7B**

balcony terraza *f.* **4B:** balcón *m.* **4B**

Balearic Islands Islas Baleares *f. pl.* **4B**

ball pelota *f.* **18A:** (dance) baile *m.* **5A**

ballpoint pen bolígrafo *m.* **3B**

ballroom dance baile de salón *m.* **17B**

banana banana *f.* **15A**

band: rubber band goma elástica *f.* **8A**

bandoneón (type of accordion) bandoneón *m.* **17B: bandoneón player** bandoneonista *m. y f.* **17B**

bank banco *m.* **0: bank transfer** transferencia bancaria *f.* **7B**

baptism bautizo *m.* **5B**

bar bar *m.* **0**

barbecue asado *m.* **1A**

bargain regatear *v.* **4A**

barrel: oil barrel barril de petróleo *m.* **14A**

barrier barrera *f.* **12B**

baseball béisbol *m.* **18A: baseball player** beisbolista *m./f.* **18A**

based: based on sobre la base de *loc. prep.* **16A**

basket cesta *f.* **7B**

basketball baloncesto *m.*

Basque vasco/a *adj.* **18A:** (language) euskera *m.* **1B**

Basque Country País Vasco *m.* **1B**

bath: to take a bath darse un baño *v.* **10A**

bathroom baño *m.* **4B**

battery batería *f.* **7B**

bazaar bazar *m.* **8B**

be ser *v.* **1A:** estar *v.* **2A: Be careful!** ¡Ojo! *exp.* **0: How are you?** ¿Qué tal? *exp.* **0: How is/are…?** ¿Qué tal está(n)…? *exp.* **2B: How much is it?** ¿Cuánto es? *exp.* **2B: I am…** (Yo) soy… *exp.* **0: I'm OK.** Estoy bien. *exp.* **7B: I'm sorry.** Lo siento. *exp.* **3B: I'm sure (that)…** Seguro que… *exp.* **9A: Is Carmen there?** ¿Está Carmen? *exp.* **6B: It's 9 euros.** Son 9 euros. *exp.* **2B: It's my turn.** Me toca a mí. *exp.* **4A: it's possible** es posible *loc. adv.* **4A: it's sunny** hace sol *v.* **10A: to be a great communicator** ser un(a) gran comunicador(a) *v.* **13B: to be a supporter of** ser hincha de *v.* **17B: to be about** tratar *v.* **14B: to be adapted** estar adaptado/a *v.* **12B: to be aimed at** estar dirigido/a a *v.* **6A: to be all ears** ser todo oídos *exp.* **9A: to be at peace** estar en paz *v.* **10B: to be away** estar de viaje *v.* **7A: to be bad (at something)** ser malo/a (en algo) *v.* **17B: to be beyond one's (our) means** estar fuera del (de nuestro) alcance *exp.* **15B: to be born** nacer *v.* **5A: to be cold/hot** tener frío/calor *v.* **10A: to be cold/hot out** hacer frío/calor *v.* **10A: to be common** ser moneda corriente *exp.* **13B: to be self-confident** estar seguro/a de sí mismo/a *v.* **18A: to be connected** estar en conexión *v.* **6A: to be delighted** estar encantado/a *v.* **11A: to be difficult** costar *v.* **14B: to be doing something** estar haciendo algo *v.* **7A: to be excited** estar ilusionado/a *v.* **12A: to be glad (that)** alegrarse (de) *v.* **11A: to be good (at something)** ser bueno/a (en algo) *v.* **17B: to be good for** servir para *v.* **4B: to be held** celebrarse *v.* **4A: to be impressed** estar impresionado/a *v.* **18A: to be in (good) shape** estar en forma *v.* **7A: to be in love (with)** estar enamorado/a (de) *v.* **12A: to be under someone's control** estar en manos de alguien *exp.* **17A: to be in touch** estar en contacto *v.* **12B:**

to be integrated integrarse *v.* **12B: to be interested in** estar interesado/a en *v.* **17A: to be of interest** interesar *v.* **7A: to be on vacation** estar de vacaciones *v.* **7B: to be reachable** estar localizable *v.* **13B: to be right** tener razón *v.* **10B: to be self-sufficient** valerse *v.* **5B: to be sensitive to** ser sensible a *v.* **10A: to be silent** estar callado/a *v.* **9A: to be the highest rated** ser líder de audiencia *v.* **14B: to be true** ser verdad *v.* **10B: to be under construction** estar en obras *v.* **11A: to be worth it** valer la pena *v.* **11B: to be… kilometers from…** estar a… kilómetros de… *exp.* **2A: What is it like?** ¿Cómo es? *exp.* **4B: What is it used for?** ¿Para qué sirve? *exp.* **4B: What is it?** ¿Qué es? *exp.* **1A: What time is it?** ¿Qué hora es? *exp.* **3A: where is…?** ¿dónde está…? *exp.* **2A: Who is it?** ¿Quién es? *exp.* **1A: I'm from Madrid.** Yo soy de Madrid. *exp.* **1A: to be called** denominarse *v.* **17A: to be motivated** estar motivado/a *v.* **13B: to be used to** estar acostumbrado/a a *v.* **13B: What's the weather like?** ¿Qué tiempo hace? *exp.* **10A**

beach playa *f.* **1A**
bean frijol *m.* **4A**
beard barba *f.* **12A**
beat batir *v.* **8A**
beautiful bello/a *adj.* **16B**
beauty belleza *f.* **4B**
because porque *conj.*
become convertirse en *v.* **7A:** hacerse *v.* **8B:** tornarse *v.* **17A: to become a vegetarian** hacerse vegetariano/a *v.* **7B: to become confused** confundirse *v.* **16B: to become happy** ponerse contento/a *v.* **18B: to become independent** independizarse *v.* **15B: to become sad** ponerse triste *v.* **18B**
bed cama *f.* **4B: double bed** cama de matrimonio *f.* **4B: to go to bed** acostarse *v.* **7A: to make the bed** hacer la cama *v.* **3A**
bedroom dormitorio *m.* **4B**
beer cerveza *f.* **2B**
beet remolacha *f.* **15A**
before antes *adv.* **9A:** antes de que *conj.* **18A**
beginning: at the beginning of the 20th century a principios del siglo XX *loc. adv.* **8B**
behind detrás de *loc. prep.* **3B: lagging behind** rezagado/a *adj.* **17A**
Beijing Pekín *m.* **1B**
being: human being ser humano *m.* **8A**
Belgium Bélgica *f.* **10B**
bell campana *f.* **18B: peal of a bell** campanada *f.* **18B**
belong pertenecer *v.* **3B**
belt cinturón *m.* **8A**
bench banco *m.* **0**
benefit redundar en *v.* **17A**
Berlin Wall Muro de Berlín *m.* **10B**
best mejor *adj., adv.* **4A: best-known** más conocido/a *adj.* **4A: the best** el/la mejor *m./f.* **9A: the best (thing)** lo mejor *m.* **4B**

better mejor *adv.* **6A**
between entre *prep.* **2A**
beverage bebida *f.* **2B**
beyond: to be beyond one's (our) means estar fuera del (de nuestro) alcance *exp.* **15B**
bicycle bicicleta *f.* **6B**
big grande *adj.* **4B**
bike bici(cleta) *f.* **6B**
Bilbao: from Bilbao bilbaíno/a *adj.* **17A**
bilingual bilingüe *adj.* **18A: bilingual school** escuela bilingüe *f.* **15B**
bill cuenta *f.* **2B**
biography biografía *f.* **5A**
biologist biólogo/a *m./f.* **11B: marine biologist** biólogo/a marino/a *m./f.* **11B**
biology biología *f.* **1B**
birth nacimiento *m.* **5A**
birthday cumpleaños *m.* **5A: fifteenth birthday party** fiesta de quince años *f.* **18B: to have one's birthday** cumplir años *v.* **18B**
birthplace lugar de nacimiento *m.* **11B**
bitter amargo/a *adj.* **10B**
black negro/a *adj.* **3B: black coffee** café solo *m.* **2B: black gold** oro negro *m.* **14A**
bland soso/a *adj.* **2B**
blank: to draw a blank quedarse en blanco *v.* **15B**
blanket frazada *f.* **13A**
blind ciego/a *adj.* **12B**
blocked bloqueado/a *adj.* **7B**
blog blog *m.* **3A**
blond(e) rubio/a *adj.* **12A**
blood sangre *f.* **17A**
blue azul *adj.* **3B: light blue** celeste *adj.* **9A**
board: on board a bordo *loc. adv.* **13A**
boarding embarque *m.* **13A: boarding gate** puerta de embarque *f.* **13A: boarding time** hora de embarque *f.* **13A**
boat lancha *f.* **9A: by boat** en barco *loc. adv.* **5A**
body cuerpo *m.* **6A**
Bolivia Bolivia *f.* **0**
bone hueso *m.* **9A**
book libro *m.* **0: book** reservar *v.* **6B: to book the tickets** reservar los billetes *v.* **13A**
bookstore librería *f.* **3B**
boot bota *f.* **3B**
booth: lottery ticket booth agencia de lotería *f.* **9B**
border frontera *f.* **7A**
bore aburrir *v.* **17B**
bored: to get bored aburrirse *v.* **17B: to get tired/bored of (something)** cansarse de (algo) *v.* **9B**
boredom aburrimiento *m.* **17B**
boring aburrido/a *adj.* **1B**
boss jefe/a *m./f.* **12B**
both los/las dos *pron.* **6B: both … and** tanto … como *conj.* **7A**
bother molestar *v.* **15B**
bottle botella *f.* **2B**
bouquet ramo *m.* **9B**
box caja *f.* **8A:** recuadro *m.* **0**
boxer boxeador(a) *m./f.* **18A**
boy niño *m.* **3A: young boy** el pibe *m.* **17B**
boyfriend novio *m.* **5A**
brand marca *f.* **3B**

Brazil Brasil *m.* **1A**
Brazilian brasileño/a *adj.*
bread pan *m.* **2B**
break romper *v.* **16A: to break a record** batir un récord *v.* **18A: break down** averiarse *v.* **13A**
breakfast desayuno *m.* **2B: to eat breakfast** desayunar *v.* **2B**
breakthrough avance *m.* **17A**
breathe respirar *v.* **7B**
bride novia *m./f.* **5A**
bright alegre *adj.* **4B:** brillante *adj.* **9A**
brilliant brillante *adj.* **14B**
bring traer *v.* **7B: to bring up to date** poner al día *v.* **7B**
broadcast emitir *v.* **14B: to broadcast the television series** pasar la serie de televisión *v.* **14B**
broccoli brócoli *m.* **15A**
brochure folleto *m.* **0**
bronze bronce *m.* **12B**
brother hermano *m.* **5A**
brown castaño/a *adj.* **12A:** (color) café *adj.* **3B:** marrón *adj.* **3B**
Buenos Aires: Buenos Aires slang lunfardo *m.* **17B: of/from the city of Buenos Aires** porteño/a *adj.* **17B**
build construir *v.* **0**
building edificio *m.* **2A**
bunch of flowers ramo de flores *m.* **18B**
bungee jumping puenting *m.* **18A**
burn quemar *v.* **18B**
bus autobús *m.* **4B:** colectivo *m.* **17B:** ómnibus *m.* **13A**
business negocio *m.* **7B: business card** tarjeta de visita *f.* **18B: businessperson** empresario/a *m./f.* **8B: business trip** viaje de negocios *m.* **3A: businesswoman** mujer empresaria *f.* **5A: to expand a business** ampliar un negocio *v.* **15A: to open a business** abrir un negocio *v.* **15A**
busy ocupado/a *adj.* **2A**
but pero *conj.* **2A**
butter mantequilla *f.* **2B**
button botón *m.* **4B**
buy comprar *v.* **3B: to buy lottery tickets** comprar (billetes de) lotería *v.* **9B**
by en, por *prep.* **5A: by boat** en barco *loc. adv.* **5A: by chance** casualmente *adv* **17B: by means of** por medio de *loc. prep.* **14B: by the way** por cierto *exp.* **10A: by vocation** por vocación *loc. adv.* **7A: day by day** día a día *loc. adv.* **14B: surrounded by** rodeado/a de *loc. adv.* **6B: to go by (means of transportation)** ir en… *v.* **6B: to go by car** ir en coche *v.* **3A: by the way** a propósito *exp.* **10A**
Bye. Chau. *exp.* **0**

C
---

cabbage col *f.* **15A**
cabin cabaña *f.* **6B**
cable cable *m.* **18A: steel cable** cable de acero *m.* **18A**
café confitería *f.* **4A:** cafetería *f.* **1B:** bar *m.* **2B: Internet café** cibercafé *m.* **4A: Internet café** locutorio *m.* **8B**

caffeine cafeína f. **2B**
cake pastel m. **18B**
calamari calamares m. pl. **2B**
calculate calcular v. **0**
calendar calendario m. **3A**
call llamada f. **3A:** (to action) convocatoria f. **16A: call center** locutorio m. **8B**
calm tranquilo/a adj. **2A**
calorie caloría m. **15A: low-calorie** bajo en calorías adj. **15A**
cameraperson camarógrafo/a m./f. **9A**
campaign campaña f. **12B: conciliation campaign** campaña de conciliación f. **15B: electoral campaign** campaña electoral f. **16A: promotional campaign** campaña de promoción f. **16B: to launch a campaign** lanzar una campaña v. **16B**
campsite campamento m. **6B:** camping m. **6B**
can (to be able to) poder v. **3B: Can I see them?** ¿Los puedo ver? exp. **3B: I can...** Yo puedo v. **0: You/One can't...** No se puede... v. **7B**
Canada Canadá m. **0**
Canadian canadiense adj. **1B**
cancelled cancelado/a adj. **13A**
candidate candidato/a m./f. **16A**
candle vela f. **5A**
candy dulce m. **2B; nougat candy** turrón m. **18B**
cannot: cannot be forgotten no puede olvidarse v. **10B**
canoeing canotaje m. **18A**
cap gorro m. **10A**
capacity capacidad f. **13B: to have (storage) capacity** tener capacidad v. **13B**
capita: per capita income renta per cápita f. **14A**
capital capital f. **2A**
caption pie de foto m. **5A**
captivate conquistar v. **15A:** fascinar v. **14A**
car auto m. **6B:** coche m. **3A:** carro m. **5B: to go by car** ir en coche v. **3A: race car driver** piloto m. y f. **18A**
carbohydrate hidrato de carbono m. **15A**
card tarjeta f. **3B:** (soccer) trading card el cromo (de fútbol) m. **9B: credit card** tarjeta de crédito f. **3B: greeting card** tarjeta de felicitación f. **5A: national identity card** DNI m. **3A: with a credit card** con tarjeta loc. adv. **3B**
cardiovascular cardiovascular adj. **17A**
care: day care guardería f. **5B: health care** asistencia sanitaria f. **10A: to take care of** cuidar (a/de) v. **5B: to take care of the details** ocuparse de los detalles v. **18B**
career carrera f. **1B: career counselor** orientador(a) profesional m./f. **13B**
caress acariciar v. **9A**
Caribbean caribeño/a adj. **4B: Caribbean Sea** mar Caribe m. **4B**
Carmelite carmelita adj. **11A**
carnation clavel m. **18B**
carpenter carpintero/a m./f. **12B**
carpentry carpintería f. **8A**
carry cargar v. **9A:** llevar v. **3A: carry out** llevar a cabo v. **18A**
cartoon panel viñeta (cómica) f. **0**

case estuche m. **13A**
cash: in cash en efectivo loc. adv. **3B**
cashier cajero/a m./f. **1B**
castle castillo m. **6B**
Catalan catalán/catalana adj. **1B:** catalán m. **1B**
catch atrapar v. **18A: to catch one's attention** llamar la atención v. **14A**
cathedral catedral f. **2A**
Catholic católico/a adj. **5A**
celebrate celebrar v. **5A**
celebration celebración f. **18B**
celiac celíaco/a adj. **15A**
cell phone (teléfono) celular m. **1B**
center centro m. **1A: call center** locutorio m. **8B: in the center of town** céntrico/a adj. **7B**
century siglo m. **8B: at the beginning of the 20th century** a principios del siglo XX loc. adv. **8B: toward the end of the 19th century** a finales del siglo XIX loc. adv. **8B**
cereal cereales m. pl. **2B**
ceremony ceremonia f. **14A: master of ceremonies** maestro/a de ceremonias m./f. **18B**
certainty certeza f. **15A**
certified certificado/a adj. **16B**
ceviche (marinated seafood dish) ceviche m. **1A**
cha-cha chachachá m. **17B**
chair silla f. **4B**
challenge reto m. **18A: to overcome challenges** superar retos v. **18A**
chamomile (tea) manzanilla f. **10A**
chance casualidad f. **16A**
change cambio m. **11A:** cambiar v. **7B: change of scenery** cambio de aires m. **11A: seat change** cambio de asiento m. **13A: to change jobs** cambiar de trabajo v. **7B: to change one's life** cambiar de vida v. **7B**
channel canal m. **9A**
character personaje m. **1A:** carácter m. **12A**
characteristic cualidad f. **17B:** rasgo m. **14A**
charisma carisma m. **18A**
charitable caritativo/a adj. **16A**
charm encanto m. **11A**
charming con encanto loc. adj. **6B**
chart tabla f. **0**
chat charlar v. **14A:** charla f. **9A: chat room** chat m. **3A: to chat (on the Internet)** chatear v. **6B**
cheap barato/a adj. **4B**
check comprobar v. **13A: check off** marcar v. **0**
checkbox casilla f. **0**
check-in facturación f. **11A: check-in counter** mostrador de facturación m. **13A**
cheese queso m. **2B**
chemist químico/a m./f. **8B**
chemistry química f. **1B**
cherry cereza f. **: wild cherry** guinda f. **16B**
chewing gum chicle m. **9B**
child niño/a m./f. **8B: to have a child** tener un hijo v. **8B**

childhood infancia f. **9A: since childhood** desde niño(s)/a(s) loc. adv. **8B: since childhood** desde pequeño/a loc. adv. **5B**
children: children's fashion moda infantil f. **3B**
Chile Chile m. **0**
Chilean chileno/a adj.
chimney chimenea f. **8B**
Chinese chino/a adj. **1B:** chino m. **1B**
chip chip m. **17A: potato chips** patatas fritas f. **4A**
chocolate chocolate m. **0**
choose elegir v. **7A: Which... do you choose?** ¿Qué... eliges? exp. **1A**
chorizo (sausage) chorizo m. **2B**
Christmas Navidad f. **5B**
chronologically cronológicamente adv. **5B**
church iglesia f. **2A**
churros churros m. **2B**
cigar: Cuban cigar puro habano m. **3B**
circle círculo m. **18A:** rodear v. **0**
circulation circulación f. **10A**
cited citado/a adj. **17A**
citizen ciudadano/a m./f. **8B: distinguished citizen** ciudadano/a ilustre m./f. **17B**
city ciudad f. **0: city hall** ayuntamiento m. **2A**
Civics Educación ético-cívica f. **15B**
civil war guerra civil f. **8B**
civilization civilización f. **11B**
claim: baggage claim entrega de equipaje f. **13A**
class clase f. **1B:** curso m. **3A: graduating class** promoción f. **9A: middle class** clase media f. **14B: music class** clase de música f. **3A: the rest of the class** el resto de la clase f. **0: to have class** tener clase v. **3A: to give (subject) ... classes** dar clases (de algo) v. **8A**
classic clásico/a adj. **4B:** clásico m. **9A**
classify clasificar v. **0**
classmate compañero/a (de clase) m./f. **0**
clay arcilla f. **16B**
clean limpio/a adj. **3A:** limpiar v. **3A**
clear evidente adj. **17A**
cliché tópico m. **16B**
click hacer clic v. **13B**
client cliente m. y f. **2A**
climate clima m. **2A**
climb ascender v. **18A:** subir v. **5A:** (a mountain) escalar v. **18A**
climber: mountain climber montañista m. y f. **18A**
climbing escalada f. **18A:** montañismo m. **18A**
clinic clínica f. **10A**
clock reloj m. **3A: alarm clock** despertador m. **3B**
close cerrar v. **17A: to close the gap** cerrar la brecha v. **17A**
closet armario m. **4B**
cloth tela f. **8A: piece of cloth** tela f. **8A**
clothing ropa f. **3B: clothing store** tienda de ropa f. **3B**
cloudy nublado/a adj. **10A**
clumsy person manazas m. y f. **8A**
coach entrenador(a) m./f. **18A**
coast costa f. **4B**

coat chaqueta *f.* **3B: coat of arms** escudo *m.* **18B**

cocktail cóctel *m.* **16B**

cocoa cacao *m.* **15A: cocoa powder** cacao en polvo *m.* **15A**

coconut coco *m.* **15A**

cod bacalao *m.* **2B: cod with sauce** bacalao en salsa *m.* **2B**

code código *m.* **13B**

coexist (with) convivir (con) *v.* **14A**

coexistence convivencia *f.* **14A**

coffee café *m.* **0: black coffee** café solo *m.* **2B: decaf coffee** descafeinado *m.* **2B**

coin moneda *f.* **0**

cold frío *m.* **2A: to be cold** tener frío *v.* **10A: to be cold out** hacer frío *v.* **10A: to have a cold** estar resfriado/a *v.* **10A**

collaborate colaborar *v.* **10B**

colleague colega *m. y f.* **7B**

collect coleccionar *v.* **9B:** reunir *v.* **15A**

collection colección *f.* **3B**

collective colectivo/a *adj.* **8A**

college universidad *f.* **2A: college dropouts** deserción universitaria *f.* **15B: college student** universitario *adj.; m./f.* **2A**

collide chocar *v.* **14B**

Colombia Colombia *f.* **0**

Colombian colombiano/a *adj.* **3B**

colonial colonial *adj.* **3A: the colonial area** zona colonial *f.* **3A**

colonizer colonizador(a) *m./f.* **18B**

colony colonia *f.* **14A**

color color *m.* **3B: What color?** ¿De qué color? *exp.* **3B**

colorant colorante *m.* **15A**

coloring colorante *m.* **15A**

column columna *f.*; **advice column** consultorio *m.* **10A**

comb peine *m.* **8A**

combine compaginar *v.* **7A**

come venir *v.* **3B: Come on!** ¡Anda ya! *exp.* **9B: Come on!** ¡Dale!/¡Venga! /¡Sale! *exp.* **8A: Come on!** ¡Pero, hombre/mujer! *exp.* **17A: to come from** provenir de *v.* **16B: to make (his/her) dreams come true** cumplir (sus) sueños *v.* **15B: to come up** surgir *v.* **15A**

comfortable cómodo/a *adj.* **2A**

comforts comodidades *f. pl.* **7B**

comic strip historieta *f.* **14B**

comics cómics *m.* **7A**

command dominio *m.* **13B**

commemorate conmemorar *v.* **17A**

commerce comercio *m.* **8B**

commitment compromiso *m.* **5A**

common frecuente *adj.* **2B: point in common** punto común *m.* **5B: to be common** ser moneda corriente *exp.* **13B: to have a lot in common** ser afín *v.* **17B**

communal comunitario/a *adj.* **17A**

communication comunicación *f.* **3B: lack of communication** falta de comunicación *f.* **15B**

communicative comunicativo/a *adj.* **16B**

communicator: to be a great communicator ser un(a) gran comunicador(a) *v.* **13B**

community comunidad *f.* **1A: immigrant community** comunidad inmigrante *f.* **8B**

company empresa *f.* **6A:** compañía *f.* **7A: (to keep) company** (hacer) compañía *v.* **7A: courier company** mensajería *f.* **7B: in good company** en buena compañía *loc. adv.* **16B: messenger company** mensajería *f.* **7B: to keep company** acompañar *v.* **9A**

compare comparar *v.* **0**

compass brújula *f.* **18A**

compatible compatible *adj.* **5B**

compete competir *v.* **18A**

competence competencia *f.* **2**

complain quejarse *v.* : protestar *v.* **11A**

complaint queja *f.* **11A: complaint form** libro de quejas *m.* **11A**

complete completo/a *adj.* **9A:** completar *v.* **0**

complex complejo/a *adj.* **16B**

compose componer *v.* **7A**

composition composición *f.* **15A**

computer computadora *f.* **4B:** ordenador *m.* **7B: computer science** informática *f.* **1B: computer technician** técnico/a informático/a *m./f.* **1B**

concern preocupación *f.* **7A: preocupar** *v.* **7A**

concert concierto *m.* **1A: to give a concert** dar un concierto *v.* **7A**

conciliation: conciliation campaign campaña de conciliación *f.* **15B**

condition: physical condition estado físico *m.* **10A**

conditioning: air conditioning aire acondicionado *m.* **11A**

conference congreso *m.* **12B: press conference** rueda de prensa *f.* **12B**

confidence confianza *f.* **18A**

confident: to be self-confident estar seguro/a de sí mismo/a *v.* **18A**

confirm confirmar *v.* **6B**

confirmation confirmación *f.* **13A**

conflict conflicto *m.* **7A: conflict resolution** resolución de conflictos *f.* **13B**

confused confundido/a *adj.* **16B: to become confused** confundirse *v.* **16B**

Congratulations! ¡Felicidades! *exp.* **5A:** ¡Felicitaciones! *exp.* **6A:** ¡Enhorabuena! *exp.* **18B**

conjugate conjugar *v.* **0**

connected: to be connected estar en conexión *v.* **6A to be connected (to the Internet)** estar conectado *v.* **13B**

conscience conciencia *f.* **17A**

consensus consenso *m.* **16A**

consequence consecuencia *f.* **12B**

construction obras *f.* **2A: to be under construction** estar en obras *v.* **11A**

consultant: labor consultant asesor(a) laboral *m./f.* **13B**

consume consumir *v.* **15A**

consumer consumidor(a) *m./f.* **3B**

consumption consumo *m.* **3B**

contact contacto *m.* **17B**

container envase *m.* **15A: plastic container** envase de plástico *m.* **15A: recyclable container** envase reciclable *m.* **15A: recycling container** contenedor *m.* **15A**

contemporary contemporáneo/a *adj.* **3B**

content contenido *m.* **14B: table of contents** sumario *m.* **1B**

contest certamen *m.* **16B**

continent continente *m.* **11B**

continue seguir *v.* **9B**

contract: employment contract contrato de trabajo *m.* **13B**

control controlar *v.* **15B: passport control** control de pasaportes *m.* **13A: to be under someone's control** estar en manos de alguien *exp.* **17A**

convenient cómodo/a *adj.* **17A**

convent convento *m.* **6B**

conventional convencional *adj.* **16A**

conversation conversación *f.* **1A**

conviction convicción *f.* **16A**

convince convencer *v.* **16A**

cook cocinero/a *m./f.* : cocinar *v.* **3A**

cooked cocido/a *adj.* **15A**

cookie galleta *f.* **2B**

cooking cocina *f.* **8A**

coordinator coordinador(a) *m./f.* **16A**

corn choclo *m.* **15A:** maíz *m.* **2B**

cornmeal harina de maíz *f.* **15A**

correct correcto/a *adj.* **0**

corruption corrupción *f.* **16A**

cosmetics: perfume/cosmetics shop perfumería *f.* **3B**

cosmopolitan cosmopolita *adj.* **16B**

cost costar *v.* **4A: How much does/do… cost?** ¿Cuánto cuesta(n)…? *exp.* **4A**

Costa Rica Costa Rica *f.* **0**

Costa Rican costarricense *adj.* **14B: tico/a** (fam.) *adj.; m./f.* **18B: costarricense** *m. y f.* **14B**

cotton algodón *m.* **9A**

counselor: career counselor orientador(a) profesional *m./f.* **13B**

country país *m.* **0: (countryside)** campo *m.* **3A: country house** masía (Cataluña) *f.* **7B: host country** país receptor *m.* **8B**

countryman/countrywoman compatriota *m. y f.* **10B**

coup d'état golpe de estado *m.* **10B**

couple pareja *f.* **5B**

courage valentía *f.* **16B**

courier company mensajería *f.* **7B**

course curso *m.* **3A: first course** primer plato *m.* **2B: main course** plato principal *m.* **2B**

court cancha *f.* **18A**

cousin primo/a *m./f.* **5B**

cover portada *f.* **3B: cover letter** carta de presentación *f.* **13B**

cow vaca *f.* **0**

coworker compañero/a de trabajo *m./f.* **5B**

crafts artesanía *f.* **3B**

crane grulla *f.* **16A**

crazy loco/a *adj.* **7B**

cream crema de leche *f.* **15A: ice cream** helado *m.* **2B**

create crear *v.* **0:** construir *v.* **0:** elaborar *v.* **0:** formar *v.* **0**

credit card tarjeta de crédito *f.* **3B: to pay with a credit card** pagar con tarjeta *v.* **3B**

crime delito *m.* **17B**

crisis crisis *f.* **12B**

critic evaluador(a) *m./f.* **17A: literary critic** crítico/a literario/a *m./f.* **10B**
criticize criticar *v.* **17B**
croissant cruasán *m.* **2B**
cross cruzar *v.* **18A: to cross out** tachar *v.* **0**
cross-border transfronterizo/a *adj.* **14A**
cruise crucero *m.* **16B**
cry llorar *v.* **14B**
Cuba Cuba *f.* **0**
Cuban cubano/a *adj., m./f.* **13A: Cuban cigar** puro habano *m.* **3B**
cucumber pepino *m.* **8A**
cuisine cocina *f.* **8A:** gastronomía *f.* **4B**
culinary gastronómico/a *adj.* **2B**
cultivate cultivar *v.* **7B**
cultural cultural *adj.* **6A**
culture shock choque cultural *m.* **14B**
cumbia (dance typical of the Caribbean coast of Colombia) cumbia *f.* **17B**
cup taza *f.* **2B**
cure cura *f.* **17A**
curiosity curiosidad *f.* : objeto curioso *m.* **4A**
curly rizado/a *adj.* **12A**
currency moneda *f.* **10B: foreign currency** divisas *f. pl.* **13A: foreign currency exchange** cambio de dinero *m.* **13A**
currently actualmente *adv.* **7A**
curse maldición *f.* **16A**
custody: joint custody custodia compartida *f.* **12A**
custom uso *m.* **16B**
cycling ciclismo *m.* **18A**
cyclist ciclista *m. y f.* **18A**

D

dad papá *m.* **5B**
daily diario/a *adj.* **13A: daily life** día a día *m.* **7A: daily routine** rutina diaria *f.* **3A**
daisy margarita *f.* **18B**
dance baile *m.* **5A:** bailar *v.* **6A: ballroom dance** baile de salón *m.* **17B: flamenco dance** baile flamenco *m.* **7A**
dancer bailarín/bailarina *m./f.* **7A: flamenco dancer** bailaor(a) *m./f.* **7A**
dangerous peligroso/a *adj.* **10A**
dare atreverse *v.* **17A**
dark oscuro/a *adj.* **16B: dark-haired** moreno/a *adj.* **12A**
data datos *m. pl.* **0**
date fecha *f.* **5A:** (appointment) cita *f.* **14B: expiration date** fecha de caducidad *f.* **15A: to bring up to date** poner al día *v.* **7B**
daughter hija *f.* **5A**
day día *m.* **3A: all day** todo el día *loc. adv.* **6A: day by day** día a día *loc. adv.* **14B: day care** guardería *f.* **5B: day of the week** día de la semana *m.* **3A: day off** día libre *m.* **14A: each day** cada día *loc. adv.* **14A: every day** todos los días *loc. adv.* **3A: Mother's Day** Día de la Madre *m.* **18B: the day after tomorrow** pasado mañana *loc. adv.* **11B: the other day** el otro día *loc. adv.* **9B: Those were the days!** ¡Qué tiempos aquellos! *exp.* **5B**
deaf sordo/a *adj.* **12B**

dear estimado/a *adj.* **6B: Dear sirs:** Estimados señores: *exp.* **6B**
death muerte *f.* **10B**
debate debate *m.* **16A**
decade década *f.* **14B**
decaf coffee descafeinado *m.* **2B**
December diciembre *m.* **3A**
decent digno/a *adj.* **3B**
decide decidir *v.* **6A**
decisive decisivo/a *adj.* **10B**
declaration of love declaración de amor *f.* **18B**
declare declarar *v.* **16A**
decorate adornar(se) *v.* **18B**
decoration decoración *f.* **3B**
decorator decorador(a) *m./f.* **11B**
dedicate dedicar *v.* **6A**
dedication dedicación *f.* **15A**
defend defender *v.* **12B**
defense defensa *f.* **16A**
degree título *m.* **13B: to study for a degree** estudiar una carrera *v.* **15B**
delay retraso *m.* **11A**
delayed con retraso *loc. adv.* **13A**
delicious exquisito/a *adj.* **13A**
delighted encantado/a *adj.* **11A**
deliver repartir *v.* **7B:** entregar *v.* **7B**
delivery entrega *f.* **7B: home delivery** reparto a domicilio *m.* **7B**
demand demanda *f.* **15A:** exigir *v.* **16B: labor demand** demanda laboral *f.* **14A**
democracy democracia *f.* **14B**
democratic democrático/a *adj.* **10B: democratic transition** transición democrática *f.* **14B**
demolish derribar *v.* **10B**
denounce denunciar *v.* **16A**
dense denso/a *adj.* **16B**
densely densamente *adv.* **16B**
dentist dentista *m. y f.* **10A**
depart salir *v.* **13A**
department secretaría *f.* **16A:** ministerio *m.* **16A**
departure salida *f.* **6A: departure time** hora de salida *f.* **13A**
depend depender *v.* **10A**
descend descender *v.* **18A**
describe describir *v.* **0**
desert desierto *m.* **5A: desert-like** desértico/a *adj.* **5A**
design diseño *m.* **4B:** diseñar *v.* **0: graphic design** diseño gráfico *m.* **7A**
designer diseñador(a) *m./f.* **3B: fashion designer** diseñador(a) de moda *m./f.* **11B**
desk mostrador *m.* **13A**
despotism caciquismo *m.* **16A**
dessert postre *m.* **2B**
destination destino *m.* **13A: tourist destination** destino turístico *m.* **4B**
detail detalle *m.* **18B: to take care of the details** ocuparse de los detalles *v.* **18B**
determine condicionar *v.* **14A**
develop desarrollar *v.* **15B**
developing en vías de desarrollo *adj.* **3B**
development desarrollo *m.* **14A**
device aparato *m.* **4B**
devour devorar *v.* **18B**
diabetes diabetes *f.* **17A**
diabetic diabético/a *adj.* **17A**

dialect dialecto *m.* **17B**
dialogue diálogo *m.* **0**
diarrhea diarrea *f.* **10A**
diary diario *m.* **5A**
dictator dictador(a) *m./f.* **16A**
dictatorship dictadura *f.* **10B**
die morir *v.* **10B**
die: roll the die tiren el dado *exp.* **10A**
diet dieta *f.* **7B**
difference diferencia *f.* **16B**
different diferente *adj.* **2A:** distinto/a *adj.* **4A: to be different from** diferenciarse *v.* **17B**
difficult difícil *adj.* **7A: extremely difficult** superdifícil *adj.* **11B: to be difficult** costar *v.* **14B**
difficulty dificultad *f.* **6B**
digital digital *adj.* **9B**
diminutive diminutivo *m.* **12A**
dine cenar *v.* **2B**
dining: dining hall comedor *m.* **15B: dining room** comedor *m.* **4B: living room-dining room** salón-comedor *m.* **4B**
diplomat diplomático/a *m./f.* **16A**
director director(a) *m./f.* **1A**
dirt tierra *f.* **9A**
disability discapacidad *f.* **12B**
disabled discapacitado/a *adj.* **12B**
disadvantage desventaja *f.* **9B**
disagree estar en desacuerdo *v.* **5B**
disagreement desacuerdo *m.* **10B**
disappear desaparecer *v.* **10B**
disappoint decepcionar *v.* **17B**
disappointment decepción *f.* **10B**
disaster desastre *m.* **16A**
disciple discípulo/a *m./fem.* **17A**
disco discoteca *f.* **2A**
disconnect (oneself) desconectarse *v.* **7B**
discount rebaja *f.* **3B:** descuento *m.* **6A**
discover descubrir *v.* **17A**
discovery descubrimiento *m.* **17A**
discus thrower lanzador(a) de disco *m./f* **17A**
discuss comentar *v.* **0**
dish plato *m.* **8A: to do the dishes** lavar los platos *v.* **5A**
disinfectant desinfectante *m.* **10A**
dispenser dispensador *m.* **9B**
display exponer *v.* **0**
disposable desechable *adj.* **17A**
distance distancia *f.* **2A: long-distance love** amor a distancia *m.* **6B**
distinguished: distinguished citizen ciudadano/a ilustre *m./f.* **17B**
distraction distracción *f.* **13B**
distribute repartir *v.* **12B**
diversity diversidad *f.* **7A**
diving: scuba diving submarinismo *m.* **11B**
divorce divorcio *m.* **12A: to get divorced** divorciarse *v.* **12A**
divorced divorciado/a *adj.* **5B**
do hacer *v.* **3A:** realizar *v.* **5A: to be doing something** estar haciendo algo *v.* **7A: to do ... again** volver a *v.* **11B: to do something for a living** dedicarse a (hacer) algo *v.* **7A: to do overtime** hacer horas extras *v.* **13B: to do something at home** hacer algo en casa *v.* **3A: to do the dishes** lavar los platos *v.* **5A: to do the shopping** hacer las compras *v.* **3A: to**

usually do something soler *v.* **14A: What do you do (for work)?** ¿A qué te dedicas? *exp.* **1B**

doctor doctor(a) *m./f.* **10A:** médico/a *m./f.* **1B: doctor's office** consultorio *m.* **10A: family doctor** médico/a de familia *m./f.* **10A**

documentary documental *m.* **9A**

dog perro/a *m./f.* **12B: guide dog** perro/a guía *m. y f.* **12B**

do-it-yourself bricolaje *m.* **8A**

dolphin delfín *m.* **5A**

domestic nacional *adj.* **13A: domestic service** servicio doméstico *m.* **8B: gross domestic product (GDP)** producto interior bruto (PIB) *m.* **11A**

dominate dominar *v.* **17A**

Dominican Republic República Dominicana *f.* **0**

donation donación *f.* **9A**

donkey burro *m.* **9A**

dorm residencia de estudiantes *f.* **12A**

dose dosis *f.* **17A**

double doble *m.* **2B: double bed** cama de matrimonio *f.* **4B: double room** habitación doble *f.* **6B**

doubt duda *f.* **16A:** dudar *v.* **16A**

downtown centro *m.* **1A**

dozen docena *f.* **4A: half a dozen** media docena *f.* **4A**

draw dibujar *v.* **0: to draw a blank** quedarse en blanco *v.* **15B**

drawback inconveniente *m.* **13B**

drawer cajón *m.* **8A**

drawing dibujo *m.* **3B:** sorteo *m.* **9B**

dreadful pésimo/a *adj.* **11A**

dream sueño *m.* **8B:** soñar *v.* **8B: the man/ woman of my dreams** el hombre/la mujer de mi vida *exp.* **12A: to make (his/her) dreams come true** cumplir (sus) sueños *v.* **15B**

dress vestido *m.* **3B: to get dressed** vestirse *v.* **7A**

drink bebida *f.* **2B:** beber *v.* **2B: soft drink** refresco *m.* **4A: soft drink** gaseosa *f.* **13A**

drive conducir *v.* **7A:** manejar *v.* **17B**

driver: race car driver piloto *m. y f.* **18A: taxi driver** taxista *m. y f.* **2A: truck driver** camionero/a *m./f.* **7A**

drop gota *f.* **2B**

dropouts: college dropouts deserción universitaria *f.* **15B**

drug droga *f.* **16A**

dry seco/a *adj.* **15A**

duck pato/a *m./f.* **18A**

duration duración *f.* **6B**

dusk atardecer *m.* **14A**

DVD DVD *m.* **9B: movie on DVD** película en DVD *f.* **4B**

dynamism dinamismo *m.* **16B**

E

each cada *adj.* **14A: each day** cada día *loc. adv.* **14A**

each other: far from each other alejados entre sí *loc. adv.* **17B: to greet each other** saludarse *v.* **17B: to hug each other** abrazarse *v.* **17B: to kiss each**

other besarse *v.* **17B: to look at each other** mirarse *v.* **17B: to love each other** quererse *v.* **17B: to tell each other** contarse *v.* **17B: to write to each other** escribirse *v.* **17B**

ear (inner) oído *m.* **10A:** (outer) oreja *f.* **10A: to be all ears** ser todo oídos *exp.* **9A**

early temprano *adv.* **7A: to get up early** madrugar *v.* **7A**

earn ganar *v.* **11B**

easily: easily accessible bien comunicado/a *loc. adv.* **4B**

east este *m.* **2A**

Easter Semana Santa *f.* **5A**

easy fácil *adj.* **6B: to make life easier** hacer la vida más fácil *v.* **17A**

eat comer *v.* **2B: to eat breakfast** desayunar *v.* **2B: to eat lunch** almorzar *v.* **2B: to eat supper** cenar *v.* **2B: to eat tapas** tapear *v.* **2B**

ecological ecológico/a *adj.* **17A:**

economic resource recurso económico *m.* **14A**

economics economía *f.* **1B**

ecotourism ecoturismo *m.* **11A**

Ecuador Ecuador *m.* **0**

Ecuadorian ecuatoriano/a *adj.*

edit editar *v.* **7A**

edition: special edition edición especial *f.* **3B**

editor: letter to the editor carta al director *f.* **2A**

educate educar *v.* **12B**

educated culto/a *adj.* **12A**

education educación *f.* **8A:** formación *f.* **6A: Physical Education** Educación física *f.* **15B**

effect efecto *m.* **6A**

effective eficaz *adj.* **13B**

efficient eficaz *adj.* **13B**

effort esfuerzo *m.* **8A**

egg huevo *m.* **2B**

eight ocho *adj.* **1A**

eighteen dieciocho *adj.* **1B**

eighty ochenta *adj.* **1B**

either o *conj.* **: not . . . either** tampoco *adv.* **10B**

El Salvador El Salvador *m.* **0**

elderly people las personas mayores *f.* **6A**

election elección *f.* **10B**

electoral campaign campaña electoral *f.* **16A**

electricity electricidad *f.* **8A**

elegant elegante *adj.* **4B**

elementary school escuela primaria *f.* **9A**

eleven once *adj.* **1A**

eliminate eliminar *v.* **16A**

elimination eliminación *f.* **12B**

else: Anything else? ¿Algo más? *exp.* **2B: Nothing else, thanks.** Nada más, gracias. *exp.* **2B**

e-mail correo electrónico *m.* **4B:** e-mail *m.* **4B**

embassy embajada *f.* **10A**

emergency emergencia *f.* **12B**

emigrant emigrante *m. y f.* **8B**

emigration emigración *f.* **8B**

emotional: emotional environment entorno afectivo *m.* **13B: emotional intelligence** inteligencia emocional *f.* **13B**

empanada empanada *f.* **17B**

empathy empatía *f.* **13B**

employee empleado/a *m./f.* **3A**

employment empleo *m.* **11B: employment contract** contrato de trabajo *m.* **13B**

empty vacío/a *adj.* **4B**

encounter encuentro *m.* **6A**

encourage fomentar *v.* **14A:** incentivar *v.* **14A**

encouragement incentivo *m.* **17A: to offer encouragement** dar ánimos *v.* **13A**

end final *m.* **0:** fin *m.* **: terminar *v.* **3A: toward the end of the 19th century** a finales del siglo XIX *loc. adv.* **8B**

ending terminación *f.* **0**

enemy enemigo/a *m./f.* **17B**

energy energía *f.* **7A: energy sector** sector energético *m.* **14A**

engineer ingeniero/a *m./f.* **1B**

engineering ingeniería *f.* **8A**

English inglés/inglesa *adj.* **1B:** inglés *m.* **1B**

enjoy disfrutar (de) *v.* **4A: Enjoy your flight!** ¡Que disfruten a bordo! *exp.* **13A: Enjoy your meal.** ¡Buen provecho! *exp.* **8A**

enough suficiente *adj.* **6A**

enroll inscribir *v.* **15B**

enrollment period plazo de inscripción *m.* **18A**

enter entrar en *v.* **3A**

enterprising emprendedor(a) *adj.* **8B**

entertainment entretenimiento *m.* **8B**

enthusiasm entusiasmo *m.* **10B**

environment entorno *m.* **11A:** medio ambiente *m.* **4B: emotional environment** entorno afectivo *m.* **13B: work environment** ambiente laboral *m.* **13B**

episode capítulo *m.* **14B**

equality igualdad *f.* **8B**

equation ecuación *f.* **15B**

Equatorial Guinea Guinea Ecuatorial *f.* **0: from Equatorial Guinea** ecuatoguineano/a *adj.* **14A**

equestrian hípico/a *adj.* **18A**

equipment equipo *m.* **18A**

equipped acondicionado/a *adj.* **6B**

ERASMUS: ERASMUS scholarship beca ERASMUS *f.* **14A**

e-reader lector de libros electrónicos *m.* **13B**

error error *m.* **11A**

especially en especial *loc. adv.* **7B**

establish establecer *v.* **6A**

establishment establecimiento *m.* **9B**

estate: real-estate agency inmobiliaria *f.* **4B**

estimate cotización *f.* **18B**

ethnic étnico/a *adj.* **16B: ethnic group** grupo étnico *m.* **16B**

euphoric eufórico/a *adj.* **15B**

euro euro *m.* **2B: It's 9 euros.** Son 9 euros. *exp.* **2B**

Europe Europa *f.*

European europeo/a *adj.* **6A: European Union** Unión Europea *f.* **10B**

evaluation puntuación *f.* **11A**

evening noche *f.* **3A: Good evening.** Buenas noches. *exp.* **0: in the evening** por la noche *loc. adv.* **3A**

event acontecimiento *m.* **5A:** evento *m.* **18B:** hecho *m.* **10B**

ever: hardly ever casi nunca *loc. adv.* **6A**

every day todos los días *loc. adv.* **3A**

everything todo *pron.* **2A: Everything is OK.** No pasa nada. *exp.* **13B: in spite of everything** a pesar de todo *exp.* **13B**

evolution evolución *f.* **16B**

ex ex *pref.:* **ex-husband** ex esposo *m.* **12A: ex-wife** ex esposa *f.* **12A**

exact exacto/a *adj.* **6A**

exaggerate exagerar *v.* **15B**

examine (a patient) atender *v.* **10A**

example ejemplo *m.* **0: to give an example** dar un ejemplo *v.* **7A**

excellent excelente *adj.* **13A**

excessive altísimo/a *adj.* **11B**

exchange intercambio *m.* **1B:** intercambiar *v.* **8A: exchange program** programa de intercambio *m.* **14A: in exchange for** a cambio de *loc. adv.* **8A: stock exchange** bolsa (de comercio) *f.* **3A**

excited emocionado/a *adj.* **10B:** ilusionado/a *adj.* **12A**

excitement ilusión *f.* **12B**

exciting emocionante *adj.* **10B**

excursion excursión *f.* **6A**

excuse perdonar *v.* **9B: excuse me** perdone (*form.*) *exp.* **9B: Excuse me, … Perdona,…** *exp.* **5A: Excuse me?** ¿Cómo? *exp.* **14A**

executive ejecutivo/a *m./f.* **13B: sales executive** ejecutivo/a de ventas *m./f.* **13B**

exercise ejercicio *m.* **10A:** hacer deporte *v.* **3A:** hacer ejercicio *v.* **6A:** hacer gimnasia *v.* **10A**

exhibition exposición *f.* **6A**

exile exilio *m.* **8B: to go into exile** exiliarse *v.* **10B**

exodus éxodo *m.* **14B**

exotic exótico/a *adj.* **4A**

expand: to expand a business ampliar un negocio *v.* **15A**

expectation expectativa *f.* **15A**

expel expulsar *v.* **14A**

expense gasto *m.* **15B**

expensive caro/a *adj.* **3B**

experience experiencia *f.* **4B: My experience** Mi experiencia *exp.* **0: professional experience** experiencia profesional *f.* **11B**

experiment experimento *m.* **17A**

experimentation experimentación *f.* **17A**

expiration date fecha de caducidad *f.* **15A**

explain explicar *v.* **14B**

exploit explotar *v.* **14A**

exploitation aprovechamiento *m.* **16A**

explore explorar *v.* **11B**

explosion explosión *f.* **14B**

export exportar *v.* **7B**

exporter exportador(a) *m./f.* **18B**

express expresar *v.* **18B**

extinction extinción *f.* **14A**

extra extra *adj.* **15A: extra virgin olive oil** aceite de oliva virgen extra *m.* **15A**

extraordinary extraordinario/a *adj.* **11B**

extremely super- *pref.* **11B:** -ísimo/a *suf.* **11B**

eye ojo *m.* **9A**

F

fabric tela *f.* **8A: piece of fabric** tela *f.* **8A**

face cara *f.* **5A:** enfrentarse a/con *v.* **18A**

facility instalación *f.* **11A**

fact hecho *m.* **7A: in fact** de hecho *exp.* **7A: in spite of the fact that** a pesar de que *conj.* **7A**

factor factor *m.* **6A**

factory fábrica *f.* **8B**

failure aplazo *m.* **15B:** suspenso *m.* **15B**

fair justo/a *adj.* **3B: fair trade** comercio justo *m.* **3B: International Fashion Fair** Salón Internacional de la Moda *m.* **3B:** feria *f.* **16B**

fairness equidad *f.* **17A**

faith fe *f.* **8A: matter of faith** acto de fe *m.* **8A**

fall otoño *m.* **10A:** caerse *v.* **: to fall in love** enamorarse *v.* **12A**

false falso/a *adj.* **0: True or false?** ¿Verdadero o falso? *exp.* **0**

family familia *f.* **2A: among family** en el ámbito familiar *m.* **12A: family doctor** médico/a de familia *m./f.* **10A: family tree** árbol genealógico *m.* **5B: the royal family** Familia Real *f.* **4B**

famous famoso/a *adj.* **2A**

fan aficionado/a *m./f.* **14B:** (hand-held) abanico *m.* **3B**

fantastic fantástico/a *adj.* **2A**

far: far from each other alejados entre sí *loc. adv.* **17B:** lejos *adv.* **2A: far from** lejos de *prep.* **2A**

fare tarifa *f.* **13A**

farewell despedida *f.* **0**

farm finca *f.* **8B**

farmer agricultor(a) *m./f.* **7B**

farming: organic farming agricultura ecológica *f.* **15A**

fascinated fascinado/a *adj.* **14B**

fashion moda *f.* **3B: children's fashion** moda infantil *f.* **3B: fashion designer** diseñador(a) de moda *m./f.* **11B: International Fashion Fair** Salón Internacional de la Moda *m.* **3B**

fast rápido/a *adj.* **17A**

fasten abrocharse *v.* **13A**

fat gordo/a *adj.* **9B:** grasa *f.* **15A**

father padre *m.* **5B**

favor favorecer *v.* **11A: in favor of** a favor de *loc. adv.* **12B**

favorite preferido/a *adj.* **3B:** favorito/a *m./f.* **9B**

fax fax *m.* **7B**

fear miedo *m.* **10B:** tener miedo *v.*

February febrero *m.* **5A**

feel encontrarse *v.* **10A:** sentirse *v.* **9A: to feel accompanied** sentirse acompañado/a *v.* **9A: to feel at home** sentirse como en casa *v.* **16B: to feel fulfilled** sentirse realizado/a *v.* **13B**

feeling sentimiento *m.* **18B: to express a feeling** expresar un sentimiento *v.* **18B**

feminine femenino/a *adj.* **0: Masculine or feminine?** ¿Masculino o femenino? *exp.* **0**

ferry ferry *m.* **3A: to take the ferry** tomar el ferry *v.* **3A**

fertilize abonar *v.* **8A**

festival fiesta *f.* **2A:** fiesta popular *f.* **6A**

fever fiebre *f.* **10A: yellow fever** fiebre amarilla *f.* **10A**

few pocos/as *adj.* **2A**

fiber fibra *f.* **10A**

fiction ficción *f.* **14B:** narrativa *f.* **10B**

field campo *m.* **17A: scientific field** campo científico *m.* **17A: sports field** cancha *f.* **17B: track and field** atletismo *m.* **18A**

fifteen quince *adj.* **1B: fifteen-year-old girl** quinceañera *f.* **5A**

fifteenth: fifteenth birthday party fiesta de quince años *f.* **18B**

fifth quinto/a *adj.* **14A**

fifty cincuenta *adj.* **1B**

fighter luchador(a) *adj.; m./f.* **5A**

figure muñeco *m.* **18B**

file archivo *m.* **7B**

fill in rellenar *v.* **0**

filled relleno/a *adj.* **16B**

fillet: fillet of veal filete de ternera *m.* **2B**

film rodar *v.* **9B**

finalist finalista *m. y f.* **9B**

finance financiar *v.* **4B: world of finance** mundo de las finanzas *m.* **3A**

financial financiero/a *adj.* **11B: financial press** prensa económica *f.* **3A**

find encontrar *v.* **4A:** localizar *v.* **0: to find out** averiguar *v.* **0: to find out** enterarse de *v.* **17A**

fire fuego *m.* **8A:** incendio *m.* **7A**

firefighter bombero/a *m./f.* **7A**

first primero/a *adj.* **14A: first course** primer plato *m.* **2B: first name** nombre de pila *m.* **12A: first prize** gordo *m.* **9B: first-aid kit** botiquín *m.* **10A: firstborn** primogénito/a *m./f.* **12A**

fish pez *m.* **:** (food) pescado *m.* **2B: fish soup** sopa de pescado *f.* **2B**

fisherman/fisherwoman pescador(a) *m./f.* **14A**

fit: to be fit estar en forma *v.* **7A: to fit into** integrarse *v.* **12B**

five cinco *adj.* **1A**

fixed: fixed-price menu menú del día *m.* **2B**

fjord fiordo *m.* **6B**

flag bandera *f.* **8B**

flamenco: flamenco dance baile flamenco *m.* **7A: flamenco dancer** bailaor(a) *m./f.* **7A**

flan (custard) flan *m.* **2B**

flavor sabor *m.* **15A**

flexibility: schedule flexibility flexibilidad horaria *f.* **6A**

flexible flexible *adj.* **6A: flexible workday** jornada flexible *f.* **6A: to make flexible** flexibilizar *v.* **6A**

flight vuelo *m.* **6B: Enjoy your flight!** ¡Que disfruten a bordo! *exp.* **13A: flight attendant** auxiliar de vuelo *m. y f.* **13A: Have a good flight!** ¡Que tengan un feliz vuelo! *exp.* **13A: to miss a flight** perder un vuelo *v.* **13A**

flip dar la vuelta *v.* **8A**

floating flotante *adj.* **9A**

floor piso *m.* **8A**

florist florista *m. y f.* **18B: florist shop** floristería *f.* **9B**

flower: bunch of flowers ramo de flores *m.* **18B: flower arrangement** arreglo floral *m.* **18B**

flowerpot maceta *f.* **8A**

fluorescent fluorescente *adj.* **11A**

fly volar *v.* **5A**

folded plegado/a *adj.* **13A**

folklore folclore *m.* **14A**

folks: my folks mi gente *exp.* **5B**

following siguiente *adj.* **0**

fond: fond of joking bromista *adj.* **13B**

food comida *f.* **1A:** alimentos *m. pl.* **2B: food product** producto de alimentación *m.* **15A: fresh food** producto fresco *m.* **15A: genetically modified food** alimento transgénico *m.* **15A: junk food** comida basura *f.* **10A: natural food** alimento natural *m.* **15A**

foot pie *m.* **10A**

for para *prep.* **4B:** por *prep.* **15B: appropriate/safe for** apto/a para *loc. adj.* **15A: as for** en cuanto a *loc. prep.* **16A: for (your) own good** por (tu) bien *loc. adv.* **15B: for free** gratarola *adv.* **17B: for sale** a la venta *loc. adv.* **4B: for young people** juvenil *adj.* **7A: in exchange for** a cambio de *loc. adv.* **8A: time for oneself** tiempo para uno/a mismo/a *m.* **3A: to ask for help** pedir ayuda *v.* **5B: to do something for a living** dedicarse a (hacer) algo *v.* **7A: to go for a walk** pasear *v.* **3A: to talk for the sake of it** hablar por hablar *v.* **14B: What is it used for?** ¿Para qué sirve? *exp.* **4B:** (and until now) desde hace *loc. prep.* **5B**

forces: armed forces fuerzas armadas *f.* **16A**

forecast: weather forecast pronóstico *m.* **9A**

forehead frente *f.* **17B**

foreign extranjero/a *adj.* **2A: foreign currency** divisas *f.* **13A: foreign currency exchange** cambio de dinero *m.* **13A: foreign language** lengua extranjera *f.* **15B**

forest bosque *m.* **5A: forest ranger** guarda forestal *m. y f.* **14A: virgin forest** bosque virgen *m.* **6B**

forever para siempre *loc. adv.* **8B**

forget olvidar(se) *v.* **5B: cannot be forgotten** no puede olvidarse *v.* **10B**

form formulario *m.* **16A:** formar *v.* **0: complaint form** libro de quejas *m.* **11A**

format formato *m.* **14B**

Formula 1 Fórmula 1 *f.* **18A**

fort fuerte *m.* **11A**

fortress fortaleza *f.* **11A**

fortune: to make a fortune hacer fortuna *v.* **8B**

forty cuarenta *adj.* **1B**

forum foro *m.* **1B**

foster potenciar *v.* **15A**

founder fundador(a) *m./f.* **4B**

four cuatro *adj.* **1A: four-star hotel** hotel de cuatro estrellas *m.* **11A**

fourteen catorce *adj.* **1B**

fourth cuarto/a *adj.* **14A**

fragrance fragancia *f.* **16B**

frame marco *m.* **3B**

Francoist franquista *adj.* **14B**

frankly abiertamente *adv.* **17A**

free libre *adj.* **16A: free time** tiempo libre *m.* **5B:** gratuito/a *adj.* **9B**

freedom libertad *f.* **13B: to set free** liberar *v.* **16A**

French francés/francesa *adj.* **1B:** francés *m.* **1B**

frequency frecuencia *f.* **13A**

fresh natural *adj.* **2B:** fresco/a *adj.* **15A: fresh food** producto fresco *m.* **15A**

Friday viernes *m.* **3A**

friend amigo/a *m./f.* **3A:** cuate/a *(fam.) m./f.* **12A: to go out with friends** salir con amigos *v.* **3A**

friendliness simpatía *f.* **2B**

friendly simpático/a *adj.* **2B: very friendly** amabilísimo/a *adj.* **13A**

friendship amistad *f.* **5B**

frighten asustar *v.* **7A**

frightened asustado/a *adj.* **12A**

from a partir de (que) *conj.* **12B:** de *prep.* **8B:** desde *prep.* **2A: arriving from** procedente de *loc. adv.* **13A: far from each other** alejados entre sí *loc. adv.* **17B: from San Juan** sanjuanero/a *m./f* **11A: from time to time** de vez en cuando *loc. adv.* **14A: from… until/ to** desde/de… hasta/a *loc. prep.* **8B: to come from** provenir de *v.* **16B: to be… kilometers from…** estar a… kilómetros de… *exp.* **2A**

frozen congelado/a *adj.* **16B**

fruit fruta *f.* **2B: fruit seller** frutero/a *m./f.* **9B: fruit shop** frutería *f.* **9B**

frustrating frustrante *adj.* **12B**

frying pan sartén *f.* **8A**

fulfill cumplir *v.* **13A: to feel fulfilled** sentirse realizado/a *v.* **13B**

fun divertido/a *adj.* **1B:** diversión *f.* **6A: to have fun** divertirse *v.* **17B**

function función *f.* **4B:** funcionar *v.* **7B: function hall** salón de fiestas *m.* **18B**

functional funcional *adj.* **4B**

funny gracioso/a *adj.* **9A**

furnished amueblado/a *adj.* **4B**

furnishings objetos domésticos *m.* **4B**

furniture: piece of furniture mueble *m.* **8A**

future futuro/a *adj.* **12B:** futuro *m.* **8B**

G

Galician gallego *m.* **1B**

game juego *m.* **0: Olympic Games** Juegos Olímpicos *m.* **12B: Pan-American Games** Juegos Panamericanos *m.* **18A: Paralympic Games** Juegos Paralímpicos *m.* **12B**

gap: to close the gap cerrar la brecha *v.* **17A**

garage garaje *m.* **4B**

garbage basura *f.* **8A**

gardening jardinería *f.* **8A**

garlic ajo *m.* **8A**

garment prenda *f.* **3B**

gastronomic gastronómico/a *adj.* **2B**

gastronomy gastronomía *f.* **4B**

gate: boarding gate puerta de embarque *f.* **13A**

gather reunir *v.* **0: reunirse** *v.* **6A**

GDP: gross domestic product (PIB) producto interior bruto *m.* **11A**

generally generalmente *adv.* **7B: en general** *loc. adv.* **4A**

generation generación *f.* **10B**

generational: generacional *adj.* **15B**

genetic: genetic modification manipulación genética *f.* **7B**

genius genio *m.* **15B**

gentleman caballero *m.* **13A**

geographic geográfico/a *adj.* **16B**

Geology Geología *f.* **15B**

German alemán/alemana *adj.* **1B:** alemán *m.* **1B**

get conseguir *v.* **4A:** obtener *v.* **0: (Let's) Get to work!** manos a la obra *exp.* **8A: to get a kick out of** encantar *v.* **5B: to get along** llevarse bien *v.* **12A: to get angry** enfadarse *v.* **17B: to get angry** enojarse *v.* **17B: to get bored** aburrirse *v.* **17B: to get divorced** divorciarse *v.* **12A: to get dressed** vestirse *v.* **7A: to get in line** hacer fila *v.* **13A: to get married** casarse *v.* **8B: to get someone hooked** enganchar *v.* **14B: to get tired/bored of** cansarse de *v.* **9B: to not get along** llevarse mal *v.* **12A: to get hold of** localizar *v.* **13B: to get up** levantarse *v.* **7A: to get up early** madrugar *v.* **7A**

gift regalo *m.* **3B: gift shop** tienda de regalos *f.* **3B: gift voucher** cheque-regalo *m.* **3B**

girl niña *f.* **3A: fifteen-year-old girl** quinceañera *f.* **5A: young girl** la piba *f.* **17B**

girlfriend novia *f.* **5A**

give dar *v.* **4A: Give me . . .** Me da/pone... *exp.* **4A: to give [subject] classes** dar clases (de algo) *v.* **8A: to give a concert** dar un concierto *v.* **7A: to give an example** dar un ejemplo *v.* **7A: to give good results** redundar en *v.* **17A: to give oneself (a present)** regalarse *v.* **6B: to give oneself an injection** inyectarse *v.* **17A: to give up** abandonar *v.* **7B: to give up** dejar *v.* **5A: to give up** renunciar a *v.* **16A**

glacier glaciar *m.* **11B**

glad alegre *adj.* **11A: to be glad that** alegrarse de *v.* **11A**

glass vaso *m.* : vidrio *m.* **8A: pane of glass** vidrio *m.* **8A**

glasses gafas *f.* **3B: sunglasses** gafas de sol *f.* **3B**

glide deslizarse *v.* **18A**

glider: hang glider ala delta *f.* **18A**

global mundial *adj.* **7B**

globetrotter trotamundos *m. y f.* **9A**

gloves guantes *m. pl.* **18A**

glucose glucosa *f.* **17A**

gluten gluten *m.* **15A**

go ir *v.* **3A: How are you going there?** ¿Cómo vas? *exp.* **6B: to go around the world** dar la vuelta al mundo *v.* **18A:**

to go beyond traspasar *v.* **14B: to go by (means of transportation)** ir en… *v.* **6B: to go by car** ir en coche *v.* **3A: to go down** bajar *v.* **15A: to go for a walk** pasear *v.* **3A: to go hungry** pasar hambre *v.* **15A: to go into exile** exiliarse *v.* **10B: to go on** seguir *v.* **11B: to go out (with friends)** salir (con amigos) *v.* **3A: to go to bed** acostarse *v.* **7A: to go to work** ir a trabajar *v.* **3A: to go via** pasar por *v.* **6B: to go wrong** ir mal *v.* **7B: to go away** marcharse *v.* **18B**

goal meta *f.* **18A:** objetivo *m.* **3B**

God Dios *m.* **8A**

gold oro *m.* **12B: black gold** oro negro *m.* **14A**

golf golf *m.* **1A**

good bueno/a *adj.* **0: (good) luck** suerte *f.* **8B: for (your) own good** por (tu) bien *exp.* **15B: Good afternoon.** Buenas tardes. *exp.* **0: Good evening.** Buenas noches. *exp.* **0: Good morning.** Buenos días. *exp.* **0: Good night.** Buenas noches. *exp.* **0: good weather** buen tiempo *m.* **2A: good-looking** guapo/a *adj.* **9A: Have a good flight!** ¡Que tengan un feliz vuelo! *exp.* **13A: in a good mood** de buen humor *loc. adv.* **12A: in good company** en buena compañía *loc. adv.* **16B: the good thing** lo bueno *m.* **12B: there is good weather** hace buen tiempo *exp.* **10A: to be good (at something)** ser bueno/a (en algo) *v.* **17B: to be good for…** servir para… *v.* **4B: to be in (good) shape** estar en forma *v.* **7A: to give good results** redundar en *v.* **17A: to have a good time** pasarla bien *v.* **17B: to have a good time** pasarlo bien *v.* **17B**

Goodbye. Adiós. *exp.* **0**

gossip: piece of gossip chisme *m.* **17B: gossip magazine** revista del corazón *f.* **9B: gossip press** prensa rosa *f.* **9B**

government gobierno *m.* **16A**

governmental: NGO (non-governmental organization) ONG (organización no gubernamental) *f.* **5A**

GPS navegador GPS *m.* **13B**

grab agarrar *v.* **17B**

grade calificación *f.* **15B:** nota *f.* **15B**

graduate egresar *v.* **9A:** graduarse *v.* **12A**

graduating class promoción *f.* **9A**

graduation graduación *f.* **18B**

grand piano piano de cola *m.* **10B**

grandchildren nietos *m.* **5B**

granddaughter nieta *f.* **5B**

grandfather abuelo *m.* **5B**

grandmother abuela *f.* **5B**

grandparents abuelos *m.* **5B**

grandson nieto *m.* **5B**

grant beca *f.* **8B**

grape uva *f.* **18B**

graphic design diseño gráfico *m.* **7A**

gray gris *adj.* **3B: to have gray hair** tener canas *v.* **17B**

great bárbaro/a *adj.* **11B:** genial *adj.* **6B:** gran (grande) *adj.* **5B: to be a great communicator** ser un(a) gran comunicador(a) *v.* **13B**

Great! ¡Pura vida! *exp.* **18B**

green verde *adj.* **3B**

greet saludar *v.* **17B: to greet each other** saludarse *v.* **17B**

greeting saludo *m.* **0: greeting card** tarjeta de felicitación *f.* **5A**

grocery store tienda de alimentación *f.* **4A**

groom novio *m.* **5A**

gross domestic product (GDP) producto interior bruto (PIB) *m.* **11A**

group agrupar *v.* **0: ethnic group** grupo étnico *m.* **16B: In groups** En grupos *loc. adv.* **0: marginalized group** grupo marginado *m.* **12B: music group** grupo musical *m.* **14B**

grow crecer *v.* **7B:** cultivar *v.* **7B: to grow up** crecer *v.* **9B**

growing creciente *adj.* **16B**

growth crecimiento *m.* **16A**

guacamole guacamole *m.* **1A**

Guarani guaraní *m.* **1B**

guarantee garantía *f.* **11A:** garantizar *v.* **3B**

guard: night security guard vigilante nocturno/a *m./f.* **3A**

Guatemala City Ciudad de Guatemala *f.* **0**

Guatemalan guatemalteco/a *adj.* **2A**

guerrilla guerrilla *f.* **16A**

guess adivinar *v.* **0**

guest invitado/a *m./f.* **18B: guest of honor** agasajado/a *m./f.* **18B**

guide: guide dog perro/a guía *m./f.* **12B: guidebook** guía *f.* **1B: tour guide** guía (turístico) *m. y f.* **1B**

guitar guitarra *f.* **8A**

guitarist guitarrista *m. y f.* **7A**

gum: chewing gum chicle *m.* **9B**

gunpowder pólvora *f.* **18A**

gym gimnasio *m.* **3A**

gymnast gimnasta *m. y f.* **18A**

gymnastics gimnasia *f.* **18A**

gypsy gitano/a *m./f.* **16A**

H

habit costumbre *f.* **15A:** hábito *m.* **7A**

hair pelo *m.* **9A: dark-haired** moreno/a *adj.* **12A: hair salon** peluquería *f.* **8B: red-haired** pelirrojo/a *adj.* **12A: to have gray hair** tener canas *v.* **17B**

half mitad *f.* **: half a dozen** media docena *f.* **4A: half a kilogram** medio kilo *m.* **4A**

hall: city hall ayuntamiento *m.* **2A: dining hall** comedor *m.* **15B: function hall** salón de fiestas *m.* **18B**

ham jamón *m.* **0: Serrano ham** jamón serrano *m.* **2B**

hand mano *f.* **8A: on the other hand** por otro lado/por otra parte *loc. adv.* **13B**

handkerchief pañuelo *m.* **3B**

handle asa *f.* **18A**

handyperson manitas *m. y f.* **8A**

hang glider ala delta *f.* **18A: to hang out** janguear (*fam.*) *v.* **11A**

happen pasar *v.* **8B:** suceder *v.* **14A: to make something happen** hacer realidad *v.* **8B**

happy alegre *adj.* **5B:** contento/a *adj.* **11A:** feliz *adj.* **5A: to become happy** ponerse contento/a *v.* **18B**

hard duro/a *adj.* **7B**

hardly ever casi nunca *loc. adv.* **6A**

harmony concordia *f.* **16A**

harness arnés *m.* **18A**

Havana La Habana *f.* **0**

have tener *v.* **2A: Have a good flight!** ¡Que tengan un feliz vuelo! *exp.* **13A: Have a nice stay!** ¡Feliz estancia! *exp.* **11A: How long have/has?** ¿Cuánto tiempo (hace)…? *exp.* **8B: to have (storage) capacity** tener capacidad *v.* **13B: to have a child** tener un hijo *v.* **8B: to have a cold** estar resfriado/a *v.* **10A: to have a good time** pasarla bien *v.* **17B: to have a good time** pasarlo bien *v.* **17B: to have a lot in common** ser afín *v.* **17B: to have (at one's disposal)** disponer *v.* **18B: to have class** tener clase *v.* **3A: to have fun** divertirse *v.* **17B: to have gray hair** tener canas *v.* **17B: to have one's birthday** cumplir años *v.* **18B: to have to** tener que *v.* **6A**

he él *pron.* **1A: he is…** él es… *exp.* **0**

head cabeza *f.* **10A**

headline titular *m.* **0**

headquarters sede *f.* **9A**

healer curandero/a *m./f.* **14A**

health salud *f.* **7A: health care** asistencia sanitaria *f.* **10A**

healthy sano/a *adj.* **5B**

hear oír *v.* **13B: I'm sorry to hear that.** Siento oír eso. *exp.* **13B**

heart corazón *m.* **2A**

heartrending desgarrador(a) *adj.* **16A**

heat calor *m.* **2A:** fuego *m.* **8A**

Hebrew hebreo *m.* **7A**

hectare hectárea *f.* **6B**

Hello. Hola. *exp.* **0: (when answering the phone)** ¿Diga?; ¿Dígame?; ¿Hola?; ¿Bueno? *exp.* **6B**

helmet casco *m.* **18A**

help ayuda *f.* **5B:** auxilio *m.* **18A:** socorro *m.* **12B:** ayudar *v.* **5B: self-help** autoayuda *f.* **6A: to ask for help** pedir ayuda *v.* **5B**

hepatitis hepatitis *f.* **10A**

her su(s) *adj.* **2A**

herb hierba *f.* **6A**

here aquí *adv.* **3B:** acá *adv.* **6B**

heritage: World Heritage Patrimonio Mundial *m.* **11B: World Heritage (Site)** Patrimonio de la Humanidad *m.* **8A**

hesitate: Don't hesitate to… No dude en… *exp.* **13B**

Hi. Buenas. *exp.* **0:** Hola. *exp.* **0**

hidden escondido/a *adj.* **6B**

hide esconder *v.* **6B:** ocultar *v.* **16B**

high alto/a *adj.* **8A: high school** secundaria *f.*, instituto *m.* **15B: high school studies** bachillerato *m.* **14A: high season** temporada alta *f.* **4B: to be the highest rated** ser líder de audiencia *v.* **14B: very high** altísimo *adj.* **11B**

hiking senderismo *m.* **11B:** trekking *m.* **6B**

hip-hop hip-hop *m.* **1A**

his su(s) *adj.* **2A**

Hispanic hispano/a *adj.*

historic histórico/a *adj.* **6B: historic neighborhood** casco viejo *m.* **12B**

history historia *f.* **1B**

hobby afición *f.* **11B**

hold sujetar *v.* **8A: to be held** tener lugar *v.* **16B: to hold** celebrarse *v.* **4A**
holiday día festivo *m.* **3A**
Holy Week Semana Santa *f.* **5A**
home vivienda *f.* **11B:** hogar *m.* **8A: at home** en casa *loc. adv.* **2B: home address** domicilio *m.* **2A: home delivery** reparto a domicilio *m.* **7B: ideal home** vivienda ideal *f.* **4B: private home** casa particular *f.* **13A: to arrive home** llegar a casa *v.* **3A: to do something at home** hacer algo en casa *v.* **3A: to feel at home** sentirse como en casa *v.* **16B**
homemaker el amo/a de casa *m./f.* **1B**
homesickness nostalgia *f.* **10B**
homework tarea *f.* **0:** deberes *m. pl.* **15B**
homogeneous homogéneo/a *adj.* **16B**
Honduran hondureño/a *adj.* **14B**
Honduras Honduras *f.* **0**
honey miel *f.* **7B**
honeymoon viaje de novios *m.* **13A**
honor: guest of honor agasajado/a *adj.* **18B**
hooked: to get someone hooked enganchar *v.* **14B**
hoop aro *m.* **18A**
hope esperanza *f.* **10B:** ilusión *f.* **12B:** esperar *v.* **12B**
hopeful esperanzado/a *adj.* **14A**
horizon horizonte *m.* **8B**
horrible horrible *adj.* **2A**
horse caballo *m.* **6B: horseback ride** paseo a caballo *m.* **6B: horseback riding** cabalgata *f.* **18A**
hospitable hospitalario/a *adj.* **13A**
hospital hospital *m.* **1B**
hospitality hospitalidad *f.* **14A**
host country país receptor *m.* **8B**
hostel albergue *m.* **6B:** hostal *m.* **11A**
hot caliente *adj.* : calor *m.* **10A: hot sauces** picantes *m. pl.* **15A: hot springs** termas *f. pl.* **6B: to be hot** tener calor *v.* **10A: to be hot out** hacer calor *v.* **10A**
hotel hotel *m.* **0: four-star hotel** hotel de cuatro estrellas *m.* **11A: hotel manager** hotelero/a *m./f.* **4B: state-run hotel in Spanish historic building** el parador nacional *m.* **6B: state-run hotel in Spanish historic buildings** Parador de Turismo de España *m.* **11A**
house casa *f.* **4B: country house** masía (*Cataluña*) *f.* **7B: house salad** ensalada de la casa *f.* **2B**
housewarming inauguración *f.* **12A**
housing vivienda *f.* **11B**
how cómo *interrog.* **1A: How are you going there?** ¿Cómo vas? *exp.* **6B: How interesting!** ¡Qué interesante! *exp.* **1B: How is/are...?** ¿Qué tal está(n)...? *exp.* **2B: How long have/has?** ¿Cuánto tiempo (hace)...? *exp.* **8B: how many?** ¿cuántos/as? *interrog.* **4B: How much is it?** ¿Cuánto es? *exp.* **2B: How often?** ¿Con qué frecuencia? *exp.* **3A**
however sin embargo *conj.* **5A**
HR: Human Resources (HR) Recursos Humanos (RR.HH.) *m., pl.* **13B**
hug abrazo *m.* **2A:** abrazar *v.* **17B: to hug each other** abrazarse *v.* **17B**
huge enorme *adj.* **16A**

human: human being ser humano *m.* **8A: Human Resources (HR)** Recursos Humanos (RR.HH.) *m.* **13B: human rights** derechos humanos *m.* **16A**
Humanities Filosofía y Letras *f.* **5A**
humankind humanidad *f.* **17A**
hundred: one hundred cien *adj.* **1B: one hundred percent** cien por ciento *adj.* **12A**
hungry: to be hungry tener hambre *v.* : **to go hungry** pasar hambre *v.* **15A**
hurt doler *v.* **10A:** herir *v.* **15B**
husband esposo *m.* **5B:** marido *m.* **5B: ex-husband** ex esposo *m.* **12A**
hygiene higiene *f.* **15A**

I

I yo *pron.* **1A: I think so/not.** Creo que sí/no. *exp.* **7B: I'm OK.** Estoy bien. *exp.* **7B: I am...** (Yo) soy... *exp.* **0: I meant...** quería decir... *exp.* **12B**
ice hielo *m.* **2B: ice cream** helado *m.* **2B: ice sheet** manto de hielo *m.* **11B**
icon: Hispanic icon referente latino *m.* **1A**
idea idea *f.* **4B**
ideal ideal *adj.* **2A**
identity identidad *f.* **18B: national identity card** DNI *m.* **3A**
idol ídolo *m.* **18A**
ill enfermo/a *adj.* **10A**
illiteracy analfabetismo *m.* **16A**
illness enfermedad *f.* **10A**
image imagen *f.* **1A**
imagine imaginarse *v.* **0**
immediate inmediato/a *adj.* **17A**
immensity inmensidad *f.* **11B**
immigrant inmigrante *m. y f.* **5B: immigrant community** comunidad inmigrante *f.* **8B**
immigration control de pasaportes *m.* **13A**
immune system sistema inmunológico *m.* **17A**
impatient impaciente *adj.* **13B**
import importar *v.* **15A**
important importante *adj.* **2A: important figure** personaje *m. y f.* **1A**
impressed impresionado/a *adj.* **18A**
impressive impresionante *adj.* **5A**
impromptu espontáneo/a *adj.* **14B**
improve mejorar *v.* **6A**
improvement perfeccionamiento *m.* **14A**
in dentro de *loc. prep.* **17A:** en *prep.* **3B: all in all** en definitiva *loc. adv.* **18B: in (good) shape** en forma *loc. adv.* **7A: in a good/bad mood** de buen/mal humor *loc. adv.* **12A: in exchange for** a cambio de *loc. adv.* **8A: in fact** de hecho *exp.* **7A: in favor of** a favor de *loc. adv.* **12B: In my opinion, ...** En mi opinión, ... *exp.* **10B: in need** sin recursos *adj.* **15A: in other words** es decir *exp.* **8B: in particular** en concreto *loc. adv.* **7B: in return** a cambio *loc. adv.* **12B: in short** en resumen *loc. adv.* **18B: in spite of everything** a pesar de todo *exp.* **13B: in spite of the fact that** a pesar de que *conj.* **7A: in the afternoon** de la tarde *loc. adv.* **3A: in the afternoon** por la

tarde *loc. adv.* **3A: in the evening** por la noche *loc. adv.* **3A: in the long term** a largo plazo *loc. adv.* **9A: in the mid sixties** a mediados de los 60 *loc. adv.* **14B: in the process** de paso *loc. adv.* **14B: in time** a tiempo *loc. adv.* **7B: Is Carmen there?** ¿Está Carmen? *exp.* **6B: point in common** punto común *m.* **to be in touch** estar en contacto *v.* **12B: to be interested in** estar interesado/a en *v.* **17A: to fall in love** enamorarse *v.* **12A: to participate in** participar en *v.* **3A: to trust in** tener confianza en *v.* **5B: in addition** además *adv.* **2A: in advance** con antelación *loc. adv.* **11A: in front of** delante de *loc. prep.* **3B: in love with** enamorado/a de *adj.* **2A: in order** en regla *loc. adv.* **11A: in the morning** de la mañana *loc. adv.* **3A: in the morning** por la mañana *loc. adv.* **3A: specializing in** especializado/a en *adj.* **2B**
inaugurate inaugurar *v.* **12A**
inbox bandeja de entrada *f.* **14A**
incidentally a propósito *conj.* **10A**
include contar con *v.* **9A:** incluir *v.* **11A:** incorporar *v.* **18A: tax included** IVA incluido *loc. adv.* **2B**
income ingresos *m.* **11A: per capita income** renta per cápita *f.* **14A**
incorrect incorrecto/a *adj.* **0**
incredible increíble *adj.* **5B**
indeed efectivamente *adv.* **15B**
independence independencia *f.* **12B**
independent independiente *adj.* **12A: to become independent** independizarse *v.* **15B**
India India *f.* **6A**
Indian indio/a *adj.* **4A**
indicate señalar *v.* **0**
indifference indiferencia *f.* **16A**
indigenous indígena *adj. invar.* **1B**
indispensable imprescindible *adj.* **13B**
industrial industrial *adj.* **8B**
industry industria *f.* **14A: oil industry** industria petrolera *f.* **14A: service industry** industria de servicios *f.* **14A**
inequality desigualdad *f.* **16A**
infection infección *f.* **10A**
infinite infinito/a *adj.* **18A**
influential influyente *adj.* **7A**
inform informar *v.* **16A**
information datos *m. pl.* **0: nutritional information** información nutricional *f.* **15A**
informed informado/a *adj.* **9B**
infrastructure infraestructura *f.* **17A**
infusion infusión *f.* **6A: mate** (infusion) yerba mate *f.* **3B**
ingredient ingrediente *m.* **15A**
inhabitant habitante *m. y f.* **2A**
inherit heredar *v.* **9B**
inhospitable inhóspito/a *adj.* **11B**
injection: to give oneself an injection inyectarse *v.* **17A**
injury herida *f.* **10A**
inn posada *f.* **11B**
innocence inocencia *f.* **18B**
innovation novedad *f.* **17A**

innovative innovador(a) *adj.* **13B**
insomnia insomnio *m.* **14B**
install instalar *v.* **14B**
insulin insulina *f.* **17A**
integrated: to be integrated integrarse *v.* **12B**
integration integración *f.* **12B**
intellectual intelectual *adj.* **17B**
intelligence inteligencia *f.* **13B: emotional intelligence** inteligencia emocional *f.* **13B**
intelligent inteligente *adj.* **12A**
intense intenso/a *adj.* **3A**
interact relacionarse *v.* **13B**
interaction trato *m.* **12B**
interactive interactivo/a *adj.* **17A**
interest inquietud *f.* **9A: interés** *m.* **1A: morbid interest** morbo *m.* **14B: to be of interest** interesar *v.* **7A: to stir up interest** despertar la inquietud *v.* **9A**
interested: to be interested in estar interesado/a en *v.* **17A**
interesting interesante *adj.* **1B: How interesting!** ¡Qué interesante! *exp.* **1B**
intern pasante *m. y f.* **13B**
international internacional *adj.* **1B: International Fashion Fair** Salón Internacional de la Moda *m.* **3B: International Relations** Relaciones Internacionales *f. pl.* **11B**
Internet Internet *m.* **4A: Internet café** cibercafé *m.* **4A: Internet café** locutorio *m.* **8B: Internet user** internauta *m./f.* **6A: to be connected (to the Internet)** estar conectado *v.* **13B: to surf the Internet** navegar por Internet *v.* **6A**
internship: summer internship pasantía de verano *f.* **13B**
interview entrevista *f.* **3A**
introduce presentar *v.* **0**
invade invadir *v.* **16A**
investigator investigador(a) *m./f.* **14B**
investment inversión *f.* **14B**
invite invitar *v.* **17B**
is: that is o sea *exp.* **8B**
island isla *f.* **1A: Balearic Islands** Islas Baleares *f.* **4B**
isolation aislamiento *m.* **13B**
issue número *m.* **15A**
it lo/la *pron.* **3B: It's my turn.** Me toca a mí. *exp.* **4A: it's possible** es posible *v.* **4A: to be worth it** valer la pena *v.* **11B: to talk for the sake of it** hablar por hablar *exp.* **14B: What is it like?** ¿Cómo es? *exp.* **4B: What is it used for?** ¿Para qué sirve? *exp.* **4B: What time is it?** ¿Qué hora es? *exp.* **3A**
Italian italiano/a *adj.* **1B: italiano** *m.* **1B**
itch picazón *f.* **10A**

jacket chaqueta *f.* **3B**
jackpot gordo *m.* **9B**
jai-alai court frontón *m.* **18A**
jam mermelada *f.* **2B**
January enero *m.* **5A**
Japanese japonés *m.* **1B**
jar frasco *m.* **8A**

jargon jerga *f.* **17B**
jazz jazz *m.* **7A**
jeans jeans *m.* **3B**
Jew judío/a *m./f.* **7A**
job actividad laboral *f.* **7B: puesto (de trabajo)** *m.* **4B: trabajo** *m.* **1B: having more than one job** pluriempleo *m.* **14B: job placement office** bolsa de trabajo *f.* **13B: to change jobs** cambiar de trabajo *v.* **7B**
join adherirse, afiliarse *v.* **16A**
joint custody custodia compartida *f.* **12A**
joke chiste *m.* **5B: fond of joking** bromista *adj.* **13B: to tell jokes** contar chistes *v.* **17B**
journal diario *m.* **5A**
journalist periodista *m. y f.* **10B**
juice: orange juice jugo (*m.*) de naranja, zumo de naranja (*Esp.*) *m.* **2B**
July julio *m.* **3A**
jump: bungee jumping puenting *m.* **18A**
June junio *m.* **5A**
jungle jungla *f.* **5A: selva** *f.* **16A**
junk food comida basura *f.* **10A**
just recién *adv.* **17B**
justice justicia *f.* **16A: social justice** justicia social *f.* **16A**

karate karate *m.* **3A**
kayak kayak *m.* **6B**
keep conservar *v.* **8A: mantener** *v.* **5B: to keep company** hacer compañía *v.* **7A: to keep company** acompañar *v.* **9A: to keep on** seguir *v.* **9B: to keep going** seguir *v.* **9B**
keeper: lighthouse keeper farero/a *m./f.* **14A**
key clave *f.*: llave *f.* **6A**
kick: to get a kick out of encantar *v.* **5B**
kid chamaquito/a *m./f.* **12A: to take the kids to school** llevar a los niños al colegio *v.* **3A**
kidnapping secuestro *m.* **16A: kidnapping victim** secuestrado/a *m./f.* **16A**
kill matar *v.* **18B**
kilogram kilo *m.* **4A: half a kilogram** medio kilo *m.* **4A**
kilometer kilómetro *m.* **2A: to be... kilometers from...** estar a... kilómetros de... *exp.* **2A**
kindergarten kínder *m.* **5B**
kiosk quiosco *m.* **9B: kiosk attendant** quiosquero/a *m./f.* **9B**
kiss beso *m.* **2A: besar** *v.* **17B: to kiss each other** besarse *v.* **17B**
kit: first-aid kit botiquín *m.* **10A**
kitchen cocina *f.* **4B**
knickknack objeto curioso *m.* **4A**
  knock down derribar *v.* **10B**
know conocer *v.* **5A: saber** *v.* **8A: best-known** más conocido/a *adj.* **4A: to know (something) (about)** saber (algo) (de) *v.* **8A: to make known** dar a conocer *v.* **16B**
Korean coreano/a *adj.* **1B: coreano** *m.* **1B**

label etiqueta *f.* **15A: record label** sello discográfico *m.* **17B**
labor: labor consultant asesor(a) laboral *m./f.* **13B: labor demand** demanda laboral *f.* **14A**
lack falta *f.* **11B: carecer de** *v.* **17B: lack of communication** falta de comunicación *f.* **15B: lacking salt** soso/a *adj.* **2B**
lady: young lady señorita *f.* **0**
lagging behind rezagado/a *adj.* **17A**
lake lago *m.* **6B**
lamp lámpara *f.* **3B**
land tierra *f.* **9A**
landmark lugar clave *m.* **4A**
landscape paisaje *m.* **6B**
language lengua *f.* **1B: idioma** *m.* **1B: foreign language** lengua extranjera *f.* **15B: Language and Literature** Lengua y literatura *f.* **15B: native language** lengua nativa *f.* **16A: official language** lengua oficial *f.* **14A: What languages do you speak?** ¿Qué lenguas hablas? *exp.* **1B**
last pasado/a *adj.* **5A: último/a** *adj.* **5A: at last** por fin *exp.* **10A: last minute** último minuto *m.* **12B: last month** el mes pasado *m.* **5A: last name** apellido *m.* **1B: last night** anoche *adv.* **5A: last week** la semana pasada *loc. adv.* **5A: two last names** doble apellido *m.* **12A**
late tarde *adv.* **7A: to be late** retrasarse *v.*
lately últimamente *adv.* **7A : to be late** retrasarse *v.*
later luego *adv.* **0: más tarde** *loc. adv.* **17B: See you later.** Hasta luego. *exp.* **0**
laugh reír *v.* **6A: reírse** *v.* **17B**
launch: to launch a campaign lanzar una campaña *v.* **16B**
lawyer abogado/a *m./f.* **1B**
layer: ozone layer capa de ozono *f.* **17A**
lead estar a la cabeza *exp.* **16A: to lead a... life** llevar una vida... *v.* **10A**
leader líder *m. y f.* **16A: gobernante** *m./f.* **12B: world leaders** líderes mundiales *m. y f.* **16A**
leaf hoja *f.* **8A**
learn aprender *v.* **3A: descubrir** *v.* **0: to learn Spanish** aprender español *v.* **3A**
least: the least el/la menos *m./f.* **9A**
leather cuero *m.* **8A**
leave abandonar *v.* **7B: irse** *v.* **12B: salir de** *v.* **3A: maternity leave** baja por maternidad *f.* **7B: maternity leave** licencia por maternidad *f.* **7B: to leave behind** dejar *v.* **7B**
left izquierda *f.* **9B: to the left** a la izquierda *loc. adv.* **9B: to the left of** a la izquierda de *loc. adv.* **3B**
leg pierna *f.* **10A**
legend leyenda *f.* **18A**
legume legumbre *f.* **2B**
leisure ocio *m.* **6A**
lend prestar *v.* **9A**
lentil lenteja *f.* **2B: lentils with chorizo** lentejas with chorizo *f.* **2B**
less menos *adv.* **6A: less than** menos que *adj.* **3A**

lesson lección *f.* **0: private lesson** clase particular *f.* **17B**
let permitir *v.* **6B: (Let's) Get to work!** manos a la obra *exp.* **8A: let's see...** a ver... *exp.* **6A**
letter letra *f.* **0:** carta *f.* **2A: cover letter** carta de presentación *f.* **13B: letter to the editor** carta al director *f.* **2A**
level nivel *m.* **16A**
library biblioteca *f.* **1A**
license licencia *f.* **2A**
life vida *f.* **2A: academic life** vida académica *f.* **14A: daily life** día a día *m.* **7A: pace of life** ritmo de vida *m.* **3A: quality of life** calidad de vida *f.* **2A: to change one's life** cambiar de vida *v.* **7B: to lead a... life** llevar una vida... *v.* **10A: to make life easier** hacer la vida más fácil *exp.* **17A: to make someone's life miserable** amargarle la vida a alguien *exp.* **17A: way of life** medio de vida *m.* **11B**
lifeguard salvavidas (*invar.*) *m. y f.* **10A**
lifestyle: sedentary lifestyle sedentarismo *m.* **16B**
light claro/a *adj.* **16B:** luz *f.* : **light blue** celeste *adj.* **9A: lights off** luz apagada *f.* **6A**
lighthouse faro *m.* **14A: lighthouse keeper** farero/a *m./f.* **14A**
like gustar *v.* **4A: desert-like** desértico/a *adj.* **5A: I'm sorry to see you like this.** Siento verte así. *exp.* **13B: to look like somebody** parecerse a alguien *v.* **12A: What is it like?** ¿Cómo es? *exp.* **2A: What would you like (to have)?** ¿Qué desean tomar? *exp.* **2B**
limit límite *m.* : limitar *v.* **6A**
limousine limusina *f.* **18B**
line línea *f.* **4A: to get/wait in line** hacer fila *v.* **13A:** cola *f.* **15A**
lion león *m.* **14A: lion tamer** domador(a) de leones *m./f.* **14A**
list lista *f.* **0: shopping list** lista de compras *f.* **4A**
listen escuchar *v.* **0: to listen to the radio** escuchar la radio *v.* **2A**
listener oyente *m. y f.* **14B**
literary critic crítico/a literario/a *m./f.* **10B**
literature letras *f.* **16A:** literatura *f.* **1B: Language and Literature** Lengua y Literatura *f.* **15B**
little pequeño/a *adj.* **4B:** poco/a *adj.* **2B: a little** un poco *loc. adv.* **2B**
live en directo *loc. adv.* **4A:** vivir *v.* **2A: Long live...** ¡Viva! *exp.* **2A: to live abroad** vivir afuera *v.* **10B**
living: living room salón *m.* **4B: living room-dining room** salón-comedor *m.* **4B: to do something for a living** dedicarse a (hacer) algo *v.* **7A**
load cargar *v.* **9A**
loan: to ask for a loan pedir un crédito *v.* **5B**
locate localizar *v.* **13B**
located ubicado/a *adj.* **11A**
location ubicación *f.* **15A**
locked bloqueado/a *adj.* **7B**
lodging alojamiento *m.* **6B**
logo logo *m.* **16B**

London Londres *m.* **1A**
long largo/a *adj.* **12A: How long have/has?** ¿Cuánto tiempo (hace)...? *exp.* **8B: in the long term** a largo plazo *loc. adv.* **9A: Long live...** ¡Viva! *exp.* **2A: long term** a largo plazo *loc. adv.* **17A: long weekend** puente *m.* **6B: long-distance love** amor a distancia *m.* **6B**
look: Look, Mira... *v.* **8A: to look at** fijarse en *v.* **0: to look at** mirar *v.* **6A: to look at each other** mirarse *v.* **17B: to look like somebody** parecerse a alguien *v.* **12A: to look for** buscar *v.* **1B**
Los Angeles Los Ángeles *m.* **1A**
lose perder *v.* **7B**
lot: a lot mucho/a *adj.* **2A:** mucho *adv.* **6A: parking lot** aparcamiento *m.* **11A: quite a lot** bastante *adv.* **5B: to have a lot in common** ser afín *v.* **17B**
lottery lotería *f.* **9B:** sorteo *m.* **12B: lottery ticket booth** agencia de lotería *f.* **9B: lottery ticket seller** vendedor(a) de lotería *m./f.* **9B: to buy lottery tickets** comprar (billetes de) lotería *v.* **9B: to play the lottery** jugar a la lotería *v.* **9B**
loudspeaker altavoz *m.* **13A**
lounge: arrival lounge sala de llegada *f.* **13A**
love amor *m.* **6B:** encantar *v.* **5B: (un) requited love** amor (no) correspondido *m.* **12A: declaration of love** declaración de amor *f.* **18B: long-distance love** amor a distancia *m.* **6B: to fall in love** enamorarse *v.* **12A: to love each other** quererse *v.* **17B: to love someone** querer a alguien *v.* **12A**
lovely hermoso/a *adj.* **13A:** precioso/a *adj.* **2A:** lindo/a *adj.* **11B**
low bajo/a *adj.* **4A: low-calorie** bajo en calorías *adj.* **15A**
luck suerte *f.* **8B: to try one's luck** probar suerte *v.* **5A**
lunch: to eat lunch almorzar *v.* **2B**
luxurious lujoso/a *adj.* **11A**
lyrics letra *f.* **7A**

M

madam señora *f.* **6B**
made up of compuesto/a por *adj.* **16B**
magazine revista *f.* **9B: gossip magazine** revista del corazón *f.* **9B**
magic mágico/a *adj.* **18B**
mahogany tree caoba *f.* **18B**
main principal *adj.* **4B: main course** plato principal *m.* **2B: main office** central *f.* **2A**
maintenance mantenimiento *m.* **4B**
major (academic) carrera *f.* **1B**
majority mayoría *f.* **5B**
make elaborar *v.* **0:** hacer *v.* **3A: to make (his/her) dreams come true** cumplir (sus) sueños *v.* **15B: to make a fortune** hacer fortuna *v.* **8B: to make aware** hacer consciente *v.* **3B: to make flexible** flexibilizar *v.* **6A: to make known** dar a conocer *v.* **16B: to make life easier** hacer la vida más fácil *v.* **17A: to make pottery** hacer cerámica *v.* **6A: to make someone's life miserable** amargarle

la vida a alguien *exp.* **17A: to make something happen** hacer realidad *v.* **8B: to make the bed** hacer la cama *v.* **3A**
makeup maquillaje *m.* **7A: to put makeup on** maquillarse *v.* **7A**
malaria paludismo *m.* **10A**
mall: shopping mall centro comercial *m.* **2A**
mallorca (Puerto Rican pastry) mallorca *f.* **1A**
man hombre *m.* **3B: the man of my dreams** el hombre de mi vida *exp.* **12A**
manage dirigir *v.* **6A:** manejar *v.* **13B**
management gestión *f.* **13B**
manager directivo/a *m./f.* **8B: hotel manager** hotelero/a *m./f.* **4B: managerial position** puesto directivo *m.* **13B**
manifesto manifiesto *m.* **12B**
many muchos/as *adj.* **2A: as many** tantos/as *adj.* **8B: as much/many... as** tan/tanto... como *conj.* **8B: how many?** ¿cuántos/as? *interrog.* **4B**
map mapa *m.* **4B**
marathon maratón *m.* **18A: to run a marathon** correr un maratón *v.* **18A**
march marcha *f.* **16A**
March marzo *m.* **5A**
marginalization marginación *f.* **12B**
marginalized marginado/a *adj.* **12B**
marinade adobo *m.* **15A**
marine marino/a *adj.* **11B: marine biologist** biólogo/a marino/a *m./f.* **11B**
marital status estado civil *m.* **5B**
mark marcar *v.* **0**
market mercado *m.* **0: market research** investigación de mercado *f.* **15A: produce market** agromercado *m.* **4A: stand (in a market)** puesto *m.* **4A**
marketing *marketing m.* **13B: marketing analyst** analista de *marketing m. y f.* **13B**
marmalade mermelada *f.* **2B**
marriage matrimonio *m.* **5B**
married casado/a *adj.* **5B: married couple** matrimonio *m.* **11B: to get married** casarse *v.* **8B**
Mars Marte *m.* **17A**
masculine masculino/a *adj.* **0: Masculine or feminine?** ¿Masculino o femenino? *exp.* **0**
Mass misa *f.* **5A**
mass-produce fabricar en serie *v.* **13B**
massive descomunal *adj.* **18A**
master maestro/a *m./f.* **6A: master of ceremonies** maestro/a de ceremonias *m./f.* **18B**
match cerilla *f.* **8A:** partido *m.* **18A:** relacionar *v.* **0**
mate (infusion) yerba mate *f.* **3B**
material material *m.* **8A: raw material** materia prima *f.* **15A**
maternity leave baja por maternidad *f.* **7B:** licencia por maternidad *f.* **7B**
math matemáticas *f. pl.* **15B**
matter asunto *m.* : **matter of faith** acto de fe *m.* **8A**
mature maduro/a *adj.* **17B**
May mayo *m.* **2A**
maybe a lo mejor *loc. adv.* **17A:** tal vez *loc. adv.* **17A**

meadow prado *m.* **9A**

meal comida *f.* **2B: Enjoy your meal.** ¡Buen provecho! *exp.* **8A**

mean significar *v.* **0: What does … mean?** ¿Qué significa…? *exp.* **0**

means medios *m.* **15A:** recursos *m. pl.* **12B: by means of** por medio de *loc. prep.* **14B: means of transportation** medio de transporte *m.* **4A: to be beyond one's (our) means** estar fuera del (de nuestro) alcance *exp.* **15B: to go by (means of transportation)** ir en… *v.* **6B**

measure medida *f.* **16A:** medir *v.* **17A**

meat carne *f.* **2B**

meatball albóndiga *f.* **2B**

mechanic mecánico/a *adj.*; *m./f.* **7B**

mechanics mecánica *f.* **8A**

medal medalla *f.* **12B**

media medios de comunicación *m.* **9A**

medication medicación *f.* **10A**

medicine medicina *f.* **10A:** fármaco *m.* **17A:** medicamento *m.* **10A**

mediocrity pobreza *f.* **13B**

meditation meditación *f.* **6A**

medium: in the medium term a medio plazo *loc. adv.* **17A**

meet quedar *v.* **8A:** cumplir con *v.* **15A:** conocer *v.* **5A:** reunir(se) *v.* **6A: Pleased to meet you.** Encantado/a. *exp.* **0: to meet again** reencontrar *v.* **9A: to meet the requirements** reunir los requisitos *v.* **13B**

meeting reunión *f.* **7B: meeting point** punto de encuentro *m.* **9A**

member miembro *m.* **5A**

memoir memorias *f. pl.* **10B**

memorize aprender de memoria *v.* **14B**

memory memoria *f.* **10B:** recuerdo *m.* **5B**

mental mental *adj.* **12B**

mention comentar *v.* **14B:** mencionar *v.* **0**

menu menú *m.* **2B: fixed-price menu** menú del día *m.* **2B**

merengue merengue *m.* **17B**

messenger company mensajería *f.* **7B**

metabolism metabolismo *m.* **17A**

metal metal *m.* **8A**

meter metro *m.* **4B: square meters** metros cuadrados (m²) *m. pl.* **4B**

method método *m.* **17A: scientific method** método científico *m.* **17A**

methodical metódico/a *adj.* **13B**

Mexican mexicano/a *adj.* **2B**

Mexico México *m.* **0**

Mexico City México, D.F. *m.* **0**

mid a mediados de *loc. adv.* **14B: in the mid-sixties** a mediados de los 60 *loc. adv.* **14B**

middle class clase media *f.* **14B**

migrant population población migrante *f.* **8B**

migration migración *f.* **8B**

milk leche *f.* **0: skim milk** leche descremada *f.* **15A: whole milk** leche entera *f.* **15A**

millennium milenio *m.* **10B**

million millón *m.* **8B**

mind mente *f.* **6A: state of mind** estado anímico *m.* **10A: state of mind** estado de ánimo *m.* **12A: Would you mind…?**

¿Le importaría…? *exp.* **13A**

minister ministro/a *m./f.* **16A**

ministry secretaría *f.* **16A:** ministerio *m.* **16A**

minority minoría *f.* **14A**

minute minuto *m.* **1A: last minute** último minuto *m.* **12B**

mirror espejo *m.* **9A**

Miss señorita *f.* **0**

miss echar de menos *v.* **14B:** extrañar *v.* **13A: Don't miss…** No se pierda *exp.* **11B: to miss a flight** perder un vuelo *v.* **13A: to miss out** perdérselo *v.* **16B**

missile misil *m.* **17A**

missing que faltan *adj.* **0**

mission misión *f.* **10A**

mistaken equivocado/a *adj.* **14A**

misunderstanding malentendido *m.* **14A**

mix mezcla *f.* **14A:** mezclar *v.* **14A**

mobile móvil *adj.* **17A**

mobility movilidad *f.* **13B**

mobilization: social mobilization movilización social *f.* **16A**

model modelo *m.* **0: fashion model** modelo *m. y f.* **3B**

moderate moderado/a *adj.* **6B**

modern moderno/a *adj.* **2A**

modernity modernidad *f.* **17A**

modernization modernización *f.* **17A**

modification: genetic modification manipulación genética *f.* **7B**

molar muela *f.* **10A**

mom mamá *f.* **5B**

moment momento *m.* **5A**

Monday lunes *m.* **3A**

money plata (*fam.*) *f.* **11B:** dinero *m.* **6B**

monitor controlar *v.* **17A**

monkey mono/a *m./f.* **16B: spider monkey** mono/a araña *m./f.* **16B**

Monterrey: born in Monterrey regiomontano/a *adj.* **12A**

month mes *m.* **5A: last month** el mes pasado *loc. adv.* **5A: next month** el próximo mes *loc. adv.* **5B: this month** este mes *loc. adv.* **6A: twice a month** dos veces al mes *loc. adv.* **6A: two months ago** hace dos meses *loc. adv.* **5A**

monument monumento *m.* **1A**

mood estado de ánimo *m.* **12A: in a good/ bad mood** de buen/mal humor *loc. adv.* **12A**

moonlighting pluriempleo *m.* **14B**

morbid: morbid interest morbo *m.* **14B**

more más *adv.* **3A: more than** más que *adj.* **3A**

morning mañana *f.* **3A: Good morning.** Buenos días. *exp.* **0: in the morning** de la mañana *loc. adv.* **3A: in the morning** por la mañana *loc. adv.* **3A**

Moroccan marroquí *adj.* **4A**

Morocco Marruecos *m.*

mosquito mosquito *m.* **10A**

most mayoría *f.* **5B: the most** el/la más *m./f.* **9A**

mother madre *f.* **5B: mother tongue** lengua materna *f.* **14A: Mother's Day** Día de la Madre *m.* **18B: working mother** madre trabajadora *f.* **7B**

motion movimiento *m.* **14A: a world**

in motion un mundo en movimiento *exp.* **14A: set in motion** poner en marcha *exp.* **16A**

motorcade caravana de coches *f.* **5A**

motto lema *m.* **3B**

mountain montaña *f.* **3A: mountain climber** montañista *m. y f.* **18A: mountain climbing** montañismo *m.* **18A**

mouse ratón *m.* **7B**

mouth boca *f.* **9A**

move cambiar de casa *v.* **5A:** mudanza *f.* **14A: (from home)** mudarse *v.* **7B**

movie película *f.* **1A: movie on DVD** película en DVD *f.* **4B: movie theater** cine *m.* **3A: to watch movies** ver películas *v.* **3A**

moving emocionante *adj.* **10B**

MP3 player reproductor de MP3 *m.* **13B**

Mrs. señora (Sra.) *f.* **2A**

much mucho/a *adj.* **2A: as much/many… as** tan/tanto… como *conj.* **8B: How much is it?** ¿Cuánto es? *exp.* **2B**

multilingual políglota *adj.* **1B**

multimedia multimedia (*invar.*) *adj.* **9B**

multinational multinacional (firm) *f.* **16A**

museum museo *m.* **0**

mushroom hongo *m.* **11A**

music música *f.* **1A: music class** clase de música *f.* **3A: music group** grupo musical *m.* **14B: music store** tienda de discos *f.* **3B**

musician músico/a *m./f.* **3A**

must deber *v.* **: a must** excluyente *adj.* **13B**

mustache bigote *m.* **12A**

my mi(s) *adj.* **2A:** mío/a(s) *pron.* **: In my opinion, …** En mi opinión, … *exp.* **10B: It's my turn.** Me toca a mí. *exp.* **4A: my folks** mi gente *exp.* **5B**

mysticism misticismo *m.* **16B**

N

Nahuatl náhuatl *m.* **12A**

nail clavo *m.* **8A: to nail down** clavar *v.* **8A**

naïveté inocencia *f.* **18B**

name nombre *m.* **1B:** nombrar *v.* **0: first name** nombre de pila *m.* **12A: His/Her name is…** (Él/Ella) se llama *exp.* **0: last name** apellido *m.* **1B: My name is…** (Yo) me llamo… *exp.* **0: two last names** doble apellido *m.* **12A: What is your name?** ¿Cómo se llama? *exp.* **0: What is your name?** ¿Cómo te llamas? *exp.* **0**

namesake tocayo/a *m./f.* **12A**

nap siesta *f.* **6A: to take a nap** dormir la siesta *v.* **6A**

nasal nasal *adj.* **10B**

national nacional *adj.* **12B: national airline** aerolínea abanderada *f.* **13A: national identity card** DNI *m.* **3A**

nationality nacionalidad *f.* **1B**

native oriundo/a *adj.* **16B:** indígena *adj. invar.* **1B: native language** lengua nativa *f.* **16A: native people** pueblo indígena *m.* **16A**

natural natural *adj.* **14A: natural food** alimento natural *m.* **15A: natural resource** recurso natural *m.* **14A**

nature naturaleza *f.* **4B**

near cerca de *prep.* **2A**
necessary necesario/a *adj.* **: to be necessary** hacer falta *v.* **16A**
need necesidad *f.* **13B: in need** sin recursos *loc. adv.* **15A**
negative negativo/a *adj.* **2B**
neighbor vecino/a *m./f.* **4A**
neighborhood barrio *m.* **1A: historic neighborhood** casco viejo *m.* **12B: rural neighborhood** vereda *f.* **9A**
neither tampoco *adv.* **10B**
nephew sobrino *m.* **18A**
nerd cerebrito *m./f.* **15B**
nervous nervioso/a *adj.* **10A**
network red *f.* **9A: radio network** cadena de radio *f.* **14B: social network** red social *f.* **13B: Wi-Fi network** red Wi-Fi *f.* **13B**
never nunca *adv.* **6A**
new nuevo/a *adj.* **1A: New Year** Año Nuevo *m.* **18B**
New Orleans Nueva Orleans *f.* **1A**
New York Nueva York *f.* **1A**
news noticia *f.* **4A: news and talk show** magacín *m.* **9A: news program** informativo *m.* **9A**
newspaper periódico *m.* **7A**
next próximo/a *adj.* **5B:** siguiente *adj.* **0: next month** el próximo mes *m.* **5B: next to** al lado de *loc. adv.* **3B**
NGO (non-governmental organization) ONG (organización no gubernamental) *f.* **5A**
Nicaragua Nicaragua *f.* **0**
Nicaraguan nicaragüense *adj.*
nice simpático/a *adj.* **2A: Have a nice stay!** ¡Feliz estancia! *exp.* **11A**
nickname diminutivo *m.* **12A**
niece sobrina *f.* **18A**
night noche *f.* **3A: at night** por la noche *loc. adv.* **3A: at night** de la noche *loc. adv.* **3A: Good night.** Buenas noches. *exp.* **0: last night** anoche *adv.* **5A: night security guard** vigilante nocturno/a *m. y f.* **3A: to spend the night** pasar la noche *v.* **6B**
night club discoteca *f.* **2A**
nine nueve *adj.* **1A**
nineteen diecinueve *adj.* **1B**
ninety noventa *adj.* **1B**
no ningún *adj.* **9A: no** *adv.* **1A: (none)** ninguno/a *adj.* **9A: No problem!** ¡No hay problema! *exp.* **7B**
Nobel Prize Premio Nobel *m.* **10B**
nobody nadie *pron.* **8A**
noise ruido *m.* **2A**
none ninguno/a *pron., adj.* **9A**
non-violence no violencia *f.* **16A**
normally normalmente *adv.* **2B**
north norte *m.* **2A: North Pole** Polo Norte *m.* **18A**
nose nariz *f.* **9A**
nostalgia nostalgia *f.* **10B**
not no *adv.* **1A: Don't worry.** No te preocupes. *exp.* **13B: I think not.** Creo que no. *exp.* **7B: not . . . either, neither** tampoco *adv.* **10B: not to be able to stand** no soportar *v.* **15B: not yet** todavía no *loc. adv.* **6A: You/One can't...** No se puede... *exp.* **7B**

notable destacado/a *adj.* **5A**
note nota *f.* **4A**
noteworthy destacable *adj.* **14A**
nothing nada *adv.* **2B: Nothing else, thanks.** Nada más, gracias. *exp.* **2B**
nougat candy turrón *m.* **18B**
November noviembre *m.* **5A**
nowadays en la actualidad *loc. adv.* **8B:** hoy en día *loc. adv.* **15B**
nuclear weapon arma nuclear *f.* **16A**
number nº (número) *m.* **2A:** número *m.* **0**
nurse enfermero/a *m./f.* **12B**
nut nuez *f.* **18B**
nutrient nutriente *m.* **15A**
nutritional information información nutricional *f.* **15A**
nutritious nutritivo/a *adj.* **15A**

O

object objeto *m.* **3B:** oponerse *v.* **15B**
objective objetivo *m.* **3B**
obligation obligación *f.* **5B**
observe observar *v.* **0**
obtain conseguir *v.* **4A:** obtener *v.* **0**
obvious obvio/a *adj.* **17A:** evidente *adj.* **17A**
occasion ocasión *f.* **: on the occasion of** con motivo de *exp.* **12B**
ocean océano *m.* **18A**
octopus pulpo *m.* **2B**
of de *prep.* **2B: by means of** por medio de *loc. prep.* **14B: day of the week** día de la semana *m.* **3A: fillet of veal** filete de ternera *m.* **2B: in favor of** a favor de *loc. adv.* **12B: means of transportation** medio de transporte *m.* **4A: of the** del (= de + el) *contrac.* **3B: on the occasion of** con motivo de *exp.* **12B: on top of** encima de *loc. prep.* **3B: outside of class** fuera de clase *loc. prep.* **3A: piece of advice** consejo *m.* **6A: place of worship** lugar de culto *m.* **8A: the rest of** el resto de *m.* **12B: time of year** época *f.* **6B: to be of interest** interesar *v.* **7A: to get a kick out of** encantar *v.* **5B: to take care of** cuidar a/de *v.* **5B: to the left of** a la izquierda de *loc. adv.* **3B: to the right of** a la derecha de *loc. adv.* **3B: work of art** obra (de arte) *f.* **8A: world of finance** mundo de las finanzas *m.* **3A: of course** claro *exp.* **1B**
off: day off día libre *m.* **14A: lights off** luz apagada *f.* **6A**
offense atentado *m.* **12B**
offer ofrecer *v.* **4B: to offer encouragement** dar ánimos *v.* **13A**
office oficina *f.* **6A: doctor's office** consultorio *m.* **10A: job placement office** bolsa de trabajo *f.* **13B: main office** central *f.* **2A: press office** oficina de prensa *f.* **16A**
official oficial *adj.* **14A: official language** lengua oficial *f.* **14A**
often a menudo *loc. adv.* **: How often?** ¿Con qué frecuencia? *exp.* **3A**
oil aceite *m.* **8A:** petróleo *m.* **14A: extra virgin olive oil** aceite de oliva virgen extra *m.* **15A: oil barrel** barril de petróleo *m.* **14A: oil industry** industria petrolera

f. **14A: oil rig** plataforma petrolera *f.* **14A: olive oil** aceite de oliva *m.* **2B**
OK ¡Vale! *exp.* **2B:** De acuerdo. *exp.* **2B: Everything is OK.** No pasa nada. *exp.* **13B: I'm OK.** Estoy bien. *exp.* **7B**
old antiguo/a *adj.* **2A:** viejo/a *adj.* **5B: an 80-year-old person** una persona de 80 años *f.* **3A: fifteen-year-old girl** quinceañera *f.* **5A**
older mayor *adj.* **9A**
olive aceituna *f.* **2B: extra virgin olive oil** aceite de oliva virgen extra *m.* **15A: olive oil** aceite de oliva *m.* **2B**
on en *prep.* **3B: Come on!** ¡Anda ya! *exp.* **9B: movie on DVD** película en DVD *f.* **4B: on (top of)** encima de *loc. prep.* **3B: on board** a bordo *loc. adv.* **13A: on the occasion of** con motivo de *exp.* **12B: on the other hand** por otro lado/por otra parte *loc. adv.* **13B: on time** a tiempo *loc. adv.* **7B: on weekends** los fines de semana *loc. adv.* **5B: to be on vacation** estar de vacaciones *v.* **7B: to depend on** depender de *v.* **10A: to put makeup on** maquillarse *v.* **7A: on the one hand** por un lado/por una parte *loc. adv.* **13B**
once: once a week una vez a la semana *loc. adv.* **6A**
one uno/a *adj.* **1A: on the one hand** por un lado/por una parte *loc. adv.* **13B: one hundred percent** cien por ciento *adj.* **12A: which one(s)?** ¿cuál(es)? *interrog.* **4B: You/One can't...** No se puede... *exp.* **7B**
one hundred cien *adj.* **1B**
oneself uno/a mismo/a *m./f.* **3A: time for oneself** tiempo para uno/a mismo/a *m.* **3A: to amuse oneself** entretenerse *v.* **9A: to outdo oneself** superarse *v.* **18A**
online en línea *loc. adv.* **9B**
only nomás *adv.* **17B:** solo/solamente *adv.* **13B:** únicamente *adv.* **13B**
open abierto/a *adj.* **3A:** abrir *v.* **3A:** inaugurar *v.* **12A: to open a business** abrir un negocio *v.* **15A**
opening apertura *f.* **15A**
openly abiertamente *adv.* **17A**
opinion opinión *f.* **10B: In my opinion, ...** En mi opinión, ... *exp.* **10B**
opponent contrincante *m. y f.* **18A**
opportunity oportunidad *f.* **8B**
opt optar *v.* **18B**
optimism optimismo *m.* **10B**
optimistic optimista *adj.* **12A**
or o *conj.* **: or otherwise** o bien *exp.* **12A:** u (before **o** or **ho**) *conj.* **11B**
orange anaranjado/a *adj.* **3B:** naranja *f.* **2B: orange juice** jugo de naranja *m.* **2B: orange juice** zumo de naranja *m.* **2B**
orchid orquídea *f.* **11A**
order pedido *m.* **7B:** pedir *v.* **7B: in order** en regla *loc. adv.* **11A: put in order** ordenar *v.* **0**
organic ecológico/a *adj.* **7B:** orgánico/a *adj.* **7B: organic farming** agricultura ecológica *f.* **15A: organic product** producto ecológico *m.* **15A**
organism organismo *m.* **17A**

organization organización *f.* **3B: NGO (non-governmental organization)** ONG (organización no gubernamental) *f.* **5A**

organize agrupar *v.* **0:** organizar *v.* **6A: to organize a trip** preparar un viaje *v.* **13A**

organized ordenado/a *adj.* **13B**

oriental oriental *adj.* **6A**

origin procedencia *f.* **8B:** origen *m.* **1A**

original original *adj.* **3B**

other otro/a *adj.* **: in other words** es decir *exp.* **8B: on the other hand** por otro lado/ por otra parte *loc. adv.* **13B: the other day** el otro día *loc. adv.* **9B**

otherwise: or otherwise o bien *conj.* **12A**

Ottawa Ottawa *f.* **1A**

our nuestro/a(s) *adj.* **5B**

out fuera *adv.* **2B: to get a kick out of** encantar *v.* **5B: to go out** salir *v.* **3A**

outdo: to outdo oneself superarse *v.* **18A**

outdoors al aire libre *loc. adv.* **3A**

outside fuera *prep.* **3A: outside of class** fuera de clase *loc. adv.* **3A**

outskirts afueras *f. pl.* **11B**

overcome superar *v.* **18A**

overnight de un día para el otro *loc. adv.* **16A**

overprotect sobreproteger *v.* **15B**

overtime horas extras *f. pl.* **13B: to do overtime** hacer horas extras *v.* **13B**

own propio/a *adj.* **: for (your) own good** por (tu/su) bien *loc. adv.* **15B**

owner dueño/a *m./f.* **8B:** propietario/a *m./f.* **8B**

oxygen oxígeno *m.* **18A**

ozone layer capa de ozono *f.* **17A**

P

p.m. de la noche *loc. adv.* **3A:** de la tarde *loc. adv.* **3A: 6 p.m.** 18:00 h *f.* **1B**

pace: pace of life ritmo de vida *m.* **3A**

pacifist pacifista *m. y f.* **16A**

pack hacer las maletas *v.* **8B**

package envase *m.* **15A:** paquete *m.* **4A: package tour** viaje organizado *m.* **13A**

packaged envasado/a *adj.* **15A**

page página *f.* **0: Web page** página web *f.* **14B**

pain dolor *m.* **10A**

painful amargo/a *adj.* **10B**

painkiller analgésico *m.* **10A**

paint pintar *v.* **6A**

painter pintor(a) *m./f.* **12B**

painting pintura *f.* **3A**

pair par *m.* **5A: In pairs** En parejas *loc. adv.* **0**

Pakistani paquistaní *adj.* **4A**

pal cuate/a *(fam.) m./f.* **12A**

pan: frying pan sartén *f.* **8A**

Panama Panamá *m.* **0**

Panama City Ciudad de Panamá *f.* **0**

Panamanian panameño/a *adj.* **2A**

Pan-American: Pan-American Games Juegos Panamericanos *m.* **18A**

panel: panel of judges jurado *m.* **16B**

panoramic panorámico/a *adj.* **18B**

pants pantalones *m. pl.* **3B**

paradise paraíso *m.* **4B**

paragliding parapente *m.* **18A**

paragraph párrafo *m.* **0**

Paraguay Paraguay *m.* **0**

Paraguayan paraguayo/a *adj.*

Paralympic Games Juegos Paralímpicos *m.* **12B**

parasite parásito *m.* **8A**

parents padres *m. pl.* **5B**

park parque *m.* **2A:** aparcar *v.* **11A**

parking lot aparcamiento *m.* **11A**

participate colaborar *v.* **3A:** participar *v.* **3A**

particular: in particular en concreto *loc. adv.* **7B**

partner pareja *f.* **5B:** compañero/a *m./f.* **2B**

party fiesta *f.* **: bachelor(ette) party** despedida de soltero/a *f.* **18B: fifteenth birthday party** fiesta de quince años *f.* **18B: political party** partido político *m.* **16A**

pasodoble (Spanish march-like dance) pasodoble *m.* **17B**

pass aprobar *v.* **14A:** pasar *v.*

passenger pasajero/a *m./f.* **13A: passengers/ladies and gentlemen** señores pasajeros *exp.* **13A**

passive pasivo/a *adj.* **6A**

passport pasaporte *m.* **13A: passport control** control de pasaportes *m.* **13A**

past pasado *m.*

pasta pasta *f.* **2B**

pastime pasatiempo *m.* **7A**

pastries bollería *f.* **2B**

Patagonia Patagonia *f.* **6B**

patent patentar *v.* **17A**

patience paciencia *f.* **15A**

patient paciente *m. y f.* **10A**

patron saint patrono/a *m./f.* **16B**

paw pata *f.* **5A**

pay pagar *v.* **3B: pay attention (to)** poner atención (a) *v.* **0: to pay attention (to somebody)** hacer caso (a alguien) *v.* **15B**

payment pago *m.* **7B**

peace paz *f.* **2A:** tranquilidad *f.* **2A: ambassador for peace** embajador(a) de la paz *m./f.* **16A: to be at peace** estar en paz *v.* **10B**

peaceful pacífico/a *adj.* **16A:** tranquilo/a *adj.* **2A**

peach durazno *m.* **16B:** melocotón *m.* **15A**

peal: peal of a bell campanada *f.* **18B**

peanut cacahuate *m.* **12A**

peel pelar *v.* **8A**

pen bolígrafo *m.* **3B**

people gente *f.* **2A: for young people** juvenil *adj.* **7A: native people** pueblo indígena *m.* **16A: to talk to people** hablar con la gente *v.* **2A: unity of the people** unidad popular *f.* **16A: young people** jóvenes *m. pl.* **2A**

pepper pimienta *f.* **: bell pepper** pimiento *m.* **2B**

per: per capita income renta per cápita *f.* **14A: per se** propiamente dicho/a *exp.* **16B**

percent por ciento *loc. adv.*: **one hundred percent** cien por ciento *adj.* **12A**

perfect perfecto/a *adj.* **2A**

perfectly: I understand you perfectly. Te entiendo perfectamente. *exp.* **13B**

perform interpretar *v.* **7A:** realizar *v.* **5A:** rendir *v.* **6A**

performance interpretación *f.* **5A:** rendimiento *m.* **13B**

perfume fragancia *f.* **16B:** perfume *m.* **3B: perfume/cosmetics shop** perfumería *f.* **3B**

perhaps quizá(s) *adv.* **17A**

period época *f.* **9A:** período *m.* **: enrollment period** plazo de inscripción *m.* **18A: postwar period** posguerra *f.* **14B**

permission: to ask permission pedir permiso *v.* **12B**

person persona *f.* **1B: an 80-year-old person** persona de 80 años *f.* **3A: businessperson** empresario/a *m./f.* **8B: person in charge** responsable *m. y f.* **13A: person of mixed race** mestizo/a *m./f.* **16A**

personal personal *adj.* **3B: personal satisfaction** satisfacción personal *f.* **13B**

personality carácter *f.* **12A**

personalized personalizado/a *adj.* **11A**

Peru Perú *m.* **0**

Peruvian peruano/a *adj.*

pessimistic pesimista *adj.* **12A**

pesticide pesticida *m.* **15A**

petrified petrificado/a *adj.* **11B**

pharmaceutical farmacéutico/a *adj.* **17A**

Philadelphia Filadelfia *f.* **1A**

philosophy filosofía *f.* **5A**

phone teléfono *m.* **1B: cell phone** (teléfono) celular *m.* **1B: phone service** telefonía *f.* **9B: What is your phone number?** ¿Cuál es tu número de teléfono? *exp.* **1B**

photo foto *f.* **0: photo story** fotonovela *f.* **12A**

photocopier (foto)copiadora *f.* **7B**

photograph fotografía *f.* **1B**

photographer fotógrafo/a *m./f.* **11B**

photographic fotográfico/a *adj.* **11B**

phrase frase *f.* **0**

physical físico/a *adj.* **6A: physical appearance** aspecto físico *m.* **12A: physical condition** estado físico *m.* **10A: Physical Education** Educación física *f.* **15B**

physics física *f.* **15B**

piano piano *m.* **8A: grand piano** piano de cola *m.* **10B**

pick up recoger *v.* **5B**

picked recogido/a *adj.* **15A**

pickup recepción *f.* **11A**

picture imagen *f.* **1A: picture frame** marco *m.* **3B: to take pictures** tomar fotos *v.* **6B**

piece: piece of advice consejo *m.* **6A: piece of furniture** mueble *m.* **8A: piece of gossip** chisme *m.* **17B**

pig cerdo/a *m./f.*

pigeon paloma *f.* **: pigeon pea** gandul *m.* **15A**

pilgrim peregrino/a *m./f.* **11A**

pineapple piña *f.* **15A**

pink rosado/a *adj.* **18B**

place lugar *m.* **2A:** sitio *m.* **11B:** rincón *m.* **11A:** colocar *v.* **9B: place of worship** lugar de culto *m.* **8A**

plan plano *m.* **8A: planificar** *v.* **18B: programar** *v.* **3A**

plane avión *m.* **6B: plane ticket** pasaje de avión *m.* **6B**

planner: (weekly) planner agenda semanal *f.* **3A**

plant planta *f.* **8A**

plastic plástico *m.* **8A: plastic container** envase de plástico *m.* **15A**

plate plato *m.* **8A**

platform andén *m.* **13A**

play jugar *v.* **7A: to play the lottery** jugar a la lotería *v.* **9B: (an instrument) tocar** *v.* **8A**

player jugador(a) *m./f.* : **bandoneón player** bandoneonista *m. y f.* **17B: baseball player** beisbolista *m. y f.* **18A: MP3 player** reproductor de MP3 *m.* **13B: soccer player** futbolista *m. y f.* : **tennis player** tenista *m. y f.* **14A**

pleasant agradable *adj.* **2A**

please por favor *exp.* **2B**

pleased: Pleased to meet you. Encantado/a. *exp.* **0: Pleased to meet you.** Mucho gusto. *exp.* **0**

pleasure placer *m.* **5B**

plentiful abundante *adj.* **17A**

pocket bolsillo *m.* **13B**

poem poema *m.* **10B**

poet poeta *m./f.* **10B: poetisa** *f.* **10B**

point punto *m.* **5B: meeting point** punto de encuentro *m.* **9A: point in common** punto común *m.* **5B**

pole bastón *m.* **18A**

police policía *f.* **0**

policy política *f.* **6A**

political político/a *adj.* **1B: political party** partido político *m.* **16A: political science** ciencias políticas *f.* **1B**

politician político/a *m./f.* **16A**

politics política *f.* **16A**

pool alberca *f.* **5B: piscina** *f.* **3A**

popular popular *adj.* **2B**

populated poblado/a *adj.* **16B**

population población *f.* **2A: migrant population** población migrante *m.* **8B**

pork carne de cerdo *f.* **18B**

Port-au-Prince Puerto Príncipe *m.* **12B**

portion ración *f.* **2B**

portrait retrato *m.* **14B**

Portugal Portugal *m.* **1A**

Portuguese portugués/portuguesa *adj.* **1B: portugués** *m.* **1B**

position cargo *m.* **17A: puesto** *m.* **4B: managerial position** puesto directivo *m.* **13B**

positive positivo/a *adj.* **2B**

possibility posibilidad *f.* **6A**

possible posible *adj.* **4A: as... as possible** lo más... posible *m.* **17A: it's possible** es posible *exp.* **4A**

post exponer *v.* **0**

postcard postal *f.* **9B**

poster cartel *m.* **0: póster** *m.* **4A**

postpone postergar *v.* **17B: posponer** *v.* **18A**

postwar: postwar period posguerra *f.* **14B**

potato papa *f.* **2B: patata** *f.* **2B: potato chips** patatas fritas *f.* **4A: Spanish potato omelet** tortilla española *f* **2B**

pottery cerámica *f.* **6A: to make pottery** hacer cerámica *f.* **6A**

powder polvo *m.* **15A: cocoa powder** cacao en polvo *m.* **15A: powdered skim milk** leche descremada en polvo *f.* **15A**

power fuerza *f.* **16A**

practical práctico/a *adj.* **3B**

practice practicar *v.* **0**

prediction predicción *f.* **17A**

premiere estrenarse *v.* **14B**

prepare preparar *v.* **7A**

presence presencia *f.* **8B**

present regalo *m.* **3B: presentar** *v.* **0: to give oneself a present** regalarse *v.* **6B**

preservation conservación *f.* **15A**

preservative conservante *m.* **15A**

preserve preservar *v.* **15A**

president presidente/a *m./f.* **16A**

press prensa *f.* **9B: financial press** prensa económica *f.* **3A: gossip press** prensa rosa *f.* **9B: press conference** rueda de prensa *f.* **12B: press office** oficina de prensa *f.* **16A: press release** nota de prensa *f.* **10B**

pressure presión *f.* **4B**

prestigious prestigioso/a *adj.* **10A**

pretext pretexto *m.* **16A**

pretty bonito/a *adj.* **2A**

prevent impedir *v.* **12B**

prevention prevención *f.* **10A**

previous anterior *adj.* **14B**

price precio *m.* **4A: fixed-price menu** menú del día *m.* **2B**

prick pinchazo *m.* **17A**

print imprimir *v.* **7B**

printer impresora *f.* **7B**

prisoner preso/a *m./f.* **16A**

privacy privacidad *f.* **17A**

private privado/a *adj.* **4B: private home** casa particular *f.* **13A: private lesson** clase particular *f.* **17B: private school** escuela privada *f.* **15B**

privatized privatizado/a *adj.* **13A**

privileged: privileged person privilegiado/a *m./f.* **2A**

prize premio *m.* **2B: first prize** gordo *m.* **9B: Nobel Prize** Premio Nobel *m.* **10B**

probability probabilidad *f.* **15A**

probable probable *adj.* **17A**

probably probablemente *adv.* **4A**

problem problema *m.* **2A: No problem!** ¡No hay problema! *exp.* **7B**

process proceso *m.* : **in the process** de paso *loc. adv.* **14B**

procession procesión *f.* **16B**

produce: produce market agromercado *m.* **4A: to mass-produce** fabricar en serie *v.* **13B**

producer productor(a) *m./f.* **3B**

product producto *m.* **3B: organic product** producto ecológico *m.* **15A: food product** producto de alimentación *m.* **15A: gross domestic product (GDP)** producto interior bruto (PIB) *m.* **11A**

production elaboración *f.* **15A**

productivity productividad *f.* **6A**

profession profesión *f.* **1B**

professional profesional *adj.* **2B:**

profesional *m. y f.* **3A: professional experience** experiencia profesional *f.* **11B: professional training** formación profesional *f.* **14A**

professionalism profesionalidad *f.* **2B**

profile perfil *m.* **14A**

program programa *m.* **9A: exchange program** programa de intercambio *m.* **14A: radio program** programa de radio *m.* **3A**

project proyecto *m.* **4B**

promotion promoción *f.* **9B**

promotional: promotional campaign campaña de promoción *f.* **16B**

pronounce pronunciar *v.* **0**

property propiedad *f.* **6A**

propose proponer *v.* **13A**

prospect perspectiva *f.* **13B**

protagonist protagonista *m. y f.* **0**

protect proteger *v.* **3B**

protein proteína *f.* **15A**

protest protesta *f.* **11A**

proud orgulloso/a *adj.* **2A**

prove demostrar *v.* **17A**

provide aportar *v.* **15A**

province provincia *f.* **7B**

proximity cercanía *f.* **16B**

psychologist psicólogo/a *m./f.* **1B**

psychology psicología *f.* **6A**

public público/a *adj.* **15B: public school** escuela pública *f.* **15B**

publicist publicista *m. y f.* **14B**

Puerto Rican boricua *adj.* **11A: puertorriqueño/a** *m./f.* **1A**

Puerto Rico Puerto Rico *m.* **0**

pump bomba *f.* **17A**

punctual puntual *adj.* **13B**

punctuality puntualidad *f.* **11A**

puppy cachorro/a *m./f.* **12B**

pupusa (Salvadoran filled tortilla) pupusa *f.* **8B**

pure puro/a *adj.* **7B**

purity pureza *f.* **18B**

purple morado/a *adj.* **16B**

purpose finalidad *f.* **14B**

purser jefe/a de cabina *m./f.* **13A**

put meter *v.* **8A: poner** *v.* **4A: put in order** ordenar *v.* **0: put out** apagar *v.* **7A: to put makeup on** maquillarse *v.* **7A**

pyramid pirámide *f.* **2A**

Q

qualify habilitar *v.* **13B**

quality calidad *f.* **2A: quality of life** calidad de vida *f.* **2A**

quantity cantidad *f.* **4A**

Quechua quechua *m.* **1B**

question pregunta *f.* **0: consulta** *f.* **6B: to question** plantearse preguntas *v.* **14B**

questionnaire cuestionario *m.* **6A**

quiet tranquilo/a *adj.* **2A**

quit dejar *v.* **5A: to quit smoking** dejar de fumar *v.* **12B**

quite: quite a lot bastante *adv.* **5B**

quoted citado/a *adj.* **17A**

R

racket raqueta *f.* **18A**

radio radio *f.* **4B: radio network** cadena de radio *f.* **14B: radio program** programa de radio *m.* **3A: radio station** emisora *f.* **14B: to listen to the radio** escuchar la radio *v.* **2A**

rafting rafting *m.* **18A**

rain lluvia *f.* **6A:** llover *v.* **10A**

raincoat impermeable *m.* **10A**

raise: to raise awareness sensibilizar *v.* **16A**

ranch estancia *f.* **3A**

range gama *f.* **16B**

ranger: forest ranger guarda forestal *m. y f.* **14A**

raspberry frambuesa *f.* **15A**

rated: to be the highest rated ser líder de audiencia *v.* **14B**

rational racional *adj.* **16A**

raw material materia prima *f.* **15A**

reach cumplir *v.* **13A**

read leer *v.* **0**

reading lectura *f.* **0:** texto *m.* **0**

real verdadero/a *adj.* **12B: real-estate agency** inmobiliaria *f.* **4B**

realistic realista *adj.* **12A**

Really? ¿De verdad? *exp.* **9B**

reason razón *f.* **:** porqué *m.* **17B**

rebel rebelde *adj.* **15B**

receive recibir *v.* **2B**

reception recepción *f.* **:** banquete *m.* **5A**

recipe receta (de cocina) *f.* **8A: recipe collection** recetario *m.* **15A**

recommend recomendar *v.* **13A**

recommendation recomendación *f.* **6A**

recommended recomendado/a *adj.* **4A**

reconcile conciliar *v.* **6A**

record: record label sello discográfico *m.* **17B: vinyl record** disco de vinilo *m.* **13B**

recyclable container envase reciclable *m.* **15A**

recycle reciclar *v.* **11B**

recycled reciclado/a *adj.* **8A**

recycling reciclaje *m.* **15A**

red rojo/a *adj.* **3B: red-haired** pelirrojo/a *adj.* **12A**

reduce reducir *v.* **16A**

refrigerator frigorífico *m.* **7B:** refrigerador *m.* **8A**

regarding con respecto a *loc. prep.* **16A**

region zona *f.* **5A**

rehearsal ensayo *m.* **7A**

reject rechazar *v.* **16A**

relate relacionar *v.* **0**

relation: International Relations Relaciones Internacionales *f.* **11B**

relationship relación *f.* **5B**

relative familiar *m.* **5B**

relaxation relajación *f.* **6A**

relaxed relajado/a *adj.* **3A**

relaxing relajante *adj.* **6A**

release: press release nota de prensa *f.* **10B:** (music) editar *v.* **17B**

reliable fiable *adj.* **17A:** serio/a *adj.* **13B**

religion religión *f.* **8A**

religious religioso/a *adj.* **8A**

relive revivir *v.* **14B**

remark observación *f.* **13A**

remedy remedio *m.* **10A**

remember acordarse de *v.* **18B:** recordar *v.* **5A**

remove retirar *v.* **13A**

renewable renovable *adj.* **17A**

rent alquiler *m.* **4B**

rental de alquiler *adj.* **11B:** alquiler *m.* **4B**

repair arreglar *v.* **7B: repair shop** taller (mecánico) *m.* **7B**

repeat repetir *v.* **0**

repellent repelente *m.* **10A**

replace sustituir *v.* **14A**

reporter reportero/a *m./f.* **7B**

represent representar *v.* **10B**

representative representante *m. y f.* **10B**

request petición *f.* **12B:** pedido *m.* **7B:** solicitar *v.* **4A**

require exigir *v.* **13A: to require sacrifices** exigir sacrificios *v.* **13A**

required excluyente *adj.* **13B**

requirement requisito *m.* **13B: to meet the requirements** reunir los requisitos *v.* **13B**

requited: requited love amor correspondido *m.* **12A**

rescue rescatar *v.* **18B**

research investigación *f.* **8B:** investigar *v.* **8B: market research** investigación de mercado *f.* **15A**

researcher investigador(a) *m./f.* **17A**

resemblance parecido *m.* **12A**

reservation reserva *f.* **6B**

reserve reservar *v.* **6B**

resolution: conflict resolution resolución de conflictos *f.* **13B**

resource recurso *m.* **12B: economic resource** recurso económico *m.* **14A: Human Resources (HR)** Recursos Humanos (RR.HH.) *m.* **13B: natural resource** recurso natural *m.* **14A**

respect respeto *m.* **14A:** respetar *v.* **8A**

respectful respetuoso/a *adj.* **12A**

responsibility responsabilidad *f.* **9A**

responsible responsable *adj.* **3B**

rest descanso *m.* **3A:** descansar *v.* **5B: the rest of** el resto de *m.* **12B**

restate reformular *v.* **8B**

restaurant restaurante *m.* **0**

restore restaurar *v.* **11A**

result resultado *m.* **12B: to give good results** redundar en *v.* **17A**

résumé currículum vítae *m.* **11B**

retire jubilarse *v.*

retired jubilado/a *adj.* **5B**

retirement jubilación *f.* **18B**

return devolución *f.* **9A:** devolver *v.* **16B:** regresar *v.* **8B:** volver *v.* **6B: in return** a cambio *loc. adv.* **12B**

reunion reencuentro *m.* **6B**

review reseña *f.* **9A:** revisar *v.* **0**

revolt revuelta *f.* **14A**

revolution revolución *f.* **13B**

reward recompensa *f.* **8B**

rewarding gratificante *adj.* **11A**

rhythm ritmo *m.* **17B**

rice arroz *m.* **2B: rice with vegetables**

arroz con verduras *m.* **2B**

rich rico/a *adj.* **7A**

richness riqueza *f.* **11B**

ride montar *v.* **9A: horseback ride** paseo a caballo *m.* **6B: horseback riding** cabalgata *f.* **18A**

ridiculous ridículo/a *adj.* **15B**

rig: oil rig plataforma petrolera *f.* **14A**

right correcto/a *adj.* **:** derecho *m.* **3B: human rights** derechos humanos *m.* **16A: to be right** tener razón *v.* **10B: to the right** a la derecha *loc. adv.* **9B: to the right of** a la derecha de *loc. adv.* **3B**

right? ¿verdad? *exp.* **4A**

rise aumentar *v.* **5A**

risk riesgo *m.* **7A**

ritual rito *m.* **6A:** ritual *m.* **14A**

river río *m.* **3A: Amazon River** Amazonas *m.* **5A**

robe bata *f.* **5A**

role papel *m.* **5B**

role-play escenificar *v.* **0:** representar *v.* **0**

roll the die tiren el dado *exp.* **10A**

romantic romántico/a *adj.* **2A**

romanticism romanticismo *m.* **12A**

room habitación *f.* **4B:** sitio *m.* **9B: chat room** chat *m.* **3A: dining room** comedor *m.* **4B: double room** habitación doble *f.* **6B: living room** salón *m.* **4B: living room-dining room** salón-comedor *m.* **4B: single room** habitación individual *f.* **6B**

rose rosa *f.* **18B**

round redondo/a *adj.* **: round-trip** ida y vuelta *exp.* **6B**

roundtable tertulia *f.* **9A**

route ruta *f.* **6B:** trayecto *m.* **13A**

routine rutina *f.* **7A: daily routine** rutina diaria *f.* **3A**

rowboat bote de remos *m.* **18A**

royal: the royal family la Familia Real *f.* **4B**

rubber band goma elástica *f.* **8A**

rug alfombra *f.* **4B**

ruins ruinas *f.* **2A**

rule norma *f.* **15B**

ruler gobernante *m./f.* **12B**

run correr *v.* **18A:** dirigir *v.* **6A: to run a marathon** correr un maratón *v.* **18A: to run in the same circles** relacionarse *v.* **10B: to run a business** llevar un negocio *v.* **9B**

runner corredor(a) *m./f.* **18A**

running shoes zapatillas (de deporte) *f.* **3B**

rural rural *adj.* **11A: rural neighborhood** vereda *f.* **9A: rural worker** campesino/a *m./f.* **9A**

S

sack bolsa *f.* **4A**

sacrifice el sacrificio *m.* **13A: to require sacrifices** exigir sacrificios *v.* **13A**

sad apenado/a *adj.* **17B:** triste *adj.* **12A: to become sad** ponerse triste *v.* **18B**

sadden entristecer *v.* **17B:** dar pena *v.* **18B**

sadness tristeza *f.* **10B**

safe seguro/a *adj.* **: safe for** apto/a para *adj.* **15A**

safety seguridad *f.* **13A**

saint santo/a *m./f.* : **patron saint** patrono/a *m./f.* **16B**

sake: to talk for the sake of it hablar por hablar *exp.* **14B**

salad ensalada *f.* **2B: house salad** ensalada de la casa *f.* **2B**

salary sueldo *m.* **14B**

sale venta *f.* **4B: for sale** a la venta *loc. adv.* **4B: sales executive** ejecutivo/a de ventas *m./f.* **13B**

salon: hair salon peluquería *f.* **8B**

salsa salsa *f.* **1A**

salt sal *f.* **8A: lacking salt** soso/a *adj.* **2B**

salty salado/a *adj.* **2B**

Salvadoran salvadoreño/a *adj.* **8B**

same mismo/a *adj.* **7A: at the same time** al mismo tiempo *loc. adv.* **7A**

San Juan: from San Juan sanjuanero/a *adj.* **11A**

sandwich sándwich *m.* **2B**

satisfaction satisfacción *f.* **11A: personal satisfaction** satisfacción personal *f.* **13B**

Saturday sábado *m.* **3A**

sauce salsa *f.* **2B: sauce similar to Thousand Island dressing** salsa golf *f.* **17A: tomato sauce** tomate frito *m.* **15A**

sausage salchicha *f.* **4A: chorizo sausage** chorizo *m.* **2B**

save ahorrar *v.* **12B:** guardar *v.* **7B:** salvar *v.* **9B: to save (songs/photos)** guardar (canciones/fotos) *v.* **13B**

savings ahorros *m. pl.* **8B**

savor saborear *v.* **16B**

say decir *v.* **7A: How do you say…?** ¿Cómo se dice...? *exp.* **0: You don't say!** ¡No me digas! *exp.* **9B**

scale escala *f.* **15B**

scarf pañuelo *m.* **3B**

scenery paisaje *m.* **6B: change of scenery** cambio de aires *m.* **11A**

scent aroma *m.* **16B**

schedule calendario *m.* **3A:** horario *m.* **3A: schedule flexibility** flexibilidad horaria *f.* **6A: work schedule** horario de trabajo *m.* **3A**

scholarship beca (escolar) *f.* **8B, 12B: ERASMUS scholarship** beca ERASMUS *f.* **14A**

school escuela *f.* **3B:** colegio *m.* **3A: bilingual school** escuela bilingüe *f.* **15B: elementary school** escuela primaria *f.* **9A: high school** secundaria *f.*, instituto *m.* **15B high school studies** bachillerato *m.* **15B: private school** escuela privada *f.* **15B: public school** escuela pública *f.* **15B: school subject** asignatura *f.* **15B: to take the kids to school** llevar a los niños al colegio *v.* **3A**

science ciencia *f.* **6A: computer science** informática *f.* **1B: political science** ciencias políticas *f.* **1B**

scientific científico/a *adj.* **17A: scientific field** campo científico *m.* **17A: scientific method** método científico *m.* **17A**

score puntuación *f.* **11A**

Scottish escocés/escocesa *adj.* **7B**

screen pantalla *f.* **13A**

screening: baggage screening control de equipaje *m.* **13A**

screw top tapa de rosca *f.* **8A**

scuba diving submarinismo *m.* **11B**

sculptor escultor(a) *m./f.* **16A**

sea mar *m.* **4B: Caribbean Sea** mar Caribe *m.* **4B**

sea bream (type of fish) dorada *f.* **2B**

season estación (del año) *f.* **10A: high season** temporada alta *f.* **4B**

seat plaza *f.* **13A:** asiento *m.* **13A: seat back** respaldo del asiento *m.* **13A: seat change** cambio de asiento *m.* **13A**

seat belt cinturón de seguridad *m.* **13A**

secretary secretario/a *m./f.* **1B**

section sección *f.* **8B**

sector sector *m.* **8B: energy sector** sector energético *m.* **14A**

security seguridad *f.* **17A: night security guard** vigilante nocturno/a *m./f.* **3A**

sedentary: sedentary lifestyle sedentarismo *m.* **16B**

see ver *v.* **3B: Can I see them?** ¿Los puedo ver? *exp.* **3B: I'm sorry to see you like this.** Siento verte así. *exp.* **13B: let's see…** a ver… *exp.* **6A: See you later.** Hasta la vista. *exp.* **0: See you tomorrow.** Hasta mañana. *exp.* **0: See you!** ¡Nos vemos! *exp.* **0: to see a patient** atender *v.* **10A**

seem parecer *v.* **5B: to seem strange** parecer raro *v.* **15B**

select seleccionar *v.* **0**

self: self-help autoayuda *f.* **6A: self-sufficient** autosuficiente *adj.* **7B: to be self-sufficient** valerse *v.* **5B: to be self-confident** estar seguro/a de sí mismo/a *v.* **18A**

sell vender *v.* **8B**

semi-: semi-sleeper semi-cama *adj.* **13A**

send enviar *v.* **7B:** mandar *v.* **7B**

sensitive sensible *adj.* **10A**

sentence oración *f.* **0**

separate separarse *v.* **12A**

separated separado/a *adj.* **12A**

September septiembre *m.* **5A**

series serie *f.* : **television series** serie de televisión *f.* **14B: to broadcast the television series** pasar/emitir la serie de televisión *v.* **14B**

serious serio/a *adj.* **12A**

Serrano ham jamón serrano *m.* **2B**

service servicio *m.* **5B: at your service** a tu/su servicio *loc. adv.* **7B: domestic service** servicio doméstico *m.* **8B: phone service** telefonía *f.* **9B: service industry** industria de servicios *f.* **14A: Social Services** Servicios Sociales *m. pl.* **5B**

serving porción *f.* **15A**

set: television set televisor *m.* **4B: to set aside** reservar *v.* **6A: set free** liberar *v.* **16A: set in motion** poner en marcha *exp.* **16A**

setback adversidad *f.* **18A**

seven siete *adj.* **1A**

seventeen diecisiete *adj.* **1B**

seventy setenta *adj.* **1B**

shaggy peludo/a *adj.* **9A**

shape: to be in (good) shape estar en forma *v.* **7A**

share compartir *v.* **5A**

she ella *pron.* **1A**

sheet: ice sheet manto de hielo *m.* **11B: sheet of paper** hoja (de papel) *f.* **8A**

shirt camisa *f.* **3B**

shock: culture shock choque cultural *m.* **14B**

shoe zapato *m.* **3B: running shoes** zapatillas (de deporte) *f. pl.* **3B: shoe store** zapatería *f.* **3B: shoes** calzado *m.* **10A**

shoot (film) rodar *v.* **9B**

shop tienda *f.* **3B: fruit shop** frutería *f.* **9B: gift shop** tienda de regalos *f.* **3B: perfume/cosmetics shop** perfumería *f.* **3B: repair shop** taller (mecánico) *m.* **7B: shop window** escaparate *m.* **3B: tobacconist shop** estanco *m.* **9B**

shopping: shopping list lista de compras *f.* **4A: shopping mall** centro comercial *m.* **2A: to do the shopping** hacer las compras *v.* **3A**

shore orilla *f.* **6B**

short bajo/a *adj.* **12A:** corto/a *adj.* **12A: (in the) short term** a corto plazo *loc. adv.* **17A: in short** en resumen *exp.* **18B: short story** cuento *m.* **9B**

shorthand taquigrafía *f.* **13B**

show espectáculo *m.* **4A:** enseñar *v.* **5B:** mostrar *v.* **0: news and talk show** magacín *m.* **9A: talk show** tertulia *f.* **9A: to show affection** mostrar afecto *v.* **18B**

shower ducha *f.* **7A:** ducharse *v.* **7A**

shrimp gamba *f.* **2B:** camarón *m.* **16B**

shy tímido/a *adj.* **12A**

siblings hermanos *m. pl.* **5B**

sick enfermo/a *adj.* **5B**

side lado *m.* **13B: bad side** lado malo *m.* **13B**

sign firmar *v.* **16A: sign up for** apuntarse a *v.* **13A**

signing firma *f.* **16A**

silence silencio *m.* **6A**

silent: to be silent estar callado/a *v.* **9A**

silver plata *f.* **12B: silver wedding anniversary** bodas de plata *f. pl.* **18B**

since desde que *conj.* **8B:** desde *prep.* **2A: since childhood** desde niño(s)/a(s) *loc. adv.* **8B: since childhood** desde pequeño/a *loc. adv.* **5B: since then** desde entonces *loc. adv.* **7A**

Sincerely, Atentamente, *exp.* **6B**

sing cantar *v.* **17B**

singer cantante *m. y f.* **5A: singer-songwriter** cantautor(a) *m./f.* **7A**

single soltero/a *adj.* **5B: single room** habitación individual *f.* **6B**

sir señor *m.* **6B: Dear sirs:** Estimados señores: *exp.* **6B**

sister hermana *f.* **5A**

six seis *adj.* **1A**

sixteen dieciséis *adj.* **1B**

sixty sesenta *adj.* **1B: in the mid sixties** a mediados de los 60 *loc. adv.* **14B: the sixties** los años 60 *m.* **8B**

size talla *f.* **3B: What size?** ¿De qué talla? *exp.* **3B**

ski esquiar *v.*

skiing esquí *m.* **1A**

skim milk leche descremada *f.* **15A**
skin piel *f.* **10A**
skirt falda *f.* **3B**
sleeper: (semi-)sleeper (semi-)cama *adj.* **13A**
slogan eslogan *m.* **11A**
slope pendiente *f.* **18A**
slow lento/a *adj.* **7B**
slower: Slower, please. Más despacio, por favor. *exp.* **0**
slowly despacio *adv.* **10A**
small chico/a *adj.* **11B:** pequeño/a *adj.* **4B**
smart listo/a *adj.*
smartphone teléfono inteligente *m.* **13B**
smile sonrisa *f.* **10A:** sonreír *v.* **13A**
smoke fumar *v.* **12B: to quit smoking** dejar de fumar *v.* **12B**
snack: afternoon snack merienda *f.* **16B**
snail caracol *m.* **2B**
sneakers zapatillas (de deporte) *f.* **3B**
snow nieve *f.* **10A:** nevar *v.* **10A**
so entonces *adv.* **7A:** así (es) que *conj.* **17A:** **I think so.** Creo que sí. *exp.* **7B**
soap jabón *m.* **8A: soap opera** telenovela *f.* **5A**
soccer fútbol *m.* **1A: soccer player** futbolista *m./f.*
social social *adj.* **6A: social justice** justicia social *f.* **16A: social network** red social *f.* **13B: social mobilization** movilización social *f.* **16A: Social Services** Servicios Sociales *m.* **5B: social studies** ciencias sociales *f.* **15B**
society sociedad *f.* **9A**
sofa sofá *m.* **4B**
soft blando/a *adj.* **9A: soft drink** refresco *m.* **4A: soft drink** gaseosa *f.* **13A**
solve solucionar *v.* **10A**
some algún, alguno/a *adj.* **9A:** algunos/as *pron.* **5A**
somebody alguien *pron.* **5B**
someone alguien *pron.* **5B**
something algo *pron.* **2B: to be doing something** estar haciendo algo *v.* **7A: to do something at home** hacer algo en casa *v.* **3A: to do something (for a living)** dedicarse a (hacer) algo *v.* **7A**
sometimes a veces *loc. adv.* **2B**
son hijo *m.* **5A**
song canción *f.* **7A**
sonnet soneto *m.* **10B**
soon pronto *adv.* **0: See you soon.** Hasta pronto. *exp.* **0**
sorry: I'm sorry to hear that. Siento oír eso. *exp.* **13B: I'm sorry to see you like this.** Siento verte así. *exp.* **13B: I'm sorry.** Lo siento. *exp.* **3B**
so-so regular *adv.* **8A**
soufflé suflé *m.* **15A**
soul alma *f.* **6A**
sound sonido *m.* **: sound track** banda sonora *f.* **17B**
soup sopa *f.* **2B: fish soup** sopa de pescado *f.* **2B**
south sur *m.* **2A: South American** sudamericano/a *adj.* **18A**
souvenir recuerdo *m.* **5B:** souvenir *m.* **4A**
space espacio *m.* **13B:** sitio *m.* **9B: to take up space** ocupar espacio *v.* **13B**

Spain España *f.* **0**
Spanish español(a) *adj.* **1B:** español *m.* **1B: Spanish-speaking** hispanohablante *adj.* **14A: to learn Spanish** aprender español *v.* **3A: Spanish National Organization for the Blind** ONCE *f.* **12B: Spanish potato omelet** tortilla española *f.* **2B**
speak hablar *v.* **1B: is/are spoken** se habla(n) *v.* **1B: What languages do you speak?** ¿Qué lenguas hablas? *exp.* **1B**
special especial *adj.* **2B: special edition** edición especial *f.* **3B**
specialist especialista *m. y f.* **10A**
specializing: specializing in especializado/a en *adj.* **2B**
specially especialmente *adv.* **7A**
specifically concretamente *adv.* **7B**
spectacular espectacular *adj.* **11B**
speech discurso *m.* **16A**
speed velocidad *f.* **13B**
spell: How do you spell...? ¿Cómo se escribe? *exp.* **0**
spend ocupar *v.* **5B:** (money) gastar *v.* **: to spend one's vacation** pasar las vacaciones *v.* **4B: to spend the night** pasar la noche *v.* **6B**
spicy picante *adj.* **2B**
spider araña *f.* **16B: spider monkey** mono/a araña *m./f.* **16B**
spill derramarse *v.* **18B**
spirit espíritu *m.* **6A**
spiritual espiritual *adj.* **14A**
split up separarse *v.* **12A**
spokesperson portavoz *m. y f.* **12B**
sport deporte *m.* **3A: sports challenge** reto deportivo *m.* **18A: sports center** polideportivo *m.* **2A**
sporting deportivo/a *adj.* **6A**
sportsman/woman deportista *m. y f.* **18A**
spot rincón *m.* **11A**
spring primavera *f.* **10A**
sprinkle espolvorear *v.* **15A**
square plaza *f.* **1B: square meters** metros cuadrados (m²) *m.* **4B**
squid calamares *m. pl.* **2B**
stability estabilidad *f.* **13B**
stable estable *adj.* **12B**
staff personal *m.* **11A**
stage etapa *f.* **9A:** fase *f.* **17A**
stand (in a market) puesto *m.* **4A**
stand: not to be able to stand no soportar *v.* **15B**
standard estándar *adj.* **7B**
stanza estrofa *f.* **17B**
star estrella *f.* **5A: four-star hotel** hotel de cuatro estrellas *m.* **11A**
start comenzar *v.* **8B:** empezar *v.* **5A**
starting a partir de *conj.* **12B**
state estado *m.* **5B:** declarar *v.* **16A: state of mind** estado anímico *m.* **10A: state of mind** estado de ánimo *m.* **12A**
station estación *f.* **4A: radio station** emisora *f.* **14B**
stationery store papelería *f.* **9B**
status: marital status estado civil *m.* **5B**
stay estancia *f.* **11A:** alojarse *v.* **13A:** quedarse *v.* **8B: Have a nice stay!** ¡Feliz estancia! *exp.* **11A**

steel acero *m.* **: steel cable** cable de acero *m.* **18A**
step paso de baile *m.* **17B**
still aún, todavía *adv.* **15B**
stimulate estimular *v.* **16A**
stimulating estimulante *adj.* **6A**
stir: to stir up interest despertar la inquietud *v.* **9A**
stock: stock exchange la bolsa (de comercio) *f.* **3A: to take stock of** hacer balance de *v.* **12B**
stomach estómago *m.* **10A**
stop dejar de *v.* **10B:** parar *v.* **3A:** impedir *v.* **12B: to stop over** hacer escala *v.* **13A**
storage: to have (storage) capacity tener capacidad *v.* **13B**
store tienda *f.* **2A:** establecimiento *m.* **9B: clothing store** tienda de ropa *f.* **3B: grocery store** tienda de alimentación *f.* **4A: music store** tienda de discos *f.* **3B: shoe store** zapatería *f.* **3B: stationery store** papelería *f.* **9B: toy store** juguetería *f.* **9B: store where pupusas are sold** pupusería *f.* **8B**
store (songs/photos) guardar (canciones/fotos) *v.* **13B**
storekeeper comerciante *m./f.* **14A**
storm tormenta *f.* **10B**
story historia *f.* **5A:** piso *m.* **8A: photo story** fotonovela *f.* **12A: short story** cuento *m.* **9B**
straight recto *adv.* **9B:** (hair) liso/a *adj.* **12A**
strange: to seem strange parecer raro *v.* **15B**
strategy estrategia *f.* **0**
strawberry fresa *f.* **15A**
street calle *f.* **2A**
strength fuerza *f.* **16A**
strengthen fortalecer *v.* **18A**
stress estrés *m.* **3A**
stressful estresante *adj.* **1B**
strip: comic strip historieta *f.* **14B**
strong resistente *adj.* **17A:** fuerte *adj.*
student estudiante *m. y f.* **:** alumno/a *m./f.* **0**
studies estudios *m. pl.* **5A: high school studies** bachillerato *m.* **14A: social studies** ciencias sociales *f.* **15B**
studio: studio apartment estudio *m.* **4B**
study cursar *v.* **14A:** estudiar *v.* **1B: to study for a degree** estudiar una carrera *v.* **15B**
stuffed relleno/a *adj.* **16B**
style estilo *m.* **4B**
subject asunto *m.* **: school subject** asignatura *f.* **15B**
sub-Saharan: sub-Saharan Africa África subsahariana *f.* **14A**
subtle sutil *adj.* **18B**
suburbs periferia *f.* **2A:** afueras *f. pl.*
subway metro *m.* **0:** subte(rráneo) *m.* **4A**
success éxito *m.* **5A**
successful exitoso/a *adj.* **5A**
suddenly de repente *loc. adv.* **9B**
suffer sufrir *v.* **12B**
sugar azúcar *m.* **0**
suggest proponer *v.* **13A**
suit traje *m.* **3B**
suitable adecuado/a *adj.* **5B**
suitcase maleta *f.* **8B**
summarize resumir *v.* **0**
summary reseña *f.* **9A**

summer verano *m.* **2A: summer internship** pasantía de verano *f.* **13B**
sun sol *m.* **4B**
sunbathe tomar el sol *v.* **10A**
Sunday domingo *m.* **3A: Sunday supplement** suplemento dominical *m.* **9B**
sunny: to be sunny hacer sol *v.* **10A**
sunscreen crema solar protectora *f.* **10A**
supervisor supervisor(a) *m./f.* **13A**
supper cena *f.* **2B: to eat supper** cenar *v.* **2B**
supplement suplemento *m.* **9B**
support adhesión *f.* **16A:** apoyar *v.* **13A: (someone)** solidarizarse (con) *v.* **14B**
supporter: to be a supporter of ser hincha de *v.* **17B**
sure seguro/a *adj.* **9A: I'm sure (that)…** Seguro que… *exp.* **9A**
surf: to surf the Internet navegar por Internet *v.* **6A**
surfer surfista *m. y f.* **16B**
surmount remontar *v.* **18A**
surprise sorpresa *f.* **17B:** chocar *v.* **14B:** extrañar *v.* **15B:** sorprender *v.* **15B**
surprising sorprendente *adj.* **18A**
surrounded rodeado/a *adj.* **6B**
surroundings entorno *m.* **11A**
survey encuesta *f.* **18B**
survive sobrevivir *v.* **13B**
sustainable sostenible *adj.* **17A**
sweater suéter *m.* **3B**
sweet dulce *adj.* **2B**
sweeten endulzar *v.* **15A**
sweethearts novios *m. pl.* **6B**
swim bañarse *v.* **10A:** nadar *v.* **5A**
swimmer nadador(a) *m./f.* **18A**
swimming natación *f.* **10A: swimming pool** piscina *f.* **3A**
sword espada *f.* **18A**
symbol emblema *m.* **18A:** símbolo *m.* **8A**
symbolize simbolizar *v.* **18B**
symptom síntoma *m.* **10A**
synchronized: synchronized swimmer nadador(a) de sincronizada *m./f.* **18A: synchronized swimming** nado sincronizado *m.* **18A**
synthesize sintetizar *v.* **13B**
syringe jeringa *f.* **17A**
syrup jarabe *m.* **15A**
system sistema *m.* **17A: immune system** sistema inmunológico *m.* **17A**

T

table mesa *f.* **3B:** tabla *f.* **0: table of contents** sumario *m.* **1B**
taco taco *m.* **2B**
tai chi taichí *m.* **8A**
take asumir *v.* **12B:** llevar *v.* **5B:** tomar *v.* **9B: to take a bath** darse un baño *v.* **10A: to take a nap** dormir la siesta *v.* **6A: to take a walk** dar un paseo *v.* **6A: to take advantage of** aprovechar *v.* **15A: to take away** quitar *v.* **16A: to take care of** cuidar (a/de) *v.* **5B: to take care of the details** ocuparse de los detalles *v.* **18B: to take into account** tener en cuenta *v.* **16B: to take pictures** tomar fotos *v.* **6B: to take stock of** hacer balance de *v.* **12B: to take the ferry** tomar el ferry

v. **3A: to take the kids to school** llevar a los niños al colegio *v.* **3A: to take up** ocupar *v.* **5B: to take up space** ocupar espacio *v.* **13B**
talent talento *m.* **11B**
talk hablar *v.* **2A: news and talk show** magacín *m.* **9A: talk show** tertulia *f.* **9A: to talk for the sake of it** hablar por hablar *v.* **14B: to talk to people** hablar con la gente *v.* **2A**
tall alto/a *adj.* **8A**
tamer: lion tamer domador(a) de leones *m./f.* **14A**
tapa tapa *f.* **2B: to eat tapas** tapear *v.* **2B**
tapestry tapiz (*pl.* tapices) *m.* **3B**
task labor *f.* **12B**
taste gusto *m.* **15A:** probar *v.* **16B**
tasty rico/a *adj.* **2B:** sabroso/a *adj.* **15A**
tax impuesto *m.* **4B: ecotax** ecotasa *f.* **4B: tax included** IVA incluido *loc. adv.* **2B**
taxi taxi *m.* **0**
tea té *m.* **2B**
tearoom tetería *f.* **8B**
teach enseñar *v.* **5B**
teacher maestro/a *m./f.* **6A:** profesor(a) *m./f.* **1B**
teaching enseñanza *f.* **7A**
team equipo *m.* **7A: as a team** en equipo *loc. adv.* **7A: work team** equipo de trabajo *m.* **13B**
technician técnico/a *m./f.* **1B: computer technician** técnico/a informático/a *m./f.* **1B**
technological tecnológico/a *adj.* **17A**
technology tecnología *f.* **8A**
teenager adolescente *m./f.* **9A**
television tele *f.* **3A:** televisión *f.* **3A: television series** serie de televisión *f.* **14B: television set** televisor *m.* **4B: television viewer** telespectador(a) *m./f.* **14B: to broadcast a television series** pasar/emitir la serie de televisión *v.* **14B**
tell contar *v.* **14B:** decir *v.* **7A:** informar *v.* **0: to tell each other** contarse *v.* **17B: to tell jokes** contar chistes *v.* **17B: to tell the truth** decir la verdad *v.* **17B: to tell the truth …,** la verdad *exp.* **2A**
temperature temperatura *f.* **10A: the temperature is 30º C** hace 30 ºC de temperatura *v.* **10A**
temporarily temporalmente *adv.* **8B**
ten diez *adj.* **1A**
tennis tenis *m.* **1A: tennis player** tenista *m. y f.* **14A**
tense tenso/a *adj.* **10A**
tent carpa *f.* **9A:** tienda de campaña *f.* **18A**
tenth décimo/a *adj.* **12B**
term plazo *m.* **9A: (in the) long term** a largo plazo *loc. adv.* **9A: (in the) medium term** a medio plazo *loc. adv.* **17A: (in the) short term** a corto plazo *loc. adv.* **17A**
terminal terminal *f.* **13A**
terrain relieve *m.* **18B**
terrible terrible *adj.* **15B**
territory territorio *m.* **16A**
terrorism terrorismo *m.* **16A**
test prueba *f.* **0:** test *m.* **1A**
testimony testimonio *m.* **8B**
text texto *m.* **0**

textbook texto *m.* **0**
Thai tailandés *m.* **7A**
Thailand Tailandia *f.* **7A**
than: less than menos que *adj.* **3A: more than** más que *adj.* **3A: older than** mayor de *adj.* **9A**
thank: Nothing else, thanks. Nada más, gracias. *exp.* **2B: Thank you!** ¡Gracias! *exp.* **0: thank goodness** menos mal *exp.* **10A: thanks to…** gracias a… *loc. prep.* **5B**
that ese/a *adj.* **3A:** que *conj.* **: eso** *pron.* **13B: I'm sorry to hear that.** Siento oír eso. *exp.* **13B: that is** o sea *exp.* **8B: that one** ese/a *pron.* **3A**
the el/la/los/las *art.* **2A**
theater teatro *m.* **1A: movie theater** cine *m.* **3A**
them ellos/as *pron.* **1B:** los/las *pron.* **3B: Can I see them?** ¿Los puedo ver? *exp.* **3B**
then entonces *adv., conj.* **7A, 9B: since then** desde entonces *loc. adv.* **7A**
then… luego… *adv.* **0**
therapy terapia *f.* **3A**
there allá *adv.* **6B:** allí *adv.* **2A: How are you going there?** ¿Cómo vas? *exp.* **6B: there is/there are** hay *v.* **3B**
therefore por eso *conj.* **17A:** por lo tanto *conj.* **17A**
these estos/as *adj.* **3A: these (ones)** estos/as *pron.* **3A**
they ellos/as *pron.* **1B**
thing cosa *f.* **4A: the bad/good thing** lo malo/bueno *m.* **12B: the best (thing)** lo mejor *m.* **4B**
think pensar *v.* **4A: I think so/not.** Creo que sí/no. *exp.* **7B: to think of** pensar de *v.* **4A: to think of/remember** ocurrirse *v.* **18B: to think about** pensar en *v.* **0**
third tercero/a *adj.* **14A:** tercio *m.* **16B**
thirteen trece *adj.* **1B**
thirty treinta *adj.* **1B**
this este/a *adj.* **3A:** esto *pron.* **: this month** este mes *loc. adv.* **6A: this one** este/a *pron.* **3A: this week** esta semana *loc. adv.* **6A: this year** este año *loc. adv.* **6A**
those esos/as *adj.* **3A: those (ones)** esos/as *pron.* **3A: Those were the days!** ¡Qué tiempos aquellos! *exp.* **5B**
thousands miles *m. pl.* **6B**
thrashing paliza *f.* **18A**
thread hilo *m.* **14B**
three tres *adj.* **1A: three times a year** tres veces al año *loc. adv.* **3A**
throat garganta *f.* **10A**
through a través de *loc. prep.* **14B**
throw lanzar *v.* **18A**
Thursday jueves *m.* **3A**
ticket entrada *f.* **7B:** pasaje *m.* **6B:** billete *m.* **6B: lottery ticket** cupón *m.* **12B: lottery ticket booth** agencia de lotería *f.* **9B: lottery ticket seller** vendedor(a) de lotería *m./f.* **9B: plane ticket** pasaje de avión *m.* **6B: to book the tickets** reservar los billetes *v.* **13A: to buy lottery tickets** comprar (billetes de) lotería *v.* **9B**
tie corbata *f.* **3B**
time época *f.* **9A:** vez (*pl.* veces) *f.* **3A:** tiempo *m.* **3A: at the same time** al mismo

tiempo *loc. adv.* **7A: At what time…?**
¿A qué hora…? *exp.* **3A: boarding time**
hora de embarque *f.* **13A: departure**
time hora de salida *f.* **13A: free time**
tiempo libre *m.* **5B: from time to time**
de vez en cuando *loc. adv.* **14A: in/on**
time a tiempo *loc. adv.* **7B: three times a**
year tres veces al año *loc. adv.* **3A: time**
for oneself tiempo para uno/a mismo/a
m. **3A: arrival time** hora de llegada
f. **13A: time of year** época *f.* **6B: to have**
a good time pasarla bien *v.* **17B: to have**
a good time pasarlo bien *v.* **17B: What**
time is it? ¿Qué hora es? *exp.* **3A**
tiny pequeñísimo/a *adj.* **11B: tiny apartment**
minipiso *m.* **11B**
tired cansado/a *adj.* **6A: to get tired of**
(something) cansarse de (algo) *v.* **9B**
tiredness cansancio *m.* **14B**
tireless incansable *adj.* **14B**
title título *m.* : titular *v.* **0**
to a *prep.* : **from time to time** de vez en
cuando *loc. adv.* **14A: from… until/**
to desde/de… hasta/a *loc. prep.* **8B:**
next to al lado de *loc. adv.* **3B: thanks**
to… gracias a… *loc. prep.* **5B: to be**
sensitive to ser sensible a *v.* **10A: to go**
to bed acostarse *v.* **7A: to go to work** ir a
trabajar *v.* **3A: to take the kids to school**
llevar a los niños al colegio *v.* **3A: to the**
left of a la izquierda de *loc. adv.* **3B: to**
the right of a la derecha de *loc. adv.* **3B**
toast tostada *f.* **2B**
tobacconist: tobacconist shop estanco
m. **9B**
today hoy *adv.* **6A:** en la actualidad *loc.*
adv. **8B**
together juntos/as *adj.* **5A**
Toledo Toledo *f.* **1A**
tolerance tolerancia *f.* **14A**
tomato tomate *m.* **4A: tomato sauce** tomate
frito *m.* **15A**
tomorrow mañana *adv.* **0: See you**
tomorrow. Hasta mañana *exp.* **0: the**
day after tomorrow pasado mañana *loc.*
adv. **11B**
tongue: mother tongue lengua materna
f. **14A: tongue twister** trabalenguas
m. **6A**
too demasiado *adv.* **13A:** también *adv.* **1B**
top: on top of encima de *loc. prep.* **3B:**
screw top tapa de rosca *f.* **8A**
topic tópico *m.* **16B**
toucan tucán *m.* **16B**
touch contacto *m.* **17B:** toque *m.* **15A: to**
be in touch estar en contacto *v.* **12B**
tough duro/a *adj.* **7B:** resistente *adj.* **17A**
tour: package tour viaje organizado *m.* **13A:**
tour guide el/la guía turístico/a *m. y f.* **1B**
tourism turismo *m.* **14A**
tourist turístico/a *adj.* **16B:** turista *m.*
y f. **1B: tourist destination** destino
turístico *m.* **4B**
tournament torneo *m.* **10B**
toward hacia *prep.* : **toward the end of the**
19th century a finales del siglo XIX *loc.*
adv. **8B**
town pueblo *m.* **1A: in the center of town**
céntrico/a *adj.* **7B**

toy juguete *m.* **8B: toy store** juguetería
f. **9B**
track: sound track banda sonora *f.* **17B:**
track and field atletismo *m.* **18A**
track-and-field: track-and-field athlete
atleta *m. y f.* **12B**
trade oficio *m.* **14A: arms trade** tráfico de
armas *m.* **16A: fair trade** comercio justo
m. **3B**
trading: (soccer) trading card el cromo (de
fútbol) *m.* **9B**
tradition tradición *f.* **2B**
traditional tradicional *adj.* **4A**
traffic tráfico *m.* **2A**
train tren *m.* **6B:** educar *v.* **12B**
trainer (of dogs) educador(a) *m./f.* **12B**
training entrenamiento *m.* **18A:**
professional training formación
profesional *f.* **14A**
tranquility tranquilidad *f.* **2A**
transfer: bank transfer transferencia
bancaria *f.* **7B**
transform transformar *v.* **0**
transformation transformación *f.* **14B**
transition: democratic transition transición
democrática *f.* **14B**
translate traducir *v.* **7A**
transparent transparente *adj.* **9A**
transport transportar *v.* **7A:** trasladar
v. **13A**
transportation: means of transportation
medio de transporte *m.* **4A**
travel recorrer *v.* **5A:** viajar *v.* **3A: travel**
agency agencia de viajes *f.* **4B**
traveler viajero/a *m./f.* **11A**
traveling: traveling library biblioteca
ambulante *f.* **9A**
treasure tesoro *m.* **10A**
treatment tratamiento *m.* **12B**
treaty tratado *m.* **16A**
tree árbol *m.* **5B: coral tree** ceibo *m.* **18B:**
family tree árbol genealógico *m.* **5B:**
mahogany tree caoba *f.* **18B**
trend tendencia *f.* **17A**
trick truco *m.* **8A**
trip viaje *m.* **3B: business trip** viaje de
negocios *m.* **3A: round-trip** ida y vuelta
exp. **6B: to organize a trip** preparar un
viaje *v.* **13A**
trot trotar *v.* **9A**
troubadour trovador(a) *m./f.* **7A**
truck camión *m.* **7A: truck driver**
camionero/a *m./f.* **7A**
true cierto/a *adj.* : verdadero/a *adj.* **0: to be**
true ser verdad *v.* **10B: to make (his/her)**
dreams come true cumplir (sus) sueños
v. **15B: True or false?** ¿Verdadero o falso?
exp. **0**
trumpet trompeta *f.* **7A**
trust: to trust in tener confianza en *v.* **5B**
truth verdad *f.* **17B: to tell the truth** decir
la verdad *v.* **17B: to tell the truth** …, la
verdad *exp.* **17B**
try intentar *v.* : **to try one's luck** probar
suerte *v.* **5A: to try to** pretender *v.* **15B: to**
try to procurar *v.* **14B**
T-shirt camiseta *f.* **3B**
tú: to address somebody as tú hablarse de
tú *v.* **7B: use of tú** tuteo *m.* **7B: to use the**

tú form of address tutearse *v.* **17B**
Tuesday martes *m.* **3A**
tulip tulipán *m.* **18B**
turn girar *v.* **9B: It's my turn.** Me toca a mí.
exp. **4A: to turn 15 years old** cumplir
15 años *v.* **5A: to turn over** dar la vuelta
v. **8A: Whose turn is it?** ¿A quién le toca?
exp. **4A: to turn on** encender *v.* **4B**
TV tele *f.* **3A: TV** *f.* **9A: TV viewer**
televidente *m.* **9A**
twelve doce *adj.* **1A**
twenty veinte *adj.* **1B**
twice: twice a month dos veces al mes *loc.*
adv. **6A**
two dos *adj.* **1A: two last names** doble
apellido *m.* **12A: two months ago** hace
dos meses *loc. adv.* **5A**
type tipo *m.* **12A**
typical típico/a *adj.* **2A**
tyrant tirano/a *m./f.* **13B**

U

ugly feo/a *adj.* **3B**
umbrella paraguas *m.* **3B**
unbearable insoportable *adj.* **2A**
Unbelievable! ¡Increíble! *exp.* **9B**
uncle tío *m.* **5B**
uncomfortable incómodo/a *adj.* **11B:**
extremely uncomfortable
incomodísimo/a *adj.* **11B**
under debajo de *loc. prep.* **3B: to be under**
construction estar en obras *v.* **11A: to be**
under someone's control estar en manos
de alguien *exp.* **17A**
underline subrayar *v.* **0**
underneath debajo *adv.* **3B**
underprivileged desfavorecido/a *adj.* **16A**
understand entender *v.* **13B:** comprender
v. **13B: I don't understand.** No entiendo.
exp. **0: I understand you perfectly.** Te
entiendo perfectamente. *exp.* **13B**
understanding comprensivo/a *adj.* **13B**
unemployed desocupado/a *adj.* **11B**
unforgettable inolvidable *adj.* **5B**
uninterruptedly ininterrumpidamente
adv. **18A**
union: European Union Unión Europea *f.* **10B**
unique único/a *adj.* **2A**
United Kingdom Reino Unido *m.* **8B**
United States (U.S.A.) Estados Unidos (EE.
UU.) *m.* **0**
unity unidad *f.* **16A**
universal universal *adj.* **17A**
universe universo *m.* **9B**
university universidad *f.* **2A**
unlimited ilimitado/a *adj.* **8A**
unpleasant desagradable *adj.* **13B**
unrequited: unrequited love amor no
correspondido *m.* **12A**
unstoppable imparable *adj.* **14A**
until hasta *prep.* **8B**
up arriba *adv.* : **to bring up to date** poner al
día *v.* **7B: What's up?** ¿Qué pasa? *exp.* **0**
update actualizar *v.* **7B:** poner (a alguien)
al día *v.* **17B**
upon: based upon sobre la base de *loc.*
prep. **16A: to be agreed upon** a convenir
loc. adv. **13B**

upright vertical *adj.* **13A**
uranium uranio *m.* **14A**
Uruguay Uruguay *m.* **0**
Uruguayan uruguayo/a *adj.* **7A**
us nosotros/as *pron.* **1B: let's see…** a ver… *exp.* **6A**
use usar *v.* **0:** utilizar *v.* **0: What is it used for?** ¿Para qué sirve? *exp.* **4B: use of tú** tuteo *m.* **7B**
useful útil *adj.* **9A**
useless inútil *adj.*
user: Internet user internauta *m. y f.* **6A**
usted: to address somebody as usted hablarse de usted *v.* **7B**
usually normalmente *adv.* **14A: to usually do something** soler *v.* **14A**
utensil utensilio *m.* **15A**

V

vacation vacaciones *f. pl.* **3A: to be on vacation** estar de vacaciones *v.* **7B: to spend one's vacation** pasar las vacaciones *v.* **4B**
vaccinate vacunar *v.* **10A**
vaccine vacuna *f.* **12B**
valid en regla *loc. adv.* **11A**
validate validar *v.* **14A**
valley valle *m.* **11B**
variety variedad *f.* **7A**
various diverso/a *adj.* **5B**
vast extenso/a *adj.* **16B**
veal ternera *f.* **2B: fillet of veal** filete de ternera *m.* **2B**
vegetable hortaliza *f.* **7B**
vegetables verduras *f.* **2B**
vegetarian vegetariano/a *adj.* **15A: to become a vegetarian** hacerse vegetariano/a *v.* **7B**
vegetation vegetación *f.* **6B**
venerate venerar *v.* **16B**
Venezuela Venezuela *f.* **0**
Venezuelan venezolano/a *adj.*
version versión *f.* **9**
very muy *adv.* **2A: very friendly** amabilísimo/a *adj.* **13A: very high** altísimo *adj.* **11B: very well** rebién *adv.* **17B: very well** muy bien *adv.* **1A**
veteran veterano/a *adj.* **14B**
veterinarian veterinario/a *m./f.* **3A**
via: to go via pasar por *v.* **6B**
victim: kidnapping victim secuestrado/a *m./f.* **16A**
view vista *f.* **11A**
viewer: television viewer televidente *m./f.* **9A: television viewer** telespectador(a) *m./f.* **14B**
viewing: wildlife viewing observación de flora y fauna *f.* **6B**
village aldea *f.* **9A**
vinyl: vinyl record disco de vinilo *m.* **13B**
violence violencia *f.* **16A**
virgin: extra virgin olive oil aceite de oliva virgen extra *m.* **15A: virgin forest** bosque virgen *m.* **6B**
visit visitar *v.* **4A**
visitor visitante *m. y f.* **8B**
vital vital *adj.* **7A**
vocation vocación *f.* **7A: by vocation** por

vocación *loc. adv.* **7A**
voice voz (*pl.* voces) *f.* **6A**
volcano volcán *m.* **6B**
volume volumen *m.* **14A**
volunteer voluntario/a *m./f.* **12B: volunteer work** trabajo voluntario *m.* **7A**
vote votar *v.* **10B**
voucher: gift voucher cheque-regalo *m.* **3B**
vowel vocal *f.* **13B**

W

wages sueldo *m.* **3B**
wait: to wait for esperar *v.* **12B:** esperar *v.* **12B: to wait in line** hacer fila *v.* **13A**
waiter camarero *m.* **2B:** mesero *m.* **13A**
waitress camarera *f.* **2B:** mesera *f.* **13A**
wake up despertarse *v.* **7A**
walk caminar *v.* **5B: to go for a walk** pasear *v.* **3A: to take a walk** dar un paseo *v.* **6A:** pasear *v.* **5B**
walkway paseo *m.* **2A**
wall pared *f.* **: Berlin Wall** Muro de Berlín *m.* **10B**
wallet billetero *m.* **18B**
waltz vals *m.* **17B**
wander: to wander aimlessly caminar sin rumbo fijo *v.* **17B**
want querer *v.* **3B**
war guerra *f.* **8B: civil war** guerra civil *f.* **8B: World War II** Segunda Guerra Mundial *f.*
ward sala *f.* **10A**
waste desperdiciar *v.* **15B**
watch reloj *m.* **3A:** mirar *v.* **6A: to watch movies** ver películas *v.* **3A**
waterfall cascada *f.* **6B**
wave ola *f.* **16B**
way manera *f.* **5A: by the way** por cierto *conj.* **10A: by the way** a propósito *exp. conj.* **10A: way of life** medio de vida *m.* **11B**
we nosotros/as *pron.* **1B**
wealth riqueza *f.* **14A**
weapon arma *f.* **16A: nuclear weapon** arma nuclear *f.* **16A**
wear llevar *v.* **3B**
weather tiempo *m.* **10A: good weather** buen tiempo *m.* **2A: there is bad weather** hace mal tiempo *exp.* **10A: there is good weather** hace buen tiempo *exp.* **10A: weather forecast** pronóstico *m.* **9A: What's the weather like?** ¿Qué tiempo hace? *exp.* **10A**
Web: Web page página web *f.* **14B: Web site** sitio web *m.* **14B**
webcam cámara web *f.* **6B**
wedding boda *f.* **5A: silver wedding anniversary** bodas de plata *f. pl.* **18B: to have one's wedding anniversary** cumplir años de casados *v.* **18B**
Wednesday miércoles *m.* **3A**
week semana *f.* **2B: day of the week** día de la semana *m.* **3A: Holy Week** Semana Santa *f.* **5A: last week** la semana pasada *loc. adv.* **5A: once a week** una vez a la semana *loc. adv.* **6A: this week** esta semana *loc. adv.* **6A**
weekend fin de semana *m.* **2B: long weekend** puente *m.* **6B: (on) weekends** los fines de semana *loc. adv.* **5B**

weekly semanal *adj.* **3A**
welcome bienvenida *f.* **11A:** dar la bienvenida *v.* **11A: You're welcome.** Con gusto. *exp.* **18B**
Welcome! ¡Bienvenido/a(s)! *exp.* **11A**
well bien *adv.* **1A:** pues *exp.* **6A: as well as** así como *conj.* **16B: very well** muy bien *adv.* **1A: very well** rebién *adv.* **17B: well-being** bienestar *m.* **6A**
well… bueno… *exp.* **2A**
west oeste *m.* **2A**
what qué *interrog.* **1A: At what time…?** ¿A qué hora…? *exp.* **3A: What color?** ¿De qué color? *exp.* **3B: What is it used for?** ¿Para qué sirve? *exp.* **4B: What is it?** ¿Qué es? *exp.* **1A: What is… like?** ¿Cómo es…? *exp.* **2A: What size?** ¿De qué talla? *exp.* **3B: What time is it?** ¿Qué hora es? *exp.* **3A: What would you like (to have)?** ¿Qué desean tomar? *exp.* **2B: What's the weather like?** ¿Qué tiempo hace? *exp.* **10A: What's wrong?** ¿Qué te/ le pasa? (*fam./form.*) *exp.* **10A**
What? ¿Cómo? *exp.* **14A**
wheat trigo *m.* **15A**
when cuándo *interrog.* **0**
where dónde *interrog.* **1A: Where are you from?** ¿De dónde eres? *exp.* **1A: Where are you from?** ¿De dónde es usted? *exp.* **1A: where is…?** ¿dónde está…? *exp.* **2A**
which: which one(s)? ¿cuál(es)? *interrog.* **4B**
white blanco/a *adj.* **3B**
who quién *interrog.* **1A: Who is it?** ¿Quién es? *exp.* **1A**
whole: whole milk leche entera *f.* **15A**
whose cuyo/a *adj.* **10B**
why por qué *interrog.* **6A: Why don't you…?** ¿Por qué no…? *exp.* **6A**
wide ancho/a *adj.* **4B**
wife esposa *f.* **5B:** mujer *f.* **3A: ex-wife** ex esposa *f.* **12A**
Wi-Fi: Wi-Fi network red Wi-Fi *f.* **13B**
wild silvestre *adj.* **18B: wild cherry** guinda *f.* **16B**
wildlife: wildlife viewing observación de flora y fauna *f.* **6B**
win ganar *v.* **5A: to win tournaments** ganar torneos *v.* **18A**
window ventana *f.* **: shop window** escaparate *m.* **3B**
wine vino *m.* **2B**
winning ganador(a) *adj.* **14B**
winter invierno *m.* **2A**
wisdom sabiduría *f.* **17B**
wish desear *v.* **11A: I/We wish.** Ojalá. *exp.* **15A**
with con *prep.* **2B: with a credit card** con tarjeta *loc. adv.* **3B: with me** conmigo *prep. + pron.* **5A: with you** contigo *prep. + pron.* **5A**
within dentro de *loc. prep.* **17A**
witness testigo *m. y f.* **10B**
woman mujer *f.* **3A: businesswoman** mujer empresaria *f.* **5A: the woman of my dreams** la mujer de mi vida *exp.* **12A**
wonderful estupendo/a *adj.* **6B:** maravilloso/a *adj.* **5A**
wonderfully de maravilla *loc. adv.* **17B**

wood madera *f.* **8A**

word palabra *f.* **0: in other words** es decir *exp.* **8B**

work labor *f.* **12B:** trabajo *m.* **1B:** funcionar *v.* **7B:** trabajar *v.* **1B: to go to work** ir a trabajar *v.* **3A: to work as** trabajar como *v.* **11B: volunteer work** trabajo voluntario *m.* **7A: What do you do (for work)?** ¿A qué te dedicas? *exp.* **1B: work environment** ambiente laboral *m.* **13B: work schedule** horario de trabajo *m.* **3A: to work out** hacer ejercicio *v.* **6A: work of art** obra (de arte) *f.* **8A: work team** equipo de trabajo *m.* **13B**

workday: flexible workday jornada flexible *f.* **6A**

worker trabajador(a) *adj.; m./f.* **3A:** obrero/a *m./f.* **8B: rural worker** campesino/a *m./f.* **9A**

working laboral *adj.* **7B: working mother** madre trabajadora *f.* **7B**

world mundo *m.* **4A: a world in motion** un mundo en movimiento *exp.* **14A: to go around the world** dar la vuelta al mundo *v.* **18A: World Heritage** Patrimonio Mundial *m.* **11B: World Heritage (Site)** Patrimonio de la Humanidad *m.* **8A: world leaders** líderes mundiales *m. y f. pl.* **16A: world of finance** mundo de las finanzas *m.* **3A**

worldwide mundial *adj.* **7B**

worried preocupado/a *adj.* **12A**

worry preocupación *f.* **7A:** preocupar *v.* **7A**

worship: place of worship lugar de culto *m.* **8A**

worth valía *f.* **18A: to be worth it** valer la pena *v.* **11B**

would: What would you like (to have)? ¿Qué desean tomar? *exp.* **2B: Would you mind...?** ¿Le importaría...? *exp.* **13A**

wound herida *f.* **10A**

wrap up abrigarse *v.* **13A**

wristwatch reloj de pulsera *m.* **3B**

write escribir *v.* **0:** redactar *v.* **0: to write to each other** escribirse *v.* **17B: to write down** anotar *v.* **0**

writer escritor(a) *m./f.* **1A**

wrong equivocado/a *adj.* **: to go wrong** ir mal *v.* **7B**

Y

yard jardín *m.* **4B**

year año *m.* **2B: fifteen-year-old girl** quinceañera *f.* **5A: New Year** Año Nuevo *m.* **18B: this year** este año *loc. adv.* **6A: three times a year** tres veces al año *loc. adv.* **3A: time of year** época *f.* **6B: to turn 15 years old** cumplir 15 años *v.* **5A**

yellow amarillo/a *adj.* **3B: yellow fever** fiebre amarilla *f.* **10A**

yes sí *adv.* **1A**

yesterday ayer *adv.* **5A**

yet aún *adv.* **15B: not yet** todavía no *loc. adv.* **6A**

yoga yoga *m.* **3A**

yogurt yogur *m.* **2B**

you tú (*sing. fam.*) *pron.* **1A:** usted (*sing. form.*) *pron.* **1A:** ustedes (*pl.*) *pron.* **1A:** vosotros/as (*pl. fam.*) *pron.* **1B: And**

you? ¿Y tú/usted? *exp.* **1A: with you** contigo *pron.* **5A: You/One can't...** No se puede... *exp.* **7B**

young joven (*pl.* jóvenes) *adj.; m. y f.* **2A: for young people** juvenil *adj.* **7A: young boy/girl** pibe/a *m./f.* **17B: young people** jóvenes *m.* **2A**

youngster chamaquito/a *m./f.* **12A**

your tu(s) (*sing. fam.*) *adj.* **2A:** su(s) (*form.*) *adj.* **2A:** vuestro/a(s) (*pl. fam.*) *adj.* **5B: at your service** a tu/su servicio *loc. adv.* **7B**

youth juventud *f.* **9A**

yucca yuca *f.* **4A**

Z

zip-lining tirolesa *f.* **18A**

Cultural Index

Note: For a complete listing of grammar topics, see pp. A17–A18.

Comic Credits

135 Courtesy of Cristian Zwonik.
202 © 2016 Artists Rights Society (ARS), New York / VEGAP, Madrid
298 Courtesy of Fernando Javier Sendra.
345 © Joaquín Salvador Lavado (QUINO) Déjenme inventar -Ediciones de La Flor, 1983
389 © Joaquín Salvador Lavado (QUINO) Déjenme inventar -Ediciones de La Flor, 1983
413 © Joaquín Salvador Lavado (QUINO) Déjenme inventar -Ediciones de La Flor, 1983

Text Credits

330 © Formularios by Juan José Millás. El País Internacional (PRISACOM).
382 "Oda al tomate", Odas elementales. ©1954, Fundación Pablo Neruda.
434 Courtesy of Cristina Fernández Cubas.

Song Credits

428 "Volver" Words and Music by CARLOS GARDEL and ALFREDO LE PERA. Copyright © 1961, 1982 WARNER CHAPPELL MUSIC ARGENTINA (SADAIC) All Rights Reserved. Used By Permission of ALFRED MUSIC.

Photo and Art Credits

All images © Vista Higher Learning and Ediciones SM, Madrid unless otherwise noted.

Cover: (background) Wataru Ebiko/500px; (tl) TT Studio/Shutterstock; (tr) Cavan Images/Offset; (b) SIME/eStockphoto.

IAE FM: IAE-35 (t) Fancy Photography/Veer; (t, inset) Fancy Photography/Veer; (b) Corbis/Veer; (b, inset) Corbis/Veer.

Preliminary Unit: 1 (tl) Jim Ruymen/UPI/Landov; (tmr) Dream Pictures/Media Bakery; (ml) J.D. Dallet/AGE Fotostock; (mr) Juan Manuel Silva/AGE Fotostock; (r) Paula Díez; (bl) Diego Santacruz, Archivo el Espectador, Comunican S. A; **2** (tl) Tinseltown/Shutterstock; (tml) Rafael Ríos; (tmr) Media Bakery; (tr) Plainpicture/AGE Fotostock; (bl) Agencia el Universal/Newscom; (blm) Masterfile; (brm) Cover/Getty Images; **3** (tlm) Scott Dalton/The New York Times/Redux; (tr) LWA-Dann Tardif/Corbis; (bl) Cover/Getty Images; (blm) Exactostock/SuperStock; (brm) Stock 4B/Getty Images; **4** (tl) George Shelley/AGE Fotostock; (tmr) Paula Díez; (bl) Klaus Tiedge/AGE Fotostock; **5** (tml) MK/Newscom; (bml) BW Media Photoagentur/AGE Fotostock; (bmr) Antoine Couvercelle/DPPI/Icon SMI 547/Newscom.

Unit One: 9 (t) Jim Ruymen/UPI/Landov; (b) Ali Burafi; **10** (tml) Album/Newscom; **11** (l) Katie Wade; (r) Janet Dracksdorf; **13** (tl) Rido/Fotolia; (bm) Martín Bernetti; (br) Apeloga/Media Bakery; **14** (tl) Jim Ruymen/UPI/Landov; (tcl) Media Bakery; (tcr) Max Messerli/AGE Fotostock; (tr) AKG-Images/The Image Works; (bcl) José Blanco; (bcr) Ángel Luis Garcia/El Nuevo Día de Puerto Rico/Newscom; (br) AF Archive/Alamy; **15** (tl) Katie Wade; (tr) Tifonimages/Shutterstock; (tcl) Villorejo/Fotolia; (tcr) Ali Burafi; (cr) Pascal Pernix; (bl) Foodstories/AGE Fotostock; (br) Tinseltown/Shutterstock; (tc) Ali Burafi; (cl) Oscar Artavia Solano; (cr) José Blanco; (bc) Tramonto/AGE Fotostock; (b) Anne Loubet; **21** Thomas Northcut/Getty Images; **23** (tl) José Blanco; (tm) Janet Dracksdorf; (tr) Janet Dracksdorf; (bl) Janet Dracksdorf; (bm) José Blanco; (br) José Blanco; **25** (t) J.D. Dallet/AGE Fotostock; (b) Paola Ríos; **26** (tl) VHL; (tr) VHL; (c) Katie Wade; (bl) Annie Pickert Fuller; (br) Martín Bernetti; **28** VHL; **30** Javier Larrea/AGE Fotostock; **32** (t) Paula Díez; (bl) VHL; (bc) Janet Dracksdorf; (br) Stephen Coburn/Shutterstock; **33** (b) Hans Georg Roth/Corbis; **34** (t) Ali Burafi.

Unit Two: 35 (t) Dream Pictures/Media Bakery; (m) J.D. Dallet/AGE Fotostock; (b) Martín Bernetti; **36** Gg/eStock Photo; **37** VHL; **38** Jose Fuste Raga/Corbis; **39** (tl) Lauren Krolick; (tc) Maria Eugenia Corbo; (tr) Javier Larrea/AGE Fotostock; (ml) Martín Bernetti; (mc) Javier Larrea/AGE Fotostock; (mr) Dusan Kostic/Fotolia; **40** Dream Pictures/Media Bakery; **41** Rubén Varela; **42** (m) José Blanco; (b) Christian Mueller/Shutterstock; **49** (tr) Media Bakery; **50** J.D. Dallet/AGE Fotostock; **51** (t) Red 2/AGE Fotostock; **58** Martín Bernetti.

Unit Three: 59 (t) Juan Manuel Silva/AGE Fotostock; (m) Diego Santacruz, Archivo el Espectador, Comunican S. A; (b) Maxisport/Shutterstock; **60** Daloiso/Giino/Ropi/Zuma Press/Newscom; **62** Digital Vision/Getty Images; **64** (t) Juan Manuel Silva/AGE Fotostock; (br) María Eugenia Corbo; **65** (l) Marka/AGE Fotostock; (m) Karl Weatherly/AGE Fotostock; (r) Álvaro Leiva/AGE Fotostock; **66** (t) Aspen Stock/AGE Fotostock; (m) Rido/Fotolia; (bl) Noam/Fotolia; (br) Andrés Rodríguez/Big Stock Photo; **70** P. Narayan/AGE Fotostock; **71** (cl) Martín Bernetti; (cr) Paula Diez; (r) Kagenmi/Fotolia; **72** (rt) Marcos Welsh/AGE Fotostock; (rb) Mauritius Images/Superstock; **73** (l) Javier Larrea/AGE Fotostock; (r) Pascal Pernix; **74** Diego Santacruz, Archivo el Espectador, Comunican S. A; **75** (bml) Emilio Ereza /Alamy; (bmr) Francesco de Marco/Shutterstock; (br) Katie Wade; **80** Javier Larrea/AGE Fotostock; **82** Javier Soriano/AFP/Getty Images; **83** VHL; **84** (t) Maxisport/Shutterstock; (logo) LatinContent/STR/Getty Images.

Unit Four: 85 (m) Paula Díez; (b) Oscar Artavia Solano; **86-87** Katie Wade; **91** (t) Ali Burafi; **92** (t) Padchas/Shutterstock; **95** Javier Larrea/AGE Fotostock; **96** (t) Matyas Rehak/Shutterstock; (m) José Blanco; (b) Javier LarreaAGE Fotostock; **98** TasfotoNL/Shutterstock; **99** (l) Ali Burafi; (c) Photographee.eu/Shutterstock; (r) Lauren Krolick; **100** (tl) Red Cover/Masterfile; (tcl) Paula Díez; (tc) Paula Díez; (tr) Pix11/Shutterstock; (cl) Eduardo Sánchez Gatell/123RF; (bl) Karammiri/123RF; (br) VHL; **101** (tl) Hywit Dimyadi/Shutterstock; (ml) Martín Bernetti; (mr) ZTS/Shutterstock; (r) Arina Zaiachin/123RF; **102** (l) Paula Díez; (r) Eugene Sergeev/Shutterstock; **104** (t) Aleksey Sergeychik/Fotolia; (tm) Vadim70 Ovthinnikov/Fotolia; (bm) Fotosearch RF; (b) Anne Loubet; **108** (l) Skodonnell/iStockphoto; (r) VHL; **109** (ml) Jon Le-Bon/Fotolia; (rc) Margo Harrison/123RF; (r) Bilder/Shutterstock; **110** Oscar Artavia Solano.

Unit Five: 111 (t) Tinseltown/Shutterstock; (m) Rafael Ríos; **112** (l) Chederros/AGE Fotostock; **113** (tl) John Van Hasselt/Sygma/Corbis; (m) Olivier Tabary/Shutterstock; **114** (t) Mónica M. González; (mr) Rossy Llano; (mm) Sam Bloomberg-Rissman/AGE Fotostock; (br) Graziano Arici/AGE Fotostock; (bl) Media Bakery; **116** (l) Tinseltown/Shutterstock; (r) Miramax/Dimension Films/The Kobal Collection; **117** (tl) Chema Moya/EPA/Corbis; (tm) Antoine Couvercelle/DPPI/Icon SMI 547/Newscom; (tr) Jim Ruymen/UPI/Landov; (bl) Dinno Kovic/Southcreek Global/ZUMApress/Newscom; (bm) A11/Zuma Press/Newscom; (br) Micheline Pelletier/Sygma/Corbis; **118** (ml) Jaume Gual/AGE Fotostock; **122** (t) Comstock/Fotosearch; (m) Corbis; (b) Andresr/Shutterstock; **124** Arthur Klonsky/Corbis; **128** Rafael Ríos; **129** Janet Dracksdorf; **130** (t) Godfer/Fotolia; (bl) Cathy Yeulet/Big Stock Photo; (bmr) Pixtal/AGE Fotostock.

Unit Six: 137 (t) Media Bakery; (m) Plainpicture RM/AGE Fotostock; **138** VHL; (inset) Battroid; **139** (l) Lindsay Hebberd/Corbis; (lc) Aquasolid/iStockphoto; (ml) Doco Dalfiano/AGE Fotostock; (mr) Pete Saloutos/ Shutterstock; (r) Tonobalaguerf/Shutterstock; **140** VHL; **142** Media Bakery; **143** Ali Burafi; **144** (t) RJ Lerich/Shutterstock; (ml) Galyna Andrushko/Shutterstock; (bl) Martín Bernetti; (bm) Ali Burafi; **147** Oscar Artavia Solano; **148** Pascal Pernix; **151** Paula Diez; **153** (tl) Paula Diez; (tr) Paula Diez; (b) Hidalgo & Lopesino/AGE Fotostock; **154** (t) Plainpicture RM/AGE Fotostock; (b) StockLite/Shutterstock; **156** (t) Galyna Andrushko/Shutterstock; (br) Pelonmaker/Shutterstock; (bl) Celso Diniz/Shutterstock.

Unit Seven: 163 (t) El Universal/Newscom; (m) Masterfile; **164** (tl) Bikeriderlondon/Shutterstock; (bl) Speedkingz/Shutterstock; (br) AFP/Getty Images; **165** (tl) Paul Maguire/Shutterstock; (tr) Taka/AGE Fotostock; (bl) Leo Himsl/AGE Fotostock; (br) Jenny Cundy/Image Source; **166** (tml) Media Bakery; (tmr) Design Pics Inc/Alamy; (tr) Aspen Stock/AGE Fotostock; (bl) VHL; (bm) Martín Bernetti; **168** El Universal/Newscom; **169** (t) Archivo/Newscom; (m) Sun/Newscom; (b) AFP/Getty Images; **170** (ml) Noam/Fotolia; (mr) Thomas Northcut/Getty Images; (bl) Tetra Images/Alamy; **176** Hagg + Kropp/AGE Fotostock; **177** Superstock/AGE Fotostock; **178** Superstock/AGE Fotostock; **180** Masterfile; **181** VHL; **182** (l) Juan Bernal/123RF; (m) Katie Wade; (r) VHL; **186** PhotoAlto/Alamy; **187** VHL.

Unit Eight: 189 (t) Cover/Getty Images; **191** (tl) Guysal/Shutterstock; (tr) Jean Dominique Dallet; (bl) VHL; (br) Eduardo Huelin/123RF; **194** Cover/Getty Images; **195** (tl) José Blanco; (tr) Lee Torrens/Shutterstock; (bl) Heeb Christian/Age Fotostock; (bm) Rob Wilson/Shutterstock; (br) Cortesia Notimex/Newscom; **200** Carlos Perez de Rozas/EFE/Corbis; **201** (l) Newscom; (mr) Nicolás Corbo; (r) VHL; **202** (b) José Blanco; **203** (l) Paul Springett/Alamy; (br) Javier Lizón/EFE/Corbis; **205** (l) María Eugenia Corbo; (ml) María Eugenia Corbo; (mr) María Eugenia Corbo; (r) María Eugenia Corbo; **206** (tr) Katie Wade; (ml) P.J. Sharpe/Corbis; (mm) Andrey Gontarev/Shutterstock; (mr) Lars Rosen Gunnilstam; (bml) Katie Wade; (br) VHL; **211** Martín Bernetti.

Unit Nine: 213 (t) Scott Dalton/The New York Times/Redux; **214** Pablo Corral V/Corbis; **215** (all) Jorgensen Fernandez; **216** (l) Ana Cabezas Martín; **217** Ivan Smuk/123RF; **218** Scott Dalton/The New York Times/Redux; **219** (l) Vanessa Bertozzi; (r) Bettmann/Corbis; **220** (tl) Oscar Artavia Solano; (tml) Oscar Artavia Solano; (tr) Martín Bernetti; (bml) Kuzma/Big Stock Photo; (bmr) VHL; (br) Shock/Fotolia; **224** (r) Juan Martin/EFE/Corbis; **225** (t) Janet Dracksdorf; (b) Javier Lizon/EFE/Corbis; **227** Emilio Naranjo/EFE/Corbis; **229**-230:(l) JuanJo Martin/EFE/Newscom; (m) Paul White/AP Images; (r) Paula Diez; **234** Photooiasson/Fotolia; **235** PictureNet/Corbis.

Unit Ten: 237 (t) LWA-Dann Tardif/Media Bakery; (m) Cover/Getty Images; **238** (mr) Katie Wade; **239** (cl) Grafton Marshall Smith/Corbis; **241** (t) Michael Jung/Fotolia; (b) VHL; **242** LWA-Dann Tardif/Media Bakery; **248** (l) Archivo Particular/El Tiempo de Colombia/Newscom; (r) Oronoz/Newscom; **249** (l) Antonio Scorza/AFP/Newscom; (m) Nathalie Koulischer/Reuters/Newscom; (r) Kyodo/Landov; **250** (t) Paula Diez; (b) Rafael Ríos; **252** Cover/Getty Images; **253** (l) Time & Life Images/Getty Images; **256** Martín Bernetti.

Unit Eleven: 261 (t) Exactostock/SuperStock; (m) Stock 4B/Getty Images; **262** (l) Oscar Artavia Solano; (m) María Eugenia Corbo; **263** (t) Maria Eugenia Corbo; (b) Goodluz/Fotolia; **265** Wicki58/iStockphoto; **266** Exactostock/SuperStock; **267** (l) VHL; (m) José Blanco; (r) José Blanco; **272** (l) Javier Larrea/AGE Fotostock; (r) Rafael Ríos; **273** Paula Diez; **274** (l) Jerry Whaley/AGE Fotostock; (mr) Mikhail Lavrenov/123RF; (r) Janet Dracksdorf; **275** (t) Evok20/Fotolia; (tml) Ali Burafi; (tmr) Harry Neave/Fotolia; (bml) Martín Bernetti; (bmr) Andy Dean/Fotolia; (b) Fred Goldstein/Fotolia; **276** Stock4B/Getty Images; **277** Kathryn Alena Korf; **280** Lauren Krolick; **282** Paola Ríos.

Unit Twelve: 285 (t) George Shelley/AGE Fotostock; **286** Laszlolorik/Fotolia; **287** Andrey Arkusha/Shutterstock; **288** (all) Paula Díez; **289** (all) Paula Díez; **290** George Shelley/AGE Fotostock; **291** Wavebreak Media/Fotolia; **292** Topham/The Image Works; **296** (m) Ulises Rodríguez/EFE/Corbis; (r, logo) Courtesy of Cimientos; (r) Sarah Meghan Lee/The Image Works; **297** Getty Images; **298** (l) Brian Mitchell/Getty Images; **299** Mika/Getty Images; **301** (dog) Getty Images; (tl) Graziano Arici/AGE Fotostock; (tr) Louisa Gouliamaki/EPA/Newscom; (br) Zuma Press/Newscom; **307** (tl) José Blanco; (tr) Robert Lerich/Fotolia; (bl) VHL; (br) Anne Loubet.

Unit Thirteen: 309 (t) Paula Díez; **310** (tl) Rob Wilson/Shutterstock; (tr) Michael Weber/Media Bakery; (bl) DPA Picture Alliance/Alamy; **314** Paula Díez; **316** (t) Lauren Krolick; (b) Katie Wade; **320** (tl) Igor Mojzes/Fotolia; (tr) Corund/Fotolia; (bl) Hitdelight/Shutterstock; **322** (ml) Paula Diez; **325** (l) Orange Line Media/Shutterstock; (m) Sean Prior/Shutterstock; (r) Monkey Business Images/Shutterstock; **326** Hero Images/500PX; **331** NuStock/iStock Photo.

Unit Fourteen: 334 (r) Michel Renaudeau/AGE Fotostock; **336** (b) Christine Nesbitt/AP Images; **339** (b) Jose Lucas/Alamy; **344** (m) KRT/Newscom; (b) Jochen Luebke/Newscom; **345** Photography Firm/Fotolia; **350** (tl) Katie Wade; (tm) Valet/Fotolia; (tr) JeffWQC/Fotolia; (bl) Mariusz Prusaczyk/Fotolia.

Unit Fifteen: 357 (t) Andy Sotiriou/Getty Images; **359** (3, logo) Colin Underhill/Alamy; (b) Paula Díez; **360** (l) Janet Dracksdorf; (mlc) Sandra Cunningham/Shutterstock; (mr) Eddie Berman/iStockphoto; (r) Vanessa Bertozzi; **363** (mr) Janet Dracksdorf; (b) José Blanco; **364** (t) Javier Etcheverry/Alamy; (b) Aizar Raldes/AFP/Getty Images; **365** Katie Wade; **368** (t) Paula Diez; (mt) Dario Eusse Tobon; (mb) Paula Diez; (b) VHL; **371** (all) VHL; **372** (t) Andresr/Shutterstock; (b) Digital Vision/Getty Images; **376** (all) VHL; **382** Pedro León.

Unit Sixteen: 385 (t) MK/Newscom; (m) Don Mason/AGE Fotostock; **387** David Fernandez/EFE/Newscom; **390** MK/Newscom; **391** KO/The Grosby Group/Newscom; **392** (b) Gg/AGE Fotostock; **396** (tmr) Louis Held/AGE Fotostock; **397** Sidney Deal Media/Fotolia; **398** (t) Epic Stock Media/123RF; (b) Royalty-Free/Corbis; **400** Don Mason/AGE Fotostock; **401** (t) Courtesy of María Teresa González; **406** (t) Lauren Krolick; (m) Ali Burafi; (b) AGE Fotostock; **409** VG Stock Studio/Shutterstock.